Presented by,

THE WILLIAM R. HIGGINS,
JR. FOUNDATION, INC.

DECEMBER 2006

Iowa National Bank Notes

A Comprehensive Census of the Notes and History of the Banks

by

James C. Ehrhardt and **Steven J. Sweeney**

published by

The William J. Higgins, Jr., Foundation
Okoboji, Iowa

Dean Oakes, President

Copyright 2006 by the William R. Higgins, Jr., Foundation

1507 Sanborn Ave.
Okoboji, Iowa 51355

All rights reserved.

First Edition

First Printing

Printed in the United States of America
Printed by Edwards Bros., Inc., Ann Arbor, MI

Library of Congress Control Number 2006905000

ISBN 0-9786633-0-6

Dedication

I am very pleased to dedicate this book to my father, Leroy J. Ehrhardt. A life-long resident of Elkader, Iowa, Dad was a lawyer, a banker, and a collector, and was devoted to his family. He bestowed upon me his appreciation and pleasure in numismatics and especially in Iowa National Bank notes. Thanks, Dad.

Jim Ehrhardt

To my great-grandmother, Nora McCarthy, whose stories of growing up in Iowa in the early part of the 20th century instilled in me an appreciation and admiration for local history.

Steve Sweeney

Acknowledgements

The authors gratefully acknowledge the support, encouragement, and essential contributions of the Board of Directors of the William R. Higgins, Jr. Foundation and Museum.

Rick Hickman	Don Mark	Clifford Mishler
Don Jensen	Mike McGinnis	Dean Oakes, President

A core group of individuals interested in Iowa National Bank notes was part of this Iowa Nationals project from its inception and provided support in numerous ways without which this book would have been impossible.

Carl Allen	Jim Jackson	Alan Moser
Bill Bagwell	Don Mark	Dean Oakes
Gene Bright	Larry Miller	Dean Peterson

The people listed below supplied information and/or assistance which made this a better book and for which we are very grateful. We would like especially to acknowledge the significant assistance of Don Kelly and Peter Huntoon who freely shared their encyclopedic knowledge and data on Iowa notes and banks. Numerous individuals made contributions to our work and we apologize for any that we have not acknowledged here.

Larry Adams	Ronald Hedglin	Allen Mincho
Jeff Arbogast	Peter Huntoon	Dave Noble
Donald Atkin	John Jackson	Jim Potter
Fred Ayer	Robert James	Duane Rice
Phil Chinitz	Glen Jorde	Tom Robertson
Sparky Duroe	Don Kelly	Michael Scacci
Flinton Eitzen	Lyn Knight	Michael Sharkey
Tom Flynn	Bob Liddell	Glenn Wright
Peter Fritz	Jerry Lorenzen	
Dave Hanson	Glenn McConnell	

The encouragement, assistance and graphic design skills of Pamela Ehrhardt were vital to success of this project.

Also, we would like to acknowledge all the early collectors and dealers who helped to preserve Iowa notes and their history for our appreciation.

About the Authors

James C. Ehrhardt, Ph.D.

Steven J. Sweeney, CFA

Jim was born and raised in Elkader, IA. He received a B.A. degree from the Univ. of Iowa and a Ph.D. in Physics from the Univ. of California, Berkeley. He returned to his home state and spent his professional career as a medical physicist in the Dept. of Radiology at the Univ. of Iowa, retiring as a Professor Emeritus. Iowa National Bank notes come naturally to Jim. As a student he worked in the Elkader Post Office in the old First National Bank building. His mother had worked in the First National Bank of Milford, Iowa. His father was President of the successor bank to the First National Bank of Elkader and collected Iowa notes. Jim shared his father's interest and was fortunate to receive his father's collection of notes, two of which are pictured in this volume. Later Jim's collecting suddenly became more active when he spotted a Strawberry Point note at Dean Oakes' table at a local coin show. He hasn't looked back since.

Steve grew up on a farm in western Iowa. He received his B.S. degree from Iowa State University and his M.B.A. from the Univ. of Iowa. He is currently an officer of an Iowa-based investment management company with over $20 billion in assets under management. Like so many others, he began his collecting interest by collecting wheat pennies as a kid. As an adult he "discovered" paper money. Soon thereafter, he met John Hickman who inspired him to pursue Iowa national bank notes. Ultimately, it was the local historical connection these notes represented that captured his attention. Steve has been the primary "census keeper" for this project.

Foreword

When I first wrote a letter to twelve Iowa National Bank Note collectors six years ago, I knew the goal I had in mind was to honor John Hickman. John and I had been business partners in buying and selling National Bank Notes for many years. The board of the Higgins Bank Note Museum quickly agreed to underwrite the cost of the book. They were wholeheartedly in favor of the goal. We all wished it could be published tomorrow. We wanted to produce a book that would honor John by listing all the known Iowa National Bank Notes and as much as possible about each bank's history. Time and pages were the two constraints that held the project in its grip. More time could be taken and additional notes would be found, bank histories could be enlarged but at some point we have to end the project as far as this book is concerned. The count of known notes will go on as long as anyone collects Iowa Nationals. When the count reached approximately double what John had compiled from 1966-96 we felt we were ready to publish.

Circulated large size currency in the late 1950's and early 1960's was hardly worth a 10 percent premium and Federal Reserve Notes of 1914 were not. Notes that were not Federals sold for about a $3 premium on $5's, $2 to $3 premium on $10's, and $20's not more than 10 percent unless there were few $20's compared to the $5's and $10's being offered. No one thought it wise to buy any larger denominations at more than $3-$5 over face. In fact why tie money up with them at all. I mention this so you can understand when in 1960 I was faced with a note that I wanted, a $10 used National that was priced at $20. I could hardly believe it. I told Dick Rudolf he was out of his mind. About 4 hours later I came back to buy the note and it had been sold to the fellow who still has the note today. I couldn't believe it a Coin, Iowa note selling for double face, $20.

I started buying and selling Nationals in the late 1950's and had the pleasure of selling to many collectors including Author Jim Ehrhardt's father. My early source of notes and coins was the Lawrence Bros. of Anamosa, Iowa. For eighteen years John Hickman and I sold Nationals to collectors from coast to coast via lists and mail bid and later live auctions. We handled a high percentage of the notes making up the Higgins Museum collection.

This book, dedicated to John's memory and published by the Higgins Museum Foundation, will be another step in helping collectors make educated, informed decisions as they pursue their collecting intents. There has been great cooperation among collectors and dealers who made this project possible as well as the great amount of time devoted to the book by its authors. A big thanks to all who helped make this possible.

Happy Hunting,

Dean Oakes

Preface

What started out as a simple conversation on the way to Memphis in June of 1999 turned into a multi-year project to compile a definitive census of surviving Iowa national bank notes. This census became the basis for a comprehensive book on Iowa national banks that will become the essential reference to anyone with an interest in these historical pieces of paper money.

While pioneering researchers like John Hickman and Don Kelly have worked to compile census data on surviving national bank notes, this is the first such study to focus exclusively on Iowa. Continuing where John left off, we have nearly doubled the number of surviving Iowa bank notes recorded, from nearly 6,000 to over 11,000 notes.

But, the notes are only part of the story. The banks themselves and the bank officers who individually signed these notes are fascinating in their own right. In many of Iowa's small towns the bank was often the heart of the community and the bank founders and officers influential civic leaders. As such, we felt it important to include a listing of the bank officers.

Many banks failed in the late 1920s and early 1930s, prompting President Roosevelt to declare a bank holiday on March 6, 1933, closing all U.S. banks. One progressive Iowa community had successfully implemented a similar strategy several years earlier.

Nothing excites a bank note collector more than the discovery of a new note or group of notes. Iowa has seen its share of interesting and unusual hoards. We share a few of them with you in the pages to follow.

A project of this scale is never truly complete. As such, we encourage you to provide us with new information as we continue to update the Iowa bank note census. Your contribution and support is greatly appreciated. We hope you enjoy the book.

Contents

Dedication i
Acknowledgements ii
About the Authors iii
Foreword iv
Preface v
Chapter One
    Introduction 1
        William R. Higgins, Jr. 1
        The Higgins Museum 1
        The Census and Book Project 2
Chapter Two
    Survival and Recovery 5
        Sentimental Keepsakes 5
        The Bayard Hoard 5
        The Oat Bin Hoard 6
        The Estherville Hoard 7
        The Davenport Bank & Trust Accumulation 9
        The "first" Lazy Deuce 9
Chapter Three
    A Census of Iowa National Bank Notes and their Banks 11
Chapter Four
    Summary and Analysis of the Census 157
        Type Notes 157
        Treasury Signatures and Friedberg Numbers 158
        Varieties 159
        Banks, Towns, and Counties 160
Chapter Five
    Illustrations of Iowa National Bank notes 165
Chapter Six
    The Abram Rutt National Bank of Casey 197
Chapter Seven
    Nevada's Bank Holiday 201
Chapter Eight
    Non-issuing Iowa National Banks 203
Chapter Nine
    Index to Bank Officers 207

Chapter One
Introduction

The national banking system had been established by the National Currency Act of Feb. 25, 1863, to provide a ready market for United States bonds issued to finance the Civil War and to provide a soundly based circulating currency that could replace the more or less insecure jumble of state and local issues then in circulation. The resulting National Bank Note issues became the country's effective circulating currency during the fifty-year period from the Civil War to World War I.

No state in the nation hosted more National Bank Note issuing banks on a per capita basis than did Iowa. It provided the preeminent example of main street, or hometown banking, in the words of the late John Hickman, a leading cataloger and dealer in National Bank Note issues, who trumpeted the merits of the notes as "history in your hand." Hickman spent 20 years in service to the Higgins Museum, from 1975 to 1995, initially in the capacity of acquisitions agent and subsequently as curator of the collection.

William R. Higgins, Jr.
The Higgins Museum stands as a legacy of the late William R. Higgins, Jr. (1913 to 1991) who grew up in Clay and Dickinson counties and who served as mayor of Okoboji for 14 years from 1960 to 1974. Over a three decade span from the early 1940s to the early 1970s his collecting interest was focused on silver dollar size coins of the world, building the world's largest such collection in private hands. His 7,000 coin collection was auctioned in 1973 and 1974, with the proceeds from the sales providing the funding to build the collections which provided the nucleus for the opening of the Museum in 1978.

While Higgins' interests were focused on the National Bank Note issues of Iowa, he actively accumulated notes from the adjoining states of Minnesota and Missouri as well. The Museum's holdings and displays today also feature significant representations for the states of Nebraska and South Dakota. Special displays incorporated in the Museum include a collection of 1902 Red Seal issues featuring one of these rare issues from each state, a comprehensive presentation of the types and denominations of issue for the National Bank Note series, and representative notes issued in U.S. territories, other states, the District of Columbia and Puerto Rico.

Bill Higgins (left, below) developed many lasting friendships through the years, one of the most enduring of which was with Ronald Reagan that spanned nearly 60 years. He became acquainted with Reagan, then an announcer at WHO radio, while attending Drake University in the early 1930s, where friends knew them as "Spook" and "Dutch." Fifty years later, President Reagan arranged for the Bureau of Engraving and Printing to loan one of their historic antique *spider* currency printing presses for display at the Higgins Museum.

The Higgins Museum
Visitors to the Higgins Museum at 1507 Sanborn Ave., Okoboji, Iowa have the opportunity to view and enjoy the largest collection of National Bank Note issues on permanent exhibit anywhere in the country. The Museum opened in 1978; its stated purpose being the acquisition, preservation and display of the notes, related artifacts

and pertinent reference materials relating to the National Bank Note issuance era for educational purposes.

Development of the Higgins Museum has been focused on the issues of Iowa and its adjacent states. The Iowa galleries display the most complete state collection of National Bank Note issues ever assembled for a major state, with 278 of the state's 300 communities of issue represented. The first National Bank to open for business anywhere in the country, on June 29, 1863, was the First National Bank of Davenport, assigned charter number 15 based on its June 22, 1863, organization date; 495 banks were subsequently chartered in Iowa, with every one of the 99 counties boasting at least one.

Among the featured displays in the lobby area is one dedicated to the first and last notes issued under the laws that authorized National Bank Note issuance. A vintage bank teller cage built by a Charles City, Iowa bank equipment manufacturer is also set up in the lobby, having been restored to its century old original quality. Other major relics of the hometown bank note era on display include an original bullet safe that served the First National Bank of Everly from 1905 to 1933, a bank signature printing and note cutting device employed at the First National Bank of Mason City for preparing notes for circulation, a vault door from the First National Bank of Iowa City, a spider printing press and an outstanding display of Iowa bank and main street photo postcards.

The Iowa display is replete with rare and unusual offerings. They include the only known $100 First Charter note for Iowa, issued by the Des Moines National Bank, and the unusual Series of 1875 *Black Charter* $5 note from the First National Bank of Red Oak. There are also unique notes from Dike, Ida Grove, Lineville, Renwick and Richland, along with the only known notes to have survived from the banks in Blanchard and Lansing. The museum's holdings also include one of only two known surviving notes from the banks in Belmond, Corwith, Hudson and Lisbon. Then, there is the Third Charter, Plain Back uncut sheet of $5 notes from the Marion County National Bank of Knoxville, a unique presentation sheet bearing representative signatures of all the bank's officers.

Perhaps the most significant National Bank Note displayed at the Higgins Museum is the $100 issue of The First National Bank of Spirit Lake. Higgins' opportunity to purchase this note from Amon Carter in 1972, at the urging of John Hickman, was instrumental in his decision to form a collection of Iowa National Bank Note issues, a development that ultimately led to the establishment of the William R. Higgins, Jr. Foundation and the building of this museum to share his acquisitions and love of the hometown bank note era with others. The only known Second Charter $100 note to have survived on this bank, it was once held in the incredible Albert Grinnell Collection that was dispersed by auction in 1945 and 1946. At that time it was among the most expensive regular issue National Bank Note offerings sold, being hammered at $135, an astounding price at the time. This note is illustrated in our chapter of color illustrations.

The Census and Book Project

The Board of Directors of the Higgins Museum and Foundation decided to embark on a substantial project to preserve and extend our knowledge of the National Bank system in Iowa. John Hickman had pioneered this area with his detailed record keeping of then-known Iowa notes and his publications which led to a blossoming of interest in the field. The Board decided to obtain and publish an up-to-date census of Iowa notes and related information on Iowa National Banks. They secured the invaluable cooperation of all the major collectors of Iowa notes who each contributed information on notes with which they were familiar. Also, dealers and other authors were very helpful in supplying information on Iowa notes. Advertising and canvassing collectors yielded additional previously unknown notes. The result of an intensive six-year campaign to identify notes has produced the current census of 11,058 notes. This is the most complete census ever compiled of any state's notes. The total is more than twice as large as John Hickman's original census, and almost forty percent greater than another recently published census.

This book also provides vignettes on the history of many notes and banks, as well as data on the notes that each bank originally issued. An important and unique feature is the inclusion of the officers of each bank and their tenure. Two bank officers signed each note, and the inclusion of their names will enable much historical research. The names of the officers are fully indexed to provide easy access.

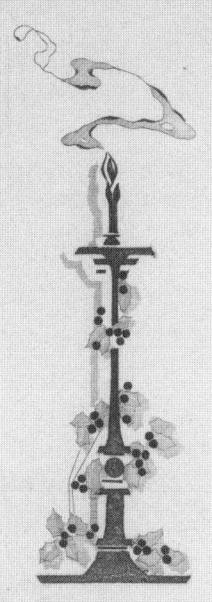

The Officers and Directors
of
The First National Bank
Elkader, Iowa
extend to their depositors and friends
a Merry Christmas and a
Happy New Year

Chapter Two
Survival and Recovery

The survival of so many national bank notes is rather remarkable. Why do such large numbers of these flimsy pieces of paper exist today? Each note that we hold in our hands has a story to tell of its travels through time and space, if only we could learn it. Some notes were saved for sentimental reasons, others because of distrust of the banking system, and more because of government efforts to increase that trust through its regulatory system. We present here some anecdotes about the survival of Iowa notes to provide a background for those interested in the history of these fascinating objects.

Sentimental Keepsakes

Bankers were proud of the notes their banks issued. For many bank founders it was a significant personal achievement to organize and operate their banks. Also, every note was personally signed by two bank officers. Notes were saved by bankers or their families as mementoes of their accomplishments. Even today, descendants of bankers may still hold dear an old note that a grandfather or great-grandfather may have signed, and some of these may be rare notes of which the collecting community is unaware. One example is a Crisp Uncirculated $10 1902 Plain Back note found in the estate of the daughter of Laverne A. Erickson, an assistant cashier of the First National Bank of Newell, #10191. The family stated that it was the only note that Mr. Erickson had been allowed to sign. Many existing serial number 1 notes were saved for similar reasons. A different kind of keepsake is represented by an Original Series ace from the First National Bank of Elkader, #1815. A family member found a leather bag nailed to the back of his great-grandmother's bedstead. In the bag was the banknote and a lock of hair. The family member speculated that the lock of hair was from his great-grandmother's nine-year old son who died in 1871, the same year that the note was issued, and that somehow the note was connected to the event.

Hoards

Citizens had learned hard lessons over the previous century that banks were a dangerous place to keep your life's savings. Even after the advent of the Federal Deposit Insurance Corporation in 1933, many people did not trust bank deposits to keep their money safe. Some individuals kept substantial amounts of cash in safety deposit boxes. When these boxes would be opened after the owner's death, national bank notes would be among the valuables found. Other people wanted nothing to do with a bank and used their ingenuity to safeguard their assets, hiding cash where no one would find it and sometimes taking their secret to the grave. Fortunately, a few of these hoards have been recovered.

The Bayard Hoard

> "Twelve hearts pounded and 24 hands dug feverishly into the damp earth Tuesday morning after a couple of Bayard 'Space Cadets' struck gold on the property owned by Fred and Ella Beardsley.
> It was the first day of vacation (June 1) and the twelve neighborhood kids had started their summer project of building a clubhouse and space laboratory. At almost 11:30 a.m. Marty Nissen and Rusty McAlister struck something hard. When they dug it out, they discovered a jar full of money.
> They were joined then by other club members and before they were through digging they had uncovered five jars filled with money and other containers with old coins and paper money.
> The money was turned over to local authorities and Wednesday morning (June 2) a count was made of the find. Face value of the hidden treasure was $11,585.51"

The above paragraphs were taken from the Bayard News, Bayard, Guthrie County, Iowa, Thursday, June 3, 1965.

The property had been sold after the death of Ella Beardsley who walked in front of a Milwaukee freight train January 29, 1958. The house and out buildings had been torn down and cleared but the foundation of the garage was not disturbed and it was under the flooring of the garage that the boys made their discovery.

There were twelve boys in all, including several brothers. The find included gold coins $2 1/2 to $20 and silver dollars down to pennies. The latest coin was a 1937 cent. The paper money was large size and small size, a lot of it being gold certificates and federal reserve notes both large and small. There were twenty-four Buffalo bills, one Indian Head bill, one 1923 Lincoln bill, and a lot of national bank notes.

Several claims were made against the cash, including the Red Cross as they were one of the beneficiaries of the original estate. Public opinion ran high in favor of the boys and over the next year all claims were dropped. The boys would get all the proceeds. The sale was held on November 2, 1968.

Boys Hidden Treasure Auction
BAYARD, IOWA
AMERICAN LEGION HALL
November 2, 1968
10:00 A. M. CST   Lunch on Grounds
By District Court Decree

One of the main problems was that the notes were soft and damp when found. The authorities who had the notes wouldn't talk to collectors about the notes or show them the notes. They were locked away. In three years the notes that were rolled up together became dry and brittle. I remember John Hickman telling me that if they had just unrolled the notes and dried each one, most would have been okay; but as it was, many lost pieces or split.

Pages 4 and 5 of the sale listed forty-two national bank notes. Nine of these were Iowa's. These were listed alone. Pages 12, 13, and 14 were National Bank notes listed "with numismatic value" so these were the better condition notes. Eighty-one notes were listed on these pages with forty-six being Iowa notes. There were only five $5 nationals and sixteen 1929 nationals in the hoard. The notes listed on pages 4 and 5 were notes that dried out still rolled up. When they were flattened to put in holders, pieces of the notes fell off. Others cracked and shed corners or edges. After the sale a cigar box of pieces was sent to the federal reserve for redemption value. Probably a few puzzle piece notes were contained in the box, along with fragments of many other notes. The Treasury Department sent a check for $1,608.00. for these pieces.

The day of the sale arrived; and although I did not attend, I've talked with several who did. The sale was well attended. There was standing room only as it started. Almost without exception the coins, especially, and the notes sold at prices almost precluding any collectors from buying. The total amount raised from the sale was $16,168.00, A judge's decree divided the money three ways. Forty percent went to the boys, thirty percent to the property owners, and thirty percent to the heir of Miss Beardsley, the former owner. Each of the eleven boys received a check for $478.35, and Iowa National Bank Note collectors had a newly discovered group of 50+ notes to appreciate over the years.

Pictured above is a unique $10 1902 Red Seal note from the Citizens National Bank of Guthrie Center that was recovered in the Bayard hoard. Its poor condition is typical of many of the notes.
by Dean Oakes

The Oat Bin Hoard

The Oat Bin Hoard was brought to numismatic attention by Howard Carter, M.D. "Doc" Carter lived in a suburb of Kansas City but had his practice in the small town of Hamilton, Missouri. He was a collector of Missouri national bank notes and president of the Kingston Bank at Kingston, MO. In this position he became known to many fellow bankers as someone to contact if old types of currency were found in an estate. Dr. Carter died in April 1974.

Dr. Carter received a call from a fellow banker in 1966 about a cash hoard that had just been brought in to the bank. Some of the bills were so worn that they would have to be turned in "if the Federal Reserve would even take them." Doc related that he seldom cancelled appointments but that morning he did. He assured the banker he would be at his bank later in the day and he would help determine which notes should be kept and which should be turned in. "Some of the notes were very old, if indeed real, and some had a smell to them," were the closing remarks of that conversation. Dr. Carter must have been as amazed as many of us were who later looked at this accumulation of old "horse blanket" bills.

Doc said that when he arrived at the bank, he was greeted and taken to a back room where, on a table, were various small to large stacks of currency. At first glance, he noted some were new and these were National Bank Notes. Other notes were dirty and almost oval in shape from wear. Lying on the table beside the older bills was an old money belt.

The banker said that they had hired some men to clean up the farmstead of an estate they were settling near Lone Jack, MO, which is about 25 miles southeast of Kansas City. Most of the buildings on the farm were falling down and the men were going through and cleaning anything of use out of there. A few sheds had been pushed over and burned. They had been working on a building built to hold small bins of grain and one bin was full of oats. It looked as though it had been there a number of years from the appearance of the grain. They were scooping the oats out by hand onto a wagon and as they were working one fellow hit something with a scoop, and pulling oats away from it, saw that it was a large crock with a lid still on it He tipped the crock over and as the oats spilled out they found a large container. It was full of what looked like rolls of paper, but it was U.S. paper money, some over one hundred years old. Also present was an old money belt, well worn and containing more bills than it was design to hold. Having so many bills in the belt resulted in the outside notes, five or six deep, being worn into an oval from the friction of the leather against the paper. The men brought the money to the banker with the explanation, "Look what we found in that old oat bin at the farm."

THE OAT BIN HOARD WAS DISCOVERED. Dr. Carter never said what he paid for the notes which had about $40,000 face value, but it must have been only a small percentage over face as some notes had to be redeemed because of their poor condition. In the hoard were 954 notes, all but 25 in large size. There were 482 national bank notes from about 37 different states and Washington D.C., as well as 3 territorial notes. Missouri and Kansas accounted for 229, twenty-five of which were consecutively numbered. Eleven large sized notes were from Iowa. Face value of all the nationals was nearly $29,000. There were one hundred fifteen first charter notes with a face value of $1,475, thirty-nine second charter notes of face value $545, three hundred twenty-nine third charter notes with a face value of nearly $14,000 and an uncut sheet of 1929 notes. The $500 Gallatin and $1,000 Morris U.S. notes of 1862 were the key notes in the hoard and both are unique. They were described by Dr. Carter as having good color and were in fine to very fine condition. He valued them at three times face value in 1967; the $1,000 note, Fr. 186c, sold at auction in October 2005 for $747,000.

Legal tender notes consisted of series 1862 (31), 1869 (85), 1878 (16), 1880 (61), and 1907 (3). There were 29 Buffalo notes.. Silver certificates were Series 1878 (1), 1880 (29), 1886 (42), 1891 (45) and 1923 (11). Gold certificates were series 1882 (8), 1905 (3), 1906 (3), 1907 (46), 1913 (1), 1922 (16), and 1928 (19). There were 13 Coin notes, series 1890 and 1891. The condition of the notes varied from a surprising XF and UNC on down.

Key Iowa notes in the hoard included a Jewell Junction $20 Plain Back now in the Higgins Museum and shown in our color illustrations, $5 Original notes from the FNBs of Clarinda and Washington, a $10 Original from Burlington (see color illustrations), and a $50 1902 Date Back from Marshalltown.

by Larry Miller and Dean Oakes

The Estherville Hoard

In 1985 I had the 'Thrill of a Lifetime', as far as a collector of national currency is concerned. Most collectors of all types of financial papers no doubt have fond memories of discovering a hoard or accumulation of various size and worth. The hoard of currency described here is the largest of which I am aware to surface in Iowa in recent times. The hoard, which I shall call the Estherville Hoard, is named for the northwest Iowa city of 7500 where the collection rested for the past six decades. Credit for the modern-day discovery of this group lies with John Hickman and the Higgins Museum in nearby Okoboji. In the summer of 1979, John was the guest of honor on a local talk radio program. One of the moderator's questions concerned what note representing a missing town was most wanted by the Higgins Museum. John replied that several northwest Iowa towns were not represented, but one of the closest and most important was Estherville. This was understandable as The First National Bank of Estherville, #4700, only issued $50 & $100 large size notes in the second and third charter periods before failing in early 1926. To drive home his point, John offered a $500 cash reward for anyone who could produce one of the elusive Estherville bank notes.

On that fateful day in the summer of 1979, John's comments were heard by an elderly farmer on a tractor radio in the field. He subsequently made contact with Mr. Hickman, only to ask "How much would you pay to see TWO Estherville national bank notes?" The Higgins Museum was able the following year to purchase the two Estherville notes, but little else, from the elderly farmer, Fred Clayton. Several rare Iowa notes, including two red seals, and the scarce Colusa, California, large size note pictured on p. 68 of the *Standard Catalog of National Banks*, by Hickman & Oakes, were sold at this time, serving to drive the imaginations of those knowing of this hoard wild wondering what else was there. The large bank box was never inventoried by knowledgeable collectors, and with Mr. Clayton's death a couple years later, the fate of this hoard was uncertain. Nothing happened until May, 1985, when the bank and heirs to the estate decided to obtain bids on the value of the 'old currency', as they referred to it.

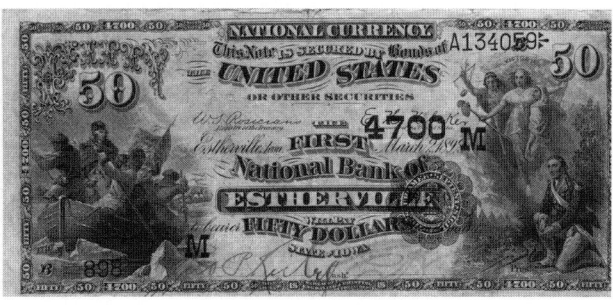

On the evening of May 8, 1985, I returned home from another currency 'research' trip, following up on a lead in another part of the state, to be greeted by my wife's telephone message about a banker calling with a hoard of over $13,000 face value in large size bills, and would I be interested? Lets just say I made short order of establishing a time to view the collection.

On the day I was finally able to view the hoard in its entirety, a funny sense of relief came over me. We collectors would now know what was, or more significantly, was NOT in this hoard. Little time was available then, however, for celebration, as I had to prepare to bid against a couple long-time friends and 'Kings' of national currency, John Hickman and Dean Oakes. Patience and perseverance paid off the Friday before the Memphis show when I finally was able to acquire this accumulation.

So, what was represented in this currency? As far as we can tell, it represents money in circulation in northwest Iowa during the period from about World War I until about 1928. The total face value of the hoard was $13,628.00. Taking out the small size currency, which comprised $2215, gave a breakdown of the large horse blanket currency as follows:

Silver Certificates $1, 2 and 5 .... $533.00
Legal Tender & Fed. Reserve Bk. notes ... $605.00
Gold Certificates $10,20 & 50 .... $2130.00
Federal Reserve Notes $5, 10 & 20 .... $3800.00
National Bank Notes $5, 10, 20 ....$4345.00

The hoard represented the complete spectrum of grades. There were many uncirculated and about uncirculated Silver Certificates and Federal Reserve Notes, but vast majority were dirty and soiled and grading fine or less. More exciting to an Iowa national bank note collector such as myself was the breakdown of the National Bank Note group.

The National section consisted of 73 - $5 bills, 170.- $10 bills and 114 - $20 bills. Of that total, seventeen fives, ninety two tens and fifty three twenties were Iowa nationals. Not bad! Another statistic was interesting. From this group, thirty seven different states were represented. However, from a type standpoint, there were no first charters and no hundred dollar denominations. Out of the 357 pieces of nationals, only six Red Seals, plus the three previously sold in 1980, for a total of nine, were present. That should say something about the relative rarity of Red Seals! The $10 red seal from Deep River, Iowa, is only the fifth note known note from this east-central Iowa town and the only Red Seal on the bank. Several scarce and desirable out-of-state notes were also in the hoard.

The owner of this currency was given the money upon the passing of his mother in the late 1920's. She and her husband had sold cream, eggs, and produce in the area for many years. Many rural Iowa bank failures occurred during the early to mid-1920's, no doubt creating a distrust of banks in the elder Mr. and Mrs. Clayton's minds. A sad portion of this story involves a robbery at the time this currency was being accumulated. Thieves robbed the husband and wife, severely beat him, but failed to locate the cash stored in a flour sack in the pantry. The elder Mr. Clayton died a week later from the injuries and complications suffered in the beating. Apparently the couple was known to local residents as a source for loans, at moderate interest, and therefore the dishonest also knew of this currency. When the elder Mrs. Clayton passed this money on to her young son, he apparently kept it for reasons unknown, but a few years afterward, with Roosevelt's call-in of gold and gold certificates, Fred Clayton apparently became reluctant to touch this hoard. Just a few years before his death, in 1980, he was under the impression it was highly illegal to own or even show gold certificates. John Hickman and I both feel that the presence of the gold certificates 'saved' this entire hoard for collectors today and in the future to appreciate.

Working with such a group of notes gives me a real sense of appreciation. Appreciation for the quirks of fate to allow me to handle such a hoard, appreciation for the sacrifices others in the past made for the money, and most importantly, an appreciation for the need or duty to preserve notes for others to enjoy in the future. It has been said that we really do not own collectables such as coins and currency, but merely are safekeepers for posterity. I agree with that premise, and hope we all take the job seriously.
by Don Mark.

The Davenport Bank & Trust Accumulation

The Davenport Bank & Trust Co. coin and cash accumulation was sold with the bank assets to Northwest Bank in 1992. Thus ended the chairmanship and ownership of V. O. Figgie and his family. Mr. Figgie had guided the bank for sixty years to its status of the largest private bank in the state of Iowa.

Of interest to collectors of U.S. Currency and National Bank notes is that the cash accumulation held many rare bank notes, especially in the $5,000 face value representing the cash reserve of the First National Bank of Davenport. These notes were in bank straps dated 1868-1871 with a pin holding each band together. About five Fr. #61 came from that group. A major rarity was the $20 Santa Barbara, California Gold Bank note.

Iowa National Bank note collectors will appreciate that the $100 Red Seal notes of the First National Bank of Davenport were in these cash holdings. I can only assume that when the assets of the Charter 15 were obtained many of the bank's Red Seal $100's had been held out by the bank as they passed through their hands and put in vault cash. Along with the $100's were a single $50 and $20 Red Seal and about thirty De Witt, Iowa $10 Red Seals. (Our census currently lists only three of these De Witt Red Seals plus one from the Bayard hoard.) All these notes had seen circulation, unlike the 1929 issue that had been held and never issued. Several # 1 Charter 15 notes were among the 1929 issue.

I was able to determine from a letter with the notes that two Davenport residents and collectors had on occasion bought notes out of this vault cash. This ended in the 1950's but not before a few of the $100 Red Seals were offered to collectors.

The dispersal of this great accumulation of bank notes was one of the last great bank holdings of heretofore unknown notes. Included beside the $50 Red Seal was the unique Brighton, Iowa National. Several $50 & $100 Blue Seal notes on Charter 15 were also in the group. Approximately $100,000 of face value of notes was included.

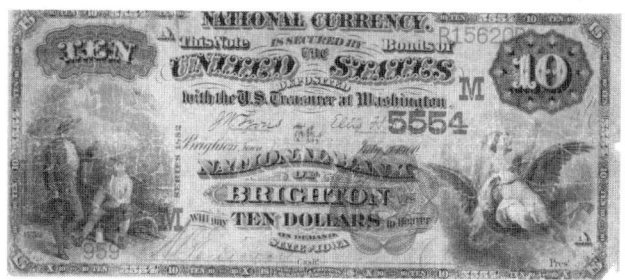

I'm sure that the cashier noted and laid aside notes that were unusual as they came in after banks reopened in 1933 and on. These notes were then compared and the common notes were discretely sold. When the vault cash was dispersed there were no common notes in any quantity in the holdings. The cash contained a rather complete type set of notes that may have been started in the later 1890's. Several banks did do this to have an example of real notes in case of being offered a counterfeit note. National bank notes as such were not collected by the bank as I assume they were too common. Only notes of different types were kept. I assume that notes that came in during the late 1930's and war years were kept as their appearance became less frequent. Notes of the new series 1928 were kept with foresight to the future. Although it is not known who had the collector's instinct to keep these notes, we have V. O. Figgie to thank for holding it together for our collecting enjoyment.
by Dean Oakes

The "first" Lazy Deuce

The Lazy Deuce, or $2 note, from Iowa has not been known to collectors for a very long time. Thinking about that fact I remember a meeting of the Iowa Numismatic Association in Cedar Rapids, I believe, in October 1965. After the show closed at probably 7 or 8 p.m., several of us went over to the Flame Room, a steak restaurant near the hotel, for our evening meal. There were six or seven dealers at the table including myself, Glenn Wright, John Hickman, and Ben Marlenee. The talk of course was about the events of the day. National Bank notes of Iowa came up and John was expounding on the various towns that he had seen notes from. I would always remind John that collecting by type was the easy way to go. It was interesting, you only needed 32 or so types, it was easier as competition was less, and you ended up with all the designs. John would reply that collecting by county or notes from your home county would be the way to go. Anyhow, at some point the Lazy Deuce from Iowa was mentioned. Now it was well known among Iowa collectors of Nationals that no one knew of a Lazy Deuce. Harold Baker had never seen one, Bill Fisher had never seen one (both Iowa National collectors going back into the 1950's). It was only speculation that it even existed. At about that time Glenn Wright said, "I believe I have one," and John, without a pause, threw out his bank bag and said, "I'll bet you don't." After all, who was this young kid, just out of college, not known for collecting currency anyway? Glenn replied that no, he wouldn't bet that amount whatever it was, it was John's bankroll, but he would bet $20. John accepted and Glenn reached in his suit pocket and extracted a limp, very well used $2 note on The First National Bank of Davenport, #15, serial no. 95 A. John looked it over and I'm sure exclaimed a few choice words upon realizing that he had been a victim of his own doing. Memories of 40-plus years are not too clear but I think John said then and later, "I would have paid $20 just to see a Lazy Two from Iowa."

This bet came about because Glenn had purchased this note at a small show in Muscatine, Iowa a few weeks before and, as he was working for my shop, A&A Coins, Inc., brought the note back for inventory. As I remember it, he asked to borrow the note for the evening at the Iowa show and of course it hadn't been shown or talked about. After that evening Glenn did purchase the note for his collection.

Since then of course many Iowa Two's have found their way to Iowa collectors. Harold Baker did indeed buy two or three pieces from Amon Carter who had acquired them from the Harley Freeman collection of First Charter notes. I will bet that in forty more years we will not double the known number of Two's known on Iowa.
by Dean Oakes

Chapter Three
A Census of Iowa National Bank Notes and their Banks

This chapter presents detailed information about all 11,058 known Iowa National Bank notes and the banks that issued them. Data for each bank includes: in bold print, the bank title, number of known large and small size notes, charter number, and county. Following that are organizational data, bank officers (President, Vice-President, Cashier, and Assistant Cashier), and serial number ranges of the types of notes each bank issued. Designations such as 10-10-10-20 or 6-10's indicate the number and denomination of notes in each sheet printed.

Finally the census of each of the known notes from the bank is listed. The census includes charter number, region letter "M", denomination, note type, Friedberg number, bank plate or serial number including plate position letter, treasury serial number, condition, and comments. The note types are designated as follows: ORIG and 1875 for Original Series and Series of 1875; 1882BB, 1882DB, 1882VB for Series of 1882 Brown Backs, Date Backs, and Value Backs, respectively; and 1902RS, 1902DB, 1902PB for Series of 1902 Red Seals, Date Backs, and Plain Backs, respectively.

Comments include notes on the bank officers' signatures, such as whether they are in pen or stamped, faded or gone, asst. cashier or vice-president; special conditions such as stains or missing corners; and information on the prior or current ownership that may be of interest to the reader. These pedigrees include notes currently in the Higgins Museum, Federal Reserve Bank collections, or the Smithsonian Institution, as well as notes that were in the Grinnell collection auctions, Bayard hoard, Oat Bin hoard, and the Davenport Bank & Trust holdings.

Caution should be used when interpreting the note conditions and comments recorded here because they reflect the varying standards of many contributors over more than thirty years. Data on the range of serial numbers issued were taken with permission from Hickman/Oakes "Standard Catalog of National Bank Notes" published by Krause Publications and from information provided by Peter Huntoon.

THE FIRST NATIONAL BANK OF ACKLEY   16 L   12 S
8762   HARDIN
Organized on May 30, 1907 with a capital of $50,000. Placed in receivership on August 10, 1932 with a capital of $50,000.
Officers: Pres. John C Lusch 1908-10, SY Eggert 1911-26, FE Trainer 1927-32; **VP** SY Eggert 1909-10, Fred E Trainer 1922-26; **Cash.** SY Eggert 1908-10, SS Trainer 1911-32; **AC** SS Trainer 1909-10, Fred S Eggert 1911-32, GL Heney 1927-32.

Third Charter, Red Seal	Ser #	# Notes
10-10-10-20	1-360	1,080
Third Charter, Date Back, Blue Seal		
10-10-10-20	1-1600	6,400

Sheets numbered 1 to 1400 were 02-08 backs. Sheets numbered 1401 to 1600 were delivered on November 4, but no year given. Sheets numbered 1601 to 2908 were plain back blue seals.

Third Charter, Plain Back, Blue Seal		
10-10-10-20	1601-2908	5,232
1929, Type 1		
6-10's	1-294	1,764
6-20's	1-78	468

Total amount of issued = $190,400. Large outstanding at close = $16,390.
13,072 Large   2,232 Small   15,304 Total

Charter	Reg	Denom	Type	Fr#	Plate/Ser #	Treasury #	Cond	Comments
8762	M	$20	1902DB	644	1046 B	T491090A	VG	stain on face
8762	M	$10	1902PB	626	2146 E	E801138E	CU	Higgins Museum
8762	M	$10	1902PB	626	2146 F	E801138E	F	
8762	M	$10	1902PB	626	2147 F	E801139E	CU	stamp/stamp
8762	M	$10	1902PB	626	2217 F	E801209E	AU	stamp/stamp
8762	M	$10	1902PB	626	2219 D	E801211E	AU+	
8762	M	$10	1902PB	626	2220 D	E801212E	CU	
8762	M	$10	1902PB	626	2267 D	E801259E	AU	stamp/stamp
8762	M	$10	1902PB	626	2268 D	E801260E	XF+	stamps Pinholes
8762	M	$10	1902PB	626	2269 F	E801261E	CU	
8762	M	$10	1902PB	626	2286 F	E801278E	CU	
8762	M	$10	1902PB	626	2287 F	E801279E	XF	
8762	M	$10	1902PB	626	2480 E	A317712H	VG+	faded/faded
8762	-	$10	1902PB	626	2673 D	2673 D	XF	stamp/stamp
8762	-	$10	1902PB	626	2673 F	2673 F	XF	
8762	-	$20	1902PB	652	2766 B	2766 B	F	
8762		$10	1929T1		D000011A		F	
8762		$10	1929T1		C000033A		F	
8762		$10	1929T1		A000046A		VG	
8762		$10	1929T1		C000148A		F/VF	Higgins Mus.
8762		$10	1929T1		A000160A		VF	
8762		$10	1929T1		D000165A		F	
8762		$10	1929T1		A000239A		XF	
8762		$10	1929T1		E000241A		CU	
8762		$10	1929T1		F000275A		G/VG	
8762		$20	1929T1		E000010A		F	
8762		$20	1929T1		A000048A		AU	
8762		$20	1929T1		E000069A		G	

FIRST NATIONAL BANK OF ADAIR   0 L
8699   ADAIR
Banknote proofs and the original charter demonstrate that the above bank title is correct. Previously published listings erroneously included the word "The" in the title.
Organized on April 29, 1907 with a capital of $25,000. Placed in receivership on December 27, 1926; capital of $35,000. Reason for failure: incompetent management & local depression.
Officers: Pres. MH Welton 1908-16, ML McManus 1917-25, FL Miller 1925-26; **VP** Thos. Robinson 1909-10, ML McManus 1910-19, HC Westergaard 1920-25, Ernest Freese 1925-1926; **Cash.** Roy R Welton 1908-1915, MI Westergaard 1916-26; **AC** DH Mueller 1909-10, JF McManus 1911-26

Third Charter, Red Seal	Ser #	# Notes
5-5-5-5	1-156	624
10-10-10-20	1-125	500
Third Charter, Date Back, Blue Seal		
5-5-5-5	1-700	2,800
10-10-10-20	1-560	2,240
Third Charter, Plain Back, Blue Seal		
5-5-5-5	701-1249	2,196
10-10-10-20	561-907	1,388

Total amount issued = $79,700. Amount outstanding at close = $8,750.
9,748 Large   0 Small   9,748 Total

THE FIRST NATIONAL BANK OF ADEL   18 L
8981   DALLAS
Chartered in January 1908 with a capital of $50,000. Placed in voluntary liquidation on August 7, 1928; capital of $50,000. Absorbed by the Adel State Bank, Adel.
Officers: Pres. J. W. Russell 1908-14, Wm. Roberts 1915-28; **VP** D.A. Blanchard 1909-19, D.E. King 1920-23, Lloyd R. Roberts 1924-28; **Cash.** Wm. Roberts 1908-14, Lloyd R. Roberts 1915-28; **AC** V.M. Miller 1909-13,

D.R. Roberts 1909-10, Lloyd R.Roberts 1914-21, C.E. Russell 1922-28.

Third Charter, Red Seal	Ser #	# Notes
5-5-5-5	1-300	1,200
10-10-10-20	1-240	960
Third Charter, Date Back, Blue Seal		
5-5-5-5	1-3400	13,600
10-10-10-20	1-2500	10,000
Third Charter, Plain Back, Blue Seal		
5-5-5-5	3401-9395	23,980
10-10-10-20	2501-6528	16,112

Total amount issued = $532,300. Amount outstanding in 1928 = $50,000.

65,852 Large   0 Small   65,852 Total

8981	M	$5 1902RS	589	96 C	R892214	VF	gone Higg. Mus.
8981	M	$5 1902DB	592	2698 F	U552235A	G	gone Soiling
8981	M	$5 1902PB	601	5510 H	R689396D	G/VG	
8981	M	$5 1902PB	601	6264 F	B294660E	F+	faded/faded
8981	M	$5 1902PB	601	6982 G	U754463E	AU	
8981	M	$5 1902PB	601	6983 G	U754464E	CU	gone/gone
8981	M	$5 1902PB	601	7489 E	D873925H	?	gone/gone
8981	M	$5 1902PB	601	7490 E	D873926H	CU	gone/gone
8981	M	$10 1902PB	626	2881 E	V493931B	F	stamp/stamp
8981	M	$10 1902PB	626	3081 F	A890958D	XF	
8981	-	$10 1902PB	626	5309 F	V17861H	F	faded/faded
8981	-	$10 1902PB	626	5574 E	A73556K	CU	gone/gone
8981	-	$10 1902PB	626	5575 F	A73557K	CU	gone Higg. Mus.
8981	-	$10 1902PB	626	6219 F	6219 F	VF	
8981	M	$20 1902PB	652	3120 B	A890997D	VG	faded Resigned
8981	-	$20 1902PB	652	5582 B	A73564K	?	Bayard
8981	-	$20 1902PB	652	5644 B	?	G	
8981	-	$20 1902PB	652	6333 B	6333 B	VG/F	gone/gone

THE FIRST NATIONAL BANK OF AFTON 0 L
2326   UNION

Chartered on February 23, 1876 with a capital of $50,000. Placed in voluntary liquidation on August 15, 1879; capital of $50,000.

Officers: Pres. J.T. Beebe 1876-79; **Cash.** O.E. Davis 1876-79.

First Charter, Series of 1875	Ser #	# Notes
5-5-5-5	1-1505	6,020

Total amount of circulation issued = $30,100. Amount outstanding at close = $26,500. Amount outstanding in 1910 = $265.

6,020 Large   0 Small   6,020 Total

THE FIRST NATIONAL BANK OF AKRON 6 L 11 S
7322   PLYMOUTH

Organized in 1904; succeeded the Farmers Loan & Trust Co.

Officers: Pres. James F. Toy 1904-11, W.H. Eddleman 1912, James F. Toy 1913-34, Frank Wakeman 1935; **VP** M.A. Agnes 1904-08, Frank Wakeman 1908-35, H. Shoulberg 1921-22, 1928-35; **Cash.** J.H. Alexander 1906-07, Geo. C. Eyland, Jr. 1908-11, H. Shoulberg 1912-21, A.C. Hauck 1912, H. Shoulberg 1923-27, H.H. Wetzeler 1928-1935; **AC** Henning Shoulberg 1907-12, Francis J. Lorge 1911-16, Ielco Bloem 1917-19, A.L. Bennett 1920, H.H. Wetzeler 1921-27, W.E. Mellen 1928-35, W.R. Chicoine 1928-30.

Third Charter, Red Seal	Ser #	# Notes
10-10-10-20	1-307	1,228
Third Charter, Date Back, Blue Seal		
10-10-10-20	1-2400	9,600
Third Charter, Plain Back, Blue Seal		
10-10-10-20	2401-5804	13,616
1929, Type I		
6-10's	1-622	3,732
6-20's	1-212	1,272
1929, Type II		
10's	1-227	227
20's	1-56	56

Total amount issued = $371,000. Amount outstanding in 1934 = $30,000. Amount of large outstanding on July 26, 1935 = $1,760.

24,444 Large   5,287 Small   29,371 Total

7322	M	$10 1902DB	616	70 D	B15105	F	
7322	M	$10 1902DB	616	641 D	M943934	VF	pen/pen vp
7322	M	$10 1902PB	624	3987 E	U668929E	VG	pen/pen
7322	-	$10 1902PB	624	5208 F	5208 F	VF	
7322	-	$10 1902PB	624	5674 D	5674 D	CU	Higgins Mus.
7322	M	$20 1902PB	650	3441 B	A264493E	VF/XF	pen/pen
7322		$10 1929T1		C000086A		VG	
7322		$10 1929T1		A000152A		VF	Mark on face
7322		$10 1929T1		E000170A		F	
7322		$10 1929T1		F000253A		F	
7322		$20 1929T1		E000036A		VF	
7322		$20 1929T1		C000085A		VF	
7322		$20 1929T1		B000093A		VF	
7322		$20 1929T1		C000117A		VF/XF	
7322		$20 1929T1		E000117A		CU	
7322		$20 1929T1		F000117A		CU	Higgins Mus.
7322		$20 1929T1		A000152A		VF	

THE ALBIA NATIONAL BANK 0 L
3012   MONROE

Chartered in 1883. Placed in voluntary liquidation on December 16, 1884; capital of $50,000.

Officers: Pres. William Bradley 1883-84; **VP** J.R. Hays 1883-84

Second Charter, Brown Backs	Ser #	# Notes
5-5-5-5	1-562	2,248

Total amount of circulation issued = $11,240. Amount outstanding at close = $11,240. Amount outstanding in 1910 = $105.

2,248 Large   0 Small   2,248 Total

THE FIRST NATIONAL BANK OF ALBIA 10 L 5 S
1799   MONROE

Chartered on March 2, 1871. Placed in voluntary liquidation on June 18, 1930; capital of $50,000. Succeeded by the First Iowa State Bank of Albia.

Officers: Pres. John H. Drake 1872-98, F.M. Drake 1899-1902, Caroline B.Drake 1904-10, Nannie M. Mabry 1911-23, J.C. Mabry 1924-30; **VP** 1896-1901; C.B. Drake 1902-03, L.T. Richmond 1904-19, Herman Snow 1920-24, L.B. Edwards 1926-30; **Cash.** Benj. F. Elbert 1872-84, Tom D. Lockman 1885-98, L.T. Richmond 1899-1914, Roy T. Alford 1915-30; **AC** Roy T. Alford 1900-1919, F.A. Wilkinson 1920-23, Frank Wilkinson 1924-30.

First Charter, Original Issue	Ser #	# Notes
1-1-1-2	1-1500	6,000
5-5-5-5	1-1875	7,500
10-10-10-20	1-1650	6,600
First Charter, Series of 1875		
10-10-10-20	1-1026	4,104
Second Charter, Brown Backs		
50-100	1-1520	3,040
Second Charter, Date Back		
50-100	1-5	10
Third Charter, Date Back, Blue Seal		
50-50-50-100	1-920	3,680
Third Charter, Plain Back, Blue Seal		
50-50-50-100	921-1109	756
1929, Type I		
6-50's	1-58	348
6-100's	1-2	12

Total amount of circulation = $703,400. Amount of large outstanding at close = $27,750. Amount of small outstanding at close = $18,600.

31,690 Large   360 Small   32,050 Total

1799		$5	ORIG	399	1 B	H68020	F/VF	Higgins Mus.
1799		$5	ORIG	399	1 D	H68020	G	Higgins Mus.
1799	M	$50	1902DB	670	52 A	A3926	VF	ac/vp Higg. Mus.
1799	M	$50	1902DB	670	156 A	A4030	F	pen ac/pen vp
1799	M	$50	1902DB	670	207 B	A4081	F	ac/vp
1799	M	$100	1902DB	692	493 A	A778839	F	gone/gone
1799	M	$100	1902DB	692	570 A	A815192	VF	Higgins Mus.
1799	M	$100	1902DB	692	763 A	B7457	F+	faded/pen
1799	-	$50	1902PB	678	951 C	951 C	VF	Higgins Mus.
1799	-	$50	1902PB	678	1070 B	1070 B	G	UR corner gone
1799		$50	1929T1		E000002A		F	
1799		$50	1929T1		E000007A		XF	
1799		$50	1929T1		E000019A		VF/XF	
1799		$50	1929T1		D000020A		F+	Higgins Mus.
1799		$50	1929T1		B000056A		VG	

THE PEOPLES NATIONAL BANK OF ALBIA 14 L 11 S
8603   MONROE

Chartered in March 1907

Officers: Pres. Lafe S. Collins 1908-11, D.M. Anderson 1912-13, Lafe S. Collins 1914-19, J.A. Canning 1920-35, J.E. King 1935; **VP** J.S. Moon 1909-12, E.E. Elder 1913-19, A.E. Bellman 1914-27, J.T. Coady 1920-35, J.L. Reddish 1928-35; **Cash.** B.P. Castner 1908-11, J.A. Canning 1912-19, F.S. Nelsen 1920-22, E.W. Baxter 1923-35; **AC** Scott Collins 1809, E.E. Elder 1910-19, E.W. Baxter 1920-22, W.M. Peterson 1922-35, C.C. Woodcock 1929-35.

Third Charter, Red Seal	Ser #	# Notes
5-5-5-5	1-1000	4,000
10-10-10-20	1-1000	4,000
Third Charter, Date Back, Blue Seal		
5-5-5-5	1-1700	6800
10-10-10-20	1-1200	4800
Third Charter, Plain Back, Blue Seal		
5-5-5-5	1701-9192	29,968
10-10-10-20	1201-5804	18,416
1929, Type I		

6-5's	1-526	3,156
6-10's	1-262	1,572
6-20's	1-86	516
1929, Type II		
6-5's	1-842	842
6-10's	1-404	404
6-20's	1-111	111

Total amount in circulation issued = $596,330. Amount of large outstanding in 1935 = $1,920. Amount of small outstanding in 1935 = $18,080.

67,984 Large   6,601 Small   74,585 Total

8603 M	$5 1902RS 589	297 D	M210761	F	Higgins Mus.
8603 M	$20 1902DB 644	685 B	E961741A	VG/F	
8603 M	$5 1902PB 600	3083 G	Y453234B	F	
8603 M	$5 1902PB 600	4641 E	R726227D	G/VG	
8603 M	$5 1902PB 600	5006 G	R726592D	F	
8603 M	$5 1902PB 600	5676 E	B204097E	VG	Bayard
8603 M	$5 1902PB 600	8043 H	D507854H	VG	pen/pen
8603 -	$5 1902PB 600	8796 F	T327507H	VG/F	pen ac/pen
8603 -	$5 1902PB 600	9100 E	9100 E	XF	pen/pen
8603 M	$10 1902PB 626	4467 E	A964499H	VG	
8603 M	$10 1902PB 626	4795 E	E796467H	VG	Higgins Mus.
8603 -	$10 1902PB 626	5252 D	U629334H	G	pen/pen
8603 M	$20 1902PB 652	4743 B	E796415H	F	pen Tight bottom
8603 -	$20 1902PB 652	5715 B	5715 B	F	
8603	$5 1929T1	B000177A		VG/F	
8603	$5 1929T1	F000177A		F/VF	Higgins Mus.
8603	$10 1929T1	E000100A		F/VF	
8603	$10 1929T1	B000103A		VG	
8603	$10 1929T1	C000243A		VF	
8603	$20 1929T1	F000025A		F/VF	
8603	$20 1929T1	D000038A		VG	
8603	$20 1929T1	C000062A		VF	
8603	$10 1929T2	A000185		F	
8603	$20 1929T2	A000010		F/VF	
8603	$20 1929T2	A000023		VF	

THE FIRST NATIONAL BANK OF ALGONA   7 L
3197   KOSSUTH

Organized on May 15, 1884 with a capital of $50,000. Succeeded the Bank of Algona. Placed in receivership on November 24, 1924; capital of $50,000. Reason for failure: incompetent management.

Officers: **Pres**. Ambrose A Call 1884-1908, Wm. K Ferguson 1908-17; **VP** DH Hutchins 1884-1909; EE Connor 1910-13, EV Swetting 1913-17; **Cash**. Frank R Lewis 1884-85, JC Blackford 1886-91, Wm. K Ferguson 1892-1908, CA Palmer 1909-11, EE Conner 1913-16, LC Seward 1916-17; **AC** CD Smith 1896-99, CA Palmer 1900-08, EL Vincent 1913-14, OJ Stephensen 1915-17.

Second Charter, Brown Backs	Ser #	# Notes
5-5-5-5	1-4381	17,524
10-10-10-20	1-1095	4,380
Third Charter, Red Seal		
10-10-10-20	1-1700	6,800
Third Charter, Date Back, Blue Seal		
10-10-10-20	1-3460	13,840
Third Charter, Plain Back, Blue Seal		
10-10-10-20	3461-6745	13,140

Total amount issued = $564,620. Amount outstanding at close = $49,600.

55,684 Large   0 Small   55,684 Total

3197	$10 1882BB 480	609 ?	B606889B	VF/XF	
3197	$20 1882BB 494	827 A	D690693D	F/VF	Higgins Mus.
3197 M	$20 1902RS 639	86 A	B865278	VF	faded/stamp
3197 M	$20 1902RS 639	404 A	B865596	VG/F	
3197 M	$10 1902DB 616	11 E	D251792	F+	
3197 M	$10 1902DB 616	1754 E	D487125A	VG/F	
3197	$20 1902PB 650	5658 B	H127081E	G/VG	Higgins Mus.

THE FARMERS NATIONAL BANK OF ALLERTON   5 L
9231   WAYNE

Chartered in August 1908. Placed in voluntary liquidation on June 19, 1926; capital of $40,000. Absorbed by the Security State Bank of Allerton.

Officers: **Pres**. Jasper McCoy 1908-09, J.M. Shelton 1910-17, D.E. Williams 1918-24, J.E. Bracewell 1925-25; **VP** B. Bracewell 1909-19, J.W. Garratt 1920-26; **Cash**. H.B. Bracewell 1908, D.T. Sollenbarger 1909-17, H.S. Shields 1918-24, Geo. W. Cox 1925-26; **AC** R.W. Kaster 1911-19, F.H. Duncan 1920-26.

Third Charter, Date Back, Blue Seal	Ser #	# Notes
10-10-10-20	1-2350	9,400
Third Charter, Plain Back, Blue Seal		
10-10-10-20	2351-4787	9,748

Total amount issued = $239,350. Amount outstanding at close = $30,000.

19,148 Large   0 Small   19,148 Total

9231 M	$10 1902PB 626	2523 A	U372831B	VG/F	Higgins Mus.
9231 M	$10 1902PB 626	2555 A	Y332786B	VG/F	pen/pen
9231 M	$10 1902PB 626	4232 A	A226584H	VG	pen/pen Ink
9231 -	$10 1902PB 626	4771 C	B135283K	VG	pen/pen
9231 -	$10 1902PB 626	4772 A	B135284K	G	lt. pen sigs

THE FIRST NATIONAL BANK OF ALLERTON   1 L
2191   WAYNE

Chartered on September 29, 1874. Placed in voluntary liquidation on December 6, 1886; capital of $50,000.

Officers: **Pres**. William Bradley 1876-86, **VP** Tyler P. Walden 1876-86

First Charter, Original Issue	Ser #	# Notes
5-5-5-5	1-3250	13,000
First Charter, Series of 1875		
5-5-5-5	1-3057	12,228

Total amount of circulation issued = $126,140. Amount outstanding at close = $11,250. Amount outstanding in 1910 = $590.

25,228 Large   0 Small   25,228 Total

2191 -	$5 1875 . 401	65 B	B220780	F	Higgins Mus.

THE FIRST NATIONAL BANK OF ALTA   7 L
7126   BUENA VISTA

Organized on January 21, 1904 with a capital of $50,000. Placed in receivership on December 3, 1926, capital of $50,000. Reason for failure: local depression.

Officers: **Pres**. James F. Toy 1904-15, A.R. Browne 1916-22, C. Holtz 1923-26; **VP** Aaron Conner 1904-08, Geo. A. Dalziel 1909-10, W.H. Crowell 1911-12, C.C. Childs 1913-19, L.C. Anderson 1920-21, C. Holtz 1922, J.M. Rehnstrom 1923-26, Nels Anderson 1926; **Cash**. A.R. Browne 1904-1915, J.L. Reynolds 1916, A.O. Cannon 1918-19, H.F. Reeder 1920-25, H.I. Ferguson 1926; **AC** A. Gulemanson 1907-08, H.V. Chase 1909, C.M. Wolf 1911-13, F.A. Oldon 1914-19, Mildred Browne 1920-22, J.C. Lightfoot 1923-24, L.J. Larson 1923-26, C.G. Kislingbury 1926.

Third Charter, Red Seal	Ser #	# Notes
10-10-10-20	1-630	2,520
Third Charter, Date Back, Blue Seal		
10-10-10-20	1-3340	13,360

Sheets numbered 1 to 3100 were 02-08 back notes. Sheets numbered 3101 to 3340 were delivered on October 19, but not marked to type. Sheets numbered 3341 to 7757 were plain back blue seals.

Third Charter, Plain Back, Blue Seal		
10-10-10-20	3341-7757	17,668

Total amount issued = $419,350. Amount outstanding at close = $48,695.

33,548 Large   0 Small   33,548 Total

7126 M	$10 1902DB 616	331 D	D250912	VG	
7126 M	$10 1902DB 616	985 E	V698225	F	pen/pen vp
7126 M	$10 1902DB 616	2052 E	T874864A	F	
7126 M	$10 1902PB 624	4386 E	H345042D	F	
7126 M	$10 1902PB 624	4698 D	N384070D	VF	pen/pen
7126 M	$10 1902PB 624	6735 H	M950597H	VF	pen/pen
7126 M	$10 1902PB 624	6866 G	M950728H	XF	pen, Higgins Mus.

THE AMES NATIONAL BANK   14 L   12 S
10408   STORY

Chartered on June 14, 1913 with a capital of $50,000. Placed in voluntary liquidation on March 31, 1933; capital of $50,000. Absorbed by the Ames Trust & Savings Bank, Ames.

Officers: **Pres**. W.D. Meltzer 1914, H.W. Stafford 1915-33; **VP** L.B. Spinney 1914-33; **Cash**. (I.O.) H. Hasbrouck 1914, I.O. Hasbrouck 1915-21, Clay W. Stafford 1922-33; **AC** C.T. Simmon 1914-19, Clay W. Stafford 1920-21, G.R. Alley 1923-33.

Third Charter, Date Back, Blue Seal	Ser #	# Notes
10-10-10-10	1-2600	10,400
Third Charter, Plain Back, Blue Seal		

10-10-10-10		2601-12856	41,024		

1929, Type I

6-10's		1-1764	10,584	

Total amount of circulation issued = $620,080. Amount of large outstanding at close = $3,620. Amount of small outstanding at close = $46,380.

51,424 Large   10,584 Small   62,008 Total

Bank	Denom	Type	Plate	Serial	Grade	Notes
10408M	$10	1902DB	622	1168 D H632196	VG	
10408M	$10	1902DB	622	2134 C K561107	?	
10408M	$10	1902PB	630	2931 ? ?	?	
10408M	$10	1902PB	630	2938 A N439928	VG	
10408M	$10	1902PB	630	3295 A N440285	F	
10408M	$10	1902PB	630	3338 A N705428	XF	Rust spots
10408M	$10	1902PB	630	5826 B T520856	F	stamp/pen
10408M	$10	1902PB	630	7607 B V401557	F+	stamp Higg. Mus.
10408M	$10	1902PB	630	7676 A V401626	VG	
10408M	$10	1902PB	630	7764 D V401714	VG/F	pen/faded
10408 -	$10	1902PB	630	9507 A Y207102	VF	pen/pen
10408 -	$10	1902PB	630	10968 C 10968 C	F/VF	
10408 -	$10	1902PB	630	11645 C 11645 C	VG	faded/gone
10408 -	$10	1902PB	630	11748 C 11748 C	VG/F	
10408	$10	1929T1		E000151A	G	
10408	$10	1929T1		E000515A	F/VF	Higgins Mus.
10408	$10	1929T1		C000809A	F	
10408	$10	1929T1		B000847A	VF	
10408	$10	1929T1		F001085A	?	
10408	$10	1929T1		F001219A	VG	
10408	$10	1929T1		A001305A	VG/F	
10408	$10	1929T1		D001485A	F	
10408	$10	1929T1		D001536A	F	
10408	$10	1929T1		A001588A	?	
10408	$10	1929T1		E001736A	F	
10408	$10	1929T1		A001746A	VF	

THE UNION NATIONAL BANK OF AMES   18 L   10 S
3017   STORY

Chartered in 1883. Succeeded the Union Bank. Placed in voluntary liquidation on July 12, 1932; capital of $100,000. Succeeded by the Union Story Trust & Savings Bank, Ames.

Officers: **Pres**. Wallace M. Greeley 1883-1916, C.L. Siverly 1917-19, S.A. Knapp 1920-1926, J.G. Tilden 1927-31; **VP** Henry Wilson 1902, Daniel McCarthy 1903-06, E.W. Stanton 1907-21, Geo. Judisch 1920-31, Don W. Atkinson 1927-31, A.J. Martin 1928-31; **Cash**. E.R. Chamberlain 1883-94, Henry Wilson 1895-1901, G.H. Tilden 1902, Henry Wilson 1903-12, C.L. Siverly 1913-16, S.A. Knapp 1917-19, A.J. Martin 1920-27, E.J. Engelginder 1928-31; **AC** T.A. Dodds 1907-08, C.L. Siverly 1909-12, S.A. Knapp 1913, M.E. Fowler 1920-24, B.M. Wheelock 1925-31, Geo. Richardson 1930-31.

	Ser #	# Notes
Second Charter, Brown Backs		
5-5-5-5	1-3762	15,048
10-10-10-20	1-1200	4,800
Third Charter, Red Seal		
10-10-10-20	1-2000	8,000
Third Charter, Date Back, Blue Seal		
10-10-10-20	1-3540	14,160

Sheets numbered 1 to 3300 were 02-08 backs. Sheets numbered 3301 to 3540 were delivered on October 16, but not marked at to type. Sheets numbered 3541 to 10021 were plain backs.

Third Charter, Plain Back, Blue Seal

10-10-10-20	3541-10021	25,924

1929, Type I

6-10's	1-769	4,614
6-20's	1-222	1,332

Total amount of circulation issued = $809,070. Amount of large outstanding at close = $7,290. Amount of small outstanding at close = $42,710.

67,932 Large   5,946 Small   73,878 Total

Bank	Denom	Type	Plate	Serial	Grade	Notes
3017 -	$5	1882BB	467	2233 B U612034	VF	pen/pen
3017 -	$5	1882BB	467	2298 A U612099	XF	pen/pen
3017	$20	1882BB	494	197 A V886870	VF/XF	
3017	$20	1882BB	494	595 A V887268	XF	Higgins Mus.
3017 M	$10	1902DB	616	992 D N256673	VG	pen/pen
3017 M	$10	1902DB	616	1575 E Y541349	F/VF	pen/pen
3017 M	$10	1902DB	616	2483 E V154189A	F	pen/pen
3017 M	$20	1902DB	642	548 B D310309	VG/F	
3017 M	$20	1902DB	642	2508 B V154214A	VF	
3017 M	$10	1902PB	624	3673 ?	?	
3017 M	$10	1902PB	624	5133 E R908675D	VF	stamp/stamp
3017 M	$10	1902PB	624	6687 E Z274639E	F	
3017 M	$10	1902PB	624	7176 D H111948H	F	Higgins Mus.
3017 -	$10	1902PB	624	7469 E N517901H	F	stamp/stamp
3017 -	$10	1902PB	624	8099 D ?	VG	
3017 -	$10	1902PB	624	8198 D 8198 D	VF	gone Stained
3017 -	$20	1902PB	650	9833 B 9833 B	F	stamp/stamp
3017 -	$20	1902PB	650	9945 B 9945 B	VF	stamp/stamp
3017	$10	1929T1		D000001A	VG	
3017	$10	1929T1		B000306A	VG/F	
3017	$10	1929T1		E000359A	VG	
3017	$10	1929T1		F000488A	VG	
3017	$10	1929T1		A000638A	XF+	
3017	$10	1929T1		D000718A	VF	
3017	$20	1929T1		E000158A	VF	Higgins Mus.
3017	$20	1929T1		A000159A	F	
3017	?	1929T1		B000206A	?	
3017	$20	1929T1		A000219A	F	

THE ANAMOSA NATIONAL BANK   18 L   32 S
4696   JONES

Organized on February 4, 1892 with a capital of $50,000. Placed in receivership on January 27, 1932; capital of $100,000.

Officers: **Pres**. Charles H. Lull 1892-96, L. Schoonover 1897-1907, Geo. L. Schoonover 1908-24, W.N. Dearborn 1925-26; **VP** W.N. Dearborn 1896-1906, Park Chamberlain 1907-08, W.N. Dearborn 1909-24, Park Chamberlain 1909-26; **Cash**. C.B. Millard 1892-1903, Geo. L. Schoonover 1904-07, Park Chamberlain 1908-09, E. Webbles 1910-13, R.C. Walters 1914-16, C.H. Brown 1917-13, R.C. Walters 1924-26; **AC** Jno. Z. Lull 1896-98, H.D. Myrick 1902-06, J.N. Ramsey 1907-09, L.A. Miller 1920-26, C.J. Tyler 1920-25, H.H. Gee 1922.

	Ser #	# Notes
Second Charter, Brown Backs		
10-10-10-20	1-6180	24,720
Second Charter, Date Back		
10-10-10-20	1-2340	9,360
Third Charter, Date Back, Blue Seal		
10-10-10-20	1-3800	15,200
Third Charter, Plain Back, Blue Seal		
10-10-10-20	3801-16804	52,012

sheet #16446 not issued

1929, Type I

6-10's	1-1592	9,552
6-20's	1-451	2,706

Total amount of circulation issued = $1,415,840. Amount of large outstanding at close = $13,000. Amount of small outstanding at close = $85,740.

101,292 Large   12,258 Small   113,550 Total

Bank	Denom	Type	Plate	Serial	Grade	Notes
4696 M	$10	1882BB	485	6020 C V31877V	F/VF	
4696 M	$20	1882BB	499	3822 A N888507N	XF	
4696 M	$20	1882BB	499	3876 A N890661N	F	
4696 M	$20	1882BB	499	4822 A R903309R	VG	Higgins Mus.
4696 M	$10	1882DB	540	965 D B384955	VG	pen/pen
4696 M	$10	1882DB	540	2011 E E857649	F+	pen/pen
4696 M	$10	1902DB	620	2563 C U946169A	VG/F	
4696 M	$10	1902PB	628	3827 A R930806B	VF	Higgins Mus.
4696 M	$10	1902PB	628	7979 B A416136E	XF	stamp/stamp
4696 M	$10	1902PB	628	8334 A A416491E	VF	stamp/stamp
4696 -	$10	1902PB	628	11511 A R622493H	F	
4696 -	$10	1902PB	628	11541 A R622523H	VG	LL gone; ttape
4696 -	$10	1902PB	628	11696 C V792088H	F	
4696 -	$10	1902PB	628	14100 B 14100 B	F	faded/pen
4696 -	$10	1902PB	628	14342 C 14342 C	F	
4696 -	$10	1902PB	628	15174 C 15174 C	VF	pen/pen
4696 M	$20	1902PB	654	4609 A V484859B	F+	
4696 -	$20	1902PB	654	12865 A ?	VG	
4696	$10	1929T1		A000122A	F/VF	
4696	$10	1929T1		D000125A	F+	
4696	$10	1929T1		A000175A	VG	
4696	$10	1929T1		B000577A	VG/F	
4696	$10	1929T1		B000607A	VG/F	
4696	$10	1929T1		A000838A	VG/F	
4696	$10	1929T1		D000993A	F	
4696	$10	1929T1		E001148A	VG	
4696	$10	1929T1		C001162A	VG	
4696	$10	1929T1		B001292A	VG	
4696	$10	1929T1		A001311A	F/VF	
4696	$10	1929T1		E001324A	F	
4696	$10	1929T1		F001577A	CU	
4696	$10	1929T1		A001580A	AU	
4696	$10	1929T1		B001581A	AU	
4696	$20	1929T1		B000055A	F	
4696	$20	1929T1		F000156A	F+	
4696	$20	1929T1		A000192A	F	
4696	$20	1929T1		E000226A	VF	
4696	$20	1929T1		F000249A	F	
4696	$20	1929T1		A000315A	VG/F	
4696	$20	1929T1		A000321A	XF	
4696	$20	1929T1		B000332A	F	

4696	$20	1929T1	C000373A		VF	
4696	$20	1929T1	E000392A		VG/F	
4696	$20	1929T1	A000430A		VG	Rust on back
4696	$20	1929T1	B000434A		?	
4696	$20	1929T1	E000442A		XF	
4696	$20	1929T1	B000444A		XF	Higgins Mus.
4696	$20	1929T1	C000444A		F/VF	
4696	$20	1929T1	C000446A		VF	
4696	$20	1929T1	F000446A		CU	

THE FIRST NATIONAL BANK OF ANAMOSA 1 L
1813   JONES
Chartered on April 22, 1871. Placed in voluntary liquidation on December 14, 1878; capital of $50,000. Succeeded by H.C. Metcalf's Bank.
Officers: **Pres.** Horace C. Metcalf 1872-76, E. Bakeslee 1877, Horace C. Metcalf 1878; **Cash.** Thomas W. Shapely 1872-78.

First Charter, Original Issue	Ser #	# Notes
1-1-1-2	1-2500	10,00
10-10-10-20	1-1360	5,440
First Charter, Series of 1875		
1-1-1-2	1-180	720
10-10-10-20	1-236	944

Total amount of circulation issued = $93,200. Amount outstanding at close = $44,500. Amount outstanding in 1910 = $457.

17,104   0 Small   17,104 Total

1813	-	$1	ORIG 382	2001 A E414081	VG	pen/pen vp

THE GERMAN-AMERICAN NATIONAL BANK OF ARLINGTON 3 L
9664 (FIRST TITLE)   FAYETTE

Arlington was platted in 1856 and was originally called "Brush Creek". When the Chicago, Milwaukee, & St. Paul Railroad came to town in 1895, the name was changed to "Arlington". In 1910 its population was 678. Despite the fact that a strong 15 year old state bank was already in town, the German-American National Bank was formed to serve the local ethnic community. It became one of 60 so-called "ethnic national banks" nationally (of which 53 were Germanic) and the only one in Iowa. It also was a classic example of small town citizens taking advantage of the federal Act of March 14, 1900, which permitted formation of national banks in towns smaller than 3,000 with a reduced capital of only $25,000. The bank opened for business on July 1, 1910. By Sept. 1, 1910 the bank had secured currency worth $6,500, slightly more than the statutory minimum of $6,250.

World War I was a stressful time for people and institutions with a German background. Many churches and publications dropped the use of the German language. Citizen groups were formed to investigate "disloyal utterances". German farmers in the Arlington area found their gates painted yellow. The bank had been running patriotic ads in the newspaper during the war, but finally in late June 1918 the bank quietly changed its name to the American National Bank. The only notice of the change in the local paper was a name change in the bank's continuing advertisements. It was one of the last of the ethnic national banks to abandon its name. At time of the change it still had $25,000 capital and $25,000 national currency outstanding.

Organized on September 28, 1909 with a capital of $25,000. Title changed to The American National Bank of Arlington in July 1918.
Officers: **Pres.** GL Rawson 1910, TJ Ainsworth 1911-18; **VP** John C Wilken 1910-18; **Cash** TJ Ainsworth 1910, GL Rawson 1911-13, EJ Engeldinger 1914-1915, HR Young 1916-18; **AC** HR Young 1914-18

Third Charter, Date Back, Blue Seal	Ser #	# Notes
5-5-5-5	1-600	2,400
10-10-10-20	1-480	1,920
Third Charter, Plain Back, Blue Seal		
5-5-5-5	601-1100	2,000
10-10-10-20	481-880	1,600

7,920 Large   0 Small   7,920 Total

9664	M	$10	1902PB	626	320 A U792876	VF
9664	M	$10	1902PB	626	606 A V563676B	F/VF
9664	M	$20	1902PB	652	747 A V563817B	F/VF Higgins Mus.

THE AMERICAN NATIONAL BANK OF ARLINGTON 8 L   22 S
9664 (SECOND TITLE)   FAYETTE
Succeeded The German-American National Bank of Arlington in July 1918. Placed in conservatorship on March 20, 1933; licensed on May 19, 1933.
Officers: **Pres.** TJ Ainsworth 1918-35; **VP** John C Wilken 1918-19, Carl Meisgeier 1920-28, WE Anderson 1929-35; **Cash** HR Young 1918, NA Buck 1919, HR Young 1920-35; **AC** HR Young 1918-19, JH St. John 1920-26, Opal A Sackett 1932-35

Third Charter, Plain Back, Blue Seal	Ser #	# Notes
5-5-5-5	1-8120	32,480
1929, Type I		
6-5's	1-2664	15,984
1929, Type II		
6-5's	1-4596	4,596

Total amount of circulation issued = $331,300. Amount of large outstanding at close = $3,750. Amount of small outstanding in 1935 = $20,800.

32,480 Large   20,580 Small   53,060 Total

9664	M	$5	1902PB	606	1852 C	B387098E	Fr/G	gone/gone
9664	M	$5	1902PB	606	3200 B	Z651286E	VG/F	
9664	M	$5	1902PB	606	3511 B	D995797H	VG	
9664	-	$5	1902PB	606	4151 C	R975237H	VF+	gone Higg. Mus.
9664	-	$5	1902PB	606	4929 ?	4929 ?	F	Piece missing LL
9664	-	$5	1902PB	606	5046 D	5046 D	F+	weak stamp Rust
9664	-	$5	1902PB	606	7359 D	7359 D	?	
9664	-	$5	1902PB	606	8080 A	8080 A	F/VF	
9664		$5	1929T1	E000561A			VG	
9664		$5	1929T1	E000786A			VG	
9664		$5	1929T1	A001081A			F/VF	
9664		$5	1929T1	F001389A			VG/F	
9664		$5	1929T1	B001461A			F	
9664		$5	1929T1	A001480A			VG	
9664		$5	1929T1	F001583A			?	
9664		$5	1929T1	E001866A			F/VF	
9664		$5	1929T1	B001955A			VF	
9664		$5	1929T1	D002054A			F+	
9664		$5	1929T1	C002073A			VG	
9664		$5	1929T1	C002074A			VG	
9664		$5	1929T1	D002251A			VG	
9664		$5	1929T1	F002393A			F	
9664		$5	1929T1	C002593A			F	
9664		$5	1929T2	A000005			?	
9664		$5	1929T2	A000006			CU	
9664		$5	1929T2	A001006			VF	Higgins Mus.
9664		$5	1929T2	A001017			Fr/G	
9664		$5	1929T2	A001422			F/VF	Spot
9664		$5	1929T2	A001911			F/VF	
9664		$5	1929T2	A002519			F/VF	

THE FIRST NATIONAL BANK OF ARMSTRONG 9 L
5442   EMMET
Organized on May 1, 1900 with a capital of $50,000. Succeeded the Armstrong Bank. Placed in receivership on November 17, 1926; capital of $50,000. Reason for failure: local depression.
Officers: **Pres.** B.F. Robinson 1900-01, John Dows 1902-19, F.S. Robinson 1920-23, H.A. Kingston 1924-26, W.H. Bailey 1926; **Cash.** L.P. Gjermo 1900-01, B.F. Robinson 1902-26; **AC** S.O. Sofholm 1904-06, Ira D. Lyle 1910-19, Florence D. Olson 1920-24, W.H. Bailey 1925, John F. O'Niel 1925-26.

Second Charter, Brown Backs	Ser #	# Notes
10-10-10-20	1-1830	7,320
Second Charter, Date Back		
10-10-10-20	1-3440	13,760
Second Charter, Value Back		
10-10-10-20	3441-4740	5200
Third Charter, Plain Back, Blue Seal		
10-10-10-20	1-3444	13,776

Total circulation issued = $500,700. Amount outstanding at close =$49,500.

40,056 Large   0 Small   40,056 Total

5442	-	$10	1882BB	490	1 A	X427734	F/VF	
5442	M	$20	1882DB	555	2946 B	R184504	XF	pen/pen
5442	M	$20	1882DB	555	3302 B	T384580	VF	Higgins Mus.
5442	M	$20	1882VB	581	3913 B	U188191	VG	
5442	M	$10	1902PB	633	1208 A	H503340E	VF	
5442	M	$10	1902PB	633	1373 B	T494965E	F	
5442	M	$20	1902PB	659	276 A	?	F	
5442	M	$20	1902PB	659	2050 A	Z841112E	VG/F	pen Higgins Mus.
5442	M	$20	1902PB	659	2063 A	Z841125E	VG	pen/pen Soiled

THE ATLANTIC NATIONAL BANK   21 L   19 S
2762   CASS

Chartered in 1882 with a capital of $50,000. Succeeded J. McDaniels. Placed in voluntary liquidation on March 15, 1933; capital of $100,000. Succeeded by the Atlantic State Bank, Atlantic.

Officers: Pres. John McDaniels 1882-87, M.L. Stearns 1888-90, J.A. McWaid 1891-1913, Chas. R. Hunt 1914-26, L.W. Niles 1927-31, Fred R. Hunt 1932-33; **VP** John W. Winslow 1882-1895, H.L. Henderson 1896-1906, Chas R. Hunt 1907-1913, C.P. Meredith 1914-30, L.W. Niles 1920-26, Fred R. Hunt 1931, T.P. Breheney 1932-33; **Cash.** Clinton McDaniels 1882-86, H.M. Boorman 1887-89, F.M. Nichols 1890-94, T.G. Turner 1895-99, L.W. Niles 1900-19, T.P. Breheny 1920-31, W.R. Remien 1932-33; **AC** J.W. Winslow, L.W. Niles 1896-99, T.P. Breheney 1900-19, W.R. Remien 1920-31, H.R. Gunderman 1932-33.

	Ser #	# Notes
First Charter, Series of 1875		
10-10-10-20	1-1285	5,140
Third Charter, Red Seal		
10-10-10-20	1-925	3,700
Third Charter, Date Back, Blue Seal		
10-10-10-20	1-4300	17,200

Sheets numbered 1 to 3800 were 02-08 backs. Sheets numbered 3801 to 4300 were delivered on September 24, but not marked as to type. Sheets 4301 to 8897 were plain backs.

	Ser #	# Notes
Third Charter, Plain Back, Blue Seal		
10-10-10-20	4301-8897	18,388
1929, Type I		
6-10's	1-866	5,196
6-20's	1-229	1,374

Total amount of circulation issued = $634,790. Amount of large outstanding at close = $5,670. Amount of small outstanding at close = $44,330.
44,428 Large   6,570 Small   50,998 Total

Charter		Denom	Type	Plate	Ser/Treasury		Grade	Notes
2762	-	$10	1875	420	1140 A	K767269	F	
2762	M	$10	1902RS	613	384 A	H69822	VF	
2762	M	$20	1902RS	639	465 A	R200242	VF	Higgins Mus.
2762	M	$10	1902DB	616	3809 D	H929775B	XF	
2762	M	$10	1902PB	624	5575 E	U577517D	F	Washed
2762	M	$10	1902PB	624	6136 F	K754248E	VG/F	pen/pen
2762	M	$10	1902PB	624	6278 E	K754390E	VF	
2762	M	$10	1902PB	624	6476 E	K754588E	XF	vp
2762	M	$10	1902PB	624	6664 F	Z503656E	VG	pen vp Washed
2762	M	$10	1902PB	624	6939 E	K834421H	?	
2762	M	$10	1902PB	624	7045 D	K834527H	?	
2762	M	$10	1902PB	624	7080 D	K834562H	?	
2762	M	$10	1902PB	624	7099 F	K834581H	F	
2762	-	$10	1902PB	624	7279 E	U930371H	?	
2762	-	$10	1902PB	624	7340 F	U930432H	VF/XF	pen/pen
2762	-	$10	1902PB	624	7473 F	U930565H	?	
2762	-	$10	1902PB	624	7760 E	B462402K	VG	pen ac/pen
2762	-	$10	1902PB	624	7889 D	7889 D	AU	pen ac Higg Mus.
2762	-	$10	1902PB	624	8180 D	8180 D	F	
2762	-	$10	1902PB	624	8473 F	8473 F	?	
2762	M	$20	1902PB	650	6548 B	Z503540E	F	vp
2762		$10	1929T1		E000016A		VF+	
2762		$10	1929T1		C000090A		F	
2762		$10	1929T1		D000215A		VF/XF	
2762		$10	1929T1		D000310A		VG	
2762		$10	1929T1		E000387A		VF	
2762		$10	1929T1		B000420A		?	
2762		$10	1929T1		F000523A		F	
2762		$10	1929T1		A000722A		F	
2762		$10	1929T1		F000741A		?	
2762		$10	1929T1		A000789A		F/VF	
2762		$20	1929T1		E000020A		F/VF	
2762		$20	1929T1		B000044A		VG	
2762		$20	1929T1		F000075A		AU	
2762		$20	1929T1		C000077A		AU	
2762		$20	1929T1		A000128A		CU	
2762		$20	1929T1		B000155A		?	
2762		$20	1929T1		C000173A		XF	
2762		$20	1929T1		B000214A		?	
2762		$20	1929T1		D000214A		AU	Higgins Mus.

THE FIRST NATIONAL BANK OF ATLANTIC   3 L
1836   CASS

Chartered on June 21, 1871 with a capital of $50,000. Placed in voluntary liquidation on March 7, 1876; capital of $50,000. Succeeded by the Bank of Atlantic.

Officers: Pres. Franklin H. Whitney 1871-73, B.F. Allen 1874-76; **Cash.** John P. Gerberich 1871-72, Norman Haskins 1872-73, F.H. Whitney 1874-76

	Ser #	# Notes
First Charter, Original Issue		
1-1-1-2	1-2500	10,000
5-5-5-5	1-2625	10,500
First Charter, Series of 1875		
5-5-5-5	1-573	2,292

Total amount of circulation issued = $76,460. Amount outstanding at close = $45,000. Amount outstanding in 1910 = $417.
22,792 Large   0 Small   22,792 Total

1836	-	$1	ORIG	382	433 A	C587838	F/VF	pen/pen
1836	-	$1	ORIG	382	837 C	C588242	F	pen Higgins Mus.
1836	-	$1	ORIG	382	1257 ?	?	?	

THE FIRST NATIONAL BANK OF AUDUBON   11 L   9 S
4891   AUDUBON

Chartered in 1882 with a capital of $50,000. Succeeded J. McDaniels. Placed in voluntary liquidation on March 15, 1933; capital of $100,000. Succeeded by the Atlantic State Bank, Atlantic.

Officers: Pres. Chas. Van Gorder 1893-1911, E.S. Van Gorder 1912-1933; **VP** Theo F. Morrow 1896-1908, H.A. Arnold 1909-1912, 1914-33, Chas Van Gorder 1913-24, Mrs. L.V. Kirk 1933; **Cash.** Frank S. Watts 1893-1919, H.E. Laubender 1920-23, C.E. Nelson 1924-33; **AC** E.S. Van Gorder 1896-1912, C.P. Christensen 1913-19, C.E. Nelson 1920-23, Peter Hansen 1923-26, A.N. Christensen 1925-26, E.S. Van Gorder, Jr. 1927-33, A.A. Kruse 1927-33.

	Ser #	# Notes
Second Charter, Brown Backs		
5-5-5-5	1-3950	15,800
10-10-10-20	1-1940	7,760
Second Charter, Date Back		
5-5-5-5	1-2002	8,008
10-10-10-20	1-1208	4,832
Third Charter, Date Back, Blue Seal		
10-10-10-20	1-1900	7,600
Third Charter, Plain Back, Blue Seal		
10-10-10-20	1901-4212	9,248
1929, Type I		
6-10's	1-487	2,922
6-20's	1-103	618

Total amount of circulation issued = $528,620. Amount of large outstanding at close = $3,680. Amount of small outstanding at close = $21,320.
53,348 Large   3,540 Small   56,788 Total

4891	M	$10	1882BB	485	980 A	N669893N	F	
4891	M	$10	1882BB	485	1387 A	T615007T	F	Higgins Mus.
4891	M	$10	1902DB	621	1269 B	X631584A	F	pen/stamp
4891	M	$10	1902DB	621	1563 ?	M895089B	VG	
4891	M	$10	1902PB	629	2614 B	E453296E	VF	light stamps
4891	M	$10	1902PB	629	2779 B	A241861N	F+	faded/gone
4891	M	$10	1902PB	629	2928 A	E523860H	VG/F	
4891	M	$10	1902PB	629	3152 C	M519454N	VF	pen/stamp
4891	-	$10	1902PB	629	3760 A	3760 A	F/VF	
4891	-	$10	1902PB	629	4121 C	4121 C	VF	
4891	M	$20	1902PB	655	1987 A	K333879D	AU	Higgins Mus.
4891		$10	1929T1		F000023A		G	
4891		$10	1929T1		B000040A		VG	
4891		$10	1929T1		A000135A		VF	
4891		$10	1929T1		E000159A		VF/XF	
4891		$10	1929T1		C000277A		VF	
4891		$10	1929T1		F000334A		F	
4891		$20	1929T1		B000023A		F+	
4891		$20	1929T1		A000029A		F	
4891		$20	1929T1		D000073A		F/VF	Higgins Mus.

THE FARMERS NATIONAL BANK OF AURELIA   **13 L   19 S**
9724   **CHEROKEE**
Chartered in 1910.
Officers: **Pres**. O.E. Yokum 1910-14, P.D. Wine 1915-28, E.L. Yokum 1929-31, L.E. Christensen 1932-35; **VP** P.D. Wine 1910-19, E.L. Yokum 1920-29, A.J. Whinnery 1920-24, T.G. Ohlson 1925-27, 1932, L.B. Christensen 1928-31, Chas. Nelson 1933-35; **Cash**. J.A. Johnson 1910-16, H.F. Reeder 1917, A.F. Capper 1918-19, L.E. Christensen 1920-27, E.L. Brummer 1928-35; **AC** G.R. Wharton 1910-19, C.A. Pankow 1920-22, E.L. Brummer 1922-27, Ray J. Parrott 1922-29, Edna M.Gearke 1930

Third Charter, Date Back, Blue Seal	Ser #	# Notes
10-10-10-20	1-3740	14,960

Sheets numbered 1 to 3500 were 02-08 backs. Sheets numbered 3501 to 3740 were delivered on October 15 but not marked as to type. Sheets numbered 3741 to 9571 were plain back blue seals.

Third Charter, Plain Back, Blue Seal		
10-10-10-20	3741-9571	23,324
1929, Type I		
6-10's	1-1093	6,558
6-20's	1-318	1,908

Total amount of circulation issued = $582,290. Amount outstanding in 1934 = $25,000. Amount of large outstanding July 17, 1935 = $3,070.

38,284 Large   8,466 Small   46,750 Total

9724	M	$10	1902DB	619	618 C	V387600	XF/AU	pen/pen
9724		$10	1902DB	619	2394 B	N46861A	F	
9724	M	$20	1902DB	645	950 A	V387932	VG+	pen/pen vp
9724	M	$20	1902DB	645	3048 A	V4884A	F/VF	Higgins Mus.
9724	M	$10	1902PB	627	3399 A	B25565B	VF	
9724	M	$10	1902PB	627	4077 B	Y459778B	G/VG	faded/faded
9724	M	$10	1902PB	627	5397 B	Y294739D	VG	pen/pen
9724		$10	1902PB	627	7351 C	T756983H	VG	Higgins Mus.
9724	-	$10	1902PB	627	7567 A	X827979H	VF/XF	pen ac/pen
9724	-	$10	1902PB	627	8688 C	8688 C	VF	
9724	-	$10	1902PB	627	9194 C	9194 C	F/VF	
9724	-	$10	1902PB	627	9480 B	9480 B	VG/F	
9724	M	$20	1902PB	653	5865 A	E606957E	F	pen/pen vp
9724		$10	1929T1	F000359A			XF	Higgins Mus.
9724		$10	1929T1	F000376A			?	
9724		$10	1929T1	E000378A			VF	
9724		$10	1929T1	B000421A			VG/F	
9724		$10	1929T1	E000645A			VG	
9724		$10	1929T1	B000722A			AU	
9724		$10	1929T1	E000724A			XF/AU	
9724		$10	1929T1	E000876A			VF+	
9724		$10	1929T1	B000964A			F	
9724		$10	1929T1	D001028A			VG	
9724		$10	1929T1	C001034A			VF	
9724		$10	1929T1	F001037A			VG	
9724		$20	1929T1	A000058A			F/VF	
9724		$20	1929T1	F000115A			F/VF	
9724		$20	1929T1	C000128A			VG/F	
9724		$20	1929T1	C000138A			F	
9724		$20	1929T1	F000262A			VG	
9724		$20	1929T1	C000269A			VG/F	Rust; stains
9724		$20	1929T1	C000313A			?	

THE FIRST NATIONAL BANK OF AURELIA   **5 L   11 S**
7108   **CHEROKEE**
Chartered in 1904. Placed in voluntary liquidation on May 11, 1935; capital of $25,000. Succeeded by the First Trust & Savings Bank of Aurelia.
Officers: **Pres**. James F. Toy 1904-35; **VP** W.P. Miller 1904-19, Moses Mummert 1920-27, J.M. Whitney 1927-35, H.H. Deyloff, 1927; **Cash**. A.J. Whinery 1904-06, W.H. Bischell 1907-35; **AC** W.H. Bischel 1904-06, Wm. Lenmann 1907-08, R.A. Edens 1909-10, J.P. Morgan 1909-10, D.R. Whitney 1911-14, A.D. Coffman 1911-14, E.S. Kiernan 1920-30, Clyde M. Mummert 1925-27, H.H. Deyloff 1925-35.

Third Charter, Red Seal	Ser #	# Notes
10-10-10-20	1-300	1,200
Third Charter, Date Back, Blue Seal		
10-10-10-20	1-1840	7,360
Third Charter, Plain Back, Blue Seal		
10-10-10-20	1841-4782	11,768
1929, Type I		
6-10's	1-518	3,108
6-20's	1-146	876
1929, Type II		
10's	1-599	599
20's	1-100	100

Total amount issued = $310,690. Amount outstanding in 1934 = $25,000.

20,328 Large   4,683 Small   25,011 Total

7108	M	$10	1902DB	616	853 E		?	AU
7108	M	$10	1902DB	616	1362 E	U267780A	F	
7108	M	$10	1902PB	624	3012 E	B114604E	?	
7108		$10	1902PB	624	3595 D	K355687H	F/VF	Higgins Mus.
7108	-	$10	1902PB	624	4573 E	4573 E	F/VF	pen/pen
7108		$10	1929T1	A000001A			AU	Paper clip stain
7108		$10	1929T1	E000246A			F	
7108		$10	1929T1	B000310A			?	
7108		$10	1929T1	E000386A			?	
7108		$20	1929T1	A000018A			F	
7108		$20	1929T1	E000043A			VF	Higgins Mus.
7108		$20	1929T1	C000057A			VG/F	
7108		$20	1929T1	A000059A			?	
7108		$20	1929T1	A000101A			XF	
7108		$10	1929T2	A000045			XF	
7108		$10	1929T2	A000187			F	

THE FIRST NATIONAL BANK OF AYRSHIRE   **9 L   1 S**
5479   **PALO ALTO**
Organized on June 9, 1900 with a capital of $25,000. Placed in receivership on August 12, 1930; capital of $25,000. Reason for failure: local depression.
Officers: **Pres**. M.L. Brown 1900-1929, Earl Brown 1930; **VP** George Barfoot 1900-06, John Sherlock 1907-19, M. Daily 1920-21, J.M. Daily 1922-20; **Cash**. E.P. Barringer 1901-05, J.M. Kelly 1906-30; **AC** J.M. Kelly 1900-06, Maude Jacobsen 1920-22, J.E. Daily 1925-30

Second Charter, Brown Backs	Ser #	# Notes
10-10-10-20	1-600	2,400
Second Charter, Date Back		
10-10-10-20	1-680	2,720
Second Charter, Value Back		
10-10-10-20	681-716	144
Third Charter, Plain Back, Blue Seal		
5-5-5-5	1-2222	8,888
1929, Type I		
6-5's	1-234	1,404

Total amount of circulation issued = $117,260. Amount outstanding at close = $8,000. Amount of large outstanding July 1, 1931 = $1,680.

14,152 Large   1,404 Small   15,556 Total

5479	M	$20	1882DB	555	448 B	K476866	XF	vp
5479	M	$20	1882DB	555	450 B	K476868	AU	Higgins Mus.
5479	M	$20	1882DB	555	451 B	K476869	XF	
5479	M	$20	1882DB	555	472 B	M818960	AU	pen/pen vp
5479	M	$20	1882DB	555	475 B	M818963	AU	stamp sigs vp
5479	M	$5	1902PB	607	890 B	E692726H	F	stamp/stamp
5479	M	$5	1902PB	607	970 B	E692806H	F	gone/gone
5479	-	$5	1902PB	607	2083 A	2083 A	VF	vp
5479	-	$5	1902PB	607	2205 A	2205 A	F+	ac Higgins Mus.
5479		$5	1929T1	D000058A			VG	Higgins Mus.

THE FIRST NATIONAL BANK OF BAGLEY   **7 L   7 S**
6995   **GUTHRIE**
Organized on October 5, 1903 with a capital of $25,000. Placed in receivership on July 3, 1931; capital of $25,000. Reason for failure: incompetent management.
Officers: **Pres**. HL Moore 1904-26, Geo. B Vaux 1927-31; **VP** S Jasinsky 1904-26, HH Russell 1927-31; **Cash**. Freeman H Jenkins 1904-13, Chas. W Cain 1914-31; **AC** Chas. W Cain 1907-1913, Ralph H Cain 1914-19, John M Hamilton 1920-31, Velma A Porter 1922-27, Lloyd Berry 1930-31

Third Charter, Red Seal	Ser #	# Notes
10-10-10-20	1-350	1,400
Third Charter, Date Back, Blue Seal		
10-10-10-20	1-1660	6,640
Third Charter, Plain Back, Blue Seal		
10-10-10-20	1661-4126	9,864
1929, Type I		
6-10's	1-284	1,704
6-20's	1-55	330

Total amount of circulation issued = $247,440. Amount of large outstanding at close = $3,420. Amount of small outstanding at close = $16,100.

17,904 Large   2,034 Small   19,938 Total

6995	M	$10	1902PB	624	2119 D	B677416D	F+	
6995	M	$10	1902PB	624	2984 F	V708776E	F/VF	Higgins Mus.
6995	-	$10	1902PB	624	3261 D	V228763H	VF/XF	pen/lt stamp
6995	-	$10	1902PB	624	3482 D	A213324K	VF	pen/gone Bayard
6995	M	$20	1902PB	650	2975 B	V708767E	F	pen/faded
6995	-	$20	1902PB	650	3467 B	A213309K	F/VF	Bayard
6995	-	$20	1902PB	650	3488 B	A213330K	?	Bayard
6995		$10	1929T1	F000043A			G	
6995		$10	1929T1	B000181A			?	
6995		$10	1929T1	B000209A			F/VF	
6995		$10	1929T1	B000223A			F	

6995		$10 1929T1	D000232A		?	
6995		$20 1929T1	E000040A		F	
6995		$20 1929T1	A000041A		VF	Higgins Mus.

THE FIRST NATIONAL BANK OF BANCROFT — 14 L
5643 — KOSSUTH

Organized on November 10, 1900 with a capital of $50,000. Chartered on December 15, 1900. Placed in receivership on October 20, 1927; capital of $50,000. Reason for failure: incompetent management.

Officers: Pres. RN Bruer 1900-27; **VP** JB Monel 1902-03, GS Ringland 1904-08, Tom Sherman 1909-10, JB Monel 1911-23, JW Sullivan 1924-27; **Cash.** Tom Sherman 1900-07, Jos. J Sherman 1908-27; **AC** WP Johnson 1902-08, Chas. Nelson 1909-19, EV Zigrang 1920-21, AH Rowe 1920-21, AJ Rohe 1923-27

Second Charter, Brown Backs	Ser #	# Notes
10-10-10-20	1-2650	10,600
Second Charter, Date Back		
10-10-10-20	1-3440	13,760
Second Charter, Value Back		
10-10-10-20	3441-4993	6,212
Third Charter, Plain Back, Blue Seal		
10-10-10-20	1-3426	13,704

Total amount issued = $553,450. Amount outstanding at close = $50,000.

44,276 Large   0 Small   44,276 Total

5643	M	$10 1882DB	545	1226 F	E31820	VF	Higgins Mus.
5643	M	$10 1882DB	545	2771 D	N825479	VF+	pen/pen vp
5643	M	$10 1882DB	545	3287 E	U133765	?	
5643	M	$20 1882DB	555	445 B	B207005	VG	pen ac/faded
5643	M	$20 1882DB	555	449 B	B207009	?	
5643	M	$20 1882VB	581	4366 B	U813424	XF	Higgins Mus.
5643	M	$20 1882VB	581	4496 B	U813554	F	pen/faded
5643		$10 1902PB	633	2364 A	X623326H	XF	Higgins Mus.
5643		$10 1902PB	633	2427 B	X623389H	F	
5643	-	$10 1902PB	633	3313 A	3313 A	VG	
5643	M	$20 1902PB	659	436 A	Y19428D	VG/F	
5643		$20 1902PB	659	2130 A	?	?	
5643	-	$20 1902PB	659	2428 A	X623390H	VG/F	pen/gone
5643	-	$20 1902PB	659	3073 A	3073 A	F	

THE BEDFORD NATIONAL BANK — 22 L 22 S
5165 — TAYLOR

Chartered on December 29, 1898; succeeded the Bedford Bank.

Officers: Pres. Wm. E Crum 1899-1914, WE Crum, Jr. 1915-31; **VP** FE Walker 1900-12, Chas. G Martin 1913-19, NV Crum 1920-26, Chas. V Dinges 1929-30; **Cash.** Chas. G Martin 1900-11, HR Reynolds 1912-14, Chas. G Martin 1915-21, JF Longfellow 1922-31; **AC** Chas. B Baily 1900-03, HR Reynolds 1904-12, JF Longfellow 1913-21, DJ Grant 1925-31, CH Cummings 1927-35, MP Borrusch 1934-35

Second Charter, Brown Backs	Ser #	# Notes
5-5-5-5	1-3775	15,100
10-10-10-20	1-1680	6,720
Second Charter, Date Back		
5-5-5-5	1-2500	10,000
10-10-10-20	1-1860	7,440
Second Charter, Value Back		
5-5-5-5	2501-3178	2,712
10-10-10-20	1861-2324	1,856
Third Charter, Plain Back, Blue Seal		
5-5-5-5	1-4940	19,760
10-10-10-20	1-3554	14,216
1929, Type I		
6-5's	1-1288	7,728
6-10's	1-810	4,860
6-20's	1-230	1,380
1929, Type II		
5's	1-1340	1,340
10's	1-822	822
20's	1-128	128

Total amount of circulation issued = $748,080. Amount of large outstanding in June 1935 = $4,570. Amount of small outstanding in June 1935 = $45,430.

77,804 Large   16,258 Small   94,062 Total

5165		$5 1882BB	477	2615 D	A713740A	XF	Higgins Mus.
5165	M	$10 1882BB	490	1308 C	T89601	VF+	
5165	M	$20 1882DB	504	924 A	E33353E	VG	pen/pen vp
5165	M	$20 1882DB	555	1091 B	M238809	F/VF	faded/faded
5165	M	$20 1882DB	555	1451 B	N756059	VF	
5165	M	$20 1882VB	581	2188 B	U392546	VG	gone/gone
5165		$5 1902PB	606	121 A	B413817D	VG/F	
5165		$5 1902PB	606	3339 B	R857575H	VG	
5165	-	$5 1902PB	606	3363 D	X962474H	VG	stamp/stamp
5165	-	$5 1902PB	606	3545 A	X962656H	VF	stamp/stamp
5165	M	$10 1902PB	632	1024 A	R858436E	G/VG	stamp/stamp
5165	M	$10 1902PB	632	1724 A	M86H	F+	
5165		$10 1902PB	632	1783 A	?	VF	
5165	-	$10 1902PB	632	2102 C	Z134534H	F/VF	
5165	-	$10 1902PB	632	2495 B	2495 B	VG	stamp/stamp
5165	-	$10 1902PB	632	3365 B	3365 B	VG/F	
5165	M	$20 1902PB	658	137 A	D925896D	AU	stamp Higg. Mus.
5165	M	$20 1902PB	658	405 A	R100567D	VF	stamp/stamp
5165	M	$20 1902PB	658	1193 A	R858605E	VF	stamp Rust
5165	M	$20 1902PB	658	1674 A	M36H	VF+	stamp/stamp
5165	-	$20 1902PB	658	2711 A	2711 A	F	
5165	-	$20 1902PB	658	3115 A	3115 A	F	
5165		$5 1929T1	A000758A			XF	Higgins Mus.
5165		$5 1929T1	A001002A			VF	
5165		$5 1929T1	C001180A			VG	
5165		$5 1929T1	C001181A			VG	
5165		$5 1929T1	A001199A			VF	
5165		$5 1929T1	F001276A			VF+	
5165		$10 1929T1	C000175A			?	
5165		$10 1929T1	E000327A			F/VF	
5165		$10 1929T1	F000420A			?	
5165		$10 1929T1	C000425A			G/VG	
5165		$10 1929T1	C000501A			VF	
5165		$10 1929T1	C000612A			?	
5165		$20 1929T1	C000045A			VF	
5165		$20 1929T1	B000067A			?	
5165		$20 1929T1	C000083A			VG	
5165		$20 1929T1	C000091A			VF	
5165		$20 1929T1	C000107A			VF	
5165		$20 1929T1	F000137A			F/VF	
5165		$20 1929T1	D000191A			F	
5165		$20 1929T1	B000210A			?	
5165		$5 1929T2	A000076			F	
5165		$10 1929T2	A000620			G/VG	

THE FIRST NATIONAL BANK OF BEDFORD — 0 L
2298 — TAYLOR

Chartered on September 18, 1875 with a capital of $50,000. Succeeded the Taylor County Bank. Placed in receivership on February 1, 1876; capital of $30,000. Reason for failure: incompetent management.

First Charter, Series of 1875	Ser #	# Notes
10-10-10-20	1-540	2,160

Total amount of circulation issued = $27,000. Amount outstanding at close = $27,000. Amount outstanding in 1915 = $90.

2,160 Large   0 Small   2,160 Total

THE CITIZENS NATIONAL BANK OF BELLE PLAINE — 19 L 18 S
4754 — BENTON

Organized on May 18, 1892 with a capital of $50,000. Succeeded the Bank of Belle Plaine. Placed in conservatorship on March 20, 1933. Placed in voluntary liquidation on April 23, 1934; capital of $50,000. Succeeded by #14069; circulation assumed by #14069 which did not issue notes of its own..

Officers: Pres. EE Hughes 1892-96, Chas. A Blossom 1897-1918, AE Fedderson 1919-24, E Nichols 1925-30, Laverne Clark 1931-34; **VP** JJ Mosnat 1896-1903, S Wertheim 1904-34, SR Van Dyke 1909, E Nichols 1914-24, Laverne Clark 1930, Anna G Luedtke 1931; **Cash.** Chas. A Blossom 1892-96, SP Van Dyke 1897-1906, JE Miller 1907-10, WO Brand 1912-34; **AC** SP Van Dyke 1896-99, JF Miller 1904-06, WO Brand 1907-12, WR Blossom 1913-19, TH Malcolm 1920-24

Second Charter, Brown Backs	Ser #	# Notes
10-10-10-20	1-4470	17,880
Second Charter, Date Back		
10-10-10-20	1-1296	5,184
Third Charter, Date Back, Blue Seal		
10-10-10-20	1-1700	6,800
Third Charter, Plain Back, Blue Seal		
10-10-10-20	1701-7695	23,980
1929, Type I		
6-10's	1-946	5,676
6-20's	1-290	1,740

Total amount of circulation issued = $764,610. Amount of large outstanding at close = $4,370. Amount of small outstanding at close = $45,630. Circulation assumed by #14069 which was then responsible for redeeming the outstanding notes of #4754.

53,844 Large   7,416 Small   61,260 Total

4754	M	$20 1882BB	499	3451 A	N962066N	VG	3451A or 3151A ?
4754	M	$10 1902DB	620	1013 A	V767388A	VF	pen Higgins Mus.
4754	M	$10 1902DB	620	1657 C	Z524291A	F+	
4754	M	$20 1902DB	646	1005 A	V767380A	F/VF	pen/pen
4754	M	$10 1902PB	628	4326 B	D225208E	G	pen/pen
4754	-	$10 1902PB	628	6175 B	Z887987H	VG	Bayard

4754	-	$10 1902PB	628	6262 C	6262 C	CU
4754	-	$10 1902PB	628	6749 A	6749 A	XF pen/pen
4754	-	$10 1902PB	628	6863 B	6863 B	AU pen/pen
4754	-	$10 1902PB	628	6863 C	6863 C	AU pen/pen
4754	-	$10 1902PB	628	7014 A	7014 A	G/VG
4754	-	$10 1902PB	628	7239 A	7239 A	CU
4754	-	$10 1902PB	628	7239 B	7239 B	CU
4754	-	$10 1902PB	628	7242 ?	7242 ?	CU
4754	-	$10 1902PB	628	7595 B	7595 B	VG
4754	M	$20 1902PB	654	3034 A	E587488D	XF
4754	M	$20 1902PB	654	4381 A	D225263E	VG
4754	-	$20 1902PB	654	6091 A	Z887903H	VF
4754	-	$20 1902PB	654	7220 A	7220 A	F
4754		$10 1929T1		C000026A		F/VF
4754		$10 1929T1		E000035A		?
4754		$10 1929T1		E000543A		F
4754		$10 1929T1		A000553A		?
4754		$10 1929T1		F000820A		F/VF
4754		$10 1929T1		D000852A		G/VG
4754		$10 1929T1		D000862A		VG
4754		$10 1929T1		F000906A		VG
4754		$10 1929T1		A000937A		Fr
4754		$20 1929T1		C000043A		F
4754		$20 1929T1		A000055A		F/VF
4754		$20 1929T1		B000091A		VG/F
4754		$20 1929T1		F000095A		VG
4754		$20 1929T1		A000123A		VG Dark
4754		$20 1929T1		B000144A		F
4754		$20 1929T1		A000191A		F/VF
4754		$20 1929T1		D000192A		XF Higgins Mus.
4754		$20 1929T1		E000281A		?

THE FIRST NATIONAL BANK OF BELLE PLAINE   **20 L**
2012   **BENTON**
Organized on May 31, 1872; capital of $50,000. Chartered on July 12, 1872. Placed in receivership on March 3, 1927; capital of $60,000. Reason for failure: incompetent management & local depression.
Officers: **Pres.** DW Read 1872-73, WA Scott 1874-75, JA Durand 1876, Sidney S Sweet 1877-1908, Geo. R Ahrens 1909-27; **VP** FE Zalesky 1900-27; **Cash.** Sidney S Sweet 1872-76, Lewis T Sweet 1877-1900, Geo. R Ahrens 1901-08, CA Sweet 1909-27; **AC** Geo. R Ahrens 1900, WA Mall 1902-19, CW Housman 1920-27

First Charter, Original Issue	Ser #	# Notes
1-1-1-2	1-2152	8,608
5-5-5-5	1-2625	10,500
First Charter, Series of 1875		
5-5-5-5	1-6232	24,928
Second Charter, Brown Backs		
10-10-10-20	1-6090	18,270
Second Charter, Date Back		
10-10-10-20	1-1285	5,140
Third Charter, Date Back, Blue Seal		
10-10-10-20	1-2200	8,800
Third Charter, Plain Back, Blue Seal		
10-10-10-20	2201-7542	21,368

Total amount of circulation issued = $933,750. Amount of above outstanding at close = $59,100.
103,704 Large   0 Small   103,704 Total

2012	-	$1	ORIG	382	1 A	D210741	XF pen/pen
2012	-	$1	ORIG	382	765 C	D211505	VG/F pen Higgins Mus.
2012	-	$1	ORIG	382	1600 A	D785684	VF Rev. tape
2012	-	$1	ORIG	382	2041 B	D786125	AU
2012	-	$5	ORIG	399	531 D	K389689	VG $1 or $5 ?
2012	-	$10	1882BB	485	2688 B	V929203	F pen/pen
2012	M	$10	1882BB	485	5871 C	V610180V	VG/F pen/pen
2012		$20	1882BB	499	4525 A	N912200N	VF
2012	M	$20	1882DB	550	1061 B	H927769	F/VF
2012	M	$10	1902DB	620	731 C	K358134A	CU
2012	M	$10	1902DB	620	1815 B	A695877B	VG/F
2012	M	$20	1902DB	646	730 A	K358133A	VF pen Higgins Mus.
2012	M	$20	1902DB	646	1486 B	?	F
2012	M	$10	1902PB	628	2891 ?	X348688D	F
2012	M	$10	1902PB	628	5807 B	A163899H	VG lt. pen/pen
2012	-	$10	1902PB	628	7013 B	7013 B	CU pen/pen
2012	-	$10	1902PB	628	7355 A	7355 A	VG pen/pen
2012	M	$10	1902PB	654	4952 A	?	F
2012	M	$20	1902PB	654	4982 A	D366764E	F/VF
2012	-	$20	1902PB	654	7469 A	7469 A	VF pen/pen

THE FIRST NATIONAL BANK OF BELMOND   **2 L**
8748   **WRIGHT**
Chartered in June 1907. Placed in voluntary liquidation on April 11, 1921; capital of $30,000. Absorbed by the State Bank of Belmond.
Officers: **Pres.** TB Kaufman 1908, GH Richardson 1909-13, WI Rosecrans 1914-18, WT Gfeller 1919, AO Hauge 1920-21; **VP** N Reese 1909-11, RL Foreseth 1911-19, WT Gfeller 1920-21; **Cash.** Bernard Mennenga 1908-19, AS Lund 1919-21; **AC** John P Rule 1909, JT Rule 1910-12, John Greenlander 1913-19

Third Charter, Red Seal	Ser #	# Notes
5-5-5-5	1-250	1,000
10-10-10-20	1-200	800
Third Charter, Date Back, Blue Seal		
5-5-5-5	1-775	3,100
10-10-10-20	1-600	2,400
Third Charter, Plain Back, Blue Seal		
5-5-5-5	776-1075	1,200
10-10-10-20	601-745	580

Total amount issued = $73,750. Amount outstanding in 1920 = $10,000.
9,080 Large   0 Small   9,080 Total

8748	M	$5	1902DB	592	684 F	U862521A	?
8748	M	$10	1902PB	626	694 D	R644216D	F pen Higgins Mus.

THE FIRST NATIONAL BANK OF BLANCHARD   **3 L**
4902   **PAGE**
Chartered in 1893 with a capital of $50,000. Succeeded the Blanchard Bank (Monk & Anderson). Placed in voluntary liquidation on June 30, 1914; capital of $50,000. Succeeded by the First Trust & Savings Bank, Blanchard.
Officers: **Pres.** Chas. G Anderson 1893-1902, FM Byrkit 1903-14; **VP** Isaac Monk 1896-1902, JH Walkinshaw 1903-14; **Cash.** Frank Hooker 1893-1914; **AC** SC Henn 1896-99, F Meredith 1900-11, Walter Hooker 1913-14

Second Charter, Brown Backs	Ser #	# Notes
10-10-10-20	1-3220	12,880
Second Charter, Date Back		
10-10-10-20	1-1568	6,272
Third Charter, Date Back, Blue Seal		
10-10-10-20	1-346	1,384

Total amount of circulation issued = $256,700. Amount outstanding at close = $35,600. Amount outstanding in October 1914 = $31,050.
20,536 Large   0 Small   20,356 Total

4902		$10	1882BB		2804 A	V475973V	VF+ Higgins Mus.
4902	M	$10	1882DB	540	1501 E	K931109	F Higgins Mus.
4902	M	$10	1902DB	617	304 A	T234534A	? Higgins Mus.

THE FIRST NATIONAL BANK OF BLOCKTON   **4 L**   **1 S**
8211   **TAYLOR**
Organized on May 3, 1906 with a capital of $25,000. Placed in receivership on October 22, 1931; capital of $25,000. Reason for failure: local depression.
Officers: **Pres.** WM Wright 1906-21, UI Willson 1922-26, CH Eaton 1927-29, ME Roof 1930-31; **VP** US Wright 1907-12, IV Wright 1913-21, CH Eaton 1922-26, UI Willson 1927-29, Geo. A Schoenmann 1930-31; **Cash.** IV Wright 1906-19, WV Wright 1920-21, ME Roof 1922-29, WG Florea 1930-31; **AC** ME Roof 1907-21, FS Roof 1931

Third Charter, Red Seal	Ser #	# Notes
10-10-10-20	1-200	800
Third Charter, Date Back, Blue Seal		
10-10-10-20	1-600	2,400

Sheets numbered 1 to 500 were 02-08 backs. Sheets numbered 501 to 600 were delivered on August 20, but not marked as to type. Sheets numbered 601 to 1102 were plain backs.

Third Charter, Plain Back, Blue Seal	Ser #	# Notes
10-10-10-20	601-1102	2,008
1929, Type I		
6-10's	1-94	564
6-20's	1-11	66

Total amount of circulation issued = $72,060. Amount of large outstanding at close = $1,610. Amount of small outstanding at close = $4,640.
5,208 Large   630 Small   5,838 Total

8211	-	$10	1902PB	625	931 D	A724333K	VF+
8211	-	$10	1902PB	625	932 F	A724334K	VF vp
8211	-	$10	1902PB	625	934 E	A724336K	XF
8211	-	$10	1902PB	625	1042 E	1042 E	VG pen/pen
8211		$10	1929T1		B000078A		F Higgins Mus.

THE FIRST NATIONAL BANK OF BLOOMFIELD   **1 L**
1299   **DAVIS**
Chartered in 1865. Placed in voluntary liquidation on February 5, 1876; capital of $55,000. Succeeded by the Bloomfield Bank.
Officers: **Pres.** JW Ellis 1867-71, WD Evans 1872-76; **Cash.** John B Glenn 1867-76

First Charter, Original Issue	Ser #	# Notes
5-5-5-5	1-4825	19,300
First Charter, Series of 1875		
5-5-5-5	1-451	1,804

Total amount of circulation issued = $105,520. Amount outstanding at close = $49,500. Amount outstanding in 1910 = $850.

21,104 Large   0 Small   21,104 Total
1299   - $5   ORIG 397   3919 C   N80042   Fr   Higgins Mus.

THE NATIONAL BANK OF BLOOMFIELD   16 L   4 S
9303   DAVIS

Chartered in January 1909. Placed in voluntary liquidation on February 26, 1930; capital of $55,000. Absorbed by The State Bank of David County, Bloomfield.

Officers: Pres. Henry C Taylor 1909-30; **VP** SS Standley 1909-26, WB Taylor 1927-30; **Cash.** SF McConnell 1909-30; **AC** SE Rowe 1909-30

Third Charter, Date Back, Blue Seal	Ser #	# Notes
10-10-10-20	1-4500	18,000
Third Charter, Plain Back, Blue Seal		
10-10-10-20	4501-10920	25680
1929, Type I		
6-10's	1-399	2,394
6-20's	1-20	120

Total amount of circulation issued = $572,340. Amount of large outstanding at close = $27,220. Amount of small outstanding at close = $26,340.

43,680 Large   2,514 Small   46,194 Total

9303 M	$10 1902DB	618	1 ?	?	?	
9303 M	$10 1902DB	618	164 B	H916140	VG	pen/pen
9303 M	$10 1902DB	618	4002 A	A710464B	F	vp
9303 M	$20 1902DB	644	1 A	?	?	
9303 M	$10 1902PB	626	4988 A	Y161969B	VF	pen/gone Stained
9303 -	$10 1902PB	626	9832 A	9832 A	?	
9303 -	$10 1902PB	626	9991 B	9991 B	XF	Higgins Mus.
9303 -	$10 1902PB	626	10034 B	10034 B	VG	LR corner gone
9303 -	$10 1902PB	626	10879 B	10879 B	AU	pen/faded
9303 -	$20 1902PB	652	6452 A	X98314D	F	pen/stamp
9303 -	$20 1902PB	652	8618 A	X330700H	VF	
9303 -	$20 1902PB	652	9352 A	?	?	
9303 -	$20 1902PB	652	9577 A	9577 A	VF	pen/stamp
9303 -	$20 1902PB	652	9897 A	9897 A	F	pen/gone
9303 -	$20 1902PB	652	10197 A	10197 A	VF	
9303 -	$20 1902PB	652	10463 A	10463 A	VG+	
9303	$10 1929T1		E000051A		?	
9303	$10 1929T1		B000265A		VG	
9303	$10 1929T1		B000323A		VG	
9303	$10 1929T1		C000356A		VG/F	Higgins Mus.

THE FIRST NATIONAL BANK OF BODE   2 L   2 S
10371   HUMBOLDT

Organized on March 29, 1913 with a capital of $25,000. Placed in receivership on October 1, 1931; capital of $25,000. Reason for failure: incompetent management & local depression.

Officers: Pres. OT Gullixson 1914-15, Henry Hanson 1916-17, OT Gullixson 1918-22, OE Halsrud 1923-31; **VP** Peter Kirsch 1914-19, EJ Erickson 1920-21, JO Dale 1922-29, AJ Oasheim 1929, Wm. F Littler 1930-31; **Cash.** LL Watson 1914-15, OT Gullixson 1916-17, WO Kirsland 1918, AC Larson 1919-21, Oscar Grefstad 1922-26, JM Rood 1917-31; **AC** CE Hanson 1920-21, BN Kinseth 1923-24, JM Rood 1925-26, Edna Christianson 1930-31

Third Charter, Date Back, Blue Seal	Ser #	# Notes
10-10-10-10	1-625	2,500
Third Charter, Plain Back, Blue Seal		
10-10-10-10	626-1450	3,300
1929, Type I		
6-10's	1-133	798

Total amount of circulation issued = $65,980. Amount of large outstanding at close = $970. Amount of small outstanding at close = $5,820.

5,800 Large   798 Small   6,598 Total

10371M	$10 1902PB	629	890 B	U911170	VG	Higgins Mus.
10371M	$10 1902PB	629	989 A	V353319	F	pen/pen
10371	$10 1929T1		A000074A		F	Higgins Mus.
10371	$10 1929T1		C002833A		AU	

THE BOONE NATIONAL BANK   11 L
6838   BOONE

Chartered in June 1903. Placed in voluntary liquidation on March 24, 1925; capital of $100,000. Absorbed by the Boone State Bank, Boone.

Officers: Pres. EE Hughes 1903-11, John Cooper 1912-19, EM Duroe 1920-25; **VP** FM Ballou 1903, FC Farrow 1904, John Cooper 1907-12, HH Canfield 1913-25; **Cash.** AJ Wilson 1903-04, TL Ashford 1905-10, ED Carter 1911, Geo. B Irick 1912-23; **AC** AM Burnside 1907-13, PG Osgood 1911, CA Ray 1920, WH Miller 1922, FC Murdock 1922, FW Murdock 1923, Joe Snover

1924

Third Charter, Red Seal	Ser #	# Notes
10-10-10-20	1-4550	18,200
Third Charter, Date Back, Blue Seal		
10-10-10-20	1-7500	30,000
Third Charter, Plain Back, Blue Seal		
10-10-10-20	7501-10458	11,832

Total amount issued = $750,400. Amount outstanding in 1924 = $48,395.

60,032 Large   0 Small   60,032 Total

6838 M	$10 1902RS	613	3498 B	H850784	CU	Higgins Mus.
6838 M	$20 1902RS	639	762 A	B128178	F	
6838 M	$20 1902RS	639	1868 A	D276762	F	pen/pen
6838 M	$10 1902DB	616	1189 D	A993568	G	
6838 M	$10 1902DB	616	1276 D	A993655	VG	pen/pen Stain
6838 M	$10 1902DB	616	1851 E	M638185	F	Higgins Mus.
6838 M	$10 1902DB	616	7064 E	H789310B	G	faded/faded
6838 M	$20 1902DB	642	5600 B	T344380A	F	stamp/stamp
6838 M	$10 1902PB	624	7867 E	E271396D	?	nice sigs
6838	$10 1902PB	624	9440 E	R680642E	?	faded/faded
6838	$10 1902PB	624	10167 F	M30139H	VG	Higgins Mus.

THE CITIZENS NATIONAL BANK OF BOONE   19 S
13817   BOONE

Chartered in October 1933 with a capital of $100,000. Succeeded #3273; assumed the circulation of #3273.

Officers: Pres. John H Georingger 1933-35; **VP** John H Abbott 1934-35; **Cash.** Harry A Laird 1933-35, RH Barber 1935

1929, Type II	Ser #	# Notes
10's	1-1635	1,635
20's	1-445	445

Total amount of circulation issued = $25,250. Amount of small outstanding on July 31, 1935 = $58,550. Includes the unredeemed notes of #3273.

0 Large   2,080 Small   2,080 Total

13817	$10	1929T2	A000533	F	
13817	$10	1929T2	A000700	F/VF	
13817	$10	1929T2	A000729	VF	
13817	$10	1929T2	A000856	F	
13817	$10	1929T2	A000890	F	
13817	$10	1929T2	A001186	F	
13817	$10	1929T2	A001588	VF	
13817	$10	1929T2	A001621	?	
13817	$20	1929T2	A000001	CU	
13817	$20	1929T2	A000029	F/VF	
13817	$20	1929T2	A000030	F/VF	
13817	$20	1929T2	A000155	VG	
13817	$20	1929T2	A000178	VF+	
13817	$20	1929T2	A000198	F/VF	
13817	$20	1929T2	A000275	XF	
13817	$20	1929T2	A000284	F	Higgins Mus.
13817	$20	1929T2	A000319	VG/F	
13817	$20	1929T2	A000320	VG/F	
13817	$20	1929T2	A000404	CU	

THE FIRST NATIONAL BANK OF BOONE   1 L
2051   BOONE

Chartered on September 26, 1872 with a capital of $50,000. Placed in voluntary liquidation on January 22, 1878; capital of $50,000. Succeeded by the City Bank.

Officers: Pres. William F Clark 1872-78; **Cash.** CJA Ericson 1872-78

First Charter, Original Issue	Ser #	# Notes
5-5-5-5	1-1600	6,400
10-10-10-20	1-700	2,800
First Charter, Series of 1875		
5-5-5-5	1-95	380

Total amount of circulation issued = $68,900. Amount outstanding at close = $32,400. Amount outstanding in 1910 = $350.

9,580 Large   0 Small   9,580 Total
2051 $5   ORIG 399   76 D   K555568   F   Higgins Mus.

THE NATIONAL BANK OF BOONE   3 L
3273 (FIRST TITLE)   BOONE

Organized on November 24, 1884 with a capital of $50,000. Title changed to The First National Bank of Boone in April 1888.

Officers: Pres. Samuel L Moore 1884-88; **VP** JM Herman 1884-88; **Cash.** James Hazlett 1884-88; **AC** TE Moore 1884-88

Second Charter, Brown Backs	Ser #	# Notes
5-5-5-5	1-169	676
10-10-10-20	1-225	900

1,576 Large   0 Small   1,576 Total

3273 -	$5 1882BB	467	28 C	B162159	?	pen/pen
3273 -	$10 1882BB	480	1 A	B22676	F/VF	Higgins Mus.

3273	-	$10 1882BB	480	1 B	B22676	?	pen/pen

THE FIRST NATIONAL BANK OF BOONE 24 L 46 S
3273 (SECOND TITLE) BOONE

Succeeded The National Bank of Boone on April 7, 1888. In conservatorship on April 5, 1933. Placed in voluntary liquidation on January 5, 1934; capital of $200,000. Succeeded by #13817; circulation assumed by #13817.
Officers: **Pres.** Samuel L Moore 1888-21, CC Quinn 1922-32, JH Herman 1933-34; **VP** JM Herman 1888-99, EE Hughes 1900-02, JE Carlson 1909, FP McDonald 1920-32, HR Eaton 1922-23, JH Herman 1926-32, CO Craig 1926-28, WH Crooks 1933-34; **Cash.** James Hazlett 1888, JH Herman 1889-1918, 1920-23, FP McDonald 1924-34; **AC** TE Moore 1888-95, SJ Jayne 1900-02, EB Arthur 1903-08, HR Eaton 1909-21, 1924-34, JE Carlson 1911-34, EC Ehlers 1919-34

Second Charter, Brown Backs	Ser #	# Notes
10-10-10-20	1-3057	12,228
Third Charter, Red Seal		
10-10-10-20	1-3600	14,400
Third Charter, Date Back, Blue Seal		
10-10-10-20	1-7100	28,400
Third Charter, Plain Back, Blue Seal		
10-10-10-20	7101-12549	21,796
1929, Type I		
6-10's	1-1328	7,968
6-20's	1-388	2,328

Total amount of circulation issued = $1,101,170. Amount of large outstanding at close = $5,600. Amount of small outstanding at close = $64,400. Circulation liability assumed by #13817 which was then responsible for redeeming the outstanding circulation of #3273. Since #13817 did not issue any large, the large outstanding for #13817 are actually notes of #3273. Therefore, the amount of large size outstanding on July 31, 1935 was $4,800.
76,824 Large   10,296 Small   87,120 Total

3273	M	$10	1902DB	616	180 F	E580745	VG/F	
3273	M	$10	1902DB	616	5536 ?	V809331A	?	
3273	M	$10	1902DB	616	6217 E	Z834885A	VG/F	
3273	M	$10	1902DB	616	6410 D	Z835078A	VG	gone/gone Rust
3273	M	$10	1902DB	616	6503 D	Z835171A	VF	nice sigs
3273	M	$20	1902DB	642	2348 B	X901814	VF	faded/faded
3273	M	$20	1902DB	642	5536 B	V809351A	VG	faded/faded
3273	M	$10	1902PB	624	7785 D	Y314667D	?	
3273	M	$10	1902PB	624	7843 E	Y314725D	VF	Higgins Mus.
3273	M	$10	1902PB	624	8481 D	H17143E	VG/F	faded/faded
3273	M	$10	1902PB	624	8694 E	T221236E	VG	
3273	M	$10	1902PB	624	8724 F	T221266E	VF	nice sigs
3273	M	$10	1902PB	624	9045 D	Z505837E	VG	
3273	-	$10	1902PB	624	10208 D	Y29260H	VG/F	faded/faded
3273	-	$10	1902PB	624	10708 F	10708 F	F	
3273	-	$10	1902PB	624	10934 F	10934 F	VG	nice sigs
3273	-	$10	1902PB	624	11985 D	11985 D	G	
3273	-	$10	1902PB	624	12112 E	12112 E	F	
3273	-	$10	1902PB	624	12378 F	12378 F	XF	stamp/stamp
3273	M	$20	1902PB	650	7581 B	Y314463D	F	sigs
3273	M	$20	1902PB	650	7881 B	Y314763D	VG	gone/gone
3273	M	$20	1902PB	650	8226 B	H16888E	VG/F	stamp/stamp
3273	-	$20	1902PB	650	9930 B	T447612H	F	stamp/stamp
3273	-	$20	1902PB	650	10027 B	Y29079H	VG	faded/faded
3273		$10	1929T1		C000096A	F+		
3273		$10	1929T1		D000121A	XF		
3273		$10	1929T1		C000182A	VG		
3273		$10	1929T1		E000205A	VG		
3273		$10	1929T1		D000245A	F		
3273		$10	1929T1		B000281A	F/VF		
3273		$10	1929T1		C000359A	F		
3273		$10	1929T1		B000482A	?		
3273		$10	1929T1		A000523A	VG		
3273		$10	1929T1		A000571A	F		
3273		$10	1929T1		D000643A	F/VF		
3273		$10	1929T1		B000657A	F		
3273		$10	1929T1		A000663A	G/VG		
3273		$10	1929T1		C000785A	?		
3273		$10	1929T1		B001031A	VG		
3273		$10	1929T1		A001054A	G/VG		
3273		$10	1929T1		B001057A	F		
3273		$10	1929T1		E001071A	F		
3273		$10	1929T1		F001122A	F/VF		
3273		$10	1929T1		C001127A	F		
3273		$10	1929T1		A001184A	AU		
3273		$10	1929T1		D001217A	VF		
3273		$10	1929T1		D001243A	VF		
3273		$10	1929T1		B001246A	F/VF		
3273		$10	1929T1		F001308A	F		
3273		$20	1929T1		C000059A	F		
3273		$20	1929T1		B000061A	?		
3273		$20	1929T1		E000081A	F		
3273		$20	1929T1		F000100A	F		
3273		$20	1929T1		B000165A	F/VF		
3273		$20	1929T1		A000170A	VG		
3273		$20	1929T1		D000187A	VF		
3273		$20	1929T1		C000224A	F/VF		
3273		$20	1929T1		D000224A	VG		
3273		$20	1929T1		A000266A	F		
3273		$20	1929T1		C000266A	F		
3273		$20	1929T1		D000271A	F/VF		
3273		$20	1929T1		D000278A	F/VF		
3273		$20	1929T1		A000281A	VF	Higgins Mus.	
3273		$20	1929T1		F000292A	VG		
3273		$20	1929T1		B000327A	VG/F		
3273		$20	1929T1		E000337A	F		
3273		$20	1929T1		B000338A	XF		
3273		$20	1929T1		C000345A	AU		
3273		$20	1929T1		B000363A	?		
3273		$20	1929T1		D000371A	G/VG		

THE BRIGHTON NATIONAL BANK 0 L
2033 WASHINGTON

Chartered on August 24, 1872. Placed in voluntary liquidation on December 15, 1881; capital of $50,000. Succeeded by the Brighton Bank.
Officers: **Pres.** RC Risk 1874-77, John W Prizer 1878-81; **VP** John W Prizer 1877; **Cash.** John W Prizer 1874-76, William H Lloyd 1877-81

First Charter, Original Issue	Ser #	# Notes
1-1-1-2	1-1500	6,000
5-5-5-5	1-2625	10,500
First Charter, Series of 1875		
5-5-5-5	1-2615	10,460

Total amount of circulation issued = $112,300. Amount outstanding at close = $45,000. Amount outstanding in 1910 = $710.
26,960 Large   0 Small   26,960 Total

THE NATIONAL BANK OF BRIGHTON 1 L
5554 WASHINGTON

Chartered on August 25, 1900. Placed in voluntary liquidation on December 31, 1906; capital of $25,000. Absorbed by The Savings Bank of Brighton.
Officers: **Pres.** MC Terry 1901-06; **VP** JL Downs 1902, JH Bull 1903-06; **Cash.** Frank R Sage 1901-02, AB Endicott 1903-06

Second Charter, Brown Backs	Ser #	# Notes
10-10-10-20	1-1020	4,080

Total amount of circulation issued = $51,000. Amount outstanding at close = $20,000. Amount outstanding in 1910 = $3,370.
4,080 Large   0 Small   4,080 Total

5554	M	$10 1882BB	490	959 A	R15620R	VG	Davenport B&T

THE FIRST NATIONAL BANK OF BRITT 5 L
5020 HANCOCK

Organized on August 23, 1895, with a capital of $50,000. Placed in receivership on February 1, 1927; capital of $50,000. Reason for failure: local depression.
Officers: **Pres.** PM Joice 1896-98, Lewis Larson 1899-1913, CP Lewis 1914-17, HC Armstrong 1918-27; **VP** CP Lewis 1896-99, PM Joice 1900-03, Webb Vincent 1904-08, CP Lewis 1909-27; **Cash.** Lewis Larson 1896-98, EF Larson 1899-1909, HA Early 1911-12, ER Haines 1913, JP Spalla 1914-27; **AC** EF Larson 1896-98, CL Larson 1900-08, 1910, HD Larson 1911-19, EH Pittman 1920-21, ME Fox 1922-27

Second Charter, Brown Backs	Ser #	# Notes
5-5-5-5	1-4800	19,200
50-100	1-770	1,540
Second Charter, Date Back		
5-5-5-5	1-2503	10,012
50-100	1-300	600
50-50-50-100	1-124	496
Third Charter, Plain Back, Blue Seal		
5-5-5-5	1-4910	19,640
10-10-10-20	1-3340	13,360

Total amount issued = $602,760. Amount outstanding at close = $44,300.
64,848 Large   0 Small   64,848 Total

5020		$50 1882BB	515	53 A	A980250	F	
5020	M	$100 1882BB	527	639 A	B556560	CU	pen/pen ac
5020	M	$50 1882DB	560	256 B	A153457	VG/F	Higgins Mus.
5020		$5 1902PB	606	3416 A	V559567E	VF	Higgins Mus.
5020	M	$10 1902PB	632	1809 C	R180283E	VG	stamp Soiled

THE FIRST NATIONAL BANK OF BROOKLYN 2 L
3284 **POWESHIEK**
Organized on December 22, 1884 with a capital of $50,000. Placed in receivership on December 4, 1925; capital of $50,000. Reason for failure: local depression.
Officers: Pres. TJ Holmes 1885-1907, BM Talbott 1908-19; **VP** AB Talbott 1896-1914; **Cash.** BM Talbott 1885-1907, NH Wright 1908-1915, AB Talbott 1916-17, Edw. H Talbott 1918-19; **AC** NH Wright 1885-1907, EH Talbott 1909-19

Second Charter, Brown Backs	Ser #	# Notes
50-100	1-536	1,072
Third Charter, Red Seal		
10-10-10-20	1-570	2,280
Third Charter, Date Back, Blue Seal		
10-10-10-20	1-1145	4,580
Third Charter, Plain Back, Blue Seal		
10-10-10-20	1146-2168	4,092

Total amount issued = $217,300. Amount outstanding at close = $14,700.
12,024 Large   0 Small   12,024 Total

| 3284 | M | $10 | 1902PB | 624 | 1379 F | V689396D | VG | Higgins Mus. |
| 3284 | M | $10 | 1902PB | 624 | 1729 D | M836811E | VG | nice sigs |

THE FIRST NATIONAL BANK OF BUFFALO CENTER 28 L 26 S
5154 **WINNEBAGO**
Organized on October 20, 1898 with a capital of $50,000. Placed in receivership on January 20, 1933; capital of $50,000. Reason for failure: not available from reports.
Officers: Pres. PM Joice 1899-1904, CW Gadd 1905-1931, HA Wagner 1932; **VP** BJ Thompson 1900-03, CW Gadd 1904-09, BJ Thompson 1910, JB Thompson 1911-12, JW Woodcock 1913-32; **Cash.** AW Winden 1899-1903, RC Ballstadt 1903-04, JJ Guyer 1904-32; **AC** John P Young 1902, CW Gadd 1903, CH Galagan 1910, Bessie McDermott 1913-32, MO Brickey 1922-26, CH Galagan 1927-32

Second Charter, Brown Backs	Ser #	# Notes
5-5-5-5	1-3850	15,400
10-10-10-20	1-2520	10,080
Second Charter, Date Back		
5-5-5-5	1-3250	13,000
10-10-10-20	1-2340	9,360
Second Charter, Value Back		
5-5-5-5	3251-4165	3,660
10-10-10-20	2341-2805	1,860
Third Charter, Plain Back, Blue Seal		
5-5-5-5	1-5237	20,948
10-10-10-10	1-850	3,400
10-10-10-20	1-3097	12,388
1929, Type I		
6-5's	1-1255	7,530
6-10's	1-579	3,474
6-20's	1-173	1,038

Total amount of circulation issued = $813,290. Amount of large outstanding at close = $5,917. Amount of small outstanding at close = $44,080.
90,096 Large   12,042 Small   102,138 Total

5154		$5	1882BB	477	1054 A	M578939	VG	
5154	-	$10	1882BB	490	1292 A	W779798	F/VF	pen/stamp Higgins Mus.
5154	-	$20	1882BB	504	689 A	W779195	VG/F	
5154	M	$5	1882DB	537	2024 H	N241566	?	
5154	M	$5	1882DB	537	2107 H	K994869	G	lt stamp sigs
5154	M	$5	1882DB	537	2544 H	N241566	VF+	stamp/stamp
5154	M	$10	1882DB	545	337 E	D163467	VG	gone/gone
5154	M	$10	1882DB	545	2190 F	T314748	F	stamp/stamp
5154	M	$5	1882VB	574	3402 E	R945664	VG	
5154	M	$5	1882VB	574	3787 F	T320624	VF	
5154	M	$5	1882VB	574	4020 G	T659082	VG	gone/gone Washed and pressed
5154	M	$5	1882VB	574	4023 F	T659085	G/VG	gone/gone
5154	M	$5	1902PB	606	1111 D	X65907D	F	pen/stamp
5154	M	$5	1902PB	606	2143 D	T879149E	VG	
5154	M	$5	1902PB	606	2413 D	T879419E	F/VF	
5154	M	$5	1902PB	606	2501 D	X300457E	F	faded/faded
5154	-	$5	1902PB	606	4250 A	4250 A	F	stamp/stamp
5154	-	$5	1902PB	606	4438 B	4438 B	VF	stamp/stamp
5154	M	$10	1902PB	632	236 G	R804021	F	Ink
5154	M	$10	1902PB	632	308 E	?	CU	
5154	M	$10	1902PB	632	402 E	T279632	XF	gone/gone
5154	M	$10	1902PB	632	780 A	V168830	VF+	Higgins Mus.
5154	-	$10	1902PB	632	2206 B	2206 B	F/VF	
5154	-	$10	1902PB	632	2331 A	2331 A	F	
5154	M	$20	1902PB	658	1464 A	M155626H	?	
5154	-	$20	1902PB	658	2026 A	2026 A	VF	
5154	-	$20	1902PB	658	2346 A	2346 A	F	
5154	-	$20	1902PB	658	2834 A	2834 A	VF	
5154		$5	1929T1		E000334A		F	
5154		$5	1929T1		D000939A		VG/F	
5154		$5	1929T1		A001049A		VG/F	
5154		$10	1929T1		A000072A		?	Higgins Mus.
5154		$10	1929T1		A000073A		AU	
5154		$10	1929T1		A000164A		G+	
5154		$10	1929T1		F000302A		XF/AU	
5154		$10	1929T1		E000303A		AU	Higgins Mus.
5154		$10	1929T1		A000329A		F+	
5154		$10	1929T1		E000390A		VF/XF	
5154		$10	1929T1		A000414A		F	
5154		$10	1929T1		D000459A		?	
5154		$10	1929T1		D000511A		VF	
5154		$10	1929T1		E000558A		F	
5154		$20	1929T1		F000004A		?	
5154		$20	1929T1		F000012A		VG/F	
5154		$20	1929T1		B000013A		VF	
5154		$20	1929T1		A000055A		F	
5154		$20	1929T1		E000080A		VG	
5154		$20	1929T1		F000094A		?	
5154		$20	1929T1		E000104A		F	Ink (teller stamp)
5154		$20	1929T1		E000106A		VG	
5154		$20	1929T1		A000118A		F	
5154		$20	1929T1		F000135A		F	
5154		$20	1929T1		D000140A		?	
5154		$20	1929T1		D000141A		XF	

THE FIRST NATIONAL BANK OF BURLINGTON 10 L
351 (FIRST TITLE) **DES MOINES**
Chartered in 1864. Assumed #751 by consolidation on September 25, 1919 with a title change to First National Bank of Burlington; assumed the circulation of #751.
Officers: Pres. Lyman Cook 1864-98, William Carson 1899-1901, 1904-19, ; **VP** AW Carpenter 1864, Geo. C Lauman 1879, Wm. P Foster 1900-19; **Cash.** Geo. C Lauman 1864-73, JC Osgood 1874-76, William P Foster 1877-1913, LC Wallbridge 1914-19; **AC** LC Wallbridge 1900-12, EA Kohrs 1914

First Charter, Original Issue	Ser #	# Notes
5-5-5-5	1-3500	14,000
10-10-10-20	1-2400	9,600
First Charter, Series of 1875		
10-10-10-20	1-534	2,136
Second Charter, Brown Backs		
10-10-10-20	1-5359	21,436
Third Charter, Red Seal		
10-10-10-20	1-4600	18,400
Third Charter, Date Back, Blue Seal		
10-10-10-20	1-6200	24,800
Third Charter, Plain Back, Blue Seal		
10-10-10-20	6201-10400	16,800

107,172 Large   0 Small   107,172 Total

351	-	$5	ORIG	?	347 B	56537	Fr	Davenport B&T
351	-	$10	1882BB	479	3557 C	R654363	VG	
351	-	$10	1882BB	479	3981 C	Y83656	F+	
351	M	$10	1902RS	613	601 C	A601266	VF	
351	M	$20	1902RS	639	2803 A	K938137	F	pen/pen
351	M	$10	1902DB	624	5134 D	Y850494A	F/VF	pen/stamp
351	M	$10	1902PB	624	6986 E	X713827B	F	
351	M	$20	1902PB	650	6918 B	X713759B	VF	Higgins Mus.
351	M	$20	1902PB	650	7488 B	X714329B	G	gone/faded
351		$20	1902PB	650	8168 B	B299925D	VG	

FIRST NATIONAL BANK OF BURLINGTON 5 L
351 (SECOND TITLE) **DES MOINES**
Succeeded The First National Bank of Burlington on September 28, 1919. Placed in voluntary liquidation on October 15, 1923; capital of $400,000. Absorbed by The First Iowa State Trust & Savings Bank of Burlington.
Officers: Pres. William Carson 1919, CE Perkins 1920-21, Emil Webbles 1922-23; **VP** Wm. P Foster 1919-22, MC Stelle 1920-23, LC Wallbridge 1920-23; **Cash.** LC Wallbridge 1919, PH Augsburger 1920-23; **AC** MR Brooks 1920-23, CS Rich 1920-22, Lester Wilson 1923, Leo Panther 1923, CT Simmons 1923

Third Charter, Plain Back, Blue Seal	Ser #	# Notes
10-10-10-20	1-9139	36,556

Total amount of circulation issued = $1,691,600. Amount outstanding at close = $249,995. This figure includes the outstanding circulation of #351 and #751 since #351 assumed the circulation of #751.
36,556 Large   0 Small   36,556 Total

| 351 | M | $10 | 1902PB | 624 | 1000 D | V740182D | F | gone Washed |

351	M	$10 1902PB 624	3203 D	A782685E	VG		
351	M	$10 1902PB 624	5316 D	H848268E	VF	stamp Pressed	
351	M	$10 1902PB 624	7355 E	T624137E	VF+	stamp/stamp	
351	M	$20 1902PB 650	7778 B	T624560E	VF	Higgins Mus.	

THE MERCHANTS NATIONAL BANK OF BURLINGTON
1744 DES MOINES 41 L 3 S

Organized on November 7, 1870 with a capital of $100,000. Chartered on December 2, 1870. Placed in voluntary liquidation on May 12, 1930; capital of $100,000. Absorbed by The First Iowa State Trust & Savings Bank, The Burlington Savings Bank, The American Savings Bank and Trust Company, and The Farmers and Merchants Savings Bank, all of Burlington, Iowa. Placed in receivership on December 2, 1930; reason: deficiency in assets sold.

Officers: **Pres.** Theo. W Barhydt 1870-1905, JL Edwards 1906-29; **VP** John Patterson 1896, WE Blake 1900-14, Alex Moir 1909-24, James Moir 1909-24, Geo. S Tracy 1920-29, FL Houke 1920-29, CL Fulton 1920-29; **Cash.** Edw. McKitterick 1870-78, Henry C Garrett 1879-96, JL Edwards 1897-1905, HJ Hungerford 1906-17, EW Wichhart 1919-29; **AC** HJ Hungerford 1897-1905, FL Houke 1907-14, CL Fulton 1909-14, CA Daniels 1920, AA Willem 1920-29, A Daniels 1922-29

First Charter, Original Issue	Ser #	# Notes
1-1-1-2	1-1500	6,000
5-5-5-5	1-2375	9,500
10-10-10-20	1-2500	10,000
First Charter, Series of 1875		
5-5-5-5	1-1040	4,160
10-10-10-20	1-2652	10,608
Second Charter, Brown Backs		
50-100	1-2473	4,946
Second Charter, Date Back		
5-5-5-5	1-1825	7,300
Third Charter, Date Back, Blue Seal		
5-5-5-5	1-5000	20,000
50-50-50-100	1-950	3,800
Third Charter, Plain Back, Blue Seal		
5-5-5-5	5001-26294	85,176
50-50-50-100	951-1172	888
1929, Type I		
6-5's	1-1506	9,036
6-50's	1-29	174
6-100's	1-1	6

Total amount of circulation issued = $1,614,210. Amount of large outstanding at close = $308,080. Amount of small outstanding at close = $54,480.
162,378 Large 9,216 Small 171,594 Total

1744	-	$2 ORIG 389	1 A	C204736	pen/pen	
1744	M	$50 1902DB 670	341 B	A341	AU	
1744	M	$50 1902DB 670	894 C	B119228	F/VF	
1744	M	$100 1902DB 692	907 A	B119241	VF	
1744	-	$100 1902DB 692	938 A	938 A	F	stamp/stamp
1744	M	$5 1902PB 600	6991 C	E564247D	F	stamp Stains
1744	M	$5 1902PB 600	12263 C	E898334E	CU	stamp/stamp
1744	M	$5 1902PB 600	12264 C	E898335E	?	
1744	M	$5 1902PB 600	12265 C	E898336E	CU	
1744	M	$5 1902PB 600	12266 C	E898337E	CU	
1744	M	$5 1902PB 600	12269 A	E898340E	CU	stamp/stamp
1744	M	$5 1902PB 600	12269 B	E898340E	CU	stamp/stamp
1744	M	$5 1902PB 600	14651 A	E950272E	CU	stamp/stamp
1744	M	$5 1902PB 600	14651 B	E950272E	CU	
1744	M	$5 1902PB 600	14652 A	E950273E	CU	stamp/stamp
1744	M	$5 1902PB 600	14653 C	E950274E	CU	stamp/stamp
1744	M	$5 1902PB 600	14654 A	E950275E	CU	
1744	M	$5 1902PB 600	14655 A	E950276E	CU	
1744	M	$5 1902PB 600	14655 B	E950276E	CU	
1744	M	$5 1902PB 600	14656 A	E950277E	CU	
1744		$5 1902PB 600	18121 C	M518132H	CU	Higgins Mus.
1744		$5 1902PB 600	19906 B	X581517H	CU	
1744		$5 1902PB 600	22266 ?	?	CU	
1744	-	$5 1902PB 600	22353 D	22353 D	CU	stamp/stamp
1744		$5 1902PB 600	22392 B	22392 B	VG	
1744	-	$5 1902PB 600	22527 ?	22527 ?	F	
1744		$5 1902PB 600	22665 C	22665 C	CU	
1744		$5 1902PB 600	22666 C	22666 C	CU	stamp/stamp
1744		$5 1902PB 600	22672 C	22672 C	CU	
1744		$5 1902PB 600	22673 C	22673 C	CU	
1744		$5 1902PB 600	23794 B	23794 B	VG	stamp/stamp
1744		$5 1902PB 600	23808 B	23808 B	XF	faded/faded
1744		$5 1902PB 600	23893 C	23893 C	VG	stamp/stamp
1744		$5 1902PB 600	24266 C	24266 C	AU	
1744		$5 1902PB 600	24703 B	24703 B	VG	
1744	-	$5 1902PB 600	24729 A	24729 A	VG/F	
1744	-	$5 1902PB 600	24970 A	24970 A	AU	
1744	-	$5 1902PB 600	24971 A	24971 A	AU	
1744	-	$5 1902PB 600	25172 D	25172 D	F	stamp/stamp
1744	-	$5 1902PB 600	26082 A	26082 A	F	Washed
1744	-	$100 1902PB 701	1132 A	1132 A	F	stamp/stamp
1744		$5 1929T1	F001244A		VG/F	Higgins Mus.
1744		$5 1929T1	E001460A		VF	
1744		$100 1929T1	F000001A		F	

THE NATIONAL STATE BANK OF BURLINGTON 24 L
751 DES MOINES

Chartered in 1865. Closed; consolidated with #351 on September 25, 1919; capital of $150,000. Circulation assumed by #351.

Officers: **Pres.** WF Coolbaugh 1865-66, FW Brooks 1867-69, ED Rand 1870-71, Jas. C Peasley 1872-82, Jno. T Remey 1883-1918, CF Brook 1919; **VP** Chas. Starker 1896, JW Brooks 1900-14; **Cash.** FW Brooks 1865-66, Jas. C Peasley 1867-71, Jno. T Remey 1872-82, TG Foster 1883-86, John J Fleming 1887-1900, JW Brooks 1901-16, MC Stelle 1917-19; **AC** JW Brooks 1896, MC Stelle 1902-14, Geo. W Roth 1909, Chase E Brooks 1909-14

First Charter, Original Issue	Ser #	# Notes
1-1-1-2	1-1000	4,000
5-5-5-5	1-1500	6,000
10-10-10-20	1-4960	19,840
First Charter, Series of 1875		
10-10-10-20	1-2250	9,000
Second Charter, Brown Backs		
10-10-10-20	1-7968	31,872
Third Charter, Red Seal		
10-10-10-20	1-5000	20,000
Third Charter, Date Back, Blue Seal		
10-10-10-20	1-9800	39,200
Third Charter, Plain Back, Blue Seal		
10-10-10-20	9801-12902	12,408

Total amount of circulation issued = $1,689,000. Amount outstanding at close = $143,600. Circulation assumed by #351 which was then responsible for redeeming the outstanding circulation of #751.
142,320 Large 0 Small 142,320 Total

751	-	$1 ORIG 380	436 C	330096	XF+	
751	-	$1 ORIG 380	701 A	330361	CU	Higgins Mus.
751	-	$1 ORIG 380	701 C	330361	CU	
751	-	$1 ORIG 380	723 A	330383	CU	
751	-	$1 ORIG 380	723 B	330383	CU	pen/pen
751	-	$1 ORIG 380	740 C	330400	CU	
751	-	$1 ORIG 380	888 A	330548	AU	pen/pen
751	-	$1 ORIG 380	888 B	330548	CU	
751	-	$10 ORIG 412	2941 B	B327000	F/VF	Oat Bin Hoard
751		$10 1882BB 480	4331 B	X901816	VG/F	Higgins Mus.
751		$10 1882BB 480	5553 C	X911159	F	
751	M	$10 1882BB 480	6962 B	D656424D	CU	ac Rust spots
751	M	$10 1902RS 613	1884 A	E180529	F	
751	M	$10 1902DB 616	6048 E	K783759A	CU	
751	M	$10 1902DB 616	6048 F	K783759A	CU	
751	M	$10 1902DB 616	6050 D	K783761A	CU	Higgins Mus.
751	M	$20 1902DB 642	6359 B	N519799A	VF	Soiled back
751	M	$10 1902PB 624	?	X911159	?	
751	M	$10 1902PB 624	7689 E	X239914A	VG/F	pen/pen ac
751	M	$10 1902PB 624	9638 D	B42644B	VF+	pen/pen ac Rust
751	M	$10 1902PB 624	10454 D	U19172B	XF/AU	
751	M	$10 1902PB 624	10868 D	U19586B	F	ac
751	M	$10 1902PB 624	11951 E	Y597660B	VF	
751	M	$20 1902PB 650	10924 B	U19642B	F	pen/pen

THE BURT NATIONAL BANK 7 L
5703 KOSSUTH

Chartered on February 6, 1901 with a capital of $40,000. Succeeded The Burt Bank. Placed in voluntary liquidation on September 5, 1927; capital of $50,000. Absorbed by #5685.

Officers: **Pres.** CC Chubb 1901-11, EJ Murtagh 1912-27; **VP** Thomas F Cooke 1902-08, EJ Murtagh 1909-11, CC Chubb 1913-27, CH Blossom 1923-27; **Cash.** CH Blossom 1901-22, Lloyd Elston 1923-27; **AC** HO Buell 1902-09, EC Nelson 1913-14, Lloyd Elston 1920-22, CO Bailey 1923-27

Second Charter, Brown Backs	Ser #	# Notes
10-10-10-20	1-2100	8,400
Second Charter, Date Back		
10-10-10-20	1-2500	10,000
Second Charter, Value Back		
10-10-10-20	2501-3905	5,620
Third Charter, Plain Back, Blue Seal		
10-10-10-20	1-2526	10,104

Total amount issued = $426,550. Amount outstanding in 1926 = $40,000.
34,124 Large 0 Small 34,124 Total

5703	M	$10 1882DB	?	1600 F	M195658	VG/F	DB or BB ?
5703	M	$20 1882DB	555	1063 B	K296811	XF	Higgins Mus.
5703	M	$10 1882VB	577	2646 D	T723644	VG	pen/gone Ink
5703	M	$20 1882VB	581	2588 B	T723586	VF	pen/stamp
5703	M	$10 1902PB	633	225 B	Y817187D	F/VF	Higgins Mus.
5703	M	$10 1902PB	633	684 A	E919266E	G/VG	pen ac/gone
5703	-	$20 1902PB	659	2414 A	2414 A	VF	pen/stamp

THE FIRST NATIONAL BANK OF BURT 18 L 3 S
5685 KOSSUTH

Organized on January 5, 1901 with a capital of $25,000. Chartered on January 18, 1901; succeeded The Farmers Savings Bank. Absorbed #5702 on September 5, 1927. Placed in receivership on September 5, 1930; capital of $40,000. Reason for failure: local depression.

Officers: Pres. Jos. W Wadsworth 1901-08, SE McMahon 1909-27, HO Buell 1928-30; **VP** LC Smith 1902-22, HO Buell 1923-27, JR Mawdsley 1928-29, BH Marlow 1930; **Cash.** Chas. D Smith 1901-08, HO Buell 1909-22, HA Thompson 1923-30; **AC** FJ Mann 1904-08, Kirby Smith 1909, HA Thompson 1920-22, CO Bailey 1928-30

Second Charter, Brown Backs	Ser #	# Notes
10-10-10-20	1-1280	5,120
Second Charter, Date Back		
10-10-10-20	1-1780	7,120
Second Charter, Value Back		
10-10-10-20	1781-2580	3,200
Third Charter, Plain Back, Blue Seal		
10-10-10-20	1-1983	7,932
1929, Type I		
6-10's	1-235	1,410
6-20's	1-29	174

Total amount of circulation issued = $309,730. Amount of large outstanding at close = $7,760. Amount of small outstanding at close = $17,240.

23,372 Large   1,584 Small   24,956 Total

5685	M	$20 1882DB	555	48 B	B542618	VG/F	
5685	M	$20 1882DB	555	1227 B	N71295	F/VF	pen/pen vp Stains
5685	M	$10 1882VB	577	2070 D	U293928	F/VF	
5685	M	$10 1882VB	577	2562 F	V307000	VG	Higgins Mus.
5685	M	$20 1882VB	581	2205 B	U676223	VG	
5685	M	$10 1902PB	633	754 B	E31906H	CU	
5685	M	$10 1902PB	633	754 C	E31906H	?	
5685	M	$10 1902PB	633	755 A	E31907H	CU	pen/pen vp
5685	M	$10 1902PB	633	755 B	E31907H	AU	
5685	M	$10 1902PB	633	755 C	E31907H	CU	
5685	M	$10 1902PB	633	756 A	E31908H	AU	
5685	M	$10 1902PB	633	756 C	E31908H	CU	pen/pen
5685	M	$10 1902PB	633	874 A	M524186H	AU	pen/pen vp
5685	M	$10 1902PB	633	874 B	M524186H	AU	pen vp Higg Mus.
5685	M	$10 1902PB	633	875 A	M524187H	XF	
5685	M	$10 1902PB	633	875 C	M524187H	CU	Higgins Mus.
5685	-	$10 1902PB	633	1490 A	1490 A	G	
5685	-	$10 1902PB	633	1513 A	1513 A	F+	pen/pen
5685		$10 1929T1		F000084A		VG/F	
5685		$10 1929T1		A000183A		F/VF	Higgins Mus.
5685		$10 1929T1		A000188A		VG	

THE FIRST NATIONAL BANK OF CAMBRIDGE 17 L
9014 STORY

Organized on October 25, 1907 with a capital of $25,000. Placed in receivership on May 22, 1926; capital of $80,000. Reason for failure: incompetent management & dishonesty.

Officers: Pres. EP Healy 1908-11, BF Scott 1912-13, SJ Severson 1914-15, FW Larson 1916-20, WH Heggen 1923-24, FW Larson 1925-26; **VP** CW Erwin 1909-12,1914, SJ Severson 1913, JS Osness 1914-19, WH Heggen 1920-22, JL Osness 1920-24, CH Alders 1925-26; **Cash.** RF Erwin 1908-12, HA Early 1913-24; **AC** CO Fatland 1910, WC Walker 1911-12, T John Hill 1913-19, N Beck 1920-21, AW Erwin 1920-21, T John Hill 1922-26

Third Charter, Red Seal	Ser #	# Notes
5-5-5-5	1-400	1,600
10-10-10-20	1-340	1,360
Third Charter, Date Back, Blue Seal		
5-5-5-5	1-2125	8,500
10-10-10-20	1-1640	6,560
Third Charter, Plain Back, Blue Seal		
5-5-5-5	2126-11890	39,060
10-10-10-20	1641-7468	23,312

Total amount issued = $636,200. Amount outstanding at close = $78,700.

80,392 Large   0 Small   80,392 Total

9014	M	$5 1902PB	600	4154 F	A833845D	XF	
9014	M	$5 1902PB	600	5397 E	H381098D	G/VG	
9014	M	$5 1902PB	600	7116 ?	?	Fr/G	
9014	M	$5 1902PB	600	7508 H	D436779E	F	
9014	M	$5 1902PB	600	9281 E	B440867H	F/VF	gone Higg. Mus.
9014	-	$5 1902PB	600	10738 G	U633724H	F	light stamps
9014	-	$5 1902PB	600	11561 E	11561 E	VF/XF	stamp/stamp
9014	-	$5 1902PB	600	11742 F	11742 F	F	stamp/stamp
9014	M	$10 1902PB	626	4225 F	A133707E	VG	Tape stains
9014	M	$10 1902PB	626	4295 ?	?	?	
9014	M	$10 1902PB	626	5442 F	Z20324E	VG/F	faded/faded
9014	-	$10 1902PB	626	7060 D	Z987852H	VG	
9014	M	$20 1902PB	652	3337 B	K163729D	?	
9014	M	$20 1902PB	652	5330 B	Z20212E	VF	sig/gone
9014		$20 1902PB	652	6376 B	T172208H	VG/F	
9014	-	$20 1902PB	652	6903 B	Z987695H	VF	gone/sig
9014	-	$20 1902PB	652	7282 B	7282 B	F	stamp/stamp

THE FIRST NATIONAL BANK OF CARROLL 7 L
3969 CARROLL

Organized on January 25, 1889 with a capital of $50,000. Succeeded The Farmers Bank. Merged with The Citizens State Bank in 1893. Consolidated with The Bank of Carroll in 1895. Placed in receivership on October 21, 1908; capital of $100,000. Reason for failure: incompetent management.

Officers: Pres. GW Wattles 1889-91, CD Boynton 1892-93, CA Mast 1894, WL Culbertson 1895-1908; **VP** HW Macomber 1896-1908; **Cash.** RG Smith 1889-90, CL Wattles 1891-94, RE Coburn 1895-1908; **AC** LG Bang 1896

Second Charter, Brown Backs	Ser #	# Notes
10-10-10-20	1-7028	28,112

Total amount of circulation issued = $351,400. Amount outstanding at close = $85,000. Amount outstanding in 1915 = $6,960.

28,112 Large   0 Small   28,112 Total

3969	M	$10 1882BB	483	5157 B	K715511K	F+	vp Higgins Mus.
3969	M	$10 1882BB	483	5223 B	K715577K	F	
3969	M	$10 1882BB	483	6678 A	U271958U	VG/F	
3969	M	$10 1882BB	483	6829 A	U272109U	VG/F	gone/pen vp
3969	-	$20 1882BB	497	? A	E87770	?	
3969	-	$20 1882BB	497	3076 A	V53369	VG	pen/pen
3969	M	$20 1882BB	497	6143 A	T320090T	F	pen/pen vp

THE ABRAM RUTT NATIONAL BANK OF CASEY 24 L 0 S
8099 GUTHRIE

Named after founder and President, Abram Rutt, this bank was one of four "private name" national banks in Iowa.

Chartered in February 1906 with a capital of $25,000. Placed in voluntary liquidation on February 1, 1930; capital of $50,000. Absorbed by The Citizens Savings Bank, Casey.

Officers: Pres. Abram Rutt 1906-13, S Lincoln Rutt 1914-1929; **VP** Wm Valentine 1907-14, John F Thompson 1922-28, Peter Ludwig 1929; **Cash.** S Lincoln Rutt 1906-13, Harlie E Smith 1914-29; **AC** Harlie E Smith 1907-13, ST Lawler 1920-29

Third Charter, Red Seal	Ser #	# Notes
10-10-10-20	1-895	3,580
Third Charter, Date Back, Blue Seal		
10-10-10-20	1-3450	13,800
Third Charter, Plain Back, Blue Seal		
10-10-10-20	3451-9895	25,780
1929, Type I		
6-10's	1-67	400

$10 type 1 = $4,000 worth; serials E000067A and F000067A were not issued. Total amount of circulation issued = $543,500. Amount outstanding at close = $33,600. Amount of small outstanding at close = $4,000.

43,160 Large   400 Small   43,560 Total

8099	M	$10 1902DB	617	1839 D	A648577A	F	Sig. Abram Rutt
8099	M	$10 1902DB	617	2732 D	V790817A	VF/XF	pen/pen
8099	M	$10 1902DB	617	3412 F	Z871856A	G	gone/faded
8099	M	$20 1902DB	643	2068 B	H607059A	VF/XF	pen/pen
8099	M	$10 1902PB	625	6215 D	K381107E	VF	Washed, Pressed
8099	M	$10 1902PB	625	6699 D	U509301E	F/VF	
8099	M	$10 1902PB	625	6775 F	U509377E	VF	
8099	M	$10 1902PB	625	7001 D	B264893H	XF/AU	Higgins Mus.
8099		$10 1902PB	625	7179 ?	?	?	
8099	-	$10 1902PB	625	8106 F	B81188K	G	
8099	-	$10 1902PB	625	8383 E	8383 E	VF	pen/pen ac
8099	-	$10 1902PB	625	8415 D	8415 D	F	Water Stain
8099	-	$10 1902PB	625	8537 D	8537 D	F	
8099	-	$10 1902PB	625	8917 F	8917 F	VG/F	
8099	-	$10 1902PB	625	9052 E	9052 E	?	
8099	-	$10 1902PB	625	9143 E	9143 E	VG/F	pen/pen
8099	-	$10 1902PB	625	9325 E	9325 E	XF	pen/pen ac
8099	-	$10 1902PB	625	9791 D	9791 D	VF	pen/pen
8099	M	$20 1902PB	651	3957 B	U705315B	F	
8099	M	$20 1902PB	651	5579 B	U367051D	VG	pen/faded
8099	M	$20 1902PB	651	5698 B	A448045E	VG/F	gone Trimmed
8099	-	$20 1902PB	651	8576 B	8576 B	VG	pen/pen

8099	-	$20 1902PB	651	9599 B	9599 B	VF	pen/pen
8099	-	$20 1902PB	651	9889 B	9889 B	VF	pen/pen Pressed

THE CEDAR FALLS NATIONAL BANK   21 L   8 S
3871   BLACK HAWK

Chartered on April 4, 1888 with a capital of $50,000. Placed in voluntary liquidation on June 30, 1933; capital of $100,000. Succeeded by The Cedar Falls Trust and Savings Bank, Cedar Falls.

Officers: Pres. James Miller 1888-1900, CH Rodenbach 1901-10, HS Gilkey 1901-04, FB Miller 1905-33; **VP** JJ Tollerton 1896-99, CH Rodenbach 1900 & 1911-20, Henry Johnson 1902-1908, Roger Leavitt 1909-33, HS Gilkey 1909-10, CA Rownd 1922-27, WH Merner 1922-33, HH Seerley 1928-29; **Cash.** Roger Leavitt 1888-1907, Frank B Miller 1908-13 & 1915-17, Harry W Johnson 1914, HC Smith 1918-33; **AC** WN Holstrop 1896-99, FB Miller 1900-04, Harry W Johnson 1907- 1913, WH Bedford 1910, JJ Kyhl 1920-33

Second Charter, Brown Backs	Ser #	# Notes
5-5-5-5	1-7199	28,796
10-10-10-20	1-3423	13,692
Third Charter, Red Seal		
5-5-5-5	1-625	2,500
10-10-10-20	1-500	2,000
Third Charter, Date Back, Blue Seal		
5-5-5-5	1-6850	27,400
10-10-10-20	1-5300	21,200
Third Charter, Plain Back, Blue Seal		
5-5-5-5	6851-28372	86,088
10-10-10-20	5301-6020	2,880
1929, Type I		
6-10's	1-486	2,916
6-20's	1-165	990

Total amount of circulation issued = $1,270,030. Amount of large outstanding at close = $4,772. Amount of small outstanding at close = $25,225.
184,556 Large   3,906 Small   188,462 Total

3871		$5 1882BB	470	450 B	E993614	CU	Higgins Mus.
3871		$10 1882BB	483	1928 C	Y541778	F	Higgins Mus.
3871	M	$10 1882BB	483	2539 C	E617630E	F	
3871	M	$10 1882BB	483	3399 A	U322529U	XF/AU	U322528U ?
3871	M	$20 1902RS	641	154 A	X641139	F	light stamps
3871	M	$20 1902RS	641	156 A	X641141	F	
3871	M	$5 1902DB	592	5653 G	Y772420A	VG/F	
3871	M	$5 1902DB	592	5678 G	Y772445A	F+	nice sigs vp
3871	M	$10 1902DB	618	2924 E	H826970A	F/VF	nice sigs
3871	M	$5 1902PB	600	8226 H	Y341802B	F	
3871	M	$5 1902PB	600	8248 H	Y341824B	F	pen ac/stamp
3871	M	$5 1902PB	600	9565 H	Z399701B	VG	pen/faded
3871	M	$5 1902PB	600	11417 H	D987293D	Fr/G	gone/gone
3871	M	$5 1902PB	600	12415 H	N47741D	VG	gone/gone
3871	M	$5 1902PB	600	16235 H	Y274606D	G	
3871	M	$5 1902PB	600	20589 F	K948385E	VG	Laminated
3871	M	$5 1902PB	600	22749 F	U123255E	VG	gone/gone
3871	M	$5 1902PB	600	23890 F	Z288576E	F	
3871	M	$5 1902PB	600	24817 H	D93378H	?	
3871		$5 1902PB	600	25598 H	D246959H	G	
3871	M	$10 1902PB	626	5714 E	Y354775B	VG	
3871		$10 1929T1		D000170A		F	
3871		$10 1929T1		B000300A		VF	Tight R corner
3871		$10 1929T1		D000401A		F	Rust spots
3871		$10 1929T1		F000444A		VG	
3871		$10 1929T1		D000457A		F	Higgins Mus.
3871		$20 1929T1		A000028A		VF	
3871		$20 1929T1		C000149A		VF	
3871		$20 1929T1		A000152A		F/VF	

THE CITIZENS NATIONAL BANK OF CEDAR FALLS   1 L
5507   BLACK HAWK

Chartered on July 19, 1900. Succeeded The Citizens Bank. Placed in voluntary liquidation on December 16, 1905; capital of $50,000. Reorganized under State Savings System.

Officers: Pres. LH Severin 1900-05; **VP** Adam Boysen 1900-05; **Cash.** WN Hostrop 1900-05; **AC** WE Albertson 1900-03, OH Leonard 1904-05

Second Charter, Brown Backs	Ser #	# Notes
10-10-10-20	1-1964	7,856

Total amount of circulation issued = $98,200. Amount outstanding at close = $49,400. Amount outstanding in 1910 = $6,170.
7,856 Large   0 Small   30,876 Total

5507		$10 1882BB	477	46 C	X519558	VF	Higgins Mus.

THE FIRST NATIONAL BANK OF CEDAR FALLS   2 L
2177   BLACK HAWK

Chartered on September 1, 1874 with a capital of $50,000. Suspended on May 16, 1893. Placed in receivership on June 13, 1893; capital of $50,000. Reason for failure: incompetent management.

Officers: Pres. William M Fields 1876-93; **Cash.** Charles J Fields 1876-93; AC AW Mason 1878-93

First Charter, Original Issue	Ser #	# Notes
1-1-1-2	1-1000	4,000
5-5-5-5	1-1500	6,000
10-10-10-20	1-200	800
First Charter, Series of 1875		
1-1-1-2	1-280	1,120
5-5-5-5	1-3520	14,080
10-10-10-20	1-1219	4,876

Total amount of circulation issued = $177,750. Amount outstanding at close = $11,250. Amount outstanding in 1915 = $1,112.
30,876 Large   0 Small   30,876 Total

2177	-	$1	ORIG 382	338 C	E1353	VF	pen/pen
2177	-	$2	ORIG 389	544 A	E1559	AU	Higgins Mus.

THE CEDAR RAPIDS NATIONAL BANK   103 L   70 S
3643   LINN

Organized on February 28, 1887 with a capital of $100,000. Succeeded G.F. Van Vechten. Assumed #9168 by consolidation on December 15, 1914. Placed in voluntary liquidation on August 3, 1932; capital of $600,000. Absorbed by #2511. Placed in receivership on January 23, 1934; reason: deficiency in assets sold.

Officers: Pres. Arthur T Averill 1887-1910, Ralph Van Vechten 1911-14, Geo B Douglas 1915, Ralph Van Vechten 1916-21, Glenn M Averill 1922-31; **VP** GF Van Vechten 1896-1909, Ralph Van Vechten 1907-10, Geo B Douglas 1911-22, EH Smith 1914, GM Averill 1914-2121, Karl H Rhenberg 1922-24, Geo F Miller 1922-28, EM Scott 1929-32, Chas C Kuning 1929-32, Peter F Bailey 1929-30; **Cash.** Ralph Van Vechten 1887-1904, JH Ingwersen 1905-07, Kent C Ferman 1908-14, 1916-19, Ed H Smith 1915, Chas C Kuning 1922-32; **AC** Kent C Ferman 1904-07, John Fletcher 1904-08, Louis Visha 1909-12, Martin Newcomer 1909-21, Chas C Kuning 1920-21, KH Rehnberg 1920-21, Geo F Miller 1920-21, AR Smouse 1920-24, Peter F Bailey 1922-28, MR Selden 1922-32, Geo W Swab 1922-32, BM Wolf 1922-32, MW Carpenter 1929-32, RD Brown 1929-32, OA Kearney 1930-32

Second Charter, Brown Backs	Ser #	# Notes
5-5-5-5	1-12975	51,900
10-10-10-20	1-3941	15,764
Third Charter, Red Seal		
10-10-10-20	1-1000	4,000
Third Charter, Date Back, Blue Seal		
10-10-10-20	1-16500	66,000
Third Charter, Plain Back, Blue Seal		
10-10-10-20	16501-81276	259,104
1929, Type I		
6-10's	1-6938	41,628
6-20's	1-2034	12,204

Total amount of circulation issued = $5,230,710. Amount of large outstanding at close = $58,712. Amount of small outstanding at close = $441,285.
396,768 Large   53,832 Small   450,600 Total

3643	-	$5 1882BB	469	1345 D	H133984	VG	pen/pen
3643	-	$5 1882BB	469	6340 D	?	XF/AU	
3643	-	$5 1882BB	469	6427 D	Y5570	CU	
3643	-	$5 1882BB	469	6428 D	Y5571	CU	
3643	-	$5 1882BB	469	6429 D	Y5572	CU	Yellow spot; torn R corner
3643	-	$5 1882BB	469	6430 D	Y5573	AU	Higgins Mus.
3643	-	$5 1882BB	469	7329 C	?	VF	Fed. Res. Bk.,

San Fran.

Bank	M	Denom	Plate	Serial	Serial2	Grade	Notes
3643		$5 1882BB 469	10055 A	?		G	
3643	M	$10 1882BB 482	3244 B	K712408K		F	
3643		$20 1882BB 496	1292 A	Y112807		VG/F	
3643	M	$20 1882BB 496	2752 A	D429164D		VF+	pen/pen vp
3643	M	$10 1902DB 618	4474 F	E964780A		AU	
3643	M	$10 1902DB 618	8560 E	R374404A		CU	
3643	M	$10 1902DB 618	8584 E	R374428A		XF	
3643	M	$10 1902DB 618	8586 E	R374430A		CU	
3643	M	$10 1902DB 618	8586 F	R374430A		CU	
3643	M	$10 1902DB 618	8588 E	R374432A		CU	8588 F ?
3643	M	$10 1902DB 618	8591 E	R374435A		CU	stamp/stamp
3643	M	$10 1902DB 618	8592 E	R374436A		CU	stamp/stamp
3643	M	$10 1902DB 618	8596 E	R374440A		CU	
3643	M	$10 1902DB 618	8599 E	R374443A		AU	
3643	M	$10 1902DB 618	8601 E	R374445A		CU	Higgins Mus.
3643	M	$10 1902DB 618	8602 E	R374446A		CU	stamp/stamp
3643	M	$10 1902DB 618	8603 E	R374447A		CU	
3643	M	$10 1902DB 618	8604 E	R374448A		CU	
3643	M	$10 1902DB 618	8607 E	R374451A		CU	stamp/stamp
3643	M	$10 1902DB 618	8609 E	R374453A		CU	
3643	M	$10 1902DB 618	8610 E	R374454A		CU	stamp/stamp
3643	M	$10 1902DB 618	8611 E	R374455A		CU	
3643	M	$10 1902DB 618	13336 F	X737501A		VG	
3643	M	$10 1902DB 618	15195 E	B847857B		CU	Davenport B&T
3643	M	$10 1902DB 618	15196 E	B847858B		CU	Davenport B&T
3643	M	$10 1902DB 618	16092 F	?		XF/AU	
3643	M	$20 1902DB 644	7063 B	R351847A		F	
3643	M	$20 1902DB 644	12018 B	X722683A		F	stamp/stamp
3643	M	$10 1902PB 626	16561 F	R740466B		XF	stamp/stamp
3643	M	$10 1902PB 626	18490 ?	?		CU	Davenport B&T
3643	M	$10 1902PB 626	19267 ?	?		?	
3643	M	$10 1902PB 626	22358 D	?		F+	Davenport B&T
3643	M	$10 1902PB 626	22814 F	X268251B		VG	stamp/stamp
3643	M	$10 1902PB 626	24121 D	X451912B		AU	
3643	M	$10 1902PB 626	26311 F	B124588D		XF	Davenport B&T
3643	M	$10 1902PB 626	32025 F	H31189D		CU	Davenport B&T
3643	M	$10 1902PB 626	35269 D	U387361D		VG/F	
3643	M	$10 1902PB 626	36716 ?	U388808D		AU	
3643	M	$10 1902PB 626	40234 I	A12196E		F	nice sigs
3643	M	$10 1902PB 626	43766 C	K403158E		VF	
3643	M	$10 1902PB 626	43773 H	K403165E		PR	tape
3643	M	$10 1902PB 626	45834 L	M70336E		VG	
3643	M	$10 1902PB 626	51826 J	B375348H		F	
3643	M	$10 1902PB 626	55167 K	K155039H		VG	nice sigs
3643		$10 1902PB 626	55240 K	K173872H		VG+	
3643		$10 1902PB 626	57688 K	T450570H		CU	Davenport B&T
3643	-	$10 1902PB 626	60587 L	Z381659H		VG/F	pen/pen
3643	-	$10 1902PB 626	60604 ?	?		?	
3643	-	$10 1902PB 626	61542 K	Z639514H		VF	
3643	-	$10 1902PB 626	63757 J	A884389K		VG	nice sigs
3643	-	$10 1902PB 626	64418 ?	A885050K		VG	
3643	-	$10 1902PB 626	64448 J	A885080K		VG	
3643	-	$10 1902PB 626	64962 J	64962 J		XF	Davenport B&T
3643	-	$10 1902PB 626	66112 L	66112 L		VG	
3643	-	$10 1902PB 626	66316 J	66316 J		VF	Davenport B&T
3643	-	$10 1902PB 626	67486 J	67486 J		F	Tear
3643	-	$10 1902PB 626	68521 K	68521 K		VF	stamp/stamp
3643	-	$10 1902PB 626	68555 L	68555 L		VF	stamp/stamp
3643	-	$10 1902PB 626	68744 J	68744 J		?	
3643	-	$10 1902PB 626	68907 J	68907 J		XF	pen/pen
3643	-	$10 1902PB 626	68929 K	68929 K		VG	
3643	-	$10 1902PB 626	70332 J	70332 J		VF	
3643	-	$10 1902PB 626	71592 L	71592 L		VF	
3643	-	$10 1902PB 626	72933 J	72933 J		VF	
3643	-	$10 1902PB 626	76271 J	76271 J		F	
3643	-	$10 1902PB 626	77541 L	77541 L		F/VF	
3643	-	$10 1902PB 626	78585 L	78585 L		F	stamp/stamp
3643	-	$10 1902PB 626	80456 K	80456 K		F	
3643	-	$10 1902PB 626	81194 K	81194 K		VF	stamp/stamp
3643	M	$20 1902PB 652	18108 B	?		VF	
3643	M	$20 1902PB 652	18281 B	T135631B		G	gone/stamp
3643	M	$20 1902PB 652	18602 B	?		F	
3643	M	$20 1902PB 652	26170 B	B124447D		F	
3643	M	$20 1902PB 652	33859 B	?		VF	
3643	M	$20 1902PB 652	34001 B	M906493D		AU	
3643	M	$20 1902PB 652	42496 C	?		AU	
3643	M	$20 1902PB 652	42625 C	A66857E		F	
3643	M	$20 1902PB 652	44721 D	M50163E		XF	
3643	M	$20 1902PB 652	50504 D	U953246E		VF	
3643	M	$20 1902PB 652	51501 D	B375023H		?	
3643	M	$20 1902PB 652	53767 D	B436369H		VF	
3643	M	$20 1902PB 652	54249 D	K154121H		VF	
3643		$20 1902PB 652	57884 D	T450766H		VG	
3643		$20 1902PB 652	60587 D	Z381659H		F	sigs
3643		$20 1902PB 652	62154 D	A831146K		VG	
3643	-	$20 1902PB 652	67056 D	67056 D		F	
3643	-	$20 1902PB 652	70498 D	70498 D		?	
3643	-	$20 1902PB 652	71725 D	71725 D		F	stamp/stamp
3643	-	$20 1902PB 652	71958 D	71958 D		CU	
3643	-	$20 1902PB 652	72299 D	72299 D		VF	
3643	-	$20 1902PB 652	72300 D	72300 D		AU	
3643	-	$20 1902PB 652	74190 D	74190 D		VG	stamp/stamp
3643	-	$20 1902PB 652	74454 D	74454 D		F	
3643	-	$20 1902PB 652	75766 D	75766 D		F/VF	stamp/stamp
3643	-	$20 1902PB 652	78448 D	78448 D		F	stamp/stamp
3643	-	$20 1902PB 652	78979 D	78979 D		G	
3643		$10 1929T1	C000379A			VG	
3643		$10 1929T1	B000438A			F/VF	
3643		$10 1929T1	C000489A			F	
3643		$10 1929T1	B000595A			F+	
3643		$10 1929T1	D000634A			F	
3643		$10 1929T1	E000655A			VG	
3643		$10 1929T1	B000730A			VF	
3643		$10 1929T1	B001299A			VF	
3643		$10 1929T1	D001471A			VG	
3643		$10 1929T1	A001568A			VF	
3643		$10 1929T1	C002046A			VG	
3643		$10 1929T1	A002171A			VG	
3643		$10 1929T1	B002452A			G/VG	
3643		$10 1929T1	A002936A			VG	Rust spots
3643		$10 1929T1	C003756A			VG	
3643		$10 1929T1	A004156A			VG	
3643		$10 1929T1	A004760A			VG	
3643		$10 1929T1	C004791A			VG	
3643		$10 1929T1	C004801A			F	
3643		$10 1929T1	B004830A			CU	
3643		$10 1929T1	B004838A			CU	Higgins Mus.
3643		$10 1929T1	E004864A			F	
3643		$10 1929T1	E004895A			VF	
3643		$10 1929T1	F005118A			VG	
3643		$10 1929T1	A005258A			VG/F	
3643		$10 1929T1	C005450A			XF/AU	
3643		$10 1929T1	A005559A			VG/F	
3643		$10 1929T1	A005700A			?	
3643		$10 1929T1	D006049A			F	
3643		$10 1929T1	C006060A			F/VF	
3643		$10 1929T1	B006093A			G	
3643		$10 1929T1	D006240A			AU	
3643		$10 1929T1	F006559A			F	
3643		$10 1929T1	F006616A			F	
3643		$10 1929T1	B006761A			F	
3643		$10 1929T1	B006819A			VF	
3643		$10 1929T1	E006842A			VG	
3643		$10 1929T1	E006865A			VG	"820" written
3643		$20 1929T1	C000042A			VF	
3643		$20 1929T1	C000106A			VG	
3643		$20 1929T1	B000160A			VF	
3643		$20 1929T1	A000208A			F	
3643		$20 1929T1	F000260A			F	
3643		$20 1929T1	C000303A			F	
3643		$20 1929T1	E000331A			XF/AU	
3643		$20 1929T1	F000396A			?	
3643		$20 1929T1	B000442A			XF	
3643		$20 1929T1	A000500A			VG/F	
3643		$20 1929T1	A000501A			VG	
3643		$20 1929T1	A000552A			AU	
3643		$20 1929T1	A000697A			G/VG	
3643		$20 1929T1	A000736A			VG	
3643		$20 1929T1	D000741A			F	
3643		$20 1929T1	E000861A			F	
3643		$20 1929T1	D000989A			F	
3643		$20 1929T1	C001137A			VF	
3643		$20 1929T1	A001256A			F/VF	
3643		$20 1929T1	B001259A			F	
3643		$20 1929T1	F001314A			G	
3643		$20 1929T1	A001335A			F	
3643		$20 1929T1	C001495A			VG	
3643		$20 1929T1	A001583A			VF	
3643		$20 1929T1	E001585A			F	
3643		$20 1929T1	A001702A			VG/F	
3643		$20 1929T1	F001741A			XF	

3643	$20	1929T1	F001833A		VF	
3643	$20	1929T1	A001948A		VF	
3643	$20	1929T1	F001967A		AU	
3643	$20	1929T1	A001986A		VF	
3643	$20	1929T1	F001992A		VF	

THE CITIZENS NATIONAL BANK OF CEDAR RAPIDS   2 L
5113   **LINN**
Chartered on March 14, 1898. Succeeded #483. Placed in voluntary liquidation on June 20, 1908; capital of $200,000. Consolidated with #2511.
Officers: Pres. Jas L Bever 1898-1905, Jno R Amidon 1906-08; **VP** John R Amidon 1900-06, TC Munger 1907-08, CE Putnam 1907-08; **Cash.** JW Bowdish 1898-03, RT Forbes 1904-06, JS Broeksmit 1907-08

Second Charter, Brown Backs	Ser #	# Notes
10-10-10-20	1-7526	30,104

Total amount of circulation issued = $376, 300. Amount outstanding at close = $150,000. Amount outstanding in 1910 = $48,895.

30,104 Large   0 Small   30,104 Total

5113	M	$10	1882BB	489	5590 A	N763733N	VF	
5113	M	$10	1882BB	489	6565 C	T907539T	AU	Higgins Mus.

THE CITY NATIONAL BANK OF CEDAR RAPIDS   2 L
483   **LINN**
Chartered on July 19, 1864. Placed in voluntary liquidation on March 28, 1898; capital of $100,000. Succeeded by #5113.
Officers: Pres. Sampson C Bever 1867-92, Jas L Bever 1893-98; **Cash.** Jas L Bever 1867-92, John B Bever 1893-95, JR Amidon 1896-98

First Charter, Original Issue	Ser #	# Notes
1-1-1-2	1-3000	12,000
5-5-5-5	1-3150	12,600
10-10-10-20	1-1500	6,000
First Charter, Series of 1875		
1-1-1-2	1-680	2,720
5-5-5-5	1-1090	4,360
10-10-10-20	1-1090	4,360
Second Charter, Brown Backs		
10-10-10-20	1-1959	7,836

Total amount of circulation issued = $330,650. Amount outstanding at close = $27,000. Amount outstanding in 1910 = $2,677.

49,876 Large   0 Small   49,876 Total

483	-	$1	ORIG	380	808 A	637230	Fair	637220 ?
483	-	$2	ORIG	387	2621 A	D853800	VF	Higgins Mus.

THE COMMERCIAL NATIONAL BANK OF CEDAR RAPIDS   4 L
9168   **LINN**
Chartered in June 1908. Placed in voluntary liquidation on December 15, 1914; capital of $100,000. Consolidated with #3643.
Officers: Pres. Jas L Bever 1908-14; **VP** WC La Tourette 1909-14, JL Bever, Jr. 1910-14; **Cash.** JL Bever, Jr. 1908-09, Homer Pitner 1910-12, EB Zbanek 1913, Homer Pitner 1914; **AC** EB Zbanek 1910, FD Snakenberg 1911-12, Geo F Miller 1913-14

Third Charter, Date Back, Blue Seal	Ser #	# Notes
5-5-5-5	1-6900	27,600
10-10-10-20	1-4724	18,896

Total amount of circulation issued = $374,200. Amount outstanding at close = $91,547. Amount outstanding in October 1915 = $52,647.

46,496 Large   0 Small   46,496 Total

9168	M	$5	1902DB	592	1079 A	A46752	VG	weak sigs
9168	M	$10	1902DB	618	4467 C	V182565A	VG	faded/faded
9168	M	$20	1902DB	644	226 A	A37654	F	
9168	M	$20	1902DB	644	3354 A	D27639A	VF	

THE FIRST NATIONAL BANK OF CEDAR RAPIDS   4 L
500   **LINN**
Chartered on August 23, 1864. Closed on May 15, 1886. Placed in voluntary liquidation on May 28,1886; capital of $100,000.
Officers: Pres. William W Walker 1867-74, John Weare 1874-86; **Cash.** John Weare 1867-73, John F Dean 1874-86; **AC** EE Weare 1885-86

First Charter, Original Issue	Ser #	# Notes
1-1-1-2	1-3300	13,200
5-5-5-5	1-9000	36,000
First Charter, Series of 1875		
5-5-5-5	1-1760	7,040
Second Charter, Brown Backs		
5-5-5-5	1-1128	4,512

Total amount of circulation issued = $254,260. Amount outstanding at close = $35,490. Amount outstanding in 1910 = $2,130.

60,752 Large   0 Small   60,752 Total

500	-	$1	ORIG	380	1180 B	536867	CU	
500	-	$1	ORIG	380	1923 A	537610	AU	
500	-	$1	ORIG	380	2462 C	C14397	AU	Higgins Mus.
500	-	$5	ORIG	397	5480 A	H656604	VG	pen/pen

THE MERCHANTS NATIONAL BANK OF CEDAR RAPIDS
2511   **LINN**   **55 L   113 S**
Chartered in 1881. Assumed #5113 by consolidation on June 20, 1908. Absorbed #3643 on August 3, 1932.
Officers: Pres. Redman D Stephens 1881-82, MA Higley 1883-98, John T Hamilton 1899-1918, JM Dinwiddie 1919-22, Jas E Hamilton 1923-33, SE Coquilette 1934-35; **VP** JW Henderson 1896-99, PC Frick 1900-08, Jas E Hamilton 1909-22, PC Frick 1913-35, Furrow 1922-31, Boyson 1922-35, Folsom 1922-31, Myers 1935, MR Selden 1935, GF Miller 1935; **Cash.** Charles E Putnam 1881-1904, Jas E Hamilton 1905-07, J S Broeksmit 1908-11, EH Furrow 1912-21, Mark J Myers 1922-35; **AC** Jas E Hamilton 1902-06, Edwin H Furrow 1907-11, HN Boyson 1913- 20, RC Folsom 1913-20, MJ Myers 1913-20, FA Groeltz 1920-22, SE Coquilette 1922-24, EB Zbanek 1922-24, Fred W Smith 1925-35, LW Broulik 1925-35, RD Brown 1935, OA Kearney 1935, RW Mannatt 1935, Peter Bailey 1935

First Charter, Series of 1875	Ser #	# Notes
5-5-5-5	1-10600	42,400
50-100	1-108	216
Second Charter, Brown Backs		
50-100	1-1200	2,400
Second Charter, Date Back		
10-10-10-20	1-10000	40,000
50-50-50-100	1-2048	8,192
Second Charter, Value Back		
10-10-10-20	10001-10630	2,520
Third Charter, Plain Back, Blue Seal		
10-10-10-20	1-19577	78,308
50-50-50-100	1-2554	10,216
1929, Type I		
6-10's	1-5624	33,744
6-20's	1-1796	10,776
6-50's	1-700	4,200
6-100's	1-164	984
1929, Type II		
10's	1-96	96

Total amount of circulation issued = $3,931,370. Amount of large outstanding in 1935 = $33,550. Amount of small outstanding in 1935 = $466,450.

184,252 Large   49,800 Small   234,052 Total

2511	-	$5	1875	404	1708 D	N363753	VG/F	weak sigs
2511	-	$5	1875	404	7459 C	Y88802	VF+	
2511	-	$5	1875	404	8214 D	Y203917	AU	pen/pen
2511	-	$5	1875	404	9749 D	Y513017	F	
2511	-	$5	1875	404	10579 B	Y546582	VF	Grinnell # 3143, Higgins Mus.
2511	-	$50	1875	446	92 A	A461857	XF	
2511	M	$10	1882DB	545	2810 C	A144412	F	
2511	M	$10	1882DB	545	8684 B	M653342	F	
2511	M	$20	1882DB	555	971 A	A133973	VG+	
2511	M	$20	1882DB	555	3744 A	?	G	
2511	M	$20	1882DB	555	5025 A	D954319	VG/F	Corner missing
2511	M	$20	1882DB	555	6241 A	D960835	F	
2511	M	$20	1882DB	555	7074 A	K72989Z	VG	
2511	M	$20	1882DB	555	9392 A	M654050	XF	Bottom tight
2511	M	$50	1882DB	563	521 ?	A52443	?	
2511	M	$50	1882DB	563	525 C	A52447	XF	
2511	M	$50	1882DB	563	1160 D	A157734	F+	lt. stamp sigs
2511	M	$50	1882DB	563	1910 E	?	CU	Fed. Res. Bk., San Fran.
2511	M	$50	1882DB	563	1965 E	A169084	F	faded/faded
2511	M	$100	1882DB	571	619 C	A52541	XF	stamp/stamp
2511		$10	1902PB	633	64 C	Z288386D	G/VG	
2511		$10	1902PB	633	698 B	Z289020D	VF	
2511	-	$10	1902PB	633	1857 B	R460919H	VG	
2511	-	$10	1902PB	633	4943 C	R506615H	F	
2511	-	$10	1902PB	633	5526 B	R507198H	AU	stamp Higg. Mus.
2511	-	$10	1902PB	633	7951 B	V816123H	VG/F	
2511	-	$10	1902PB	633	8175 A	?	VG	
2511	-	$10	1902PB	633	9070 B	9070 B	VG/F	R corner missing
2511	-	$10	1902PB	633	9988 B	9988 B	CU	
2511	-	$10	1902PB	633	10884 A	10884 A	F	gone/faded
2511	-	$10	1902PB	633	11746 A	11746 A	VF	gone/gone
2511	-	$10	1902PB	633	12027 A	12027 A	VF	$10 or $20 ?
2511	-	$10	1902PB	633	12494 B	12494 B	VG	
2511	-	$10	1902PB	633	12631 C	12631 C	VG	
2511	-	$10	1902PB	633	17259 C	17259 C	F	faded/faded
2511	-	$10	1902PB	633	19499 B	19499 B	CU	
2511	-	$10	1902PB	633	19500 B	19500 B	VF	stamp/stamp
2511	-	$20	1902PB	659	6741 A	V785633H	VF	
2511	-	$20	1902PB	659	8017 A	8017 A	F	stamp/stamp

2511	-	$20	1902PB	659	10884 A	10884 A	VG/F		2511		$50	1929T1	B000112A	F+	
2511	-	$20	1902PB	659	12238 A	12238 A	F		2511		$50	1929T1	A000114A	F/VF	
2511	-	$20	1902PB	659	12531 A	12531 A	VG	Tight bottom	2511		$50	1929T1	C000119A	F/VF	
2511	-	$20	1902PB	659	16423 A	16423 A	AU	stamp/stamp	2511		$50	1929T1	D000126A	F	
2511	M	$50	1902PB	683	370 B	A874772	VG	stamp/stamp	2511		$50	1929T1	C000128A	F	
2511	M	$50	1902PB	683	724 C	A938838	VG/F		2511		$50	1929T1	D000129A	?	
2511	M	$50	1902PB	683	947 B	A999721	AU+		2511		$50	1929T1	E000132A	VF	
2511	M	$50	1902PB	683	984 A	A999758	F	light stamps	2511		$50	1929T1	D000219A	F	
2511	M	$100	1902PB	705	714 A	A938828	G/VG	gone/gone	2511		$50	1929T1	A000284A	VG	
2511	-	$100	1902PB	705	1401 A	B72975	VF+	stamp/stamp	2511		$50	1929T1	B000290A	VG	Rust on back
2511	-	$100	1902PB	705	1495 A	B73069	?	Bayard	2511		$50	1929T1	C000311A	XF	
2511	-	$100	1902PB	705	1522 A	B73096	VG		2511		$50	1929T1	C000355A	VF	
2511	-	$100	1902PB	705	1847 A	?	F/VF		2511		$50	1929T1	F000387A	XF	
2511	-	$100	1902PB	705	1891 A	1891 A	F	light stamps	2511		$50	1929T1	A000450A	AU	
2511	-	$100	1902PB	705	2186 A	2186 A	?		2511		$50	1929T1	D000456A	VF+	
2511	-	$100	1902PB	705	2534 A	2534 A	VG		2511		$50	1929T1	B000472A	VG/F	
2511		$10	1929T1		B000275A		VG		2511		$50	1929T1	F000478A	VF+	
2511		$10	1929T1		E000346A		VG		2511		$50	1929T1	E000490A	XF	
2511		$10	1929T1		F000741A		F		2511		$50	1929T1	C000513A	F+	
2511		$10	1929T1		C001047A		AU		2511		$50	1929T1	B000521A	VF	
2511		$10	1929T1		B001299A		VF+		2511		$50	1929T1	A000523A	F	
2511		$10	1929T1		A001426A		F		2511		$50	1929T1	A000528A	F	
2511		$10	1929T1		E001444A		XF		2511		$50	1929T1	D000545A	VF	
2511		$10	1929T1		C001583A		XF		2511		$50	1929T1	E000578A	XF	
2511		$10	1929T1		D001892A		VG/F		2511		$50	1929T1	B000605A	?	
2511		$10	1929T1		D002623A		?		2511		$50	1929T1	C000625A	F	
2511		$10	1929T1		E002907A		F/VF		2511		$50	1929T1	B000632A	?	
2511		$10	1929T1		E002944A		VF		2511		$50	1929T1	A000653A	VF	
2511		$10	1929T1		C002959A		CU		2511		$50	1929T1	E000664A	F	
2511		$10	1929T1		B003204A		G		2511		$50	1929T1	A000666A	VF	
2511		$10	1929T1		F003259A		F+		2511		$50	1929T1	D000691A	G	Stained
2511		$10	1929T1		D003437A		VF/XF		2511		$50	1929T1	E000692A	XF	
2511		$10	1929T1		D003874A		CU		2511		$50	1929T1	C000670A	VF/XF	
2511		$10	1929T1		A003883A		AU		2511		$100	1929T1	F000001A	VF	
2511		$10	1929T1		B003924A		VF		2511		$100	1929T1	C000010A	AU	
2511		$10	1929T1		D003996A		VF		2511		$100	1929T1	E000015A	F/VF	
2511		$10	1929T1		D004087A		F		2511		$100	1929T1	F000029A	VF	
2511		$10	1929T1		C004113A		CU		2511		$100	1929T1	F000050A	VF	
2511		$10	1929T1		B004179A		VF		2511		$100	1929T1	C000062A	VF	
2511		$10	1929T1		B004293A		F/VF		2511		$100	1929T1	F000069A	XF	
2511		$10	1929T1		E004369A		?		2511		$100	1929T1	D000070A	VF	
2511		$10	1929T1		B004382A		VF/XF		2511		$100	1929T1	C000075A	F	
2511		$10	1929T1		C004411A		VG		2511		$100	1929T1	A000098A	VF	
2511		$10	1929T1		D004470A		VF		2511		$100	1929T1	F000128A	VF	
2511		$10	1929T1		B004540A		F		2511		$100	1929T1	C000143A	VF	
2511		$10	1929T1		B004567A		VG		2511		$10	1929T2	A000033	VF	
2511		$10	1929T1		E004864A		F	Tight bottom	2511		$10	1929T2	A000051	F	
2511		$10	1929T1		E004955A		VG		2511		$10	1929T2	A000096	F	
2511		$10	1929T1		D005047A		VG	
2511		$10	1929T1		F005161A		F	
2511		$20	1929T1		B000196A		VG	
2511		$20	1929T1		D000314A		VF	
2511		$20	1929T1		B000779A		F/VF	
2511		$20	1929T1		B000797A		F	
2511		$20	1929T1		B000818A		VG	
2511		$20	1929T1		C000866A		F	
2511		$20	1929T1		F000895A		VG/F	
2511		$20	1929T1		E000976A		VF+	
2511		$20	1929T1		B001108A		F	
2511		$20	1929T1		E001110A		VG	Stains
2511		$20	1929T1		C001111A		AU	
2511		$20	1929T1		B001196A		F	
2511		$20	1929T1		B001254A		XF	
2511		$20	1929T1		B001256A		VG	
2511		$20	1929T1		D001307A		F	Paper clip rust
2511		$20	1929T1		A001326A		AU	
2511		$20	1929T1		A001399A		VF	
2511		$20	1929T1		C001421A		F	
2511		$20	1929T1		D001426A		F	
2511		$20	1929T1		D001520A		VF	
2511		$20	1929T1		A001522A		XF/AU	Higgins Mus.
2511		$20	1929T1		F001544A		VG	
2511		$20	1929T1		A001573A		F	
2511		$20	1929T1		B001611A		VF	
2511		$20	1929T1		B001630A		F	
2511		$20	1929T1		F001640A		CU	Rust stains
2511		$20	1929T1		D001765A		VF	
2511		$50	1929T1		B000010A		F+	
2511		$50	1929T1		D000038A		F	
2511		$50	1929T1		F000080A		VG	
2511		$50	1929T1		B000106A		F	

THE CENTERVILLE NATIONAL BANK 12 L 15 S
2841 APPANOOSE
Chartered in 1882; succeeded the Appanoose County Bank.

Officers: Pres. FM Drake 1883-1903, JL Sawyers 1904-1913, JD Sawyers 1914-18, JL Sawyers 1919, GM Barnett 1920-24, Frank S Payne 1925-32, FL Sawyers 1933-35; **VP** Joseph Goss 1896-1919, Jennie D Sawyers 1920-22, FL Sawyers 1923-33, JB Taylor 1925-35, GW McDonald 1925-27, 1933; **Cash.** WL Selby 1883-35, JC Bevington 1885-94, Geo M Barnett 1895-1919, FD Sargent 1920-23, WM Evans 1925-27, CA Peatman 1928-35; **AC** Guy G Gilcrest 1904-06, FD Sargent 1909-19, HR Joiner 1920-24, RE Packard 1925-27, SH Mehrhoff 1928-35, Pearl Johnston 1929-31, 1933-35

Second Charter, Brown Backs	Ser #	# Notes
5-5-5-5	1-3324	13,296
10-10-10-20	1-841	3,364

Third Charter, Red Seal

5-5-5-5		1-1000	4,000
50-100		1-600	1,200

Third Charter, Date Back, Blue Seal

5-5-5-5		1-3200	12,800
50-100		1-300	600
50-50-50-100		1-427	1,708

Third Charter, Plain Back, Blue Seal

5-5-5-5		3201-15099	47,596
50-50-50-100		428-488	244

1929, Type I

6-5's		1-1660	9,960
6-50's		1-86	516
6-100's		1-32	192

1929, Type II

5's		1-1948	1,948

Total amount of circulation issued = $792,050. Amount of large outstanding in 1935 = $5,167. Amount of small outstanding in 1935 = $44,830.

84,808 Large   12,616 Small   97,424 Total

2841	-	$5 1882BB	466	2970 D	Y906388	VG	pen Higgins Mus.
2841	-	$100 1902DB	689	407 C	407 C	VF/XF	faded/faded
2841	M	$5 1902PB	598	4940 F	K754941D	VG	
2841	M	$5 1902PB	598	8035 E	K66656E	VG	Pinholes
2841	-	$5 1902PB	598	10032 ?	?	VG	
2841	-	$5 1902PB	598	11450 F	Z500761H	F	plate pos. letter ?
2841	-	$5 1902PB	598	12440 H	12440 H	F	faded/faded
2841	-	$5 1902PB	598	12498 F	12498 F	VG	ac vp Higg. Mus.
2841	-	$5 1902PB	598	13176 F	13176 F	VG/F	
2841	-	$5 1902PB	598	14712 F	14712 F	VG/F	pen/pen
2841	-	$5 1902PB	598	14972 G[	14972 G	?	pen Higgins Mus.
2841	-	$5 1902PB	598	14972 H[	14972 H	?	pen Higgins Mus.
2841		$5 1929T1		B000007A		VF	
2841		$5 1929T1		C000257A		G	
2841		$5 1929T1		A001059A		VG	
2841		$5 1929T1		A001360A		VG/F	
2841		$5 1929T1		B001572A		VG	
2841		$50 1929T1		F000007A		F	Ink on face
2841		$50 1929T1		F000038A		F/VF	Higgins Mus.
2841		$50 1929T1		C000042A		XF	
2841		$50 1929T1		D000046A		VF+	
2841		**$50** 1929T1		F000085A		VG/F	$5 or $50
2841		$100 1929T1		D000012A		F/VF	
2841		$100 1929T1		A000019A		VF	
2841		$100 1929T1		C000032A		VF	Last sheet
2841		$5 1929T2		A000817		VG/F	Aged
2841		$5 1929T2		A001583		F	

THE FARMERS NATIONAL BANK OF CENTERVILLE   0 L
2197   APPANOOSE
Chartered on October 27, 1874. Placed in voluntary liquidation on February 27, 1879; capital of $50,000. Succeeded by The Citizens Bank.
Officers: Pres. DC Campbell 1874-79; **Cash.** SW Wright 1874-79

First Charter, Original Issue   Ser #   # Notes
5-5-5-5   1-2250   9,000

First Charter, Series of 1875
5-5-5-5   1-1665   6,660

Total amount of circulation issued = $78,300. Amount outstanding at close = $41,500. Amount outstanding in 1910 = $447.
15,660 Large   0 Small   15,660 Total

THE FIRST NATIONAL BANK OF CENTERVILLE   11 L   31 S
337   APPANOOSE
Chartered in 1864. 1929 notes have the same bank title as above, but the spelling of the town was changed to Centerville to reflect a change in the town name.
Officers: Pres. William Bradley 1867-96, AT Bradley 1896-1900, DC Bradley 1901-10, JA Bradley 1911-16, DC Bradley 1917-26, JA Bradley 1927-33, WO Steel 1934-35; **VP** CW Lewis 1900-01, CM Crego 1902-03, AT Bradley 1904-06, JA Bradley 1907-10, DC Bradley 1911-19, JA Bradley 1920-26, JB Bruckshaw 1920-27, AD Crawford 1928-35; **Cash.** DC Campbell 1867-69, CW Bowen 1870-71, Jno R Hayes 1872-80, William Evans 1881-86, JR Hays 1887-91, JA Bradley 1892-1906, WM Evans 1907-14, OA Tweedy 1916-24, HR Joiner 1925-27, GD Argo 1928-29, RE Oughten 1932-35, **AC** Edward Shutts 1913, WR Krapfel 1914-19, Wm S Bradley 1920-25, RE Oughten 1926-31, Colin F Senior 1934-35

First Charter, Original Issue   Ser #   # Notes
5-5-5-5   1-4500   18,000

First Charter, Series of 1875
5-5-5-5   1-3295   13,180

Second Charter, Brown Backs
5-5-5-5   1-2758   11,032
10-10-10-20   1-192   768

Third Charter, Red Seal

5-5-5-5		1-1500	6,000
10-10-10-20		1-2000	8,000

Third Charter, Date Back, Blue Seal

5-5-5-5		1-3050	12,200

$5 sheets numbered 2801 to 3050 were delivered in September, but not marked as to type. Type uncertain.

10-10-10-20		1-2200	8,800

Sheets 2041-2200 type uncertain.

Third Charter, Plain Back, Blue Seal

5-5-5-5		3051-9420	25,480

Sheets 2801-3050 type uncertain.

10-10-10-20		2201-6329	16,516

Sheets 2041-2200 type uncertain.

1929, Type I
For 1929 notes, the bank name is unchanged at "The First National Bank of Centreville", but the town name is Centerville.

6-5's		1-1232	7,392
6-10's		1-756	4,536
6-20's		1-246	1,476

1929, Type II

5's		1-1484	1,484
10's		1-842	842
20's		1-155	155

Total amount of circulation issued = $986,290. Amount of large outstanding in 1935 = $4,280. Amount of small outstanding in 1935 = $45,720.

119,976 Large   15,885 Small   135,861 Total

337	-	$5 1882BB	466	1114 H	H781556E	G	Oat Bin Hoard
337	-	$20 1882BB	493	33 A	X236739	VG	
337	M	$5 1902PB	598	4998 F	R597334D	G/VG	pen Higgins Mus.
337	M	$5 1902PB	598	7087 G	B224948H	VG	pen/pen
337	M	$5 1902PB	598	7127 E	B224988H	VF+	pen/pen Foxing
337	-	$5 1902PB	598	8084 E	8084 E	VG/F	
337	-	$5 1902PB	598	8830 E	8830 E	F+	pen/pen
337	-	$5 1902PB	598	9090 H	9090 H	VG/F	
337	M	$10 1902PB	624	3418 E	Y795850D	F+	pen/pen
337	M	$20 1902PB	650	1844 B	A405558B	VF	pen/pen
337	-	$20 1902PB	650	5168 B	5168 B	VG+	pen/gone
337		$5 1929T1		E000820A		?	
337		$10 1929T1		E000119A		VG/F	
337		$10 1929T1		A000249A		F	
337		$10 1929T1		F000284A		F/VF	
337		$10 1929T1		D000376A		F	
337		$10 1929T1		A000414A		G/VG	
337		$10 1929T1		C000614A		?	
337		$10 1929T1		A000649A		VG/F	
337		$10 1929T1		B000649A		VF	Stain
337		$10 1929T1		D000649A		XF/AU	
337		$10 1929T1		A000650A		CU	
337		$10 1929T1		E000650A		CU	Higgins Mus.
337		$10 1929T1		F000650A		VG	Ink
337		$10 1929T1		E000651A		F	
337		$10 1929T1		F000731A		F/VF	
337		$20 1929T1		A000032A		VG/F	
337		$20 1929T1		A000036A		?	
337		$20 1929T1		F000063A		F	
337		$20 1929T1		B000119A		VG/F	
337		$20 1929T1		A000172A		F	
337		$20 1929T1		A000178A		F/VF	
337		$20 1929T1		B000205A		F	Washed
337		$10 1929T2		A000348		VF	
337		$10 1929T2		A000519		F	
337		$10 1929T2		A000666		F	
337		$10 1929T2		A000731		AU	
337		$10 1929T2		A000733		CU	
337		$10 1929T2		A000734		AU	
337		$10 1929T2		A000735		AU	
337		$10 1929T2		A000751		VF	
337		$10 1929T2		A000778		F	

THE CHARITON NATIONAL BANK   8 L
6014   LUCAS
Chartered in November 1901. Closed; consolidated with #9024 on October 15, 1921; capital of $50,000.
Officers: Pres. WC Penick 1902-07, HD Copeland 1908-11, JC Copeland 1912-16, EH Perry 1917-21; **VP** Calvin Manning 1902-03, HO Penick 1904-06, JA Penick 1907-12, GW Larimer 1913-19, JA Penick 1920-21; **Cash.** HO Penick 1902, Will Culbertson 1903-04, JC Copeland 1905-11, EL Gookin 1912-21; **AC** GF Trotter 1902-03, Lloyd Penick 1904-09, EL Gookin 1909-10, LB Gittinger 1911-19, JC Bennett 1920-21, MO Johnson 1920-21

Second Charter, Brown Backs   Ser #   # Notes

10-10-10-20	1-3300	13,200

Second Charter, Date Back

10-10-10-20	1-3140	12,560

Second Charter, Value Back

10-10-10-20	3141-5305	8,660

Total amount of circulation issued = $430,250. Amount outstanding in 1921 report = $49,600. Circulation assumed by #9024, which was then responsible for redeeming the outstanding notes of #6014.

34,420 Large   0 Small   34,420 Total

6014	-	$10 1882BB	490	292 C	Z581418	VG/F
6014	M	$10 1882BB	490	1307 B	D668189D	VG pen/lt. pen
6014	M	$10 1882BB	490	1948 A	N407680N	F
6014	M	$10 1882BB	490	3197 C	V604536V	F/VF Higgins Mus.
6014	M	$10 1882VB	577	3797 E	U62355	VG
6014	M	$10 1882VB	577	4628 D	V145536	XF Higgins Mus.
6014	M	$20 1882VB	581	3365 B	T708983	VG
6014	M	$20 1882VB	581	3572 B	U62130	VG

THE FIRST NATIONAL BANK OF CHARITON   2 L
1724   LUCAS

Chartered on October 20, 1870 with a capital of $50,000. Placed in receivership on October 31, 1907; capital of $50,000. Reason for failure: incompetent management.

Officers: Pres. Smith H Mallory 1872-1903, Joseph Braden 1904-05, AL Mallory 1906-07; **VP** Jos Braden 1896-1903, Frank R Crocker 1904-07, JM Thayer 1904-06; **Cash.** Edward A Temple 1872-83, Frank R Crocker 1884-07; **AC** WP Beem 1896-1907

First Charter, Original Issue	Ser #	# Notes
10-10-10-20	1-2000	8,000

First Charter, Series of 1875

10-10-10-20	1-925	3,700

Second Charter, Brown Backs

10-10-10-20	1-2887	11,548

Total amount of circulation issued = $290,600. Amount outstanding at close = $50,000. Amount outstanding in 1915 = $2,840.

23,248 Large   0 Small   23,248 Total

1724	-	$20 1882BB	498	1106 A	T409747	F/VF Higgins Mus.
1724	M	$20 1882BB	498	2556 A	N539898N	VG+ pen/gone

THE LUCAS COUNTY NATIONAL BANK OF CHARITON   11 L
9024 (FIRST TITLE)   LUCAS

Chartered in February 1908. Assumed #6014 by consolidation on October 15, 1921 with a change in title to The Chariton and Lucas County National Bank of Chariton.

Officers: Pres. Samuel McKlveen 1908-21; **VP** WA Eikenberry 1909-21; **Cash.** LH Busselle 1908-21; **AC** Fred O Derrough 1911-13, BR Van Dyke, Jr. 1914-21, JH Collins 1920-21, AR Hass 1920-21

Third Charter, Red Seal	Ser #	# Notes
10-10-10-20	1-375	1,500

Third Charter, Date Back, Blue Seal

5-5-5-5	1-3500	14,000
10-10-10-20	1-2440	9,760

Third Charter, Plain Back, Blue Seal

5-5-5-5	3501-6750	13,000
10-10-10-20	2441-4180	6,960

45,220 Large   0 Small   45,220 Total

9024	M	$20 1902RS	641	1 A	X604578	AU Higgins Mus.
9024	M	$5 1902DB	592	1 A	N718516	AU+
9024	M	$5 1902DB	592	1 B	N718516	F/VF pen Grade ?
9024	M	$5 1902DB	592	3308 D	Y801325	VG
9024	M	$10 1902DB	618	1486 F	E283771A	VG
9024	M	$5 1902PB	600	4052 C	R417500B	F+ nice sigs
9024	M	$5 1902PB	600	5433 D	H595159D	XF pen Higgins Mus.
9024	M	$5 1902PB	600	6118 B	U58729D	VG
9024	M	$10 1902PB	626	2869 D	Y150510B	XF pen/pen
9024	M	$10 1902PB	626	4077 F	B67959E	F
9024		$20 1902PB	652	?	?	AU Hickman-Oakes 11/88 lot #374

THE CHARITON AND LUCAS COUNTY NATIONAL BANK OF CHARITON
9024 (SECOND TITLE)   LUCAS   77 L   4 S

Succeeded The Lucas County National Bank of Chariton on October 15, 1921. Assumed the circulation of #6014. Placed in voluntary liquidation on April 19, 1930; capital of $100,000. Succeeded by #13458; circulation assumed by #13458.

Officers: Pres. LH Busselle 1922-30; **VP** WA Eikenberry 1922-30, EH Perry 1922-30; **Cash.** EL Gookin 1922-30; **AC** BR Van Dyke, Jr. 1922-30, JH Collins 1922-23, AR Hass 1922, MO Johnson 1922-27, HF Barnes 1927-30, WG Shore 1927-30, DE Yost 1927-30

Third Charter, Plain Back, Blue Seal	Ser #	# Notes
5-5-5-5	1-7430	29,720
10-10-10-20	1-5406	21,624

1929, Type I

6-5's	1-1241	7,446
6-10's	1-470	2,820
6-20's	1-92	552

Total amount of circulation issued = $858,120. Amount of large outstanding at close = $27,340. Includes the large outstanding of #6014 and #9024. Amount of small outstanding at close = $72,570. Circulation assumed by #13458, which was then responsible for redeeming the outstanding notes of #9024 and #6014 since #9024 assumed circulation of #6014.

51,334 Large   10,818 Small   62,162 Total

9024	M	$5 1902PB	600	1 A	K265822E	F	
9024	M	$5 1902PB	600	533 B	K266354E	VG	Davenport B&T
9024	M	$5 1902PB	600	4052 C	?	F/VF	
9024	-	$5 1902PB	600	5038 B	5038 B	F	stamp/pen vp
9024	-	$5 1902PB	600	5660 B	5660 B	VG	
9024	-	$5 1902PB	600	6417 B	6417 B	AU	
9024	-	$5 1902PB	600	6729 D	6729 D	VF	
9024	-	$5 1902PB	600	7233 A	7233 A	VF	
9024	-	$5 1902PB	600	7242 D	7242 D	XF/AU	stamp/pen
9024	-	$10 1902PB	626	2185 C	2185 C	Fr/G	
9024	-	$10 1902PB	626	2762 C	2762 C	CU	stamp/pen
9024	-	$10 1902PB	626	2762 C	2762 C	CU	
9024	-	$10 1902PB	626	2763 B	2763 B	?	
9024	-	$10 1902PB	626	2763 C	2763 C	CU	
9024	-	$10 1902PB	626	2766 B	2766 B	CU	
9024	-	$10 1902PB	626	2766 C	2766 C	CU	
9024	-	$10 1902PB	626	2767 ?	2767 ?	CU	
9024	-	$10 1902PB	626	2768 C	2768 C	CU	
9024	-	$10 1902PB	626	2769 A	2769 A	CU	
9024	-	$10 1902PB	626	2770 A	2770 A	CU	
9024	-	$10 1902PB	626	2770 C	2770 C	CU	Higgins Mus.
9024	-	$10 1902PB	626	2771 B	2771 B	CU	stamp/pen
9024	-	$10 1902PB	626	2772 A	2772 A	CU	
9024	-	$10 1902PB	626	2772 C	2772 C	CU	
9024	-	$10 1902PB	626	2773 A	2773 A	AU	Tight bottom
9024	-	$10 1902PB	626	2773 B	2773 B	CU	stamp/pen Orig sigs, not resigned
9024	-	$10 1902PB	626	2773 C	2773 C	CU	stamp/pen Orig sigs, not resigned
9024	-	$10 1902PB	626	2774 A	2774 A	CU	stamp/pen Orig sigs, not resigned
9024	-	$10 1902PB	626	2774 B	2774 B	AU	
9024	-	$10 1902PB	626	2774 C	2774 C	CU	
9024	-	$10 1902PB	626	2776 B	2776 B	VF	
9024	-	$10 1902PB	626	2776 C	2776 C	VF	
9024	-	$10 1902PB	626	2777 C	2777 C	XF/AU	
9024	-	$10 1902PB	626	2778 A	2778 A	VF	
9024	-	$10 1902PB	626	2778 B	2778 B	VF	
9024	-	$10 1902PB	626	2778 C	2778 C	?	
9024	-	$10 1902PB	626	2784 A	2784 A	VF	
9024	-	$10 1902PB	626	2784 B	2784 B	VF	
9024	-	$10 1902PB	626	2784 C	2784 C	AU	
9024	-	$10 1902PB	626	2785 C	2785 C	XF	
9024	-	$10 1902PB	626	2787 ?	2787 ?	AU	
9024	-	$10 1902PB	626	2788 A	2788 A	CU	stamp/pen
9024	-	$10 1902PB	626	2788 B	2788 B	CU	stamp/pen Retraced signature
9024	-	$10 1902PB	626	2789 C	2789 C	CU	
9024	-	$10 1902PB	626	2790 C	2790 C	CU	
9024	-	$10 1902PB	626	2791 C	2791 C	CU	
9024	-	$10 1902PB	626	2829 A	2829 A	CU	
9024	-	$10 1902PB	626	3134 A	3134 A	VG/F	
9024	-	$10 1902PB	626	3252 A	3252 A	VG	Fed. Res. Bk., San Fran.
9024	-	$10 1902PB	626	3768 ?	3768 ?	?	
9024	-	$10 1902PB	626	4884 C	4884 C	VF/XF	
9024		$20 1902PB	652	1871 A	U278223H	?	
9024	-	$20 1902PB	652	2263 A	Z407775H	F	stamp/pen
9024	-	$20 1902PB	652	2490 A	Z408002H	VG	
9024	-	$20 1902PB	652	2768 A	2768 A	?	
9024	-	$20 1902PB	652	2771 A	2771 A	CU	stamp/pen
9024	-	$20 1902PB	652	2777 A	2777 A	CU	
9024	-	$20 1902PB	652	2780 A	2780 A	CU	stamp/pen
9024	-	$20 1902PB	652	2782 A	2782 A	CU	
9024	-	$20 1902PB	652	2784 A	2784 A	CU	
9024	-	$20 1902PB	652	2786 A	2786 A	AU	
9024	-	$20 1902PB	652	2787 A	2787 A	CU	stamp/pen
9024	-	$20 1902PB	652	2788 A	2788 A	AU	stamp/pen
9024	-	$20 1902PB	652	2789 A	2789 A	CU	
9024	-	$20 1902PB	652	2790 A	2790 A	CU	

9024	- $20 1902PB	652	2791 A	2791 A	CU	
9024	- $20 1902PB	652	2823 A	2823 A	CU	
9024	- $20 1902PB	652	2825 A	2825 A	CU	
9024	- $20 1902PB	652	2826 A	2826 A	CU	
9024	- $20 1902PB	652	2827 A	2827 A	CU	Orig sigs, not resigned
9024	- $20 1902PB	652	2828 A	2828 A	CU	
9024	- $20 1902PB	652	2829 A	2829 A	AU	
9024	- $20 1902PB	652	2835 A	2835 A	CU	
9024	- $20 1902PB	652	2836 A	2836 A	XF	
9024	- $20 1902PB	652	2837 A	2837 A	CU	stamp/pen
9024	- $20 1902PB	652	2856 A	2856 A	CU	
9024	- $20 1902PB	652	5101 A	5101 A	VG	stamp/faded
9024	$5 1929T1		F000064A		F	
9024	$5 1929T1		B000755A		VF	Higgins Mus.
9024	$20 1929T1		E000049A		G	
9024	$20 1929T1		E000068A		F	

NATIONAL BANK AND TRUST COMPANY OF CHARITON
13458   LUCAS   **32 S**

Chartered in April 1930. Succeeded #9024. Assumed the circulation of #9024 and thus the circulation of #6014.

Officers: Pres. LH Busselle 1930-35; **VP** WA Eikenberry 1930-35, EH Perry 1930-35; **Cash.** EL Gookin 1930-35; **AC** BR Van Dyke 1930-35, HF Barnes 1930, DE Yost 1930, 1931-35, AR Hass 1930, 1931-35

1929, Type I	Ser #	# Notes
6-5's	1-1562	9,372
6-10's	1-1018	6,108
6-20's	1-256	1,536
1929, Type II		
5's	1-2278	2,278
10's	1-740	740
20's	1-200	200

Total amount of circulation issued = $161,450. Amount of large outstanding in 1935 = $8,520. Includes the large outstanding of #6014 and #9024. Amount of small outstanding in 1935 = $41,480. Includes the small outstanding of #9024 and #13458.

0 Large   20,234 Small   20,234 Total

13458	$5 1929T1	B000175A	VG/F	
13458	$5 1929T1	E000242A	VF	
13458	$5 1929T1	A000245A	?	
13458	$5 1929T1	E000533A	G	
13458	$5 1929T1	C000762A	F+	
13458	$10 1929T1	D000004A	?	
13458	$10 1929T1	A000150A	G+	
13458	$10 1929T1	A000184A	VF	
13458	$10 1929T1	D000250A	VG/F	
13458	$10 1929T1	B000289A	?	
13458	$10 1929T1	E000406A	VG/F	
13458	$10 1929T1	E000485A	?	
13458	$10 1929T1	C000506A	VF/XF	
13458	$10 1929T1	F000768A	VG	
13458	$10 1929T1	B000829A	VF	
13458	$10 1929T1	C000931A	VG/F	Rust
13458	$10 1929T1	C001003A	VG	
13458	$10 1929T1	E001003A	F	
13458	$10 1929T1	E001005A	AU	Higgins Mus.
13458	$10 1929T1	F001005A	F+	
13458	$20 1929T1	C000051A	F	
13458	$20 1929T1	F000112A	VF+	
13458	$20 1929T1	D000170A	F	
13458	$20 1929T1	F000176A	F	
13458	$20 1929T1	B000234A	XF+	
13458	$10 1929T2	A000250	F	
13458	$10 1929T2	A000391	F/VF	
13458	$20 1929T2	A000027	?	
13458	$20 1929T2	A000041	AU	
13458	$20 1929T2	A000083	F+	
13458	$20 1929T2	A000093	F	
13458	$20 1929T2	A000139	F/VF	

THE CHARLES CITY NATIONAL BANK
2579   FLOYD   **5 L**

Chartered on October 25, 1881. Succeeded The Charles City Bank. Placed in voluntary liquidation Oct. 8, 1901; capital of $50,000. Succeeded by #5979.

Officers: Pres. JP Taylor 1883-87, SF Farnham 1888-92, JH Owen 1893-95, Robt G Reiniger 1896-01; **Cash.** SF Farnham 1883-87, JH Owen 1888-92, Geo E May 1893-1901

First Charter, Series of 1875	Ser #	# Notes
5-5-5-5	1-5704	22,816
10-10-10-20	1-138	552

Total amount of circulation issued = $120,980. Amount outstanding at close = $12,500. Amount outstanding in 1910 = $935.

23,368 Large   0 Small   23,368 Total

2579	- $5	1875 405	2309 C	V850308	VG/F	Higgins Mus.
2579	- $5	1875 405	5238 C	Y190461	XF	Wm. Philpott
2579	- $5	1875 405	5280 D	Y190503	VG	
2579	- $5	1875 405	5283 D	Y190503	?	
2579	- $20	1875 435	81 A	K963819	VG	pen/pen 61 A ?

THE CITIZENS NATIONAL BANK OF CHARLES CITY   14 L   25 S
4677   FLOYD

Organized on January 2, 1892 with a capital of $50,000. Placed in conservatorship on April 1, 1933. Licensed on November 27, 1932.

Officers: Pres. HC Baldwin 1892-1917, AL Olds 1918-33, Horace B Olds 1934-35; **VP** Avery Brush 1896-1922, HM Walleser 1923-25, FB Miner 1926-33, Russell B Olds 1933, WA Loosbrock 1934-35; **Cash.** FB Miner 1892-1925, Russell B Olds 1926-32, Horace B Olds 1933, WA Loosbrock 1934-35; **AC** CF Dinkel 1922-24, RB Olds 1922-26, JR Jackson 1922-31, Horace B Olds 1926-32, JH Nelson 1933-35, EA Toepfer 1933-35

Second Charter, Brown Backs	Ser #	# Notes
10-10-10-20	1-1900	7,600
Second Charter, Date Back		
10-10-10-20	1-1170	4,680
Third Charter, Date Back, Blue Seal		
10-10-10-20	1-1700	6,800
Third Charter, Plain Back, Blue Seal		
10-10-10-20	1701-7403	22,812
1929, Type I		
6-10's	1-1162	6,972
6-20's	1-322	1,932
1929, Type II		
5's	1-324	324
10's	1-431	431
20's	1-153	153

Total amount of circulation issued = $641,000. Amount of large outstanding in 1935 = $2,425. Amount of small outstanding in 1935 = $47,575.

41,892 Large   9,812 Small   51,704 Total

4677	$10 1882BB	485	843 A		?	G
4677	$10 1882BB	485	1367 A	K412624K	G	Higgins Mus.
4677 M	$20 1902DB	646	521 A	E339776A	F/VF	
4677	$10 1902PB	628	?	B486727B	?	
4677 M	$10 1902PB	628	2240 C	D332497D	F	
4677 M	$10 1902PB	628	2645 C	K479387D	F	stamp/stamp
4677	$10 1902PB	628	3042 M	V798184D	F	
4677 -	$10 1902PB	628	6206 A	6206 A	F	
4677 -	$10 1902PB	628	6949 B	6949 B	?	
4677 -	$10 1902PB	628	7163 B	7163 B	F/VF	
4677 M	$20 1902PB	654	2354 A	D332611D	F	nice sigs
4677 -	$20 1902PB	654	5419 A	A259391K	Fr/G	gone/gone
4677 -	$20 1902PB	654	5436 A	A259408K	CU	Higgins Mus.
4677 -	$20 1902PB	654	5487 A	A259459K	VG+	
4677	$10 1929T1		D000028A		VG+	
4677	$10 1929T1		A000258A		F/VF	
4677	$10 1929T1		C000283A		VF	
4677	$10 1929T1		F000521A		F/VF	
4677	$10 1929T1		F000909A		F	
4677	$10 1929T1		F001087A		VF	Rust spots
4677	$20 1929T1		D000019A		VF	
4677	$20 1929T1		A000042A		VG	
4677	$20 1929T1		A000148A		VG	
4677	$20 1929T1		F000148A		VF	
4677	$20 1929T1		B000169A		VF	
4677	$20 1929T1		C000220A		?	
4677	$20 1929T1		C000221A		VF	
4677	$20 1929T1		A000232A		F	
4677	$20 1929T1		F000235A		VF	
4677	$20 1929T1		F000247A		F	
4677	$20 1929T1		C000263A		VG	
4677	$20 1929T1		C000268A		VF/XF	
4677	$20 1929T1		C000286A		VG	LL missing
4677	$20 1929T1		A000289A		VF	
4677	$20 1929T1		A000294A		CU	Higgins Mus.
4677	$20 1929T1		D000296A		VG	
4677	$20 1929T1		F000309A		VF	
4677	$5 1929T2		A000323		CU	
4677	$20 1929T2		A000001		VF	

THE COMMERCIAL NATIONAL BANK OF CHARLES CITY
5979   FLOYD   **17 L   29 S**

Chartered in September 1901; succeeded #2579.

Officers: Pres. Geo E May 1902-17, Geo W Johnson 1918, IN Snyder 1919,

Geo W Johnson 1920-21, Carl C Magdsick 1922-35, **VP** Jos Hecht 1903-34, AM Hauser 1919-35, CC Magdsick 1920-21; **Cash.** FC Fisher 1902-03, IN Snyder 1908-22, SN Snyder 1923, AM Hauser 1924-35; **AC** Clarence Seaman 1907-08, AM Hauser 1909-10, Edgar Ball 1922-35, W Loren Parr 1924-35, Marvin P Martens 1934-35

Second Charter, Brown Backs	Ser #	# Notes
10-10-10-20	1-1650	6,600
Second Charter, Date Back		
10-10-10-20	1-2200	8,800
Second Charter, Value Back		
10-10-10-20	2201-4326	8,504
Third Charter, Plain Back, Blue Seal		
10-10-10-20	1-3921	15,684
1929, Type I		
6-10's	1-992	5,952
6-20's	1-294	1,764
1929, Type II		
10's	1-1305	1,305
20's	1-145	145

Total amount of circulation issued = $605,600. Amount of large outstanding in 1935 = $3,180. Amount of small outstanding in 1935 = $46,470.

39,588 Large   9,166 Small   48,754 Total

5979	M	$10	1882BB	490	868 C	U643686U	XF	
5979	M	$10	1882BB	490	1303 B	U644121U	VG	Higgins Mus.
5979	M	$20	1882BB	504	912 A	U643730U	CU	
5979	M	$10	1882DB	545	12 D	D179972	AU	pen/pen
5979	M	$10	1882DB	545	1832 E	R273980	XF	Higgins Mus.
5979	M	$20	1882DB	555	653 B	D180613	F	pen/pen
5979	M	$20	1882DB	555	1342 B	N444550	F	pen/pen
5979	M	$10	1882VB	577	2484 D	T873572	XF	
5979	M	$10	1882VB	577	3291 E	?	VF	
5979	M	$10	1882VB	577	3480 E	V92278	CU	Higgins Mus.
5979	M	$10	1902PB	634	127 C	H44989E	AU	Higgins Mus.
5979	M	$10	1902PB	634	1385 C	M384317H	F	
5979	M	$10	1902PB	634	1415 A	M384347H	VG	pen ac/pen
5979	-	$10	1902PB	634	1753 B	V255005H	VF	
5979	-	$10	1902PB	634	2998 C	2998 C	?	
5979	M	$20	1902PB	660	20 A	H44882E	F	pen/pen vp
5979	-	$20	1902PB	660	3299 A	3299 A	VF	
5979		$10	1929T1		A000049A		F	
5979		$10	1929T1		C000568A		?	
5979		$10	1929T1		B000661A		VF	Pinholes
5979		$10	1929T1		E000712A		F/VF	
5979		$10	1929T1		B000756A		?	
5979		$20	1929T1		D000002A		VF	
5979		$20	1929T1		A000029A		VG	
5979		$20	1929T1		E000040A		VF	
5979		$20	1929T1		F000040A		F	
5979		$20	1929T1		B000057A		CU	
5979		$20	1929T1		E000058A		VF	
5979		$20	1929T1		B000089A		VF	
5979		$20	1929T1		A000109A		F	
5979		$20	1929T1		E000137A		VG/F	
5979		$20	1929T1		B000176A		F	
5979		$20	1929T1		C000191A		VF	
5979		$20	1929T1		A000241A		CU	Higgins Mus.
5979		$20	1929T1		C000241A		CU	
5979		$20	1929T1		E000241A		CU	
5979		$20	1929T1		F000241A		CU	
5979		$20	1929T1		A000242A		CU	
5979		$20	1929T1		B000242A		CU	
5979		$20	1929T1		C000242A		?	
5979		$20	1929T1		D000242A		CU	
5979		$20	1929T1		E000242A		CU	
5979		$20	1929T1		F000242A		CU	
5979		$20	1929T1		A000243A		?	
5979		$20	1929T1		F000246A		VF	
5979		$20	1929T1		E000254A		F	

THE FIRST NATIONAL BANK OF CHARLES CITY   46 L
1810   FLOYD

Chartered on April 7, 1871. Placed in voluntary liquidation on September 28, 1929; capital of $100,000. Absorbed by The Security Trust & Savings Bank, Charles City.

Officers: Pres. Almon G Case 1872-1904, JA Case 1905, CD Ellis 1906-29; **VP** HC Raymond 1896-1908, Wm Hausberg 1909-10, AE Ellis 1911-19, HM Wallaser 1920-22, 1927-29 MW Ellis 1923-29; **Cash.** Charles C Siver 1872, Horace C Baldwin 1872-90, SB Hall 1891-1900, JA Case 1901-04, HM Walleser 1906-17, RV McCammond 1918-29; **AC** Jas A Case 1896-1900, Arthur Bailey 1904-06, RV McCammond 1907-19, Merten J Klaus 1920-29, MM Raymond 1920-29

First Charter, Original Issue	Ser #	# Notes
1-1-1-2	1-1500	6,000
5-5-5-5	1-3875	15,500
First Charter, Series of 1875		
5-5-5-5	1-3657	14,628
Second Charter, Brown Backs		
5-5-5-5	1-3450	13,800
10-10-10-20	1-1600	6,400
Second Charter, Date Back		
5-5-5-5	1-752	3,008
10-10-10-20	1-598	2,392
Third Charter, Date Back, Blue Seal		
5-5-5-5	1-2400	9,600
10-10-10-20	1-1880	7,520
Third Charter, Plain Back, Blue Seal		
5-5-5-5	2401-7767	21,468
10-10-10-20	1881-5243	13,452

Total amount of circulation issued = $769,570. Amount outstanding at close = $43,547.

113,768 Large   0 Small   113,768 Total

1810	-	$1	ORIG	382	3 B	C481765	AU	
1810	-	$1	ORIG	382	145 B	C481907	F	pen/pen
1810	-	$2	ORIG	389	1 A	C481763	VF	Higgins Mus.
1810	-	$2	ORIG	389	245 A	C482007	Fr	Tape back left
1810	-	$2	ORIG	389	1421 A	C483183	F	pen/pen
1810	-	$5	1875	401	1352 ?	?	AU	
1810	-	$5	1875	401	1357 A	H686327	VF/XF	pen/pen
1810	-	$5	1875	401	1357 B	H686327	CU	vp Higgins Mus.
1810	-	$5	1875	401	1357 C	H686327	XF	
1810	-	$5	1875	401	1357 D	H686327	XF	
1810	-	$5	1875	401	1362 A	H686332	AU	Higgins Mus.
1810	-	$5	1875	401	1362 B	H686332	AU	Higgins Mus.
1810	-	$5	1875	401	1362 C	H686332	AU	
1810	-	$5	1875	401	1362 D	H686332	AU	
1810	-	$5	1875	401	1375 A	H686345	CU	Blue end paper
1810	-	$5	1875	401	1375 B	H686345	CU	Blue end paper
1810	-	$5	1875	401	1375 C	H686345	CU	Blue end paper
1810	-	$5	1875	401	1375 D	H686345	CU	Blue end paper
1810	-	$5	1875	401	1974 B	H686944	AU+	
1810	-	$5	1882BB	471	512 C	K434988	AU	
1810	-	$5	1882BB	471	1558 B	M947133	F	
1810	M	$5	1882BB	471	1935 A	K429870K	VF/XF	
1810	M	$5	1882BB	471	2054 A	K429989K	XF	pen/pen
1810	M	$5	1882BB	471	?	K430122K	?	
1810	M	$5	1882BB	471	2677 D	K430612K	CU	
1810	M	$5	1882BB	471	3266 D	U366619U	VF	pen/pen vp
1810	M	$5	1882BB	471	3300 B	U366653U	CU	Higgins Mus.
1810	M	$10	1882BB	484	498 B	H435102H	XF/AU	pen/pen
1810	M	$10	1882BB	484	743 B	H435347H	F+	
1810	M	$10	1882BB	484	751 B	H435355H	AU	Higgins Mus.
1810	M	$5	1882DB	532	6 F	B242501	VF+	pen/pen
1810	M	$5	1882DB	532	15 E	B242510	CU	Higgins Mus.
1810	M	$10	1882DB	539	14 F	B466084	CU	pen/pen
1810	M	$5	1902DB	593	1 A	Y462161	AU	
1810	M	$5	1902DB	593	104 A	Y462264	CU	pen/pen
1810	M	$5	1902DB	593	104 B	Y462264	CU	pen/pen
1810	M	$5	1902DB	593	980 D	Z394920	VG	vp 980 B ?
1810	M	$10	1902DB	619	1 C	Z150237	F	
1810	M	$10	1902DB	619	941 C	D627067A	F+	
1810	M	$20	1902DB	645	253 A	Z150489	?	
1810		$5	1902PB	601	4428 B	A472824E	XF	Higgins Mus.
1810		$5	1902PB	601	6673 B	?	VG	
1810	-	$5	1902PB	601	6845 B	6845 B	F	
1810	-	$5	1902PB	601	7224 B	7224 B	VG	
1810	-	$10	1902PB	627	4043 C	Z865005H	F	lt. stamp sigs
1810	-	$10	1902PB	627	5172 A	5172 A	XF	

THE FIRST NATIONAL BANK OF CHARTER OAK   10 L   20 S
4376   CRAWFORD

Chartered in 1890. Succeeded H.N. Moore & Co.

Officers: Pres. HN Moore 1890-98, GN Sweetser 1899-1905, James F Toy 1906-35; **VP** CL Van Patten 1896-99, Martin Neal 1900-01, Chas Robertson 1902-21, EW Timm 1922-35; **Cash.** JG Shumaker 1890-91, WT Bradford 1892, JG Shumaker 1893-98, EE Springer 1899-03, AJ Eggen 1904, PF Fiene 1904-1921, BH Runge 1922-29, Clyde M Mummert 1930, BH Runge 1930-33, EJ Knebel 1934-35; **AC** FL Shumaker 1896-99, PF Fiene 1900-01, Chas C Jacobson 1903-06, CA Mains 1907-12, BH Runge 1913-20, HC Bierwirth 1920, Helen Amstein 1922-25, EW Schreiber 1926-29, HA Schultz 1930-32, EA Dethlefs 1933-35

Second Charter, Brown Backs	Ser #	# Notes
50-100	1-493	986

Second Charter, Date Back
50-100   1-114   228
Third Charter, Date Back, Blue Seal
10-10-10-20   1-2100   8,400
Third Charter, Plain Back, Blue Seal
10-10-10-20   2101-4962   11,448
1929, Type I
6-10's   1-604   3,624
6-20's   1-210   1,260
1929, Type II
10's   1-355   355
20's   1-51   51
Total amount of circulation issued = $405,160. Amount of large outstanding on May 23, 1935 = $2,140. Amount of small outstanding on May 23, 1935 = $27,860.
21,062 Large   5,290 Small   26,352 Total

4376		$100 1882BB	527	387 A	B318555	XF	Higgins Mus.
4376	M	$10 1902DB	619	1150 A	U405096A	AU	stamp sigs vp
4376	M	$10 1902DB	619	1721 B	N59747B	F	stamp/stamp
4376	M	$10 1902DB	619	1914 C	N59940B	VG	faded, Pinholes
4376	M	$10 1902PB	627	3319 A	N977631E	VF	nice sigs vp
4376	M	$10 1902PB	627	4376 B	M174054H	F/VF	vp
4376	-	$10 1902PB	627	4382 A	4382 A	?	
4376	M	$20 1902PB	653	3244 A	N977556E	VG/F	
4376	M	$20 1902PB	653	3544 A	B476406H	F/VF	Higgins Mus.
4376	M	$20 1902PB	653	3901 A	X28123H	F+	
4376		$10 1929T1		A000206A		VG/F	
4376		$10 1929T1		D000234A		F	
4376		$10 1929T1		A000401A		AU	Higgins Mus.
4376		$10 1929T1		F000403A		F+	
4376		$10 1929T1		F000512A		AU	
4376		$10 1929T1		F000521A		AU	
4376		$20 1929T1		A000005A		F	
4376		$20 1929T1		C000059A		VF	2 pinholes
4376		$20 1929T1		A000071A		F	
4376		$20 1929T1		E000110A		VG/F	
4376		$20 1929T1		A000132A		F	
4376		$20 1929T1		F000132A		F	
4376		$20 1929T1		B000134A		VF	
4376		$20 1929T1		A000198A		XF	
4376		$10 1929T2		A000193		AU	
4376		$10 1929T2		A000194		AU	
4376		$10 1929T2		A000195		AU	
4376		$10 1929T2		A000196		AU	
4376		$10 1929T2		A000197		AU	
4376		$10 1929T2		A000198		AU	

THE FIRST NATIONAL BANK OF CHELSEA   10 L   19 S
5412   TAMA

Organized on May 17, 1900 with a capital of $25,000. Chartered on June 9, 1900. Placed in conservatorship on March 25, 1933. Placed in receivership on October 30, 1933; capital of $40,000.
Officers: Pres. DO Wilcox 1900-04, FJ Nowak 1905-13, EP Willey 1914-33; **VP** JH Mercer 1900-03, FJ Nowak 1904, WR Loutzenheiser 1907-12, JC Johnston 1913-19, LP Wilkenson 1920-22, Albert Ulch 1923-27, JW Ryan 1928-33; **Cash.** JW Shaler 1900-02, EP Willey 1903-11, Jos F Weaver 1912-18, Jos Benesh 1919-33; **AC** EP Willey 1902, HC Loutzenheiser 1909, Jos R Ulch 1913-33, EW Kesl 1924-33

Second Charter, Brown Backs	Ser #	# Notes
10-10-10-20	1-1000	4,000
Second Charter, Date Back		
10-10-10-20	1-1620	6,480
Second Charter, Value Back		
10-10-10-20	1621-2277	2,628
Third Charter, Plain Back, Blue Seal		
10-10-10-20	1-2097	8,388
1929, Type I		
6-10's	1-439	2,634
6-20's	1-122	732

Total amount of circulation issued = $309,680. Amount of large outstanding at close = $2,950. Amount of small outstanding at close = $22,060.
21,496 Large   3,366 Small   24,862 Total

5412		$10 1882BB	490	328 A	X398271	VG/F	Davenport B&T
5412	M	$10 1882DB	545	625 E	H433733	F+	pen/pen
5412	M	$20 1882DB	555	1068 B	N96416	VG	Higgins Mus.
5412	M	$20 1882DB	555	1182 B	N96530	F	
5412	M	$20 1882DB	555	1248 B	N425156	F	
5412		$10 1902PB	633	1749 A	1749 A	VF	pen Rust spot
5412	M	$20 1902PB	659	557 A	M468774E	F	
5412	M	$20 1902PB	659	877 A	Z502339E	VG	
5412	-	$20 1902PB	659	1588 A	1588 A	F	
5412	-	$20 1902PB	659	1929 A	1929 A	VF	
5412		$10 1929T1		F000137A		F	
5412		$10 1929T1		B000157A		?	
5412		$10 1929T1		D000205A		F	
5412		$10 1929T1		F000234A		VG	
5412		$10 1929T1		D000271A		VF	
5412		$10 1929T1		F000281A		F	
5412		$20 1929T1		A000038A		VF	
5412		$20 1929T1		D000046A		?	
5412		$20 1929T1		?000052A		VG	
5412		$20 1929T1		E000055A		VG/F	
5412		$20 1929T1		D000060A		?	
5412		$20 1929T1		A000063A		VF	
5412		$20 1929T1		D000073A		F+	
5412		$20 1929T1		B000077A		VF	
5412		$20 1929T1		E000078A		AU	Higgins Mus.
5412		$20 1929T1		F000078A		VF	
5412		$20 1929T1		E000096A		F/VF	
5412		$20 1929T1		F000102A		XF	
5412		$20 1929T1		E000118A		VG/F	

THE FIRST NATIONAL BANK OF CHEROKEE   9 L   14 S
3049   CHEROKEE

Organized on August 11, 1883 with a capital of $50,000. Succeeded Scribner & Burroughs. Placed in receivership on January 31, 1931; capital of $100,000.
Officers: Pres. Nelson T Burroughs 1883-1911, WA Sanford 1912-21, LF Parker 1922-30; **VP** WA Sanford 1883-1922, Roy H King 1920, Fred W Johansen 1922-30, Robert Gracey 1922-24, Fred W Johansen 1925-30; **Cash.** Roderick H Scribner 1883-1913, Cornelius Sullivan 1914-23, RG Rodman 1925, Fred W Johansen 1926-28, JM Redfield 1929, HB Adkins 1929-30; **AC** Cornelius Sullivan 1883-1913, RG Rodman 1914-1925, FC Bordewick 1922, JM Redfield 1925-29, HB Adkins 1926-29, TW Jones 1929-30

Second Charter, Brown Backs	Ser #	# Notes
10-10-10-20	1-1754	7,016
Third Charter, Red Seal		
10-10-10-20	1-1150	4,600
Third Charter, Date Back, Blue Seal		
10-10-10-20	1-1750	7,000
Third Charter, Plain Back, Blue Seal		
10-10-10-20	1751-6735	19,940
1929, Type I		
6-10's	1-530	3,180
6-20's	1-130	780

Total amount of circulation issued = $529,350. Amount outstanding at close = $46,280. Amount of large outstanding on February 4, 1931 = $10,320.
38,556 Large   3,960 Small   42,516 Total

3049	M	$10 1902DB	616	54 D	K295810	F/VF	
3049	M	$10 1902DB	616	1480 E	X624885A	F+	Higgins Mus.
3049	M	$10 1902DB	616	1483 D	X624888A	VF	Higgins Mus.
3049	M	$10 1902PB	624	1762 F	A665999D	VF	pen/gone
3049	M	$10 1902PB	624	3556 E	N712358E	F	
3049	M	$10 1902PB	624	4150 A	H143502H	F	pen/pen
3049	M	$10 1902PB	624	4242 H	H143594H	VF	pen/stamp
3049	-	$20 1902PB	650	5200 B	5200 B	VF+	
3049	-	$20 1902PB	650	5271 B	5271 B	F	Pressed
3049		$10 1929T1		E000039A		VG	
3049		$10 1929T1		C000048A		F	
3049		$10 1929T1		F000118A		VF	Higgins Mus.
3049		$10 1929T1		A000138A		VG	
3049		$10 1929T1		A000199A		F	
3049		$10 1929T1		D000201A		VF	
3049		$10 1929T1		A000455A		VG	
3049		$10 1929T1		A000457A		VF/XF	
3049		$10 1929T1		D000465A		F+	
3049		$20 1929T1		B000026A		VF	
3049		$20 1929T1		B000040A		VG	LL corner missing

3049	$20	1929T1	A000045A		F	Rust spots
3049	$20	1929T1	D000117A		F	
3049	$20	1929T1	C000124A		VF	

THE SECURITY BANK OF CHEROKEE   12 L   6 S
10711   CHEROKEE

Organized on February 10, 1915 with a capital of $50,000. Placed in receivership on March 17, 1930; capital of $50,000. Reason for failure: incompetent management.

Officers: Pres. GW Johns 1915-21, WP Goldie 1922-30; **VP** Ray Adsit 1920, RP Will 1920, JH Spinharney 1922-30; **Cash.** Geo E Long 1915-20, IE Baumgardner 1922-24, WE Spinharney 1925-30; **AC** JF Wanberg 1920-21, WE Spinharney 1922-24

Third Charter, Date Back, Blue Seal	Ser #	# Notes
10-10-10-20	1-1100	4,400
Third Charter, Plain Back, Blue Seal		
10-10-10-20	1101-7907	27,228
1929, Type I		
6-10's	1-382	2,292
6-20's	1-40	240

Total amount of circulation issued = $423,070. Amount outstanding at close = $48,920. Amount of large outstanding on July 1, 1931 = $21,400.

31,628 Large   2,532 Small   34,160 Total

10711M	$10	1902PB	631	3194 A	R742076D	VF	stamp Rust
10711M	$10	1902PB	631	3994 A	E859606E	VG	
10711 -	$10	1902PB	631	5364 C	R832056H	VG/F	
10711 -	$10	1902PB	631	5773 B	X941055H	VG	
10711 -	$10	1902PB	631	6361 C	6361 C	VG/F	lt stamp/pen
10711 -	$10	1902PB	631	6540 ?	6540 ?	VG	
10711 -	$10	1902PB	631	7023 B	7023 B	CU	Higgins Mus.
10711 -	$10	1902PB	631	7525 C	7525 C	F	
10711M	$20	1902PB	657	4643 A	B176575H	VG/F	pen/pen
10711 -	$20	1902PB	657	5679 A	X940961H	VG	
10711 -	$20	1902PB	657	6853 A	6853 A	F	
10711 -	$20	1902PB	657	7734 A	7734 A	VG/F	
10711	$10	1929T1	B000123A			F/VF	
10711	$10	1929T1	A000138A			VG	
10711	$10	1929T1	A000139A			F/VF	AU ?
10711	$10	1929T1	F000349A			VG	
10711	$10	1929T1	A000361A			VG/F	
10711	$10	1929T1	A000374A			VF+	Higgins Mus.

THE FIRST NATIONAL BANK OF CHURDAN   6 L   15 S
6737   GREENE

Organized on April 7, 1903 with a capital of $25,000. Licensed after the Banking Holiday on March 23, 1933.

Officers: Pres. CJ Martin 1903-14, RT West 1915-27, DE Whitney 1928-35; **VP** Joseph Carroll 1904-10, OC Lohr 1911-12, 1914, 1931-35, RT West 1913-14, 1928-31; **Cash.** MF Coons 1903-07, DE Whitney 1908-20, Yates E Allen 1922-35; **AC** YE Allen 1911-21, Josephine Fitzpatrick 1923, Jno R Wherry 1926, Joseph Hunt 1926-35

Third Charter, Red Seal	Ser #	# Notes
10-10-10-20	1-1450	5,800
Third Charter, Date Back, Blue Seal		
10-10-10-20	1-1680	6,720
Third Charter, Plain Back, Blue Seal		
10-10-10-20	1681-4657	11,908
1929, Type I		
6-10's	1-588	3,528
6-20's	1-138	828
1929, Type II		
10's	1-348	348
20's	1-33	33

Total amount of circulation issued = $361,330. Amount of large outstanding in June 1935 = $1,340. Amount of small outstanding in June 1935 = $23,660.

24,428 Large   4,737 Small   29,165 Total

6737 M	$10	1902DB	616	1063 D	M515526A	VG/F	pen/pen
6737 M	$10	1902DB	616	1663 E	D154865B	F	pen/pen
6737 M	$10	1902PB	624	1900 D	U692058B	VF	ac Higgins Mus.
6737 M	$10	1902PB	624	2523 D	T986465D	VG	
6737	$10	1902PB	624	3603 D	V256425H	F	
6737 -	$20	1902PB	650	4456 B	4456 B	F	gone/faded
6737	$10	1929T1	B000030A			VG/F	
6737	$10	1929T1	B000058A			F	
6737	$10	1929T1	F000059A			F	
6737	$10	1929T1	C000061A			F	
6737	$10	1929T1	D000174A			F	
6737	$10	1929T1	E000250A			AU	
6737	$10	1929T1	F000506A			F	Rust, tight top
6737	$20	1929T1	D000054A			VG	
6737	$20	1929T1	E000072A			VF/XF	
6737	$20	1929T1	C000079A			AU	
6737	$20	1929T1	D000081A			AU	
6737	$20	1929T1	F000083A			F	
6737	$20	1929T1	F000085A			F	
6737	$20	1929T1	F000111A			F+	
6737	$20	1929T1	D000138A			F+	Higgins Mus.

THE FIRST NATIONAL BANK OF CLARENCE   11 L   8 S
7682   CEDAR

Chartered in April 1905. Placed in voluntary liquidation on June 19, 1931; capital of $30,000. Absorbed by The Clarence Savings Bank, Clarence.

Officers: Pres. WDG Cottrell 1905, MB Cottrell 1906-23, CE Read 1924-31; **VP** CE Read 1907-23, E Kirkpatrick 1923-25, AE Kelly 1924-26, JR Claney 1925-31, John Pruess 1926-27; **Cash.** MB Cottrell 1905, RO Hoyer 1906-19, CJ Birdsall 1920-21, RO Hoyer 1922-25, Robert M Harder 1925-26, EC Hasselbusch 1926-31; **AC** HI Decker 1912-19, EC Hasselbusch 1920-26, CZ Mack 1926-29, C Wayne Saunders 1929-30

Third Charter, Red Seal	Ser #	# Notes
10-10-10-20	1-1100	4,400
Third Charter, Date Back, Blue Seal		
10-10-10-20	1-1610	6,440
Third Charter, Plain Back, Blue Seal		
10-10-10-20	1611-4787	12,708
1929, Type I		
6-10's	1-315	1,890
6-20's	1-81	486

Total amount of circulation issued = $322,970. Amount of large outstanding at close = $4,920. Amount of small outstanding at close = $20,080.

23,548 Large   2,376 Small   25,924 Total

7682 M	$20	1902DB	642	899 B	A381722A	AU	
7682 M	$20	1902DB	642	900 B	A381723A	AU	Higgins Mus.
7682 M	$20	1902DB	642	1339 B	V628174A	VF	pen/faded
7682 M	$10	1902PB	624	2348 D	A787300E	?	
7682 M	$10	1902PB	624	2622 D	U859804E	VG	
7682 M	$10	1902PB	624	2880 D	A787332E	VF+	pen/stamp
7682 M	$10	1902PB	624	3206 F	V567648E	VF	Higgins Mus.
7682	$10	1902PB	624	3610 ?	V81932H	PR	
7682 -	$10	1902PB	624	4066 F	4066 F	AU	nice sigs
7682 M	$20	1902PB	650	2216 B	H23070D	XF	
7682 M	$20	1902PB	650	2801 B	A787253E	F	
7682	$10	1929T1	E000074A			VG	Staining
7682	$20	1929T1	B000011A			VF	
7682	$20	1929T1	F000015A			F	Dark
7682	$20	1929T1	F000059A			F	
7682	$20	1929T1	F000071A			VG/F	
7682	$20	1929T1	C000074A			VF	
7682	$20	1929T1	?000075A			VF	Dark
7682	$20	1929T1	F000077A			XF	Higgins Mus.

THE CLARINDA NATIONAL BANK   11 L
3112   PAGE

Organized on December 26, 1883 with a capital of $50,000. Succeeded The Valley Bank. Placed in receivership on November 29, 1926; capital of $50,000. Reason for failure: incompetent management.

Officers: Pres. Frank W Parish 1884-1904, HE Parslow 1905, ED F Rose 1906-13, JT Harrell 1914-1918, AW Palmer 1920-26; **VP** HL Cokenower 1896-99, A Nienstedt 1900-01, HE Parslow 1902-12, JT Harrell 1913, EG Day 1914, HE Parslow 1914, EG Day 1920, CE Blair 1920-22, IW Shambaugh 1922-23, LJ Sunderman 1924-26; **Cash.** Isaac J Poley 1884, WW Newlon 1885-91, HR Spry 1892-1903, CD Brown 1903-05, Elmer G Day 1906-13, AW Palmer 1914-18, JD Loudon 1920-24, WK Swanson 1925-26; **AC** JL Brown 1885, CF Butler 1904-24, WA Sayler 1910-11, RE Thorn 1920-23, WK Swanson 1924, RE Freudenberg 1925-26

Second Charter, Brown Backs	Ser #	# Notes
10-10-10-20	1-1830	7,320
Third Charter, Red Seal		
10-10-10-20	1-2000	8,000
Third Charter, Date Back, Blue Seal		
10-10-10-20	1-2900	11,600
Third Charter, Plain Back, Blue Seal		
10-10-10-20	2901-7691	19,164

Total amount issued = $576,050. Amount outstanding at close = $49,500.

46,084 Large   0 Small   46,084 Total

3112 M	$10	1902RS	613	674 A	E860444	XF	
3112 M	$10	1902RS	613	681 A	E860451	VF	
3112 M	$10	1902DB	616	998 E	Z433556	F/VF	pen/pen
3112 M	$10	1902DB	616	1660 E	K221333A	AU	
3112 M	$10	1902DB	616	1849 E	T477893A	VG	pen/pen ac
3112 M	$20	1902DB	642	1748 B	K221421A	F	
3112 M	$10	1902PB	624	4894 F	V169586D	VG	gone/pen Soiled
3112 M	$10	1902PB	624	6185 F	D614237H	VG	

3112	-	$10 1902PB	624	7621 D	7621 D	F stamp sigs ac
3112	M	$20 1902PB	650	5716 B	N448128E	F
3112	-	$20 1902PB	650	7538 B	7538 B	F/VF gone Higg. Mus.

THE FIRST NATIONAL BANK OF CLARINDA　　4 L
2028　　PAGE
Chartered on August 19, 1872 with a capital of $50,000. Merged with Read & Farnham in 1875. Assumed West, Morsman & Co. by consolidation in 1877. Placed in voluntary liquidation on March 1, 1879; capital of $50,000. Succeeded by Webster, Linderman & Co.
Officers: Pres. Napoleon B Moore 1873-75, Watson E Webster 1876-79; **Cash.** AB Cramer 1873-75, Solomon West 1876-79; **AC** Thomas Boston 1878

First Charter, Original Issue	Ser #	# Notes
1-1-1-2	1-1500	6,000
5-5-5-5	1-4125	16,500
First Charter, Series of 1875		
1-1-1-2	1-240	960
5-5-5-5	1-120	480

Total amount of circulation issued = $93,600. Amount outstanding at close = $45,000. Amount outstanding in 1910 = $656.
23,940 Large　　0 Small　　23,940 Total

2028	-	$1	ORIG 382	1 ?	D248537	XF Faded
2028	-	$1	ORIG 382	370 B	D248906	F Higgins Mus.
2028	-	$2	ORIG 389	233 A	D248769	F pen/pen Tear
2028	-	$5	ORIG 399	219 C	K499878	G/VG Oat Bin Hoard

THE FIRST NATIONAL BANK OF CLARION　　7 L 15 S
3796　　WRIGHT
Organized on August 29, 1887 with a capital of $50,000. Succeeded The Wright County Bank. Placed in conservatorship on March 20, 1933. Licensed on May 26, 1933.
Officers: Pres. GS Ringland 1887-1916, UB Tracy 1917-35, Thos H Crowe 1935; **VP** LL Estes 1896-1902, MA Michelson 1903-33, Thos H Crowe 1933-35, CJ Birdsall 1935; **Cash.** Ed Hartsock 1887, NF Weber 1888-91, UB Tracy 1892-1916, FW Walker 1917-19, CJ Birdsall 1920-35; **AC** JM Overbaugh 1896-99, FW Walker 1900-19, Verne Tracy 1922, AL Tracy 1923-24, HH Lumbarge 1926-27, WW Linebarger 1927-33, AH Tracy 1932-35, Hazel Kuver 1935

Second Charter, Brown Backs	Ser #	# Notes
50-100	1-1034	2,068
Third Charter, Red Seal		
50-100	1-334	668
Third Charter, Date Back, Blue Seal		
50-100	1-240	480
50-50-50-100	1-958	3,832
Third Charter, Plain Back, Blue Seal		
50-50-50-100	959-1087	516
1929, Type I		
6-50's	1-150	900
6-100's	1-25	150

Total amount of circulation issued = $572,950. Amount outstanding in 1934 = $50,000. Amount of large outstanding in 1935 = $6,200.
7,564 Large　　1,050 Small　　8,614 Total

3796		$50 1882BB	?	627 A	B323590	F 877 A ?
3796	M	$50 1902DB	669	54 D	A10794	F/VF vp Pinholes
3796	M	$50 1902DB	669	769 E	B60023	VF pen/pen
3796	-	$50 1902PB	677	989 C	989 C	F Heavy stain
3796	-	$50 1902PB	677	1053 D	1053 D	AU Higgins Mus.
3796	-	$50 1902PB	677	1057 E	1057 E	VG/F pen/pen Stain
3796	-	$100 1902PB	700	1055 C	1055 C	?
3796		$50 1929T1		C000008A		VF
3796		$50 1929T1		C000026A		?
3796		$50 1929T1		E000056A		G Dark
3796		$50 1929T1		D000071A		CU
3796		$50 1929T1		?000081A		AU
3796		$50 1929T1		D000099A		CU
3796		$50 1929T1		D000100A		CU
3796		$50 1929T1		F000100A		CU
3796		$50 1929T1		D000109A		XF/AU Higgins Mus.
3796		$50 1929T1		E000124A		AU
3796		$100 1929T1		A000009A		CU
3796		$100 1929T1		B000009A		CU
3796		$100 1929T1		C000009A		
3796		$100 1929T1		D000009A		AU
3796		$100 1929T1		E000009A		AU

THE WRIGHT COUNTY NATIONAL BANK OF CLARION　　0 L
3788　　WRIGHT
Chartered on September 9, 1887. Placed in voluntary liquidation on June 19, 1889; capital of $50,000. Succeeded by The Bank of Clarion.
Officers: Pres. Duane Young 1887-88; **Cash.** Charles Duane Young 1887-88

Second Charter, Brown Backs	Ser #	# Notes
10-10-10-20	1-246	984

Total amount of circulation issued = $12,300. Amount outstanding at close = $11,250. Amount outstanding in 1910 = $100.
984 Large　　0 Small　　984 Total

THE FIRST NATIONAL BANK OF CLEAR LAKE　　9 L 26 S
7869　　CERRO GORDO
Organized on July 10, 1905 with a capital of $35,000. Placed in conservatorship on March 28, 1933. Placed in voluntary liquidation on May 10, 1934; capital of $60,000. Succeeded by #14085.

Officers: Pres. FM Rogers 1905-16, FL Rogers 1917-24, A Roenfanz, HN Halvorson; **VP** JK Hill 1907, CR Hamstreet 1909-13, EH Rich 1920-23, RR Rogers 1920, A Roenfanz 1924, CA Knutson 1925-33; **Cash.** FL Rogers 1905-16, RR Rogers 1917-19, FP Walker 1920-34; **AC** RR Rogers 1907-14, CS Hamstreet 1920-25, MS Rogers 1920, RR Rogers 1922, HH Crane 1925-26, LW Sherman 1926-33

Third Charter, Red Seal	Ser #	# Notes
10-10-10-20	1-1400	5,600
Third Charter, Date Back, Blue Seal		
10-10-10-20	1-2250	9,000
Third Charter, Plain Back, Blue Seal		
10-10-10-20	2251-6631	17,524
1929, Type I		
6-10's	1-1063	6,378
6-20's	1-310	1,860

Total amount of circulation issued = $502,530. Amount of large outstanding at close = $3,510. Amount of small outstanding at close = $56,940.
32,124 Large　　8,238 Small　　40,362 Total

7869	M	$10 1902PB	625	2589 F	U626187B	VF	pen/pen
7869	M	$10 1902PB	625	2938 F	B544015D	VF	
7869	M	$10 1902PB	625	4117 E	E512159E	F	
7869	M	$10 1902PB	625	4474 F	U347836E	XF	
7869	M	$10 1902PB	625	5079 E	M34441H	VG	gone/gone
7869		$10 1902PB	625	5561 F	?	VG	Fed. Res. Bk., San Fran.
7869	-	$10 1902PB	625	5686 D	5686 D	CU	
7869	-	$10 1902PB	625	6290 F	6290 F	F/VF	gone, Higg. Mus.
7869	M	$20 1902PB	652	2341 B	R506395B	G	Soiled
7869		$10 1929T1		F000020A		VF	
7869		$10 1929T1		E000109A		F	
7869		$10 1929T1		E000116A		F	
7869		$10 1929T1		A000384A		XF	
7869		$10 1929T1		B000665A		F/VF	
7869		$10 1929T1		C000843A		VG/F	
7869		$10 1929T1		E000843A		XF	
7869		$10 1929T1		B000849A		VF	
7869		$10 1929T1		B000893A		AU	Higgins Mus.
7869		$10 1929T1		C001032A		F	
7869		$20 1929T1		?000004A		F	
7869		$20 1929T1		E000011A		F	
7869		$20 1929T1		F000032A		XF	
7869		$20 1929T1		C000046A		F/VF	
7869		$20 1929T1		D000083A		VF	
7869		$20 1929T1		F000084A		F/VF	
7869		$20 1929T1		F000091A		VF	
7869		$20 1929T1		D000108A		VF	
7869		$20 1929T1		C000114A		VF	
7869		$20 1929T1		B000120A		F	
7869		$20 1929T1		D000203A		VF/XF	
7869		$20 1929T1		A000249A		XF	
7869		$20 1929T1		E000262A		XF	

7869	$20	1929T1	D000264A		VF	
7869	$20	1929T1	D000283A		F	
7869	$20	1929T1	C000300A		F	

THE FIRST NATIONAL BANK OF CLEARFIELD   6 L   1 S
9549   TAYLOR

Organized on August 19, 1909 with a capital of $25,000. Placed in conservatorship on March 21, 1933. Placed in receivership on September 5, 1933; capital of $25,000.

Officers: Pres. Grant McPherrin 1910-11, CW Edwards 1912-16, JS Walton 1917-1930, HS Duncan 1931-33; **VP** CW Edwards 1910-12, Grant McPherrin 1913-1930, WB Duncan 1930-33; **AC** AH Edwards 1911, Paul Wilson 1914, Geo Fosmire 1920

Third Charter, Date Back, Blue Seal	Ser #	# Notes
10-10-10-20	1-700	2,800
Third Charter, Plain Back, Blue Seal		
10-10-10-20	701-1193	1,972
1929, Type I		
6-10's	1-142	852
6-20's	1-21	126

Total amount of circulation issued = $70,690. Amount of large outstanding at close = $680. Amount of small outstanding at close = $5,570.

4,772 Large   978 Small   5,750 Total

9549	M	$10	1902DB	618	1 A	T108014	?
9549	M	$20	1902DB	644	157 A	T108170	VG	pen/pen
9549	M	$20	1902DB	644	445 A	U329888	VF
9549	-	$10	1902PB	626	1174 C	1174 C	F
9549		$20	1902PB	652	772 A	M301704E	G/VG	Higgins Mus.
9549		$20	1902PB	652	773 A	M301705E	AU
9549		$10	1929T1	D000104A		VG

THE CITY NATIONAL BANK OF CLINTON   86 L   128 S
2469   CLINTON

Chartered on March 31, 1880. Succeeded Stone & Smith. Absorbed #66 (#2733) on October 7, 1930. Absorbed #3736 on June 4, 1931; assumed the circulation of #3736.

Officers: Pres. Augustus L Stone 1880-1900, AG Smith 1901-19, AC Smith 1920-29, GL Curtis 1930-32, WA Anderson 1933-35; **VP** Geo M Curtis 1896-1914, GL Curtis 1920-29, HW Seaman 1920-25, OP Petty 1930-35, Milo J Gabriel 1930-35, WA Anderson 1931, AR Thurn 1932-35; **Cash.** Alfred G Smith 1880-1990, AC Smith 1901-19, OP Petty 1920-31, JH Nissen 1932-35; **AC** AC Smith 1900, AW Hansen 1913-14, John H Nissen 1920-31, Henry G Kramer 1920-31, HM Olney 1930-32, FE Conover 1931-35, FH Hamann 1931-35, Emil Johannsen 1933-35, ME McCrabb 1933-35

First Charter, Series of 1875	Ser #	# Notes
10-10-10-20	1-7080	28,320
Second Charter, Brown Backs		
5-5-5-5	1-3500	14,000
10-10-10-20	1-7500	30,000
Second Charter, Date Back		
5-5-5-5	1-9750	39,000
10-10-10-20	1-6700	26,800
Second Charter, Value Back		
5-5-5-5	9751-16195	25,780
10-10-10-20	6701-9836	12,544
Third Charter, Plain Back, Blue Seal		
5-5-5-5	1-36070	144,280
10-10-10-20	1-19891	79,564
1929, Type I		
6-5's	1-11980	71,880
6-10's	1-5600	33,600
6-20's	1-1420	8,520
1929, Type II		
5's	1-7778	7,778
10's	1-4930	4,930
20's	1-1576	1,576

Total amount of circulation issued = $4,316,160. Amount of large outstanding in 1935 = $20,810. Includes the large outstanding of #2469 and #3736. Amount of small outstanding in 1935 = $376,090. Includes the small outstanding of #2469 and #3736.

400,288 Large   128,284 Small   528,572 Total

2469	-	$10	1875	419	53 C	?	F/VF
2469	-	$10	1875	419	4179 C	K533307	F+
2469	-	$10	1875	419	6157 A	K831656	F/VF
2469	-	$10	1875	419	6783 B	K832681	CU
2469	-	$10	1875	419	6786 A	K832684	AU	Higgins Mus.
2469	-	$10	1875	419	6786 B	K832684	CU
2469	-	$10	1875	419	6787 B	K832685	CU
2469	-	$10	1875	419	6789 C	K832687	CU	pen/pen
2469	-	$10	1875	419	6931 A	K832829	F
2469	-	$20	1875	434	5113 A	K830311	?
2469	-	$20	1875	434	6786 A	K832684	CU
2469	-	$20	1875	434	6806 A	K832704	CU
2469	M	$5	1882BB	477	1 A	T419994T	CU	Higgins Mus.
2469	M	$5	1882BB	477	1 B	T419994T	CU
2469	M	$5	1882BB	477	1 C	T419994T	CU	pen/pen
2469	M	$5	1882BB	477	2197 C	?	VG
2469	M	$5	1882BB	477	2421 A	U816579U	CU
2469	-	$10	1882BB	490	1 A	U900392	CU	pen ac/pen
2469	-	$10	1882BB	490	1 B	U900392	CU	pen ac/pen
2469	-	$10	1882BB	490	1 C	U900392	CU	pen ac/pen
2469	-	$10	1882BB	490	14 B	U900405	VF
2469	-	$10	1882BB	490	2197 C	Z416983	VG
2469	-	$10	1882BB	490	2351 C	Z417137	VF	pen/pen
2469	-	$20	1882BB	504	1 A	U900392	AU	pen ac/pen
2469		$20	1882BB	504	7024 A	T111801T	VF/XF
2469		$20	1882BB	504	7417 A	T112194T	F/VF	Davenport B&T
2469		$20	1882BB	504	7455 A	T112232T	VF/XF
2469	M	$5	1882DB	537	3344 E	H582581	VG
2469	M	$5	1882DB	537	5032 H	K573419	CU	pen Higgins Mus.
2469	M	$5	1882DB	537	8195 H	N125632	F+
2469	M	$5	1882DB	537	8290 F	N125727	XF
2469	M	$10	1882DB	545	2420 F	H908508	XF
2469	M	$10	1882DB	545	?	M843412	F
2469	M	$20	1882DB	555	1086 B	B442456	XF
2469	M	$20	1882DB	555	3533 B	M362161	PR	light pen sigs
2469	M	$20	1882DB	555	5976 B	T287874	VF
2469	M	$20	1882DB	555	6163 B	T288061	F/VF
2469	M	$5	1882VB	574	11587 E	T373574	F
2469	M	$5	1882VB	574	12367 G	T678579	VG
2469	M	$5	1882VB	574	12565 E	T678777	VF
2469	M	$10	1882VB	577	7142 D	T786320	VG
2469	M	$10	1882VB	577	7242 ?	T786420	VG
2469	M	$20	1882VB	581	7432 B	T786610	F
2469	M	$20	1882VB	581	9391 B	U955519	F	pen ac, Washed
2469	M	$5	1902PB	607	1339 A	R410375D	AU
2469	M	$5	1902PB	607	2457 B	?	CU
2469	M	$5	1902PB	607	2578 A	?	AU
2469	M	$5	1902PB	607	6157 A	D243603E	AU
2469	M	$5	1902PB	607	6158 D	D243604E	CU
2469	M	$5	1902PB	607	6294 D	D243740E	VG
2469	M	$5	1902PB	607	6648 C	D244094E	F
2469	M	$5	1902PB	607	10734 A	T99740E	G
2469	M	$5	1902PB	607	10779 D	T99785E	F/VF	pen ac/stamp
2469	M	$5	1902PB	607	14894 B	H375630H	VF	pen ac/stamp
2469	-	$5	1902PB	607	19128 A	U897689H	AU
2469	-	$5	1902PB	607	19380 C	U897941H	F	pen ac/stamp
2469	-	$5	1902PB	607	20133 C	Y719944H	VF	pen/stamp
2469	-	$5	1902PB	607	22271 D	?	F+	Davenport B&T
2469	-	$5	1902PB	607	24578 A	24578 A	CU
2469	-	$5	1902PB	607	27908 D	27908 D	?
2469	-	$5	1902PB	607	28046 D	28046 D	XF/AU	pen ac/stamp
2469	-	$5	1902PB	607	28083 A	28083 A	VG/F
2469	-	$5	1902PB	607	30556 A	30556 A	VF
2469	-	$5	1902PB	607	32061 D	32061 D	AU	pen ac/stamp Higgins Mus.
2469	-	$5	1902PB	607	33117 B	33117 B	?
2469	-	$5	1902PB	607	33134 A	33134 A	VG/F
2469	-	$5	1902PB	607	34494 A	34494 A	VF
2469	-	$5	1902PB	607	34729 A	34729 A	XF
2469	-	$5	1902PB	607	34885 C	34885 C	XF
2469	M	$10	1902PB	633	617 B	V191869K	XF
2469	M	$10	1902PB	633	3136 B	H313618E	F
2469	M	$10	1902PB	633	3270 A	H313752E	XF	pen ac/stamp
2469		$10	1902PB	633	6308 A	B961490H	F/VF
2469		$10	1902PB	633	6579 A	B961761H	VF
2469	-	$10	1902PB	633	12400 C	12400 C	F/VF	ac pressed
2469	-	$10	1902PB	633	14979 A	14979 A	VG
2469	-	$10	1902PB	633	18305 B	18305 B	VF
2469	-	$10	1902PB	633	18377 A	18377 A	F
2469	-	$10	1902PB	633	19020 C	19020 C	VF/XF
2469	-	$20	1902PB	659	2530 A	B470882E	XF
2469	-	$20	1902PB	659	11018 A	A63030K	VG
2469	-	$20	1902PB	659	12118 A	12118 A	VF	pen ac/stamp
2469	-	$20	1902PB	659	12467 A	12467 A	F	Davenport B&T
2469	-	$20	1902PB	659	14172 A	14172 A	VG
2469	-	$20	1902PB	659	16247 A	16247 A	XF	pen ac/stamp
2469	-	$20	1902PB	659	19783 A	19783 A	VG/F
2469		$5	1929T1	A000977A		VF
2469		$5	1929T1	C001548A		VF
2469		$5	1929T1	B002887A		VF
2469		$5	1929T1	B003535A		VG/F

2469	$5	1929T1	F004028A		VG		2469	$20	1929T1	A000541A		VF
2469	$5	1929T1	E004722A		F/VF		2469	$20	1929T1	B000545A		?
2469	$5	1929T1	A005989A	[	CU		2469	$20	1929T1	F000619A		F/VF
2469	$5	1929T1	B005989A	[	CU		2469	$20	1929T1	B000660A		F
2469	$5	1929T1	C005989A	[	CU		2469	$20	1929T1	D000710A		VF
2469	$5	1929T1	D005989A	[	CU		2469	$20	1929T1	D000773A		VF/XF
2469	$5	1929T1	E005989A	[	CU		2469	$20	1929T1	C000779A		VG
2469	$5	1929T1	F005989A	[	CU		2469	$20	1929T1	B000827A		F/VF
2469	$5	1929T1	E007277A		VG Stain		2469	$20	1929T1	B000852A		F/VF
2469	$5	1929T1	D007370A		VF/XF		2469	$20	1929T1	C000879A		XF/AU
2469	$5	1929T1	C007404A		F+		2469	$20	1929T1	A001060A		VG+
2469	$5	1929T1	C008261A		F		2469	$20	1929T1	C001072A		VF
2469	$5	1929T1	B008596A		AU		2469	$20	1929T1	D001086A		AU
2469	$5	1929T1	D008624A		F		2469	$20	1929T1	B001108A		VF
2469	$5	1929T1	C008683A		F/VF		2469	$20	1929T1	F001119A		F
2469	$5	1929T1	C008699A		VG+		2469	$20	1929T1	E001143A		VF
2469	$5	1929T1	F009612A		F		2469	$20	1929T1	F001218A		F
2469	$5	1929T1	A009881A		VF		2469	$20	1929T1	C001223A		F+
2469	$5	1929T1	D010055A		VF		2469	$20	1929T1	A001297A		F/VF
2469	$5	1929T1	B010183A		F/VF		2469	$20	1929T1	E001336A		?
2469	$5	1929T1	B010848A		CU		2469	$20	1929T1	D001347A		VG
2469	$5	1929T1	B011120A		F		2469	$20	1929T1	C001355A		AU
2469	$10	1929T1	B000022A		F+		2469	$20	1929T1	C001365A		XF
2469	$10	1929T1	B000064A		G		2469	$20	1929T1	B001366A		VF/XF Some ink bleed
2469	$10	1929T1	C000294A		F+		2469	$20	1929T1	D001367A		CU
2469	$10	1929T1	A000521A		VG		2469	$20	1929T1	E001367A		CU
2469	$10	1929T1	A000899A		F		2469	$20	1929T1	F001367A		CU
2469	$10	1929T1	C001408A		VF		2469	$20	1929T1	A001368A		CU
2469	$10	1929T1	E001459A		F		2469	$20	1929T1	D001368A		VF
2469	$10	1929T1	C001676A		VG		2469	$20	1929T1	A001370A		VF
2469	$10	1929T1	D001682A		VG/F		2469	$20	1929T1	F001378A		VG
2469	$10	1929T1	F001779A		F/VF		2469	$20	1929T1	F001419A		VF/XF
2469	$10	1929T1	E001883A		VF+		2469	$5	1929T2	A001604		F
2469	$10	1929T1	D001916A		VG		2469	$5	1929T2	A001737		VG Soiled
2469	$10	1929T1	D001917A		XF		2469	$5	1929T2	A005128		F/VF
2469	$10	1929T1	F002197A		VG/F		2469	$10	1929T2	A000187		F/VF
2469	$10	1929T1	A002279A		VG		2469	$10	1929T2	A000736		VF
2469	$10	1929T1	A002363A		XF/AU		2469	$10	1929T2	A000856		VG
2469	$10	1929T1	B002515A		F/VF		2469	$10	1929T2	A002489		VF
2469	$10	1929T1	C002834A		VF		2469	$10	1929T2	A003522		AU
2469	$10	1929T1	E002911A		F/VF		2469	$20	1929T2	A000055		F
2469	$10	1929T1	D003362A		VG		2469	$20	1929T2	A000087		VF Rust spot on top
2469	$10	1929T1	A003374A		F		2469	$20	1929T2	A000510		F
2469	$10	1929T1	C003403A		CU							
2469	$10	1929T1	C003404A		CU							
2469	$10	1929T1	C003405A		CU							
2469	$10	1929T1	D003405A		CU							
2469	$10	1929T1	D003406A		CU							
2469	$10	1929T1	E003406A		CU							
2469	$10	1929T1	B003462A		F/VF							
2469	$10	1929T1	C003622A		VG/F							
2469	$10	1929T1	D003642A		F/VF							
2469	$10	1929T1	F003661A		XF Higgins Mus.							
2469	$10	1929T1	F003887A		XF							
2469	$10	1929T1	F004071A		F/VF							
2469	$10	1929T1	A004120A		VF							
2469	$10	1929T1	C004126A		VF							
2469	$10	1929T1	A004227A		F							
2469	$10	1929T1	D004348A		VF							
2469	$10	1929T1	F004556A		VF							
2469	$10	1929T1	A004637A		VF							
2469	$10	1929T1	E004670A		F							
2469	$10	1929T1	C004843A		VF							
2469	$10	1929T1	E005082A		F							
2469	$10	1929T1	A005086A		VF							
2469	$10	1929T1	E005304A		CU							
2469	$10	1929T1	D005323A		F							
2469	$10	1929T1	C005506A		?							
2469	$10	1929T1	D005506A		?							
2469	$10	1929T1	E005506A		?							
2469	$20	1929T1	A000075A		XF							
2469	$20	1929T1	A000123A		VG							
2469	$20	1929T1	E000129A		F							
2469	$20	1929T1	F000129A		F							
2469	$20	1929T1	F000183A		F/VF							
2469	$20	1929T1	E000294A		F							
2469	$20	1929T1	D000390A		?							
2469	$20	1929T1	C000428A		VG							
2469	$20	1929T1	?000432A		VF							
2469	$20	1929T1	B000439A		VG							
2469	$20	1929T1	C000447A		VG							

THE CLINTON NATIONAL BANK   24 L   29 S
994   **CLINTON**
Chartered in 1865.
Officers: Pres. William F Coan 1867-85, John C Weston 1887-94, CC Coan 1896-1923, EA Young 1924-32, WJ Young, Jr. 1932-33, LJ Schuster 1934-35; **VP** JC Bucner 1868, WJ Young, Jr. 1896-14, EA Young 1920-23, CH Young 1924-31, AL Schuyler 1932-35, FO Kershner 1932-34, LJ Derflinger 1935; **Cash.** James A Townsend 1867-69, John C Weston 1870-85, CC Coan 1887-95, WF Coan 1896-1917, Albert B Rathburn 1918-29, Roy Hutchinson 1930-33, LJ Derflinger 1933-35; **AC** CC Coan 1885, AF Bohnson 1914-35, AB Rathburn 1914, Roy Hutchinson 1929

First Charter, Original Issue	Ser #	# Notes
1-1-1-2	1-1800	7,200
5-5-5-5	1-1100	4,400
10-10-10-20	1-1560	6,240
First Charter, Series of 1875		
10-10-10-20	1-1540	6,160
Second Charter, Brown Backs		
10-10-10-20	1-5708	22,832
Third Charter, Red Seal		
5-5-5-5	1-2150	8,600
10-10-10-20	1-1360	5,440
Third Charter, Date Back, Blue Seal		
5-5-5-5	1-2650	10,600
10-10-10-20	1-2520	10,080
Third Charter, Plain Back, Blue Seal		
5-5-5-5	2651-10852	32,808
10-10-10-20	2521-7429	19,636
1929, Type I		
6-5's	1-1882	11,292
6-10's	1-936	5,616
6-20's	1-272	1,632
1929, Type II		
5's	1-1414	1,414
10's	1-728	728
20's	1-130	130

Total amount of circulation issued = $1,333,100. Amount of large outstanding in 1935 = $4,460. Amount of small outstanding in 1935 = $55,540.

133,966 Large   20,812 Small   154,808 Total

994	-	$1 ORIG	380	1 B	952838	F	
994	-	$1 ORIG	380	1275 B	954112	VF	
994	-	$10 1875	416	1507 C	H949091	CU	
994		$10 1882BB	480	14 A	B138917	AU	
994		$10 1882BB	480	2789 C	K332780	VG	
994		$10 1882BB	480	4725 C	W590138	VF	W590139 ?
994	M	$5 1902RS	587	1 A	B483112	CU	Grinnell # 1673
994	M	$5 1902RS	587	980 A	M97664	AU+	
994	M	$10 1902RS	613	1 A	E414177	CU	
994	M	$20 1902RS	639	1 A	E414177	CU	Grinnell # 1674
994	M	$10 1902DB	616	?	A191959A	VG/F	
994	M	$5 1902PB	598	3308 F	U66384B	XF+	
994	M	$5 1902PB	598	5442 F	Y923088D	XF/AU	pen/pen
994		$5 1902PB	598	7492 E	E139078H	VF	
994		$5 1902PB	598	7663 F	N214874H	VG	
994		$5 1902PB	598	9017 ?	?	F	
994	-	$5 1902PB	598	10068 G	10068 G	XF	stamp/stamp
994	-	$5 1902PB	598	10235 G	10235 G	F	stamp/stamp
994	-	$5 1902PB	598	10575 G	10575 G	F	
994	-	$10 1902PB	624	6368 D	6368 D	F	
994	-	$10 1902PB	624	6417 F	6417 F	F	
994	-	$10 1902PB	624	6588 ?	6588 ?	G	
994	-	$10 1902PB	624	6681 F	6681 F	XF	Higgins Mus.
994	-	$20 1902PB	650	7379 B	7379 B	VG/F	
994		$5 1929T1		A000003A		?	
994		$5 1929T1		B000003A		?	
994		$5 1929T1		C000003A		?	
994		$5 1929T1		D000003A		?	
994		$5 1929T1		E000003A		?	
994		$5 1929T1		F000003A		?	
994		$5 1929T1		A001478A		F	
994		$10 1929T1		A000001A		CU	Higgins Mus.
994		$10 1929T1		B000001A		CU	Sheet cut 1972
994		$10 1929T1		C000001A		CU	Sheet cut 1972
994		$10 1929T1		D000001A		CU	Sheet cut 1972
994		$10 1929T1		E000001A		CU	Sheet cut 1972
994		$10 1929T1		F000001A		CU	Sheet cut 1972
994		$10 1929T1		B000127A		VG	
994		$10 1929T1		C000383A		F/VF	
994		$10 1929T1		D000549A		AU	
994		$10 1929T1		C000720A		VG/F	
994		$10 1929T1		F000916A		VG/F	
994		$20 1929T1		A000035A		XF	
994		$20 1929T1		E000083A		G	Rust
994		$20 1929T1		D000121A		VF	stains; small tear
994		$20 1929T1		D000182A		VG/F	
994		$20 1929T1		C000186A		F	
994		$20 1929T1		B000258A		F/VF	
994		$5 1929T2		A000282		VF	Tear LL corner
994		$5 1929T2		A000685		VF	
994		$5 1929T2		A000788		F	
994		$5 1929T2		A001332		VG	
994		$5 1929T2		A001376		CU	

FIRST NATIONAL BANK OF LYONS AT CLINTON   3 L
66 (2ND TITLE)   CLINTON

Succeeded The First National Bank of Lyons on August 8, 1911. Title changed to First National Bank of Lyons at Clinton on June 6, 1922. Placed in voluntary liquidation on October 7, 1930; capital of $100,000. Absorbed by #2469.

Officers: Pres. JH Peters 1922-27, David B Ogden 1928-29, Otto Rockrohr 1930; **VP** Otto Rockrohr 1922-29, SC Rand 1923-30; **Cash.** AL Holmes 1922-30; **AC** EE Matthiesen 1922-29, JW Campbell 1922-30, DT Eells 1930

Third Charter, Plain Back, Blue Seal	Ser #	# Notes
10-10-10-10 (plate dated 1922)	1-3418	13,672

Total amount of circulation issued = $1,036,020. Amount outstanding in 1924 = $99,600. Amount outstanding at close in 1930 = $8,515.

13,672 Large   0 Small   13,672 Total

66	M	$10 1902PB	635	103 C	V191278	VF	
66	M	$10 1902PB	635	1681 C	V738171	VF	
66	M	$10 1902PB	635	2974 D	X374729	VG+	Higgins Mus.

THE MERCHANTS NATIONAL BANK OF CLINTON   38 L   18 S
3736   CLINTON

Organized on June 7, 1887 with a capital of $100,000. Placed in voluntary liquidation on June 4, 1931; capital of $100,000. Absorbed by #2469; circulation assumed by #2469. Placed in receivership on September 9, 1933; reason: deficiency in assets sold.

Officers: Pres. BHA Henningsen 1887-88, ES Bailey 1889-91, L Lamb 1893-1902, WT Joyce 1903-07, Geo E Wilson 1908-17, CD May 1918-23, EL Miller 1925-30; **VP** Lafayette Lamb 1892-95, Simon Shoecraft 1896-1912, Fred Rixon 1913-19, Geo E Wilson, Jr. 1920-23; **Cash.** RC Van Kuran 1887-95, CD May 1896-1917, JW Streib 1918-19, VG Coe 1920, 1924-30, JF Wilson 1923; **AC** John W Streib 1904-17, AD Wilson 1920, JF Burke 1920-30, JF Stich 1922-25, CB Bickle 1926-30

Second Charter, Brown Backs	Ser #	# Notes
10-10-10-20	1-2639	10,556
Third Charter, Red Seal		
5-5-5-5	1-1000	4,000
10-10-10-20	1-1000	4,000
Third Charter, Date Back, Blue Seal		
5-5-5-5	1-7000	28,000
10-10-10-20	1-5180	20,720
Third Charter, Plain Back, Blue Seal		
5-5-5-5	7001-20470	53,880
10-10-10-20	5181-14101	35,684
1929, Type I		
6-10's	1-1332	7,992
6-20's	1-391	2,346

Total amount of circulation issued = $1,443,240. Amount of large outstanding at close = $12,220. Amount of small outstanding at close = $87,780. Circulation assumed by #2469 which was then responsible for redeeming the outstanding notes of #3736. Note: ten sheets numbered 1204 to 1213 of the Brown Back 10-10-10-20 issue were sent by error to The Clinton, Minnesota Bank.

156,840 Large   10,338 Small   167,178 Total

3736	-	$10 1882BB	483	609 A	E298250	?	
3736	-	$10 1882BB	483	609 B	E298252	?	
3736	-	$10 1882BB	483	1643 C	W311592	F/VF	pen/pen
3736	M	$5 1902RS	589	1 ?	?	CU	
3736	M	$5 1902RS	589	282 C	R703964	AU	Higgins Mus.
3736	M	$10 1902RS	615	1 A	T994430	CU	
3736	M	$10 1902RS	615	1 B	T994430	AU	Grinnell # 1660
3736	M	$5 1902DB	592	1 E	B567584	CU	
3736	M	$5 1902DB	592	2734 H	Y600534	VG	
3736	M	$5 1902DB	592	3908 F	A547921A	CU	pen/pen vp
3736	M	$5 1902DB	592	5793 F	X581045A	F	stamp/stamp
3736	M	$10 1902DB	618	1 D	B256276	CU	Grinnell # 1710
3736	M	$10 1902DB	618	1 E	B256276	CU	
3736	M	$10 1902DB	618	1 F	B256276	CU	Grinnell # 1711
3736	M	$10 1902DB	618	2 D	B256277	CU	light handling
3736	M	$10 1902DB	618	2 E	B256277	XF	Higgins Mus.
3736	M	$10 1902DB	618	2 F	B256277	AU	pen/pen
3736	M	$10 1902DB	618	4558 D	Z99918A	F/VF	nice sigs
3736	M	$5 1902PB	600	9286 F	Z876672B	AU	pen/pen
3736	M	$5 1902PB	600	12191 E	A843912E	AU	pen/pen
3736	M	$5 1902PB	600	12191 F	A843912E	AU	pen/pen
3736	M	$5 1902PB	600	12191 G	A843912E	AU	pen/pen
3736	M	$5 1902PB	600	12191 H	A843912E	AU	pen/pen
3736	-	$5 1902PB	600	16871 H	16871 H	AU	?VF?
3736	-	$5 1902PB	600	17715 H	17715 H	VG/F	
3736	-	$5 1902PB	600	17857 G	17857 G	AU	
3736	-	$5 1902PB	600	18806 H	18806 H	VF	Pressed
3736	-	$5 1902PB	600	18869 E	18869 E	VG	stamp/stamp
3736	-	$5 1902PB	600	19382 G	19382 G	F	stamp/stamp
3736	M	$10 1902PB	626	7353 D	N449185D	AU	pen/pen ac
3736	M	$10 1902PB	626	9180 F	V606112E	VG	
3736	M	$10 1902PB	626	9320 F	V606252E	VF	stamp/stamp
3736	-	$10 1902PB	626	11292 E	Z787904H	?	
3736	-	$10 1902PB	626	12448 E	?	F+	Davenport B&T
3736	M	$20 1902PB	652	5470 B	T475600B	?	
3736	M	$20 1902PB	652	5496 B	T475626B	VG	
3736	M	$20 1902PB	652	6469 B	?D	F/VF	
3736	-	$20 1902PB	652	13251 B	13251 B	F/VF	
3736		$10 1929T1		C000225A		VG	
3736		$10 1929T1		C000434A		F+	
3736		$10 1929T1		A000531A		G/VG	
3736		$10 1929T1		D000598A		VF	
3736		$10 1929T1		F000756A		XF	
3736		$10 1929T1		D000811A		VF	
3736		$10 1929T1		F000850A		F/VF	
3736		$10 1929T1		E000987A		F	
3736		$10 1929T1		D001141A		F	
3736		$10 1929T1		F001152A		AU	Higgins Mus.
3736		$10 1929T1		D001211A		CU	
3736		$20 1929T1		F000164A		VG	
3736		$20 1929T1		C000280A		XF	
3736		$20 1929T1		C000299A		XF	
3736		$20 1929T1		F000318A		VG	Tear; stains
3736		$20 1929T1		E000349A		VG/F	

3736	$20	1929T1	A000367A		VF
3736	$20	1929T1	A000375A		?

THE FIRST NATIONAL BANK OF CLUTIER 0 L
5366   TAMA
Chartered on May 22, 1900. Placed in voluntary liquidation on October 12, 1908; capital of $25,000. Purchased by The Clutier State Bank.
Officers: Pres. SG Hawks 1900-02, John Skrable 1903-08; **VP** Henry Holst 1902, Frank Meggers 1904-08; **Cash.** Henry Mohr 1900-02, Wm Benesh 1903-08; **AC** JP Novak 1907

Second Charter, Brown Backs	Ser #	# Notes
5-5-5-5	1-800	3,200
10-10-10-20	1-700	2,800
Second Charter, Date Back		
5-5-5-5	1-20	80
10-10-10-20	1-10	40

Total amount of circulation issued = $51,900. Amount outstanding at close = $20,000. Amount outstanding in 1910 =$6,307.
6,120 Large   0 Small   6,120 Total

THE FIRST NATIONAL BANK OF COIN   2 L   1 S
7309   PAGE

Organized on June 3, 1904 with a capital of $25,000. Placed in receivership on September 8, 1931; capital of $50,000. Reason for failure: local depression.
Officers: Pres. TH Read 1904-26, CH Henderson 1926-31; **VP** Elbert A Read 1907-24, JF Schick 1922-24, RO Gamble 1922-26, LS McCracken 1925-27, Jas F Monzingo 1927-31, PM Cadwell 1927-28; **Cash.** JF Schick 1904-20, GF Mitchell 1922-27, PM Cadwell 1928-31; **AC** MF Utter 1909-11, AW Liston 1920, CH Waldruff 1922-29, Nelle Woods 1930-31

Third Charter, Red Seal	Ser #	# Notes
10-10-10-20	1-1140	4,560
Third Charter, Date Back, Blue Seal		
10-10-10-20	1-1370	5,480
Third Charter, Plain Back, Blue Seal		
10-10-10-20	1371-2370	4,000
1929, Type I		
6-10's	1-163	978
6-20's	1-19	114

Total amount of circulation issued = $187,560. Amount of large outstanding at close = $1,600. Amount of small outstanding at close = $8,400.
14,040 Large   1,092 Small   15,312 Total

7309	M	$10 1902DB	616	141 D	K291447	VF pen/gone vp
7309	-	$10 1902PB	624	2210 E	2210 E	VG+
7309		$10 1929T1	B000131A			G

THE FIRST NATIONAL BANK IN COLFAX   5 S
13686   JASPER
Chartered in May 1933. Succeeded #7114; assumed the circulation of #7114.
Officers: Pres. FE Boyd 1933-35; **VP** FM Gagle 1933-35; **Cash.** HE Bell 1933-35; **AC** RE Cummings 1933-35, JH Cairns 1933-35

1929, Type II	Ser #	# Notes
5's	1-1564	1,564
10's	1-635	635
20's	1-180	180

Total amount of circulation issued = $17,770. Amount of large outstanding in 1935 = $1,820. Includes the amount of large outstanding for #7114. Amount of small outstanding in 1935 = $23,030. Includes the amount of small outstanding for #7114 and #13686.
0 Large   2,379 Small   2,379 Total

13686	$5	1929T2	A001524		VF
13686	$10	1929T2	A000031		G/VG Higgins Mus.
13686	$10	1929T2	A000043		?
13686	$10	1929T2	A000123		AU
13686	$20	1929T2	A000104		?

THE FIRST NATIONAL BANK OF COLFAX   7 L   10 S
7114   JASPER
Organized on January 2, 1904 with a capital of $25,000. Placed in conservatorship on March 22, 1933. Placed in voluntary liquidation on June 24, 1933; capital of $50,000. Succeeded by #13686; circulation assumed by #13686.
Officers: Pres. WW Lyons 1904-07, FM Gagle 1908-10, JB Johannsen 1911, FE Boyd 1912-33; **VP** RA Crawford 1907, FE Boyd 1909-11, FM Gagle 1913-33; **Cash.** GH York 1905, EE Dotson 1906-07, PE Johannsen 1908-11, RD Aitchison 1912-15, CR Wick 1916-25, HE Bell 1927-33; **AC** RE Cummings 1909-33, HE Bell 1920-25, JH Cairns 1927-33

Third Charter, Red Seal	Ser #	# Notes
5-5-5-5	1-875	3,500
10-10-10-20	1-657	2,628
Third Charter, Date Back, Blue Seal		
5-5-5-5	1-1900	7,600
10-10-10-20	1-1380	5,520
Third Charter, Plain Back, Blue Seal		
5-5-5-5	1901-5495	14,380
10-10-10-20	1381-3488	8,432
1929, Type I		
6-5's	1-752	4,512
6-10's	1-316	1,896
6-20's	1-104	624

Total amount of circulation issued = $388,650. Amount of large outstanding at close = $2,200. Amount of small outstanding at close = $22,800. Circulation assumed by #13686 which was then responsible for redeeming the outstanding circulation of #7114.
42,060 Large   7,032 Small   49,092 Total

7114		$20 1902RS	639	208 A	D161243	VG/F	
7114	M	$5 1902PB	598	2492 E	H62188D	Fr/G	
7114		$5 1902PB	598	3753 H	Z706939E	VF	
7114		$5 1902PB	598	4675 H	4675 H	HG	stamp/stamp
7114		$5 1902PB	598	4824 G	4824 G	XF+	stamp/stamp
7114		$10 1902PB	624	2711 ?	?	VG	
7114	-	$10 1902PB	624	3198 F	3198 F	F/VF	Higgins Mus.
7114		$5 1929T1	B000432A			F	
7114		$5 1929T1	A000683A			VF	Higgins Mus.
7114		$10 1929T1	B000200A			F	
7114		$10 1929T1	C000236A			?	
7114		$10 1929T1	A000271A			F	
7114		$20 1929T1	F000001A			VG	
7114		$20 1929T1	B000044A			VF	Ink
7114		$20 1929T1	C000060A			VG/F	
7114		$20 1929T1	F000070A			F	
7114		$20 1929T1	A000085A			VG/F	

THE FIRST NATIONAL BANK OF COLLEGE SPRINGS   0 L
11295   PAGE
Chartered in January 1919 with a capital of $50,000. Placed in voluntary liquidation on November 25, 1929; capital of $50,000. Absorbed by The Citizens Bank of Clarinda.
Officers: Pres. WS Farguhar 1919-29; **VP** Hugh Miller 1920-29, JD Loudon 1920-21; **Cash.** JD Loudon 1919, L Wallace Farquhar 1920-26, OJ Miller 1926-29; **AC** Veda H Loudon 1920, OJ Miller 1923-26

Third Charter, Plain Back, Blue Seal	Ser #	# Notes
10-10-10-20	1-92	368

Total amount issued = $4,600. Amount outstanding at close = $800.
368 Large   0 Small   368 Total

THE LOUISA COUNTY NATIONAL BANK OF COLUMBUS JUNCTION
2032   LOUISA   16 L   25 S
Chartered on August 24, 1872.
Officers: Pres. Andrew Gamble 1872-76, SC Curtis 1877, George W Merrill 1878, Jarrat W Garner 1880-95, RS Johnston 1896, FG Coffin 1897-1917, ER Lacey 1918-28, RS Johnston 1928-31, JD Buser 1932-35; **VP** WG Allen 1880, FG Coffin 1896, W Dougherty 1900-12, JW Garner 1913-20, CB Dougherty 1923-28, JD Buser 1928-32, JC Ritchie 1932-35; **Cash.** John W True 1872-77, William A Colton 1878-98, ER Lacey 1899-1917, WC Hall 1920-32, FJ Iwert 1932-33, JE Henson 1935; **AC** ER Lacey 1885-96, FM Colton 1900-07, WC Hall 1909-14, FC Spaethe 1920-35, JE Henson 1920-34

First Charter, Original Issue	Ser #	# Notes
1-1-1-2	1-2200	8,800
5-5-5-5	1-2875	11,500
First Charter, Series of 1875		
5-5-5-5	1-4744	18,976
Second Charter, Brown Backs		
5-5-5-5	1-3756	15,024
10-10-10-20	1-2200	8,800
Second Charter, Date Back		
5-5-5-5	1-1509	6,036

10-10-10-20			1-1129		4,516

Third Charter, Date Back, Blue Seal
10-10-10-20			1-1900		7,600

Third Charter, Plain Back, Blue Seal
10-10-10-20			1901-8048		24,592

1929, Type I
6-10's			1-1042		6,252
6-20's			1-294		1,764

1929, Type II
10's			1-509		509
20's			1-105		105

Total amount of circulation issued = $942,520. Amount of large outstanding in 1935 = $4,739. Amount of small outstanding in 1935 = $7,760.

105,844 Large   8,630 Small   114,474 Total

2032	-	$5 1875	401	4690 C	Z700113	VG+ Higgins Mus.
2032		$5 1882BB	472	1976 A	B199065B	VG
2032		$5 1882BB	472	2823 B	N960315N	VG
2032	M	$10 1882BB	485	1483 A	N902998N	VG Davenport B&T
2032	M	$10 1882BB	485	1484 A	N902999N	F
2032	-	$20 1882BB	499	375 A	W120708	F nice sigs
2032	M	$20 1902DB	646	578 A	K946274A	VF
2032	M	$10 1902PB	628	2241 B	X789942B	VG
2032	M	$10 1902PB	628	4684 B	T307036E	VG
2032	M	$10 1902PB	628	5591 C	H650743H	VG
2032	-	$10 1902PB	628	6160 A	X168202H	G
2032	-	$10 1902PB	628	6347 C	B149609K	XF stamp/stamp
2032	-	$10 1902PB	628	7907 C	7907 C	VF Pinholes
2032	-	$20 1902PB	654	4898 A	T307250E	VG stamp/stamp
2032	-	$20 1902PB	654	7531 A	7531 A	F Higgins Mus.
2032	-	$20 1902PB	654	7779 A	7779 A	F/VF
2032		$10 1929T1		E000102A		F
2032		$10 1929T1		D000217A		G/VG
2032		$10 1929T1		F000500A		F
2032		$10 1929T1		C000517A		VF
2032		$10 1929T1		C000730A		VF/XF
2032		$10 1929T1		A000777A		F+
2032		$10 1929T1		C000800A		VF
2032		$10 1929T1		E000967A		VG/F
2032		$10 1929T1		C001034A		VG
2032		$20 1929T1		?000092A		VF
2032		$20 1929T1		B000111A		VG UR corner torn
2032		$20 1929T1		D000197A		VF Higgins Mus.
2032		$20 1929T1		F000222A		VG/F
2032		$20 1929T1		E000239A		F/VF
2032		$20 1929T1		C000240A		CU VF ?
2032		$20 1929T1		B000243A		CU
2032		$20 1929T1		C000243A		CU
2032		$20 1929T1		D000243A		AU Higgins Mus.
2032		$20 1929T1		E000243A		CU
2032		$20 1929T1		B000269A		VG
2032		$10 1929T2		A000066		G+ Stains
2032		$10 1929T2		A000436		F/VF
2032		$20 1929T2		A000001		F
2032		$20 1929T2		A000017		VF
2032		$20 1929T2		A000031		F

THE FIRST NATIONAL BANK OF CONRAD   8 L   2 S
9447   GRUNDY

Organized on April 24, 1909 with a capital of $25,000. Placed in voluntary liquidation on November 5, 1931; capital of $25,000. Absorbed by The First State Bank of Conrad. Placed in receivership on March 28, 1934; reason: deficiency in assets sold.

Officers: Pres. AB Reynolds 1910, Homer S Thomas 1911-19, EO Ecklund 1920-24, WR Stewart 1925, JF Wheeler 1925-31; **VP** Samuel Bockes 1910-14, WR Stewart 1920-24, FW Cartwright 1925, WR Stewart 1925-31; **Cash.** Homer S Thomas 1910, EO Ecklund 1911-19, JF Wheeler 1920-24, FW Cartwright 1925-31; **AC** EO Ecklund 1910

Third Charter, Date Back, Blue Seal   Ser #   # Notes
10-10-10-20   1-1930   7,720

Third Charter, Plain Back, Blue Seal
10-10-10-20   1931-4798   11,472

1929, Type I
6-10's   1-332   1,992
6-20's   1-83   498

Total amount of circulation issued = $269,780. Amount of large outstanding at close = $4,620. Amount of small outstanding at close = $20,380.

19,192 Large   2,490 Small   21,682 Total

9447	-	$20 1902PB	644	1068 A	E189333	XF pen/pen
9447	M	$10 1902PB	626	2732 A	V163094D	VF
9447	-	$10 1902PB	626	4729 C	4729 C	CU Higgins Mus.
9447	-	$10 1902PB	626	4737 A	4737 A	XF pen/pen
9447	-	$20 1902PB	652	4141 A	4141 A	VF
9447	-	$20 1902PB	652	4204 A	4204 A	XF
9447	-	$20 1902PB	652	4206 A	4206 A	VF
9447	-	$20 1902PB	652	4508 A	4508 A	F
9447		$10 1929T1		B000073A		AU
9447		$10 1929T1		A000243A		VG+ Higgins Mus.

THE COON RAPIDS NATIONAL BANK   1 L
6080   CARROLL

Chartered in January 1902 with a capital of $25,000. Succeeded The Valley Bank. Placed in voluntary liquidation on December 3, 1912; capital of $50,000.

Officers: Pres. John Lee 1902-10, A Brutsche 1911, CP McDonald 1912; **VP** TR Lambert 1902-09, WW Wine 1910, E Conner 1911; **Cash.** Dana Reed 1902, CH Stockwell 1903-05, WA Storm 1906-07, MF Strauser 1908, TC Lundy 1910, WR Prettyman; **AC** JW Smith

Second Charter, Brown Backs   Ser #   # Notes
10-10-10-20   1-1120   4,480

Second Charter, Date Back
10-10-10-20   1-749   2,996

Total amount of circulation issued = $93,450. Amount outstanding at close = $24,500. Amount outstanding in October 1913 = $13,200.

7,476 Large   0 Small   7,476 Total

6080	M	$10 1882DB	545	733 F	K690131	VF pen/pen

THE FIRST NATIONAL BANK OF COON RAPIDS   15 L   19 S
5514   CARROLL

Chartered on July 23, 1900 with a capital of $25,000. Succeeded The State Savings Bank. Placed in voluntary liquidation on April 11, 1933; capital of $25,000. Succeeded by The First State Bank of Coon Rapids.

Officers: Pres. Abraham Dixon 1900-09, Edward McDonald 1910-33; **VP** Edward McDonald 1900-09, J Dixon 1910-12, MB Keister 1913-33; **Cash.** John A Dixon 1900-05, George H Dixon 1906-09, AF Greenwaldt 1910-33; **AC** CA Baker 1902-05, ME Wallace 1907, BE Friend 1920, WA Jaeger 1923, Paul H Kinnick 1924-33

Second Charter, Brown Backs   Ser #   # Notes
10-10-10-20   1-1410   5,640

Second Charter, Date Back
10-10-10-20   1-1740   6,960

Sheets numbered 1611 to 1740 were delivered on September 23, but not marked as to type. Type uncertain.

Second Charter, Value Back
10-10-10-20   1741-2407   2,668

Sheets 1611-1740 type uncertain.

Third Charter, Plain Back, Blue Seal
10-10-10-20   1-2124   8,496

1929, Type I
6-10's   1-438   2,628
6-20's   1-104   624

Total amount of circulation issued = $335,810. Amount of large outstanding at close = $3,010. Amount of small outstanding at close = $21,990.

23,764 Large   3,242 Small   27,016 Total

5514	-	$10 1882BB	490	146 B	X521458	VF pen/pen
5514	-	$10 1882BB	490	147 B	X521459	VF pen Higgins Mus.
5514		$10 1882DB	504	346 A	?	VG
5514	M	$10 1882DB	545	?	D175529	? Bayard
5514	M	$10 1882DB	545	1495 F	R437533	VF pen/pen
5514	M	$20 1882DB	555	998 B	M343156	VG/F

Charter		Denom	Type	Plate	Ser#	Treas#	Grade	Notes
5514	M	$10	1882VB	577	1794 F	T846402	VG	Rust
5514	M	$10	1882VB	577	1844 F	T846452	VF	Higgins Mus.
5514	M	$10	1902PB	633	491 C	A981573E	AU	pen/pen
5514	-	$10	1902PB	633	?	V846776H	VG+	Bayard
5514	M	$20	1902PB	659	882 A	A353564H	VF	pen/pen
5514		$20	1902PB	659	? A	B163624K	VF+	Bayard
5514	-	$20	1902PB	659	1711 A	1711 A	F	pen/pen
5514	-	$20	1902PB	659	2041 A	2041 A	AU	
5514	-	$20	1902PB	659	2068 A	2068 A	VF+	Higgins Mus.
5514		$10	1929T1		E000094A		F/VF	Stained
5514		$10	1929T1		B000125A		VG	Rust; small hole
5514		$10	1929T1		C000273A		F	
5514		$10	1929T1		A000276A		F	
5514		$10	1929T1		C000329A		?	Bayard
5514		$10	1929T1		B000362A		VF	
5514		$20	1929T1		E000006A		VG	
5514		$20	1929T1		D000033A		F	Higgins Mus.
5514		$20	1929T1		B000094A		VG+	
5514		$20	1929T1		A000102A		XF	
5514		$20	1929T1		B000102A		AU	
5514		$20	1929T1		D000102A		AU	
5514		$20	1929T1		E000102A		AU	
5514		$20	1929T1		F000102A		CU	
5514		$20	1929T1		C000103A		AU	
5514		$20	1929T1		D000103A		CU	
5514		$20	1929T1		E000103A		AU	Stain & washed
5514		$20	1929T1		C000104A		CU	
5514		$20	1929T1		D000104A		AU	Minor stain

THE FARMERS NATIONAL BANK OF CORNING   8 L
8100   ADAMS

Chartered in February 1906 with a capital of $25,000. Placed in voluntary liquidation on November 3, 1925; capital of $25,000. Absorbed by #8725.
Officers: Pres. Chas C Norton 1906-13, SC Scott 1914-25; **VP** SC Scott 1907-13, WH Cochrane 1914, James Roach 1920-25; **Cash.** Nelle Belding 1906-13, JJ Hogan 1914-15, Harry Scott 1916-25; **AC** HW Kergsen, WA McKelry 1920-25, Violet Tracey 1920, Florence Brown 1922, Florence Bixler 1923-25

Third Charter, Red Seal	Ser #	# Notes
10-10-10-20	1-687	2,748
Third Charter, Date Back, Blue Seal		
10-10-10-20	1-1610	6,440
Third Charter, Plain Back, Blue Seal		
10-10-10-20	1611-3924	9,256

Total amount issued = $230,550. Amount outstanding at close = $25,000.
18,444 Large   0 Small   18,444 Total

Charter		Denom	Type	Plate	Ser#	Treas#	Grade	Notes
8100	M	$10	1902RS	614	276 C	Y212048	F	
8100	M	$20	1902RS	640	665 A	Y310790	VF	pen Higgins Mus.
8100	M	$20	1902DB	643	1488 B	A478532B	AG	
8100	M	$10	1902PB	625	1709 F	R651510B	PR	pen/pen
8100	M	$10	1902PB	625	1836 D	U617744B	VF	
8100	M	$10	1902PB	625	3422 E	D687224H	XF	gone Higg. Mus.
8100	M	$10	1902PB	625	3553 F	M99825H	VG	
8100	M	$20	1902PB	651	2403 B	H903553D	F/VF	pen/pen

THE FIRST NATIONAL BANK OF CORNING   2 L
2936   ADAMS

Organized on April 26, 1883 with a capital of $50,000. Succeeded George W. Frank & Darrow. Purchased #4268 on November 10, 1896. Placed in receivership on June 22, 1914; capital of $50,000. Reason for failure: incompetent management.
Officers: Pres. Lew E Darrow 1883-91, FM Widner 1892-1911, Ralph Newcomb 1912-14; **VP** Ralph Newcomb 1896-1911, WW Runyon 1913-14; **Cash.** Charles C Norton 1883-1905, B Newcomb 1906-14; **AC** EF Miner 1896-1904, FB Miner 1907, RE Phillips 1911

Second Charter, Brown Backs	Ser #	# Notes
10-10-10-20	1-1240	4,960
Third Charter, Red Seal		
10-10-10-20	1-3135	12,540
Third Charter, Date Back, Blue Seal		
10-10-10-20	1-4227	16,908

Total amount of circulation issued = $430,100. Amount outstanding at close = $57,245. Amount outstanding in October 1915 = $26,44.
34,408 Large   0 Small   34,408 Total

Charter		Denom	Type	Plate	Ser#	Treas#	Grade	Notes
2936		$10	1882BB	480	933 C	N876492	F	
2936	M	$10	1902DB	616	69 D	E726484	G	faded Higg. Mus.

THE NATIONAL BANK OF CORNING   0 L
4268   ADAMS

Chartered on March 21, 1896. Succeeded The Bank of Corning. Placed in voluntary liquidation on November 10, 1896; capital of $50,000. Purchased by #2936.
Officers: Pres. DS Sigler 1890-91, WS Hefling 1892-96; **Cash.** Charles T Cole 1890-96

Second Charter, Brown Backs	Ser #	# Notes
10-10-10-20	1-574	2,296

Total amount of circulation issued = $28,700. Amount outstanding at close = $11,250. Amount outstanding in 1910 = $300.
2,296 Large   0 Small   2,296 Total

THE OKEY-VERNON NATIONAL BANK OF CORNING   20 L   89 S
8725   ADAMS

Founders A. F. Okey and C. H. Vernon gave this bank its name, one of four private name national banks in Iowa.
Chartered in June 1907 with a capital of $50,000. Absorbed #8100 on November 3, 1925.
Officers: Pres. AF Okey 1908-09, CH Vernon 1910-20, CE Okey 1922-35; **VP** CH Vernon 1909, FC Okey 1910-21, EM Vernon 1922-31; **Cash.** CE Okey 1908-21, FC Okey 1922-35; **AC** EM Vernon 1909-20, WB Stephenson 1922-35, CL Rogers 1922-35

Third Charter, Red Seal	Ser #	# Notes
5-5-5-5	1-900	3,600
10-10-10-10	1-1100	4,400
Third Charter, Date Back, Blue Seal		
5-5-5-5	1-3500	14,000
10-10-10-10	1-3000	12,000
Third Charter, Plain Back, Blue Seal		
5-5-5-5	3501-10246	26,984
10-10-10-10	3001-8787	23,148
1929, Type I		
6-5's	1-2192	13,152
6-10's	1-1162	6,972
1929, Type II		
5's	1-2734	2,734
10's	1-1404	1,404

Total amount of circulation issued = $781,590. Amount of large outstanding in June 1935 = $3,235. Amount of small outstanding in June 1935 = $46,765.
84,132 Large   24,262 Small   108,394 Total

Charter		Denom	Type	Plate	Ser#	Treas#	Grade	Notes
8725	M	$5	1902RS	589	350 D	N859073	VG	stamp/stamp
8725	M	$5	1902DB	592	1197 F	T405806	XF	stamp/stamp
8725	M	$10	1902DB	618	2270 H	H546423	VG/F	
8725	M	$5	1902PB	600	3541 G	M893548B	AU	
8725	M	$5	1902PB	600	4048 E	T980224B	VG/F	
8725	M	$5	1902PB	600	4094 H	T980270B	F/VF	stamp/stamp
8725	M	$5	1902PB	600	6937 H	M275683E	F+	gone/gone
8725	-	$5	1902PB	600	8353 H	Z491714H	VF	stamp/faded
8725	-	$5	1902PB	600	9726 G	9726 G	VF+	stamp/stamp
8725	M	$10	1902PB	626	3860 G	R93825	XF/AU	stamp/stamp
8725	M	$10	1902PB	626	3861 G	R93826	VG	faded stamps
8725	M	$10	1902PB	626	3865 F	R93830	VF+	stamp/stamp
8725	M	$10	1902PB	626	4755 F	T96660	XF+	stamp/stamp
8725	-	$10	1902PB	626	6687 G	Y74772	XF/AU	stamp/stamp
8725	-	$10	1902PB	626	6973 G	Y515018	F	stamp, trimmed
8725	-	$10	1902PB	626	7438 F	7438 F	F	stamp/stamp
8725	-	$10	1902PB	626	8346 H	8346 H	F	
8725	-	$10	1902PB	626	8568 F	8568 F	F	stamp/stamp
8725	-	$10	1902PB	626	8745 G	8745 G	XF	stamp Higg. Mus.
8725	-	$10	1902PB	626	8765 E	8765 E	F	
8725		$5	1929T1		B000737A		VG	
8725		$5	1929T1		C000737A		VG/F	
8725		$5	1929T1		D001246A		?	
8725		$5	1929T1		D001689A		VF	
8725		$5	1929T1		C001930A		F	
8725		$10	1929T1		C000346A		XF	
8725		$10	1929T1		A000347A		?	
8725		$10	1929T1		C000367A		VF	
8725		$10	1929T1		F000391A		VG	
8725		$10	1929T1		E000429A		VG	
8725		$10	1929T1		F000441A		VF	
8725		$10	1929T1		D000581A		VG	
8725		$10	1929T1		D000582A		VG	
8725		$10	1929T1		B000611A		F	
8725		$10	1929T1		D000792A		VF	
8725		$10	1929T1		A000995A		VG	
8725		$10	1929T1		F001043A		VG	
8725		$5	1929T2		A000001	[	CU	
8725		$5	1929T2		A000002	[	CU	
8725		$5	1929T2		A000003	[	CU	
8725		$5	1929T2		A000004	[	CU	
8725		$5	1929T2		A000005	[	CU	
8725		$5	1929T2		A000006	[	CU	
8725		$5	1929T2		A000996		?	

8725	$5	1929T2	A001988		CU	
8725	$5	1929T2	A001989		CU	
8725	$5	1929T2	A001993		?	
8725	$5	1929T2	A001999		CU	
8725	$5	1929T2	A002000		CU	
8725	$5	1929T2	A002001		AU	
8725	$5	1929T2	A002002		CU	
8725	$5	1929T2	A002003		CU	
8725	$5	1929T2	A002004		CU	
8725	$5	1929T2	A002008		CU	
8725	$5	1929T2	A002010		CU	
8725	$5	1929T2	A002011		CU	
8725	$5	1929T2	A002012		CU	
8725	$5	1929T2	A002016		CU	
8725	$5	1929T2	A002020		CU	
8725	$5	1929T2	A002021		CU	
8725	$5	1929T2	A002022		CU	
8725	$5	1929T2	A002023		AU	
8725	$5	1929T2	A002024		CU	
8725	$5	1929T2	A002025		CU	
8725	$5	1929T2	A002026		CU	
8725	$5	1929T2	A002027		CU	
8725	$5	1929T2	A002028		AU	
8725	$5	1929T2	A002029		CU	
8725	$5	1929T2	A002030		?	
8725	$5	1929T2	A002031		CU	
8725	$5	1929T2	A002034		CU	
8725	$5	1929T2	A002035		CU	
8725	$5	1929T2	A002037		CU	
8725	$5	1929T2	A002041		?	
8725	$5	1929T2	A002042		?	
8725	$5	1929T2	A002044		CU	
8725	$5	1929T2	A002045		CU	
8725	$5	1929T2	A002046		CU	
8725	$5	1929T2	A002048		CU	
8725	$5	1929T2	A002049		CU	
8725	$5	1929T2	A002051		CU	
8725	$5	1929T2	A002054		CU	Higgins Mus.
8725	$5	1929T2	A002056		CU	
8725	$5	1929T2	A002057		CU	
8725	$5	1929T2	A002059		CU	
8725	$5	1929T2	A002061		CU	
8725	$5	1929T2	A002062		CU	
8725	$5	1929T2	A002065		CU	
8725	$5	1929T2	A002066		CU	
8725	$5	1929T2	A002068		?	
8725	$5	1929T2	A002071		CU	
8725	$5	1929T2	A002072		CU	
8725	$5	1929T2	A002073		CU	
8725	$5	1929T2	A002074		CU	
8725	$5	1929T2	A002075		CU	
8725	$5	1929T2	A002079		CU	
8725	$5	1929T2	A002080		CU	
8725	$5	1929T2	A002081		?	
8725	$5	1929T2	A002082		CU	
8725	$5	1929T2	A002084		CU	
8725	$5	1929T2	A002085		CU	
8725	$10	1929T2	A000001	[	CU	
8725	$10	1929T2	A000002	[	CU	
8725	$10	1929T2	A000003	[	CU	
8725	$10	1929T2	A000004	[	CU	
8725	$10	1929T2	A000005	[	CU	
8725	$10	1929T2	A000006	[	CU	
8725	$10	1929T2	A000575		XF	
8725	$10	1929T2	A000739		CU	

THE FIRST NATIONAL BANK OF CORWITH   2 L
5775   HANCOCK

Chartered in April 1901. Succeeded The Corwith State Bank. Placed in voluntary liquidation on January 12, 1910; capital of $25,000.

Officers: Pres. Thomas A Way 1901-06, Ben Major 1907-10; **VP** Thomas Daylor 1902-06, Peter Hatterscheid 1907-10; **Cash.** HE Paul 1901-04, Hugo C Hatterscheid 1905-10; **AC** AA Miller 1902-04, EB Applegate, WL Monlux 1909-10

Second Charter, Brown Backs	Ser #	# Notes
10-10-10-20	1-1800	7,200
Second Charter, Date Back		
10-10-10-20	1-30	120

Total amount of circulation issued = $91,500. Amount outstanding at close = $25,000. Amount outstanding in October 1910 = $16,160.

7,320 Large   0 Small   7,320 Total

5775	M	$10 1882BB	490	1180 A R57191R	VG	gone/gone
5775	M	$20 1882BB	504	1594 A U179970U	F/VF	Higgins Mus.

THE FIRST NATIONAL BANK OF CORYDON   12 L
10146   WAYNE

Organized on February 16, 1912 with a capital of $75,000. Placed in receivership on August 18, 1927; capital of $75,000.

Officers: Pres. CW Steele 1912-27; **VP** Lemuel Kimple 1913-22, FR Fry 1923-27; **Cash.** FB Fry 1912-17, JT Rogers 1919-27; **AC** JT Rogers 1913-17, RW Kaster 1920-24, JL Young 1925-27

Third Charter, Date Back, Blue Seal	Ser #	# Notes
10-10-10-20	1-4000	16,000
Third Charter, Plain Back, Blue Seal		
10-10-10-20	4001-11969	31,876

Total amount issued = $598,450. Amount outstanding at close = $72,900.

47,876 Large   0 Small   47,876 Total

10146M	$10	1902DB	620	998 A	H653359A	F	
10146M	$10	1902DB	620	3963 A	N651811B	VF	Higgins Mus.
10146M	$20	1902DB	646	3839 A	N651687B	VF	
10146M	$10	1902PB	628	4157 A	T288727B	VG	Soiled
10146M	$10	1902PB	628	6509 C	N446881D	VG/F	
10146M	$10	1902PB	628	9213 B	D733825H	F	pen/pen
10146	$10	1902PB	628	10317 B	V486859H	VF	
10146 -	$10	1902PB	628	11335 C	11335 C	F	
10146M	$20	1902PB	654	6297 A	N446669D	VG/F	pen/pen Rust
10146M	$20	1902PB	654	7393 A	D200485E	F	
10146M	$20	1902PB	654	9057 A	V572679E	VG	pen/pen
10146M	$20	1902PB	654	9507 A	H550919H	VF	pen/pen

THE CITY NATIONAL BANK OF COUNCIL BLUFFS   33 L   39 L
9306   POTTAWATTAMIE

Chartered on December 5, 1908 with a capital of $120,000. Licensed after Banking Holiday on March 17, 1933.

Officers: Pres. TG Turner 1909-26, Robert W Turner 1927-35; **VP** Oscar Keeline 1909-35, JG Wadsworth 1909-32, RDM Turner 1921-35; **Cash.** Chas R Hannan, Jr. 1909-13, RDM Turner 1914-19, Chas W Parks 1920-35; **AC** RDM Turner 1910-13, PJ McBride 1910-35

Third Charter, Date Back, Blue Seal	Ser #	# Notes
10-10-10-20	1-7500	30,000
Third Charter, Plain Back, Blue Seal		
10-10-10-20	7501-21002	54,008
1929, Type I		
6-5's	1-4736	28,416
6-10's	1-2570	15,420
1929, Type II		
5's	1-9582	9,582
10's	1-3536	3,536

Total amount of circulation issued = $1,429,650. Amount of large outstanding in June 1935 = $6,440. Amount of small outstanding in June 1935 = $113,560.

84,008 Large   56,954 Small   140,962 Total

9306	M	$10 1902DB	618	1 A	H873797	VF	
9306	M	$10 1902DB	618	1552 A	H894448	F	
9306	M	$20 1902DB	644	608 A	H874404	VG/F	lt stamp/pen
9306	M	$10 1902PB	626	11224 C	V694446D	F	
9306	M	$10 1902PB	626	14192 B	X959234E	VF	stamp Higg. Mus.
9306	M	$10 1902PB	626	14906 A	K741118H	F	
9306	M	$10 1902PB	626	15019 A	K741231H	F	
9306	M	$10 1902PB	626	15145 A	K741357H	VG	stamp/stamp
9306		$10 1902PB	626	16277 B	V288659H	?	
9306	-	$10 1902PB	626	16780 A	16780 A	F	stamp/stamp
9306	-	$10 1902PB	626	16807 B	16807 B	VG/F	
9306	-	$10 1902PB	626	16995 C	16995 C	G	
9306	-	$10 1902PB	626	17517 C	17517 C	F	stamp/stamp
9306	-	$10 1902PB	626	18769 C	18769 C	VG	stamp/stamp
9306	-	$10 1902PB	626	19133 A	19133 A	VG+	
9306	-	$10 1902PB	626	19395 A	19395 A	G/VG	faded/faded
9306	-	$10 1902PB	626	19779 ?	19779 ?	VG	
9306	-	$10 1902PB	626	20547 A	20547 A	CU	
9306	-	$10 1902PB	626	20909 A	20909 A	VG	
9306	M	$20 1902PB	652	14443 A	D665565H	VG	stamp/stamp
9306		$20 1902PB	652	16435 A	V288817H	XF+	
9306	-	$20 1902PB	652	16995 C	16995 C	Fr/G	
9306	-	$20 1902PB	652	17248 A	17248 A	XF	stamp/stamp
9306	-	$20 1902PB	652	17884 A	17884 A	G	
9306	-	$20 1902PB	652	20528 A	20528 A	CU	stamp/stamp
9306	-	$20 1902PB	652	20537 A	20537 A	CU	
9306	-	$20 1902PB	652	20538 A	20538 A	CU	stamp/stamp
9306	-	$20 1902PB	652	20540 A	20540 A	CU	
9306	-	$20 1902PB	652	20541 A	20541 A	CU	stamp/stamp
9306	-	$20 1902PB	652	20544 A	20544 A	AU	stamp/stamp

9306	- $20	1902PB	652	20545 A	20545 A	CU
9306	- $20	1902PB	652	20546 A	20546 A	CU
9306	- $20	1902PB	652	20547 A	20547 A	CU
9306	$5	1929T1		D000050A		VG
9306	$5	1929T1		E000208A		VF
9306	$5	1929T1		B002256A		F
9306	$5	1929T1		C002554A		?
9306	$5	1929T1		C002799A		VG
9306	$5	1929T1		C003386A		?
9306	$5	1929T1		A004058A		F
9306	$5	1929T1		C004058A		F
9306	$5	1929T1		D004104A		VF
9306	$5	1929T1		E004321A		VF
9306	$5	1929T1		E004550A		VG
9306	$5	1929T1		F004560A		VG
9306	$5	1929T1		B004666A		F
9306	$10	1929T1		C000413A		F/VF
9306	$10	1929T1		B000454A		F/VF
9306	$10	1929T1		F000456A		F
9306	$10	1929T1		F000554A		VF
9306	$10	1929T1		D000825A		F
9306	$10	1929T1		F001173A		VG/F
9306	$10	1929T1		F001175A		VG/F
9306	$10	1929T1		C001404A		VG	$5 or $10 ?
9306	$10	1929T1		E001415A		?
9306	$10	1929T1		B001492A		?
9306	$10	1929T1		D001603A		F
9306	$10	1929T1		D001697A		XF
9306	$10	1929T1		E002092A		F/VF
9306	$10	1929T1		E002264A		F/VF
9306	$10	1929T1		E002325A		VF
9306	$5	1929T2		A000001	[	CU	Grinnell # 5392
9306	$5	1929T2		A000002	[	CU	Grinnell # 5392
9306	$5	1929T2		A000003	[	CU	Grinnell # 5392
9306	$5	1929T2		A000004	[	CU	Grinnell # 5392
9306	$5	1929T2		A000005	[	CU	Grinnell # 5392
9306	$5	1929T2		A000006	[	CU	Grinnell # 5392
9306	$5	1929T2		A001208		VG
9306	$5	1929T2		A004429		XF
9306	$5	1929T2		A006414		VG
9306	$10	1929T2		A000375		CU
9306	$10	1929T2		A002942		CU	Higgins Mus.

THE COMMERCIAL NATIONAL BANK OF COUNCIL BLUFFS
5838   POTTAWATTAMIE   11 L

Chartered in May 1901 with a capital of $100,000. Placed in voluntary liquidation on September 10, 1927; capital of $100,000. Absorbed by The State Savings Bank of Council Bluffs.

Officers: Pres. Jos R Reed 1901-11, CE Price 1912-24, WA Maurer 1925-27; **VP** Louis Hammer 1902-10, FC Loucee 1907, RH Bloomer 1909, JF Wilcox 1910-11, WA Maurer 1911-24, L Hammer 1914-22, JL Blanchard 1923, RB Barnum 1924, JC Jensen 1925-27; **Cash.** CE Price 1901-10, C Konigmacher 1911-24, BB Barnum 1925-27; **AC** CE Walters 1902-03, F Konigmacher 1904, C Konigmacher 1907-10, WB Price 1909-22, GW Bernhardi 1914-22, DC Morgan 1923, HW Hazleton 1923, HC Hattenhauer 1923, LE Albreti 1925-27

Second Charter, Brown Backs	Ser #	# Notes
5-5-5-5	1-2750	11,000
10-10-10-20	1-3220	12,880
Second Charter, Date Back		
5-5-5-5	1-6700	26,800
10-10-10-20	1-4600	18,400
Second Charter, Value Back		
5-5-5-5	6701-11610	19,640
10-10-10-20	4601-7473	11,492
Third Charter, Plain Back, Blue Seal		
10-10-10-20	1-6086	18,258

Total amount issued = $1,126,150. Amount outstanding in 1925 = $100,000.
124,556 Large   0 Small   124,556 Total

5838	M	$5	1882DB	537	6442 E	R110829	F
5838	M	$10	1882DB	545	4566 F	T65854	F	Higgins Mus.
5838	M	$5	1882VB	574	8061 E	T246648	VF/XF	stamp/stamp
5838	M	$10	1882VB	577	6619 D	V26377	VF
5838	M	$10	1882VB	577	5363 F	U168721	F/VF
5838	M	$10	1902PB	633	1907 C	T500099E	VG/F
5838	M	$10	1902PB	633	2469 C	T500661E	VF	stamp/stamp
5838	M	$10	1902PB	633	3937 B	K160059H	AU	Higgins Mus.
5838	-	$10	1902PB	633	5768 C	5768 C	F
5838	-	$10	1902PB	633	5902 B	5902 B	VG/F	Paper skinned
5838	-	$20	1902PB	659	4941 A	X746383H	F/VF	stamp/stamp

THE COUNCIL BLUFFS NATIONAL BANK   0 L
3427   POTTAWATTAMIE

Chartered on December 30, 1885. Merged with The Iowa State Savings Institution in 1886. Placed in voluntary liquidation on May 5, 1887; capital of $100,000. Succeeded by Burnham, Tulleys & Co.

Second Charter, Brown Backs	Ser #	# Notes
5-5-5-5	1-1157	4,628

Total amount of circulation issued = $23,140. Amount outstanding at close = $22,500. Amount outstanding in 1910 = $195.
4,628 Large   0 Small   4,628 Total

FIRST NATIONAL BANK IN COUNCIL BLUFFS   22 S
14028   POTTAWATTAMIE

Chartered in February 1934 with a capital of $100,000.
Officers: Pres. CG Ouren 1934-35; **VP** Geo W Woods 1934-35, DB Stoufer 1934-35; **Cash.** Geo W Woods 1934-35; **AC** Roy Maxfield 1934-35

1929, Type II	Ser #	# Notes
5's	1-4970	4,970
10's	1-2480	2,480
20's	1-840	840

Total amount of circulation issued = $66,450. Amount outstanding on June 5, 1935 = $50,000.
0 Large   8,290 Small   8,290 Total

14028	$5	1929T2	A000001	CU
14028	$5	1929T2	A000113	CU
14028	$5	1929T2	A000626	F
14028	$5	1929T2	A001238	?
14028	$5	1929T2	A002531	VG
14028	$5	1929T2	A002906	G/VG
14028	$5	1929T2	A003876	VG/F	Ink
14028	$10	1929T2	A000003	CU
14028	$10	1929T2	A000005	CU
14028	$10	1929T2	A000257	VF
14028	$10	1929T2	A001587	VG/F
14028	$10	1929T2	A002115	F
14028	$20	1929T2	A000001	CU
14028	$20	1929T2	A000002	CU
14028	$20	1929T2	A000003	CU
14028	$20	1929T2	A000004	CU
14028	$20	1929T2	A000005	CU
14028	$20	1929T2	A000006	CU
14028	$20	1929T2	A000217	VG
14028	$20	1929T2	A000797	F
14028	$20	1929T2	A000804	F/VF	Higgins Mus.

THE FIRST NATIONAL BANK OF COUNCIL BLUFFS   69 L   47 S
1479   POTTAWATTAMIE

The First National Bank of Council Bluffs is one of two Iowa banks with reported notes bearing Bruce/Jordan Treasury signatures.

Organized on June 1, 1865 with a capital of $50,000. The January 1899 issue of The Bankers Magazine said that the bank was purchased by The Citizens State Bank, but that The First National Bank continued in business. Placed in conservatorship on March 16, 1933. Placed in receivership on April 20, 1934; capital of $300,000.

Officers: Pres. AL Deming 1867-71, MH Deming 1922, James F Evans 1872-89, Geo P Sanford 1890-91, JF Evans 1892, Geo P Sanford 1893-96, Lucius Wells 1896-98, JD Edmundson 1899-1900, Chas R Hannan 1901, Ernest E Hart 1902-12, JP Greenshields 1913-22, EA Wickham 1923-24, FF Everest 1925-34; **VP** Chas R Hannan 1900, JP Greenshields 1902-12, EA Wickham 1913-22, FF Everest 1923-24, Roy Maxfield 1925-34, EB Wilson 1925; **Cash.** MH Deming 1867-69, Shepard Farnsworth 1870-90, AW Riekman 1891-95, Jas A Patton 1896-98, Chas R Hannan 1899, TG Turner 1902-07, John J Spindler 1908-17, GF Spooner 1918-34; **AC** WJ Leverett 1896, Geo F Spooner 1902, 1904-17, FA Buckman 1903, CA Wiley 1904-05, Roy Maxfield 1920-24, JS Watson 1920-34, Perry Badollet 1920, FM Scarr 1926-34

First Charter, Original Issue	Ser #	# Notes
1-1-1-2	1-2200	8,800
5-5-5-5	1-5500	22,000
First Charter, Series of 1875		
5-5-5-5	1-4030	16,120
Second Charter, Brown Backs		
5-5-5-5	1-7270	29,080
10-10-10-20	1-5439	21,756
Third Charter, Red Seal		
10-10-10-20	1-6800	27,200
Third Charter, Date Back, Blue Seal		
5-5-5-5	1-16080	64,320
10-10-10-20	1-8900	35,600
Third Charter, Plain Back, Blue Seal		

5-5-5-5			16081-69037	211,828		
10-10-10-20			8901-17600	34,800		

1929, Type I

6-5's		1-12756	76,536
6-10's		1-2278	13,668
6-20's		1-584	3,504

1929, Type II

5's		1-2074	2,074
10's		1-1085	1,085
20's		1-233	233

Total amount of circulation issued = $3,835,010. Amount of large outstanding at close = $15,185. Amount of small outstanding at close = $184,815.

471,504 Large   97,100 Small   568,604 Total

Charter		Denom	Series	Plate	Treas #	Bank #	Grade	Notes
1479	-	$1	ORIG	380	1649 ?	E76735	G	
1479	-	$1	ORIG	380	1906 A	E76992	F	
1479	-	$2	ORIG	387	1 A	B313397	G	Higgins Mus.
1479	-	$5	ORIG	?	249 D	D8792	F	pen/pen
1479	-	$5	1875	401	1265 A	B981310	VG	pen, Higgins Mus.
1479	-	$5	1882BB	468	6254 D	D511037D	VF	
1479	-	$5	1882BB	468	6746 C	D511529D	F/VF	stamp/stamp
1479	-	$10	1882BB	481	1648 B	V598131	VG	
1479	-	$10	1882BB	481	1748 A	V598231	VF	
1479	-	$20	1882BB	495	2085 A	?	AU	Fed. Res. Bk., San Fran.
1479	M	$20	1882BB	495	3768 A	H548904H	VG	Higgins Mus.
1479	M	$20	1882BB	495	4198 A	H924276H	VF	stamp/stamp
1479	M	$10	1902RS	613	?	?	CU	Grinnell # 2823
1479	M	$10	1902RS	613	5987 A	X804531	G/VG	gone/gone
1479	M	$20	1902RS	639	5156 A	X169959	F+	stamp/stamp
1479	M	$20	1902RS	639	5310 A	X803854	F	faded/faded Washed
1479	M	$20	1902RS	639	6767 A	X805311	F/VF	
1479	M	$5	1902DB	590	4058 C	X928503	?	
1479	M	$5	1902DB	590	13113 C	Y814965A	VG+	gone/gone LR corner missing
1479	M	$5	1902DB	590	15574 B	K80276B	F	lt. stamp sigs
1479	M	$5	1902DB	590	15970 B	K80672B	VG/F	gone/gone
1479	M	$10	1902DB	616	372 F	D818561	VG	gone/gone
1479	M	$10	1902DB	616	2700 E	A196663A	VF	
1479	M	$10	1902DB	616	3500 E	E327655A	F	lt. stamp sigs
1479	M	$10	1902DB	616	3506 E	E327661A	VG/F	gone/stamp
1479	M	$10	1902DB	616	4609 F	T483853A	VG	gone/gone
1479	M	$20	1902DB	642	532 B	D818721	F	faded Cut tight
1479	M	$20	1902DB	642	6845 B	A756761B	VG	gone/gone
1479	M	$20	1902DB	642	8824 B	M521110B	F	faded/faded
1479	M	$5	1902PB	598	17375 B	V851756B	G/VG	gone/gone
1479	M	$5	1902PB	598	23838 A	T472544D	G	stamp/stamp
1479	M	$5	1902PB	598	26725 A	D237841E	G	stamp/stamp
1479	M	$5	1902PB	598	28098 A	M456264E	?	
1479	-	$5	1902PB	598	36947 H	N429028H	VG	stamp/stamp
1479	-	$5	1902PB	598	38064 G	N454545H	VG	
1479	-	$5	1902PB	598	39980 G	V192811H	VF	stamp/stamp
1479	-	$5	1902PB	598	40676 F	V209009H	VG	
1479	-	$5	1902PB	598	41222 H	V209553H	G/VG	
1479	-	$5	1902PB	598	43495 H	Z354426H	VG	
1479	-	$5	1902PB	598	43579 H	Z354510H	VG	
1479	-	$5	1902PB	598	44845 H	Z397176H	AU	
1479	-	$5	1902PB	598	45799 F	45799 F	CU	stamp/stamp
1479	-	$5	1902PB	598	45966 G	45966 G	VG	
1479	-	$5	1902PB	598	48939 F	48939 F	VG/F	
1479	-	$5	1902PB	598	50121 F	50121 F	F	
1479	-	$5	1902PB	598	50360 H	50360 H	VF	
1479	-	$5	1902PB	598	52032 F	52032 F	VG/F	
1479	-	$5	1902PB	598	56493 E	56493 E	F	
1479	-	$5	1902PB	598	57108 E	57108 E	F	
1479	-	$5	1902PB	598	57650 ?	57650 ?	VG	
1479	-	$5	1902PB	598	57907 E	57907 E	F	stamp/stamp
1479	-	$5	1902PB	598	58535 E	58535 E	VG/F	stamp/stamp
1479	-	$5	1902PB	598	58650 G	58650 G	F+	stamp/stamp
1479	-	$5	1902PB	598	59268 F	59268 F	VG/F	
1479	-	$5	1902PB	598	60485 G	60485 G	VG	stamp/stamp
1479	-	$5	1902PB	598	60931 G	60931 G	VG	
1479	-	$5	1902PB	598	60973 G	60973 G	VG	stamp/stamp
1479	-	$5	1902PB	598	63107 E	63107 E	VG/F	
1479	-	$5	1902PB	598	64504 E	64504 E	F+	
1479	-	$5	1902PB	598	64595 G	64595 G	?	
1479	-	$5	1902PB	598	65224 F	65224 F	VF/XF	stamp/stamp
1479	-	$5	1902PB	598	65690 G	65690 G	AU	stamp/stamp
1479	M	$10	1902PB	624	14889 E	H360261E	VF	stamp/stamp
1479	-	$10	1902PB	624	65224 F	65224 F	VF	stamp/stamp
1479	M	$20	1902PB	650	13857 B	Z821689D	VF/XF	
1479	M	$20	1902PB	650	16965 B	B553467H	VF	stamp/stamp
1479	M	$20	1902PB	650	16989 B	B553491H	VF	
1479	M	$20	1902PB	650	17389 B	B553891H	CU	Higgins Mus.
1479	M	$20	1902PB	650	17391 B	B553893H	AU	
1479		$5	1929T1			E001029A	VG/F	
1479		$5	1929T1			D001261A	VG	Soiled
1479		$5	1929T1			B002045A	XF	
1479		$5	1929T1			D002333A	VF	
1479		$5	1929T1			A002370A	F	
1479		$5	1929T1			E004283A	VG/F	
1479		$5	1929T1			B004396A	G	
1479		$5	1929T1			A004577A	VG	
1479		$5	1929T1			A004979A	VG/F	
1479		$5	1929T1			C006389A	VG	
1479		$5	1929T1			F006552A	VG	
1479		$5	1929T1			A006906A	XF/AU	
1479		$5	1929T1			F007297A	VG/F	
1479		$5	1929T1			D009172A	VG	
1479		$5	1929T1			E009589A	F	
1479		$5	1929T1			D010314A	VG	
1479		$5	1929T1			F011023A	?	
1479		$5	1929T1			A011242A	F	
1479		$5	1929T1			A011304A	F	
1479		$5	1929T1			A011323A	AU	Cut tight bottom
1479		$5	1929T1			D011723A	?	
1479		$5	1929T1			B012508A	VF+	
1479		$10	1929T1			B000602A	?	
1479		$10	1929T1			A000662A	F+	
1479		$10	1929T1			E000972A	VF	
1479		$10	1929T1			C001324A	AU	
1479		$10	1929T1			B001363A	VG/F	
1479		$10	1929T1			A001395A	F	
1479		$10	1929T1			A001617A	VG	
1479		$10	1929T1			A001707A	?	
1479		$10	1929T1			C002098A	VF	
1479		$10	1929T1			E002242A	F	
1479		$20	1929T1			E000254A	F+	
1479		$20	1929T1			F000345A	F	
1479		$20	1929T1			D000364A	G	
1479		$20	1929T1			F000399A	?	
1479		$20	1929T1			F000403A	XF	
1479		$20	1929T1			C000406A	F+	
1479		$20	1929T1			F000423A	F/VF	
1479		$20	1929T1			C000424A	VG/F	Rust stain
1479		$20	1929T1			A000449A	VF	
1479		$20	1929T1			E000458A	VG	
1479		$20	1929T1			A000461A	VG+	
1479		$20	1929T1			A000488A	AU	Higgins Mus.
1479		$20	1929T1			F000559A	?	
1479		$20	1929T1			E000578A	F	
1479		$10	1929T2			A000979	F	

THE PACIFIC NATIONAL BANK OF COUNCIL BLUFFS   4 L
1684   POTTAWATTAMIE

This is the only bank in Iowa to have reported notes bearing the Treasury signatures of Noah L. Jeffries and Francis E. Spinner. Bank President Grenville M. Dodge was a Civil War Major General and the Chief Engineer for the Union Pacific Railroad's construction of the first transcontinental railroad.

Chartered in September 1868 with a capital of $100,000. Succeeded #485 of Des Moines. Placed in voluntary liquidation on November 30, 1878; capital of $100,000.

Officers: Pres. John T Baldwin 1868-71, Grenville M Dodge 1872-77; **Cash.** Albert West 1868-73, John Beresheim 1874-75, WM Siedentopf 1876-77

First Charter, Original Issue   Ser #   # Notes
1-1-1-2   1-4000   16,000
5-5-5-5   1-7250   29,000

First Charter, Series of 1875
5-5-5-5   1-680   2,720

Total amount of circulation issued = $178,600. Amount outstanding at close = $45,000. Amount outstanding in 1910 = $1,011.

47,720 Large   0 Small   47,720 Total

1684	-	$1	ORIG	381	1773 C	B995825	VG/F	pen/faded
1684	-	$5	ORIG	398	165 C	E171751	VG	pen/pen vp
1684	-	$5	ORIG	398	540 C	E465383	XF	Higgins Mus.
1684	-	$5	ORIG	398	745 D	E465588	VF/XF	Higgins Mus.

THE FIRST NATIONAL BANK OF CRESCO   10 L   15 S
4897   HOWARD

Organized on April 7, 1893 with a capital of $50,000. Placed in conservation on March 21, 1933. Placed in receivership on October 30, 1933; capital of $50,000.

Cresco, Ia.

Officers: Pres. SA Converse 1893-1919, AB Converse 1920-23, Carl W Reed 1924-26, CC Burgess 1926-33; **VP** SB Carpenter 1896-1909, HC Burgess 1910-19, Ole Natvig 1920-33, EJ Thomas 1927-32; **Cash.** CA Crawford 1893-95, OG Wanless 1896-1900, Abbie J Converse 1901-09, EJ Thomas 1910-30, MZ Daily 1931-33; **AC** Abbie J Converse 1900, EJ Thomas 1902-09, AB Converse 1910-14, John Kakac 1914-29, AJ Bird 1932-33

	Ser #	# Notes
Second Charter, Brown Backs		
10-10-10-20	1-1870	7,480
Second Charter, Date Back		
10-10-10-20	1-1370	5,480
Third Charter, Date Back, Blue Seal		
10-10-10-20	1-1800	7,200
Third Charter, Plain Back, Blue Seal		
10-10-10-20	1801-6526	18,904
1929, Type I		
6-10's	1-880	5,280
6-20's	1-276	1,656

Total amount of circulation issued = $574,220. Amount of large outstanding at close = $4,170. Amount of small outstanding at close = $45,830.

			39,064 Large		6,936 Small		46,000 Total
4897	M	$20 1882BB	499	1206 A	N553704N	F	pen/pen
4897	M	$20 1902DB	621	1563 A	M895089B	G/VG	pen/faded Tape
4897	M	$10 1902DB	647	1385 A	T102725A	VG	pen/pen
4897	M	$10 1902PB	629	1845 C	X464836B	F	pen/faded
4897	M	$10 1902PB	629	2745 A	K452027D	VG	
4897	M	$10 1902PB	629	3217 A	B1839E	VG	pen/pen
4897	M	$10 1902PB	629	4331 A	A12513H	AU	
4897	-	$10 1902PB	629	6479 B	6479 B	AU	pen/pen
4897	-	$20 1902PB	655	4974 A	X355076H	VF	
4897	-	$20 1902PB	655	5090 A	X355192H	XF	Higgins Mus.
4897		$10 1929T1		E000068A		?	
4897		$10 1929T1		F000264A		AU	Higgins Mus.
4897		$10 1929T1		F000472A		F/VF	
4897		$10 1929T1		A000501A		F+	
4897		$10 1929T1		C000555A		VF/XF	
4897		$20 1929T1		C000010A		F	
4897		$20 1929T1		B000024A		F/VF	
4897		$20 1929T1		B000092A		?	
4897		$20 1929T1		C000121A		?	
4897		$20 1929T1		E000157A		VG/F	
4897		$20 1929T1		F000173A		F/VF	
4897		$20 1929T1		C000191A		AU	
4897		$20 1929T1		D000209A		?	
4897		$20 1929T1		E000237A		VG	
4897		$20 1929T1		A000240A		VF	

THE CRESTON NATIONAL BANK   18 L   3 S
2833   UNION

Chartered in 1882 with a capital of $100,000. Succeeded J.B. Harsh & Co. Placed in voluntary liquidation on January 2, 1930; capital of $100,000. Absorbed by #12636; circulation assumed by #12636.
Officers: Pres. James B Harsh 1883-1923, AF Harsh 1924-27, HF Harsh 1928-30; **VP** Ed A Aldrich 1896-1909, 1913, Scott Skinner 1910-22, HF Harsh 1923-24, GS Harsh 1926-30; **Cash.** Addison V Scott 1883-84, RE Boyer 1885-1916, HF Harsh 1917-21, 1925-27, JW McCue 1922-24, HW Brown 1928-30; **AC** WJ Donlin 1896-1902, LG Armstrong 1903-09, JW McCue 1920-21, HW Brown 1920-27, Z Ohlschlager 1928-29

	Ser #	# Notes
Second Charter, Brown Backs		
10-10-10-20	1-2510	10,040
Third Charter, Red Seal		
10-10-10-20	1-1130	4,520
Third Charter, Date Back, Blue Seal		
10-10-10-20	1-2500	10,000
Third Charter, Plain Back, Blue Seal		
10-10-10-20	2501-12548	40,192
1929, Type I		
6-10's	1-621	3,726
6-20's	1-36	216

Total amount of circulation issued = $850,980. Amount of large outstanding at close = $53,200. Amount of small outstanding at close = $41,580. There is a later outstanding figure for the large size because #12636 assumed the large and small size notes of #2833 and #12636 never issued large size, so any large size listed as outstanding on #12636 are actually notes of #2833. Therefore, amount of large outstanding is $5,345 in June 1935.

			64,752 Large		3,942 Small		68,694 Total
2833	M	$10 1902PB	624	5340 F	N99077E	F	stamp Higg. Mus.
2833	M	$10 1902PB	624	5488 F	X329500E	F	
2833	M	$10 1902PB	624	6347 F	D470769H	F	nice sigs
2833	M	$10 1902PB	624	6429 E	D470851H	VG/F	
2833	M	$10 1902PB	624	7031 D	H295243H	VF	
2833	-	$10 1902PB	624	10196 F	10196 F	VG	
2833	-	$10 1902PB	624	10687 D	10687 D	F	
2833	-	$10 1902PB	624	11080 D	11080 D	VF	
2833	-	$10 1902PB	624	11120 F	11120 F	VG/F	
2833	-	$10 1902PB	624	11123 F	11123 F	VG/F	
2833	M	$20 1902PB	650	4833 B	N98570E	F	N87570E ?
2833	M	$20 1902PB	650	5736 B	X329748E	F	
2833	M	$20 1902PB	650	6279 B	D470701H	?	
2833		$20 1902PB	650	8022 B	U595304H	VG/F	Washed
2833		$20 1902PB	650	8936 B	?	VG/F	
2833	-	$20 1902PB	650	10906 B	10906 B	VG/F	
2833	-	$20 1902PB	650	11301 B	11301 B	VG/F	
2833	-	$20 1902PB	650	11677 B	11677 B	XF	pen/pen
2833		$10 1929T1		B000038A		F/VF	
2833		$10 1929T1		D000125A		F+	
2833		$10 1929T1		A000145A		F	Higgins Mus.

THE FIRST NATIONAL BANK IN CRESTON   52 S
12636   UNION

Organized on February 2, 1925 with a capital of $100,000. Succeeded #2586. Absorbed #2833 on January 2, 1930; assumed the circulation of #2833. Placed in conservatorship on March 20, 1933. Licensed again on May 12, 1933.
Officers: Pres. Frank A Ide 1925-33, Will Recknor 1934-35; **VP** DG Wiley 1925-28, GA Mosely 1929, Will Recknor 1929-33, HF Harsh 1930-35, AE Jensen 1931-35; **Cash.** Bert Tallman 1925-35; **AC** RI Pinkerton 1925-35, GR Heflen 1929-35, OE Markitan 1931

	Ser #	# Notes
1929, Type I		
6-5's	1-2712	16,272
6-10's	1-1302	7,812
6-20's	1-358	2,148
1929, Type II		
5's	1-2658	2,658
10's	1-1460	1,460
20's	1-565	565

Total amount of circulation issued = $241,630. Amount outstanding in June 1935 = $99,400. Includes large and small outstanding of #2833.

			0 Large		30,915 Small		30,915 Total
12636		$5 1929T1		E000085A		VF	
12636		$5 1929T1		E000241A		VG+	
12636		$5 1929T1		C000840A		VG/F	
12636		$5 1929T1		C000906A		VG	
12636		$5 1929T1		D001301A		VG	
12636		$5 1929T1		D001364A		F/VF	
12636		$5 1929T1		C001416A		?	
12636		$5 1929T1		A001596A		F	
12636		$5 1929T1		E001872A		?	
12636		$5 1929T1		F001942A		F	
12636		$5 1929T1		A001967A		F/VF	
12636		$5 1929T1		C002273A		G/VG	
12636		$10 1929T1		E000008A		VF	
12636		$10 1929T1		A000016A		F	
12636		$10 1929T1		B000187A		VG/F	
12636		$10 1929T1		C000328A		VG	
12636		$10 1929T1		D000438A		VF	
12636		$10 1929T1		B000630A		F	
12636		$10 1929T1		C000752A		AU	

12636	$10	1929T1	E000755A	XF		
12636	$10	1929T1	C000854A	VF		
12636	$10	1929T1	E000941A	F+		
12636	$10	1929T1	C001038A	CU		
12636	$10	1929T1	A001203A	VG/F		
12636	$10	1929T1	E001295A	VF		
12636	$20	1929T1	F000007A	VG/F		
12636	$20	1929T1	B000034A	XF		
12636	$20	1929T1	F000086A	VG		
12636	$20	1929T1	A000103A	?		
12636	$20	1929T1	A000112A	?		
12636	$20	1929T1	A000125A	F/VF		
12636	$20	1929T1	E000127A	?		
12636	$20	1929T1	C000142A	VF		
12636	$20	1929T1	B000198A	F		
12636	$20	1929T1	E000245A	F		
12636	$20	1929T1	E000289A	XF		
12636	$20	1929T1	E000298A	CU		
12636	$20	1929T1	A000300A	XF		
12636	$5	1929T2	A000318	VF		
12636	$10	1929T2	A000367	VG/F		
12636	$10	1929T2	A000419	CU		
12636	$10	1929T2	A000425	CU		
12636	$10	1929T2	A000450	CU		
12636	$10	1929T2	A000473	XF	Higgins Mus.	
12636	$10	1929T2	A000479	AU+		
12636	$10	1929T2	A000516	AU		
12636	$10	1929T2	A000528	AU	Spotted	
12636	$10	1929T2	A000980	?		
12636	$20	1929T2	A000156	VG		
12636	$20	1929T2	A000189	AU		
12636	$20	1929T2	A000436	XF		
12636	$20	1929T2	A000499	VG		

THE FIRST NATIONAL BANK OF CRESTON 2 L
2586   **UNION**

Chartered on October 22, 1881 with a capital of $50,000. Succeeded S.H. Mallory & Co. Merged with The Bank of Creston in 1886. Placed in voluntary liquidation on March 26, 1925; capital of $50,000. Succeeded by #12636. Placed in receivership on December 12, 1925. Reason for failure: deficiency in assets sold.

Officers: Pres. SH Mallory 1883-86, HS Clarke 1887-02, SW Richardson 1902-10, MD Smith 1911-15; **VP** AB Devoe 1896, Chas L Bullard 1902-19, Will Recknor 1920-24, JV Richardson 1920-24, DG Wiley 1925, MD Smith 1925; **Cash.** FD Ball 1883-85, EJ Bush 1887-88, FW Clarke 1889-99, MD Smith 1900-10, JV Richardson 1911-16, FA Fariday 1918-24, Bert Tallman 1925; **AC** MD Smith 1896-99, RI Pinkerton 1907-25, Bert Tallman 1911-24

First Charter, Series of 1875	Ser #	# Notes
10-10-10-20	1-2352	9,408
Second Charter, Brown Backs		
50-100	1-480	960
Second Charter, Date Back		
50-100	1-300	600
50-50-50-100	1-190	7600
Third Charter, Plain Back, Blue Seal		
50-50-50-100	1-119	476

Total amount issued = $311,850. Amount of outstanding in 1924 = $30,000.
12,204 Large   0 Small   12,204 Total

2586	M	$50	1882BB	518	462 A	B566774	F	Smithsonian
2586	M	$100	1882BB	530	296 A	B448132	VF+	pen/pen

THE FARMERS NATIONAL BANK OF CRYSTAL LAKE 8 L 7 S
9853   **HANCOCK**

Organized on September 22, 1910 with a capital of $25,000. Succeeded #5305. Placed in conservatorship on March 30, 1933. Placed in receivership on May 23, 1934; capital of $25,000. Reason for failure: not available from reports.

Officers: Pres. HR Kluver 1911-23, FA Gabrielson 1924-26, Guy George Gabrielson 1927-34; **VP** EP Nelson 1911, JC Nelson 1911, Ed Peterson 1913-34, Nels Matson 1914-25, WF Jones 1929-31; **Cash.** WP Jones 1911, CN Brones 1912-14, Chas Nelson 1915, JE Hansen 1916-17, HP Stahr 1918-23, John Potgeter 1924-29, Rush Gabrielson 1929-34; **AC** JP Johnson 1913, HP Stahr 1914, John Potgeter 1920-22, Tilla M Stahr 1923, Rush Gabrielson 1923-29, Chas Ausharm 1925, AR Jansson 1929, AJ Janssen 1929-34

Third Charter, Date Back, Blue Seal	Ser #	# Notes
10-10-10-20	1-1660	6,6400
Third Charter, Plain Back, Blue Seal		
10-10-10-20	1661-4834	12,696
1929, Type I		
6-10's	1-548	3,288
6-20's	1-138	828
1929, Type II		
10's	1-146	146
20's	1-35	35

Total amount of circulation issued = $293,300. Amount of large outstanding at close = $1,690. Amount of small outstanding at close = $23,310.
19,336 Large   4,297 Small   23,633 Total

9853	M	$20	1902DB	645	968 A	H458471A	F/VF	pen/pen
9853	M	$10	1902PB	627	2226 C	B696523?	VG/F	
9853	M	$10	1902PB	627	3416 B	Z191738E	F	pen ac/stamp
9853	-	$10	1902PB	627	4168 C	4168 C	VF	pen/stamp
9853	-	$10	1902PB	627	4657 A	4657 A	VG	
9853	-	$10	1902PB	627	4674 A	4674 A	PR	
9853	-	$20	1902PB	653	3676 A	N632126H	?	
9853	-	$20	1902PB	653	3683 A	N632135H	F/VF	Higgins Mus.
9853		$10	1929T1	F000045A			F	
9853		$10	1929T1	E000185A			VG	
9853		$10	1929T1	E000302A			F	
9853		$20	1929T1	F000008A			VG/F	Rust spot
9853		$20	1929T1	D000077A			F	
9853		$20	1929T1	C000080A			F	
9853		$20	1929T1	D000120A			VG	Higgins Mus.

THE FIRST NATIONAL BANK OF CRYSTAL LAKE 3 L
5305   **HANCOCK**

Chartered on April 25, 1900. Placed in voluntary liquidation on September 23, 1910; capital of $25,000. Succeeded by #9853.

Officers: Pres. Josiah Little 1900-03, WB Vaughan 1904-07, JO Osmundson 1908-10; **VP** JO Osmundson 1900-08, LC Larsen 1909-10; **Cash.** Edward C Haga 1900-04, FA Keup 1905, John C Preston 1906-10; **AC** O Erickson 1902, FA Keup 1903-04, El Levong

Second Charter, Brown Backs	Ser #	# Notes
5-5-5-5	1-1465	5,860
10-10-10-20	1-1274	5,096
Second Charter, Date Back		
5-5-5-5	1-210	840
10-10-10-20	1-190	760

Total amount of circulation issued = $106,700. Amount outstanding at close = $12,000. Amount outstanding in 1911 = $2,095.
12,556 Large   0 Small   12,556 Total

5305	-	$20	1882BB	504	285 A	Y134960	VG	gone/faded
5305		$20	1882BB	504	1257 A	V598902V	F	Higgins Mus.
5305	M	$5	1882DB	537	199 E	?	VG	

THE FIRST NATIONAL BANK OF CUMBERLAND 2 L
7326   **CASS**

Organized on June 7, 1904 with a capital of $25,000. Placed in receivership on July 22, 1926; capital of $25,000. Reason for failure: local depression.

Officers: Pres. P Pettinger 1905-19, DP Becker 1920-21, JW Reihman 1922-23, TE Ostrus 1924-26; **VP** E Euken 1905-14, Chas E Studley 1920, 1924-26, OR Patrick 1922-23; **Cash.** PH Pettinger 1905-17, WH Bell 1918-20, Geo E Wollenhaupt 1922-26; **AC** WT Pettinger 1905-10, FC Williams 1914, Grace M Read 1920, Hillary H Studley 1922-26, LM Wollenhaupt 1924-25

Third Charter, Red Seal	Ser #	# Notes
10-10-10-20	1-376	1,504
Third Charter, Date Back, Blue Seal		
10-10-10-20	1-860	3,440
Third Charter, Plain Back, Blue Seal		
10-10-10-20	861-960	400

Total amount issued = $66,800. Amount outstanding at close = $5,950.
5,344 Large   0 Small   5,344 Total

7326	M	$10	1902DB	616	833 F	N54399B	XF	vp Higgins Mus.
7326	M	$20	1902DB	642	494 B	Y517294A	VF	

THE CITIZENS NATIONAL BANK OF DAVENPORT 20 L
1671   **SCOTT**

All of the known Iowa notes with Allison/Gilfillan signatures are from the Citizens National Bank of Davenport.

Chartered on May 4, 1867. Placed in voluntary liquidation on October 15, 1906; capital of $300,000. Consolidated with The German Savings Bank, Davenport.

Officers: Pres. Moses Kelley 1867, WC Wadsworth 1868-69, C Steward Ellis 1870-73, Francis H Griggs 1874-1906; **VP** R Krause 1896, Jens Lorenzen 1900; **Cash.** Andrew O Butler 1867, JC Conklin 1868-69, Hugo Schmidt 1870-75, Ernst S Carl 1876-99, Aug A Balluff 1900-06, **AC** A Priester 1885-99, FC Kroeger 1900

First Charter, Original Issue	Ser #	# Notes
1-1-1-2	1-5600	22,400
5-5-5-5	1-4350	17,400
10-10-10-20	1-1100	4,400
First Charter, Series of 1875		
1-1-1-2	1-1000	4,000

5-5-5-5			1-4305	17,220		
10-10-10-20			1-2047	8,188		

Second Charter, Brown Backs

50-100			1-5284	10,568		

Total amount of circulation issued = $1,156,050. Amount outstanding at close = $245,200. Amount outstanding in 1910 = $71,210.

84,176 Large   0 Small   84,176 Total

1671	-	$1	ORIG	380	2075 C	C12190	VG	
1671	-	$1	ORIG	380	4186 A	C446413	VG/F	pen/pen
1671	-	$1	ORIG	380	4186 C	C446413	G	vp
1671	-	$2	ORIG	387	610 A	B358803	VG	Higgins Mus.
1671	-	$2	ORIG	387	5316 A	D922361	F	
1671	-	$10	ORIG	414	137 B	A147815	F	
1671	-	$5	1875	403	3863 D	Z28629	F/VF	Davenport B&T
1671	-	$10	1875	418	443 A	B722479	AU	Higgins Mus.
1671	-	$10	1875	418	446 ?	?	?	Reinforced
1671	-	$10	1875	418	1401 C	E383131	?	Eroded
1671	-	$10	1875	418	1427 A	E383157	XF/AU	pen/pen Tight cut
1671	-	$50	1882BB	510	1459 A	A514093	VF	Davenport B&T
1671	-	$50	1882BB	510	1649 A	A584181	F/VF	Davenport B&T
1671	-	$50	1882BB	510	1666 A	A584198	VF	
1671	-	$50	1882BB	510	1984 A	A707163	F/VF	Davenport B&T
1671	-	$50	1882BB	510	2010 A	?	F+	Davenport B&T
1671	-	$50	1882BB	510	3168 A	B15929	F+	
1671	M	$50	1882BB	510	4894 B	B479249	F	
1671	-	$100	1882BB	522	1298 A	A513932	F	Davenport B&T
1671	-	$100	1882BB	522	3024 A	B15785	VF	Davenport B&T

THE DAVENPORT NATIONAL BANK   **1 L**
848   SCOTT

Chartered on March 1, 1865. Placed in voluntary liquidation on December 4, 1901; capital of $100,000. Consolidated with The Union Savings Bank.
Officers: Pres. George L Davenport 1867-75, BB Woodward 1876-78, ES Ballord 1879-91, SF Smith 1891-93, WC Hayward 1894-01; **VP** Henry Egbert 1896; **Cash.** BB Woodward 1867-75, GE Maxwell 1879-87, SD Bawden 1888-1901; **AC** Chas A Mast 1876-79, SD Bawden 1885

First Charter, Original Issue	Ser #	# Notes
5-5-5-5	1-10800	43,200
10-10-10-20	1-2000	8,000

First Charter, Series of 1875		
5-5-5-5	1-4500	18,000
10-10-10-20	1-2658	10,632

Second Charter, Brown Backs		
5-5-5-5	1-1595	6,380
50-100	1-1468	2,936

Total amount of circulation issued = $791,000. Amount outstanding at close = $100,000. Amount outstanding in 1910 = $8,877.

89,148 Large   0 Small   89,148 Total

848	-	$5	1882BB	467	1459 A	D210599D	VF	Davenport B&T

THE FIRST NATIONAL BANK OF DAVENPORT   **16 L**
2695   SCOTT

All of the reported $100 1902 Red Seal notes from Iowa were issued by this bank.

Chartered in 1882. Succeeded #15. Received permission on May 22, 1911 to retake original charter #15. Placed in voluntary liquidation on April 25, 1931; capital of $400,000. Absorbed by The Union Savings Bank and Trust Company of Davenport.
Officers: Pres. James Thompson 1883-93, Anthony Burdick 1894-1911; **VP** John L Dow 1896, C Mueller 1900, Joe R Lane 1902-11, Jno P Van Patten 1904-10; **Cash.** John B Fidlar 1883-94, CA Mast 1895-1903, Geo Hoehn 1904-05, Lew J Yaggy 1906-11; **AC** Geo Hoehn 1896-1903, LJ Yaggy 1904-05, Will J Housman 1907-11

Second Charter, Brown Backs	Ser #	# Notes
5-5-5-5	1-2300	9,200
10-10-10-20	1-2025	8,100
50-100	1-1811	3,622

Third Charter, Red Seal		
10-10-10-20	1-3300	13,200
50-100	1-2127	4,254

Third Charter, Date Back, Blue Seal		
10-10-10-20	1-4500	18,000
50-100	1-4	8

2695	-	$20	1882BB	493	1589 A	N968157	F/VF	Davenport B&T
2695		$50	1882BB	507	1772 A	?	CU	Davenport B&T
2695		$100	1882BB	519	1529 A	B91196	VF	Davenport B&T
2695	M	$10	1902RS	613	376 B	A179939	XF	Davenport B&T
2695	M	$20	1902RS	639	362 A	A179925	XF	Davenport B&T
2695	M	$50	1902RS	664	10 A	A8812	VF	Davenport B&T
2695	M$100	1902RS	686	21 A	A8823	VF	Davenport B&T
2695	M$100	1902RS	686	1216 A	A135635	VF	Davenport B&T
2695	M$100	1902RS	686	1441 A	A135860	VF	Higgins Mus.
2695	M$100	1902RS	686	1642 A	A284926	F/VF	vp Pinholes
2695	M$100	1902RS	686	1684 A	A284968	F	
2695	M$100	1902RS	686	1785 A	A285069	F	Davenport B&T
2695	M$100	1902RS	686	1838 A	A350632	VF+	Davenport B&T
2695	M$100	1902RS	686	1906 A	A350700	VF	Ink
2695	M$100	1902RS	686	1922 A	A350716	XF	
2695	M	$10	1902DB	616	1499 F	D832188	F	pen/pen

THE FIRST NATIONAL BANK OF DAVENPORT   **4 L**
15 **(FIRST ORGANIZATION)**   SCOTT

The First National Bank of Davenport, charter #15, was the first national bank in the nation to open its doors for business, beating the next bank into operatoin by one day.

Organized on June 22, 1863; opened on June 29, 1863. Placed in voluntary liquidation on May 9, 1882; capital of $100,000. Succeeded by #2695.
Officers: Pres. Ira M Gifford 1867-73, Hiram Price 1874-75, Tristram T Dow 1876-82; **Cash.** Hugo Schmidt 1867-69, DC Porter 1870-74, Lloyd G Gage 1876-77, John B Fidlar 1878-82; **AC** Charles F Meyer 1878-82

First Charter, Original Issue	Ser #	# Notes
1-1-1-2	1-3500	14,000
5-5-5-5	1-3690	14,760
10-10-10-20	1-2400	9,600

First Charter, Series of 1875		
10-10-10-20	1-62	248

Total amount issued = $214,400. Amount outstanding at close = $45,000. Amount outstanding in 1910 = $2,009.

38,608 Large   0 Small   38,608 Total

15	-	$2	ORIG	387	95 A	791871	Fr	gone/gone
15	-	$2	ORIG	387	1079 A	792855	VG	
15	-	$2	ORIG	387	2002 A	793778	VG	Torn in two
15	-	$5	ORIG	397	2295 A	E873499	?	

THE FIRST NATIONAL BANK OF DAVENPORT   **69 L 127 S**
15 **(2ND ORGANIZATION)**   SCOTT

Received permission on May 22, 1911 to retake original charter #15.
Officers: Pres. Anthony Burdick 1911, Albert F Dawson 1912-28, Irvin J Green 1928-31; **VP** Joe R Lane 1911-31, Irvin J Green 1928; **Cash.** Lew J Yaggy 1911-19, Irvin J Green 1920-28, Wm M Brandon 1928-31; **AC** Will J Housman 1911-19, CF Schmidt 1913-31, PA Tornquist 1920-31, AA Georgen 1928-31, AL Sessler 1928-31

Third Charter, Date Back, Blue Seal	Ser #	# Notes
10-10-10-20	1-8300	33,200
50-50-50-100	1-1455	5,820

Third Charter, Plain Back, Blue Seal		
10-10-10-20	8301-34694	105,576
50-50-50-100	1456-2011	2,224

1929, Type I		
6-10's	1-3573	21,438
6-20's	1-1007	6,042
6-50's	1-319	1,914
6-100's	1-69	414

Total amount of circulation issued = $3,838,320. Amount of large outstanding at close = $72,720. Amount of small outstanding at close = $322,840.

116,940 Large   29,808 Small   146,748 Total

15	M	$10	1902DB	616	1 B	D185328A	CU	Davenport B&T
15	M	$10	1902DB	616	1876 ?	?	?	
15	M	$10	1902DB	616	1977 C	R81791A	VG	
15	M	$10	1902DB	616	4208 C	A445722B	VF	
15	M	$10	1902DB	616	6880 A	M70916B	F/VF	stamp/stamp
15	M	$10	1902DB	616	7734 B	M100190B	XF	Davenport B&T
15	M	$20	1902DB	642	1458 A	R81272A	VG	

15	M	$50	1902DB	667	192 B	A39622	XF	Davenport B&T	15	$10	1929T1	C000005A	CU	Davenport B&T
15	-	$50	1902DB	667	1248 B	1248 B	F+	faded Higg. Mus.	15	$10	1929T1	D000005A	CU	Davenport B&T
15	-	$50	1902DB	667	1291 A	1291 A	XF		15	$10	1929T1	E000005A	CU	Davenport B&T
15	-	$50	1902DB	667	1427 B	1427 B	VF	Davenport B&T	15	$10	1929T1	F000005A	CU	Davenport B&T
15	M	$100	1902DB	689	255 A	?	VF	Davenport B&T	15	$10	1929T1	A000006A	CU	Davenport B&T
15	M	$100	1902DB	689	259 A	?	VF+	Davenport B&T	15	$10	1929T1	B000006A	CU	Davenport B&T
15	M	$100	1902DB	689	264 A	A699958	VF+	Davenport B&T	15	$10	1929T1	C000006A	CU	Davenport B&T
15	M	$100	1902DB	689	267 A	A699961	F/VF	Davenport B&T	15	$10	1929T1	D000006A	CU	Davenport B&T
15	M	$100	1902DB	689	424 A	A700118	XF	Davenport B&T	15	$10	1929T1	E000006A	CU	Davenport B&T
15	M	$100	1902DB	689	465 A	B120489	VF/XF	Grinnell # 4276	15	$10	1929T1	F000006A	CU	Davenport B&T
15	M	$100	1902DB	689	1164 A	B121188	VG+	Higgins Mus.	15	$10	1929T1	A000007A	CU	Davenport B&T
15	-	$100	1902DB	689	1313 A	1313 A	XF	Davenport B&T	15	$10	1929T1	B000007A	CU	Davenport B&T
15	M	$10	1902PB	624	13880 C	U889302D	VG	lt. stamp sigs	15	$10	1929T1	C000007A	CU	Davenport B&T
15	M	$10	1902PB	624	14399 B	D440371E	F	lt. stamp sigs	15	$10	1929T1	D000007A	CU	Davenport B&T
15	M	$10	1902PB	624	16503 ?	N514006E	G		15	$10	1929T1	E000007A	CU	Davenport B&T
15	M	$10	1902PB	624	18506 C	B287948H	VG		15	$10	1929T1	F000007A	CU	Davenport B&T
15	M	$10	1902PB	624	18563 B	B288005H	CU	pen/pen	15	$10	1929T1	A000008A	CU	Davenport B&T
15		$10	1902PB	624	21443 C	U676445H	CU		15	$10	1929T1	B000008A	CU	Davenport B&T
15		$10	1902PB	624	22214 C	Z448766H	VG+		15	$10	1929T1	C000008A	CU	Davenport B&T
15		$10	1902PB	624	23154 B	?	VF	Davenport B&T	15	$10	1929T1	D000008A	CU	Davenport B&T
15	-	$10	1902PB	624	23458 B	Z477420H	VG		15	$10	1929T1	E000008A	CU	Davenport B&T
15	-	$10	1902PB	624	24105 C	Z478067H	VF	Grinnell # 4275	15	$10	1929T1	F000008A	CU	Davenport B&T
15	-	$10	1902PB	624	25961 A	25961 A	VF		15	$10	1929T1	A000009A	CU	Davenport B&T
15	-	$10	1902PB	624	28024 B	28024 B	AU	stamp/stamp	15	$10	1929T1	B000009A	CU	Davenport B&T
15	-	$10	1902PB	624	28248 F	28248 F	VF+	Higgins Mus.	15	$10	1929T1	C000009A	CU	Davenport B&T
15	-	$10	1902PB	624	28435 E	28435 E	F	stamp/stamp	15	$10	1929T1	D000009A	CU	Davenport B&T
15	-	$10	1902PB	624	29465 ?	29465 ?	?	Small split on top	15	$10	1929T1	F000009A	AU+	
15	-	$10	1902PB	624	29525 E	29525 E	AU		15	$10	1929T1	A000010A	CU	Davenport B&T
15	-	$10	1902PB	624	29939 E	29939 E	AU		15	$10	1929T1	B000010A	CU	Davenport B&T
15	-	$10	1902PB	624	30156 F	30156 F	F		15	$10	1929T1	C000010A	CU	Davenport B&T
15	-	$10	1902PB	624	30551 D	30551 D	F		15	$10	1929T1	D000010A	CU	Davenport B&T
15	-	$10	1902PB	624	33648 E	33648 E	XF	Davenport B&T	15	$10	1929T1	A000066A	VG	
15	-	$10	1902PB	624	33945 F	33945 F	VF	Davenport B&T	15	$10	1929T1	A000388A	VF	
15	-	$10	1902PB	624	34294 F	34294 F	F	gone/gone	15	$10	1929T1	F000521A	XF/AU	
15	M	$20	1902PB	650	13137 A	U888559D	AU		15	$10	1929T1	D000604A	G	
15	M	$20	1902PB	650	16144 A	N486776E	VG+		15	$10	1929T1	A000618A	VG	
15	M	$20	1902PB	650	18567 A	B288009H	CU	pen/pen	15	$10	1929T1	F001036A	F	
15	M	$20	1902PB	650	18671 A	B288113H	VG/F		15	$10	1929T1	B001221A	F	
15		$20	1902PB	650	19567 A	?	CU		15	$10	1929T1	C001891A	?	
15		$20	1902PB	650	19637 A	E507059H	F/VF		15	$10	1929T1	D002166A	CU	
15		$20	1902PB	650	21443 A	U676445H	CU		15	$10	1929T1	A002654A	F	
15	-	$20	1902PB	650	24886 A	24886 A	VG		15	$10	1929T1	D002664A	VG	
15	-	$20	1902PB	650	26197 A	26197 A	VF		15	$10	1929T1	D002910A	CU	
15	-	$20	1902PB	650	27608 A	27608 A	XF	Davenport B&T	15	$10	1929T1	E002956A	VG	Rust
15	-	$20	1902PB	650	28383 B	28383 B	VF	Davenport B&T	15	$10	1929T1	F003259A	CU	
15	-	$20	1902PB	650	29788 B	29788 B	AU	nice sigs	15	$10	1929T1	A003294A	CU	
15	-	$20	1902PB	650	32800 B	32800 B	VG/F		15	$20	1929T1	B000001A	CU	
15	-	$20	1902PB	650	34027 B	34027 B	Fr	Ink	15	$20	1929T1	C000001A	CU	
15	-	$20	1902PB	650	34366 B	34366 B	VF	Davenport B&T	15	$20	1929T1	D000001A	CU	
15	-	$50	1902PB	675	1515 C	1515 C	F		15	$20	1929T1	E000001A	CU	
15	-	$50	1902PB	675	1872 A	1872 A	VG/F		15	$20	1929T1	F000001A	CU	
15	-	$50	1902PB	675	1929 A	1929 A	F/VF	lt. stamp sigs	15	$20	1929T1	D000097A	?	
15	-	$100	1902PB	698	1497 A	1497 A	CU		15	$20	1929T1	B000212A	?	Higgins Mus.
15	-	$100	1902PB	698	1525 A	1525 A	CU	stamp/stamp	15	$20	1929T1	D000280A	VG/F	
15	-	$100	1902PB	698	1526 A	1526 A	AU	Davenport B&T	15	$20	1929T1	C000416A	CU	Davenport B&T
15	-	$100	1902PB	698	1527 A	1527 A	AU	Davenport B&T	15	$20	1929T1	C000417A	CU	Davenport B&T
15	-	$100	1902PB	698	1528 A	1528 A	?		15	$20	1929T1	C000418A	CU	Davenport B&T
15	-	$100	1902PB	698	1549 A	1549 A	AU	Davenport B&T	15	$20	1929T1	C000419A	CU	Davenport B&T
15	-	$100	1902PB	698	1597 A	1597 A	XF	Davenport B&T	15	$20	1929T1	C000420A	CU	Davenport B&T
15	-	$100	1902PB	698	1718 A	1718 A	F/VF	Davenport B&T	15	$20	1929T1	B000421A	AU	Davenport B&T
15	-	$100	1902PB	698	1719 A	1719 A	XF/AU	Repair, Dav. B&T	15	$20	1929T1	C000421A	CU	Davenport B&T
15	-	$100	1902PB	698	1766 A	1766 A	VF	gone, Dav. B&T	15	$20	1929T1	B000422A	CU	Davenport B&T
15		$10	1929T1	B000001A			CU	Davenport B&T	15	$20	1929T1	C000422A	CU	Davenport B&T
15		$10	1929T1	C000001A			CU	Davenport B&T	15	$20	1929T1	B000423A	CU	Davenport B&T
15		$10	1929T1	D000001A			CU	Davenport B&T	15	$20	1929T1	C000423A	CU	Davenport B&T
15		$10	1929T1	E000001A			CU	Davenport B&T	15	$20	1929T1	B000424A	CU	Davenport B&T
15		$10	1929T1	F000001A			CU	Davenport B&T	15	$20	1929T1	C000424A	CU	Davenport B&T
15		$10	1929T1	F000002A			AU		15	$20	1929T1	B000425A	CU	Davenport B&T
15		$10	1929T1	A000003A	[		CU	4 uncut notes	15	$20	1929T1	C000425A	CU	Davenport B&T
15		$10	1929T1	B000003A	[		CU	4 uncut notes	15	$20	1929T1	B000426A	CU	Davenport B&T
15		$10	1929T1	C000003A	[		CU	4 uncut notes	15	$20	1929T1	B000427A	CU	Davenport B&T
15		$10	1929T1	D000003A	[		CU	4 uncut notes	15	$20	1929T1	C000428A	CU	Davenport B&T
15		$10	1929T1	E000003A			CU		15	$20	1929T1	B000429A	CU	Davenport B&T
15		$10	1929T1	A000004A			CU	Davenport B&T	15	$20	1929T1	B000430A	CU	Davenport B&T
15		$10	1929T1	B000004A			CU	Davenport B&T	15	$20	1929T1	B000431A	CU	Davenport B&T
15		$10	1929T1	C000004A			CU	Davenport B&T	15	$20	1929T1	B000432A	CU	Davenport B&T
15		$10	1929T1	D000004A			CU	Davenport B&T	15	$20	1929T1	B000433A	CU	Davenport B&T
15		$10	1929T1	E000004A			CU	Davenport B&T	15	$20	1929T1	B000434A	CU	
15		$10	1929T1	F000004A			AU	Davenport B&T	15	$20	1929T1	C000434A	CU	Davenport B&T
15		$10	1929T1	A000005A			AU+	Davenport B&T	15	$20	1929T1	B000435A	CU	Davenport B&T
15		$10	1929T1	B000005A			CU		15	$20	1929T1	E000478A	F	

15	$20	1929T1	F000572A		F+	
15	$20	1929T1	B000768A		XF/AU	
15	$20	1929T1	E000850A		?	
15	$20	1929T1	B000923A		VG	
15	$20	1929T1	B000954A		F	
15	$20	1929T1	F000960A		F/VF	Small tear
15	$20	1929T1	C000983A		F	
15	$20	1929T1	C000990A		VG	
15	$50	1929T1	E000001A		CU	Davenport B&T
15	$50	1929T1	C000029A		VG	
15	$50	1929T1	F000105A		F	
15	$50	1929T1	A000148A		VF+	Pressed
15	$50	1929T1	B000212A		?	Higgins Mus.
15	$50	1929T1	A000217A		VG/F	
15	$50	1929T1	F000252A		VG/F	
15	$50	1929T1	E000264A		F	
15	$50	1929T1	D000272A		CU	
15	$50	1929T1	D000274A		CU	
15	$50	1929T1	D000290A		F	
15	$50	1929T1	D000293A		VF	Higgins Mus.
15	$50	1929T1	F000300A		F	
15	$50	1929T1	A000308A		CU	Davenport B&T
15	$100	1929T1	?000001A		?	
15	$100	1929T1	?000001A		?	
15	$100	1929T1	A000023A		F	
16	$100	1929T1	D000052A		AU	Davenport B&T
15	$100	1929T1	F000057A		VG+	

THE IOWA NATIONAL BANK OF DAVENPORT   39 L
4022   SCOTT

Chartered in 1889. Placed in voluntary liquidation on October 31, 1927; capital of $150,000. Absorbed by The American Commercial & Savings Bank of Davenport.

Officers: Pres. Charles Beiderbecke 1889-1901, AP Doe 1902-10, JE Burmeister 1911, Chas Shuler 1912-23; **VP** AP Doe 1896-1901, John D Brockman 1902-10, Wm H Gehrmann 1913-23, Frank B Yetter 1920-23; **Cash.** DH Veiths 1889-91, 1889-92, Chas N Voss 1892, Charles Pasche 1893-1902, JE Burmeister 1903-10, FB Yetter 1911-19, Louis G Bein 1920-23; **AC** WH Crecelius 1900, JE Burmeister 1902, FB Yetter 1909-10, Louis G Bein 1911-09, Herman Staak 1920-23

	Ser #	# Notes
Second Charter, Brown Backs		
5-5-5-5	1-6651	26,604
10-10-10-20	1-2492	9,968
Second Charter, Date Back		
5-5-5-5	1-40	160
10-10-10-20	1-20	80
Third Charter, Date Back, Blue Seal		
5-5-5-5	1-8750	35,000
10-10-10-20	1-6300	25,200
Third Charter, Plain Back, Blue Seal		
5-5-5-5	8751-27570	75,280
10-10-10-20	6301-17726	45,704

Total amount issued = $1,697,120. Amount outstanding in 1927 = $147,700.
217,996 Large   0 Small   217,996 Total

4022	-	$5 1882BB	470	1 D	H569068	VF	Davenport B&T
4022	-	$5 1882BB	470	2933 A	V623101	VG	pen/pen
4022	M	$5 1882BB	470	5869 B	R15367R	F+	pen/pen
4022	M	$5 1882BB	470	6639 A	V297742V	VF	pen ac/pen vp
4022	-	$10 1882BB	483	483 C	W475242	F	
4022	-	$10 1882BB	483	788 C	W859354	CU	Grinnell # 1213?
4022	-	$10 1882BB	483	789 C	W859355	CU	Grinnell # 1213?
4022	-	$10 1882BB	483	791 B	W859357	AU	pen ac/pen
4022	-	$10 1882BB	483	794 B	W859360	XF	
4022	-	$10 1882BB	483	794 C	W859360	CU	Grinnell # 1213?
4022	-	$10 1882BB	483	796 B	W859362	XF	Higgins Mus.
4022	M	$5 1902DB	592	4960 D	K252996A	VG	faded/faded
4022	M	$5 1902DB	592	6086 B	R484213A	VG/F	faded/faded
4022	M	$5 1902DB	592	7287 B	X147129A	VF	stamp/stamp
4022	M	$5 1902PB	600	11342 D	Z596903B	VG	
4022	M	$5 1902PB	600	12682 B	E631083D	F	pen/faded
4022	M	$5 1902PB	600	12727 B	?	VG	Davenport B&T
4022	M	$5 1902PB	600	16373 C	A230519E	VG	stamp/stamp
4022	M	$5 1902PB	600	19564 ?	?	F/VF	
4022	M	$5 1902PB	600	20414 A	B434325H	VG/F	
4022	M	$5 1902PB	600	20671 C	H230457H	VG	stamp/stamp
4022	M	$5 1902PB	600	20803 A	H230589H	VG	stamp/stamp
4022	M	$5 1902PB	600	20805 D	H230591H	F	
4022	-	$5 1902PB	600	26316 C	26316 C	AU	Higgins Mus.
4022	-	$5 1902PB	600	26530 A	26530 A	VF/XF	stamp/stamp
4022	-	$5 1902PB	600	26739 D	26739 D	VG	
4022	-	$5 1902PB	600	27316 D	27316 D	XF	Wm. Philpott
4022	-	$5 1902PB	600	27568 B	27568 B	?	
4022	M	$10 1902PB	626	10685 A	B794107E	F/VF	
4022	M	$10 1902PB	626	12091 C	Y601393E	F	stamp/stamp
4022	M	$10 1902PB	626	13444 C	Y601936E	F	
4022	M	$10 1902PB	626	14396 A	K932978H	F	
4022	-	$10 1902PB	626	16393 A	16393 A	F	Hole, Dav. B&T
4022	M	$20 1902PB	652	8020 A	X578291B	VG	stamp/stamp
4022	M	$20 1902PB	652	11729 A	K542431E	XF+	Davenport B&T
4022	-	$20 1902PB	652	16393 A	16393 A	F	
4022	-	$20 1902PB	652	17498 A	17498 A	XF+	
4022	-	$20 1902PB	652	17513 A	17513 A	F/VF	Davenport B&T
4022	-	$20 1902PB	652	17526 A	17526 A	AU	stamp Dav. B&T

THE FIRST NATIONAL BANK OF DAYTON   11 L   22 S
5302   WEBSTER

Chartered on April 24, 1900.

	Ser #	# Notes
Second Charter, Brown Backs		
10-10-10-20	1-1880	7,520
Second Charter, Date Back		
10-10-10-20 (2451-2650 type uncertain)	1-2650	10,600
Second Charter, Value Back		
10-10-10-20	2651-3508	3,432
Third Charter, Plain Back, Blue Seal		
10-10-10-20	1-3208	12,832
1929, Type I		
6-10's	1-764	4,584
6-20's	1-234	1,404
1929, Type II		
10's	1-456	456
20's	1-124	124

Total amount of circulation issued = $510,760. Amount of large outstanding in 1935 = $2,230. Amount of small outstanding in 1935 = $32,770.
34,384 Large   6,568 Small   40,952 Total

5302		$20 1882BB	504	1877 A	U437827U	F	
5302	M	$10 1882BB	545	2298 F	R395290	?	
5302	M	$10 1882VB	577	2697 E	T926545	F/VF	
5302	M	$10 1882VB	577	2945 D	U328253	F/VF	pen/pen
5302	M	$10 1882VB	577	3365 D	U965783	F+	
5302	M	$20 1882VB	581	2880 B	T926728	VG/F	Higgins Mus.
5302	M	$10 1902PB	633	344 A	Y912606D	?	
5302	M	$10 1902PB	633	1107 ?	U123069E	VF/XF	
5302	-	$10 1902PB	633	2294 C	2294 C	F/VF	pen Higgins Mus.
5302	-	$10 1902PB	633	2684 C	2684 C	VF	pen/pen
5302	-	$10 1902PB	633	2840 C	2840 C	VF+	sigs
5302		$10 1929T1		D000033A		F	
5302		$10 1929T1		E000087A		VG	Stains
5302		$10 1929T1		C000197A		VG/F	
5302		$10 1929T1		A000276A		VG	
5302		$10 1929T1		E000545A		G/VG	
5302		$10 1929T1		E000611A		CU	Higgins Mus.
5302		$20 1929T1		E000018A		VF	
5302		$20 1929T1		E000023A		F	
5302		$20 1929T1		E000053A		?	
5302		$20 1929T1		E000078A		VF	
5302		$20 1929T1		C000087A		VG	Staining
5302		$20 1929T1		F000120A		VF	
5302		$20 1929T1		C000141A		VF	Paper clip rust stain
5302		$20 1929T1		B000165A		F/VF	
5302		$20 1929T1		D000168A		F/VF	
5302		$20 1929T1		B000170A		?	
5302		$20 1929T1		B000192A		XF	
5302		$20 1929T1		F000197A		VG	Soiled/stains
5302		$20 1929T1		D000204A		VF+	
5302		$20 1929T1		E000220A		VF/XF	
5302		$10 1929T2		A000437		?	
5302		$10 1929T2		A000438		AU	

THE FIRST NATIONAL BANK OF DE WITT   28 L   34 S
3182   CLINTON

Chartered in 1884.

Officers: Pres. NA Merrell 1884-96, WH Talbot 1897-1914, AM Price 1915-23, LN Williams 1924-27, Geo Myers 1928-35; **VP** WH Talbot 1896, Wm Lee 1900-14, CH Arthur 1920-34, Geo Myers 1924-34, Paul Siegmund 1935; **Cash.** JH Price 1884-87, EW Price 1888-90, AM Price 1891-1914, LN Williams 1915-23, Paul Siegmund 1924-27, TE Bell 1928-32, Paul Siegmund 1933-34, Harold J Kriebs 1935; **AC** EW Price 1885, LN Williams 1907-14, Paul Siegmund 1920-23, AF Deke 1933-34

	Ser #	# Notes
Second Charter, Brown Backs		
10-10-10-20	1-1220	4,880
Third Charter, Red Seal		

10-10-10-20			1-1750	7,000		

Third Charter, Date Back, Blue Seal
10-10-10-20   1-3400   13,600

Third Charter, Plain Back, Blue Seal
10-10-10-20   3401-9796   25,584

1929, Type I
6-10's   1-1152   6,912
6-20's   1-290   1,740

1929, Type II
10's   1-1017   1,017
20's   1-272   272

Total amount of circulation issued = $757,830. Amount of large outstanding in 1935 = $3,140. Amount of small outstanding in 1935 = $46,860.

51,064 Large   9,941 Small   61,005 Total

Charter		Denom	Type	Plate	Serial	Ser2	Grade	Notes
3182	-	$20	1882BB	494	622 A	H623944	F	
3182	M	$10	1902RS	613	315 C	N772138	F/VF	Davenport B&T
3182	M	$10	1902RS	613	336 C	N772159	F	Davenport B&T
3182	M	$10	1902RS	613	983 ?	N772806	?	Bayard, a "Dog"
3182	M	$10	1902RS	613	1214 B	N773037	AU	
3182	M	$10	1902DB	616	2835 E	V497160A	F	Davenport B&T
3182	M	$10	1902DB	616	2963 D	B901205B	F+	
3182	M	$10	1902PB	624	4052 F	V551522B	VF	pen Dav. B&T
3182	M	$10	1902PB	624	5884 D	K99946E	CU	
3182	M	$10	1902PB	624	5887 F	K99949E	VF+	pen/pen
3182	M	$10	1902PB	624	6613 D	?	F	Davenport B&T
3182	M	$10	1902PB	624	6732 E	A705424H	AU	Higgins Mus.
3182	M	$10	1902PB	624	6907 D	A705599H	VF	pen/pen vp
3182	M	$10	1902PB	624	7226 E	M151478H	CU	
3182	M	$10	1902PB	624	8421 D	?	F+	Davenport B&T
3182	-	$10	1902PB	624	8711 D	8711 D	F/VF	pen/pen vp
3182	-	$10	1902PB	624	9524 F	9524 F	VF	faded/faded
3182	M	$20	1902PB	650	4524 B	E49333D	VG	pen/pen Stains
3182	M	$20	1902PB	650	6140 B	K100202E	XF	pen Dav. B&T
3182	M	$20	1902PB	650	6141 B	K100203E	XF	Davenport B&T
3182	M	$20	1902PB	650	6142 B	K100203E	XF/AU	
3182	M	$20	1902PB	650	6294 B	T927066E	VG	pen/pen
3182	M	$20	1902PB	650	6548 B	?	F+	Davenport B&T
3182	M	$20	1902PB	650	6598 B	?	XF	
3182	M	$20	1902PB	650	6601 B	A705293H	XF	pen Dav. B&T
3182	M	$20	1902PB	650	7006 B	?	AU	Davenport B&T
3182	-	$20	1902PB	650	8468 B	8468 B	F	lt. stamp sigs
3182	-	$20	1902PB	650	8690 B	8690 B	XF	Davenport B&T
3182		$10	1929T1		D000291A		VG/F	Stains
3182		$10	1929T1		A000361A		CU	
3182		$10	1929T1		B000361A		CU	
3182		$10	1929T1		E000361A		CU	
3182		$10	1929T1		F000361A		AU	
3182		$10	1929T1		A000362A		CU	
3182		$10	1929T1		B000362A		CU	
3182		$10	1929T1		C000362A		CU	
3182		$10	1929T1		D000362A		CU	
3182		$10	1929T1		E000362A		CU	
3182		$10	1929T1		F000362A		AU	
3182		$10	1929T1		A000363A		AU	
3182		$10	1929T1		A000364A		CU	
3182		$10	1929T1		B000364A		CU	
3182		$10	1929T1		C000364A		CU	
3182		$10	1929T1		A000366A		VF+	Higgins Mus.
3182		$10	1929T1		D000366A		CU	Davenport B&T
3182		$10	1929T1		E000367A		VF	Davenport B&T
3182		$10	1929T1		A000368A		VG	
3182		$10	1929T1		A000426A		AU	Writing on face
3182		$10	1929T1		D000912A		VG	
3182		$10	1929T1		F000940A		F/VF	
3182		$10	1929T1		F001090A		VF	
3182		$10	1929T1		E001104A		F+	
3182		$10	1929T1		A001148A		XF	
3182		$20	1929T1		D000086A		F	
3182		$20	1929T1		D000106A		F	
3182		$20	1929T1		F000126A		F/VF	
3182		$20	1929T1		A000149A		VG	"46" inked on face
3182		$20	1929T1		D000203A		F	
3182		$20	1929T1		B000242A		VG/F	
3182		$20	1929T1		C000270A		VG	
3182		$10	1929T2		A000950		VG/F	
3182		$20	1929T2		A000196		VG	

THE FIRST NATIONAL BANK OF DECORAH   1 L
493   **WINNESHIEK**

Organized on August 6, 1864 with a capital of $75,000. Closed on November 10, 1896; capital of $75,000. Placed in receivership on November 24, 1896. Reason for failure: incompetent management.

Officers: Pres. James H Easton 1867-96; **Cash.** Theo W Burdick 1867-83, George Q Gardner 1884-93, ER Baker 1894-96; **AC** Geo Q Gardner 1878-83, Eldred R Baker 1885, WH Nelson 1896

First Charter, Original Issue   Ser #   # Notes
5-5-5-5   1-7375   29,500

First Charter, Series of 1875
5-5-5-5   1-5040   20,160

Second Charter, Brown Backs
5-5-5-5   1-3669   14,676

Total amount of circulation issued = $321,680. Amount outstanding at close = $17,320. Amount outstanding in 1915 = $1,800.

64,336 Large   0 Small   64,336 Total

493   - $5   1875   402   518 B   B624458   VG   Higgins Mus.

THE NATIONAL BANK OF DECORAH   14 L   8 S
5081   **WINNESHIEK**

Chartered in 1897. Placed in voluntary liquidation on January 28, 1932; capital of $50,000. Absorbed by The Decorah State Bank.

Officers: Pres. LB Whitney 1897-1923, OL Wennes 1924-25, LB Whitney 1925-26, OL Wennes 1926-29; **VP** OC Johnson 1900-23, GF Heuser 1924-29, OL Wennes 1925-26, WF Baker 1925-29; **Cash.** HC Hjerleid 1897-27, Oscar Helgerson 1928-29; **AC** WF Baker 1902-25, RC Hjerleid 1920-27, NE Haugen 1920-29

Second Charter, Brown Backs   Ser #   # Notes
10-10-10-20   1-3450   13,800

Second Charter, Date Back
10-10-10-20   1-2800   11,200

Second Charter, Value Back
10-10-10-20   2801-2993   772

Third Charter, Plain Back, Blue Seal
10-10-10-20   1-4909   19,636

1929, Type I
6-10's   1-713   4,278
6-20's   1-183   1,098

Total amount of circulation issued = $632,340. Amount of large outstanding at close = $6,810. Amount of small outstanding at close = $43,190.

45,408 Large   5,376 Small   50,784 Total

Charter		Denom	Type	Plate	Serial	Ser2	Grade	Notes
5081		$10	1882BB	488	2806 C	R140127R	?	
5081		$20	1882BB	502	3299 A	V56306V	F/VF	
5081		$20	1882BB	502	3424 A	V56431V	VG	
5081	M	$10	1882DB	543	1142 D	H505540	AU	pen Higgins Mus.
5081	M	$10	1882DB	543	1934 E	M696542	VG	
5081	M	$20	1882DB	553	485 B	D205595	VG/F	
5081	M	$10	1902PB	632	7 C	Y766876B	F/VF	
5081	M	$10	1902PB	632	1467 A	A161399E	F+	
5081	M	$10	1902PB	632	2748 A	E756080H	VF+	Higgins Mus.
5081	-	$10	1902PB	632	2784 C	R403816H	VF+	pen/pen
5081	-	$10	1902PB	632	3723 A	3723 A	AU+	pen/pen
5081	-	$10	1902PB	632	3765 A	3765 A	G	pen/pen
5081	-	$10	1902PB	632	3797 A	3797 A	F	
5081	-	$10	1902PB	632	4755 A	4755 A	VF	
5081		$10	1929T1		F000293A		F	
5081		$10	1929T1		D000559A		F	
5081		$20	1929T1		F000006A		VG	
5081		$20	1929T1		E000025A		VF	
5081		$20	1929T1		D000083A		VG+	
5081		$20	1929T1		E000116A		?	
5081		$20	1929T1		D000122A		XF	Higgins Mus.
5081		$20	1929T1		F000146A		XF/AU	

THE FIRST NATIONAL BANK OF DEEP RIVER   5 L
6705   **POWESHIEK**

Organized on March 14, 1903 with a capital of $25,000. Placed in receivership on March 25, 1926; capital of $25,000. Reason for failure: incompetent management.

Officers: Pres. JR Morris 1904-20, HW Hatter 1922-25; **VP** RJ McLain 1904-14, ET Whitney 1920-24, M Holderness 1925; **Cash.** HW Hatter 1904-1920, RP Wilhite 1922-25; **AC** Otto Emal 1904-05, Eva M Stackhouse 1910-14, RP Wilhite 1920-21

Third Charter, Red Seal   Ser #   # Notes
10-10-10-20   1-1400   5,600

Third Charter, Date Back, Blue Seal
10-10-10-20   1-1560   6,240

Third Charter, Plain Back, Blue Seal
10-10-10-20   1561-3708   8,592

Total amount issued = $255,400. Amount outstanding at close = $24,600.

20,432 Large   0 Small   20,432 Total

6705	M	$10	1902RS	613	1365 A	Y355417	F+	faded/pen
6705	M	$10	1902DB	616	731 F	D467712A	F+	pen/pen
6705	M	$10	1902PB	624	1680 E	T294640B	F	Washed

6705	M	$20 1902PB	650	2051 B A327578D	?		Photo in Deep River newspaper
6705		$20 1902PB	650	3614 B A685796K	G+		Higgins Mus.

THE FIRST NATIONAL BANK OF DENISON
4784 CRAWFORD 30 L 69 S

Chartered in 1892. Succeeded W.A. McHenry Bank.
Officers: Pres. WA McHenry 1892-1920, Sears McHenry 1922-25, Wm Adams 1926-35; **VP** Mary S McHenry 1896-1909, Geo McHenry 1910-27, Chas D Saunders 1927-28, WA Glotfelty 1929-30; **Cash.** Sears McHenry 1892-1920, Louis Seeman 1922-24, Chas D Saunders 1926-28, WA Glotfelty 1929-35, Henry Linduski 1935; **AC** Louis Seeman 1896-1921, Geo McHenry 1910, WH McHenry 1922-24, WE Terry 1929-35

	Ser #	# Notes
Second Charter, Brown Backs		
5-5-5-5	1-11600	46,400
10-10-10-20	1-5400	21,600
Second Charter, Date Back		
5-5-5-5	1-2260	9,040
10-10-10-20	1-1746	6,984
Third Charter, Date Back, Blue Seal		
5-5-5-5	1-3900	15,600
10-10-10-20	1-3040	12,160
Third Charter, Plain Back, Blue Seal		
5-5-5-5	3901-16025	48,500
10-10-10-20	3041-10841	31,204
1929, Type I		
6-5's	1-3242	19,452
6-10's	1-1474	8,844
6-20's	1-374	2,244
1929, Type II		
5's	1-1421	1,421
10's	1-1503	1,503
20's	1-390	390

Total amount of circulation issued = $1,757,565. Amount of large outstanding in May 1935 = $8,540. Amount of small outstanding in May 1935 = $91,460.
191,488 Large   33,854 Small   225,342 Total

4784		$5 1882BB	472	8139 ?		AU	
4784	M	$5 1882BB	472	8189 G H474539H	Fr/G		pen/pen
4784	M	$5 1882BB	472	10235 F T739393T	VF		
4784	M	$5 1882BB	472	11464 H U519507U	F		gone Higg. Mus.
4784	M	$5 1882BB	472	11497 G U519540U	VG		
4784		$10 1882BB	485	4154 A R707606R	?		
4784	M	$10 1882BB	485	4659 ? U551263U	?		Bayard
4784	-	$20 1882BB	499	1836 A X776903	F		pen/stamp
4784	M	$20 1882BB	499	5040 A U551644U	F/VF		
4784	M	$5 1882DB	533	1 ? ?	CU		cut across top
4784	M	$10 1882DB	540	1 D B479251	CU		stamp/stamp
4784	M	$10 1902DB	617	1 D M13217A	CU		
4784	M	$5 1902PB	602	5229 A U806945B	XF+		
4784	M	$5 1902PB	602	8247 A X468293D	G		gone/gone
4784	M	$5 1902PB	602	? N46285E	XF		
4784	M	$5 1902PB	602	10786 A X402642E	VG		
4784	-	$5 1902PB	602	11672 C M387633H	VG/F		
4784	-	$5 1902PB	602	12379 C U930540H	XF		
4784	-	$5 1902PB	602	14304 B 14304 B	XF+		
4784	-	$5 1902PB	602	14574 D 14574 D	VG/F		
4784	-	$5 1902PB	602	14811 B 14811 B	?		
4784	M	$10 1902PB	628	7194 C Z105006E	F		
4784	-	$10 1902PB	628	8922 C 8922 C	F		gone/gone
4784	-	$10 1902PB	628	8989 C 8989 C	VG		
4784	-	$10 1902PB	628	9701 B 9701 B	VF		Higgins Mus.
4784	-	$10 1902PB	628	9818 B 9818 B	VF+		stamp/stamp
4784	M	$20 1902PB	654	5280 A Z21672D	F+		
4784	M	$20 1902PB	654	5559 A Z21951D	VG		lt. stamp sigs
4784	-	$20 1902PB	654	8293 A A68105K	F		Stain now wash
4784	-	$20 1902PB	654	10330 A 10330 A	VF		
4784		$5 1929T1		B001462A	VF/XF		
4784		$5 1929T1		E001872A	?		
4784		$5 1929T1		B001938A	VF		
4784		$5 1929T1		C001949A	VG+		
4784		$5 1929T1		E002263A	VG		Staining
4784		$5 1929T1		C002274A	VG/F		
4784		$5 1929T1		B003169A	?		
4784		$5 1929T1		B003237A	XF		
4784		$10 1929T1		B000077A	?		
4784		$10 1929T1		B000086A	VG		
4784		$10 1929T1		A000330A	VF		
4784		$10 1929T1		D000337A	VF		
4784		$10 1929T1		D000354A	XF		
4784		$10 1929T1		A000377A	VF		
4784		$10 1929T1		B000411A	VG		
4784		$10 1929T1		C000412A	F/VF		
4784		$10 1929T1		F000435A	VF/XF		Light mildew
4784		$10 1929T1		B000577A	XF/AU		
4784		$10 1929T1		B000580A	F+		
4784		$10 1929T1		F000601A	VF		
4784		$10 1929T1		D000609A	VF		
4784		$10 1929T1		D000699A	F/VF		
4784		$10 1929T1		A000779A	VF		
4784		$10 1929T1		A000861A	F		
4784		$10 1929T1		E000906A	XF		
4784		$10 1929T1		F000911A	AU		
4784		$10 1929T1		C000915A	F		
4784		$10 1929T1		A000944A	XF		
4784		$10 1929T1		C000979A	VF/XF		
4784		$10 1929T1		E000985A	VF		
4784		$10 1929T1		C001027A	?		
4784		$10 1929T1		B001053A	AU		Higgins Mus.
4784		$10 1929T1		B001083A	F		
4784		$10 1929T1		F001113A	XF		
4784		$10 1929T1		F001233A	?		
4784		$10 1929T1		D001239A	F		
4784		$10 1929T1		D001255A	F		
4784		$10 1929T1		F001448A	F		
4784		$20 1929T1		F000011A	F		
4784		$20 1929T1		A000014A	F/VF		
4784		$20 1929T1		D000061A	?		
4784		$20 1929T1		E000064A	VG/F		
4784		$20 1929T1		C000097A	XF		
4784		$20 1929T1		C000124A	VG/F		
4784		$20 1929T1		A000125A	F		Tear
4784		$20 1929T1		C000135A	F		
4784		$20 1929T1		B000147A	F/VF		
4784		$20 1929T1		B000161A	XF		
4784		$20 1929T1		F000232A	CU		
4784		$20 1929T1		A000233A	AU		Cut tight
4784		$20 1929T1		B000233A	AU		
4784		$20 1929T1		C000233A	AU		
4784		$20 1929T1		D000233A	AU		
4784		$20 1929T1		E000233A	AU		
4784		$20 1929T1		F000233A	AU		
4784		$20 1929T1		B000234A	AU		
4784		$20 1929T1		A000243A	F		
4784		$20 1929T1		B000257A	VG/F		
4784		$20 1929T1		D000297A	F		
4784		$20 1929T1		A000309A	F/VF		
4784		$20 1929T1		B000340A	VG		Spotting
4784		$5 1929T2		A001295	VF/XF		
4784		$10 1929T2		A000297	F		
4784		$10 1929T2		A000497	VG		
4784		$10 1929T2		A000509	AU		
4784		$10 1929T2		A001234	VF		
4784		$10 1929T2		A001357	F		Pressed
4784		$10 1929T2		A001473	XF		
4784		$20 1929T2		A000123	F/VF		

CENTRAL NATIONAL BANK AND TRUST COMPANY OF DES MOINES
13321 POLK 102 S

Chartered on May 15, 1929 with a capital of $25,000. Succeeded a state bank.
Officers: Pres. Grant McPherrin 1929-35; **VP** Leland Windsor 1929-34, Lynn G Fuller 1929-35, Chas W Oxborrow 1929-34, John W Hawk 1929-35, Frank R Warden 1929-35, D Boyd Brann 1929-34, WC Garst 1931-32, EF Buckley 1935, Donhowe 1935; **Cash.** Lynn G Fuller 1929-33, CW Oxborrow 1934, JR Capps 1935; **AC** Emmet E Johns 1929-35, FE Quiner 1929-35, AT Donhowe 1929-34, , Geo L Nissley 1929-35, Warren C Garst 1929-30

	Ser #	# Notes
1929, Type I		
6-5's	1-5434	32,604
6-10's	1-2560	15,360
6-20's	1-726	4,356
1929, Type II		
5's	1-10862	10,682
10's	1-4980	4,980
20's	1-1230	1,230

Total amount of circulation issued = $532,450. Amount outstanding on July 30, 1935 = $219,100.
0 Large   69,392 Small   69,392 Total

13321	$5 1929T1	A000001A	[	CU	Uncut Sheet
13321	$5 1929T1	B000001A	[	CU	Uncut Sheet
13321	$5 1929T1	C000001A	[	CU	Uncut Sheet
13321	$5 1929T1	D000001A	[	CU	Uncut Sheet
13321	$5 1929T1	E000001A	[	CU	Uncut Sheet

13321	$5	1929T1	F000001A	[	CU	Uncut Sheet	13321	$10	1929T2	A000002	[	CU	Uncut Sheet
13321	$5	1929T1	E000229A		CU	Higgins Mus.	13321	$10	1929T2	A000003	[	CU	Uncut Sheet
13321	$5	1929T1	D000391A		VG/F		13321	$10	1929T2	A000004	[	CU	Uncut Sheet
13321	$5	1929T1	A000876A		VG		13321	$10	1929T2	A000005	[	CU	Uncut Sheet
13321	$5	1929T1	B000888A		F		13321	$10	1929T2	A000006	[	CU	Uncut Sheet
13321	$5	1929T1	D001140A		G		13321	$10	1929T2	A000245		G/VG	
13321	$5	1929T1	D001145A		F		13321	$10	1929T2	A001210		F/VF	
13321	$5	1929T1	A002197A		G		13321	$10	1929T2	A002869		VG	
13321	$5	1929T1	A002476A		F		13321	$20	1929T2	A000001	[	CU	Uncut Sheet
13321	$5	1929T1	A002657A		?		13321	$20	1929T2	A000002	[	CU	Uncut Sheet
13321	$5	1929T1	A002829A		VG/F		13321	$20	1929T2	A000003	[	CU	Uncut Sheet
13321	$5	1929T1	C002964A		AG		13321	$20	1929T2	A000004	[	CU	Uncut Sheet
13321	$5	1929T1	E003495A		XF		13321	$20	1929T2	A000005	[	CU	Uncut Sheet
13321	$5	1929T1	E003506A		VF/XF		13321	$20	1929T2	A000006	[	CU	Uncut Sheet
13321	$5	1929T1	D003648A		VG/F		13321	$20	1929T2	A000801		VF	
13321	$5	1929T1	E004670A		VF		13321	$20	1929T2	A000946		F	
13321	$5	1929T1	C004774A		VG								
13321	$10	1929T1	A000001A	[	CU	Uncut Sheet							
13321	$10	1929T1	B000001A	[	CU	Uncut Sheet							
13321	$10	1929T1	C000001A	[	CU	Uncut Sheet							
13321	$10	1929T1	D000001A	[	CU	Uncut Sheet							
13321	$10	1929T1	E000001A	[	CU	Uncut Sheet							
13321	$10	1929T1	F000001A	[	CU	Uncut Sheet							
13321	$10	1929T1	A000157A		VF								
13321	$10	1929T1	C000329A		F								
13321	$10	1929T1	C000365A		VG								
13321	$10	1929T1	C000727A		VF								
13321	$10	1929T1	D000852A		F								
13321	$10	1929T1	B001049A		F								
13321	$10	1929T1	A001153A		VG/F								
13321	$10	1929T1	D001201A		XF								
13321	$10	1929T1	D001202A		XF								
13321	$10	1929T1	D001205A		CU								
13321	$10	1929T1	D001208A		CU								
13321	$10	1929T1	E001334A		VG								
13321	$10	1929T1	E001352A		AU								
13321	$10	1929T1	E001353A		CU								
13321	$10	1929T1	C001415A		F								
13321	$10	1929T1	D001522A		?								
13321	$10	1929T1	A001730A		VG/F								
13321	$10	1929T1	F002036A		F/VF								
13321	$10	1929T1	F002107A		VF								
13321	$20	1929T1	A000001A	[	CU	Uncut Sheet							
13321	$20	1929T1	B000001A	[	CU	Uncut Sheet							
13321	$20	1929T1	C000001A	[	CU	Uncut Sheet							
13321	$20	1929T1	D000001A	[	CU	Uncut Sheet							
13321	$20	1929T1	E000001A	[	CU	Uncut Sheet							
13321	$20	1929T1	F000001A	[	CU	Uncut Sheet							
13321	$20	1929T1	A000014A		VF/XF								
13321	$20	1929T1	C000024A		VF								
13321	$20	1929T1	A000035A		F								
13321	$20	1929T1	A000046A		F+								
13321	$20	1929T1	D000063A		XF								
13321	$20	1929T1	D000069A		F								
13321	$20	1929T1	E000069A		F								
13321	$20	1929T1	B000122A		F								
13321	$20	1929T1	A000129A		VF/XF								
13321	$20	1929T1	C000133A		F								
13321	$20	1929T1	F000141A		F								
13321	$20	1929T1	F000225A		F								
13321	$20	1929T1	C000265A		VF	Mark on face							
13321	$20	1929T1	D000269A		VF								
13321	$20	1929T1	F000283A		F								
13321	$20	1929T1	C000335A		?								
13321	$20	1929T1	B000429A		VG+								
13321	$20	1929T1	F000473A		XF/AU								
13321	$20	1929T1	A000586A		AU								
13321	$20	1929T1	D000631A		F/VF								
13321	$20	1929T1	F001057A		VF								
13321	$20	1929T1	A001153A		?								
13321	$5	1929T2	A000001	[	CU	Uncut Sheet							
13321	$5	1929T2	A000002	[	CU	Uncut Sheet							
13321	$5	1929T2	A000003	[	CU	Uncut Sheet							
13321	$5	1929T2	A000004	[	CU	Uncut Sheet							
13321	$5	1929T2	A000005	[	CU	Uncut Sheet							
13321	$5	1929T2	A000006	[	CU	Uncut Sheet							
13321	$5	1929T2	A000050		F/VF								
13321	$5	1929T2	A000927		XF								
13321	$5	1929T2	A001981		VG								
13321	$5	1929T2	A007026		VG/F								
13321	$10	1929T2	A000001	[	CU	Uncut Sheet							

THE CITIZENS NATIONAL BANK OF DES MOINES   16 L
1970   POLK

Chartered on April 24, 1872. Placed in voluntary liquidation on June 30, 1917; capital of $300,000. Consolidated with #2307; circulation assumed by #2307.

Officers: Pres. Samuel Merrill 1872-88, JH Merrill 1889-95, JG Rounds 1896-1917; **VP** A Lederer 1896, J Callanan 1900-06, SA Merrill 1907-17; **Cash.** John W Ulm 1872-73, JA Elliot 1874-75, Joseph G Rounds 1876-95, Geo E Pearsall 1896-1917; **AC** HT Blackburn 1896, Geo Cooper 1900-08, Wm W Maish 1909-17, LJ Merrill 1914-17, J Burson 1914-17

First Charter, Original Issue		Ser #	# Notes
5-5-5-5		1-2500	10,000
10-10-10-20		1-1200	4,800
First Charter, Series of 1875			
5-5-5-5		1-3350	13,400
10-10-10-20		1-1657	6,628
Second Charter, Brown Backs			
10-10-10-20		1-10640	42,560
Second Charter, Date Back			
5-5-5-5		1-2415	9,660
10-10-10-20		1-2630	10,520
Third Charter, Date Back, Blue Seal			
10-10-10-20		1-7636	30,544

Total amount of circulation issued = $1,353,450. Amount outstanding in 1916 report = $140,000. Circulation liability assumed by #2307 which was then responsible for redeeming the outstanding circulation of #1970.

128,112 Large   0 Small   745,524 Total

1970	-	$10 1882BB	485	2605 B		?	G Torn
1970	-	$10 1882BB	485	4423 C	W53688	?	
1970	M	$10 1882BB	485	8923 B	T940167T	F	pen/stamp
1970	M	$10 1882BB	485	8959 B	T940203T	VG	pen/stamp
1970	M	$10 1882BB	485	10437 A	V509746V	VG	pen/weak
1970	-	$20 1882BB	499	5088 A	W54353	F/VF	Higgins Mus.
1970	-	$20 1882BB	499	5097 A	W54362	F	Davenport B&T
1970	M	$5 1882DB	533	1 A	D792191	CU	
1970	M	$5 1882DB	533	1429 A	D808794	VF	Higgins Mus.
1970	M	$10 1882DB	540	416 F	A507468	G	gone Washed
1970	M	$10 1882DB	540	1592 E	A537946	F	stamp/stamp
1970	M	$10 1882DB	540	?	B65232R	?	
1970	M	$10 1902DB	617	2713 B	H465406A	VG	Higgins Mus.
1970	M	$10 1902DB	617	3665 B	H479928A	F	
1970	M	$10 1902DB	617	5050 C	Y214243A	VG/F	stamp/stamp
1970	M	$10 1902DB	617	5071 A	Y214264A	CU	

THE DES MOINES NATIONAL BANK   113 L
2583   POLK

Chartered in 1881 with a capital of $400,000. Assumed The Polk County Savings Bank in 1897. Closed; consolidated with #2307 on September 20, 1929; capital of $1,000,000. Circulation assumed by #2307.

Officers: Pres. John Wyman 1883-87, RT Wellslager 1888-93, WW Lyons 1894, GM Reynolds 1895-97, Arthur Reynolds 1898-1919, JA Cavanaugh 1920-22, HR Howell 1923, John H Hogan 1924-26, Louis C Kurtz 1927-29; **VP** EA Lynd 1896-1901, FM Hubbell 1902-03, John H Blair 1904-09, HR Howell 1920-22, 1924-26, JH Hogan 1922-23, HE Rumsey 1923-26, AJ Huglin 1925-29, WJ Roberts 1926, Clarence A Diehl 1926, HL Horton 1927-29; **Cash.** WE Hazen 1883-85, RT Wellslager 1887, VF Newell 1888-92, GM Reynolds 1893-94, Arthur Reynolds 1895-97, AJ Zwart 1901-09, CA Barr 1910-16, JH Hogan 1917-20, Andrew J Huglin 1922-25, Herbert L Horton 1925-26, Geo D Thompson 1927-29; **AC** CM Spencer 1896, AJ Zwart 1900, CA Barr 1907-09, AJ Zwart 1910-14, CH Diehl 1920, Geo C Williams 1920, Otis L Jones 1920-23, AJ Huglin 1920-21, RH Collins 1920-26, Otis L Jones 1922-23, Carl Hummell 1922-23, Edwin F Buckley 1922-26, Geo D Thompson 1924-26, Owen P McDermott 1927-28, Leland J Andereck 1927-28, Owen P McDonald 1929

First Charter, Series of 1875   Ser #   # Notes

5-5-5-5			1-17381	69,524	
50-100			1-596	1,192	
Second Charter, Brown Backs					
5-5-5-5			1-6000	24,000	
10-10-10-10			1-3000	12,000	
50-100			1-2000	4,000	
Second Charter, Date Back					
5-5-5-5			1-21750	87,000	
10-10-10-10			1-20500	82,000	
Second Charter, Value Back					
5-5-5-5			21751-71248	197,992	
10-10-10-10			20501-52745	128,980	
Third Charter, Plain Back, Blue Seal					
5-5-5-5			1-18045	72,180	
10-10-10-20			1-16664	66,656	

Total amount of circulation issued = $5,705,880. Amount outstanding in 1922 = $1,000,000. Amount outstanding at close = $56,392. Circulation liability assumed by #2307 which was then responsible for redeeming the outstanding circulation of #2583.

745,524 Large   0 Small   745,524 Total

Bank		Denom	Year	Plate	Sheet	Pos	Serial	Grade	Notes
2583	-	$5	1875	405	11710	C	Z596473	XF	
2583	-	$5	1875	405	15558	B	Y180211	XF	pen/pen
2583	-	$5	1875	405	15576	B	Y180229	XF	
2583	-	$5	1875	405	15501	B	Y180244	CU	
2583	-	$5	1875	405	15592	B	Y180245	VF	pen Higgins Mus.
2583	-	$50	1875	447	478	A	A457656	XF	Higgins Mus.
2583	-	$100	1875	460	213	A	A457391	XF	Higgins Mus.
2583	M	$5 1882BB	477		3313	C	U623651U	F/VF	
2583	M	$5 1882BB	477		4252	D	U630590U	F	gone/faded
2583	M	$5 1882BB	477		4382	A	U630720U	VG/F	Higgins Mus.
2583	M	$5 1882BB	477		5015	D	U643053U	VG	gone/gone
2583		$50 1882BB	518		921	A	B244747	VF	Higgins Mus.
2583	M	$5 1882DB	537		2039	H	A430769	?	
2583	M	$5 1882DB	537		10470	H	K445432	VF	
2583	M	$5 1882DB	537		14756	G	M66143	F	stamp/stamp
2583	M	$5 1882DB	537		15488	G	M66875	VG	
2583	M	$5 1882DB	537		15500	F	M66887	F	
2583	M	$5 1882DB	537		15621	E	M67008	VF	Higgins Mus.
2583	M	$5 1882DB	537		19160	F	R73647	VG/F	stamp/stamp
2583	M	$5 1882DB	537		20303	E	?	VG	
2583	M	$10 1882DB	545		5005	A	A407510	?	
2583	M	$10 1882DB	545		6499	?	?	VG/F	
2583	M	$10 1882DB	545		6783	H	A411288	F	light pen sigs
2583	M	$10 1882DB	545		9665	E	A549720	F	stamp/stamp
2583	M	$10 1882DB	545		10765	G	A629695	F	faded/faded
2583	M	$10 1882DB	545		11092	A	A630022	VG/F	faded/faded
2583	M	$10 1882DB	545		11822	F	A630752	F+	
2583	M	$10 1882DB	545		11982	E	A630912	XF	stamp Pinholes
2583	M	$10 1882DB	545		12084	H	A651864	G	gone/gone
2583	M	$10 1882DB	545		14234	F	A654014	F+	stamp/stamp
2583	M	$10 1882DB	545		14413	F	A654193	VG	
2583	M	$10 1882DB	545		14718	G	A750748	VG	gone/gone
2583	M	$10 1882DB	545		17115	E	A944645	VG	
2583	M	$10 1882DB	545		17836	F	A945366	CU	
2583	M	$10 1882DB	545		17970	E	A945500	VF	stamp/stamp
2583	M	$10 1882DB	545		18335	E	A947865	F	
2583	M	$10 1882DB	545		19141	E	A954671	VG	
2583	M	$10 1882DB	545		19351	H	A954861	VG/F	
2583	M	$10 1882DB	545		20769	F	B101949	F	gone/gone
2583	M	$10 1882DB	545		21277	E	B102457	VG/F	stamp/stamp
2583	M	$10 1882DB	545		21827	E	B135407	VF	stamp/stamp
2583	M	$10 1882DB	545		23185	F	B148465	F	stamp/stamp
2583	M	$10 1882DB	545		24975	F	B159255	VG	
2583	M	$10 1882DB	545		25036	G	B159316	VG	
2583	M	$10 1882DB	545		25963	E	B160243	F	
2583	M	$10 1882DB	545		26626	?	B160906	VG	
2583	M	$10 1882DB	545		28311	F	B162591	VG	
2583	M	$10 1882DB	545		28581	F	B162861	VF	stamp, Tight top
2583	M	$10 1882DB	545		35167	H	B176147	G/VG	
2583	M	$10 1882DB	545		35967	G	B176947	F/VF	stamp
2583	M	$10 1882DB	545		39180	F	B180160	VG	Washed
2583	M	$10 1882DB	545		39638	H	B180618	VG/F	
2583	M	$10 1882DB	545		39991	G	B180971	?	
2583	M	$10 1882DB	545		41381	?	B182361	F/VF	
2583	M	$10 1882DB	545		45209	F	B189789	VF	stamp/stamp
2583	M	$10 1882DB	545		45710	G	B190290	F	stamp/stamp
2583	M	$10 1882DB	545		46998	F	B191578	VG	
2583	M	$10 1882DB	545		47305	E	B192385	VF	faded/faded
2583	M	$10 1882DB	545		49620	F	B194700	AU	Higgins Mus.
2583	M	$10 1882DB	545		50646	E	B197476	VF/XF	
2583	M	$10 1882DB	545		52655	F	B199485	VG	
2583	M	$5 1882VB	574		21928	E	T119065	VG	
2583	M	$5 1882VB	574		24306	H	T458493	VG	
2583	M	$5 1882VB	574		24986	G	T459173	VG	
2583	M	$5 1882VB	574		29898	F	U126010	F	pen/pen
2583	M	$5 1882VB	574		31065	G	U128177	XF	Smithsonian
2583	M	$5 1882VB	574		30949	B	U128961	VG	
2583	M	$5 1882VB	574		32170	F	U154682	F+	stamp/stamp
2583	M	$5 1882VB	574		43798	?	U166310	?	
2583	M	$5 1882VB	574		37866	G	U200078	CU	
2583	M	$5 1882VB	574		39077	F	U201589	G	gone/gone
2583	M	$5 1882VB	574		39938	E	U202450	?	
2583	M	$5 1882VB	574		40735	H	U203247	VG	
2583	M	$5 1882VB	574		43322	F	U218034	VG	
2583	M	$5 1882VB	574		43402	F	U218114	VG	lt stamp sigs
2583	M	$5 1882VB	574		46123	H	U232635	VG/F	faded; washed
2583	M	$5 1882VB	574		46210	H	U232722	VG	
2583	M	$5 1882VB	574		47665	E	U409877	F+	stamp/stamp
2583	M	$5 1882VB	574		47803	H	?	?	
2583	M	$5 1882VB	574		52938	G	U417700	G	gone/gone
2583	M	$5 1882VB	574		53215	F	U417977	CU	stamp/stamp
2583	M	$5 1882VB	574		54975	G	U421237	VG	gone/gone
2583	M	$5 1882VB	574		56461	E	U424923	VF	
2583	M	$5 1882VB	574		64218	E	U509780	VG	
2583	M	$5 1882VB	574		64756	G	U622218	XF	stamp/stamp
2583	M	$5 1882VB	574		65260	G	U622722	VF	Higgins Mus.
2583	M	$5 1882VB	574		65590	H	U623052	VG	
2583	M	$5 1882VB	574		66521	G	U623983	XF	
2583	M	$5 1882VB	574		69439	E	U655901	F	stamp/stamp
2583	M	$5 1882VB	574		69789	H	U656251	VG	gone/gone
2583	M	$5 1882VB	574		69938	?	U656400	G	
2583	M	$5 1882VB	574		70153	G	U656615	AU	stamp/stamp
2583	M	$5 1902PB	608		1273	B	K18144E	VG	
2583	M	$5 1902PB	608		4572	D	K105593E	VG	
2583	M	$5 1902PB	608		4926	C	K105947E	F/VF	
2583	M	$5 1902PB	608		15881	C	X158237E	G	
2583	M	$10 1902PB	634		476	A	M887613E	VF	Higgins Mus.
2583	M	$10 1902PB	634		724	C	M887861E	VG	
2583	M	$10 1902PB	634		5737	B	N12054E	F	
2583	M	$10 1902PB	634		9607	B	T514549E	VG/F	gone/gone
2583	M	$10 1902PB	634		11194	A	T583346E	?	
2583	M	$10 1902PB	634		11225	B	T583377E	VG	gone, Washed
2583	M	$10 1902PB	634		12399	C	T827851E	VG	
2583	M	$10 1902PB	634		13704	C	Y900266E	VG/F	light stamps
2583	M	$10 1902PB	634		15168	A	Y948440E	VG/F	stamp/stamp
2583	M	$20 1902PB	660		399	A	M887536E	VG	faded stamps
2583	M	$20 1902PB	660		1862	A	M928599E	F	faded/faded
2583	M	$20 1902PB	660		7083	A	N49360E	VF	stamp/stamp
2583	M	$20 1902PB	660		8417	A	T475879E	VG	
2583	M	$20 1902PB	660		9283	A	T514225E	VG	
2583	M	$20 1902PB	660		12915	A	T828367E	VG	
2583	M	$20 1902PB	660		14522	A	Y901084E	VG	faded, Trimmed
2583		$20 1902PB	660		14941	A	Y901503E	VG	

THE FIRST NATIONAL BANK OF DES MOINES   **0 L**
389   **POLK**
Chartered on April 18, 1864 with a capital of $50,000. Placed in voluntary liquidation on March 25, 1871; capital of $100,000.
Officers: Pres. Joseph B Stewart 1867, FW Palmer 1868-69, BF Allen 1870-71; **Cash.** Chas Mosher 1867-69, Wm S Pritchard 1870-71

First Charter, Original Issue	Ser #	# Notes
5-5-5-5	1-2500	10,000
10-10-10-20	1-996	3,984

Total amount of circulation issued = $99,800. Amount outstanding at close = $90,000. Amount outstanding in 1910 = $727.

13,984 Large   0 Small   13,984 Total

THE IOWA NATIONAL BANK OF DES MOINES   **60 L**
2307 (FIRST TITLE)   **POLK**
Chartered on October 26, 1875 with a capital of $100,000. Assumed #1970 by consolidation on June 30, 1917; assumed circulation of #1970. Assumed #2583 and The Des Moines Savings Bank & Trust Co. by consolidation on September 20, 1929 with a change in title to The Iowa-Des Moines National Bank & Trust Company, Des Moines; assumed circulation of #2583.
Officers: Pres. Henry K Love 1876-91, BP Kaufman 1892-93, SA Robertson 1894-98, EH Hunter 1899, HS Butler 1901-07, Homer A Miller 1908-28, Clyde E Brenton 1928-29; **VP** HS Butler 1900, HT Blackburn 1902-04, JH Cownie 1907, GC Prouty 1907, HS Butler 1909-14, Clyde E Brenton 1920-26, JH Blair 1920, HT Blackburn 1920-26, Geo E Pearsall 1920-29, AJ Robertson 1923-29, WH Brenton 1929, AJ Huglin 1929, RL Horton 1929, JR Capps 1929, Clarence Diehl 1929; **Cash.** George H Maish 1876-87, CB Worthington 1888-93, Geo A Dissmore 1894-99, HT Blackburn 1900, Leland Windsor

53

1901-05, HT Blackburn 1906-16; JR Capps 1917-29, Harry G Wilson 1929-35; **AC** Geo A Dissmore 1900, GA Nelson 1907, RL Chase, Jr. 1913-29, JF Hart 1914-29, CH Stephenson 1914, J Burson 1920-29, CH Nutt 1920-24, SW Fowler 1920-29, Walter H Miller 1922-29, Wm M Brandon 1927-29, AJ Warnke 1927-29, Winfield W Scott 1927-29, Harry G Wilson 1927-29

First Charter, Series of 1875   Ser #   # Notes
5-5-5-5   1-11455   45,820

Second Charter, Brown Backs
5-5-5-5   1-9600   38,400
10-10-10-20   1-6500   26,000

Second Charter, Date Back
5-5-5-5   1-36160   144,640
10-10-10-20   1-23054   92,216

Third Charter, Plain Back, Blue Seal
5-5-5-5   1-25195   100,780
10-10-10-20   1-18257   73,028

520,884 Large   0 Small   520,884 Total

Bank		Denom	Series	Plate	Ser #	Check	Grade	Notes
2307	-	$5	1875	401	5172 A	K314862	VG+	Higgins Mus.
2307	-	$5	1875	401	6739 A	U497394	F	
2307		$5	1882BB	474	1821 C	?	VF/XF	
2307	M	$5	1882BB	474	5050 A	N619290N	F/VF	stamp/pen
2307	M	$5	1882BB	474	7772 B	U781665U	F+	stamp/stamp
2307	M	$10	1882BB	487	892 C	Y395545	F+	Higgins Mus.
2307	M	$5	1882DB	534	19948 E	D594393	VG/F	
2307	M	$5	1882DB	534	22811 E	D666986	VG/F	stamp/stamp
2307	M	$5	1882DB	534	27345 H	H481982	F/VF	light stamps
2307	M	$10	1882DB	542	3034 E	A911234	VG+	Higgins Mus.
2307	M	$10	1882DB	542	3672 D	E443852	F/VF	
2307	M	$10	1882DB	542	12700 F	D827844	VG	Repaired
2307	M	$10	1882DB	542	13733 F	E813278	F	
2307	M	$10	1882DB	542	15629 D	E93023	XF	faded/faded Ink
2307	M	$10	1882DB	542	17859 H	K162297	VF	stamp, Pressed
2307	M	$20	1882DB	552	1551 B	A899651	VG	gone, Bleached
2307	M	$20	1882DB	552	10535 B	D785859	?	
2307	M	$20	1882DB	552	11826 B	D812050	VF	bold stamps
2307	M	$5	1902PB	606	1469 B	N87061B	G	gone/gone
2307	M	$5	1902PB	606	2321 B	N98463B	F/VF	
2307	M	$5	1902PB	606	2371 B	?	F	Davenport B&T
2307	M	$5	1902PB	606	7132 C	A595028E	F	
2307	M	$5	1902PB	606	9044 C	K535590E	CU	
2307	M	$5	1902PB	606	9618 A	K560964E	VF+	stamp/stamp
2307	M	$5	1902PB	606	11705 C	B137516H	VG	
2307		$5	1902PB	606	14414 C	N47825H	AU	
2307	-	$5	1902PB	606	15004 B	U659515H	VG	stamp/stamp D ?
2307	-	$5	1902PB	606	15758 A	Z678969H	VG	
2307	-	$5	1902PB	606	15953 A	Z679164H	?	
2307	-	$5	1902PB	606	18132 B	18132 B	F	
2307	-	$5	1902PB	606	18609 B	18609 B	VG	
2307	-	$5	1902PB	606	18426 ?	18426 ?	XF	
2307	-	$5	1902PB	606	21796 A	21796 A	F/VF	stamp/stamp
2307	-	$5	1902PB	606	22547 B	22547 B	VG	
2307	-	$5	1902PB	606	23229 A	23229 A	F	
2307	-	$5	1902PB	606	23230 A	23230 A	F	stamp/faded
2307	-	$5	1902PB	606	23244 B	23244 B	CU	faded/faded
2307	-	$5	1902PB	606	24291 D	24291 D	VG	
2307	M	$10	1902PB	632	5735 A	N395207E	Fr	gone/gone
2307	M	$10	1902PB	632	7623 B	Y484925E	F/VF	faded/faded
2307	M	$10	1902PB	632	7627 B	Y484929E	AU	stamp/stamp
2307	M	$10	1902PB	632	7629 B	Y484931E	XF	stamp/stamp Higgins Mus.
2307	-	$10	1902PB	632	8??? ?	K44144H	?	Bayard
2307	-	$10	1902PB	632	10584 C	V897606H	VG	
2307	-	$10	1902PB	632	10954 ?	V897976H	?	Bayard
2307	-	$10	1902PB	632	11124 C	V898146H	VF	stamp/stamp
2307	-	$10	1902PB	632	12111 B	A670223K	VG/F	
2307	-	$10	1902PB	632	13394 C	13394 C	F	Davenport B&T
2307	-	$10	1902PB	632	13859 B	13859 B	VG	
2307	-	$10	1902PB	632	14291 C	14291 C	VF/XF	stamp/stamp
2307	-	$10	1902PB	632	15240 A	15240 A	F	
2307	-	$10	1902PB	632	17253 B	17253 B	CU	gone/gone
2307	-	$10	1902PB	632	17254 B	17254 B	VF	
2307	-	$20	1902PB	658	10711 A	V897733H	VG	
2307	-	$20	1902PB	658	11141 A	?	VF+	
2307	-	$20	1902PB	658	11370 A	A669482K	F	faded/faded
2307	-	$20	1902PB	658	11400 A	A669512K	F	stamp/stamp
2307	-	$20	1902PB	658	12281 A	A670393K	V	
2307	-	$20	1902PB	658	16904 A	16904 A	VF/XF	faded/stamp
2307	-	$20	1902PB	658	16908 A	16908 A	F	

IOWA-DES MOINES NATIONAL BANK & TRUST COMPANY 230 S 2307 (2ND TITLE)   POLK

Succeeded The Iowa National Bank of Des Moines on September 20, 1929.
Officers: Pres. Clyde E Brenton 1929-30, WH Brenton 1931-33, Herbert L Horton 1934-35; **VP** Geo E Pearsall 1929-35, AJ Robertson 1929-35, WH Brenton 1929-30, AJ Huglin 1929-35, RL Horton 1929-35, JR Capps 1929-35, Clarence Diehl 1929-35, EW Jones 1935, John DeJong 1935, Harry H Sivright 1935, Winfield W Scott 1935, RL Chase, Jr.; **Cash.** JR Capps 1929, Harry G Wilson 1929-35; **AC** RL Chase, Jr. 1929, JF Hart 1929, J Burson 1929, SW Fowler 1929, Walter H Miller 1929, Wm M Brandon 1929, AJ Warnke 1929, Winfield W Scott 1929, Harry G Wilson 1929

1929, Type I   Ser #   # Notes
6-5's   1-11717   70,302
6-10's   1-11397   68,382
6-20's   1-5783   34,698
6-50's   1-416   2,496
6-100's   1-314   1,884

Total amount of circulation issued = $6,182,140. Amount of large outstanding in 1935 =$44,695. Amount of small outstanding in 1935 = $955,305. Includes large outstanding of #1970 and #2583 whose circulation was assumed by #2307.

0 Large   177,762 Small   177,762 Total

Bank	Denom	Series	Ser #	Grade	Notes
2307	$5	1929T1	F000237A	VG/F	
2307	$5	1929T1	D000961A	VG	
2307	$5	1929T1	A001007A	F	
2307	$5	1929T1	D002644A	VG	
2307	$5	1929T1	A003297A	VG	
2307	$5	1929T1	D003356A	VG	
2307	$5	1929T1	E003391A	F	
2307	$5	1929T1	B003697A	?	Bayard
2307	$5	1929T1	F004150A	VF/XF	
2307	$5	1929T1	F004151A	VF	
2307	$5	1929T1	E004798A	VG	
2307	$5	1929T1	A005073A	F	
2307	$5	1929T1	B005073A	F	
2307	$5	1929T1	E005699A	XF	
2307	$5	1929T1	E005982A	XF	
2307	$5	1929T1	E007026A	F	
2307	$5	1929T1	B007256A	XF	
2307	$5	1929T1	F007991A	VF/XF	
2307	$5	1929T1	A008014A	VG	
2307	$5	1929T1	B008861A	VG	
2307	$5	1929T1	D009033A	G	
2307	$5	1929T1	B009509A	F	
2307	$5	1929T1	E009636A	F/VF	
2307	$5	1929T1	E010350A	VF	
2307	$5	1929T1	C010604A	VG	
2307	$5	1929T1	F011589A	VF	
2307	$10	1929T1	E000170A	CU	
2307	$10	1929T1	B000216A	VF	
2307	$10	1929T1	C000429A	?	Bayard
2307	$10	1929T1	F000569A	F	
2307	$10	1929T1	E001158A	F	
2307	$10	1929T1	E001227A	CU	
2307	$10	1929T1	E001282A	F	Higgins Mus.
2307	$10	1929T1	A001388A	F	
2307	$10	1929T1	D002176A	?	
2307	$10	1929T1	D002320A	?	
2307	$10	1929T1	A002373A	F	
2307	$10	1929T1	C002398A	CU	
2307	$10	1929T1	E002473A	F	
2307	$10	1929T1	E002554A	VG/F	
2307	$10	1929T1	F002575A	VG	
2307	$10	1929T1	A002910A	VG/F	
2307	$10	1929T1	E003363A	VF	
2307	$10	1929T1	C003736A	F	
2307	$10	1929T1	A003821A	CU	
2307	$10	1929T1	B004531A	G/VG	
2307	$10	1929T1	C004621A	VG	
2307	$10	1929T1	E004770A	VF/XF	
2307	$10	1929T1	F004911A	?	
2307	$10	1929T1	B005062A	F/VF	
2307	$10	1929T1	D005072A	F	
2307	$10	1929T1	D005080A	F	
2307	$10	1929T1	B005143A	F/VF	
2307	$10	1929T1	A005173A	F	
2307	$10	1929T1	D005278A	VG	
2307	$10	1929T1	E005299A	F	
2307	$10	1929T1	C005371A	F	
2307	$10	1929T1	C005376A	F/VF	

2307	$10	1929T1	D005434A	PR		2307	$20	1929T1	B001995A	VF	
2307	$10	1929T1	E005443A	AU+	Bottom tight	2307	$20	1929T1	E002084A	F/VF	
2307	$10	1929T1	C005613A	VG		2307	$20	1929T1	B002129A	VG	
2307	$10	1929T1	D005649A	CU	Autographed	2307	$20	1929T1	A002284A	VG	Notched top
2307	$10	1929T1	C006027A	VF		2307	$20	1929T1	D002332A	F/VF	
2307	$10	1929T1	B006056A	F/VF		2307	$20	1929T1	E002452A	VF	
2307	$10	1929T1	D006502A	F		2307	$20	1929T1	D002504A	?	
2307	$10	1929T1	A006890A	?		2307	$20	1929T1	D002524A	F	
2307	$10	1929T1	A007074A	VF/XF		2307	$20	1929T1	E002540A	?	
2307	$10	1929T1	D007093A	AU		2307	$20	1929T1	F002554A	XF	
2307	$10	1929T1	C007131A	XF		2307	$20	1929T1	A002562A	F	
2307	$10	1929T1	E007238A	F		2307	$20	1929T1	C002613A	F	
2307	$10	1929T1	E007279A	XF		2307	$20	1929T1	D002631A	VG	
2307	$10	1929T1	C007334A	F+		2307	$20	1929T1	E002660A	AU	
2307	$10	1929T1	D007488A	VG		2307	$20	1929T1	F002932A	VF/XF	
2307	$10	1929T1	C007745A	F+		2307	$20	1929T1	D002952A	VG	
2307	$10	1929T1	B008059A	VG		2307	$20	1929T1	D003061A	F+	
2307	$10	1929T1	E008195A	F		2307	$20	1929T1	D003082A	XF/AU	
2307	$10	1929T1	B008253A	F		2307	$20	1929T1	D003083A	CU	
2307	$10	1929T1	F008425A	F+		2307	$20	1929T1	D003084A	CU	
2307	$10	1929T1	F008719A	VF		2307	$20	1929T1	D003085A	CU	
2307	$10	1929T1	A008847A	F		2307	$20	1929T1	D003086A	CU	
2307	$10	1929T1	B008859A	VG		2307	$20	1929T1	D003087A	CU	
2307	$10	1929T1	D009147A	?		2307	$20	1929T1	D003088A	CU	
2307	$10	1929T1	E009261A	F		2307	$20	1929T1	D003089A	CU	
2307	$10	1929T1	A009376A	F		2307	$20	1929T1	D003090A	CU	
2307	$10	1929T1	D010133A	F		2307	$20	1929T1	D003091A	CU	
2307	$10	1929T1	A010630A	F/VF		2307	$20	1929T1	D003092A	CU	
2307	$10	1929T1	B010734A	?		2307	$20	1929T1	A003189A	G	
2307	$10	1929T1	E010761A	VG		2307	$20	1929T1	D003196A	XF	
2307	$10	1929T1	D011065A	F		2307	$20	1929T1	A003270A	AU	
2307	$10	1929T1	E011113A	F		2307	$20	1929T1	D003310A	AU	
2307	$10	1929T1	F011140A	F		2307	$20	1929T1	A003316A	F/VF	
2307	$20	1929T1	C000029A	XF		2307	$20	1929T1	F003412A	AU	
2307	$20	1929T1	B000083A	F/VF		2307	$20	1929T1	F003413A	AU	
2307	$20	1929T1	E000109A	F		2307	$20	1929T1	E003468A	F	
2307	$20	1929T1	E000115A	VF		2307	$20	1929T1	B003496A	XF	
2307	$20	1929T1	F000123A	F		2307	$20	1929T1	B003499A	F/VF	
2307	$20	1929T1	F000283A	XF	Higgins Mus.	2307	$20	1929T1	E003511A	F	
2307	$20	1929T1	F000342A	VG/F		2307	$20	1929T1	B003532A	VF/XF	
2307	$20	1929T1	C000429A	G		2307	$20	1929T1	D003771A	VG/F	
2307	$20	1929T1	E000467A	VG/F		2307	$20	1929T1	D003857A	VG	
2307	$20	1929T1	F000467A	VF		2307	$20	1929T1	A003967A	VF	
2307	$20	1929T1	D000490A	XF		2307	$20	1929T1	B004213A	CU	
2307	$20	1929T1	D000568A	?		2307	$20	1929T1	E004319A	F	
2307	$20	1929T1	E000647A	F+		2307	$20	1929T1	F004355A	XF	
2307	$20	1929T1	B000834A	XF		2307	$20	1929T1	B004498A	G	
2307	$20	1929T1	A000926A	CU		2307	$20	1929T1	F004519A	XF/AU	
2307	$20	1929T1	A000927A	CU		2307	$20	1929T1	C004539A	F/VF	stamp on back
2307	$20	1929T1	A000928A	CU		2307	$20	1929T1	B004761A	F	
2307	$20	1929T1	A000929A	CU		2307	$20	1929T1	B004822A	F	
2307	$20	1929T1	A000930A	CU		2307	$20	1929T1	C004831A	XF	
2307	$20	1929T1	A000931A	CU		2307	$20	1929T1	A004891A	F/VF	
2307	$20	1929T1	A000932A	CU		2307	$20	1929T1	F005042A	VF	
2307	$20	1929T1	A000933A	CU		2307	$20	1929T1	A005062A	AU	
2307	$20	1929T1	A000934A	CU		2307	$20	1929T1	F005078A	F/VF	
2307	$20	1929T1	A000935A	CU		2307	$20	1929T1	C005305A	F	
2307	$20	1929T1	A000936A	CU		2307	$20	1929T1	D005325A	AU	
2307	$20	1929T1	A000937A	CU		2307	$20	1929T1	C005371A	VF	
2307	$20	1929T1	A000940A	CU		2307	$20	1929T1	B005375A	F/VF	
2307	$20	1929T1	A000941A	CU		2307	$20	1929T1	E005416A	VG	
2307	$20	1929T1	A000942A	CU		2307	$20	1929T1	C005601A	F	
2307	$20	1929T1	A000943A	CU		2307	$20	1929T1	D005626A	F/VF	
2307	$20	1929T1	A000944A	CU		2307	$20	1929T1	E005678A	VG	
2307	$20	1929T1	A000945A	CU		2307	$20	1929T1	D005747A	XF/AU	Higgins Mus.
2307	$20	1929T1	A000948A	CU		2307	$20	1929T1	B005769A	AU	
2307	$20	1929T1	A000949A	CU		2307	$20	1929T1	C007131A	?	
2307	$20	1929T1	A000973A	?		2307	$50	1929T1	C000046A	VG/F	
2307	$20	1929T1	F000977A	VF		2307	$50	1929T1	A000054A	F/VF	
2307	$20	1929T1	A001092A	F		2307	$50	1929T1	F000066A	F/VF	
2307	$20	1929T1	E001109A	F		2307	$50	1929T1	B000119A	F	
2307	$20	1929T1	C001132A	?		2307	$50	1929T1	F000123A	VF	
2307	$20	1929T1	E001158A	F		2307	$50	1929T1	B000145A	VF	
2307	$20	1929T1	B001537A	VG		2307	$50	1929T1	D000200A	XF	
2307	$20	1929T1	C001604A	?		2307	$50	1929T1	A000294A	VF+	
2307	$20	1929T1	B001658A	VG		2307	$50	1929T1	E000308A	F	
2307	$20	1929T1	E001679A	VF		2307	$50	1929T1	E000322A	F	
2307	$20	1929T1	F001764A	F		2307	$50	1929T1	C000361A	VG	
2307	$20	1929T1	C001773A	F		2307	$50	1929T1	C000373A	XF	
2307	$20	1929T1	A001855A	VG		2307	$50	1929T1	C000377A	VF	
2307	$20	1929T1	B001956A	F		2307	$100	1929T1	F000014A	F/VF	

2307		$100	1929T1	?000061A		VG/F		2886	-	$10 1882BB	479	3829 B	N797400	F	Davenport B&T
2307		$100	1929T1	C000078A		AU		2886	-	$10 1882BB	479	9096 E	W87570	VG	pen/pen
2307		$100	1929T1	F000128A		XF/AU		2886	-	$20 1882BB	493	6444 A	T922809	G/VG	
2307		$100	1929T1	F000170A		VG/F		2886	M	$5 1902RS	587	1007 B	B347621	VF	pen/faded
2307		$100	1929T1	D000180A		VF	Pin Holes	2886	M	$5 1902RS	587	2631 A	B350950	CU	stamp/stamp
2307		$100	1929T1	A000187A		VF/XF	Rust	2886	M	$5 1902RS	587	3802 A	B354121	F	
2307		$100	1929T1	E000213A		VF		2886	M	$5 1902RS	587	4233 C	D962218	AU	stamp/stamp
2307		$100	1929T1	C000289A		VG		2886	M	$10 1902RS	613	1 A	A701768	CU	pen/pen
2307		$100	1929T1	E000294A		VF/XF		2886	M	$10 1902RS	613	631 A	A702398	F	pen vp Higg. Mus
2307		$100	1929T1	F000297A		F	Light ink on back	2886	M	$5 1902DB	590	828 H	B881121	VF	

THE MERCHANTS NATIONAL BANK OF DES MOINES 1 L
2631   POLK

Chartered on February 16, 1882 with a capital of $100,000. Succeeded The Merchants Bank. Placed in voluntary liquidation on March 1, 1889; capital of $100,000.

Officers: Pres. Thomas Mitchell 1883, FM Mills 1884-86, A Howell 1887, WR Graham 1888; **Cash.** Rufus L Chase 1883, HJ Ransom 1884-88

First Charter, Series of 1875	Ser #	# Notes
10-10-10-20	1-1403	5,612

Total amount of circulation issued = $70,150. Amount outstanding at close = $22,500. Amount outstanding in 1910 = $375.

5,612 Large	0 Small	5,612 Total
2631 - $10 1875 420	1379 A E583750	VG

THE NATIONAL STATE BANK OF DES MOINES 0 L
950   POLK

Chartered in March 1865. Placed in voluntary liquidation on June 21, 1876; capital of $100,000. Succeeded by F.R. West & Sons.

Officers: Pres. Benj F Allen 1867-76; **Cash.** Francis R West 1867-76

First Charter, Original Issue	Ser #	# Notes
5-5-5-5	1-2800	11,200
10-10-10-20	1-1786	7,144

Total amount of circulation issued = $145,300. Amount outstanding at close = $50,795. Amount outstanding in 1910 = $1,080.

18,344 Large   0 Small   18,344 Total

THE SECOND NATIONAL BANK OF DES MOINES 0 L
485   POLK

Chartered on July 22, 1864 with a capital of $50,000. Placed in voluntary liquidation on August 5, 1868; capital of $50,000. Succeeded by #1684 of Council Bluffs.

Officers: Pres. Benj. F Allen 1867-68; **Cash.** WS Pritchard 1867-68

First Charter, Original Issue	Ser #	# Notes
5-5-5-5	1-1350	5,400
10-10-10-20	1-310	1,240

Total amount of circulation issued = $42,500. Amount outstanding at close = $42,500. Amount outstanding in 1910 = $337.

6,640 Large   0 Small   6,640 Total

THE VALLEY NATIONAL BANK OF DES MOINES 110 L   39 S
2886   POLK

Chartered in 1883 with a capital of $150,000. Succeeded The Valley Bank.

Officers: Pres. JJ Town 1883-98, NW Johnson 1899-1900, RA Crawford 1901-31, JH Cownie 1932-33; **VP** CH Dilworth 1896-1904, DS Chamberlain 1907-33, CT Cole, Jr 1909-33, DS Chamberlain 1913-33, CT Cole, Jr. 1911-33, CO Craig 1929-33, AR Thompson 1929-31, CW Enyart 1930-33; **Cash.** William D Lucas 1883-91, MM Crookshank 1892, RA Crawford 1893-1900, WE Barrett 1901-30, CT Cole, Jr. 1931-33; **AC** WE Barrett 1896-1900, HS Hollingsworth 1909-10, John H Ginsberg 1920-29, Clarence M Cornwell 1920-30

Second Charter, Brown Backs	Ser #	# Notes
5-5-5-5	1-3375	13,500
10-10-10-20	1-10539	42,156
Third Charter, Red Seal		
5-5-5-5	1-8500	34,000
10-10-10-20	1-7400	29,600
Third Charter, Date Back, Blue Seal		
5-5-5-5	1-17250	69,000
10-10-10-20	1-13000	52,000
Third Charter, Plain Back, Blue Seal		
5-5-5-5	17251-63862	186,448
10-10-10-20	13001-41944	115,776
1929, Type I		
6-5's	1-4347	26,082
6-10's	1-2050	12,300
6-20's	1-642	3,852

Total amount issued = $4,847,840. Amount outstanding in 1932 = $124,040. Amount of large outstanding in June 1935 = $19,850.

542,480 Large   42,234 Small   584,714 Total

2886	-	$5 1882BB	466	2388 A	K412754	F/VF	pen/pen

2886	M	$5 1902DB	590	9956 F	D137512A	VG	fake sigs
2886	M	$5 1902DB	590	9971 G	D137527A	VF	stamp/stamp
2886	M	$5 1902DB	590	1024 A	D249370E	VF	
2886	M	$5 1902DB	590	13704 H	V566801A	VG	
2886	M	$10 1902DB	616	?	B639280	?	Bayard
2886	M	$10 1902DB	616	6354 E	D913480A	VG/F	
2886	M	$10 1902DB	616	11172 E	?	F/VF	
2886	M	$10 1902DB	616	12584 D	K606710B	XF	stamp/stamp
2886	M	$20 1902DB	642	10509 B	Y220702A	F	
2886	M	$20 1902DB	642	11949 B	K539195B	F	stamp/stamp
2886	M	$5 1902PB	598	?	N330478B	F	
2886	M	$5 1902PB	598	19341 G	R722906B	F	
2886	M	$5 1902PB	598	19437 F	R723002B	VF	gone/gone
2886	M	$5 1902PB	598	20542 G	V155063B	F/VF	
2886	M	$5 1902PB	598	23090 H	Y594191B	VG	
2886	M	$5 1902PB	598	31247 H	Y187718D	XF	
2886	M	$5 1902PB	598	31366 G	Y187837D	G	
2886	M	$5 1902PB	598	31756 F	Y188227D	?	
2886	M	$5 1902PB	598	31757 F	Y188228D	CU	gone/gone
2886	M	$5 1902PB	598	32936 H	Y189407D	CU	gone/gone
2886	M	$5 1902PB	598	33017 F	D195163E	F	
2886	M	$5 1902PB	598	34881 G	D242327E	CU	gone Pressed
2886	M	$5 1902PB	598	34884 E	D242330E	CU	fake sigs
2886	M	$5 1902PB	598	35102 E	D294948E	AU	gone/gone
2886	M	$5 1902PB	598	36127 F	M839773E	VG	gone/gone
2886	M	$5 1902PB	598	43774 H	E201510H	VG	
2886	M	$5 1902PB	598	44470 F	H880206H	VG	
2886	M	$5 1902PB	598	45506 G	K142142H	VG	stamp/stamp
2886		$5 1902PB	598	48040 K	N285851H	G/VG	
2886	-	$5 1902PB	598	48366 L	R237352H	F/VF	engraved
2886	-	$5 1902PB	598	48462 K	R237448H	G	engraved
2886	-	$5 1902PB	598	48870 L	R237856H	F	engraved
2886	-	$5 1902PB	598	48994 L	R237980H	VG/F	engraved
2886	-	$5 1902PB	598	49554 I	R267740H	XF	eng. XF or CU ?
2886	-	$5 1902PB	598	49555 J	R267741H	AU	engraved
2886	-	$5 1902PB	598	50234 K	R268420H	VG	engraved
2886	-	$5 1902PB	598	50345 J	R294231H	F	engraved
2886	-	$5 1902PB	598	?	T523933H	?	engraved
2886	-	$5 1902PB	598	51097 I	51097 I	F/VF	engraved Bayard
2886	-	$5 1902PB	598	53063 J	53063 J	F/VF	engraved
2886	-	$5 1902PB	598	53147 K	53147 K	F	engraved
2886	-	$5 1902PB	598	53224 J	53224 J	CU	eng. Higgins Mus.
2886	-	$5 1902PB	598	53829 I	53829 I	VG	engraved
2886	-	$5 1902PB	598	55068 J	55068 J	F/VF	engraved
2886	-	$5 1902PB	598	55710 L	55710 L	VF	engraved
2886	-	$5 1902PB	598	56616 K	56616 K	F	engraved
2886	-	$5 1902PB	598	57227 L	57227 L	VF	engraved
2886	-	$5 1902PB	598	58279 I	58279 I	VG/F	engraved
2886	-	$5 1902PB	598	61210 J	61210 J	G	engraved
2886	-	$5 1902PB	598	61316 J	61316 J	VF	engraved
2886	-	$5 1902PB	598	62172 J	62172 J	XF	engraved
2886	-	$5 1902PB	598	63533 H	63533 H	F+	engraved H ?
2886	-	$5 1902PB	598	88822 ?	88822 ?	CU	engraved
2886	M	$10 1902PB	624	14449 E	4688977B	F	
2886	M	$10 1902PB	624	16291 D	A811918D	VG	
2886	M	$10 1902PB	624	17175 ?	A812802D	?	
2886	M	$10 1902PB	624	20113 ?	U875235D	VG/F	
2886	M	$10 1902PB	624	20444 D	U923576D	XF	
2886	M	$10 1902PB	624	21525 E	Z704567D	G/VG	
2886	M	$10 1902PB	624	23555 D	H165377E	AU	
2886	M	$10 1902PB	624	25346 B	R833788E	AU	
2886	M	$10 1902PB	624	26071 F	Y658053E	CU	faded/faded
2886		$10 1902PB	624	26072 E	Y658054E	CU	
2886		$10 1902PB	624	26888 F	D364380H	VF	
2886		$10 1902PB	624	27261 F	D364753H	F/VF	
2886		$10 1902PB	624	27925 E	E24679H	F	
2886		$10 1902PB	624	28648 D	H481930H	VF	
2886		$10 1902PB	624	30809 ?	M351841H	?	
2886	-	$10 1902PB	624	33049 G	T505311H	VF	
2886		$10 1902PB	624	33144 G	T505406H	F	
2886	-	$10 1902PB	624	33500 I	T523312H	CU	engraved

2886	-	$10	1902PB	624	33579 ?	T523391H	?	engraved Bayard
2886	-	$10	1902PB	624	33726 G	T523538H	CU	engraved
2886	-	$10	1902PB	624	34119 G	T523931H	VF	engraved Bayard
2886	-	$10	1902PB	624	34120 G	T523932H	XF	engraved Bayard
2886	-	$10	1902PB	624	34121 G	T523933H	XF	engraved Bayard
2886	-	$10	1902PB	624	34124 G	T523936H	VF	engraved Bayard
2886	-	$10	1902PB	624	34125 I	T523937H	VF	engraved Bayard
2886	-	$10	1902PB	624	36112 I	36112 I	F	engraved
2886	-	$10	1902PB	624	36533 H	36533 H	F/VF	engraved
2886	-	$10	1902PB	624	36731 I	36731 I	VF/XF	engraved
2886	-	$10	1902PB	624	36781 I	36781 I	VF/XF	engraved
2886	-	$10	1902PB	624	38929 H	38929 H	F	engraved
2886	-	$10	1902PB	624	39004 I	39004 I	F	engraved
2886	-	$10	1902PB	624	40705 G	40705 G	CU	engraved
2886	M	$20	1902PB	650	15085 B	U689613B	F	
2886	M	$20	1902PB	650	17921 B	E663955D	XF	
2886	M	$20	1902PB	650	17922 B	E663956D	AU	gone/gone
2886	M	$20	1902PB	650	17940 B	E663974D	?	
2886	M	$20	1902PB	650	18597 B	N408909D	AU	gone/gone
2886	M	$20	1902PB	650	21566 B	Z704608D	F	
2886	M	$20	1902PB	650	24832 B	R788134E	VG	gone BR missing
2886	M	$20	1902PB	650	25345 B	R833787E	XF	faded Pressed
2886	M	$20	1902PB	650	25346 B	R833788E	AU	
2886	M	$20	1902PB	650	28716 B	H481998H	G	gone/gone
2886		$20	1902PB	650	32212 C	R758294H	VG	
2886	-	$20	1902PD	050	38166 C	38166 C	VF	engraved
2886		$20	1902PB	650	38692 C	38692 C	F/VF	engraved
2886	-	$20	1902PB	650	41154 C	41154 C	VF	engraved
2886		$5	1929T1		D000162A		F	
2886		$5	1929T1		E000453A		F	
2886		$5	1929T1		F000800A		XF	
2886		$5	1929T1		D002901A		VG	
2886		$5	1929T1		D003076A		VG	
2886		$5	1929T1		A003200A		VG/F	
2886		$5	1929T1		C003349A		AU	Higgins Mus.
2886		$5	1929T1		A003694A		VF	
2886		$5	1929T1		D003908A		VF	
2886		$5	1929T1		F003934A		?	
2886		$5	1929T1		A004300A		VF	
2886		$10	1929T1		F000569A		VG/F	
2886		$10	1929T1		C000861A		VG+	
2886		$10	1929T1		A001492A		F	
2886		$10	1929T1		A001656A		VF+	
2886		$10	1929T1		A001658A		F/VF	
2886		$10	1929T1		D001663A		CU	
2886		$10	1929T1		B001809A		CU	
2886		$10	1929T1		B001838A		F	
2886		$10	1929T1		A001896A		F	Pressed
2886		$10	1929T1		A002047A		XF	
2886		$20	1929T1		E000019A		F	
2886		$20	1929T1		A000167A		VG/F	
2886		$20	1929T1		B000279A		VG	
2886		$20	1929T1		C000310A		?	
2886		$20	1929T1		E000316A		VG	
2886		$20	1929T1		C000325A		XF	
2886		$20	1929T1		C000331A		VG	
2886		$20	1929T1		D000368A		F/VF	
2886		$20	1929T1		D000424A		AU	
2886		$20	1929T1		A000471A		F/VF	
2886		$20	1929T1		A000486A		F	
2886		$20	1929T1		C000516A		XF	
2886		$20	1929T1		C000562A		VF/XF	Stain top edge
2886		$20	1929T1		C000576A		VF	
2886		$20	1929T1		A000633A		VF/XF	
2886		$20	1929T1		B000634A		VF	Washed
2886		$20	1929T1		C000861A		F	
2886		$20	1929T1		A003291A		XF	

THE FIRST NATIONAL BANK OF DEXTER 7 L
10030   DALLAS

Chartered in June 1911 with a capital of $25,000. Placed in voluntary liquidation on May 31, 1920; capital of $25,000. Succeeded by The Iowa State Bank of Dexter.
Officers: Pres. Geo Lowis 1912-19; **VP** FF Winsell 1913-14; **Cash.** MF Palmer 1912-14, Rex Spooner 1915-19; **AC** PC Monroe 1913, FC Repass 1914

Third Charter, Date Back, Blue Seal	Ser #	# Notes
10-10-10-20	1-1160	4,640
Third Charter, Plain Back, Blue Seal		
10-10-10-20	1161-1654	1,976

Total amount issued = $82,700. Amount outstanding in 1920 = $18,750.
6,616 Large   0 Small   6,616 Total

10030M	$10	1902DB	619	1 A	B730113A	?	
10030M	$10	1902DB	619	532 A	M38776A	VF	pen/pen
10030M	$10	1902DB	619	710 C	N589500A	VF	pen/pen
10030M	$10	1902DB	627	1106 B	M29802B	F/VF	Higgins Mus.
10030M	$10	1902PB	627	1486 C	B685043D	VG	pen/stamp ac
10030M	$10	1902PB	627	1545 A	B685102D	VG/F	
10030M	$10	1902PB	627	1578 A	K448860D	VG/F	sigs

THE FIRST NATIONAL BANK OF DIAGONAL 6 L 12 S
9125   RINGGOLD
Chartered in May 1908 with a capital of $25,000.

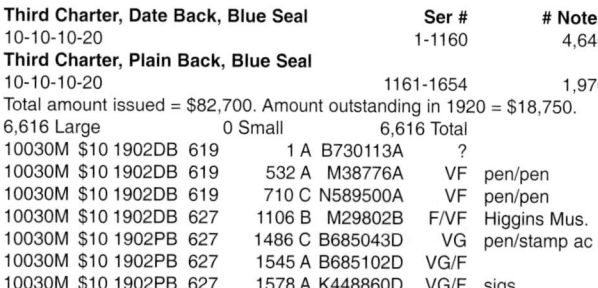

Officers: Pres. ET Dufur 1908-35; **VP** ASA Bailey 1909-14, D Eastman 1920-35; **Cash.** DV Ferris 1908-35; **AC** Jessie N Talley 1909-35, Bessie Dufur Ferris 1920-35

Third Charter, Date Back, Blue Seal	Ser #	# Notes
10-10-10-20	1-2200	8,800
Third Charter, Plain Back, Blue Seal		
10-10-10-20	2201-5358	12,632
1929, Type I		
6-10's	1-546	3,276
6-20's	1-136	816
1929, Type II		
10's	1-591	591
20's	1-160	160

Total amount of circulation issued = $326,090. Amount of large outstanding in 1935 = $1,710. Amount of small outstanding in 1935 = $23,290.
21,432 Large   4,843 Small   26,275 Total

9125	M	$10	1902DB	618	48 B	A1773	VF	pen/pen
9125	M	$10	1902DB	618	1826 C	X644701A	G	faded/faded
9125	-	$10	1902PB	626	5016 A	5016 A	XF	Higgins Mus.
9125	-	$20	1902PB	652	4192 A	V437024H	VF+	pen/pen ac
9125	-	$20	1902PB	652	4796 A	?	CU	
9125	-	$20	1902PB	652	4813 A	4813 A	XF	
9125		$10	1929T1		B000141A		F	
9125		$10	1929T1		E000257A		F+	
9125		$10	1929T1		C000309A		VG/F	
9125		$10	1929T1		D000313A		VG/F	
9125		$10	1929T1		F000468A		G	
9125		$20	1929T1		E000043A		VF	Higgins Mus.
9125		$20	1929T1		E000049A		VF	
9125		$20	1929T1		C000068A		F	
9125		$20	1929T1		A000070A		VG+	
9125		$20	1929T1		F000071A		F	
9125		$20	1929T1		A000086A		VG	
9125		$20	1929T1		A000131A		F	

THE FIRST NATIONAL BANK OF DIKE 1 L
5372   GRUNDY
Chartered on May 25, 1900. Placed in voluntary liquidation on April 5, 1909; capital of $25,000. Succeeded by The Farmers Savings Bank of Dike.
Officers: Pres. Hans J Boysen 1900-03, RH Rehder 1904-08; **VP** Henry Johnson 1900, Marshall Rugg 1902, MW Roadman 1903-07; **Cash.** MA Buchan 1900-03, JJ Schultz 1904-08; **AC** Jeppe J Schultz

Second Charter, Brown Backs	Ser #	# Notes
10-10-10-20	1-1631	6,524

Total amount of circulation issued = $81,550. Amount outstanding at close = $25,000. Amount outstanding in 1910 = $10,280.
6,524 Large   0 Small   6,524 Total
5372 $20 1882BB 504   1264 A R666410R   VG/F   Higgins Mus.

THE FIRST NATIONAL BANK OF DOON   14 L   11 S
6764   LYON

Organized on April 15, 1903 with a capital of $25,000. Succeeded The Doon Savings Bank. Placed in receivership on Oct. 22, 1931; capital of $50,000.
Officers: Pres. OP Miller 1903-28, AG Miller 1929-31; **VP** JKP Thompson 1903, E Huntington 1904-14, CR McDowell 1920-31; **Cash.** CR McDowell 1903-19, RH Armistead 1920-25, CR McDowell 1926-31; **AC** HD Kenyon 1904, WC Bentley 1907, RH Armistead 1909-14, LJ Denn 1925-31, Frances McDowell 1925-26

Third Charter, Red Seal	Ser #	# Notes
10-10-10-20	1-986	3,944
Third Charter, Date Back, Blue Seal		
10-10-10-20	1-1730	6,920
Third Charter, Plain Back, Blue Seal		
10-10-10-20	1731-7681	23,804
1929, Type I		
6-10's	1-769	4,614
6-20's	1-186	1,116

Total amount of circulation issued = $501,810. Amount outstanding at close = $49,995. Amount of large outstanding on October 19, 1931 = $8,035.
34,668 Large   5,730 Small   40,398 Total

6764	M	$10 1902DB	616	1299 F	T610023A	VG/F	gone/gone
6764	-	$10 1902PB	624	3351 D	T955783D	VG	faded/faded
6764	-	$10 1902PB	624	5767 F	Y818409H	VG	Tear
6764	-	$10 1902PB	624	5935 E	Y818577H	F/VF	
6764	-	$10 1902PB	624	6375 E	6375 E	VG	gone/gone
6764	-	$10 1902PB	624	6398 E	6398 E	VF	Higgins Mus.
6764	-	$10 1902PB	624	7170 F	7170 F	VG	
6764	-	$10 1902PB	624	7360 E	7360 E	VF	stamp sigs vp
6764	M	$20 1902PB	650	3663 B	T956095D	F+	faded/faded
6764	M	$20 1902PB	650	4279 B	H974601E	VG	
6764	M	$20 1902PB	650	5241 B	K247033H	VF+	stamp/stamp
6764	-	$20 1902PB	650	5844 B	Y818486H	VF	light stamps
6764	-	$20 1902PB	650	6103 B	?	VG/F	weak sigs
6764	-	$20 1902PB	650	7364 B	7364 B	F	gone/stmp vp
6764		$10 1929T1		E000140A		?	
6764		$10 1929T1		D000608A		XF	
6764		$10 1929T1		B000718A		?	
6764		$10 1929T1		C000723A		F	
6764		$20 1929T1		E000032A		F/VF	
6764		$20 1929T1		D000089A		XF	
6764		$20 1929T1		B000110A		?	
6764		$20 1929T1		F000135A		F+	
6764		$20 1929T1		B000148A		F+	
6764		$20 1929T1		C000161A		F	Higgins Mus.
6764		$20 1929T1		D000163A		F	

THE FIRST NATIONAL BANK OF DOUGHERTY   2 L   5 S
5576   CERRO GORDO

Organized on July 30, 1900 with a capital of $25,000. Chartered on Sept. 13, 1900. Placed in receivership on December 14, 1931; capital of $25,000.
Officers: Pres. CH McNider 1901-16, Wm J Christians 1917-24, CH Christians 1925-31; **VP** Chas. Christians 1902, AH Gale 1903, Robt Mullin 1904-14, Peter Gorman 1920-31, JJ Beecher 1925-31; **Cash.** Wm J Christians 1901-16, CH Christians 1917-24, WJ Lalor 1925-31; **AC** FL Christians 1909-10, CH Christians 1911-14, WJ Lalor 1920-24, ME Burke 1925-27

Second Charter, Brown Backs	Ser #	# Notes
10-10-10-20	1-800	3,200
Second Charter, Date Back		
10-10-10-20	1-740	2,960
Second Charter, Value Back		
10-10-10-20	741-971	924
Third Charter, Plain Back, Blue Seal		
10-10-10-20	1-1091	4,364
1929, Type I		
6-10's	1-197	1,182
6-20's	1-30	180

Total amount of circulation issued = $158,520. Amount of large outstanding at close = $2,270. Amount of small outstanding at close = $9,780.
11,448 Large   1,362 Small   12,810 Total

5576	-	$10 1882BB	490	394 A	X589821	VG	pen/pen
5576	-	$20 1882BB	504	384 A	X589811	VF	pen Higgins Mus.
5576		$10 1929T1		F000006A		F	
5576		$10 1929T1		F000112A		?	
5576		$20 1929T1		C000012A		VF	
5576		$20 1929T1		E000021A		CU	
5576		$20 1929T1		D000027A		VF	Higgins Mus.

THE DUBUQUE NATIONAL BANK   11 L
3140   DUBUQUE

Chartered in 1884. Closed; consolidated with #2327 on January 23, 1923; capital of $125,000. Circulation assumed by #2327.
Officers: Pres. BB Richards 1884-90, DD Myers 1891-1916, Geo W Myers 1918-22; **VP** Fred O'Donnell 1896, JG Bailey 1900, CH Berg 1902-14, JF Harragan 1914, NJ Schrup 1920-22, John W Schwind 1920-22; **Cash.** James Harragan 1884-1908, Joseph F Harragan 1909-13, DD Myers 1910-12, Geo J Homan 1913-15, Jos W Meyer 1916-22; **AC** EJ McLaughlin 1896-1907, JF Harragan 1904, 1910, GJ Homan 1911, JJ Sullivan 1920-22, JA Behnke 1920-22, OB Kuhl 1922

Second Charter, Brown Backs	Ser #	# Notes
5-5-5-5	1-2535	10,140
10-10-10-20	1-1381	5,524
Third Charter, Red Seal		
50-100	1-300	600
Third Charter, Date Back, Blue Seal		
50-100	1-1000	2,000
50-50-50-100	1-480	1,920
Third Charter, Plain Back, Blue Seal		
5-5-5-5	1-9096	36,384

Total amount of circulation issued = $616,670. Amount outstanding at close = $99,300. Circulation assumed by #2327 which was then responsible for redeeming the outstanding notes of #3140.
56,568 Large   0 Small   56,568 Total

3140	M	$5 1902PB	598	1316 A	M675143B	VF+	stamp/stamp
3140	M	$5 1902PB	598	1557 B	M675384B	AU	
3140	M	$5 1902PB	598	1559 D	M675386B	CU	stamp/pen
3140	M	$5 1902PB	598	1571 B	M675398B	AU	Higgins Mus.
3140	M	$5 1902PB	598	1605 C	M675432B	CU	stamp/stamp
3140	M	$5 1902PB	598	1808 C	X151894B	VG/F	stamp
3140	M	$5 1902PB	598	1827 D	X151913B	VF/XF	
3140	M	$5 1902PB	598	1980 B	X152066B	F	
3140	M	$5 1902PB	598	2957 B	B585078D	XF	
3140	M	$5 1902PB	598	3135 B	B585256D	CU	pen/pen
3140		$5 1902PB	598	4546 B	U103307D	VG	

THE COMMERCIAL NATIONAL BANK OF DUBUQUE   4 L
1801   DUBUQUE

Chartered on March 11, 1871 with a capital of $100,000. Merged with The Peoples Bank in 1875. Placed in receivership on April 2, 1888; capital of $100,000. Reason for failure: incompetent management.
Officers: Pres. Rufus E Graves 1872-88; **VP** HL Stout 1878-79; **Cash.** Henry M Kingman 1872-80, Clarence H Harris 1881-88

First Charter, Original Issue	Ser #	# Notes
1-1-1-2	1-2400	9,600
5-5-5-5	1-5400	21,600
First Charter, Series of 1875		
1-1-1-2	1-2780	11,120
5-5-5-5	1-10533	42,132

Total amount of circulation issued = $344,560. Amount outstanding at close = $62,170. Amount outstanding in 1915 = $2,081.
84,452 Large   0 Small   84,452 Total

1801	-	$5	ORIG	?	4311 D	K311854	F/VF	pen/pen
1801	-	$1	1875	384	1282 B	B181586	VF	
1801	-	$1	1875	384	1308 C	B181612	XF	Higgins Mus.
1801	-	$1	1875	384	1334 A	B181638	CU	pen/pen

THE FIRST NATIONAL BANK OF DUBUQUE   65 L   71 S
317   DUBUQUE

Chartered in 1864. Assumed #1540 by consolidation on March 9, 1867. Suspended on August 17, 1893; resumed on August 30, 1893.
Officers: Pres. RE Graves 1867-71, Dennis Cooley 1872-90, CH Eighmey 1891-1921, EM Hetherton 1922-26, Wm Lawther, Jr. 1927-38; **VP** BW Lacy 1896, EA Engler 1902-03, JC Collier 1911-32, Wm Hetherton 1920, WM Lanther 1924-27, JW Wiwali 1932; **Cash.** Wm Hyde Clark 1867-71, Chas H Eighmey 1872-84, OF Guernsey 1885-1902, BF Blocklinger 1905, HA Koester 1916-31, JV Keppler 1932-38; **AC** OF Guernsey 1878, BF Blocklinger

1900-01, HA Koester 1910, HCW Scholz 1922-31, Jos V Keppler 1924-31, JF Kircher 1934

First Charter, Original Issue	Ser #	# Notes
1-1-1-2	1-9700	38,800
10-10-10-20	1-4100	16,400
10-10-10-20	5101-6900	7,200
20 (Cut from the 10-10-10-20 plate)	4101-5100	1,000
First Charter, Series of 1875		
1-1-1-2	1-1370	5,480
10-10-10-20	1-2704	10,816
Second Charter, Brown Backs		
5-5-5-5	1-13677	54,708
50-100	1-883	1,766
Third Charter, Red Seal		
10-10-10-20	1-8300	33,200
Third Charter, Date Back, Blue Seal		
10-10-10-20	1-11000	44,000
Third Charter, Plain Back, Blue Seal		
10-10-10-20	11001-33530	90,120
1929, Type I		
6-10's	1-4002	24,012
6-20's	1-1240	7,440
1929, Type II		
10's	1-10042	10,042
20's	1-2402	2,402

Total amount of circulation issued = $3,540,420. Amount of large outstanding in 1935 = $15,830. Amount of small outstanding in 1935 = $284,170.
306,490 Large   43,896 Small   350,386 Total

317	-	?	ORIG	?	347 B	56537	Fr
317	-	$1	ORIG 380	1 A	B347642	VF	
317	-	$1	1875 386	168 A	B378972	P	
317	-	$1	1875 386	345 B	B379149	XF	pen/pen
317	-	$1	1875 386	348 C	B379152	XF	
317	-	$1	1875 386	1264 C	B382468	F/VF	Higgins Mus.
317	-	$10	1875 419	1741 B	B994243	VG	Grinnell # 2821
317	-	$5	1882BB 466	1336 B	T433099	VG	pen/pen
317	-	$5	1882BB 466	4867 A	A668326A	F	
317	M	$10	1902RS 613	172 A	A577092	VG	
317	M	$10	1902RS 613	4056 A	H584732	VF	pen/pen vp
317	M	$10	1902RS 613	4291 A	H584967	VG	pen/lt stamp
317	M	$10	1902RS 613	5847 A	N199304	VG/F	pen/pen Ink
317	M	$20	1902RS 639	5507 A	N185424	VF	Higgins Mus.
317	M	$10	1902DB 616	3093 D	R443154	F	stamp/stamp
317	M	$10	1902DB 616	6095 D	D488266A	?	
317	M	$10	1902DB 616	8716 F	U507892A	VF	stamp sigs vp
317	M	$10	1902DB 616	8946 F	U508122A	VG	stamp/stamp
317	M	$10	1902DB 616	9806 D	Z910600A	CU	nice sigs
317	M	$10	1902DB 616	9806 E	Z910600A	CU	
317	M	$10	1902DB 616	9807 D	Z910601A	CU	nice sigs
317	M	$10	1902DB 616	9807 E	Z910601A	CU	
317	M	$10	1902DB 616	9808 E	Z910602A	CU	
317	M	$10	1902DB 616	9808 F	Z910602A	CU	stamp/stamp
317	M	$10	1902DB 616	10220 E	Z943324A	AU	stamp/stamp
317	M	$10	1902DB 616	10221 E	Z943325A	CU	
317	M	$10	1902DB 616	10910 E	Z944014A	F+	
317	M	$20	1902DB 642	?	B965493	?	Bayard
317	M	$20	1902DB 642	5448 B	D458959A	F	stamp/stamp
317	M	$20	1902DB 642	10029 B	Z943133A	F/VF	stamp/stamp
317	M	$20	1902DB 642	10825 B	Z943929A	VG	lt stamp sigs
317	M	$20	1902DB 642	10872 B	Z943976A	CU	
317	M	$10	1902PB 624	14656 E	K857678D	VF	stamp/stamp
317	M	$10	1902PB 624	15471 E	?	VF	weak sigs
317	M	$10	1902PB 624	17061 B	T78543D	VG/F	
317	M	$10	1902PB 624	17077 F	T78559D	G	
317	M	$10	1902PB 624	21995 E	B710387H	F	
317	M	$10	1902PB 624	22324 F	B710716H	F	stamp/stamp
317	M	$10	1902PB 624	22840 E	B711232H	VF	
317	M	$10	1902PB 624	23560 E	K562452H	AU	gone/gone
317	M	$10	1902PB 624	23563 D	K562455H	XF	UR corner gone
317	M	$10	1902PB 624	23927 E	K562819H	VG/F	stamp/stamp
317	-	$10	1902PB 624	24657 E	T988459H	VG	
317	-	$10	1902PB 624	24791 F	T988593H	F/VF	Davenport B&T
317	-	$10	1902PB 624	25260 D	Y650322H	VG	stamp/stamp
317	-	$10	1902PB 624	25326 D	Y650388H	VG	
317	-	$10	1902PB 624	26023 E	Y651085H	VG/F	
317	-	$10	1902PB 624	26028 ?	Y651090H	VF	
317	-	$10	1902PB 624	26897 E	26897 E	Fr/G	
317	-	$10	1902PB 624	27476 ?	27476 ?	VF	
317	-	$10	1902PB 624	29314 F	29314 F	VF	stamp/stamp
317	-	$10	1902PB 624	31198 H	31198 H	VF	
317	-	$10	1902PB 624	31725 I	31725 I	F	stamp/stamp
317	-	$10	1902PB 624	32507 I	32507 I	F	
317	-	$10	1902PB 624	32811 H	32811 H	XF	stamp/stamp
317	-	$10	1902PB 624	32879 G	32879 G	F	
317	M	$20	1902PB 650	15854 B	T77336D	VF+	
317	M	$20	1902PB 650	16550 B	T78032D	VF	stamp/stamp
317	M	$20	1902PB 650	17061 B	T78543D	F	
317	M	$20	1902PB 650	19548 B	N925010E	F/VF	Higgins Mus.
317	M	$20	1902PB 650	20574 B	N926036E	VG/F	
317	M	$20	1902PB 650	20683 B	N926145E	VF	stamp/stamp
317	-	$20	1902PB 650	24686 B	T988488H	VF	stamp/stamp
317	-	$20	1902PB 650	27072 B	27072 B	F	
317	-	$20	1902PB 650	30100 C	30100 C	F	stamp/stamp
317		$10	1929T1	F000163A		XF	
317		$10	1929T1	C001023A		VF/XF	
317		$10	1929T1	C001581A		VG/F	
317		$10	1929T1	B001672A		XF/AU	
317		$10	1929T1	C001674A		VF	
317		$10	1929T1	C001676A		XF/AU	
317		$10	1929T1	E001981A		F/VF	Paper clip stain
317		$10	1929T1	D002522A		VF	
317		$10	1929T1	E002638A		VF+	
317		$10	1929T1	D002719A		XF+	
317		$10	1929T1	D002789A		F	
317		$10	1929T1	F002823A		F	
317		$10	1929T1	B002921A		VG	
317		$10	1929T1	D002932A		VG/F	
317		$10	1929T1	E003023A		XF/AU	
317		$10	1929T1	A003150A		AU	
317		$10	1929T1	E003202A		VF	
317		$10	1929T1	D003206A		?	
317		$10	1929T1	E003259A		VG	
317		$10	1929T1	?003398A		XF	
317		$10	1929T1	F003541A		?	
317		$10	1929T1	C003582A		VF	
317		$10	1929T1	F003695A		VG	
317		$10	1929T1	E003843A		VG	
317		$20	1929T1	B000009A		VG/F	
317		$20	1929T1	E000013A		F	
317		$20	1929T1	E000018A		VF	
317		$20	1929T1	D000104A		VG	
317		$20	1929T1	B000308A		F	
317		$20	1929T1	E000388A		CU	
317		$20	1929T1	F000390A		?	
317		$20	1929T1	B000460A		F	
317		$20	1929T1	B000493A		F	
317		$20	1929T1	C000495A		?	
317		$20	1929T1	F000510A		F/VF	
317		$20	1929T1	B000660A		CU	
317		?	1929T1	F000712A		XF	
317		$20	1929T1	F000751A		F	
317		$20	1929T1	D000776A		VF/XF	
317		$20	1929T1	C000830A		?	
317		$20	1929T1	F000899A		F/VF	
317		$20	1929T1	D001001A		VF/XF	
317		$20	1929T1	E001017A		VG	
317		$20	1929T1	F001087A		F+	
317		$20	1929T1	D001101A		VG	
317		$20	1929T1	B001133A		CU	
317		$20	1929T1	A001227A		F/VF	
317		$20	1929T1	F001229A		F/VF	
317		$10	1929T2	A000073		F	
317		$10	1929T2	A000969		XF	
317		$10	1929T2	A001060		F	
317		$10	1929T2	A001171		XF	
317		$10	1929T2	A001729		VG	Stains
317		$10	1929T2	A003513		F/VF	
317		$10	1929T2	A003674		VG	
317		$10	1929T2	A004467		XF	
317		$10	1929T2	A006439		VF	
317		$10	1929T2	A006979		F/VF	
317		$10	1929T2	A009082		?	
317		$10	1929T2	A009651		XF	
317		$10	1929T2	A009687		?	
317		$20	1929T2	A000005		CU	Higgins Mus.
317		$20	1929T2	A000133		VF	
317		$20	1929T2	A000602		VF/XF	
317		$20	1929T2	A000735		AU	
317		$20	1929T2	A001347		VF	
317		$20	1929T2	A001420		F	
317		$20	1929T2	A001649		XF/AU	
317		$20	1929T2	A002237		AU	

317	$20 1929T2	A002316		F	
317	$20 1929T2	A002333		F	

THE MERCHANTS NATIONAL BANK OF DUBUQUE   0 L
846   DUBUQUE

Chartered on February 27, 1865. Placed in voluntary liquidation on September 30, 1873; capital of $200,000.
Officers: Pres. Fred WH Sheffield 1867-73; **Cash.** Richard A Babbage 1867-73

First Charter, Original Issue	Ser #	# Notes
1-1-1-2	1-6000	24,000
5-5-5-5	1-5275	21,100
10-10-10-20	1-2300	9,200
50-100	1-100	200

Total amount of circulation issued = $265,500. Amount outstanding at close = $180,000. Amount outstanding in 1910 = $3,093.

54,502 Large   0 Small   54,502 Total

THE NATIONAL STATE BANK OF DUBUQUE   0 L
1540   DUBUQUE

Chartered on August 28, 1865. Placed in voluntary liquidation on March 9, 1867; capital of $150,000. Consolidated with #317.

First Charter, Original Issue	Ser #	# Notes
5-5-5-5	1-2500	10,000
10-10-10-20	1-902	3,608
50-100	1-216	432

Total amount of circulation issued = $127,500. Amount outstanding at close = $127,500. Amount outstanding in 1910 = $1,135.

14,040 Large   0 Small   14,040 Total

THE SECOND NATIONAL BANK OF DUBUQUE   17 L
2327 (FIRST TITLE)   DUBUQUE

Chartered on March 20, 1876 with a capital of $100,000. Assumed #3140 by consolidation on January 23, 1923, with a change in title to The Consolidated Bank of Dubuque.
Officers: Pres. Wm L Bradley 1876-83, George B Burch 1884-1900, JK Deming 1901-1923; **VP** JK Deming 1900, WH Day 1902-13, James M Burch 1914-23, Geo W Myers 1923, Herman Eschen 1923; **Cash.** GV Smock 1876-78, Louis Boisot 1880-85, JK Deming 1887-1900, Herm Eschen 1901-22; **AC** JK Deming 1885, Herman Eschen 1896-1900, AP Melchior 1922-23, A Wharton 1922-23, JA Behnke 1923, John Wagner 1923, MJ Grace 1927

First Charter, Series of 1875	Ser #	# Notes
5-5-5-5	1-15865	63,460
Second Charter, Brown Backs		
10-10-10-20	1-8000	32,000
50-100	1-2476	4,952
Second Charter, Date Back		
10-10-10-20	1-11225	44,900
50-100	1-67	134
Third Charter, Plain Back, Blue Seal		
50-50-50-100	1-880	3,520

148,966 Large   0 Small   148,966 Total

2327	-	$5 1875 401	9457 C	?	VG/F	
2327	-	$5 1875 401	14818 C	Y93711	VF	Grinnell # 2820
2327	-	$5 1875 401	15412 C	Y209295	Fr/G	pen/pen
2327	M	$10 1882BB 487	3981 A	R816938R	VG/F	
2327	M	$10 1882BB 487	4575 A	R817862R	Fr/G	
2327	M	$10 1882BB 487	6106 C	V453655V	VG	lt. stamp sigs
2327	M	$10 1882BB 487	7819 B	V458368V	F/VF	Higgins Mus.
2327		$20 1882BB 501	241 A	K913137K	VG/F	
2327	M	$10 1882DB 542	1655 E	A571311	VG	Soiled
2327	M	$10 1882DB 542	2355 D	A572011	VF	lt. stamp sigs
2327	M	$10 1882DB 542	5078 D	E443852	F	gone/gone
2327	M	$10 1882DB 542	5225 D	E443999	Fr/G	gone/gone
2327	M	$10 1882DB 542	6975 F	K813093	XF	faded/faded
2327	M	$10 1882DB 542	10899 E	N265637	VG/F	
2327	M	$20 1882DB 552	5359 B	E444133	F	
2327	M	$100 1902PB 704	551 A	A852623	F	Davenport B&T
2327	M	$100 1902PB 704	876 A	B9480	F/VF	lt. stamp sigs

THE CONSOLIDATED NATIONAL BANK OF DUBUQUE
2327 (2ND TITLE)   DUBUQUE   37 L   13 S

Succeeded The Second National Bank of Dubuque on January 23, 1923. Assumed the circulation of #3140. Placed in receivership on July 14, 1932; capital of $500,000.
Officers: Pres. JK Deming 1923-1932; **VP** James M Burch 1923-27, Geo W Myers 1923-32, Herman Eschen 1923-24; **Cash.** Jos W Meyer 1923-32; **AC** AP Melchior 1923-32, A Wharton 1923-32, JA Behnke 1923-28, John J Sullivan 1923-32, John Wagner 1923-32, MJ Grace 1927-32

Third Charter, Plain Back, Blue Seal	Ser #	# Notes
5-5-5-5	1-27239	108,956

1929, Type I

6-5's	1-2995	17,970

Total amount of circulation issued = $2,514,630. Amount of large outstanding at close = 25,970. Includes large outstanding of #2327 and #3140. Amount of small outstanding at close = $23,370.

108,956 Large   17,970 Small   126,926 Total

2327	M	$5 1902PB 606	251 A	D90362H	VF	
2327	M	$5 1902PB 606	691 C	D90802H	G/VG	engraved sigs.
2327	M	$5 1902PB 606	4938 B	M872349H	AU	engraved
2327		$5 1902PB 606	5507 ?	?	CU	engraved
2327	-	$5 1902PB 606	6663 B	X560374H	F/VF	engraved
2327	-	$5 1902PB 606	8123 D	8123 D	VG	engraved
2327	-	$5 1902PB 606	10209 B	10209 B	VF	engraved
2327	-	$5 1902PB 606	10433 A	10433 A	VG	engraved
2327	-	$5 1902PB 606	11430 B	11430 B	Fr	engraved
2327	-	$5 1902PB 606	11527 C	11527 C	CU	engraved
2327	-	$5 1902PB 606	11698 B	11698 B	VF	engraved
2327	-	$5 1902PB 606	13497 B	13497 B	VF/XF	engraved
2327	-	$5 1902PB 606	14300 B	14300 B	F	engraved
2327	-	$5 1902PB 606	14435 A	14435 A	VG	engraved
2327	-	$5 1902PB 606	15558 B	15558 B	AU+	engraved
2327	-	$5 1902PB 606	16414 A	16414 A	F+	engraved
2327	-	$5 1902PB 606	17992 B	17992 B	VG	engraved
2327	-	$5 1902PB 606	18355 C	18355 C	CU	engraved
2327	-	$5 1902PB 606	18356 C	18356 C	CU	engraved
2327	-	$5 1902PB 606	19209 B	19209 B	VF/XF	engraved
2327	-	$5 1902PB 606	19233 D	19233 D	VG	engraved
2327	-	$5 1902PB 606	19251 D	19251 D	XF	engraved
2327	-	$5 1902PB 606	19688 A	19688 A	XF+	engraved
2327	-	$5 1902PB 606	19690 C	19690 C	CU	eng. Higgins Mus.
2327	-	$5 1902PB 606	19690 D	19690 D	CU	engraved
2327	-	$5 1902PB 606	19695 D	19695 D	XF	engraved
2327	-	$5 1902PB 606	20949 C	20949 C	F/VF	engraved
2327	-	$5 1902PB 606	20986 C	20986 C	VF/XF	engraved
2327	-	$5 1902PB 606	21594 B	21594 B	VG/F	engraved
2327	-	$5 1902PB 606	21599 B	21599 B	F+	engraved
2327	-	$5 1902PB 606	23005 D	23005 D	F/VF	engraved
2327	-	$5 1902PB 606	23031 B	23031 B	VF/XF	engraved
2327	-	$5 1902PB 606	25009 C	25009 C	G	engraved
2327	-	$5 1902PB 606	25965 D	25965 D	F/VF	engraved Stain
2327	-	$5 1902PB 606	26447 A	26447 A	F	engraved
2327	-	$5 1902PB 606	26750 B	26750 B	F+	engraved
2327	-	$5 1902PB 606	26897 A	26897 A	?	eng. High grade
2327		$5 1929T1	F000188A		VF+	Higgins Mus.
2327		$5 1929T1	C000207A		VG	Major rust
2327		$5 1929T1	B000431A		F+	
2327		$5 1929T1	A000477A		VG	
2327		$5 1929T1	F000918A		VF	
2327		$5 1929T1	E001380A		AU	
2327		$5 1929T1	D001382A		?	
2327		$5 1929T1	C001808A		VG	
2327		$5 1929T1	C001920A		VF	
2327		$5 1929T1	F001921A		VF	
2327		$5 1929T1	D002091A		F	
2327		$5 1929T1	E002179A		XF	
2327		$5 1929T1	A002196A		VF/XF	

THE FIRST NATIONAL BANK OF DUNKERTON   10 L   13 S
6722   BLACK HAWK

Organized on April 1, 1903 with a capital of $30,000. Succeeded The Bank of Dunkerton. Placed in conservatorship on March 28, 1933. Placed in receivership on October 31, 1933; capital of $40,000.
Officers: Pres. CH Dunkerton 1904-11, GS Kleckner 1912-33; **VP** GS Kleckner 1904-12, John Keane 1913-27, 1932, FP Davis 1926-33; **Cash.** MT Blake 1904, WW Beal, Jr. 1905-06, FC Braniger 1907, FP Davis 1908-26, EJ Kleckner 1926-33; **AC** EJ Kleckner 1923-26

Third Charter, Red Seal	Ser #	# Notes
10-10-10-20	1-1468	5,872
Third Charter, Date Back, Blue Seal		
10-10-10-20	1-2310	9,240
Third Charter, Plain Back, Blue Seal		
10-10-10-20	2311-6031	14,884
1929, Type I		
6-10's	1-764	4,584
6-20's	1-242	1,452

Total amount of circulation issued = $449,830. Amount of large outstanding at close = $2,760. Amount of small outstanding at close = $37,240.

29,996 Large   6,036 Small   36,032 Total

6722	M	$10 1902DB 616	1852 D	A516544B	VF+	
6722	M	$10 1902DB 616	2146 D	M891862B	VF	pen/stamp
6722	M	$20 1902DB 642	2174 B	M891890B	Fr	gone/gone

6722	-	$10	1902PB	624	4638 F	4638 F	F+
6722	-	$10	1902PB	624	4709 F	4709 F	VG
6722	-	$10	1902PB	624	4857 E	4857 E	F
6722	-	$10	1902PB	624	5450 E	5450 E	AU Higgins Mus.
6722	M	$20	1902PB	650	3262 B	A474824E	F
6722	M	$20	1902PB	650	3953 B	D508695H	F+
6722	-	$20	1902PB	650	4730 B	4730 B	VG/F stamp/stamp
6722		$10	1929T1		F000143A		VG
6722		$10	1929T1		E000315A		F
6722		$10	1929T1		C000478A		F+
6722		$10	1929T1		F000557A		F
6722		$10	1929T1		D000560A		VG/F
6722		$10	1929T1		A000683A		VG
6722		$20	1929T1		F000010A		F
6722		$20	1929T1		B000015A		VF Top tight cut
6722		$20	1929T1		E000129A		XF Higgins Mus.
6722		$20	1929T1		E000164A		?
6722		$20	1929T1		F000209A		VG/F
6722		$20	1929T1		A000237A		VF
6722		$20	1929T1		D000239A		XF

THE FIRST NATIONAL BANK OF DUNLAP 7 L
4139   HARRISON
Chartered in 1889. Placed in voluntary liquidation on February 23, 1926; capital of $40,000. Absorbed by The Dunlap Savings Bank.
Officers: Pres. James H Patterson 1890-93, TF Jordan 1894-1923; **VP** WT Preston 1896-1909, HL Preston 1910, LE Jordan 1911, Frank Wettengel 1913-21, LE Wright 1923; **Cash.** Henry A Moore 1890-1906, AN Jordan 1907-23; **AC** AN Jordan 1896, Geo G Cronkelton 1900-05, GF Haas 1907-09, RW Wettengel 1913-23, WJ Wettengel 1920-23

Second Charter, Brown Backs	Ser #	# Notes
5-5-5-5	1-3828	15,312
10-10-10-20	1-1208	4,832
Third Charter, Date Back, Blue Seal		
5-5-5-5	1-2250	9,000
10-10-10-20	1-1740	6,960
Third Charter, Plain Back, Blue Seal		
5-5-5-5	2251-5085	11,340
10-10-10-20	1741-3520	7,120

Total amount issued = $414,660. Amount outstanding at close = $30,000.
54,564 Large   0 Small   56,564 Total

4139	-	$5	1882BB	470	307 C	H741739	XF pen/pen
4139	-	$5	1882BB	470	961 D	R874	F pen/pen
4139		$10	1882BB	483	484 ?	?	F Tight top margin
4139		$5	1902PB	600	4303 A	Y646709E	VG
4139	-	$5	1902PB	600	4566 C	M638327H	VG/F gone Higg. Mus.
4139	M	$10	1902PB	626	2998 A	A380210H	VF stamp/stamp
4139	M	$20	1902PB	652	2201 A	M296653D	F+

THE FIRST NATIONAL BANK OF DYERSVILLE 12 L 7 S
9555   DUBUQUE
Chartered in October 1909. Placed in voluntary liquidation on May 21, 1931; capital of $50,000. Succeeded by #13508.
Officers: Pres. Frank L Drexler 1910-30; **VP** AM Cloud 1910-15, Conrad May 1920-30; **Cash.** HB Willenborg 1910-30; **AC** FH Deutmeyer 1910-14, AL Vogl 1920, LL Gloden 1922-23, AL Vogl 1924-30

Third Charter, Date Back, Blue Seal	Ser #	# Notes
10-10-10-20	1-2550	10,200
Third Charter, Plain Back, Blue Seal		
10-10-10-20	2551-6577	16,108
1929, Type I		
6-10's	1-376	2,256
6-20's	1-68	408

Total amount of circulation issued = $359,570. Amount of large outstanding at close = $6,150. Amount of small outstanding at close = $28,850.
26,308 Large   2,664 Small   28,972 Total

9555	M	$20	1902DB	644	1594 B	B762745A	VG stamp/stamp
9555	M	$20	1902DB	644	2315 A	A516067B	XF stamp/stamp
9555	M	$10	1902PB	626	3072 B	E657196D	VG stamp/stamp
9555	M	$10	1902PB	626	4349 A	V806221E	F/VF stamp/stamp
9555	M	$10	1902PB	626	4565 B	D793807H	VG stamp/stamp
9555	-	$10	1902PB	626	4776 A	N144398H	VF stamps Rust
9555	-	$10	1902PB	626	4813 C	N144435H	F Bayard
9555	-	$10	1902PB	626	5237 B	A238579K	CU Higgins Mus.
9555	-	$10	1902PB	626	5719 A	5719 A	XF stamp/stamp
9555	-	$10	1902PB	626	6069 A	6069 A	VG
9555	-	$20	1902PB	652	5165 A	A238507K	F stamp/stamp rust
9555	-	$20	1902PB	652	6078 A	6078 A	XF
9555		$10	1929T1		E000126A		F
9555		$10	1929T1		A000208A		VG UL corner gone
9555		$10	1929T1		B000287A		F
9555		$10	1929T1		F000318A		F
9555		$10	1929T1		F000329A		F/VF
9555		$20	1929T1		B000022A		VF+ Higgins Mus.
9555		$20	1929T1		A000046A		F/VF

THE FIRST NATIONAL BANK OF DYSART 13 L
5934   TAMA
Chartered in August 1901. Assumed The Dysart Savings Bank on March 10, 1928 with a change in title to Dysart National Bank, Dysart.
Officers: Pres. Oscar Casey 1901-03, HJ Von Lackum 1904-09, Oscar Casey 1910-11, CP Fedderson 1912-25, Herm Schroeder 1926-27, HP Jensen 1928-34, Dan Lally 1935; **VP** Conrad Brandan 1902-11, EF Douglass 1913-27, Dan Lally 1928-29, FH Schmidt 1928-35, Ervin Moeller 1928-34; **Cash.** JH Lunemann 1901, CJ Miller 1902-03, Oscar Casey 1904-09, FH Schmidt 1910-27, JC Marsau 1928-34; **AC** FH Schmidt 1907, JR Casey 1911, Chas I Creps 1913-20, LC Schmidt 1922, Wesley T Hecht 1922-25, Elsie Richardson 1923-24, Lester Thiel 1926, Ralph Schroeder 1926-27

Second Charter, Brown Backs	Ser #	# Notes
10-10-10-20	1-2600	10,400
Second Charter, Date Back		
10-10-10-20	1-3040	12,160
Second Charter, Value Back		
10-10-10-20	3041-4708	6,672
Third Charter, Plain Back, Blue Seal		
10-10-10-20	1-3259	13,036

Total amount of circulation issued = $528,350. Amount outstanding in 1927 = $49,500. Amount outstanding in 1935 = $3,270.
42,268 Large   0 Small   42,268 Total

5934	M	$10	1882BB	490	2541 B	V185344V	VG Davenport B&T
5934	M	$10	1882DB	545	736 F	D284786	VG
5934	M	$20	1882DB	555	2470 B	N270648	?
5934	M	$10	1882VB	577	2038 ?		?
5934	M	$10	1882VB	577	3136 E	T641984	VF Higgins Mus.
5934	M	$10	1882VB	577	3345 D	U6343	VG Rust on Portrait
5934	M	$10	1882VB	577	4343 E	V30261	F/VF pen/pen
5934	M	$20	1882VB	581	3550 B	U6548	VF
5934	M	$10	1902PB	632	665 A	H333487E	VF pen ac/pen
5934	M	$10	1902PB	632	1835 C	H717657H	F+ Higgins Mus.
5934	-	$10	1902PB	632	3038 B	3038 B	F lt. stamp sigs
5934	M	$20	1902PB	659	1371 A	U98373E	F/VF
5934	M	$20	1902PB	659	1583 A	D506885H	VG/F pen ac/pen

THE FIRST NATIONAL BANK OF EAGLE GROVE 0 L
3439   WRIGHT
Chartered on January 22, 1886. Succeeded Odenheimer, Miller & Co. Placed in voluntary liquidation on January 20, 1890; capital of $50,000. Succeeded by The Citizens State Bank.
Officers: Pres. HA Miller 1887-90; **Cash.** AN Olenheimer 1887-90

Second Charter, Brown Backs	Ser #	# Notes
5-5-5-5	1-1021	4,084

Total amount of circulation issued = $20,420. Amount outstanding at close = $11,250. Amount outstanding in 1910 = $140.
4,084 Large   0 Small   4,084 Total

THE MERCHANTS NATIONAL BANK OF EAGLE GROVE 2 L
4694 (FIRST TITLE)   WRIGHT
Chartered in 1892. Title changed to First National Bank in Eagle Grove on October 26, 1920.
Officers: Pres. J Fitzmaurice 1892-94, WS Worthington 1895-98, J Fitzmaurice 1899-1911, LG Focht 1912-17; **VP** FW Pellsbury 1896, Thos. Collins 1900-02, Henry Dersheid 1903-04, JL Slade 1907, M Armbruster 1909-17; **Cash.** WS Worthington 1892-93, JP Clarke 1894-97, JH Howell 1898, EC Platt 1899-1900, LJ Clarke 1901-17; **AC** EC Platt 1896

Second Charter, Brown Backs	Ser #	# Notes
10-10-10-20	1-1535	6,140
Second Charter, Date Back		
10-10-10-20	1-306	1,224
Third Charter, Date Back, Blue Seal		
50-50-50-100	1-670	2,680

10,044 Large   0 Small   10,044 Total

4694	-	$20	1882BB	499	1631 A	Y394029	VG
4694	M	$100	1902DB	693	445 A	A754085E	F/VF pen/pen

FIRST NATIONAL BANK IN EAGLE GROVE 1 L
4694 (SECOND TITLE)   WRIGHT
Succeeded The Merchants National Bank of Eagle Grove on October 26, 1920. Placed in voluntary liquidation on July 15, 1924; capital of $50,000. Absorbed by The Citizens State Bank of Eagle Grove.

Third Charter, Plain Back, Blue Seal	Ser #	# Notes
10-10-10-20	1-877	3,508

Total amount issued = $303,400. Amount outstanding in 1922 = $50,000.

3,508 Large		0 Small		3,508 Total		
4694 M $20 1902PB	?	410 A	Y839012D	VF/XF	Higgins Mus.	

THE FIRST NATIONAL BANK OF ELDON   11 L   27 S
5342   WAPELLO

Chartered on May 8, 1900.
Officers. Pres. DC Bradley 1900-09, JA Bradley 1910-32; **VP** JO Hunnell 1900-20, D McHaffey 1922-25, HE Ritz 1926, FW Davis 1927-32; **Cash.** HE Ritz 1900-06, CW Finney 1907-20, KC Finney 1922-23, VD Koons 1924-27, LN Frescoln 1928-32; **AC** MH Ritz 1907-08, KC Finney 1909-14, Nora S Kittle 1922-32, Leone Mead 1930-32

Second Charter, Brown Backs	Ser #	# Notes
10-10-10-20	1-1850	7,400
Second Charter, Date Back		
10-10-10-20	1-1600	6,400
Second Charter, Value Back		
10-10-10-20	1601-2324	2,896
Third Charter, Plain Back, Blue Seal		
10-10-10-20	1-2640	10,560
1929, Type I		
6-10's	1-562	3,372
6-20's	1-148	888
1929, Type II		
10's	1-574	574
20's	1-143	143

Total amount of circulation issued = $400,780. Amount of large outstanding in 1935 = $1,660. Amount of small outstanding in 1935 = $23,340.

27,256 Large		4,977 Small		32,233 Total		
5342	$20 1882BB	504	? A	Z755722E	F/VF	
5342 -	$20 1882BB	504	910 A	E24605	XF	?/pen
5342 M	$10 1882DB	545	1416 E	6172444	VF	Higgins Mus.
5342 M	$10 1882VB	577	1849 E	U61887	F	pen/pen
5342 M	$10 1902PB	633	852 C	V836584E	VF	Higgins Mus.
5342 M	$10 1902PB	633	1081 A	D351553H	F	pen/pen vp
5342 -	$10 1902PB	633	1898 C	1898 C	VG/F	pen/pen vp
5342 -	$10 1902PB	633	2096 A	2096 A	F	
5342 -	$20 1902PB	659	2500 A	2500 A	VG	
5342 -	$20 1902PB	659	2561 A	2561 A	VF	pen/pen
5342 -	$20 1902PB	659	2564 A	2564 A	VF	pen/pen
5342	$10 1929T1		F000094A		VG/F	
5342	$10 1929T1		C000205A		F	
5342	$10 1929T1		C000218A		VG	Stained
5342	$10 1929T1		A000239A		F	
5342	$10 1929T1		B000283A		VG	
5342	$10 1929T1		A000285A		AU	Ink; toned paper
5342	$10 1929T1		A000286A		XF/AU	Ink; toned paper
5342	$10 1929T1		A000287A		VF	
5342	$10 1929T1		A000288A		CU	F ?
5342	$10 1929T1		A000362A		CU	
5342	$10 1929T1		F000463A		F+	
5342	$10 1929T1		A000466A		VF+	
5342	$10 1929T1		E000540A		F	
5342	$20 1929T1		D000004A		G/VG	
5342	$20 1929T1		C000038A		VG/F	
5342	$20 1929T1		E000066A		F/VF	Washed
5342	$20 1929T1		C000078A		VF	
5342	$20 1929T1		F000092A		XF	
5342	$20 1929T1		A000115A		VF	
5342	$20 1929T1		F000117A		F+	
5342	$20 1929T1		C000121A		VF	Higgins Mus.
5342	$20 1929T1		E000121A		VF	
5342	$20 1929T1		D000122A		F	
5342	$10 1929T2		A000061		VF+	
5342	$10 1929T2		A000289		VF	Corner tear
5342	$10 1929T2		A000397		VF	
5342	$20 1929T2		A000001		VG	

THE FIRST NATIONAL BANK OF ELDORA   9 L   14 S
5140   HARDIN

Organized on August 22, 1898 with a capital of $50,000. Succeeded The City State Bank. Placed in receivership on August 10, 1932; capital of $50,000.
Officers: Pres. JH Bales 1898-1907, WJ Murray 1908-22, WE Rathbone 1923-32; **VP** DE Byam 1900-07, WJ Moir 1909-13, WE Rathbone 1914-22, WJ Murray 1923-27, AW Crosson 1928-32, GL Marks 1928-32, WJ Murray 1932; **Cash.** WJ Murray 1898-1907, WE Rathbone 1908-11, AW Crosson 1912-32; **AC** WE Rathbone 1900-07, AW Crosson 1909-10, OM Barnes 1913-14, FR Price 1920-32, VE Miller 1923-27, OM Barnes 1928-32, GO Guenther 1929-32

Second Charter, Brown Backs	Ser #	# Notes
10-10-10-20	1-1600	6,400
Second Charter, Date Back		
10-10-10-20	1-2500	10,000
Second Charter, Value Back		
10-10-10-20	2501-3017	2,068
Third Charter, Plain Back, Blue Seal		
10-10-10-20	1-3954	15,816
1929, Type I		
6-5's	1-1022	6,132
6-10's	1-426	2,556
6-20's	1-65	390

Total amount of circulation issued = $492,570. Amount of large outstanding at close = $5,735. Amount of small outstanding at close = $29,985.

34,284 Large		9,078 Small		43,362 Total		
5140 M	$10 1882BB	490	808 B	T121145T	F	pen/pen
5140 M	$10 1882BB	490	977 C	U658925U	F	
5140 M	$10 1882DB	545	1056 F	H333284	VG/F	Higgins Mus.
5140 M	$10 1882DB	545	2217 E	R437165	VF	
5140 M	$10 1882DB	545	2257 D	R437205	VG	retraced sigs
5140 -	$10 1902PB	632	2654 A	2654 A	F	
5140 -	$20 1902PB	658	2310 A	R961392H	F+	stamp/pen
5140 -	$20 1902PB	658	2530 A	X716692H	VG	Higgins Mus.
5140 -	$20 1902PB	658	2881 A	2881 A	VF	pen/pen
5140	$5 1929T1		D000105A		VF	
5140	$5 1929T1		D000151A		?	
5140	$5 1929T1		F000717A		VF	
5140	$5 1929T1		D000722A		VF	
5140	$5 1929T1		F000846A		F/VF	
5140	$10 1929T1		F000053A		VF	
5140	$10 1929T1		F000161A		VG	
5140	$10 1929T1		B000120A		F	
5140	$10 1929T1		E000199A		F	
5140	$10 1929T1		A000270A		VF	
5140	$10 1929T1		C000337A		?	Bayard
5140	$10 1929T1		C000387A		AU	
5140	$10 1929T1		F000391A		VG	
5140	$20 1929T1		D000013A		VF	Higgins Mus.

THE HARDIN COUNTY NATIONAL BANK OF ELDORA
9233   HARDIN   18 L   23 S

Chartered in September 1908. Placed in voluntary liquidation on February 14, 1935; capital of $50,000. Succeeded by #14286; circulation assumed by #14286.
Officers: Pres. C McKeen Duren 1908-11, DM Moser 1912-35; **VP** JD Newcomer 1909-10, Alice D Hubbard 1911, CS Newcomer 1913, PS Davis 1914-29, HH Turner 1930-35, James Nuckolls 1930-35; **Cash.** Ellis D Robb 1908-11, HH Turner 1912-22, 1925-29, EW Nuckolls 1930-35; **AC** James Nuckolls 1909-29, FH Diehl 1914, TP Guenther 1920, EW Nuckolls 1925-29

Third Charter, Red Seal	Ser #	# Notes
5-5-5-5	1-2975	11,900
10-10-10-20	1-2280	9,120
Third Charter, Plain Back, Blue Seal		
5-5-5-5	2976-9094	24,476
10-10-10-20	2281-6288	16,032
1929, Type I		
6-5's	1-1422	8,532
6-10's	1-724	4,344
6-20's	1-182	1,092
1929, Type II		
5's	1-300	300
10's	1-375	375
20's	1-55	55

Total amount of circulation issued = $610,570. Amount of large outstanding at close = $3,610. Amount of small outstanding at close = $46,390. Circulation assumed by #14286 which was then responsible for redeeming the outstanding notes of #9233.

61,528 Large		14,698 Small		76,226 Total		
9233 M	$5 1902DB	592	74 D	D358797	VF/XF	pen/pen
9233 M	$5 1902DB	592	1545 A	D687091A	VG	
9233 M	$5 1902PB	600	3074 C	N477266B	G/VG	
9233 M	$5 1902PB	600	3892 ?	V345513B	VG	
9233 M	$5 1902PB	600	6343 B	R970424E	XF	pen/pen
9233 M	$5 1902PB	600	7059 D	E980920H	VG	
9233 -	$5 1902PB	600	7137 A	R182048A	VF	pen/pen
9233 -	$5 1902PB	600	7669 A	7669 A	F/VF	Bayard, Higg Mus
9233 -	$5 1902PB	600	7884 A	7884 A	F/VF	pen/pen
9233 -	$5 1902PB	600	8153 D	8153 D	F	
9233 -	$5 1902PB	600	8355 A	8355 A	F	
9233 -	$5 1902PB	600	8733 B	8733 B	VG/F	
9233 -	$5 1902PB	600	8761 D	8761 D	F+	
9233	$10 1902PB	626	2562 B	V198764B	VG	
9233	$10 1902PB	626	4990 A	X780612H	VG/F	
9233 -	$10 1902PB	626	5915 C	5915 C	F	pen/pen

9233	-	$10	1902PB	626	6280 C	6280 C	CU	Grinnell # 1385
9233	M	$20	1902PB	652	2471 A	T182081B	G/VG	stamp/stamp
9233		$5	1929T1		B000065A		VF+	
9233		$5	1929T1		F000131A		AU	
9233		$5	1929T1		E000561A		VG/F	
9233		$5	1929T1		B000685A		F	
9233		$5	1929T1		F000853A		VG	
9233		$5	1929T1		C001096A		F/VF	
9233		$10	1929T1		D000199A		F/VF	
9233		$10	1929T1		C000346A		VF	
9233		$10	1929T1		B000360A		XF	
9233		$10	1929T1		C000495A		VF	
9233		$10	1929T1		B000685A		F/VF	
9233		$10	1929T1		E000693A		VF	
9233		$10	1929T1		B000704A		F	
9233		$20	1929T1		B000093A		F	
9233		$20	1929T1		B000109A		F	
9233		$20	1929T1		F000109A		F	Foxing
9233		$20	1929T1		F000111A		VF/XF	
9233		$20	1929T1		F000115A		F/VF	
9233		$20	1929T1		D000137A		VF	
9233		$20	1929T1		E000156A		VG/F	
9233		$20	1929T1		E000170A		VF+	Higgins Mus.
9233		$20	1929T1		C000554A		AU	
9233		$5	1929T2		A000009		XF	

THE FIRST NATIONAL BANK OF ELKADER   20 L   12 S
1815   CLAYTON

Elkader was first settled in 1836 and became the county seat in 1860. However, it wasn't until a narrow gauge railroad penetrated the surrounding hills that several leading citizens decided to form a bank in the town. The First National Bank of Elkader received its charter on May 11, 1871 and commenced business on May 24. One of the bank's first acts was to obtain a 5,000 pound safe brought up the river from Dubuque. Then construction was started on a new stone building to house the bank (see 1872 photo). The building was enlarged and remodeled in 1916-1917. When the bank liquidated on Nov. 12, 1931 it merged with the two year old Elkader State Bank to become the Central State Bank & Trust Co. All checks and certificates of deposit from the former banks were honored. After the bank's closure in 1931, the Post Office occupied the building, followed by other businesses. The building still stands with much of its 1917 appearance.

Chartered in 1871. Placed in voluntary liquidation on November 12, 1931; capital of $50,000. Succeeded by The Central State Bank & Trust Co. of Elkader. William Larrabee was the 12th Governor of the State of Iowa from 1886 to 1890 and signed notes as the bank President during this period.
Officers: Pres. Henry B Carter 1872-82, William Larrabee 1883-1903, Realto E Price 1904-23, CC Oehring 1924-29, VT Price 1930-32; **VP** Anton Kramer 1896-1901, RE Price 1902-23, William Larrabee 1904-09, Joseph Lamm 1910-13, CC Oehring 1920-23, RE Price 1924, VT Price 1925-29, HL Swenson 1930-31, John O Glesne 1930-31; **Cash.** Frank H Carter 1872-81, Henry Meyer 1883-97, AJ Carpenter 1898-1923, HL Swenson 1924-31; **AC** GM Gifford 1896, 1909, Geo Witt 1902-08, JF Maley 1910-14, HL Swenson 1920-23, WH Schmidt 1920-21, EF Seifert 1927-31, Marjorie Richardson 1930-31

	Ser #	# Notes
First Charter, Original Issue		
1-1-1-2	1-2700	10,800
5-5-5-5	1-2725	10,900
First Charter, Series of 1875		
5-5-5-5	1-4040	16,160
Second Charter, Brown Backs		
5-5-5-5	1-1632	6,528
10-10-10-20	1-1380	5,520
Second Charter, Date Back		
10-10-10-20	1-180	720
Third Charter, Date Back, Blue Seal		
10-10-10-20	1-1150	4,600
Third Charter, Plain Back, Blue Seal		
10-10-10-20	1151-2800	6,600
1929, Type I		
6-10's	1-298	1,788
6-20's	1-68	408

Total amount of circulation issued = $425,480. Amount of large outstanding at close = $4,382. Amount of small outstanding at close = $18,110.
61,828 Large   2,196 Small   64,024 Total

1815	-	$1	ORIG	?	175 B	C535022	VG	
1815	-	$5	1875	401	2933 C	U344080	VG	
1815	-	$5	1875	401	3296 C	U344443	VG	
1815	-	$5	1875	401	3933 B	Z517916	XF+	pen/pen
1815	-	$5	1875	401	3966 E	Z517949	VF	Grinnell # 3262, Higgins Mus.
1815	-	$5	1875	401	3966 F	Z517949	VF	pen/pen
1815	-	$5	1875	401	3966 H	Z517949	VF	
1815	-	$5	1875	401	3968 H	Z517951	XF/AU	pen/pen
1815	M	$10	1902DB	619	1004 B	V217130A	VF	
1815	M	$10	1902DB	619	1012 B	V217138A	F	pen ac/pen vp
1815	M	$10	1902PB	627	1170 B	B789587D	VF	Higgins Mus.
1815	M	$10	1902PB	627	1708 E	E704420E	VG	
1815	M	$10	1902PB	627	1944 C	U7245E	VG	Bleached
1815	M	$10	1902PB	627	2037 A	E512959H	VG	pen/pen
1815	-	$10	1902PB	627	2351 A	?	G	
1815	M	$20	1902PB	653	234 A	A475746K	VG/F	
1816	M	$20	1902PB	653	1951 A	E512873H	VG	
1815	-	$20	1902PB	653	2234 A	A475746K	VG/F	
1815	-	$20	1902PB	653	2395 A	2395 A	XF	pen/pen
1815	-	$20	1902PB	653	2532 A	2532 A	VG	
1815		$10	1929T1		A000065A		VG	
1815		$10	1929T1		E000178A		VG/F	
1815		$10	1929T1		A000201A		VF	
1815		$10	1929T1		F000262A		F	Ink
1815		$10	1929T1		D000282A		F	
1815		$20	1929T1		D000009A		F	
1815		$20	1929T1		E000018A		VG	
1815		$20	1929T1		D000041A		F	
1815		$20	1929T1		E000046A		VG	
1815		$20	1929T1		B000047A		XF	
1815		$20	1929T1		F000059A		VF+	Higgins Mus.
1815		$20	1929T1		D000066A		CU	

THE FIRST NATIONAL BANK OF ELLIOTT   4 L   6 S
6857   MONTGOMERY

Organized on June 15, 1903 with a capital of $25,000. Succeeded The Bank of Elliott. Placed in receivership on July 2, 1931; capital of $50,000.
Officers: Pres. FM Byrkit 1904-05, JW Manker 1906-09, HE Manker 1910-11, OJ Powell 1912-31; **VP** JW Manker 1904-05, WH Kennedy 1907-30, WL DeWitt 1931; **Cash.** HE Manker 1904-09, CF Cadwell 1910-31; **AC** JJ Manker 1904-05, JM Logan 1907, CF Cadwell 1909, FH Osborn 1911-14, DH Fortune 1920-23, DC Perley 1925-30

	Ser #	# Notes
Third Charter, Red Seal		
10-10-10-20	1-520	2,080
Third Charter, Date Back, Blue Seal		
10-10-10-20	1-2250	9,000
Third Charter, Plain Back, Blue Seal		
10-10-10-20	2251-4201	7,804
1929, Type I		
6-10's	1-263	1,578
6-20's	1-64	384

Total amount of circulation issued = $259,510. Amount outstanding at close = $20,000. Amount of large outstanding on July 1, 1931 = $3,110.
18,884 Large   1,962 Small   20,846 Total

6857	M	$10	1902DB	616	440 E	A987719	F	Higgins Mus.
6857	M	$10	1902DB	616	1936 E	B917468B	?	
6857	M	$10	1902DB	616	2113 E	B917645B	VG/F	pen/pen
6857	M	$10	1902PB	624	2634 F	E705046E	G	
6857		$10	1929T1		F000003A		VG+	Higgins Mus.
6857		$10	1929T1		F000044A		F	
6857		$10	1929T1		E000134A		G/VG	
6857		$10	1929T1		B000219A		F	
6857		$10	1929T1		D000243A		F	
6857		$20	1929T1		E000047A		F	

THE EMMETSBURG NATIONAL BANK   4 L
8035   PALO ALTO

Organized on December 23, 1905 with a capital of $50,000. Placed in receivership on March 11, 1921; capital of $50,000. Reason for failure: local depression.
Officers: Pres. ML Brown 1906-15, WT Branagan 1916-18, JH Wilson 1919, Starr G Wilson 1920; **VP** Geo E Pearsall 1907-13, WI Branagan 1914, Martin Ausland 1920; **Cash.** WJ Brown 1906-14, JH Wilson 1915-18, HL Irvine 1919, LH Jackson 1920; **AC** PS Brown 1907-11, Earl Brown 1913-14, WR Eagan

1920
Third Charter, Red Seal   Ser #   # Notes
10-10-10-20   1-1100   4,400
Third Charter, Date Back, Blue Seal
10-10-10-20   1-1250   5,000
Sheets numbered 1 to 1050 were 02-08 backs. Sheets numbered 1051 to 1250 were delivered on February 27, but not marked as to type. Sheets numbered. 1251 to 1870 were plain back blue seals.
Third Charter, Plain Back, Blue Seal
10-10-10-20   1251-1870   2,480
Total amount issued = $148,500. Amount outstanding at close = $22,000.
11,880 Large   0 Small   11,880 Total

8035	M	$10 1902RS	614	609 A	V210272	F	
8035	M	$10 1902RS	614	948 C	V210611	F	
8035	M	$10 1902DB	617	511 D	K710637	F	Higgins Mus.
8035	M	$20 1902DB	643	760 B	K710886	XF	Higgins Mus.

THE FIRST NATIONAL BANK OF EMMETSBURG   14 L
3337   PALO ALTO

Chartered in 1885. Succeeded Ormsby Bros. & Co. Placed in voluntary liquidation on June 10, 1927; capital of 80,000. Succeeded by #13059.
Officers: Pres. ES Ormsby 1885-96, EB Soper 1897-1918; **VP** EB Soper 1896, JJ Watson 1900-12, Jas Dunigan 1903-11, MF Kerwick 1913-14; **Cash.** AL Ormsby 1885, JJ Watson 1887-94, AH Keller 1894—7, Robt Laughlin 1907-18; **AC** OW Hodgkinson 1896, Robt Laughlin 1902-04, Leo C Streator 1909-11, Geo A Freeman 1913-14

Second Charter, Brown Backs   Ser #   # Notes
5-5-5-5   1-4675   18,700
10-10-10-20   1-600   2,400
Third Charter, Red Seal
10-10-10-20   1-1400   5,600
Third Charter, Date Back, Blue Seal
10-10-10-20   1-4900   19,600
Third Charter, Plain Back, Blue Seal
10-10-10-20   4901-12819   31,676
Total amount of issued = $834,450. Amount outstanding at close = $79,000.
77,976 Large   0 Small   77,976 Total

3337		$5 1882BB	467	2659 ?	N921372	VG	
3337		$5 1882BB	467	3995 C	Z105888	G	Higgins Mus.
3337	M	$10 1902DB	616	342 F	H633240	F	Ink; margin tear
3337	M	$20 1902DB	642	2817 B	H566120A	VG	stamp/stamp
3337	M	$10 1902PB	624	6291 F	Z507234B	F	Higgins Mus.
3337	M	$10 1902PB	624	8329 F	Z967331D	F	
3337	M	$10 1902PB	624	9544 F	V5396E	VG	gone/gone Soiled
3337	M	$10 1902PB	624	9674 E	V5526E	VG/F	
3337	M	$10 1902PB	624	10952 D	K871644H	VG/F	
3337	-	$10 1902PB	624	12376 D	12376 D	VG	faded/faded
3337	-	$10 1902PB	624	12492 F	12492 F	VG	
3337	M	$20 1902PB	650	8784 B	H933246E	F	stamp/stamp
3337	M	$20 1902PB	650	9106 B	H933568E	F	stamp/stamp
3337	-	$20 1902PB	650	11180 B	X54492H	Fr	Pieces missing

THE COMMERCIAL NATIONAL BANK OF ESSEX   15 L   9 S
5803   PAGE

Organized on April 22, 1901 with a capital of $50,000. Chartered in May 1901; succeeded The Commercial State Bank. Placed in receivership on May 5, 1931; capital of $50,000. Reason for failure: incompetent management & local depression.
Officers: Pres. RA Sanderson 1901-04, A Wenstrand 1905, Levi Baker 1906-19, Abe Lindburg 1920-28, J Fridolph 1929-30; **VP** A Hallberg 1902-03, Oliver Bussard 1904, CJ Johnson 1907-11, Abe Lindburg 1913-19, J Fridolph 1920-27, 1928-29; WJ Knox 1920-27, AT Johnson 1929-30; **Cash.** TK Elliott 1901-03, JF Ekeroth 1904, EG Day 1905, Arthur Lindburg 1906-26, Victor Freed 1926-31; **AC** JJ Ekeroth 1902-03, A Lindburg 1904, CW Fredrickson 1907-30, ML Sederburg 191423, Joe Lindburg 1927, HC Overbeck 1929-30

Second Charter, Brown Backs   Ser #   # Notes
10-10-10-20   1-3000   12,000
Second Charter, Date Back
10-10-10-20   1-3550   14,200
Sheets numbered 1 to 3300 were 82-08 backs. Sheets numbered 3301 to 3550 were delivered on September 28, but not marked as to type. Sheets numbered 3551 to 5142 are denominational back notes.
Second Charter, Value Back
10-10-10-20   3551-5142   6,368
Third Charter, Plain Back, Blue Seal
10-10-10-20   1-4050   16,200
1929, Type I
6-10's   1-640   3,840
6-20's   1-192   1,152
Total amount of circulation issued = $671,040. Amount of large outstanding at close = $8,170. Amount of small outstanding at close = $41,830.

48,768 Large   4,992 Small   53,760 Total

5803	M	$10 1882BB	490	1324 C	D283690D	?	
5803	M	$20 1882BB	504	2259 A	N765832N	F	
5803	M	$10 1882DB	545	2173 E	M231051	VG/F	Higgins Mus.
5803	M	$10 1882DB	545	2886 F	R56934	VG	gone/gone
5803	M	$20 1882DB	555	3136 B	R57184	G	gone/gone Ink
5803	M	$20 1882VB	581	3846 C	T863304	VF	
5803	M	$20 1882VB	581	4297 B	U621575	XF/AU	ac Higgins Mus.
5803		$10 1902PB	633	1678 B	N390780H	VF	
5803	-	$10 1902PB	633	3168 B	3168 B	VG	stamp sigs ac
5803	-	$10 1902PB	633	3171 A	3171 A	F	stamp sigs ac
5803	-	$10 1902PB	633	3351 B	3351 B	VF+	
5803	M	$20 1902PB	659	864 A	K581426E	F	
5803	-	$20 1902PB	659	2797 A	2797 A	F/VF	stamp/stamp
5803	-	$20 1902PB	659	3630 A	3630 A	VF	pen/pen vp
5803	-	$20 1902PB	659	3653 A	3653 A	F/VF	pen/pen vp
5803		$10 1929T1		B000029A		VF	
5803		$10 1929T1		D000269A		XF/AU	
5803		$10 1929T1		F000379A		?	Higgins Mus.
5803		$10 1929T1		A000557A		VG	
5803		$20 1929T1		B000048A		VF	
5803		$20 1929T1		C000115A		F	
5803		$20 1929T1		E000143A		F	
5803		$20 1929T1		C000160A		?	
5803		$20 1929T1		F000185A		VF	

THE FIRST NATIONAL BANK OF ESSEX   17 L   26 S
5738   PAGE

Chartered in March 1901 with a capital of $25,000.
Officers: Pres. A Brodeen 1901-28, RA Sanderson 1929-35; **VP** HI Foskett 1902, NC Nelson 1903-13, RA Sanderson 1920-28, GJ Liljedahl 1929-35; **Cash.** GJ Liljedahl 1903-29, CJ Liljedahl 1930-35; **AC** JP Nye 1902-06, John GE Carlson 1909-30, JJ Exeroth 1913-22, CJ Liljedahl 1924-28, De Los Quist 1931-35

Second Charter, Brown Backs   Ser #   # Notes
10-10-10-20   1-1300   5,200
Second Charter, Date Back
10-10-10-20   1-3490   13,960
Second Charter, Value Back
10-10-10-20   3491-5297   7,228
Third Charter, Plain Back, Blue Seal
10-10-10-20   1-4352   17,408
1929, Type I
6-10's   1-1212   7,272
6-20's   1-312   1,872
1929, Type II
10's   1-36   36
Total amount of circulation issued = $657,970. Amount of large outstanding in 1935 = $2,790. Amount of small outstanding in 1935 = $22,210.
43,796 Large   9,180 Small   52,976 Total

5738	M	$20 1882DB	555	363 B	D236993	VG	ac Higgins Mus.
5738	M	$20 1882DB	555	2917 B	N720895	VG	Ink
5738	M	$10 1882VB	577	4349 D	U615217	F/VF	pen ac/stamp
5738	M	$10 1882VB	577	4501 F	?	VG	
5738	M	$10 1882VB	577	5117 E	V213855	F	faded/faded
5738	M	$20 1882VB	581	3850 B	T862828	F/VF	pen/stamp
5738	M	$10 1902PB	633	1443 C	D506285H	VG	
5738	M	$10 1902PB	633	1676 C	H765138H	?	
5738	M	$10 1902PB	633	1682 C	H765144H	VG	faded/faded
5738		$10 1902PB	633	2861 A	?	VG/F	
5738	-	$10 1902PB	633	3416 A	3416 A	F/VF	Higgins Mus.
5738	-	$10 1902PB	633	3797 B	3797 B	F/VF	stamp/stamp
5738	M	$20 1902PB	659	523 A	H179035E	F/VF	lt. stamp sigs
5738		$20 1902PB	659	1899 A	?	F	
5738	-	$20 1902PB	659	3078 A	3078 A	VG	gone/gone
5738	-	$20 1902PB	659	3181 A	3181 A	VG	gone/gone
5738	-	$20 1902PB	659	4147 A	4147 A	F	
5738		$10 1929T1		C000070A		F+	
5738		$10 1929T1		A000126A		VF	
5738		$10 1929T1		D000136A		F	
5738		$10 1929T1		D000405A		F	
5738		$10 1929T1		B000700A		VG+	
5738		$10 1929T1		C000829A		F/VF	
5738		$10 1929T1		E000877A		VF	
5738		$10 1929T1		A000944A		VG	
5738		$10 1929T1		B000947A		G/VG	
5738		$10 1929T1		B000997A		VG	
5738		$10 1929T1		D001032A		VG	
5738		$10 1929T1		F001056A		VG	Some foxing
5738		$10 1929T1		C001082A		VG	
5738		$10 1929T1		D001126A		F	

5738	$20	1929T1	C000096A	VG/F	
5738	$20	1929T1	D000110A	F	
5738	$20	1929T1	D000136A	F	
5738	$20	1929T1	B000142A	VG	
5738	$20	1929T1	A000152A	?	
5738	$20	1929T1	F000172A	VG	
5738	$20	1929T1	D000195A	?	
5738	$20	1929T1	C000196A	XF	Higgins Mus.
5738	$20	1929T1	E000289A	?	
5738	$20	1929T1	F000296A	VF	
5738	$20	1929T1	E000305A	?	
5738	$20	1929T1	F000308A	VG	

THE FIRST NATIONAL BANK OF ESTHERVILLE 6 L
4700   EMMET

Organized on January 23, 1892 with a capital of $50,000. Succeeded The Emmett County State Bank. Placed in receivership on February 27, 1926; capital of $100,000. Reason for failure: local depression.

Officers: Pres. FE Allen 1892-98, EB Sofer 1899-14, John P Kirby 1915-25; **VP** Webb Vincent 1896-1911, John P Kirby 1913-14, MK Whelan 1920-25; **Cash.** John P Kirby 1893-1914, RH Miller 1916-20, CB Graham 1922, Don J Kirby 1925; **AC** WA Streater 1902-03, FH Allen 1907-13, BA Gronstal 1914, RH Miller 1914, Don J Kirby 1922-24, RS Knight 1922-25, Geo Lorimer, Jr. 1922, AA Herrick 1923-26

Second Charter, Brown Backs	Ser #	# Notes
50-100	1-663	1,326

Second Charter, Date Back
	Ser #	# Notes
50-100	1-898	1,796

Third Charter, Date Back, Blue Seal
	Ser #	# Notes
50-50-50-100	1-1615	6,460

Total amount issued = $637,900. Amount outstanding at close = $97,000.
9,582 Large   0 Small   9,582 Total

4700	M	$50 1882DB	559	898 B	A134059	F	Higgins Mus.
4700	M	$50 1902DB	671	451 A	A254205	F	
4700	M	$50 1902DB	671	633 C	A698027	F	Higgins Mus.
4700	M	$50 1902DB	671	813 C	A774723	VG/F	light pen/pen
4700	M	$50 1902DB	671	1389 C	A974683	G	pen/pen
4700	M	$100 1902DB	693	719 A	A698113	F	

THE FIRST NATIONAL BANK OF EVERLY   11 L   6 S
7828   CLAY

Organized on June 17, 1905 with a capital of $25,000. Placed in conservatorship on March 27, 1933. Placed in receivership on August 3, 1933; capital of $25,000.
Officers: Pres. AW Sleeper 1905-08, HE Jones 1909-11, Peter Kettelsen 1912-31, John AM Heuck 1931-32, FP Ketelson 1933; **VP** Peter Ketelsen 1907-11, John Lorensen 1913-22, Lewis Scharnberg 1914-33, John AM Heuck 1923-31, AP Cronk 1931-33; **Cash.** Lewis Scharnberg 1905-13, AP Cronk 1914-31, CM Cronk 1931-33; **AC** WH Sleeper, Jr. 1907-08, EF Scharnberg 1909-12, GD Cronk 1913-14, CM Cronk 1920-31, E Brugman 1920-33, CH Sartorius 1920-22

Third Charter, Red Seal
	Ser #	# Notes
10-10-10-20	1-500	2,000

Third Charter, Date Back, Blue Seal
	Ser #	# Notes
10-10-10-20	1-1730	6,920

Third Charter, Plain Back, Blue Seal
	Ser #	# Notes
10-10-10-20	1731-4957	12,908

1929, Type I
	Ser #	# Notes
6-10's	1-547	3,282
6-20's	1-110	660

Total amount of circulation issued = $318,870. Amount outstanding at close = $25,000. Amount of large outstanding on July 27, 1933 = $2,050.
21,828 Large   3,942 Small   25,770 Total

7828	M	$10 1902DB	616	541 F	U255684	VG/F	
7828	M	$10 1902DB	616	793 E	Z927546	F	pen/pen
7828	M	$10 1902DB	616	964 F	E100564A	VG/F	pen/pen Edge nick
7828	M	$20 1902DB	642	1635 B	B904547B	VF	pen/stamp
7828	M	$20 1902DB	642	1676 B	B904588B	VG	pen/stamp
7828	M	$10 1902PB	624	3579 D	D956501H	XF	Higgins Mus.
7828	M	$10 1902PB	624	3589 E	D956511H	VG	
7828	-	$10 1902PB	624	4264 D	4264 D	VG	
7828	-	$10 1902PB	624	4578 D	4578 D	VG	
7828	-	$10 1902PB	624	4884 F	4884 F	VF	weak sigs
7828	M	$20 1902PB	650	2686 B	V589438D	F	pen/stamp Stained; paper pull on face
7828		$10 1929T1		E000045A		XF	Higgins Mus.
7828		$10 1929T1		A000115A		VF	
7828		$10 1929T1		B000328A		XF	
7828		$10 1929T1		F000359A		VG/F	
7828		$10 1929T1		C000482A		VG/F	
7828		$20 1929T1		E000036A		VG/F	

THE FIRST NATIONAL BANK OF EXIRA   7 L   5 S
6870   AUDUDON

Organized on June 11, 1903 with a capital of $35,000. Succeeded The Farmers & Merchants Bank. Placed in conservatorship on April 3, 1933. Placed in receivership on November 3, 1933; capital of $35,000.
Officers: Pres. FM Leet 1904, Jas E Bruce 1905-10, Soren Madsen 1911-32; **VP** A Boysen 1904, FM Hensley 1907, A Voorhees 1909, CW Bruce 1909-10, Oscar Hunt 1911-14, TO Hester 1920-23, Chas Hensley 1920-32; **Cash.** JE McGuire 1904, WE Wissler 1905, A Voorhees 1906-07, MB Nelson 1908-09, AW Harvey 1910-11, JM Carlson 1912-17, CH Townsend 1918-20, HM Mortensen 1922-27, HP Hansen, Jr. 1928-33; **AC** WE Wissler 1904, AW Harvey 1907-09, FC Wilken 1909, Glen E Hunt 1913-14, Hans Hansen 1922-27, Iva Ancraux 1924-27, EC Rasmussen 1928-32

Third Charter, Red Seal
	Ser #	# Notes
10-10-10-20	1-525	2,100

Third Charter, Date Back, Blue Seal
	Ser #	# Notes
10-10-10-20	1-860	3,440

Sheets numbered 1 to 800 were 02-08 backs. The sheets numbered 801 to 860 were not marked as to type. Sheets numbered 861 to 1634 were plain backs.

Third Charter, Plain Back, Blue Seal
	Ser #	# Notes
10-10-10-20	861-1634	3,096

1929, Type I
	Ser #	# Notes
6-10's	1-215	1,290
6-20's	1-41	246

Total amount of circulation issued = $125,770. Amount of large outstanding at close = $920. Amount of small outstanding at close = $8,080.
8,636 Large   1,536 Small   10,172 Total

6870	M	$10 1902DB	616	622 E	T628590A	VF/XF	pen Higgins Mus.
6870	M	$20 1902DB	642	112 B	K729308	VG	
6870	M	$10 1902PB	624	1094 F	X202246E	F	vp Stained
6870	-	$10 1902PB	624	1314 F	T510866H	F	pen/pen
6870	-	$10 1902PB	624	1480 D	1480 D	F	pen/pen
6870	M	$20 1902PB	650	870 B	U859132D	VG	
6870	-	$20 1902PB	650	1341 B	B304933K	F	pen/pen
6870		$10 1929T1		F000101A		F	
6870		$10 1929T1		E000156A		?	Bayard
6870		$10 1929T1		E000160A		XF	
6870		$20 1929T1		B000026A		?	
6870		$20 1929T1		E000031A		VF+	Higgins Mus.

THE FIRST NATIONAL BANK OF FAIRFIELD   32 L   42 S
1475   JEFFERSON

The First National Bank of Fairfield is one of two Iowa banks with reported notes bearing Bruce/Jordan Treasury signatures.
Organized on May 9, 1865 with a capital of $50,000. Placed in conservatorship on March 25, 1933. Placed in voluntary liquidation on April 26, 1934; capital of $100,000. Succeeded by #13991.
Officers: Pres. James F Wilson 1867-94, BS McElhinny 1895-1905, Rollin J Wilson 1906-28, WH Bangs 1929-34; **VP** John A Spielman 1896, Rollin J Wilson 1900-05, JA Spielman 1907-14, WH Bangs 1920-28, LJ Marcy 1920, Leroy Williams 1930-34; **Cash.** Samuel C Farmer 1867-73, George D Temple 1874-85, BS McElhinny 1887-94, John Daviel 1895, Frank Light 1896-1914, Frank S Boies 1915-18, AR Carlson 1919, WP Starr 1920, 1922-34; **AC** FJL Black 1896, Samuel L Dana 1902, RF Wilson 1903-14, EG Linder 1920-28, WP Starr 1922, GL Peebler 1922, HA Berg 1925-34, Glenn A Sherman 1930-34, Glenn A Sherman 1930-34

First Charter, Original Issue
	Ser #	# Notes
1-1-1-2	1-5603	22,412

5-5-5-5		1-4700	18,800	
10-10-10-20		1-1730	6,920	

First Charter, Series of 1875

5-5-5-5	1-2405	9,620	
10-10-10-20	1-1370	5,480	

Second Charter, Brown Backs

5-5-5-5	1-2344	9,376	
10-10-10-20	1-2634	10,536	

Third Charter, Red Seal

10-10-10-20	1-2000	8,000

Third Charter, Date Back, Blue Seal

10-10-10-20	1-6400	25,600

Third Charter, Plain Back, Blue Seal

10-10-10-20	6401-18454	48,216

1929, Type I

6-10's	1-2208	13,248
6-20's	1-570	3,420

1929, Type II

10's	1-869	869
20's	1-135	135

Total amount of circulation issued = $1,738,665. Amount of large outstanding at close = $7,750. Amount of small outstanding at close = $92,250.

164,960 Large   17,672 Small   182,632 Total

Bank		Series	Plate	Sheet	Serial	Grade	Notes
1475	- $1	ORIG 380	4670 C		E499255	Fr/G	pen/pen
1475	- $1	ORIG 380	5040 A		E499625	VG	
1475	- $1	ORIG 380	5080 A		E499665	G	pen/pen
1475	- $2	ORIG 387	4675 A		E499260	G/VG	Ink
1475	- $2	ORIG 387	4816 A		E499401	?	
1475	- $2	ORIG 387	4823 A		E499408	F	
1475	- $10	1882BB 481	1728 A		R276851	VG	
1475	M $10	1902DB 616	1153 D		E711068	F	
1475	M $10	1902DB 616	6128 E		K354394B	VG	pen/pen
1475	M $20	1902DB 642	2914 B		Y666221	F	
1475	M $20	1902DB 642	4481 B		N327843A	G	Davenport B&T
1475	M $20	1902DB 642	4614 B		N327976A	VG	nice sigs
1475	M $10	1902PB 624	7820 E		B340967D	VG/F	
1475	$10	1902PB 624	10565 F		?	VG	
1475	$10	1902PB 624	12357 F		Z545069E	F/VF	
1475	$10	1902PB 624	13222 D		H618274H	F	
1475	$10	1902PB 624	13276 E		H618328H	AU	Higgins Mus.
1475	$10	1902PB 624	14499 D		V680851H	VG	
1475	$10	1902PB 624	14711 D		A780153K	F	pen/stamp
1475	- $10	1902PB 624	15233 D	15233 D		?	
1475	- $10	1902PB 624	15500 D	15500 D		F	
1475	- $10	1902PB 624	15525 D	15525 D		VF	pen ac/stamp
1475	- $10	1902PB 624	15604 E	15604 E		VG	faded stamps
1475	- $10	1902PB 624	15629 E	15629 E		F	nice sigs
1475	- $10	1902PB 624	15788 F	15788 F		F	
1475	- $10	1902PB 624	16274 E	16274 E		XF	pen/stamp
1475	- $10	1902PB 624	16365 E	16365 E		F+	pen/stamp
1475	M $20	1902PB 650	7993 B		B341140D	F	pen/pen Stained
1475	$20	1902PB 650	12687 B		Z545399	VG/F	
1475	$20	1902PB 650	14234 B		V680586H	VF	
1475	- $20	1902PB 650	16493 B	16493 B		VF	Davenport B&T
1475	- $20	1902PB 650	17597 B	17597 B		G/VG	
1475	$10	1929T1			F000109A	VG	
1475	$10	1929T1			C000827A	VG	
1475	$10	1929T1			B000876A	G	
1475	$10	1929T1			E000916A	VG/F	
1475	$10	1929T1			E001140A	XF	
1475	$10	1929T1			A001252A	VG/F	
1475	$10	1929T1			B001416A	F	
1475	$10	1929T1			D001464A	F/VF	
1475	$10	1929T1			D001638A	AU	
1475	$10	1929T1			E001638A	AU	
1475	$10	1929T1			E001639A	AU	
1475	$10	1929T1			E001640A	AU	
1475	$10	1929T1			E001641A	AU	
1475	$10	1929T1			E001642A	AU	
1475	$10	1929T1			F001643A	CU	
1475	$10	1929T1			C001738A	CU	
1475	$10	1929T1			E001743A	AU	
1475	$10	1929T1			E001744A	AU	
1475	$10	1929T1			E001746A	CU	
1475	$10	1929T1			F001854A	VF	
1475	$10	1929T1			A001904A	F	
1475	$10	1929T1			D001917A	VF	
1475	$10	1929T1			E001935A	F	Ink on back
1475	$10	1929T1			B001941A	VG	
1475	$10	1929T1			F001975A	XF+	Higgins Mus.
1475	$10	1929T1			E002084A	VF	
1475	$10	1929T1			D002174A	VG/F	
1475	$20	1929T1			E000025A	?	
1475	$20	1929T1			?000078A	VF/XF	
1475	$20	1929T1			C000148A	F	
1475	$20	1929T1			B000155A	F+	
1475	$20	1929T1			E000426A	F	
1475	$20	1929T1			C000429A	AU	
1475	$20	1929T1			A000448A	CU	
1475	$20	1929T1			D000455A	CU	
1475	$20	1929T1			E000460A	AU	
1475	$20	1929T1			B000471A	F+	
1475	$20	1929T1			B000488A	VF	
1475	$20	1929T1			B000489A	F+	
1475	$20	1929T1			E000516A	F	
1475	$20	1929T1			B000527A	VF	
1475	$10	1929T2			A000332	VF	

THE FAIRFIELD NATIONAL BANK   2 L
8986   **JEFFERSON**

Organized on December 24, 1907 with a capital of $60,000. Placed in voluntary liquidation on June 1, 1922; capital of $60,000. Absorbed by The Iowa Loan & Trust Company of Fairfield. Placed in receivership on August 30, 1923. Reason for failure: incompetent management.

Officers: Pres. DC Bradley 1908-13, RB Louden 1914-20; **VP** RB Louden 1909-13, Ellsworth Turney 1914, L Thoma 1920; **Cash.** SK West 1908-13, Roscoe P Thoma 1914-15, FJL Black 1916, JH McCarty 1917, CU Emry 1919, CN Emry 1919-20; **AC** Frank S West 1909-14, Elmer Ramsey 1920

Third Charter, Red Seal	Ser #	# Notes
10-10-10-20	1-1800	7,200
Third Charter, Date Back, Blue Seal		
10-10-10-20	1-3540	14,160
Third Charter, Plain Back, Blue Seal		
10-10-10-20	3541-6534	11,976

Total amount issued = $416,700. Amount outstanding at close = $57,100.

33,336 Large   0 Small   33,336 Total

8986	M $10	1902DB 618	1273 F		Z420251	XF	Higgins Mus.
8986	M $10	1902PB 626	6407 F		K383699E	VG	

THE FIRST NATIONAL BANK OF FARMINGTON   7 L
5579   **VAN BUREN**

Chartered on September 19, 1900. Placed in voluntary liquidation on September 6, 1926; capital of $100,000. Succeeded by The First Trust & Savings Bank of Farmington.

Officers: Pres. WB Seeley 1901-25; **VP** Kirk Meek 1902-07, John Lightfoot 1909-10, BF Ketcham 1911-25; **Cash.** BF Ketcham 1901-10, M Harnagel 1911-20, EH Wiegner 1922-25; **AC** WB Welch 1902, M Harnagel 1903-10, EH Wiegner 1911-20

Second Charter, Brown Backs	Ser #	# Notes
10-10-10-20	1-1100	4,400
Second Charter, Date Back		
10-10-10-20 (1381-1480 type uncertain)	1-1480	5,920
Second Charter, Value Back		
10-10-10-20	1481-2174	2,776
Third Charter, Plain Back, Blue Seal		
10-10-10-20	1-990	3,960

Total amount issued = $213,200. Amount outstanding at close = $25,000.

17,056 Large   0 Small   17,056 Total

5579	M $20	1882BB 504	521 A		H374113H	F	Stained
5579	M $10	1882DB 545	416 F		D292246	F	
5579	M $20	1882DB 555	675 B		K138373	VG/F	pen/pen
5579	M $20	1882VB 581	2115 B		U891623	AU+	Higgins Mus.
5579	M $20	1882VB 581	2116 B		U891624	XF	
5579	M $10	1902PB 633	224 A		X863426D	XF	Higgins Mus.
5579	M $10	1902PB 633	883 B		N181900E	F/VF	pen/pen Tight top

THE FIRST NATIONAL BANK OF FARNHAMVILLE   11 L   12 S
11907   **CALHOUN**

Organized on December 6, 1920 with a capital of $40,000. Placed in conservatorship on March 29, 1933. Placed in receivership on July 28, 1933; capital of $40,000. Reason for failure: not available from reports.

Officers: Pres. Chas Beacham 1922-33; **VP** HW Beacham 1922-33; **Cash.** MB Flesher 1922-24, Herbert Gustofson 1925-33; **AC** Herbert Gustofson 1922-24, CR Reynolds 1925-33

Third Charter, Plain Back, Blue Seal	Ser #	# Notes
10-10-10-20	1-4051	16,204
1929, Type I		
6-5's	1-3144	18,864
6-10's	1-156	936
6-20's	1-54	324

Total amount of circulation issued = $312,710. Amount of large outstanding in 1933 = $2,210. Amount of small outstanding in 1933 = $37,790.

16,204 Large		20,124 Small		36,328 Total		
11907 -	$10 1902PB	633	1450 A	A140442H	F+	pen/pen vp
11907 -	$10 1902PB	633	3282 A	3282 A	VG	pen/gone
11907 -	$10 1902PB	633	3452 B	3452 B	VG+	
11907M	$20 1902PB	659	384 A	Z680826D	VG	
11907M	$20 1902PB	659	635 A	Z681077D	F	pen Higgins Mus.
11907M	$20 1902PB	659	1033 A	M452410E	F	
11907M	$20 1902PB	659	1574 A	A140566H	VG	
11907 -	$20 1902PB	659	2381 A	Z798273H	F/VF	pen/lt stamp
11907 -	$20 1902PB	659	2908 A	2908 A	Fr/G	
11907 -	$20 1902PB	659	3119 A	3119 A	XF	
11907 -	$20 1902PB	659	3670 A	3670 A	VF	pen/lt stamp
11907	$5 1929T1		C001034A		VG/F	
11907	$5 1929T1		C001473A		F+	
11907	$5 1929T1		F001507A		F	Higgins Mus.
11907	$5 1929T1		D001587A		VF/XF	
11907	$5 1929T1		F001944A		?	
11907	$5 1929T1		F002035A		F	
11907	$5 1929T1		B002221A		F	
11907	$5 1929T1		C002829A		F+	
11907	$10 1929T1		C000102A		?	
11907	$20 1929T1		C000005A		VG	Washed
11907	$20 1929T1		B000039A		VG	
11907	$20 1929T1		B000054A		?	

THE FIRST NATIONAL BANK OF FARRAGUT 5 L 5 S
6700   FREMONT

Chartered on March 14, 1903 with a capital of $30,000. Licensed after the Banking Holiday on April 28, 1933.

Officers: Pres. TH Read 1904-26, William Rogers 1926-35; **VP** RO Henstorf 1909, H Rogers 1910-25, Wm Rogers 1923-26, C Anderson 1926-32; **Cash.** H Rogers 1904-08, Wm Rogers 1909-22, RO Henstorf 1923-35; **AC** Wm Rogers 1904-07, RO Henstorf 1910-22

Third Charter, Red Seal	Ser #	# Notes
10-10-10-20	1-1200	4,800
Third Charter, Date Back, Blue Seal		
5-5-5-5	1-1850	7,400
10-10-10-20	1-1120	4,480
Third Charter, Plain Back, Blue Seal		
5-5-5-5	1851-2589	2,956
10-10-10-20	1121-1608	1,952
1929, Type I		
6-5's	1-354	2,124
6-10's	1-177	1,062
6-20's	1-53	318

Total amount of circulation issued = $219,780. Amount of large outstanding in June 1935 = $1,190. Amount of small outstanding in June 1935 = $8,810.

21,558 Large		3,504 Small		25,092 Total		
6700 M	$5 1902DB	590	1849 D	U950036A	F/VF	pen/pen
6700 M	$10 1902DB	616	881 D	R171835A	G+	stamp/stamp
6700 M	$20 1902DB	642	850 B	R171804A	F	faded/faded
6700 -	$5 1902PB	598	2171 C	R177907H	F	
6700 -	$5 1902PB	598	2584 B	2584 B	F/VF	Higgins Mus.
6700	$5 1929T1		C000312A		XF+	
6700	$10 1929T1		A000045A		?	
6700	$20 1929T1		B000016A		VG/F	Taped edge
6700	$20 1929T1		B000026A		F	
6700	$20 1929T1		E000040A		XF	Higgins Mus.

THE FIRST NATIONAL BANK OF FAYETTE 5 L
9592   FAYETTE

Chartered in November 1909. Placed in voluntary liquidation on June 8, 1928; capital of $25,000. Absorbed by The State Bank of Fayette.

Officers: Pres. WN Clothier 1910-27; **VP** MJ Hartman 1910-14, GS Hartman 1920-27; **Cash.** FE Finch 1910-27; **AC** WD Brown 1913, BE Stansbury 1914, RA Mieke 1920-22, GH Finch 1923-24, RA Mieke 1925-26, AC Hanson 1927

Third Charter, Date Back, Blue Seal	Ser #	# Notes
10-10-10-20	1-1540	6,160

Sheets numbered 1 to 1410 were 02-08 backs. Sheets numbered 1411 to 1540 were delivered on September 24, but not marked as to type. Sheets numbered 1541 to 3198 were plain backs.

Third Charter, Plain Back, Blue Seal	Ser #	# Notes
10-10-10-20	1541-3198	6,632

Total amount issued = $159,900. Amount outstanding at close = $5,950.

12,792 Large		0 Small		12,792 Total		
9592 M	$10 1902DB	618	740 B	E282275A	F+	
9592 M	$10 1902DB	618	882 C	R172446A	VG	
9592 M	$20 1902DB	644	128 A	U58336	AU	pen/pen
9592 M	$10 1902PB	626	2749 B	N316311E	?	
9592 M	$10 1902PB	626	2797 B	V645039E	VF	pen Higgins Mus.

THE FIRST NATIONAL BANK OF FLOYD 5 L 1 S
9821   FLOYD

Organized on June 16, 1910 with a capital of $25,000. Placed in receivership on January 9, 1931; capital of $25,000.

Officers: Pres. Geo H Jackson 1911-15, Robt Hanf 1916-27, Dennis Holland 1928-30; **VP** AS Griffith 1911-14, FB Schaffer 1920-26, Dennis Holland 1927, Robt Hanf 1928-30; **Cash.** OC Kindig 1911-15, Ward E Kepple 1916, HJ Thompson 1917-31; **AC** MM Raymond 1911-13, Ward E Kepple 1914, DE Morse 1920-27, HC Dinkel 1927-29

Third Charter, Date Back, Blue Seal	Ser #	# Notes
10-10-10-20	1-1740	6,960
Third Charter, Plain Back, Blue Seal		
10-10-10-20	1741-4711	11,884
1929, Type I		
6-10's	1-280	1,680
6-20's	1-69	414

Total amount of circulation issued = $260,630. Amount of large outstanding at close = $4,830. Amount of small outstanding at close = $19,870.

18,844 Large		2,094 Small		20,938 Total		
9821 M	$20 1902DB	645	281 A	X528393	VG/F	
9821 M	$10 1902DB	627	2325 G	E669249D	VG	pen/stamp
9821 -	$20 1902PB	653	4130 A	4130 A	AU	Higgins Mus.
9821	$20 1902PB	653	1146 A	1146 A	XF	
9821 -	$20 1902PB	653	4158 A	4158 A	XF+	
9821	$20 1929T1		B000035A		F/VF	Higgins Mus.

THE FIRST NATIONAL BANK OF FONDA 6 L 23 S
6550   POCAHONTAS

Organized on December 15, 1902. Chartered in 1902.

Officers: Pres. James F Toy 1902-33; **VP** Lee S Straight 1903-14, Guy F Wilde 1920-33; **Cash.** LA Rothe 1902-06, JW Martin 1907, Melvin Royer 1909-19, IC Brubacher 1920-27, RC Brogmus 1928-31, LE Eckerson 1932-33; **AC** Melvin Royer 1903, JW Martin 1907, Ira A Moore 1909-11, CA Mains 1913, IC Brubacher 1914, Geo F Patterson 1920, Ned Kearney 1922-23, EC Kearney 1924-26, LE Eckerson 1926-31, WK Wiewel 1933

Third Charter, Red Seal	Ser #	# Notes
10-10-10-20	1-356	1,424
Third Charter, Date Back, Blue Seal		
10-10-10-20	1-2030	8,120
Third Charter, Plain Back, Blue Seal		
10-10-10-20	2031-5111	12,324
1929, Type I		
6-10's	1-440	2,640
6-20's	1-138	828
1929, Type II		
10's	1-577	577
20's	1-103	103

Total amount of circulation issued = $324,140. Amount outstanding in 1934 = $25,000. Amount of large outstanding on July 23, 1935 = $1,270.

21,868 Large		4,148 Small		26,016 Total		
6550 M	$10 1902DB	616	528 F	M944121	CU	
6550 M	$10 1902DB	616	529 E	M944122	AU	pen/gone
6550 M	$10 1902PB	624	2457 F	A528534D	XF	pen/pen vp
6550 M	$10 1902PB	624	3647 F	T527999E	F/VF	Higgins Mus.
6550 -	$10 1902PB	624	4473 D	4473 D	F	vp
6550 -	$20 1902PB	650	4891 B	4891 B	VF	stamp/stamp
6550	$10 1929T1		C000125A		CU	
6550	$10 1929T1		D000200A		?	
6550	$10 1929T1		E000200A		?	
6550	$10 1929T1		E000242A		VF	Higgins Mus.
6550	$10 1929T1		F000269A		CU	
6550	$10 1929T1		D000273A		F/VF	
6550	$10 1929T1		C000283A		AU	
6550	$10 1929T1		E000302A		CU	
6550	$10 1929T1		C000328A		F	
6550	$10 1929T1		C000376A		VF	
6550	$20 1929T1		B000001A		VF	
6550	$20 1929T1		E000011A		F/VF	
6550	$20 1929T1		F000039A		VG+	Soiled
6550	$20 1929T1		B000046A		HG	
6550	$20 1929T1		E000046A		?	
6550	$20 1929T1		C000094A		?	
6550	$20 1929T1		E000120A		F/VF	
6550	$20 1929T1		A000127A		AU+	
6550	$20 1929T1		C000127A		XF+	
6550	$20 1929T1		B000128A		AU	
6550	$20 1929T1		C000128A		XF/AU	
6550	$10 1929T2		A000090		VF+	Higgins Mus.
6550	$10 1929T2		A000341		VG/F	

THE FIRST NATIONAL BANK OF FONTANELLE   9 L   4 S
7061   ADAIR

Chartered in December 1903 with a capital of $25,000. Placed in voluntary liquidation on August 12, 1930; capital of $25,000. Absorbed by The State Savings Bank, Fontanelle.

Officers: Pres. JS Hulbert 1904-10, WF Johnston 1911, JF Bandler 1912-30; **VP** JH Hulbert 1904-10, ER Faurote 1911-30, ED Wallsworth 1914-27; **Cash.** WF Johnston 1904-05, RR Tuttle 1906-07, WA Addison 1908-30; **AC** RR Tuttle 1904-05, GF Faurote 1907-10, RA Bates 1909-10, ED Wallsworth 1911, Mina A Addison 1913-14, L Bess Currier 1920-30, BG Davis 1923-24, CL Butler 1925-30

Third Charter, Red Seal	Ser #	# Notes
5-5-5-5	1-730	2,920
10-10-10-20	1-544	2,176
Third Charter, Date Back, Blue Seal		
5-5-5-5	1-1500	6,000
10-10-10-20	1-1160	4,640
Third Charter, Plain Back, Blue Seal		
5-5-5-5	1501-4642	12,568
10-10-10-20	1161-3112	7,808
1929, Type I		
6-5's	1-258	1,548
6-10's	1-125	750
6-20's	1-16	96

Total amount of circulation issued = $307,400. Amount of large outstanding at close = $6,280. Amount of small outstanding at close = $17,160.

36,112 Large   2,394 Small   38,506 Total

7061	M	$10 1902DB	616	88 F	E988923	VF	pen/pen
7061	M	$10 1902DB	616	494 E	Z502672	F+	pen/pen Washed
7061	M	$5 1902PB	598	2983 H	D291479E	F	ac
7061	M	$10 1902PB	624	1525 F	Z798238B	VG	
7061	M	$10 1902PB	624	1807 F	U39599D	F/VF	pen ac/pen vp
7061	M	$10 1902PB	624	1867 D	Z88929D	VF	pen Higgins Mus.
7061	-	$10 1902PB	624	2870 E	2870 E	VF	pen/pen vp
7061	M	$20 1902PB	650	1909 B	Z88971D	?	
7061	M	$20 1902PB	650	2264 B	E794496H	VG+	pen ac/pen
7061		$5 1929T1		F000114A		VG	Higgins Mus.
7061		$10 1929T1		A000064A		F	
7061		$10 1929T1		C000073A		F+	
7061		$10 1929T1		A000105A		VG	

THE FIRST NATIONAL BANK OF FOREST CITY   10 L
4889   WINNEBAGO

Organized on February 20, 1892 with a capital of $50,000. Succeeded The City Bank (Plummer, Secors & Hanson). Placed in receivership on November 14, 1925; capital of $75,000. Reason for failure: incompetent management and dishonesty.

Officers: Pres. BA Plummer 1893-1919, John Olson 1920-25; **VP** Eugene Secor 1896, MJ Plumer 1900-13, RC Plummer 1913-14, WO Hanson 1920-23, Maude Olson 1920-23, Edwin A Pinckney 1924-25; **Cash.** WO Hanson 1893-98, RC Plummer 1899-1911, John Olson 1912-19, Otto Beckjorden 1920-25, FE Taylor 1925; **AC** RC Plummer 1896, FL Wacholz 1900-10, WC Haugland 1914, Bessie Harstedt 1920-23, Lovillia Harstedt 1920-23, AT Ambrason 1924-25

Second Charter, Brown Backs	Ser #	# Notes
5-5-5-5	1-4055	16,220
10-10-10-20	1-1668	6,672
Second Charter, Date Back		
5-5-5-5	1-1778	7,112
10-10-10-20	1-1207	4,828
Third Charter, Date Back, Blue Seal		
50-50-50-100	1-1247	4,988

Total amount issued = $572,160. Amount outstanding at close = $73,998.

39,820 Large   0 Small   39,820 Total

4889	M	$10 1882BB	485	1347 C	R533623R	G	Bayard, Ink; torn
4889	M	$50 1902DB	672	3 A	A198701	VG	pen UR corner off
4889	M	$50 1902DB	672	369 C	A722073	F	stamp/stamp
4889	M	$50 1902DB	672	516 A	A759886	VG+	
4889	M	$50 1902DB	672	796 B	?	CU	Fed. Res. Bk., San Fran.
4889	M	$50 1902DB	672	866 B	A875068	VF	pen/stamp
4889	M	$50 1902DB	672	1007 A	A934349	F	
4889	M	$50 1902DB	672	1034 C	A934376	XF	ac Higgins Mus.
4889	M	$100 1902DB	694	836 A	?	XF	Fed. Res. Bk., San Fran.
4889	M	$100 1902DB	694	1054 A	A934396	F	Higgins Mus.

THE FOREST CITY NATIONAL BANK   10 L   17 S
5011   WINNEBAGO

Chartered in 1895.

Officers: Pres. CJ Thompson 1895-1903, GS Gilbertson 1904-13, WS Wadsworth 1914, GN Haugen 1915-32, HR Cleophas 1933-35; **VP** CH Kelley 1896-1902, BH Thomas 1903-04, CA Isaacs 1905-13, RW Stephenson 1914, HR Cleophas 1915-32, CH Kelley 1920-32, OE Gunderson 1926-28, HN Rye 1933-35; **Cash.** GS Gilbertson 1895-1902, BH Thomas 1903-04, CA Isaacs 1905-13, RW Stephenson 1914, HR Cleophas 1915-28, HN Rye 1929-35; **AC** CA Isaacs 1896-1904, WO Hanson 1904, MJ Johnson 1907-11, JP Spalla 1913, OE Gunderson 1914-26, Henry Gjellefald 1926-35, CO Nerby 1931-35

Second Charter, Brown Backs	Ser #	# Notes
10-10-10-20	1-2650	10,600
Second Charter, Date Back		
10-10-10-20	1-3076	12,304
Third Charter, Plain Back, Blue Seal		
10-10-10-20	1-5938	23,752
1929, Type I		
6-10's	1-954	5,724
6-20's	1-298	1,788
1929, Type II		
10's	1-1158	1,158
20's	1-294	294

Total amount of circulation issued = $693,660. Amount of large outstanding in June 1935 = $3,640. Amount of small outstanding in June 1935 = $46,360.

46,656 Large   8,964 Small   55,620 Total

5011	-	$10 1882BB	487	495 C	T737050	F	pen; staining
5011	M	$10 1882BB	487	1053 C	E258416E	VG/F	
5011	M	$10 1882DB	542	2866 D	R57574	VF/XF	light stamps
5011	M	$20 1882DB	552	2863 B	R57571	VF+	Higgins Mus.
5011	M	$20 1882DB	552	2867 B	R57575	F/VF	
5011	M	$10 1902PB	632	1022 C	B795609D	VG	faded/faded
5011	M	$10 1902PB	632	3829 C	K306021H	F+	stamp/stamp
5011	-	$10 1902PB	632	4296 A	Z868588H	VG	faded/faded
5011	-	$10 1902PB	632	4805 B	4805 B	F+	Higgins Mus.
5011	-	$20 1902PB	658	5490 A	5490 A		
5011		$10 1929T1		D000039A		VG/F	
5011		$10 1929T1		A000215A		VG	
5011		$10 1929T1		C000432A		VG/F	
5011		$10 1929T1		C000517A		VF	Higgins Mus.
5011		$10 1929T1		B000538A		VF/XF	
5011		$10 1929T1		E000648A		VF	
5011		$10 1929T1		D000713A		VG	
5011		$10 1929T1		D000731A		VG	
5011		$10 1929T1		C000806A		F	
5011		$10 1929T1		A000858A		F	
5011		$10 1929T1		C000869A		F	
5011		$20 1929T1		D000023A		F	
5011		$20 1929T1		D000144A		?	
5011		$20 1929T1		D000167A		VF	
5011		$20 1929T1		A000224A		F/VF	
5011		$20 1929T1		C000294A		?	
5011		$10 1929T2		A000728		F	Stains

THE COMMERCIAL NATIONAL BANK OF FORT DODGE
4566   WEBSTER   35 L   11 S

Chartered in 1891. Placed in voluntary liquidation on August 5, 1930; capital of $100,000. Absorbed by #2763.

Officers: Pres. SJ Bennett 1891-1911, RM Wright 1912-24, CA Garlock 1925-29; **VP** H Norton 1896-1903, J Garmoe 1904-07, Thos H Wright 1909-10, Wm E Haviland 1911-20, ER Campbell 1923, SN Magowan 1924-25, Walter L Casteel 1926-29, Loran M Martin 1926-29; **Cash.** JW Campbell 1891-1915, ER Campbell 1916-19, Quintus Blomgren 1920-25, CA Garlock 1926, Fred R Kaufman 1927-29; **AC** JH Pearsons 1896-1901, ER Campbell 1902-14, Geo A Knigge 1920, Geo E Porter 1920-26, FR Kaufman 1926, AE Rasch 1926-30

Second Charter, Brown Backs	Ser #	# Notes
10-10-10-20	1-3600	14,400
Second Charter, Date Back		
10-10-10-20	1-2113	8,452
Third Charter, Date Back, Blue Seal		
10-10-10-20	1-4900	19,600
Third Charter, Plain Back, Blue Seal		
10-10-10-20	4901-17626	50,904
1929, Type I		
6-10's	1-889	5,334
6-20's	1-119	714

Total amount of circulation issued = $1,234,570. Amount outstanding in 1929 = $100,000. Amount of large outstanding at close = $28,280.

93,356 Large   6,048 Small   99,404 Total

4566		$10 1882BB	485	2984 A	V3872??	Fr/G	Bayard
4566	M	$10 1882DB	540	1252 F	B543322	F	stamp/stamp
4566	M	$10 1902DB	619	2622 C	R202236A	F/VF	stamp/stamp
4566	M	$10 1902PB	627	5609 C	X36813B	?	

4566	M	$10 1902PB 627	5965 C	X37169B	F		
4566	M	$10 1902PB 627	10180 B	E819512E	VG/F		
4566	M	$10 1902PB 627	11538 A	Z543450E	VF+	stamp/stamp	
4566	M	$10 1902PB 627	11854 B	Z543766E	F	gone/gone	
4566		$10 1902PB 627	12503 C	H396685H	VG		
4566		$10 1902PB 627	13619 C	V195001H	HG		
4566		$10 1902PB 627	14277 ?	A230079K	?		
4566		$10 1902PB 627	14572 ?	?	?		
4566	-	$10 1902PB 627	14574 B	14574 B	AU		
4566	-	$10 1902PB 627	15099 B	15099 B	F/VF	gone/gone	
4566	-	$10 1902PB 627	16246 B	16246 B	VG	faded/faded	
4566	-	$10 1902PB 627	16551 A	16551 A	F		
4566	-	$10 1902PB 627	16776 C	16776 C	VF		
4566	-	$10 1902PB 627	17425 B	17425 B	VG		
4566	M	$20 1902PB 653	6319 A	A311186D	VG		
4566	M	$20 1902PB 653	7517 A	M319609D	?		
4566	M	$20 1902PB 653	11189 A	R750691E	VG		
4566	-	$20 1902PB 653	16318 A	16318 A	HG		
4566	-	$20 1902PB 653	16357 A	16357 A	F	gone/gone	
4566	-	$20 1902PB 653	17193 A	17193 A	F		
4566	-	$20 1902PB 653	17434 A	17434 A	Fr/G		
4566	-	$20 1902PB 653	17518 A	17518 A	XF	lt stamp/stamp	
4566	-	$20 1902PB 653	17524 A	17524 A	VF		
4566	-	$20 1902PB 653	17530 A	17530 A	XF/AU		
4566	-	$20 1902PB 653	17531 A	17531 A	VF		
4566		$20 1902PB 653	17534 A	17534 A	AU	Toned paper	
4566	-	$20 1902PB 653	17535 A	17535 A	VF+	Higgins Mus.	
4566	-	$20 1902PB 653	17536 A	17536 A	XF		
4566	-	$20 1902PB 653	17537 A	17537 A	AU	Toned paper	
4566	-	$20 1902PB 653	17538 A	17538 A	CU		
4566	-	$20 1902PB 653	17539 A	17539 A	CU		
4566		$10 1929T1	B000044A		F/VF		
4566		$10 1929T1	E000270A		F		
4566		$10 1929T1	B000537A		?		
4566		$10 1929T1	D000650A		AU		
4566		$5 1929T1	B000793A		G/VG		
4566		$10 1929T1	B000850A		F	Higgins Mus.	
4566		$20 1929T1	A000009A		VF	Higgins Mus.	
4566		$20 1929T1	A000025A		XF		
4566		$20 1929T1	A000059A		VG		
4566		$20 1929T1	E000095A		F/VF		
4566		$20 1929T1	F000101A		?		

THE FIRST NATIONAL BANK OF FORT DODGE   70 L   23 S
1661   WEBSTER

Chartered in 1866. Placed in voluntary liquidation on Feb. 10, 1931; capital of $300,000. Succeeded by The First State Bank & Trust Co., Fort Dodge.
Officers: Pres. Charles B Richards 1867-73, Erastus G Morgan 1874-75, Leander Blanden 1876-89, ST Meservey 1890-1901, Webb Vincent 1902-15, EH Rich 1916-30; **VP** JM Mulroney 1896-1914, OM Oleson 1920-30, Geo L Rich 1923-28, Chas D Case 1923-30, CW Gadd 1929-30; **Cash.** Erastus G Morgan 1867-69, Edward DG Morgan 1870-81, JB Scott 1883, CG Blanden 1884-85, JB Scott 1887, CG Blanden 1888-89, JW Campbell 1890, Harry Jones 1891, EH Rich 1892-1915, Geo L Rich 1916-22, J Floyd Rich 1923-30; **AC** Geo L Rich 1896-1915, CD Case 1920-22, J Floyd Rich 1920-22, WF Rich 1920-31, EH Moore 1923-30.

	Ser #	# Notes
First Charter, Original Issue		
1-1-1-2	1-2300	9,200
5-5-5-5	1-3450	13,800
First Charter, Series of 1875		
1-1-1-2	1-200	800
5-5-5-5	1-5765	23,060
Second Charter, Brown Backs		
5-5-5-5	1-19275	77,100
10-10-10-20	1-8528	34,112
Third Charter, Red Seal		
5-5-5-5	1-4540	18,160
10-10-10-20	1-3684	14,736
Third Charter, Date Back, Blue Seal		
5-5-5-5	1-16415	65,660
10-10-10-20	1-13834	55,336
Third Charter, Plain Back, Blue Seal		
5-5-5-5	16416-28915	50,000
10-10-10-20	13835-42617	115,132
1929, Type I		
6-10's	1-3345	20,070
6-20's	1-768	4,608

Total amount of circulation issued = $4,285,710. Amount of large outstanding at close = $65,780. Amount of small outstanding at close = $234,220.
477,096 Large   24,678 Small   501,774 Total

1661	-	$1 ORIG 380	1907 B	E103113	XF	Higgins Mus.	
1661	-	$1 ORIG 380	2108 A	E103113	AG	pen/pen	
1661	-	$2 ORIG 387	436 A	B8558	XF	Higgins Mus.	
1661	-	$2 ORIG 387	1113 A	C428426	G	Repaired	
1661	-	$5 1875 401	4172 C	N870117	VG		
1661	-	$5 1875 401	4352 C	X79806	AU	Higgins Mus.	
1661		$5 1882BB 469	3727 A	N156049	VG	Oat Bin Hoard	
1661		$10 1882BB 482	696 B	K810274	VG		
1661		$10 1882BB 482	1547 B	W24302	VF		
1661		$10 1882BB 482	6536 C	E518361E	VG		
1661	M	$5 1902RS 589	3814 A	N761432	VG		
1661	M	$10 1902RS 615	2883 A	V180468	G/VG	stamp/stamp	
1661	M	$5 1902DB 592	9945 G	Y627422A	F		
1661	M	$5 1902DB 592	13933 E	D928025B	VF		
1661	M	$10 1902DB 618	3016 E	X889408	VG/F		
1661	M	$10 1902DB 618	5722 E	M565681A	F	stamp/stamp	
1661	M	$10 1902DB 618	9380 D	H391472B	G	stamp/stamp	
1661	M	$10 1902DB 618	9450 F	H391542B	F	Repaired	
1661	M	$10 1902DB 618	10634 F	H489026B	F		
1661	M	$10 1902DB 618	13136 D	H637028B	VG		
1661	M	$10 1902DB 618	13575 D	H637467B	F	stamp/stamp	
1661	M	$20 1902DB 644	2137 B	R787194	F/VF	faded/faded Aged	
1661	M	$20 1902DB 644	3272 B	X889664	F+	Washed	
1661	M	$20 1902DB 644	13039 B	H636931B	F	stamp/stamp	
1661	M	$20 1902DB 644	13593 B	H637485B	F+		
1661	M	$5 1902PB 600	16797 G	Z30083B	F/VF		
1661	M	$5 1902PB 600	19491 G	E721772D	G		
1661	M	$5 1902PB 600	21842 E	E768873D	VF	stamp/stamp	
1661	M	$5 1902PB 600	24526 F	U353572D	G	pen/pen	
1661	M	$10 1902PB 626	18773 D	Y597011D	VG	stamp/stamp	
1661	M	$10 1902PB 626	24543 E	X854771E	?		
1661	M	$10 1902PB 626	24623 E	X854851E	?		
1661	M	$10 1902PB 626	24742 E	X854970E	VF	stamp/stamp	
1661	M	$10 1902PB 626	29225 F	M546103H	F	stamp/stamp	
1661	M	$10 1902PB 626	29729 ?	M546607H	?	Bayard	
1661	-	$10 1902PB 626	31760 F	U958998H	F+	stamp/stamp	
1661	-	$10 1902PB 626	34947 F	34947 F	F/VF	stamp/stamp	
1661	-	$10 1902PB 626	35099 ?	35099 ?	F		
1661	-	$10 1902PB 626	37266 E	37266 E	?		
1661	-	$10 1902PB 626	38092 E	38092 E	VF	Stains	
1661	-	$10 1902PB 626	38363 D	38363 D	F	stamp/stamp	
1661	-	$10 1902PB 626	39246 E	39246 E	F	stamp/stamp	
1661	-	$10 1902PB 626	39947 F	39947 F	F		
1661	-	$10 1902PB 626	40726 E	40726 E	F		
1661	M	$20 1902PB 652	16078 B	R232166D	VF		
1661	M	$20 1902PB 652	18089 B	Y579447D	F	stamp/stamp	
1661	M	$20 1902PB 652	21130 B	D606858E	VF		
1661	M	$20 1902PB 652	24073 B	N855951E	F/VF		
1661	M	$20 1902PB 652	25325 B	X855553E	VG	retraced sigs	
1661	M	$20 1902PB 652	28592 B	M269520H	VG		
1661	M	$20 1902PB 652	28752 B	M269680H	VG/F		
1661	M	$20 1902PB 652	28981 B	M545859H	VG		
1661	-	$20 1902PB 652	30383 B	U659261H	?		
1661	-	$20 1902PB 652	31310 B	U958548H	CU	stamp/stamp	
1661	-	$20 1902PB 652	31503 B	U958741H	VG	stamp/stamp	
1661	-	$20 1902PB 652	32785 B	A575193K	VF		
1661	-	$20 1902PB 652	32880 B	A575288K	VG/F		
1661	-	$20 1902PB 652	33044 B	A780652K	VG	stamp/stamp	
1661	-	$20 1902PB 652	33049 B	A780657K	VF	stamp/stamp	
1661	-	$20 1902PB 652	34781 B	34781 B	?		
1661	-	$20 1902PB 652	35743 B	35743 B	F		
1661	-	$20 1902PB 652	35940 B	35940 B	XF	stamp Higg. Mus.	
1661	-	$20 1902PB 652	37115 B	37115 B	VF+	stamp/stamp	
1661	-	$20 1902PB 652	38753 B	38753 B	F	stamp/stamp	
1661	-	$20 1902PB 652	38824 B	38824 B	F/VF	stamp/stamp	
1661	-	$20 1902PB 652	39531 B	39531 B	VF		
1661	-	$20 1902PB 652	40308 B	40308 B	?		
1661	-	$20 1902PB 652	40536 B	40536 B	?		
1661	-	$20 1902PB 652	41375 B	41375 B	F/VF		
1661	-	$20 1902PB 652	41722 B	41722 B	XF		
1661		$10 1929T1	C000128A		VF		

1661	$10 1929T1	B000573A	XF		
1661	$10 1929T1	D000663A	VG/F		
1661	$10 1929T1	E000724A	G		
1661	$10 1929T1	D000748A	VF		
1661	$10 1929T1	A000772A	?		
1661	$10 1929T1	E001327A	VG		
1661	$10 1929T1	D001654A	?		
1661	$10 1929T1	E001676A	PR		
1661	$10 1929T1	C001705A	VF		
1661	$10 1929T1	A002022A	F		
1661	$10 1929T1	B002549A	VG		
1661	$10 1929T1	B002772A	XF	Higgins Mus.	
1661	$10 1929T1	C003132A	F/VF		
1661	$10 1929T1	A003142A	VG		
1661	$20 1929T1	C000144A	F		
1661	$20 1929T1	B000194A	F/VF		
1661	$20 1929T1	A000198A	F+		
1661	$20 1929T1	D000293A	F		
1661	$20 1929T1	A000509A	VF		
1661	$20 1929T1	D000532A	VF?		
1661	$20 1929T1	B000615A	VF		
1661	$20 1929T1	C000656A	F		

THE FORT DODGE NATIONAL BANK   51 L   53 S
2763   **WEBSTER**

Organized on July 8, 1882 with a capital of $50,000. Absorbed #4566 on August 5, 1930. Placed in conservation on March 23, 1933. Licensed on June 21, 1933.

Officers: Pres. JC Cheney 1883-87, AF Guenther 1888-97, JC Cheney 1898-1913, FE Seymour 1914-22, LE Armstrong 1923-35; **VP** AE Haskell 1896, FE Seymour 1900-13, Chas Stayman 1914-33, Geo Schnurr 1927-35, HE Laufer 1933-34; **Cash.** George B Wheeler 1883-87, JC Cheney 1888-97, John T Cheney 1898-1915, GB Wheeler 1916-20, FC Moeller 1922-35; **AC** JT Cheney 1896, GB Wheeler 1907-14, FC Moeller 1920, EH Zuerrer 1920-35

First Charter, Series of 1875	Ser #	# Notes
5-5-5-5	1-6201	24,804
10-10-10-20	1-1309	5,236
Third Charter, Red Seal		
10-10-10-20	1-5200	20,800
Third Charter, Date Back, Blue Seal		
10-10-10-20	1-6300	25,200
Third Charter, Plain Back, Blue Seal		
10-10-10-20	6301-18992	50,768
1929, Type I		
6-10's	1-2204	13,224
6-20's	1-614	3,684
1929, Type II		
10's	1-1609	1,609
20's	1-392	392

Total amount of circulation issued = $1,628,920. Amount of large outstanding in 1935 = $7,297. Amount of small outstanding in 1935 = $92,700.
126,808 Large   8,909 Small   145,717 Total

2763	-	$5	1875 405	4898 A	Y226001	VF
2763	-	$5	1875 405	4901 D	Y226004	AU Higgins Mus.
2763	-	$5	1875 405	5400 B	Y347896	XF
2763	-	$5	1875 405	5401 D	Y347897	XF
2763	-	$5	1875 405	5403 A	Y347899	VF
2763	-	$5	1875 405	5403 B	Y347896	XF
2763	-	$5	1875 405	5404 C	Y347897	XF pen/pen vp
2763	-	$5	1875 405	5404 D	Y347897	F/VF
2763	-	$5	1875 405	5405 D	Y347898	XF
2763	-	$5	1875 405	5406 A	Y347902	XF
2763	-	$5	1875 405	5494 ?	?	XF
2763	-	$10	1875 420	696 B	K816274	G/VG pen/pen
2763	-	$10	1875 420	1259 C	K996607	F+ Higgins Mus.
2763	-	$20	1875 435	1281 A	K996629	VG Fed. Res. Bk., San Fran.
2763	M	$10	1902RS 613	?	?	F Grinnell # 3300
2763	M	$20	1902RS 639	1171 A	B276858	VG nice sigs
2763	M	$10	1902DB 616	575 E	E647310	PR Bayard
2763	M	$10	1902DB 616	4982 F	T672124A	G/VG
2763	M	$10	1902PB 624	6972 D	V374642B	F
2763	M	$10	1902PB 624	10287 E	Y935769D	VG
2763	M	$10	1902PB 624	12280 D	N956692E	AU stamp/stamp
2763	M	$10	1902PB 624	12280 E	N956692E	AU+ mach stamps
2763	M	$10	1902PB 624	12281 D	N956693E	AU mach stamps
2763	M	$10	1902PB 624	12281 E	N956693E	AU mach stamps
2763	M	$10	1902PB 624	12281 F	N956693E	AU mach stamps
2763	M	$10	1902PB 624	12282 D	N956694E	AU mach stamps
2763	M	$10	1902PB 624	12282 E	N956694E	AU
2763	M	$10	1902PB 624	12282 F	N956694E	?
2763	M	$10	1902PB 624	12283 E	N956695E	CU
2763	M	$10	1902PB 624	12283 F	N956695E	?
2763	M	$10	1902PB 624	12285 D	N956697E	?
2763	M	$10	1902PB 624	12285 E	N956697E	CU
2763	M	$10	1902PB 624	12285 F	N956697E	AU+
2763	M	$10	1902PB 624	12291 F	N956703E	?
2763	M	$10	1902PB 624	12292 F	N956704E	?
2763	M	$10	1902PB 624	12472 F	Y423842E	?
2763	M	$10	1902PB 624	12475 F	Y423824E	?
2763		$10	1902PB 624	13196 E	D628708H	F
2763	-	$10	1902PB 624	16462 D	16462 D	VG+ Higgins Mus.
2763	-	$10	1902PB 624	18522 B	18522 B	F
2763	-	$10	1902PB 624	18942 E	18942 E	VF stamp/stamp
2763	M	$20	1902PB 650	7673 B	Z289926B	VG
2763	M	$20	1902PB 650	7939 B	Z290192B	F/VF
2763	M	$20	1902PB 650	7974 B	Z290227B	VF
2763	M	$20	1902PB 650	12292 B	N956704E	AU stamp/stamp Aged paper
2763	M	$20	1902PB 650	12293 B	N956705E	AU mach stamps Aged paper
2763	M	$20	1902PB 650	12294 B	N956706E	AU Aged paper
2763	M	$20	1902PB 650	12295 B	N956707E	VF Repaired
2763	M	$20	1902PB 650	12296 B	N956708E	AU
2763	-	$20	1902PB 650	16246 B	16246 B	VG/F stamp/stamp
2763	-	$20	1902PB 650	18522 B	18522 B	?
2763		$10	1929T1	A000195A		VG
2763		$10	1929T1	E000272A		VG
2763		$10	1929T1	C000338A		VG
2763		$10	1929T1	F000446A		VF
2763		$10	1929T1	B000452A		G/VG
2763		$10	1929T1	F000506A		F/VF
2763		$10	1929T1	A001192A		XF
2763		$10	1929T1	F001298A		VG
2763		$10	1929T1	C001497A		VF
2763		$10	1929T1	E001681A		?
2763		$10	1929T1	E001698A		VF
2763		$10	1929T1	A001721A		VF
2763		$10	1929T1	C001793A		F
2763		$10	1929T1	E001834A		?
2763		$10	1929T1	C001873A		VG
2763		$10	1929T1	D001873A		VF Stain/spotting
2763		$10	1929T1	E001873A		CU
2763		$10	1929T1	B001874A		CU
2763		$10	1929T1	A001875A		CU
2763		$10	1929T1	B001875A		CU
2763		$10	1929T1	A001876A		CU
2763		$10	1929T1	C001877A		CU
2763		$10	1929T1	D001878A		VF
2763		$10	1929T1	F001878A		CU
2763		$10	1929T1	A001880A		?
2763		$10	1929T1	E001880A		CU cut tight
2763		$10	1929T1	F001880A		F
2763		$10	1929T1	C001921A		F/VF
2763		$20	1929T1	D000050A		VG
2763		$20	1929T1	E000133A		F/VF
2763		$20	1929T1	A000134A		CU
2763		$20	1929T1	C000155A		VG/F
2763		$20	1929T1	C000228A		VF
2763		$20	1929T1	E000288A		VF
2763		$20	1929T1	C000365A		VF
2763		$20	1929T1	E000373A		VF/XF
2763		$20	1929T1	B000378A		F/VF
2763		$20	1929T1	A000401A		CU Higgins Mus.
2763		$20	1929T1	A000402A		CU
2763		$20	1929T1	A000403A		CU
2763		$20	1929T1	C000407A		F/VF
2763		$20	1929T1	B000440A		VG
2763		$20	1929T1	F000440A		F
2763		$20	1929T1	C000454A		VG
2763		$20	1929T1	C000462A		VG/F
2763		$20	1929T1	E000479A		VF/F
2763		$20	1929T1	D000488A		VF
2763		$20	1929T1	D000569A		F+
2763		$20	1929T1	C000592A		F
2763		$10	1929T2	A000140		F
2763		$10	1929T2	A000161		VF
2763		$20	1929T2	A000129		F/VF
2763		$20	1929T2	A000385		XF

THE MERCHANTS NATIONAL BANK OF FORT DODGE 1 L
1947   WEBSTER
Chartered on March 20, 1872. Placed in voluntary liquidation on December 31, 1891; capital of $100,000.
Officers: Pres. Harry Strong 1872-76, John M Mulroney 1877-80, Webb Vincent 1881, Angus McBane 1883-85, Webb Vincent 1887-91; **Cash.** JM Bell 1872-76, Edward H Rich 1877-91; **AC** Geo L Rich 1885

First Charter, Original Issue	Ser #	# Notes
1-1-1-2	1-1500	6,000
5-5-5-5	1-2625	10,500
First Charter, Series of 1875		
5-5-5-5	1-7243	28,972

Total amount of circulation issued = $204,860. Amount outstanding at close = $22,500. Amount outstanding in 1910 = $1,150.
45,472 Large   0 Small   45,472 Total
1947 - $1   ORIG 382   503 C   D33246   VG   Higgins Mus.

THE WEBSTER COUNTY NATIONAL BANK OF FORT DODGE
11304   WEBSTER   9 L
Chartered in February 1919. Placed in voluntary liquidation on October 29, 1923; capital of $250,000. Succeeded by The Webster County Trust & Savings Bank, Fort Dodge.
Officers: Pres. JB Butler 1919-23; **VP** OM Thatcher 1920-22, DG Stiles 1920, MF Healy 1920-23; **Cash.** JL Hanrahan 1919-23; **AC** CW Goodrich 1922-23, Orin Thatcher 1923

Third Charter, Plain Back, Blue Seal	Ser #	# Notes
10-10-10-20	1-11746	46984

Total amount of circulation issued = $587,300. Amount outstanding in 1922 = $184,995.
46,984 Large   0 Small   46,984 Total

11304M	$10	1902PB	632	1 A	E942295D	?
11304M	$10	1902PB	632	1107 ?	E965101D	?
11304M	$10	1902PB	632	6656 B	Z330678D	VF stamp/stamp
11304M	$10	1902PB	632	7084 C	Z331106D	CU stamp/stamp
11304M	$10	1902PB	632	10257 B	U730889E	F
11304M	$10	1902PB	632	10565 B	Z609867E	VF stamp/stamp
11304M	$10	1902PB	632	10712 B	Z610014E	?
11304M	$10	1902PB	632	11139 A	Z610441E	F+ Higgins Mus.
11304M	$20	1902PB	658	5597 A	X933939D	VF stamp/stamp

THE FIRST NATIONAL BANK OF FORT MADISON   1 L
3974   LEE
Chartered on February 2, 1889. Succeeded The Bank of Fort Madison. Placed in voluntary liquidation on October 8, 1895; capital of $100,000.
Officers: Pres. Joseph B Morrison 1889-90, Chas Brewster 1891, DA Morrison 1892-95; **Cash.** WH Miller 1889-90, JC Brewster 1891-93, JAS Pollard 1894-95

Second Charter, Brown Backs	Ser #	# Notes
10-10-10-20	1-993	3,972

Total amount of circulation issued = $49,650. Amount outstanding at close = $22,500. Amount outstanding in 1910 = $485.
3,972 Large   0 Small   3,972 Total
3974 $10 1882BB 483   993 C   K999747   CU

THE FORT MADISON NATIONAL BANK   1 L
1611   LEE
Chartered on November 20, 1865. Placed in voluntary liquidation on December 26, 1871; capital of $75,000.
Officers: Pres. JH Winterbotham 1867, Clark R Wever 1868-71; **Cash.** Clark R Wever 1867, JR Winterbotham 1868-71

First Charter, Original Issue	Ser #	# Notes
5-5-5-5	1-1750	7,000
10-10-10-20	1-650	2600

Total amount of circulation issued = $67,500. Amount outstanding at close = $67,500. Amount outstanding in 1910 = $430.
9,600 Large   0 Small   9,600 Total
1611 - $10   ORIG   ?   650 ?   ?   AU

THE FIRST NATIONAL BANK OF FREDERICKSBURG 35 L   2 S
10541   CHICKASAW
Chartered in May 1914. Placed in voluntary liquidation on January 15, 1930; capital of $30,000. Absorbed by The First State Bank, Fredericksburg.
Officers: Pres. Tim Donovan 1914-19, Guy M Padden 1920-26, Wm Drape 1927, WH Mohling 1928-29; **VP** HJ Kroninger 1914-26, JA Eygabroad 1920-30; **Cash.** Guy M Padden 1914-19, CE Leach 1920-26, Guy M Padden 1927-28, CE Leach 1929; **AC** CE Leach 1914, LW Sampson 1920-24, Evelyn Sloan 1925-29

Third Charter, Date Back, Blue Seal	Ser #	# Notes
5-5-5-5	1-850	3,400
10-10-10-20	1-680	2,720

Third Charter, Plain Back, Blue Seal

	Ser #	# Notes
5-5-5-5	851-4922	16,288
10-10-10-20	681-3029	9,396

1929, Type I

6-5's	1-60	360
6-10's	1-16	96
6-20's	1-8	48

Total amount of circulation issued = $253,610. Amount of large outstanding at close = $24,980. Amount of small outstanding at close = $3,720.
31,804 Large   504 Small   32,208 Total

10541M	$5	1902DB	597	114 C	Y672356A	F/VF	pen/pen
10541M	$5	1902PB	605	1418 C	Y139194B	Fr	gone/gone
10541M	$5	1902PB	605	1644 C	Y139420B	HG	
10541M	$5	1902PB	605	1646 B	Y139422B	AU	
10541M	$5	1902PB	605	1945 A	M288421D	CU	stamp/stamp
10541M	$5	1902PB	605	1945 B	M288421D	CU	stamp/stamp
10541M	$5	1902PB	605	1945 C	M288421D	CU	stamp/stamp
10541M	$5	1902PB	605	1945 D	M288421D	CU	stamp/stamp
10541M	$5	1902PB	605	1946 C	M288422D	CU	stamp/stamp
10541M	$5	1902PB	605	1946 D	M288422D	CU	
10541M	$5	1902PB	605	1963 B	M288439D	AU	stamp/stamp
10541M	$5	1902PB	605	1964 A	M288440D	CU	stamp Higg. Mus.
10541M	$5	1902PB	605	1965 A	M288441D	CU	nice sigs
10541M	$5	1902PB	606	2833 A	N052029E	VF+	
10541M	$5	1902PB	605	3014 A	?	VG+	
10541M	$5	1902PB	605	3319 C	H6255H	XF	stamp/stamp
10541M	$5	1902PB	605	3540 A	K31626H	XF	
10541 -	$5	1902PB	605	3610 A	X949371H	CU	
10541 -	$5	1902PB	605	3610 C	X949371H	AU	lt. stamp sigs Washed
10541 -	$5	1902PB	605	3898 B	3898 B	F/VF	lt. stamp sigs
10541 -	$5	1902PB	605	4001 B	4001 B	F	
10541 -	$5	1902PB	605	4077 A	4077 A	AU	
10541 -	$5	1902PB	605	4148 D	4148 D	CU	
10541 -	$5	1902PB	605	4153 A	4153 A	CU	
10541 -	$5	1902PB	605	4164 A	4164 A	XF	
10541 -	$5	1902PB	605	4464 B	4464 B	HG	
10541M	$10	1902PB	631	1283 C	N473675D	CU	stamp/stamp
10541M	$10	1902PB	631	1575 C	A176217E	HG	
10541 -	$10	1902PB	631	2352 A	Z118514H	VG/F	
10541 -	$10	1902PB	631	2888 A	2888 A	VF	
10541M	$20	1902PB	657	1274 A	N473666D	VF	gone/gone
10541M	$20	1902PB	657	1617 A	A176259E	HG	
10541M	$20	1902PB	657	1869 A	T891731E	F	gone/gone
10541 -	$20	1902PB	657	2725 A	?	VG/F	
10541 -	$20	1902PB	657	2909 A	2909 A	HG	
10541	$10	1929T1		D000002A		VG	
10541	$10	1929T1		D000004A		F/VF	Higgins Mus.

THE FIRST NATIONAL BANK OF GALVA   9 L
10501   IDA
Organized on March 23, 1914; capital of $25,000. Placed in receivership on March 6, 1928; capital of $50,000. Reason for failure: deficiency in assets.
Officers: Pres. Geo W Johns 1914-22, Wm Schmidt 1923, RB Clemens 1924-28; **VP** Wm Schmidt 1914-22, 1924-28, RB Clemens 1923, IE Baumgardner 1924-28; **Cash.** FH Schleiter 1914-16, JW Marmet 1917-23, Geo E Missildine 1924-28; **AC** Geo E Missildine 1914-23

Third Charter, Date Back, Blue Seal	Ser #	# Notes
10-10-10-20	1-860	3,440

Third Charter, Plain Back, Blue Seal		
10-10-10-20	861-6250	21,560

Total amount issued = $312,500. Amount outstanding at close = $41,050.
25,000 Large   0 Small   25,000 Total

10501M	$10	1902PB	631	2926 C	Y683658D	VG/F	nice sigs vp
10501M	$10	1902PB	631	4631 B	H469653H	F	pen/stamp
10501M	$10	1902PB	631	4650 C	H469672H	F	
10501 -	$10	1902PB	631	5426 B	A372348K	VG/F	pen/faded
10501 -	$10	1902PB	631	5512 B	5512 B	F	
10501 -	$10	1902PB	631	5533 C	5533 C	VG/F	pen/stamp
10501M	$20	1902PB	649	3239 A	D978821E	VG/F	Soiling; washed
10501 -	$20	1902PB	649	5213 A	A372135K	F	
10501 -	$20	1902PB	649	5532 A	5532 A	VF	Higgins Mus.

THE FIRST NATIONAL BANK OF GARDEN GROVE   0 L
5464   DECATUR
Chartered on June 28, 1900 with a capital of $25,000. Placed in voluntary liquidation on June 11, 1913; capital of $25,000. Succeeded by C.S. Stearns Commercial Bank, Garden Grove.
Officers: Pres. CS Stearns 1900-13; **VP** FE Stearns 1900-13; **Cash.** GM Russell 1900-06, JW Stearns 1907-10, Laura Aten 1912-13; **AC** GM Russell 1907, Laura Aten 1909-11, HJ Culver 1913

Second Charter, Brown Backs	Ser #	# Notes
5-5-5-5	1-1550	6,200
10-10-10-20	1-1100	4,400
Second Charter, Date Back		
5-5-5-5	1-980	3,920
10-10-10-20	1-632	2,528

Total amount of circulation issued = $137,200. Amount outstanding at close = $24,200. Amount outstanding in October 1913 = $20,050.

17,048 Large   0 Small   17,048 Total

THE FARMERS NATIONAL BANK OF GARNER   7 L   5 S
8367   HANCOCK

Organized on August 22, 1906 with a capital of $25,000. Placed in conservatorship on March 21, 1933. Placed in receivership on March 20, 1934; capital of $50,000. Reason for failure: not available from reports.

Officers: Pres. CK Moe 1907-10, CH Nelson 1911-12, Isaac Sweigard 1913-24, JN Sprole 1925-32, Chas Welik 1933; **VP** CS Terwilliger 1907, GE Troeger 1909-10, A Kelly 1911, FE Blackstone 1913-33, JN Sprole 1923-24; **Cash.** Isaac Sweigard 1907-11, CR Sweigard 1912-20, Chas Wellik 1922-32, HL Ollenburg 1933; **AC** MR Pollock 1907-09, CR Sweigard 1909-11, EC Ford 1914, Chas Wellik 1920, RW Newton 1920, Earl C Conway 1922-23, FM Miller 1930-32, HL Ollenburg 1931-32, WL Baggs 1933

Third Charter, Red Seal	Ser #	# Notes
10-10-10-20	1-750	3,000
Third Charter, Date Back, Blue Seal		
10-10-10-20	1-1930	7,720
Third Charter, Plain Back, Blue Seal		
10-10-10-20	1931-4767	11,348
1929, Type I		
6-10's	1-531	3,186
6-20's	1-136	816

Total amount of circulation issued = $324,030. Amount of large outstanding at close = $1,870. Amount of small outstanding at close = $23,130.

22,068 Large   4,002 Small   26,070 Total

8367	M	$10	1902DB	618	1436 ?	A249860B	?	
8367	M	$10	1902DB	618	1669 D	M494845B	F/VF	Higgins Mus.
8367	M	$20	1902DB	644	1184 B	U528700A	F/VF	pen/pen
8367	M	$10	1902PB	626	2392 D	D670949D	VF	pen/pen
8367	M	$10	1902PB	626	2755 E	U40167D	F/VF	Higgins Mus.
8367	M	$10	1902PB	626	2873 E	A471465E	VG	pen Tape Stains
8367		$20	1902PB	652	4221 B	?	VG	
8367		$10	1929T1		D000121A		F	
8367		$10	1929T1		D000318A		F	
8367		$10	1929T1		F000363A		VG	
8367		$10	1929T1		D000507A		VG+	
8367		$20	1929T1		C000021A		F	Higgins Mus.

THE FIRST NATIONAL BANK OF GARNER   12 L
4810   HANCOCK

Organized on August 24, 1892 with a capital of $50,000. Succeeded The Hancock County Bank and The City Bank. Placed in receivership on December 4, 1928; capital of $50,000. Reason for failure: deficiency in assets.

Officers: Pres. JM Elder 1893-97, Wm Shattuck 1898-1911, AC Ripley 1912-13, FM Hanson 1914-25; **VP** Wm Shattuck 1896, AC Ripley 1900-11, JE Wichman 1913-25, FM Hansen 1924, Chris Jacobs 1923-25; **Cash.** JJ Upton 1893, Chas W Knoop 1894-1901, FM Hanson 1902, 1905-11, Chas W Knoop 1902-04, JFW Vrba 1912-25; **AC** Clarence B Cassill 1904, JFW Vrba 1909-11, RW Newton 1922-25

Second Charter, Brown Backs	Ser #	# Notes
10-10-10-20	1-4100	16,400
Second Charter, Date Back		
10-10-10-20	1-1316	5,264
Third Charter, Date Back, Blue Seal		
10-10-10-20	1-2000	8,000
Third Charter, Plain Back, Blue Seal		
10-10-10-20	2001-7025	20,100

Total amount issued = $622,050. Amount outstanding in 1927 = $49,700.

49,764 Large   0 Small   49,764 Total

4810		$10	1882BB	485	1 B	H31769E	F/VF	
4810	M	$10	1882BB	485	3908 A	V609807V	F	Higgins Mus.
4810	M	$20	1882BB	499	3897 A	V609796V	VF	pen/stamp
4810	M	$10	1902DB	620	1509 C	M767135B	VG	faded/pen
4810	M	$10	1902PB	628	2054 A	Y66096B	F	sigs Washed
4810	M	$10	1902PB	628	3305 C	T181707E	VG	
4810	M	$10	1902PB	628	3717 C	A162049E	F	stamp Higg. Mus.
4810	M	$20	1902PB	628	4529 B	U479291E	VF	
4810		$10	1902PB	628	6141 B	A978043K	VG	
4810	-	$10	1902PB	628	6976 C	6976 C	VG	faded/gone
4810	-	$20	1902PB	654	6796 A	6796 A	G	
4810	-	$20	1902PB	654	6839 A	6839 A	?	

THE FIRST NATIONAL BANK OF GEORGE   11 L   9 S
9910   LYON

Organized on December 5, 1910 with a capital of $25,000. Placed in receivership on January 4, 1933; capital of $25,000.

Officers: Pres. Ben Hoeven 1911-32; **VP** WC Collman 1911-22, Fred Marschall 1923-32; **Cash.** OC Collman 1911-22, WC Collman 1923-24, MC Ennor 1925-32; **AC** JA Parden 1911-14, FC Jordan 1920, JH Klinkenborg 1920, J Oltmann 1923, 1924-32, CO Lehmann 1925-32

Third Charter, Date Back, Blue Seal	Ser #	# Notes
10-10-10-20	1-1550	6,200
Third Charter, Plain Back, Blue Seal		
10-10-10-20	1551-4232	10,728
1929, Type I		
6-10's	1-409	2,454
6-20's	1-103	618

Total amount of circulation issued = $248,500. Amount outstanding at close = $24,640. Amount of large outstanding on January 10, 1933 = $2,890.

16,928 Large   3,072 Small   20,000 Total

9910	M	$10	1902PB	627	1949 C	B364806D	XF	
9910	M	$10	1902PB	627	2664 C	H542346E	CU	pen/pen
9910	M	$10	1902PB	627	3074 C	Z562876E	AU	pen/pen
9910		$10	1902PB	627	3183 A	K105785H	F	
9910	-	$10	1902PB	627	3411 B	U847203H	VF	pen Higgins Mus.
9910	-	$10	1902PB	627	3500 C	A542722K	VG	pen/gone Bayard
9910	-	$10	1902PB	627	3807 B	3807 B	VG/F	
9910	-	$10	1902PB	627	3944 A	3944 A	F	
9910	-	$10	1902PB	627	4087 B	4087 B	XF/AU	pen/pen vp
9910	-	$20	1902PB	653	3534 A	A542756K	VG/F	
9910	-	$20	1902PB	653	4179 A	4179 A	VF	
9910		$10	1929T1		A000115A		F	Higgins Mus.
9910		$10	1929T1		B000153A		?	
9910		$10	1929T1		F000187A		G/VG	
9910		$20	1929T1		C000011A		G+	
9910		$20	1929T1		E000040A		VG	
9910		$20	1929T1		D000051A		F+	
9910		$20	1929T1		A000062A		F	
9910		$20	1929T1		A000067A		F/VF	
9910		$20	1929T1		F000079A		VF	

THE FIRST NATIONAL BANK OF GILMORE   1 L
6611   POCAHONTAS

Organized on Dec. 2, 1902 with a capital of $25,000. Placed in receivership on Jan. 18, 1926; capital of $25,000. Reason for failure: local depression.

Officers: Pres. CP Bratnober 1903-04, TJ Calligan 1905-25; **VP** JJ McEvoy 1903, GW Black 1904-07, R Conwell 1909-13, RL Van Alstine 1914, CW Edgington 1920-25; **Cash.** CB Fitch 1903-16, AL Allen 1917-18, Lorenz Lorenzen 1919-25; **AC** Lorenz Lorenzen 1914, BW Rademacher 1920-25, EL Freeman 1920-25

Third Charter, Red Seal	Ser #	# Notes
5-5-5-5	1-350	1,400
10-10-10-20	1-280	1,120
Third Charter, Date Back, Blue Seal		
5-5-5-5	1-500	2,000
10-10-10-20	1-400	1,600
Third Charter, Plain Back, Blue Seal		
5-5-5-5	501-860	1,440
10-10-10-20	401-654	1,016

Total amount issued = $70,900. Amount outstanding at close = $6,200.

8,576 Large   0 Small   8,576 Total

6611		$10	1902PB	624	647 D	A945439K	F/VF	Higgins Mus.

THE FIRST NATIONAL BANK OF GLADBROOK   15 L   24 S
5461   TAMA

Chartered in June 1900.

Officers: Pres. William Mee 1900-13, Martin Mee 1914-32, Wm Mee, Jr. 1933-35; **VP** Marx Heinrich Rehder 1900-21, Henry Ludwig 1922-25, JL Glass 1925-32, Wm C Wiese 1933-35; **Cash.** Martin Mee 1900-13, EW Branch 1921-33, JH Dye 1934-35; **AC** JG Branch 1907, EW Branch 1909-11, Frank Kelley 1909-20, WC Moldenschardt 1922, AC Loepp 1930-32, Kent J Wiloth 1930, AF Agena 1931-35

Second Charter, Brown Backs	Ser #	# Notes
10-10-10-20	1-1800	7,200
Second Charter, Date Back		
10-10-10-20	1-3500	14,000
Second Charter, Value Back		
10-10-10-20	3501-4970	5,880
Third Charter, Plain Back, Blue Seal		
10-10-10-20	1-4138	16,552
1929, Type I		
6-10's	1-956	5,736

		6-20's		1-253	1,518		

Total amount of circulation issued = $633,120. Amount of large outstanding in 1935 = $2,480. Amount of small outstanding in 1935 = $42,520.

43,632 Large			7,254 Small		50,886 Total		
5461	M	$10 1882BB	490	1499 B	U721187U	F/VF	pen/pen
5461	M	$10 1882DB	?	952 E	E245566	?	Bayard, Ink
5461	M	$10 1882VB	?	3532 ?	T564180	VG	
5461	M	$10 1902PB	633	671 A	D391673E	F	gone Higg. Mus.
5461	M	$10 1902PB	633	1308 A	X545720E	VF/XF	stamp/stamp
5461	M	$10 1902PB	633	1922 B	M204274H	VF	
5461	M	$10 1902PB	633	2437 A	A210129K	F/VF	
5461	-	$10 1902PB	633	3349 A	3349 A	F/VF	stamp/stamp
5461	-	$10 1902PB	633	3433 B	3433 B	VF	gone/gone
5461	-	$10 1902PB	633	3655 A	3655 A	F/VF	
5461	-	$10 1902PB	633	3708 B	3708 B	G	gone/gone
5461	-	$10 1902PB	633	4096 A	4096 A	F	
5461	M	$20 1902PB	659	557 A	?	F/VF	
5461	-	$20 1902PB	659	2437 A	A210129K	F/VF	
5461	-	$20 1902PB	659	3655 A	3655 A	F/VF	stamp/stamp
5461		$10 1929T1		D000028A		F	$10 or $20 ?
5461		$10 1929T1		B000049A		F	
5461		$10 1929T1		E000049A		VG/F	
5461		$10 1929T1		A000179A		VG	
5461		$10 1929T1		B000191A		?	
5461		$10 1929T1		A000225A		F	
5461		$10 1929T1		B000449A		F+	
5461		$10 1929T1		D000541A		VG	
5461		$10 1929T1		F000592A		?	
5461		$10 1929T1		B000723A		VG	
5461		$10 1929T1		C000767A		XF	Rust spots
5461		$20 1929T1		E000026A		F	Spot
5461		$20 1929T1		C000064A		?	
5461		$20 1929T1		E000081A		?	
5461		$20 1929T1		D000098A		VG	
5461		$20 1929T1		D000134A		?	
5461		$20 1929T1		D000143A		F	
5461		$20 1929T1		F000146A		VG+	
5461		$20 1929T1		D000151A		VG/F	
5461		$20 1929T1		D000162A		G/VG	
5461		$20 1929T1		A000171A		VF	Higgins Mus.
5461		$20 1929T1		A000179A		VF	
5461		$20 1929T1		B000196A		VG	
5461		$20 1929T1		A000225A		F	

THE MILLS COUNTY NATIONAL BANK OF GLENWOOD
1862   **MILLS**   **7 L   10 S**

Organized on August 11, 1871 with a capital of $65,000. Chartered on August 16, 1871. Placed in receivership on December 27, 1932; capital of $65,000.
Officers: Pres. Joseph V Hinchman 1872-81, BF Buffington 1883-93, Geo Mickelwait 1894-97, DL Heinsheimer 1898-1911, AJ Gettler 1912-14, HH Cheyney 1915-27, WC Rathke 1928-30, CR Buffington 1930-32; **VP** FM Buffington 1896-1909, AD French 1910-11, HH Cheyney 1913-14, WC Rathke 1920-27, CH Cheyney 1928-30, FJ Wallace 1930-32, TQ Records 1932, SF Vinton 1932; **Cash.** William H Anderson 1872-90, AC Sabin 1891-98, AD French 1899-1909, HA French 1910-32; **AC** Geo A Bailey 1878, HA French 1900-09, WC Rathke 1910-14, Mary Rathke 1922-24, Lydia Kupka 1926-28, BH Hamilton 1929-32

First Charter, Original Issue	Ser #	# Notes
1-1-1-2	1-1800	7,200
5-5-5-5	1-3975	15,900
First Charter, Series of 1875		
5-5-5-5	1-5051	20,204
Second Charter, Brown Backs		
10-10-10-20	1-3510	14,040
Second Charter, Date Back		
10-10-10-20	1-801	3,204
Third Charter, Date Back, Blue Seal		
50-50-50-100	1-750	3,000
Third Charter, Plain Back, Blue Seal		
50-50-50-100	751-920	680
1929, Type I		
6-50's	1-110	660
6-100's	1-14	84

Total amount of circulation issued = $676,470. Amount of large outstanding at close = $9,200. Amount of small outstanding at close = $32,050.

64,228 Large			744 Small		64,972 Total		
1862		$10 1882BB	485	1355 B	U945186	VG+	Higgins Mus.
1862	M	$20 1882BB	499	2479 A	N299643N	F/VF	pen/pen
1862	M	$20 1882BB	499	2630 A	N299794N	VF	pen/pen
1862	M	$50 1902DB	671	668 C	B53272	F/VF	Washed; pressed
1862	-	$50 1902PB	679	879 B	879 B	F+	pen/gone
1862	-$100	1902PB	702	759 A	759 A	XF	Higgins Mus.
1862	-$100	1902PB	702	774 A	774 A	AU	
1862		$50 1929T1		D000013A		VF/XF	
1862		$50 1929T1		D000020A		F	
1862		$50 1929T1		B000045A		F/VF	pinholes
1862		$50 1929T1		B000071A		VF	
1862		$50 1929T1		E000081A		F/VF	
1862		$50 1929T1		E000090A		VF	
1862		$50 1929T1		E000103A		F/VF	
1862		$100 1929T1		E000008A		VF	Higgins Mus.
1862		$100 1929T1		E000012A		CU	
1862		$100 1929T1		F000012A		CU	

THE FIRST NATIONAL BANK OF GLIDDEN
4814   **CARROLL**   **19 L   22 S**

Organized on November 1, 1892 with a capital of $50,000. Succeeded The Glidden Bank. Placed in conservatorship on March 22, 1933; licensed on September 2, 1933. Placed in voluntary liquidation on February 28, 1935; capital of $50,000. Succeeded by #14326; circulation assumed by #14326.
Officers: Pres. SC Dunkle 1893-1905, LM Lyons 1906-19, A Moorhouse 1920-23, DE Waldron 1924-26; **VP** WH Badeau 1896-1907, WA Badeau 1909, A Moorhouse 1909-14, Chas U Fisher 1920-26, DE Waldron 1920-23; **Cash.** DE Waldron 1893-1915, HW Porter 1916-26; **AC** J Coder 1896, HW Porter 1902-14, WF Shove 1920-26

Second Charter, Brown Backs	Ser #	# Notes
10-10-10-20	1-3200	12,800
Second Charter, Date Back		
10-10-10-20	1-1511	6,044
Third Charter, Date Back, Blue Seal		
10-10-10-20	1-1700	6,800
Third Charter, Plain Back, Blue Seal		
10-10-10-20	1701-7550	23,400
1929, Type I		
6-10's	1-1028	6,168
6-20's	1-278	1,668
1929, Type II		
10's	1-1186	1,186
20's	1-235	235

Total amount of circulation issued = $724,650. Amount of large outstanding at close = $3,090. Amount of small outstanding at close = $46,910. Circulation liability assumed by #14326 which was then responsible for redeeming the outstanding circulation of #4814.

49,044 Large			9,257 Small		58,301 Total		
4814	-	$20 1882BB	499	630 A	U818575	F+	pen Higgins Mus.
4814		$20 1882BB	499	1581 A	W40354D	VF	
4814	M	$20 1882BB	499	2971 A	V538930V	F/VF	faded/pen
4814	M	$10 1882DB	540	116 F	D436006	CU	Higgins Mus.
4814	M	$10 1882DB	540	1447 E	K63615	VG	
4814	M	$20 1902DB	646	1110 A	Y698120A	VG	gone/sig
4814	M	$10 1902PB	628	1825 A	U118833B	VG	
4814	M	$10 1902PB	628	2295 A	Y187916A	VG/F	Pres. sig stamped upside down
4814	M	$10 1902PB	628	4254 B	M413571E	F/VF	pen/pen
4814	-	$10 1902PB	628	5250 B	R376682H	VF	pen/pen
4814	-	$10 1902PB	628	?	B336223K	?	Bayard
4814	-	$10 1902PB	628	6282 C	6282 C	VG	pen/pen
4814	-	$10 1902PB	628	6752 B	6752 B	F	pen/pen
4814	-	$10 1902PB	628	6855 C	6855 C	VF	pen/pen
4814	-	$10 1902PB	628	6954 A	6954 A	F	
4814	-	$10 1902PB	628	7350 B	7350 B	VG	
4814	-	$10 1902PB	628	7447 C	7447 C	VF	
4814	-	$20 1902PB	654	5198 A	R376630H	VF+	pen Higgins Mus.
4814	-	$20 1902PB	654	5314 A	R376746H	VG	
4814		$10 1929T1		D000033A		VF	
4814		$10 1929T1		D000116A		G/VG	
4814		$10 1929T1		B000212A		VG+	
4814		$10 1929T1		D000230A		VG	
4814		$10 1929T1		A000616A		?	
4814		$10 1929T1		E000677A		VF/XF	
4814		$10 1929T1		E000842A		AU	
4814		$10 1929T1		F000951A		CU	Higgins Mus.
4814		$10 1929T1		E000956A		F	Small puncture
4814		$20 1929T1		C000010A		F+	
4814		$20 1929T1		E000044A		?	

4814	$20	1929T1	F000070A	F	
4814	$20	1929T1	F000082A	F+	
4814	$20	1929T1	C000101A	F	
4814	$20	1929T1	F000102A	F/VF	
4814	$20	1929T1	C000130A	F	
4814	$20	1929T1	C000178A	F	
4814	$20	1929T1	F000207A	F	
4814	$20	1929T1	C000231A	XF	
4814	$10	1929T2	A000012	VG/F	
4814	$10	1929T2	A000037	F	Rust spots
4814	$20	1929T2	A000174	VF	

THE FIRST NATIONAL BANK OF GOLDFIELD 0 L
5373 WRIGHT
Chartered on May 26, 1900. Succeeded The Bank of Goldfield. Placed in voluntary liquidation on September 20, 1900; capital of $30,000. (According to treasury dept. records, by the time the bank received its notes the bank had contemplated liquidation and all the currency returned to Washington—hence none outstanding.)
Officers: Pres. John Henderson 1900; **VP** JS Braden 1900; **Cash.** WV Palmer 1900

Second Charter, Brown Backs	Ser #	# Notes
10-10-10-20	1-150	600

Total amount of circulation issued = $7,500. According to the reports, the entire issue was redeemed.
600 Large   0 Small   600 Total

THE FIRST NATIONAL BANK OF GOWRIE 10 L   12 S
5707 WEBSTER
Organized on January 15, 1901 with a capital of $25,000. Chartered on February 9, 1901; succeeded The Webster County State Bank. Placed in conservatorship on March 28, 1933. Licensed on February 14, 1934.
Officers: Pres. NA Lindquist 1901-22, FW Lindquist 1923-33, Warner Larson 1934-35; **VP** AR Daugenbaugh 1902-10, GG Lindquist 1909-11, AF Daugenbaugh 1913-33, CO Bowman 1934, FW Lindquist 1935; **Cash.** GG Lindquist 1901-07, FW Lindquist 1908-22, 1934, AE Lindquist 1923-33,; **AC** FW Lindquist 1904-07, AE Lindquist 1909-22, 1934

Second Charter, Brown Backs	Ser #	# Notes
10-10-10-20	1-1020	4,080
Second Charter, Date Back		
10-10-10-20	1-1730	6,920
Second Charter, Value Back		
10-10-10-20	1731-2691	3,844
Third Charter, Plain Back, Blue Seal		
10-10-10-20	1-2126	8,504
1929, Type I		
6-10's	1-546	3,276
6-20's	1-150	900
1929, type II		
10's	1-489	489
20's	1-85	85

Total amount of circulation issued = $349,200. Amount of large outstanding in 1935 = $2,290. Amount of small outstanding in 1935 = $22,710.
23,348 Large   4,750 Small   28,098 Total

5707		$10 1882BB	490	1 A	Y461323	?
5707	M	$10 1882DB	545	1629 ?	?	?
5707	M	$20 1882DB	555	835 B	K117093	VG
5707	-	$10 1902PB	633	1074 B	X294146H	VF Higgins Mus.
5707	-	$10 1902PB	633	1208 B	X294280H	VF pen/pen
5707	-	$10 1902PB	633	2088 B	2088 B	F
5707	-	$20 1902PB	659	1361 A	B409033K	VG/F
5707	-	$20 1902PB	659	1379 A	B409051K	?
5707	-	$20 1902PB	659	1572 A	1572 A	F+
5707	-	$20 1902PB	659	1905 A	1905 A	VG
5707		$10 1929T1		E000349A		?
5707		$10 1929T1		F000413A		?
5707		$10 1929T1		A000438A		F/VF Higgins Mus.
5707		$10 1929T1		B000499A		VG+
5707		$20 1929T1		D000026A		VF
5707		$20 1929T1		A000049A		F
5707		$20 1929T1		C000086A		VG
5707		$20 1929T1		D000094A		VG/F
5707		$20 1929T1		E000121A		F
5707		$10 1929T2		A000249		CU
5707		$10 1929T2		A000346		VG
5707		$20 1929T2		A000078		?

THE FIRST NATIONAL BANK OF GRAETTINGER 6 L   3 S
5571 PALO ALTO
Organized on July 13, 1900 with a capital of #25,000. Placed in conservatorship on March 27, 1933. Placed in receivership on October 30, 1933; capital of $25,000.
Officers: Pres. ML Brown 1900-29, Fred Spies 1929-33; **VP** EC Kent 1900-02, LC Christensen 1903-11, DC Tipp 1913-14, AJ Johnson 1920, John O Jertson 1922, Fred Spies 1923-29, AJ Johnson 1929-33; **Cash.** PH Donlon 1900-01, EC Kent 1903, CS George 1904-14, John O Jertson 1915-20, Fred Spies 1922, John O Jertson 1923, HB Hetzler 1924-28, HA Elsenbast 1929-33; **AC** Elizabeth Jensen 1920-31, 1933

Second Charter, Brown Backs	Ser #	# Notes
10-10-10-20	1-500	2,000
Second Charter, Date Back		
10-10-10-20	1-960	3,840
Second Charter, Value Back		
10-10-10-20	961-1225	1,060
Third Charter, Plain Back, Blue Seal		
10-10-10-20	1-1028	4,112
1929, Type I		
6-10's	1-254	1,524
6-20's	1-60	360

Total amount of circulation issued = $160,090. Amount outstanding at close = $12,000. Amount of large outstanding on November 3, 1933 = $1,000.
11,012 Large   1,884 Small   12,896 Total

5571	M	$10 1882BB	490	448 E	E953646	VG/F	
5571	M	$10 1882DB	545	484 D	N322392	XF	
5571	M	$10 1882DB	545	928 F	R130286	VF	
5571	M	$10 1882VB	577	1064 E	U574672	G/VG	Higgins Mus.
5571	M	$10 1902PB	633	343 B	X711875D	CU	pen ac/pen vp
5571	-	$10 1902PB	633	962 B	962 B	VG	gone/gone
5571		$10 1929T1		A000087A		VG	
5571		$10 1929T1		E000149A		VF	Higgins Mus.
5571		$20 1929T1		B000017A		VG/F	

THE FIRST NATIONAL BANK OF GRAFTON 0 L
6610 WORTH
Chartered on February 5, 1903. Succeeded The Farmers Exchange Bank. Placed in voluntary liquidation on December 23, 1904; capital of $25,000.
Officers: Pres. Charles Christians 1903-04; **VP** SM Mann 1903-04; **Cash.** OH Christians 1903-04; **AC** EA Heimke 1903-04

Third Charter, Red Seal	Ser #	# Notes
10-10-10-20	1-167	668

Total amount of circulation issued = $8,350. Amount outstanding at close = $6,250. Amount outstanding in 1910 = $520.
668 Large   0 Small   668 Total

THE FIRST NATIONAL BANK OF GRAND RIVER 9 L   7 S
9737 DECATUR
Organized on March 10, 1910 with a capital of $25,000. Placed in conservatorship on March 24, 1933. Placed in receivership on October 30, 1933; capital of $25,000.
Officers: Pres. AL Ackerley 1911-19, Peter Brennaman 1920-22, B Brennaman 1923, Fred Bone 1924-25, Joseph Brown 1925-28, Blair Brennaman 1928-33; **VP** Patrick K Griffin 1911-14, R Brennaman 1920-22, Fred Bone 1923, 1928-33, Joseph Brown 1923-24, B Brennaman 1924-26, ER Gord 1925-26, CH Robbins 1926-29, Orval Burchett 1931-32; **Cash.** JC Brothers 1911-13, Cary O Andrew 1916, JC Brothers 1917-28, Florence E Madison 1928-33; **AC** JE Fierce 1911, Charles Kelley 1914, FE Brennaman 1920-24, BL Brothers 1925-26, John C Madison 1929-33

Third Charter, Date Back, Blue Seal	Ser #	# Notes
10-10-10-20	1-1850	7,400

Sheets numbered 1 to 1730 were 02-08 backs. Sheets numbered 1731 to 1850 were not marked as to type. Sheets numbered 1851 to 4430 were plain backs.

Third Charter, Plain Back, Blue Seal		
10-10-10-20	1851-4430	10,320
1929, Type I		
6-10's	1-496	2,976
6-20's	1-121	726

Total amount of circulation issued = $265,780. Amount of large outstanding at close = $2,300. Amount of small outstanding at close = $22,700.
17,720 Large   3,702 Small   21,422 Total

9737	M	$10 1902DB	619	254 ?	?	?	
9737	M	$20 1902DB	645	488 A	V496840	Fr/G	Bayard
9737	M	$20 1902DB	645	794 A	Z433402	VF	Higgins Mus.
9737	M	$10 1902PB	627	2811 B	A967933E	G/VG	pen/gone Soiled
9737	M	$10 1902PB	627	2941 A	T15563E	F+	pen/lt stamp
9737	M	$10 1902PB	627	3099 B	X239071E	F	
9737	-	$10 1902PB	627	4102 B	4102 B	F	pen/pen
9737	M	$20 1902PB	653	2643 A	U40575D	VG+	
9737	M	$20 1902PB	653	2941 A	T15563E	F	
9737		$10 1929T1		D000025A		F	
9737		$10 1929T1		A000129A		F+	
9737		$10 1929T1		E000183A		VG/F	

9737	$10	1929T1	D000342A		?	
9737	$20	1929T1	B000027A		VG	
9737	$20	1929T1	C000060A		VF	Higgins Mus.
9737	$20	1929T1	D000082A		VF	

THE FIRST NATIONAL BANK OF GREENE   0 L
3071   BUTLER
Chartered on November 2, 1883. Succeeded The Shell Rock Valley Bank. Placed in voluntary liquidation on December 15, 1887; capital of $50,000.
Officers: Pres. A Slimmer 1884-85, J Perrin 1887; **Cash.** CH Wilcox 1884-85, M Hartness 1887

Second Charter, Brown Backs	Ser #	# Notes
10-10-10-20	1-321	1,284

Total amount of circulation issued = $16,050. Amount outstanding at close = $10,590. Amount outstanding in 1910 = $70.

1,284 Large   0 Small   1,284 Total

THE MERCHANTS NATIONAL BANK OF GREENE   6 L
6880   BUTLER
Organized on June 23, 1903 with a capital of $50,000. Succeeded Soesbe, Shepardson & Company. Placed in receivership on June 4, 1927; capital of $50,000. Reason for failure: incompetent management.
Officers: Pres. EW Soesbe 1904-05, JB Shepardson 1906-15, CW Soesbe 1916-24, GA Carney 1925-27; **VP** JB Shepardson 1904-05, Ed Morrill 1907, CW Soesbe 1909-14, WS Shepardson 1920-24, Wm Meyne 1925-27; **Cash.** CW Soesbe 1904-08, DH Ellis 1909, BN Mead 1910-11, GA Carney 1912-16, RP Palmer 1917-19, AH Nolterieke 1920-27; **AC** DH Ellis 1904-07, CH Williams 1904-05, BN Mead 1909, RS Walker 1914, CH Kahuda 1920-24

Third Charter, Red Seal	Ser #	# Notes
10-10-10-20	1-2500	10,000
Third Charter, Date Back, Blue Seal		
10-10-10-20	1-3200	12,800
Third Charter, Plain Back, Blue Seal		
10-10-10-20	3201-7012	15,248

Total amount of circulation issued = $475,600. Amount outstanding in 1924 report = $49,500. Note: the bank quit issuing notes in 1924, therefore the amount outstanding at close would be less than the $49,500.

38,048 Large   0 Small   38,048 Total

6880	M	$10	1902RS	613	1509 A	H859570	VG	vp Higgins Mus.
6880	M	$10	1902DB	616	1847 E	D900673A	VF	
6880	M	$10	1902PB	624	3437 D	T535367B	VG	pen/pen
6880	M	$10	1902PB	624	4165 E	A769482D	VG	pen/pen Bayard
6880	M	$10	1902PB	624	4335 D	E397304D	VG/F	pen/pen
6880	M	$20	1902PB	650	5889 B	M748896E	F/VF	pen Higgins Mus.

THE FIRST NATIONAL BANK OF GREENFIELD   15 L
5334   ADAIR
Organized on April 23, 1900 with a capital of $25,000. Chartered on May 7, 1900; succeeded The Citizens Bank. Placed in receivership on March 21, 1928; capital of $50,000. Reason for failure: local depression.
Officers: Pres. AP Littleton 1900-11, Guy A Lee 1912-28; **VP** Lewis Linebarger 1900-04, WW Burrell 1907-11, JH Hoyt 1913, JC Hoyt 1914, Jas F Lande 1920, S Kreps 1922-27; **Cash.** HN Linebarger 1900-04, WW Burrell 1905, CD Myers 1906-11, John A Barr 1912-27; **AC** Vern C Littleton 1900-02, CD Myers 1904, John A Barr 1909-11, RH Murray 1913, AL Dorsey 1920-27

Second Charter, Brown Backs	Ser #	# Notes
10-10-10-20	1-800	3,200
Second Charter, Date Back		
10-10-10-20	1-1760	7,040
Second Charter, Value Back		
10-10-10-20	1761-2501	2,964
Third Charter, Plain Back, Blue Seal		
10-10-10-20	1-3394	13,576

Total amount issued = $334,750. Amount outstanding at close = $24,995.

26,780 Large   0 Small   26,780 Total

5334		$10	1882BB	490	1 B	X303441	AU	
5334	M	$10	1882DB	545	398 F	D409468	VG/F	pen/pen
5334	M	$10	1882DB	545	956 E	K265314	F+	pen/pen
5334	M	$10	1882DB	545	1643 F	R604951	VG	Ink; tape spot
5334	M	$20	1882DB	555	1101 B	M206009	VG	pen/pen
5334	M	$20	1882VB	581	1986 B	T896044	VG	Higgins Mus.
5334	M	$10	1902PB	633	870 B	Y893122B	VG	pen/stamp
5334	M	$10	1902PB	633	1073 C	Y893325D	?	
5334	M	$10	1902PB	633	1308 A	K98370E	VG	
5334	M	$10	1902PB	633	1963 C	T223005E	VG	
5334	M	$10	1902PB	633	2322 C	Z621744E	VF+	Higgins Mus.
5334	M	$10	1902PB	633	2349 B	Z621771E	F	
5334	-	$10	1902PB	633	3182 A	V345504H	F	
5334	M	$20	1902PB	659	160 A	V494352D	F+	pen/stamp
5334	-	$20	1902PB	659	3337 A	3337 A	VF	pen/faded Nice

THE POWESHIEK COUNTY NATIONAL BANK OF GRINNELL   31 S
13473   POWESHIEK
Chartered in June 1930. Absorbed #7439 on July 31, 1930.
Officers: Pres. WH Brenton 1932-34, CE Brenton 1935; **VP** GC Kelly 1932-34, CE Child 1932-35, WP Wilson 1935; **Cash.** RS Kinsey 1932-35; **AC** AR McMurray 1932-35

1929, Type I	Ser #	# Notes
6-5's	1-734	4,404
6-10's	1-376	2,256
6-20's	1-122	732

Total amount issued = $59,220. Amount outstanding in 1935 = $26,900.

0 Large   7,392 Small   7,392 Total

13473	$5	1929T1	A000001A	[	CU	Grinnell # 5793
13473	$5	1929T1	B000001A	[	CU	Grinnell # 5793
13473	$5	1929T1	C000001A	[	CU	Grinnell # 5793
13473	$5	1929T1	D000001A	[	CU	Grinnell # 5793
13473	$5	1929T1	E000001A	[	CU	Grinnell # 5793
13473	$5	1929T1	F000001A	[	CU	Grinnell # 5793
13473	$5	1929T1	C000191A		XF	Higgins Mus.
13473	$5	1929T1	A000388A		F	
13473	$5	1929T1	D000476A		VG	
13473	$5	1929T1	D000700A		F	
13473	$5	1929T1	C000723A		AU	
13473	$10	1929T1	A000001A	[	CU	Grinnell # 5794
13473	$10	1929T1	B000001A	[	CU	Grinnell # 5794
13473	$10	1929T1	C000001A	[	CU	Grinnell # 5794
13473	$10	1929T1	D000001A	[	CU	Grinnell # 5794
13473	$10	1929T1	E000001A	[	CU	Grinnell # 5794
13473	$10	1929T1	F000001A	[	CU	Grinnell # 5794
13473	$10	1929T1	E000110A		VF	
13473	$10	1929T1	E000113A		VG	
13473	$10	1929T1	A000174A		?	
13473	$10	1929T1	D000348A		VG	
13473	$20	1929T1	A000001A	[	CU	Grinnell # 5795
13473	$20	1929T1	B000001A	[	CU	Grinnell # 5795
13473	$20	1929T1	C000001A	[	CU	Grinnell # 5795
13473	$20	1929T1	D000001A	[	CU	Grinnell # 5795
13473	$20	1929T1	E000001A	[	CU	Grinnell # 5795
13473	$20	1929T1	F000001A	[	CU	Grinnell # 5795
13473	$20	1929T1	E000046A		XF/AU	
13473	$20	1929T1	A000061A		F+	
13473	$20	1929T1	A000076A		F+	Ink
13473	$20	1929T1	A000106A		F/VF	

THE CITIZENS NATIONAL BANK OF GRINNELL   10 L   2 S
7439   POWESHIEK
Chartered on September 15, 1904. Placed in voluntary liquidation on July 31, 1930; capital of $75,000. Absorbed by #13473. Placed in receivership on September 6, 1930.
Officers: Pres. HW Spaulding 1905-14, John Goodfellow 1915-29, Carl E Child 1930; **VP** Wm F Vogt 1907-30, GH McMurray 1920-29, GO Watland 1930; **Cash.** HF Lanphere 1905-14, HM Harris 1915-19, Carl E Child 1920-29, AR McMurray 1930; **AC** A Shadbolt 1907, HM Harris 1909-14, AR McMurray 1920-29, Mary Dennison 1920-29

Third Charter, Red Seal	Ser #	# Notes
10-10-10-20	1-1400	5,600
Third Charter, Date Back, Blue Seal		
10-10-10-20	1-700	2,800
Third Charter, Plain Back, Blue Seal		
10-10-10-20	701-6891	24,764
1929, Type I		
6-10's	1-400	2,400
6-20's	1-85	510

Total amount of circulation issued = $448,750. Amount of large outstanding at close = $13,780. Amount of small outstanding at close = $34,200.

33,164 Large   2,910 Small   36,074 Total

7439	M	$10	1902PB	624	821 D	V836981B	G	stamp/stamp
7439	M	$10	1902PB	624	2253 D	R814175D	F	
7439	M	$10	1902PB	624	2377 D	R814299D	F+	Higgins Mus.
7439		$10	1902PB	624	3178 F	E243060E	G	Faded
7439	-	$10	1902PB	624	6338 F	6338 F	F	gone/gone
7439	-	$10	1902PB	624	6377 D	6377 D	F	
7439	-	$10	1902PB	624	6561 F	6561 F	VF	
7439		$20	1902PB	650	?	?	CU	Grinnell # 1398
7439	-	$20	1902PB	650	6056 B	6056 B	VF+	
7439	-	$20	1902PB	650	6391 B	6391 B	VG	faded/faded

Pieces missing on bottom

7439	$10	1929T1	B000149A		VF/XF	
7439	$10	1929T1	A000366A		VG	Higgins Mus.

THE FIRST NATIONAL BANK OF GRINNELL   **4 L**
1629   **POWESHIEK**
Organized on January 15, 1866 with a capital of $50,000. Placed in receivership on July 27, 1904; capital of $100,000. Reason for failure: incompetent management.
Officers: Pres. Erastus Snow 1867, JB Grinnell 1868-71, Thomas Holyoke 1872-75, Alonzo Steele 1876-80, JP Lyman 1881-85, Charles F Craver 1887-90, HK Edson 1891-97, JP Lyman 1898-1900; **Cash.** Chas H Spencer 1867-92, HC Spencer 1893-1900; **AC** Henry C Spencer 1878-79, 1885

First Charter, Original Issue	Ser #	# Notes
1-1-1-2	1-3400	13,600
5-5-5-5	1-2250	9,000
10-10-10-20	1-1460	5,840
First Charter, Series of 1875		
5-5-5-5	1-500	2,000
10-10-10-20	1-1092	4,368
Second Charter, Brown Backs		
50-100	1-801	1,602

Total amount of circulation issued = $319,750. Amount outstanding at close = $25,000. Amount outstanding in 1915 = $3,661.
36,410 Large   0 Small   36,410 Total

1629	-	$1	ORIG	380	1232 B	A871543	?	Higgins Mus.
1629	-	$1	ORIG	380	1404 B	C408400	VF	pen/pen
1629	-	$1	ORIG	380	1539 A	C408535	VG	pen/pen
1629	-	$1	ORIG	380	2395 A	C409391	G	

THE MERCHANTS NATIONAL BANK OF GRINNELL   **7 L**
2953   **POWESHIEK**
Organized on April 28, 1883 with a capital of $50,000. Placed in receivership on Nov. 12, 1924; capital of $100,000. Reason for failure: local depression.
Officers: Pres. Samuel F Cooper 1883-95, CR Morse 1896-99, SA Cravath 1900-11, Geo H Hamlin 1912-24; **VP** SA Cravath 1896, R McDonald 1896, 1900, EW Clark 1902-10, LF Parker 1909, JF Wilson 1910-11, SA Cravath 1913-14, JC Goodrich 1920, BJ Carney 1922-24, BJ Ricker 1922; **Cash.** George H Hamlin 1883-1911, Hallie C Burd 1914, WC Staat 1917-22, John H Horn 1923-24; **AC** WC Staat 1907-09, SA Mac Eachron 1913-14, Hallie C Burd 1913,1920-22, HB Westlake 1923-24, Harvey B Adkins 1923-24

Second Charter, Brown Backs	Ser #	# Notes
50-100	1-866	1,732
Third Charter, Red Seal		
50-100	1-1067	2,134
Third Charter, Date Back, Blue Seal		
50-100	1-800	1,600
50-50-50-100	1-1339	5,356

Total amount issued = $744,700. Amount outstanding at close = $100,000.
10,822 Large   0 Small   10,822 Total

2953	M	$50 1902RS	664	756 A	A213053	VG	Repair, Higg. Mus
2953	M	$50 1902DB	667	750 D	A758840	F	pen/pen
2953	M	$50 1902DB	667	904 E	A817476	VG	pen/pen ac
2953	M	$50 1902DB	667	1007 D	A853099	VF	Higgins Mus.
2953	M	$50 1902DB	667	1038 D	A853130	VF	
2953	M	$50 1902DB	667	1163 D	A928885	VG	Ink stains
2953	M	$50 1902DB	667	1310 D	B40784	VG	ac/vp

THE FIRST NATIONAL BANK OF GRISWOLD   **0 L**
3048   **CASS**
Organized on September 15, 1883 with a capital of $50,000. Succeeded The Bank of Griswold. Closed on February 3, 1897; placed in receivership on February 17, 1897. Reason for failure: incompetent management; capital at close of $50,000.
Officers: Pres. Theodore H Brown 1883-97; **Cash.** Frank L Brown 1883, RL Brown 1887-89, WL Mote 1890, RL Brown 1891-96; **AC** Frank L Brown

Second Charter, Brown Backs	Ser #	# Notes
5-5-5-5	1-2472	9,888

Total amount of circulation issued = $49,440. Amount outstanding at close = $10,887. Amount outstanding in 1915 = $272.
9,888 Large   0 Small   9,888 Total

THE GRISWOLD NATIONAL BANK   **17 L**
8915   **CASS**
Organized on September 2, 1907 with a capital of $50,000. Placed in receivership on December 13, 1929; capital of $50,000. Reason for failure: incompetent management.
Officers: Pres. Hamilton Wilcox 1908-11, Jas Boiler 1912-13, WL Edwards 1914-16, RR Bell 1917-20, WT Kirkpatrick 1922-29; **VP** Jas Boiler 1909-11, WL Edwards 1913, AG Arrasmith 1914-29; **Cash.** AG Arrasmith 1908-17, RH Bell 1918-20, Fred S DeWitt 1922-29; **AC** Fred B DeWitt 1909-20

Third Charter, Red Seal	Ser #	# Notes
10-10-10-10	1-450	1,800
Third Charter, Date Back, Blue Seal		
10-10-10-10	1-3100	12,400
Third Charter, Plain Back, Blue Seal		
10-10-10-10	3101-8363	21,052
1929, Type I		
6-10's	1-101	606

Total amount of circulation issued = $358,580. Amount of large outstanding at close = $23,940. Amount of small outstanding at close = $6,060.
35,252 Large   606 Small   35,858 Total

8915	M	$10 1902DB	618	1213 G	B256321	XF	ac vp Higg. Mus.
8915	M	$10 1902PB	626	3128 H	N196661	?	
8915	M	$10 1902PB	626	3214 G	N196747	VG	
8915	M	$10 1902PB	626	4300 E	R852695	?	
8915	M	$10 1902PB	626	4897 E	T898342	G/VG	pen/pen
8915	M	$10 1902PB	626	5263 G	U322553	VF	pen/pen
8915	M	$10 1902PB	626	5417 E	U888682	VG	
8915	M	$10 1902PB	626	6044 E	X243394	VG	
8915	M	$10 1902PB	626	6154 H	X243504	F+	faded/pen
8915	-	$10 1902PB	626	6420 E	Y98505	?	Bayard
8915	-	$10 1902PB	626	6940 F	6940 F	VF	pen/pen
8915	-	$10 1902PB	626	7020 E	7020 E	G/VG	
8915	-	$10 1902PB	626	7063 F	7063 F	F	Edge trimmed
8915	-	$10 1902PB	626	7225 H	7225 H	CU	pen/pen
8915	-	$10 1902PB	626	7543 F	7543 F	?	
8915	-	$10 1902PB	626	7543 G	7543 G	F	pen/pen
8915	-	$10 1902PB	626	8190 F	8190 F	F/VF	pen Tight bottom

THE FIRST NATIONAL BANK OF GRUNDY CENTER   **14 L**
3225   **GRUNDY**
Chartered in 1884. Succeeded The Grundy County Bank. Suspended on June 16, 1893; resumed on September 1, 1893. Placed in voluntary liquidation on August 27, 1929; capital of $50,000. Succeeded by The First Trust & Savings Bank, Grundy Center. Placed in receivership on April 11, 1934; reason: deficiency in assets sold.
Officers: Pres. George Wells 1884-1905, RM Finlayson 1906-29; **VP** Eug A Crouse 1896-1929, WC Sargent 1913-14, WC Morrison 1914-29; **Cash.** Chris C Shuler 1884-92, RM Finlayson 1893-1905, WC Sargent 1906-11, JJ Dalgliesh 1912-19, Walter C Morrison 1920-25, GD Harberts 1926-29; **AC** JL Wetzel 1885, WF McLane 1896, WC Sargent 1900-04, Chas T Rogers 1907, EW Allison 1909-10, JJ Dalgliesh 1911, Harold D Finlayson 1913, WC Morrison 1914, GD Harberts 1920-26, Claus P Dudden

Second Charter, Brown Backs	Ser #	# Notes
5-5-5-5	1-3306	13,224
50-100	1-87	174
Third Charter, Red Seal		
10-10-10-20	1-1130	4,520
Third Charter, Date Back, Blue Seal		
10-10-10-20	1-3300	13,200
Third Charter, Plain Back, Blue Seal		
10-10-10-20	3301-9335	24,140

Total amount issued = $602,420. Amount outstanding at close = $50,000.
55,258 Large   0 Small   55,258 Total

3225	M	$10 1902DB	616	254 D	H521112	F	pen/pen
3225	M	$10 1902DB	616	654 D	H521512	VG	pen/pen
3225	M	$20 1902DB	642	57 B	H520915	VF	
3225	M	$20 1902DB	642	2751 B	X270156A	VF	pen/pen
3225	M	$10 1902PB	624	?	V533054	?	
3225	M	$10 1902PB	624	3588 D	U816156B	F	
3225	M	$10 1902PB	624	5292 F	V883004D	VG	faded/faded
3225	M	$10 1902PB	624	6450 E	Y660782E	VF	stamp Higg. Mus.
3225		$10 1902PB	624	7177 D	U635609H	VG	
3225	-	$10 1902PB	624	7603 D	Z962195H	VG	faded/faded
3225	-	$10 1902PB	624	8967 E	8967 E	VF	
3225	-	$10 1902PB	624	9089 F	9089 F	F	
3225	M	$20 1902PB	650	4065 B	Y377336B	XF	
3225	-	$20 1902PB	650	9104 B	9104 B	?	

THE GRUNDY COUNTY NATIONAL BANK OF GRUNDY CENTER
3396   **GRUNDY**   **12 L   15 S**
Organized on September 16, 1885 with a capital of $50,000. Succeeded C. Beckman & The Bank of Morrison (Raymond & Allison). Placed in conservatorship on March 20, 1933. Placed in voluntary liquidation on April 20, 1934; capital of $50,000. Succeeded by #14066.
Officers: Pres. SR Raymond 1887-1904, HS Beckman 1905-13, GC Allison 1914, WD Wilson 1914-33; **VP** JS King 1896, EM Sargent 1900-03, WD Wilson 1907-13, GC Allison 1914-33; **Cash.** Roger Leavitt 1887, HD Beckman 1888-1904, George M Rea 1905-10, Vernon H Wilson 1911-18, RJ Ruehl 1919-33; **AC** DM Moser 1896, George M Rea 1903-04, Naomi C Tomkins 1907-10, VH Wilson 1910, GC Allison 1910, RJ Kuehl 1914, BD Lane 1920, DC Scott 1922-28, Wm Groote 1930-33

Second Charter, Brown Backs	Ser #	# Notes
5-5-5-5	1-5306	21,224

10-10-10-20	1-1508	6,032
Third Charter, Red Seal		
10-10-10-20	1-1000	4,000
Third Charter, Date Back, Blue Seal		
10-10-10-20	1-3200	12,800
Third Charter, Plain Back, Blue Seal		
10-10-10-20	3201-9057	23,428
1929, Type I		
6-10's	1-956	5,736
6-20's	1-278	1,668
1929, Type II		
10's	1-157	157
20's	1-14	14

Total amount of circulation issued = $776,940. Amount of large outstanding at close = $3,577. Amount of small outstanding at close = $46,420.

67,484 Large   7,575 Small   75,059 Total

3396	-	$10 1882BB	482	240 C	V721733E	F+	pen/pen
3396	-	$20 1882BB	496	990 A	X310270	F+	
3396	M	$10 1902DB	617	124 D	A178648	VF	Higgins Mus.
3396	M	$10 1902DB	617	1233 E	R337544	VG	
3396	M	$20 1902DB	643	3085 B	Z155045A	F	faded/faded
3396	M	$10 1902PB	625	3230 F	N866108B	F+	stamp sigs vp
3396	M	$10 1902PB	625	3788 E	X244425B	F/VF	stamp sigs vp
3396	M	$10 1902PB	625	5443 F	A959255E	F/VF	
3396	M	$10 1902PB	625	6322 E	X206144F	F	
3396	-	$10 1902PB	625	8666 D	8666 D	F/VF	stamp sigs vp
3396	M	$20 1902PB	651	4079 B	X244716B	XF	
3396	M	$20 1902PB	651	6503 B	X206325E	AU	stamp/stamp
3396		$10 1929T1		C000155A		F	
3396		$10 1929T1		F000175A		F	
3396		$10 1929T1		A000420A		VG	Rust
3396		$10 1929T1		B000581A		VG	
3396		$10 1929T1		C000672A		VF	
3396		$10 1929T1		C000715A		F	
3396		$10 1929T1		D000803A		VG	
3396		$10 1929T1		D000867A		F	
3396		$20 1929T1		D000038A		F	
3396		$20 1929T1		D000057A		VF	
3396		$20 1929T1		A000101A		F	
3396		$20 1929T1		F000136A		F+	
3396		$20 1929T1		F000191A		F/VF	
3396		$10 1929T2		A000006		F+	Higgins Mus.
3396		$10 1929T2		A000153		VG	

THE CITIZENS NATIONAL BANK OF GUTHRIE CENTER
7736   **GUTHRIE**   **1 L**

Chartered in May 1905 with a capital of $25,000. Placed in voluntary liquidation on March 23, 1912; capital of $25,000. Consolidated with #5424; circulation assumed by #5424.

Officers: Pres. John W Foster 1905-11; **VP** TJ Foster 1907-11; **Cash.** OD Williams 1905, Fred R Jones 1906-09, CS Foster 1910-11; **AC** FC Roberts 1907, RM Sayre 1909-11, RF Long 1911

Third Charter, Red Seal	Ser #	# Notes
10-10-10-20	1-760	3,040
Third Charter, Date Back, Blue Seal		
10-10-10-20	1-312	1,248

Total amount of circulation issued = $53,600. Amount outstanding at close = $20,000. Circulation liability assumed by #5424 which was then responsible for redeeming the outstanding notes of #7736.

4,288 Large   0 Small   4,288 Total

7736	M	$10 1902RS	613	691 A	V442774	G	Bayard

THE FIRST NATIONAL BANK OF GUTHRIE CENTER
5424   **GUTHRIE**   **15 L   5 S**

Organized on May 4, 1900 with a capital of $30,000. Chartered on June 14, 1900. Assumed #7736 by consolidation on March 23, 1912l; assumed the circulation of #7736. Placed in voluntary liquidation on June 23, 1930; capital of $75,000. Absorbed by The Peoples State Bank of Guthrie Center. Placed in receivership on Sept. 15, 1930. Reason for failure: deficiency in assets sold.

Officers: Pres. EC Lane 1900-11; Jno W Foster 1912-29; **VP** FM Hopkins 1900-11, Carl H Lane 1911-13, CS Foster 1914, Carl S Foster 1920-29, TJ Foster 1922-28, WL Reed 1922-29; **Cash.** Carl H Lane 1900-10, Will A Lane 1911-13, Carl H Lane 1914-15, GW Cook 1917-22, CH Sayre 1923-29; **AC** KB O'Dair 1900-05, Will A Lane 1907-10, Roy F Long 1913-14, CH Sayre 1920-22, HA Miller 1920-22, C Flanery 1922

Second Charter, Brown Backs	Ser #	# Notes
10-10-10-20	1-1590	6,360
Second Charter, Date Back		
10-10-10-20	1-3550	14,200
Second Charter, Value Back		
10-10-10-20	3551-4507	3,828
Third Charter, Plain Back, Blue Seal		
10-10-10-20	1-4672	18,688
1929, Type I		
6-10's	1-358	2,148
6-20's	1-45	270

Total amount of circulation issued = $565,330. Amount of large outstanding at close = $15,920. Includes the unredeemed notes of #7736. Amount of small outstanding at close = $26,880.

43,076 Large   2,418 Small   45,494 Total

5424	M	$10 1882BB	490	?	U94341U	?	Bayard
5424	M	$20 1882BB	504	1343 A	U94417U	XF	Reverse Stains
5424	M	$10 1882DB	545	2667 D	R190415	VF	Higgins Mus.
5424	M	$20 1882DB	555	3161 B	T251739	VG/F	
5424	M	$20 1882VB	581	3576 B	U243724	XF	pen/pen Stain
5424	-	$10 1902PB	633	2409 B	R80751H	F	Bayard; staining
5424	-	$10 1902PB	633	2691 A	V819073H	VF	pen/pen vp
5424	-	$10 1902PB	633	2995 B	B258477K	F	vp Bayard
5424	-	$10 1902PB	633	3039 C	B258521K	VF	Bayard, Tears
5424	-	$10 1902PB	633	3126 C	3126 C	?	
5424	-	$10 1902PB	633	3168 B	3168 B	XF	vp Higgins Mus.
5424	-	$10 1902PB	633	3582 A	3582 A	VF	pen/pen vp
5424	-	$10 1902PB	633	4408 C	4408 C	F/VF	pen/pen
5424	-	$20 1902PB	659	2856 A	B258338K	VG	
5424	-	$20 1902PB	659	3004 A	B258486K	VF	pen/pen vp
5424		$10 1929T1		C000017A		F/VF	
5424		$10 1929T1		B000226A		VG	
5424		$10 1929T1		A000331A		F	
5424		$10 1929T1		A000335A		F	
5424		$20 1929T1		A000026A		F	Higgins Mus.

THE FARMERS NATIONAL BANK OF HAMBURG   4 L
6017   FREMONT

Chartered in November 1901 with a capital of $50,000. Succeeded The Farmers & Merchants State Bank. Placed in voluntary liquidation on August 27, 1910; capital of $50,000.

Officers: Pres. A Hydinger 1902-10; **VP** GM Beal 1902-07, MM Payne 1904-05, HH Clayton 1909, Hos F Miller 1909, CD Butterfield 1910; **Cash.** CD Butterfield 1902-09, EA Brittain 1910; **AC** BG Franklin 1902-07, CB Clayton 1909, SB Cunningham 1909, FS Miller 1909-10

Second Charter, Brown Backs	Ser #	# Notes
5-5-5-5	1-1480	5,920
10-10-10-20	1-1188	4752
Second Charter, Date Back		
5-5-5-5	1-395	1,580
10-10-10-20	1-293	1,172

Total amount of circulation issued = $111,500. Amount outstanding at close = $50,000. Amount outstanding in October 1910 = $39,100.

13,428 Large   0 Small   13,428 Total

6017	M	$5 1882BB	477	1063 D	T576511T	VF+	pen ac/pen vp
6017	M	$5 1882BB	477	1064 D	T576512T	VF+	pen ac/pen vp
6017	M	$5 1882BB	477	1067 D	T576515T	VF	Higgins Mus.
6017	M	$5 1882BB	477	1104 B	T576552T	G	

THE FIRST NATIONAL BANK OF HAMBURG   0 L
2364   FREMONT

Chartered on June 28, 1877 with a capital of $50,000. Placed in voluntary liquidation on December 31, 1886; capital of $50,000. Succeeded by The Bank of Hamburg.

Officers: Pres. Joel N Cornish 1877-85; **Cash.** John H Hertsche 1877-86

First Charter, Series of 1875	Ser #	# Notes
5-5-5-5	1-3161	12,644

Total amount of circulation issued = $63,220. Amount outstanding at close = $13,500. Amount outstanding in 1910 = $345.

12,644 Large   0 Small   12,644 Total

THE CITIZENS NATIONAL BANK OF HAMPTON   23 L   40 S
7843   FRANKLIN

Organized on July 20, 1905 with a capital of $100,000. Placed in conservatorship on March 22, 1933. Placed in voluntary liquidation on January 20, 1934; capital of $100,000. Succeeded by #13842.

Officers: Pres. TJB Robinson 1906-22, WL Robinson 1923-33; **VP** NW Beebe 1907-33, WL Robinson 1920-22, WT Robinson 1932-33; **Cash.** WL Robinson 1906-19, Walter T Robinson 1920-32, JM Boots 1932-33; **AC** Chas Krag 1907-11, OW Maxwell 1911-13, Walter T Robinson 1914, WE Clinton 1920-26, LC Robinson 1920-30, JM Boots 1923-32, Wm L Robinson, Jr 1932, JH Boehmler 1932-33

Third Charter, Red Seal	Ser #	# Notes
10-10-10-20	1-3800	15,200
Third Charter, Date Back, Blue Seal		
10-10-10-20	1-6100	24,400
Third Charter, Plain Back, Blue Seal		

10-10-10-20			6101-18377		49,108	
1929, Type I						
6-10's			1-1867		11,202	
6-20's			1-568		3,408	

Total amount of circulation issued = $1,289,030. Amount of large outstanding at close = $8,540. Amount of small outstanding at close = $91,460.
88,708 Large   14,610 Small   103,318 Total

7843	M	$10	1902RS	614	2360 A	N525756	F	Higgins Mus.
7843	M	$10	1902DB	617	2357 E	U726853	F	
7843	M	$10	1902DB	617	2701 D	A586444A	VF	stamp/stamp
7843	M	$10	1902DB	617	3453 E	H859969A	VG+	stamp/stamp
7843	M	$10	1902DB	617	4832 D	X290852A	VG	
7843	M	$20	1902DB	643	1527 B	?	G	
7843	M	$20	1902DB	643	5649 B	A604461B	AU	stamp/stamp
7843	M	$20	1902DB	643	5650 B	A604462B	CU	
7843	M	$20	1902DB	643	5651 B	A604463B	CU	Higgins Mus.
7843	M	$10	1902PB	625	7614 F	Y367035B	G	Tape on back
7843	M	$10	1902PB	625	8760 F	E672764D	XF	stamp/stamp
7843	M	$10	1902PB	625	12780 D	X520892E	F	
7843	-	$10	1902PB	625	14763 E	A736445K	VG	
7843	-	$10	1902PB	625	14947 F	A736629K	VG	gone/gone
7843	-	$10	1902PB	625	14970 E	A736652K	Fr/G	
7843	-	$10	1902PB	625	15531 D	15531 D	F	
7843	-	$10	1902PB	625	15835 E	15835 E	VG	
7843	-	$10	1902PB	625	17114 E	17114 E	F/VF	stamp/stamp
7843	-	$10	1902PB	625	18001 E	18001 E	F	stamp/stamp
7843	-	$20	1902PB	651	15235 B	15235 B	F/VF	retraced sigs
7843	-	$20	1902PB	651	15646 B	15646 B	F	
7843	-	$20	1902PB	651	17438 B	17438 B	F	
7843	-	$20	1902PB	651	18103 B	18103 B	AU	Grinnell # 1400
7843		$10	1929T1		B000085A		?	
7843		$10	1929T1		A000202A		VG	
7843		$10	1929T1		B000283A		F	
7843		$10	1929T1		C000349A		F	
7843		$10	1929T1		A000522A		VG	
7843		$10	1929T1		C000643A		F	
7843		$10	1929T1		C000744A		F/VF	
7843		$10	1929T1		B000987A		F	Ink
7843		$10	1929T1		B001012A		VF	
7843		$10	1929T1		B001119A		?	
7843		$10	1929T1		D001225A		VG/F	
7843		$10	1929T1		C001266A		VF	
7843		$10	1929T1		B001287A		VG/F	
7843		$10	1929T1		C001307A		VF	
7843		$10	1929T1		D001322A		F+	
7843		$10	1929T1		B001344A		AU	Higgins Mus.
7843		$10	1929T1		B001427A		F	
7843		$10	1929T1		E001430A		VG	
7843		$10	1929T1		B001437A		G	
7843		$10	1929T1		C001437A		VG	
7843		$10	1929T1		A001439A		?	
7843		$10	1929T1		C001440A		F	
7843		$10	1929T1		E001501A		F	
7843		$10	1929T1		B001514A		VF	
7843		$10	1929T1		C001780A		VG	
7843		$10	1929T1		A001788A		VF	
7843		$10	1929T1		B001800A		F	
7843		$20	1929T1		A000011A		F/VF	
7843		$20	1929T1		D000034A		F	
7843		$20	1929T1		F000046A		VG/F	
7843		$20	1929T1		A000262A		VF+	
7843		$20	1929T1		D000263A		F	
7843		$20	1929T1		E000273A		F	
7843		$20	1929T1		A000296A		F	
7843		$20	1929T1		F000309A		VG	Some stains
7843		$20	1929T1		C000387A		?	
7843		$20	1929T1		F000435A		VG/F	
7843		$20	1929T1		E000460A		F/VF	
7843		$20	1929T1		F000480A		F	
7843		$20	1929T1		E000529A		AU	

FIRST NATIONAL BANK OF HAMPTON   36 S
13842   FRANKLIN

Chartered in November 1933. Succeeded #7843.
Officers: Pres. WK Bramwell 1934-35; **VP** DD Bramwell 1934-35; **Cash.** JH Boehmler 1934-35; **AC** Fred Keepf 1934-35

1929, Type II	Ser #	# Notes
10's	1-3090	3,090
20's	1-1380	1,380

Total amount issued = $58,500. Amount outstanding on July 31, 1935 = $44,300.
0 Large   4,470 Small   4,470 Total

13842	$10	1929T2	A000771	VF/XF	
13842	$10	1929T2	A001222	AU	
13842	$10	1929T2	A001228	CU	
13842	$10	1929T2	A001234	AU+	
13842	$10	1929T2	A001240	XF+	
13842	$10	1929T2	A001463	F	
13842	$10	1929T2	A001970	VG	
13842	$20	1929T2	A000114	F+	
13842	$20	1929T2	A000148	F/VF	
13842	$20	1929T2	A000308	CU	
13842	$20	1929T2	A000398	CU	
13842	$20	1929T2	A000404	CU	
13842	$20	1929T2	A000410	XF	
13842	$20	1929T2	A000416	AU	
13842	$20	1929T2	A000422	XF	
13842	$20	1929T2	A000560	CU	
13842	$20	1929T2	A000572	XF/AU	
13842	$20	1929T2	A000578	CU	
13842	$20	1929T2	A000584	AU	
13842	$20	1929T2	A000594	CU	
13842	$20	1929T2	A000596	CU	
13842	$20	1929T2	A000602	AU	
13842	$20	1929T2	A000608	?	
13842	$20	1929T2	A000614	CU	
13842	$20	1929T2	A000632	CU	
13842	$20	1929T2	A000638	CU	
13842	$20	1929T2	A000644	CU	
13842	$20	1929T2	A000650	XF/AU	
13842	$20	1929T2	A000656	XF/AU	
13842	$20	1929T2	A000662	XF/AU	
13842	$20	1929T2	A000675	CU	
13842	$20	1929T2	A001110	AU	Higgins Mus.
13842	$20	1929T2	A001143	?	
13842	$20	1929T2	A001185	CU	
13842	$20	1929T2	A001191	CU	
13842	$20	1929T2	A001197	CU	

THE FIRST NATIONAL BANK OF HAMPTON   1 L
2573   FRANKLIN

Chartered on October 13, 1881. Succeeded Latimer & Inglis. Placed in voluntary liquidation on February 1, 1888; capital of $50,000. Succeeded by The Bank of Hampton.
Officers: Pres. JF Latimer 1883-85; **Cash.** DD Inglis 1883-85; **AC** NW Beebe 1885

First Charter, Series of 1875	Ser #	# Notes
10-10-10-10	1-847	3,388

Total amount of circulation issued = $33,880. Amount outstanding at close = $11,250. Amount outstanding in 1910 = $180.
3,388 Large   0 Small   3,388 Total

2573	-	$10	1875	420	835 D	A878904	AU+	Higgins Mus.

THE FIRST NATIONAL BANK OF HARLAN   0 L
5207   SHELBY

Chartered on July 11, 1899. Placed in voluntary liquidation on March 22, 1906; capital of $50,000. Absorbed by The Shelby County State Bank, Harlan.
Officers: Pres. LF Potter 1899-1905; **VP** WH Freeman 1899-1905; **Cash.** Thomas N Franklin 1899-1905

Second Charter, Brown Backs	Ser #	# Notes

10-10-10-20		1-878	3,512

Total amount of circulation issued = $43,900. Amount outstanding at close = $25,000. Amount outstanding in 1910 = $3,700.

3,512 Large   0 Small   3,512 Total

THE HARLAN NATIONAL BANK   9 L
10354   SHELBY

Chartered in April 1913 with a capital of $50,000.
Officers: Pres. JE Davis 1913-14, FW Ouren 1915-19, Wm J Lewis 1920-35; **VP** James Bisgard 1914-35, JJ Norgaard; **Cash.** Gottlieb Walters 1913, Harry E Lewis 1914-17, Wm J Lewis 1918-19, EA Schell 1920, JJ Norgaard 1922-33, EA Howe 1934-35; **AC** DL Shaw 1914, Glenn Myatt 1920-22, EA Howe 1920-33, HW Ouren 1923-29, VL Christensen 1932-34, Andrew Arent, Jr 1934-35

Third Charter, Date Back, Blue Seal	Ser #	# Notes
5-5-5-5	1-750	3,000
10-10-10-20	1-700	2,800
Third Charter, Plain Back, Blue Seal		
5-5-5-5	751-1165	1,660
10-10-10-20	701-1148	1,792

Total amount of circulation issued = $80,700. Amount outstanding in 1925 = $12,500. Amount outstanding in 1935 = $430.

9,252 Large   0 Small   9,252 Total

10354M	$5 1902DB	595	629 A R669981A	XF	vp Higgins Mus.
10354M	$10 1902DB	621	411 C T770543A	VG	
10354M	$10 1902DB	621	629 A R669981A	AU	
10354M	$20 1902DB	647	493 A T770625A	CU	pen/pen vp
10354M	$20 1902DB	647	499 A T770631A	CU	pen/pen vp
10354M	$20 1902DB	647	501 A T770633A	CU	pen/pen vp
10354M	$10 1902PB	629	961 B Y935083D	VF+	pen/pen
10354M	$10 1902PB	629	1027 ?	? VF/XF	
10354M	$20 1902PB	655	1123 A Y935245D	VG/F	pen/pen

THE FIRST NATIONAL BANK OF HARRIS   0 L
6949   OSCEOLA

Organized on September 8, 1903. Placed in voluntary liquidation on April 1, 1906; capital of $25,000. Succeeded by The Savings Bank, Harris.
Officers: Pres. Frank Y Locke 1904-05; **VP** Geo W Burnside 1904; **Cash.** CH Royce 1904-05

Third Charter, Red Seal	Ser #	# Notes
10-10-10-20	1-416	1,664

Total amount of circulation issued = $20,800. Amount outstanding at close = $12,500. Amount outstanding in 1910 = $1,730.

1,664 Large   0 Small   1,664 Total

THE FIRST NATIONAL BANK OF HARTLEY   8 L
4881   O'BRIEN

Organized on February 22, 1893 with a capital of $50,000. Succeeded The Security State Bank. Placed in receivership on March 22, 1927; capital of $75,000. Reason for failure: local depression & incompetent management.
Officers: Pres. JP Gross 1893-96, JW Walter 1897, Oliver Evans 1898-1900, EE Hall 1901-05, EF Broders 1906-14, WJ Davis 1915-26; **VP** WM Smith 1896, Oliver Evans 1902-11, WJ Davis 1913-14, EE Burns 1920-26, HT Broders 1923-26; **Cash.** EE Hall 1893-1900, WJ Davis 1901-10, HT Broders 1911-120, RO Bumann 1922-26; **AC** JC Nordling 1896, WJ Davis 1900, Henry Hesse 1902, JH Bordewick 1903-13, HF Broders 1910-13, RO Bumann 1914, AF Hansen 1923-26

Second Charter, Brown Backs	Ser #	# Notes
10-10-10-20	1-1920	7,680
Second Charter, Date Back		
10-10-10-20	1-1730	6,920
Third Charter, Date Back, Blue Seal		
10-10-10-20	1-1500	6,000
Third Charter, Plain Back, Blue Seal		
10-10-10-20	1501-6414	19,656

Total amount issued = $503,200. Amount outstanding at close = $49,600.

40,256 Large   0 Small   40,256 Total

4881	M	$10 1882BB	485	1450 A H217590H	F	
4881	M	$20 1882DB	550	1149 B E385643	VG/F	stamp sigs vp
4881	M	$20 1882DB	550	1337 B K53325	F/VF	
4881	M	$20 1902DB	643	935 A R266409A	F	
4881	M	$10 1902PB	629	2624 A E669828D	VG	stamp/pen
4881	M	$10 1902PB	629	3804 A A793456E	VG	stamp/stamp
4881	M	$10 1902PB	629	4463 A U832505E	VG	
4881	-	$20 1902PB	655	6003 A 6003 A	F/VF	Higgins Mus.

THE FIRST NATIONAL BANK OF HARVEY   14 L 18 S
6936   MARION

Chartered in August 1903. Placed in voluntary liquidation on August 23, 1935; capital of $25,000. Succeeded by The Marion County State Bank, Harvey.
Officers: Pres. Herman Rietveld 1904, RG Harvey 1905-07, AL Harvey 1908-22, WG Harvey 1923-32, KH Bean 1932-35; **VP** Elisha Hardin 1904, TJ Neiswanger 1905-09, FA Converse 1910-21, RG Harvey 1922-27, KH Bean 1928-32, WG Harvey 1932-35; **Cash.** Robt G Emmel 1904-07, WG Maddy 1908-14, WG Harvey 1915-22, KH Bean 1923-27, Wm J Johns 1928-35; **AC** JB Roovaart 1904, KH Bean 1922

Third Charter, Red Seal	Ser #	# Notes
5-5-5-5	1-310	1,240
10-10-10-20	1-246	984
Third Charter, Date Back, Blue Seal		
5-5-5-5	1-1925	7,700
10-10-10-20	1-1410	5,640
Third Charter, Plain Back, Blue Seal		
5-5-5-5	1926-5759	15,336
10-10-10-20	1411-3671	9,044
1929, Type I		
6-5's	1-770	4,620
6-10's	1-380	2,280
6-20's	1-86	516
1929, Type II		
5's	1-3228	3,228

Total amount of circulation issued = $389,590. Amount of large outstanding at close = $1,165. Amount of small outstanding at close = $23,835.

39,944 Large   10,644 Small   50,588 Total

6936	M	$5 1902PB	598	3908 F Z64544E	VG	Higgins Mus.
6936	M	$5 1002PB	590	4221 E K6415/H	G	
6936	-	$5 1902PB	598	4996 H 4996 H	G	pen/pen
6936	-	$5 1902PB	598	5098 G 5098 G	?	
6936	-	$5 1902PB	598	5386 F 5386 F	VG	nice sigs
6936	-	$5 1902PB	598	5737 F 5737 F	CU	pen/pen
6936	-	$5 1902PB	598	5759 A[5759 A	AU+	Last sheet
6936	-	$5 1902PB	598	5759 B[5759 B	AU+	Last sheet
6936	-	$5 1902PB	598	5759 C[5759 C	AU+	Last sheet
6936	-	$5 1902PB	598	5759 D[5759 D	AU+	Last sheet
6936	M	$10 1902PB	624	1728 F B461915D	VG	pen/pen
6936	M	$10 1902PB	624	2239 D E838101E	VG	
6936	M	$10 1902PB	624	2437 E V134999E	F/VF	
6936	-	$10 1902PB	624	3330 F 3330 F	XF	
6936		$5 1929T1		D000366A	VF	
6936		$5 1929T1		F000472A	F+	
6936		$5 1929T1		E000726A	VG/F	
6936		$10 1929T1		E000012A	F	
6936		$10 1929T1		A000272A	F+	
6936		$10 1929T1		B000277A	F	
6936		$20 1929T1		B000035A	VG	
6936		$20 1929T1		E000050A	F/VF	
6936		$20 1929T1		F000060A	VF	
6936		$20 1929T1		A000069A	VF	
6936		$5 1929T2		A000001 [	AU	
6936		$5 1929T2		A000002 [	AU	
6936		$5 1929T2		A000003 [	AU	
6936		$5 1929T2		A000004 [	AU	
6936		$5 1929T2		A000005 [	AU	
6936		$5 1929T2		A000006 [	AU	
6936		$5 1929T2		A000371	VG	
6936		$5 1929T2		A002842	F	Higgins Mus.

THE FIRST NATIONAL BANK OF HAVELOCK   9 L
7294   POCAHONTAS

Organized on April 30, 1904 with a capital of $25,000. Placed in receivership on November 5, 1927; capital of $25,000. Reason for failure: incompetent management.
Officers: Pres. JP Farmer 1904-07, AG Obrecht 1908-09, JG Obrecht 1910-19, AG Obrecht 1920-27; **VP** SH Gill 1907-14, Fred Hauswirth 1920-26, Thos Edge 1926-27; **Cash.** WH Harris 1905-06, AF Clarke 1907-11, AG Obrecht 1912-19, WC Wood 1920, CC Johnson 1922-26, Lillian Hauswirth 1926, HE Bachman 1927; **AC** AG Obrecht 1907, WM Obrecht 1913, C Elwood Miller 1914, Dena Hauswirth 1920, Marie Glenn 1922, Lola Pope 1923,1925, Lillian Hauswirth 1924, 1926, Alice Rodda 1927

Third Charter, Red Seal	Ser #	# Notes
10-10-10-20	1-300	1,200
Third Charter, Date Back, Blue Seal		
10-10-10-20	1-1610	6,440
Third Charter, Plain Back, Blue Seal		
10-10-10-20	1611-4223	10,452

Total amount issued = $226,150. Amount outstanding in 1927 = $25,000.

18,092 Large   0 Small   18,092 Total

7294	M	$20 1902DB	642	1349 B Y961799A	VG	
7294	M	$10 1902PB	624	3107 F Y738239E	F	lt. stamp sigs
7294	M	$10 1902PB	624	3314 ?	? ?	
7294	M	$10 1902PB	624	3366 F E693218H	VG	very faded
7294		$10 1902PB	624	3816 E A593828K	XF	Higgins Mus.

7294	-	$10 1902PB	624	3925 D	3925 D	F	ac/gone
7294	-	$10 1902PB	624	4026 E	4026 E	F	faded/gone
7294	-	$10 1902PB	624	4145 F	4145 F	F	gone/gone
7294	-	$20 1902PB	650	4186 B	4186 B	VF	stamp/stamp

FIRST NATIONAL BANK IN HAWARDEN 7 S
13939 SIOUX
Chartered in 1934. Succeeded #4594. Assumed the circulation of #4594.
Officers: Pres. BT French 1934-35; **VP** MR Stone 1934-35; **Cash.** H Van Der Stoep 1934, Henry Visser 1935; **AC** John L Klay 1934-35

1929, Type II	Ser #	# Notes
5's	1-748	748
10's	1-417	417

Includes the circulation of #4594 that was still outstanding. Total amount of circulation issued = $7,910. Amount outstanding in 1935 = $25,000.
0 Large 1,165 Small 1,165 Total

13939	$5	1929T2	A000668		G	
13939	$10	1929T2	A000001	cut	CU	Higgins Mus.
13939	$10	1929T2	A000002	[	CU	
13939	$10	1929T2	A000003	[	CU	
13939	$10	1929T2	A000004	[	CU	
13939	$10	1929T2	A000005	[	CU	
13939	$10	1929T2	A000006	[	AU	Torn

THE FIRST NATIONAL BANK OF HAWARDEN 5 L 14 S
4594 SIOUX
Organized on June 15, 1891 with a capital of $75,000. Succeeded The First State Bank. Suspended on August 24, 1893; restored on September 25, 1893. Placed in receivership on September 15, 1927; capital of $50,000. Reason for failure: incompetent management & local depression. Restored to solvency on September 26, 1927. Placed in conservatorship on March 24, 1933. Placed in voluntary liquidation on February 12, 1934; capital of $50,000. Succeeded by #13939.
Officers: Pres. Wm W Hall 1891-95, FE Watkins 1896-1908, John Smith 1909-21, AD Coffman 1922-24; **VP** JA Moody 1896-1900, A Melrose 1902, John Smith 1903, S Brunskill 1904-14, RW Snell 1920-22, WS Randall 1923-24; **Cash.** FE Watkins 1891-95, TA Greiner 1896-99, AD Horton 1901-18, AD Coffman 1919-20, Dan Whitney 1922-24; **AC** AD Horton 1900, RL Brooks 1909, 1914 Dan Whitney 1920, EH Jacobs 1922-24, Alice Jacobs 1922-24

Second Charter, Brown Backs	Ser #	# Notes
10-10-10-20	1-2585	10,340
Second Charter, Date Back		
10-10-10-20	1-496	1,984
Third Charter, Date Back, Blue Seal		
10-10-10-20	1-2040	8,160
Third Charter, Plain Back, Blue Seal		
10-10-10-20	2041-3806	7,064
1929, Type I		
6-10's	1-558	3,348
6-20's	1-132	792

Total amount of circulation issued = $423,670. Amount outstanding at close = $25,000. Amount of large outstanding at close = $2,040. Amount of small outstanding at close = $22,960. Amount of large outstanding on July 22, 1935 = $1,730. Liability for redemption of circulation assumed by #13939.
27,548 Large 4,140 Small 31,688 Total

4594	M	$10 1882BB	485	2118 C	R256096R	VG/F	pen/pen
4594	M	$20 1882BB	485	2576 A	U444431U	F	pen Higgins Mus.
4594	M	$10 1902PB	628	2560 A	V471892E	VF	pen/pen
4594	-	$10 1902PB	628	3358 C	3358 C	VG/F	Stain on back
4594	-	$20 1902PB	654	3489 A	3489 A	VF	Higgins Mus.
4594		$10 1929T1		B000081A		VF	
4594		$10 1929T1		D000112A		VG	
4594		$10 1929T1		F000152A		VG	
4594		$10 1929T1		B000155A		VG/F	
4594		$10 1929T1		F000231A		XF	
4594		$10 1929T1		E000344A		VF	
4594		$10 1929T1		B000400A		VG/F	
4594		$10 1929T1		B000558A		?	Last sheet of $10s
4594		$20 1929T1		D000011A		F	
4594		$20 1929T1		E000037A		F/VF	
4594		$20 1929T1		C000048A		VF	
4594		$20 1929T1		B000064A		F/VF	
4594		$20 1929T1		F000100A		VG	
4594		$20 1929T1		C000107A		XF	Higgins Mus.

THE FIRST NATIONAL BANK OF HAWKEYE 13 L 9 S
8900 FAYETTE
Organized on September 16, 1907 with a capital of $25,000. Placed in conservatorship on March 31, 1933. Placed in receivership on November 3, 1933; capital of $25,000.
Officers: Pres. Chas W Bopp 1908-16, Will E Bopp 1917-24, John G Bopp 1925-33; **VP** Will E Bopp 1909-14, John G Bopp 1920-24, JF Ungerer 1925-33; **Cash.** EL Bopp 1908-16, LE Bopp 1917-33; **AC** Clyde A Munson 1913-14, HR Hiams 1923, AJ Hockberger 1924-26, AJ Begalske 1930-31, Bertha Lippert 1932, AJ Hochberger 1933

Third Charter, Red Seal	Ser #	# Notes
5-5-5-5	1-525	2,100
10-10-10-20	1-510	2,040
Third Charter, Date Back, Blue Seal		
5-5-5-5	1-1475	5,900
10-10-10-20	1-990	3,960
Third Charter, Plain Back, Blue Seal		
5-5-5-5	1476-4562	12,348
10-10-10-20	991-2853	7,452
1929, Type I		
6-5's	1-634	3,804
6-10's	1-341	2,046
6-20's	1-85	510

Total amount of circulation issued = $319,570. Amount of large outstanding at close = $2,120. Amount of small outstanding at close = $22,880.
33,800 Large 6,360 Small 40,160 Total

8900	M	$5 1902PB	600	1561 E	N725893B	VF	pen/stamp
8900	M	$5 1902PB	600	3155 H	X14261E	F/VF	vp
8900	-	$5 1902PB	600	3356 E	M591667H	G	pen/pen
8900	-	$5 1902PB	600	3483 G	M591794H	VF	
8900	-	$5 1902PB	600	4221 H	4221 H	VF+	
8900	-	$5 1902PB	600	4374 G	4374 G	VF	pen/gone
8900	-	$5 1902PB	600	4446 G	4446 G	XF	pen Higgins Mus.
8900	-	$5 1902PB	600	4522 F	4522 F	CU	
8900	-	$5 1902PB	600	4535 E	4535 E	XF/AU	
8900	M	$10 1902PB	627	1486 F	R825018D	VG	
8900	M	$10 1902PB	627	1581 F	Z132303D	F	
8900		$10 1902PB	627	2168 F	R160600H	F+	
8900		$20 1902PB	653	1757 B	H326329E	VG/F	
8900		$5 1929T1		A000051A		VF	
8900		$5 1929T1		D000102A		F/VF	
8900		$10 1929T1		A000001A		?	
8900		$10 1929T1		A000073A		PR	
8900		$10 1929T1		F000120A		VG	
8900		$20 1929T1		D000001A		F	
8900		$20 1929T1		B000047A		VG/F	Higgins Mus.
8900		$20 1929T1		B000051A		VG	
8900		$20 1929T1		E000078A		VG	

THE FIRST NATIONAL BANK OF HEDRICK 4 L
5540 KEOKUK
Organized on August 11, 1900 with a capital of $25,000. Placed in receivership on April 24, 1925; capital of $25,000.
Officers: Pres. WH Young 1900-07, JT Brooks 1908-13, WH Young 1914-24; **VP** Frank S Yerger 1902-03, William Hursey 1904-06, Wade Kirkpatrick 1907-11, WW Young 1913-14, JG McWilliams 1920-24; **Cash.** JT Brooks 1900-07, Harry C Lynn 1908-15, WW Young 1916-24; **AC** D Snakenberg 1900-05, Harry C Lynn 1907, WW Young 1909-10, FL Hinton 1920, Anna M Bowlin 1922

Second Charter, Brown Backs	Ser #	# Notes
10-10-10-20	1-1800	7,200
Second Charter, Date Back		
10-10-10-20 (1601-1720 type uncertain)	1-1720	6,880
Second Charter, Value Back		
10-10-10-20	1721-2443	2,892
Third Charter, Plain Back, Blue Seal		
10-10-10-20	1-1270	5,080

Total amount issued = $275,650. Amount outstanding at close = $19,800.
22,052 Large 0 Small 22,052 Total

5540		$10 1882BB	490	46 B	X549753	XF	Higgins Mus.
5540	M	$10 1882DB	545	1053 D	M889881	VG	
5540	M	$10 1882VB	577	1813 E	T845961	VG/F	Higgins Mus.
5540		$10 1902PB	633	1025 A	K436876H	VF+	Higgins Mus.

THE HEDRICK NATIONAL BANK 11 L 6 S
12656 KEOKUK
Chartered in March 1925. Placed in voluntary liquidation on October 14, 1932; capital of $40,000. Succeeded by The Hedrick Savings Bank.
Officers: Pres. CA Dickey 1925-32, Wm Wright 1932; **VP** RL Jamison 1925-32; **Cash.** TT Warren 1925-28, Laban E Fleak 1929-32; **AC** Jno M Brady 1926-27, SR Stroud 1928, CT Lindberg 1929, CP Weldin 1929-32

Third Charter, Plain Back, Blue Seal	Ser #	# Notes
5-5-5-5	1-4742	18,968
1929, Type I		
6-5's	1-2257	13,542

Total amount of circulation issued = $162,550. Amount of large outstanding at

close = $860. Amount of small outstanding at close = $24,140.
18,968 Large   13,542 Small   32,510 Total
12656 - $5 1902PB 609   1417 D   A147128K   F/VF
12656 - $5 1902PB 609   1509 A   A147220K   ?
12656 - $5 1902PB 609   2124 B   2124 B   VF
12656 - $5 1902PB 609   2210 B   2210 B   F   gone/pen vp
12656 - $5 1902PB 609   2841 C   2841 C   VG
12656 - $5 1902PB 609   2998 C   2998 C   VG   Higgins Mus.
12656 - $5 1902PB 609   3536 C   3536 C   VG
12656 - $5 1902PB 609   3800 ?   3800 ?   ?
12656 - $5 1902PB 609   3810 D   3810 D   F   stamp/stamp
12656 - $5 1902PB 609   4069 B   4069 B   G/VG stamp/stamp
12656 - $5 1902PB 609   4241 D   4241 D   VG   faded/faded
12656 $5 1929T1   F000987A   VG
12656 $5 1929T1   E001130A   AU
12656 $5 1929T1   D001236A   VG+   Higgins Mus.
12656 $5 1929T1   A001528A   F
12656 $5 1929T1   D001732A   G+
12656 $5 1929T1   B001988A   F/VF

THE FARMERS NATIONAL BANK OF HENDERSON   6 L   10 S
7382   MILLS

Organized on March 7, 1904; capital of $25,000. Placed in conservatorship on Mar. 23, 1933. Placed in receivership on July 28, 1933; capital of $25,000.
Officers: Pres. AS Paul 1905-33, **VP** CE Irwin 1907-26, WE Sowers 1927-33; **Cash.** MC Turner 1905-08, RD Turner 1909-10, JG Loving 1911-17, CH Amick 1918-33; **AC** WA Phelps 1913-14, Arthur Phelps 1920-28, Jno Rainbow 1928-32

Third Charter, Red Seal	Ser #	# Notes
10-10-10-20	1-1150	4,600
Third Charter, Date Back, Blue Seal		
10-10-10-20	1-1680	6,720
Third Charter, Plain Back, Blue Seal		
10-10-10-20	1681-4926	12,984
1929, Type I		
6-10's	1-528	3,168
6-20's	1-148	888

Total amount of circulation issued = $353,240. Amount of large outstanding at close = $2,030. Amount of small outstanding at close = $22,970.
24,304 Large   4,056 Small   28,360 Total
7382 M $20 1902DB 642   921 B   D661447A   F/VF stamp/stamp
7382 M $10 1902PB 624   3193 D R828015E   VF   pen/stamp
7382 M $10 1902PB 624   3453 D Z428525E   F   pen/faded Ink
7382 - $10 1902PB 624   3752 D T622004H   VF   Higgins Mus.
7382 - $10 1902PB 624   4477 D 4477 D   VG   pen/faded
7382 $20 1902PB 650   2021 B Z154204B   F
7382 $10 1929T1   E000072A   F
7382 $10 1929T1   F000253A   F
7382 $10 1929T1   D000281A   F+
7382 $20 1929T1   A000008A   VG/F
7382 $20 1929T1   A000086A   AU
7382 $20 1929T1   A000087A   CU   Higgins Mus.
7382 $20 1929T1   A000088A   AU
7382 $20 1929T1   E000095A   VF
7382 $20 1929T1   F000101A   XF
7382 $20 1929T1   F000114A   VF

THE FIRST NATIONAL BANK OF HOLSTEIN   0 L
4553   IDA
Chartered on April 15, 1891. Succeeded The German State Bank. Placed in voluntary liquidation on July 1, 1898; capital of $50,000. Succeeded by E.H. McCutchen & Co.
Officers: Pres. FC Knepper 1892, FS Manson 1893-96, JC Edgar 1897; **Cash.** EH McCutchen 1891, Chr Haas 1892, EH McCutchen 1893-97

Second Charter, Brown Backs	Ser #	# Notes
10-10-10-20	1-565	2,260

Total amount of circulation issued = $28,250. Amount outstanding at close = $11,250. Amount outstanding in 1910 = $350.
2,260 Large   0 Small   2,260 Total

THE FIRST NATIONAL BANK OF HUBBARD   6 L   14 S
8970   HARDIN
Organized on December 3, 1907 with a capital of $25,000. Absorbed #6435 on December 30, 1931; assumed the circulation of #6435. Placed in conservatorship on March 23, 1933. Placed in receivership on October 30, 1933; capital of $50,000.
Officers: Pres. Geo R Long 1908-16, HR Long 1917-20, SH Boeke 1922-33; **VP** WE Long 1909-20, John Foust 1922, FJ Miller 1923-24, John Foust 1925-33; **Cash.** HR Long 1908-16, FJ Miller 1917-22, Theo P Guenther 1923-33; **AC** WO Reed 1909-11, FJ Miller 1913-14, Theo P Guenther 1922, Ida M Willig 1925-26, WA Marshman 1925-30, Ida M Cox 1927, EE Wiemer 1932-33

Third Charter, Red Seal	Ser #	# Notes
10-10-10-20	1-300	1,200
Third Charter, Date Back, Blue Seal		
10-10-10-20	1-1730	6,920
Third Charter, Plain Back, Blue Seal		
10-10-10-20	1731-4854	12,496
1929, Type I		
6-5's	1-668	4,008
6-10's	1-393	2,358
6-20's	1-116	696

Total amount of circulation issued = $315,240. Amount of large outstanding at close = $4,160. Amount of small outstanding at close = $33,340. Includes notes of #8970 and #6435.
20,616 Large   7,062 Small   27,678 Total
8970 M $10 1902DB 618   107 F   K498423   F   pen ac/faded
8970 M $20 1902DB 644   38 I B K498697   F/VF Higgins Mus.
8970 M $10 1902PB 626   1929 D V213841B   F   pen/pen
8970 $10 1902PB 626   2145 D Z226268B   VG/F
8970 - $10 1902PB 626   4409 D 4409 D   VG
8970 - $20 1902PB 652   4334 B 4334 B   VF   Higgins Mus.
8970 $5 1929T1   C000274A   F+
8970 $5 1929T1   F000304A   F
8970 $10 1929T1   B000180A   F
8970 $10 1929T1   E000190A   G
8970 $10 1929T1   C000217A   VF
8970 $10 1929T1   D000226A   AU
8970 $10 1929T1   C000234A   VG
8970 $10 1929T1   A000266A   F
8970 $10 1929T1   D000273A   G/VG
8970 $10 1929T1   B000287A   F   Stains
8970 $20 1929T1   D000019A   F
8970 $20 1929T1   F000046A   VF
8970 $20 1929T1   D000048A   F/VF Higgins Mus.
8970 $20 1929T1   F000054A   F

THE FIRST NATIONAL BANK OF HUDSON   2 L
5659   BLACK HAWK
Chartered on December 29, 1900. Placed in voluntary liquidation on July 1, 1912; capital of $25,000. Consolidated with The Hudson Savings Bank.
Officers: Pres. John A Leavitt 1901-04, Thomas Loonan 1905-11; **VP** Thomas Loonan 1902-04, Frank R Hollis 1905-11; **Cash.** CW Bedford 1901-11; **AC** WJ Glenny 1904, CD Bedford 1909-11

Second Charter, Brown Backs	Ser #	# Notes
10-10-10-20	1-1720	6,880
Second Charter, Date Back		
10-10-10-20	1-728	2,912

Total amount of circulation issued = $122,400. Amount outstanding at close = $24,200. Amount outstanding in October 1912 = $21,200.
9,792 Large   0 Small   9,792 Total
5659 $10 1882BB 490   936 A   E668009E   XF   Higgins Mus.
5659 $10 1882BB 490   1023 A E668096E   ?

THE FIRST NATIONAL BANK OF HULL   6 L   11 S
6953   SIOUX
Organized on August 14, 1903 with a capital of $35,000. Succeeded a state bank. Placed in conservatorship on March 24, 1933. Placed in receivership on December 20, 1933; capital of $35,000.
Officers: Pres. Henry H Wyatt 1904-05, MD Gibbs 1906-25, Jno De Koster 1926-33; **VP** MD Gibbs 1904, John Van De Berg 1907, BF Hawkins 1909-13, Jno DeKoster 1914-25, DH Wissink 1922-33, JM De Koster 1926-33; **Cash.** JS Wilson 1904-19, EC Dunkelberg 1920-25, CB Schaap 1926-33; **AC** JC Wilson 1904-10, 1914, Jno De Koster 1909-13, JM De Koster 1920-25, John W De Haan 1926-33

Third Charter, Red Seal	Ser #	# Notes
10-10-10-20	1-1990	7,960
Third Charter, Date Back, Blue Seal		
10-10-10-20	1-1700	6,800
Third Charter, Plain Back, Blue Seal		
10-10-10-20	1701-5824	16,496
1929, Type I		
6-10's	1-711	4,266

6-20's			1-201	1,206		

Total amount of circulation issued = $457,480. Amount outstanding at close = $35,000. Amount of large outstanding on December 13, 1933 = $2,920.

31,256 Large			5,472 Small		36,728 Total		
6953	M	$10 1902DB	616	1458 E	Z176548A	XF	
6953	-	$10 1902PB	624	4692 D	4692 D	F	stamp/stamp
6953	-	$10 1902PB	624	5555 E	5555 E	VG/F	stamp/stamp
6953		$20 1902PB	650	1777 B	R101629B	F	Repaired
6953	-	$20 1902PB	650	4417 B	V824229H	F	
6953		$20 1902PB	650	5557 B	5557 B	AU	stamp Higg. Mus.
6953		$10 1929T1		C000105A		F	
6953		$10 1929T1		C000119A		VF	
6953		$10 1929T1		D000486A		?	
6953		$10 1929T1		F000608A		F	
6953		$10 1929T1		F000619A		VG	
6953		$10 1929T1		C000655A		CU	Higgins Mus.
6953		$10 1929T1		C000661A		F+	Teller stamp
6953		$20 1929T1		B000060A		XF	
6953		$20 1929T1		E000094A		F+	
6953		$20 1929T1		D000160A		F	
6953		$20 1929T1		C000195A		VG/F	

THE FIRST NATIONAL BANK IN HUMBOLDT 11 S
13766 HUMBOLDT

Chartered in September 1933.
Officers: Pres. CW Garfield 1933-35; **VP** HE Passig 1933, JD Berkhimer 1934-35, EO Nervig 1935; **Cash.** BB Watson 1933-35; **AC** RD Leland 1933

1929, Type II	Ser #	# Notes
5's	1-7162	7,162
10's	1-3792	3,792

Total amount issued = $73,730. Amount outstanding in July 1935 = $49,300.

0 Large		10,954 Small	10,954 Total			
13766	$5 1929T2	A004917		?		
13766	$5 1929T2	A006199		VF	Higgins Mus.	
13766	$10 1929T2	A000378		F		
13766	$10 1929T2	A000769		VG		
13766	$10 1929T2	A001097		F+		
13766	$10 1929T2	A001330		F/VF		
13766	$10 1929T2	A002239		VF		
13766	$10 1929T2	A002350		F		
13766	$10 1929T2	A003252		VG		
13766	$10 1929T2	A003788		F		
13766	$10 1929T2	A003792		F/VF	Last sheet of $10s	

THE FIRST NATIONAL BANK OF HUMBOLDT 8 L 18 S
8277 HUMBOLDT

Organized on May 24, 1906 with a capital of $25,000. Placed in conservatorship on March 22, 1933. Placed in receivership on October 24, 1933; capital of $50,000. Reason for failure: not available from reports.
Officers: Pres. EA Wilder 1906-07, DA Ray 1908-20, EA Wilder 1922-28, EO Nervig 1929-33; **VP** HE Passig 1907-32, CW Garfield 1932-33; **Cash.** EO Nervig 1906-28, BB Watson 1929-33; **AC** RD Leland 1929-32

Third Charter, Red Seal	Ser #	# Notes
10-10-10-20	1-900	3,600

Third Charter, Date Back, Blue Seal

10-10-10-20	1-1620	6,480

Third Charter, Plain Back, Blue Seal

10-10-10-20	1621-5421	15,204

1929, Type I

6-5's	1-1460	8,760
6-10's	1-704	4,224
6-20's	1-202	1,212

1929, Type II

5's	1-60	60
10's	1-108	108

Total amount of circulation issued = $427,710. Amount of large outstanding at close = $2,370. Amount of small outstanding at close = $47,630.

25,284 Large			14,364 Small		39,648 Total		
8277	M	$20 1902RS	640	758 A	Y318830	F	Washed
8277	M	$10 1902PB	625	3250 F	V26992E	F	pen/pen
8277	-	$10 1902PB	625	4461 F	4461 F	?	
8277	-	$10 1902PB	625	4824 E	4824 E	VF	Higgins Mus.
8277	-	$10 1902PB	625	5279 E	5279 E	VG	
8277	-	$20 1902PB	651	4325 B	4325 B	VF	pen/pen
8277	-	$20 1902PB	651	4459 B	4459 B	F+	pen/pen
8277	-	$20 1902PB	651	5307 B	5307 B	VF	pen/pen
8277		$5 1929T1		A000594A		XF	
8277		$5 1929T1		A000801A		XF	
8277		$5 1929T1		B001006A		?	
8277		$5 1929T1		C001006A		AU	Higgins Mus.
8277		$5 1929T1		A001315A		AU	
8277		$10 1929T1		B000364A		VG	
8277		$10 1929T1		E000559A		?	
8277		$10 1929T1		E000668A		G	
8277		$20 1929T1		C000085A		VG/F	
8277		$20 1929T1		E000102A		F+	
8277		$20 1929T1		F000104A		F	
8277		$20 1929T1		C000123A		?	
8277		$20 1929T1		A000143A		F	
8277		$20 1929T1		C000153A		F/VF	
8277		$20 1929T1		D000184A		CU	
8277		$20 1929T1		C000185A		XF	
8277		$20 1929T1		E000185A		CU	
8277		$10 1929T2		A000030		F/VF	

THE FIRST NATIONAL BANK OF IDA GROVE 1 L
3930 IDA

Chartered on October 10, 1888 with a capital of $100,000. Purchased The Ida County Bank in late 1888. Placed in voluntary liquidation on May 1892; capital of $150,000. Succeeded by The Ida County Savings Bank, Inc. Placed in receivership on June 4, 1895. Reason for failure: deficiency in assets sold.
Officers: Pres. EM Donaldson 1889-92; **Cash.** Edwin Coles 1889, HM Whinery 1890-92

Second Charter, Brown Backs	Ser #	# Notes
10-10-10-20	1-1192	4,768

Total amount of circulation issued = $59,600. Amount outstanding at close = $32,650. Amount outstanding in 1915 = $360.

4,768 Large		0 Small		4,768 Total		
3930	$10 1882BB	483	705 B	D940635	F/VF	Higgins Mus.

THE FIRST NATIONAL BANK OF IMOGENE 0 L 7 S
8295 FREMONT

Chartered in July 1906 with a capital of $25,000.
Officers: Pres. TH Read 1906-25, JL Gwynn 1925-35; **VP** JL Gwynn 1907-25, Jas Laughlin 1927-35, OF Howard 1934-35; **Cash.** Elbert A Read 1906-15, LS McCracken 1916-20, Jas A Gleason 1922-26, JW Bowman 1927-29, WH Drake 1930-35; **AC** LS McCracken 1907-14, Anna C McCargill 1920-23; Wayne H Drake 1927-29, Ruth Howard 1931-35

Third Charter, Red Seal	Ser #	# Notes
10-10-10-20	1-600	2,400

Third Charter, Date Back, Blue Seal

10-10-10-20	1-1470	5,880

Sheets numbered 1 to 1310 were 02-08 backs. Sheets numbered 1311 to 1470 were delivered on October 15, but not marked as to type. Sheets numbered 1471 to 2442 were plain backs.

Third Charter, Plain Back, Blue Seal

10-10-10-20	1471-2442	3,888

1929, Type I

6-10's	1-252	1,512
6-20's	1-80	480

Total amount of circulation issued = $176,820. Amount of large outstanding in June 1935 = $650. Amount of small outstanding in June 1935 = $9,350.

12,168 Large		1,992 Small		14,160 Total		
8295	$10 1929T1		D000001A		?	
8295	$10 1929T1		A000210A		F	
8295	$20 1929T1		B000004A		VG	
8295	$20 1929T1		F000023A		F/VF	
8295	$20 1929T1		A000031A		F	
8295	$20 1929T1		F000049A		F/VF	Higgins Mus.
8295	$20 1929T1		D000060A		VF	

THE FIRST NATIONAL BANK OF THE CITY OF INDEPENDENCE
1581 BUCHANAN 0 L

Chartered in 1865. Placed in voluntary liquidation on October 31, 1884; capital of $100,000. Succeeded by #3263. Previously published title was incorrect. See image of proof below courtesy of Peter Huntoon.

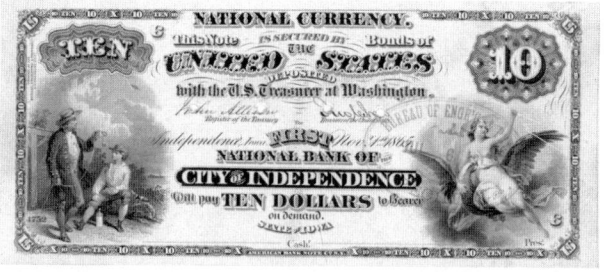

Officers: Pres. Richard Campbell 1867-84; **Cash.** Horatio P Browne 1867-

81, George B Warne 1883-84

First Charter, Original Issue　　　　　　Ser #　　　　# Notes
5-5-5-5　　　　　　　　　　　　　　　　1-3525　　　　14,100
10-10-10-20　　　　　　　　　　　　　　1-1800　　　　　7,200
First Charter, Series of 1875
5-5-5-5　　　　　　　　　　　　　　　　1-1000　　　　　4,000
10-10-10-20　　　　　　　　　　　　　　1-2086　　　　　8,344

Total amount of circulation issued = $284,800. Amount outstanding at close = $90,000. Amount outstanding in 1910 = $1,600.
33,644 Large　　　　0 Small　　　　33,644 Total

THE FIRST NATIONAL BANK OF THE CITY OF INDEPENDENCE
3263 (FIRST TITLE)　　　BUCHANAN　　　2 L
Organized on October 27, 1884 with a capital of $100,000. Succeeded #1581. Title changed at extension in 1904 to The First National Bank of Independence.
Officers: Pres. Richard Campbell 1885-1900, Z Stout 1901-03, WG Donnan 1903-04; **VP** Ephriam Leach 1896-1900, LV Tabor 1902-04; **Cash.** George B Warne 1885-87, Wm W Donnan 1888-1901, RB Raines 1902-04; **AC** WB Stevenson 1902, WG Stevenson 1903-04

Second Charter, Brown Backs　　　　Ser #　　　　# Notes
5-5-5-5　　　　　　　　　　　　　　　　1-4320　　　　17,280
10-10-10-20　　　　　　　　　　　　　　1-2842　　　　11,368
20,648 Large　　　　0 Small　　　　28,648 Total

3263	-	$5 1882BB	467	2793 D	X534306	VG	vp Higgins Mus.
3263		$10 1882BB	480	2751 A	B732729B	VF+	Higgins Mus.

THE FIRST NATIONAL BANK OF INDEPENDENCE　　44 L
3263 (SECOND TITLE)　　　BUCHANAN
Succeeded The First National Bank of the City of Independence on Oct. 28, 1904. Placed in receivership on July 5, 1928; capital of $100,000.
Officers: Pres. WG Donnan 1904-08, Robert B Raines 1909-27; **VP** LV Tabor 1904, RM Campbell 1907-23, Jed Lake 1909-13, MW Harmon 1920-24, AH Wallace 1924-27; **Cash.** RB Raines 1904-08, WG Stevenson 1909-27, JM Gemmel 1927; **AC** WG Stevenson 1904-07, JM Gemmel 1914-27, EE Cole 1927

Third Charter, Red Seal　　　　　　Ser #　　　　# Notes
5-5-5-5　　　　　　　　　　　　　　　　1-1340　　　　　5,360
10-10-10-20　　　　　　　　　　　　　　1-1074　　　　　4,296
Third Charter, Date Back, Blue Seal
5-5-5-5　　　　　　　　　　　　　　　　1-6350　　　　25,400
10-10-10-20　　　　　　　　　　　　　　1-4660　　　　18,640
Third Charter, Plain Back, Blue Seal
5-5-5-5　　　　　　　　　　　　　　　　6351-17270　　　43,680
10-10-10-20　　　　　　　　　　　　　　4661-11983　　　29,292

Total amount issued = $1,253,550. Amount outstanding at close = $98,997.
126,668 Large　　　　0 Small　　　　126,668 Total

Charter	M/-	Denom/Series	Plate	Bank Ser	Treasury Ser	Grade	Notes
3263	M	$5 1902RS	587	946 D	N161192	VF	ac Higgins Mus.
3263	M	$5 1902RS	587	1111 A	N161357	VF+	Grinnell # 3401, Higgins Museum
3263	M	$10 1902RS	613	54 A	D413680	AU	
3263	M	$10 1902RS	613	850 B	U435666	AU	Higgins Mus.
3263	M	$5 1902DB	590	3691 F	B615042A	VF	
3263	M	$5 1902DB	590	3940 E	N339717A	?	
3263	M	$5 1902DB	590	4163 E	N339940A	VF	
3263	M	$10 1902DB	616	2556 E	D237043A	VF+	
3263	M	$10 1902DB	616	2898 E	D237385A	F/VF	
3263	M	$10 1902DB	616	4274 F	M659230B	CU	Higgins Mus.
3263	M	$20 1902DB	642	1684 B	T165383	F+	pen/gone
3263	M	$20 1902DB	642	2797 B	D237284A	F	
3263	M	$20 1902DB	642	2907 B	D237394A	G/VG	
3263	M	$20 1902DB	642	4597 B	M659553B	?	
3263	M	$5 1902PB	598	7046 G	?	F	
3263	M	$5 1902PB	598	7641 F	T995567B	VF	
3263	M	$5 1902PB	598	8162 F	X785138B	VF	stamp/stamp
3263	M	$5 1902PB	598	13018 F	N271169T	VG	
3263	M	$5 1902PB	598	13884 F	E996420H	F	stamp/stamp
3263	-	$5 1902PB	598	16812 F	16812 F	VF	
3263	M	$10 1902PB	624	6235 E	K947697D	XF/AU	
3263	M	$10 1902PB	624	6395 ?	?	VG	
3263	M	$10 1902PB	624	7975 D	B292457E	AU	
3263	M	$10 1902PB	624	8525 E	T268627E	VF	pen/pen
3263	M	$10 1902PB	624	8673 F	A166305H	F/VF	
3263	M	$10 1902PB	624	8900 E	A166532H	VG	
3263	M	$10 1902PB	624	9178 ?	K321460H	CU	
3263	M	$10 1902PB	624	9180 E	K321462H	XF	
3263	M	$10 1902PB	624	9181 E	K321463H	?	
3263	M	$10 1902PB	624	9182 E	K321464H	XF	
3263	M	$10 1902PB	624	9365 F	K321647H	CU	stamp/stamp
3263	M	$10 1902PB	624	9371 D	K321653H	VG	
3263	M	$10 1902PB	624	9558 D	K321840H	XF	
3263	-	$10 1902PB	624	10422 E	B175694K	F/VF	plate pos. letter ?
3263	-	$10 1902PB	624	11161 F	11161 F	F	stamp/stamp
3263	-	$10 1902PB	624	11173 D	11173 D	F/VF	gone/gone
3263	M	$20 1902PB	650	5058 B	T640648B	VG/F	
3263	M	$20 1902PB	650	5718 B	A190765D	F	
3263	M	$20 1902PB	650	9195 B	K321477H	CU	mach stamps
3263	M	$20 1902PB	650	9196 B	K321478H	XF	stamp/stamp
3263	M	$20 1902PB	650	9405 B	K321687H	VF	lt stamp sigs
3263	M	$20 1902PB	650	9513 B	K321795H	F	
3263	-	$20 1902PB	650	10835 B	10835 B	VF	
3263	-	$20 1902PB	650	10881 B	10881 B	F	

THE PEOPLES NATIONAL BANK OF INDEPENDENCE
2187　　　BUCHANAN　　　53 L
Organized on July 30, 1874 with a capital of $50,000. Chartered on September 17, 1874. Placed in receivership on July 5, 1928; capital of $75,000.
Officers: Pres. Edward Ross 1876-90, Thomas Edwards 1891-99, SF Fisher 1900-01, SJ Fisher 1902, Thos Edwards 1902-05, RF Clarke 1906-27; **VP** Lyman J Curtis 1896-1900, Thos Edwards 1902, Thos Scarcliff 1903-14, E Buchanan 1922, MS Carver 1923-27; **Cash.** Justus F Coy 1876-99, RF Clarke 1900-05, CM Roberts 1906-27, EE Everett 1922-25

First Charter, Original Issue　　　　Ser #　　　　# Notes
10-10-10-20　　　　　　　　　　　　　　1-900　　　　　3,600
First Charter, Series of 1875
10-10-10-20　　　　　　　　　　　　　　1-2427　　　　　9,708
Second Charter, Brown Backs
10-10-10-20　　　　　　　　　　　　　　1-2600　　　　10,400
Second Charter, Date Back
10-10-10-20　　　　　　　　　　　　　　1-3523　　　　14,092
Third Charter, Date Back, Blue Seal
10-10-10-20　　　　　　　　　　　　　　1-1500　　　　　6,000
Third Charter, Plain Back, Blue Seal
10-10-10-20　　　　　　　　　　　　　　1501-9019　　　30,076

Total amount of issued = $923,450. Amount outstanding at close = $65,050.
73,876 Large　　　　0 Small　　　　73,876 Total

Charter	M/-	Denom/Series	Plate	Bank Ser	Treasury Ser	Grade	Notes
2187	M	$10 1882BB	487	1383 A	H768291H	VF	
2187	M	$10 1882BB	487	1389 B	H768297H	AU	
2187	M	$10 1882BB	587	1389 C	H768297H	XF	
2187	M	$10 1882BB	487	1391 B	H768299H	CU	pen/pen
2187	M	$10 1882BB	487	1391 C	H768299H	XF/AU	pen/pen
2187	M	$10 1882BB	487	1397 A	H768305H	AU	
2187	M	$10 1882BB	487	1407 C	H768315H	CU	pen Higgins Mus.
2187	M	$10 1882BB	487	1410 C	H768318H	CU	
2187	M	$10 1882BB	487	1522 B	H768430H	AU	
2187	M	$10 1882BB	487	1553 A	H768461H	VF	pen/pen
2187	M	$10 1882BB	487	2056 A	R930593R	?	
2187	-	$20 1882BB	501	510 A	R608096	VG	pen UR missing
2187	M	$20 1882BB	501	1407 A	H768315H	CU	
2187	M	$20 1882BB	501	1534 A	H768442H	VF	
2187	M	$10 1882DB	542	225 E	B988175	F	
2187	M	$10 1882DB	542	815 F	B988765	F+	
2187	M	$10 1882DB	542	849 F	B988799	XF+	
2187	M	$10 1882DB	542	884 F	B988834	VF+	
2187	M	$10 1882DB	542	906 E	B988856	XF	Higgins Mus.
2187	M	$10 1882DB	542	1066 F	B989016	XF	stamp/stamp
2187	M	$10 1882DB	542	1340 F	K185318	VF	
2187	M	$10 1882DB	542	1890 D	K659668	XF	
2187	M	$10 1882DB	542	3363 F	N289791	F	pen/pen
2187	M	$10 1902DB	623	402 A	B370270B	AU	pen/pen
2187	M	$10 1902DB	623	617 A	B370485B	VF	
2187	M	$10 1902DB	623	810 B	B370678B	?	
2187	M	$20 1902DB	649	1452 A	B371320B	F/VF	
2187	M	$10 1902PB	631	3909 A	Y934291D	VG	pen/pen
2187	M	$10 1902PB	631	5385 A	U237577E	XF/AU	
2187	M	$10 1902PB	631	5385 B	U237577E	VF	
2187	M	$10 1902PB	631	6142 B	B765584H	F	
2187	M	$10 1902PB	631	6150 A	B765592H	CU	
2187	M	$10 1902PB	631	6699 C	?	XF/AU	
2187	M	$10 1902PB	631	6700 A	M379572H	XF/AU	pen/pen
2187	-	$10 1902PB	631	6734 ?	U327156H	G	faded/faded
2187	-	$10 1902PB	631	6782 C	U327204H	VF	pen/pen
2187	-	$10 1902PB	631	7462 B	Z636534H	XF	
2187	-	$10 1902PB	631	7724 ?	?	?	
2187	-	$10 1902PB	631	8039 B	8039 B	XF/AU	pen/pen
2187	-	$10 1902PB	631	8410 A	8410 A	CU	pen/pen
2187	-	$10 1902PB	631	8410 B	8410 B	AU	
2187	-	$10 1902PB	631	8411 C	8411 C	AU	Higgins Mus.
2187	M	$20 1902PB	657	1882 A	U376290B	F	
2187	M	$20 1902PB	657	3100 A	H567260D	F	gone/gone tear
2187	M	$20 1902PB	657	3497 A	N921759D	CU	

2187	M	$20 1902PB	657	3502 A	N921764D	CU	
2187	M	$20 1902PB	657	3528 A	N921790D	AU	pen/pen
2187	M	$20 1902PB	657	5174 A	E247756E	F	pen/pen
2187	M	$20 1902PB	657	6634 A	M379506H	F	
2187	-	$20 1902PB	657	7103 A	Z636175H	F	
2187	-	$20 1902PB	657	7173 A	Z636245H	VF	
2187	-	$20 1902PB	657	7174 A	Z636246H	AU	
2187	-	$20 1902PB	657	8096 A	8096 A	VG	

THE FIRST NATIONAL BANK OF INDIANOLA   12 L
1811   WARREN

Organized on November 15, 1870 with a capital of $50,000. Chartered on April 13, 1871. Placed in receivership on August 30, 1932; capital of $50,000.
Officers: Pres. David Hallam 1872-73, Archibald R Henry 1874-82, JG Sandy 1883-97, John A Shuler 1898-99, JM Harlan 1900-14, Edgar C Lane 1915, Carl H Lane 1916-32; **VP** John A Shuler 1896, AF Schimelfenig 1909-14, GE Johnson 1920-32, Will A Lane 1920-32; **Cash.** Thomas W Hallam 1872, AS Moncrief 1872-73, Gorham A Worth 1874-97, JF Samson 1898-1913, Will A Lane 1914-19, Ray Lane 1920, Louis C Pendry 1922-27, Stoddard M Robinson 1928-32; **AC** JF Samson 1896, FH McClure 1909-14, LC Pendry 1920, Helen Igo 1922, Wayne F Jones 1923-27, Rena M Dewey 1925-26, Helen Ogan 1927, Stoddard M Robinson 1927, Georgia Snodgrass 1928-32

First Charter, Original Issue	Ser #	# Notes
1-1-1-2	1-2820	11,280
5-5-5-5	1-3025	12,100
First Charter, Series of 1875		
5-5-5-5	1-4669	18,676
Second Charter, Brown Backs		
5-5-5-5	1-3900	15,600
10-10-10-20	1-2340	9,360
Second Charter, Date Back		
5-5-5-5	1-686	2,744
10-10-10-20	1-529	2,116
Third Charter, Date Back, Blue Seal		
10-10-10-20	1-2600	10,400
Third Charter, Plain Back, Blue Seal		
10-10-10-20	2601-6447	15,388

Total amount of circulation issued = $725,500. Amount outstanding in 1924 report = $50,000. Amount outstanding at close = $4,543.
97,664 Large   0 Small   97,664 Total

1811	-	$1	ORIG 382	1452 B	C463293	G	
1811	-	$1	ORIG 382	1767 C	D408001	F/VF	Higgins Mus.
1811	-	$2	ORIG 389	1808 A	D408042	Fr	Higgins Mus.
1811	-	$2	ORIG 389	2241 A	D408475	XF	pen/gone
1811	M	$5	1882BB 471	2692 C	K209592K	F	pen Higgins Mus.
1811	M	$5	1882BB 471	3434 B	R80682R	VG	
1811	M	$10	1882BB 484	1936 B	R143267R	F/VF	pen/pen
1811	-	$20	1882BB 498	718 A	X605945	VG/F	pen/pen
1811	M	$10	1902PB 627	3901 A	M399013D	F	faded/pen vp
1811	M	$10	1902PB 627	4244 B	T957366D	VG	pen/faded Soiling
1811	M	$10	1902PB 627	4279 C	T957401D	VF	stamp/stamp
1811		$10	1902PB 627	5180 A	M207462E	XF	Higgins Mus.

THE FARMERS NATIONAL BANK OF INWOOD   12 L   9 S
8257   LYON

Organized on March 19, 1906 with a capital of $40,000. Placed in receivership on December 20, 1930; capital of $40,000.
Officers: Pres. Chas Shade 1906-30; **VP** GM Anderson 1907-10, GA Manwaring 1911-14, GM Anderson 1920-23, Delbert Brown 1924-30; **Cash.** GA Manwaring 1906-10, GM Anderson 1911-19, DH Vander Stoep 1920-28, J Van Steenbergen 1929-30; **AC** GM Larsen 1907, EL Davenport 1909-10, A Chambers 1914, Lena Schemmel 1920-22, J Van Steenbergen 1924-26, Geo O Anderson 1926-30

Third Charter, Red Seal	Ser #	# Notes
10-10-10-20	1-900	3,600
Third Charter, Date Back, Blue Seal		
10-10-10-20	1-2920	11,680
Third Charter, Plain Back, Blue Seal		
10-10-10-20	2921-7329	17,636
1929, Type I		
6-10's	1-384	2,304
6-20's	1-88	528

Total amount of circulation issued = $445,050. Amount outstanding at close = $40,000. Amount of large outstanding on July 1, 1931 = $11,400.
32,916 Large   2,832 Small   35,748 Total

8257	M	$20 1902RS	640	105 A	R232170	VG	pen/pen
8257	M	$20 1902RS	640	468 A	V765109	F/VF	Higgins Mus.
8257	M	$10 1902DB	617	2100 E	R463544A	VG/F	pen/faded
8257	M	$20 1902DB	643	1281 B	Z928374	F/VF	Higgins Mus.
8257	M	$10 1902PB	625	3062 B	U590950B	F	
8257	M	$10 1902PB	625	3900 D	M398812D	VG	
8257		$10 1902PB	625	5254 D	?	VG	
8257	-	$10 1902PB	625	5925 F	U133827H	VF	lt stamp sigs
8257		$20 1902PB	651	5648 B	K820530H	CU	
8257		$20 1902PB	651	?-B	R984096H	?	Smithsonian
8257	-	$20 1902PB	651	6296 B	Z928578H	F	
8257	-	$20 1902PB	651	6488 B	6488 B	F	stamp/stamp
8257		$10 1929T1		D000262A		VG	
8257		$10 1929T1		F000331A		VF	
8257		$10 1929T1		D000367A		XF	
8257		$10 1929T1		E000383A		F	
8257		$20 1929T1		E000038A		F	
8257		$20 1929T1		D000049A		VF+	Higgins Museum
8257		$20 1929T1		D000050A		AU	
8257		$20 1929T1		D000072A		VG/F	
8257		$20 1929T1		A000079A		F	Washed

THE FIRST NATIONAL BANK OF INWOOD   10 L
7304   LYON

Organized on May 23, 1904 with a capital of $25,000. Succeeded The Peoples Savings Bank. Placed in receivership on September 6, 1927; capital of $50,000. Reason for failure: incompetent management & local depression.
Officers: Pres. E Renshaw 1905-07, Herbert Renshaw 1908-13, Chris Erickson 1914-19, HJ Hanson 1920-27; **VP** H Renshaw 1907, HJ Hanson 1909-14, GE Holland 1920-23, 1926-27, FA Bucknam 1924-27; **Cash.** Chris Erickson, Jr. 1905-13, Hugo Reimers 1914-25, Ben H Weberg 1925-27; **AC** Hugo Reimers 1907, Ben H Weberg 1920-25

Third Charter, Red Seal	Ser #	# Notes
10-10-10-20	1-1150	4,600
Third Charter, Date Back, Blue Seal		
10-10-10-20	1-1910	7,640

Sheets numbered 1 to 1610 were 02-08 backs. Sheets numbered 1611 to 1910 were delivered on August 10, but not marked as to type. Sheets numbered 1911 to 4132 were plain back notes.

Third Charter, Plain Back, Blue Seal		
10-10-10-20	1911-4132	8,888

Total amount issued = $264,100. Amount outstanding at close = $25,000.
21,128 Large   0 Small   21,128 Total

7304	M	$10 1902DB	616	795 E	A662293A	F	pen/pen
7304	M	$20 1902DB	642	918 B	H959664A	VG/F	pen/pen
7304	M	$20 1902DB	642	1281 B	?	VF	
7304	M	$10 1902PB	624	2275 F	K686107D	VG	faded/pen
7304	M	$10 1902PB	624	3362 D	A284944H	VF	stamp Higg. Mus.
7304	M	$10 1902PB	624	3368 F	A284950H	VF	stamp Staining
7304	-	$10 1902PB	624	3637 F	U205969H	VG	gone/gone
7304	M	$20 1902PB	650	3231 B	A284813H	VG	Ink
7304	-	$20 1902PB	650	3928 B	3928 B	XF	stamp/stamp
7304	-	$20 1902PB	650	4053 B	4053 B	VF	faint stamps

THE FIRST NATIONAL BANK OF IOWA CITY   1 L
18 (FIRST ORGANIZATION)   JOHNSON

Chartered in July 1863; opened on July 13, 1863. Placed in voluntary liquidation on June 24, 1882; capital of $100,000. Succeeded by #2738.
Officers: Pres. MJ Morsman 1867-69, Peter A Dey 1870-78, De Witt C Clapp 1878-82; **Cash.** WH Hubbard 1867-71, LM Sedgwick 1872-75, Wm M Anderson 1876-79, JB Haddock 1881; **AC** CS Welch 1880-81

First Charter, Original Issue	Ser #	# Notes
5-5-5-5	1-5750	23,000
10-10-10-20	1-1350	5,400
First Charter, Series of 1875		
5-5-5-5	1-1950	7,800
10-10-10-20	1-602	2,408

Total amount of circulation issued = $251,600. Amount outstanding at close = $88,400. Amount outstanding in 1910 = $1,610.
38,608 Large   0 Small   38,608 Total

18	-	$5	ORIG 394	2295 A	E873499	VF	

THE FIRST NATIONAL BANK OF IOWA CITY   26 L   32 S
18 (2ND ORGANIZATION)   JOHNSON

Received permission to retake #18 as its charter number on December 2, 1911.
Officers: Pres. Peter A Dey 1911, WJ McChesney 1912-31; **VP** Geo W Ball 1911-1919, WP Hohenschuh 1920, Chas M Dutcher 1922-31; **Cash.** Lovell Swisher 1911, Thomas Farrell 1912-31; **AC** GS Krouth 1911, Thomas Farrell 1911, RL Parsons 1914-28, JE Gatens 1928-31, GR Griffith 1928-31

Third Charter, Date Back, Blue Seal	Ser #	# Notes
10-10-10-20	1-1400	5,600
Third Charter, Plain Back, Blue Seal		
10-10-10-20	1401-11081	38,724
1929, Type I		
6-10's	1-1642	9,852
6-20's	1-438	2,628

44,324 Large   12,480 Small   56,804 Total

18	M	$10 1902PB	624	2009 B	N916671D	VG/F	
18	M	$10 1902PB	624	4009 A	U698221D	VF	lt stamp sigs
18	M	$10 1902PB	624	5822 B	X427724E	G+	
18	M	$10 1902PB	624	7291 C	M708163H	F/VF	lt. stamp sigs
18	M	$10 1902PB	624	7586 C	M708458H	F+	faded/faded
18	-	$10 1902PB	624	8357 C	8357 C	VF	
18	-	$10 1902PB	624	8378 B	8378 B	XF+	
18	-	$10 1902PB	624	8790 B	8790 B	G	
18	-	$10 1902PB	624	9468 B	9468 B	F	Davenport B&T
18	-	$10 1902PB	624	10057 C	10057 C	XF/AU	stamp/stamp
18	-	$10 1902PB	624	10321 C	10321 C	VF	
18	-	$10 1902PB	624	10836 B	10836 B	VF	stamp/stamp
18	-	$10 1902PB	624	10849 C	10849 C	CU	
18	-	$10 1902PB	624	10968 C	10968 C	AU	Higgins Museum
18	-	$10 1902PB	624	10983 B	10983 B	CU	
18	M	$20 1902PB	650	2119 A	N916781D	VG/F	
18	M	$20 1902PB	650	3480 A	U697692D	VF	
18	M	$20 1902PB	650	3948 A	U698160D	VG/F	
18	M	$20 1902PB	650	6361 A	X428263E	VG	
18	M	$20 1902PB	650	6632 A	D961914H	VG	
18	M	$20 1902PB	650	6730 A	D962012H	F/VF	
18	-	$20 1902PB	650	8710 A	8710 A	VF	stamp/stamp
18	-	$20 1902PB	650	8942 A	8942 A	VG	
18	-	$20 1902PB	650	9501 A	9501 A	VF	gone/gone
18	-	$20 1902PB	650	9887 A	9887 A	VG	
18	-	$20 1902PB	650	10108 A	10108 A	VF	
18		$10 1929T1		A000001A		CU	
18		$10 1929T1		B000001A		CU	
18		$10 1929T1		C000001A		?	
18		$10 1929T1		D000001A		?	
18		$10 1929T1		E000001A		CU	
18		$10 1929T1		F000001A		AU	
18		$10 1929T1		A000124A		VG	
18		$10 1929T1		E000169A		VG	Stain on top
18		$10 1929T1		F000481A		?	
18		$10 1929T1		E000813A		?	
18		$10 1929T1		D000817A		VG	
18		$10 1929T1		B001119A		VG/F	
18		$10 1929T1		C001196A		F+	
18		$10 1929T1		E001496A		CU	
18		$10 1929T1		A001585A		VG	
18		$20 1929T1		D000158A		F	
18		$20 1929T1		F000199A		VF	
18		$20 1929T1		B000205A		F	
18		$20 1929T1		D000207A		VG	
18		$20 1929T1		E000221A		VF	
18		$20 1929T1		B000231A		VF	
18		$20 1929T1		F000249A		VG+	
18		$20 1929T1		D000269A		VG	
18		$20 1929T1		D000277A		CU	Higgins Museum
18		$20 1929T1		C000299A		VG/F	
18		$20 1929T1		D000347A		VG/F	
18		$20 1929T1		F000350A		F	
18		$20 1929T1		B000354A		XF	
18		$20 1929T1		C000389A		F/VF	
18		$20 1929T1		C000400A		F+	
18		$20 1929T1		E000421A		F	
18		$20 1929T1		E000429A		VF/XF	

THE FIRST NATIONAL BANK OF IOWA CITY   4 L
2738   **JOHNSON**

Organized on June 12, 1882 with a capital of $100,000. Succeeded #18. Received permission to retake #18 as its charter number on December 2, 1911. Placed in receivership on January 22, 1932; capital of $100,000.
Officers: Pres. DWC Clapp 1883, Lyman Parsons 1884-94, Peter A Dey 1895-1911; **VP** Geo W Ball 1896-1911; **Cash.** JB Haddock 1883, Lovell Swisher 1884-1911; **AC** John Lasheck 1885-1900, John U Plank 1903-10, GS Krouth 1911, Thomas Farrell 1911

Second Charter, Brown Backs	Ser #	# Notes
10-10-10-20	1-3218	12,872
Third Charter, Red Seal		
10-10-10-20	1-3000	12,000
Third Charter, Date Back, Blue Seal		
10-10-10-20	1-1700	6,800

Total amount of circulation issued = $1,101,030. Amount of large outstanding at close = $14,390. Amount of small outstanding at close = $83,630.
31,672 Large   0 Small   31,672 Total

2738	M	$10 1902RS	613	2971 A	V677034	VF	pen/pen
2738	M	$10 1902RS	613	85 C	A97906	VG	Stained
2738	M	$10 1902DB	616	775 F	E691930	VF	
2738	M	$20 1902DB	642	1220 B	E730875	VF	

THE IOWA CITY NATIONAL BANK   0 L
977   **JOHNSON**

Chartered on April 5, 1865. Placed in voluntary liquidation on April 14, 1875; capital of $125,000.
Officers: Pres. E Clark 1867-75; **Cash.** TJ Cox 1867-75

First Charter, Original Issue	Ser #	# Notes
1-1-1-2	1-3200	12,800
5-5-5-5	1-2575	10,300
10-10-10-20	1-1600	6,400

Total amount of circulation issued = $147,500. Amount outstanding at close = $112,500. Amount outstanding in 1910 = $1,426.
29,500 Large   0 Small   29,500 Total

THE IOWA CITY NATIONAL BANK   1 L
2821   **JOHNSON**

Chartered on November 14, 1882 with a capital of $200,000. Succeeded The Iowa City Bank. Placed in voluntary liquidation on February 7, 1889; capital of $200,000. Succeeded by The Iowa State Bank.
Officers: Pres. Samuel J Kirkwood 1883-88; **Cash.** John N Coldren 1883-88; **AC** JC Switzer 1885

Second Charter, Brown Backs	Ser #	# Notes
5-5-5-5	1-1083	4,332
10-10-10-20	1-661	2,644
50-100	1-215	430

Total amount of circulation issued = $86,960. Amount outstanding at close = $45,000. Amount outstanding in 1910 = $1,426.
7,406 Large   0 Small   7,406 Total

2821		$5 1882BB	466	894 C	E442148	VF	Higgins Museum

THE FIRST NATIONAL BANK OF IOWA FALLS   12 L   27 S
3252   **HARDIN**

Organized on August 28, 1884 with a capital of $50,000. Succeeded The Commercial Bank. Placed in receivership on December 27, 1932; capital of $50,000.
Officers: Pres. John H Carleton 1885-95, ES Ellsworth 1896-1907, WH Woods 1908-14, EO Ellsworth 1915-32; **VP** JH Carleton 1896-1911, EO Ellsworth 1914, John J Carleton 1920-22, FW Crockett 1923-24, JL Welden 1925-32; **Cash.** WH Woods 1885-1904, CH Burlingame 1905, WH Woods 1906-07, CH Burlingame 1908-20, CE Foote 1922-32; **AC** FD Peet 1896-1900, CH Burlingame 1902-07, TE Bell 1913-14, CE Foote 1920, PM Nelson 1922-32, LL Winterfield 1925-32

Second Charter, Brown Backs	Ser #	# Notes
10-10-10-20	1-1316	5,264
Third Charter, Red Seal		
10-10-10-20	1-450	1,800
Third Charter, Date Back, Blue Seal		
10-10-10-20	1-4100	16,400
Third Charter, Plain Back, Blue Seal		
10-10-10-20	4101-10607	26,028

1929, Type I

6-10's		1-925	5,550
6-20's		1-223	1,338

Total amount of circulation issued = $700,910. Amount of large outstanding at close = $5,350. Amount of small outstanding at close = $44,230.

49,492 Large   6,888 Small   56,380 Total

3252	M	$10 1902DB	616	1209 D	K680965	F/VF	
3252	M	$10 1902DB	616	2653 E	H841149A	F/VF	Higgins Museum
3252	M	$10 1902DB	616	2851 E	R464015A	VG/F	pen/pen
3252	M	$10 1902DB	616	3661 D	A232875B	VG/F	
3252		$10 1902PB	624	7928 D	H315610H	G/VG	
3252	-	$10 1902PB	624	8664 D	A87416K	F	stamp/pen
3252	-	$10 1902PB	624	8700 E	A87452K	XF+	stamp/pen
3252	-	$10 1902PB	624	9333 F	9333 F	G	gone/pen
3252	-	$10 1902PB	624	10153 E	10153 E	VF	faded/pen
3252		$20 1902PB	650	4414 B	U967552B	?	
3252	-	$20 1902PB	650	10147 B	10147 B	F/VF	gone/gone
3252	-	$20 1902PB	650	10372 B	10372 B	AU	stamp/pen
3252		$10 1929T1		F000098A		VG/F	
3252		$10 1929T1		E000121A		VF	
3252		$10 1929T1		A000157A		F/VF	
3252		$10 1929T1		D000621A		XF	Higgins Museum
3252		$10 1929T1		E000639A		AU	
3252		$10 1929T1		A000660A		CU	
3252		$10 1929T1		C000660A		CU	
3252		$10 1929T1		E000660A		?	
3252		$10 1929T1		A000661A		CU	
3252		$10 1929T1		E000753A		AU	
3252		$10 1929T1		E000755A		CU	
3252		$10 1929T1		F000756A		AU	
3252		$10 1929T1		C000757A		CU	
3252		$10 1929T1		E000772A		?	
3252		$20 1929T1		D000020A		VF	Rust on back
3252		$20 1929T1		?000085A		XF	
3252		$20 1929T1		B000107A		?	
3252		$20 1929T1		F000115A		G	
3252		$20 1929T1		A000183A		CU	
3252		$20 1929T1		B000183A		AU	
3252		$20 1929T1		C000183A		?	
3252		$20 1929T1		D000183A		CU	
3252		$20 1929T1		F000184A		CU	
3252		$20 1929T1		E000198A		VG	Washed
3252		$20 1929T1		A000199A		F	
3252		$20 1929T1		E000204A		VF	
3252		$20 1929T1		E000211A		F	

THE STATE NATIONAL BANK OF IOWA FALLS   14 L   13 S
7521   HARDIN

Organized on August 20, 1904 with a capital of $50,000. Placed in receivership on July 7, 1932; capital of $50,000.

Officers: Pres. SR Cross 1905-11, FD Peet 1912-32; **VP** BH Thomas 1907-11, Robt Wright 1913-14, CH Cross 1920-28, MD Boddy 1928, HS Powers 1928-32; **Cash.** Frank D Peet 1905-11, EE Benedict 1912-32; **AC** Cyrus B Richmond 1907-09, EE Benedict 1911, Ray E Miller 1913-32, VA Gerhardt 1924-28, EP Kickels 1929-30

Third Charter, Red Seal	Ser #	# Notes
10-10-10-20	1-1260	5,040

Third Charter, Date Back, Blue Seal		
10-10-10-20	1-3300	13,200

Third Charter, Plain Back, Blue Seal		
10-10-10-20	3301-9938	26,552

1929, Type I

6-10's		1-823	4,938
6-20's		1-214	1,284

Total amount of circulation issued = $634,960. Amount of large outstanding at close = $6,840. Amount of small outstanding at close = $42,620.

44,792 Large   6,222 Small   56,380 Total

7521	M	$10 1902RS	613	520 C	E937332	VG	
7521	M	$10 1902RS	613	696 B	E937508	CU	Higgins Museum
7521	M	$10 1902DB	616	169 F	?	PR	gone, Bayard
7521	M	$10 1902DB	616	601 D	K811572	VG	
7521	M	$10 1902DB	616	1651 E	B617032A	VG/F	
7521	M	$10 1902DB	616	1962 E	K598713A	F+	pen/pen
7521	M	$20 1902DB	642	256 B	K811227	VF	pen/pen
7521	M	$10 1902PB	624	4257 D	A169764D	F/VF	pen/pen
7521	M	$10 1902PB	624	4423 F	A169930D	F/VF	Higgins Mus.
7521	-	$10 1902PB	624	8343 F	8343 F	VF	Davenport B&T
7521	-	$10 1902PB	624	9176 E	9176 E	VG+	
7521	-	$10 1902PB	624	9258 F	9258 F	F	
7521	M	$20 1902PB	650	3682 B	T664992B	VG/F	
7521	-	$20 1902PB	650	9563 B	9563 B	VG+	
7521		$10 1929T1		D000162A		VG	
7521		$10 1929T1		D000245A		VF	
7521		$10 1929T1		A000632A		?	
7521		$10 1929T1		C000665A		?	
7521		$10 1929T1		C000666A		CU	
7521		$10 1929T1		E000669A		CU	
7521		$10 1929T1		F000750A		?	
7521		$10 1929T1		C000759A		VG/F	
7521		$20 1929T1		E000083A		F/VF	Higgins Museum
7521		$20 1929T1		A000091A		VG/F	
7521		$20 1929T1		A000163A		VF+	
7521		$20 1929T1		C000187A		XF	
7521		$20 1929T1		D000210A		F	

THE FIRST NATIONAL BANK OF IRETON   0 L
4794   SIOUX

Organized on August 31, 1892. Succeeded The Bank of Northwestern Iowa. Placed in voluntary liquidation on September 1, 1894; capital of $50,000.
Officers: Pres. N Kessey 1892-93; **Cash.** AP Owens 1892-93

Second Charter, Brown Backs	Ser #	# Notes
10-10-10-20	1-297	1,188

Total amount of circulation issued = $14,850. Amount outstanding at close = $11,350. Amount outstanding in 1910 = $180.

1,188 Large   0 Small   1,188 Total

THE FARMERS AND MERCHANTS NATIONAL BANK OF JEFFERSON
10123   GREENE   2 L

Organized on December 28, 1911 with a capital of $40,000. Placed in receivership on April 27, 1923; capital of $40,000. Reason for failure: local depression.
Officers: Pres. Jno McCarthy 1912-14, ZA Church 1915, SC Culbertson 1916-19, JM Wiggins 1920, Joseph Mehan 1923; **VP** ZA Church 1913-14, FJ Forbes 1923; **Cash.** SC Culbertson 1912-15, G Wm Dunlop 1916-17, CL Brock 1918-20, JL Reynolds 1923; **AC** PB Osgood, George Johns 1920-23

Third Charter, Date Back, Blue Seal	Ser #	# Notes
10-10-10-20	1-2340	9,360

Sheets numbered 1 to 2140 were 02-08 backs. Sheets numbered 2141 to 2340 were delivered on October 1, but not marked as to type. Sheets numbered 2341 to 4705 were plain backs.

Third Charter, Plain Back, Blue Seal		
10-10-10-20	2341-4705	9,460

Total amount issued = $235,250. Amount outstanding at close = $40,000.

18,820 Large   0 Small   18,820 Total

10123	M	$10 1902DB	617	1393 A	T63985A	F+	stamp/stamp
10123	M	$10 1902PB	628	2776 B	X992857B	VG	gone Higg. Mus.

THE FIRST NATIONAL BANK OF JEFFERSON   2 L
8262   GREENE

Organized on March 26, 1906 with a capital of $50,000. Placed in receivership on December 23, 1925; capital of $50,000. Reason for failure: incompetent management.
Officers: Pres. Albert Head 1906-07, MM Head 1908-25; **VP** RC Head 1907-25, Albert Head 1909, TR Watts 1914-25; **Cash.** MM Head 1906-07, CE Marquis 1908-22, OG Wynkoop 1924, RS Kinsey 1925; **AC** CE Marquis 1907, SC Culbertson 1909-11, OG Wynkoop 1920-22, RS Kinsey 1924, Fanny Johnson 1924

Third Charter, Red Seal	Ser #	# Notes
10-10-10-20	1-900	3,600
50-100	1-200	400

Third Charter, Date Back, Blue Seal		
10-10-10-20	1-2540	10,160
50-100	1-100	200

Third Charter, Plain Back, Blue Seal		
10-10-10-20	2541-3083	2,172

Total amount issued = $244,150. Amount outstanding at close = $12,100.

16,532 Large   0 Small   16,532 Total

8262	M	$10 1902DB	617	271 D	M76352	F	faded Higg. Mus.
8262		$10 1902PB	625	3032 F	M496914H	AU	

THE FIRST NATIONAL BANK OF JESUP   0 L
2856   BUCHANAN

Chartered on January 10, 1883 with a capital of $50,000. Succeeded The Farmers Bank. Closed on April 15, 1886. Placed in voluntary liquidation on April 20, 1886; capital of $50,000. Succeeded by The Farmers Bank.
Officers: Pres. Thomas Taylor 1883-85; **Cash.** George S Murphey 1883-85

Second Charter, Brown Backs	Ser #	# Notes
5-5-5-5	1-2250	9,000

Total amount of circulation issued = $45,000. Amount outstanding at close = $25,760. Amount outstanding in 1910 = $325.

9,000 Large   0 Small   9,000 Total

THE FIRST NATIONAL BANK OF JEWELL JUNCTION 2 L 10 S
5743 HAMILTON

Organized on February 28, 1901 with a capital of $25,000. Chartered on March 15, 1901; succeeded The Farmers and Traders Bank. Placed in conservatorship on March 24, 1933. Placed in receivership on November 3, 1933; capital of $25,000. Reason for failure: not available in reports.
Officers: Pres. HC Smith 1901-33; **VP** Jas B Thompson 1902-07, JS Smith 1909-33; **Cash.** A Alexander 1901-20, Sterling Alexander 1923-25, Lester L Billings 1926-33; **AC** FH Alexander 1902, 1909, Lester L Billings 1920-25, Cora E Alexander 1926-33

	Ser #	# Notes
Second Charter, Brown Backs		
10-10-10-20	1-640	2,560
Second Charter, Date Back		
10-10-10-20	1-700	2,800
Second Charter, Value Back		
10-10-10-20	701-775	300
Third Charter, Plain Back, Blue Seal		
10-10-10-20	1-676	2,704
1929, Type I		
6-5's	1-356	2,136
6-10's	1-286	1,716
6-20's	1-74	444

Total amount of circulation issued = $141,270. Amount of large outstanding at close = $850. Amount of small outstanding at close = $24,150.

8,364 Large 4,296 Small 12,660 Total

5743	M	$10	1882VB	577	744 D	V75482	F/VF	pen/pen ac
5743		$20	1902PB	659	158 A	K577370E	F	Oat Bin Hoard, Higgins Museum
5743		$5	1929T1	C000214A			VF	Higgins Museum
5743		$5	1929T1	D000225A			G	Soiled
5743		$5	1929T1	B000252A			F	
5743		$10	1929T1	E000123A			F	
5743		$10	1929T1	D000170A			F	
5743		$10	1929T1	E000250A			F+	
5743		$20	1929T1	B000009A			VG	
5743		$20	1929T1	C000029A			F	
5743		$20	1929T1	C000037A			F	
5743		$20	1929T1	C000038A			VG/F	

THE FIRST NATIONAL BANK OF KANAWHA 6 L 11 S
9018 HANCOCK

Organized on December 14, 1907 with a capital of $25,000. Placed in conservatorship on March 28, 1933. Placed in receivership on October 7, 1933; capital of $50,000. Reason for failure: not available from reports.
Officers: Pres. JE Wichman 1908-20, FL Bush 1922-33; **VP** OT Rikansrud 1909-10, CC Lucas 1911-33; FL Bush 1908-20, FN Knudsen 1922-33; **Cash.** LD Perisho 1909-10, FN Knudson 1913-20, Clara B Show 1925, CB Fosen 1925-26, Omar Maland 1927-29

	Ser #	# Notes
Third Charter, Red Seal		
10-10-10-20	1-700	2,800
Third Charter, Date Back, Blue Seal		
10-10-10-20	1-1870	7,480
Third Charter, Plain Back, Blue Seal		
10-10-10-20	1871-4808	11,752
1929, Type I		
6-10's	1-548	3,288
6-20's	1-116	696

Total amount of circulation issued = $322,200. Amount of large outstanding at close = $1,570. Amount of small outstanding at close = $23,430.

22,032 Large 3,984 Small 26,016 Total

9018	M	$10	1902PB	626	?	A655851D	?	
9018	M	$10	1902PB	626	2731 E	V450153D	?	
9018	-	$10	1902PB	626	4022 D	4022 D	VG	
9018	-	$10	1902PB	626	4268 E	4268 E	XF	Higgins Museum
9018	-	$10	1902PB	626	4472 ?	4472 ?	G/VG	
9018	M	$20	1902PB	652	2972 B	M746589E	F+	pen/gone
9018		$10	1929T1	D000027A			F	
9018		$10	1929T1	D000046A			VG	
9018		$10	1929T1	A000082A			?	
9018		$10	1929T1	A000267A			?	
9018		$10	1929T1	F000438A			F	
9018		$10	1929T1	A000456A			VG	
9018		$10	1929T1	A000546A			F	
9018		$20	1929T1	C000048A			F	Trimmed on top
9018		$20	1929T1	C000055A			?	
9018		$20	1929T1	F000061A			F+	
9018		$20	1929T1	C000083A			VF+	Higgins Museum

THE FIRST NATIONAL BANK OF KEOKUK 0 L
80 LEE

Organized on September 9, 1863 with a capital of $50,000. Placed in receivership on March 3, 1868; capital of $100,000. Reason for failure: incompetent management. The first Iowa national bank failure.
Officers: Pres. HK Love 1867; **Cash.** RB Foote 1867

	Ser #	# Notes
First Charter, Original Issue		
5-5-5-5	1-4600	18,400

Total amount of circulation issued = $92,000. Amount outstanding at close = $90,000. Amount outstanding in 1915 = $330.

18,400 Large 0 Small 18,400 Total

KEOKUK NATIONAL BANK 0 S
14309 LEE

Chartered in December 1934. Succeeded #1992 and assumed circulation of #1992. The highest Iowa charter number to issue currency. The total circulation issued, $2,400, was less than that issued by any other bank in Iowa that issued.
Officers: Pres. JA Dunlap 1935; **VP** ER Cochrane 1935; **Cash.** ER Cochrane 1935; **AC** JR Baur 1935, LA Whetstone 1935

	Ser #	# Notes
1929, Type II		
10's	1-30	30
20's	1-105	105

Total amount of circulation issued = $2,400. Amount of small outstanding in 1935 = $39,430. Includes small #1992 since #14309 assumed circulation of #1992.

0 Large 135 Small 135 Total

THE KEOKUK NATIONAL BANK 17 L 17 S
1992 LEE

Chartered on June 1, 1872. Placed in voluntary liquidation on Jan. 8, 1935; capital of $150,000. Succeeded by #14309; circulation assumed by #14309.
Officers: Pres. William Patterson 1872-82, SP Pond 1883-1904, ES Baker 1905-25, JA Dunlap 1925-34; **VP** WA Brownell 1896-1900, Edwin F Brownell 1902, ES Baker 1903-04, AE Matless 1907-14, Ira W Wills 1909-23, JA Dunlap 1920-24, E Ross Baker 1924-25, MF Baker 1925-30, CR Joy 1925-29, LJ Montgomery 1930-31, ER Cochrane 1930-34; **Cash.** Edwin F Brownell 1872-1904, John A Dunlap 1905-15, ER Cochrane 1916-33, 1934, JR Bauer 1933; **AC** ER Cochrane 1907-14, JR Baur 1920-34, LA Whetstone 1932-34

	Ser #	# Notes
First Charter, Original Issue		
1-1-1-2	1-2900	11,600
5-5-5-5	1-2750	11,000
10-10-10-20	1-400	1,600
First Charter, Series of 1875		
5-5-5-5	1-5250	21,000
10-10-10-20	1-1220	4,880
Second Charter, Brown Backs		
10-10-10-20	1-7840	31,360
Second Charter, Date Back		
10-10-10-20	1-1811	7,244
Third Charter, Date Back, Blue Seal		
10-10-10-20	1-2600	10,400
Third Charter, Plain Back, Blue Seal		
10-10-10-20	2601-6955	17,420
1929, Type I		
6-10's	1-848	5,088
6-20's	1-285	1,710

Total amount of circulation issued = $1,170,880. Amount of large outstanding in 1935 = $4,570. Amount of small outstanding in 1935 = $39,890. Circulation assumed by #14309.

116,504 Large 6,798 Small 123,302 Total

1992	-	$1	ORIG	380	661 A	D138308		VF+	pen Higg. Mus.
1992	-	$1	ORIG	380	2308 B	D139955		PR	pen/pen
1992	-	$1	ORIG	380	2434 B	D140081		?	pen Higgins Mus.
1992	-	$1	ORIG	380	2443 C	D140090		G+	pen/pen
1992	-	$2	ORIG	389	1656 A	D139303		F	Grinnell # 3439, Higgins Museum
1992	-	$2	ORIG	389	2480 A	D140127		G	pen/pen
1992	M	$10	1882BB	485	4876 A	E229345E		F	pen/pen vp
1992	M	$10	1882BB	485	5525 C	N162295N		VG/F	pen/pen
1992	M	$10	1882BB	485	5620 B	N162390N		F	
1992	M	$10	1882BB	485	6765 E	U257475U		F	Higgins Museum
1992	M	$10	1902DB	620	2103 C	Y584943A		F	Higgins Museum
1992		$10	1902PB	628	4467 B	T564729E		VG	
1992		$10	1902PB	628	4551 C	T564813E		VG/F	
1992		$10	1902PB	628	5585 C	A504787K		VG+	
1992	-	$10	1902PB	628	6481 B	6481 B		F	faded/pen
1992	-	$20	1902PB	654	6547 A	6547 A		VF	stamp/stamp
1992	-	$20	1902PB	654	6953 A	6953 A		CU	Grinnell # 1403

1992	$10	1929T1	D000018A	AU	
1992	$10	1929T1	F000021A	VG	
1992	$10	1929T1	A000180A	CU	
1992	$10	1929T1	A000248A	VG	
1992	$10	1929T1	D000290A	VG	
1992	$10	1929T1	F000294A	VG	
1992	$10	1929T1	F000330A	VG	
1992	$10	1929T1	C000535A	VG	
1992	$10	1929T1	C000608A	VF	
1992	$10	1929T1	E000668A	XF	
1992	$10	1929T1	B000837A	VF	
1992	$20	1929T1	A000057A	VF/XF	
1992	$20	1929T1	A000087A	?	
1992	$20	1929T1	D000089A	VF	Higgins Museum
1992	$20	1929T1	D000105A	VG	Red stamp face
1992	$20	1929T1	D000196A	VF	
1992	$20	1929T1	F000282A	?	

THE STATE NATIONAL BANK OF KEOKUK   2 L
1441   LEE

Chartered in 1865. Placed in voluntary liquidation on May 23, 1885; capital of $150,000. Succeeded by a state bank.
Officers: Pres. James F Cox 1867-76, Arthur Hosmer 1877-84; **Cash.** Oscar C Hale 1867-79, A Bridgman, Jr 1880-84

First Charter, Original Issue	Ser #	# Notes
5-5-5-5	1-2100	8,400
10-10-10-20	1-3700	14,800
50-100	1-100	200
First Charter, Series of 1875		
10-10-10-20	1-1078	4,312

Total amount of circulation issued = $295,900. Amount outstanding at close = $45,000. Amount outstanding in 1910 = $1,910.
27,712 Large   0 Small   27,712 Total

| 1441 | - | $5 | ORIG | 397 | 1226 D | L703280 | F | |
| 1441 | - | $5 | ORIG | 397 | 2082 C | L704136 | VG+ | Higgins Museum |

THE LANDMANDS NATIONAL BANK OF KIMBALLTON
9619   AUDUBON   7 L   12 S

Kimballton has a strong Danish heritage. Landmand is the Danish word for farmer.
Chartered in December 1909 with a capital of $25,000.
Officers: Pres. Hans Madsen 1910-27, SC Pedersen 1928-35; **VP** HJ Jorgensen 1910-13; Christ Christensen 1914-28, Dr. P Soe 1929-35; **Cash.** Alma Madsen 1910-22, Alma Madsen Halst 1924-26; Herlup E Madsen 1926-27, Victor H Trukken 1927-35; **AC** Math Nissager 1922-26, SC Pedersen 1927, Folmer Faaborg 1929-35

Third Charter, Date Back, Blue Seal	Ser #	# Notes
5-5-5-5	1-950	3,800

Sheets numbered 1 to 850 were 02-08 backs. Sheets numbered 851 to 950 were delivered on September 24 but not marked as to type. Sheets numbered 951 to 2430 were plain backs.

| 10-10-10-20 | 1-760 | 3,040 |

Sheets numbered 1 to 680 were 02-08 backs. Sheets numbered 681 to 760 were delivered on September 25, but not marked as to type. Sheets numbered 761 to 1723 were plain backs.

Third Charter, Plain Back, Blue Seal		
5-5-5-5	951-2430	5,920
10-10-10-20	761-1723	3,852
1929, Type I		
6-5's	1-414	2,484
6-10's	1-206	1,236
6-20's	1-64	384
1929, Type II		
5's	1-36	36
10's	1-881	881
20's	1-219	219

Total amount of circulation issued = $180,580. Amount of large outstanding in June 1935 = $1,330. Amount of small outstanding in June 1935 = $23,670.
16,612 Large   5,240 Small   21,852 Total

9619	M	$5	1902DB	592	1 A	T909810	VF	pen/pen
9619	M	$20	1902DB	644	467 B	?	XF	
9619	M	$20	1902DB	644	517 A	B874342A	F/VF	stamp/pen
9619	M	$20	1902DB	644	618 A	X413723A	AU	stamp/pen
9619	-	$10	1902PB	626	1344 A	X628826H	XF	Higgins Museum
9619	-	$10	1902PB	626	1412 B	1412 B	?	
9619	-	$20	1902PB	652	1686 A	1686 A	?	pen/pen
9619		$5	1929T1	A000104A			F	
9619		$5	1929T1	B000268A			VG/F	Light ink
9619		$10	1929T1	B000043A			VG	
9619		$10	1929T1	F000059A			VG	
9619		$10	1929T1	?000081A			F/VF	
9619		$10	1929T1	D000170A			VF/XF	
9619		$10	1929T1	F000177A			F	
9619		$20	1929T1	C000017A			F	
9619		$20	1929T1	E000040A			VG	
9619		$20	1929T1	D000060A			XF/AU	Higgins Museum
9619		$20	1929T2	A000106			F	
9619		$20	1929T2	A000136			?	

THE FARMERS NATIONAL BANK OF KINGSLEY   4 L   11 S
9116   PLYMOUTH

Organized on April 6, 1908 with a capital of $25,000. Placed in conservatorship on March 20, 1933. Placed in receivership on October 30, 1933; capital of $25,000.
Some (all?) of the 1929 notes had the engraved signature of Assistant Cashier W. L. Karlson, the only known instance of an assistant cashier's signature engraved on Iowa notes and perhaps also nationally.
Officers: Pres. Mason J Foft 1908-13, FA Gates 1914-33; **VP** Allen Harrod 1909, LA Dugan 1910-11, Allen Harrod 1913, MD Gates 1914-22, MF Rathbun 1923-31, Val Sitzmann 1932-33, WM Feeney 1932-33; **Cash.** RB Lyle 1908-11, G Lindeman 1912, Frank Lindeman 1913, LF Kliebenstein 1914-28; **AC** LA Dugan 1913, Walter L Karlson 1920-33, RE Tool 1928-33

Third Charter, Red Seal	Ser #	# Notes
5-5-5-5	1-150	600
10-10-10-20	1-120	480
Third Charter, Date Back, Blue Seal		
5-5-5-5	1-500	2,000
10-10-10-20	1-380	1,520
Third Charter, Plain Back, Blue Seal		
5-5-5-5	501-1545	4,180
10-10-10-20	381-1028	2,592
1929, Type I		
6-5's	1-694	4,164
6-10's	1-410	2,460
6-20's	1-128	768
1929, Type II		
5's	1-42	42

Total amount of circulation issued = $152,290. Amount outstanding at close = $25,000. Amount of large outstanding on October 27, 1933 = $660.
11,372 Large   7,434 Small   18,806 Total

9116	M	$5	1902RS	589	1 A	T669033	VF	pen/pen Rust
9116	M	$20	1902DB	644	313 B	E404062A	VF	pen/pen
9116	M	$5	1902PB	600	580 F	E769126D	AU	
9116		$10	1902PB	626	542 D	X354274E	F	Higgins Museum
9116		$10	1929T1	F000016A			?	
9116		$10	1929T1	D000091A			VG	Higgins Museum
9116		$10	1929T1	C000111A			F/VF	
9116		$10	1929T1	A000221A			F	
9116		$10	1929T1	A000335A			XF	
9116		$10	1929T1	E000350A			F	
9116		$10	1929T1	C000376A			F	
9116		$20	1929T1	D000027A			VG/F	
9116		$20	1929T1	E000055A			VG	
9116		$20	1929T1	B000070A			F/VF	Higgins Mus.
9116		$20	1929T1	E000122A			VG	

THE FIRST NATIONAL BANK OF KLEMME   7 L   16 S
6659   HANCOCK

Chartered in March 1903. Succeeded The State Savings Bank, Klemme.
Officers: Pres. Fred Arnold 1904-07, CH Wiegman 1908-23, FA Arnold 1924-35; **VP** CH Wiegman 1904-07, August Lau 1909-25, August Barz 1925-34, Fred Greiman 1935; **Cash.** FA Arnold 1904-23, CG Waterman 1924-35; **AC** MH Crissman 1904, MI Parker 1909-10, CF Bier 1914, CG Waterman 1920-23, AJ Kudje 1935

Third Charter, Red Seal	Ser #	# Notes
10-10-10-20	1-1006	4,024
Third Charter, Date Back, Blue Seal		
10-10-10-20	1-1610	6,440
Third Charter, Plain Back, Blue Seal		
10-10-10-20	1611-4645	12,140
1929, Type I		
6-10's	1-540	3,240
6-20's	1-140	840
1929, Type II		
5's	1-312	312

10's			1-380	380	
20's			1-151	151	

Total amount of circulation issued = $340,130. Amount of large outstanding in 1935 = $1,225. Amount of small outstanding in 1935 = $23,745.

22,604 Large   4,923 Small   27,527 Total

6659	M	$20 1902DB 642	116 B	H22491	VG	
6659	M	$20 1902DB 642	467 B	H22842	F	lt pen sigs
6659		$10 1902PB 624	1824 F	U410762B	F+	Higgins Museum
6659		$10 1902PB 624	3225 E	B939277H	F	Repaired
6659	-	$10 1902PB 624	3989 D	3989 D	F	faded/faded
6659	-	$10 1902PB 624	4125 E	4125 E	VG	stamp/stamp
6659	-	$10 1902PB 650	4553 B	4553 B	VF	
6659		$10 1929T1	C000059A		?	
6659		$10 1929T1	E000068A		VG/F	
6659		$10 1929T1	F000097A		VG	
6659		$10 1929T1	E000106A		F+	
6659		$10 1929T1	E000249A		XF	
6659		$10 1929T1	C000310A		AU	
6659		$10 1929T1	A000522A		?	
6659		$20 1929T1	C000003A		VG	
6659		$20 1929T1	A000014A		XF	
6659		$20 1929T1	E000015A		F	Small rust spot
6659		$20 1929T1	B000025A		VF	
6659		$20 1929T1	C000045A		VF	
6659		$20 1929T1	C000129A		XF	
6659		$5 1929T2	A000120		F+	
6659		$10 1929T2	A000209		VF	Higgins Museum
6659		$20 1929T2	A000135		VG	

THE CITIZENS NATIONAL BANK OF KNOXVILLE   19 L   25 S
4633   **MARION**

Chartered in 1891. Placed in voluntary liquidation on January 21, 1932; capital of $100,000. Absorbed by #12849; circulation assumed by #12849.

Officers: Pres. SL Collins 1891-1904, Lafe S Collins 1905-27, JL Collins 1928, JC Collins 1929-31; **VP** John McMillan 1896-1904, AJ Hanna 1907, WR Myers 1909-14, AJ Hanna, Jr 1920-31; **Cash.** Lafe S Collins 1891-1904, LB Myers 1905-09, JC Collins 1910-28, EL Job 1929; **AC** LB Myers 1896-1904, Joy C Collins 1907-09, NG Fast 1910-11, Gilbert Dutton 1920-28, LJ Martin 1920, JR Dyer 1922-31, EL Job 1928

Second Charter, Brown Backs	Ser #	# Notes
5-5-5-5	1-7875	31,500
10-10-10-20	1-1640	6,560
Second Charter, Date Back		
5-5-5-5	1-911	3,644
10-10-10-20	1-690	2,760
Third Charter, Date Back, Blue Seal		
10-10-10-20	1-3000	12,000
Third Charter, Plain Back, Blue Seal		
10-10-10-20	3001-15170	48,680
1929, Type I		
6-10's	1-1525	9,150
6-20's	1-462	2,772

Total amount of circulation issued = $1,217,660. Amount of large outstanding at close = $12,137. Amount of small outstanding at close = $87,860. Circulation assumed by #12849 which was then responsible for redeeming the outstanding notes of #4633.

105,144 Large   11,922 Small   117,066 Total

4633		$5 1882BB 472	7189 C	N54724N	VG/F	
4633	M	$20 1882BB 499	653 A	A581726A	AU	
4633	M	$20 1902DD 499	654 A	A581727A	VF/XF	
4633	M	$20 1882BB 499	655 A	A581728A	CU	
4633	M	$20 1882BB 499	656 A	A581729A	AU	Higgins Museum
4633	M	$10 1902PB 628	3287 B	Y4428B	F/VF	pen/pen vp
4633	M	$10 1902PB 628	3842 A	?	?	Higgins Museum
4633	M	$10 1902PB 628	5384 C	V361886D	F	
4633	M	$10 1902PB 628	8371 C	Y161753E	XF	pen ac/stamp
4633	M	$10 1902PB 628	8401 ?		?	
4633	M	$10 1902PB 628	8688 C	D632700H	VF+	
4633	M	$10 1902PB 628	9135 A	D633147H	F	pen ac/pen
4633	M	$10 1902PB 628	9654 C	K459556H	VF	Higgins Museum
4633	-	$10 1902PB 628	12565 B	12565 B	G	pen/pen
4633	-	$10 1902PB 628	12997 C	12997 C	XF+	pen/pen ac
4633	-	$10 1902PB 628	13554 B	13554 B	F/VF	pen/pen ac
4633	-	$10 1902PB 628	14349 B	14349 B	F	ac
4633	-	$10 1902PB 628	15129 A	15129 A	F/VF	Higgins Museum
4633	M	$20 1902PB 654	4439 A	V350921D	VG/F	
4633		$10 1929T1	E000024A		F	
4633		$10 1929T1	D000124A		?	
4633		$10 1929T1	A000319A		VG	
4633		$10 1929T1	F000967A		VG/F	
4633		$10 1929T1	F001043A		VG	
4633		$10 1929T1	C001095A		VF	
4633		$10 1929T1	D001295A		VG	
4633		$10 1929T1	B001432A		XF	
4633		$20 1929T1	A000062A		F/VF	
4633		$20 1929T1	F000066A		F/VF	
4633		$20 1929T1	C000075A		VG	Ink on back
4633		$20 1929T1	A000102A		F/VF	
4633		$20 1929T1	D000162A		VG/F	
4633		$20 1929T1	F000175A		?	
4633		$20 1929T1	F000229A		VF	
4633		$20 1929T1	A000259A		VG/F	
4633		$20 1929T1	B000259A		VF	
4633		$20 1929T1	B000271A		F/VF	
4633		$20 1929T1	D000271A		F	
4633		$20 1929T1	E000298A		F	
4633		$20 1929T1	A000366A		F/VF	
4633		$20 1929T1	D000415A		F/VF	
4633		$20 1929T1	F000443A		XF	Higgins Museum
4633		$20 1929T1	B000455A		F	
4633		$20 1929T1	E000462A		F	Last sheet of $20s

THE COMMUNITY NATIONAL BANK & TRUST COMPANY OF KNOXVILLE
13707   **MARION**   **12 S**

Chartered in June 1933.

Officers: Pres. EL Job 1933-35; **VP** JL Collins 1933-35; **Cash.** JR Dyer 1933-35; **AC** Ed M Butterfield 1933-35

1929, Type II, Brown Serial Numbers	Ser #	# Notes
10's	1-4225	4,225
20's	1-1314	1,314

Total amount issued = $68,530. Amount outstanding in 1935 = $48,750.

0 Large   5,539 Small   5,539 Total

13707	$10 1929T2	A001561		VF/XF	
13707	$10 1929T2	A001876		F	Higgins Museum
13707	$10 1929T2	A002283		VG	
13707	$10 1929T2	A002355		VG	Ink
13707	$10 1929T2	A002369		F	
13707	$10 1929T2	A002655		F	
13707	$10 1929T2	A002887		VG	
13707	$10 1929T2	A003602		VG/F	
13707	$20 1929T2	A000424		F	
13707	$20 1929T2	A000606		VF+	
13707	$20 1929T2	A000660		G/VG	
13707	$20 1929T2	A001216		G+	

THE KNOXVILLE NATIONAL BANK   29 L
1871   **LEE**

Chartered on September 7, 1871. Placed in voluntary liquidation on December 17, 1925; capital of $100,000. Succeeded by #12849.

Officers: Pres. Larken Wright 1872-73, Adgate W Collins 1874-94, EH Amos 1895-96, JH Auld 1897-98, EH Amos 1899-1902, JS Cunningham 1903-10, John B Elliott 1911-25; **VP** JS Cunningham 1896-1902, E Hardin 1903-06, CC Cunningham 1907-24, FM Butcher 1925; **Cash.** Abington J Briggs 1872-81, Henry L Bousquiet 1883, John B Elliott 1884-1910, JJ Roberts 1911-25; **AC** WL Collins 1885, CC Cunningham 1896, JJ Roberts 1900-10, Ed M Butterfield 1911-25, CC Cunningham 1925

First Charter, Original Issue	Ser #	# Notes
1-1-1-2	1-1000	4,000
10-10-10-20	1-2799	11,106
50-100	1-167	334
First Charter, Series of 1875		
10-10-10-20	1-2733	10,932
Second Charter, Brown Backs		
5-5-5-5	1-10430	41,720
10-10-10-20	1-4560	18,240
Second Charter, Date Back		
5-5-5-5	1-2331	9,324
10-10-10-20	1-1525	6,100
Third Charter, Date Back, Blue Seal		
5-5-5-5	1-4850	19,400
10-10-10-20	1-3760	15,040
Third Charter, Plain Back, Blue Seal		
5-5-5-5	4851-13415	34,260
10-10-10-20	3761-9582	23,288

Total amount issued = $1,613,520. Amount outstanding at close = $100,000.

193,834 Large   0 Small   193,834 Total

1871	M	$5 1882BB 472	7993 A	K690083K	F+	pen/pen
1871	M	$5 1882BB 472	8709 C	R144297R	VG	pen/pen
1871	M	$10 1882BB 485	2371 B	B631047R	F/VF	
1871	M	$10 1882BB 485	2377 B	?	VF	
1871	M	$20 1882DB 555	60 B	B424330	VF+	Higgins Museum

1871	M	$5 1902DB	594	884 B	B142125A	F	pen ac/pen vp
1871	M	$5 1902DB	594	2832 B	U681144A	VG	
1871	M	$5 1902DB	594	2896 C	U681208A	F	
1871	M	$5 1902DB	594	4433 A	K424895B	G	pen/pen
1871	M	$10 1902DB	620	360 C	B675181A	F	
1871	M	$20 1902DB	646	820 A	B675641A	VF	pen/pen
1871	M	$5 1902PB	602	6310 C	X787786B	F	pen/pen
1871	M	$5 1902PB	602	9277 A	B959473E	F/VF	
1871	M	$5 1902PB	602	10839 D	V515070E	VG/F	
1871	M	$5 1902PB	602	12283 D	K295919H	F	corner tears
1871	M	$5 1902PB	602	12463 A	K296099H	VG	faded/faded
1871	-	$5 1902PB	602	13005 B	T312966H	F/VF	stamp/stamp
1871	M	$10 1902PB	628	4916 B	M402948D	VF	
1871	M	$10 1902PB	628	8090 C	H62442H	XF	
1871		$10 1902PB	628	8423 C	M997495H	VG	
1871	-	$10 1902PB	628	9215 A	Y786077H	G/VG	
1871		$10 1902PB	628	9301 A	Y786163H	F	
1871	M	$20 1902PB	654	7989 A	H62341H	F/VF	gone/gone
1871	M	$20 1902PB	654	7990 A	H62342H	CU	Higgins Museum
1871	M	$20 1902PB	654	7993 A	H62345H	XF	
1871	M	$20 1902PB	654	7995 A	H62347H	AU	stamp/stamp
1871	M	$20 1902PB	654	7996 A	H62348H	AU	
1871	M	$20 1902PB	654	8000 A	H62352H	XF/AU	
1871	M	$20 1902PB	654	8001 A	H62353H	AU	

KNOXVILLE-CITIZENS NATIONAL BANK & TRUST COMPANY
12849 (SECOND TITLE)   MARION   7 S

Succeeded The Knoxville National Bank and Trust Company #12849 (First Title), which issued no notes, on January 21, 1932. Assumed the circulation of #4633. Placed in conservatorship on March 14, 1933. Placed in receivership on October 10, 1933; capital of $100,000.

Officers: Pres. John B Elliott 1925-26, OM Bundy 1927-28, ER Jordan 1929, CC Cooper 1930-31, EL Job 1932-33; **VP** FM Butcher 1925-26, RJ Harrison 1927-28, JA Bundy 1928, ER Jordan 1928, CC Cooper 1929, 1932-33, SL Walker 1929-33, WJ Casey 1930-31, Ed M Butterfield 1932-33; **Cash.** JJ Roberts 1925-27, SL Walker 1928, Ed M Butterfield 1929-31, JC Collins 1932-33; **AC** Ed Butterfield 1925-28, CC Cunningham 1925-33, JJ Roberts 1928, Lenore E Swinehart 1929-31, JR Dyer 1932-33

1929, Type I	Ser #	# Notes
6-10's	1-586	3,516
6-20's	1-125	750

Total amount of circulation issued = $50,160. Amount of large outstanding at close = $6,580. Includes the large outstanding for #4633. Amount of small outstanding at close= $93,420. Includes the small outstanding for #4633 & #12849 since #12849 assumed the circulation of #4633.

0 Large		4,266 Small		4,266 Total	
12849	$10 1929T1	A000123A		F	
12849	$10 1929T1	B000243A		F	
12849	$10 1929T1	B000291A		XF	
12849	$10 1929T1	A000294A		VF	
12849	$20 1929T1	C000014A		VG/F	Higgins Museum
12849	$20 1929T1	E000059A		G	Tear
12849	$20 1929T1	A000078A		VF	

THE MARION COUNTY NATIONAL BANK OF KNOXVILLE
1986   MARION   21 L

Organized on April 12, 1872 with a capital of $50,000. Placed in receivership on February 1, 1927; capital of $60,000. Reason for failure: local depression.

Officers: Pres. Jairus E Neal 1872-73, Larkin Wright 1874-89, Charles Perry 1890, Charles Perrin 1891, Oliver P Wright 1892-1926; **VP** LO Donley 1896, Charles Perry 1900-14, Jas D Gamble 1920-26; **Cash.** Oliver P Wright 1872-91, OL Wright 1892-1926; **AC** Chas E Grant 1885, Lou Donley 1896-1900, Agnes White 1902-13, HH Browne 1914-26, Pattie Slayman 1923-24, EL Job 1923-26

First Charter, Original Issue	Ser #	# Notes
1-1-1-2	1-2000	8,000
5-5-5-5	1-4200	16,800
First Charter, Series of 1875		
1-1-1-2	1-999	3,996
5-5-5-5	1-7286	29,144
Second Charter, Brown Backs		
5-5-5-5	1-5075	20,300
50-100	1-900	1,800
Second Charter, Date Back		
5-5-5-5	1-1390	5,560
50-100	1-259	518
Third Charter, Date Back, Blue Seal		
5-5-5-5	1-1900	7,600
10-10-10-20	1-1440	5,760
Third Charter, Plain Back, Blue Seal		
5-5-5-5	1901-8405	26,020
10-10-10-20	1441-5182	14,968

Total amount issued = $974,065. Amount outstanding at close = $57,095.

140,466 Large		0 Small		140,466 Total		
1986	-	$2 ORIG	389	795 A	D135435	PR	D135736 ?
1986	-	$1 1875	384	14 A	A490218	Fr	Blue end paper, Higgins Museum
1986	-	$2 1875	391	938 A	A505292	VG/F	
1986	M	$5 1882DB	533	1074 G	E505161	VG/F	pen/pen
1986	M	$5 1902DB	591	965 B	E970521A	VF	
1986		$5 1902PB	602	6078 A	[	CU	Higgins Mus.
1986		$5 1902PB	602	6078 B	[	CU	Higgins Mus.
1986		$5 1902PB	602	6078 C	[	CU	Higgins Mus.
1986		$5 1902PB	602	6078 D	[	CU	Higgins Mus.
1986	-	$5 1902PB	602	6992 D	K898478H	G/VG	
1986	-	$5 1902PB	602	7138 B	K898624H	?	
1986	-	$5 1902PB	602	7168 C	T595079H	VG	
1986	-	$5 1902PB	602	7699 B	X884160H	F	stamp/stamp
1986	-	$5 1902PB	602	8054 B	8054 B	HG	stamp/stamp
1986	-	$5 1902PB	602	8197 B	8197 B	VG	stamp/stamp
1986		$10 1902PB	628	3373 B	T176905E	VF	Higgins Mus.
1986		$10 1902PB	628	3730 A	Z881162E	F+	Repaired
1986		$10 1902PB	628	4??? ?	M997495H	?	
1986	-	$10 1902PB	628	4440 C	U893072H	VF	pen/pen
1986	-	$10 1902PB	628	4761 C	Z105203H	?	
1986	-	$20 1902PB	654	5073 A	5073 A	F	

THE FIRST NATIONAL BANK OF LA PORTE CITY   17 L
4114   BLACK HAWK

Organized on August 12, 1889 with a capital of $50,000. Placed in receivership on February 15, 1928; capital of $75,000. Reason for failure: incompetent management & local depression.

Officers: Pres. James F Camp 1889-1893, RA Perkins 1894-1907, JH Lunemann 1908-09, CE Ashley 1910-28; **VP** E Simpson 1896-1900, WD Wagoner 1902-07, RA Perkins 1909-24, JH Luneman 1914-24, CA Brust 1925-27; **Cash.** FE Wettstein 1889-1902, JH Lunemann 1902-07, CB Gingrich 1908-09, GE Stebbins 1910-24, Roy E Ashley 1925-27; **AC** John J Large 1896, GE Stebbins 1900-04, 1909, Roy E Ashley 1907-24, LJ Bitterley 1914, ML Haven 1920-27

Second Charter, Brown Backs	Ser #	# Notes
10-10-10-20	1-4892	19,568
Third Charter, Date Back, Blue Seal		
10-10-10-20	1-4600	18,400
Third Charter, Plain Back, Blue Seal		
10-10-10-20	4601-12748	32,592

Total amount issued = $882,000. Amount outstanding at close = $75,000.

70,560 Large		0 Small		70,560 Total		
4114	M	$10 1882BB	490	2626 A	E574281E	VG/F	
4114	M	$20 1882BB	498	3078 A	N33432N	CU	pen/pen
4114	M	$20 1882BB	498	4273 A	U228111U	F+	pen/stamp
4114	M	$10 1902DB	618	2890 C	K439007A	VF	
4114	M	$10 1902DB	618	3725 B	X530410A	VF	nice sigs
4114	M	$20 1902DB	644	2465 A	N281726	F+	pen/pen
4114	M	$10 1902PB	626	5544 C	Y8405B	F	
4114	M	$10 1902PB	626	6741 C	N520043D	F	pen/pen Spot
4114	M	$10 1902PB	626	8506 B	M822413E	VG/F	
4114	M	$10 1902PB	626	8819 C	M822726E	F	sigs Ragged Top
4114	M	$10 1902PB	626	8850 A	M822757E	F	
4114	M	$10 1902PB	626	8860 ?	M822787E	VG	
4114	-	$10 1902PB	626	11686 B	11686 B	XF	

4114	M	$20 1902PB	652	4659 ?	?	F
4114	M	$20 1902PB	652	5269 A	Y8130B	VF pen/pen
4114		$20 1902PB	652	9207 A	X313479E	AU Higgins Mus.
4114	-	$20 1902PB	652	11822 A	11822 A	VG/F

THE FIRST NATIONAL BANK OF LAKE CITY   15 L   7 S
4966   CALHOUN
Organized on June 21, 1894 with a capital of $50,000. Placed in receivership on October 22, 1931; capital of $50,000. Reason for failure: incompetent management & local depression.

Officers: Pres. ST Hutchison 1894-1913, LF Danforth 1914-24, GG Hutchison 1925-27; **VP** LF Danforth 1896-1913, Walter Jacobs 1914-27; **Cash.** C Korslund 1894, GB Wheeler 1895-1905, GG Hutchison 1906-23, Walter Jacobs 1924-27; **AC** AO Wick 1896-1903, GG Hutchison 1904, Walter Jacobs 1907-12, LE Nokes 1920, ST Hutchison 1923, Harold D Miner 1924-27

Second Charter, Brown Backs	Ser #	# Notes
5-5-5-5	1-3825	15,300
10-10-10-20	1-2580	10,320
Second Charter, Date Back		
5-5-5-5	1-2558	10,232
10-10-10-20	1-1752	7,008
Third Charter, Date Back, Blue Seal		
5-5-5-5	1-750	3,000
10-10-10-20	1-700	2,800
Third Charter, Plain Back, Blue Seal		
5-5-5-5	751-7269	26,076
10-10-10-20	701-4976	17,104
1929, Type I		
6-5's	1-953	5,718
6-10's	1-429	2,574
6-20's	1-121	726

Total amount of circulation issued = $807,290. Amount of large outstanding at close = $8,120. Amount of small outstanding at close = $40,680.
91,840 Large   9,018 Small   100,858 Total

4966	M	$10 1882DB	542	1592 D	M694030	F/VF pen/pen
4966	M	$10 1882DB	542	1725 E	N441793	VF+ pen Higgins Mus.
4966		$5 1902PB	607	5564 A	X637475H	VF/F Higgins Mus.
4966	-	$5 1902PB	607	6702 A	6702 A	F/VF red sigs
4966	M	$10 1902PB	631	2615 C	U932617E	VG
4966	-	$10 1902PB	631	2853 ?	B321365H	F/VF
4966	-	$10 1902PB	631	2980 C	B321492H	F/VF lt. stamp/pen
4966	-	$10 1902PB	631	3803 C	3803 C	?
4966	-	$10 1902PB	631	4151 A	4151 A	F+ stamp/stamp
4966	-	$10 1902PB	631	4418 A	4418 A	VF stamp/stamp
4966	-	$10 1902PB	631	4902 A	4902 A	XF stamp/stamp
4966	M	$20 1902PB	657	879 A	U154127B	G/VG gone/pen
4966	M	$20 1902PB	657	2853 A	B321365H	F/VF gone/pen
4966	-	$20 1902PB	657	3974 A	3974 A	VG/F stamp/stamp
4966	-	$20 1902PB	657	4621 A	4621 A	VG Ink
4966		$5 1929T1		D000871A		VG
4966		$10 1929T1		C000221A		VF
4966		$10 1929T1		A000393A		XF/AU Higgins Mus.
4966		$10 1929T1		A000056A		G/VG
4966		$20 1929T1		C000071A		VF
4966		$20 1929T1		D000107A		VG/F
4966		$20 1929T1		E000117A		F

THE FIRST NATIONAL BANK OF LAKE MILLS   8 L
5123   WINNEBAGO
Organized on February 21, 1898 with a capital of $50,000. Placed in receivership on April 8, 1927; capital of $50,000. Reason for failure: incompetent management & local depression.

Officers: Pres. JC Williams 1898-1901, PM Joice 1902-09, Chas E Paulson 1910-16, OV Eckert 1917, LJ Paulson 1918-20, OJ Sheldon 1922-26; **VP** GS Gilbertson 1900-02, JC Williams 1903-13, HM Martinson 1910-11, HH Dorland 1920, OV Eckert 1920-24, NL Sheldon 1923-26; **Cash.** BH Thomas 1898-1901, SH Larson 1902-04, AE Pfiffner 1905, AW Winden 1906-1908, JM Tapager 1909-23, TJ Severson 1924-26; **AC** SH Larson 1900-01, AE Pfiffner 1903-04, JM Tapager 1907, Oscar Horvel 1909-11, TJ Severson 1920-23, G Ulve 1920-26

Second Charter, Brown Backs	Ser #	# Notes
5-5-5-5	1-4325	17,300
10-10-10-20	1-1960	7,840
Second Charter, Date Back		
5-5-5-5	1-3200	12,800
10-10-10-20	1-2180	8,720
Second Charter, Value Back		
5-5-5-5	3201-3923	2,892
10-10-10-20	2181-2609	1,716
Third Charter, Plain Back, Blue Seal		
5-5-5-5	1-4575	18,300
10-10-10-20	1-2799	11,196

Total amount issued = $624, 860. Amount outstanding at close = $49,497.
80,764 Large   0 Small   80,764 Total

5123	-	$5 1882BB	476	425 D	?	VG
5123	-	$5 1882BB	476	3009 D	B627279B	VG/F gone/gone
5123	M	$10 1882BB	489	1369 B	N442731N	F faded Higg. Mus.
5123	M	$5 1882DB	536	560 E	B410055	VF stamp/pen Rust
5123	M	$20 1882DB	554	911 B	H880779	F Higgins Mus.
5123		$10 1902PB	632	1223 B	?	?
5123	-	$10 1902PB	632	2684 A	2684 A	G/VG A or D ?
5123	-	$20 1902PB	658	2260 A	X716392H	VG

THE FIRST NATIONAL BANK OF LANSING   2 L
405   ALLAMAKEE
Chartered in 1864. Placed in voluntary liquidation on February 25, 1881; capital of $50,000.

Officers: Pres. Gustav Kerndt 1867-75, Moritz Kerndt 1876-80; **Cash.** James W Thomas 1867-80

First Charter, Original Issue	Ser #	# Notes
1-1-1-2	1-2940	11,760
5-5-5-5	1-4500	18,000
First Charter, Series of 1875		
5-5-5-5	1-2040	8,160

Total amount of circulation issued = $145,500. Amount outstanding at close = $45,000. Amount outstanding in 1910 = $1,084.
37,920 Large   0 Small   37,920 Total

405	-	$1 ORIG	380	860 A	B350001	VF pen Higgins Mus.
405	-	$2 ORIG	387	1215 A	C377547	VG/F pen Higgins Mus.

THE FIRST NATIONAL BANK OF LAURENS   7 L   3 S
4795   POCAHONTAS
Chartered in 1892. Succeeded The Bank of Laurens. Placed in voluntary liquidation on June 6, 1930; capital of $50,000. Absorbed by The State Bank of Laurens.

Officers: Pres. FH Helsell 1892-1926, MW Shaner 1927-29; **VP** JP Farmer 1892-1910, HL Farmer 1911-26, WA McNee 1920-29; **Cash.** WA McNee 1892-1919, AD Claussen 1920-29; **AC** LD Beardsley 1892, GE McKinnon 1892, CE Narey 1896-1902, EP Lowry 1903-11, AD Claussen 1913-14, EF Reid 1920-28, Cecil Lund 1928-29

Second Charter, Brown Backs	Ser #	# Notes
10-10-10-20	1-1310	5,240
Second Charter, Date Back		
10-10-10-20	1-335	1,340
Third Charter, Date Back, Blue Seal		
10-10-10-20	1-750	3,000
Third Charter, Plain Back, Blue Seal		
10-10-10-20	751-1895	4580
1929, Type I		
6-10's	1-117	702
6-20's	1-9	54

Total amount of circulation issued = $185,100. Amount outstanding in 1929 = $12,500. Amount of large outstanding on November 10, 1930 = $3,000.
14,160 Large   756 Small   14,916 Total

4795		$10 1882BB	472	1 A	H248050	AU+ Higgins Mus.
4795	M	$10 1902DB	620	1 A	M176314A	CU Higgins Mus.
4795	M	$10 1902DB	620	115 C	M176428A	VF pen/pen
4795	M	$10 1902DB	620	686 A	M176999A	CU Higgins Mus.
4795	M	$10 1902PB	628	1106 B	N373398E	VF+ Higgins Mus.
4795	-	$10 1902PB	628	1500 B	B38502K	F/VF stamp/pen vp
4795	-	$20 1902PB	654	1862 A	1862 A	VG/F vp
4795		$10 1929T1		A000002A		F

4795	$10	1929T1	?000003A		AU	
4795	$10	1929T1	C000013A		VG/F	Higgins Mus.

THE FIRST NATIONAL BANK OF LAWLER 12 L
10599 CHICKASAW

Chartered in August 1914. Placed in voluntary liquidation on April 7, 1928; capital of $50,000. Absorbed by The State Savings Bank, Lawler.

Officers: Pres. CM Parker 1914-20, FB Shaffer 1922-27; **VP** Ettie Parker 1914-20, FE Eickhoff 1922-27; **Cash.** GE Himes 1914-20, OB Taylor 1922-27; **AC** AW Clapham 1914, CP Galligan 1920-27

Third Charter, Plain Back, Blue Seal	Ser #	# Notes
10-10-10-20	1-4262	17,048

Total amount issued = $213,100. Amount outstanding at close = $49,500.

17,048 Large   0 Small   17,048 Total

10599M	$10	1902PB	631	1A Z950283D	VF	retraced sigs
10599M	$10	1902PB	631	1963 B Y661545E	F/VF	
10599 -	$10	1902PB	631	3533 B 3533 B	AU	Higgins Mus.
10599 -	$10	1902PB	631	3533 C 3533 C	CU	
10599 -	$10	1902PB	631	3534 B 3534 B	CU	
10599 -	$10	1902PB	631	3534 C 3534 C	VF	
10599 -	$10	1902PB	631	3537 A 3537 A	CU	pen/stamp
10599 -	$10	1902PB	631	3538 A 3538 A	CU	
10599 -	$10	1902PB	631	3539 A 3539 A	CU	
10599 -	$10	1902PB	631	3540 A 3540 A	CU	
10599 -	$10	1902PB	631	4160 A 4160 A	XF	pen/stamp
10599 -	$20	1902PB	657	3775 A 3775 A	F	pen/stamp

THE FIRST NATIONAL BANK OF LE MARS 23 L 19 S
2728 PLYMOUTH

Organized on May 23, 1882 with a capital of $75,000. Succeeded The Plymouth County Bank. Suspended on August 18, 1893. Restored September 11, 1893. Placed in conservatorship on March 28, 1893. Placed in receivership on October 31, 1933. Restored on August 27, 1934. Placed in voluntary liquidation on September 27, 1934; capital of $100,000. Succeeded by #14253.

Officers: Pres. PF Dalton 1882-1920, EA Dalton 1922-33; **VP** FE Shaw 1882, CD Hoffman 1896-1900, GL Wernli 1902-33, JA Hoffman 1914-33; **Cash.** JW Myers 1882-84, MH Finney 1885-88, GL Wernli 1889-1901, EA Dalton 1902-20, RB Dalton 1922-33; **AC** EA Dalton 1896-1900, JA Hoffman 1902-1911, RB Dalton 1913-20, CL Eastman 1922-33, JM Hays 1922-27

First Charter, Series of 1875	Ser #	# Notes
10-10-10-20	1-4784	19,136
Third Charter, Red Seal		
10-10-10-20	1-4900	19,600
Third Charter, Date Back, Blue Seal		
10-10-10-20	1-5700	22,800
Third Charter, Plain Back, Blue Seal		
10-10-10-20	5701-17207	46,028
1929, Type I		
6-5's	1-2334	14,004
6-10's	1-1758	10,548
6-20's	1-378	2,268

Total amount of circulation issued = $1,565,410. Amount outstanding at close (1933) = $100,000. By 1935, this was reduced to $57,380. Amount of small outstanding in 1935 = $51,050. Amount of large outstanding on June 26, 1935 = $6,330. Liability for redemption of circulation assumed by #14253.

107,564 Large   26,820 Small   134,384 Total

2728 -	$20	1875	435	2729 A K892827	F	pen/pen Pinholes
2728 -	$20	1875	435	3661 A K932459	AU	
2728 -	$20	1875	435	4276 A K933074	VF	Higgins Mus.
2728 M	$10	1902DB	616	3930 D T977972A	CU	Cut sheet, Grinnell lot # 1545
2728 M	$10	1902DB	616	3930 E T977972A	CU	Grinnell # 1545
2728 M	$10	1902DB	616	3930 F T977972A	CU	Grinnell # 1545
2728 M	$10	1902DB	616	3950 D T977992A	CU	
2728 M	$10	1902DB	616	3950 E T977992A	AU	
2728 M	$10	1902DB	616	3951 F T977993A		
2728 M	$10	1902DB	616	4589 F X425474A	F/VF	stamp/stamp
2728 M	$10	1902DB	616	5450 F A828886B	VG	gone/gone
2728 M	$20	1902DB	642	3930 B T977972A	CU	Grinnell # 1545
2728 M	$20	1902DB	642	3951 B T977993A	AU	Higgins Mus.
2728 -	$10	1902PB	624	10359 D E886521E	VG	
2728 -	$10	1902PB	624	11929 F X549421E	G/VG	tear, pinholes
2728	$10	1902PB	624	12893 F N57385H	?	
2728 -	$10	1902PB	624	14407 D 14407 D	VG	
2728 -	$10	1902PB	624	14751 D 14751 D	VG	
2728	$10	1902PB	624	15699 G 15699 G	AU	gone/gone
2728 M	$20	1902PB	650	8619 B R167751D	F	faded/faded
2728 -	$20	1902PB	650	13305 B U929897H	F/VF	
2728 -	$20	1902PB	650	15670 C 15670 C	VG	gone/gone
2728 -	$20	1902PB	650	16015 C 16015 C	XF	stamp/stamp
2728	$5	1929T1		B000804A	VF	
2728	$5	1929T1		E001050A	VF	
2728	$5	1929T1		F001886A	F	Washed, pressed
2728	$5	1929T1		D002004A	G/VG	
2728	$10	1929T1		C001150A	VF	
2728	$20	1929T1		E000002A	VF	
2728	$20	1929T1		C000030A	F	
2728	$20	1929T1		D000045A	F	
2728	$20	1929T1		F000074A	XF	Higgins Mus.
2728	$20	1929T1		F000080A	AU	
2728	$20	1929T1		C000111A	VG/F	
2728	$20	1929T1		E000219A	CU	
2728	$20	1929T1		C000261A	VG	
2728	$20	1929T1		F000304A	VF	
2728	$20	1929T1		F000305A	CU	
2728	$20	1929T1		B000325A	?	
2728	$20	1929T1		E000339A	AU	
2728	$20	1929T1		F000341A	AU	
2728	$20	1929T1		A000342A	CU	

THE LE MARS NATIONAL BANK 0 L
2818 PLYMOUTH

Chartered on November 13, 1882 with a capital of $100,000. Succeeded The Le Mars Bank. Suspended on August 18, 1893. Restored September 16, 1893. Placed in receivership on April 17, 1901; capital of $100,000. Reason for failure: incompetent management.

Officers: Pres. William H Dent 1882-95, Gilbert C Maclagan 1896-1900; **VP** R Morton 1882, TF Ward 1896-1900; **Cash.** Gilbert C Maclagan 1882-95, JD Simpson 1896-97, Frank Koob 1898-1900; **AC** Frank Koob 1896

Second Charter, Brown Backs	Ser #	# Notes
5-5-5-5	1-1155	4,620
50-100	1-654	1,308

Total amount of circulation issued = $121,200. Amount outstanding at close = $23,900. Amount outstanding in 1915 = $510.

5,928 Large   0 Small   5,928 Total

THE FIRST NATIONAL BANK OF LEHIGH 6 L 9 S
5868 WEBSTER

Organized on June 15, 1901 with a capital of $25,000. Chartered on June 21, 1901. Placed in receivership on August 17, 1931; capital of $25,000. Reason for failure: local depression.

Second Charter, Brown Backs	Ser #	# Notes
10-10-10-20	1-1600	6,400
Second Charter, Date Back		
10-10-10-20 (1131-1330 type uncertain)	1-1330	5,320
Second Charter, Value Back		
10-10-10-20	1331-2064	2,936
Third Charter, Plain Back, Blue Seal		
10-10-10-20	1-1770	7,080
1929, Type I		
6-10's	1-278	1,668
6-20's	1-63	378

Total amount of circulation issued = $295,940. Amount of large outstanding at close = $3,300. Amount of small outstanding at close = $16,700.

21,736 Large   2,046 Small   23,782 Total

5868 M	$20	1882VB	581	1666 B U530874	F/VF	pen/pen
5868 M	$10	1902PB	633	138 C B492090E	VF	pen/pen 1/2" tear
5868 -	$10	1902PB	633	810 C T975372H	G	
5868 -	$10	1902PB	633	1678 C 1678 C	F	
5868 -	$10	1902PB	633	1741 A 1741 A	VF	Higgins Mus.
5868 -	$20	1902PB	659	1419 A 1419 A	VF	
5868	$10	1929T1		A000043A	F/VF	
5868	$10	1929T1		C000266A	F/VF	
5868	$20	1929T1		F000020A	F	
5868	$20	1929T1		D000050A	CU	
5868	$20	1929T1		B000060A	AU	
5868	$20	1929T1		C000060A	XF	Higgins Mus.
5868	$20	1929T1		D000060A	F	
5868	$20	1929T1		E000060A	CU	
5868	$20	1929T1		B000062A	CU	

FIRST NATIONAL BANK IN LENOX 2 S
14040 TAYLOR

Chartered in March 1934 with a capital of $50,000. Succeeded #5517 and assumed the circulation of #5517.

Officers: Pres. WH Madden 1934-35; **VP** JE Cameron 1934-35; **Cash.** Retta Goodale 1934-35

1929, Type II	Ser #	# Notes
5's	1-934	934
10's	1-390	390
20's	1-185	185

Total amount issued = $12,270. Amount of small size outstanding in June 1935 = $37,000. Includes unredeemed small size issues of #5517.

0 Large		1,509 Small		1,509 Total	
14040	$5 1929T2	A000700		XF	Higgins Mus.
14040	$20 1929T2	A000014		VG	

THE FIRST NATIONAL BANK OF LENOX   25 L   16 S
5517   TAYLOR

Organized on June 25, 1900 with a capital of $30,000. Chartered on July 26, 1900. Placed in conservatorship on March 25, 1933. Placed in voluntary liquidation on April 30, 1934; capital of $50,000. Succeeded by #14040; circulation assumed by #14040.

Officers: Pres. Phil Ridgeway 1900-05, LB Wilson 1906-10, Fran Wilkin 1911-15, JW Walter 1916-17, JJ Walter 1918-28, WH Madden 1929-34; **VP** Jacob H Bennison 1900-10, TW Bennett 1911-14, Fred A Childs 1920-33; **Cash.** Walter S Bennison 1900-10, Fred A Childs 1911-17, BF Wurster 1918-34; **AC** BF Wurster 1913-14, Ray V Anderson 1920, Retta Goodale 1930-33

	Ser #	# Notes
Second Charter, Brown Backs		
10-10-10-20	1-1870	7,480
Second Charter, Date Back		
5-5-5-5	1-2850	11,400
10-10-10-20	1-1940	7,760
Second Charter, Value Back		
5-5-5-5	2851-4715	7,460
10-10-10-20	1941-2995	4,220
Third Charter, Plain Back, Blue Seal		
5-5-5-5	1-4402	17,608
10-10-10-20	1-2958	11,832
1929, Type I		
6-5's	1-1473	8,838
6-10's	1-712	4,272
6-20's	1-192	1,152

Total amount of circulation issued = $633,440. Amount of large outstanding in 1934 = $5,237. Amount of small outstanding in 1934 = $44,760. Circulation liability was assumed by #14040 which was then responsible for redeeming the outstanding circulation of #5517. The amount of large size by June 1935 had been reduced to $5,047 outstanding. A later figure is not available on the small size because #14040 issued small size and it is impossible to separate the small size issues of #5517 from #14040.

63,760 Large		14,262 Small		78,022 Total		
5517	-	$10 1882BB 490	1 A	?	VF	
5517	-	$10 1882BB 490	104 C	X523316	AU	
5517	M	$10 1882BB 490	419 C	H158169H	VG	
5517	-	$20 1882BB 504	98 A	X523307	CU	
5517	-	$20 1882BB 504	104 A	X523316	AU	pen/pen vp
5517	M	$5 1882DB 537	1 C	D958538	VF/XF	
5517	M	$5 1882DB 537	2 A	D958539	XF	pen/pen vp
5517	M	$5 1882DB 537	2 D	D958539	VF	Higgins Mus.
5517	M	$5 1882DB 537	1641 ?	M230878	F	
5517	M	$5 1882DB 537	2716 D	N270778	F	
5517	M	$10 1882DB 545	42 E	D307822	F	pen/pen
5517	M	$10 1882DB 545	505 E	H413083	VF	
5517	M	$10 1882DB 545	1455 D	?	VG	
5517	M	$20 1882DB 555	1764 B	R232072	XF/AU	lt stamp sigs
5517	M	$5 1882VB 574	4189 B	T997776	VG	
5517	M	$5 1902PB 607	542 C	?	XF	
5517	M	$5 1902PB 607	1597 D	N713193E	VG/F	stamp Higg. Mus.
5517	-	$5 1902PB 607	2834 D	V833695H	F	gone/gone
5517	-	$5 1902PB 607	2858 A	2858 A	VG	
5517	M	$10 1902PB 633	992 B	A356004H	VG/F	
5517	-	$10 1902PB 633	1898 A	1898 A	F/VF	
5517	-	$10 1902PB 633	2194 A	2194 A	G	gone/gone
5517	-	$10 1902PB 633	2316 C	2316 C	G/VG	gone/gone
5517	-	$10 1902PB 633	2820 A	2820 A	?	
5517	-	$20 1902PB 659	2743 A	2743 A	VG	Fed. Res. Bk., San Fran.
5517		$5 1929T1	B000804A		F	
5517		$5 1929T1	C000843A		F	
5517		$10 1929T1	F000271A		F	
5517		$10 1929T1	F000359A		VG/F	Higgins Mus.
5517		$10 1929T1	B000436A		F	
5517		$10 1929T1	E000486A		VG/F	Rust spots
5517		$10 1929T1	B000600A		VF	
5517		$10 1929T1	A000603A		VF	
5517		$10 1929T1	F000704A		F	
5517		$20 1929T1	A000018A		?	
5517		$20 1929T1	A000033A		F	
5517		$20 1929T1	B000036A		F	
5517		$20 1929T1	B000039A		HG	
5517		$20 1929T1	F000083A		VG	$10 or $20 ?
5517		$20 1929T1	?000093A		VF	Small rust spot
5517		$20 1929T1	F000184A		F	

THE EXCHANGE NATIONAL BANK OF LEON   12 L
5489   DECATUR

Organized on June 20, 1900 with a capital of $35,000. Chartered on July 8, 1900. Placed in receivership on March 9, 1927; capital of $35,000. Reason for failure: local depression.

Officers: Pres. ED Dorn 1900-04, JP Hamilton 1905-11, AL Ackerley 1912-19, EG Monroe 1920-24, OE Hull 1925-26; **VP** IN Clark 1900, S Vargaa 1902-04, Harry J Vogt 1905-13, OE Hull 1914-24, JF Garber 1925-26; **Cash.** WA Boone 1900-04, ED Dorn 1905-07, AL Ackerley 1908-11, EG Monroe 1912-19, Carl Monroe 1920-26, JF Rush 1926; **AC** WJ Edwards 1900-04, AE Dorn 1905-07, Carl Monroe 1909-10, 1913-14, SG Mitchell 1909-11, JF Rush 1920-26, LL Hutchinson 1920-23

	Ser #	# Notes
Second Charter, Brown Backs		
5-5-5-5	1-1415	5,660
10-10-10-20	1-1134	4,536
Second Charter, Date Back		
5-5-5-5	1-1950	7,800
10-10-10-20	1-1500	6,000
Second Charter, Value Back		
5-5-5-5	1951-3251	5,204
10-10-10-20	1501-2220	2,880
Third Charter, Plain Back, Blue Seal		
10-10-10-20	1-2204	8,816

Total amount issued = $371,220. Amount outstanding at close = $34,500.

40,896 Large			0 Small		40,896 Total		
5489	M	$10 1882DB 545	737 E	K248385		VG	pen/pen
5489	M	$10 1902PB 633	1169 A	Z678191E		CU	
5489	M	$10 1902PB 633	1170 A	Z678192E		CU	
5489	M	$10 1902PB 633	1170 B	Z678192E		CU	
5489	M	$10 1902PB 633	1170 C	Z678192E		CU	
5489	M	$10 1902PB 633	1171 C	Z678193E		CU	
5489	M	$10 1902PB 633	1174 A	Z678196E		CU	pen/pen
5489	M	$10 1902PB 633	1174 B	Z678196E		CU	
5489	M	$10 1902PB 633	1174 C	Z678196E		CU	Higgins Mus.
5489	M	$20 1902PB 659	270 A	X411372		F+	
5489	M	$20 1902PB 659	1170 A	Z678192E		CU	
5489	M	$20 1902PB 659	1174 A	Z678196E		CU	

THE FIRST NATIONAL BANK OF LEON   1 L
1696   DECATUR

Organized in December 1869 with a capital of $60,000. Merged with The Farmers and Traders Bank in 1874. Placed in voluntary liquidation on July 11, 1876; capital of $60,000. Succeeded by The Farmers and Traders Bank.

Officers: Pres. John Clarke 1870-75; **Cash.** JL Young 1870-71, LP Sigler 1872-75

	Ser #	# Notes
First Charter, Original Issue		
1-1-1-2	1-1900	7,600
5-5-5-5	1-2350	9,400
50-100	1-200	400
First Charter, Series of 1875		
50-100	1-25	50

Total amount of circulation issued = $90,250. Amount outstanding at close = $45,000. Amount outstanding in 1910 = $655.

17,450 Large		0 Small		17,450 Total		
1696	-	$2 ORIG 389	831 A	C68569	F/VF	pen/pen

THE FIRST NATIONAL BANK OF LIME SPRINGS   6 L   20 S
6750   HOWARD

Chartered in April 1903. Succeeded Bank of Lime Springs. Placed in voluntary liquidation on June 20, 1934; capital of $25,000. Absorbed by The Exchange State Bank of Lime Springs.

Officers: Pres. ER Morris 1904-05, WW Williams 1906-15, DW Davis 1916-28, RJ Hughes 1928-34; **VP** WW Williams 1904-05, JA Williams 1907-34, RJ Hughes 1923-28; **Cash.** DH Thomas 1904-22, CE Anderson 1923-34; **AC** Clarence W Lee 1904-05, CE Anderson 1920-22, AG Buchanan 1923-33

	Ser #	# Notes
Third Charter, Red Seal		
10-10-10-20	1-356	1,424
Third Charter, Date Back, Blue Seal		
10-10-10-20	1-1830	7,320
Third Charter, Plain Back, Blue Seal		
10-10-10-20	1831-4563	10,932
1929, Type I		
6-10's	1-526	3,156
6-20's	1-130	780
1929, Type II		
10's	1-42	42
20's	1-54	54

Total amount of circulation issued = $294,610. Amount of large outstanding at close = $1,650. Amount of small outstanding at close = $23,350.
19,676 Large   4,032 Small   23,708 Total

6750	M	$10	1902DB	616	1664 D	A823130B	F/VF	gone/faded
6750	M	$10	1902PB	624	3147 F	M405334E	VG/F	faded/pen
6750	-	$10	1902PB	624	3962 D	3962 D	F	
6750	-	$10	1902PB	624	4041 F	4041 F	VG	stamp/stamp
6750	-	$10	1902PB	624	4365 F	4365 F	F/VF	
6750	-	$20	1902PB	650	3796 B	B551658K	VF	Higgins Mus.
6750		$10	1929T1		C000019A		VG	?Denomination?
6750		$10	1929T1		E000086A		AU	Higgins Mus.
6750		$10	1929T1		F000185A		F	
6750		$10	1929T1		D000192A		VF	
6750		$10	1929T1		B000244A		F	
6750		$10	1929T1		A000344A		F	
6750		$10	1929T1		?000363A		VF	
6750		$10	1929T1		D000366A		?	
6750		$10	1929T1		D000369A		XF/AU	
6750		$10	1929T1		A000371A		F	
6750		$10	1929T1		F000375A		VF/XF	
6750		$10	1929T1		A000506A		VF	
6750		$20	1929T1		B000007A		VF	
6750		$20	1929T1		C000019A		VG	Pinholes
6750		$20	1929T1		D000026A		XF/AU	
6750		$20	1929T1		F000026A		VF	
6750		$20	1929T1		E000044A		F	Washed
6750		$20	1929T1		E000049A		VG	
6750		$20	1929T1		F000117A		VF	
6750		$10	1929T2		A000019		F/VF	

THE FIRST NATIONAL BANK OF LINEVILLE   1 L
7261   WAYNE
Organized on April 23, 1904 with a capital of $25,000. Placed in receivership on April 9, 1927; capital of $25,000. Reason for failure: local depression.
Officers: Pres. JP Jordan 1905-07, Geo Rockhold 1908-13, WB Wasson 1914-17, RE Molleston 1918-26; **VP** Geo Rockhold 1907, WB Wasson 1909-13, Alex Mardis 1914, CW Steele 1920-26; **Cash.** DT Sollenbarger 1905-09, RE Molleston 1910-12, DT Sollenbarger 1913, RE Molleston 1914-17, GW Molleston 1918-26; **AC** Gerald W Molleston 1907-14, GW Molleston 1923-24

Third Charter, Red Seal	Ser #	# Notes
10-10-10-20	1-300	1,200
Third Charter, Date Back, Blue Seal		
10-10-10-20	1-1780	7,120
Third Charter, Plain Back, Blue Seal		
10-10-10-20	1781-4439	10,636

Total amount issued = $236,950. Amount outstanding at close = $24,300.
18,956 Large   0 Small   18,956 Total

7261	M	$10	1902PB	624	3455 E	T841157E	F	Higgins Mus.

THE FIRST NATIONAL BANK OF LINN GROVE   5 L   5 S
7137   BUENA VISTA
Chartered in 1904. Placed in voluntary liquidation on August 25, 1930; capital of $50,000. Succeeded by The First State Bank, Linn Grove.
Officers: Pres. CB Mills 1904-14, OE Anderson 1915-30; **VP** JH McCord 1904, JJ Spindler 1907, EM Duroe 1909-14, AO Anderson 1920-25, NP Nelson 1926-30; **Cash.** A Tymeson, Jr. 1904, NO Monserud 1905-08, EO Loe 1909-17, WG Anderson 1919, AR Mickelson 1923-28, AJ Scott 1929-30; **AC** Jean A Norris 1910-11, CR Cate 1913-14, AR Mickelson 1920-22, AJ Scott 1923-28

Third Charter, Red Seal	Ser #	# Notes
10-10-10-20	1-732	2,928
Third Charter, Date Back, Blue Seal		
10-10-10-20	1-1250	5,000

Sheets numbered 1 to 1090 were 02-08 backs. Sheets numbered 1091 to 1250 were delivered on October 13 but not marked as to type. Sheets numbered 1251 to 3788 were plain back blue seals.

Third Charter, Plain Back, Blue Seal		
10-10-10-20	1251-3788	10,152
1929, Type I		
6-10's	1-180	1,080
6-20's	1-13	78

Total amount of circulation issued = $238,360. Amount outstanding in 1929 = $19,000. Amount of large outstanding on July 1, 1931 = $5,430.
18,080 Large   1,158 Small   19,238 Total

7137	M	$20	1902DB	642	469 B	T807756	VG	lt stamps vp
7137		$10	1902PB	624	1708 F	R127580D	?	Holes
7137		$10	1902PB	624	1827 D	U376099D	F	
7137	M	$10	1902PB	650	1902 B	U376174D	VG/F	nice sigs
7137	-	$20	1902PB	650	3436 B	3436 B	F/VF	pen/pen Higgins Mus.
7137		$10	1929T1		D000065A		XF	Higgins Mus.
7137		$10	1929T1		?000080A		AU	
7137		$10	1929T1		C000134A		XF	
7137		$10	1929T1		F000161A		VG	
7137		$20	1929T1		E000004A		VG/F	

THE FIRST NATIONAL BANK OF LISBON   2 L
2182   LINN
Chartered on September 10, 1874. Placed in voluntary liquidation on November 1, 1881; capital of $50,000. Succeeded by Stuckslager & Auracher.
Officers: Pres. Harrison Stuckslager 1876-81; **Cash.** Godlieb Auracher 1876-81

First Charter, Original Issue	Ser #	# Notes
5-5-5-5	1-2250	9,000
First Charter, Series of 1875		
5-5-5-5	1-2245	8,980

Total amount of circulation issued = $89,900. Amount outstanding at close = $45,000. Amount outstanding in 1910 = $580.
17,980 Large   0 Small   17,980 Total

2182	-	$5	ORIG	?	1811 C	N570549	F	
2182	-	$5	1875	401	2214 A	N126494	VG	Higgins Mus.

THE FIRST NATIONAL BANK OF LITTLE ROCK   8 L   7 S
8119   LYON

Organized on January 24, 1906 with a capital of $25,000. Placed in conservatorship on March 31, 1933. Placed in receivership on October 31, 1933; capital of $25,000.
Officers: Pres. MD Bilsborough 1906-11, Aug GF Ross 1912-15, H Soenke 1916-19, A Christians 1920-29, Henry Block 1929-33; **VP** WB Burton 1907, Aug GF Ross 1909-11, ND Kruse 1913-24, Henry Block 1925-29, EE Bowen 1929-33; **Cash.** Chas C Armour 1906-08, H Soenke 1911-15, A Christians 1916-19, WJ Lindaman 1920-33; **AC** HL Bilsborough 1909-10, A Christians 1914, Philip Odens 1920-33

Third Charter, Red Seal	Ser #	# Notes
10-10-10-20	1-900	3,600
Third Charter, Date Back		
10-10-10-20	1-1560	6,240
Third Charter, Plain Back, Blue Seal		
10-10-10-20	1561-4531	11,884
1929, Type I		
6-10's	1-452	2,712
6-20's	1-132	792

Total amount of circulation issued = $314,510. Amount outstanding at close = $25,000. Amount of large outstanding on November 3, 1933 = $2,540.
21,724 Large   3,504 Small   25,228 Total

8119	M	$10	1902DB	617	1??? D	A42670B	AU	pen/pen
8119	M	$20	1902DB	643	376 B	K965207	VG	pen/pen
8119	-	$10	1902PB	625	4033 E	4033 E	XF	pen/pen
8119	-	$10	1902PB	625	4109 ?	4109 ?	AU	
8119	-	$10	1902PB	625	4112 D	4112 D	?	pen/pen
8119	-	$10	1902PB	625	4183 F	4183 F	VF	Higgins Mus.
8119	M	$10	1902PB	651	3594 B	M854636H	F/VF	pen/pen
8119	-	$20	1902PB	651	4458 B	4458 B	VF	pen/pen
8119		$10	1929T1		E000028A		F/VF	
8119		$10	1929T1		E000079A		F	
8119		$10	1929T1		F000395A		XF	Higgins Mus.
8119		$20	1929T1		D000029A		F/VF	
8119		$20	1929T1		B000114A		XF	
8119		$20	1929T1		B000119A		AU	
8119		$20	1929T1		A000125A		VF	

THE FIRST NATIONAL BANK OF LOGAN   15 L   16 S
6771   HARRISON
Chartered in May 1903 with a capital of $50,000.
Officers: Pres. Jno W Wood 1904-23, CN Wood 1924-35; **VP** CN Wood 1904-23, WH Wood 1924-26, EJ Wood 1927-31, FQ Wood 1931-34, LM Wood 1935; **Cash.** WH Wood 1904, BJ Wood 1905-35; **AC** BJ Wood 1904, EJ Wood 1907-26

Third Charter, Red Seal	Ser #	# Notes
5-5-5-5	1-1775	7,100
10-10-10-20	1-2040	8,160
Third Charter, Date Back, Blue Seal		
5-5-5-5	1-3575	14,300
10-10-10-20	1-2320	9,280
Third Charter, Plain Back, Blue Seal		
5-5-5-5	3576-10320	26,980

			10-10-10-20		2321-6721	17,604

1929, Type I

6-5's					1-1754	10,524
6-10's					1-806	4,836
6-20's					1-204	1,224

1929, Type II

5's					1-312	312
10's					1-299	299
20's					1-30	30

Total amount of circulation issued = $810,560. Amount of large outstanding in June 1935 =$3,397. Amount of small outstanding in June 1935 = $21,600.

83,424 Large   17,225 Small   100,649 Total

6771	M	$20	1902DB	642	1257 B	E190802A	?	Stained back
6771	M	$5	1902PB	598	5059 E	B673655D	F	pen/gone
6771	M	$5	1902PB	598	5762 H	?	?	
6771		$5	1902PB	598	5885 E	R757746D	VF	Higgins Mus.
6771	-	$5	1902PB	598	9663 G	9663 G	F	pen/pen
6771	-	$10	1902PB	624	4706 D	?	F+	
6771	-	$10	1902PB	624	5461 E	5461 E	VF	
6771	-	$10	1902PB	624	5659 E	5659 E	F/VF	nice sigs
6771	-	$10	1902PB	624	6344 F	6344 F	F	pen/pen stain
6771	-	$10	1902PB	624	6361 D	6361 D	F	
6771	-	$10	1902PB	624	6459 F	6459 F	F/VF	pen/pen
6771	-	$10	1902PB	624	6472 E	6472 E	F+	pen/pen
6771	-	$10	1902PB	624	6503 E	6503 E	F/VF	pen/pen
6771	-	$10	1902PB	624	6700 ?	6700 ?	F	
6771	M	$20	1902PB	650	4086 B	R390998E	VG	
6771		$5	1929T1		D000032A		VF	Higgins Mus.
6771		$5	1929T1		B000048A		VG	
6771		$5	1929T1		C000961A		VG	
6771		$5	1929T1		C001322A		?	
6771		$5	1929T1		F001661A		F	
6771		$10	1929T1		C000105A		VG	
6771		$10	1929T1		D000133A		VF	
6771		$10	1929T1		E000151A		VF	
6771		$10	1929T1		F000197A		?	Denomination?
6771		$10	1929T1		F000458A		VG/F	
6771		$10	1929T1		D000461A		F	Stains
6771		$10	1929T1		B000732A		F	
6771		$10	1929T1		B000778A		VF+	
6771		$20	1929T1		D000002A		VG	
6771		$20	1929T1		D000139A		F	
6771		$10	1929T2		A000183		F/VF	

THE FIRST NATIONAL BANK OF LORIMOR   7 L   27 S
12248   UNION

Organized on August 7, 1922 with a capital of $35,000. Placed in conservatorship on April 11, 1933. Placed in receivership on September 5, 1933; capital of $35,000.

Officers: Pres. ET Dufur 1922-33; **VP** Geo W Austin 1922-33, ES Gilbert 1925-33; **Cash.** MG Bacon 1922-33; **AC** Clarence Hausz 1922-33, Clyde E Wilson 1922-33, Marie Keys 1922-23

Third Charter, Plain Back, Blue Seal	Ser #	# Notes
10-10-10-20	1-3178	12,712

1929, Type I

6-10's	1-742	4,452
6-20's	1-226	1,356

Total amount of circulation issued = $230,540. Amount of large outstanding at close = $1,260. Amount of small outstanding at close = $33,740.

12,712 Large   5,808 Small   18,520 Total

12248M		$10	1902PB	635		1 B	X746883E	CU	
12248M		$10	1902PB	635		1069 C	K85751H	VF	Higgins Mus.
12248M		$10	1902PB	635		1199 A	K85881H	F	pen/pen tear
12248	-	$10	1902PB	635		2236 A	2236 A	VG	
12248M		$20	1902PB	661		280 A	X747162E	VG	pen/pen
12248	-	$20	1902PB	661		1262 A	R280554H	VG/F	gone/gone
12248	-	$20	1902PB	661		1390 A	V519522H	VG	Stain paper skins
12248		$10	1929T1			F000061A		F	
12248		$10	1929T1			C000338A		CU	
12248		$10	1929T1			E000338A		F	
12248		$10	1929T1			B000372A		VF	
12248		$10	1929T1			B000374A		VG/F	
12248		$10	1929T1			D000431A		AU	
12248		$10	1929T1			D000435A		AU	
12248		$10	1929T1			A000436A		XF	
12248		$10	1929T1			C000510A		VF	Higgins Mus.
12248		$10	1929T1			C000522A		VF	
12248		$10	1929T1			D000569A		Fr/G	
12248		$10	1929T1			B000576A		?	Stained
12248		$10	1929T1			D000606A		VF	
12248		$10	1929T1			F000712A		XF	
12248		$10	1929T1			A000713A		VF	
12248		$10	1929T1			B000741A		F	
12248		$20	1929T1			E000066A		F	Paper clip stain
12248		$20	1929T1			F000087A		F+	
12248		$20	1929T1			A000093A		?	
12248		$20	1929T1			F000093A		XF	
12248		$20	1929T1			D000112A		F	
12248		$20	1929T1			C000115A		F/VF	
12248		$20	1929T1			E000116A		VG	
12248		$20	1929T1			E000154A		VG	
12248		$20	1929T1			D000158A		VG+	
12248		$20	1929T1			E000160A		F+	
12248		$20	1929T1			E000192A		F/VF	

THE FIRST NATIONAL BANK OF LOST NATION   4 L   8 S
5402   CLINTON

Organized on May 2, 1900 with a capital of $25,000. Chartered on June 6, 1900. Placed in receivership on January 11, 1932; capital of $40,000.

Officers: Pres. AH Gish 1900-04, MW Burnett 1905-25, MH Drake 1926-31; **VP** Emil Ruggeberg 1900-04, JD Busch 1905-14, V Willimack 1920-28, EH Balster 1928-30, JE Gilroy 1930-31, MC Sweney 1931; **Cash.** AL Cook 1900-03, HA Mohl 1904, AL Cook 1905-13, FW Dickman 1914-19, MH Dake 1920-25, WJ Schultz 1926-28, WC Rutenbeck 1930; **AC** WS Hill 1900-04, Fred W Dickman 1905-13, HF Burrichter 1914-31, FW Dickman 1920-22, WJ Schultz 1923-25

Second Charter, Brown Backs	Ser #	# Notes
5-5-5-5	1-400	1,600
10-10-10-20	1-320	1,280

Second Charter, Date Back

5-5-5-5 (851-950 type uncertain)	1-950	3,800
10-10-10-20 (681-760 type uncertain)	1-760	3,040

Second Charter, Value Back

5-5-5-5	951-1070	480
10-10-10-20	761-830	280

Third Charter, Plain Back, Blue Seal

10-10-10-20	1-1075	4,300

1929, Type I

6-10's	1-200	1,200
6-20's	1-34	204

Total amount of circulation issued = $156,730. Amount outstanding at close = $11,010. Amount of large outstanding at close = $1,640. Amount of small outstanding at close = $9,370.

14,780 Large   1,404 Small   16,184 Total

5402	-	$5	1882BB	477	188 D	B936683B	XF	pen/pen
5402	-	$10	1902PB	633	609 B	U489501H	VG	pen/pen vp
5402	-	$10	1902PB	633	655 C	U489547H	VG	
5402	-	$20	1902PB	659	189 A	Z88871D	F/VF	Higgins Mus.
5402		$10	1929T1		D000050A		VG	
5402		$10	1929T1		F000167A		VG	
5402		$10	1929T1		F000194A		Fr	
5402		$20	1929T1		C000017A		F	
5402		$20	1929T1		B000020A		VF	Pinholes
5402		$20	1929T1		C000024A		VF+	
5402		$20	1929T1		D000029A		VG	Higgins Mus.
5402		$20	1929T1		D000032A		VF	

THE FIRST NATIONAL BANK OF LYONS   3 L
66 (FIRST ORGANIZATION)   CLINTON

Chartered in 1863. Placed in voluntary liquidation on June 15, 1882; capital of $100,000. Succeeded by #2733.

Officers: Pres. James P Gage 1867-80, Oliver McMahon 1881; **Cash.** RN Rand 1867-71, William Holmes 1872-81

First Charter, Original Issue	Ser #	# Notes
1-1-1-2	1-2000	8,000
5-5-5-5	1-2250	9,000
10-10-10-10	1-1675	6,700
20-20-20-20	1-750	3,000

First Charter, Series of 1875

20-20-20-20	1-758	3,032

Total amount of circulation issued = $242,640. Amount outstanding at close = $90,000. Amount outstanding in 1910 = $1,620.

29,732 Large   0 Small   29,732 Total

66	-	$1	ORIG	380	1185 C	C465526	F	
66	-	$1	ORIG	380	1559 C	C465900	VG/F	Grinnell # 2218, Higgins Museum
66	-	$2	ORIG	387	1887 A	C466228	AG	Corner missing

THE FIRST NATIONAL BANK OF LYONS (FIRST TITLE)
66 (2ND ORGANIZATION)   CLINTON   5 L

Received permission to retake #66 as its charter number on August 8, 1911.
Officers: Pres. Stephen Briggs 1911, JH Peters 1912-22; **VP** JH Peters

1911, JL Wilson 1913-20, Otto Rockrohr 1922; **Cash.** Milo J Gabriel 1911-13, AL Holmes 1914-22; **AC** AL Holmes 1911-13, EE Matthiesen 1914-22, JW Campbell 1920-22

Third Charter, Date Back, Blue Seal	Ser #	# Notes
10-10-10-10	1-1500	6,000
Third Charter, Plain Back, Blue Seal		
10-10-10-10	1501-8750	29,000
Fourth Charter, 1922		
10-10-10-20	1-2500	10,000
45,000 Large	0 Small	45,000 Total

66	M	$10 1902DB	616	166 D	E721452	F	
66	M	$10 1902DB	616	1072 D	H930115	VF	
66	M	$10 1902DB	616	2218 C	K521891	VF	
66	M	$10 1902PB	624	3907 D	R134147	VF	Grinnell # 4332
66		$10 1902PB	624	5251 C	R726326	AU	Higgins Mus.

THE CITIZENS' NATIONAL BANK OF LYONS   1 L
4536   **CLINTON**

This is the only bank in Iowa with an apostrophe in its title.
Chartered on March 23, 1891. Placed in voluntary liquidation on June 11, 1900; capital of $100,000. Consolidated with #2733 (#66).
Officers: Pres. Leroi B Wadleigh 1891-99; **Cash.** Virtus Lund 1891-99

Second Charter, Brown Backs	Ser #	# Notes
10-10-10-20	1-1307	5,228

Total amount of circulation issued = $65,530. Amount outstanding at close = $25,000. Amount outstanding in 1910 = $1,000.
5,228 Large   0 Small   36,344 Total

4536	$10 1882BB	484	836 A	K619600	F	Higgins Mus.

THE FIRST NATIONAL BANK OF LYONS   4 L
2733   **CLINTON**

Chartered in 1882. Succeeded #66. Assumed #4536 by consolidation June 11, 1900. Received permission to retake #66 as its charter number Aug. 8, 1911. Title change to First National Bank of Lyons at Clinton on June 6, 1922.
Officers: Pres. Oliver McMahan 1883-92, D Joyce 1893-94, DJ Batchelder 1895-1904, WT Joyce 1905-07, Stephen Briggs 1908-11; **VP** WT Joyce 1896-1900, Wm Holmes 1902-04, JH Peters 1907-11; **Cash.** William Holmes 1883-1900, JH Peters 1901-06, Milo J Gabriel 1907-11; **AC** JH Peters 1896-1900, AL Holmes 1902-11, MJ Gabriel 1904

Second Charter, Brown Backs	Ser #	# Notes
5-5-5-5	1-1000	4,000
10-10-10-20	1-5686	22,744
Third Charter, Red Seal		
10-10-10-20	1-2400	9,600
Third Charter, Date Back, Blue Seal		
10-10-10-20	1-2500	10,000
46,344 Large	0 Small	46,344 Total

2733	-	$10 1882BB	479	3755 A	K321626	VF	pen/pen
2733	-	$10 1882BB	479	4616 A	N855518	XF	N855519 ?
2733	-	$10 1882BB	479	5663 C	U178519	VG/F	pen Higgins Mus.
2733	M	$20 1902RS	?	1803 A	X765454	F/VF	Higgins Mus.

THE MACKSBURG NATIONAL BANK   1 L
6852   **MADISON**

Organized on May 13, 1903 with a capital of $25,000. Succeeded The Macksburg Bank. Placed in voluntary liquidation on May 15, 1930; capital of $25,000. Absorbed by #2002, Madison County State Bank, and Winterset Savings Bank. These three banks absorbed #6852 jointly. Placed in receivership on Dec. 22, 1931. Reason for failure: deficiency in assets sold.
Officers: Pres. JM Wilson 1904-10, LT Townsend 1911-13, Eugene Wilson 1914-29; **VP** LT Townsend 1904, JH Mack 1907, LT Townsend 1909-10, ID Harrison 1911, Martin Rowe 1913-14, EB Marsh 1920, Mamie B Walker 1922-26, Onie B Hixon 1927-29, FC Herren 1929; **Cash.** OE Klingaman 1904-05, WW Walker 1906-20, Rex M Wilder 1922-24, Carl L Conway 1925-29, HM Sexton 1929; **AC** RH Walker 1910-11, Rex M Wilder 1920

Third Charter, Red Seal	Ser #	# Notes
10-10-10-20	1-357	1,428
Third Charter, Date Back, Blue Seal		
10-10-10-20	1-660	2,640
Third Charter, Plain Back, Blue Seal		
10-10-10-20	661-1208	2,192
1929, Type I		
6-10's	1-46	276
6-20's	1-10	60

Total amount of circulation issued = $82,210. Amount of large outstanding at close= $2,050. Amount of small outstanding at close = $3,960.
6,260 Large   336 Small   6,596 Total

6852	M	$10 1902DB	616	346 E	K887557	VG	

THE FARMERS NATIONAL BANK OF MALVERN   0 L
4834   **MILLS**

Chartered on January 5, 1893. Placed in voluntary liquidation on August 6, 1896; capital of $50,000.
Officers: Pres. JC Taylor 1893-94, AJ Chantry 1895; **Cash.** Wm M Evans 1893-95

Second Charter, Brown Backs	Ser #	# Notes
50-100	1-120	240

Total amount of circulation issued = $18,000. Amount outstanding at close = $11,250. Amount outstanding in 1910 = $250.
240 Large   0 Small   240 Total

THE FIRST NATIONAL BANK OF MALVERN   4 L
2247   **MILLS**

Organized on February 9, 1875 with a capital of $50,000. Chartered on April 10, 1875. Placed in receivership on December 10, 1926; capital of $50,000. Reason for failure: incompetent management.
Officers: Pres. James M Strahan 1876-1907, ML Evans 1908, WL Summers 1909-26; **VP** SD Davis 1900-03, ML Evans 1904-07, CB Christy 1904, ML Evans 1907, Geo Mellor 1909-10, Sherman Jones 1911-26, JJ Wilson 1925; **Cash.** Leander Bentley 1876-92, James J Wilson 1893-24, GO Lowe 1925, PT Betz 1926; **AC** OA Strahan 1896-1907, Harry Wilson 1911-13, FH Kruse 1926, Fannie Clark 1926

First Charter, Original Issue	Ser #	# Notes
5-5-5-5	1-2500	10,000
First Charter, Series of 1875		
5-5-5-5	1-3498	13,992
Second Charter, Brown Backs		
10-10-10-20	1-1112	4,448
Second Charter, Date Back		
5-5-5-5	1-580	2,320
10-10-10-20	1-391	1,564
Third Charter, Date Back, Blue Seal		
10-10-10-20	1-500	2,000
Third Charter, Plain Back, Blue Seal		
10-10-10-20	501-1281	3,124

Total amount issued = $170,760. Amount outstanding at close = $12,500.
37,448 Large   0 Small   37,448 Total

2247	-	$5	1875	404	2471 A	U433751	G/VG	Higgins Mus.
2247		$20 1882BB	501	988 A	T607354T	F	Higgins Mus.	
2247	M	$10 1882DB	542	314 E	D333104	XF	stamp/pen	
2247	M	$10 1902DB	631	88 C	M976254B	F/VF	vp Higgins Mus.	

THE MALVERN NATIONAL BANK   1 L
8057   **MILLS**

Chartered in January 1906 with a capital of $50,000. Placed in voluntary liquidation on December 6, 1929; capital of $50,000. Succeeded by The Malvern Trust & Savings Bank.
Officers: Pres. CB Christy 1906-27, Fred Durbin 1928-29; **VP** James Durbin 1907-13, JO Laird 1914, GW Strohl 1920-24, FR Chantry 1925-29; **Cash.** Fred Durbin 1906-27, RW Criswell 1928-29; **AC** Lottie Deardorff 1910-14, Iowa Deardorff 1920, RS Criswell 1920-27

Third Charter, Red Seal	Ser #	# Notes
10-10-10-20	1-460	1,840
Third Charter, Date Back, Blue Seal		
10-10-10-20	1-1220	4,880
Third Charter, Plain Back, Blue Seal		
10-10-10-20	1221-2432	4,848
1929, Type I		
6-10's	1-33	198
6-20's	1-5	30

Total amount of circulation issued = $147,180. Amount of large outstanding at close = $10,330. Amount of small outstanding at close = $2,170.
11,568 Large   228 Small   11,796 Total

8057	-	$10 1902PB	625	1915 F	V350027H	VG/F	stamp Higg. Mus.

THE FIRST NATIONAL BANK OF MANCHESTER   15 L
4221   **DELAWARE**

Organized on January 17, 1890 with a capital of $50,000. Placed in receivership on February 13, 1929; capital of $50,000. Reason for failure: incompetent management.
Officers: Pres. AR Loomis 1890-95, JW Miles 1896-1900, MF Le Roy 1901-13, AR Le Roy 1914-20, Don A Preussner 1922, RD Graham 1923-24; **VP** WH Norris 1896, RR Robinson 1900, AH Blake 1902, RR Robinson 1903, HA Von Oven 1904-07, LL Hoyt 1909, AH Blake 1909-14, H Carr

1910-14, DA Preussner 1920-24, EH Hoyt 1922, Don E Preussner 1923-24, EH Hoyt 1923-24, Hubert Carr 1923-24; **Cash.** MF Le Roy 1890-1900, HA Granger 1901-07, AR Le Roy 1912-13, Don A Preussner 1914-18, RD Graham 1919-20, FB Wilson 1922-24; **AC** BF Miles 1896-1900, Elmer C Hesner 1902-03, Don A Preussner 1907-13, FE Dutton 1909-11, CS Bing 1920-24, PA Klaus 1922-24

Second Charter, Brown Backs	Ser #	# Notes
5-5-5-5	1-2350	9,400
10-10-10-20	1-620	2,480
Second Charter, Date Back		
5-5-5-5	1-33	132
10-10-10-20	1-49	196
Third Charter, Date Back, Blue Seal		
10-10-10-20	1-2750	11,000
Third Charter, Plain Back, Blue Seal		
10-10-10-20	2751-7760	20,040

Total amount issued = $469,110. Amount outstanding at close = $39,447.
43,248 Large   0 Small   43,248 Total

4221	-	$5 1882BB	471	1 B	H894453	VF/XF	Grinnell # 1616
4221	-	$5 1882BB	471	2 A[	H894454	CU	Partial sheet
4221	-	$5 1882BB	471	2 B[	H894454	CU	Partial sheet
4221	-	$10 1882BB	484	117 C	X464310	VF	
4221	-	$10 1882BB	484	163 B	X464356	VG	
4221	M	$10 1902DB	619	1848 A	M516021A	F	
4221	M	$10 1902PB	627	2791 C	U482179B	?	good sigs
4221	M	$10 1902PB	627	2979 B	U842367B	XF	Higgins Mus.
4221	M	$10 1902PB	627	3242 C	B572359D	F	stamp/stamp
4221	-	$10 1902PB	627	6650 B	6650 B	VF	light stamps
4221	-	$10 1902PB	627	7577 C	7577 C	F	
4221	-	$10 1902PB	627	7704 A	7704 A	XF/AU	stamp Pinholes
4221	M	$20 1902PB	653	4294 A	U724136D	F+	gone/gone
4221	M	$20 1902PB	653	5042 A	M178364E	F	gone/faded
4221	-	$20 1902PB	653	7749 A	7749 A	AU	stamp Pinholes

THE FIRST NATIONAL BANK OF MANILLA   7 L   15 S
5873   CRAWFORD
Organized on June 14, 1901 with a capital of $25,000. Succeeded The Commercial Bank. Placed in receivership on January 30, 1935; capital of $25,000.
Officers: Pres. AT Bennett 1901-10, Edward Saunders 1911-32; **VP** Frank M Leet 1902, Hans Rief 1903-05, Edward Saunders 1907-10, Frank A Brown 1911-32; **Cash.** WH Hart 1901-06, RC Jackson 1907-32; **AC** Alfred Bohlander 1902, JG Rief 1903-05, CL Breckenridge 1907-10, JA Saunders 1913

Second Charter, Brown Backs	Ser #	# Notes
10-10-10-20	1-400	1,600
Second Charter, Date Back		
10-10-10-20	1-1640	6,560
Second Charter, Value Back		
10-10-10-20	1641-2720	4,320
Third Charter, Plain Back, Blue Seal		
10-10-10-20	1-1989	7,956
1929, Type I		
6-10's	1-409	2,454
6-20's	1-121	726

Total amount of circulation issued = $294,510. Amount of large outstanding at close= $3,540. Amount of small outstanding at close = $21,460.
20,436 Large   3,180 Small   23,616 Total

5873	M	$10 1882VB	?	1753 F	T611731	VG	Higgins Mus.
5873	M	$10 1882VB	?	1933 ?	T977651	F	
5873	-	$10 1902PB	633	1498 A	1498 A	VG	
5873	-	$10 1902PB	633	1810 B	1810 B	VG	stamp sigs vp
5873	-	$10 1902PB	633	1814 A	1814 A	F	stamp sigs vp
5873	-	$20 1902PB	659	1311 A	1311 A	XF	
5873	-	$20 1902PB	659	1312 A	1312 A	XF	vp Higgins Mus.
5873		$10 1929T1		F000009A		VF+	
5873		$10 1929T1		B000074A		F/VF	
5873		$10 1929T1		E000286A		VF	
5873		$10 1929T1		E000311A		VG/F	
5873		$10 1929T1		F000353A		VG	
5873		$20 1929T1		F000009A		VG/F	
5873		$20 1929T1		C000039A		VF/XF	
5873		$20 1929T1		A000061A		AU	Higgins Mus.
5873		$20 1929T1		A000062A		VF	Edge nick
5873		$20 1929T1		A000063A		F/VF	
5873		$20 1929T1		?000072A		XF	
5873		$20 1929T1		D000078A		VF	
5873		$20 1929T1		B000086A		VF	Stained
5873		$20 1929T1		A000088A		F	
5873		$20 1929T1		C000119A		?	

THE MANILLA NATIONAL BANK   2 L
6041   CRAWFORD
Organized on November 12, 1901 with a capital of $25,000. Placed in receivership on October 20, 1925; capital of $25,000. Reason for failure: incompetent management & dishonesty.
Officers: Pres. LM Shaw 1902, DW Shaw 1903-04, Carl F Kuehnle 1905-24; **VP** LW Shaw 1902, Carl F Kuehnle 1903, JC Ruby 1904-07, Chas Wenzel 1909-13, John G Hamann 1914-25; **Cash.** FL Van Slyke 1902-25; **AC** Edw Theobald 1907-25

Second Charter, Brown Backs	Ser #	# Notes
10-10-10-20	1-400	1,600
Second Charter, Date Back		
10-10-10-20	1-1120	4,480
Second Charter, Value Back		
10-10-10-20	1121-2050	3,720
Third Charter, Plain Back, Blue Seal		
10-10-10-20	1-780	3,120

Total amount issued = $161,500. Amount outstanding at close = $18,450.
12,920 Large   0 Small   12,920 Total

6041	M	$10 1902PB	634	356 A	A740378H	F/VF	very faded
6041		$20 1902PB	660	751 A	Z156533H	G/VG	Higgins Mus.

THE FIRST NATIONAL BANK OF MANNING   14 L   36 S
3455   CARROLL
Chartered on February 12, 1886 with a capital of $50,000. Succeeded The Farmers & Traders Bank. Licensed after the Banking Holiday on March 23, 1933.
Officers: Pres. Donald W Sutherland 1887-1926, RG Sutherland 1926-35; **VP** LC Sutherland 1900; **Cash.** Orson E Dutton 1887-91, LC Sutherland 1892, WE Sweesy 1893-94, Orson E Dutton 1895-1907, RG Sutherland 1908-26, ED Sutherland 1926-35; **AC** RG Sutherland 1900-07, ED Sutherland 1909-26, Harry Hinz 1925-35

Second Charter, Brown Backs	Ser #	# Notes
5-5-5-5	1-4270	17,080
50-100	1-550	1,100
Third Charter, Red Seal		
10-10-10-20	1-900	3,600
Third Charter, Date Back, Blue Seal		
10-10-10-20	1-4740	18,960
Third Charter, Plain Back, Blue Seal		
10-10-10-20	4741-12514	31,096
1929, Type I		
6-10's	1-1574	9,444
6-20's	1-446	2,676
1929, Type II		
10's	1-1318	1,318
20's	1-308	308

Total amount of circulation issued = $1,005,900. Amount of large outstanding in June 1935 = $4,580. Amount of small outstanding in June 1935 = $70,420.
71,836 Large   13,746 Small   85,582 Total

3455	M	$20 1902DB	643	1554 B	Z784637	XF	pen Higgins Mus.
3455	M	$20 1902DB	643	1556 B	Z784639	AU	
3455	M	$20 1902DB	643	1561 B	Z784644	VF	
3455	M	$20 1902DB	643	1562 B	Z784645	VF/XF	pen/pen
3455	M	$20 1902DB	643	1564 B	Z784647	VF+	pen/pen
3455	M	$10 1902PB	625	5614 F	Y7935B	F	pen/pen
3455	M	$10 1902PB	625	5750 D	B54377D	F	
3455	M	$10 1902PB	625	8265 E	E882387E	CU	
3455	M	$10 1902PB	625	8580 E	U941342 E	VF	

Charter	M/-	Denom	Type	Plate	Sheet	Serial	Grade	Notes
3455	M	$10	1902PB	625	8919 D	U941681E	VG	
3455	M	$10	1902PB	625	9080 F	U941842E	PR	gone/gone
3455	M	$10	1902PB	625	9774 E	M872686H	F	
3455	M	$20	1902PB	651	5806 B	B54433D	VG	
3455	M	$20	1902PB	651	7090 B	R321492D	CU	
3455		$10	1929T1			C000182A	VF	
3455		$10	1929T1			A000301A	F/VF	
3455		$10	1929T1			D000416A	?	?Denomination?
3455		$10	1929T1			A000487A	VF	
3455		$10	1929T1			D000557A	VF	
3455		$10	1929T1			D000580A	VF/XF	
3455		$10	1929T1			B000651A	F	
3455		$10	1929T1			F000904A	F	
3455		$10	1929T1			E000937A	XF	
3455		$10	1929T1			E000984A	?	
3455		$10	1929T1			B001070A	VF	
3455		$10	1929T1			E001095A	F	
3455		$10	1929T1			E001130A	VG	
3455		$10	1929T1			F001236A	?	
3455		$10	1929T1			F001359A	F/VF	
3455		$10	1929T1			E001449A	VG	
3455		$10	1929T1			D001465A	F	
3455		$20	1929T1			E000089A	VF	
3455		$20	1929T1			F000092A	F+	
3455		$20	1929T1			D000129A	F	
3455		$20	1929T1			E000162A	F/VF	
3455		$20	1929T1			C000263A	VG	
3455		$20	1929T1			D000297A	VF	
3455		$20	1929T1			F000324A	?	
3455		$20	1929T1			D000326A	VF	
3455		$20	1929T1			C000352A	XF	Higgins Mus.
3455		$20	1929T1			C000374A	VF	
3455		$20	1929T1			D000416A	VF	
3455		$20	1929T1			C000435A	VG+	Ink on face
3455		$10	1929T2			A000175	VF	
3455		$10	1929T2			A000192	?	
3455		$10	1929T2			A000909	F	
3455		$10	1929T2			A000926	F/VF	
3455		$10	1929T2			A001051	VF	Pinholes
3455		$20	1929T2			A000048	VF	
3455		$20	1929T2			A000274	F	

THE FIRST NATIONAL BANK OF MAQUOKETA 6 L 12 S
999 JACKSON

Organized on February 20, 1865 with a capital of $50,000. Placed in receivership on June 28, 1932; capital of $50,000.

Officers: Pres. LB Dunham 1867, DM Hubbell 1868-71, Otto V Schrader 1872-75, Peirce Mitchell 1876-82, Thomas E Cannell 1883-88, JE Squires 1889-1910, Chas Von Schrader 1911-19, Geo L Mitchell 1920-32; **VP** MS Dunn 1907-09, AB Bowen 1909-26, OH Cuddy 1927-32; **Cash.** Otto V Schrader 1867-69, Henry Reigart 1870-81, Matthew Dalzell 1883-87, Chas Von Schrader 1888-1911, Geo L Mitchell 1912-15, 1918, OC Kucheman 1916-17, OH Cuddy 1920-32; **AC** Chas. Von Schrader 1885, M Dalzell 1896, Geo L Mitchell 1900-10, Burr Von Schrader 1920-32, EJ Kuhlmer 1920-22, JC Ellis 1924-28

	Ser #	# Notes
First Charter, Original Issue		
5-5-5-5	1-2450	9,800
10-10-10-20	1-840	3,360
First Charter, Series of 1875		
5-5-5-5	1-370	1,480
10-10-10-20	1-1086	4,344
Second Charter, Brown Backs		
10-10-10-20	1-1800	7,200
Third Charter, Red Seal		
10-10-10-20	1-1250	5,000
Third Charter, Date Back, Blue Seal		
10-10-10-20	1-700	2,800
Third Charter, Plain Back, Blue Seal		
10-10-10-20	701-3556	11,424
1929, Type I		
6-10's	1-468	2,808
6-20's	1-111	666

Total amount of circulation issued = $524,400. Amount of large outstanding at close = $3,740. Amount of small outstanding at close = $23,580.

45,408 Large 3,474 Small 48,882 Total

Charter	M/-	Denom	Type	Plate	Sheet	Serial	Grade	Notes
999	-	$20	1882BB	494	1713 A	V775096	VF	
999	M	$10	1902RS	613	803 B	V211976	F	pen/pen
999	M	$10	1902DB	616	238 F	K891409	F	Higgins Mus.
999	M	$10	1902DB	616	539 E	K891710	VG	stamp/stamp
999	M	$20	1902DB	642	256 B	K891427	VF	
999	-	$10	1902PB	624	3397 ?	3397 ?	?	
999		$10	1929T1			E000001A	?	? $10 or $20 ?
999		$10	1929T1			F000056A	?	
999		$10	1929T1			E000231A	VG+	
999		$10	1929T1			B000238A	VG	Higgins Mus.
999		$10	1929T1			E000264A	VG	
999		$20	1929T1			E000001A	VF	
999		$20	1929T1			E000052A	?	
999		$20	1929T1			B000071A	F	
999		$20	1929T1			C000075A	VG+	
999		$20	1929T1			E000083A	VG	
999		$20	1929T1			C000089A	VF+	
999		$20	1929T1			F000105A	VG	

THE FIRST NATIONAL BANK OF MARATHON 3 L 6 S
4789 BUENA VISTA

Organized on August 1, 1892 with a capital of $50,000. Succeeded The Marathon. Placed in conservatorship on March 22, 1933. Placed in receivership on October 31, 1933; capital of $25,000.

Officers: Pres. JP Farmer 1892-1909, FH Helsell 1910-13, GF Tincknell 1914-20, AA Wells 1922-26, K Sandine 1927-33; **VP** WW Wells 1896, AA Wells 1900, FH Helsell 1902-09, HL Farmer 1910-13, AA Wells 1914-20, JR Howe 1922-23, HL Farmer 1924, EE Peterson 1925-26, FW Heiny 1927-33, A Dahlberg 1927-33; **Cash.** ST Goltry 1892-1900, JE Allison 1901-12, EP Lowry 1913, JH Wegersley 1914-22, EP Lomen 1923-26, FW Heiny 1927-35, A Dahlberg 1927-33

	Ser #	# Notes
Second Charter, Brown Backs		
10-10-10-20	1-1270	5,080
Second Charter, Date Back		
10-10-10-20	1-333	1,332
Third Charter, Date Back, Blue Seal		
10-10-10-20	1-750	3,000
Third Charter, Plain Back, Blue Seal		
10-10-10-20	751-1871	4,484
1929, Type I		
6-10's	1-277	1,662
6-20's	1-58	348

Total amount of circulation issued = $197,280. Amount outstanding at close = $12,500. Amount of large outstanding on October 30, 1933 = $1,420.

13,896 Large 2,010 Small 15,906 Total

Charter	M/-	Denom	Type	Plate	Sheet	Serial	Grade	Notes
4789	-	$10	1902PB	628	1608 C	1608 C	XF+	pen/pen
4789	-	$10	1902PB	628	1798 A	1798 A	VF+	pen/pen
4789	-	$20	1902PB	654	1825 A	1825 A	F	Higgins Mus.
4789		$10	1929T1			E000018A	XF	Higgins Mus.
4789		$10	1929T1			E000059A	VG/F	
4789		$10	1929T1			C000110A	VF	
4789		$20	1929T1			D000006A	VG/F	
4789		$20	1929T1			F000025A	VF+	
4789		$20	1929T1			E000045A	F	

THE FIRST NATIONAL BANK OF MARCUS 2 L
9819 CHEROKEE

Organized on June 22, 1910; capital of $100,000. Placed in receivership on May 18, 1921; capital of $50,000. Reason for failure: local depression.

Officers: Pres. FS Barnes 1911, Dan Melter 1912-13, WP Manley 1914, AR Kenney 1914-17, EL Lundquist 1918-20; **VP** CW Rowe 1911, AR Kenney 1914, 1920, CR McConnell 1914, Dan Melter 1914; **Cash.** DH Smith 1911, EL Lundquist 1912-14, RW Moore 1915-19, M Bruns 1920; **AC** FS Barnes, Jr 1911, Floyd Barnes 1913-14, CL Ellis 1920

	Ser #	# Notes
Third Charter, Date Back, Blue Seal		
10-10-10-20	1-2350	9,400
Third Charter, Plain Back, Blue Seal		
10-10-10-20	2351-2794	1,776

Total amount issued = $139,700. Amount outstanding at close = $21,800.

11,176 Large 0 Small 11,176 Total

Charter	M/-	Denom	Type	Plate	Sheet	Serial	Grade	Notes
9819	M	$10	1902DB	619	2102 A	D221899A	VG	vp Higgins Mus.
9819	M	$20	1902DB	645	1729 A	B762830A	VG	pen/stamp

THE FIRST NATIONAL BANK OF MARENGO 18 L
2484 IOWA

Organized on May 25, 1880 with a capital of $50,000. Placed in receivership on Feb. 18, 1927; capital of $65,000. Reason for failure: local depression.

Officers: Pres. JH Branch 1880-1906, Frank Cook 1907-16, 1920-26, DH Mueller 1917-19; **VP** JH Feenan 1896, Thos Stapleton 1902-23, JH Lewis 1924, Thos Stapleton 1924, FC Lindenmayer 1925-26; **Cash.** C Baumer 1880-81, Lewis Haas 1883-85, CE Bingham 1887-89, QP Reno 1891-1900, Frank Cook 1901-06, HE Oldaker 1907-09, SE Roland 1910-12, CC Clements 1913, DH Mueller 1920-26, FW Goldthwaite 1926; PR Lacolli 1913, FW Goldthwaite 1914-26, John H Rusch 1922-26, Margaret Hogan 1922-25

	Ser #	# Notes
First Charter, Series of 1875		
5-5-5-5	1-2163	8,652

10-10-10-20		1-1675	6,700

Second Charter, Brown Backs

10-10-10-20		1-2800	11,200

Second Charter, Date Back

10-10-10-20		1-2740	10,960

Second Charter, Value Back

10-10-10-20		2741-3993	5,012

Third Charter, Plain Back, Blue Seal

10-10-10-20		1-2960	11,840

Total amount issued = $614,660. Amount outstanding at close = $49,600.

| 54,364 Large | 0 Small | 54,364 Total | |

2484	- $5	1875 404	1267 B	K734207	CU	Unc 3 folds?
2484	- $5	1875 404	2076 B	Y457369	VF	Grinnell # 3521, Higgins Museum
2484	- $10	1875 419	532 B	D694552	F/VF	pen/pen
2484	- $10	1875 419	1483 A	K897251	VG	Higgins Mus.
2484	- $20	1875 434	1304 A	K897072	VF	Grinnell # 1168
2484	M $10	1882BB 490	572 A	A520007A	F+	Davenport B&T
2484	M $10	1882BB 490	1161 A	D514527D	VG/F	pen/pen
2484	M $10	1882BB 490	1264 C	?	F	Davenport B&T
2484	M $10	1882BB 490	1954 B	T228506T	F/VF	pen Higgins Mus.
2484	M $10	1882BB 490	2001 B	T228553T	VF	Davenport B&T
2484	M $10	1882BB 490	2294 B	U322224U	AU+	pen/pen Grinnell lot # 1168
2484	M $10	1882DB 545	1161 A	?	F	
2484	M $10	1882VB 577	3520 E	U638268	F	pen/pen
2484	M $10	1882VB 577	3008 ?		VF	
2484	M $10	1902PB 633	1137 A	M684354E	VF	pen/pen
2484	- $10	1902PB 633	2756 B	2756 B	VG	
2484	- $10	1902PB 633	2829 A	2829 A	F	pen, Odd color
2484	M $20	1902PB 659	235 A	V110827D	VF+	Higgins Mus.

THE FIRST NATIONAL BANK OF MARION 2 L
117 (FIRST ORGANIZATION) LINN

Chartered in 1863. Placed in voluntary liquidation on July 11, 1882; capital of $50,000. Succeeded by #2753.
Officers: Pres. Redman D Stephens 1867-81; **Cash.** FS Winslow 1867, Amos W Crandell 1870-75, Jackson W Bowdish 1876-80, Jay J Smyth 1881

First Charter, Original Issue		Ser #	# Notes
1-1-1-2		1-1040	4,160
5-5-5-5		1-6350	25,400

First Charter, Series of 1875

5-5-5-5		1-3115	12,460

Total amount of circulation issued = $194,500. Amount outstanding at close = $45,000. Amount outstanding in 1910 = $1,479.

| 42,020 Large | 0 Small | 42,020 Total | |

117	- $1	ORIG 380	251 C	B447756	VG	Higgins Mus.
117	- $5	ORIG 397	2394 C	559686	G	

THE FIRST NATIONAL BANK OF MARION 0 L
2753 LINN

Chartered in 1882. Succeeded #117. Received permission to retake #117 as its charter # on May 27, 1911.
Officers: Pres. LB Stephens 1883-84, Jay J Smyth 1885-95, JS Alexander 1896-1907, CH Kurtz 1908, TJ Davis 1909-11; **VP** AJ McKean 1896, EA Vaughn 1900-07, WW Vaughn 1909-11; **Cash.** Jay J Smyth 1883-84, Samuel N Goodhue 1885-92, JS Alexander 1893-95, CH Kurtz 1896-1907, JW Bowman 1908-11; **AC** BF Mentzer 1911

Second Charter, Brown Backs		Ser #	# Notes
5-5-5-5		1-4991	19,964
10-10-10-20		1-183	732

Third Charter, Red Seal

10-10-10-20		1-645	2,580

Third Charter, Date Back, Blue Seal

10-10-10-20		1-700	2,800

Total amount of circulation issued = $696,680. Amount outstanding in 1935 = $50,000. Amount of large outstanding in 1935 = $4,790. Amount of small outstanding in 1935 = $45,210.

| 26,076 Large | 0 Small | 26,076 Total | |

THE FIRST NATIONAL BANK OF MARION 20 L 26 S
117 (2ND ORGANIZATION) LINN

Received permission to retake #117 as its charter # on May 27, 1911.
Officers: Pres. TJ Davis 1911-17, JW Bowman 1918-25, RN Fitzgerald 1926-35; **VP** WW Vaughn 1911-14, WG Lillie 1920, RN Fitzgerald 1922-25, WB Sebern 1926-35; **Cash.** JW Bowman 1911-17, HF Lockwood 1919-35; **AC** BF Mentzer 1911-14, Bertha Petro 1914, Mabel Davidson 1920-23, Emery J Miller 1926-35

Third Charter, Date Back, Blue Seal		Ser #	# Notes
10-10-10-20		1-2100	8,400

Third Charter, Plain Back, Blue Seal

10-10-10-20		2101-8087	23,948

1929, Type I

6-10's		1-1176	7,056
6-20's		1-308	1,848

1929, Type II

10's		1-619	619
20's		1-120	120

| 32,348 Large | 9,643 Small | 41,991 Total | |

117	M	$10 1902DB	616	1743 C	A564145B	CU	Davenport B&T
117	M	$10 1902DB	616	1756 C	A564158B	CU	Davenport B&T
117	M	$10 1902DB	616	1929 B	X549421B	F	
117	M	$20 1902DB	642	689 B	A205532A	?	
117	M	$10 1902PB	624	2978 B	B731155D	VG+	pen/pen
117	M	$10 1902PB	624	4466 B	E603948E	XF	
117	M	$10 1902PB	624	4672 B	E604154E	VG+	gone/gone
117	M	$10 1902PB	624	4809 A	R679761E	XF	faded Higg. Mus.
117	M	$10 1902PB	624	5014 B	R679966E	VG	
117	M	$10 1902PB	624	5733 C	K63405H	AU	
117	M	$10 1902PB	624	5848 B	R679490H	VF/XF	pen/pen
117	-	$10 1902PB	624	5907 B	R679549H	VG/F	
117	-	$10 1902PB	624	5923 B	R679595H	VF	pen/pen
117	-	$10 1902PB	624	6624 B	B291006K	VG	faded/faded
117	-	$10 1902PB	624	7425 A	7425 A	F/VF	
117	-	$10 1902PB	624	7742 A	7742 A	?	pen/pen
117	-	$10 1902PB	624	8038 B	8038 B	XF/AU	pen Higgins Mus.
117	-	$20 1902PB	650	6529 A	B290911K	XF	
117	-	$20 1902PB	650	7139 A	7139 A	VG/F	
117	-	$20 1902PB	650	7590 A	7590 A	F	
117		$10 1929T1		F000017A		VF	
117		$10 1929T1		F000259A		F	
117		$10 1929T1		F000347A		G	Rust
117		$10 1929T1		D000348A		F	
117		$10 1929T1		E000462A		F	
117		$10 1929T1		B000607A		VG+	
117		$10 1929T1		E000777A		VF	
117		$10 1929T1		A000861A		VF	
117		$10 1929T1		D000867A		F/VF	
117		$10 1929T1		C001011A		F	
117		$10 1929T1		B001014A		F	Higgins Mus.
117		$10 1929T1		C001040A		VG/F	
117		$10 1929T1		C001096A		F	
117		$10 1929T1		F001133A		F	
117		$10 1929T1		D001150A		VF/XF	
117		$10 1929T1		B001162A		VG	
117		$20 1929T1		F000015A		VG	
117		$20 1929T1		?000029A		VG	
117		$20 1929T1		D000061A		VF/XF	
117		$20 1929T1		A000064A		VF	
117		$20 1929T1		B000103A		F	
117		$20 1929T1		B000170A		VF/XF	Edge dark
117		$20 1929T1		A000242A		VG	
117		$20 1929T1		A000294A		F	
117		$10 1929T2		A000230		G	
117		$20 1929T2		A000011		VG	

THE CITY NATIONAL BANK OF MARSHALLTOWN 0 L
4359 MARSHALLTOWN

Chartered on July 8, 1890. Succeeded The City Bank. Placed in voluntary liquidation on May 4, 1908; capital of $100,000. Consolidated with #411.
Officers: Pres. James L Williams 1890-94, DT Denmead 1895-1907; **VP** GF Capron 1896-1903, JL Carney 1907; **Cash.** DT Denmead 1890-93, CC St. Clair 1894-1907, Fred S Williams 1896, HS Lawrence 1904-07

Second Charter, Brown Backs		Ser #	# Notes
5-5-5-5		1-4478	17,912
10-10-10-20		1-980	3,920

Total amount of circulation issued = $138,560. Amount outstanding at close = $25,000. Amount outstanding in 1910 = $7,022.

| 21,832 Large | 0 Small | 21,832 Total | |

THE COMMERCIAL NATIONAL BANK OF MARSHALLTOWN
2971 MARSHALL 0 L

Chartered on June 9, 1883. Succeeded The Commercial Bank (Lyon & McFaden). Placed in voluntary liquidation on October 25, 1886; capital of $100,000. Succeeded by The Commercial Banking Company.
Officers: Pres. Elijah L Lyon 1883-85; **Cash.** AA McFadon 1883-85

Second Charter, Brown Backs		Ser #	# Notes
10-10-10-20		1-587	2,348

Total amount of circulation issued = $29,350. Amount outstanding at close = $22,500. Amount outstanding in 1910 = $150.

| 2,348 Large | 0 Small | 2,348 Total | |

THE FARMERS NATIONAL BANK OF MARSHALLTOWN
2115 MARSHALL **1 L**

Chartered on June 30, 1873 with a capital of $50,000. Succeeded The Marshall County Bank. Placed in voluntary liquidation on September 18, 1875; capital of $50,000.

Officers: Pres. HEJ Boardman 1874-75; **Cash.** John Turner 1874-75

First Charter, Original Issue	Ser #	# Notes
5-5-5-5	1-1590	6,360

Total amount of circulation issued = $31,800. Amount outstanding at close = $27,000. Amount outstanding in 1910 = $125.

6,360 Large   0 Small   6,360 Total

| 2115 | - | $5 | ORIG | 399 | 1398 A | L134097 | F | Higgins Mus. |

THE FIRST NATIONAL BANK OF MARSHALLTOWN **8 L**
411 MARSHALL

Organized on April 25, 1864 with a capital of $50,000. Assumed #4359 by consolidation on May 4, 1908. Placed in receivership on June 11, 1928; capital of $200,000. Reason for failure: local depression & incompetent management.

Officers: Pres. Greenleaf M Woodbury 1867-73, George Glick 1874-93, JP Woodbury 1894-1907, DT Denmead 1908-11, CC St. Clair 1912-28; **VP** George Glick 1896-1907, Jas L Denmead 1909-11, AM Friend 1913-24, TJ Shoemaker 1925-28; **Cash.** CW Fracker 1867-69, George Glick 1870-72, CW Fracker 1872-76, Thomas J Fletcher 1877-81, AG Glick 1883-89, TJ Fletcher 1891-1907, CC St. Clair 1908-11, James L Denmead 1912-13, HK Denmead 1914-28; **AC** H Gerhart 1896-1927, HS Lawrence 1909-11

First Charter, Original Issue	Ser #	# Notes
1-1-1-2	1-4190	16,760
5-5-5-5	1-10450	41,800
First Charter, Series of 1875		
1-1-1-2	1-500	2,000
5-5-5-5	1-1452	5,808
Second Charter, Brown Backs		
50-100	1-902	1,804
Third Charter, Red Seal		
50-100	1-644	1,288
Third Charter, Date Back, Blue Seal		
50-100	1-800	1,600
50-50-50-100	1-450	1,800
Third Charter, Plain Back, Blue Seal		
50-50-50-100	451-507	228

Total amount issued = $740,140. Amount outstanding at close = $49,750.

73,088 Large   0 Small   73,088 Total

411	-	$1	ORIG	?	1957 C	348338	F	
411	M	$50	1902DB	667	99 D	A31909	F	Higgins Mus.
411	M	$50	1902DB	667	156 C	A233260	VG+	
411	M	$50	1902DB	667	280 B	A140739	CU	Oat Bin Hoard
411	-	$50	1902DB	667	385 D	B94469	F	pen/lt pen
411	-	$50	1902DB	667	448 E	448 E	F	faded/lt pen
411	M$100	1902DB	689	117 C	A233221	XF	gone/pen
411	M$100	1902DB	689	789 C	A141248	VG/F	

THE CITY NATIONAL BANK OF MASON CITY **10 L**
4587 CERRO GORDO

Placed in voluntary liquidation on February 19, 1921; capital of $200,000. Purchased by The Commercial Savings Bank.

Officers: Pres. James Rule 1891-95, HA Merrill 1896-1905, JS Wheeler 1906-11, AH Gale 1912-15, James E Blythe 1916-18, WV Escher 1919, EG Dunn 1920; **VP** JEE Markley 1896-1904, AH Gale 1907-11, JEE Markley 1913-14, HM Gilmore 1920, JA Parden 1920; **Cash.** HA Merrill 1891-92, AH Gale 1893-1905, WR Daggett 1906-07, John F Shaible 1908-18, JA Parden 1919, RP Palmer 1920; **AC** Geo W Hill 1900-14, Lynn A Merrill 1904, CE Brooks 1920, LW Sherman 1920

Second Charter, Brown Backs	Ser #	# Notes
10-10-10-20	1-6940	27,760
Second Charter, Date Back		
10-10-10-20	1-1861	7,444
Third Charter, Date Back, Blue Seal		
10-10-10-20	1-5600	22,400
Third Charter, Plain Back, Blue Seal		
10-10-10-20	5601-13180	30,320

Total amount issued = $1,099,050. Amount outstanding at close = $197,500.

87,924 Large   0 Small   87,924 Total

4587		$10	1882BB	485	866 A	T779401	F	Higgins Mus.
4587		$10	1882BB	485	2931 B	D346681D	?	
4587	M	$10	1902DB	619	4188 ?	K145464B	VG	
4587	M	$10	1902PB	627	6891 B	Y790460B	F	
4587	M	$10	1902PB	627	7259 C	Y984022B	VG	
4587	M	$10	1902PB	627	7843 A	Y984606B	VF+	nice sigs vp
4587	M	$10	1902PB	627	8032 C	Y984795B	VG	vp Dark
4587	M	$10	1902PB	627	9206 C	D149343D	F/VF	stamp sigs vp
4587	M	$10	1902PB	627	10693 C	K49675D	G	nice sigs vp
4587		$10	1902PB	627	12513 B	U62425D	CU	Higgins Mus.

THE FIRST NATIONAL BANK OF MASON CITY **55 L 68 S**
2574 CERRO GORDO

On March 13, 1934 John Dillinger led a gang of seven, including Baby Face Nelson, in a violent robbery of the First National Bank of Mason City. About $52,000 was stolen. The gang took hostages and made their escape amidst gunfire in a Buick sedan. No serial numbers of stolen national bank notes were recorded, but there must have been some included in the loot.

Chartered in 1881. Succeeded The Cerro Gordo County Bank (Montague & Smith).

Officers: Pres. Henry I Smith 1883-1900, CH McNider 1901-28, WGC Bagley 1929-35; **VP** Wm D Balch 1896, OT Dennison 1909-10, FE Keeler 1911-14, WGC Bagley 1920-28, CA Parker 1920-35, FE Keeler 1922-30, Hanford McNider 1922-29, RP Smith 1929-35, FC Heneman 1931-35; **Cash.** JVW Montague 1883-84, CH McNider 1887-1900, FE Keeler 1901-02, WGC Bagley 1909-19, RP Smith 1920-28, HV Bull 1929-33, Wm W Boyd 1934-35; **AC** CH McNider 1885, FE Keeler 1896-1902, WGC Bagley 1903-07, CA Parker 1904-14, HV Bull 1920-28, HC Fisher 1923-35, WW Boyd 1922-33, RB Johnson 1925-31, RE Wiley 1929-35

First Charter, Series of 1875	Ser #	# Notes
10-10-10-20	1-3643	14,572
Second Charter, Brown Backs		
10-10-10-20	1-7300	29,200
Second Charter, Date Back		
10-10-10-20	1-14900	59,600
Second Charter, Value Back		
10-10-10-20	14901-26138	44,952
Third Charter, Plain Back, Blue Seal		
10-10-10-20	1-20492	81,968
1929, Type I		
6-10's	1-5426	32,556
6-20's	1-1544	9,264
1929, Type II		
10's	1-2737	2,737
20's	1-360	360

Total amount of circulation issued = $3,424,060. Amount of large outstanding in 1935 = $15,290. Amount of small outstanding in 1935 = $184,710.

229,932 Large   44,917 Small   274,849 Total

2574	-	$10	1875	420	1245 A	K743853	XF	Higgins Mus.
2574	-	$20	1875	435	2080 A	K835246	VG	pen/gone
2574	-	$20	1875	435	2417 A	K877945	F	pen/gone
2574		$10	1882BB	490	?	N216140N	?	
2574	M	$10	1882BB	490	5937 A	T939721T	G	
2574	M	$10	1882BB	490	6942 A	V457191V	VF	pen/pen
2574	M	$10	1882BB	490	7257 C	?	F+	
2574	M	$20	1882BB	504	4468 A	N758871N	Fr	gone/gone
2574	M	$20	1882BB	504	4770 A	N759173N	AU	Higgins Mus.
2574	M	$20	1882BB	504	6149 A	T939931T	F	
2574	M	$20	1882BB	504	6399 A	V456648V	F/VF	pen/pen
2574	M	$10	1882DB	545	3809 ?	H348271	VG	
2574	M	$10	1882DB	545	4676 E	H947484	F	gone Higg. Mus.
2574	M	$10	1882DB	545	10992 D	M216140	F+	
2574	M	$10	1882DB	545	14107 E	T428805	F	pen/pen
2574	M	$10	1882DB	545	14428 D	T429126	VG+	pen/pen
2574	M	$10	1882DB	545	14584 F	T429282	F+	
2574	M	$20	1882DB	555	6467 B	K628125	VG/F	
2574	M	$20	1882DB	555	9149 B	M446977	VG/F	
2574	M	$20	1882DB	555	9922 B	N208760	VG	
2574	M	$10	1882VB	577	16160 E	T687928	VG	pen/pen
2574	M	$10	1882VB	577	19688 F	U554636	VG	pen/pen
2574	M	$10	1882VB	577	21423 D	U984851	F	faded/faded
2574	M	$10	1882VB	577	23081 E	V273529	CU	Higgins Mus.
2574	M	$10	1882VB	577	24123 E	V277771	F	
2574	M	$20	1882VB	581	16716 B	T688484	VG/F	
2574	M	$20	1882VB	581	21899 B	U985327	G	gone/gone
2574	M	$20	1882VB	581	24106 B	V277754	VG	stamp/stamp
2574	M	$20	1882VB	581	25611 B	V572539	F	
2574	M	$20	1882VB	581	26120 B	V573048	VG	
2574		$5	1902PB	608	1920 B	?	VG	

Charter		Denom	Series	Plate	Sheet/Pos	Serial	Grade	Notes
2574	M	$10	1902PB	634	806 C	H940668E	VF	stamp/stamp
2574	M	$10	1902PB	634	1303 A	K1315E	VF+	Higgins Mus.
2574	M	$10	1902PB	634	1920 B	K1932E	F	
2574	M	$10	1902PB	634	3901 B	T441193E	VG/F	close at bottom
2574	M	$10	1902PB	634	4559 A	Z446661E	F	stamp/stamp
2574		$10	1902PB	634	6875 ?	?	VG	
2574	-	$10	1902PB	634	14010 A	14010 A	G	Stains and splits
2574	-	$10	1902PB	634	14019 B	14019 B	F	stamp/stamp
2574	-	$10	1902PB	634	14213 A	14213 A	F	stamp/stamp
2574	-	$10	1902PB	634	14399 B	14399 B	VG+	
2574	-	$10	1902PB	634	14754 A	14754 A	VG	faded/faded
2574	-	$10	1902PB	634	15083 A	15083 A	VF/XF	
2574	-	$10	1902PB	634	15671 C	15671 C	?	
2574	-	$10	1902PB	634	16082 C	16082 C	VG	
2574	-	$10	1902PB	634	16701 C	16701 C	F	
2574	-	$10	1902PB	634	16850 ?	16850 ?	VG	
2574	-	$10	1902PB	634	17677 B	17677 B	F+	stamp/stamp
2574	-	$10	1902PB	634	18542 A	18542 A	VF	
2574	-	$10	1902PB	634	20277 C	20277 C	CU	
2574	M	$20	1902PB	660	3615 A	T440907E	VF	
2574	M	$20	1902PB	660	4338 A	T441630E	VG/F	nice sigs
2574	M	$20	1902PB	660	4581 A	Z446683E	F/VF	Yellowed
2574	M	$20	1902PB	660	5107 A	Z447209E	F	
2574	-	$20	1902PB	660	19086 A	19086 A	VG	
2574		$10	1929T1			F000288A	G/VG	
2574		$10	1929T1			D000389A	F+	
2574		$10	1929T1			B000574A	F/VF	
2574		$10	1929T1			C000659A	VG	
2574		$10	1929T1			D001195A	VF	
2574		$10	1929T1			D001353A	F	
2574		$10	1929T1			F001440A	VG	
2574		$10	1929T1			C001697A	VG	
2574		$10	1929T1			C002145A	CU	
2574		$10	1929T1			A002398A	VG/F	
2574		$10	1929T1			B002399A	?	
2574		$10	1929T1			D002587A	F	
2574		$10	1929T1			B002589A	?	
2574		$10	1929T1			C002624A	VG	
2574		$10	1929T1			C002668A	F	
2574		$10	1929T1			C002689A	F	
2574		$10	1929T1			A003330A	CU	
2574		$10	1929T1			C003342A	VF	
2574		$10	1929T1			D003745A	VG	
2574		$10	1929T1			D003764A	VF	
2574		$10	1929T1			F003776A	?	
2574		$10	1929T1			B003813A	F	
2574		$10	1929T1			E003837A	XF	Higgins Mus.
2574		$10	1929T1			A003893A	F	
2574		$10	1929T1			E004077A	VG	
2574		$10	1929T1			E004079A	?	
2574		$10	1929T1			F004204A	VF/XF	
2574		$10	1929T1			A004206A	F	
2574		$10	1929T1			C004287A	VG	
2574		$10	1929T1			D004361A	F	
2574		$10	1929T1			A004377A	?	
2574		$10	1929T1			C004407A	VF	
2574		$10	1929T1			A004479A	XF	
2574		$10	1929T1			F004635A	F/VF	
2574		$10	1929T1			C004702A	VF	
2574		$10	1929T1			C004744A	F	
2574		$10	1929T1			F004909A	XF	
2574		$10	1929T1			C004919A	F	
2574		$10	1929T1			A004987A	F/VF	
2574		$10	1929T1			F005328A	VF/XF	
2574		$10	1929T1			D005417A	AU	
2574		$20	1929T1			B000184A	VG	
2574		$20	1929T1			A000209A	?	
2574		$20	1929T1			E000232A	VG/F	
2574		$20	1929T1			E000289A	F	
2574		$20	1929T1			C000324A	VF	
2574		$20	1929T1			C000343A	F	
2574		$20	1929T1			E000463A	VG/F	
2574		$20	1929T1			E000494A	F	
2574		$20	1929T1			B000590A	VG	
2574		$20	1929T1			D000604A	VG/F	
2574		$20	1929T1			B000642A	F	
2574		$20	1929T1			A000681A	G/VG	
2574		$20	1929T1			F000718A	CU	
2574		$20	1929T1			F000719A	CU	Ink on back
2574		$20	1929T1			F000720A	CU	
2574		$20	1929T1			E001004A	XF	
2574		$20	1929T1			F001005A	VF	
2574		$20	1929T1			A001006A	VF	
2574		$20	1929T1			C001209A	F+	
2574		$20	1929T1			F001244A	VG/F	
2574		$20	1929T1			F001295A	VG	
2574		$20	1929T1			B001355A	?	
2574		$20	1929T1			B001396A	VF	
2574		$20	1929T1			B001447A	VF	
2574		$20	1929T1			C001490A	F	
2574		$10	1929T2			A001117	XF/AU	
2574		$10	1929T2			A001385	VF	

THE SECURITY NATIONAL BANK OF MASON CITY   14 L
10428   CERRO GORDO

Organized on July 16, 1913; capital of $100,000. Placed in receivership on Dec. 29, 1925; capital of $100,000. Reason for failure: local depression.
Officers: Pres. John A Senneff 1914-25; **VP** T Donovan 1914, SA Schneider 1914, JF Shaible 1920-22, Tim Donovan 1923-25, JF Shaible 1923-25; **Cash.** EW Clark 1914-25; **AC** CR Hendrikson 1923-25, Agnes Ginthner 1925

Third Charter, Date Back, Blue Seal	Ser #	# Notes
5-5-5-5	1-3700	14,800
10-10-10-20	1-2760	11,040
Third Charter, Plain Back, Blue Seal		
5-5-5-5	3701-13395	38,780
10-10-10-20	2761-9323	26,252

Total amount issued = $734,050. Amount outstanding at close = $97,900.
90,872 Large   0 Small   90,872 Total

Charter		Denom	Series	Plate	Sheet/Pos	Serial	Grade	Notes
10428	M	$10	1902DB	622	2538 C	M284844B	F/VF	stamp/stamp
10428	M	$10	1902DB	622	3510 D	H815292B	F	gone/gone
10428	M	$20	1902DB	648	57 A	V870072A	VF	
10428	M	$5	1902PB	604	3510 D	H815292B	?	
10428	M	$5	1902PB	604	3809 A	N949111B	VG	stamp/stamp
10428	M	$5	1902PB	604	11345 C	Z355131E	F	gone/gone
10428	-	$5	1902PB	604	12328 B	K613014H	CU	gone/gone
10428	-	$5	1902PB	604	12924 B	T668285H	VG	gone/gone
10428	-	$5	1902PB	604	13055 B	Y592766H	VF	gone/gone
10428	M	$10	1902PB	630	3798 B	Z571411B	F/VF	light sigs
10428		$10	1902PB	630	4741 ?	K44743D	VG	
10428		$10	1902PB	630	6341 ?	B845033E	VG	
10428		$10	1902PB	630	7393 C	B235535H	VG	
10428	-	$10	1902PB	630	9315 B	9315 B	F/VF	Higgins Mus.

THE FIRST NATIONAL BANK OF MCGREGOR   21 L   19 S
323   CLAYTON

Chartered on December 19, 1863 with a capital of $50,000. Placed in voluntary liquidation on May 29, 1933; capital of $50,000. Absorbed by The Marquette Savings Bank, Marquette.
Officers: Pres. Samuel Merrill 1867, JH Merrill 1868-71, Frank Larrabee 1872-1907, Thos Updegraff 1908-10, Wm R Kinnaird 1911-13, WF Daubenberger 1914-33; **VP** Wm Larrabee 1896-1900, Thos Updegraff 1902-07, Wm R Kinnaird 1909-10, DS Baird 1911 Albert Clemens 1913, CJ Weiser 1914, Henry Reeves 1914, FG Bell 1920, Albert Clemens 1922-33; **Cash.** Oley Aulverson 1867-71, William R Kinnaird 1872-1907, Fred S Richards 1908-33; **AC** Fred S Richards 1896-1902, RA Clemens 1911-13

First Charter, Original Issue	Ser #	# Notes
1-1-1-2	1-2600	10,400
5-5-5-5	1-5500	22,000
10-10-10-20	1-1190	4,760
First Charter, Series of 1875		
1-1-1-2	1-660	2,640
5-5-5-5	1-2705	10,820
10-10-10-20	1-1000	4,000
Second Charter, Brown Backs		
10-10-10-20	1-3824	15,296
Third Charter, Red Seal		
10-10-10-20	1-1000	4,000
Third Charter, Date Back, Blue Seal		
10-10-10-20	1-1400	5,600
Third Charter, Plain Back, Blue Seal		
10-10-10-20	1401-3528	8,512
1929, Type I		
6-10's	1-410	2,460
6-20's	1-104	624

Total amount of circulation issued = $744,580. Amount of large outstanding at close = $4,910. Amount of small outstanding at close = $20,090.
88,028 Large   3,084 Small   91,112 Total

Charter		Denom	Series	Plate	Sheet/Pos	Serial	Grade	Notes
323	-	$1	ORIG	380	119 ?	286955	?	
323	-	$1	ORIG	380	558 A	?	F	
323	-	$1	ORIG	380	1395 A	D318969	VG	pen/pen
323	-	$2	ORIG	387	401 A	287237	G	pen/pen

323	-	$2	ORIG	387	1284 A	D318858	VG	pen Higgins Mus.
323	M	$20	1902RS	639	98 A	A703665	VG	
323	M	$20	1902RS	639	388 A	A703955	?	
323	M	$20	1902RS	639	390 A	A703957	VF	Higgins Mus.
323	M	$20	1902RS	639	392 A	?	AU	
323	M	$20	1902RS	639	393 A	?	AU	
323	M	$20	1902RS	639	441 A	A704008	F/VF	
323	M	$10	1902DB	616	1028 ?	U30500A	VG	
323	M	$20	1902DB	642	1354 B	A318088B	F	
323	M	$10	1902PB	624	1624 B	H948244D	F/VF	
323	M	$10	1902PB	624	1707 ?	H948327D	F/VF	
323		$20	1902PB	624	2671 D	V887973H	XF	
323	M	$20	1902PB	650	1624 ?	H948244D	F+	pen/pen
323	M	$20	1902PB	650	1932 B	H388854E	VG	sigs Stained
323	M	$20	1902PB	650	2010 B	H388932E	F	
323	M	$20	1902PB	650	2648 B	M344430H	VF	pen/pen
323	M	$20	1902PB	650	2665 B	M344447H	XF	Higgins Mus.
323		$10	1929T1		B000001A		CU	
323		$10	1929T1		C000001A		CU	
323		$10	1929T1		D000001A		CU	
323		$10	1929T1		F000001A		CU	
323		$10	1929T1		A000124A		XF+	
323		$10	1929T1		D000234A		F	
323		$10	1929T1		F000289A		F	
323		$10	1929T1		E000341A		F/VF	Higgins Mus.
323		$10	1929T1		C000347A		F/VF	
323		$20	1929T1		B000001A		XF	
323		$20	1929T1		C000001A		CU	
323		$20	1929T1		D000001A		CU	
323		$20	1929T1		E000001A		CU	
323		$20	1929T1		E000039A		VF	
323		$20	1929T1		C000064A		VG/F	Foxing spot
323		$20	1929T1		F000070A		VF	
323		$20	1929T1		E000084A		F	
323		$20	1929T1		C000089A		F	
323		$20	1929T1		E000089A		VF	Soiled back

THE FIRST NATIONAL BANK OF MELVIN 4 L
5616 OSCEOLA

Organized on October 9, 1900 with a capital of $25,000. Placed in receivership on February 12, 1929; capital of $25,000. Reason for failure: incompetent management.

Officers: Pres. Frank Y Locke 1900-05, HL Emmert 1906-09, JF Mattert 1910-29; **VP** Carrol Wright 1902-03, JF Mattert 1907, WT Steiner 1909-20, JJ Ellerbroek 1922-28; **Cash.** EB Townsend 1900-05, Geo A Romey 1906-17, HI Ramsey 1918-28, BB Abels 1907-09, Art M Evans 1913-14, AC Graves 1920-25, FF Fairbrother 1920, Geo W Bauman 1926-28

Second Charter, Brown Backs	Ser #	# Notes
10-10-10-20	1-920	3,680
Second Charter, Date Back		
10-10-10-20	1-940	3,760
Second Charter, Value Back		
10-10-10-20	941-1183	972
Third Charter, Plain Back, Blue Seal		
5-5-5-5	1-3259	13,036

Total amount issued = $170,330. Amount outstanding at close = $12,500.
21,448 Large   0 Small   21,448 Total

5616	M	$5	1902PB	607	898 D	V580854E	VG+	vp Higgins Mus.
5616	-	$5	1902PB	607	2464 D	2464 D	VF/XF	gone/faded
5616	-	$5	1902PB	607	2806 B	2806 B	VG	
5616	-	$5	1902PB	607	3200 D	3200 D	F/VF	stamp/stamp

THE FIRST NATIONAL BANK OF MILFORD 7 L
5539 DICKINSON

Succeeded The Commercial Savings Bank. Organized on August 3, 1900 with a $35,000. Placed in receivership on July 8, 1926; capital of $35,000.

Officers: Pres. Pete Rasmussen 1900-16, CF Mauss 1917-26; **VP** ML Brown 1900-02, C Torstenson 1903-14, PO Bjorenson 1917-20, AL Lodge 1922-24, Eugene Dodge 1925-26; **Cash.** HS Abbott 1900-03, CF Mauss 1904-16, LD Daily 1917-24, MO Hanson 1925-26; **AC** SA Schneider 1900-02, CF Mauss 1903, LO Pillsbury 1904, VD Flemming 1907-10, PO Bjorenson 1911-13, LD Daily 1914, PO Bjorenson 1914-16, OC Holcomb 1920-25, LL Groff 1922-26

Second Charter, Brown Backs	Ser #	# Notes
10-10-10-20	1-1080	4,320
Second Charter, Date Back		
10-10-10-20	1-2160	8,640
Second Charter, Value Back		
10-10-10-20	2161-2594	1,736
Third Charter, Plain Back, Blue Seal		
10-10-10-20	1-1608	6,432

Total amount of issued = $264,100. Amount outstanding at close =$24,000.
21,128 Large   0 Small   21,128 Total

5539	M	$10	1882DB	545	1645 F	T188353	F	Higgins Mus.
5539	M	$10	1882DB	545	2141 D	T310079	F	pen/pen
5539	M	$20	1882DB	555	167 B	D472717	VF/XF	pen/pen
5539	M	$20	1882DB	555	720 B	H934258	F+	pen/pen
5539	M	$20	1882DB	555	1555 B	T188263	XF	Higgins Mus.
5539	M	$10	1882VB	577	2373 E	U853111	F+	Higgins Mus.
5539	M	$20	1882VB	581	2329 B	U853067	F+	Higgins Mus.

THE MILFORD NATIONAL BANK 5 L
9298 (FIRST TITLE) DICKINSON

Organized on November 27, 1908 with a capital of $25,000. Title changed to The Security National Bank of Milford on October 10, 1921.

Officers: Pres. Milton S Dewey 1909-11, HH Overocker 1912-17, JF May 1918-21; **VP** HH Overocker 1909-11, JF May 1913-14, QC Fuler 1918-21; **Cash.** HS Abbott 1909-11, FA Heldridge 1912-16, EL Ewen 1917, CT Stevens 1918-21; **AC** FA Heldridge 1909-11, EL Ewen 1913-14, Grace E House 1918, WG Anderson 1918, CE Menor 1919-20, VH Downey 1920-21

Third Charter, Date Back, Blue Seal	Ser #	# Notes
10-10-10-20	1-2120	8,480
Third Charter, Plain Back, Blue Seal		
10-10-10-20	2121-3360	4,960

13,440 Large   0 Small   13,440 Total

9298	M	$10	1902DB	618	958 A	U782014	F/VF	stamp/stamp
9298	M	$10	1902DB	618	1152 C	A61315A	XF	gone/pen
9298	M	$10	1902DB	618	1991 C	Z591925A	VF+	Higgins Mus.
9298	M	$10	1902PB	626	3321 C	A515803E	AU	pen/pen vp
9298	M	$10	1902PB	626	3329 C	A515811E	VF	pen/pen vp

THE SECURITY NATIONAL BANK OF MILFORD 2 L 3 S
9298 (2ND TITLE) DICKINSON

Succeeded The Milford National Bank on October 10, 1921. Placed in receivership on May 11, 1931; capital of $25,000.

Officers: Pres. JF May 1921, Wm R Gillette 1922-31; **VP** QC Fuler 1921, WC Meyers 1922-25, CC Fuller 1922, JF Ewen 1923-25, JF Yager 1927-31; **Cash.** CT Stevens 1921, Richard S Davis 1922-30; **AC** VH Downey 1921, AP Meyers 1922-24, HL Burk 1925-27, CW Moeller 1927-30

Third Charter, Date Back, Blue Seal	Ser #	# Notes
10-10-10-20	1-1990	7,960
1929, Type I		
6-10's	1-318	1,908
6-20's	1-84	504

Total amount of circulation issued = $296,660. Amount outstanding at close = $25,000. Amount of large outstanding at close = $4,380.

7,960 Large	2,412 Small		10,372 Total			
9298	- $10 1902PB	626	1318 C	1318 C	VF+	Higgins Mus.
9298	- $20 1902PB	652	1669 A	1669 A	VF/XF	stamp/pen
9298	$10 1929T1	E000021A			F	
9298	$20 1929T1	B000021A			VG	Red mark
9298	$20 1929T1	C000061A			VG+	Higgins Mus.

THE NATIONAL BANK OF MILTON   4 L   4 L
10243   VAN BUREN

Organized on August 9, 1912 with a capital of $25,000. Placed in receivership on June 25, 1932; capital of $25,000.

Officers: Pres. Henry C Taylor 1912-30, SF McConnell 1930-32; **VP** EE Hoskins 1913-14, SF McConnell 1920-30, R Townsend 1930-32; **Cash.** UG Rice 1912-32; **AC** DM Rowe 1920, HC Huddleston 1923-32

Third Charter, Date Back, Blue Seal	Ser #	# Notes
10-10-10-20	1-510	2,040
Third Charter, Plain Back, Blue Seal		
10-10-10-20	511-1115	2,420
1929, Type I		
6-10's	1-120	720
6-20's	1-15	90

Total amount of circulation issued = $64,750. Amount of large outstanding at close = $1,550. Amount of small outstanding at close = $5,450.

4,460 Large	810 Small		5,270 Total			
10243M	$10 1902DB	620	165 B	M528588A	AU	Higgins Mus.
10243M	$10 1902PB	628	671 A	B817943E	VF	pen/pen
10243	- $10 1902PB	628	889 A	889 A	VF	pen/stamp
10243M	$20 1902PB	654	696 A	B817968E	Fr	
10243	$10 1929T1	D000063A			F	
10243	$10 1929T1	F000084A			VG/F	Higgins Mus.
10243	$20 1929T1	B000010A			CU	
10243	$20 1929T1	F000011A			XF/AU	

THE FIRST NATIONAL BANK OF MISSOURI VALLEY   12 L   17 S
3189   HARRISON

Chartered in 1884.

Officers: Pres. Orson B Dutton 1884-89, LM Kellogg 1890-1900, George A Kellogg 1901-18, JS McGavern 1919, Geo A Kellogg 1920-35; **VP** EW Hibbard 1896-1900, JE Blenkiron 1902-11, CH Deur 1913-22, JM O'Connor 1923-32, Robert W Harvey 1932-35; **Cash.** Jay G Dutton 1884-89, Jno S McGavren 1890-1919, HF Foss 1920-35; **AC** Geo A Kellogg 1896-1900, HF Foss 1902-35, GW Johnson 1914-19, HM Silsby 1920-35

Second Charter, Brown Backs	Ser #	# Notes
5-5-5-5	1-5715	22,860
50-100	1-398	796
Third Charter, Red Seal		
10-10-10-20	1-1900	7,600
Third Charter, Date Back, Blue Seal		
10-10-10-20	1-3040	12,160
Third Charter, Plain Back, Blue Seal		
10-10-10-20	3041-9329	25,156
1929, Type I		
6-10's	1-1196	71,176
6-20's	1-309	1,854

Total amount of circulation issued = $844,290. Amount of large outstanding in June 1935 = $4,170. Amount of small outstanding in June 1935 = $25,830.

68,572 Large	9,030 Small		77,602 Total			
3189	- $5 1882BB	467	1433 H	H198772	F	pen/pen
3189	$5 1882BB	467	5532 H	A727017A	F	
3189 M	$10 1902RS	613	364 C	B829763	F	
3189 M	$10 1902PB	624	6709 F	K503391H	VG+	
3189	- $10 1902PB	624	8531 E	8531 E	VG/F	Higgins Mus.
3189	- $10 1902PB	624	8612 E	8612 E	VG	faded/faded
3189	- $10 1902PB	624	9065 H	9065 H	G+	LR corner gone
3189 M	$20 1902PB	650	3477 B	V806387B	G+	
3189 M	$20 1902PB	650	4651 B	T288253D	VG	
3189 M	$20 1902PB	650	5466 B	H505508E	F/VF	faded/faded
3189	- $20 1902PB	650	7542 B	7542 B	VG	
3189	- $20 1902PB	650	9035 C	9035 C	VG/F	faded/faded
3189	$10 1929T1	F000235A			F	Pinholes
3189	$10 1929T1	B000290A			VG	
3189	$10 1929T1	B000384A			VG	
3189	$10 1929T1	F000510A			VF	
3189	$10 1929T1	A000561A			VG	
3189	$10 1929T1	A000584A			VF	
3189	$10 1929T1	A000699A			VG/F	
3189	$10 1929T1	F000949A			VF	Higgins Mus.
3189	$10 1929T1	A001005A			F	
3189	$10 1929T1	E001055A			F/VF	
3189	$10 1929T1	A001182A			VF	
3189	$10 1929T1	C001187A			F	
3189	$20 1929T1	F000005A			VG	Ink stains
3189	$20 1929T1	B000137A			?	Bayard
3189	$20 1929T1	C000238A			F/VF	
3189	$20 1929T1	E000282A			VG	
3189	$20 1929T1	F000303A			F	

THE FIRST NATIONAL BANK OF MONROE   2 L
2215   JASPER

Chartered on January 9, 1875. Succeeded by The Bank of Monroe.
Officers: Pres. Tunis Schenck 1876-77; **Cash.** RC Anderson 1876-77

First Charter, Original Issue	Ser #	# Notes
1-1-1-2	1-1000	4,000
5-5-5-5	1-1000	4,000
10-10-10-20	1-400	1,600

Total amount of circulation issued = $45,000. Amount outstanding at close = $35,700. Amount outstanding in 1910 = $184.

9,600 Large	0 Small		9,600 Total			
2215	- $1 ORIG	382	1 C	E191568	VF	Grinnell # 1596, Higgins Museum
2215	- $2 ORIG	389	1 A	E191568	VF	Grinnell # 1597, Higgins Museum

THE MONROE NATIONAL BANK   2 L   1 S
7357   JASPER

Chartered in August 1904. Placed in voluntary liquidation on August 7, 1931; capital of $50,000. Succeeded by The Monroe State Bank.

Officers: Pres. AJ Porter 1905-13, Fred Whitehead 1914-16, Geo H Orcutt 1917-22, CB Livingston 1923-30; **VP** Fred Whitehead 1907-13, Geo H Orcutt 1914, CB Livingston 1920-22, HL Orcutt 1923-27, Frank Chipps 1928-30; **Cash.** Chas T Schenck 1905-09, FB Kingdon 1910-28, Ulrie Clevenger 1930; **AC** FB Kingdon 1907-09, AG Warren 1910-11, Frank Chipps 1913-20, RO Kingdon 1920-30

Third Charter, Red Seal	Ser #	# Notes
10-10-10-20	1-400	1,600
Third Charter, Date Back, Blue Seal		
10-10-10-20	1-600	2,400
Third Charter, Plain Back, Blue Seal		
10-10-10-20	601-1168	2,272
1929, Type I		
6-10's	1-92	552
6-20's	1-11	66

Total amount of circulation issued = $85,240. Amount of large outstanding at close = $1,480. Amount of small outstanding at close = $5,520.

6,272 Large	618 Small		6,890 Total			
7357	$10 1902PB	624	738 F	B219010E	VF+	Higgins Mus.
7357	$10 1902PB	624	792 F	X401834E	VF+	Higgins Mus.
7357	$20 1929T1	C000009A			F	

THE FIRST NATIONAL BANK OF MONTEZUMA   12 L
2961   POWESHIEK

Organized on May 21, 1883 with a capital of $50,000. Succeeded The Bank of Montezuma. Placed in receivership on September 16, 1929; capital of $50,000. Reason for failure: incompetent management.

Officers: Pres. John Hall 1883-96, John Hall, Sr. 1897-98, Thomas Harris 1899-1902, John Hall, Jr. 1902-04, Charles R Clark 1905-07, AF Rayburn 1908-11, John H Porter 1912-17, ED Rayburn 1918-20, JM Grimes 1922, ED Rayburn 1923-29; **VP** CAC Harris 1896, AF Rayburn 1900-07, John H Porter 1909-11, ED Rayburn 1913-14, Edw B Williams 1920-29; **Cash.** George W Kieruilff 1883-96, John Hall, Jr. 1897-1911, ED Rayburn 1902-11, Arthur C Heath 1912-29; **AC** John Hall, Jr. 1885-96, ED Rayburn 1900-02, Arthur C Heath 1904-11, Sadie E Smith 1913-25, Bertha K McDonald 1928-29

Second Charter, Brown Backs	Ser #	# Notes
10-10-10-20	1-2580	10,320
Third Charter, Red Seal		
10-10-10-20	1-2300	9,200
Third Charter, Date Back, Blue Seal		
10-10-10-20	1-2980	11,920
Third Charter, Plain Back, Blue Seal		
10-10-10-20	2981-9174	24,776
1929, Type I		
6-10's	1-21	125

$10 type 1 = $1,250 worth; serial # F000001A not issued. Total amount of circulation issued = $703,950. Amount of large outstanding at close =

$47,000. Amount of small outstanding at close = $1,250.
56,216 Large   125 Small   56,341 Total

2961	-	$10 1882BB	480	2118 A	X699895	VF	
2961	-	$20 1882BB	494	1364 A	V38877	VG	
2961	M	$10 1902DB	616	2161 D	M673438A	VG	pen/pen
2961	M	$20 1902DB	642	1519 B	D503210A	F+	
2961	M	$10 1902PB	624	3303 D	U51391B	G/VG	LR corner gone
2961	M	$10 1902PB	624	4133 E	B13820D	VG	
2961	M	$10 1902PB	624	5816 E	K235548E	F/VF	pen/pen
2961	M	$10 1902PB	624	6259 F	U999531E	VF+	Higgins Mus.
2961	M	$20 1902PB	650	5454 B	A518396E	F	
2961	M	$20 1902PB	650	5747 B	K235479E	VG	
2961	M	$20 1902PB	650	6784 B	K45536H	VG	
2961	-	$20 1902PB	650	7805 B	7805 B	VG	pen/pen

THE MONTICELLO NATIONAL BANK   3 L
2080   JONES
Chartered on February 3, 1873. Succeeded The Monticello State Bank. The firm of Carpenter & Lovell merged on January 1875. Placed in voluntary liquidation on March 30, 1875; capital of $100,000. Succeeded by The Monticello Bank.
Officers: Pres. SC Langworthy 1874-75; **Cash.** John O Duer 1874-75

First Charter, Original Issue	Ser #	# Notes
1-1-1-2	1-1500	6,000
10-10-10-20	1-823	3,292

Total amount of circulation issued = $48,650. Amount outstanding at close = $45,000. Amount outstanding in 1910 = $121.
9,292 Large   0 Small   9,292 Total

2080	-	$1	ORIG 382	2 ?	D462592	?	
2080	-	$2	ORIG 389	1 A	D462591	VF+	Higgins Mus.
2080	-	$2	ORIG 389	999 A	D463589	VF	pen/pen Split

THE FIRST NATIONAL BANK OF MONTOUR   10 L 16 S
7469   TAMA
Organized on October 25, 1904 with a capital of $25,000. Placed in conservatorship on April 1, 1933. Placed in receivership on November 16, 1933; capital of $30,000.
Officers: Pres. AB Taplin 1905-1907, RM Tenny 1908-1911, HG Stiger 1912-16, ES Smith 1917-31; **VP** HG Stiger 1907-1911, RM Tenny 1913-14, OL Millard 1920-31; **Cash.** RE Austin, Jr. 1905-1919, GS Buchanan 1920-26, ER Cronk 1927-31; **AC** RW Adair 1907-1913, GL Franks 1914, 1920, ER Cronk 1920-1927, CE Webb 1924-26, Walter Dahl 1927, H Kubicek 1927, Walter E. Dahl 1927-31

Third Charter, Red Seal	Ser #	# Notes
10-10-10-20	1-796	3,184
Third Charter, Date Back, Blue Seal		
10-10-10-20	1-1910	7,640
Third Charter, Plain Back, Blue Seal		
10-10-10-20	1911-5524	14,456
1929, Type I		
6-10's	1-578	3,468
6-20's	1-178	1,068

Total amount of circulation issued = $372,040. Amount of large outstanding at close = $2,390. Amount of small outstanding at close = $27,610.
25,280 Large   4,536 Small   29,816 Total

7469	M	$10 1902RS	613	262 C	E54335	F/VF	pen/pen Rust
7469	M	$20 1902RS	639	299 A	E54372	VG/F	
7469		$10 1902PB	624	3201 D	E280293E	F/VF	
7469		$10 1902PB	624	4387 F	A604899K	VF	
7469	-	$10 1902PB	624	4619 D	4619 D	F	
7469	-	$10 1902PB	624	4945 E	4945 E	VG	
7469	-	$10 1902PB	624	5236 D	5236 D	VG	
7469	-	$10 1902PB	624	5266 D	5266 D	F	pen/pen
7469		$20 1902PB	650	3967 B	A253839H	F+	Higgins Mus.
7469	-	$20 1902PB	650	4746 B	4746 B	F/VF	pen Higgins Mus.
7469		$10 1929T1		F000104A		VF	
7469		$10 1929T1		D000182A		CU	
7469		$10 1929T1		E000182A		AU	
7469		$10 1929T1		F000182A		CU	Higgins Mus.
7469		$10 1929T1		E000185A		AU	
7469		$10 1929T1		E000188A		AU	
7469		$10 1929T1		D000243A		AU	
7469		$10 1929T1		B000246A		?	Bayard
7469		$10 1929T1		D000430A		CU	
7469		$10 1929T1		F000484A		F	
7469		$10 1929T1		B000542A		XF/AU	
7469		$20 1929T1		A000018A		VG/F	
7469		$20 1929T1		D000049A		F	
7469		$20 1929T1		D000066A		VF	
7469		$20 1929T1		E000078A		F	
7469		$20 1929T1		F000108A		F	

THE FIRST NATIONAL BANK OF MOULTON   5 L
5319   APPANOOSE

Organized on April 5, 1900 with a capital of $25,000. Chartered on May 1, 1900; succeeded Bradleys Bank. Placed in receivership on January 14, 1927; capital of $35,000. Reason for failure: local depression.
Officers: Pres. JA Bradley 1900-11, August Post 1912-1, JS Gregory 1917-19, S Richardson 1920-26; **VP** GW Blosser 1900-04, August Post 1905-07, JS Gregory 1909, GR Holbert 1910, JS Gregory 1911-14, WT Daniels 1920-24, JP Stansberry 1925-26; **Cash.** WC Stickney 1900-04, EL Stickney 1905-16, JJ James 1917, EL Stickney 1918-19, JJ James 1920-26; **AC** EL Stickney 1900-04, JJ James 1913-14, Paul Callen 1920-25, Lydia Blosser 1925-26

Second Charter, Brown Backs	Ser #	# Notes
10-10-10-20	1-1700	6,800
Second Charter, Date Back		
10-10-10-20	1-2480	9,920
Second Charter, Value Back		
10-10-10-20	2481-3566	4,344
Third Charter, Plain Back, Blue Seal		
10-10-10-20	1-3490	13,960

Total amount issued = $402,900. Amount outstanding at close = $33,800.
35,024 Large   0 Small   35,024 Total

5319	M	$10 1882BB	490	991 A	E167160E	VG	Tape on bank; ink
5319	-	$20 1882BB	504	764 A	Z707881	VG	pen/pen vp
5319	M	$10 1882DB	545	431 E	B571481	VF	
5319	M	$10 1882DB	545	2156 F	N953764	VG	Higgins Mus.
5319	M	$10 1902PB	633	2044 C	X88044	F	pen/pen

THE FIRST NATIONAL BANK OF MT. PLEASANT   33 L 12 S
299   HENRY
Chartered in 1864. Absorbed #922 on March 10, 1922. Placed in voluntary liquidation on January 13, 1931; capital of $100,000. Absorbed by The Henry County Savings Bank, Mount Pleasant.

First Charter, Original Issue	Ser #	# Notes
1-1-1-2	1-3700	14,800
5-5-5-5	1-2900	11,600
10-10-10-20	1-1730	6,920
First Charter, Series of 1875		
10-10-10-20	1-648	2,592
Second Charter, Brown Backs		
10-10-10-20	1-4762	19,048
Third Charter, Red Seal		
10-10-10-20	1-4500	18,000
Third Charter, Date Back, Blue Seal		
5-5-5-5	1-7715	30,860
10-10-10-20	1-4600	18,400
Third Charter, Plain Back, Blue Seal		
5-5-5-5	7716-18835	44,480
10-10-10-20	4601-12128	30,112
1929, Type I		
6-5's	1-1369	8,214
6-10's	1-602	3,612
6-20's	1-165	990

Total amount of circulation issued = $1,738,590. Amount of large outstanding at close = $19,197. Amount of small outstanding at close = $80,800.
196,812 Large   12,816 Small   209,628 Total

299	-	$1 ORIG	380	2510 B	B665223	F	Higgins Mus.
299	-	$10 1882BB	479	3138 B	U769073	VG+	Higgins Mus.
299	-	$20 1882BB	493	3504 A	U769439	F/VF	pen/pen
299	M	$20 1902RS	639	3358 A	R936943	VF	pen/pen
299	M	$20 1902RS	639	3060 A	R936645	F/VF	
299	M	$5 1902DB	590	4581 D	H631982A	VF/XF	
299	M	$5 1902DB	590	6421 B	H341138B	VG	gone/gone
299	M	$10 1902DB	616	2541 D	R639219A	G/VG	
299	M	$10 1902DB	616	2687 D	R639359A	VG/F	
299	M	$10 1902DB	616	3525 D	Y324211A	F	
299	M	$5 1902PB	598	8766 C	V5917B	F	
299	M	$5 1902PB	598	9025 D	V6176B	F+	
299	M	$5 1902PB	598	10466 A	B867147D	F	pen/stamp
299	M	$5 1902PB	598	12794 D	D575525E	VG	pen/faded
299	M	$5 1902PB	598	14198 C	N322504E	XF/AU	
299		$5 1902PB	598	16120 C	X426666H	?	
299		$5 1902PB	598	17523 D	?	VG	
299	-	$5 1902PB	598	17560 B	17560 B	Fr	Ink

Bank		Denom	Series	Plate	Ser # (start)	Ser # (end)	Grade	Notes
299	-	$5	1902PB	598	17619 B	17619 B	VF	
299	-	$5	1902PB	598	17648 A	17648 A	G	gone ac/gone
299	-	$5	1902PB	598	17781 A	17781 A	VF	stmp ac/gone
299	M	$10	1902PB	624	5156 D	Y390577B	G	pen/gone
299	M	$10	1902PB	624	5601 E	E272830D	VF	pen ac/stamp
299	M	$10	1902PB	624	9121 D	K803163H	VF	stamp/stamp
299	M	$10	1902PB	624	9186 E	K803228H	F	
299	-	$10	1902PB	624	9890 D	Y629672H	F	pen/stamp
299	-	$10	1902PB	624	10432 F	10432 F	VF	pen ac/stamp
299	-	$10	1902PB	624	10554 E	10554 E	F/VF	Higgins Mus.
299	-	$10	1902PB	624	11189 D	11189 D	Fr	
299	-	$10	1902PB	624	11476 F	11476 F	VG	
299	-	$20	1902PB	650	9653 B	Y629435H	F	
299	-	$20	1902PB	650	9807 B	Y629589H	VG	gone/gone
299	-	$20	1902PB	650	11865 B	11865 B	F	gone/gone
299		$5	1929T1		C000215A		VF+	
299		$10	1929T1		E000021A		XF	Higgins Mus.
299		$10	1929T1		A000031A		VG	
299		$10	1929T1		D000183A		?	
299		$10	1929T1		D000271A		VG	
299		$10	1929T1		E000287A		XF	
299		$10	1929T1		B000309A		VG	
299		$10	1929T1		E000337A		F	Stained
299		$20	1929T1		A000080A		F	
299		$20	1929T1		D000080A		G	
299		$20	1929T1		F000125A		?	
299		$20	1929T1		F000136A		VF/XF	

THE NATIONAL STATE BANK OF MT. PLEASANT   15 L
922   HENRY

Chartered in 1865. Placed in voluntary liquidation on March 10, 1922; capital of $100,000. Absorbed by #299.

	Ser #	# Notes
First Charter, Original Issue		
1-1-1-2	1-2910	11,640
5-5-5-5	1-3300	13,200
10-10-10-20	1-2100	8,400
First Charter, Series of 1875		
5-5-5-5	1-483	1,932
10-10-10-20	1-2187	8,748
Second Charter, Brown Backs		
10-10-10-20	1-6449	25,796
Third Charter, Red Seal		
10-10-10-20	1-3400	13,600
Third Charter, Date Back, Blue Seal		
10-10-10-20	1-5800	23,200
Third Charter, Plain Back, Blue Seal		
10-10-10-20	5801-10646	19,384

Total amount issued = $1,329,210. Amount outstanding at close = $97,700.
125,900 Large   0 Small   125,900 Total

Bank		Denom	Series	Plate	Ser #	Ser #	Grade	Notes
922	-	$20	1875	432	588 A	B124166	F	Blue end paper
922	-	$10	1882BB	480	4260 B	W487949	VG	pen/pen Pinholes
922	M	$10	1902RS	613	640 B	E405263	?	
922	M	$10	1902RS	613	1510 A	R167775	F	pen/pen
922	M	$10	1902RS	613	3169 B	X122576	VG	
922	M	$20	1902RS	639	499 A	E405122	VF	pen/pen
922	M	$10	1902DB	616	5364 F	Z357538A	F	
922	M	$10	1902DB	616	5429 F	N795527B	XF	Higgins Mus.
922	M	$20	1902DB	642	2286 B	X957992	VG	pen/pen
922	M	$20	1902DB	642	3074 B	D812410A	VG/F	pen/pen
922	M	$10	1902PB	624	6588 E	X436119B	G	
922	M	$10	1902PB	624	7763 D	A955300D	F/VF	
922	M	$10	1902PB	624	10460 E	A838132E	CU	pen/pen
922	M	$20	1902PB	650	6808 B	X436339B	F	lt. pen/pen
922	M	$20	1902PB	650	10282 B	A837954E	VG	lt. pen/pen

THE MERCHANTS EXCHANGE NATIONAL BANK OF MUSCATINE
1577 (FIRST TITLE)   MUSCATINE   1 L

Chartered in 1865. Title changed to The First National Bank of Muscatine on June 8, 1886.

Officers: Pres. Simon G Stein 1867-86; **Cash.** Peter Jackson 1867-78, Frank R Lewis 1878-82, TN Brown 1883-86

	Ser #	# Notes
First Charter, Original Issue		
5-5-5-5	1-1825	7,300
10-10-10-20	1-820	3,280
First Charter, Series of 1875		
5-5-5-5	1-100	400
10-10-10-20	1-1070	4,280
Second Charter, Brown Backs		
5-5-5-5	1-141	564
10-10-10-20	1-46	184
50-100 (All were redeemed.)	1-13	26

16,034 Large   0 Small   16,034 Total

1577		$10	1875	416	1066 C	H809010	F	Higgins Museum

THE FIRST NATIONAL BANK OF MUSCATINE   6 L   84 S
1577 (SECOND TITLE)   MUSCATINE

Succeeded The Merchants Exchange National Bank of Muscatine on June 8, 1886. Assumed The First Trust & Savings Bank of Muscatine by consolidation on July 29, 1930. Placed in voluntary liquidation on July 8, 1933; capital of $200,000. Succeeded by The First Trust & Savings Bank of Muscatine.

Officers: Pres. Simon G Stein 1886-91, HW Moore 1892-93, Simon G Stein 1894-1932; **VP** DV Jackson 1896-1930, RK Smith 1920-22, SG Stein, Jr. 1924-26, WF Bishop 1928-31, TC Clark 1930-32; **Cash.** TN Brown 1886-93, SM Hughes 1894-1914, TC Clark 1917-30, EE Bloom 1930-32; **AC** TC Clark 1910-14, AH Steinmetz 1920-27, HE Schroeder 1920-23, SG Stein, Jr. 1922-23, Geo F Hudson 1928-32, RJ Diercks 1930-32

	Ser #	# Notes
Second Charter, Brown Backs		
5-5-5-5	1-2590	10,360
10-10-10-20	1-1601	6,404
Third Charter, Red Seal		
5-5-5-5	1-700	2,800
10-10-10-20	1-390	1,560
Third Charter, Date Back, Blue Seal		
5-5-5-5	1-2015	8,060
10-10-10-20	1-1614	6,456
Third Charter, Plain Back, Blue Seal		
5-5-5-5	2016-4618	10,412
10-10-10-20	1615-3123	6,036
1929, Type I		
6-5's	1-2119	12,714
6-10's	1-1753	10,518
6-20's	1-460	2,760

Total amount of circulation issued = $777,880. Amount of large outstanding at close = $3,415. All of the old title Brown Back $50's and $100's were redeemed. Amount of small outstanding at close = $196,585.
52,088 Large   25,992 Small   78,080 Total

Bank		Denom	Series	Plate	Ser #	Ser #	Grade	Notes
1577	M	$5	1902DB	591	1257 F	Z435807	F	pen/pen
1577	M	$5	1902DB	591	1777 G	V801189A	F	
1577	-	$5	1902PB	599	3791 G	3791 G	VF	Davenport B&T
1577	M	$10	1902PB	625	1935 D	A619523E	CU	pen/pen
1577	-	$10	1902PB	625	2492 F	Y372590H	G/VG	vp Stained
1577	-	$10	1902PB	625	2650 F	2650 F	VF	Higgins Mus.
1577		$5	1929T1		A000001A		CU	
1577		$5	1929T1		B000001A		CU	
1577		$5	1929T1		C000001A		CU	
1577		$5	1929T1		D000001A		CU	
1577		$5	1929T1		E000001A		CU	
1577		$5	1929T1		F000001A		CU	
1577		$5	1929T1		F000543A		VG	
1577		$5	1929T1		F000604A		VG	
1577		$5	1929T1		D001113A		VG	
1577		$5	1929T1		D001116A		?	
1577		$5	1929T1		F001294A		F	
1577		$5	1929T1		E001693A		XF+	
1577		$5	1929T1		D001808A		?	
1577		$10	1929T1		D000001A		CU	
1577		$10	1929T1		F000100A		VG	
1577		$10	1929T1		A000175A		?	
1577		$10	1929T1		C000237A		F/VF	Spots on edge
1577		$10	1929T1		E000248A		VF+	
1577		$10	1929T1		D000484A		VF/XF	
1577		$10	1929T1		A000501A		?	
1577		$10	1929T1		F000505A		VG/F	
1577		$10	1929T1		F000671A		AU	
1577		$10	1929T1		D000677A		F/VF	
1577		$10	1929T1		F000686A		VF	
1577		$10	1929T1		F000737A		CU	
1577		$10	1929T1		F000754A		CU	Higgins Mus.
1577		$10	1929T1		A000793A		F	
1577		$10	1929T1		A000795A		F	
1577		$10	1929T1		F000816A		AU	
1577		$10	1929T1		B000821A		VG	
1577		$10	1929T1		E000931A		VG	
1577		$10	1929T1		F000967A		XF	
1577		$10	1929T1		A000975A		G	
1577		$10	1929T1		F000981A		F	
1577		$10	1929T1		F000984A		XF	
1577		$10	1929T1		D000995A		VG/F	
1577		$10	1929T1		F001000A		VG	
1577		$10	1929T1		E001020A		VF	
1577		$10	1929T1		E001037A		F	
1577		$10	1929T1		A001059A		F/VF	Washed

1577	$10	1929T1	B001258A	VG	
1577	$10	1929T1	A001317A	VG	Staining
1577	$10	1929T1	C001402A	VG/F	
1577	$10	1929T1	C001404A	F	
1577	$10	1929T1	F001431A	?	
1577	$10	1929T1	F001437A	AU	
1577	$10	1929T1	A001451A	XF	
1577	$10	1929T1	F001467A	VG	
1577	$10	1929T1	F001506A	F	
1577	$10	1929T1	F001511A	AU	
1577	$10	1929T1	C001528A	F	
1577	$10	1929T1	C001572A	XF	
1577	$10	1929T1	E001572A	AU	
1577	$10	1929T1	E001573A	CU	
1577	$10	1929T1	E001574A	CU	
1577	$10	1929T1	E001575A	?	
1577	$10	1929T1	E001576A	CU	
1577	$10	1929T1	E001577A	CU	
1577	$10	1929T1	E001578A	CU	
1577	$10	1929T1	D001735A	VG/F	
1577	$20	1929T1	A000001A	CU	
1577	$20	1929T1	B000001A	CU	
1577	$20	1929T1	C000001A	CU	
1577	$20	1929T1	D000001A	CU	
1577	$20	1929T1	E000001A	CU	
1577	$20	1929T1	F000001A	CU	
1577	$20	1929T1	F000016A	?	
1577	$20	1929T1	D000063A	XF	
1577	$20	1929T1	B000166A	VF/XF	Paper clip stain
1577	$20	1929T1	A000180A	VG	Writing and dark
1577	$20	1929T1	C000185A	VF	Tear
1577	$20	1929T1	C000191A	VF/XF	
1577	$20	1929T1	C000192A	VF/XF	
1577	$20	1929T1	C000194A	XF/AU	
1577	$20	1929T1	E000265A	?	
1577	$20	1929T1	A000340A	XF	
1577	$20	1929T1	D000358A	?	
1577	$20	1929T1	D000381A	F	Pinholes
1577	$20	1929T1	C000403A	AU	
1577	$20	1929T1	C000409A	VF	
1577	$20	1929T1	D000426A	AU	
1577	$20	1929T1	A000459A	CU	
1577	$20	1929T1	C000459A	CU	
1577	$20	1929T1	F000460A	CU	Last sheet of $20s

THE MUSCATINE NATIONAL BANK   **1 L**
692   **MUSCATINE**
Chartered in 1865. Placed in voluntary liquidation on September 2, 1878; capital of $100,000. Succeeded by G.A. Garrettson & Co.
Officers: Pres. JB Dougherty 1867-69, Jacob Butler 1870-73, JB Dougherty 1874-75, GA Garrettson 1876-78; **Cash.** Jos. Richardson 1867-69, FL Underwood 1870-73, AB Brown 1874-78

First Charter, Original Issue	Ser #	# Notes
5-5-5-5	1-2500	10,000
10-10-10-20	1-2220	8,880
First Charter, Series of 1875		
10-10-10-20	1-144	576

Total amount of circulation issued = $168,200. Amount outstanding at close = $44,200. Amount outstanding in 1910 = $1,215.
19,456 Large   0 Small   19,456 Total
692 - $5   ORIG   394   2091 C   N259968   F   Higgins Museum

THE FIRST NATIONAL BANK OF NASHUA   **0 L**
2411   **CHICKASAW**
Another publication reported a $10 1882 Brown Back from Nashua, but apparently that was an erroneous listing.
Chartered on February 15, 1879. Succeeded A.J. Felt. Consolidated with The Bank of Nashua in 1880. Placed in voluntary liquidation on November 1, 1894; capital of $50,000. Succeeded by A.G. Case & Company.
Officers: Pres. Almon G Case 1879-94; **Cash.** Andrew J Felt 1879, Amos Case 1880-89, EH Barnes 1890-94

First Charter, Series of 1875	Ser #	# Notes
10-10-10-20	1-2203	8,812

Total amount of circulation issued = $110,150. Amount outstanding at close = $11,250. Amount outstanding in 1910 = $570.
8,812 Large   0 Small   8,812 Total

THE FIRST NATIONAL BANK OF NEVADA   **22 L**
2555   **STORY**
Organized on August 3, 1881 with a capital of $50,000. Succeeded The Nevada City Bank. Placed in receivership on January 10, 1927; capital of $75,000. Reason for failure: local depression.
Officers: Pres. Elijah L Lyon 1881-82, RJ Silliman 1883-95, Wm Lockridge 1896-99, JA Fitchpatrick 1900-20, Fred C McCall 1922-23, JE Drybread 1924-26; **VP** JA Fitchpatrick 1896, James Dillin 1900, WF Swayze 1902, James D Ferner 1903-04, EP Zwilling 1907-13, FC McCall 1914-20, JE Drybread 1922-23, SM McHose 1924-26; **Cash.** Wilber F Swayze 1881-1901, Edgar John 1902-09, Edgar A Fawcett 1910-27; **AC** JA Fitchpatrick 1885, FH Greenwalt 1900-02, Willard John 1903-07, Edgar A Fawcett 1909, Geo A Klove 1910-26, Carl E Stone 1924-26

First Charter, Series of 1875	Ser #	# Notes
10-10-10-20	1-3332	13,328
Second Charter, Brown Backs		
50-100	1-827	1,654
Second Charter, Date Back		
5-5-5-5	1-5330	21,320
50-100	1-500	1,000
50-50-50-100	1-504	2,016
Second Charter, Value Back		
5-5-5-5	5331-8680	13,400
Third Charter, Plain Back, Blue Seal		
5-5-5-5	1-13194	52,776

Total amount issued = $895,810. Amount outstanding at close = $73,300.
105,494 Large   0 Small   105,494 Total

2555	-	$10	1875	420	2037 A	A956218	VF	pen/pen
2555	-	$10	1875	420	2363 A	A977929	F	pen sigs Washed
2555	-	$10	1875	420	2640 B	A979451	F+	pen/pen ac
2555	-	$10	1875	420	3304 B	A980115	VG	Higgins Mus.
2555		$50	1882BB	518	373 A	B416082	F+	Davenport B&T
2555	M	$50	1882BB	518	816 A	B584261	XF	
2555	M	$5	1882DB	537	1746 B	H117053	F	stamp Higg. Mus.
2555	M	$5	1882DB	537	2414 B	H117721	VF	stamp/stamp
2555	M	$5	1882DB	537	3262 B	M467444	VF	
2555	M	$5	1882DB	537	4621 B	R502278	VG	gone/gone
2555	M	$5	1882DB	537	4658 D	R502315	VG	
2555	M	$50	1882DB	563	440 D	A159114	F	
2555	M	$50	1882DB	563	478 B	A160899	VF	stamp/stamp
2555	M	$5	1882VB	574	8601 C	U573883	G/VG	gone/gone
2555	M	$5	1902PB	608	209 C	D631755E	VG	stamp/stamp
2555	M	$5	1902PB	608	1253 C	D679949E	F	
2555	M	$5	1902PB	608	4903 A	X237959E	VG	stamp/stamp
2555	M	$5	1902PB	608	6238 C	H397524H	VG	stamp/stamp
2555	-	$5	1902PB	608	9163 A	Y702124H	VF	
2555	-	$5	1902PB	608	9387 C	Y702348H	VG/F	
2555	-	$5	1902PB	608	10612 A	10612 A	?	gone/gone
2555	-	$5	1902PB	608	11663 B	11663 B	VF	Higgins Mus.

NEVADA NATIONAL BANK   **4 S**
14065   **STORY**
Chartered in March 1934 with a capital of $50,000. Succeeded #13083.
Officers: Pres. SM McHose 1934-35; **VP** HW Bowers 1934-35; **Cash.** LR Bassett 1934-35; **AC** Agnes Jacobsen 1934-35, GL Henry 1935

1929, Type II	Ser #	# Notes
5's	1-2460	2,460
10's	1-1260	1,260
20's	1-300	300

Total amount of circulation issued = $30,900. Amount outstanding on June 5, 1935 = $25,000.
0 Large   4,020 Small   4,020 Total

14065	$5	1929T2	A001974	F+	
14065	$10	1929T2	A000405	F	
14065	$10	1929T2	A000806	F/VF	
14065	$20	1929T2	A000279	VG	

THE FIRST NATIONAL BANK OF NEW HAMPTON   **14 L**
2588   **CHICKASAW**
Organized on May 3, 1881 with a capital of $50,000. Succeeded The Chickasaw County Bank (Easton & Bigelow) and The Bank of New Hampton. Placed in receivership on December 9, 1926; capital of $50,000.
Officers: Pres. Alfred E Bigelow 1883-87, OB Sherman 1888-89, Alfred E Bigelow 1890-1906, Grant M Bigelow 1907-23, Tim Donovan 1924-26; **VP** H Gurley 1896, JW Sandusky 1900-04, 1925-26, Tim Donovan 1907-23, John H Kolthoff 1924-26; **Cash.** Samuel J Kenyon 1883-89, Tim Donovan 1890-1905, CA Larson 1906-13, CH Kenyon 1914-24, Jos W Krieger 1925-26; **AC** Grant M Bigelow 1896-1904, CH Kenyon 1907-13, Jos W Krieger 1914-24, AC Klatt 1920-26, TJ McCarthy 1924-26

First Charter, Series of 1875	Ser #	# Notes
5-5-5-5	1-4502	18,008
Second Charter, Brown Backs		
5-5-5-5	1-1525	6,100
10-10-10-20	1-1120	4,480

Second Charter, Date Back
5-5-5-5	1-2900	11,600
10-10-10-20	1-2060	8,240

Second Charter, Value Back
5-5-5-5	2901-4398	5,992
10-10-10-20	2061-2914	3,416

Third Charter, Plain Back, Blue Seal
5-5-5-5	1-2937	11,748
10-10-10-10	1-2704	10,816

Total amount issued = $577,100. Amount outstanding at close = $43,200.
80,400 Large 0 Small 80,400 Total

2588	-	$5	1875	405	4269 D	Y431252	F	pen/pen vp
2588	-	$5	1875	405	4497 C	Y541150	XF	Higgins Mus.
2588	-	$5	1875	405	4500 D	Y541153	XF	vp
2588	M	$5 1882DB	537	1036 F	H114223	VG	Higgins Mus.
2588	M	$10 1882DB	545	1604 F	N633732	VG	
2588	M	$5 1882VB	574	3379 E	T99266	CU	Small hole UR
2588	M	$5 1882VB	574	3396 E	T99283	XF	faded/faded
2588	M	$5 1882VB	574	3478 G	T99365	VF+	
2588	M	$5 1882VB	574	3549 E	T506236	CU	
2588	M	$5 1902PB	607	864 D	D249210E	F	gone Higg. Mus.
2588	M	$5 1902PB	607	1024 A	D249370E	HG	gone/gone
2588	M	$5 1902PB	607	2015 B	H339701H	VF	pen/pen
2588	-	$10 1902PB	633	1863 C	X793298	F	pen/pen Tear
2588	-	$10 1902PB	633	2104 B	Y233749	G/VG	pen/pen

THE SECOND NATIONAL BANK OF NEW HAMPTON   25 L   14 S
7607   CHICKASAW

Organized on January 3, 1905 with a capital of $50,000. Placed in receivership on July 14, 1931; capital of $100,000. Reason for failure: incompetent management & local depression.

Officers: Pres. WG Shaffer 1905-22, WH Shaffer 1923, WG Shaffer 1924-26, GM Bailey 1926-30, SE Johnston 1930-31; **VP** TK Young 1907-26, LM Utley 1926, SE Johnston 1927-30, Thomas Dowd 1930-31; **Cash.** AH Shaffer 1905-26, CB Phillips 1926-31; **AC** TK Young 1909, J Reilly 1911, CB Phillips 1913-26, Vida L Sewell 1922-30, LC Shaffer 1925-26, WG Greenwald 1926-28, Alva Griffith 1929-31

Third Charter, Red Seal	Ser #	# Notes
10-10-10-20	1-2100	8,400

Third Charter, Date Back, Blue Seal
10-10-10-20	1-6100	24,400

Third Charter, Plain Back, Blue Seal
10-10-10-20	6101-17422	45,288

1929, Type I
6-10's	1-1138	6,828
6-20's	1-313	1,878

Total amount of circulation issued = $1,081,940. Amount of large outstanding at close = $19,670. Amount of small outstanding at close = $80,330.
78,088 Large   8,706 Small   86,794 Total

7607	M	$10 1902RS	613	390 C	E198918	F	
7607	M	$10 1902RS	613	1161 B	E938533	VG+	sigs
7607	M	$10 1902RS	613	1324 B	R971927	VF	gone/gone
7607	M	$10 1902DB	616	2009 D	A404532A	VG	
7607	M	$10 1902DB	616	2038 F	A404561A	XF+	gone Higg. Mus.
7607	M	$10 1902DB	616	2110 D	A404633A	VG	gone/gone
7607	M	$10 1902DB	616	5645 D	B142139B	F/VF	
7607	M	$20 1902DB	642	2710 A	A405233A	VF	stamp UR torn
7607	M	$10 1902PB	624	7295 F	X626946B	F	Rust, holes
7607	M	$10 1902PB	624	8303 D	H762713D	F/VF	
7607	M	$10 1902PB	624	9435 D	R363597D	VF	stamp/stamp
7607	M	$10 1902PB	624	9593 D	Y665465D	VG	stamp/stamp
7607	M	$10 1902PB	624	12333 E	A111275H	VG/F	stamp/stamp
7607	-	$10 1902PB	624	13686 D	U431798H	VF	stamp/stamp
7607	-	$10 1902PB	624	13917 F	A72359K	F	
7607	-	$10 1902PB	624	14909 D	14909 D	VG	
7607	-	$10 1902PB	624	15000 E	15000 E	VF	pen/pen
7607	-	$10 1902PB	624	16339 E	16339 E	Fr/G	gone/gone
7607	-	$10 1902PB	624	16698 D	16698 D	VG	gone/gone
7607	-	$10 1902PB	624	17266 E	17266 E	F	
7607	-	$20 1902PB	650	? M128429H	?	Bayard	
7607	-	$20 1902PB	650	13489 B	U431601H	F	stamp Bayard
7607	-	$20 1902PB	650	14287 B	A72729K	F/VF	stamp/stamp
7607	-	$20 1902PB	650	15068 B	15068 B	VG	stamp/stamp
7607	-	$20 1902PB	650	15694 B	15694 B	VF	stamp/stamp
7607		$10 1929T1		A000066A		F	
7607		$10 1929T1		A000077A		VF	
7607		$10 1929T1		F000100A		VG/F	Higgins Mus.
7607		$10 1929T1		D000243A		VG	
7607		$10 1929T1		E000306A		F	
7607		$10 1929T1		E000360A		VF	
7607		$10 1929T1		B000590A		F/VF	
7607		$10 1929T1		C000923A		G/VG	
7607		$10 1929T1		D000999A		F	
7607		$10 1929T1		D001105A		?	
7607		$20 1929T1		C000128A		VG	
7607		$20 1929T1		E000182A		F/VF	Pressed
7607		$20 1929T1		D000232A		F	
7607		$20 1929T1		E000250A		VF	

THE FIRST NATIONAL BANK OF NEW LONDON   1 L
5420   HENRY

Chartered on June 13, 1900. Placed in voluntary liquidation on December 31, 1909; capital of $25,000.

Officers: Pres. Robt. S Gillis 1900-07, JE Peterson 1908-09; **VP** JE Peterson 1900-07, Jas T Whiting 1909; **Cash.** VH Shields 1900-07, WH Bangs 1908, HL McGrew 1909; **AC** HE Walker 1903, Virgil Breneman 1907

Second Charter, Brown Backs	Ser #	# Notes
10-10-10-20	1-1800	7,200

Second Charter, Date Back
10-10-10-20	1-48	192

Total amount of circulation issued = $92,400. Amount outstanding at close = $25,000. Amount outstanding in 1910 = $14,870.
7,392 Large   0 Small   7,392 Total

5420	M	$10 1882BB	490	1598 C	U103868H	VF	Higgins Museum

THE NEW LONDON NATIONAL BANK   7 L   10 S
8352   HENRY

Organized on August 22, 1906 with a capital of $25,000. Placed in conservatorship on June 1, 1933. Placed in receivership on October 30, 1933; capital of $25,000.

Officers: Pres. WJ Francy 1907-14, FN Smith 1915-27, EF Hasenclever 1928-33; **VP** Sam'l. Keiser 1907-14, JM Crawford 1920-24, Geo W Nugen 1925, Ira Redfearn 1925-26, JM Crawford 1926-27, Ira Redfearn 1928-33, EE McKee 1930-33; **Cash.** TL White 1907-08, OH Tyner 1909-13, EE McKee 1914-30, FW Goldthwaite 1930-33; **AC** Jesse Walker 1909-11, EE McKee 1913, Charles E Walker 1914, Chas M Hodgson 1920-25, Sevella Petzinger 1920-33, JP Hemmings 1925-29, EJ Olson 1933

Third Charter, Red Seal	Ser #	# Notes
10-10-10-10	1-775	3,100

Third Charter, Date Back, Blue Seal
10-10-10-10	1-1925	7,700

Third Charter, Plain Back, Blue Seal
10-10-10-10	1926-5377	13,808

1929, Type I
6-10's	1-686	4,116

Total amount of circulation issued = $287,240. Amount of large outstanding at close = $1,570. Amount of small outstanding at close = $18,430.
24,608 Large   4,116 Small   28,724 Total

8352	M	$10 1902PB	626	1980 H	N442245	VG/F	pen ac/pen vp
8352	M	$10 1902PB	626	2460 G	R126050	F	ac/vp Higg. Mus.
8352	-	$10 1902PB	626	4320 F	Y395765	VG+	pen/pen
8352	-	$10 1902PB	626	4670 H	4670 H	CU	pen/pen
8352	-	$10 1902PB	626	4903 F	4903 F	F	pen ac/pen
8352	-	$10 1902PB	626	4937 F	4937 F	?	
8352	-	$10 1902PB	626	5182 ?	5182 ?	?	
8352		$10 1929T1		B000037A		G	Tear, tape
8352		$10 1929T1		B000087A		F/VF	
8352		$10 1929T1		B000101A		VF	
8352		$10 1929T1		A000386A		AU	Higgins Mus.
8352		$10 1929T1		F000393A		F/VF	
8352		$10 1929T1		B000401A		XF	
8352		$10 1929T1		F000427A		VG	
8352		$10 1929T1		B000505A		VF	
8352		$10 1929T1		F000546A		F	
8352		$10 1929T1		B000583A		VG	

THE FIRST NATIONAL BANK OF NEW SHARON   5 L
8950   MAHASKA

Chartered in November 1907. Placed in voluntary liquidation on June 1, 1926; capital of $50,000. Absorbed by The Citizens State Bank, New Sharon.

Officers: Pres. Geo H Barbour 1908-13, M Bainbridge 1914, GM Garner 1915-25, PT Cope 1925-26; **VP** GM Garner 1909-11, TR Osborne 1913-14, WE Patterson 1920-26; **Cash.** M Bainbridge 1908-13, JB Heitsman 1914, BB Watson 1915-26; **AC** ER Raffety 1909-11, Lena Sexton 1913-14, Verah Schlegel 1920, FW Else 1922-23, Phillip Patterson 1925-26

Third Charter, Red Seal	Ser #	# Notes
5-5-5-5	1-667	2,668
10-10-10-10	1-635	2,540

Third Charter, Date Back, Blue Seal
5-5-5-5	1-3250	13,000
10-10-10-10	1-2950	11,800

Third Charter, Plain Back, Blue Seal

5-5-5-5			3251-8399		20,596	
10-10-10-10			2951-6885		15,740	

Total amount issued = $482,120. Amount outstanding at close = $50,000.

66,344 Large 0 Small 66,344 Total

8950	M	$5 1902DB	592	1971 G	M72422A	G+	pen/pen
8950	M	$10 1902DB	618	2491 E	K85899	VF+	Higgins Mus.
8950	M	$5 1902PB	601	3887 F	U289303B	VG	faded/faded
8950	M	$10 1902PB	626	4315 H	T65555	VG/F	
8950	M	$10 1902PB	626	5819 G	V362219	F/VF	

THE FIRST NATIONAL BANK OF NEWELL   7 L   18 S
10191   BUENA VISTA

Organized on April 23, 1912 with a capital of $25,000. Placed in conservatorship on June 1, 1933. Placed in receivership on September 18, 1933; capital of $25,000. Restored to solvency on November 27, 1934. The $10 1902PB note s/n 2104A came from the estate of the daughter of Assistant Cashier Laverne A Erickson. The family stated that it was the only note he was ever allowed to sign.

Officers: Pres. JM Brooks 1912-17, LF Parker 1918-30, Henry Sievers 1931-33, FC Foley 1935; **VP** PC Bodholdt 1913-33, HA Vogel 1922-33, AJ Hill 1935; **Cash.** LF Parker 1912-17, ER Norton 1918-19, RS Geiger 1920-33, Laverne A Erickson 1935; **AC** ER Norton 1913-14, LA Erickson 1920-33

	Ser #	# Notes
Third Charter, Date Back, Blue Seal		
10-10-10-20	1-1200	4,800
Third Charter, Plain Back, Blue Seal		
10-10-10-20	1201-4251	12,204
1929, Type I		
6-10's	1-487	2,922
6-20's	1-123	738

Total amount of circulation issued = $256,530. Amount outstanding in 1933 = $25,000. Amount of large outstanding on September 19, 1933 = $1,950.

17,004 Large 3,660 Small 20,664 Total

10191M	$20 1902DB	646	338 A	K898799A	F		
10191M	$10 1902PB	628	1369 B	T432939B	VF		
10191M	$10 1902PB	628	2104 B	N474936D	CU	pen ac/pen	
10191M	$10 1902PB	628	2702 C	M204354E	F		
10191 -	$10 1902PB	628	3323 C	U913035H	VG	pen/pen vp	
10191 -	$10 1902PB	628	4157 A	4157 A	XF	Higgins Mus.	
10191M	$20 1902PB	654	1219 A	N986147B	F	pen/stamp	
10191	$10 1929T1		?000008A		F		
10191	$10 1929T1		C000153A		VG		
10191	$10 1929T1		A000242A		VG		
10191	$10 1929T1		D000336A		XF		
10191	$10 1929T1		C000350A		F		
10191	$10 1929T1		C000436A		F	Ink spot of face	
10191	$10 1929T1		E000446A		VF	Higgins Mus.	
10191	$20 1929T1		D000008A		VF		
10191	$20 1929T1		D000024A		VF+		
10191	$20 1929T1		A000066A		VG		
10191	$20 1929T1		D000069A		XF		
10191	$20 1929T1		D000083A		F		
10191	$20 1929T1		?000090A		F		
10191	$20 1929T1		A000093A		F		
10191	$20 1929T1		C000093A		F		
10191	$20 1929T1		D000104A		?		
10191	$20 1929T1		A000113A		VG	UR corner gone	
10191	$20 1929T1		E000118A		AU		

THE FIRST NATIONAL BANK OF NEWTON   23 L   10 S
2644   JASPER

Chartered in 1882. Placed in receivership on October 8, 1931. Restored to solvency on March 31, 1932. Placed in voluntary liquidation on August 1, 1932; capital of $100,000. Succeeded by #13609; circulation assumed by #13609.

Officers: Pres. Frank T Campbell 1883-85, JH Lyday 1887-91, Chester Sloanaker 1892-1904, WC Bergman 1905-25, AH Bergman 1926-32; **VP** Chas Jasper 1896-1904, Chester Sloanaker 1907-11, HB Allfree 1909-26, AH Bergman 1925, LA Russell 1926-31; **Cash.** Chester Sloanaker 1883-91, EE Lyday 1892-1905, RL Arnold 1906-13, OF Ecklund 1914-22, LA Russell 1923-31; **AC** Lee E Brown 1896-1904, LA Russell 1914-22, MG Addicks 1922-31, Wesley McClary 1926-31, RM Roberts 1929-31

	Ser #	# Notes
First Charter, Series of 1875		
50-50	1-1321	2,642
Second Charter, Brown Backs		
5-5-5-5	1-1450	5,800
50-100	1-523	1,026
Second Charter, Date Back		
5-5-5-5	1-3875	15,500
50-100	1-300	600
50-50-50-100	1-328	1,312
Second Charter, Value Back		
5-5-5-5	3876-8904	20,116
Third Charter, Plain Back, Blue Seal		
5-5-5-5	1-5860	23,440
10-10-10-20	1-3322	13,288
1929, Type I		
6-5's	1-1273	7,638
6-10's	1-627	3,762
6-20's	1-174	1,044

Total amount of circulation issued = $934,470. Amount of large outstanding at close = $9,550. Amount of small outstanding at close = $55,450. Circulation assumed by #13609.

83,744 Large 12,444 Small 96,188 Total

2644	-	$50	1875	447	685 A	A17886	VF	Grinnell # 1180
2644	-	$50	1875	447	?	A22878	?	Fed. Res. Bk., Chicago
2644	M	$5 1882BB	477	244 A	T544742T	VG	light sigs	
2644	M	$5 1882DB	537	2111 E	M468248	F	stamp 2211 E ?	
2644	M	$5 1882DB	537	3230 E	R539342	F	stamp/stamp	
2644	M	$5 1882DB	537	3588 E	R539700	F		
2644	M	$50 1882DB	563	152 C	A41074	VF		
2644	M	$5 1882VB	574	5240 E	T563502	VG		
2644	M	$5 1882VB	574	5409 E	U250396	XF		
2644	M	$5 1882VB	574	5798 E	U250785	VG/F	faded/faded	
2644	M	$5 1882VB	574	5881 F	U250868	VG/F	faded/faded	
2644	M	$5 1882VB	574	8817 G	U638104	F/VF	Higgins Mus.	
2644	M	$5 1902PB	608	1429 A	A820140H	XF	stamp/stamp	
2644	-	$5 1902PB	608	1841 ?	M75927H	?		
2644	-	$5 1902PB	608	2011 B	M76097H	F/VF	mach stamps	
2644	-	$5 1902PB	608	2137 B	T536448H	XF+	stamp/stamp Higgins Mus.	
2644	-	$5 1902PB	608	4135 ?	?	F		
2644	-	$5 1902PB	608	4281 D	4281 D	G		
2644	-	$5 1902PB	608	4766 D	4766 D	VG	Stain on back	
2644	-	$5 1902PB	608	5488 A	5488 A	VF		
2644	-	$10 1902PB	634	2301 B	2301 B	VG+	gone/gone	
2644	M	$20 1902PB	660	968 A	H592490H	F		
2644	-	$20 1902PB	660	2251 A	2251 A	?		
2644		$5 1929T1		C000202A		VG+		
2644		$5 1929T1		B000872A		F/VF		
2644		$5 1929T1		D001044A		F		
2644		$5 1929T1		D001239A		VG/F		
2644		$10 1929T1		D000084A		VG+		
2644		$10 1929T1		C000216A		F	Rust	
2644		$10 1929T1		A000357A		G/VG	Higgins Mus.	
2644		$10 1929T1		C000414A		VG		
2644		$20 1929T1		C000030A		F		
2644		$20 1929T1		C000171A		?		

THE FIRST NATIONAL BANK OF NEWTON   3 L
650   JASPER

Chartered in 1864. Placed in voluntary liquidation on December 16, 1876; capital of $50,000. Succeeded by The Bank of Newton.

Officers: Pres. DL Clark 1867-71, Jesse Long 1872-75, William Vaughan 1876; **Cash.** Thomas Arthur 1867-69, CG Bulkley 1870-71, Thomas Arthur 1872-76

	Ser #	# Notes
First Charter, Original Issue		
1-1-1-2	1-2500	10,000
5-5-5-5	1-1500	6,000
10-10-10-20	1-1028	4,112

Total amount of circulation issued = $93,900. Amount outstanding at close = $45,000. Amount outstanding in 1910 = $844.

20,112 Large 0 Small 20,112 Total

650	-	$1	ORIG 380	403 B	638822	G/VG	Higgins Mus.
650	-	$1	ORIG 380	1265 B	639684	VG	pen/pen
650	-	$2	ORIG 387	2075 A	E70061	Fr	

THE NEWTON NATIONAL BANK   31 S
13609   JASPER

Chartered in March 1932; succeeded #2644 and assumed its circulation.

Officers: Pres. HC McCardell 1932-35; **VP** CA Peck 1932-35, OL Karsten 1935; **Cash.** OL Karsten 1932-35, Walter T Robinson 1935; **AC** MG Addicks 1935

	Ser #	# Notes
1929, Type I		
6-5's	1-810	4,860
6-10's	1-394	2,364
6-20's	1-108	648
1929, Type II		
5's	1-1394	1,394
10's	1-1054	1,054
20's	1-307	307

Total amount of circulation issued = $84,550. Amount of large outstanding in

1935 = $4,310. Amount of large outstanding is from bank #2644 since #13609 assumed the circulation of #2644. Amount of small outstanding in 1935 = $60,090. Amount of small outstanding includes #2644 and #13609 since #13609 assumed the circulation of #2644.

0 Large   10,627 Small   10,627 Total

Bank	Denom	Type	Serial		Grade	Notes
13609	$5	1929T1	C000033A		F/VF	
13609	$5	1929T1	E000078A		VF+	
13609	$5	1929T1	C000425A		?	
13609	$5	1929T1	C000426A		?	
13609	$10	1929T1	A000001A	[	AU	
13609	$10	1929T1	B000001A	[	AU	
13609	$10	1929T1	C000001A	[	AU	
13609	$10	1929T1	D000001A	[	AU	
13609	$10	1929T1	E000001A	[	AU	
13609	$10	1929T1	F000001A	[	AU	
13609	$10	1929T1	B000016A		F	
13609	$10	1929T1	D000117A		F	
13609	$20	1929T1	A000042A		F+	
13609	$20	1929T1	B000049A		VF	
13609	$20	1929T1	A000053A		CU	Higgins Mus.
13609	$20	1929T1	A000060A		VG	
13609	$20	1929T1	D000104A		?	
13609	$5	1929T2	A001351	[	AU	Sheet cut Tear
13609	$5	1929T2	A001352	[	CU	Sheet cut
13609	$5	1929T2	A001353	[	CU	Sheet cut
13609	$5	1929T2	A001354	[	AU	Sheet cut Tear
13609	$5	1929T2	A001355	[	CU	Sheet cut
13609	$5	1929T2	A001356	[	AU	Sheet cut
13609	$10	1929T2	A000094		F/VF	
13609	$10	1929T2	A000268		VF	
13609	$10	1929T2	A000357		VG	
13609	$10	1929T2	A001031		?	
13609	$10	1929T2	A001032		VF/XF	
13609	$20	1929T2	A000236		?	
13609	$20	1929T2	A000259		VF+	
13609	$20	1929T2	A000265		VF+	

THE FIRST NATIONAL BANK OF NORA SPRINGS   6 L   14 S
4761   FLOYD

Chartered in 1892. Succeeded The Nora Springs Bank.
Officers: Pres. Louis H Piehn 1892-1909, HC Hamilton 1910-14, HF Schnedler 1915-26; **VP** JG Gaylord 1896, JG Cutler 1900-09, JG Schmidt 1910-19, JG Schnedler 1922, JG Schmidt 1923-26; **Cash.** HF Schnedler 1892-1914, RI Pollock 1915-19, John Husting 1920-22, John R Adams 1923-26; **AC** M Jean Wilkinson 1896-1909, RI Pollock 1910, M Jean Wilkinson 1911, RI Pollock 1913-14, Stella Johnson 1920, JR Adams 1922, Selby Russell 1923-26

	Ser #	# Notes
Second Charter, Brown Backs		
10-10-10-20	1-1300	5,200
Second Charter, Date Back		
10-10-10-20	1-795	3,180
Third Charter, Date Back, Blue Seal		
10-10-10-20	1-1200	4,800
Third Charter, Plain Back, Blue Seal		
10-10-10-20	1201-3858	10,632
1929, Type I		
6-10's	1-583	3,498
6-20's	1-155	930

Total amount of circulation issued = $351,230. Amount of large outstanding in 1935 = $1,730. Amount of small outstanding in 1935 = $23,270.

23,812 Large   4,428 Small   28,240 Total

Bank		Denom	Type	Plate	Serial	Treas Serial	Grade	Notes
4761	M	$10	1882BB	485	1049 A	N823350N	F	pen/pen vp
4761	M	$10	1882BB	485	1087 A	N823382N	VG/F	
4761	M	$10	1882BB	485	1239 A	U255989U	F	pen Higgins Mus.
4761	M	$10	1882DB	540	70 F	D350820	XF	pen/pen
4761	M	$10	1882DB	540	562 D	D351212	VF+	Higgins Mus.
4761	-	$10	1902PB	628	3674 B	3674 B	PR	faded/pen
4761		$10	1929T1		A000463A		VF	
4761		$10	1929T1		D000558A		F	
4761		$20	1929T1		D000005A		VG+	
4761		$20	1929T1		F000018A		VF	
4761		$20	1929T1		A000044A		?	
4761		$20	1929T1		E000050A		F/VF	
4761		$20	1929T1		C000053A		F/VF	
4761		$20	1929T1		E000055A		F	
4761		$20	1929T1		E000090A		VF	
4761		$20	1929T1		A000098A		AU	Higgins Mus.
4761		$20	1929T1		E000112A		VF	
4761		$20	1929T1		F000116A		?	
4761		$20	1929T1		F000131A		F/VF	
4761		$20	1929T1		F000145A		VF+	

THE FIRST NATIONAL BANK OF NORTHBORO   12 L   6 S
9015   PAGE

Organized on January 17, 1908. Placed in receivership on September 16, 1932; capital of $25,000.
Officers: Pres. HJ Scott 1908-32; **VP** Alex Harris 1909-20, James Mackey 1914, JB Mackey 1920-22, LE Harris 1923-32; **Cash.** JR Harris 1908-11, Frank T Nye 1912-20, RB Murphy 1922-32; **AC** HH Harris 1909-11, WH Longman 1920-23, WC Rorebeck 1924-29, Robt E Ricker 1930, TL Reynolds 1931-32

	Ser #	# Notes
Third Charter, Red Seal		
10-10-10-10	1-468	1,872
Third Charter, Date Back, Blue Seal		
10-10-10-10	1-2525	10,100
Third Charter, Plain Back, Blue Seal		
10-10-10-10	2526-7297	19,088
1929, Type I		
6-5's	1-338	2,028
6-10's	1-707	4,242

Total amount of circulation issued = $363,160. Amount of large outstanding at close = $1,970. Amount of small outstanding at close = $23,030.

31,060 Large   6,270 Small   37,330 Total

Bank		Denom	Type	Plate	Serial	Treas Serial	Grade	Notes
9015	M	$10	1902DB	623	2290 H	K318718	VG	faded stamps
9015	M	$10	1902PB	626	2739 H	N616144	VG/F	
9015	M	$10	1902PB	626	4139 D	?	VG	
9015	M	$10	1902PB	626	4604 G	U737729	VG	
9015		$10	1902PB	626	4842 G	V161667	F	Higgins Mus.
9015	-	$10	1902PB	626	5400 E	X446505	?	UR corner gone
9015	-	$10	1902PB	626	5457 G	X446562	VG	faded/gone
9015	-	$10	1902PB	626	5473 E	X446578	VG	
9015	-	$10	1902PB	626	6140 F	6140 F	F	faded stamps
9015	-	$10	1902PB	626	6389 F	6389 F	VG	
9015	-	$10	1902PB	626	7151 H	7151 H	VG	faded stamps
9015	-	$10	1902PB	626	7293 G	7293 G	VG	faded stamps
9015		$5	1929T1		D000005A		F	
9015		$5	1929T1		C000289A		F/VF	
9015		$10	1929T1		F000248A		F	
9015		$10	1929T1		B000441A		AU	
9015		$10	1929T1		E000533A		VG	Higgins Mus.
9015		$10	1929T1		D000587A		F	

THE FIRST NATIONAL BANK OF NORTHWOOD   7 L   21 S
8373   WORTH

Organized on August 20, 1906 with a capital of $50,000. Placed in receivership on August 8, 1932; capital of $50,000.
Officers: Pres. GN Haugen 1907-32; **VP** OV Eckert 1907-24, NT Christianson 1925-28, AO Johnson 1929-31, AS Lund 192932, Hans Fosnes 1931-32; **Cash.** NE Haugen 1907-08, Iver Iverson 1909-20, AS Lund 1922-32; **AC** TL Ringham 1907, TO Groe 1909-32, JOE Johnson 1909-14, NT Christianson 1920-24, SE Espeseth 1923-27, A Talle 1930-32, Arnold Talle 1932

	Ser #	# Notes
Third Charter, Red Seal		
10-10-10-20	1-1100	4,400
Third Charter, Date Back, Blue Seal		
10-10-10-20	1-3200	12,800
Third Charter, Plain Back, Blue Seal		
10-10-10-20	3201-9135	23,740
1929, Type I		
6-10's	1-837	5,022
6-20's	1-217	1,302

Total amount of circulation issued = $588,010. Amount of large outstanding at close = $5,840. Amount of small outstanding at close = $43,860.

40,940 Large   6,324 Small   47,264 Total

Bank		Denom	Type	Plate	Serial	Treas Serial	Grade	Notes
8373	M	$10	1902DB	618	1434 D	Z842267	F	lt. stamp sigs
8373	M	$10	1902PB	626	4183 E	A693350D	VF	lt. stamp sigs
8373	M	$10	1902PB	626	5682 F	B296124E	F	gone/faded
8373	M	$10	1902PB	626	6536 F	A74258H	VF+	Higgins Mus.
8373	-	$10	1902PB	626	7922 F	7922 F	VG/F	Repaired corner
8373	M	$20	1902PB	652	2369 B	T895271A	F	faded/faded
8373	-	$20	1902PB	652	7132 B	V572264H	VF	stamp/stamp
8373		$10	1929T1		A000156A		VF	
8373		$10	1929T1		F000297A		VG/F	
8373		$10	1929T1		F000459A		F	
8373		$10	1929T1		F000479A		F	
8373		$10	1929T1		C000572A		VG/F	
8373		$10	1929T1		D000580A		F	
8373		$10	1929T1		F000594A		F	
8373		$10	1929T1		B000669A		XF	Higgins Mus.
8373		$10	1929T1		F000670A		VF	
8373		$10	1929T1		D000673A		F+	
8373		$10	1929T1		D000693A		VG/F	

8373	$10	1929T1	F000699A	VG	
8373	$10	1929T1	C000713A	F	
8373	$10	1929T1	D000713A	VG/F	
8373	$10	1929T1	B000764A	F	
8373	$20	1929T1	E000030A	VG	
8373	$20	1929T1	E000071A	F/VF	
8373	$20	1929T1	?000086A	VF	Soiled back
8373	$20	1929T1	F000088A	F	
8373	$20	1929T1	A000156A	F+	
8373	$20	1929T1	E000198A	VF	

FIRST NATIONAL BANK OF NORWAY   **9 L**
7287   **BENTON**

Organized on May 23, 1904 with a capital of $25,000. Placed in receivership on March 23, 1927; capital of $25,000. Reason for failure: local depression.
Officers: Pres. CP Christianson 1905-07, CE Simpson 1908-25, Alex Melberg 1926; **VP** Geo A Doebel 1907, Jacob Hofferd 1909-23, Alex Melberg 1924-25, Henry Tuttle 1926; **Cash.** John T Smith 1905-14, LH Jurgemeyer 1915, Geo A Doebel 1916-26; **AC** LH Jurgemeyer 1909-14, NA Thomas 1920-23, Hazel A Pirie 1924-26

Third Charter, Red Seal			Ser #	# Notes
10-10-10-20			1-1320	5,280
Third Charter, Date Back, Blue Seal				
10-10-10-20			1-1600	6,400
Third Charter, Plain Back, Blue Seal				
10-10-10-20			1601-4264	10,656

Total amount of issued = $279,200. Amount outstanding at close = $25,000.
22,336 Large   0 Small   22,336 Total

7287	M	$20 1902DB	642	1425 B	A875901B	?
7287	M	$10 1902PB	624	2603 F	V309895D	VG Higg. Mus.
7287	M	$10 1902PB	624	3036 F	M170458E	VG
7287	-	$10 1902PB	624	?	M206544H	?
7287	-	$10 1902PB	624	3912 F	Z425664H	VG/F gone/pen
7287	-	$10 1902PB	624	4149 D	4149 D	XF/AU
7287	M	$20 1902PB	650	3497 B	D644129H	F
7287	-	$20 1902PB	650	4009 B	4009 B	VF stamp/pen
7287	-	$20 1902PB	650	4127 B	4127 B	F gone/pen

THE FARMERS NATIONAL BANK OF ODEBOLT   **1 L**
5817   **SAC**

Chartered on May 16, 1901 with a capital of $50,000. Succeeded The Farmers Savings Bank. Placed in voluntary liquidation on January 7, 1914; capital of $50,000. Consolidated with #4511; circulation assumed by #4511.
Officers: Pres. RW Sayre 1901-13; **VP** Albert E Cook 1902-13; **Cash.** S Ben Sayre 1901—04, AE Baker 1905-08, Wayne M Sayre 1909-13; **AC** AE Baker 1904, Wayne M Sayre 1907, Edna M Hanson 1910-13

Second Charter, Brown Backs		Ser #	# Notes
10-10-10-20		1-2500	10,000
Second Charter, Date Back			
10-10-10-20		1-2218	8,872

Total amount of circulation issued = $235,900. Amount outstanding at close = $50,000. Circulation liability assumed by #4511.
18,872 Large   0 Small   18,872 Total

5817		$10 1882BB	490	1387 B	N971132N	F+ Higgins Mus.

THE FIRST NATIONAL BANK OF ODEBOLT   **27 L   43 S**
4511   **SAC**

Chartered in 1891. Succeeded The Odebolt State Bank. Assumed #5817 by consolidation on January 7, 1914; assumed the circulation of #5817. Placed in voluntary liquidation on June 18, 1934; capital of $140,000.

Officers: Pres. WW Field 1891-1907, Joseph Mattes 1908-25, William P Adams 1925-31, Robert B Adams 1932-34; **VP** WJ Summerwill 1896, Jos. Mattes 1900-07, Henry Hanson 1909-20, John Fuchs 1922-32, GH Hanson 1932-34; **Cash.** WF Bay 1891-1918, LR Bassett 1919-33, JL Mathews 1934; **AC** W Mengis 1896, AL Hess 1900-02, EJ Gifford 1903, AH Lundberg 1904-14, AW Lewis 1920-34

Second Charter, Brown Backs	Ser #	# Notes
10-10-10-20	1-4090	16,360
Second Charter, Date Back		
10-10-10-20	1-464	1,856
Third Charter, Date Back, Blue Seal		
10-10-10-20	1-4100	16,400
Third Charter, Plain Back, Blue Seal		
10-10-10-20	4101-15754	46,616
1929, Type I		
6-5's	1-4558	27,348
6-10's	1-1230	7,380
6-20's	1-416	2,496

Total amount of circulation issued = $1,275,860. Amount outstanding in 1933 = $99,160. Amount of large outstanding at close = $8,260. Includes the unredeemed notes of #5817.
81,232 Large   37,224 Small   118,456 Total

4511	M	$10 1882BB	484	2503 A	K433700K	VF	pen Higgins Mus.
4511	M	$10 1882DB	539	101 E	B905831	XF	pen/stamp
4511	M	$10 1882DB	539	237 E	B905967	VG	retraced sigs
4511	M	$10 1902DB	619	2157 ?	U722383A	?	
4511	M	$20 1902DB	645	384 A	Z120470	VG/F	
4511	M	$20 1902DB	645	1888 A	U722114A	VF	stamp/stamp
4511	M	$20 1902DB	645	2090 A	U722316A	VG	
4511	M	$20 1902DB	645	2883 A	Y688793A	VG	Stains
4511	M	$10 1902PB	627	4581 B	V140023B	VG/F	
4511	M	$10 1902PB	627	5214 C	Z352017B	F	
4511	M	$10 1902PB	627	7757 B	V812219D	XF	Higgins Mus.
4511	M	$10 1902PB	627	10609 ?	K645010H	?	
4511	M	$10 1902PB	627	10712 C	K645114H	F	
4511	M	$10 1902PB	627	10754 B	K654156H	?	
4511	-	$10 1902PB	627	11278 B	T969910H	VF/XF	mach stamps
4511	-	$10 1902PB	627	12004 C	Z533696H	F	mach stamps
4511	-	$10 1902PB	627	12115 C	Z533807H	F	mach stamps
4511	-	$10 1902PB	627	14385 A	14385 A	F	stamp/stamp
4511	M	$20 1902PB	653	5583 A	B867390D	F/VF	
4511	M	$20 1902PB	653	10424 A	?	F/VF	
4511	M	$20 1902PB	653	11036 A	K645438H	VG/F	
4511	-	$20 1902PB	653	12218 A	Z533910H	CU	mach stamps
4511	-	$20 1902PB	653	12219 A	Z533911H	CU	mach stamps
4511	-	$20 1902PB	653	12222 A	Z533914H	CU	
4511	-	$20 1902PB	653	15399 A	?	?	
4511	-	$20 1902PB	653	15592 A	?	?	
4511	-	$20 1902PB	653	15599 A	15599 A	VF	
4511		$5 1929T1		B000057A		F	
4511		$5 1929T1		E000201A		VG	
4511		$5 1929T1		B000410A		VF	Higgins Mus.
4511		$5 1929T1		A000626A		VG	
4511		$5 1929T1		E000723A		F/VF	Stain
4511		$5 1929T1		B001913A		?	
4511		$5 1929T1		F002314A		?	
4511		$5 1929T1		D002768A		F	Foxed paper
4511		$5 1929T1		F002997A		VG	
4511		$5 1929T1		D003356A		?	
4511		$5 1929T1		F003425A		F	
4511		$5 1929T1		F004183A		VG	
4511		$5 1929T1		F004204A		VG	
4511		$5 1929T1		E004252A		F	
4511		$5 1929T1		B004350A		F	
4511		$5 1929T1		C004401A		F	
4511		$5 1929T1		C004432A		F	
4511		$5 1929T1		E004491A		F	
4511		$10 1929T1		E000124A		F	
4511		$10 1929T1		A000377A		VG	
4511		$10 1929T1		B000680A		?	
4511		$10 1929T1		C000968A		VG	
4511		$10 1929T1		B001026A		VF	
4511		$10 1929T1		C001040A		F	
4511		$20 1929T1		E000026A		VG	Paper clip rust
4511		$20 1929T1		A000070A		?	
4511		$20 1929T1		B000120A		F	
4511		$20 1929T1		B000121A		VG/F	
4511		$20 1929T1		B000128A		CU	
4511		$20 1929T1		B000142A		F	
4511		$20 1929T1		D000159A		VG	
4511		$20 1929T1		B000163A		VG	
4511		$20 1929T1		E000168A		?	
4511		$20 1929T1		B000208A		VF	
4511		$20 1929T1		C000248A		?	

Charter		Denom	Series	Plate	Serial	Treasury	Grade	Notes
4511		$20	1929T1	C000263A			VF	
4511		$20	1929T1	B000271A			VF/XF	
4511		$20	1929T1	E000278A			XF	Ink spots on back
4511		$20	1929T1	E000284A			VF	CU ?
4511		$20	1929T1	E000296A			F/VF	
4511		$20	1929T1	A000309A			XF	
4511		$20	1929T1	C000312A			?	
4511		$20	1929T1	B000338A			F	

THE FIRST NATIONAL BANK OF OELWEIN 53 L 20 S
5778 FAYETTE

Chartered in April 1901. Succeeded The Commercial Savings Bank.
Officers: Pres. TL Hanson 1901-14, A Hanson 1915-22, CB Chambers 1923—35; **VP** EC Belt 1902-07, AC Wilson 1909-11, JB Feltus 1913-20, TL Hanson 1920, CB Chambers 1922, Thomas Smith 1922-35; **Cash.** A Hanson 1901-14, CB Chambers 1915-20, George W Falk 1922-35; **AC** JW Hanson 1902-05, CB Chambers 1909-14, GW Falk 1920, Fred S Rule 1922-35, MC Hanson 1925-35

	Ser #	# Notes
Second Charter, Brown Backs		
10-10-10-20	1-1600	6,400
Second Charter, Date Back		
10-10-10-20	1-2540	10,160
Second Charter, Value Back		
10-10-10-20	2541-3866	5,304
Third Charter, Plain Back, Blue Seal		
10-10-10-20	1-3656	14,624
1929, Type I		
6-10's	1-1016	6,096
6-20's	1-282	1,692
1929, Type II		
5's	1-324	324
10's	1-1343	1,343
20's	1-181	181

Total amount of circulation issued = $569,570. Amount of large outstanding in 1935 = $3,585. Amount of small outstanding in 1935 = $46,415.
36,488 Large 9,636 Small 46,124 Total

Bank		Denom	Series	Plate	Plate2	Serial	Grade	Notes
5778	M	$10	1882BB	490	1347 C	U51161U	XF	pen/pen
5778	M	$10	1882BB	490	1520 C	V560719V	VF	
5778	M	$10	1882BB	490	1555 B	V560754V	AU	
5778	M	$20	1882BB	504	1270 A	U51084U	VF	
5778	M	$20	1882BB	504	1530 A	V560729V	XF	pen/pen Higgins Mus.
5778	M	$10	1882DB	545	151 F	D367481	AU+	pen/pen
5778	M	$10	1882DB	545	153 F	D367483	XF	
5778	M	$10	1882DB	545	233 F	D367563	AU	
5778	M	$10	1882DB	545	624 D	D367954	VG	
5778	M	$10	1882DB	545	650 D	D367980	CU	pen/pen
5778	M	$10	1882DB	545	1479 D	M555347	XF	pen/pen
5778	M	$10	1882DB	545	1947 D	N701655	VF	
5778	M	$10	1882DB	545	2038 D	N701746	XF	pen/pen Higgins Mus.
5778	M	$10	1882DB	545	2039 F	N701747	XF/AU	pen/pen
5778	M	$10	1882DB	545	2048 F	N701756	XF/AU	pen/pen
5778	M	$10	1882DB	545	2062 F	N701770	VF/XF	pen/pen
5778	M	$20	1882DB	555	650 B	D367980	CU	pen/pen
5778	M	$20	1882DB	555	706 B	D368036	VG/F	
5778	M	$20	1882DB	555	738 B	D368068	VF	
5778	M	$20	1882DB	555	762 B	D368092	F/VF	
5778	M	$20	1882DB	555	1270 A	U51084U	VF	
5778	M	$20	1882DB	555	1746 B	M555614	CU	Higgins Mus.
5778	M	$20	1882DB	555	2284 B	T177492	AU	pen/pen
5778	M	$10	1882VB	577	2554 E	T923612	?	pen/pen High grade
5778	M	$10	1882VB	577	2555 D	T923613	AU	
5778	M	$10	1882VB	577	2555 F	T923613	AU	pen/pen
5778	M	$20	1882VB	581	2556 B	T923614	AU	
5778	M	$20	1882VB	581	2558 B	T923616	CU	Higgins Mus.
5778	M	$20	1882VB	581	2566 B	T923624	F/VF	pen/pen
5778	M	$20	1882VB	581	2883 B	U363361	XF	CU ?
5778	M	$20	1882VB	581	2980 B	U363458	XF/AU	pen/lt pen
5778	M	$20	1882VB	581	2981 B	U363459	AU+	
5778	M	$20	1882VB	581	2982 B	U363460	XF	
5778	M	$10	1902PB	633	29 C	Y802841D	F	pen/pen vp
5778	M	$10	1902PB	633	918 C	X923890E	F	
5778	M	$10	1902PB	633	1230 B	D506472H	F/VF	
5778	-	$10	1902PB	633	1595 A	N977707H	VF/AU	pen/pen
5778	-	$10	1902PB	633	1823 B	V167845H	XF	pen/pen
5778	-	$10	1902PB	633	2026 A	A262838K	F	gone/gone
5778	-	$10	1902PB	633	2134 B	A262946K	VF	lt stamp sigs
5778	-	$10	1902PB	633	2181 C	2181 C	VG	
5778	-	$10	1902PB	633	2788 C	2788 C	VF+	stamp Higg. Mus.
5778	-	$10	1902PB	633	2925 C	2925 C	F/VF	stamp/stamp
5778	-	$10	1902PB	633	3052 C	3052 C	VF	AU ?
5778	-	$10	1902PB	633	3405 B	3405 B	?	
5778	M	$20	1902PB	659	1122 A	D506364H	VG	
5778	-	$20	1902PB	659	2019 A	A262831K	F	
5778	-	$20	1902PB	659	2132 A	A262944K	CU	
5778	-	$20	1902PB	659	2133 A	A262945K	CU	
5778	-	$20	1902PB	659	2134 A	A262946K	CU	gone Higg. Mus.
5778	-	$20	1902PB	659	2135 A	A262947K	CU	nice sigs
5778	-	$20	1902PB	659	2137 A	2137 A	CU	
5778	-	$20	1902PB	659	3231 A	3231 A	AU	stamp/stamp
5778		$10	1929T1	C000288A			F	
5778		$10	1929T1	C000519A			F/VF	
5778		$10	1929T1	F000520A			F	
5778		$10	1929T1	E000521A			AU	Higgins Mus.
5778		$10	1929T1	F000655A			F	
5778		$10	1929T1	F000716A			VG	
5778		$10	1929T1	A000744A			F	
5778		$10	1929T1	A001009A			VG/F	
5778		$20	1929T1	E000070A			VG	
5778		$20	1929T1	D000072A			VF	
5778		$20	1929T1	A000121A			F/VF	
5778		$20	1929T1	C000175A			F	
5778		$20	1929T1	B000263A			VF	
5778		$20	1929T1	B000264A			VF	
5778		$20	1929T1	B000270A			VF	
5778		$20	1929T1	C000275A			F	
5778		$5	1929T2	A000239			F	Rust spots
5778		$10	1929T2	A000094			?	
5778		$10	1929T2	A000578			XF	
5778		$20	1929T2	A000061			VG	

THE FIRST NATIONAL BANK OF OLIN 6 L
7585 JONES

Chartered in January 1905. Placed in voluntary liquidation on May 21, 1926; capital of $25,000. Absorbed by The Citizens Savings Bank of Olin.
Officers: Pres. Geo L Schoonover 1905-26; **VP** GW Huber 1907, LM Carpenter 1909-22, CE Walston 1911-14, HD Miller 1920-26, AB Miller 1923-26; **Cash.** MH Crissman 1905-11, RC Walters 1912-13, NC Hall 1914-26; **AC** RJ Blenn 1913-20, LS Newcomb 1922-24

	Ser #	# Notes
Third Charter, Red Seal		
10-10-10-20	1-1050	4,200
Third Charter, Date Back, Blue Seal		
10-10-10-20	1-1560	6,240
Third charter, Plain Back, Blue Seal		
10-10-10-20	1561-3813	9,012

Total amount issued = $243,150. Amount outstanding at close = $25,000.
19,452 Large 0 Small 19,452 Total

Bank		Denom	Series	Plate	Plate2	Serial	Grade	Notes
7585	M	$10	1902RS	613	579 B	K192685	G/VG	pen/pen vp
7585	M	$20	1902RS	639	477 A	K192583	F/VF	
7585	M	$10	1902PB	624	1867 D	Y417278B	F	pen/lt stamp
7585	M	$10	1902PB	624	2765 D	B269677E	VF	vp
7585		$10	1902PB	624	3421 D	K555933H	VG/F	Higgins Mus.
7585	M	$20	1902PB	650	2763 B	B269675E	XF	pen/pen vp

THE FIRST NATIONAL BANK OF ORANGE CITY 0 L
6132 SIOUX

Organized on February 10, 1902. Chartered on February 20, 1902. Placed in voluntary liquidation on November 21, 1905; capital of $25,000. Absorbed by The Northwestern State Bank, Orange City.
Officers: Pres. James F Toy 1902-05; **VP** A Bolks 1902-04; **Cash.** AJ Kuyper 1902, Ed De Mots 1903-04, Herbert Kuyper 1905; **AC** Herbert Kuyper 1903-04

	Ser #	# Notes
Third Charter, Red Seal		
10-10-10-20	1-239	956

Total amount of circulation issued = $11,950. Amount outstanding at close = $6,250. Amount outstanding in 1910 = $880.
956 Large 0 Small 956 Total

THE FARMERS NATIONAL BANK OF OSAGE 5 L
4885 (FIRST TITLE) MITCHELL

Chartered in 1893. Title changed to Osage Farmers National Bank, Osage on January 5, 1927.
Officers: Pres. John H Johnson 1893-1913, KJ Johnson 1914-27; **VP** ES Fonda 1900, Jas A Smith 1902-14, FW Annis 1920-34, Fred Crego Smith 1926-27; **Cash.** Frank W Annis 1893-97, EE Prime 1899, KJ Johnson 1900-08, Ray Roberts 1909, KJ Johnson 1910-13, EC Swanson 1916, RF Dorow 1917-19, EC Swanson 1920-26, Birchard Brush 1927; **AC** KJ Johnson 1896, RF Dorow 1900-02, RR Roberts 1910-13, HG Bartlett 1914, RF Dorow 1920-35, EC Swanson 1927

	Ser #	# Notes
Second Charter, Brown Backs		

10-10-10-20	1-1320	5,280
Second Charter, Date Back		
10-10-10-20	1-355	1,420
Third Charter, Date Back, Blue Seal		
10-10-10-20	1-700	2,800
Third Charter, Plain Back, Blue Seal		
10-10-10-20	701-1277	2,308

11,808 Large   0 Small   11,808 Total

4885	-	$10 1882BB	485	854 B	U177260	VF pen Higgins Mus.
4885	M	$10 1882BB	485	1229 C	V514066V	F
4885	M	$10 1902DB	621	337 A	R369481A	VF
4885	M	$10 1902PB	629	1084 B	Y830456E	VG
4885	M	$10 1902PB	629	1084 C	Y830456E	VF Higgins Mus.

OSAGE FARMERS NATIONAL BANK   33 S
4885 (2ND TITLE)   **MITCHELL**

Succeeded The Farmers National Bank of Osage on January 5, 1927. Absorbed #1618 on April 18, 1927.

Officers: Pres. KJ Johnson 1927-34, AT Altick 1935; **VP** FW Annis 1927-34, Fred Crego Smith 1927-35, AT Altick 1934, EJ Scofield 1935; **Cash.** Birchard Brush 1927-35; **AC** RF Dorow 1927-35, EC Swanson 1927-32, Neva C Sullivan 1929, Vera C Sullivan 1929-35

1929, Type I	Ser #	# Notes
6-10's	1-826	4,956
6-20's	1-304	1,824
6-50's	1-128	768
1929, Type II		
10's	1-1499	1,499
20's	1-305	305

Total amount of circulation issued = $293,130. Amount of large outstanding in 1935 = $540. Amount of small outstanding in 1935 = $99,460.

0 Large   9,352 Small   9,352 Total

4885	?	1929T1	F000005A	VF	
4885	$10	1929T1	F000036A	?	
4885	$10	1929T1	D000059A	?	
4885	$10	1929T1	A000508A	F	
4885	$10	1929T1	E000508A	F	
4885	$10	1929T1	A000587A	VF	
4885	$10	1929T1	E000687A	?	
4885	$10	1929T1	B000823A	VF	Higgins Mus.
4885	$20	1929T1	E000012A	F	
4885	$20	1929T1	C000015A	VG	
4885	$20	1929T1	C000107A	XF	
4885	$20	1929T1	E000116A	VG+	
4885	$20	1929T1	D000172A	F	
4885	$20	1929T1	A000213A	F	
4885	$20	1929T1	F000222A	F	
4885	$20	1929T1	A000284A	F	
4885	$20	1929T1	C000303A	VF	
4885	$50	1929T1	D000005A	F	Writing on face
4885	$50	1929T1	F000005A	VF	
4885	$50	1929T1	B000019A	F	
4885	$50	1929T1	F000045A	F	
4885	$50	1929T1	B000063A	?	
4885	$50	1929T1	E000087A	F/VF	
4885	$50	1929T1	D000106A	VG/F	Small tear at top
4885	$50	1929T1	A000117A	F+	Ink
4885	$50	1929T1	B000117A	F/VF	
4885	$50	1929T1	D000126A	F	
4885	$10	1929T2	A000476	F	
4885	$10	1929T2	A000751	F/VF	
4885	$10	1929T2	A000814	F	
4885	$10	1929T2	A000906	XF	
4885	$10	1929T2	A000946	VF	
4885	$20	1929T2	A000030	VF	

THE OSAGE NATIONAL BANK   16 L
1618   **MITCHELL**

$5 Original Series notes with serial numbers from 1751 to 2200 were stolen unissued and unsigned in a robbery of this bank on Saturday night May 5/6, 1866. Some notes were distressed and passed with forged signatures. All thirteen of the $5 notes listed below were in this stolen group.

Chartered in 1865. Placed in voluntary liquidation on April 18, 1927; capital of $50,000. Absorbed by #4885.

Officers: Pres. Arad Hitchcock 1867-69, Jacob H Brush 1870-80, Jessie P Brush 1881-83, JH Brush 1884-90, Avery Brush 1891-1923, Birchard Brush 1924-26; **VP** Julia Brush Johnson 1924-26; **Cash.** Jacob H Brush 1867-69, Jesse P Brush 1870-80, Avery Brush 1881-90, JW Annis 1891-1916, Birchard Brush 1918-23, Laura Brush Spaanum 1924-26; **AC** Avery Brush 1878-79, AL Brush 1900, Birchard Brush 1909-14

First Charter, Original Issue	Ser #	# Notes
1-1-1-2	1-1090	4,360
5-5-5-5	1-2277	9,048

Sheets numbered 2211 to 2225 were cancelled.

10-10-10-20	1-800	3,200
First Charter, Series of 1875		
10-10-10-20	1-964	3,856
Second Charter, Brown Backs		
50-100	1-714	1,428
Third Charter, Red Seal		
50-100	1-253	506
Third Charter, Date Back, Blue Seal		
50-100	1-330	660
50-50-50-100	1-273	1,092

Total amount issued = $401,690. Amount outstanding at close = $25,000.

24,150 Large   0 Small   24,150 Total

1618	-	$5	ORIG	397	1765 A	D560973	PR	pen Higgins Mus.
1618	-	$5	ORIG	397	1845 B	D561053		
1618	-	$5	ORIG	397	1852 D	D561060	VG	
1618	-	$5	ORIG	397	1872 D	D561080	G	
1618	-	$5	ORIG	397	1875 A	D561083	G	
1618	-	$5	ORIG	397	1884 B	D561092	PR	
1618	-	$5	ORIG	397	1950 C	D561158	Fr	pen/pen
1618	-	$5	ORIG	397	1951 A	D561159	Fr	
1618	-	$5	ORIG	397	1960 C	D561168	G	
1618	-	$5	ORIG	397	1963 A	D561171	PR	
1618	-	$5	ORIG	397	2001 D	D561209	G	
1618	-	$5	ORIG	397	2072 A	D561280	AG	
1618	-	$5	ORIG	397	2121 D	D561329	AG	
1618	-	$1	ORIG	380	678 B	C751521	VF	Higgins Mus.
1618	M	$100	1902DB	690	136 C	A273854	XF	Higgins Mus.
1618	M	$100	1902DB	690	199 C	A889121	AU	

THE FIRST NATIONAL BANK OF OSCEOLA   1 L
1776   **CLARKE**

Chartered on January 26, 1871 with a capital of $50,000. Placed in receivership on February 25, 1876; capital of $50,000. Reason for failure: incompetent management.

Officers: Pres. Henry C Sigler 1872-76; **Cash.** Wm Christy 1872-73, WG Kennedy 1874-76

First Charter, Original Issue	Ser #	# Notes
1-1-1-2	1-1500	6,000
5-5-5-5	1-2875	11,500
First Charter, Series of 1875		
5-5-5-5	1-340	1,360

Total amount of circulation issued = $71,800. Amount outstanding at close = $45,000. Amount outstanding in 1915 = $410.

18,860 Large   0 Small   18,860 Total

1776	-	$1	ORIG	382	716 B	C273611	F	Higgins Museum

THE OSCEOLA NATIONAL BANK   7 L
6033   **CLARKE**

Organized on October 8, 1901 with a capital of $25,000. Placed in receivership on April 22, 1925; capital of $25,000. Reason for failure: incompetent management.

Officers: Pres. Chas T Ayers 1902-25; **VP** Nathan McGrew 1902-13, CA Twyford 1914, SA Blake 1920-25, AF Williams 1922-25; **Cash.** PL Fowler 1902-07, CA Twyford 1908-13, John Ledgerwood 1914, Roy A Downs 1915-25; **AC** Amy J Fowler 1903-07, Sid Bates 1909, MI Wick 1911, Lon Williams 1920-25

Second Charter, Brown Backs	Ser #	# Notes
5-5-5-5	1-950	3,800
10-10-10-20	1-865	3,460
Second Charter, Date Back		
5-5-5-5	1-1600	6,400
10-10-10-20	1-1080	4,320
Second Charter, Value Back		
5-5-5-5	1601-2875	5,100
10-10-10-20	1081-1855	3,100
Third Charter, Plain Back, Blue Seal		
10-10-10-20	1-878	3,512

Total amount issued = $56,400. Amount outstanding at close = $25,000.

29,692 Large   0 Small   29,692 Total

6033	M	$20 1882DB	555	800 B	N188268	VG	pen/pen
6033	M	$10 1882VB	577	1082 B	T532720	XF	Dark
6033	M	$10 1882VB	577	1851 E	V622349	VG/F	tear; tight top
6033	M	$20 1882VB	581	1231 B	T822169	XF	
6033	M	$20 1882VB	581	1461 B	U851459	VG+	faded Higg. Mus.
6033	M	$10 1902PB	634	206 A	K4218E	VG/F	stamp/stamp
6033	M	$20 1902PB	660	6 A	K4018E	AU	Higgins Mus.

THE FARMERS AND TRADERS NATIONAL BANK OF OSKALOOSA
2895   MAHASKA   0 L
Chartered on March 5, 1883. Succeeded The Farmers and Traders Bank. Placed in voluntary liquidation on July 30, 1892; capital of $100,000. Succeeded by The Farmers and Traders State Bank.
Officers: Pres. John Siebel 1883-87, JG Jones 1888-92; **Cash.** John H Warren 1883-92; **AC** Jas F McNeill 1885

Second Charter, Brown Backs	Ser #	# Notes
5-5-5-5	1-1075	4,300
10-10-10-20	1-850	3,400

Total amount of circulation issued = $64,000. Amount outstanding at close = $22,500. Amount outstanding in 1910 = $380.
7,700 Large   0 Small   7,700 Total

THE FARMERS NATIONAL BANK OF OSKALOOSA   10 L
8076   MAHASKA
Organized on January 24, 1906. Placed in voluntary liquidation on February 21, 1928; capital of $100,000. Absorbed by #2417. Placed in receivership on April 9, 1930. Reason for failure: deficiency in assets sold.
Officers: Pres. WI Beans 1906-27; **VP** WH Pike 1907-25, Roy Hutchison 1925-27, Carl Mayer 1926-27; **Cash.** RK Davis 1906-19, Carl Mayer 1920-25, Leslie Jones 1926-27; **AC** HL Pike 1907-09, HA Warner 1910-11, Carl Mayer 1911-14, ER Raffety 1914-23, Leslie Jones 1922-25, Oliver Anderson 1924-25, Annabelle Gordon 1926-27

Third Charter, Red Seal	Ser #	# Notes
10-10-10-20	1-890	3,560
Third Charter, Date Back, Blue Seal		
10-10-10-20	1-3900	15,600
Third Charter, Plain Back, Blue Seal		
10-10-10-20	3901-9112	20,848

Total amount issued = $500,100. Amount outstanding at close = $50,000.
40,008 Large   0 Small   40,008 Total

8076	M	$10 1902PB	625	4990 F	M49052D	F/VF stamp/stamp
8076	M	$10 1902PB	625	5019 D	M49081D	VG/F stamp/stamp
8076	-	$10 1902PB	625	5708 E	Z673250D	VF Higgins Mus.
8076	-	$10 1902PB	625	7541 E	T531633H	VG/F stamp/stamp
8076	-	$10 1902PB	625	7808 D	X824510H	F/VF
8076	-	$10 1902PB	625	8433 D	8433 D	F pen/stamp
8076	-	$10 1902PB	625	8719 E	8719 E	VG
8076	-	$10 1902PB	625	9104 D	9104 F	VG/F stamp/stamp
8076	-	$10 1902PB	625	9110 D	9110 D	VG LR corner gone
8076	-	$20 1902PB	651	8401 B	8401 B	XF+ stamp/stamp

THE FIRST NATIONAL BANK OF OSKALOOSA   0 L
147   MAHASKA
Chartered on December 10, 1863. Placed in voluntary liquidation on December 17, 1868; capital of $75,000.
Officers: Pres. John White 1867-68; **Cash.** John H Warren 1867, GW Sheppard 1868

First Charter, Original Issue	Ser #	# Notes
1-1-1-2	1-1000	4,000
5-5-5-5	1-2525	10,100
10-10-10-20	1-270	1,080

Total amount of circulation issued = $69,000. Amount outstanding at close = $67,500. Amount outstanding in 1910 = $488.
15,180 Large   0 Small   15,180 Total

THE NATIONAL STATE BANK OF OSKALOOSA   1 L
1101   MAHASKA
Chartered in 1865. Placed in voluntary liquidation on August 13, 1881; capital of $50,000.
Officers: Pres. AC Williams 1867-69, John White 1870-71, Seth Richards 1872-81; **VP** Cyrus Beede 1867-69, TJ Fletcher 1870-71, WA Lindly 1872, ED Lindly 1872-79, RO Green 1880-81

First Charter, Original Issue	Ser #	# Notes
5-5-5-5	1-2775	11,100
10-10-10-10	1-2900	11,600
First Charter, Series of 1875		
10-10-10-10	1-1447	5,788

Total amount of circulation issued = $229,380. Amount outstanding at close = $81,665. Amount outstanding in 1910 = $1,505.
28,488 Large   0 Small   28,488 Total
1101 - $10   1875   416   545 C   A145895   VF   Higgins Mus.

THE OSKALOOSA NATIONAL BANK   15 L
2417   MAHASKA
Organized on March 6, 1879 with a capital of $50,000. Chartered on March 12, 1879; succeeded The Mahaska County Savings Bank. Absorbed #8076 on February 21, 1928. Placed in receivership on January 20, 1932; capital of $100,000.

Officers: Pres. Marsena E Cutts 1879-81, WH Seevers 1883-85, HL Spencer 1887-88, WH Seevers 1889-94, HL Spencer 1895, WH Kalbach 1896-1932; **VP** HL Spencer 1900-10, JF McNeil 1910-28, CE Lofland 1920-31, Carl Mayer 1928-32; **Cash.** William A Lindly 1879-85, CE Lofland 1887-1919, EL Butler 1920-31; **AC** EK Himes 1896, HL Lane 1904, ND Lane 1904, HD Lane 1909-13, HH Harold 1911, Ferne Roberts 1920-24, Wallace Holmes 1926-31, Leslie Jones 1928-31

First Charter, Series of 1875	Ser #	# Notes
10-10-10-20	1-1892	7,568
Second Charter, Brown Backs		
10-10-10-20	1-4420	17,680
Second Charter, Date Back		
10-10-10-20	1-6500	26,000
Second Charter, Value Back		
10-10-10-20	6501-8540	8,160
Third Charter, Plain Back, Blue Seal		
10-10-10-20	1-5964	23,856

Total amount of circulation issued = $1,040,800. Amount outstanding in 1924 = $99,100. Amount outstanding at close = $7,550.
83,264 Large   0 Small   83,264 Total

2417	-	$10 1875	419	1568 B	K549496	VG	Higgins Mus.
2417		$10 1882BB	490	500 B	X907865	XF	Higgins Mus.
2417	M	$10 1882DB	545	46 F	B803756	VF+	Higgins Mus.
2417	M	$10 1882DB	545	2285 F	E639213	F	gone/gone
2417	M	$10 1882DB	545	3923 D	M356961	F/VF	
2417	M	$10 1882DB	545	5507 F	R44195	VG	gone/gone
2417	M	$10 1882VB	577	6775 D	T535753	VG/F	Higgins Mus.
2417	M	$10 1882VB	577	6970 E	T535948	?	
2417	M	$20 1882VB	581	7311 B	T864719	G/VG	Soiled
2417	M	$20 1882VB	581	8061 B	U245359	VG	gone/gone
2417	M	$20 1882VB	581	8228 B	U593496	VF	light stamps
2417	M	$10 1902PB	632	761 B	M428153D	F+	stamp/stamp
2417	M	$10 1902PB	632	5333 A	H684215H	VG	
2417	M	$20 1902PB	658	2999 A	K55691E	F	Higgins Mus.
2417	M	$20 1902PB	658	4123 A	U303425E	G/VG	stamp/stamp

THE FIRST NATIONAL BANK OF OTTUMWA   25 L   23 S
107   WAPELLO
Chartered in 1863. Placed in voluntary liquidation on Oct. 29, 1931; capital of $200,000. Succeeded by The First Bank & Trust Company of Ottumwa.
Officers: Pres. James Hawley 1867-69, Wesley B Bonnifield 1870-1931; **VP** Geo Haw 1896-1911, MB Hutchison 1909-13, HL Waterman 1914, JB Sax 1920-31; **Cash.** Joseph B Field 1867, William A McGrew 1868-85, WT Fenton 1887-90, MB Hutchison 1892-1902, WB Bonnifield, Jr. 1903-08, PC Ackley 1912-31; **AC** WB Bonnifield, Jr. 1896-1902, SL Vest 1904-14, PC Ackley 1909-11, TK Harlan 1920-27, AW Trautwein 1920-31

First Charter, Original Issue	Ser #	# Notes
5-5-5-5	1-6500	26,000
First Charter, Series of 1875		
5-5-5-5	1-4330	17,320
Second Charter, Brown Backs		
10-10-10-20	1-5000	20,000
50-100	1-944	1,888
Third Charter, Red Seal		
50-100	1-2166	4,332
Third Charter, Date Back, Blue Seal		
50-100	1-1800	3,600
50-50-50-100	1-2856	11,424
Third Charter, Plain Back, Blue Seal		
50-50-50-100	2857-3558	2,808
1929, Type I		
6-50's	1-363	2,178
6-100's	1-102	612

Total amount of circulation issued = $2,262,700. Amount of large outstanding at close = $53,500. Amount of small outstanding at close = $146,000.
87,372 Large   2,790 Small   90,162 Total

107	-	$20 1882BB	493	4889 A	R766927	VF	pen/pen
107	M	$50 1902DB	667	377 E	A242401	VF+	pen/pen
107	M	$50 1902DB	667	702 E	?	VF	Davenport B&T
107	M	$50 1902DB	667	1032 C	A751902	VG	
107	M	$50 1902DB	667	1120 D	A808752	VG	pen/pen
107	M	$50 1902DB	667	1125 B	A808757	VG	
107	M	$50 1902DB	667	1189 C	A808821	CU	pen/pen
107	M	$50 1902DB	667	1189 E	A808821	CU	pen/pen
107	M	$50 1902DB	667	1191 E	A808823	AU	Davenport B&T
107	M	$50 1902DB	667	1585 E	A856777	F	
107	M	$50 1902DB	667	2129 D	A983183	F	pen/pen
107	M	$50 1902DB	667	2175 D	A983229	F	pen/pen
107	-	$50 1902DB	667	2334 C	B66118	VG	pen/pen
107	-	$50 1902DB	667	2564 E	B114288	VG+	pen Higgins Mus.
107	-	$50 1902DB	667	2659 D	2659 D	VG/F	pen/pen

Charter	Denom	Plate	Sheet	Serial	Treasury	Grade	Notes
107	M$100 1902DB	689	119 C	A84410		F+	Higgins Mus.
107	M$100 1902DB	689	1476 B	A241414		G/VG	faded/faded
107	M$100 1902DB	689	1846 C	A915223		VF	
107	M$100 1902DB	689	?	A982133		VG+	
107	M$100 1902DB	689	2068 C	A983122		?	
107	-$100 1902DB	689	2699 C	2699 C		VG/F	pen/pen
107	- $50 1902PB	675	3166 C	3166 C		VG	faded/faded
107	- $50 1902PB	675	3197 D	3197 D		VF+	
107	- $50 1902PB	675	3511 C	3511 C		VF	
107	-$100 1902PB	698	3451 C	3451 C		XF	pen/pen
107	$50 1929T1		B000025A			XF	
107	$50 1929T1		E000025A			F	Erased ink
107	$50 1929T1		B000045A			VF	
107	$50 1929T1		C000045A			XF	
107	$50 1929T1		D000045A			F/VF	
107	$50 1929T1		E000049A			F	Ink on face
107	$50 1929T1		D000057A			F	
107	$50 1929T1		E000086A			VG+	
107	$50 1929T1		D000102A			VG	Wallet staining
107	$50 1929T1		D000138A			VG	Corner tear UR
107	$50 1929T1		A000215A			VG/F	
107	$50 1929T1		B000216A			F+	
107	$50 1929T1		F000249A			F/VF	
107	$50 1929T1		E000302A			VF	
107	$50 1929T1		F000319A			VG+	
107	$50 1929T1		A000321A			F+	
107	$50 1929T1		F000338A			F	Pinholes
107	$50 1929T1		A000341A			AU	
107	$50 1929T1		B000341A			AU	
107	$50 1929T1		D000344A			VF	Higgins Mus.
107	$100 1929T1		A000024A			F	
107	$100 1929T1		D000075A			VF	Stains
107	$100 1929T1		D000079A			VF/XF	Stains

THE IOWA NATIONAL BANK OF OTTUMWA   6 L   11 S
1726   WAPELLO

Chartered in October 1870. Placed in voluntary liquidation on August 20, 1931; capital of $200,000. Succeeded by The Union Bank and Trust Company of Ottumwa.

Officers: Pres. LW Vale 1872-73, Charles F Blake 1874-92, Edwin Manning 1893-1900, Calvin Manning 1901-04, JH Merrill 1905-09, JC Jordan 1910-27, Cyrus K Blake 1927-30; **VP** William Daggett 1896, Calvin Manning 1900, JH Merrill 1902, John C Jordan 1907-09, JH Merrill 1910-11, Samuel Mahon 1913-14, HW Merrill 1920-26, Cyrus K Blake 1927, HW Merrill 1927-30; **Cash.** JB Field 1872-73, ES Scheffield 1874-75, John W Edgerly 1876-87, TH Eaton 1888-92, CK Blake 1893, Calvin Manning 1894-99, WR Daggett 1900-06; HC Chambers 1909-13, CF Rauscher 1914-30; **AC** WR Daggett 1896, HC Chambers 1900-07, CF Rauscher 1909-13, WC Miller 1920-30

First Charter, Original Issue	Ser #	# Notes
1-1-1-2	1-2000	8,000
5-5-5-5	1-4410	17,640

First Charter, Series of 1875
| 5-5-5-5 | 1-6685 | 26,740 |

Second Charter, Brown Backs
| 50-100 | 1-2074 | 4,148 |

Second Charter, Date Back
| 50-100 | 1-287 | 574 |

Third Charter, Date Back, Blue Seal
| 50-100 | 1-1000 | 2,000 |
| 50-50-50-100 | 1-1200 | 4,800 |

Third Charter, Plain Back, Blue Seal
| 50-50-50-100 | 1201-1579 | 1,516 |

1929, Type I
| 6-50's | 1-181 | 1,086 |
| 6-100's | 1-41 | 246 |

Total amount of circulation issued = $1,209,700. Amount of large outstanding at close = $29,350. Amount of small outstanding at close = $70,650.

65,418 Large   1,332 Small   66,750 Total

1726	- $5 1875	401	2309 A	E392909	F	pen/pen
1726	M $50 1902DB	667	638 A	A390237	VG	pen/pen UR gone
1726	M$100 1902DB	692	730 B	A909447	F/VF	pen/pen
1726	- $50 1902PB	678	1467 D	1467 D	VF	Higgins Mus.
1726	-$100 1902PB	701	1325 B	1325 B	VG/F	
1726	-$100 1902PB	701	1572 B	1572 B	XF	pen/pen
1726	$50 1929T1		F000013A		F/VF	
1726	$50 1929T1		B000055A		XF	
1726	$50 1929T1		D000084A		G	Damaged
1726	$50 1929T1		B000087A		XF	Higgins Mus.
1726	$50 1929T1		C000087A		VG	
1726	$50 1929T1		D000103A		VF	
1726	$50 1929T1		E000131A		VG/F	
1726	$50 1929T1		B000137A		F	
1726	$50 1929T1		C000154A		F	Pinholes
1726	$100 1929T1		B000022A		VF/XF	
1726	$100 1929T1		A000033A		VG/F	Writing on face

THE OTTUMWA NATIONAL BANK   29 L   16 S
2621   WAPELLO

Chartered in 1882. Placed in voluntary liquidation on October 26, 1931; capital of $100,000. Succeeded by The Union Bank and Trust Company of Ottumwa.

Officers: Pres. Joseph G Hutchison 1883-88, JB Mowrey 1889-1911, JT Hackworth 1912-19, JF Weber 1920-27, JH Anderson 1928-30; **VP** JT Hackworth 1896-1907, TD Foster 1909, JT Hackworth 1909-11, AG Harrow 1913-14, JW Nearham 1920-30, Homer H Harris 1920-30, RW Funk 1929-30; **Cash.** Arthur H Bayston 1883-84, MB Hutchison 1887-90, Charles E Boude 1891-97, LE Stevens 1898-1910, RW Funk 1911-31; **AC** MB Hutchison 1885, LE Stevens 1896, Wm S Hogue 1900-04, RW Funk 1907-10, Fred Dimmitt 1911-28, Philip Daggett 1920-22, CP Glenn 1922-30

First Charter, Series of 1875	Ser #	# Notes
10-10-10-20	1-3472	13,888

Second Charter, Brown Backs
| 10-10-10-20 | 1-4600 | 18,400 |

Second Charter, Date Back
| 5-5-5-5 | 1-6815 | 27,260 |
| 10-10-10-20 | 1-4220 | 16,880 |

Second Charter, Value Back
| 5-5-5-5 | 6816-12100 | 21,140 |
| 10-10-10-20 | 4221-7596 | 13,504 |

Third Charter, Plain Back, Blue Seal
| 50-50-50-100 | 1-1078 | 4,312 |

1929, Type I
| 6-50's | 1-182 | 1,092 |
| 6-100's | 1-39 | 234 |

Total amount of circulation issued = $1,372,900. Amount of large outstanding at close = $31,320. Amount of small outstanding at close = $68,650.

115,384 Large   1,326 Small   116,710 Total

2621	- $10 1875	420	2962 B	K880140	F	pen/pen
2621	- $10 1875	420	3258 A	K986336	XF/AU	Higgins Mus.
2621	M $20 1882BB	504	2840 A	N895605N	AU	
2621	M $5 1882DB	537	4172 D	K466869	G/VG	faded stamps
2621	M $5 1882DB	537	5131 B	M324053	F	stamp/stamp
2621	M $10 1882DB	545	2623 D	M252981	VG	stamp/stamp
2621	M $10 1882DB	545	3715 E	N918323	F	Higgins Mus.
2621	M $10 1882DB	545	3746 E	N918354	F	stamp/stamp
2621	M $20 1882DB	555	2164 B	M252622	VF	stamp Higg. Mus.
2621	M $5 1882VB	574	8789 C	T769711	F	stamp/stamp
2621	M $5 1882VB	574	9274 A	T770196	VG/F	stamp/stamp
2621	M $5 1882VB	574	9694 D	U148491	VG	
2621	M $5 1882VB	574	10819 B	U354466	VG	gone/gone
2621	M $5 1882VB	574	10922 C	U354569	F	
2621	M $5 1882VB	574	?	U498539	?	Smithsonian
2621	M $5 1882VB	574	11983 B	U595030	VG	stamp Rust
2621	M $10 1882VB	577	5273 D	U391791	F+	stamp/stamp
2621	M $10 1882VB	577	6060 F	U976108	VG	stamp/stamp
2621	M $20 1882VB	581	4612 B	T675860	VG	stamp/stamp
2621	M $20 1882VB	581	6532 B	V293520	VG/F	stamp/stamp
2621	M $20 1882VB	581	6674 B	V491322	VG	stamp/stamp
2621	M $50 1902PB	684	409 B	B27783	G	gone Washed
2621	- $50 1902PB	684	666 C	666 C	AU	
2621	- $50 1902PB	684	820 C	820 C	G/VG	faded/faded Tape
2621	- $50 1902PB	684	912 A	912 A	VG	stamp/stamp
2621	- $50 1902PB	684	1067 C	1067 C	VF	Fed. Res. Bk., San Francisco
2621	-$100 1902PB	706	536 A	B75280	F+	stamp/stamp
2621	-$100 1902PB	706	884 A	884 A	VG+	vp Higgins Mus.
2621	-$100 1902PB	706	1069 A	1069 A	F/VF	light sigs
2621	$50 1929T1		A000006A		F	
2621	$50 1929T1		C000036A		F/VF	Higgins Mus.
2621	$50 1929T1		E000039A		F/VF	Stained; Repaired
2621	$50 1929T1		A000046A		F	Ink stain on back
2621	$50 1929T1		B000049A		XF	
2621	$50 1929T1		F000063A		VF	
2621	$50 1929T1		D000082A		XF	
2621	$50 1929T1		D000093A		F	
2621	$50 1929T1		B000132A		VG	
2621	$50 1929T1		F000168A		F	
2621	$50 1929T1		F000176A		F/VF	
2621	$100 1929T1		F000002A		VG	
2621	$100 1929T1		C000017A		XF+	
2621	$100 1929T1		B000024A		XF/AU	

2621	$100 1929T1	C000031A		VF/XF	
2621	$100 1929T1	D000031A		VG/F	

THE GUTHRIE COUNTY NATIONAL BANK OF PANORA
3226   **GUTHRIE**   **16 L**

Organized on July 9, 1884 with a capital of $50,000. Succeeded The Guthrie County Bank. Placed in receivership on July 22, 1926; capital of $50,000. Reason for failure: local depression.

Officers: Pres. George H Moore 1884-98, MM Reynolds 1899-1915, HL Moore 1916-26; **VP** EJ Reynolds 1896-1907, HL Moore 1909-14, Wade Spurgin 1920-25, NW Irwin 1926; **Cash.** LJ Pentecost 1884-87, GM Reynolds 1888-92, Arthur Reynolds 1893-94, MM Reynolds 1895-98, WC Spurgin 1899-1900, Beaumont Apple 1902-03, 1907, Wade Spurgin 1905-06, 1908-15, TR Swanson 1916-26; **AC** Wade Spurgin 1904, VR Pentecost 1910-03, TR Swanson 1914, LL King 1922-23, Jos T Kilmer 1923-26

Second Charter, Brown Backs	Ser #	# Notes
10-10-10-20	1-2662	10,648
Third Charter, Red Seal		
10-10-10-20	1-1600	6,400
Third Charter, Date Back, Blue Seal		
10-10-10-20	1-3300	13,200
Third Charter, Plain Back, Blue Seal		
10-10-10-20	3301-7171	15,484

Total amount issued = $571,650. Amount outstanding at close = $49,100.
45,732 Large   0 Small   45,732 Total

3226		$10 1882BB	480	978 B	U124063	F+ Higgins Mus.
3226		$10 1882BB	480	1080 A	W341434	VG
3226		$20 1882BB	494	104 ?	?	G
3226	M	$10 1902RS	613	845 A	K59330	? Bayard, Damage
3226	M	$10 1902RS	613	845 C	K59330	Fr gone Bayard
3226	M	$10 1902DB	616	?	H307187	? Bayard
3226	M	$10 1902DB	616	2679 E	V852474A	G
3226	M	$10 1902DB	616	3113 E	A123007B	VG pen/pen
3226	M	$10 1902PB	624	4515 D	E692339D	G
3226	M	$10 1902PB	624	6047 D	R230959E	VF stamp sigs vp
3226	M	$10 1902PB	624	6191 D	D537523H	VG part'l/gone vp
3226	M	$10 1902PB	624	6273 E	D537605H	F+
3226	-	$10 1902PB	624	6859 E	X482081H	CU vp Higg. Mus.
3226	-	$10 1902PB	624	7073 D	7073 D	VG faded/pen vp
3226	M	$20 1902PB	650	4165 B	B15532D	F pen/pen
3226	M	$20 1902PB	650	4863 B	M976865D	F/VF

THE FIRST NATIONAL BANK OF PARKERSBURG   6 L
9846   **BUTLER**

Chartered in September 1910. Placed in voluntary liquidation on November 14, 1916; capital of $60,000. Absorbed by The Beaver Valley State Bank of Parkersburg.

Officers: Pres. Sander Ludemann 1911-15, CF Franke 1916; **VP** GN Clark 1911, CF Franke 1913-14; **Cash.** HEW Kaiser 1911-12, RA Ludemann 1913-16; **AC** JJ Ludemann 1911, AK Smith 1913-14

Third Charter, Date Back, Blue Seal	Ser #	# Notes
5-5-5-5	1-3300	13,200
10-10-10-20	1-2560	10,240
Third Charter, Plain Back, Blue Seal		
5-5-5-5	3301-3785	1,940
10-10-10-20	2561-2861	1,204

Total amount issued = $218,750. Amount outstanding at close = $60,000.
26,584 Large   0 Small   26,584 Total

9846	M	$5 1902DB	593	15 A	X720225	VF pen/pen
9846	M	$5 1902DB	593	1518 B	H201904A	F/VF Higgins Mus.
9846	M	$10 1902DB	619	538 C	Y368737	F+
9846	M	$10 1902DB	619	1503 C	K939784A	F 1508 C ?
9846	M	$20 1902DB	645	2291 A	Z392575A	F
9846	M	$10 1902PB	627	2848 A	U195816B	VG faded Higg. Mus.

THE CITIZENS NATIONAL BANK OF PELLA   8 L
8047 (FIRST TITLE)   **MARION**

Chartered in January 1906. Title changed to The Farmers National Bank of Pella on September 7, 1918 (Second Title) and did not issue any notes under that title.

Officers: Pres. L Kruidenier 1906-07, HD Wormhoudt 1908-17, GH Wormhoudt 1918, JH Cochrane 1919-23; **VP** A Wormhoudt 1907, AN Kuyper 1909-11, JS Rhynsburger 1913-14, Anna Van Spanckeren 1920-23, PH Van Gorp 1922-23, AC Van Houweling; **Cash.** BH Van Spanckeren, Jr. 1906-17, WH Vanderploeg 1919-23; **AC** JVD Roovaart 1909-13, 1920-23

Third Charter, Red Seal	Ser #	# Notes
10-10-10-20	1-300	1,200
Third Charter, Date Back, Blue Seal		
10-10-10-20	1-1750	7,000
Third Charter, Plain Back, Blue Seal		
10-10-10-20	1751-2270	2,080

Total amount issued = $128,500. Amount outstanding in 1922 = $4,900.
10,280 Large   0 Small   10,280 Total

8047	M	$10 1902RS	614	1 A	?	F
8047	M	$10 1902DB	617	1598 F	K542654B	VG/F
8047	M	$20 1902DB	643	1634 B	K542690B	VG Chunk missing
8047	M	$10 1902PB	625	1882 E	?	?
8047	M	$10 1902PB	625	2238 F	A998155D	VF Higgins Mus.
8047	M	$20 1902PB	651	1846 B	T559506B	VG very faded
8047	M	$20 1902PB	651	1929 B	?	VG
8047	M	$20 1902PB	651	2102 B	X597243B	F pen/pen ac

THE FIRST NATIONAL BANK OF PELLA   2 L
1891   **MARION**

Chartered on October 14, 1871 with a capital of $50,000. Placed in receivership on June 5, 1895; capital of $50,000. Reason for failure: local depression & dishonesty.

Officers: Pres. Edward R Cassatt 1872-94; **Cash.** OP Wright 1872-79, William Fisher 1872-79, JH Stubenrauch 1880-94

First Charter, Original Issue	Ser #	# Notes
1-1-1-2	1-1500	6,000
5-5-5-5	1-4375	17,500
First Charter, Series of 1875		
5-5-5-5	1-3290	13,160
Second Charter, Brown Backs		
10-10-10-20	1-282	1,128

Total amount of circulation issued = $174,900. Amount outstanding at close = $14,218. Amount outstanding in 1915 = $975.
37,788 Large   0 Small   37,788 Total

1891	-	$1	ORIG	382	163 A	C792769	VF Higgins Museum
1891	-	?	1875	?	? A	A671472	VG/F

THE PELLA NATIONAL BANK   19 L   30 S
2063   **MARION**

Chartered on November 7, 1872 with a capital of $50,000. Placed in conservatorship on March 16, 1933. Licensed on June 8, 1933.

Officers: Pres. John Rosiersz 1873-75, Pierre H Bousquet 1876-1907, RR Beard 1909-20, Geo G Gaass 1922-35; **VP** RR Beard 1896-1907, John Nollen 1909-14, Geo G Gaass 1920, ES Cook 1922-35, JH DeVries 1922-35, HH Geelhoed 1922-33; **Cash.** John Nollen 1873-1904, HP Scholte 1905-35; **AC** HL Bousquet 1878-79, Henry P Scholte 1885-1904, ES Cook 1907-14, Paul Scholte 1914, C Smorenberg 1920-35, Will Baer 1927-35

First Charter, Original Issue	Ser #	# Notes
5-5-5-5	1-1750	7,000
10-10-10-20	1-2500	10,000
First Charter, Series of 1875		
10-10-10-20	1-3410	9,640
Second Charter, Brown Backs		
10-10-10-20	1-3680	14,720
Second Charter, Date Back		
10-10-10-20	1-1564	6,256
Third Charter, Date Back, Blue Seal		
10-10-10-20	1-1500	6,000
Third Charter, Plain Back, Blue Seal		
10-10-10-20	1501-6944	21,776
1929, Type I		
6-5's	1-4242	25,452
1929, Type II		
5's	1-8936	8,936

Total amount of circulation issued = $1,111,840. Amount of large outstanding in 1935 = $4,710. Amount of small outstanding in 1935 = $43,240.
79,392 Large   34,388 Small   113,780 Total

2063	-	$10	1875 416	440 C	A638233	VF ac/vp Blue end paper
2063	M	$10 1882DB	540	718 E	B17118	VF Higgins Mus.
2063	M	$10 1882DB	540	1467 D	K99265	F pen/pen
2063	M	$10 1902DB	620	1269 A	M569062A	F+ pen/pen
2063	M	$10 1902DB	620	1341 C	M569134A	G pen/pen
2063	M	$10 1902DB	620	1342 B	M569135A	F
2063	M	$10 1902PB	628	1730 B	?	?
2063	M	$10 1902PB	628	3336 D	X241008D	XF Higgins Mus.
2063	M	$10 1902PB	628	4438 C	A159480H	VG+
2063	-	$10 1902PB	628	5842 C	5842 C	VG/F
2063	-	$10 1902PB	628	5912 C	5912 C	AU
2063	M	? 1902PB	?	1672 A	?	?
2063	M	$20 1902PB	654	1929 A	V846739B	F pen/pen
2063	M	$20 1902PB	654	3527 A	E51179E	CU
2063	M	$20 1902PB	654	3597 A	E51249E	VF
2063	M	$20 1902PB	654	3621 A	E51273E	VF pen/pen vp
2063	M	$20 1902PB	654	4214 A	R490116E	VF
2063	M	$20 1902PB	654	4538 A	A159580H	VG
2063		$20 1902PB	654	5186 A	X168478H	G/VG

2063	$5	1929T1	F000155A	VG	
2063	$5	1929T1	B000280A	VG	
2063	$5	1929T1	A000885A	F	
2063	$5	1929T1	A001173A	?	
2063	$5	1929T1	D001204A	VG	
2063	$5	1929T1	C001653A	F	
2063	$5	1929T1	D001786A	?	
2063	$5	1929T1	F001795A	HG	
2063	$5	1929T1	E001821A	?	
2063	$5	1929T1	E001831A	?	
2063	$5	1929T1	A002381A	XF	
2063	$5	1929T1	E002642A	VF	
2063	$5	1929T1	A003345A	VG/F	
2063	$5	1929T1	F003394A	VG/F	
2063	$5	1929T1	D003552A	?	
2063	$5	1929T1	F003588A	VG	
2063	$5	1929T1	D003594A	VG	
2063	$5	1929T1	E003666A	AU	Higgins Mus.
2063	$5	1929T1	D003725A	F	
2063	$5	1929T1	F003733A	VF	
2063	$5	1929T1	D003781A	VG	
2063	$5	1929T1	A004122A	VG/F	
2063	$5	1929T2	A000994	VG	
2063	$5	1929T2	A001860	?	
2063	$5	1929T2	A004090	VG/F	
2063	$5	1929T2	A007120	CU	
2063	$5	1929T2	A007348	F	
2063	$5	1929T2	A007362	CU	
2063	$5	1929T2	A007363	CU	
2063	$5	1929T2	A007824	F	

THE FIRST NATIONAL BANK OF PERRY   9 L
3026   DALLAS
Chartered in 1883; succeeded George W. Blakeslee.
Officers: Pres. George W Blakeslee 1883-85, DJ Pattee 1887-1911, HM Pattee 1912-22, JM Grimes 1923-26, WH Brenton 1926-35; **VP** Allen Breed 1896-1911, JL Blake 1913-22, WH Pattee 1922, DD McColl 1923, CR Lyon 1923-26, HA Foltz 1925-26, 1928-33, Clyde E Brenton 1926-31, JM Grimes 1926, Eva AB McColl 1932-35, GC Kelly 1932-35, Dr. EM Foltz 1935; **Cash.** Howard A Rouse 1883, Wilmot Blakeslee 1884-85, O Mosher 1887, HJ Holmes 1888-98, AS Holmes 1899, JM Woodworth 1900-07, HM Pattee 1908-11, WH Pattee 1912-20, BH Wood 1922-24, HL Thomas 1925-26, ER Burkett 1926-35; **AC** EN Swain 1885, HS Taylor 1900, HM Pattee 1904-07, WH Pattee 1909-11, RA Ridge 1913, HL Thomas 1914-24, 1926-31, JM Grimes, Jr. 1926, Nancy Underwood 1927-35, RS Kinsey 1927-30, WB Christ 1931-35

	Ser #	# Notes
Second Charter, Brown Backs		
10-10-10-20	1-2000	8,000
Third Charter, Red Seal		
10-10-10-20	1-2150	8,600
Third Charter, Date Back, Blue Seal		
10-10-10-20	1-3000	12,000
Third Charter, Plain Back, Blue Seal		
10-10-10-20	3001-7775	19,100

Total amount of circulation issued = $596,250. Amount outstanding in 1925 = $50,000. Amount outstanding in 1935 = $2,940.

47,700 Large   0 Small   47,700 Total

3026	M	$10 1882BB	480	1364 C	M913003D	VG/F
3026	M	$10 1902DB	616	829 E	K988070	AU+ stamp/stamp
3026	M	$10 1902DB	616	1487 F	E149412A	F gone Higg. Mus.
3026	M	$10 1902DB	616	2953 E	A105967B	VG+
3026	M	$10 1902PB	624	6650 ?	A386292H	VG/F
3026	M	$10 1902PB	624	5772 F	K98894E	VG gone Higg. Mus.
3026	-	$10 1902PB	624	7560 D	X947572H	VG pen/pen
3026	M	$20 1902PB	650	3420 B	U783198B	VF stamp/stamp
3026	-	$20 1902PB	650	7655 B	7655 B	VG Bayard

THE PEOPLES NATIONAL BANK OF PERRY   4 L
10130 (FIRST TITLE)   DALLAS
Organized on January 2, 1912 with a capital of $50,000. Chartered on Jan. 22, 1912. Title changed to The Perry National Bank, Perry on Feb. 23, 1917.
Officers: Pres. John P O'Malley 1912-16, WH McCammon 1917; **VP** JC O'Malley 1914; **Cash.** ED Carter 1912-16, John Carmody 1917

	Ser #	# Notes
Third Charter, Date Back, Blue Seal		
10-10-10-20	1-1055	4,220

Sheets numbered 1 to 1000 were 02-08 backs. Sheets numbered 1001 to 1055 were delivered on October 2 but not marked as to type. If they were 02-08 backs, then 55 sheets of plains would have been issued on the old title. Sheets numbered 1056 to 1120 were cancelled.

4,220 Large   0 Small   4,220 Total

10130M	$10 1902DB	617	170 C	H258155A	F	pen/pen
10130M	$20 1902DB	643	604 A	H258589A	VF	stamp/pen
10130M	$20 1902DB	643	819 A	H258804A	F/VF	pen Higg. Mus.
10130M	$20 1902DB	643	901 A	H258886A	VF	

THE PERRY NATIONAL BANK, PERRY   9 L
10130 (2ND TITLE)   DALLAS
Succeeded The Peoples National Bank of Perry on February 23, 1917. Placed in receivership on February 5, 1925; capital of $75,000. Reason for failure: incompetent management & dishonesty.
Officers: Pres. WH McCammon 1917-24; **VP** JP O'Malley 1920, JC O'Malley 1923-24, DD McColl 1920, 1922; **Cash.** John Carmody 1917-24; **AC** JE Hambright 1920-24, Geo W O'Malley 1920-24, ME Carmody 1920-24

	Ser #	# Notes
Third Charter, Plain Back, Blue Seal		
5-5-5-5	1-6270	25,080
10-10-10-20	1-4480	17,920

Total amount issued = $402,150. Amount outstanding at close = $72,300.

43,000 Large   0 Small   43,000 Total

10130M	$5 1902PB	606	4418 A	U900574E	VG	stamp/stamp
10130M	$5 1902PB	606	4821 A	U900977E	VG/F	gone/gone
10130	-	$5 1902PB	606	6109 C	M693795H	VG gone Washed
10130M	$10 1902PB	632	320 B	A726807D	VG	stamp/stamp
10130M	$10 1902PB	632	993 A	A976480D	F	stamp/stamp
10130M	$10 1902PB	632	2313 B	A959005E	F	gone/gone
10130M	$10 1902PB	632	2315 C	A959007E	F	gone/gone
10130M	$10 1902PB	632	2857 A	H504569E	XF	stamp Higg. Mus.
10130M	$20 1902PB	658	483 A	A726970D	XF	

THE FIRST NATIONAL BANK OF PETERSON   10 L   15 S
4601   CLAY
Chartered in 1891.
Officers: Pres. JP Farmer 1891, AS Weir 1892-1907, EL Mantor 1908-13, AO Anderson 1914-24; **VP** William Kirchner 1896-1911, EC Bertrom 1913-24; **Cash.** GC Allison 1891-1902, CH Staples 1902-08, HG Morrison 1909-24; **AC** AC Hastings 1896, JE Allison, Frank Steckmest 1902, EL Mantor 1903-04, Chas. Mertens 1907, PJ Toft 1920-24

	Ser #	# Notes
Second Charter, Brown Backs		
10-10-10-20	1-2290	9,160
Second Charter, Date Back		
10-10-10-20	1-481	1,924
Third Charter, Date Back, Blue Seal		
10-10-10-20	1-1400	5,600
Third Charter, Plain Back, Blue Seal		
10-10-10-20	1401-7128	22,912
1929, Type I		
6-10's	1-1024	6,144
6-20's	1-286	1,716
1929, Type II		
10's	1-478	478
20's	1-178	178

Total amount of circulation issued = $599,050. Amount outstanding in 1934 = $25,000. Amount of large outstanding on August 1, 1935 = $2,840.

39,596 Large   8,516 Small   48,112 Total

4601	-	$10 1882BB	485	770 A	U1225	VG+ pen/pen
4601		$10 1882BB	485	1277 B	W191150	VG Higgins Mus.
4601	M	$10 1882BB	485	2144 B	U444494U	G/VG Repaired
4601		$10 1902PB	628	3235 C	Y639327D	VF Higgins Mus.
4601		$10 1902PB	628	4119 C	?	F/VF
4601		$10 1902PB	628	4143 B	T454725E	VG
4601	-	$10 1902PB	628	5425 B	Z839577H	lt pen/pen
4601	-	$20 1902PB	654	5072 A	T938364H	F/VF
4601	-	$20 1902PB	654	5156 A	T938448H	F/VF stamp/stamp
4601	-	$20 1902PB	654	6528 A	6528 A	VG/F pen/pen
4601		$10 1929T1		D000034A		VG Ink; bleach, rust
4601		$10 1929T1		B000086A		F
4601		$10 1929T1		F000380A		F/VF
4601		$10 1929T1		B000450A		VF Repaired tear
4601		$10 1929T1		B000611A		HG
4601		$10 1929T1		A000616A		VF
4601		$10 1929T1		F000688A		VF
4601		$10 1929T1		F000729A		VF
4601		$10 1929T1		E000830A		VG/F
4601		$20 1929T1		B000061A		VF+
4601		$20 1929T1		E000098A		F+
4601		$20 1929T1		D000101A		?
4601		$20 1929T1		E000107A		F
4601		$20 1929T1		F000169A		F UL corner missing
4601		$20 1929T2		A000162		VF Higgins Mus.

THE FIRST NATIONAL BANK OF PLEASANTVILLE   3 L
5564   MARION
Chartered on August 30, 1900 with a capital of $25,000. Placed in receivership on February 21, 1925; capital of $25,000. Reason for failure: incompetent management.
Officers: Pres. WA Clark 1901-07, L Williams 1908-13, Charles Clark 1914-17, Reuben Core 1918-23, Charles Clark 1924; **VP** TR Brown 1902-07, AD Reynolds 1909-13, Reuben Core 1914, RS Flanagan 1920-24; **Cash.** WC Reed 1901-06, AS Flanagan 1907, FT Metcalf 1908-23, RB Farquhar 1924; **AC** Mrs. FT Metcalf 1913, 1920-23, Esther F Metcalf 1914, LS Rouze 1920-23

Second Charter, Brown Backs	Ser #	# Notes
10-10-10-20	1-1800	7,200
Second Charter, Date Back		
10-10-10-20	1-1530	6,120
Second Charter, Value Back		
10-10-10-20	1531-2417	3,548
Third Charter, Plain Back, Blue Seal		
10-10-10-20	1-1268	5,072

Total amount issued = $274,250. Amount outstanding at close = $24,700.
21,940 Large   0 Small   21,940 Total

5564	M	$20	1882VB	581	1667 B	T700245	VG/F	Higgins Mus.
5564	M	$10	1902PB	633	1 A	X719253D	CU	Higgins Mus.
5564	M	$10	1902PB	633	517 A	N176874E	VG	pen ac/pen

THE FIRST NATIONAL BANK IN POCAHONTAS   3 L
12544   POCAHONTAS
Organized on May 12, 1924 with a capital of $75,000. Succeeded #6303. Assumed the circulation of #6303. Placed in receivership on January 30, 1926; capital of $75,000. Reason for failure: local depression.
Officers: Pres. CW Bash 1924-25; **VP** PL Rivard 1925; **Cash.** FW Lindeman 1924-25; **AC** FJ Lorge 1925, R Bash 1925

Third Charter, Plain Back, Blue Seal	Ser #	# Notes
5-5-5-5	1-155	620
10-10-10-20	1-352	1,408

Total amount of circulation issued = $20,700. Amount outstanding at close = $24,300. Includes the circulation of #6303 that was still outstanding.
2,028 Large   0 Small   2,028 Total

12544	-	$5	1902PB	609	3 D	R645689H	VG/F	
12544	-	$5	1902PB	609	127 C	R645813H	XF	Higgins Mus.
12544	-	$5	1902PB	609	136 B	R645822H	VG	stamp/pen

THE FIRST NATIONAL BANK OF POCAHONTAS   8 L
6303   POCAHONTAS
Organized May 27, 1902. Chartered in 1902. Placed in voluntary liquidation on July 9, 1924; capital of $50,000. Succeeded by #12544.
Officers: Pres. LC Thornton 1902-03, JH Allen 1904-18, JM Berry 1919-20, CW Bash 1922-24; **VP** WD McEwen 1903, CS Allen 1904-11, JA Crummer 1913-14, FW Lindeman 1920-24, Theo F McCarton 1920-24, Thomas Shimon 1920; **Cash.** WS McEwen 1902-03, FW Lindeman 1904-16, Anton Mackovets 1917-24; **AC** James Bruce 1903, GW Gilchrist 1904, ET Shors 1907, James Parizer 1909-10, Anton Mackovets 1911-14, CCB McCarton 1920-24, WG Anderson 1920, LC Pattee 1920-24

Third Charter, Red Seal	Ser #	# Notes
5-5-5-5	1-825	3,300
10-10-10-20	1-660	2,640
Third Charter, Date Back, Blue Seal		
5-5-5-5	1-2125	8,500
10-10-10-20	1-1600	6,400
Third Charter, Plain Back, Blue Seal		
5-5-5-5	2126-3855	6,920
10-10-10-20	1601-2542	3,768

Total amount of circulation issued = $253,700. Amount outstanding in 1922 = $24,700. Liability for redemption of circulation assumed by #12544.
31,528 Large   0 Small   31,528 Total

6303	M	$5	1902DB	590	2026 F	?	F	pen/pen
6303	M	$10	1902DB	616	930 D	V837065A	F	pen/pen
6303	M	$10	1902DB	616	1139 E	Y370645A	VG	Higgins Mus.
6303	M	$10	1902DB	616	1309 D	Y370815A	VG	
6303	M	$5	1902PB	598	2514 G	Z803775B	F/VF	pen/pen
6303	M	$5	1902PB	598	3318 E	B841339E	F+	stamp/pen vp
6303	M	$5	1902PB	598	3728 H	A863264H	VG	gone/pen vp
6303	M	$10	1902PB	624	1852 F	T424994D	F	vp

THE FIRST NATIONAL BANK OF POMEROY   16 L   3 S
6063   CALHOUN
Organized on December 10, 1901 with a capital of $40,000. Chartered on December 26, 1901; succeeded The Pomeroy Exchange Bank. Placed in receivership on May 5, 1931; capital of $40,000. Reason for failure: local depression.

Officers: Pres. Lewis W Moody 1901-14, Mrs. Mary R Moody 1915-17, WC McCulloch 1918-31; **VP** WC McCulloch 1902-15, HJ Colburn 1920-31; **Cash.** Albert B Nixon 1901-10, AF Volberding 1911-26, HJ Colburn 1927, FJ Oehmke 1928-31; **AC** GG Pierce 1907, RM McCulloch 1909, F Johnson 1910-13, HJ Colburn 1914-15, JH Brogmus 1920, FJ Oehmke 1927, Hugo Swalin 1928-31

Second Charter, Brown Backs	Ser #	# Notes
5-5-5-5	1-1055	4,220
10-10-10-20	1-858	3,432
Second Charter, Date Back		
5-5-5-5	1-2850	11,400
10-10-10-20	1-2020	8,080
Second Charter, Value Back		
5-5-5-5	2851-5015	8,660
10-10-10-20	2021-3264	4,976
Third Charter, Plain Back, Blue Seal		
5-5-5-5	1-9522	38,088
1929, Type I		
6-5's	1-2225	13,350

Total amount of circulation issued = $584,690. Amount of large outstanding at close = $4,100. Amount of small outstanding at close = $35,900.
78,856 Large   13,350 Small   92,206 Total

6063	M	$5	1882DB	537	2646 C	N317808	G	pen/gone
6063	M	$20	1882DB	555	1980 B	R292788	AU	pen/gone
6063	M	$5	1882VB	574	3382 H	T406619	F	
6063	M	$5	1882VB	574	3410 H	T406647	VG/F	Higgins Mus.
6063	M	$20	1882VB	581	3254 B	V663217	VG/F	Higgins Mus.
6063	M	$5	1902PB	608	710 C	H763731E	F/VF	Higgins Mus.
6063	M	$5	1902PB	608	1326 A	R783607E	VG/F	stamp/stamp
6063	M	$5	1902PB	608	1425 C	R783706E	F	
6063	M	$5	1902PB	608	3354 A	K457640H	VG/F	stamp/stamp
6063	-	$5	1902PB	608	4121 C	X610782H	F	
6063	-	$5	1902PB	608	5047 C	5047 C	VG/F	gone/gone
6063	-	$5	1902PB	608	5085 C	5085 C	F	stamp sigs vp
6063	-	$5	1902PB	608	6281 A	6281 A	VG	gone/gone
6063	-	$5	1902PB	608	6984 B	6984 B	VF	stamp/stamp
6063	-	$5	1902PB	608	7508 A	7508 A	F	pen/stamp
6063	-	$5	1902PB	608	8432 C	8432 C	F/VF	
6063		$5	1929T1		D000114A		Fr	
6063		$5	1929T1		F000300A		F	Higgins Mus.
6063		$5	1929T1		E001602A		F	

THE FIRST NATIONAL BANK OF PRAIRIE CITY   5 L   16 S
6755   JASPER
Organized on April 14, 1903 with a capital of $25,000. Succeeded The Zachary Bank. Placed in conservatorship on March 23, 1933. Licensed on December 1, 1933.
Officers: Pres. JD Whisenand 1904-14, BE Moore 1915-33, WR Hayes 1934-35; **VP** James G Olmsted 1904-14, BE Moore 1909-14, JH Little 1920-22, John H McKlveen 1923-35; **Cash.** Fred S Risser 1904-07, WD Scott 1908, Hugh G Little 1909-31, John Van Steenbergen 1931-32, 1934-35, FC Turner 1933; **AC** Hugh G Little 1907, FC Turner 1913-34, Le Roy Schakel 1923-35

Third Charter, Red Seal	Ser #	# Notes
10-10-10-20	1-356	1,424
Third Charter, Date Back, Blue Seal		
10-10-10-20	1-1000	4,000
Third Charter, Plain Back, Blue Seal		
10-10-10-20	1001-4219	12,876
1929, Type I		
6-10's	1-522	3,132
6-20's	1-150	900
1929, Type II		
10's	1-519	519
20's	1-105	105

Total amount of circulation issued = $285,360. Amount of large outstanding in 1935 = $1,260. Amount of small outstanding in 1935 = $23,490.
18,300 Large   4,656 Small   22,956 Total

6755	M	$20	1902DB	642	769 B	K834650A	VG	
6755	-	$20	1902PB	650	3469 B	3469 B	VF	pen/pen
6755	-	$20	1902PB	650	4175 B	4175 B	VF	
6755	-	$20	1902PB	650	4176 B	4176 B	CU	Higgins Mus.
6755	-	$20	1902PB	650	4198 B	4198 B	VF	
6755		$10	1929T1		E000139A		F	

6755	$10	1929T1	C000156A	F/VF	
6755	$10	1929T1	E000209A	F	
6755	$10	1929T1	C000217A	F	
6755	$10	1929T1	E000217A	F	
6755	$10	1929T1	E000442A	VG/F	
6755	$10	1929T1	D000467A	VG	
6755	$20	1929T1	F000010A	VF+	Higgins Mus.
6755	$20	1929T1	A000038A	CU	
6755	$20	1929T1	B000039A	VF	
6755	$20	1929T1	E000047A	G/VG	Ink
6755	$20	1929T1	A000068A	F	
6755	$20	1929T1	B000077A	VF/XF	
6755	$20	1929T1	D000131A	F+	
6755	$10	1929T2	A000240	VF	Higgins Mus.
6755	$10	1929T2	A000322	VG	

THE FIRST NATIONAL BANK OF PRESCOTT   13 L   16 S
5912   **ADAMS**
Chartered in July 1901 with a capital of $25,000.
Officers: Pres. James C Allen 1902-07, FM Widner 1908-11, Ralph Newcomb 1912-13, FD Ball 1914-19, D Davenport 1920-34, George J Bartle 1935; **VP** JR Comstock 1902, HC Reese 1903-05, C Johnson 1907, FA Outhier 1909-13, D Davenport 1914, Scott Skinner 1920-35; **Cash.** Theo F King 1902, WP Shinn 1903-05, WA Addison 1906-07, B Newcomb 1908-13, FA Outhier 1914-35; **AC** FR Warnick 1904, WG Perkins 1909-35, Bradford Outhier 1930-35

	Ser #	# Notes
Second Charter, Brown Backs		
5-5-5-5	1-1475	5,900
10-10-10-20	1-1140	4,560
Second Charter, Date Back		
5-5-5-5	1-1575	6,300
10-10-10-20	1-1120	4,480
Second Charter, Value Back		
5-5-5-5	1576-2805	4,920
10-10-10-20	1121-1815	2,780
Third Charter, Plain Back, Blue Seal		
5-5-5-5	1-2006	8,024
10-10-10-20	1-1331	5,324
1929, Type I		
6-5's	1-776	4,656
6-10's	1-386	2,316
6-20's	1-130	780
1929, Type II		
5's	1-260	260
10's	1-341	341
20's	1-65	65

Total amount of circulation issued = $408,070. Amount of large outstanding in June 1935 = $1,557. Amount of small outstanding in June 1935 = $23,440.
42,288 Large   8,418 Small   50,706 Total

5912	M	$5 1882DB	537	1490 G	N259827	VG	stamp/stamp
5912	M	$5 1882VB	574	1925 F	T398787	F/VF	Higgins Mus.
5912	M	$5 1882VB	574	2696 E	U472583	VG/F	
5912	M	$10 1882VB	577	1282 D	T7??280	Fr	Pieces gone
5912	M	$10 1882VB	577	1449 D	U596357	CU	
5912	M	$5 1902PB	607	255 A	K285151E	AU	stamp/pen vp
5912	M	$5 1902PB	607	284 A	K285180E	AG	faded/pen Stains
5912	M	$10 1902PB	633	93 A	A872705E	AU	stamp/pen vp
5912	M	$10 1902PB	633	335 C	Y441847E	F+	Higgins Mus.
5912	M	$10 1902PB	633	383 A	Y441895E	F	
5912	-	$10 1902PB	633	725 B	A366847K	F	stamp/stamp
5912	M	$20 1902PB	659	429 A	D873791H	F	LR corner gone
5912	-	$20 1902PB	659	1005 A	1005 A	VF	stamp/stamp
5912		$5 1929T1		D000533A		VG	
5912		$10 1929T1		E000094A		VF	Higgins Mus.
5912		$10 1929T1		F000172A		VF	
5912		$10 1929T1		F000255A		VG	
5912		$10 1929T1		C000303A		VG	
5912		$10 1929T1		A000305A		F	
5912		$20 1929T1		D000002A		F	
5912		$20 1929T1		F000014A		F	
5912		$20 1929T1		B000020A		VG	
5912		$20 1929T1		F000021A		F/VF	
5912		$20 1929T1		A000038A		F	
5912		$20 1929T1		B000083A		VG/F	
5912		$20 1929T1		F000091A		VF	
5912		$10 1929T2		A000088		?	
5912		$10 1929T2		A000173		VG	
5912		$10 1929T2		A000213		?	

THE FIRST NATIONAL BANK OF PRESTON   6 L   5 S
8273   **JACKSON**
Chartered in June 1906. Placed in voluntary liquidation on August 25, 1931; capital of $25,000. Succeeded by The United Bank & Trust Company.
Officers: Pres. AL Bartholowmew 1906-14, Hugh Jenkins 1915-25, WF Schroeder 1926-31; **VP** GE Bartholowmew 1907-11, RA Countryman 1913, WF Schroeder 1914, 1920-25, John Grant 1926-31; **Cash.** Helen M Beckwith 1906-12, Fredireka Paulsen 1913-15, WF Schroeder 1916-25, JW Campbell 1926-28, CB Johnson 1929-31; **AC** JW Campbell 1922-25

	Ser #	# Notes
Third Charter, Red Seal		
5-5-5-5	1-200	800
10-10-10-20	1-160	640
Third Charter, Date Back, Blue Seal		
5-5-5-5	1-1725	6,900
10-10-10-20	1-1260	5,040
Third Charter, Plain Back, Blue Seal		
5-5-5-5	1726-5202	13,908
10-10-10-20	1261-3384	8,496
1929, Type I		
6-5's	1-457	2,742
6-10's	1-209	1,254
6-20's	1-57	342

Total amount of circulation issued = $318,330. Amount of large outstanding at close = $3,350. Amount of small outstanding at close = $21,650.
35,784 Large   4,338 Small   40,122 Total

8273	M	$5 1902PB	599	2315 H	Y549641B	VG	pen/pen Washed
8273	M	$5 1902PB	599	3860 H	H943271H	Fr/G	
8273	-	$5 1902PB	599	4414 H	4414 H	VG	
8273	M	$10 1902PB	625	2431 F	M496923H	F	pen/pen
8273	-	$10 1902PB	625	3122 E	3122		pen/pen nice sigs
8273	-	$20 1902PB	651	2598 B	U133580H	F/VF	Bayard Higg. Mus
8273		$5 1929T1		B000186A		F	
8273		$10 1929T1		D000056A		VG/F	Higgins Mus.
8273		$10 1929T1		B000099A		VG/F	
8273		$10 1929T1		D000123A		VG/F	
8273		$10 1929T1		F000148A		VG	

THE FARMERS NATIONAL BANK OF PRIMGHAR   0 L
6650   **O'BRIEN**
Chartered on February 28, 1903. Placed in voluntary liquidation on November 10, 1904; capital of $30,000. Consolidated with #4155.
Officers: Pres. GR Whitmer 1903-04; **VP** WA Sanford 1904; **Cash.** R Hinman 1903-04; **AC** Will H Eddy 1903

	Ser #	# Notes
Third Charter, Red Seal		
10-10-10-20	1-197	788

Total amount of circulation issued = $9,850. Amount outstanding at close = $7,500. Amount outstanding in 1910 = $600.
788 Large   0 Small   788 Total

THE FIRST NATIONAL BANK OF PRIMGHAR   9 L   24 S
4155   **O'BRIEN**
Organized on October 23, 1889 with a capital of $50,000. Assumed #6650 by consolidation on November 10, 1904. Licensed after the Bank Holiday of 1933 on March 20, 1933.
Officers: Pres. Frank H Robinson 1889-92, CH Slocum 1894-1904, WH Smith 1905-13, R Hinman 1914-35; **VP** HS Green 1896-1904, OH Montzheimer 1907-35; **Cash.** George R Slocum 1889-1902, LW Mittendorff 1902-04, R Hinman 1905-13, Roy M King 1914-19, FC Bordewick 1920, Bernice Stewart 1922-23, FC Bordewick 1924-35; **AC** Roy M King 1910-13, Bernice Stewart 1920, LH Jackson 1924-25, James M Metcalf 1932-35

	Ser #	# Notes
Second Charter, Brown Backs		
10-10-10-20	1-1484	5,936
Third Charter, Date Back, Blue Seal		
10-10-10-20	1-1080	4,320
Third Charter, Plain Back, Blue Seal		
10-10-10-20	1081-5406	17,304
1929, Type I		
6-10's	1-1182	7,092
6-20's	1-304	1,824
1929, Type II		
10's	1-726	726
20's	1-175	175

Total amount of circulation issued = $462,660. Amount outstanding in 1934 = $49,550. Amount of large outstanding on July 18, 1935 = $2,690.
27,560 Large   9,817 Small   37,377 Total

4155	M	$20 1902DB	644	945 A	V850900A	VF	gone/gone
4155	M	$10 1902PB	626	1015 A	V850970A	CU	Higgins Mus.
4155	M	$10 1902PB	626	2236 C	X994128E	VF	stamp/stamp
4155	M	$10 1902PB	626	2703 A	Y233445E	VF	

Bank	Type	Plate	Serial 1	Serial 2	Grade	Notes
4155	- $10 1902PB 626		3907 C	9307 C	VG/F	stamp/stamp
4155	- $10 1902PB 626		4332 A	4332 A	XF	discoloration
4155	M $20 1902PB 652		1404 A	R204516E	XF	faded/faded
4155	M $20 1902PB 652		2570 A	Y233312E	VF	
4155	- $20 1902PB 652		4764 A	4764 A	VG+	
4155	$10 1929T1		F000387A		VF	
4155	$10 1929T1		F000465A		G	
4155	$10 1929T1		E000561A		F	bank stamp
4155	$10 1929T1		E000660A		VG	
4155	$10 1929T1		F000740A		VG	Dirty
4155	$10 1929T1		A000774A		F/VF	
4155	$10 1929T1		B000827A		XF	
4155	$10 1929T1		F000850A		VG	
4155	$10 1929T1		E000852A		VF	Pinholes
4155	$10 1929T1		F000880A		VF	
4155	$10 1929T1		D000971A		F	
4155	$10 1929T1		A001005A		VG	Stained
4155	$10 1929T1		B001028A		VG/F	Odd serial # printing?
4155	$10 1929T1		B001051A		VF	
4155	$10 1929T1		F001081A		XF	Higgins Mus.
4155	$10 1929T1		A001085A		XF	
4155	$10 1929T1		E001142A		VG	
4155	$20 1929T1		A000066A		VF	
4155	$20 1929T1		F000088A		F	corner piece gone
4155	$20 1929T1		D000096A		F+	
4155	$20 1929T1		F000209A		VF	
4155	$20 1929T1		C000262A		F/VF	
4155	$20 1929T1		A000278A		VF	
4155	$20 1929T2		A000165		XF	

THE FIRST NATIONAL BANK OF RADCLIFFE   3 L   9 S
6435   HARDIN

Organized on September 15, 1902 with a capital of $50,000. Placed in voluntary liquidation on December 30, 1931; capital of $50,000. Absorbed by #8970; circulation assumed by #8970. Placed in receivership on January 30, 1934; reason: deficiency in assets.

Officers: Pres. Wm Wiemer 1903-15, CG Wiemer 1916-31; **VP** F Stukenberg 1903-13, PJ Hoffman 1920-31; **Cash.** CG Wiemer 1903-15, Wm Hoffman 1916-31; **AC** HH Lexvold 1907-09, Wm Hoffman 1910-11, ET Rorem 1913, Jewell Bockwitz 1914, MO Skrovig 1923-26, EE Wiemer 1925-31

	Ser #	# Notes
Third Charter, Red Seal		
10-10-10-20	1-730	2,920
Third Charter, Date Back, Blue Seal		
10-10-10-20	1-1200	4,800
Third Charter, Plain Back, Blue Seal		
10-10-10-20	1201-2294	4,376
1929, Type I		
6-10's	1-189	1,134
6-20's	1-36	216

Total amount of circulation issued = $166,860. Amount outstanding at close = $12,500. Amount of large outstanding at close = $2,400. Amount of small outstanding at close = $10,100. Circulation assumed by #8970 which was then responsible for redeeming the outstanding circulation of #6435.

12,096 Large   1,350 Small   13,446 Total

6435	- $10 1902PB 624	2173 D	2173 D	F+	pen/pen Cut; tape
6435	- $10 1902PB 624	2181 E	2181 E	F/VF	Higgins Mus.
6435	- $10 1902PB 624	2274 D	2274 D	VG/F	pen/pen
6435	$10 1929T1	E000015A		?	Higgins Mus.
6435	$10 1929T1	F000005A		CU	
6435	$10 1929T1	B000088A		F	
6435	$10 1929T1	A000162A		AU	
6435	$10 1929T1	F000166A		F/VF	
6435	$20 1929T1	F000004A		XF	
6435	$20 1929T1	D000005A		CU	
6435	$20 1929T1	F000005A		XF	Higgins Mus.
6435	$20 1929T1	E000015A		CU	

THE FARMERS FIRST NATIONAL BANK OF RAKE   14 S
11735   WINNEBAGO

Organized on May 12, 1920 with a capital of $25,000. Placed in conservatorship on April 10, 1933. Placed in receivership on October 30, 1933; capital of $25,000. Reason for failure: not available from reports.

Officers: Pres. Joe Larson 1920-22, Oscar C Olson 1923-26, JO Jordahl 1927-33, NT Matson 1933; **VP** AA Rake 1920-25, Joe Larson 1926, Gust Johnson 1927-33; **Cash.** TA Rake 1920-25, AM Erdahl 1925-33; **AC** AM Erdahl 1920-25, JA Sheldon 1925, EM Knutson 1926-33

	Ser #	# Notes
1929, Type I		
6-5's	1-388	2,328
6-10's	1-249	1,494

Total amount issued = $26,580. Amount outstanding at close = $16,000.
0 Large   3,822 Small   3,822 Total

11735	$5 1929T1	F000278A	VF	
11735	$5 1929T1	A000318A	F	
11735	$5 1929T1	F000330A	VF	
11735	$10 1929T1	F000001A	VG	
11735	$10 1929T1	A000041A	VG/F	
11735	$10 1929T1	A000105A	CU	
11735	$10 1929T1	D000106A	CU	Higgins Mus.
11735	$10 1929T1	D000108A	CU	
11735	$10 1929T1	E000109A	XF	
11735	$10 1929T1	F000110A	AU	
11735	$10 1929T1	F000111A	CU	
11735	$10 1929T1	A000126A	XF	
11735	$10 1929T1	B000149A	F	
11735	$10 1929T1	D000211A	F	

THE FIRST NATIONAL BANK OF RANDOLPH   5 L   4 S
7833   FREMONT

Organized on June 27, 1905 with a capital of $25,000. Placed in receivership on September 8, 1931; capital of $45,000.

Officers: Pres. HJ Failing 1905-09, AW Murphy 1910-16, CH Fichter 1917-23, MO Inman 1924-31; **VP** WA Townsend 1907-13, CH Fichter 1914, MO Inman 1920-23, HW Nieman 1924-27, Frank Kilpatrick 1928-31; **Cash.** HM Townsend 1905-13, AW Fichter 1914-23, Pearl Inman 1924, HJ Fichter 1925-31; **AC** AW Fichter 1910-13, G Gilchrist 1914, HJ Fichter 1920-23, JJ Amen 1925, Gertrude Walker 1926-31

	Ser #	# Notes
Third Charter, Red Seal		
10-10-10-20	1-860	3,440
Third Charter, Date Back, Blue Seal		
10-10-10-20	1-2030	8,120
Third Charter, Plain Back, Blue Seal		
10-10-10-20	2031-5099	12,276
1929, Type I		
6-10's	1-374	2,244
6-20's	1-100	600

Total amount of circulation issued = $332,390. Amount of large outstanding at close = $3,710. Amount of small outstanding at close = $20,930.
23,836 Large   2,844 Small   26,680 Total

7833	M $10 1902PB 624	2348 F	B215765D	VG	pen/pen
7833	M $10 1902PB 624	2488 D	H67482D	F	
7833	M $10 1902PB 624	3226 ?	?	F	
7833	- $10 1902PB 624	4129 F	Y441151H	VG/F	
7833	M $20 1902PB 650	3233 B	K304325E	XF	Higgins Mus.
7833	$10 1929T1	A000239A		?	
7833	$20 1929T1	D000044A		F	? $10 ?
7833	$20 1929T1	E000081A		VG/F	Higgins Mus.
7833	$20 1929T1	C000098A		F/VF	

THE FARMERS NATIONAL BANK OF RED OAK   17 L   1 S
6056   MONTGOMERY

Organized on November 9, 1901 with a capital of $60,000. Placed in receivership on March 27, 1924. Reason for failure: local depression. Restored to solvency on June 9, 1924. Placed in receivership on October 14, 1929; capital of $60,000. Reason for failure: incompetent management.

Officers: Pres. M Chandler 1901-05, LD Goodrich 1907-13, Paul P Clark 1914-23, LA Hatswell 1925-29; **VP** Geo C Boileah 1902-07, JF Brown 1909-13, Wright Clark 1914-23, CL Ellis 1925-27, OF Fryer 1928-29; **Cash.** OJ Gibson 1901-05, FJ Brodby 1906, JB Stair 1907-13, EA Gaukel 1914-18, Wright Clark 1919, AO Norene 1920-26, CL Ellis 1926-27, CS Fridolph 1928-29; **AC** Geo W Thomas 1903-05, VA Spicer 1911-14, CS Fridolph 1925-27, CL Anderson 1928-29, H Wetterholm 1928-29

	Ser #	# Notes
Second Charter, Brown Backs		
10-10-10-20	1-2650	10,600
Second Charter, Date Back		
10-10-10-20	1-4200	16,800
Second Charter, Value Back		
10-10-10-20	4201-7106	11,624
Third Charter, Plain Back, Blue Seal		
10-10-10-20	1-4958	19,832
1929, Type I		
6-10's	1-117	700

($10 type 1 = $7,000 worth; serials E000117A and F000117A not issued.)

	Ser #	# Notes
6-20's	1-7	40

($20 type 1 = $800 worth; serials E000007A and F000007A not issued.)

Total amount of circulation issued = $743,500. Amount outstanding at close = $58,900. Amount of large outstanding on July 1, 1930 = $51,100.
58,856 Large   744 Small   59,600 Total

6056	M $20 1882BB 504	2558 A	U509212U	VG	retraced sigs
6056	M $20 1882BB 504	2621 A	?	?	
6056	M $10 1882DB 545	446 D	B902176	F/VF	pen/pen

6056	M	$10 1882DB 545	2286 D	H61214	F/VF	Higgins Mus.
6056	M	$20 1882DB 555	1211 B	E596889	VG	partial pen sigs
6056	M	$20 1882DB 555	2621 B	M445349	VG/F	pen/pen vp
6056	M	$10 1882VB 577	5558 D	U596946	F	lt stamp/gone
6056	M	$10 1882VB 577	7005 F	V663388	VG/F	
6056	M	$10 1902PB 634	1120 ?	A501482H	VF/XF	
6056	M	$10 1902PB 634	1292 B	A501654H	VF	Higgins Mus.
6056	-	$10 1902PB 634	1988 C	T580380H	F+	Bayard
6056	-	$10 1902PB 634	3370 C	3370 C	VG	stamp/stamp
6056	-	$10 1902PB 634	3880 A	3880 A	F/VF	pen ac/pen vp
6056	-	$10 1902PB 634	4117 C	4117 C	XF	Higgins Mus.
6056	-	$10 1902PB 634	4663 A	4663 A	F	pen/pen vp
6056	M	$20 1902PB 660	1534 A	A501896H	F	stamp/stamp
6056	-	$20 1902PB 660	4347 A	4347 A	G	weak pen sigs
6056		$10 1929T1	D000085A		VG	Higgins Mus.

THE FIRST NATIONAL BANK OF RED OAK   21 L   33 S
2130   MONTGOMERY

Chartered on November 10, 1873. Succeeded F.M. Byrkit.
Officers: Pres. Charles H Lane 1873-88, FM Byrkit 1889-1908, Thos Griffith 1909-11, Chas T Schenck 1912-35; **VP** FM Byrkit 1873-88, AC Hinchman 1896-1913, HE Deemer 1914, FS Schadel 1920-35; **Cash.** Charles F Clarke 1876-1905, OJ Gibson 1906, FJ Brodby 1907-14, WJ Roberts 1915-35; **AC** WS Ellis 1902-04, WJ Roberts 1907-14, FR Iddings 1914-35

First Charter, Original Issue	Ser #	# Notes
1-1-1-2	1-1500	6,000
5-5-5-5	1-2875	11,500
First Charter, Series of 1875		
5-5-5-5	1-7092	28,368
Second Charter, Brown Backs		
10-10-10-20	1-6200	24,800
50-100	1-590	1,180
Second Charter, Date Back		
10-10-10-20	1-3262	13,048
50-100	1-101	202
Third Charter, Date Back, Blue Seal		
10-10-10-20	1-2000	8,000
Third Charter, Plain Back, Blue Seal		
10-10-10-20	2001-15603	54,412
1929, Type I		
6-10's	1-2488	14,928
6-20's	1-712	4,272
1929, Type II		
10's	1-1494	1,494
20's	1-300	300

Total amount of circulation issued = $1,819,400. Amount of large outstanding on July 29, 1935 = $7,180.
147,510 Large   20,994 Small   168,504 Total

2130	-	$1 ORIG 382	1002 A	D719126	XF	pen/pen vp
2130	-	$1 ORIG 382	1079 A	D719203	F/VF	pen/pen vp
2130	-	$5 ORIG 399	1888 B	P747280	F	Black Charter Higgins Museum
2130	-	$5 1875 401	4874 C	X971565	VG	Black Charter
2130	-	$5 1875 402	6516 A	Y20194	VG	Black Charter
2130		$10 1882BB 487	2612 C	E23177E	F+	
2130		$10 1882BB 487	5142 C	U158240U	VG	Pinholes
2130	M	$10 1882DB 542	215 E	B452725	F	pen/pen
2130	M	$10 1902DB 622	794 B	V867809A	F	faded/faded
2130	M	$10 1902PB 630	5438 A	U69250D	F	faded/faded
2130	M	$10 1902PB 630	7709 C	K546711E	AU+	Higgins Mus.
2130	-	$10 1902PB 630	9645 B	R10957H	VG	pen/stamp
2130	-	$10 1902PB 630	10986 C	?	VG	Fed. Res. Bk., San Francisco
2130	-	$10 1902PB 630	12889 A	12889 A	?	
2130	M	$20 1902PB 656	3158 A	X920319B	VF	pen/faded
2130	M	$20 1902PB 656	4562 A	E722086D	G/VG	Small hole
2130	M	$20 1902PB 656	11196 A	Z749488H	VG	
2130	-	$20 1902PB 656	12208 A	12208 A	VF	pen/stamp
2130	-	$20 1902PB 656	13430 A	13430 A	VG	LR corner gone
2130	-	$20 1902PB 656	13766 A	13766 A	XF	
2130	-	$20 1902PB 656	14305 A	14305 A	F	
2130		$10 1929T1	A000058A		F	
2130		$10 1929T1	D000060A		XF+	Higgins Mus.
2130		$10 1929T1	F000080A		XF	
2130		$10 1929T1	E001150A		VF	
2130		$10 1929T1	B001257A		VG	
2130		$10 1929T1	A001289A		F	
2130		$10 1929T1	A001350A		VG	
2130		$10 1929T1	D001408A		F	
2130		$10 1929T1	B001548A		VF	
2130		$10 1929T1	D001871A		F	Rust spots/stains
2130		$10 1929T1	A002263A		XF+	
2130		$20 1929T1	E000008A		VF	
2130		$20 1929T1	D000014A		VG	
2130		$20 1929T1	F000036A		?	
2130		$20 1929T1	E000067A		F	
2130		$20 1929T1	A000081A		VF	
2130		$20 1929T1	E000142A		VF	
2130		$20 1929T1	B000146A		F/VF	
2130		$20 1929T1	B000157A		F	
2130		$20 1929T1	E000252A		VG	
2130		$20 1929T1	D000258A		F	
2130		$20 1929T1	A000263A		F	
2130		$20 1929T1	A000320A		F+	
2130		$20 1929T1	B000360A		F/VF	
2130		$20 1929T1	A000371A		F/VF	
2130		$20 1929T1	B000384A		AU	
2130		$20 1929T1	B000468A		VF	
2130		$20 1929T1	D000634A		F+	
2130		$20 1929T1	D000641A		VF	
2130		$20 1929T1	E000677A		F	
2130		$10 1929T2	A000425		XF	
2130		$10 1929T2	A000544		VF	
2130		$10 1929T2	A001293		VG/F	

THE RED OAK NATIONAL BANK   21 L   19 S
3055   MONTGOMERY

Organized on August 29, 1883 with a capital of $100,000. Placed in conservatorship on March 22, 1933. Placed in voluntary liquidation on January 16, 1934; capital of $100,000. Succeeded by #13785 which did not issue any notes.
Officers: Pres. Justus Clark 1883-94, Ben B Clark 1895-31, Wm Cochrane 1931-33; **VP** HC Binns 1896-1911, Paul P Clark 1913, Thos D Murphy 1914-28, Wm Cochrane 1929-31, Chas E Carry 1931-33; **Cash.** Paul P Clark 1883-1911, FE Crandall 1912-33; **AC** DB Miller 1885, Gordon Hayes 1909, OR Byers 1913—14, 1933, WM Apple 1914-29, RE Shoemaker 1920-32, Chas A Reese 1930-31

Second Charter, Brown Backs	Ser #	# Notes
10-10-10-20	1-5380	21,520
Third Charter, Red Seal		
10-10-10-20	1-4400	17,600
Third Charter, Date Back, Blue Seal		
10-10-10-20	1-7100	28,400
Third Charter, Plain Back, Blue Seal		
10-10-10-20	7101-19009	47,636
1929, Type I		
6-10's	1-2086	12,516
6-20's	1-545	3,270

Total amount of circulation issued = $1,630,010. Amount outstanding at close = $100,000. Amount outstanding in 1935 = $58,690. Amount of small outstanding in 1935 = $49,300. Amount of large outstanding on July 31, 1935 = $9,390. Liability for redemption of circulation assumed by #13785.
115,156 Large   15,786 Small   130,942 Total

3055	M	$10 1902DB 616	365 D	E834920	?	
3055	M	$10 1902DB 616	6765 D	M765091B	VF	
3055	M	$10 1902PB 624	8536 E	B5483D	F	stamp/stamp
3055	M	$10 1902PB 624	10785 ?	?	AU	
3055	M	$10 1902PB 624	11255 F	B216607E	F+	
3055	M	$10 1902PB 624	13542 F	D948744H	G/VG	stamp/stamp
3055	M	$10 1902PB 624	14152 E	M462514H	F	stamp/stamp
3055	-	$10 1902PB 624	14960 E	Z785212H	F	
3055	-	$10 1902PB 624	16082 F	16082 F	F+	
3055	-	$10 1902PB 624	16089 D	16089 D	F	
3055	-	$10 1902PB 624	16148 D	16148 D	XF/AU	Higgins Mus.
3055	-	$10 1902PB 624	18165 I	18165 I	VG+	stamp/stamp
3055	-	$10 1902PB 624	18633 H	18633 H	VF/XF	stamp/stamp
3055	M	$20 1902PB 650	13117 B	X314489E	VF/XF	Wallet stained
3055	M	$20 1902PB 650	13234 B	D948436H	F+	stamp/stamp
3055	M	$20 1902PB 650	13836 B	M462198H	VF/XF	stamp/stamp
3055	-	$20 1902PB 650	16115 B	16115 B	VG	
3055	-	$20 1902PB 650	17113 C	17113 C	Fr/G	stamp/stamp
3055	-	$20 1902PB 650	18208 C	18208 C	AU	stamp Higg. Mus.
3055	-	$20 1902PB 650	18213 ?	18213 ?	XF/AU	
3055	-	$20 1902PB 650	18259 ?	18259 ?	XF/AU	
3055		$10 1929T1	B000692A		F	
3055		$10 1929T1	C000857A		VF/XF	
3055		$10 1929T1	F001131A		VF	
3055		$10 1929T1	D001181A		?	
3055		$10 1929T1	B001229A		F	
3055		$10 1929T1	F001351A		VF	
3055		$10 1929T1	D001491A		?	

3055	$10	1929T1	B001570A		?	
3055	$10	1929T1	F001697A		G/VG	
3055	$10	1929T1	A001814A		F/VF	Higgins Mus.
3055	$10	1929T1	A002035A		VG	
3055	$10	1929T1	B002042A		VG	
3055	$20	1929T1	C000096A		F	
3055	$20	1929T1	E000230A		VG	
3055	$20	1929T1	B000296A		VG	
3055	$20	1929T1	D000372A		F/VF	
3055	$20	1929T1	C000378A		?	
3055	$20	1929T1	D000432A		F	
3055	$20	1929T1	C000499A		CU	

THE VALLEY NATIONAL BANK OF RED OAK 0 L
2230 MONTGOMERY
Chartered on March 3, 1875. Placed in voluntary liquidation on October 20, 1884; capital of $50,000. Succeeded by The Valley Bank.
Officers: Pres. Henry N Moore 1876-84; **Cash.** Reuben M Roberts 1876-80, Warren H Kinkade 1881-84

First Charter, Original Issue	Ser #	# Notes
10-10-10-20	1-540	2,160
First Charter, Series of 1875		
10-10-10-20	1-634	2,536

Total amount of circulation issued = $58,700. Amount outstanding at close = $22,150. Amount outstanding in 1910 = $330.
4,696 Large 0 Small 4,696 Total

THE FIRST NATIONAL BANK OF REMSEN 16 L 21 S
6975 PLYMOUTH
Chartered in 1903.

Officers: Pres. Michael Faber 1903, JF Kriege 1904-05, WJ Kass 1906-35; **VP** JF Kriege 1903, 1907-11, FG Meinert 1904, 1913-25, Barney Bunkers 1926-35; **Cash.** MR Faber 1903-05, WG Sievers 1906-35; **AC** CJ Ahmann 1910-29, SR Nothem 1930-35

Third Charter, Red Seal	Ser #	# Notes
5-5-5-5	1-1450	5,800
10-10-10-20	1-1000	4,000
Third Charter, Date Back, Blue Seal		
5-5-5-5	1-2050	8,200
10-10-10-20	1-1540	6,160
Third Charter, Plain Back, Blue Seal		
5-5-5-5	2051-8115	24,260
10-10-10-20	1541-5621	16,324
1929, Type I		
6-5's	1-1334	8,004
6-10's	1-776	4,656
6-20's	1-226	1,356
1929, Type II		
5's	1-1294	1,294
10's	1-790	790
20's	1-200	200

Total amount of circulation issued = $654,300. Amount outstanding in 1934 = $50,000. Amount of large outstanding on July 26, 1935 = $2,660.
64,744 Large 16,300 Small 81,044 Total

6975	M	$5 1902DB	590	1364 H	?	F Mounting damage
6975	M	$20 1902DB	642	1445 B	K209701B	F pen/gone
6975	M	$5 1902PB	598	2817 F	Y40393B	F light sigs
6975	M	$5 1902PB	598	3064 H	D470785D	VG
6975	M	$5 1902PB	598	3897 H	T728408D	G/VG
6975		$5 1902PB	598	6040 E	M55426H	F
6975		$5 1902PB	598	7289 H	7289 H	XF Higgins Mus.
6975	-	$5 1902PB	598	7829 ?	7829 ?	F
6975		$5 1902PB	598	7905 H	7905 H	XF
6975	-	$10 1902PB	624	4217 E	A70449K	VF stamp/stamp
6975	-	$10 1902PB	624	4588 F	4588 F	F stamp/stamp
6975	-	$10 1902PB	624	5222 F	5222 F	VF gone/gone
6975	-	$10 1902PB	624	5415 D	5415 D	F
6975	M	$20 1902PB	650	3711 B	H428333H	? faded/faded
6975	M	$20 1902PB	650	3846 B	H428468H	VG
6975	-	$20 1902PB	650	4207 B	A70439K	G
6975		$5 1929T1		A000479A		F+
6975		$5 1929T1		C000727A		F
6975		$5 1929T1		E001245A		VG/F
6975		$10 1929T1		E000103A		VG Corner gone
6975		$10 1929T1		F000127A		F
6975		$10 1929T1		A000166A		F
6975		$10 1929T1		D000198A		F
6975		$10 1929T1		E000203A		?
6975		$10 1929T1		F000446A		F Washed
6975		$10 1929T1		B000457A		F
6975		$10 1929T1		E000486A		VF
6975		$20 1929T1		C000054A		VF
6975		$20 1929T1		B000091A		XF
6975		$20 1929T1		D000093A		VF/XF
6975		$20 1929T1		C000171A		?
6975		$20 1929T1		F000175A		F
6975		$20 1929T1		E000189A		VF
6975		$10 1929T2		A000728		F
6975		$20 1929T2		A000063		CU Higgins Mus.
6975		$20 1929T2		A000064		AU
6975		$20 1929T2		A000141		VF

THE FIRST NATIONAL BANK OF RENWICK 1 L
7988 HUMBOLDT
Organized on Nov. 24, 1905 with a capital of $25,000. Placed in receivership on Jan. 13, 1927; capital of $25,000. Reason for failure: local depression.
Officers: Pres. QM Lee 1906-10, BW McElhinney 1911-15, CA Packard 1916-25, JF Kelling 1926; **VP** FJ Weston 1907, JH Tauck 1909, WH Martin 1910-11, FJ Wenck 1913, JF Kelling 1914-25, CA Packard 1926; **Cash.** WM Hoffman 1906, HB Cole 1907, WE Harvey 1908-10, FJ Wenck 1911, CA Packard 1912-15, RM Goettsch 1916-26; **AC** WE Harvey 1907, LP Aldrich 1911, RM Goettsch 1913-14, CA Richardson 1920-25, LM Thompson 1920, JT Nervig 1926

Third Charter, Red Seal	Ser #	# Notes
10-10-10-20	1-285	1,140
Third Charter, Date Back, Blue Seal		
10-10-10-20	1-580	2,320
Third Charter, Plain Back, Blue Seal		
10-10-10-20	581-963	1,532

Total amount of issued = $62,400. Amount outstanding at close = $6,250.
4,992 Large 0 Small 4,992 Total

| 7988 | | $20 1902PB | 651 | 849 B | R828631H | VF Higgins Mus. |

THE FIRST NATIONAL BANK OF RICEVILLE 5 L 15 S
8442 MITCHELL
Chartered in November 1906.
Officers: Pres. Jas Hendricks 1907-14, BN Hendricks 1915-35; **VP** RT St. John 1907-20, BN Hendricks 1914, CE Adams 1922-35, Fred Lehaw 1922-24; **Cash.** BN Hendricks 1907-09, ER St. John 1910-35; **AC** ER St. John 1907-09, BN Hendricks 1910-11, AG Dunton 1913-22, AT Hinton 1923, AG Dunton 1924-35

Third Charter, Red Seal	Ser #	# Notes
10-10-10-10	1-861	3,444
Third Charter, Date Back, Blue Seal		
10-10-10-10	1-2000	8,000
Third Charter, Plain Back, Blue Seal		
10-10-10-10	2001-6198	16,792
1929, Type I		
6-10's	1-997	5,982
1929, Type II		
5's	1-120	120

Total amount of circulation issued = $342,780. Amount of large outstanding in 1935 = $1,645. Amount of small outstanding in 1935 = $23,350.
28,236 Large 6,102 Small 34,338 Total

8442	M	$10 1902RS	614	186 C	A243739	F+
8442	M	$10 1902RS	614	762 C	A498919	F/VF Higgins Mus.
8442	M	$10 1902DB	617	950 G	D799539	F/VF pen/pen
8442	-	$10 1902PB	625	5250 G	5250 G	F/VF Higgins Mus.
8442	-	$10 1902PB	625	5566 G	5566 G	?
8442		$10 1929T1		A000147A		VG

8442	$10	1929T1	D000299A		F	
8442	$10	1929T1	D000382A		VG	
8442	$10	1929T1	C000404A		VG	
8442	$10	1929T1	D000437A		VG/F	Trimmed into top
8442	$10	1929T1	D000472A		F	
8442	$10	1929T1	D000565A		AU	
8442	$10	1929T1	A000566A		VF/XF	
8442	$10	1929T1	B000566A		CU	Higgins Mus.
8442	$10	1929T1	E000568A		?	Nice
8442	$10	1929T1	D000576A		VF	
8442	$10	1929T1	F000817A		CU	
8442	$10	1929T1	F000890A		F	
8442	$10	1929T1	D000932A		VF	
8442	$5	1929T2	A000116		?	

THE FIRST NATIONAL BANK OF RICHLAND 2 L
5611 KEOKUK

Chartered on October 29, 1900. Placed in voluntary liquidation on August 31, 1919; capital of $25,000. Succeeded by The First Savings Bank, Richland.
Officers: Pres. Charles F Singmaster 1900-13, ES Wolcott 1914, CM Keck 1915-19; **VP** JE Wolcott 1900-06, Jacob Marz 1907, DA Boyer 1909, ES Wolcott 1910-13, CM Keck 1914; **Cash.** TF McCarty 1900-13, Geo C Reames 1914-19; **AC** GN Ranous 1904-07, RE McCarty 1909-11, Thomas D Marr 1914

Second Charter, Brown Backs	Ser #	# Notes
10-10-10-20	1-720	2,880
Second Charter, Date Back		
10-10-10-20	1-700	2,800
Second Charter, Value Back		
10-10-10-20	701-707	28

Total amount of circulation issued = $71,350. Amount outstanding at close = $9,700.
5,708 Large   0 Small   5,708 Total

5611	M	$20	1882DB	555	78 B	D470378	XF	
5611	M	$20	1882DB	555	425 B	M188763	F/VF	Higgins Museum

THE FIRST NATIONAL BANK OF RIPPEY 12 L 12 S
7609 GREENE

Chartered in February 1905 with a capital of $25,000.
Officers: Pres. WH McCammon 1905-14, DL McCammon 1915-16, WH McCammon 1917-29, Alex High 1929-31, BM Riley 1931-35; **VP** JM Woodworth 1907-14, Alex High 1920-29, OS Gilliland 1929-32, IJ Burk 1933-35; **Cash.** JH Van Scoy 1905-35; **AC** JA Haberer 1910-14, Ethel High 1920-22, Max Van Scoy 1922, James Van Scoy 1923, Howard E Jackson 1923-24, LS Burk 1925-29, Herbert Van Scoy 1930, Ferne States 1930, Fern Holmes 1931-32, Clark Bardole 1933-35, Dorotha Dugan 1933-35

Third Charter, Red Seal	Ser #	# Notes
5-5-5-5	1-1045	4,180
10-10-10-20	1-697	2,788
Third Charter, Date Back, Blue Seal		
5-5-5-5	1-1700	6,800
10-10-10-20	1-1160	4,640
Third Charter, Plain Back, Blue Seal		
5-5-5-5	1701-5569	15,476
10-10-10-20	1161-3468	9,232
1929, Type I		
6-5's	1-834	5,004
6-10's	1-424	2,544
6-20's	1-130	780
1929, Type II		
5's	1-394	394
10's	1-324	324
20's	1-60	60

Total amount of circulation issued = $413,000. Amount of large outstanding in June 1935 = $1,560. Amount of small outstanding in June 1935 = $23,440.
43,116 Large   9,106 Small   52,222 Total

7609	M	$10	1902RS	613	198 C	E271133	VG/F	
7609	M	$5	1902PB	598	3518 F	M351639E	XF+	stamp/stamp
7609		$5	1902PB	598	4130 H	?	?	
7609	-	$5	1902PB	598	4135 E	N246921H	F/VF	
7609	-	$5	1902PB	598	4824 F	4824 F	AU	stamp Higg. Mus.
7609	-	$5	1902PB	598	4979 H	4979 H	VG	stamp/stamp
7609	-	$5	1902PB	598	5140 G	5140 G	VG	
7609	M	$10	1902PB	624	1665 F	E706789D	F	gone/gone
7609	-	$10	1902PB	624	3225 E	3225 E	VG	
7609	-	$10	1902PB	624	3354 E	3354 E	AU	stamp/stamp
7609	M	$20	1902PB	650	1242 B	T419832B	F	
7609	M	$20	1902PB	650	1366 B	V593986B	VF	stamp/stamp
7609		$5	1929T1	E000624A			VF+	Higgins Mus.
7609		$5	1929T1	D000750A			VG	
7609		$10	1929T1	A000051A			F	
7609		$10	1929T1	B000175A			VG	
7609		$10	1929T1	A000192A			VG	
7609		$10	1929T1	A000243A			VG/F	
7609		$10	1929T1	B000245A			VG	
7609		$10	1929T1	D000248A			F	
7609		$10	1929T1	F000287A			?	
7609		$20	1929T1	C000049A			F	
7609		$20	1929T1	F000119A			AU	
7609		$20	1929T2	A000034			VF	

THE FIRST NATIONAL BANK OF ROCK RAPIDS 29 L 11 S
3153 LYON

Organized on March 17, 1884; capital of $50,000. Succeeded The Bank of Rock Rapids. Placed in receivership on Dec. 20, 1930; capital of $100,000.
Officers: Pres. Jeremiah Shade 1884-85, BL Richards 1886-1901, Charles Shade 1902-26, JP Buscher 1926-27, Charles Shade 1927-30; **VP** Charles Shade 1901, SS Wold 1902-13, GA Manwaring 1914-19, JP Buscher 1920-26, JW Roach 1920-28, EA Hunt 1928-30, JH Peacock 1929-30; **Cash.** BL Richards 1884-85, CH Huntington 1886, EL Partch 1887-1919, JP Buscher 1920-22, 1926, JJ Shade 1923-25, RH Rhode 1926-27, HP Jennings 1929-30; **AC** GE Davis 1907, CA Kast 1908-14, JJ Shade 1920-22, HP Jennings 1923, HA Jensen 1924-25, RM Engel 1925-30, RH Rhode 1925-26, HP Jennings 1927-28

Second Charter, Brown Backs	Ser #	# Notes
10-10-10-20	1-1267	5,068
Third Charter, Red Seal		
10-10-10-20	1-4450	17,800
Third Charter, Date Back, Blue Seal		
10-10-10-20	1-6300	25,200
Third Charter, Plain Back, Blue Seal		
10-10-10-20	6301-17351	44,204
1929, Type I		
6-10's	1-1038	6,228
6-20's	1-268	1,608

Total amount of circulation issued = $1,247,840. Amount outstanding at close = $94,100. Amount of large outstanding on July 1, 1931 = $22,160.
92,272 Large   7,836 Small   100,108 Total

3153	M	$10	1902RS	613	505 A	D772900	VF	
3153	M	$10	1902RS	613	3886 B	Y292508	VG	pen/faded
3153	M	$20	1902RS	639	214 A	B721176	VF	Higgins Mus.
3153	M	$20	1902RS	639	3304 A	U540056	VF/XF	Rough top
3153	M	$10	1902DB	616	2231 ?	U844147	Fr	Bayard
3153	M	$10	1902DB	616	2798 E	A445631A	G/VG	stamp/gone
3153	M	$10	1902DB	616	5117 ?	X469562A	VG/F	
3153	M	$10	1902DB	616	5757 D	A951203B	F	
3153	M	$10	1902PB	624	7174 E	X187151B	VG	
3153	M	$10	1902PB	624	8309 H	H413535D	G	
3153	M	$10	1902PB	624	10458 E	E403110E	VG/F	
3153	M	$10	1902PB	624	12341 E	Z203713E	VF/XF	stamp/stamp
3153	M	$10	1902PB	624	12969 D	K261091H	F	
3153		$10	1902PB	624	13266 ?	?	CU	
3153	-	$10	1902PB	624	14757 E	14757 E	VG	pen ac/stamp
3153	-	$10	1902PB	624	15386 D	15386 D	VG	
3153	-	$10	1902PB	624	15788 D	15788 D	XF	pen/stamp ac
3153	-	$10	1902PB	624	16373 F	16373 F	VF	lt. stamps ac
3153	M	$20	1902PB	650	10629 B	E403281E	?	
3153	M	$20	1902PB	650	10855 B	E403507E	VF	
3153	M	$20	1902PB	650	12001 B	Z203373E	F	stamp/stamp Tape stains
3153	M	$20	1902PB	650	12915 B	K261037H	XF	
3153	-	$20	1902PB	650	14040 B	Y585442H	VG	faded/faded
3153	-	$20	1902PB	650	15007 B	15007 B	VF	
3153	-	$20	1902PB	650	15131 B	15131 B	AU	gone/gone
3153	-	$20	1902PB	650	15134 B	15134 B	AU	faded/faded
3153	-	$20	1902PB	650	15135 B	15135 B	CU	gone/gone
3153	-	$20	1902PB	650	15137 B	15137 B	AU	nearly gone
3153	-	$20	1902PB	650	15139 B	15139 B	VF	Higgins Mus.
3153		$10	1929T1	C000093A			VG/F	Washed
3153		$10	1929T1	D000671A			F	
3153		$10	1929T1	D000923A			VG	
3153		$10	1929T1	F000987A			F	Soiled
3153		$20	1929T1	B000004A			VF	Higgins Mus.
3153		$20	1929T1	D000020A			VF	
3153		$20	1929T1	A000029A			F	
3153		$20	1929T1	B000066A			VF/XF	
3153		$20	1929T1	C000111A			VG/F	
3153		$20	1929T1	D000140A			F	
3153		$20	1929T1	C000172A			F	

THE LYON COUNTY NATIONAL BANK OF ROCK RAPIDS
7089   **LYON**   **21 L   13 S**
Organized on December 15, 1903 with a capital of $75,000. Placed in receivership on October 20, 1931; capital of $75,000.
Officers: Pres. OP Miller 1904-28, MA Cox 1929-31; **VP** MA Cox 1920-28, AG Miller 1929-31; **Cash.** MA Cox 1904-19, AG Miller 1920-28, FB Parker 1929, JT Dykhouse 1930-31; **AC** Fred B Parker 1904-15, AG Miller 1909-15, ED Van Rhee 1920-26, 1927, JT Dykhouse 1920-29, Henry Visser 1929-31

Third Charter, Red Seal	Ser #	# Notes
10-10-10-20	1-3200	12,800
Third Charter, Date Back, Blue Seal		
10-10-10-20	1-4900	19,600
Third Charter, Plain Back, Blue Seal		
10-10-10-20	4901-13649	34,996
1929, Type I		
6-10's	1-1027	6,162
6-20's	1-276	1,656

Total amount of circulation issued = $937,190. Amount outstanding at close = $74,280. Amount of large outstanding on October 26, 1931 = $12,110.
67,396 Large   7,818 Small   75,214 Total

7089	M	$20 1902RS	639	2927 A	Y299899	F	
7089	M	$10 1902DB	616	961 F	H702579	VG	stamp/stamp
7089	M	$10 1902DB	616	3278 F	U228528A	F/VF	stamp/stamp
7089	M	$10 1902DB	616	3936 D	Y797336A	VF	
7089	M	$10 1902DB	616	4150 D	Y797550A	VG/F	
7089	M	$10 1902DB	616	4496 F	M312082B	F/VF	stamp/stamp
7089	M	$20 1902DB	642	981 B	H702599	VG	faded/faded
7089	M	$20 1902DB	642	4565 B	M312151B	VG/F	
7089	M	$10 1902PB	624	4978 F	U453566B	F	
7089	M	$10 1902PB	624	4987 D	U453575B	G/VG	gone/gone
7089	M	$10 1902PB	624	7520 F	Z235342D	XF	Higgins Mus.
7089	M	$10 1902PB	624	8738 F	T226380E	VG	
7089	M	$10 1902PB	624	9057 F	T226699E	AU	gone/gone
7089	-	$10 1902PB	624	12101 E	12101 E	VG	gone/gone
7089	-	$10 1902PB	624	12921 D	12921 D	F/VF	stamp/stamp
7089	-	$10 1902PB	624	13499 E	13499 E	F/VF	
7089	M	$20 1902PB	650	6329 B	B595806D	F	
7089	-	$20 1902PB	650	12418 B	12418 B	VG	faded/gone
7089	-	$20 1902PB	650	12635 B	12635 B	AU	stamp/stamp
7089	-	$20 1902PB	650	12683 B	12683 B	VF	stamp/stamp
7089	-	$20 1902PB	650	12863 B	12863 B	VF	
7089		$10 1929T1		D000129A		F	
7089		$10 1929T1		B000431A		VF	Higgins Mus.
7089		$10 1929T1		F000644A		F	
7089		$10 1929T1		A000667A		VF	
7089		$10 1929T1		A001018A		F/VF	
7089		$20 1929T1		F000057A		G	
7089		$20 1929T1		F000068A		F	
7089		$20 1929T1		C000101A		VG+	
7089		$20 1929T1		B000160A		VG	
7089		$20 1929T1		D000162A		?	
7089		$20 1929T1		F000162A		VF+	
7089		$20 1929T1		A000182A		VF+	
7089		$20 1929T1		E000251A		F	

THE FIRST NATIONAL BANK OF ROCK VALLEY   16 L   17 S
5200   **SIOUX**
Organized on June 20, 1899 with a capital of $50,000. Succeeded The Large Bros. Placed in conservatorship on March 25, 1933. Placed in receivership on October 31, 1933; capital of $50,000.
Officers: Pres. IS Large 1899-1933; **VP** SA Mitchell 1900-13, Hans Moeller 1914-25, FT McGill 1920-33; **Cash.** John J Large 1899-1909, Frank A Large 1910-33; **AC** JA Huizenga 1904-09, Delco Bloem 1910-11, FT McGill 1913, LF Sandschulte 1920-28, WJ Heffernan 1929-33

Second Charter, Brown Backs	Ser #	# Notes
10-10-10-20	1-3650	14,600
Second Charter, Date Back		
10-10-10-20	1-2900	11,600
Second Charter, Value Back		
10-10-10-20	2901-3900	4,000
Third Charter, Plain Back, Blue Seal		
10-10-10-20	1-4766	19,064
1929, Type I		
6-10's	1-941	5,646
6-20's	1-227	1,362

Total amount of circulation issued = $699,500. Amount outstanding at close = $50,000. Amount of large outstanding on November 3, 1933 = $6,350.
49,264 Large   7,008 Small   56,272 Total

5200	M	$10 1882BB	490	3446 C	V259199V	F	Higgins Mus.
5200	M	$10 1882DB	545	2669 D	R113927	VG	lt stamp sigs
5200	M	$20 1882DB	555	2578 B	R113836	F	Higgins Mus.
5200	M	$10 1902PB	632	503 ?	?	VG+	
5200	M	$10 1902PB	632	? A	R424265D	?	
5200	M	$10 1902PB	632	1920 B	R39252E	VF/XF	stamp/stamp
5200	M	$10 1902PB	632	1931 C	R39263E	VG/F	
5200	M	$10 1902PB	632	2681 B	K284153H	VG	
5200		$10 1902PB	632	3181 B	Y562563H	F	
5200	-	$10 1902PB	632	3484 B	3484 B	VG	
5200	-	$10 1902PB	632	3919 B	3919 B	Fr	stamp/stamp
5200	-	$10 1902PB	632	4092 B	4092 B	VF	stamp/stamp
5200	-	$20 1902PB	658	3892 A	3892 A	VF+	stamp/stamp
5200	-	$20 1902PB	658	4521 A	4521 A	VF/XF	
5200	-	$20 1902PB	658	4523 A	4523 A	VF	Higgins Mus.
5200	-	$20 1902PB	658	4528 A	4528 A	XF	stamp/stamp
5200		$10 1929T1		C000195A		F/VF	
5200		$10 1929T1		F000234A		?	
5200		$10 1929T1		E000493A		VF	
5200		$10 1929T1		B000631A		VG	
5200		$10 1929T1		B000743A		XF	
5200		$10 1929T1		B000793A		VF	
5200		$10 1929T1		F000877A		VG/F	
5200		$20 1929T1		A000066A		VG/F	
5200		$20 1929T1		C000066A		F	
5200		$20 1929T1		F000080A		?	
5200		$20 1929T1		B000120A		VG	
5200		$20 1929T1		D000171A		F/VF	
5200		$20 1929T1		E000176A		F/VF	
5200		$20 1929T1		E000193A		VG/F	
5200		$20 1929T1		A000199A		CU	Higgins Mus.
5200		$20 1929T1		E000213A		F	Pressed
5200		$20 1929T1		D000222A		VF	

THE FIRST NATIONAL BANK OF ROCKFORD   6 L
3053   **FLOYD**
Organized on July 18, 1883 with a capital of $50,000. Succeeded Mathews & Lyon. Placed in receivership on February 23, 1929; capital of $50,000. Reason for failure: local depression.
Officers: Pres. Orlo H Lyon 1883-1902, RC Mathews 1903-04, ZT Mitchell 1905-19, Wm F Johannaber 1920-28; **VP** JS Childs 1896-1903, ZT Mitchell 1904, MA Hubbard 1907-11, Julius Heft 1913-14, FW Draeger 1920-27, Julius Heft 1928; **Cash.** Harry A Merrill 1883-90, HL Mitchell 1891-92, Edward Billings 1893-1903, BH Quackenbush 1903-08, Geo E Shear 1909-11, RF Bruce 1912-13, Wm F Johannaber 1914-19, Harry Bishop 1920-28; **AC** Geo A Lyon 1896-1900, RF Bruce 1909-11, AL Blumenstiel 1913-14

Second Charter, Brown Backs	Ser #	# Notes
10-10-10-20	1-1243	4,972
Third Charter, Red Seal		
10-10-10-20	1-570	2,280
Third Charter, Date Back, Blue Seal		
10-10-10-20	1-1080	4,320
Third Charter, Plain Back, Blue Seal		
10-10-10-20	1081-2041	3,844

Total amount issued = $192,700. Amount outstanding at close = $12,500.
15,416 Large   0 Small   15,416 Total

3053	M	$10 1902RS	613	451 A	Y90528	AU	
3053	M	$10 1902DB	616	98 D	M32439	AU	
3053	M	$10 1902DB	616	326 E	M32667	VG	pen/gone
3053	M	$20 1902DB	639	52 B	M32393	G	pen/pen
3053	M	$10 1902PB	624	1504 E	D488306H	VF	Davenport B&T
3053	-	$10 1902PB	624	1821 E	1821 E	VG	pen Higgins Mus.

THE FIRST NATIONAL BANK OF ROCKWELL   7 L   1 S
10217   **CERRO GORDO**
Organized on June 11, 1912 with a capital of $25,000. Placed in receivership on March 30, 1931; capital of $25,000.
Officers: Pres. Geo H Felthous 1912-20, WB Bruce 1922-24, WF McClelland 1925-30; **VP** WH Ryburn 1913-14, WB Bruce 1920, WF McClelland 1923-24, FB Tourtellott 1925-27, Frank Johnson 1926-27, WD Gibson 1928-30; **Cash.** FC Siegfried 1912-26, PW Grummon 1926-30; **AC** Frank Johnson 1913-26

Third Charter, Date Back, Blue Seal	Ser #	# Notes
5-5-5-5	1-865	3,460
10-10-10-20	1-694	2,776
Third Charter, Plain Back, Blue Seal		
5-5-5-5	866-8430	30,260
10-10-10-20	695-914	880
1929, Type I		
6-5's	1-874	5,244

Total amount of circulation issued = $240,520. Amount of large outstanding at close = $2,310. Amount of small outstanding at close = $15,960.

123

37,376 Large		5,244 Small		42,620 Total		
10217M	$5 1902DB	594	476 A	T483098A	F+	Higgins Mus.
10217M	$5 1902PB	602	4404 D	B304150H	F/VF	pen/pen vp
10217M	$5 1902PB	602	4421 A	B304167H	VG/F	
10217 -	$5 1902PB	602	5779 A	5779 A	VG	
10217 -	$5 1902PB	602	7179 D	7179 D	VF	Higgins Mus.
10217 -	$5 1902PB	602	7250 C	7250 C	VG	Fed. Res. Bk., San Francisco
10217 -	$5 1902PB	602	7596 ?	7596 ?	G/VG	
10217	$5 1929T1		E000823A		G	Higgins Mus.

THE FIRST NATIONAL BANK OF ROCKWELL CITY   27 L
5185   CALHOUN

Chartered in 1899. Placed in voluntary liquidation on September 26, 1929; capital of $50,000. Absorbed by The Union State Bank, Rockwell City.

Officers: Pres. EA Richards 1899-1910, JH Bradt 1911-25, EC Stevenson 1925-29; **VP** JC Kerr 1899-1903, FP Huff 1899, JH Bradt 1904-10, PC Holdoegel 1911, EH Rich 1913-28, WF Rich 1929; **Cash.** Chas D Case 1899, FP Huff 1900-29; **AC** JF Hutchison 1900-04, WA Sandburg 1907-15, Harry T Huff 1920-29

Second Charter, Brown Backs	Ser #	# Notes
5-5-5-5	1-3350	13,400
10-10-10-20	1-2720	10,880
Second Charter, Date Back		
5-5-5-5	1-3675	14,700
10-10-10-20	1-2560	10,240
Second Charter, Value Back		
5-5-5-5	3676-4740	4,260
10-10-10-20	2561-3111	2,204
Third Charter, Plain Back, Blue Seal		
10-10-10-20	1-5262	21,048

Total amount issued = $716,450. Amount outstanding at close = $40,800.

76,732 Large		0 Small		76,732 Total		
5185 -	$5 1882BB	477	853 G	A805178A	Fr/G	gone/pen vp
5185	$5 1882BB	477	2232 H	K924617K	VG+	Higgins Mus.
5185	$10 1882BB	490	1193 C	X369892	VG	Davenport B&T
5185 M	$10 1882BB	490	1402 A	D735193D	F	pen/stamp
5185 M	$10 1882BB	490	?	T335210T	?	Bayard
5185 M	$5 1882DB	537	1237 K	E408554	VF	
5185 M	$10 1882DB	545	2553 D	T276591	VF+	
5185 M	$20 1882DB	555	918 B	H989626	VG/F	stamp, Stained
5185 M	$10 1902PB	632	681 C	?	F	
5185 M	$10 1902PB	632	1158 B	Y278760D	AU	Higgins Mus.
5185 M	$10 1902PB	632	1799 B	E178541E	F	stamp/stamp
5185 M	$10 1902PB	632	1935 B	N660027E	VG	stamp/stamp
5185 M	$10 1902PB	632	2870 A	M254942H	F/VF	stamp/stamp
5185 -	$10 1902PB	632	3425 A	Z323767H	F	
5185 -	$10 1902PB	632	3503 B	Z323845H	VG	faded, Soiled
5185 -	$10 1902PB	632	3636 C	Z323978H	F/VF	lt stamp sigs
5185 -	$10 1902PB	632	3947 B	3947 B	XF	stamp/stamp
5185 -	$10 1902PB	632	3947 C	3947 C	?	
5185 -	$10 1902PB	632	3948 B	3948 B	AU	stamp/stamp
5185 -	$10 1902PB	632	4497 B	4497 B	VG	
5185 -	$10 1902PB	632	4865 B	4865 B	XF	stamp/stamp
5185 -	$10 1902PB	632	5055 A	5055 A	F	
5185 -	$10 1902PB	632	5061 A	5061 A	?	
5185 M	$20 1902PB	658	943 B	T335535D	F/VF	retraced sigs
5185 -	$20 1902PB	658	3628 A	Z323970H	VG/F	
5185 -	$20 1902PB	658	3630 A	Z323972H	G	faded/faded
5185 -	$20 1902PB	658	5135 A	5135 A	VF/XF	

THE ROCKWELL CITY NATIONAL BANK   2 L   11 S
11582   CALHOUN

Organized on January 13, 1920 with a capital of $50,000. Placed in conservatorship on March 21, 1933. Placed in voluntary liquidation on January 29, 1934; capital of $50,000. Succeeded by #13890 which did not issue any notes.

Officers: Pres. Henry Parsons 1920-32, Geo B Lemen 1933-34; **VP** BE Stonebraker 1920-28, Geo B Lemen 1929-32, AF Bledsoe 1933, SA Frick 1934; **Cash.** Geo B Lemen 1920-28, EB Lemen 1929-34; **AC** EB Lemen 1920-28

Third Charter, Plain Back, Blue Seal	Ser #	# Notes
10-10-10-20	1-1483	5,932
1929, Type I		
6-10's	1-283	1,698
6-20's	1-62	372

Total amount of circulation issued = $98,570. Amount outstanding in 1932 = $12,500. Amount of large outstanding at close = $710.

5,932 Large		2,070 Small		8,002 Total		
11582 -	$20 1902PB	659	1264 A	1264 A	VF	Higgins Mus.
11582 -	$20 1902PB	659	1370 A	1370 A	F	
11582	$10 1929T1		D000011A		VG	
11582	$10 1929T1		A000083A		VF	Higgins Mus.
11582	$10 1929T1		C000241A		VF	
11582	$10 1929T1		A000243A		VG+	
11582	$10 1929T1		B000253A		CU	
11582	$20 1929T1		B000020A		VF/XF	
11582	$20 1929T1		D000025A		VF/XF	
11582	$20 1929T1		A000029A		VF/XF	
11582	$20 1929T1		D000033A		VG	
11582	$20 1929T1		E000035A		VF	
11582	$20 1929T1		E000062A		G	Last sheet of $20s

THE FIRST NATIONAL BANK OF ROLAND   5 L   28 S
11249   STORY

Organized on August 17, 1918; capital of $30,000. Placed in receivership on Nov. 29, 1930; capital of $40,000. Reason for failure: local depression.

Officers: Pres. TT Henryson 1919-28, Jonas Christian 1929, NE Waugh 1930; **VP** Jonas Christian 1920-28, Oscar E Twedt 1929-30; **Cash.** Eli N Nelson 1919-30; **AC** Arnie J Johnson 1920-25, Jeffrey Michaelson 1925-30

Third Charter, Plain Back, Blue Seal	Ser #	# Notes
5-5-5-5	1-4006	16,024
10-10-10-20	1-2712	10,848
1929, Type I		
6-5's	1-470	2,820
6-10's	1-227	1,362
6-20's	1-30	180

Total amount of circulation issued = $247,040. Amount of large outstanding at close = $6,740. Amount of small outstanding at close = $23,260.

26,872 Large		4,362 Small		31,234 Total		
11249M	$10 1902PB	632	1214 A	T526616E	VF	pen/pen
11249M	$10 1902PB	632	1298 A	Z325050E	F	nice sigs
11249M	$10 1902PB	632	1556 B	K209128H	F	light sigs
11249 -	$20 1902PB	658	1938 A	1938 A	VG+	
11249 -	$20 1902PB	658	2339 A	2339 A	VF	Higgins Mus.
11249	$5 1929T1		C000005A		AU	
11249	$5 1929T1		E000012A		CU	Higgins Mus.
11249	$5 1929T1		D000014A		AU	
11249	$5 1929T1		C000019A		AU+	
11249	$5 1929T1		D000020A		CU	
11249	$5 1929T1		C000029A		AU	
11249	$5 1929T1		D000038A		F/VF	
11249	$5 1929T1		?000041A		CU	
11249	$5 1929T1		F000049A		AU	
11249	$5 1929T1		C000088A		VF	
11249	$5 1929T1		C000139A		AU	
11249	$5 1929T1		C000140A		AU	
11249	$5 1929T1		A000165A		AU	
11249	$5 1929T1		F000442A		F/VF	
11249	$10 1929T1		E000002A		F	
11249	$10 1929T1		D000007A		?	
11249	$10 1929T1		C000014A		VF	
11249	$10 1929T1		A000036A		XF	
11249	$10 1929T1		B000053A		CU	
11249	$10 1929T1		F000068A		VF/XF	Soiling on back
11249	$10 1929T1		B000073A		XF+	
11249	$10 1929T1		A000111A		VF/XF	
11249	$10 1929T1		E000120A		AU	
11249	$10 1929T1		D000158A		VF	
11249	$10 1929T1		A000207A		VF+	
11249	$10 1929T1		A000209A		?	
11249	$20 1929T1		F000022A		XF	
11249	$20 1929T1		C000026A		VF/XF	

THE FIRST NATIONAL BANK OF ROLFE   6 L
4954   POCAHONTAS

Organized on April 24, 1894; capital of $50,000. Placed in receivership on April 3, 1928; capital of $50,000. Reason for failure: local depression.

Officers: Pres. JP Farmer 1894-1906, JH Charlton 1907-11, D Brinkman 1912-28; **VP** JH Charlton 1894-1904, Diedrich Brinkman 1907-11, JH Brinkman 1913-28; **Cash.** JW Warren 1894-95, SS Reed 1896-1900, JK Lemon 1901-22, BL Green 1923-24, JH Engel 1925-28; **AC** SS Reed 1894, JK Lemon 1896-1900, CH Rolston 1902-04, JH Brinkman 1907-11, WS Taylor 1913-14, BL Green 1920-22, Ella C Taylor 1925-27

Second Charter, Brown Backs	Ser #	# Notes
10-10-10-20	1-1190	4,760
Second Charter, Date Back		
10-10-10-20	1-543	2,172
Third Charter, Date Back, Blue Seal		
10-10-10-20	1-600	2,400
Third Charter, Plain Back, Blue Seal		
10-10-10-20	601-1458	3,432

Total amount issued = $159,550. Amount outstanding at close = $12,150.
12,764 Large   0 Small   12,764 Total
4954 M $10 1882BB ?   782 B E785890E   F+   pen ac/pen
4954 M $10 1882BB ?   1021 C R247924R   AU   Higgins Mus.
4954 M $10 1902DB 623   449 B Z921003A   VF/XF
4954 M $20 1902DB 649   553 A Z921107A   VG   pen/pen vp
4954 M $10 1902PB 631   790 C A847062E   F   Higgins Mus.
4954 - $10 1902PB 631   1203 B Y640905H   AU   pen/pen

THE CITIZENS NATIONAL BANK OF ROYAL   6 L
10395   CLAY
Organized on April 10, 1913 with a capital of $25,000. Placed in receivership on January 5, 1927; capital of $35,000. Reason for failure: local depression.
Officers: Pres. JH McCord 1914-26; **VP** Wm Flindt 1914, Henry Johnson 1920-22, 1926, OB Scott 1920-26; **Cash.** OB Scott 1914-16, WG Anderson 1917-25, JP Grieve 1926-27; **AC** WG Anderson 1914, AP Rosendall 1920-25

Third Charter, Date Back, Blue Seal	Ser #	# Notes
10-10-10-20	1-520	2,080

Sheets numbered 1 to 400 were 02-08 backs. Sheets numbered 401 to 520 were delivered November 6, but not marked as to type. Sheets numbered 521 to 2643 were plain back blue seals.

Third Charter, Plain Back, Blue Seal		
10-10-10-20	521-2643	8,492

Total amount issued = $132,150. Amount outstanding at close = $23,700.
10,572 Large   0 Small   10,572 Total
10395M $10 1902PB 630   759 A D515586D   VF   Higgins Mus.
10395M $10 1902PB 630   1573 C D267115E   VG   faded/gone
10395M $10 1902PB 630   1856 C Y314868E   F   Higgins Mus.
10395M $10 1902PB 630   2145 C M500687H   F/VF lt. stamp sigs
10395M $20 1902PB 656   1076 A R375938D   XF   faded/faded Nice
10395 $20 1902PB 656   1922 A   ?   VG

THE FIRST NATIONAL BANK OF RUTHVEN   7 L
5541   PALO ALTO
Organized on July 7, 1900 with a capital of $25,000. Succeeded The Iowa Savings Bank. Placed in receivership on May 2, 1929; capital of $25,000. Reason for failure: local depression.
Officers: Pres. ML Brown 1900-28; **VP** G Baldwin 1902-22, John A Berg 1923-26, John Ruthven 1927-28; **Cash.** JH Thatcher 1900-28; **AC** AB Brown 1904-10, JO Jertson 1914, HF Cain 1920-28

Second Charter, Brown Backs	Ser #	# Notes
10-10-10-20	1-500	2,000
Second Charter, Date Back		
10-10-10-20	1-580	2,320
Second Charter, Value Back		
10-10-10-20	581-599	76
Third Charter, Plain Back, Blue Seal		
10-10-10-20	1-539	2,156

Total amount issued = $81,900. Amount outstanding at close = $7,000.
6,552 Large   0 Small   6,552 Total
5541 $10 1882BB 490   1 B X573228   AU   Higgins Mus.
5541 $10 1882BB 490   141 A X573368   VF+
5541 M $10 1882BB 490   486 A U127186U   VG   UR corner gone,
Davenport B&T
5541 M $10 1882DB 545   484 ? N322302   CU
5541 M $10 1882DB 545   484 D N322302   CU   Higgins Mus.
5541 M $10 1902PB 633   3 B X740075D   F   pen/pen vp
5541 $20 1902PB 659   152 A T136884E   VG   Higgins Mus.

THE FIRST NATIONAL BANK OF SAC CITY   16 L
4450   SAC
Organized on October 6, 1890; capital of $50,000. Placed in receivership on Dec. 2, 1925; capital of $50,000. Reason for failure: local depression.
Officers: Pres. DE Hallett 1891-1904, Geo B Perkins 1905-23; **VP** Eugene Criss 1896-1903, Phil Schaller 1909-11, CB Adams 1913-23; **Cash.** HH Allison 1891-1904, 1907, 1909, HS Barnt 1906, 1908-18, 1920-23; **AC** HS Barnt 1900-04, ED Humphries 1909-23, LE Wiseman 1920-22

Second Charter, Brown Backs	Ser #	# Notes
10-10-10-20	1-2320	9,280
Second Charter, Date Back		
10-10-10-20	1-1174	4,696
Third Charter, Date Back, Blue Seal		
10-10-10-20	1-3100	12,400
Third Charter, Plain Back, Blue Seal		
10-10-10-20	3101-7260	16,640

Total amount issued = $537,700. Amount outstanding at close = $47,500.
43,016 Large   0 Small   43,016 Total
4450 M $10 1882DB 540   679 F B377769   F+   Higgins Mus.
4450 M $10 1902DB 619   140 A Y153426   CU   Higgins Mus.
4450 M $10 1902DB 619   714 C Y154000   G
4450 M $10 1902DB 619   1224 C Y154510   G/VG pen/pen
4450 M $10 1902DB 619   2662 C M753588B   VG
4450 M $10 1902DB 619   2909 C M753835B   VG
4450 M $10 1902PB 627   4111 C K335723D   VF   stamp/stamp
4450 M $10 1902PB 627   4852 B Z42424D   VF
4450 M $10 1902PB 627   5769 B R328921E   VF   light stamps
4450 M $10 1902PB 627   6110 C Z68212E   VF   stamp/stamp
4450 M $10 1902PB 627   6432 A H536374H   VF   stamp/stamp
4450 M $10 1902PB 627   6509 A H536451H   VG/F
4450 M $20 1902PB 653   4429 A T367741D   F
4450 M $20 1902PB 653   4903 A Z42475D   F/VF
4450 - $20 1902PB 653   6803 A R942365H   VF+   stamp/stamp
4450 - $20 1902PB 653   6973 A X485595H   VG/F

THE FIRST NATIONAL BANK OF SAINT ANSGAR   8 L   13 S
10684   MITCHELL

Organized on December 9, 1914 with a capital of $25,000. Placed in conservatorship on March 28, 1933. Placed in receivership on October 31, 1933; capital of $25,000.
Officers: Pres. AN Lund 1915-33; **VP** TA Grath 1920, 1925-33, John P Lund 1930-33; **Cash.** TH Hume 1915-31, Chas Lamm 1931, MA Houg 1932 TH Hume 1932-33; **AC** EA Sponheim 1920, John P Lund 1922-30, BT Hegland 1932-33

Third Charter, Date Back, Blue Seal	Ser #	# Notes
10-10-10-20	1-800	3,200
Third Charter, Plain Back, Blue Seal		
10-10-10-20	801-3501	10,804
1929, Type I		
6-10's	1-512	3,072
6-20's	1-126	756

Total amount of circulation issued = $220,890. Amount of large outstanding at close = $1,670. Amount of small outstanding at close = $23,330.
14,004 Large   3,828 Small   17,832 Total
10684M $10 1902DB 620   659 A N359965B   VG   Soiled
10684M $20 1902DB 649   264 A N19630B   VF   pen/pen
10684M $10 1902PB 631   2382 B M107154H   F   pen/pen
10684 - $10 1902PB 631   3186 B   3186 B VG/F
10684 - $10 1902PB 631   3251 B   3251 B   XF   pen/pen
10684 - $10 1902PB 631   3309 B   3309 B VG+   pen/faded
10684 - $20 1902PB 657   3053 A   3053 A   F   lt pen sigs
10684 - $20 1902PB 657   3146 A   3146 A   VF   Higgins Mus.
10684 $10 1929T1   E000028A   VG
10684 $10 1929T1   D000063A   G/VG
10684 $10 1929T1   E000231A   VG
10684 $10 1929T1   F000235A   ?
10684 $10 1929T1   B000380A   F/VF
10684 $20 1929T1   B000012A   VG
10684 $20 1929T1   A000032A   XF/AU
10684 $20 1929T1   B000056A   F+
10684 $20 1929T1   A000072A   G/VG
10684 $20 1929T1   C000075A   F/VF
10684 $20 1929T1   A000102A   VF+
10684 $20 1929T1   C000115A   VF   Higgins Mus.
10684 $20 1929T1   A000115A   XF

THE FIRST NATIONAL BANK OF SANBORN   1 L
4824   O'BRIEN
When she assumed the presidency of the First National Bank of Sanborn, Elizabeth Harker became the first female officer of an Iowa national bank and one of the first in the nation.
Organized on December 6, 1892. Placed in voluntary liquidation on March 1, 1899; capital of $50,000. Succeeded by The Sanborn Savings Bank.
Officers: Pres. William Harker 1893-95, Elizabeth Harker 1896-98; **VP** Ezra M Brady 1896; **Cash.** JH Daly 1893-98

Second Charter, Brown Backs	Ser #	# Notes
10-10-10-20	1-521	2,084

Total amount of circulation issued = $26,050. Amount outstanding at close = $11,250. Amount outstanding in 1910 = $520.
2,084 Large   0 Small   2,084 Total
4824 $10 1882BB 485   11 A H385255   CU

THE FIRST NATIONAL BANK OF SEYMOUR   9 L   2 S
8247   WAYNE
Chartered in June 1906. Absorbed #11210 on January 2, 1926. Placed in voluntary liquidation on December 17, 1930; capital of $50,000. Absorbed by #13495.
Officers: Pres. JC Calhoun 1906-07, DC Bradley 1908-26, Wm S Bradley 1927-30, HT Long 1930; **VP** Wm Haines 1907-22, HT Long 1923-30, AE Davis 1930; **Cash.** JD Johnston 1906-25, LC Gordon 1926-30; **AC** J Walter Phillipps 1909, JW Haines 1910, JS McCord 1913, JP King 1914, Chas West 1920-22, Nora Gingerich 1923, 1925-30, Sadie E Morris 1926

Third Charter, Red Seal	Ser #	# Notes
10-10-10-20	1-1500	6,000
Third Charter, Date Back, Blue Seal		
10-10-10-20	1-3100	12,400
Third Charter, Plain Back, Blue Seal		
10-10-10-20	3101-9413	25,252
1929, Type I		
6-10's	1-459	2,754
6-20's	1-132	792

Total amount of circulation issued = $589,030. Amount of large outstanding at close = $11,010. Amount of small outstanding at close = $38,990.

43,652 Large   3,546 Small   47,198 Total

8247	M	$20 1902RS	640	624 A	R220526	G	gone/gone
8247	M	$20 1902RS	640	1468 A	R225183	AU	
8247	M	$10 1902DB	617	111 F	M111282	F	
8247	M	$10 1902DB	643	1629 B	A663727A	F	
8247	M	$20 1902PB	625	6343 E	V569265E	F/VF	stamp/stamp
8247	-	$10 1902PB	625	7660 E	7660 E	VG	pen/pen
8247	-	$10 1902PB	625	7902 F	7902 F	F	gone/stamp
8247	M	$20 1902PB	651	3305 B	R583436B	F	Higgins Mus.
8247	-	$20 1902PB	651	8803 B	8803 B	XF	Higgins Mus.
8247		$20 1929T1		F000031A		VF	Higgins Mus.
8247		$20 1929T1		B000052A		F	

THE SEYMOUR NATIONAL BANK   4 L
11210   WAYNE
Chartered in July 1918. Placed in voluntary liquidation on January 2, 1926; capital of $50,000. Absorbed by #8247.
Officers: Pres. MH Wilson 1918-26; **VP** WH McCabe 1920-26; **Cash.** AJ Davis 1918-20, LC Gordon 1922-26; **AC** LC Gordon 1920, Sadie E Morrison 1922-26

Third Charter, Plain Back, Blue Seal	Ser #	# Notes
10-10-10-20	1-4560	18,240

Total amount issued = $228,000. Amount outstanding at close = $49,995.

18,240 Large   0 Small   18,240 Total

11210	M	$10 1902PB	632	180 A	D453847D	VG/F	Higgins Mus.
11210	M	$10 1902PB	632	1583 A	N19905D	VG/F	
11210	M	$10 1902PB	632	3450 B	B324032H	VG	
11210	-	$10 1902PB	632	4029 A	V670871H	F+	pen/stamp

THE FIRST NATIONAL BANK OF SHANNON CITY   10 L   10 S
9723   UNION
Chartered in April 1910 with a capital of $25,000.
Officers: Pres. ET Dufur 1911-35; **VP** Frank Wolfe 1911, SM Tennis 1914, BL Clark 1920-35; **Cash.** MI Roberts 1911-35; **AC** LGD Roberts 1911-29, M Purviance 1920-24, Robt. Wilson 1920-23, HA Sanderson 1925-27, HO Sanderson 1925-35, WM Brown 1925-27, Bessie Orr 1929

Third Charter, Date Back, Blue Seal	Ser #	# Notes
10-10-10-20	1-1700	6,800
Third Charter, Plain Back, Blue Seal		
10-10-10-20	1701-4962	13,048
1929, Type I		
6-10's	1-522	3,132
6-20's	1-150	900
1929, Type II		
10's	1-540	540
20's	1-137	137

Total amount of circulation issued = $305,560. Amount of large outstanding in June 1935 = $1,820. Amount of small outstanding in June 1935 = $23,180.

19,848 Large   4,709 Small   24,557 Total

9723	-	$10 1902PB	627	4071 C	4071 C	F/VF	pen ac/stamp
9723	-	$10 1902PB	627	4241 C	4241 C	VG	
9723	-	$10 1902PB	627	4323 B	4323 B	G	gone/gone
9723	-	$10 1902PB	627	4599 B	4599 B	VF	pen/pen
9723	M	$20 1902PB	653	2157 A	B509174D	VF	
9723	M	$20 1902PB	653	2764 A	V549286D	?	
9723	M	$20 1902PB	653	3139 A	M272991E	VG	
9723		$20 1902PB	653	3718 A	N180000H	XF	
9723		$20 1902PB	653	3757 A	V320869H	F+	pen/pen
9723	-	$20 1902PB	653	4279 A	4279 A	F/VF	Higgins Mus.
9723		$10 1929T1		F000035A		F	
9723		$10 1929T1		D000039A		VF	
9723		$10 1929T1		F000059A		F+	Higgins Mus.
9723		$10 1929T1		B000184A		F	
9723		$20 1929T1		C000041A		F	
9723		$20 1929T1		C000058A		VG	
9723		$20 1929T1		A000059A		VG/F	
9723		$20 1929T1		E000063A		VG/F	
9723		$10 1929T2		A000453		VG	UR corner gone
9723		$20 1929T2		A000044		VF	

THE FIRST NATIONAL BANK OF SHEFFIELD   1 L   13 S
12430   FRANKLIN
Organized on August 7, 1923 with a capital of $40,000. Placed in receivership on June 11, 1932; capital of $40,000.
Officers: Pres. RG Wolf 1924-32; **VP** Dan R Edgington 1925-32, Geo F Stoll 1925-32; **Cash.** FD Williams 1924-27, KH Weltner 1928-32; **AC** KH Weltner 1924-27

Third Charter, Plain Back, Blue Seal	Ser #	#Notes
10-10-10-20	1-1847	7,388
1929, Type I		
6-10's	1-677	4,062
6-20's	1-189	1,134

Total amount of circulation issued = $155,650. Amount of large outstanding at close = $2,620. Amount of small outstanding at close = $37,080.

7,388 Large   5,196 Small   12,584 Total

12430	-	$20 1902PB	661	1832 A	1832 A	F	
12430		$10 1929T1		E000054A		G	
12430		$10 1929T1		F000172A		F	
12430		$10 1929T1		D000208A		F/VF	
12430		$10 1929T1		B000394A		XF	
12430		$10 1929T1		B000399A		CU	
12430		$10 1929T1		C000517A		F	
12430		$10 1929T1		E000533A		XF/AU	
12430		$10 1929T1		B000566A		VG	
12430		$20 1929T1		B000092A		F	
12430		$20 1929T1		A000099A		?	
12430		$20 1929T1		A000103A		VG	
12430		$20 1929T1		C000123A		VF	Higgins Mus.

THE FIRST NATIONAL BANK OF SHELDON   27 L
3848   O'BRIEN
Organized on Feb. 8, 1888 with a capital of $50,000. Placed in receivership on March 29, 1927; capital of $150,000. Reason for failure: local depression.
Officers: Pres. George W Schee 1888, CS McLaury 1889-94, Frank Frisbee 1895-1902, WM Smith 1903-10, Fred E Frisbee 1911-26; **VP** JE Van Patten 1896-1904, John H Archer 1907-25, FW Bloxham 1920-25, OJ Frey 1926; **Cash.** Charles S McLaury 1888, WM Smith 1889-1902, Fred E Frisbee 1903-10, FW Bloxham 1911-19, FL Barragar 1920-25, HC Moret 1926; **AC** Fred E Frisbee 1896-1902, FW Bloxham 1907-10, FL Barragar 1911-19, HC Moret 1920-25, LP Struyk 1920-23, LD Frisbee 1924-26, John Versteeg 1925

Second Charter, Brown Backs	Ser #	# Notes
10-10-10-20	1-4135	16,540
Third Charter, Red Seal		
10-10-10-20	1-1000	4,000
Third Charter, Date Back, Blue Seal		
10-10-10-20 (6501-7000 type uncertain)	1-7000	28,000
Third Charter, Plain Back, Blue Seal		
10-10-10-20	7001-15887	35,548

Total amount issued = $1,051,100. Amount outstanding at close = $99,000.

84,088 Large   0 Small   84,088 Total

3848	M	$10 1902DB	618	3262 D	Y465238	VG	
3848	M	$10 1902DB	618	3742 E	E812350A	VG	
3848	M	$10 1902DB	618	5509 E	X492474A	F	lt stamp/faded
3848	M	$20 1902DB	644	4079 B	E812687A	VG	
3848	M	$20 1902DB	644	4134 E	E812742A	F+	stamp/stamp
3848	M	$20 1902DB	644	5107 B	X492072A	G	
3848	M	$10 1902PB	626	7484 F	U685412B	VF+	light stamps
3848	M	$10 1902PB	626	7491 E	U685419B	VF+	Higgins Mus.
3848	M	$10 1902PB	626	7501 D	U685429B	F	Repaired
3848	M	$10 1902PB	626	7505 D	U685433B	AU	Rust
3848	M	$10 1902PB	626	9039 E	H830939D	Fr	gone/gone Taped
3848	M	$10 1902PB	626	11114 F	E885476E	XF	stamp/stamp
3848	M	$10 1902PB	626	11149 D	E885511E	VF	gone/gone
3848	M	$10 1902PB	626	11429 E	E885791E	VG	
3848	M	$10 1902PB	626	12137 D	T270999D	VG	
3848	M	$10 1902PB	626	12607 E	B431609H	VF	stamp/stamp
3848	-	$10 1902PB	626	14277 E	X664329H	VF/XF	stamp/stamp
3848	-	$10 1902PB	626	14475 E	X664527H	VF	stamp/stamp

3848	-	$10 1902PB	626	14630 F	X664682H	F+	stamp/stamp
3848	-	$10 1902PB	626	15115 E	15115 E	VF	stamp/stamp
3848	-	$10 1902PB	626	15855 E	15855 E	CU	stamp/stamp
3848	M	$20 1902PB	652	10033 B	R396745D	VG/F	stamp/stamp
3848	M	$20 1902PB	652	10524 B	Y936606D	VG	
3848	M	$20 1902PB	652	12402 B	?	VG/F	
3848	-	$20 1902PB	652	15039 B	15039 B	XF	stamp/stamp
3848	-	$20 1902PB	652	15322 B	15322 B	VG/F	pen/pen
3848	-	$20 1902PB	652	15775 B	15775 B	VG/F	

THE SHELDON NATIONAL BANK   15 L   16 S
7880   **O'BRIEN**
Chartered in 1905.
Officers: Pres. James F Toy 1906-15, AW Sleeper 1916-20, WP Iverson 1922-23, AW Sleeper 1924, WJ Hollander 1925-35; **VP** WH Myers 1907-11, WC Kimmel 1913-28, HP Mousel 192023, WP Iverson 1924-35; **Cash.** PW Hall 1906-10, WE Clagg 1911-17, WP Iverson 1918-20, HP Mousel 1922-25, WP Iverson 1926-35; **AC** EB Myers 1907-10, Delco Bloem 1913-14, EA Hoeven 1920-28, FH Cash 1926-29, EB Myers 1929-35, Fred J Pylman 1929-35

Third Charter, Red Seal	Ser #	# Notes
10-10-10-20	1-470	1,880
Third Charter, Date Back, Blue Seal		
10-10-10-20	1-3700	14,800
Third Charter, Plain Back, Blue Seal		
10-10-10-20	3701-9590	23,560
1929, Type I		
6-10's	1-1102	6,612
6-20's	1-313	1,878

Total amount of circulation issued = $606,680. Amount outstanding in 1934 = $25,000. Amount of large outstanding on July 24, 1935 = $4,000.
40,240 Large   8,490 Small   48,730 Total

7880	M	$10 1902RS	614	243 A	H984733	F	
7880	M	$10 1902DB	617	2103 ?	X571539	G/VG	LR corner gone
7880	M	$10 1902PB	625	4041 D	U347179B	VG+	Higgins Mus.
7880	M	$10 1902PB	625	5074 D	E731838D	XF	stamp sigs vp
7880		$10 1902PB	625	7025 ?	?	G	
7880		$10 1902PB	625	7857 F	V544679H	F/VF	
7880	-	$10 1902PB	625	7891 D	B182473K	F	
7880	-	$10 1902PB	625	7988 D	B182570K	F/VF	Higgins Mus.
7880	-	$10 1902PB	625	8037 E	B182619K	F+	stamp/pen
7880	-	$10 1902PB	625	8398 D	8398 D	F+	gone/gone
7880	-	$10 1902PB	625	8489 E	8489 E	XF	stamp/stamp
7880	-	$10 1902PB	625	8658 E	8658 E	VF	stamp/stamp
7880	M	$20 1902PB	651	2455 B	D879781A	VG/F	
7880	-	$20 1902PB	651	8638 B	8638 B	VG	
7880	-	$20 1902PB	651	9069 B	9069 B	VF/XF	stamp/stamp
7880		$10 1929T1		A000081A		F	
7880		$10 1929T1		C000416A		HG	
7880		$10 1929T1		E000447A		F	
7880		$10 1929T1		E000562A		VG	
7880		$10 1929T1		E000681A		F/VF	
7880		$10 1929T1		A000695A		F	
7880		$10 1929T1		C000959A		VG	
7880		$20 1929T1		D000017A		VG+	
7880		$20 1929T1		E000042A		F/VF	
7880		$20 1929T1		E000052A		F	
7880		$20 1929T1		F000066A		VG	Repaired
7880		$20 1929T1		B000161A		VF	
7880		$20 1929T1		E000201A		XF	Higgins Mus.
7880		$20 1929T1		A000216A		G	
7880		$20 1929T1		C000260A		F/VF	
7880		$20 1929T1		D000275A		?	

THE COMMERCIAL NATIONAL BANK OF SHENANDOAH
8971   **PAGE**   **0 L**
Chartered in December 1907 with a capital of $50,000. Placed in voluntary liquidation on Dec. 20, 1909; capital of $50,000. Consolidated with #2679.
Officers: Pres. HI Foskett 1908-09; **VP** AW Murphy 1909; **Cash.** JF Lake 1908-09

Third Charter, Red Seal	Ser #	# Notes
10-10-10-20	1-675	2,700
Third Charter, Date Back, Blue Seal		
10-10-10-20	1-585	2,340

Total amount of circulation issued = $63,000. Amount outstanding at close = $50,000. Amount outstanding in October 1910 = $29,680.
5,040 Large   0 Small   5,040 Total

THE FARMERS NATIONAL BANK OF SHENANDOAH
11588   **PAGE**   **1 L**
Chartered in January 1920 with a capital of $100,000. Placed in voluntary liquidation on October 2, 1924; capital of $100,000. Absorbed by #2679.
Officers: Pres. CA Wenstrand 1920-24; **VP** Fred Nordstrom 1920-22, George Jay 1923-24; **Cash.** David A Wenstrand 1920-24; **AC** Geo Wild 1920-22, MC Spry 1923-24

Third Charter, Plain Back, Blue Seal	Ser #	# Notes
5-5-5-5	1-1955	7,820

Total amount issued = $39,100. Amount outstanding in 1924 = $10,000.
7,820 Large   0 Small   7,820 Total

11588M	$5 1902PB	607	1220 A	M194016E	VG	gone/gone

THE FIRST NATIONAL BANK OF SHENANDOAH   5 L
2363   **PAGE**
Organized on May 5, 1877 with a capital of $50,000. Chartered on June 22, 1877; succeeded The Farmers & Merchants Bank. Placed in receivership on May 13, 1926; capital of $50,000. Reason for failure: local depression.
Officers: Pres. Thomas H Read 1877-1926; **VP** Elbert A Read 1910-26, TL Brown 1920-26, Henry Read 1923-26, Earl Sheets 1923-26; **Cash.** Andrew Jackson Crose 1877-81, Richard W Carey 1883-87, Frank Hooker 1888-92, TC Beard 1893-94, Elbert A Read 1899-1909, Henry Read 1910-19, DB Miller 1920-23; **AC** LA Tomkins 1896, JF Lake 1900-04, EC Fishbaugh 1907, Henry Read 1909, DB Miller 1910-13, OR Hayes 1920, WA Davidson 1920-26, FS Young 1923-26

First Charter, Series of 1875	Ser #	# Notes
10-10-10-20	1-2769	11,076
Second Charter, Brown Backs		
5-5-5-5	1-1000	4,000
10-10-10-20	1-3020	12,080
Second Charter, Date Back		
5-5-5-5	1-2295	9,180
10-10-10-20	1-1639	6,556
Third Charter, Plain Back, Blue Seal		
10-10-10-20	1-1584	6,336

Total amount issue = $516,500. Amount outstanding at close = $20,000.
49,228 Large   0 Small   49,228 Total

2363	-	$20	1875	?	2603 A	K174840	VF
2363	M	$10 1882BB	487	1723 B	D233169D	VF	Higgins Mus.
2363	M	$10 1882BB	487	2680 C	R84401R	G	gone/gone
2363	M	$5 1882DB	534	1630 E	K22042	VG/F	
2363	M	$20 1902PB	658	737 A	A817829E	VF+	stamp/stamp

SHENANDOAH NATIONAL BANK   6 L   40 S
12950   **PAGE**
Organized on June 21, 1926 with a capital of $100,000. Succeeded #2679 and assumed the circulation of #2679. Placed in conservatorship on March 21, 1933. Placed in voluntary liquidation on June 1, 1934; capital of $100,000. Succeeded by #14057 which assumed the circulation of #12950 but did not issue any of its own notes.
Officers: Pres. ES Welch 1927-30, HE Ross 1931-33; **VP** HE Ross 1927-30, RS Lake 1927-33, ES Welch 1931-33; **Cash.** FM Schneider 1927-33; **AC** RH Sawyer 1928-33

Third Charter, Plain Back, Blue Seal	Ser #	# Notes
10-10-10-20	1-3072	12,288
1929, Type I		
6-10's	1-2114	12,684
6-20's	1-638	3,828
1929, Type II		
10's	1-732	732
20's	1-138	138

Total amount of circulation issued = $367,080. Amount of large outstanding at close = $7,010. Includes the large outstanding of #2679 which was assumed by #12950. Amount of small outstanding at close = $91,970. Circulation liability assumed by #14057 which was then responsible for redeeming the outstanding circulation of #12950 (also #2679). Since the circulation was assumed, a later large outstanding is available. In July 1935, there was $6,300 worth of large still outstanding and $90,880 worth of small still outstanding.
12,288 Large   17,382 Small   29,670 Total

12950	-	$10 1902PB	635	1446 A	1446 A	VG	vp Corners gone
12950	-	$10 1902PB	635	1577 A	1577 A	G	stamp sigs vp
12950	-	$10 1902PB	635	1877 C	1877 C	F/VF	stamp/stamp
12950	-	$10 1902PB	635	2288 B	2288 B	VG	lt stamp sigs
12950	-	$10 1902PB	635	2488 A	2488 A	VG	Higgins Mus.
12950		$20 1902PB	658	1370 A		? VF/XF	
12950		$10 1929T1		A000081A		F	
12950		$10 1929T1		B000173A		F/VF	
12950		$10 1929T1		E000206A		VG/F	
12950		$10 1929T1		A000347A		?	
12950		$10 1929T1		F000374A		VG	
12950		$10 1929T1		D000410A		F	
12950		$10 1929T1		E000816A		F	
12950		$10 1929T1		B000883A		F	

12950	$10	1929T1	A000963A	VG	
12950	$10	1929T1	A001274A	?	
12950	$10	1929T1	B001339A	CU	
12950	$10	1929T1	D001419A	CU	
12950	$10	1929T1	B001488A	VG	
12950	$10	1929T1	D001597A	VF	
12950	$10	1929T1	C001652A	VG/F	
12950	$10	1929T1	B001706A	F	
12950	$10	1929T1	C001712A	?	
12950	$10	1929T1	B001760A	F	
12950	$10	1929T1	B001792A	?	
12950	$10	1929T1	A001845A	G/VG	
12950	$10	1929T1	A001963A	F	
12950	$10	1929T1	A002003A	XF	Higgins Mus.
12950	$20	1929T1	?000041A	VG	
12950	$20	1929T1	D000107A	F	
12950	$20	1929T1	E000131A	F+	
12950	$20	1929T1	B000173A	F	
12950	$20	1929T1	A000175A	F	
12950	$20	1929T1	B000178A	F	
12950	$20	1929T1	B000238A	VG/F	
12950	$20	1929T1	E000310A	VG	
12950	$20	1929T1	B000404A	VF	
12950	$20	1929T1	C000464A	XF	
12950	$20	1929T1	D000468A	F	
12950	$20	1929T1	C000479A	VG+	
12950	$20	1929T1	B000515A	F/VF	
12950	$20	1929T1	F000558A	VG/F	
12950	$20	1929T1	B000579A	?	
12950	$20	1929T1	D000602A	VF	
12950	$10	1929T2	A000077	VG/F	
12950	$10	1929T2	A000370	F	

THE SHENANDOAH NATIONAL BANK 9 L
2679 PAGE

Chartered in 1882 with a capital of $50,000. Succeeded The Page County Bank. Assumed #8971 by consolidation on December 20, 1909. Absorbed #11588 on October 2, 1924. Placed in voluntary liquidation on January 20, 1927; capital of $100,000. Succeeded by #12950 which assumed the outstanding circulation of #2679.

Officers: Pres. George Bogart 1883-14, AW Murphy 1915-26; **VP** EH Mitchell 1907-09, AW Murphy 1910-14, HI Foskett 1910-26, JF Lake 1926; **Cash.** Hamer F Wilson 1883-87, ES Ferris 1888-96, Ellis Tucker 1900-04, RM Gwynn 1906-09, John F Lake 1910-26, HE Ross 1926; **AC** ES Ferris 1885, D Van Buskirk 1896, RM Gwynn 1900-04, CJ Alden 1907, FM Schneider 1909-26, Harry E Ross 1920-26

First Charter, Series of 1875	Ser #	# Notes
10-10-10-20	1-2475	9,900
Third Charter, Red Seal		
10-10-10-20	1-3200	12,800
Third Charter, Date Back, Blue Seal		
10-10-10-20	1-7000	28,000
Third Charter, Plain Back, Blue Seal		
10-10-10-20 (plate dated 1902)	7001-12293	21,172
10-10-10-20 (plate dated 1922)	1-4364	17,456

Total amount of circulation issued = $1,116,600. Amount outstanding at close = $100,000. Circulation liability assumed by #12950, which was then responsible for the redemption of the outstanding notes of #2679
89,328 Large   0 Small   89,328 Total

2679	M	$10	1902PB	624	7478 E	R456288B	?	pen/pen
2679	M	$10	1902PB	624	10247 E	N7869D	F	lt. stamp sigs
2679	M	$10	1902PB	624	10506 F	U898038D	G/VG	faded/faded
2679	M	$20	1902PB	650	9359 B	E710943D	VG	Stains
2679	M	$20	1902PB	650	11824 B	A800976E	F+	faded/faded

Higgins Mus.

2679		$10	1902PB	634	1946 D	D927298H	VG/F	
2679	-	$10	1902PB	634	3459 C	Y430131H	VG/F	faded/faded
2679	-	$20	1902PB	660	4012 A	4012 A	VG	
2679	-	$20	1902PB	660	4062 A	4062 A	F	gone/gone

THE FIRST NATIONAL BANK OF SIBLEY 4 L 9 S
3320 OSCEOLA

Organized on February 25, 1885 with a capital of $50,000. Succeeded The Osceola County Bank. Placed in conservatorship on March 22, 1933. Licensed to reopen on April 6, 1933.

Officers: Pres. Charles E Brown 1885-1909, HL Emmert 1910-28, J Fred Mattert 1929-34, MD Brodt 1935; **VP** GE Lathrop 1896, WT Steiner 1907-25, EL Harding 1930-32, Mrs. EL Harding 1933-34, J Fred Mattert; **Cash.** HL Emmert 1885-1908, J Fred Mattert 1909-28, MD Brodt 1929-34, Geo W Bauman 1935; **AC** J Fred Mattert 1896-1907, MD Brodt 1914-28, Chas L Ramsey 1935

Second Charter, Brown Backs	Ser #	# Notes
5-5-5-5	1-3271	13,084
10-10-10-20	1-356	1,424
Third Charter, Red Seal		
10-10-10-20	1-390	1,560
Third Charter, Date Back, Blue Seal		
10-10-10-20	1-1160	4,640
Third Charter, Plain Back, Blue Seal		
10-10-10-20	1161-2123	3,852
1929, Type I		
6-10's	1-283	1,698
6-20's	1-71	426

Total amount of circulation issued = $234,370. Amount outstanding in 1934 = $12,500. Amount of large outstanding on July 31, 1935 = $1,480.
24,560 Large   2,124 Small   26,684 Total

3320		$20	1882BB	494	170 A	X286836	VG	
3320	-	$10	1902PB	624	1983 D	1983 D	VG/F	stamp/stamp
3320	-	$10	1902PB	624	2001 F	2001 F	AU	Higgins Mus.
3320	-	$10	1902PB	624	2002 F	2002 F	AU	Ink spots
3320		$10	1929T1		B000035A		VF	
3320		$10	1929T1		C000086A		G	
3320		$10	1929T1		A000203A		VF	Higgins Mus.
3320		$10	1929T1		C000229A		VG/F	
3320		$20	1929T1		F000024A		VG+	
3320		$20	1929T1		B000037A		VF	
3320		$20	1929T1		C000060A		VF	
3320		$20	1929T1		E000062A		F	
3320		$20	1929T1		D000069A		VF/XF	

THE NATIONAL BANK OF SIDNEY 20 L 13 S
5145 FREMONT

Organized on September 3, 1898 with a capital of $60,000. Succeeded Metelman & Frazer. Placed in receivership on October 15, 1931; capital of $60,000. Reason for failure: local depression.

Officers: Pres. AF Metelman 1899-1913, JT Hodges 1914-24, JC Nichols 1925-28, A Wildberger 1929-31; **VP** JT Hodges 1900-07, Geo E Draper 1909-13, L Wankel 1914, CA Metelman 1920, A Wildberger 1922-28, FA Gore 1928-31; **Cash.** WT Frazer 1899-1907, CA Metelman 1908-19, Milton Estes 1920-25, RB Farquhar 1926-30, WT Cozad 1930-31; **AC** CA Metelman 1900-07, Milton Estes 1909-14, RM Goy 1920-26, TM Wightman 1923-28, LB Foster 1928-31

Second Charter, Brown Backs	Ser #	# Notes
10-10-10-20	1-1530	6,120
Second Charter, Date Back		
10-10-10-20	1-3540	14,160
Second Charter, Value Back		
10-10-10-20	3541-4241	2,804
Third Charter, Plain Back, Blue Seal		
10-10-10-20	1-6657	26,628
1929, Type I		
6-5's	1-664	3,984
6-10's	1-724	4,344
6-20's	1-192	1,152

Total amount of circulation issued = $707,800. Amount of large outstanding at close = $10,055. Amount of small outstanding at close = $49,945.
49,712 Large   9,480 Small   59,192 Total

5145		$10	1882BB	490	130 B	T941255	VF	
5145	M	$10	1882DB	545	?	N735448	F	
5145	M	$20	1882DB	555	884 B	D31994	F	pen ac/gone
5145	M	$20	1882DB	555	1335 B	E729273	F	
5145	M	$20	1882DB	555	1612 B	K218150	VF+	Higgins Mus.
5145	M	$20	1882DB	555	3140 B	R294468	VF/XF	pen/pen
5145	M	$10	1882VB	577	4104 D	U390022	AG	

Charter	M	Denom	Series	Plate	Serial A	Serial B	Grade	Notes
5145	M	$10	1902PB	632	1413 A	Y360195D	F	pen/pen vp
5145	M	$10	1902PB	632	2660 B	R900442E	VG/F	
5145	-	$10	1902PB	632	5499 A	5499 A	F+	Higgins Mus.
5145	-	$10	1902PB	632	6329 B	6329 B	F+	Higgins Mus.
5145	-	$20	1902PB	658	3745 A	R666627H	F	Higgins Mus.
5145	-	$20	1902PB	658	3854 A	R666736H	VG	ac corner gone
5145	-	$20	1902PB	658	3909 A	X461171H	VG/F	pen ac/stamp
5145	-	$20	1902PB	658	4251 A	X461513H	VG/F	
5145	-	$20	1902PB	658	4814 A	4814 A	VG	
5145	-	$20	1902PB	658	5593 A	5593 A	VF	
5145	-	$20	1902PB	658	5822 A	5822 A	VG/F	stamp/stamp
5145	-	$20	1902PB	658	6050 A	6050 A	VG/F	stamp/stamp
5145	-	$20	1902PB	658	6258 A	6258 A	F/VF	
5145		$5	1929T1		A000607A		VG/F	
5145		$10	1929T1		B000074A		F	
5145		$10	1929T1		E000284A		VG	
5145		$10	1929T1		E000395A		?	
5145		$10	1929T1		C000510A		VG	
5145		$10	1929T1		C000009A		F+	
5145		$20	1929T1		B000033A		VG/F	
5145		$20	1929T1		A000058A		VG/F	
5145		$20	1929T1		C000065A		F+	Higgins Mus.
5145		$20	1929T1		A000085A		VG/F	
5145		$20	1929T1		E000168A		VG	
5145		$20	1929T1		B000190A		XF/AU	
5145		$20	1929T1		D000192A		VF/XF	Last sheet of $20s

THE FIRST NATIONAL BANK OF SIGOURNEY   32 L   5 S
1786   KEOKUK

Chartered on February 6, 1871. Placed in voluntary liquidation on June 10, 1930; capital of $75,000. Absorbed by The Union Savings Bank, Sigourney.

Officers: Pres. Joseph Keck 1872-81, George D Woodin 1883, JP Yerger 1884-97, GD Woodin 1898-1903, Harry G Brown 1903-20, HJ Brown 1922-23, CE Baylor 1924-30; **VP** GD Woodin 1896, E Laffer 1900-03, Thos Kelly 1904-09, Edwin Franken 1911-20, CE Baylor 1922-23, KE Wilcockson 1924-30, JR Mackey 1928-30, CC Williamson 1928-30; **Cash.** Irving A Keck 1872-83, JT Webber 1884-88, JR Mackey 1889-1927, HR White 1928-30; **AC** TC Weaver 1888-89, Edw. Bower 1896-1903, CC Williamson 1909-27, RD Painter 1914, WA Mackey 1920-30

	Ser #	# Notes
First Charter, Original Issue		
1-1-1-2	1-2500	10,000
5-5-5-5	1-3625	14,500
First Charter, Series of 1875		
5-5-5-5	1-3336	13,344
Second Charter, Brown Backs		
5-5-5-5	1-4625	18,500
10-10-10-20	1-2430	9,720
Second Charter, Date Back		
5-5-5-5	1-638	2,552
10-10-10-20	1-495	1,980
Third Charter, Date Back, Blue Seal		
5-5-5-5	1-3375	13,500
10-10-10-20	1-2600	10,400
Third Charter, Plain Back, Blue Seal		
5-5-5-5	3376-12540	36,660
10-10-10-20	2601-8178	22,312
1929, Type I		
6-5's	1-788	4,728
6-10's	1-358	2,148
6-20's	1-74	444

Total amount of circulation issued = $1,116,930. Amount of large outstanding at close = $21,790. Amount of small outstanding at close = $53,210.

153,468 Large   7,320 Small   160,788 Total

Charter	M	Denom	Series	Plate	Serial A	Serial B	Grade	Notes
1786	-	$1	ORIG	380	1 C	C306238	XF	pen/pen vp
1786	-	$5	1875	401	2902 D	U265902	VF	Higgins Mus.
1786	-	$5	1882BB	471	406 D	K953058	G	Oat Bin Hoard
1786		$5	1882BB	471	2721 B	?	G/VG	
1786	M	$5	1882BB	471	3861 B	U754929U	XF	
1786	M	$10	1882BB	484	1349 A	R790393R	CU	
1786	M	$10	1882BB	484	1349 C	R790393R	CU	
1786	M	$20	1882BB	498	1001 A	R790045R	XF+	pen/pen
1786	M	$20	1882BB	498	1069 A	R790113R	CU	
1786	M	$20	1882BB	498	1112 A	R790156R	XF	Higgins Mus.
1786	M	$20	1882BB	498	1344 A	R790388R	AU	
1786	M	$20	1882BB	498	1370 A	R790414R	XF	pen/pen
1786	M	$5	1902DB	593	1906 D	N794418A	XF	Higgins Mus.
1786	M	$10	1902DB	619	100 B	Y102926	AU	
1786	M	$10	1902DB	619	637 B	Y103463	VF	pen/pen
1786	M	$10	1902DB	619	1930 C	X484675A	VG	
1786	M	$5	1902PB	601	3454 C	M963281B	G/VG	gone/gone
1786	M	$5	1902PB	601	4031 A	R794571B	F	
1786	M	$5	1902PB	601	6972 A	Z623218D	XF	gone/gone
1786	M	$5	1902PB	601	7815 D	K78911E	G	gone/gone
1786	M	$5	1902PB	601	9296 B	H995857H	VG	
1786	-	$5	1902PB	601	9486 C	R396147H	VF	gone/gone
1786	-	$5	1902PB	601	9979 A	X85265H	G/VG	gone/gone
1786	-	$5	1902PB	601	10555 C	10555 C	VG	
1786	-	$5	1902PB	601	10980 C	10980 C	F	gone/gone
1786	-	$5	1902PB	601	11376 D	11376 D	VF+	faded/faded
1786	M	$10	1902PB	627	4476 B	V781718D	XF	
1786	M	$10	1902PB	627	5886 B	E72378H	F/VF	faded/faded
1786	M	$10	1902PB	627	5903 C	E72395H	F/VF	gone/gone
1786		$10	1902PB	627	6504 ?	?	VG	
1786	-	$10	1902PB	627	7044 C	7044 C	F	
1786	-	$20	1902PB	653	7684 A	7684 A	F/VF	nearly gone
1786		$5	1929T1		D000187A		F	
1786		$10	1929T1		F000169A		XF	
1786		$10	1929T1		B000323A		VF/XF	
1786		$10	1929T1		D000355A		F	Higgins Mus.
1786		$20	1929T1		D000036A		G/VG	

THE FIRST NATIONAL BANK OF SIOUX CENTER   2 L   13 S
7369   SIOUX

Chartered in 1904.

Officers: Pres. OP Miller 1904-10, A Van der Meide 1911-17, Neal Mouw 1918-35; **VP** Chas. Creglow 1904, MA Cox 1907-10, Anthony Te Paske 1911-35, John Boeyink 1920-34; **Cash.** Neal Mouw 1904-17, FC Aue 1918-35; **AC** Geo D Siemen 1907-10, John Boeyink 1911-14, PB Mouw 1920-35

	Ser #	# Notes
Third Charter, Red Seal		
10-10-10-20	1-854	3,416
Third Charter, Date Back, Blue Seal		
10-10-10-20	1-1590	6,360
Third Charter, Plain Back, Blue Seal		
10-10-10-20	1591-4630	12,160
1929, Type I		
6-10's	1-546	3,276
6-20's	1-126	756
1929, Type II		
10's	1-341	341
20's	1-113	113

Total amount of circulation issued = $327,750. Amount outstanding in 1934 = $24,550. Amount of large outstanding on July 24, 1935 = $1,390.

21,936 Large   4,486 Small   26,422 Total

Charter	M	Denom	Series	Plate	Serial A	Serial B	Grade	Notes
7369	M	$10	1902DB	616	1380 D	X884385A	Fr/G	gone/gone
7369	M	$10	1902PB	624	2889 D	X421741E	Fr/G	Higgins Mus.
7369		$10	1929T1		C000050A		F	
7369		$10	1929T1		B000203A		VF	Higgins Mus.
7369		$10	1929T1		A000215A		VG/F	
7369		$10	1929T1		C000271A		F	
7369		$10	1929T1		B000287A		F/VF	
7369		$10	1929T1		D000430A		F	
7369		$10	1929T1		C000455A		F	
7369		$20	1929T1		D000023A		F	
7369		$20	1929T1		A000047A		F	
7369		$20	1929T1		C000064A		F	
7369		$20	1929T1		B000101A		F	Rust hole UR
7369		$20	1929T1		A000122A		VG/F	
7369		$20	1929T2		A000014		F	1/2 inch tear

THE AMERICAN NATIONAL BANK OF SIOUX CITY   0 L
3940   WOODBURY

Chartered on November 14, 1888.

Officers: Pres. OJ Taylor 1889-90; **Cash.** Herman Russell 1889, Thos. C Pease 1890

	Ser #	# Notes
Second Charter, Brown Backs		
5-5-5-5	1-2148	8,592

Total amount of circulation issued = $42,960. Amount outstanding at close = $33,750. Amount outstanding in 1910 = $300.

8,592 Large   0 Small   8,592 Total

THE CITIZENS NATIONAL BANK OF SIOUX CITY   0 L
1976   WOODBURY

Chartered on May 6, 1872. Placed in voluntary liquidation on April 14, 1874; capital of $50,000.

Officers: Pres. Ogilvie C Tredway 1872-74; **Cash.** John A Schmidt 1872-74

	Ser #	# Notes
First Charter, Original Issue		
5-5-5-5	1-1500	6,000
10-10-10-20	1-300	1,200

Total amount of circulation issued = $45,000. Amount outstanding at close = $45,000. Amount outstanding in 1910 = $130.

7,200 Large   0 Small   7,200 Total

THE CITY NATIONAL BANK OF SIOUX CITY   **0 L**
7401   **WOODBURY**
Chartered on September 17, 1904. Placed in voluntary liquidation on April 1, 1905; capital of $100,000. Consolidated with #1757.
Officers: Pres. AT Bennett 1904; **VP** Wm Jepson 1904; **Cash.** AJ Wilson 1904; **AC** FT Wilson 1904, FW Kane 1904

Third Charter, Red Seal	Ser #	# Notes
10-10-10-20	1-500	2,000

Total amount of circulation issued = $25,000. Amount outstanding at close = $25,000. Amount outstanding in 1910 = $1,880.
2,000 Large   0 Small   2,000 Total

THE COMMERCIAL NATIONAL BANK OF SIOUX CITY   0 L
4630   **WOODBURY**
Chartered on September 16, 1891. Succeeded The Commercial State Bank. Placed in voluntary liquidation on December 1, 1892; capital of $150,000. Consolidated with #3968.
Officers: Pres. JW Brown 1891-92; **Cash.** Louis H Brown 1891-92

Second Charter, Brown Backs	Ser #	# Notes
50-100	1-250	500

Total amount of circulation issued = $37,500. Amount outstanding at close = $33,750. Amount outstanding in 1910 = $250.
500 Large   0 Small   500 Total

THE CORN EXCHANGE NATIONAL BANK OF SIOUX CITY
4235   **WOODBURY**   **0 L**
Chartered on February 15, 1890. Placed in voluntary liquidation on April 29, 1895; capital of $150,000. Consolidated with #3968.
Officers: Pres. John C French 1890-94; **Cash.** WGH Vernon 1890, C Bevan Oldfield 1891-94

Second Charter, Brown Backs	Ser #	# Notes
10-10-10-20	1-1032	4,128
50-100	1-249	498

Total amount of circulation issued = $88,950. Amount outstanding at close = $44,500. Amount outstanding in 1910 = $960.
4,626 Large   0 Small   4,626 Total

THE FIRST NATIONAL BANK OF SIOUX CITY   **84 L   29 S**
1757   **WOODBURY**
Chartered on December 28, 1870 with a capital of $100,000. Closed on November 19, 1896. Placed in receivership on January 7, 1897; capital of $100,000. (suspension) Restored to solvency on March 16, 1897. Assumed by consolidation The Farmers Loan and Trust Company in 1899. Assumed #7401 by consolidation on April 1, 1905. Absorbed #3968 on November 6, 1909. Absorbed #4209 on February 15, 1911. Placed in receivership on December 8, 1930; capital of $1,000,000. Reason for failure: local depression & incompetent management.
Officers: Pres. Asahel W Hubbard 1872-79, Hyde B Rice 1879-83, Thos J Stone 1884-98, James F Toy 1899-1907, Ackley Hubbard 1908-09, John McHugh 1910-15, John J Large 1916-24, JL Mitchell 1925-30; **VP** Geo Murphy 1896, A Groninger 1900-03, Ackley Hubbard 1907, WL Montgomery 1909-14, HG Weare 1910-13, FA McCornack 1910-23, John J Large 1911-14, HA Gooch 1919-30, JL Mitchell 1919-24, LH Henry 1919-28, HB Scott 1930; **Cash.** Thomas J Stone 1872-83, EH Stone 1884-98, TA Black 1899-1900, AS Garretson 1901, CN Lukes 1902-05, HA Gooch 1904-05, 1910-14, J Fred Toy 1906-07, Lawrence S Critchell 1908-09, OD Pettit 1915-29, JP Hainer 1930; **AC** Thos R Galbraith 1885, IC Brubacher 1900, J Fred Toy 1902-03, FB Watson 1903-04, FW Kammann 1907, FW Bland 1909, OD Pettit 1910-14, Fritz Fritzson 1910-25, Frank R Kirk 1919-30, LM Ashley 1919-30, JP Hainer 1919-29, Geo JN Smith 1925-30

First Charter, Original Issue	Ser #	# Notes
5-5-5-5	1-6750	27,000
10-10-10-20	1-500	2,000
First Charter, Series of 1875		
10-10-10-20	1-4383	17,532
Second Charter, Brown Backs		
10-10-10-20	1-7000	28,000
50-100	1-1374	2,748
Second Charter, Date Back		
5-5-5-5	1-3515	14,060
10-10-10-20	1-1455	5,820
50-100	1-210	420
Third Charter, Date Back, Blue Seal		
5-5-5-5	1-21500	86,000
10-10-10-20	1-13200	52,800
Third Charter, Plain Back, Blue Seal		
5-5-5-5	21501-61135	158,540
10-10-10-20	13201-38101	99,604
1929, Type I		
6-5's	1-4712	28,272
6-10's	1-2123	12,738
6-20's	1-570	3,420

Total amount of circulation issued = $4,574,690. Amount of large outstanding at close = $65,850. Amount of small outstanding at close = $934,150.
494,524 Large   44,430 Small   538,954 Total

Bank	Denom	Series	Plate	Serial L	Serial T	Grade	Notes
1757 M	$10	1882BB	484	2286 A	T945830T	VG	Higgins Mus.
1757 M	$10	1882BB	484	6611 B	U546975U	AU	Grinnell # 2822
1757 M	$20	1882BB	498	2290 A	T945834T	XF/AU	
1757 M	$20	1882BB	498	3955 A	U489879U	F	
1757 M	$20	1882BB	498	6078 A	U546442U	VG	
1757 M	$100	1882BB	524	1181 A	B243533	VF	pen/pen Pinholes
1757 M	$100	1882BB	524	1225 A	B243577	F	gone/gone
1757 M	$5	1882DB	532	2479 C	D693984	VG	
1757 M	$100	1882DB	566	13 B	A23579	XF/AU	Higgins Mus.
1757 M	$100	1882DB	566	74 B	A23640	CU	
1757 M	$100	1882DB	566	100 B	A23666	XF/AU	
1757 M	$100	1882DB	566	163 B	A23729	AU	
1757 M	$5	1902DB	592	1 C	V582986	XF/AU	
1757 M	$5	1902DB	592	6988 C	V685573	VG	
1757 M	$5	1902DB	592	13736 D	T155113A	VG/F	
1757 M	$10	1902DB	618	686 C	X111050	F/VF	
1757 M	$10	1902DB	618	? A	X149721	F	
1757 M	$10	1902DB	618	?	U370406A	VG	
1757 M	$10	1902DB	618	9391 A	Z284955A	F+	
1757 M	$10	1902DB	618	10689 B	Z304333A	VF	
1757 M	$10	1902DB	618	12326 B	M52562B	VG	
1757 M	$20	1902DB	644	1488 A	X111852	G/VG	
1757 M	$20	1902DB	644	3700 A	X144724	G	
1757 M	$20	1902DB	644	8598 A	U398154A	VF	
1757 M	$5	1902PB	601	22732 B	U53758B	VF	
1757 M	$5	1902PB	601	31174 A	N209600D	VF	
1757 M	$5	1902PB	601	32168 C	V269214D	F	
1757 M	$5	1902PB	601	32305 C	V269357D	F	
1757 M	$5	1902PB	601	40038 A	R553269E	VG	
1757 M	$5	1902PB	601	40719 B	R553950E	AU	Higgins Mus.
1757 M	$5	1902PB	601	42584 A	X826790E	XF	mach stamps
1757	$5	1902PB	601	?	D401993H	VG	
1757	$5	1902PB	601	45686 D	M292697H	VG	
1757 -	$5	1902PB	601	46752 B	V596713H	F/VF	mach stamps
1757 -	$5	1902PB	601	48481 A	V615842H	XF	mach stamps
1757 -	$5	1902PB	601	48611 ?	V615972H	F	
1757 -	$5	1902PB	601	49461 D	49461 D	XF	mach stamps
1757 -	$5	1902PB	601	49805 B	49805 B	F/VF	mach stamps
1757 -	$5	1902PB	601	50162 D	50162 D	G	lt. stamp sigs
1757 -	$5	1902PB	601	50334 D	50334 D	VG/F	faded/faded
1757 -	$5	1902PB	601	51125 ?	51125 ?	VF	
1757 -	$5	1902PB	601	52399 A	52399 A	F/VF	
1757 -	$5	1902PB	601	52582 B	52582 B	XF	
1757 -	$5	1902PB	601	52719 A	52719 A	VF	
1757 -	$5	1902PB	601	53378 B	53378 B	G	
1757 -	$5	1902PB	601	53618 D	53618 D	F	
1757 -	$5	1902PB	601	55360 A	55360 A	F/VF	
1757 -	$5	1902PB	601	55502 D	55502 D	AU	
1757 -	$5	1902PB	601	55518 C	55518 C	VG	
1757 -	$5	1902PB	601	55529 D	55529 D	XF	Higgins Mus.
1757 -	$5	1902PB	601	55681 A	55681 A	F	
1757 -	$5	1902PB	601	60350 D	60350 D	F/VF	stamp/stamp
1757 M	$10	1902PB	627	14243 B	?	F	
1757 M	$10	1902PB	627	15663 B	A974130D	VG	
1757 M	$10	1902PB	627	19593 B	R344235D	F+	
1757 M	$10	1902PB	627	20918 A	D442090E	VG/F	
1757 M	$10	1902PB	627	21939 D	D498671E	VF	
1757 M	$10	1902PB	627	23208 B	K179010E	CU	
1757 M	$10	1902PB	627	25048 C	U614550E	VG	
1757 M	$10	1902PB	627	26708 C	Z742160E	VF	
1757 M	$10	1902PB	627	27127 C	E928789H	VF	
1757 -	$10	1902PB	627	31248 C	31248 C	F	gone/gone
1757 -	$10	1902PB	627	31305 B	31305 B	F	
1757 -	$10	1902PB	627	31460 B	31460 B	VG	
1757 -	$10	1902PB	627	31663 B	31663 B	VG	Soiled
1757 -	$10	1902PB	627	31738 C	31738 C	VG	
1757 -	$10	1902PB	627	33787 C	33787 C	VG	
1757 -	$10	1902PB	627	33843 A	33843 A	VG	
1757 -	$10	1902PB	627	33853 B	33853 B	VF	
1757 -	$10	1902PB	627	34165 C	34165 C	VF	
1757 -	$10	1902PB	627	34915 C	34915 C	F	
1757 -	$10	1902PB	627	35654 C	35654 C	F	stamp Rust
1757 -	$10	1902PB	627	36101 C	36101 C	HG	stamp/stamp
1757 M	$20	1902PB	653	16976 A	K417528D	F/VF	
1757 M	$20	1902PB	653	17566 A	K418118D	VG	
1757 M	$20	1902PB	653	22260 A	D498992E	F	stamp Pinholes

1757	M	$20 1902PB 653	22625 A	K178427E	VF	
1757	M	$20 1902PB 653	25976 A	Z697398E	VG	stamp/stamp
1757	M	$20 1902PB 653	27614 A	E929276H	F/VF	stamp/stamp
1757	M	$20 1902PB 653	27640 A	E929302H	F/VF	
1757		$20 1902PB 653	29913 A	X851855H	F	
1757	-	$20 1902PB 653	34200 A	34200 A	VG	
1757	-	$20 1902PB 653	34392 A	34392 A	VG/F	
1757	-	$20 1902PB 653	36157 A	36157 A	F+	stamp/stamp
1757		$5 1929T1	C000176A		VG	
1757		$5 1929T1	A001056A		AU	
1757		$5 1929T1	E002333A		VG	
1757		$5 1929T1	F003857A		VF	
1757		$5 1929T1	C004357A		VF	
1757		$10 1929T1	C000237A		F/VF	
1757		$10 1929T1	A000299A		F/VF	
1757		$10 1929T1	C000364A		VF	
1757		$10 1929T1	C000510A		F/VF	
1757		$10 1929T1	C000523A		VG	
1757		$10 1929T1	C000805A		VF	
1757		$10 1929T1	C001006A		?	
1757		$10 1929T1	C001123A		G	
1757		$10 1929T1	C001185A		AU	Higgins Mus.
1757		$10 1929T1	C001254A		?	Bayard
1757		$10 1929T1	E001329A		F/VF	
1757		$10 1929T1	C001486A		F/VF	
1757		$10 1929T1	E001602A		VF	
1757		$10 1929T1	C001699A		XF	
1757		$10 1929T1	B001858A		VF	
1757		$20 1929T1	F000069A		VF	
1757		$20 1929T1	F000197A		VF	
1757		$20 1929T1	A000260A		VF	
1757		$20 1929T1	B000265A		?	
1757		$20 1929T1	A000354A		F	
1757		$20 1929T1	C000425A		VF	
1757		$20 1929T1	C000444A		F+	
1757		$20 1929T1	F000496A		VG	
1757		$20 1929T1	D000518A		VF	

THE IOWA STATE NATIONAL BANK OF SIOUX CITY   13 L
3968   WOODBURY

Chartered in 1889. Assumed #4630 by consolidation on December 1, 1892. Assumed #4235 by consolidation on April 29, 1895. Assumed Weare & Allison by consolidation in 1901. Placed in voluntary liquidation on November 6, 1909; capital of $200,000. Absorbed by #1757.

Officers: Pres. DT Gilman 1889-1900, George Weare 1901-08, John McHugh 1909; **VP** HA Jandt 1896-1907, John McHugh 1907, Henry G Weare 1909, FA McCornack 1909; **Cash.** RS Van Keuren 1889-91, HH Clark 1892-93, CM Swan 1894-95, FA McCornack 1896-99, John McHugh 1900-05, HA Gooch 1906-09; **AC** WS Gilman 1900-02, HA Gooch 1903-04, OD Pettit 1909

Second Charter, Brown Backs	Ser #	#Notes
5-5-5-5	1-14280	57,120
10-10-10-20	1-6222	24,888
Third Charter, Date Back, Blue Seal		
5-5-5-5	1-2845	11,380
10-10-10-20	1-632	2,528

Total amount of circulation issued = $685,200. Amount outstanding at close = $200,000. Amount outstanding in 1910 = $122,482.
95,916 Large   0 Small   95,916 Total

3968	-	$5 1882BB 470	9346 A	M32231	F	pen/pen
3968		$5 1882BB 470	11348 D	T215856T	F	Higgins Mus.
3968		$10 1882BB 483	225 B	W278814	F/VF	
3968		$10 1882BB 483	757 C	T169487T	F	Serial #?
3968	M	$10 1882BB 483	2865 A	H536071H	VG/F	pen/pen
3968	M	$10 1882BB 483	3842 B	R250805R	F/VF	Higgins Mus.
3968	M	$10 1882BB 483	5922 A	R769586R	G	Bayard, B or R serial number?
3968	M	$20 1882BB 497	3683 A	R250646R	F+	pen/pen
3968	M	$20 1882BB 497	4699 A	R255862R	F+	Higgins Mus.
3968	M	$5 1902DB 592	1 A	E508714	XF/AU	
3968	M	$5 1902DB 592	2552 C	E546665	G/VG	gone/gone
3968	M	$10 1902DB 618	263 D	A380837	F/VF	
3968	M	$10 1902DB 618	603 B	E747978	VF	light sigs

THE LIVE STOCK NATIONAL BANK OF SIOUX CITY
5022   WOODBURY   59 L 213 S

Chartered in 1895.
Officers: Pres. IC Elston 1896-1903, Geo H Rathman 1903-06, George S Parker 1907-09, AG Sam 1920-35; **VP** FL Eaton 1896-1925, JL Mitchell 1913, CD Haskell 1920-22, HB Scott 1924-32, CL Fredricksen 1930-35; **Cash.** Geo H Rathman 1896-1902, EC Currey 1903, Melvin E Bauer 1904-07, Walter P Dickey 1908-11, CD Van Dyke 1912-19, CL Fredricksen 1920-29, MA Wilson 1930-35; **AC** EC Currey 1900-02, JH Osborne 1903, WP Dickey 1907, CD Van Dyke 1909-11, AW Smith 1913-14, AE Rugg 1920-22, Wm Wagner, Jr. 1922, MA Wilson 1923-29, SG Eaton 1923-24, WG Nelson 1926-35, WC Schenk 1930-35

Second Charter, Brown Backs	Ser #	# Notes
5-5-5-5	1-7850	31,400
50-100	1-1140	2,280
Second Charter, Date Back		
5-5-5-5	1-6345	25,380
50-100	1-623	1,246
50-50-50-100	1-254	1,016
Third Charter, Plain Back, Blue Seal		
5-5-5-5	1-17350	69,400
10-10-10-10	1-14966	59,864
1929, Type I		
6-5's	1-8544	51,264
6-10's	1-4120	24,720
1929, Type II		
5's	1-12740	12,740
10's	1-6454	6,454

Total amount of circulation issued = $2,189,250. Amount of large outstanding in 1935 = $11,270. Amount of small outstanding in 1935 = $188,730.
190,586 Large   95,178 Small   285,764 Total

5022	-	$5 1882BB 474	1659 A	X677252	F	pen/pen vp Circus Poster layout; LR repaired
5022	M	$5 1882BB 474	6599 C	N690947N	XF	Circus Poster
5022	M	$5 1882BB 474	7349 D	T933402T	?	Circus Poster
5022		$50 1882BB 515	1 ?	?	?	
5022	M	$100 1882BB 527	1125 A	B585477	XF/AU	
5022	M	$100 1882BB 527	1127 A	B585479	AU	pen/pen
5022		$100 1882BB 527	1128 A	B585480	AU	
5022	M	$5 1882DB 534	3960 E	K250376	VG	
5022	M	$50 1882DB 560	208 B	A48506	F/VF	pen/pen
5022	M	$100 1882DB 568	53 B	A48351	XF+	pen/pen
5022	M	$100 1882DB 568	55 B	A48353	XF	pen/pen
5022	M	$100 1882DB 568	65 B	A48363	AU	
5022	M	$100 1882DB 568	81 B	A161219	F	
5022	M	$100 1882DB 568	87 B	A48385	XF/AU	
5022	M	$100 1882DB 568	143 B	A48441	CU	
5022	M	$100 1882DB 568	144 B	A48442	CU	
5022	M	$100 1882DB 568	145 B	A48443	AU	Higgins Mus.
5022	M	$100 1882DB 568	148 B	A48446	AU	
5022	M	$100 1882DB 568	152 B	A48450	AU	
5022	M	$100 1882DB 568	166 B	A48464	CU	
5022	M	$100 1882DB 568	170 B	A48468	CU	pen/pen
5022	M	$100 1882DB 568	481 B	A161219	F	
5022	M	$5 1902PB 606	2697 B	N178173D	F	
5022	M	$5 1902PB 606	2741 A	N178217D	VG/F	stamp/stamp
5022		$5 1902PB 606	5750 B	N131396E	F/VF	
5022	-	$5 1902PB 606	7980 B	U931141H	F/VF	stamp/stamp
5022	-	$5 1902PB 606	9077 D	V553288H	VF	gone/gone
5022	-	$5 1902PB 606	10262 C	Y207523H	F	
5022	-	$5 1902PB 606	11211 A [	11211 A	CU	uncut sheet
5022	-	$5 1902PB 606	11211 B [	11211 B	CU	
5022	-	$5 1902PB 606	11211 C [	11211 C	CU	see color
5022	-	$5 1902PB 606	11211 D [	11211 D	CU	illustration
5022	-	$5 1902PB 606	15696 A	15696 A	VG	
5022	-	$5 1902PB 606	15794 A	15794 A	F	
5022	-	$5 1902PB 606	15826 A	15826 A	VG	
5022	-	$5 1902PB 606	16343 C	16343 C	?	
5022		$10 1902PB 632	1243 B	N215076	VG	
5022		$10 1902PB 632	5759 D	Y106854	VG	
5022	-	$10 1902PB 632	6851 C	Y165096	VG/F	nice sigs
5022	-	$10 1902PB 632	7792 D	Y383887	F+	
5022	-	$10 1902PB 632	7891 B	Y383986	F/VF	pen/pen
5022	-	$10 1902PB 632	9237 B	9237 B	VG	
5022	-	$10 1902PB 632	9391 C	9391 C	VG	
5022	-	$10 1902PB 632	9612 B	9612 B	F	
5022	-	$10 1902PB 632	9936 C	9936 C	VF	
5022	-	$10 1902PB 632	10642 B	10642 B	VG	Rust
5022	-	$10 1902PB 632	11637 B	11637 B	VG/F	faded/faded
5022	-	$10 1902PB 632	12019 B	12019 B	VG	gone/gone
5022	-	$10 1902PB 632	12053 C	12053 C	CU	gone/gone
5022	-	$10 1902PB 632	12278 C	12278 C	VG/F	
5022	-	$10 1902PB 632	12435 C	12435 C	VG	
5022	-	$10 1902PB 632	12813 D	12813 D	VF	gone/gone
5022	-	$10 1902PB 632	13318 C	13318 C	F	gone/gone
5022	-	$10 1902PB 632	13378 C	13378 C	?	
5022	-	$10 1902PB 632	13627 A	13627 A	VG/F	faded/gone
5022	-	$10 1902PB 632	13834 A	13834 A	VF+	

5022	-	$10	1902PB	632	14159 A	14159 A	VG		5022		$10	1929T2	A003020		VF
5022	-	$10	1902PB	632	14572 D	14572 D	CU	Higgins Mus.	5022		$10	1929T2	A003039		VG
5022	-	$10	1902PB	632	15794 A	15794 A	F		5022		$10	1929T2	A003437		?
5022		$5	1929T1		B000701A		F		5022		$10	1929T2	A003885		F/VF
5022		$5	1929T1		D002203A		F		5022		$10	1929T2	A003893		F/VF
5022		$5	1929T1		C002292A		XF		5022		$10	1929T2	A003944		CU
5022		$5	1929T1		F002305A		VG		5022		$10	1929T2	A003949		F
5022		$5	1929T1		C004278A		VG		5022		$10	1929T2	A004897		VG
5022		$5	1929T1		A005154A		F/VF		5022		$10	1929T2	A005229		XF
5022		$5	1929T1		C005352A		F		5022		$10	1929T2	A006319	[	CU
5022		$5	1929T1		D006210A		VG		5022		$10	1929T2	A006320	[	CU
5022		$5	1929T1		A007054A		F		5022		$10	1929T2	A006321	[	CU
5022		$5	1929T1		F007266A		F/VF		5022		$10	1929T2	A006322	[	CU
5022		$5	1929T1		B007651A		VG		5022		$10	1929T2	A006323	[	CU
5022		$5	1929T1		E007799A		XF		5022		$10	1929T2	A006324	[	CU
5022		$5	1929T1		E007866A		F		5022		$10	1929T2	A006325	[	CU
5022		$5	1929T1		B008540A		VF/XF		5022		$10	1929T2	A006326	[	CU
5022		$5	1929T1		D008544A		CU	Last sheet of $5s	5022		$10	1929T2	A006327	[	CU
5022		$10	1929T1		E000005A		AU		5022		$10	1929T2	A006328	[	CU
5022		$10	1929T1		B000137A		VG/F		5022		$10	1929T2	A006329	[	CU
5022		$10	1929T1		B000326A		VG		5022		$10	1929T2	A006330	[	CU
5022		$10	1929T1		C000468A		G		5022		$10	1929T2	A006331	[	CU
5022		$10	1929T1		A000840A		VG/F		5022		$10	1929T2	A006332	[	CU
5022		$10	1929T1		A000881A		VG		5022		$10	1929T2	A006333	[	CU
5022		$10	1929T1		B000947A		F/VF		5022		$10	1929T2	A006334	[	CU
5022		$10	1929T1		B000957A		CU		5022		$10	1929T2	A006335	[	CU
5022		$10	1929T1		F001221A		VG/F		5022		$10	1929T2	A006336	[	CU
5022		$10	1929T1		B001673A		VG		5022		$10	1929T2	A006337	[	AU
5022		$10	1929T1		B001748A		G		5022		$10	1929T2	A006338	[	AU
5022		$10	1929T1		E001903A		F/VF		5022		$10	1929T2	A006339	[	AU
5022		$10	1929T1		E002059A		VF/XF	Stain right side	5022		$10	1929T2	A006340	[	AU
5022		$10	1929T1		B002358A		?		5022		$10	1929T2	A006341	[	AU
5022		$10	1929T1		A002402A		F		5022		$10	1929T2	A006342	[	AU
5022		$10	1929T1		A002510A		VG		5022		$10	1929T2	A006343	[	AU
5022		$10	1929T1		E003036A		VF		5022		$10	1929T2	A006344	[	AU
5022		$10	1929T1		C003099A		VG		5022		$10	1929T2	A006345	[	AU
5022		$10	1929T1		D003350A		G/VG		5022		$10	1929T2	A006346	[	AU
5022		$10	1929T1		C003438A		VF		5022		$10	1929T2	A006347	[	AU
5022		$10	1929T1		D003438A		F		5022		$10	1929T2	A006348	[	AU
5022		$10	1929T1		E003658A		F		5022		$10	1929T2	A006349	[	AU
5022		$10	1929T1		C003661A		AU		5022		$10	1929T2	A006350	[	AU
5022		$10	1929T1		B003798A		HG		5022		$10	1929T2	A006351	[	AU
5022		$10	1929T1		D003806A		VF/XF		5022		$10	1929T2	A006352	[	AU
5022		$10	1929T1		A003874A		VG		5022		$10	1929T2	A006353	[	AU
5022		$10	1929T1		E003915A		VF		5022		$10	1929T2	A006354	[	AU
5022		$10	1929T1		C004063A		AU		5022		$10	1929T2	A006355	[	AU
5022		$5	1929T2		A000007		F	Small Tear	5022		$10	1929T2	A006356	[	AU
5022		$5	1929T2		A000011		CU	Higgins Mus.	5022		$10	1929T2	A006357	[	AU
5022		$5	1929T2		A002047		F		5022		$10	1929T2	A006358	[	AU
5022		$5	1929T2		A002262		F		5022		$10	1929T2	A006359	[	AU
5022		$5	1929T2		A002554		VG		5022		$10	1929T2	A006360	[	AU
5022		$5	1929T2		A006691		XF/AU		5022		$10	1929T2	A006361	[	AU
5022		$5	1929T2		A007031		F		5022		$10	1929T2	A006362	[	AU
5022		$5	1929T2		A008967		?		5022		$10	1929T2	A006363	[	AU
5022		$5	1929T2		A012305		VG		5022		$10	1929T2	A006364	[	AU
5022		$5	1929T2		A012385		F/VF		5022		$10	1929T2	A006365	[	AU
5022		$5	1929T2		A012387		VF/XF		5022		$10	1929T2	A006366	[	AU
5022		$5	1929T2		A012388		VF/XF		5022		$10	1929T2	A006367	[	AU
5022		$5	1929T2		A012389		VF/XF		5022		$10	1929T2	A006368	[	AU
5022		$5	1929T2		A012390		VF/XF		5022		$10	1929T2	A006369	[	AU
5022		$5	1929T2		A012406		F/VF		5022		$10	1929T2	A006370	[	AU
5022		$5	1929T2		A012413		CU		5022		$10	1929T2	A006371	[	AU
5022		$5	1929T2		A012440		?		5022		$10	1929T2	A006372	[	AU
5022		$5	1929T2		A012443		G		5022		$10	1929T2	A006373	[	AU
5022		$5	1929T2		A012482		AU		5022		$10	1929T2	A006374	[	AU
5022		$5	1929T2		A012590		AU		5022		$10	1929T2	A006375	[	AU
5022		$5	1929T2		A012594		XF		5022		$10	1929T2	A006376	[	AU
5022		$5	1929T2		A012601		VF		5022		$10	1929T2	A006377	[	AU
5022		$5	1929T2		A012637		XF		5022		$10	1929T2	A006378	[	AU
5022		$5	1929T2		A012653		VF		5022		$10	1929T2	A006379	[	AU
5022		$5	1929T2		A012715		F/VF		5022		$10	1929T2	A006380	[	AU
5022		$5	1929T2		A012720		G+		5022		$10	1929T2	A006381	[	AU
5022		$10	1929T2		A000001		XF		5022		$10	1929T2	A006382	[	AU
5022		$10	1929T2		A000002		XF		5022		$10	1929T2	A006383	[	AU
5022		$10	1929T2		A000003		XF		5022		$10	1929T2	A006384	[	AU
5022		$10	1929T2		A000004		XF		5022		$10	1929T2	A006385	[	CU
5022		$10	1929T2		A000005		XF		5022		$10	1929T2	A006386	[	CU
5022		$10	1929T2		A000006		F		5022		$10	1929T2	A006387	[	CU
5022		$10	1929T2		A000484		VF/XF		5022		$10	1929T2	A006388	[	CU
5022		$10	1929T2		A000499		?		5022		$10	1929T2	A006389	[	CU
5022		$10	1929T2		A002047		F/VF		5022		$10	1929T2	A006390	[	CU

5022	$10 1929T2	A006391	[	AU	
5022	$10 1929T2	A006392	[	AU	
5022	$10 1929T2	A006393	[	AU	
5022	$10 1929T2	A006394	[	AU	
5022	$10 1929T2	A006395	[	AU	
5022	$10 1929T2	A006396	[	AU	
5022	$10 1929T2	A006397	[	AU	
5022	$10 1929T2	A006398	[	AU	
5022	$10 1929T2	A006399	[	AU	
5022	$10 1929T2	A006400	[	AU	
5022	$10 1929T2	A006401	[	AU	
5022	$10 1929T2	A006402	[	AU	
5022	$10 1929T2	A006403	[	AU	
5022	$10 1929T2	A006404	[	AU	
5022	$10 1929T2	A006405	[	AU	
5022	$10 1929T2	A006406	[	AU	
5022	$10 1929T2	A006407	[	AU	
5022	$10 1929T2	A006408	[	AU	
5022	$10 1929T2	A006409	[	AU	
5022	$10 1929T2	A006410	[	AU	
5022	$10 1929T2	A006411	[	AU	
5022	$10 1929T2	A006412	[	AU	
5022	$10 1929T2	A006413	[	AU	
5022	$10 1929T2	A006414	[	AU	
5022	$10 1929T2	A006415	[	AU	
5022	$10 1929T2	A006416	[	AU	
5022	$10 1929T2	A006417	[	AU	
5022	$10 1929T2	A006418	[	AU	
5022	$10 1929T2	A006419	[	AU	
5022	$10 1929T2	A006420	[	AU	
5022	$10 1929T2	A006421	[	AU	
5022	$10 1929T2	A006422	[	AU	
5022	$10 1929T2	A006423	[	AU	
5022	$10 1929T2	A006424	[	AU	
5022	$10 1929T2	A006425	[	AU	
5022	$10 1929T2	A006426	[	AU	
5022	$10 1929T2	A006427	[	AU	
5022	$10 1929T2	A006428	[	AU	
5022	$10 1929T2	A006429	[	AU	
5022	$10 1929T2	A006430	[	AU	
5022	$10 1929T2	A006431	[	AU	
5022	$10 1929T2	A006432	[	AU	
5022	$10 1929T2	A006433	[	AU	
5022	$10 1929T2	A006434	[	AU	
5022	$10 1929T2	A006435	[	AU	
5022	$10 1929T2	A006436	[	AU	
5022	$10 1929T2	A006437	[	AU	
5022	$10 1929T2	A006438	[	AU	
5022	$10 1929T2	A006439	[	AU	
5022	$10 1929T2	A006440	[	AU	
5022	$10 1929T2	A006441	[	AU	
5022	$10 1929T2	A006442	[	AU	
5022	$10 1929T2	A006443	[	AU	
5022	$10 1929T2	A006444	[	AU	

THE MERCHANTS NATIONAL BANK OF SIOUX CITY
4209   **WOODBURY**   **2 L**
Chartered in 1890. Succeeded The Merchants Bank. Placed in voluntary liquidation on February 15, 1911; capital of $100,000. Absorbed by #1757.
Officers: Pres. Eugene W Rice 1890-1906; **VP** EB Spaulding 1896-1904; **Cash.** George P Day 1890-1906; **AC** GN Swan 1896-1904

Second Charter, Brown Backs	Ser #	# Notes
10-10-10-20	1-2780	11,120
Second Charter, Date Back		
10-10-10-20	1-173	692
Third Charter, Date Back, Blue Seal		
10-10-10-20	1-216	864

Total amount of circulation issued = $158,450. Amount outstanding at close = $23,900. Amount outstanding in October 1911 = $15,850.
12,676 Large   0 Small   12,676 Total

| 4209 | - | $10 1882BB | 484 | 1 A | E132939 | VF | pen/pen Restored |
| 4209 | M | $10 1902DB | ? | 1 A | T695398 | XF | Restored, Higgins Museum |

THE NATIONAL BANK OF COMMERCE OF SIOUX CITY
10139 (FIRST TITLE)   **WOODBURY**   **4 L**
Chartered in February 1912. Title changed to The Toy National Bank of Sioux City on July 1, 1920.
Officers: Pres. GR Whitmer 1912, TF Harrington 1913, James F Toy 1914-20; **VP** FW Kammann 1913, FM Pelletier 1914, CB Toy 1914-20, JD Untendorfer 1920; **Cash.** JB Alexander 1912-14, FW Kammann 1915-19, RR Brubacher 1920; **AC** CB Toy 1913, N Crowell 1913-14, CC Fowler 1920, JW Van Dyke 1920, EE Erickson 1920

Third Charter, Date Back, Blue Seal	Ser #	# Notes
10-10-10-20	1-6000	24,000
Third Charter, Plain Back, Blue Seal		
10-10-10-20	6001-10000	16,000

40,000 Large   0 Small   40,000 Total

10139M	$10 1902DB	620	3750 C	U375986A	VF	Ink
10139M	$20 1902DB	646	5210 A	M608376B	VG/F	Higgins Mus.
10139M	$20 1902DB	646	5526 A	M608692B	XF	5520 A ?
10139	$10 1902PB	628	7263 C	X638334B	VF	

THE NATIONAL BANK OF SIOUX CITY   **0 L**
4431   **WOODBURY**
Chartered on October 7, 1890. Placed in voluntary liquidation on December 29, 1893; capital of $900,000. Consolidated with #3124.
Officers: Pres. OJ Taylor 1891, HL Warner 1892-93; **Cash.** CQ Chandler 1891-93

Second Charter, Brown Backs	Ser #	# Notes
50-100	1-554	1,108

Total amount of circulation issued = $83,100. Amount outstanding at close = $43,950. Amount outstanding in 1910 = $900.
1,108 Large   0 Small   1,108 Total

THE NORTHWESTERN NATIONAL BANK OF SIOUX CITY
4510 (FIRST TITLE)   **WOODBURY**   **8 L**
Organized on August 19, 1890 with a capital of $100,000. Title changed to Sioux National Bank in Sioux City on January 17, 1920.
Officers: Pres. FT Evans 1891, JF Toy 1892, Abel Anderson 1893-1906, John Scott, Jr. 1907, John A Magoun, Jr. 1908-20; **VP** PE Hoflund 1896, Chas E Hoflund 1900-07, JS Nelson 1909-11, BH Kingsbury 1913-20, IM Lyon 1920; **Cash.** EM Donaldson 1891, HA Knepper 1892-94, John Scott, Jr. 1896-1902, JA Magoun, Jr. 1903-07, CE Hoflund 1908, IM Lyon 1909-19, CM Magoun 1920; **AC** IM Lyon 1907, Kirk Kingsbury 1920

Second Charter, Brown Backs	Ser #	# Notes
5-5-5-5	1-5000	20,000
10-10-10-20	1-5040	20,160
Second Charter, Date Back		
5-5-5-5	1-1355	5,420
10-10-10-20	1-499	1,996
Third Charter, Date Back, Blue Seal		
5-5-5-5	1-6000	24,000
10-10-10-20	1-4100	16,400
Third Charter, Plain Back, Blue Seal		
5-5-5-5	6001-9550	14,200
10-10-10-20	4101-6020	7,680

109,856 Large   0 Small   109,856 Total

4510		$5 1882BB	471	4725 A	V110733V	F/VF	Davenport B&T
4510		$10 1882BB	484	2399 A	H552295H	F/VF	Higgins Mus.
4510		$10 1882BB	484	3761 C	T169487T	F	
4510	M	$10 1902DB	619	2458 C	U338844A	VG	
4510	M	$10 1902DB	619	2566 A	U338952A	VG/F	Higgins Mus.
4510	M	$10 1902DB	619	3229 A	A961355B	F	stamp/stamp
4510	M	$20 1902DB	645	2951 A	U339337A	F	
4510	M	$20 1902PB	653	?831 A	Y659303D	VG	

SIOUX NATIONAL BANK IN SIOUX CITY   **18 L   11 S**
4510 (SECOND TITLE)   **WOODBURY**
Succeeded The Northwestern National Bank of Sioux City on January 17, 1920. Absorbed #10518 on January 10, 1922. Placed in receivership on December 8, 1930; capital of $400,000. Reason for failure: incompetent management.
Officers: Pres. John A Magoun, Jr. 1920-30; **VP** BH Kingsbury 1920-30, IM Lyon 1920-28, CD Van Dyke 1922-27, TF Harrington 1922-28; **Cash.** CM Magoun 1920-30; **AC** Kirk Kingsbury 1920-29, RJ Doyle 1922-29, MI Junk 1922-30, WT Hatch 1929-30

Third Charter, Plain Back, Blue Seal	Ser #	# Notes
5-5-5-5	1-9335	37,340
10-10-10-20	1-7074	28,296
1929, Type I		
6-5's	1-1411	8,466
6-10's	1-687	4,122
6-20's	1-174	1,044

Total amount of circulation issued = $1,541,280. Amount of large outstanding at close = $21,020. Amount of small outstanding at close = $78,980.
65,636 Large   13,362 Small   79,268 Total

4510	-	$5 1902PB	601	5398 B	T930634H	VG/F	stamp/stamp
4510	-	$5 1902PB	601	5757 B	Y877118H	VF	
4510	-	$5 1902PB	601	5758 A	Y877119H	VG	
4510	M	$10 1902PB	627	775 A	Y659247D	F	
4510	M	$10 1902PB	627	1999 C	N744891E	VG	

Charter		Denom	Type	Plate	Bank #	Treasury #	Grade	Notes
4510	M	$10	1902PB	627	2804 B	B510466H	HG	stamp/stamp
4510	-	$10	1902PB	627	3604 B	V164756H	VG	stamp/stamp
4510	-	$10	1902PB	627	3860 A	V165012H	VF	
4510	-	$10	1902PB	627	4062 A	A17724K	VF+	Higgins Mus.
4510	-	$10	1902PB	627	4549 C	4549 C	F	stamp/stamp
4510	-	$10	1902PB	627	5497 B	5497 B	F	
4510	-	$10	1902PB	627	6027 B	6027 B	VG	
4510	-	$10	1902PB	627	6290 C	6290 C	VG	
4510	-	$10	1902PB	627	6580 A	6580 A	F/VF	stamp/stamp
4510	-	$10	1902PB	627	6714 ?	6714 ?	XF	
4510	M	$20	1902PB	653	831 A	Y659303D	F	stamp/stamp
4510	M	$20	1902PB	653	2680 A	B510342H	F	
4510	M	$20	1902PB	653	? A	Z533914H	?	
4510		$5	1929T1		C000111A		F/VF	
4510		$5	1929T1		E000113A		VG/F	
4510		$5	1929T1		A000604A		AU	
4510		$10	1929T1		B000017A		VG	
4510		$10	1929T1		D000047A		F	Higgins Mus.
4510		$10	1929T1		A000271A		G	
4510		$10	1929T1		A000455A		F	
4510		$10	1929T1		F000498A		VG	
4510		$10	1929T1		A000623A		VG	
4510		$10	1929T1		D000639A		HG	
4510		$20	1929T1		B000029A		CU	

THE SECURITY NATIONAL BANK OF SIOUX CITY   64 L   57 S
3124   WOODBURY

Organized on February 1, 1884 with a capital of $100,000. Assumed #4431 by consolidation on December 29, 1893. Placed in conservatorship on March 13, 1933. Licensed on May 31, 1933.

Officers: Pres. Frank H Peavey 1884, James D Spaulding 1885-90, EP Manley 1891-1923, AB Darling 1924-28, LR Manley 1929-32, HH Everist 1933-34, Edward C Palmer 1935; **VP** CL Wright 1896-1910, TA Black 1907-14, AB Darling 192023, VC Bonesteel 1920-27, Geo C Call 1924, CC Jacobsen 1928—32, CR Gossett 1931-35, Delko Bloem 1932-35, Paul Bekins 1933-35; **Cash.** Wilbur P Manley 1884-90, FM Case 1891-1900, TA Black 1901-04, CN Lukes 1904-09, CW Britton 1910-13, Clyde Cummings 1913, CW Britton 1914-18, LR Manley 1918-28, RE Brown 1929-32, CR Gossett 1933-35; **AC** HH Buckwalter 1885, FC Swan 1896-1900, CW Britton 1904-09, DM Brownlee 1910-14, RE Brown 1920-28, HB Bolks 1920, AC Eckert 1929-35, Delco Bloem 1929-31, DB Severson 1929-35, EO Smeby 1929-34

	Ser #	# Notes
Second Charter, Brown Backs		
5-5-5-5	1-11025	44,100
10-10-10-20	1-7864	31,456
Third Charter, Red Seal		
5-5-5-5	1-5500	22,000
10-10-10-20	1-6600	26,400
Third Charter, Date Back, Blue Seal		
5-5-5-5	1-17500	70,000
10-10-10-20	1-14100	56,400
Third Charter, Plain Back, Blue Seal		
5-5-5-5	17501-46964	117,856
10-10-10-20	14101-33043	73,972
1929, Type I		
6-5's	1-9048	54,288
6-10's	1-3142	18,852
6-20's	1-890	5,340
1929, Type II		
5's	1-12054	12,054
10's	1-5013	5,013
20's	1-1574	1,574

Total amount of circulation issued = $4,353,770. Amount of large outstanding in 1935 = $19,835. Amount of small outstanding in 1935 = $228,515.

443,984 Large   97,121 Small   541,105 Total

Charter		Denom	Type	Plate	Bank #	Treasury #	Grade	Notes
3124	-	$5	1882BB	467	1275 A	A674569	CU	Higgins Mus.
3124	-	$5	1882BB	467	7294 D	U845907	VG	pen/pen
3124	-	$10	1882BB	480	75 A	T513246	XF	Higgins Mus.
3124	-	$10	1882BB	480	3451 B	T527024	AG	
3124	-	$10	1882BB	480	3620 A	T527193	VF	gone/gone
3124	-	$10	1882BB	480	3992 B	T527565	VG	
3124		$20	1882BB	494	4302 A	Y973026	VF	Higgins Mus.
3124		$20	1882BB	494	5583 A	?	F/VF	
3124	M	$5	1902RS	587	73 B	H112384	VG	stamp Staining
3124	M	$5	1902RS	587	1482 A	H133293	F	
3124	M	$10	1902RS	613	1605 A	B553792	F	pen/pen
3124	M	$20	1902RS	639	828 A	B547745	F	pen/pen
3124	M	$5	1902DB	590	2274 H	B991627	VG	
3124	M	$5	1902DB	590	2782 H	M396159	VG	
3124	M	$5	1902DB	590	3049 H	M396426	VG/F	Torn in half; taped
3124	M	$5	1902DB	590	3640 H	M403567	VF	stamp/stamp
3124	M	$10	1902DB	616	1605 A	B553792	F	
3124	M	$10	1902DB	616	2153 D	N18132	F	
3124	M	$10	1902DB	616	3175 D	?	XF	
3124	M	$10	1902DB	616	?	T527024	?	
3124	M	$10	1902DB	616	12486 D	?	F	
3124	M	$10	1902DB	616	?	M930526B	VG	
3124	M	$10	1902DB	616	14095 F	M931121B	VG	stamp/stamp
3124	M	$20	1902DB	642	1394 B	B697326	VG/F	
3124	M	$20	1902DB	642	8783 B	R806913A	F	stamp Rust
3124	M	$5	1902PB	598	11530 E	V378672A	VG	
3124	M	$5	1902PB	598	22049 E	E662815D	F/VF	Higgins Mus.
3124	M	$5	1902PB	598	23565 H	N816451D	VG	
3124	M	$5	1902PB	598	28360 G	A762881E	F	
3124	M	$5	1902PB	598	30465 G	H842636E	?	stamp/stamp
3124	M	$5	1902PB	598	30914 F	H843085E	VG	stamp/stamp
3124	M	$5	1902PB	598	31787 G	T736043E	F	pen/pen
3124		$5	1902PB	598	?	D527277H	?	
3124		$5	1902PB	598	35962 F	N798998H	?	
3124	-	$5	1902PB	598	36724 H	R68210H	XF/AU	
3124	-	$5	1902PB	598	38856 H	Z705967H	VF	
3124	-	$5	1902PB	598	38898 F	Z706009H	VF	
3124	-	$5	1902PB	598	41370 F	41370 F	F	
3124	-	$5	1902PB	598	41849 H	41849 H	VF/XF	
3124	-	$5	1902PB	598	43025 F	43025 F	F	stamp/stamp
3124	-	$5	1902PB	598	44044H	44044H	F	stamp/stamp
3124	-	$5	1902PB	598	44658 G	44658 G	F	
3124	-	$5	1902PB	598	46451 E	46451 E	F	stamp/stamp
3124	M	$10	1902PB	624	23324 ?	H263976H	F	
3124		$10	1902PB	624	23358 F	H264010H	VG	
3124		$10	1902PB	624	23464 E	H264116H	F	
3124		$10	1902PB	624	26098 F	X382630H	VF	
3124	-	$10	1902PB	624	26758 E	A796380K	VG	
3124	-	$10	1902PB	624	28106 E	28106 E	F+	stamp/stamp
3124	-	$10	1902PB	624	28464 F	28464 F	CU	
3124	-	$10	1902PB	624	30368 E	30368 E	VF	
3124	-	$10	1902PB	624	31353 E	31353 E	VG	stamp/stamp
3124	-	$10	1902PB	624	31754 D	31754 D	XF	
3124	-	$10	1902PB	624	31854 D	31854 D	XF/AU	
3124	-	$10	1902PB	624	31890 D	31890 D	HG	
3124	-	$10	1902PB	624	32228 D	32228 D	VG	
3124	-	$10	1902PB	624	32984 D	32984 D	F/VF	
3124	-	$20	1902PB	650	27199 B	27199 B	F	stamp/stamp
3124	-	$20	1902PB	650	27219 B	27219 B	VG	
3124	-	$20	1902PB	650	27442 B	27442 B	F/VF	stamp/stamp
3124	-	$20	1902PB	650	28174 B	28174 B	VG/F	stamp/stamp
3124	-	$20	1902PB	650	29808 B	29808 B	F	nice sigs Rust
3124	-	$20	1902PB	650	30791 B	30791 B	?	nice sigs
3124	-	$20	1902PB	650	31421 B	31421 B	VG	
3124		$5	1929T1		C000428A		VG/F	
3124		$5	1929T1		A000549A		VG	
3124		$5	1929T1		A001315A		VG	
3124		$5	1929T1		F003877A		F	
3124		$5	1929T1		B004547A		F/VF	
3124		$5	1929T1		A005863A		F	
3124		$5	1929T1		F005872A		?	
3124		$5	1929T1		F006817A		?	
3124		$5	1929T1		E008596A		VG	
3124		$5	1929T1		C008787A		F/VF	
3124		$10	1929T1		C000321A		F	
3124		$10	1929T1		B000773A		VG	
3124		$10	1929T1		F000898A		F	
3124		$10	1929T1		C001027A		VF	
3124		$10	1929T1		A001036A		VG	
3124		$10	1929T1		F001077A		F	
3124		$10	1929T1		E001337A		F	
3124		$10	1929T1		C001515A		F	
3124		$10	1929T1		D001743A		F	
3124		$10	1929T1		E001974A		VF	
3124		$10	1929T1		A002001A		VF/XF	
3124		$10	1929T1		A002142A		F	
3124		$10	1929T1		B002233A		F	
3124		$10	1929T1		E002299A		F	
3124		$10	1929T1		E002482A		VF	
3124		$10	1929T1		A002598A		?	Higgins Mus.
3124		$10	1929T1		E002623A		VF	
3124		$10	1929T1		E002709A		VG	
3124		$10	1929T1		D003092A			
3124		$10	1929T1		C003118A		F	Pinholes
3124		$20	1929T1		D000001A			
3124		$20	1929T1		A000131A		F	
3124		$20	1929T1		D000176A		F	Minor spotting

Charter	Denom	Series	Serial	Grade	Notes
3124	$20	1929T1	A000202A	F/VF	
3124	$20	1929T1	A000306A	F/VF	
3124	$20	1929T1	D000318A	VF	Ink on face
3124	$20	1929T1	C000321A	VG/F	
3124	$20	1929T1	C000419A	VG	
3124	$20	1929T1	F000458A	VG	
3124	$20	1929T1	D000587A	VF	
3124	$20	1929T1	A000613A	VF	
3124	$20	1929T1	E000704A	VG	
3124	$20	1929T1	C000724A	CU	Higgins Mus.
3124	$20	1929T1	D000773A	AU	
3124	$5	1929T2	A004089	VG	
3124	$5	1929T2	A005864	VG/F	
3124	$5	1929T2	A010848	F	
3124	$5	1929T2	A011143	F	
3124	$10	1929T2	A002212	VG+	
3124	$10	1929T2	A002981	F	
3124	$10	1929T2	A003868	VF+	
3124	$10	1929T2	A004495	XF	
3124	$20	1929T2	A000461	VF+	Higgins Mus.
3124	$20	1929T2	A000741	VG	
3124	$20	1929T2	A000744	F	
3124	$20	1929T2	A001135	F	
3124	$20	1929T2	A001413	CU	

THE SIOUX CITY NATIONAL BANK OF SIOUX CITY
2535   WOODBURY   2 L

Organized on June 9, 1881; a capital of $100,000. Succeeded The Sioux City Savings Bank. Closed on Aug. 28, 1896. Placed in receivership on Sept. 9, 1896; capital of $300,000. Reason for failure: incompetent management.

Officers: Pres. William L Joy 1881-95; **VP** DT Hedges 1885; **Cash.** Arthur S Garretson 1881-90, TA Block 1891-95

First Charter, Series of 1875		Ser #	# Notes
10-10-10-20		1-4315	17,260

Total amount of circulation issued = $215,750. Amount outstanding at close = $44,100. Amount outstanding in 1915 = $1,120.

17,260 Large   0 Small   17,260 Total

| 2535 | - | $10 | 1875 | 420 | 3094 A | K317133 | VF | Grinnell # 3862 |
| 2535 | - | $20 | 1875 | 435 | 3651 A | K438636 | VF | |

THE TOY NATIONAL BANK OF SIOUX CITY   41 L   88 S
10139 (2ND TITLE)   WOODBURY

Named after President James F. Toy, this bank was one of four private name national banks in Iowa. Mr Toy was an officer of several Iowa banks. See the index of bank officers.

Succeeded The National Bank of Commerce of Sioux City on July 1, 1920.

Officers: Pres. James F Toy 1920-28, 1934, Carleton B Toy 1929-32, Palmer C Toy 1933, ME Toy 1935; **VP** CB Toy 1920-28, JD Untendorfer 1920-24, FM Pelletier 1923-24, Moore 1924-25, F Shenkberg 1924-30, JW Van Dyke 1924-29, 1931-35, AB Darling 1929-33, RR Brubacher 1929-35, EA Hoffman 1930-33, James T Van Dyke 1934-35; **Cash.** RR Brubacher 1920-30, EE Erickson 1931-35; **AC** CC Fowler 1920, JW Van Dyke 1920-23, EE Erickson 1920-30, CA Johnson 1923-35, HT Crouse 1923-28, Ira A Moore 1923, CC Childs 1928, Eli S Robinson 1931-35, Wm Van Dyke 1935

Third Charter, Plain Back, Blue Seal	Ser #	# Notes
10-10-10-20	1-18200	72,800
1929, Type I		
6-5's	1-6728	40,368
6-10's	1-2894	17,364
6-20's	1-734	4,404
1929, Type II		
5's	1-7562	7,562
10's	1-4235	4,235
20's	1-1151	1,151

Total amount of circulation issued = $1,976,740. Amount of large outstanding in 1935 = $12,270. Amount of small outstanding in 1935 = $17,730.

72,800 Large   75,084 Small   147,884 Total

Charter		Denom	Series		Serial		Grade	Notes
10139M		$10	1902PB	628	820 B	Z588992D	F	
10139	-	$10	1902PB	628	8008 C	N999610H	VF	faded/faded
10139	-	$10	1902PB	628	9866 C	V268388H	F	stamp/stamp
10139	-	$10	1902PB	628	10212 B	A490844K	F/VF	
10139	-	$10	1902PB	628	10281 B	A490913K	VF+	
10139	-	$10	1902PB	628	10605 ?	A491237K	?	
10139	-	$10	1902PB	628	10851 C	A491483K	VF	
10139	-	$10	1902PB	628	11226 ?	A491858K	?	
10139	-	$10	1902PB	628	12702 C	12702 C	VG	
10139	-	$10	1902PB	628	12792 C	12792 C	VG/F	gone/gone
10139	-	$10	1902PB	628	13036 C	13036 C	F	gone/gone
10139	-	$10	1902PB	628	14150 C	14150 C	VF	faded/faded
10139	-	$10	1902PB	628	14600 A	14600 A	CU	stamp/stamp
10139	-	$10	1902PB	628	14601 C	14601 C	CU	stamp/stamp
10139	-	$10	1902PB	628	14610 A	14610 A	?	
10139	-	$10	1902PB	628	14848 A	14848 A	XF	
10139	-	$10	1902PB	628	15144 B	15144 B	F	
10139	-	$10	1902PB	628	15522 A	15522 A	F	
10139	-	$10	1902PB	628	15841 A	15841 A	F/VF	stamp/stamp
10139	-	$10	1902PB	628	15883 A	15883 A	F	faded/faded
10139	-	$10	1902PB	628	16804 B	16804 B	F	
10139	-	$10	1902PB	628	17600 A	17600 A	AU	stamp/stamp
10139M		$20	1902PB	654	2712 A	K647764E	F	faded/faded
10139M		$20	1902PB	654	6893 A	N999673E	?	
10139M		$20	1902PB	654	6906 A	B729388H	VF	Oat Bin Hoard
10139M		$20	1902PB	654	6999 A	B729481H	AU	stamp/stamp
10139	-	$20	1902PB	654	8071 A	N999673H	VG	gone/gone
10139	-	$20	1902PB	654	9938 A	V268460H	VG	stamp/stamp
10139	-	$20	1902PB	654	11578 A	11578 A	F	stamp/stamp
10139	-	$20	1902PB	654	13009 A	13009 A	F	
10139	-	$20	1902PB	654	13449 A	13449 A	CU	
10139	-	$20	1902PB	654	13855 A	13855 A	CU	light stamps
10139	-	$20	1902PB	654	14368 A	14368 A	VG/F	gone/gone
10139	-	$20	1902PB	654	15173 A	15173 A	CU	stamp/stamp
10139	-	$20	1902PB	654	15174 A	15174 A	CU	stamp/stamp
10139	-	$20	1902PB	654	15176 A	15176 A	XF	
10139	-	$20	1902PB	654	15177 A	15177 A	CU	Higgins Mus.
10139	-	$20	1902PB	654	15178 A	15178 A	CU	
10139	-	$20	1902PB	654	15180 A	15180 A	XF/AU	
10139	-	$20	1902PB	654	15181 A	15181 A	CU	light stamps
10139	-	$20	1902PB	654	15993 A	15993 A	XF	
10139		$5	1929T1		E000070A		CU	
10139		$5	1929T1		B000504A		VG/F	
10139		$5	1929T1		A001430A		F/VF	
10139		$5	1929T1		C001649A		VG	
10139		$5	1929T1		B002948A		G	
10139		$5	1929T1		C003886A		F	
10139		$5	1929T1		D004050A		CU	
10139		$5	1929T1		A004513A		F/VF	
10139		$5	1929T1		D004538A		VF	
10139		$5	1929T1		A004573A		F	
10139		$5	1929T1		E004720A		AU	
10139		$5	1929T1		C005352A		F	
10139		$5	1929T1		D005852A		VG	
10139		$5	1929T1		A006035A		F/VF	
10139		$5	1929T1		F006215A		VG/F	
10139		$5	1929T1		B006322A		F/VF	
10139		$10	1929T1		B000018A		VG	
10139		$10	1929T1		C000103A		XF	
10139		$10	1929T1		C000115A		VG	
10139		$10	1929T1		F000298A		XF	
10139		$10	1929T1		E000316A		?	
10139		$10	1929T1		C000659A		XF	
10139		$10	1929T1		D000757A		VG	
10139		?	1929T1		E001032A		F+	
10139		$10	1929T1		F001484A		F	
10139		$10	1929T1		B001495A		F	
10139		$10	1929T1		F001521A		F	
10139		$10	1929T1		D001845A		VF/XF	
10139		$10	1929T1		C001907A		F	
10139		$10	1929T1		B002071A		VG	
10139		$10	1929T1		B002091A		VF/XF	
10139		$10	1929T1		D002121A		VG	
10139		$10	1929T1		D002142A		VG	
10139		$10	1929T1		E002482A		VF	
10139		$10	1929T1		C002499A		CU	
10139		$10	1929T1		C002500A		XF	
10139		$10	1929T1		C002502A		G	Stains
10139		$10	1929T1		F002503A		XF	
10139		$10	1929T1		F002505A		?	
10139		$10	1929T1		C002509A		XF/AU	
10139		$10	1929T1		F002509A		CU	Higgins Mus.
10139		$10	1929T1		C002512A		CU	
10139		$10	1929T1		C002513A		VG	
10139		$10	1929T1		C002521A		VF	
10139		$10	1929T1		C002523A		AU	
10139		$10	1929T1		D002658A		XF	
10139		$10	1929T1		D002660A		F	
10139		$10	1929T1		A002723A		VG	
10139		$10	1929T1		B002737A		F	
10139		$10	1929T1		C002816A		VG	
10139		$20	1929T1		B000076A		F	
10139		$20	1929T1		E000090A		F/VF	
10139		$20	1929T1		B000135A		VF	
10139		$20	1929T1		A000153A		VG	

10139	$20	1929T1	C000239A	VG	
10139	$20	1929T1	D000287A	F/VF	
10139	$20	1929T1	D000310A	VF	
10139	$20	1929T1	C000337A	F	
10139	$20	1929T1	C000388A	F	Higgins Mus.
10139	$20	1929T1	E000389A	?	
10139	$20	1929T1	A000514A	VG	
10139	$20	1929T1	F000515A	F	
10139	$20	1929T1	B000533A	F+	
10139	$20	1929T1	C000542A	VG/F	
10139	$20	1929T1	C000565A	XF	
10139	$20	1929T1	E000587A	?	
10139	$20	1929T1	B000633A	F	
10139	$20	1929T1	B000702A	VF	
10139	$20	1929T1	D000716A	VF	
10139	$5	1929T2	A003449	?	
10139	$5	1929T2	A003480	XF	
10139	$5	1929T2	A003725	VF	
10139	$5	1929T2	A005656	XF	
10139	$10	1929T2	A000107	F	
10139	$10	1929T2	A000510	VG/F	
10139	$10	1929T2	A000679	?	
10139	$10	1929T2	A000699	F	
10139	$10	1929T2	A000891	F	
10139	$10	1929T2	A001699	F	
10139	$10	1929T2	A001708	F	
10139	$10	1929T2	A001780	VG	
10139	$10	1929T2	A002341	XF	
10139	$20	1929T2	A000264	AU	
10139	$20	1929T2	A000394	XF/AU	
10139	$20	1929T2	A000841	F	
10139	$20	1929T2	A000891	F	
10139	$20	1929T2	A000989	VF	
10139	$20	1929T2	A000992	VF	

THE FIRST NATIONAL BANK OF SIOUX RAPIDS 14 L
9585 BUENA VISTA

Organized on October 23, 1909 with a capital of $50,000. Placed in voluntary liquidation on Jan. 30, 1930; capital of $50,000. Succeeded by #13400. Placed in receivership on Feb. 13, 1933. Reason for failure: deficiency in assets.

Officers: Pres. CB Mills 1910-19, GF Tincknell 1920, CB Mills 1922-29; **VP** EM Duroe 1910-14, FN Sipe 1920, OM Lee 1920-26, EM Duroe 1922-29, Chas Gilmore 1925-26; **Cash.** Scott W Whitehead 1910-13, FH Diercks 1914-29; **AC** BG Peterson 1910-13, WH Clark 1914, CL Sipe 1920, RH Leonard 1920-23, CB Mills, Jr. 1922-25, CR Duroe 1926-29, Hildred Smith 1929

Third Charter, Date Back, Blue Seal

	Ser #	# Notes
5-5-5-5	1-3250	13,000
10-10-10-20	1-2520	10,080

Third Charter, Plain Back, Blue Seal

5-5-5-5	3251-9918	26,672
10-10-10-20	2521-6763	16,972

Total amount of circulation issued = $536,510. Amount outstanding at close = $50,000. Amount of large outstanding on August 8, 1932 = $5,450. Liability for redemption of circulation assumed by #13400.
66,724 Large   0 Small   66,724 Total

9585	-	$5	1902PB	600	7895 A	T203406H	F	Davenport B&T
9585	-	$5	1902PB	600	8209 C	Y235770N	G/VG	faded/gone
9585	-	$5	1902PB	600	9227 D	9227 D	F	
9585	-	$5	1902PB	600	9535 A	9535 A	VF	stamp Higg. Mus.
9585	-	$5	1902PB	600	9888 C		VG+	faded/faded
9585	M	$10	1902PB	626	1861 B	R833301A	F	pen/stamp
9585	M	$10	1902PB	626	2836 B	??393??B	G	Repaired (2826B?)
9585	M	$10	1902PB	626	4687 A	Z359629E	VG	gone/gone
9585	-	$10	1902PB	626	5766 C	5766 C	VG/F	stamp/stamp
9585	-	$10	1902PB	626	5908 B	5908 B	VG/F	
9585	M	$20	1902PB	652	3475 A	N48727D	VG/F	
9585	M	$20	1902PB	652	3514 A	N48766D	VG/F	
9585	-	$20	1902PB	652	5780 A	5780 A	VG	
9585	-	$20	1902PB	652	6232 A	6232 A	F	gone/gone stain

THE FIRST NATIONAL BANK IN SIOUX RAPIDS 9 S
13400 BUENA VISTA

Organized on November 8, 1929 with a capital of $50,000. Succeeded #9585. Assumed the circulation of #9585. Placed in receivership on August 1, 1932; capital of $50,000.

Officers: Pres. CB Mills 1929-32; **VP** EM Duroe 1929-32; **Cash.** FH Diercks 1929-31, LF Pingel 1931-32; **AC** FM Duroe 1929-30, Hildred Smith 1929-32

1929, Type I

	Ser #	# Notes
6-5's	1-1109	6,654
6-10's	1-491	2,946
6-20's	1-182	1,092

Total amount of circulation issued = $84,570. Amount outstanding at close = $49,100. Amount includes circulation of #9585 that was still outstanding.
0 Large   10,692 Small   10,692 Total

13400	$5	1929T1	F000247A	VG	
13400	$5	1929T1	B000655A	VF/XF	Higgins Mus.
13400	$10	1929T1	C000133A	VG	
13400	$10	1929T1	C000202A	F/VF	
13400	$10	1929T1	D000243A	VG/F	
13400	$10	1929T1	C000304A	HG	
13400	$20	1929T1	A000084A	VG	
13400	$20	1929T1	A000107A	F	
13400	$20	1929T1	D000169A	F	Tight margin

THE FIRST NATIONAL BANK OF SIOUX RAPIDS 0 L
7189 BUENA VISTA

Organized on March 29, 1904. Placed in voluntary liquidation on July 25, 1904; capital of $25,000. (According to Treasury Dept. Records, by the time the bank received its notes the bank had contemplated liquidation and all the currency returned to Washington—hence none outstanding.)

Third Charter, Red Seal

	Ser #	# Notes
10-10-10-20	1-250	1,000

Total amount of circulation issued = $12,500. According to the ledgers, all of the bank's notes were redeemed.
1,000 Large   0 Small   1,000 Total

THE CITIZENS NATIONAL BANK OF SPENCER 20 L
6941 CLAY

Organized on August 11, 1903 with a capital of $50,000. Placed in receivership on November 19, 1926; capital of $100,000. Reason for failure: incompetent management & local depression.

Officers: Pres. Franklin Floete 1903-22, JH McCord 1923-26; **VP** Andrew R Smith 1903-13, Wm Flindt 1914, JH McCord 1918-22, PR Graham 1923-26; **Cash.** Ackley Hubbard 1903-05, JH McCord 1906-15, ER Mauss 1916-17, PR Graham 1918-22, OB Scott 1923-26; **AC** BO Tupper 1904, EJ Armstrong 1907, PC Cilley 1909-11, ER Mauss 1913-14, PR Graham 1914-17, CA Cuttell 1921-26, RH Miller 1921-24

Third Charter, Red Seal

	Ser #	#Notes
10-10-10-20	1-1120	4,480

Third Charter, Date Back, Blue Seal

10-10-10-20	1-4140	16,560

Third Charter, Plain Back, Blue Seal

10-10-10-20	4141-8803	18,652

Total amount issued = $496,150. Amount outstanding at close = $49,295.
39,692 Large   0 Small   39,692 Total

6941	M	$10	1902RS	613	979 C	B280376	F	Higgins Mus.
6941	M	$10	1902DB	616	2258 D	K988454A	XF	stamp/stamp
6941	M	$10	1902DB	616	2258 E	K988454A	XF	stamp/stamp
6941	M	$10	1902DB	616	2258 F	K988454A	XF	stamp/stamp
6941	M	$10	1902DB	616	2261 E	K988457A	VF	
6941	M	$10	1902DB	616	4060 F	M936046B	F	
6941	M	$20	1902DB	642	1176 B	V679636	VG/F	
6941	M	$20	1902DB	642	1202 B	V679662	VG	faded Washed
6941	M	$20	1902DB	642	2258 A	K988454A	VF/XF	lt stamp/stamp
6941	M	$20	1902DB	642	2261 B	K988457A	VF	
6941	M	$20	1902DB	642	2262 B	K988458A	F	stamp/stamp
6941	M	$10	1902PB	624	4429 F	X95553B	VG/F	
6941	M	$10	1902PB	624	5839 D	U145131D	VG	stamp/stamp
6941	M	$10	1902PB	624	6749 E	X554001E	VG	
6941	M	$10	1902PB	624	7590 E	H629472H	VG	
6941	-	$10	1902PB	624	7600 D	R132792H	VF	stamp/stamp
6941	-	$10	1902PB	624	8462 F	8462 F	F/VF	
6941	-	$10	1902PB	624	8469 D	8469 D	VG	
6941	-	$10	1902PB	624	8652 E	8652 E	F/VF	
6941	M	$20	1902PB	650	7862 B	T729494H	F	Higgins Mus.

THE FIRST NATIONAL BANK OF SPENCER 5 L
3898 CLAY

Organized on May 26, 1888 with a capital of $60,000. Absorbed The Clay County Bank in 1901. Placed in receivership on June 25, 1927; capital of $150,000. Reason for failure: incompetent management & local depression.

Officers: Pres. Albert W Miller 1888-92, Ackley Hubbard 1893-95, Franklin Floete 1896, Chas. McAllister 1897-1913, AC Perine 1914-19, CP Buckey 1920-26; **VP** TP Bender 1888, AR Smith 1896, AC Perine 1900, HN Smith 1902-26, JJ Cairns 1921-26; **Cash.** PE Randall 1888-89, MC Remsburg 1890, Ackley Hubbard 1891, David Painter 1892-95, Ackley Hubbard 1896, MP W Albee 1897-1900, CP Buckey 1901-19, Chas R Howe 1920-26; **AC** AF Lamar 1896-1907, Chas R Howe 1909-18, AE Anderson 1918-26, AJ

Prechel 1921-26, CC Bender 1921-26, WD Buckey 1921-24

Second Charter, Brown Backs	Ser #	# Notes
5-5-5-5	1-5139	20,556
10-10-10-20	1-947	3,788
Third Charter, Red Seal		
10-10-10-20	1-250	1,000
Third Charter, Date Back, Blue Seal		
10-10-10-20	1-2200	8,800
Third Charter, Plain Back, Blue Seal		
10-10-10-20	2201-4000	7,200

Total amount issued = $362,630. Amount outstanding at close = $24,300.
41,344 Large   0 Small   41,344 Total

3898 M	$20 1902DB	644	997 B	B940268	F	Higgins Mus.
3898 M	$20 1902DB	644	1375 B	B947146	XF	pen/pen vp
3898 M	$20 1902DB	644	1894 B	R941043	VG+	
3898 M	$10 1902PB	626	2769 E	M897776E	VG/F	gone/pen
3898	$20 1902PB	652	3107 B	V752659E	VF	

FIRST NATIONAL BANK IN SPIRIT LAKE   5 L   18 S
13020   DICKINSON

Organized in December 1926 with a capital of $50,000.
Officers: Pres. Marcus Snyder 1927-30, CE Yeutter 1931-32, Fred S Barlow 1933-34, HG Burr 1935, LP LaFontaine 1935; **VP** CE Narey 1927-30, Fred S Barlow 1927-32, FH Ehlbeck 1928, 1932-35, J Robert Cornell 1935; **Cash.** LA Price 1927-34, Gladys L Warren 1935; **AC** Gladys L Warren 1929-34, OW Parsons 1935

Third Charter, Plain Back, Blue Seal	Ser #	# Notes
10-10-10-20	1-1927	7,708
1929, Type I		
6-10's	1-1108	6,648
6-20's	1-348	45
1929, Type II		
10's	1-418	418
20's	1-45	45

Total amount of circulation issued = $209,670. Amount outstanding in 1935 = $39,400. Amount of large outstanding in 1935 = $960.
7,708 Large   9,199 Small   16,907 Total

13020 -	$10 1902PB	635	483 B	483 B	VG	
13020 -	$10 1902PB	635	927 C	927 C	VF	Higgins Mus.
13020 -	$10 1902PB	635	1331 A	1331 A	XF	stamp/stamp
13020 -	$10 1902PB	635	1627 B	1627 B	AU	stamp/stamp
13020 -	$20 1902PB	661	1590 A	1590 A	XF	
13020	$10 1929T1		E000256A		?	
13020	$10 1929T1		F000560A		XF	Higgins Mus.
13020	$10 1929T1		E000708A		VG/F	
13020	$10 1929T1		C000778A		VF	
13020	$10 1929T1		B000953A		F	
13020	$10 1929T1		D000020A		VF	
13020	$20 1929T1		E000109A		VG/F	
13020	$20 1929T1		A000123A		VF	Higgins Mus.
13020	$20 1929T1		F000196A		VG	
13020	$20 1929T1		B000199A		VF	
13020	$20 1929T1		D000213A		VG	
13020	$20 1929T1		D000222A		VG	
13020	$20 1929T1		B000228A		VF/XF	Pinhole
13020	$20 1929T1		D000259A		VG	
13020	$20 1929T1		E000274A		F	
13020	$20 1929T1		F000276A		VF	
13020	$20 1929T1		C000340A		F/VF	
13020	$10 1929T2		A000085		VG	Higgins Mus.

THE FIRST NATIONAL BANK OF SPIRIT LAKE   20 L
4758   DICKINSON

Successor to B.B. Van Steenburg and Company. Organized on June 7, 1892 with a capital of $50,000. In 1895, The Spirit Lake Savings Bank consolidated with it. Placed in receivership on August 25, 1927; capital of $50,000.
Officers: Pres. BB Van Steenburg 1892-93, Jas F Cravens 1895-1900, Jno. W Cravens 1901-09, OS Jones 1910-14, CE Narey 1915-25; **VP** A Kingman 1896, OS Jones 1900-09, JF Cravens 1910-13, Fred W Jones 1914-25; **Cash.** Samuel L Pillsbury 1892-93, VC Hemenway 1894, Jno. W Cravens 1895-1900, LD Goodrich 1901-02, CE Narey 1902-14, John H Rozema 1915-22, LA Price 1923-25; **AC** LD Goodrich 1900, GE Corson 1910-14, LA Price 1914-1922, Clem L Redden 1922-24, Eva F Phippin 1923-25

Second Charter, Brown Backs	Ser #	# Notes
5-5-5-5	1-3475	13,900
50-100	1-514	1,028
Second Charter, Date Back		
5-5-5-5	1-1038	4,152
50-100	1-271	542
Third Charter, Date Back, Blue Seal		
10-10-10-20	1-1600	6,400
Third Charter, Plain Back, Blue Seal		
10-10-10-20	1601-6178	18,312

Total amount issued = $516,910. Amount outstanding at close = $40,000.
44,334 Large   0 Small   44,334 Total

4758 -	$5 1882BB	472	1 A	N539729	XF	Higgins Mus.
4758 -	$5 1882BB	472	592 B	N540320	?	Higgins Mus.
4758 -	$5 1882BB	472	1616 B	Z627896	VF+	pen ac/pen vp
4758 -	$5 1882BB	472	2755 ?	T152943T	F	
4758	$100 1882BB	525	29 A	B52906	XF+	Grinnell #3877, Higgins Museum
4758 M	$5 1882DB	533	174 G	B962069	VG	Higgins Mus.
4758 M	$10 1902DB	620	263 C	K428530A	CU	Higgins Mus.
4758 M	$10 1902DB	620	959 B	K429226A	VF	pen/stamp
4758 M	$10 1902PB	628	2131 A	Y240532B	F	
4758 M	$10 1902PB	628	2163 C	Y240564B	?	
4758 M	$10 1902PB	628	2164 B	Y240565B	XF	
4758 M	$10 1902PB	628	2164 C	Y240565B	VF	stamp/stamp
4758 M	$10 1902PB	628	2165 A	Y240566B	?	
4758 M	$10 1902PB	628	3401 C	V608313D	F	
4758 -	$10 1902PB	628	5266 C	U269988H	VG	
4758 -	$10 1902PB	628	5972 B	5972 B	F/VF	
4758 -	$10 1902PB	628	5987 B	5987 B	VF	Higgins Mus.
4758 -	$10 1902PB	628	6089 B	6089 B	VF	stamp/stamp
4758 M	$20 1902PB	654	4936 A	K590868H	VG	stamp/stamp
4758 -	$20 1902PB	654	5813 A	5813 A	F	Higgins Mus.

THE SPIRIT LAKE NATIONAL BANK   15 L
8032   DICKINSON

Organized on December 12, 1905 with a capital of $50,000. Placed in receivership on March 23, 1926; capital of $50,000.
Officers: Pres. Marcus Snyder 1906-09, AB Funk 1910-12, BB Van Steenburg 1913-21, GC Taylor 1922-25; **VP** AW Osborne 1907-11, BB Van Steenburg 1912, Marcus Snyder 1913-19, Harry H Buck 1917-19, GC Taylor 1920-21, BB Van Steenburg 1922-25, A Hurd 1922, 1925; **Cash.** L Sperbeck 1906-10, AW Crossan 1911, Harry H Buck 1912-14, GC Taylor 1915-19, HS Pierce 1920-23, CC Gravatt 1924-25; **AC** Chas H Sperbeck 1909-14, BA Funk 1912, AD Chisholm 1914-16, Harry Kuhn 1917, HS Pierce 1918-19, OW Parsons 1920-25

Third Charter, Red Seal	Ser #	# Notes
10-10-10-20	1-1700	6,800
Third Charter, Date Back, Blue Seal		
10-10-10-20	1-3640	14,560
Third Charter, Plain Back, Blue Seal		
10-10-10-20	3641-7538	15,592

Total amount of circulation issued = $246,120. Amount outstanding at close = $25,000. Amount of large outstanding on October 27, 1933 = $1,430.
36,952 Large   0 Small   36,952 Total

8032 M	$10 1902DB	617	2204 E	U435580A	VG/F	pen/stamp
8032 M	$10 1902DB	617	2248 F	U435624A	VF	
8032 M	$10 1902DB	617	3146 D	M795332A	VF+	pen/pen
8032 M	$20 1902DB	643	1608 B	D882434A	VG	
8032 M	$20 1902DB	643	2094 B	M673991A	?	
8032 M	$10 1902PB	625	4610 E	E158679D	XF	stamp/stamp
8032 M	$10 1902PB	625	4611 F	E158680D	VF	
8032 M	$10 1902PB	625	5310 E	U144702D	F/VF	stamp/stamp
8032 M	$10 1902PB	625	5527 F	A660999E	F/VF	stamp/stamp
8032 M	$5 1902PB	625	5607 F	A661079E	CU	stamp/stamp
8032 -	$10 1902PB	625	6823 D	K102435H	VG	Bayard
8032 -	$10 1902PB	625	6913 E	K102525H	F/VF	Higgins Mus.
8032 -	$10 1902PB	625	7105 D	T144237H	VG	
8032 M	$20 1902PB	651	6372 B	U933834E	G	Corner gone tape
8032 -	$20 1902PB	651	7233 B	T144365H	F+	Higgins Mus.

THE FIRST NATIONAL BANK OF STANTON   4 L   5 S
6434   MONTGOMERY

Organized on April 23, 1902; capital of $25,000. Placed in conservatorship on March 21, 1933. Placed in receivership on Oct. 30, 1933; capital of $25,000.
Officers: Pres. CW Swanson 1902-11, LJ Newman 1912-19, JS Anderson 1920-33; **VP** CG Lind 1903-07, LJ Newman 1909-11, CV Almquist 1913-33; **Cash.** JS Anderson 1902-18, EM Coppage 1919-33; **AC** Peter Ostrom 1903-05, EM Coppage 1909-14, Lloyd Peterson 1920-33

Third Charter, Red Seal	Ser #	# Notes
10-10-10-20	1-620	2,480
Third Charter, Date Back, Blue Seal		
10-10-10-20	1-820	3,280
Third Charter, Plain Back, Blue Seal		
10-10-10-20	821-1240	1,680
10-10-10-20 (plate dated 1922)	1-2046	8,184
1929, Type I		
6-10's	1-519	3,114

6-20's			1-164		984	
Total amount of circulation issued = $246,120. Amount outstanding at close = $25,000. Amount of large outstanding on October 27, 1933 = $1,430.						
15,624 Large		4,098 Small		19,722 Total		
6434 M	$10 1902PB	635	562 B	K670034H	AU	ac/vp Higg. Mus. plate dated April 23, 1922
6434 -	$10 1902PB	635	1660 C	1660 C	VG	Stained
6434 -	$20 1902PB	661	1526 A	1526 A	F	
6434 -	$20 1902PB	661	1561 A	1561 A	F	pen ac/pen vp
6434	$10 1929T1		B000145A		G	
6434	$10 1929T1		F000459A		VG/F	
6434	$10 1929T1		E000484A		VF+	Higgins Mus.
6434	$20 1929T1		B000006A		F/VF	
6434	$20 1929T1		B000145A		Fr/G	

THE FIRST NATIONAL BANK OF STATE CENTRE 2 L 19 S
8931 MARSHALL
Chartered in October 1907 with a capital of $25,000.
Officers: Pres. JW Dobbin 1908-13, FL Dobbin 1914-35; **VP** JL McMahon 1909-35, WA Miles 1935; **Cash.** FL Dobbin 1908-13, WJ Whitehall 1914-35; **AC** WJ Whitehill 1909-13

Third Charter, Red Seal	Ser #	# Notes
10-10-10-20	1-300	1,200
Third Charter, Date Back, Blue Seal		
10-10-10-20	1-760	3,040
Third Charter, Plain Back, Blue Seal		
10-10-10-20	761-1790	4,120
1929, Type I		
6-10's	1-310	1,860
6-20's	1-106	636
1929, Type II		
10's	1-353	353
20's	1-60	60

Total amount of circulation issued = $140,550. Amount of large outstanding in June 1935 = $620. Amount of small outstanding in June 1935 = $19,380.
8,360 Large   2,909 Small   11,269 Total

8931 M	$10 1902PB	626	918 D	K60080D	XF	Higgins Mus.
8931 M	$20 1902PB	652	1144 B	K410156E	VF+	pen/pen
8931	$10 1929T1		A000107A		F/VF	
8931	$10 1929T1		E000131A		VF	
8931	$10 1929T1		A000185A		XF	
8931	$10 1929T1		E000189A		VF	
8931	$10 1929T1		F000189A		XF	
8931	$10 1929T1		A000201A		VF	
8931	$10 1929T1		D000207A		CU	
8931	$10 1929T1		D000208A		AU	Higgins Mus.
8931	$10 1929T1		E000232A		XF	
8931	$10 1929T1		F000238A		CU	
8931	$10 1929T1		E000242A		VF	
8931	$10 1929T1		F000249A		XF	
8931	$20 1929T1		E000005A		VG+	
8931	$20 1929T1		D000031A		VG	
8931	$20 1929T1		D000033A		VG/F	
8931	$20 1929T1		C000064A		F/VF	
8931	$10 1929T2		A000135		VF	
8931	$10 1929T2		A000182		XF	
8931	$20 1929T2		A000044		F/VF	Dark

THE CITIZENS NATIONAL BANK OF STORM LAKE 3 L
10034 (FIRST TITLE) BUENA VISTA
Chartered in 1911. Title changed to The Citizens First National Bank of Storm Lake on January 28, 1920.
Officers: Pres. Fred Schaller 1912-20; **VP** AD Bailie 1913-14, Geo J Schaller 1920; **Cash.** Geo J Schaller 1912-14, RA Jones 1915-20; **AC** RA Jones 1913-14, WA Myers 1920, RE Sheffield 1920

Third Charter, Date Back, Blue Seal	Ser #	# Notes
10-10-10-20	1-2250	9,000

Sheets 1 to 1950 were 02-08 backs. Sheets 1951 to 2250 were delivered on July 10, but not marked as to type. Sheets 2251 to 2690 were plain backs.

Third Charter, Plain Back, Blue Seal		
10-10-10-20	2251-2690	1,760
10,760 Large	0 Small	10,760 Total

10034M	$10 1902DB	619	87 C	B364699A	F	pen/pen
10034M	$10 1902DB	619	1168 A	B365780A	VG	
10034M	$10 1902DB	619	1763 A	X9008A	F+	pen Higg. Mus.

THE CITIZENS FIRST NATIONAL BANK OF STORM LAKE
10034 (SECOND TITLE) BUENA VISTA 2 L 15 S
Succeeded The Citizens National Bank of Storm Lake on January 28, 1920.
Officers: Pres. Fred Schaller 1920, Geo J Schaller 1922-33, HW Schaller 1934-35; **VP** Geo J Schaller 1920, RE Sheffield 1930-35, RA Jones 1930-33, HW Schaller 1930-33; **Cash.** RA Jones 1920-29, WA Myers 1930-35; **AC** WA Myers 1920-29, RE Sheffield 1920-29, HW Schaller 1927-29, ER Stock 1930-35

Third Charter, Plain Back, Blue Seal	Ser #	# Notes
10-10-10-20	1-2914	11,656
1929, Type I		
6-10's	1-620	3,720
6-20's	1-210	1,260
1929, Type II		
10's	1-362	362
20's	1-55	55

Total amount of circulation issued = $347,320. Amount outstanding in 1934 = $30,000. Amount of large outstanding on August 1, 1935 = $1,720.
11,656 Large   5,397 Small   17,053 Total

10034 -	$20 1902PB	653	2216 A	2216 A	VG+	Higgins Mus.
10034 -	$20 1902PB	653	2337 A	2337 A	F/VF	Higgins Mus.
10034	$10 1929T1		C000049A		VF	
10034	$10 1929T1		F000103A		VF	
10034	$10 1929T1		A000235A		F+	
10034	$10 1929T1		B000236A		VG/F	
10034	$10 1929T1		B000238A		F	
10034	$10 1929T1		A000497A		VF	
10034	$10 1929T1		D000576A		F/VF	
10034	$20 1929T1		F000071A		XF	
10034	$20 1929T1		C000084A		XF	
10034	$20 1929T1		C000120A		VG	
10034	$20 1929T1		B000140A		F/VF	
10034	$20 1929T1		E000173A		VF	
10034	$20 1929T1		D000204A		VF	
10034	$20 1929T1		B000209A		VF	
10034	$20 1929T2		A000009		VF	Higgins Mus.

COMMERCIAL NATIONAL BANK OF STORM LAKE 1 L
10223 BUENA VISTA
Chartered in 1912. Placed in voluntary liquidation on July 1, 1920; capital of $50,000.
Officers: Pres. Palmer C Toy 1912-20; **VP** James F Toy 1913-20, Geo Witter 1920; **Cash.** Harry J Crouse 1912-15, Albert Tymeson 1916-20; **AC** Harry H Covey 1913, Ralph R Brubacher 1914, JL DeLand 1920

Third Charter, Date Back, Blue Seal	Ser #	# Notes
10-10-10-20	1-1000	4,000
Third Charter, Plain Back, Blue Seal		
10-10-10-20	1001-1048	192

Total amount issued = $52,400. Amount outstanding at close = $12,500.
4,192 Large   0 Small   4,192 Total

10223M	$10 1902DB	620	234 B	M177297A	VG/F	vp Higgins Mus.

THE FIRST NATIONAL BANK OF STORM LAKE 6 L
2595 BUENA VISTA
Chartered on December 1, 1881 with a capital of $50,000. Succeeded The Storm Lake Bank. Placed in receivership on January 2, 1904; capital of $50,000. Reason for failure: incompetent management.
Officers: Pres. Joseph Sampson 1883-88, Zeph Chas. Felt 1889-92, AM Hutchinson 1893-95, Geo H Eastman 1896, WE Brown 1897-1903; **VP** EC Cowles 1896, LJ Metcalf 1900-03; **Cash.** George H Eastman 1883-85, RH Brown 1887-92, AH Waitt 1895-98, JB Alexander 1902-03; **AC** Zeph. Chas. Felt 1885, JB Alexander 1900, CJ Clancy 1902-03

First Charter, Series of 1875	Ser #	# Notes
5-5-5-5	1-3949	15,796
10-10-10-20	1-874	3,496
Second Charter, Brown Backs		
50-100	1-139	278

Total amount of circulation issued = $143,530. Amount outstanding at close = $50,000. Amount outstanding in 1915 = $1,782.
19,570 Large   0 Small   19,570 Total

2595 -	$5	1875	405	1 C	U314126	XF	pen Higgins Mus.
2595 -	$5	1875	405	244 B	U314369	F	pen ac/pen
2595 -	$5	1875	405	3612 A	Y416420	VF	pen ac/pen
2595 -	$5	1875	405	3641 D	Y416449	VF+	pen ac/pen
2595 -	$5	1875	405	1831 A	Z384339	VF	Z387339 ?
2595 -	$5	1875	405	2765 A	Z916958	G	pen ac/pen

THE FIRST NATIONAL BANK OF STORY CITY 24 L 34 S
9017 STORY
Organized on January 15, 1908 with a capital of $25,000. Placed in receivership on October 10, 1932; capital of $75,000.
Officers: Pres. HT Henryson 1908-13, TT Henryson 1914-32; **VP** AM Henderson 1909-13, OT Henryson 1914-23, Ole O Roe 1924-31; **Cash.** TT Henryson 1908-13, AM Henderson 1914-32; **AC** EE Sevareid 1913-14, Martin C Hanson 1923-32

Third Charter, Red Seal Ser # # Notes

5-5-5-5		1-310	1,240
10-10-10-20		1-252	1,008

Third Charter, Date Back, Blue Seal

5-5-5-5		1-4050	16,200
10-10-10-20		1-2800	11,200

Third Charter, Plain Back, Blue Seal

5-5-5-5		4051-14130	40,320
10-10-10-20		2801-8921	24,484

1929, Type I

6-5's		1-1973	11,838
6-10's		1-891	5,346
6-20's		1-254	1,524

Total amount of circulation issued = $890,580. Amount outstanding at close = $74,997. Amount of large outstanding at close = $7,447. Amount of small outstanding at close = $67,550.

94,452 Large   18,708 Small   113,160 Total

9017	M	$5 1902RS	589	1 B	T225794	XF
9017	M	$5 1902DB	592	3711 G	H541893B	F	nice sigs
9017	M	$5 1902DB	592	4011 F	H542193B	VG
9017	M	$10 1902DB	618	1278 F	R179019	VF
9017	M	$20 1902DB	644	131 B	A503941	F
9017	M	$5 1902PB	600	8998 G	Y638204E	G	UR corner gone
9017	-	$5 1902PB	600	9854 F	K978790H	VG	faded/faded
9017	-	$5 1902PB	600	10601 H	X802362H	G	gone/gone
9017	-	$5 1902PB	600	10648 ?	X802409H	F
9017	-	$5 1902PB	600	11483 H	11483 H	F	gone/gone
9017	-	$5 1902PB	600	12035 ?	12035 ?	?
9017	-	$5 1902PB	600	13569 E	13569 E	VG	faded/faded
9017	-	$5 1902PB	600	13712 G	13712 G	F/VF	stamp/stamp
9017	-	$5 1902PB	600	14025 H	14025 H	VF	stamp/stamp
9017	M	$10 1902PB	626	4083 F	X535045D	F/VF
9017	M	$10 1902PB	626	4362 E	A42624E	VG	stamp/stamp
9017	M	$10 1902PB	626	5058 E	M309545E	G	gone/gone
9017		$10 1902PB	626	5275 ?	?	?
9017	-	$10 1902PB	626	6608 D	Y994920H	VF	Higgins Mus.
9017	-	$10 1902PB	626	6609 E	Y994921H	CU	stamp/stamp
9017	-	$10 1902PB	626	7654 E	7654 E	F
9017	-	$10 1902PB	626	8490 D	8490 D	VF/XF
9017	M	$20 1902PB	652	3696 B	K393988D	F/VF	faded/stamp
9017	-	$20 1902PB	652	7490 B	7490 B	F
9017		$5 1929T1		D000153A		F
9017		$5 1929T1		A000285A		VG
9017		$5 1929T1		D000731A		VG
9017		$5 1929T1		B001066A		XF
9017		$5 1929T1		D001157A		XF/AU	Higgins Mus.
9017		$5 1929T1		A001356A		F
9017		$5 1929T1		B001505A		VF
9017		$5 1929T1		C001870A		G
9017		$5 1929T1		A001873A		XF
9017		$10 1929T1		E000062A		VF+
9017		$10 1929T1		F000118A		?
9017		$10 1929T1		F000238A		VG/F
9017		$10 1929T1		F000415A		?
9017		$10 1929T1		C000481A		CU	Higgins Mus.
9017		$10 1929T1		E000481A		F+
9017		$10 1929T1		E000486A		CU
9017		$10 1929T1		D000493A		?
9017		$10 1929T1		D000545A		VF
9017		$10 1929T1		A000638A		VF
9017		$10 1929T1		A000859A		F
9017		$10 1929T1		F000860A		VG/F
9017		$10 1929T1		E000867A		?
9017		$20 1929T1		F000052A		G/VG	Rust spots
9017		$20 1929T1		C000126A		XF
9017		$20 1929T1		D000166A		CU
9017		$20 1929T1		E000166A		CU
9017		$20 1929T1		F000166A		CU
9017		$20 1929T1		B000167A		CU
9017		$20 1929T1		C000167A		AU
9017		$20 1929T1		A000169A		CU
9017		$20 1929T1		B000169A		CU
9017		$20 1929T1		A000170A		CU
9017		$20 1929T1		A000187A		?
9017		$20 1929T1		C000251A		F/VF

THE STORY CITY NATIONAL BANK 3 L
10222 STORY

Organized on June 24, 1912 with a capital of $40,000. Placed in receivership on January 3, 1927; capital of $40,000. Reason for failure: local depression.

Officers: Pres. Joseph Marwick 1912-17, HN Donhowe 1918-19, John Donhowe 1920-23, HN Donhowe 1924-25, Edwin Olson 1925-26; **VP** HN Donhowe 1913-14, Melburn Donhowe 1920-26; **Cash.** John Donhowe 1912-19, Peter C Donhowe 1920-23, AT Donhowe 1925, Hallvard Kloster 1913, SJ Marwick 1914, CN Christensen 1920, LO Jacobson 1925-26

Third Charter, Date Back, Blue Seal	Ser #	# Notes
10-10-10-20	1-1500	6,000

Third Charter, Plain Back, Blue Seal

10-10-10-20	1501-4589	12,356

Total amount issued = $229,450. Amount outstanding at close = $29,600.
18,356 Large   0 Small   18,356 Total

10222	M	$10 1902DB	620	687 A	N251504A	F/VF
10222	-	$10 1902PB	628	3841 A	R164973H	VG	gone Higg. Mus.
10222	-	$10 1902PB	628	4038 C	V698620H	VF+

THE FIRST NATIONAL BANK OF STRAWBERRY POINT
9069 CLAYTON 8 L

Chartered in March 1908. Placed in voluntary liquidation on December 23, 1929; capital of $25,000. Succeeded by The Union Bank and Trust Company, Strawberry Point.

Officers: Pres. Alfred Hanson 1908-22, Miner F Harwood 1923-29, JW Hesner 1929; **VP** AO Kingsley 1909-14, JC Ludy 1920-22, CB Chambers 1923-25, William J Blanchard 1926-29; **Cash.** FJ Gressler 1908-13, Miner F Harwood 1914-22, Gus H Wilke 1923, Gertrude Opperman 1924-25, George Hansen 1926-29, GE Dunfrund 1929; **AC** CR Barnes 1909, RC Barnes 1910, BC Barnes 1911, MF Harwood 1913, BR Cole 1914, Ruby B Sauerbry 1920, Gertrude Opperman 1920-23, 1926-27, HL McCarty 1922, Etta Fritschel 1924-27, Ray Nicolet 1928-29, Jane Stamp 1928-29

Third Charter, Red Seal	Ser #	# Notes
10-10-10-10	1-250	1,000

Third Charter, Date Back, Blue Seal

10-10-10-10	1-700	2,800

Third Charter, Plain Back, Blue Seal

10-10-10-10	701-4517	15,268

Total amount issued = $190,680. Amount outstanding at close = $19,260.
19,068 Large   0 Small   19,068 Total

9069	M	$10 1902PB	626	1039 H	R370354	VG	gone/pen
9069	M	$10 1902PB	626	1304 H	R770004	VG
9069	M	$10 1902PB	626	1700 H	T287055	VG	gone/lt pen vp
9069	M	$10 1902PB	626	2527 G	V576982	F
9069	-	$10 1902PB	626	3076 G	X803961	VG
9069	-	$10 1902PB	626	3474 G	3474 G	VF	pen ac/gone
9069	-	$10 1902PB	626	3613 G	3613 G	VG
9069	-	$10 1902PB	626	3717 H	3717 H	VF	ac Higgins Mus.

THE FIRST NATIONAL BANK OF STUART 8 L   4 S
2721 GUTHRIE

Chartered in 1882 with a capital of $50,000.

Officers: Pres. Charles E Bates 1883-85, JR Bates 1887-96, H Lawbaugh 1897-1903, John W Foster 1903-29, Walter I Haynes 1930-32, Bard Williams 1933-35; **VP** H Lawbaugh 1896, PL Sever 1900-02, JF Blackman 1903, AC Curtis 1904-07, 1914-22, Jacob F Blackman 1909-29, Carl S Foster 1923-29, Bard Williams 1930-32, EA Cullen 1930-34, Frank Eckardt 1933-35; **Cash.** H Leighton 1883-96, JR Bates 1897-1903, MR Porter 1903, Jacob F Blackman 1904-07, AC Curtis 1908-13, Ralph M Sayre 1914-25, CL Beech 1925-35; **AC** JF Blackman 1900-02, JP McLaughlin 1904-11, RM Sayre 1913, CE Meyer 1920, SL Porter 1920-25, HC Cronkhite 1925-35

Second Charter, Brown Backs	Ser #	# Notes
5-5-5-5	1-5629	22,516
10-10-10-20	1-303	1,212

Third Charter, Red Seal

10-10-10-20	1-1000	4,000

Third Charter, Date Back, Blue Seal

10-10-10-20	1-2010	8,040

Third Charter, Plain Back, Blue Seal

10-10-10-20	2011-3623	6,452

1929, Type I

6-10's	1-204	11,224
6-20's	1-31	186

Total amount of circulation issued = $374,840. Amount of large outstanding in 1929 = $4,040. Amount of small outstanding in 1929 = $15,960. Amount of large outstanding in June 1935 = $1,940.

42,220 Large   1,410 Small   43,630 Total

2721		$5 1882BB	466	1 ?	?	?
2721		$5 1882BB	466	4997 A	Y868740	AU	Higgins Mus.
2721	M	$10 1902PB	624	2528 D	U557510E	F	pen ac/stamp
2721	-	$10 1902PB	624	2755 D	N307437H	?
2721	-	$10 1902PB	624	2902 E	Y539854H	F	ac
2721	-	$10 1902PB	624	2982 D	Y539934H	XF	ac Higgins Mus.
2721	-	$10 1902PB	624	3336 F	3336 F	VF	pen ac/stamp
2721	-	$20 1902PB	650	2872 B	Y539824H	VG	nice sigs vp
2721		$10 1929T1		E000059A		VG/F
2721		$10 1929T1		C000173A		VG	Higgins Mus.

2721	$20	1929T1	F000004A	VG/F	
2721	$20	1929T1	A000022A	VG	

THE FIRST NATIONAL BANK OF SUMNER 30 L 53 S
8198 BREMER
Organized on March 17, 1906 with a capital of $50,000. Placed in conservatorship on March 27, 1933. Licensed on December 23, 1933.
Officers: Pres. RD McCook 1906-16, Nelson McCook 1917-33, CW Pennington 1934-35; **VP** Frank Webcott 1907-29, CW Pennington 1930-33, LP Winks 1934-35; **Cash.** Nelson McCook 1906-16, WA Heyer 1917-35; **AC** WH Heyer 1907, FJ Wilharm 1909, WA Heyer 1910-14, Elmer Mohling 1920-33, PM Sorg 1920-35, JA Lease 1935

Third Charter, Red Seal	Ser #	# Notes
10-10-10-20	1-1800	7,200
Third Charter, Date Back, Blue Seal		
10-10-10-20	1-2840	10;'s
11,360		
Third Charter, Plain Back, Blue Seal		
10-10-10-20	2841-8908	24,272
1929, Type I		
6-10's	1-984	5,904
6-20's	1-264	1,584
1929, Type II		
10's	1-1042	1,042
20's	1-219	219

Total amount of circulation issued = $640,920. Amount of large outstanding in 1935 = $3,580. Amount of small outstanding in 1935 = $46,420.
42,832 Large   8,749 Small   51,581 Total

8198	M	$10	1902RS	614	213 B	R55694	VF	Higgins Mus.
8198	M	$10	1902RS	614	971 B	R56452	VG	
8198	M	$10	1902RS	614	1743 B	Y380315	VG	Soiled back
8198	M	$20	1902RS	640	1731 A	Y380303	F/VF	
8198	M	$10	1902DB	617	162 F	M132253	AU	Higgins Mus.
8198	M	$10	1902DB	617	892 E	M132983	F	gone/gone
8198	M	$10	1902DB	617	1436 E	D804672A	F	gone/gone
8198	M	$10	1902DB	617	1729 E	D804965A	VG/F	
8198	M	$10	1902DB	617	2185 D	U856931A	CU	
8198	M	$10	1902DB	617	2468 E	Z460702A	F	
8198	M	$20	1902DB	643	1007 B	?	VF	Fed. Res. Bk., San Francisco
8198	M	$20	1902DB	643	2234 B	U856980A	AU	
8198	M	$10	1902PB	625	3456 E	X587747B	VF	pen/pen
8198	M	$10	1902PB	625	3598 F	X587889B	XF	
8198	M	$10	1902PB	625	3628 ?	X587919B	VG	
8198	M	$10	1902PB	625	4569 ?	U860551D	?	
8198	M	$10	1902PB	625	4581 E	U860563D	F	gone/gone
8198		$10	1902PB	625	5789 F	M316756E	F/VF	
8198		$10	1902PB	625	6583 E	?	VG	
8198	-	$10	1902PB	625	6855 E	U978577H	F	stamp/stamp
8198	-	$10	1902PB	625	7029 D	A369941K	F+	
8198	-	$10	1902PB	625	7139 F	A370051K	VF	stamp/stamp
8198	-	$10	1902PB	625	7268 D	A370180K	CU	
8198	M	$20	1902PB	651	3706 B	A118053D	F/VF	
8198	M	$20	1902PB	651	4251 B	N75853D	CU	nice sigs
8198	M	$20	1902PB	651	45?? B	A854283E	?	
8198	-	$20	1902PB	651	6947 B	U978669H	F	
8198	-	$20	1902PB	651	8071 B	8071 B	VF	stamp/stamp Pressed
8198	-	$20	1902PB	651	8320 B	8320 B	F	
8198	-	$20	1902PB	651	8747 B	8747 B	VF	
8198		$10	1929T1		F000041A		G	
8198		$10	1929T1		F000152A		F	
8198		$10	1929T1		B000263A		F	
8198		$10	1929T1		A000295A		F	
8198		$10	1929T1		C000445A		VF	
8198		$10	1929T1		C000617A		?	
8198		$20	1929T1		F000118A		?	
8198		$20	1929T1		F000153A		VG	
8198		$20	1929T1		D000173A		F	
8198		$20	1929T1		B000193A		F	
8198		$20	1929T1		E000222A		F+	Washed
8198		$10	1929T2		A000350		VF	
8198		$10	1929T2		A000449		XF/AU	
8198		$10	1929T2		A000726		VF	
8198		$10	1929T2		A000810		CU	
8198		$10	1929T2		A000819		AU	Stain on edge
8198		$10	1929T2		A000820		CU	
8198		$10	1929T2		A000823		CU	
8198		$10	1929T2		A000830		AU+	
8198		$10	1929T2		A000831		CU	
8198		$10	1929T2		A000832		CU	
8198		$10	1929T2		A000833		AU	
8198		$10	1929T2		A000834		CU	
8198		$10	1929T2		A000835		CU	
8198		$10	1929T2		A000836		CU	
8198		$10	1929T2		A000837		CU	
8198		$10	1929T2		A000838		CU	
8198		$10	1929T2		A000839		CU	
8198		$10	1929T2		A000840		CU	
8198		$10	1929T2		A000841		CU	
8198		$10	1929T2		A000842		CU	
8198		$10	1929T2		A000843		CU	
8198		$10	1929T2		A000844		CU	
8198		$10	1929T2		A000845		CU	
8198		$10	1929T2		A000846		CU	
8198		$10	1929T2		A000847		CU	
8198		$10	1929T2		A000848		CU	Higgins Mus.
8198		$10	1929T2		A000849		CU	
8198		$10	1929T2		A000850		CU	
8198		$10	1929T2		A000851		CU	
8198		$10	1929T2		A000852		CU	
8198		$10	1929T2		A000853		CU	
8198		$10	1929T2		A000854		CU	
8198		$10	1929T2		A000855		CU	
8198		$10	1929T2		A000856		CU	
8198		$10	1929T2		A000857		CU	
8198		$10	1929T2		A000858		CU	
8198		$10	1929T2		A000860		CU	
8198		$10	1929T2		A000872		XF	
8198		$10	1929T2		A000875		CU	
8198		$10	1929T2		A000879		CU	Spot ULC
8198		$10	1929T2		A000880		CU	
8198		$10	1929T2		A000905		VF	

THE FIRST NATIONAL BANK OF SUTHERLAND 1 L
3618 O'BRIEN
Chartered on January 14, 1887. Placed in voluntary liquidation on March 15, 1897; capital of $50,000. Succeeded by The First Savings Bank.
Officers: Pres. Benjamin Thompson 1887-94, CE Achorn 1895-96; **VP** DM Sheldon 1896; **Cash.** Charles H Brintnall 1887-93, B Thompson 1894, TB Bark 1895-96; **AC** Myrtelle Gunsul 1896

Second Charter, Brown Backs	Ser #	# Notes
10-10-10-20	1-751	3,004

Total amount of circulation issued = $37,550. Amount outstanding at close = $11,250. Amount outstanding in 1910 = $360.
3,004 Large   0 Small   3,004 Total

3618	$10	1882BB	482	751 C	K872272	VF

THE FIRST NATIONAL BANK OF SWEA CITY 7 L
5637 KOSSUTH
Organized on October 24, 1900 with a capital of $25,000. Chartered on December 13, 1900. Placed in receivership on October 29, 1927; capital of $25,000. Reason for failure: local depression.
Officers: Pres. CJ Lenander 1900-02, Gardner Cowles 1903-11, EJ Murtagh 1912-27; **VP** Geo C Call 1902, EJ Murtagh 1903-11, JW Sullivan 1913-27, AT Wherry 1914, Claude Spieker 1920-23, 1925-27; **Cash.** GF Thomas 1900-01, Sam'l Mayne 1902, AT Wherry 1903-13, Claude Spieker 1914-19, WE Carlson 1920-27; **AC** PE Benson 1900-03, CF Berggren 1909-14, Harriet Anderson 1920-22, CF Berggren 1923-27

Second Charter, Brown Backs	Ser #	# Notes
10-10-10-20	1-1270	5,080
Second Charter, Date Back		
10-10-10-20	1-1640	6,560
Second Charter, Value Back		
10-10-10-20	1641-2490	3,400
Third Charter, Plain Back, Blue Seal		
10-10-10-20	1-1772	7,088

Total amount issued = $276,600. Amount outstanding at close = $24,600.
22,128 Large   0 Small   22,128 Total

5637	M	$10	1882VB	577	2199 E	U724487	AU	
5637	-	$10	1902PB	633	1397 A	A134629K	XF	Repair, Higg Mus.
5637	-	$10	1902PB	633	1762 C	1762 C	G/VG	
5637	M	$20	1902PB	659	890 A	Y905772E	F	ac, Rust
5637	-	$20	1902PB	659	1113 A	N879475H	F	Repair; rust hole
5637	-	$20	1902PB	659	1116 A	N879478H	VF	Repair; rust hole
5637	-	$20	1902PB	659	1343 A	A134575K	VG	Mold problems

THE FIRST NATIONAL BANK OF TABOR 8 L
4609 FREMONT
Chartered on July 1, 1891 with a capital of $50,000. Succeeded The Tabor Bank. Placed in voluntary liquidation on December 15, 1925; capital of $25,000. Succeeded by The First State Bank, Tabor. Placed in receivership

on September 14, 1927; reason: deficiency in assets sold.
Officers: Pres. FC Johnson 1891-92, JP Farmer 1893, FC Johnson 1894-95, SD Davis 1896-97, HR Laird 1898-17, MT Davis 1919-26; **VP** Mary E Lawrence 1896-1902, WH Wadhams 1903, TM Aistrope, Jr. 1904-14, WW Glynn 1920-26; **Cash.** LJ Nettleton 1891-1903, Ira McCormick 1903-26; **AC** CO Laird 1909-11, Dayre Williams 1920-26

Second Charter, Brown Backs	Ser #	# Notes
10-10-10-20	1-1410	5,640
Second Charter, Date Back		
10-10-10-20	1-218	872
Third Charter, Date Back, Blue Seal		
10-10-10-20	1-1140	4,560
Third Charter, Plain Back, Blue Seal		
10-10-10-20	1141-1820	2,720

Total amount of circulation issued = $172,400. Amount outstanding in 1925 = $12,500. Amount outstanding in 1927 = $4,100.

13,792 Large   0 Small   13,792 Total

4609	$10 1882BB 485	779 A	V537332	VG	Higgins Mus.	
4609 M	$10 1902DB 620	291 A	?	AU		
4609 M	$10 1902DB 620	582 C	E143277A	VF		
4609 M	$10 1902DB 620	1063 B	M936749B	AU	pen Higgins Mus.	
4609 M	$10 1902DB 620	1091 B	M936777B	CU		
4609 M	$10 1902PB 628	1337 B	Z751149D	AU	pen/pen	
4609 M	$10 1902PB 628	1371 A	H922473E	F	faded/pen	
4609 M	$10 1902PB 628	1634 A	M253446H	VF		

THE FIRST NATIONAL BANK OF TAMA CITY   4 L
1880 (FIRST TITLE)   TAMA

Organized on August 5, 1871 with a capital of $50,000. Chartered on September 19, 1871. Title changed to The First National Bank of Tama on July 11, 1891.
Officers: Pres. Benjamin A Hall 1872-79, JL Bracken 1880-1891; **Cash.** Geo H Warren 1872-79, Arthur P Starr 1880-90, TL Williamson 1891; **AC** FN Warren 1878-79

First Charter, Original Issue	Ser #	# Notes
1-1-1-2	1-2700	10,800
5-5-5-5	1-2575	10,300
First Charter, Series of 1875		
1-1-1-2	1-1280	5,120
5-5-5-5	1-4818	19,272

45,492 Large   0 Small   45,492 Total

1880 - $2	ORIG 389	1215 A	C724744	XF		
1880 - $1	1875 383	916 C	A54972	F	Blue end paper	
1880 - $1	1875 383	919 A	A54975	VF+	Higgins Mus., Blue end paper	
1880 - $2	1875 390	917 A	A54973	F	Blue end paper	

THE FIRST NATIONAL BANK OF TAMA   9 L
1880 (SECOND TITLE)   TAMA

Succeeded The First National Bank of Tama City on July 11, 1891. Placed in receivership on January 18, 1926; capital of $75,000. Reason for failure: local depression.
Officers: Pres. JL Bracken 1891-1925; **VP** EG Penrose 1920-25, CR Johnston 1924-25; **Cash.** TL Williamson 1891-1914, TJ Bracken 1916-23, Chalmers Winders 1924-25; **AC** DE Goodell 1896-1906, TJ Bracken 1907-14, Chalmers Winders 1920-23, Katherine Hartsock 1920-25, LD Carris 1920, Margaret Kearney 1922-25

Second Charter, Brown Backs	Ser #	# Notes
5-5-5-5	1-4000	16,000
10-10-10-20	1-2260	9,040
Second Charter, Date Back		
5-5-5-5	1-1044	4,176
10-10-10-20	1-850	3,400
Third Charter, Date Back, Blue Seal		
10-10-10-20	1-2140	8,560
Third Charter, Plain Back, Blue Seal		
10-10-10-20	2141-6553	17,652

Total amount issued = $751,790. Amount outstanding at close = $49,297.

58,828 Large   0 Small   58,828 Total

1880 M	$5 1882BB 472	2663 B	K549593K	VG/F	Higgins Mus.	
1880 M	$5 1882BB 472	2726 C	K549656K	VG		
1880 M	$20 1882BB 499	1244 A	B952720B	F+	pen Higgins Mus.	
1880 M	$10 1902DB 620	1818 A	Z481772A	CU	Higgins Mus.	
1880 M	$10 1902PB 628	4740 B	A958812E	VG+	pen/pen vp	
1880 M	$10 1902PB 628	5077 C	M628304E	F+		
1880 M	$10 1902PB 628	5156 B	M628383E	G/VG		
1880 M	$10 1902PB 628	5632 B	E6964H	F		
1880 -	$20 1902PB 654	6501 A	Z653H	XF		

THE FIRST NATIONAL BANK OF TERRIL   49 L
10238   DICKINSON

Organized on July 17, 1912 with a capital of $25,000. Placed in receivership on November 23, 1926; capital of $25,000.
Officers: Pres. Harry H Buck 1912-16, AW Bascom 1917-25, Frank Hildreth 1926; **VP** BB Van Steenburg 1913, AW Bascom 1914, C McNary 1920-26; **Cash.** CC Gravatt 1912-18, Max Miller 1919-26; **AC** EJ Starkey 1913-14, WM Stoakes 1920-26

Third Charter, Date Back, Blue Seal	Ser #	# Notes
10-10-10-20	1-1140	4,560
Third Charter, Plain Back, Blue Seal		
10-10-10-20	1141-3770	10,520

Total amount of circulation issued = $188,500.

15,080 Large   0 Small   15,080 Total

10238M	$10 1902DB 620	297 C	M499500A	VG	vp	
10238M	$10 1902DB 620	531 A	T702523A	VG	pen/pen	
10238M	$10 1902DB 620	618 A	T702610A	XF	pen/pen	
10238M	$10 1902DB 620	619 B	T702611A	XF	Higgins Mus.	
10238M	$10 1902DB 620	633 A	T702625A	F	gone/pen	
10238M	$10 1902DB 620	641 C	T702633A	?		
10238M	$10 1902DB 620	662 A	T702654A	?		
10238M	$10 1902DB 620	665 C	T702657A	XF/AU	ac	
10238M	$10 1902DB 620	672 C	T702664A	XF/AU	pen ac/stamp	
10238M	$10 1902DB 620	714 B	T702706A	G/VG		
10238M	$10 1902DB 620	929 C	A720311B	?		
10238M	$10 1902DB 620	930 A	A720312B	VF	pen/stamp Stain	
10238M	$10 1902DB 620	930 C	A720312B	?		
10238M	$10 1902DB 620	932 A	A720314B	?		
10238M	$10 1902DB 620	932 B	A720314B	?		
10238M	$10 1902DB 620	933 A	A720315B	?		
10238M	$20 1902DB 646	87 A	M499290A	VF	pen/pen	
10238M	$20 1902DB 646	483 A	T702475A	VG/F	pen ac/faded	
10238M	$20 1902DB 646	732 A	T702724A	VF	pen/stamp	
10238M	$20 1902DB 646	758 A	T702750A	F/VF		
10238M	$20 1902DB 646	931 A	A720313B	CU		
10238M	$20 1902DB 646	932 A	A720314B	?		
10238M	$20 1902DB 646	961 A	A720343B	AU		
10238M	$20 1902DB 646	1123 A	A720505B	VF		
10238M	$20 1902DB 646	1132 A	A720514B	?		
10238M	$10 1902PB 628	1172 C	R67050B	VF		
10238M	$10 1902PB 628	1219 C	R67097B	VF	pen/pen	
10238M	$10 1902PB 628	1489 B	V861149B	AU	pen/pen	
10238M	$10 1902PB 628	1936 B	M527748D	XF		
10238M	$10 1902PB 628	1965 B	M527777D	?		
10238M	$10 1902PB 628	1965 C	M527777D	F/VF		
10238M	$10 1902PB 628	1980 B	M527792D	VF		
10238M	$10 1902PB 628	2088 B	T951050D	?		
10238M	$10 1902PB 628	2387 B	A624089E	?		
10238M	$10 1902PB 628	2535 B	H616997E	XF/AU	Higgins Mus.	
10238M	$10 1902PB 628	2562 A	H617024E	VF/XF		
10238M	$10 1902PB 628	2609 C	H617071E	?		
10238M	$10 1902PB 628	2628 C	H617090E	VF	pen/pen	
10238M	$10 1902PB 628	2632 A	H617094E	VG/F		
10238M	$10 1902PB 628	2678 C	H617140E	VF		
10238M	$10 1902PB 628	2711 A	R961823E	XF/AU		
10238	$10 1902PB 628	2752 C	R961864E	?		
10238	$10 1902PB 628	3050 C	Z734552E	VF	Higgins Mus.	
10238M	$20 1902PB 654	1354 A	T349034B	F	pen ac/stamp	
10238M	$20 1902PB 654	1414 A	V861074B	F		
10238M	$20 1902PB 654	1419 A	V861079B	F	gone/retraced	
10238M	$20 1902PB 654	1489 A	V861149B	AU	Higgins Mus.	
10238M	$20 1902PB 654	2567 A	H617029E	VF+	pen Higgins Mus.	
10238M	$20 1902PB 654	2782 A	R961894E	F	pen/pen	

THE FIRST NATIONAL BANK OF THOMPSON   11 L   19 S
5054   WINNEBAGO

Organized on December 21, 1896 with a capital of $50,000. Succeeded The Farmers Savings Bank. Placed in receivership on June 28, 1932; capital of $50,000. Reason for failure: not available from reports.
Officers: Pres. CH Kelley 1897-1910, NE Isaacs 1911-29; **VP** James Ellickson 1900-14, Matt Carson 1920, C Carson 1922, MH Carson 1923-29; **Cash.** FW Thompson 1897-1904, NE Isaacs 1905-08, ER Alquist 1909, TE Isaacson 1910-16, SE Isaacs 1917-29; **AC** NE Isaacs 1900-04, ER Alquist 1907, SE Isaacs 1910-14, JE Helgeson 1920-24, Edith Ellickson 1920-29

Second Charter, Brown Backs	Ser #	# Notes
5-5-5-5	1-1845	7,380
50-100	1-431	862
Second Charter, Date Back		
5-5-5-5	1-2320	9,280
50-100	1-360	720

50-50-50-100			1-123	492	

Third Charter, Plain Back, Blue Seal

5-5-5-5			1-13332	53,328	
50-50-50-100			1-200	800	

1929, Type I

6-5's			1-1196	7,176	
6-10's			1-571	3,426	
6-20's			1-162	972	

Total amount of circulation issued = $638,920. Amount of large outstanding at close = $5,890. Amount of small outstanding at close = $44,110.

72,862 Large   11,574 Small   84,436 Total

Charter	Denom	Type	Plate	Serial	Grade	Notes
5054	$5 1882BB	474	1299 B	M95809	F	Higgins Mus.
5054 M	$5 1902PB	606	1757 A	E91303E	F	ac Higgins Mus.
5054 -	$5 1902PB	606	6047 D	T264758H	F	v. faded sigs
5054 -	$5 1902PB	606	6080 D	T264791H	F	light sigs
5054 -	$5 1902PB	606	6532 A	X124293H	F	stamp/stamp
5054 -	$5 1902PB	606	6653 D	X124414H	VG	Davenport B&T
5054 -	$5 1902PB	606	7410 B	7410 B	VG	gone/gone
5054 -	$5 1902PB	606	9964 A	9964 A	VF	stamp/stamp
5054 -	$5 1902PB	606	11306 D	11306 D	F	very faded, stain
5054 -	$5 1902PB	606	12005 A	12005 A	VG	gone, stain
5054 -	$5 1902PB	606	12087 D	12087 D	VF/XF	
5054	$5 1929T1		F000244A		VG	
5054	$5 1929T1		F000617A		VG	
5054	$5 1929T1		E000862A		VG	
5054	$5 1929T1		E000970A		?	
5054	$5 1929T1		A001006A		VG	
5054	$5 1929T1		F001047A		CU	
5054	$5 1929T1		D001160A		VG	
5054	$10 1929T1		B000302A		F	
5054	$10 1929T1		C000310A		VG	
5054	$10 1929T1		C000314A		VG	
5054	$10 1929T1		F000319A		XF	
5054	$10 1929T1		A000476A		VF+	Higgins Mus.
5054	$10 1929T1		C000545A		F+	
5054	$20 1929T1		C000067A		VG/F	
5054	$20 1929T1		A000076A		F	
5054	$20 1929T1		C000080A		VG/F	
5054	$20 1929T1		D000100A		?	
5054	$20 1929T1		D000109A		?	
5054	$20 1929T1		B000144A		?	

THE FIRST NATIONAL BANK OF THORNTON   3 L   19 S
8340   **CERRO GORDO**

Chartered in August 1906.

Officers: Pres. PR Engebretson 1906-11, WV Crapser 1912-35; **VP** WV Crapser 1907, Soren Peterson 1909-35; **Cash.** JL James 1906-22, Paul L James 1923-35; **AC** FE Johnson 1907, Melvin Ingebretson 1925-35

Third Charter, Red Seal   Ser #   # Notes
10-10-10-20   1-300   1,200

Third Charter, Date Back, Blue Seal
10-10-10-20   1-520   2,080

Sheets numbered 1 to 400 were 02-08 backs. Sheets numbered 401 to 520 were delivered on October 15, but not marked as to type. Sheets numbered 521 to 2124 were plain backs.

Third Charter, Plain Back, Blue Seal
10-10-10-20   521-2124   6,416

1929, Type I

6-5's	1-774	4,644
6-10's	1-430	2,580
6-20's	1-126	756

1929, Type II

5's	1-568	568
10's	1-374	374
20's	1-60	60

Total amount of circulation issued = $193,120. Amount of large outstanding in 1935 = $830. Amount of small outstanding in 1935 = $24,140.

9,696 Large   8,982 Small   18,678 Total

Charter	Denom	Type	Plate	Serial	Grade	Notes
8340 M	$10 1902RS	615	1 B	R683038	CU	
8340 -	$20 1902PB	652	1697 B	1697 B	F+	Higgins Mus.
8340 -	$20 1902PB	652	1860 B	1860 B	VG	pen/pen Edge chipping
8340	$5 1929T1		A000001A		[CU	Grinnell # 5781
8340	$5 1929T1		B000001A		[CU	Grinnell # 5781
8340	$5 1929T1		C000001A		[CU	Grinnell # 5781
8340	$5 1929T1		D000001A		[CU	Grinnell # 5781
8340	$5 1929T1		E000001A		[CU	Grinnell # 5781
8340	$5 1929T1		F000001A		[CU	Grinnell # 5781
8340	$5 1929T1		B000772A		VG	
8340	$10 1929T1		D000167A		F/VF	
8340	$10 1929T1		E000215A		VG	
8340	$10 1929T1		A000250A		G/VG	
8340	$10 1929T1		C000254A		VG+	
8340	$10 1929T1		B000266A		F	
8340	$10 1929T1		A000289A		F	
8340	$10 1929T1		D000406A		VG	Washed
8340	$20 1929T1		A000102A		VF	
8340	$20 1929T1		F000103A		F	
8340	$20 1929T1		E000116A		VF+	
8340	$5 1929T2		A000389		XF/AU	Higgins Mus.
8340	$10 1929T2		A000374		AU	Last sheet of $10s

THE CITY NATIONAL BANK OF TIPTON   29 L
6760   **CEDAR**

Chartered in May 1903. Succeeded #2983. Placed in voluntary liquidation on November 10, 1928; capital of $50,000. Succeeded by #13232.

Officers: Pres. WJ Moore 1904-23, FL Butzloff 1924, WGW Geiger 1925-28; **VP** WW Aldrich 1904, FD Wingert 1907-22, FL Butzloff 1923, LW Mathews 1926-27, Chas. Swartzlender 1927-28; **Cash.** Paul Heald 1905-06, Chas Swartzlender 1907-27, RD Swartzlender 1927-28; **AC** Paul Heald 1904, FJ Beaty 1911, Harry E Thompson 1922-25, RD Swartzlender 1926-27

Third Charter, Red Seal   Ser #   # Notes
10-10-10-20   1-1300   5,200

Third Charter, Date Back, Blue Seal
10-10-10-20   1-3240   12,960

Third Charter, Plain Back, Blue Seal
10-10-10-20   3241-9089   23,396

Total amount issued = $519,450. Amount outstanding at close = $50,000.

41,556 Large   0 Small   41,556 Total

Charter	Denom	Type	Plate	Serial	Grade	Notes
6760 M	$10 1902RS	613	793 C	D466132	XF	pen/pen
6760 M	$10 1902RS	613	794 C	D466133	?	
6760 M	$20 1902RS	639	747 A	D466086	?	
6760 M	$20 1902DB	642	1519 B	E627177A	VG	
6760 M	$10 1902PB	624	4046 D	X180683B	AU	stamp/stamp
6760 M	$10 1902PB	624	4680 E	E152669D	CU	Higgins Mus.
6760 M	$10 1902PB	624	4680 F	E152669D	F	
6760 M	$10 1902PB	624	4809 E	M141781D	F	
6760 M	$10 1902PB	624	4954 D	M141926D	F+	stamp/stamp
6760 M	$10 1902PB	624	4964 D	M141936D	F	
6760 -	$10 1902PB	624	7545 D	X121127H	F/VF	pen/pen
6760 -	$10 1902PB	624	7605 D	X121187H	F	
6760 -	$10 1902PB	624	8069 E	8069 E	VF	Small tear
6760 M	$20 1902PB	650	4323 B	A529910C	AU	pen/gone
6760 M	$20 1902PB	650	4328 B	A529915D	CU	pen/stamp
6760 M	$20 1902PB	650	4705 B	E152694D	?	
6760 M	$20 1902PB	650	4707 B	E152696D	?	
6760 M	$20 1902PB	650	4708 B	E152697D	CU	stamp/stamp
6760 M	$20 1902PB	650	4711 B	E152700D	CU	
6760 M	$20 1902PB	650	4713 B	E152702D	CU	
6760 M	$20 1902PB	650	4716 B	E152705D	?	
6760 M	$20 1902PB	650	4717 B	E152706D	CU	stamp/stamp
6760 M	$20 1902PB	650	4720 B	E152709D	CU	
6760 M	$20 1902PB	650	4722 B	E152711D	CU	stamp/stamp
6760 M	$20 1902PB	650	4723 B	E152712D	CU	stamp/stamp
6760 M	$20 1902PB	650	6807 B	A997429H	VF	pen/pen
6760 -	$20 1902PB	650	7623 B	X121205H	VG	
6760 -	$20 1902PB	650	8077 B	8077 B	VG/F	retraced/stamp
6760 -	$20 1902PB	650	8132 B	8132 B	F	pen/pen

THE FIRST NATIONAL BANK OF TIPTON   5 L
2983   **CEDAR**

Chartered on June 20, 1883. Succeeded Herbert Hammond. Placed in voluntary liquidation on June 2, 1903; capital of $50,000. Succeeded by #6760.

Officers: Pres. Herbert Hammond 1883-87, HL Dean 1888-92, JH Coutts 1893-1903; **VP** WW Aldrich 1896-1903; **Cash.** Charles A Snyder 1883-84, Clarence Jewett 1885, CW Hawley 1887-91, WJ Moore 1892-1903; **AC** Nellie M Moore 1896, W Woods 1900-02, Paul Heald 1903

Second Charter, Brown Backs   Ser #   # Notes
10-10-10-20   1-2226   8,904

Total amount of circulation issued = $111,300. Amount outstanding at close = $40,010. Amount outstanding in 1910 = $2,100.

8,904 Large   0 Small   8,904 Total

Charter	Denom	Type	Plate	Serial	Grade	Notes
2983 -	$10 1882BB	480	1425 C	U971831	CU	pen/pen one fold
2983 -	$10 1882BB	480	1426 C	U971832	AU	
2983 -	$10 1882BB	480	1921 C	Y476778	VF+	Higgins Mus.
2983 -	$10 1882BB	480	1927 C	Y476784	VF	Brown stains
2983 -	$20 1882BB	494	807 A	K598303	VF	Davenport B&T

TIPTON NATIONAL BANK   **17 S**
13232   **CEDAR**

Chartered in August 1928. Succeeded #6760. Placed in voluntary liquidation on June 8, 1933; capital of $50,000. Succeeded by The Tipton State Bank.
Officers: Pres. Chas J Lynch 1928-33; **VP** Chas Swartzlender 1928-33, LW Mathews 1929-33, WT Schwendemann 1933; **Cash.** RD Swartzlender 1928-33; **AC** Henry B Walter 1928-33, AE Rumble 1929-33

1929, Type I		Ser #	# Notes
6-5's		1-1684	10,104

Total amount issued = $50,520. Amount outstanding at close = $49,980.

		0 Large		10,104 Small		10,104 Total
13232	$5	1929T1	A000001A	[	AU	
13232	$5	1929T1	B000001A	[	AU	
13232	$5	1929T1	C000001A	[	AU	
13232	$5	1929T1	D000001A	[	AU	
13232	$5	1929T1	E000001A	[	AU	
13232	$5	1929T1	F000001A	[	AU	
13232	$5	1929T1	A000030A		F	Higgins Mus.
13232	$5	1929T1	E000058A		VG	
13232	$5	1929T1	A000130A		VG/F	
13232	$5	1929T1	F000302A		XF	
13232	$5	1929T1	F000303A		F	
13232	$5	1929T1	B000424A		?	
13232	$5	1929T1	E000574A		VG	
13232	$5	1929T1	B000644A		XF	
13232	$5	1929T1	A000837A		CU	
13232	$5	1929T1	F001481A		F	
13232	$5	1929T1	D001609A		VF	

THE FIRST NATIONAL BANK OF TITONKA   **8 L   4 S**
5597   **KOSSUTH**

Organized on August 20, 1900 with a capital of $25,000. Chartered on October 5, 1900. Placed in receivership on December 30, 1930; capital of $25,000. Reason for failure: incompetent management.
Officers: Pres. GS Gilbertson 1900-03, Stitzel X Way 1904-05, EB Soper 1906-13, JW Sullivan 1914-27, J Budlong 1927-30; **VP** HG Gardner 1900-02, Stitzel X Way 1903, CW Todd 1904, SA Schneider 1907, EV Swetting 1909-13, EJ Murtagh 1914, CB Murtagh 1920, JJ Cosgrove 1922-27, Roy Budlong 1927-30; **Cash.** GL Dalton 1900-02, SA Schneider 1903-04, FB Stevens 1905, HC Armstrong 1906-13, JJ Cosgrove 1914-20, HE Rachut 1922-30; **AC** FB Stevens 1903-04, Glen Reibsamer 1907-09, Geo W Hanson 1909-10, JJ Cosgrove 1911, Wm Boykin 1913-14, Edith Budlong 1922-30

Second Charter, Brown Backs	Ser #	# Notes
10-10-10-20	1-1800	7,200
Second Charter, Date Back		
10-10-10-20	1-1470	5,880
Second Charter, Value Back		
10-10-10-20	1471-2267	3,188
Third Charter, Plain Back, Blue Seal		
10-10-10-20	1-2194	8,776
1929, Type I		
6-10's	1-247	1,482
6-20's	1-53	318

Total amount of circulation issued = $334,230. Amount of large outstanding at close = $6,700. Amount of small outstanding at close = $18,300.

		25,044 Large		1,800 Small		26,844 Total	
5597	M	$10	1882DB	?	892 F	K755110	VF
5597	M	$10	1902PB	633	627 C	N636569E	F pen/stamp
5597	M	$10	1902PB	633	883 E	E200755H	VG faded/stamp
5597	-	$10	1902PB	633	1572 B	1572 B	VF gone/gone
5597	M	$20	1902PB	659	259 A	X629711D	VG/F gone/stamp
5597	M	$20	1902PB	659	286 A	X629738D	VG
5597	M	$20	1902PB	659	901 A	E200773H	F/VF Higgins Mus.
5597	-	$20	1902PB	659	1900 A	1900 A	F
5597		$10	1929T1	F000025A			F Higgins Mus.
5597		$10	1929T1	B000138A			F+
5597		$10	1929T1	A000155A			F
5597		$10	1929T1	E000165A			VG

THE FIRST NATIONAL BANK OF TOLEDO   **20 L**
6432   **TAMA**

Organized on August 19, 1902 with a capital of $50,000. Placed in receivership on November 3, 1926; capital of $85,000. Reason for failure: local depression.
Officers: Pres. LB Blinn 1903-23, WA Dexter 1925-26; **VP** PG Wieting 1903-04, HJ Stiger 1907-22, EC Ebersole 1909-14, HD Muckler 1920-22, GH Struble 1923-26, Chas Benesh 1923-26; **Cash.** WA Dexter 1903-24, JN Lichty 1925-26; **AC** JN Lichty 1903-20, Robert Muckles 1909-10, Ralph Johnson 1911, LF Renesh 1914-20, JW Lichty 1922, Ruth B Rines 1922-26, Georgiana Jenks 1922-26, NR McAnulty 1922-26

Third Charter, Red Seal	Ser #	# Notes
10-10-10-20	1-2360	9,440
Third Charter, Date Back, Blue Seal		
10-10-10-20	1-4800	19,200
Third Charter, Plain Back, Blue Seal		
10-10-10-20	4801-13084	33,136

Total amount issued = $772,200. Amount outstanding at close = $83,800.

		61,776 Large		0 Small		61,776 Total		
6432	M	$10	1902RS	613	1739 B	R325910	VG	Higgins Mus.
6432	M	$10	1902RS	613	1922 C	X172765	G	
6432	M	$20	1902RS	639	553 A	A368117	VF	
6432	M	$20	1902RS	639	703 A	A368267	VG	pen/pen
6432	M	$10	1902DB	616	3891 F	Z117411A	F	pen/pen
6432	M	$20	1902DB	642	3642 B	T459746A	VG/F	
6432	M	$10	1902PB	624	6117 E	Z361080B	F	pen/pen vp
6432	M	$10	1902PB	624	9211 E	D621163E	G	
6432	M	$10	1902PB	624	9579 E	N807591E	AU	
6432	M	$10	1902PB	624	10290 F	X519902E	VF+	Higgins Mus.
6432	M	$10	1902PB	624	10887 F	D910199H	VG	
6432	M	$10	1902PB	624	11419 D	K736731H	G/VG	pen/pen
6432		$10	1902PB	624	11560 ?	?	F	
6432		$10	1902PB	624	?	T816452H	?	
6432	-	$10	1902PB	624	12102 F	Z601184H	VF	pen/pen
6432	-	$10	1902PB	624	12599 ?	?	?	
6432	-	$10	1902PB	624	12745 F	12745 F	F/VF	
6432	-	$10	1902PB	624	12954 F	12954 F	VG	Fed. Res. Bk., San Francisco
6432	M	$20	1902PB	650	8511 B	X823713D	VG	
6432	-	$20	1902PB	650	12657 B	12657 B	VF	pen/pen

THE NATIONAL BANK OF TOLEDO   **30 S**
13073   **TAMA**

Chartered in May 1927.
Officers: Pres. Charles Benesh 1927-35; **VP** WB Schultz 1927-35; **Cash.** PC Welle 1927-35; **AC** WA Kaliban 1927-35, Georgiana Jenks 1928, Sara Sime 1933-35

1929, Type I	Ser #	# Notes
6-5's	1-522	3,132
6-10's	1-618	3,708
6-20's	1-190	1,140
1929, Type II		
5's	1-2210	2,210
10's	1-900	900
20's	1-190	190

Total amount issued = $99,390. Amount outstanding in 1935 = $50,000.

		0 Large		11,280 Small		11,280 Total	
13073	$5	1929T1	A000001A			CU	Light diag. crease
13073	$5	1929T1	B000001A			CU	
13073	$5	1929T1	C000001A			CU	
13073	$5	1929T1	D000001A			CU	
13073	$5	1929T1	E000001A			CU	
13073	$5	1929T1	F000001A			AU	
13073	$5	1929T1	E000045A			VF+	
13073	$10	1929T1	A000001A			AU	
13073	$10	1929T1	B000001A			CU	
13073	$10	1929T1	C000001A			CU	
13073	$10	1929T1	D000001A			CU	
13073	$10	1929T1	E000001A			AU+	
13073	$10	1929T1	F000001A			CU	
13073	$10	1929T1	E000045A			VF	
13073	$10	1929T1	A000082A			VG	
13073	$10	1929T1	F000145A			AU	
13073	$10	1929T1	E000160A			F	
13073	$10	1929T1	D000458A			VG	Stains
13073	$10	1929T1	B000469A			VF	
13073	$10	1929T1	E000492A			?	
13073	$10	1929T1	B000545A			?	
13073	$20	1929T1	F000006A			G	
13073	$20	1929T1	E000064A			XF+	Higgins Mus.
13073	$20	1929T1	D000072A			F/VF	
13073	$20	1929T1	E000072A			F/VF	
13073	$20	1929T1	B000127A			?	
13073	$20	1929T1	A000131A			F/VF	
13073	$20	1929T1	D000147A			VG/F	
13073	$5	1929T2	A000238			VG	
13073	$10	1929T2	A000814			VG/F	

THE FIRST NATIONAL BANK OF TRAER   **18 L   47 S**
5135   **TAMA**

Chartered in 1898; succeeded Brooks & Moore. Placed in voluntary

liquidation on July 17, 1934; capital of $100,000. Succeeded by #14172.
Officers: Pres. James Wilson 1898-1906, LE Wood 1907, RH Moore 1908-13, RJ Morrison 1914-34; **VP** O Gravatt 1900-05, Howard Everett 1907, John Steffen 1909-14, A Gravatt 1920-33, Lyman Wood 1933-34; **Cash.** RH Moore 1898-1907, WJ Ladd 1908-15, KP Moore 1916-34; **AC** WJ Ladd 1900-07, EE Yeliner 1909, E Rodskial 1911, KP Moore 1913-14, DH Hyland 1922-34, Anne Scharfenberg 1922-34

Second Charter, Brown Backs	Ser #	# Notes
10-10-10-20	1-1900	7,600
Second Charter, Date Back		
10-10-10-20	1-2350	9,400
Second Charter, Value Back		
10-10-10-20	2351-3490	4,560
Third Charter, Plain Back, Blue Seal		
10-10-10-20	1-11265	45,060
1929, Type I		
6-10's	1-2208	13,248
6-20's	1-594	3,564
1929, Type II		
10's	1-800	800
20's	1-178	178

Total amount of circulation issued = $1,048,070. Amount of large outstanding at close = $5,430. Amount of small outstanding at close = $93,700.
66,620 Large   17,790 Small   84,410 Total

Charter		Type				Grade	Notes
5135	-	$10 1882BB	490	407 A	T861272	F/VF	pen/pen
5135	M	$10 1902PB	632	275 C	B619902D	VF/XF	stamp/stamp
5135	M	$10 1902PB	632	826 C	K402878D	AU	Higgins Mus.
5135	M	$10 1902PB	632	2681 C	B225953E	F	
5135	M	$10 1902PB	632	4050 A	N428062E	VG	Bayard
5135	M	$10 1902PB	632	4075 C	N428087E	AU	
5135	M	$10 1902PB	632	4501 A	V872893E	F	
5135	M	$10 1902PB	632	4675 C	V873067E	AU	stamp/stamp
5135	M	$10 1902PB	632	5876 A	K609178H	F	stamp/stamp
5135	-	$10 1902PB	632	8327 C	8327 C	VG	Staining
5135	-	$10 1902PB	632	8424 A	8424 A	F/VF	
5135	M	$20 1902PB	658	1912 A	X327394D	F	
5135	M	$20 1902PB	658	1925 A	X327407D	VF	stamp/stamp Ink on face
5135	M	$20 1902PB	658	2874 A	B226146E	XF	
5135	M	$20 1902PB	658	3510 A	N427522E	F	stamp/stamp Washed; pressed
5135	M	$20 1902PB	658	4148 A	N428160E	XF	faded/faded
5135	M	$20 1902PB	658	4380 A	V872772E	VF+	faded/faded
5135	-	$20 1902PB	658	7883 A	7883 A	VF/XF	stamp/stamp
5135		$10 1929T1			D000026A	VG	
5135		$10 1929T1			E000058A	VF	
5135		$10 1929T1			D000561A	F/VF	
5135		$10 1929T1			E000586A	F	Rust stains
5135		$10 1929T1			A000983A	VF/XF	
5135		$10 1929T1			A001254A	?	
5135		$10 1929T1			F001332A	XF/AU	
5135		$10 1929T1			B001338A	F	
5135		$10 1929T1			E001353A	VF	
5135		$10 1929T1			E001382A	F	
5135		$10 1929T1			F001394A	VF	
5135		$10 1929T1			A001412A	CU	
5135		$10 1929T1			E001483A	CU	Higgins Mus.
5135		$10 1929T1			E001502A	VF	
5135		$10 1929T1			A001568A	F	
5135		$10 1929T1			F001623A	VG	
5135		$10 1929T1			F001665A	F	
5135		$10 1929T1			C001827A	?	
5135		$10 1929T1			F001873A	?	
5135		$10 1929T1			A001888A	VG	
5135		$10 1929T1			B001912A	VF	
5135		$10 1929T1			D001938A	VF	
5135		$10 1929T1			E001944A	VG	
5135		$10 1929T1			A001945A	VG	
5135		$20 1929T1			E000104A	?	
5135		$20 1929T1			F000132A	F	
5135		$20 1929T1			F000148A	AU	
5135		$20 1929T1			D000160A	VF	
5135		$20 1929T1			F000160A	XF	
5135		$20 1929T1			B000186A	VG	
5135		$20 1929T1			D000207A	F+	
5135		$20 1929T1			E000229A	VG	
5135		$20 1929T1			F000231A	?	
5135		$20 1929T1			D000278A	VG	
5135		$20 1929T1			D000309A	VF	
5135		$20 1929T1			D000309A	F	
5135		$20 1929T1			B000370A	VG/F	
5135		$20 1929T1			E000377A	F/VF	
5135		$20 1929T1			E000390A	AU	
5135		$20 1929T1			F000412A	VF/XF	
5135		$20 1929T1			A000433A	VF	
5135		$20 1929T1			B000508A	?	
5135		$20 1929T1			B000511A	VF	
5135		$20 1929T1			A000566A	F	
5135		$10 1929T2			A000009	F/VF	
5135		$10 1929T2			A000605	G	
5135		$20 1929T2			A000028	F	

THE FIRST NATIONAL BANK OF VALLEY JUNCTION
5891   POLK   4 L   18 S

Organized on June 24, 1901 with a capital of $25,000. Chartered on July 2, 1901. Placed in conservatorship on March 20, 1933. Licensed again on August 22, 1933.
Officers: Pres. LP Bennett 1901-04, Simon Casady 1906-14, JW Mullane 1914-28, WA Kinnaird 1929-34; **VP** Simon Casady 1902-04, LP Bennett 1907-24, WA Kinnaird 1926-28, Clarence M Cornwell 1929-33; **Cash.** JW Mullane 1901-14, WA Kinnaird 1914-28, BW Taylor 1929-30, CC Heenan 1931-34, Clarence M Cornwell 1935; **AC** WA Kinnaird 1907-14, BW Taylor 1920-28, MC Kolling 1929-35, CC Heenan 1929-31

Second Charter, Brown Backs	Ser #	# Notes
10-10-10-20	1-900	3,600
Second Charter, Date Back		
10-10-10-20	1-1800	7,200

Sheets numbered 1 to 1700 were 82-08 backs. Sheets numbered 1701 to 1800 were delivered on August 4, 1915, but not marked as to type. Sheets numbered 1801 to 2939 are denominational backs.

Second Charter, Value Back		
10-10-10-20	1801-2939	4,556
Third Charter, Plain Back, Blue Seal		
10-10-10-20	1-2375	9,500
1929, Type I		
6-10's	1-546	3,276
6-20's	1-160	960
1929, Type II		
10's	1-627	627
20's	1-172	172

Total amount of circulation issued = $372,370. Amount of large outstanding on July 25, 1935 = $1,750. Amount of small outstanding on July 25, 1935 = $22,850.
24,856 Large   5,035 Small   29,891 Total

Charter		Type				Grade	Notes
5891		$10 1902PB	631	719 B	D651661H	VG/F	Higgins Mus.
5891	-	$10 1902PB	631	1285 B	Y64697H	F/VF	pen/stamp ac
5891	-	$10 1902PB	631	1603 A	1603 A	AU	pen/stamp ac
5891	-	$20 1902PB	659	2061 A	2061 A	VF	vp
5891		$10 1929T1			D000257A	F	Ink
5891		$10 1929T1			D000287A	VG	LR corner gone
5891		$10 1929T1			B000373A	VG/F	
5891		$10 1929T1			B000422A	F	
5891		$10 1929T1			D000440A	VG	
5891		$10 1929T1			B000516A	AU	Higgins Mus.
5891		$20 1929T1			A000030A	F	
5891		$20 1929T1			C000045A	F+	
5891		$20 1929T1			E000073A	VG	Rust stains
5891		$20 1929T1			A000078A	XF	
5891		$20 1929T1			C000092A	F	
5891		$20 1929T1			?000123A	XF	
5891		$20 1929T1			C000132A	VG	Wallet Stained
5891		$20 1929T1			F000132A	F	
5891		$20 1929T1			C000139A	F	
5891		$20 1929T1			E000146A	VF	
5891		$10 1929T2			A000376	VF	
5891		$10 1929T2			A000543	F	

THE FIRST NATIONAL BANK OF VILLISCA   20 L   7 S
2766   MONTGOMERY

Organized on May 29, 1882 with a capital of $50,000. Succeeded W.S. Alger & Co. Placed in receivership on October 18, 1930; capital of $50,000. Reason for failure: local depression.
Officers: Pres. WS Alger 1883-1919, BF Fast 1920-30; **VP** MN McNaughton 1896-1911, BF Fast 1913-19, DE Lomas 1920-29, MB Alger 1930; **Cash.** HH McCartney 1883-84, BF Fast 1885-1911, DE Lomas 1912-19, FE Shane 1920-30; **AC** D Perrine 1900, BJ Olson 1902-03, DE Lomas 1904-11, MH Bell 1913-14, LE Gunderman 1920-30

First Charter, Series of 1875	Ser #	#Notes
5-5-5-5	1-3408	13,632
50-100	1-278	556
Third Charter, Red Seal		
10-10-10-20	1-2500	10,000

Third Charter, Date Back, Blue Seal

	Ser #	# Notes
10-10-10-20	1-2900	1,160

Third Charter, Plain Back, Blue Seal

10-10-10-20	2901-7579	18,716

1929, Type I

6-10's	1-460	2,760
6-20's	1-119	714

Total amount of circulation issued = $655,690. Amount outstanding at close = $50,000. Amount of large outstanding on July 1, 1931 = $9,690.

54,504 Large   3,474 Small   57,978 Total

2766	-	$5	1875	405	3071 B	Y556874	XF	
2766	-	$5	1875	405	3303 B	Y557106	VF	Higgins Mus.
2766	-	$5	1875	405	3335 A	Y557138	XF	pen/pen B.F. Fast (cashier)
2766	-	$5	1875	405	3392 B	Y557195	F	
2766	-	$50	1875	447	47 A	A462239	VF	pen/pen
2766	M	$20	1902RS	639	2323 A	Y387085	F	pen/pen
2766	M	$20	1902RS	639	2456 A	Y387218	F/VF	Higgins Mus.
2766	M	$10	1902DB	616	1135 E	X485637	VF	pen/pen vp
2766	M	$20	1902DB	642	1170 B	X485672	F	
2766	M	$10	1902PB	624	3103 D	R744808B	VF	pen ac/pen vp
2766	M	$10	1902PB	624	5144 D	Z983006D	?	pen/pen vp
2766	M	$10	1902PB	624	5213 ?	?	CU	
2766	M	$10	1902PB	624	5336 F	H177908E	AU	pen/pen
2766	M	$10	1902PB	624	5429 H	H178001E	F	
2766		$10	1902PB	624	6093 D	N412495H	?	
2766		$10	1902PB	624	6618 D	Y496030H	AU	Higgins Mus.
2766	-	$10	1902PB	624	6731 D	6731 D	VF	pen/pen
2766	-	$10	1902PB	624	6982 D	6982 D	VF+	pen/pen vp
2766	-	$10	1902PB	624	7559 F	7559 F	VF	pen/pen vp
2766	-	$20	1902PB	650	7154 B	7154 B	?	pen/pen vp
2766		$10	1929T1		D000161A		VG/F	Higgins Mus.
2766		$10	1929T1		B000194A		VF/XF	
2766		$10	1929T1		E000226A		F	
2766		$10	1929T1		D000228A		VG	
2766		$10	1929T1		D000229A		VG	
2766		$10	1929T1		C000273A		F	
2766		$20	1929T1		D000015A		XF	

THE NODAWAY VALLEY NATIONAL BANK OF VILLISCA
14041   MONTGOMERY   18 L

Chartered in 1934. Succeeded #7506 and assumed its outstanding circulation.
Officers: Pres. FF Jones 1934-35; **VP** SM Jolliffe 1934-35; **Cash.** JL Wheeler 1934-35; **AC** Roy B Means 1934-35

1929, Type II

	Ser #	# Notes
5's	1-714	714
10's	1-345	345
20's	1-115	115

Total amount of circulation issued = $9,320. Amount outstanding in 1935 = $30,000. Includes the circulation of #7506 that was still outstanding.

0 Large   1,174 Small   1,174 Total

14041	$5	1929T2	A000001	CU	
14041	$5	1929T2	A000002	AU	
14041	$5	1929T2	A000004	AU	
14041	$5	1929T2	A000005	AU	
14041	$5	1929T2	A000006	AU	
14041	$5	1929T2	A000113	CU	
14041	$10	1929T2	A000002	CU	
14041	$10	1929T2	A000003	CU	
14041	$10	1929T2	A000004	CU	
14041	$10	1929T2	A000005	CU	
14041	$10	1929T2	A000006	CU	
14041	$20	1929T2	A000001	AU	
14041	$20	1929T2	A000002	CU	
14041	$20	1929T2	A000003	CU	
14041	$20	1929T2	A000004	CU	
14041	$20	1929T2	A000005	CU	
14041	$20	1929T2	A000006	CU	
14041	$20	1929T2	A000026	CU	Higgins Museum

THE VILLISCA NATIONAL BANK
7506   MONTGOMERY   6 L 20 S

Organized on November 29, 1904 with a capital of $75,000. Placed in conservatorship on April 4, 1933. Placed in voluntary liquidation on March 20, 1934; capital of $60,000. Succeeded by #14041.
Officers: Pres. Amos P West 1905-11, FF Jones 1912-17, FM Dirrim 1918-33; **VP** FM Dirrim 1907-14, Hal Hausen 1920-33; **Cash.** FF Jones 1905-11, WK Finlayson 1912-19, PH Peterson 1920-23, John L Wheeler 1924-33; **AC** Chas W Hill 1913, John L Wheeler 1920-23, Roy B Means 1928-33

Third Charter, Red Seal

	Ser #	# Notes
10-10-10-20	1-990	3,960

Third Charter, Date Back, Blue Seal

10-10-10-20	1-1750	7,000

Third Charter, Plain Back, Blue Seal

10-10-10-20	1751-3800	8,200

1929, Type I

6-10's	1-314	1,884
6-20's	1-252	1,512

Total amount of circulation issued = $288,580. Amount outstanding in 1932 = $19,760. Amount of large outstanding on June 5, 1935 = $1,000.

19,160 Large   3,396 Small   22,556 Total

7506	M	$10	1902DB	616	1017 E	A771305A	F	
7506	M	$10	1902DB	616	1294 D	K198077A	XF	pen/pen
7506	M	$10	1902DB	616	1650 E	M337306B	VF	pen/pen
7506	M	$10	1902DB	624	2589 F	Z878291E	?	pen/pen vp
7506	M	$20	1902PB	650	2872 B	T511404H	VG/F	Higgins Mus.
7506	-	$20	1902PB	650	3184 B	3184 B	VG	
7506		$10	1929T1		B000002A		F	
7506		$10	1929T1		E000080A		VF	
7506		$10	1929T1		A000091A		VG/F	
7506		$20	1929T1		?000028A		VF/XF	
7506		$20	1929T1		B000034A		F+	
7506		$20	1929T1		F000062A		F	
7506		$20	1929T1		B000074A		F/VF	Higgins Mus.
7506		$20	1929T1		F000074A		VG/F	
7506		$20	1929T1		C000092A		VF	
7506		$20	1929T1		C000120A		F	
7506		$20	1929T1		A000126A		F	
7506		$20	1929T1		C000126A		F	
7506		$20	1929T1		E000147A		AU	
7506		$20	1929T1		E000154A		F/VF	
7506		$20	1929T1		B000156A		VG+	
7506		$20	1929T1		C000157A		F	
7506		$20	1929T1		E000165A		?	
7506		$20	1929T1		D000168A		AU	
7506		$20	1929T1		C000171A		VG/F	
7506		$20	1929T1		A000233A		VF	

THE FARMERS NATIONAL BANK OF VINTON
5088   BENTON   9 L

One of two Iowa banks with reported notes with the Tillman/Roberts Treasury signature combination.
Chartered in 1897. Voluntary liquidation on Jan. 10, 1929; capital of $65,000.
Officers: Pres. George Horridge 1897-1929; **VP** WC Ellis 1900-29, C Nichols 1924-29; **Cash.** CO Harrington 1897-1911, Geo D McElroy 1912-29; **AC** Geo D McElroy 1900-11, FL Gerberich 1913-29

Second Charter, Brown Backs

	Ser #	# Notes
5-5-5-5	1-2562	10,248
10-10-10-20	1-1640	6,560

Second Charter, Date Back

5-5-5-5	1-2450	9,800
10-10-10-20	1-1860	7,440

Second Charter, Value Back

5-5-5-5	2451-2735	1,140
10-10-10-20	1861-1996	544

Third Charter, Plain Back, Blue Seal

10-10-10-10	1-5219	20,876

Total amount issued = $496,500. Amount outstanding in 1927 = $36,050.

56,608 Large   0 Small   56,608 Total

5088	M	$5	1882DB	535	1258 G	H397020	VG/F	pen Higgins Mus.
5088	M	$10	1882DB	543	948 D	K55756	F+	pen/pen
5088	M	$10	1882DB	543	1079 E	K905167	F/VF	
5088	M	$10	1902PB	632	8 D	N937213	VF	pen Higgins Mus.
5088	M	$10	1902PB	632	1168 C	T345998	F	lt pen/pen
5088	M	$10	1902PB	632	1318 ?	?	VG	
5088	M	$10	1902PB	632	2805 B	V495805	F	
5088	M	$10	1902PB	632	3245 B	X365700	AU+	
5088		$10	1902PB	632	3438 A	X854148	F	

THE FIRST NATIONAL BANK OF VINTON
1593   BENTON   0 L

Chartered on October 18, 1865. Placed in voluntary liquidation on December 13, 1869; capital of $50,000.
Officers: Pres. Harvey D Gay 1867-69; **Cash.** Samuel H Watson 1867-69

First Charter, Original Issue

	Ser #	# Notes
5-5-5-5	1-1575	6,300
10-10-10-10	1-275	1,100

Total amount of circulation issued = $42,500. Amount outstanding at close = $42,500. Amount outstanding in 1910 = $177.

7,400 Large   0 Small   7,400 Total

145

THE CITIZENS NATIONAL BANK OF WASHINGTON   1 L
6122   WASHINGTON
Chartered on February 7, 1902. Succeeded #2656. Placed in voluntary liquidation on June 1, 1908; capital of $50,000.
Officers: Pres. Charles H Keck 1902-07; **VP** CM Keck 1903-07; **Cash.** Frank R Sage 1902-08

Third Charter, Red Seal	Ser #	# Notes
10-10-10-20	1-2460	9,840

Total amount of circulation issued = $123,000. Amount outstanding at close = $50,000. Amount outstanding in 1910 = $13,320.
9,840 Large   0 Small   9,840 Total

| 6122 | M | $10 | 1902RS | 613 | 1392 B | A935582 | VG | Higgins Museum |

THE FIRST NATIONAL BANK OF WASHINGTON   2 L
398   WASHINGTON
Chartered in 1864. Placed in voluntary liquidation on April 11, 1882; capital of $100,000. Succeeded by #2656.
Officers: Pres. Joseph Keck 1867-75, Norman Everson 1876-81; **Cash.** S Farnsworth 1867, Henry S Clarke 1868-73, Roland R Bowland 1874-81; **AC** WG Simmons 1878-79

First Charter, Original Issue	Ser #	# Notes
1-1-1-2	1-1698	6,792
5-5-5-5	1-7350	29,400
First Charter, Series of 1875		
5-5-5-5	1-2500	10,000
20-20-20-20	1-318	1,272

Total amount of circulation issued = $230,930. Amount outstanding at close = $88,565. Amount outstanding in 1910 = $1,650.
47,464 Large   0 Small   47,464 Total

| 398 | - | $5 | ORIG | 394 | 5387 B | L138011 | VF | Higgins Mus. |
| 398 | - | $5 | ORIG | 394 | 5641 B | L138265 | F | Oat Bin Hoard |

THE FIRST NATIONAL BANK OF WASHINGTON   1 L
2656   WASHINGTON
Chartered on April 11, 1882. Succeeded #398. Placed in voluntary liquidation on March 13, 1902; capital of #50,000. Succeeded by #6122. The first bank recharter in the nation.
Officers: Pres. Norman Everson 1883-84, Joseph Keck 1885-99, AH Wallace 1900, Wm. Blair 1901; **VP** Chas. H Keck 1896, Wm. Blair 1900; **Cash.** WG Simmons 1883-84, SA White 1885-1901; **AC** Chas. H Keck 1885, CM Keck 1896-1900

Second Charter, Brown Backs	Ser #	# Notes
10-10-10-20	1-4243	16,972

Total amount of circulation issued = $212,150. Amount outstanding at close = $50,000. Amount outstanding in 1910 = $3,250.
16,972 Large   0 Small   16,972 Total

| 2656 | - | $20 | 1882BB | 493 | 3299 A | T913404 | VG | gone Washed |

THE WASHINGTON NATIONAL BANK   24 L   29 S
1762   WASHINGTON
Chartered on January 5, 1871; capital of $50,000. Placed in conservatorship on March 13, 1933. Placed in voluntary liquidation on Dec. 15, 1933; capital of $100,000. Succeeded by #13849; circulation assumed by #13849.
Officers: Pres. Alex. W Chilcote 1872-94, WW Wells 1895-1907, AH Wallace 1908-13, John A Young 1914-20, Chas. C Cunningham 1922-26, WP Wells 1927-33, Winfield Smouse 1933; **VP** WE Chilcote 1896, Wm. A Cook 1900, 1909-14, Chas. C Cunningham 1920, Marsh W Bailey 1925-26, WA Anderson 1926-30, Winfield Smouse 1928-33, HB Knight 1930-33, RE Dougherty 1933; **Cash.** John R Richards 1872-77, John A Young 1878-1909, WF Wilson 1910-17, Harvey S Young 1918-25, HB Knight 1926-30, Walter L Graves 1930-33; **AC** John A Young 1877, RR Bowland 1885-1902, FH Smith 1903-07, WF Wilson 1908, SH White 1910, AW McCulley 1913-14, DC Bell 1917-20, 1924-25, J Louis Fifer 1920-22, OF Larkin 1920, WG Conner 1923-33, HL Tolander 1924-25, PH Weldin 1926-29, Ed Miick 1930-33

First Charter, Original Issue	Ser #	# Notes
1-1-1-2	1-1000	4,000
5-5-5-5	1-3750	15,000
20-20-20-20	1-375	1,500
First Charter, Series of 1875		
5-5-5-5	1-248	992
20-20-20-20	1-1210	4,840
Second Charter, Brown Backs		
10-10-10-20	1-6190	24,760
Second Charter, Date Back		
10-10-10-20	1-1276	5,104
Third Charter, Date Back, Blue Seal		
10-10-10-20	1-4900	19,600
Third Charter, Plain Back, Blue Seal		
10-10-10-20	4901-16502	46,408
1929, Type I		
6-10's	1-2130	12,780
6-20's	1-577	3,462

Total amount of circulation issued = $1,607,200. Amount of large outstanding at close = $8,600. Amount of small outstanding at close = $91,400. Circulation assumed by #13849 which was then responsible for redeeming the outstanding circulation of #1762.
122,204 Large   16,242 Small   138,446 Total

1762	-	$1	ORIG	382	510 C	D391916 C	F	
1762		$10	1882BB	484	2625 B	D177449D	F	
1762	M	$10	1882BB	484	3938 A	R310737R	F	
1762	M	$10	1882BB	484	4506 A	R311305R	AU+	
1762	M	$10	1882BB	484	6040 C	V568469V	F+	Davenport B&T
1762	M	$10	1902DB	619	1262 A	Z225411	F	
1762	M	$10	1902DB	619	3035 A	U880621A	F	pen/pen vp
1762	M	$10	1902PB	627	6328 B	A985525D	F	
1762	M	$10	1902PB	627	6708 B	A985905D	G	gone/gone
1762	M	$10	1902PB	627	7852 A	N57704D	VF	
1762	M	$10	1902PB	627	8369 B	U929901D	AU	Higgins Mus.
1762	M	$10	1902PB	627	8571 A	U930103D	VG	LL corner gone
1762	M	$10	1902PB	627	10124 C	M617051E	VG	
1762	M	$10	1902PB	627	10186 B	M617113E	VF	lt stamp sigs
1762	M	$10	1902PB	627	11361 A	Z715003E	VF	stamp/stamp
1762	-	$10	1902PB	627	13382 A	13382 A	F	stamp sigs vp
1762	-	$10	1902PB	627	13443 C	13443 C	VG/F	
1762	-	$10	1902PB	627	13910 C	13910 C	VG	
1762	-	$10	1902PB	627	15691 C	15691 C	VG	gone/gone vp
1762	-	$10	1902PB	627	15763 B	15763 B	F/VF	
1762	M	$20	1902PB	653	5625 A	X86489B	?	
1762	M	$20	1902PB	653	8915 A	A937367E	VG/F	
1762	M	$20	1902PB	653	9364 A	A937816E	F	stamp/stamp
1762		$20	1902PB	653	12607 A	V64179H	F	
1762		$10	1929T1		A000201A		VG	
1762		$10	1929T1		D000309A		VG/F	
1762		$10	1929T1		B000766A		F	
1762		$10	1929T1		B000767A		F	
1762		$10	1929T1		A000900A		F	
1762		$10	1929T1		F001121A		F	
1762		$10	1929T1		A001274A		F/VF	
1762		$10	1929T1		E001320A		F/VF	
1762		$10	1929T1		E001546A		XF	
1762		$20	1929T1		D000126A		F	
1762		$20	1929T1		B000166A		VG	
1762		$20	1929T1		B000217A		F	
1762		$20	1929T1		D000231A		AU+	D000213A ?
1762		$20	1929T1		C000232A		F	
1762		$20	1929T1		B000266A		F/VF	
1762		$20	1929T1		D000307A		VG	
1762		$20	1929T1		E000338A		F+	
1762		$20	1929T1		C000341A		F	Foxing
1762		$20	1929T1		F000347A		VG/F	
1762		$20	1929T1		E000366A		F	bank teller stamp
1762		$20	1929T1		B000403A		VG/F	
1762		$20	1929T1		C000416A		F	
1762		$20	1929T1		A000420A		F/VF	
1762		$20	1929T1		C000433A		F/VF	
1762		$20	1929T1		D000447A		?	Higgins Mus.
1762		$20	1929T1		B000450A		VG	
1762		$20	1929T1		A000535A		F	
1762		$20	1929T1		A000567A		VF	
1762		$20	1929T1		B000573A		?	

THE BLACK HAWK NATIONAL BANK OF WATERLOO
6854   BLACK HAWK   38 L
Organized on April 17, 1903 with a capital of $100,000. Assumed #5700 by consolidation on June 15, 1904. Placed in receivership on February 13, 1925; capital of $200,000.
Officers: Pres. FF McElhinney 1904-13, FW Powers 1914-10, GB Miller 1920, RO Hutchison 1922-24; **VP** TK Elliott 1904, Richard Holmes 1907, ED Glenny 1909, FW Powers 1909-13, AE Glenny 1910-14, James Loonan 1914-24, RO Hutchison 1920; **Cash.** Chas W Knoop 1905-24; **AC** RE Cushman 1904, Lyman D Bedfor 1907-09, EA French 1910-11, HE Rugg 1913-14, EA Schaefer 1920-24

Third Charter, Red Seal	Ser #	# Notes
10-10-10-20	1-7700	30,800
Third Charter, Date Back, Blue Seal		
10-10-10-20	1-11600	46,400
Third Charter, Plain Back, Blue Seal		
10-10-10-20	11601-26951	62,124

Total amount issued = $1,732,550. Amount outstanding at close = $189,800.
138,604 Large   0 Small   138,604 Total

6854	M	$10 1902RS 613	3064 C	B975291	VG	gone/gone	
6854	M	$10 1902RS 613	6322 B	T938009	F/VF	Higgins Mus.	
6854	M	$10 1902RS 613	6737 C	Y100044	VF		
6854	M	$10 1902RS 613	7488 C	Y100795	VG	lt pen sigs	
6854	M	$10 1902DB 616	3203 D	R433924	VG+	stamp sigs vp	
6854	M	$10 1902DB 616	4507 D	Z333077	VF	stamp sigs vp	
6854	M	$10 1902DB 616	8087 D	N950771A	VF		
6854	M	$10 1902DB 616	9389 F	X15084A	F/VF		
6854	M	$10 1902DB 616	11091 F	Z893005A	AU+	F/VF?	
6854	M	$10 1902DB 616	11406 F	Z893320A	F	stamps Pressed	
6854	M	$20 1902DB 642	163 B	E877078	VF/XF		
6854	M	$20 1902DB 642	1182 B	E899897	AU		
6854	M	$20 1902DB 642	2058 B	R390009	VG		
6854	M	$20 1902DB 642	6138 B	H232769A	VG		
6854	M	$10 1902PB 624	11693 E	?	XF		
6854	M	$10 1902PB 624	12436 D	R904285B	G		
6854	M	$10 1902PB 624	13429 E	V334059B	F	stamp/stamp	
6854	M	$10 1902PB 624	13923 F	V334553B	VG		
6854	M	$10 1902PB 624	14333 D	A81440D	VF		
6854	M	$10 1902PB 624	14773 E	A81880D	VF		
6854	M	$10 1902PB 624	16539 E	M503621D	F		
6854	M	$10 1902PB 624	18101 D	U58013D	F/VF	retraced/stamp vp	
6854	M	$10 1902PB 624	19453 F	?	VG/F		
6854	M	$10 1902PB 624	22746 F	U690718E	VG		
6854	M	$10 1902PB 624	23195 D	U691167E	F/VF		
6854	M	$10 1902PB 624	23872 F	?	Fr/G		
6854	M	$10 1902PB 624	24087 E	U739069E	VF	Oat Bin Hoard	
6854	M	$10 1902PB 624	24833 F	B438535H	VF	stamp/stamp	
6854	M	$10 1902PB 624	26086 F	K248218H	CU	Higgins Mus.	
6854	M	$10 1902PB 624	26113 F	K248245H	VG/F	stamp/stamp	
6854	M	$10 1902PB 624	26288 F	K248420H	XF		
6854		$10 1902PB 624	26902 D	?	F		
6854	M	$20 1902PB 650	12859 B	V333489B	VF	stamp/stamp	
6854	M	$20 1902PB 650	14613 B	A81720D	CU		
6854	M	$20 1902PB 650	14614 B	A81721D	CU	pen ac/stamp	
6854	M	$20 1902PB 650	15062 B	A82169D	F+	stamp/stamp	
6854	M	$20 1902PB 650	21691 B	K296533E	F		
6854		$20 1902PB 650	26410 ?	?	F		

THE COMMERCIAL NATIONAL BANK OF WATERLOO 31 L
2910 BLACK HAWK

Organized on March 16, 1883 with a capital of $50,000. Succeeded The Commercial Bank. Absorbed #792 on January 13, 1931. Placed in receivership on July 18, 1932; capital of $400,000.

Officers: Pres. John D Platt 1883-88, WW Miller 1889-1918, EW Miller 1919-32; **VP** WL Illingworth 1896, EL Johnson 1900-11, Geo E Lichty 1909-11, 1914, FC Platt 1909-14, 1920-24, EW Miller 1913-14, James M Graham 1925-32, AM Place 1931, HA Maine 1931-32, WA Lane 1931-32; **Cash.** Frank L Gilbert 1883-91, AJ Edwards 1892-95, HC Schultz 1897-1919, HW Wente 1920-32; **AC** HC Schultz 1896, CW Illingworth 1900-03, EW Miller 1904-11, HW Wente 1910-14, SC Kimm 1920-32, RL Penne 1920-32, CS McKinstry 1924-32

Second Charter, Brown Backs		Ser #	# Notes
5-5-5-5		1-3508	14,032
10-10-10-20		1-2584	10,336
Third Charter, Red Seal		
10-10-10-20		1-8500	34,000
Third Charter, Date Back, Blue Seal		
10-10-10-20		1-14900	59,600
Third Charter, Plain Back, Blue Seal		
10-10-10-20		14901-27776	51,504

Total amount of circulation issued = $2,013,160. Amount outstanding in 1924 = $197,100. Amount outstanding at close = $14,055.
169,472 Large   0 Small   167,472 Total

2910	-	$5 1882BB 466	2631 A	M955294	VG	
2910	M	$10 1902RS 613	2447 A	B557894	F/VF	Higgins Mus.
2910	M	$10 1902RS 613	3839 B	E724005	VG	stamp/stamp
2910	M	$10 1902RS 613	5094 A	?	F	Davenport B&T
2910	M	$10 1902RS 613	5595 B	N677433	F/VF	
2910	M	$10 1902DB 616	427 E	D872036	VF	stamp/stamp
2910	M	$10 1902DB 616	4496 F	X321520	XF	stamp/stamp
2910	M	$10 1902DB 616	7895 D	K184108A	F+	
2910	M	$10 1902DB 616	11613 F	R881503F	VF	
2910	M	$10 1902DB 616	13217 D	K409643B	HG	stamp/stamp
2910	M	$10 1902DB 616	13905 E	K410331B	Fr/G	corners gone
2910	M	$10 1902DB 616	13909 F	K410335B	AU	Higgins Mus.
2910	M	$10 1902DB 616	13976 F	K410402B	F+	stamp/stamp
2910	M	$10 1902DB 616	14589 F	K411015B	VG	
2910	M	$10 1902DB 616	14593 E	K411019B	VF/XF	
2910	M	$20 1902DB 642	18 B	D871627	F+	
2910	M	$20 1902DB 642	2492 B	N473573	VG	
2910	M	$20 1902DB 642	7702 B	K183915A	XF	Pin holes
2910	M	$20 1902DB 642	13916 B	K410342B	?	
2910	M	$10 1902PB 624	15575 D	Y569784B	AU	Pres. sig. twice
2910	M	$10 1902PB 624	18266 F	H996688D	VF	stamp/stamp
2910	M	$10 1902PB 624	19526 D	R455788D	VG	
2910	M	$10 1902PB 624	20928 F	Z609300D	F/VF	nice sigs
2910	M	$10 1902PB 624	22440 E	H110862E	VG	stamp/stamp
2910	M	$10 1902PB 624	23123 E	H184935E	VG	pen/pen
2910	M	$10 1902PB 624	23284 E	H185096E	F/VF	
2910	M	$10 1902PB 624	23947 F	T240379E	F/VF	
2910	M	$20 1902PB 650	15183 B	Y569392B	VG/F	
2910	M	$20 1902PB 650	17351 B	H995773D	F	stamp/stamp
2910	M	$20 1902PB 650	23300 B	H185112E	F	
2910	M	$20 1902PB 650	24369 B	T300561E	F+	stamp/stamp

THE FIRST NATIONAL BANK OF WATERLOO 16 L
792 BLACK HAWK

Chartered in 1865. Placed in voluntary liquidation on January 13, 1931; capital of $200,000. Absorbed by #2910.

Officers: Pres. Martin H Moore 1867, Henry B Allen 1868-69, Robert Manson 1870-78, Henry B Allen 1879-1902, CP Bratnober 1903, CO Balliett 1904, Frank J Fowler 1905-11, Frank J Eighmey 1912-19, JW Rath 1920, Chas A Marsh 1922-30, HA Maine 1930; **VP** John W Krapfel 1896, CO Balliett 1900-03, Frank J Fowler 1904, Frank J Eighmey 1907-11, AM Place 1913-30, James Black 1914-23, HA Maine 1924-30; **Cash.** George W Couch 1867-71, Emmons Johnson 1872-73, Cyrus A Farwell 1874-75, Henry B Allen 1876-79, John W Krapfel 1879-89, Frank J Eighmey 1890-1911, HM Cowles 1912-13, 1919, CA Larson 1914-15, Will A Lane 1920-30; **AC** JES Heath 1900-03, FB Dietrick 1904-11, FP Hurst 1904-13, VJ Rechtfertig 1914, HH Cordes 1914, Paul W Eighmey 1920-27, RS Walker 1922, OL Morris 1923-27, LR Swenson 1927-30, AJ Burk 1930

First Charter, Original Issue	Ser #	# Notes
1-1-1-2	1-3100	12,400
5-5-5-5	1-1850	7,400
10-10-10-20	1-900	3,600
First Charter, Series of 1875	
5-5-5-5	1-250	1,000
10-10-10-20	1-1020	4,080
Second Charter, Brown Backs	
10-10-10-20	1-5903	23,612
Third Charter, Red Seal	
50-100	1-1900	3,800
Third Charter, Date Back, Blue Seal	
50-100	1-1400	2,800
50-50-50-100	1-2763	11,052

Total amount of circulation issued = $1,634,400. Amount outstanding in 1924 = $198,000. Amount outstanding at close = $40,580.
69,744 Large   0 Small   69,744 Total

792	-	$1	ORIG 380	1338 B	980052	VG/F	
792	-	$1	ORIG 380	1835 C	B916955	VG	Higgins Mus.
792	-	$1	ORIG 380	2812 C	C691299	F	pen/pen
792	-	$10 1882BB 480		3358 B	X672685C	VG	
792	M	$50 1902DB 667		795 E	A238819	VG+	ac corners gone
792	M	$50 1902DB 667		1017 D	A706751	VF	Higgins Mus.
792	M	$50 1902DB 667		2003 E	A868145	VG	gone/gone
792	M	$50 1902DB 667		2190 C	A922722	F	stamp/stamp
792	M	$50 1902DB 667		2654 D	B44968	VG/F	
792	M	$100 1902DB 689		475 C	A72316	VG	

147

792	M$100 1902DB	689	1913 C	A868055	VF		
792	M$100 1902DB	689	1921 C	A868063	VF		
792	M$100 1902DB	689	2167 C	A922699	VF		
792	M$100 1902DB	689	2207 C	A922739	F		
792	M$100 1902DB	689	2209 C	A972741	AU		
792	M$100 1902DB	689	2736 C	B45050	F		

THE LEAVITT AND JOHNSON NATIONAL BANK OF WATERLOO
5120 (FIRST TITLE) BLACK HAWK 49 L

Founders J. H. Leavitt and Emmous Johnson gave this bank its name, one of four private name banks in Iowa.

Organized on April 12, 1898 with a capital of $100,000. Succeeded Leavitt & Johnson. Title changed to The Pioneer National Bank of Waterloo on May 26, 1926.

Officers: Pres. JH Leavitt 1898-1902, Emmous Johnson 1903-05, JE Sedgwick 1906-18, Ira Rodamar 1919-26; **VP** Emmous Johnson 1900, Thos. Cascaden, Jr. 1902, Elbert L Johnson 1903, JR Vaughan 1904, CE Pickett 1907-26, CL Kingsley 1910, 1914, JO Trumbauer 1910, 1914-26; **Cash.** Ira Rodamar 1898-1918, Wm C Logan 1903, Fred H Wray 1919-26; **AC** Ira J Hoover 1900-02, 1904, John La Bam 1903, Emma Rodamar 1909-11, WF McGarvey 1913, CJ McNulty 1914, RE Miller 1920-26, R Rouse 1920-24, Ira Blough 1923-26, AM Decker 1923-26

	Ser #	# Notes
Second Charter, Brown Backs		
10-10-10-20	1-10800	43,200
Second Charter, Date Back		
5-5-5-5	1-5000	20,000
10-10-10-20	1-13800	55,200
Second Charter, Value Back		
5-5-5-5	5001-6000	4,000
10-10-10-20	13801-14364	2,256
Third Charter, Plain Back, Blue Seal		
5-5-5-5	1-16129	64,516
10-10-10-20	1-11107	44,428

233,600 Large   0 Small   233,600 Total

5120	-	$10 1882BB	490	2 B	T429543	CU	ac Leavitt sig
5120	-	$10 1882BB	490	28 A	T429569	VF	Leavitt sig. Pres.
5120	M	$10 1882BB	490	3975 C	Z948223	F+	Higgins Mus.
5120	M	$10 1882BB	490	4117 B	Z948365	F	
5120	M	$10 1882BB	490	6190 C	N99680N	XF	Higgins Mus.
5120	M	$10 1882BB	490	6214 A	N99704N	XF	
5120	M	$10 1882BB	490	7359 C	R494973R	VG+	pen/pen vp
5120	M	$10 1882BB	490	7630 A	R495244R	F	pen/pen vp
5120	M	$10 1882BB	490	10618 A	U671166U	F	pen/pen
5120	M	$20 1882BB	504	7681 A	R495295R	VG+	pen/pen vp
5120	M	$20 1882BB	504	7854 A	T126891T	F	pen/pen
5120	M	$20 1882BB	504	10010 A	U652218U	F+	
5120	M	$20 1882BB	504	10361 A	U670909U	F	
5120	M	$20 1882BB	504	10496 A	U671044U	VF+	pen/pen
5120	M	$5 1882DB	537	1300 B	R359937	VG	gone/gone
5120	M	$5 1882DB	537	2246 D	R365183	F/VF	
5120	M	$10 1882DB	545	9299 F	M989427	VG	gone/gone
5120	M	$10 1882DB	545	9973 D	M993601	XF	
5120	M	$10 1882DB	545	10621 F	N804529	F/VF	gone/gone
5120	M	$20 1882DB	555	12957 B	T185985	G	gone/gone
5120	M	$20 1882DB	555	13324 B	T186352	VG	gone/gone
5120	M	$5 1882VB	574	5268 C	T335005	VF/XF	Higgins Mus.
5120	M	$5 1882VB	574	5713 B	T335450	VF	Pinholes; pressed
5120	M	$20 1882VB	581	13857 B	U226955	F	faded/faded
5120	M	$5 1902PB	606	573 B	Z408659B	VG	
5120	M	$5 1902PB	606	853 C	A747144D	VF/XF	
5120	M	$5 1902PB	606	2862 A	H549013D	F	faded/faded
5120	M	$5 1902PB	606	7306 B	D164727E	VF+	
5120	M	$5 1902PB	606	8422 C	H234318E	G	gone/gone
5120	M	$5 1902PB	606	9714 D	Y657345E	XF	stamp/stamp
5120	M	$5 1902PB	606	12441 B	N715152H	CU	Higgins Mus.
5120	M	$5 1902PB	606	13504 ?	U746540H	VG	
5120	M	$5 1902PB	606	13676 A	U746712H	F+	
5120	-	$5 1902PB	606	14586 C	Z885922H	XF	
5120	-	$5 1902PB	606	15510 C	15510 C	F	
5120	M	$10 1902PB	632	1604 A	K384436D	VG	
5120	M	$10 1902PB	632	5230 A	M300612E	F/VF	
5120	M	$10 1902PB	632	6997 C	A600539H	VF	
5120	M	$10 1902PB	632	7365 C	K390787H	VF	gone/gone
5120	-	$10 1902PB	632	11004 A	11004 A	VG	
5120	M	$20 1902PB	658	809 A	D447316D	VF	
5120	M	$20 1902PB	658	977 A	D447484D	?	
5120	M	$20 1902PB	658	4686 A	H220758E	F/VF	
5120	M	$20 1902PB	658	5934 A	M301316E	F	stamp/stamp
5120	M	$20 1902PB	658	7099 A	A600641H	F/VF	
5120	M	$20 1902PB	658	7965 A	K391387H	F	
5120		$20 1902PB	658	9602 A	A959074K	F	
5120	-	$20 1902PB	658	10580 A	10580 A	VF	stamp/stamp
5120	-	$20 1902PB	658	10971 A	10971 A	F+	stamp/stamp

THE PIONEER NATIONAL BANK OF WATERLOO 22 L 44 L
5120 (2ND TITLE) BLACK HAWK

Succeeded The Leavitt & Johnson National Bank of Waterloo on May 26, 1926. Placed in receivership on February 18, 1932; capital of $200,000.

Officers: Pres. Ira Rodamar 1926-32; **VP** CE Pickett 1926-31, JO Trumbauer 1926-32, Fred H Wray 1930-32, CA Clark 1932, JA Young 1932, DJ Walker 1932, Bert McCulloch 1932; **Cash.** Fred H Wray 1926-32; **AC** RE Miller 1926-32, Ira Blough 1926-32, AM Decker 1926-32, M Harmon 1929-32, WA Dewess 1929, Robert Stewart 1930-32, EM Greene 1931-32

	Ser #	# Notes
Third Charter, Plain Back, Blue Seal		
5-5-5-5	1-17971	71,884
1929, Type I		
6-5's	1-13510	81,060

Total amount of circulation issued = $3,020,850. Amount of large outstanding at close = $24,615. Amount of small outstanding at close = $172,325.

71,884 Large   81,060 Small   152,944 Total

5120	-	$5 1902PB	606	1 C	1 C	VF	
5120	-	$5 1902PB	606	677 B	677 B	F	
5120	-	$5 1902PB	606	1040 C	1040 C	VG	stamp/stamp
5120	-	$5 1902PB	606	3127 A	3127 A	G/VG	stamp/stamp
5120	-	$5 1902PB	606	3163 C	3163 C	VG	
5120	-	$5 1902PB	606	3869 C	3869 C	F	
5120	-	$5 1902PB	606	4039 C	4039 C	XF	stamp/stamp
5120	-	$5 1902PB	606	4449 D	4449 D	F/VF	
5120	-	$5 1902PB	606	4794 B	4794 B	F	
5120	-	$5 1902PB	606	4965 C	4965 C	XF	
5120	-	$5 1902PB	606	6434 C	6434 C	F	gone/gone
5120	-	$5 1902PB	606	6989 D	6989 D	F	Water Stains
5120	-	$5 1902PB	606	7546 D	7546 D	VG/F	stamp/stamp
5120	-	$5 1902PB	606	10232 B	10232 B	F/VF	
5120	-	$5 1902PB	606	10828 B	10828 B	CU	Higgins Mus.
5120	-	$5 1902PB	606	12468 A	12468 A	VG	stamp/stamp
5120	-	$5 1902PB	606	12777 D	12777 D	F/VF	Davenport B&T
5120	-	$5 1902PB	606	13110 D	13110 D	VF	
5120	-	$5 1902PB	606	13139 B	13139 B	G/VG	stamp/stamp
5120	-	$5 1902PB	606	13833 B	13833 B	VG	
5120	-	$5 1902PB	606	15247 B	15247 B	VG/F	stamp/stamp
5120	-	$5 1902PB	606	16316 C	16316 C	XF	stamp/stamp
5120		$5 1929T1		A000279A		VF	
5120		$5 1929T1		D000418A		F	
5120		$5 1929T1		E001094A		G/VG	
5120		$5 1929T1		F001684A		VG/F	
5120		$5 1929T1		F001949A		F	
5120		$5 1929T1		F003093A		VG	
5120		$5 1929T1		D003594A		VG	
5120		$5 1929T1		F003786A		F	
5120		$5 1929T1		B004478A		VG	
5120		$5 1929T1		C004686A		F/VF	
5120		$5 1929T1		B005091A		G	
5120		$5 1929T1		A005549A		AG	
5120		$5 1929T1		C006112A		F/VF	
5120		$5 1929T1		F007287A		G/VG	
5120		$5 1929T1		B007552A		VG/F	
5120		$5 1929T1		E008085A		?	
5120		$5 1929T1		A008477A		F/VF	
5120		$5 1929T1		B008533A		VG	LL corner torn
5120		$5 1929T1		C008594A		XF	
5120		$5 1929T1		B008673A		XF	
5120		$5 1929T1		F008697A		VG	
5120		$5 1929T1		E009113A		VG+	
5120		$5 1929T1		F009503A		VF	
5120		$5 1929T1		F009812A		F	
5120		$5 1929T1		B009824A		F	
5120		$5 1929T1		C010064A		XF	
5120		$5 1929T1		C010085A		AU	Higgins Mus.
5120		$5 1929T1		C010464A		VF	
5120		$5 1929T1		A010901A		G/VG	
5120		$5 1929T1		A011033A		F	
5120		$5 1929T1		B011521A		VG	
5120		$5 1929T1		A011635A		F/VF	
5120		$5 1929T1		D012140A		F	
5120		$5 1929T1		C012183A		F/VF	
5120		$5 1929T1		C012268A		XF/AU	
5120		$5 1929T1		A012369A		VG/F	
5120		$5 1929T1		A012452A		VF	
5120		$5 1929T1		D012476A		VF	
5120		$5 1929T1		C012527A		VG/F	
5120		$5 1929T1		C012611A		XF	

5120	$5 1929T1	B013056A		VG	Soiled	
5120	$5 1929T1	B013163A		F		
5120	$5 1929T1	B013205A		VF		
5120	$5 1929T1	F013240A		G/VG		

THE NATIONAL BANK OF WATERLOO   24 S
13702   BLACK HAWK
Chartered in June 1933.
Officers: Pres. James M Graham 1933-35; **VP** RP Lien 1933-34, Chas. S McKinstry 1935; **Cash.** Chas. S McKinstry 1933-34, RL Penne 1935; **AC** RL Penne 1933-34, HF Hoffer 1935, Lawrence Kilgore 1935

1929, Type II	Ser #	# Notes
5's	1-19040	19,040
10's	1-10329	10,329

Total amount issued = $198,490. Amount outstanding in July 1935 =$130,950
0 Large   29,369 Small   29,369 Total

13702	$5 1929T2	A004344		VF	
13702	$5 1929T2	A009694		VG	
13702	$5 1929T2	A009976		F	tight on bottom
13702	$5 1929T2	A010975		VF	
13702	$5 1929T2	A014505		VF	
13702	$5 1929T2	A015846		G/VG	
13702	$5 1929T2	A016807		F/VF	
13702	$5 1929T2	A016971		XF/AU	
13702	$5 1929T2	A017719		AU	
13702	$10 1929T2	A000005		XF	
13702	$10 1929T2	A001900		VG	
13702	$10 1929T2	A002407		F/VF	
13702	$10 1929T2	A002548		F	
13702	$10 1929T2	A004112		F	
13702	$10 1929T2	A004753		VG/F	
13702	$10 1929T2	A004840		VG	
13702	$10 1929T2	A005586		AU	Higgins Mus.
13702	$10 1929T2	A005808		F/VF	
13702	$10 1929T2	A006011		VF	
13702	$10 1929T2	A006920		VF	
13702	$10 1929T2	A007476		VF	
13702	$10 1929T2	A007549		F/VF	
13702	$10 1929T2	A007561		F	
13702	$10 1929T2	A009844		VF/XF	

THE WATERLOO NATIONAL BANK   4 L
5700   BLACK HAWK
Chartered on February 4, 1901. Succeeded The Waterloo State Bank. Placed in voluntary liquidation on June 15, 1904; capital of $100,000. Consolidated with #6854.
Officers: Pres. Richard Holmes 1901-02, JD Easton 1903, Richard Holmes 1904; **VP** JR Vaughn 1902-03, Chas Biebesheimer 1904; **Cash.** JD Easton 1901-02, GN Garrettson 1903-04; **AC** RM Knox 1902-03

Second Charter, Brown Backs	Ser #	# Notes
10-10-10-20	1-1383	5,532

Total amount of circulation issued = $69,150. Amount outstanding at close = $49,200. Amount outstanding in 1910 = $4,130.
5,532 Large   0 Small   5,532 Total

5700	- $10 1882BB	490	67 B	Y409294	AU	Higgins Mus.
5700	- $10 1882BB	490	1008 B	Y438210	CU	Smithsonian
5700	- $10 1882BB	490	1285 C	Y438487	VF	? Grinnell # 3959
5700	- $20 1882BB	504	817 A	Y410044	F/VF	Davenport B&T

THE FIRST NATIONAL BANK OF WAUKON   19 L
4921   ALLAMAKEE
Organized on April 22, 1893 with a capital of $50,000. Succeeded The Bank of Waukon. Placed in receivership on January 18, 1926; capital of $100,000. Reason for failure: local depression.
Officers: Pres. BF Boomer 1893, WJ Mitchell 1894-96, John M Barthell 1897-1901, OJ Hager 1902-25; **VP** JM Barthell 1896, HS Opfer 1900-09, E Dillenberg 1910-20, JC Ludeking 1922-25, Burt Hendrick 1923-25; **Cash.** OJ Hager 1893-1901, AT Nierling 1902-20, OH Grangaard 1922-25, JC Ludeking 1925; **AC** AT Nierling 1896-1900, JC Ludeking 1907-20, EA Allanson 1920, CF Simmons 1925

Second Charter, Brown Backs	Ser #	# Notes
5-5-5-5	1-2140	8,560
10-10-10-20	1-2294	9,176
Second Charter, Date Back		
5-5-5-5	1-2115	8,460
10-10-10-20	1-1267	5,068
Third Charter, Date Back, Blue Seal		
10-10-10-20	1-2800	11,200
Third Charter, Plain Back, Blue Seal		
10-10-10-20	2801-10287	29,948

Total amount issued = $777,500. Amount outstanding at close = $93,200.
72,412 Large   0 Small   72,412 Total

4921	M	$5 1882BB	472	1945 C	V173178V	VF	pen/pen
4921	M	$5 1882BB	472	1947 A	V173180V	F	pen/pen
4921	-	$10 1882BB	485	420 C	X717497	XF	pen/pen vp
4921	M	$10 1882BB	485	1926 B	R970973R	VF	Repair; 1928 B ?
4921	M	$20 1882BB	499	2236 A	V222635V	G+	
4921	M	$10 1882BB	540	277 E	D473827	F+	pen/pen Soiling
4921	M	$10 1902DB	622	1482 C	T347472A	F	pen/pen
4921	M	$10 1902DB	622	2235 C	B681157B	F	gone/gone
4921	M	$20 1902DB	648	1301 A	T347291A	F+	
4921	M	$10 1902PB	630	3524 C	R973729	CU	
4921	M	$10 1902PB	630	5234 C	R392946D	VF/F	pen Higgins Mus.
4921	M	$10 1902PB	630	6313 C	Z988115D	VF/XF	pen/pen
4921	M	$10 1902PB	630	7092 C	K548694E	VG	
4921	M	$10 1902PB	630	7522 B	K549124E	VF+	
4921	M	$20 1902PB	656	2935 A	U9053B	F	
4921	M	$20 1902PB	656	5069 A	H528379D	F	
4921	M	$20 1902PB	656	6867 A	K548469E	F	pen/pen
4921	M	$20 1902PB	656	7729 A	U979071E	F/VF	
4921		$20 1902PB	656	9629 A	U398591H	?	

THE PEOPLES NATIONAL BANK OF WAUKON   24 L
10207   ALLAMAKEE
Organized on May 1, 1912 with a capital of $50,000. Placed in receivership on July 19, 1927; capital of $125,000. Reason for failure: incompetent management & local depression.
Officers: Pres. Theo B Stock 1912-24, WH Hale 1926-27; **VP** LT Hermanson 1913-27, AT Nierling 1922-24, , JP Bieber 1926-27; **Cash.** PE O'Donnell 1912-24, Theo B Stock 1926-27; **AC** JP Bieber 1920-24, PE O'Donnell 1926-27

Third Charter, Date Back, Blue Seal	Ser #	#Notes
10-10-10-20	1-1500	6,000
Third Charter, Plain Back, Blue Seal		
10-10-10-20	1501-11658	40,632

Total amount issued = $582,900. Amount outstanding at close = $123,200.
46,632 Large   0 Small   46,632 Total

10207	$10 1902PB	628	?	B706??	VG	
10207M	$10 1902PB	628	1854 C	T777094B	F	
10207M	$10 1902PB	628	2062 C	T777302B	VG	pen/pen Soiled
10207M	$10 1902PB	628	2548 B	B463425D	XF	
10207M	$10 1902PB	628	2831 A	H881081D	F	
10207M	$10 1902PB	628	8014 ?	H69768H	?	
10207M	$10 1902PB	628	8510 B	H698182H	F/VF	pen/pen vp rust
10207 -	$10 1902PB	628	9005 A	R563507H	VG	
10207 -	$10 1902PB	628	9057 B	R563559H	F	
10207 -	$10 1902PB	628	9100 A	R563602H	F/VF	pen/pen
10207 -	$10 1902PB	628	10477 B	10477 B	VF	ac/vp Higg. Mus.
10207 -	$10 1902PB	628	10951 A	10951 A	CU	Cut Sheet, Grinnell lot # 1558
10207 -	$10 1902PB	628	10951 B	10951 B	CU	Grinnell # 1558
10207 -	$10 1902PB	628	10951 C	10951 C	CU	Grinnell # 1558
10207 -	$10 1902PB	628	10973 A	10973 A	CU	ac
10207 -	$10 1902PB	628	10973 C	10973 C	CU	stamp ac/pen
10207 -	$10 1902PB	628	11150 A	11150 A	F/VF	
10207 -	$10 1902PB	628	11376 A	11376 A	G/VG	
10207 -	$10 1902PB	628	11523 C	11523 C	VG/F	
10207M	$20 1902PB	654	1854 A	T777094B	F+	
10207M	$20 1902PB	654	3135 A	R381647D	VF	
10207M	$20 1902PB	654	6352 A	T214714E	VF	
10207 -	$20 1902PB	654	9198 A	R563700H	?	pen ac/pen vp
10207 -	$20 1902PB	654	10951 A	10951 A	CU	Grinnell # 1558

THE FIRST NATIONAL BANK OF WAVERLY   42 L   38 S
3105   BREMER
Chartered in 1884. Succeeded by Bank of Waverly. Consolidated with The Bremer County Bank in 1885.

Officers: Pres. JH Bowman 1884-98, HS Burr 1899, RH Sewell 1900-03, Emmons Johnson 1903-13, EL Johnson 1914-35; **VP** WD Lashbrook 1900, EH Curtis 1902-03, RH Sewell 1904-33, WH Wehrmacher 1920-35; **Cash.** HS Burr 1884-98, AF Bodeker 1899, Henry Kasemeier 1901-16, W Weiditschka 1916-30, HC Nolting 1930-35; **AC** AF Bodeker 1896, Henry Kasemeier 1900, W Weiditschka 1902-14, Roy Herrmann 1920-27, HC Nolting 1927-30, WH Ray 1930-34, Geo A

149

Stephenson 1930-35, FH Keseberg 1935

Second Charter, Brown Backs	Ser #	# Notes
5-5-5-5	1-500	2,000
10-10-10-20	1-2651	10,604
Third Charter, Red Seal		
10-10-10-20	1-3900	15,600
Third Charter, Date Back, Blue Seal		
10-10-10-20	1-5900	23,600
Third Charter, Plain Back, Blue Seal		
10-10-10-20	5901-16621	42,884
1929, Type I		
6-10's	1-2006	12,036
6-20's	1-518	3,108
1929, Type II		
10's	1-825	825
20's	1-165	165

Total amount of circulation issued = $1,361,470. Amount of large outstanding in 1935 = $7,140. Amount of small outstanding in 1935 = $42,860.
94,688 Large   16,134 Small   110,822 Total

3105	M	$10 1902RS	613	3637 C	X74171	VG/F	
3105	M	$20 1902RS	639	285 A	B475100	VF+	Higgins Mus.
3105	M	$20 1902RS	639	1626 A	E936998	F	pen/pen vp
3105	M	$10 1902DB	616	4419 D	U915615A	F/VF	pen/pen
3105	M	$10 1902DB	616	4866 D	U916062A	VG	
3105	M	$20 1902DB	642	2347 B	Z795130	F	Oat Bin Hoard
3105	M	$20 1902DB	642	4746 B	U915942A	HG	pen/faded
3105	M	$20 1902DB	642	5603 B	B372071B	F+	pen/pen vp
3105	M	$10 1902PB	624	6401 D	V161323B	F/VF	pen/stamp vp
3105	M	$10 1902PB	624	6750 E	Z202963B	?	
3105	M	$10 1902PB	624	7409 F	D664436D	VG/F	pen/gone Ink
3105	M	$10 1902PB	624	8683 F	U129155D	F	pen/pen vp
3105	M	$10 1902PB	624	8772 E	U129244D	VG	very faded vp
3105	M	$10 1902PB	624	9667 D	D277889E	VF	
3105	M	$10 1902PB	624	10660 D	M823567E	AU	
3105	M	$10 1902PB	624	11097 D	Y228419E	F	pen/gone
3105		$10 1902PB	624	11667 ?	?	F	
3105		$10 1902PB	624	13485 E	A409567K	F	
3105	-	$10 1902PB	624	13717 D	13717 D	F	
3105	-	$10 1902PB	624	14128 F	14128 F	AU	
3105	-	$10 1902PB	624	14227 E	14227 E	AU	pen/faded
3105	-	$10 1902PB	624	14236 E	14236 E	F	
3105	-	$10 1902PB	624	14302 E	14302 F	Fr/G	pen/gone
3105	-	$10 1902PB	624	14308 F	14308 F	VF	pen/gone
3105	-	$10 1902PB	624	15819 D	15819 D	CU	Higgins Mus.
3105	-	$10 1902PB	624	15820 D	15820 D	CU	pen/pen vp
3105	-	$10 1902PB	624	15820 E	15820 E	CU	
3105	-	$10 1902PB	624	15820 F	15820 F	CU	pen/pen vp
3105	-	$10 1902PB	624	16483 F	16483 F	HG	pen/pen vp
3105	M	$20 1902PB	650	6001 B	V160923B	AU	
3105	M	$20 1902PB	650	6008 B	V160930B	AU	
3105	M	$20 1902PB	650	10334 B	M823241E	VG	
3105	M	$20 1902PB	650	10445 B	M823352E	F	
3105	M	$20 1902PB	650	11473 B	D568295H	F	
3105		$20 1902PB	650	13133 B	A409215K	XF	
3105	-	$20 1902PB	650	13948 B	13948 B	VG/F	
3105	-	$20 1902PB	650	15080 B	15080 B	XF	
3105	-	$20 1902PB	650	15158 B	15158 B	CU	
3105	-	$20 1902PB	650	15571 B	15571 B	?	
3105	-	$20 1902PB	650	15822 B	15822 B	AU+	Grinnell # 3968
3105	-	$20 1902PB	650	16176 B	16176 B	HG	
3105	-	$20 1902PB	650	16522 B	16522 B	VF	
3105		$10 1929T1		F000029A		CU	
3105		$10 1929T1		E000070A		AU	Higgins Mus.
3105		$10 1929T1		A000089A		CU	A000090A ?
3105		$10 1929T1		F000092A		CU	
3105		$10 1929T1		D000093A		CU	
3105		$10 1929T1		F000093A		CU	
3105		$10 1929T1		F000094A		CU	Ink
3105		$10 1929T1		A000099A		CU	Pinholes
3105		$10 1929T1		C000522A		VG	
3105		$10 1929T1		A000665A		VF/XF	
3105		$10 1929T1		F000702A		VG	
3105		$10 1929T1		C000764A		VF	Ink on back
3105		$10 1929T1		A000791A		?	
3105		$10 1929T1		D000953A		XF	
3105		$10 1929T1		B001030A		VG/F	
3105		$10 1929T1		B001461A		F/VF	
3105		$10 1929T1		E001461A		VF	
3105		$10 1929T1		A001659A		VG	
3105		$10 1929T1		A001764A		F	
3105		$10 1929T1		C001782A		F/VF	
3105		$10 1929T1		A001787A		VF	
3105		$10 1929T1		C001787A		AU	
3105		$10 1929T1		A001809A		VF	
3105		$10 1929T1		E001927A		F	Pressed
3105		$20 1929T1		E000030A		F	
3105		$20 1929T1		B000160A		VF	
3105		$20 1929T1		E000217A		F/VF	
3105		$20 1929T1		F000256A		G+	
3105		$20 1929T1		B000260A		XF	
3105		$20 1929T1		D000269A		VF	
3105		$20 1929T1		C000273A		F	
3105		$20 1929T1		A000309A		VF+	
3105		$20 1929T1		A000311A		XF	
3105		$20 1929T1		C000413A		F	
3105		$20 1929T1		A000417A		VG	
3105		$20 1929T1		A000431A		VF	
3105		$20 1929T1		D000441A		F	
3105		$20 1929T1		B000485A		VF	

THE FARMERS NATIONAL BANK OF WEBSTER CITY
3420   **HAMILTON**   **8 L   21 S**

Organized on November 23, 1885 with a capital of $50,000. Succeeded The Farmers Bank (Miller & Mattice). Placed in conservatorship on March 30, 1933. Licensed on November 17, 1933.

Officers: Pres. BF Miller 1887-90, JM Jones 1891-1908, RE Jones 1909-35; **VP** Geo. Shipp 1896, RE Jones 1900-07, JM Jones 1909-14, HA Crandall 1920-25, Varick C Crosley 1925-33, JE Burnstedt 1934-35; **Cash.** Aug. F Hoffman 1887-91, JH Shipp 1892-1933, GE Alexander 1934-35; **AC** WG Howard 1900, SK Virtue 1904-27, MF Johnson 1920-33, BA Wilson 1920-33, GE Alexander 1927-33

Second Charter, Brown Backs	Ser #	# Notes
10-10-10-20	1-3466	13,864
Third Charter, Red Seal		
10-10-10-20	1-1000	4,000
Third Charter, Date Back, Blue Seal		
10-10-10-20 (3401-3650 type uncertain)	1-3650	14,600
Third Charter, Plain Back, Blue Seal		
10-10-10-20	3651-9533	23,532
1929, Type I		
6-10's	1-956	5,736
6-20's	1-302	1,812
1929, Type II		
10's	1-1429	1,429
20's	1-308	308

Total amount of circulation issued = $814,000. Amount of large outstanding in 1935 = $3,110. Amount of small outstanding in 1935 = $46,890.
55,996 Large   9,285 Small   65,281 Total

3420	M	$10 1902DB	617	1710 F	X832696	VG	pen ac/pen vp
3420	M	$20 1902DB	643	2044 B	E186103A	VG	
3420	M	$10 1902PB	625	6837 E	D614899H	F/VF	stamp/stamp
3420	-	$10 1902PB	625	9304 D	9304 D	F	stamp/stamp
3420	M	$20 1902PB	651	4089 B	Y420700B	F	stamp/stamp
3420	M	$20 1902PB	651	4330 B	B116087D	VG/F	gone/gone
3420	M	$20 1902PB	651	5671 B	A962133E	G/VG	Higgins Mus.
3420	-	$20 1902PB	651	7645 B	A180677K	F	
3420		$10 1929T1		C000100A		CU	
3420		$10 1929T1		A000187A		G/VG	
3420		$10 1929T1		E000638A		VG+	
3420		$10 1929T1		A000643A		F+	
3420		$10 1929T1		B000791A		VF	
3420		$20 1929T1		F000001A		F	Closed pinholes
3420		$20 1929T1		D000012A		F	Higgins Mus.
3420		$20 1929T1		A000020A		VG/F	
3420		$20 1929T1		B000020A		VG/F	
3420		$20 1929T1		F000118A		VG	Stained
3420		$20 1929T1		D000182A		VG+	
3420		$20 1929T1		D000186A		VG/F	
3420		$20 1929T1		F000186A		XF/AU	
3420		$20 1929T1		E000195A		VF	
3420		$20 1929T1		E000217A		F	
3420		$20 1929T1		D000223A		CU	
3420		$10 1929T2		A000394		F	
3420		$10 1929T2		A000967		VG/F	
3420		$20 1929T2		A000001		XF/AU	
3420		$20 1929T2		A000074		VF	Pressed
3420		$20 1929T2		A000273		F/VF	

THE FIRST NATIONAL BANK OF WEBSTER CITY   **39 L   25 S**
1874   **HAMILTON**

Organized on August 10, 1871 with a capital of $50,000. Chartered on September 8, 1871. Placed in receivership on November 30, 1932; capital of

$100,000. Reason for failure: not available from reports.
Officers: Pres. Kendall Young 1871-95, LL Estes 1896-1909, WJ Covil 1910-20, EF King 1922-26, Wesley Martin 1927-32; **VP** LL Estes 1895, WJ Covil 1900-09, Elston F King 1910-20, WC Pile 1922-24, JW Young 1925-26, EG Fardal 1927-32; **Cash.** OK Eastman 1871-75, Bradford S Mason 1876-85, BC Mason 1887-96, Wm Anderson 1897-09, HW McDonald 1900-03, Aug F Hoffman 1903-05, Elston F King 1906-09, Warren C Pile 1910-20, EE Mason 1922-32; **AC** OJ Waite 1878-79, BC Mason 1885, S Sogard 1896, HP Mason 1900-02, CL Treat 1903, Warren C Pile 1907-14, HO Cutler 1910-26, Earl E Mason 1910-20, WL Clifton 1920-29

First Charter, Original Issue	Ser #	# Notes
1-1-1-2	1-1500	6,000
5-5-5-5	1-3375	13,500
First Charter, Series of 1875		
5-5-5-5	1-5876	23,504
Second Charter, Brown Backs		
5-5-5-5	1-2400	9,600
10-10-10-20	1-3630	14,520
Second Charter, Date Back		
5-5-5-5	1-1985	7,940
10-10-10-20	1-1657	6,628
Third Charter, Date Back, Blue Seal		
10-10-10-20	1-5600	22,400
Third Charter, Plain Back, Blue Seal		
10-10-10-20	5601-16557	43,828
1929, Type I		
6-10's	1-1810	10,860
6-20's	1-492	2,952

Total amount of circulation issued = $1,570,060. Amount of large outstanding at close = $13,650. Amount of small outstanding at close = $86,350.
147,920 Large   13,812 Small   161,732 Total

Year		Denom	Type	Plate	Ser # Bank	Ser # Treasury	Grade	Notes
1874	-	$5	ORIG	399	2453 A	U52593	F	Higgins Mus.
1874		$20	1882BB	499	1580 A	W618594	VF/XF	
1874	M	$10	1882DB	540	1236 E	E378230	VG/F	
1874	M	$10	1902DB	620	4170 B	B35636B	VG	gone/gone
1874	M	$10	1902DB	620	5121 A	M946507B	F	Repaired
1874	M	$10	1902DB	620	5367 C	M946753B	F	gone/gone
1874	M	$20	1902DB	646	729 A	B476041A	VF	faded/faded
1874	M	$20	1902DB	646	4934 A	M946320B	?	Bayard
1874		$10	1902PB	628	9239 C	D785121E	VG/F	
1874		$10	1902PB	628	11589 A	D552371H	?	
1874		$10	1902PB	628	12107 C	K863899H	VG	
1874	-	$10	1902PB	628	12365 B	U392777H	VG	gone/gone
1874	-	$10	1902PB	628	12557 ?	U392969H	?	
1874	-	$10	1902PB	628	14672 A	14672 A	VG	
1874	-	$10	1902PB	628	14802 B	14802 B	F	
1874	-	$10	1902PB	628	14802 C	14802 C	XF	
1874	-	$10	1902PB	628	14868 C	14868 C	F/VF	gone/pen vp
1874	-	$10	1902PB	628	16141 A	16141 A	CU	faded/faded vp
1874	-	$10	1902PB	628	16143 B	16143 B	F	gone/gone vp
1874	-	$10	1902PB	628	16144 A	16144 A	AU	very faded vp
1874	-	$10	1902PB	628	16144 B	16144 B	AU	
1874	-	$10	1902PB	628	16146 C	16146 C	VF/XF	very faded vp
1874	-	$10	1902PB	628	16257 C	16257 C	CU	
1874	-	$10	1902PB	628	16259 A	16259 A	CU	very faded vp
1874	-	$10	1902PB	628	16260 C	16260 C	AU	faded sigs vp
1874	-	$10	1902PB	628	16261 B	16261 B	CU	
1874	-	$10	1902PB	628	16261 C	16261 C	CU	
1874	-	$20	1902PB	654	10882 A	Y367644E	VG+	
1874	-	$20	1902PB	654	16143 A	16143 A	XF	
1874	-	$20	1902PB	654	16157 A	16157 A	XF	Higgins Mus.
1874	-	$20	1902PB	654	16159 A	16159 A	CU	faded sigs vp
1874	-	$20	1902PB	654	16160 A	16160 A	CU	
1874	-	$20	1902PB	654	16161 A	16161 A	CU	gone/gone
1874	-	$20	1902PB	654	16197 A	16197 A	VF/XF	gone/gone vp
1874	-	$20	1902PB	654	16242 A	16242 A	AU	
1874	-	$20	1902PB	654	16248 A	16248 A	AU	faded sigs vp
1874	-	$20	1902PB	654	16251 A	16251 A	VG	gone/gone vp
1874	-	$20	1902PB	654	16260 A	16260 A	XF	faded/faded
1874	-	$20	1902PB	654	16263 A	16263 A	XF	faded sigs vp
1874		$10	1929T1		D000007A		VF	
1874		$10	1929T1		C000180A		VF	
1874		$10	1929T1		A000424A		F	
1874		$10	1929T1		F000941A		F+	Higgins Mus.
1874		$10	1929T1		A001014A		VG/F	
1874		$10	1929T1		F001146A		VG	
1874		$10	1929T1		E001149A		F	
1874		$10	1929T1		B001181A		F	
1874		$10	1929T1		F001506A		VF	
1874		$10	1929T1		C001525A		F	
1874		$10	1929T1		F001605A		VF+	
1874		$10	1929T1		A001689A		VF	
1874		$20	1929T1		C000015A		VG+	
1874		$20	1929T1		C000020A		?	
1874		$20	1929T1		D000048A		F	
1874		$20	1929T1		E000140A		VG	
1874		$20	1929T1		D000163A		VG	
1874		$20	1929T1		E000166A		?	
1874		$20	1929T1		C000297A		F	
1874		$20	1929T1		E000297A		?	
1874		$20	1929T1		E000299A		F	
1874		$20	1929T1		C000301A		F	
1874		$20	1929T1		D000357A		G	
1874		$20	1929T1		E000392A		VF/XF	
1874		$20	1929T1		C000406A		F	

THE HAMILTON COUNTY NATIONAL BANK OF WEBSTER CITY
2984   HAMILTON   0 L
Chartered on June 20, 1883. Succeeded The Hamilton County Bank (McMurray & Eastman). Placed in voluntary liquidation on June 30, 1890; capital of $50,000.
Officers: Pres. LA McMurray 1883-90; **VP** OK Eastman 1883-85, Cyrus Smith 1887-90

Second Charter, Brown Backs	Ser #	# Notes
5-5-5-5	1-1337	5,348

Total amount of circulation issued = $26,740. Amount outstanding at close = $11,250. Amount outstanding in 1910 = $220.
5,348 Large   0 Small   5,348 Total

THE FIRST NATIONAL BANK OF WESLEY   3 L
5457   KOSSUTH
Organized on June 26, 1900 with a capital of $25,000. Succeeded The Wesley State Bank. Placed in receivership on October 12, 1928; capital of $25,000. Reason for failure: local depression.
Officers: Pres. Nathan Studer 1900-02, Stitzel X Way 1903-05, Nathan Studer 1906-28; **VP** Thos A Way 1900-04, Julius Kunz 1907-28; **Cash.** Stitzel X Way 1900-02, Theo Doerfler 1903-11, Ihno A Gerdes 1912-28; **AC** Julius Kunz 1900-03, Inno A Gerdes 1904-11, TB Peterman 1913, WA Drewelow 1914-28

Second Charter, Brown Backs	Ser #	# Notes
10-10-10-20	1-1250	5,000
Second Charter, Date Back		
10-10-10-20 (1771-1900 type uncertain)	1-1900	7,600
Second Charter, Value Back		
10-10-10-20	1901-2460	2,240
Third Charter, Plain Back, Blue Seal		
10-10-10-20	1-2203	8,812

Total amount issued = $295,650. Amount outstanding at close = $24,600.
23,652 Large   0 Small   23,652 Total

5457	M	$10	1882DB	545	704 D	H696732	VG	Higgins Mus.
5457	M	$20	1882VB	581	2226 B	U430524	F	pen/pen
5457		$10	1902PB	?	1353 B	X643555H	G/VG	

THE FAYETTE COUNTY NATIONAL BANK OF WEST UNION
2015   FAYETTE   38 L   14 S
Organized on June 28, 1872 with a capital of $50,000. Placed in conservatorship on March 22, 1933. Placed in voluntary liquidation on March 14, 1934; capital of $50,000. Succeeded by #13978.
Officers: Pres. Joseph Hobson 1872-87, SB Zeigler 1888-1909, GD Darnall 1910-28, BD Chandler 1928-33; **VP** HB Hoyt 1896-1904, GD Darnall 1907-09, WE Fuller 1910-14, BD Chandler 1920-28, RO Woodard 1923-31, WH Antes 1931-33; **Cash.** Edward A Whitney 1872-85, EB Shaw 1887-1902, Frank Camp 1902-33; **AC** EB Shaw 1878-85, Ruel P Camp

1920-32, DR Lynch 1932-33

First Charter, Original Issue | Ser # | # Notes
1-1-1-2 | 1-1500 | 6,000
5-5-5-5 | 1-2875 | 11,500
First Charter, Series of 1875
5-5-5-5 | 1-6249 | 24,996
Second Charter, Brown Backs
5-5-5-5 | 1-6635 | 26,540
10-10-10-20 | 1-2248 | 8,992
Second Charter, Date Back
5-5-5-5 | 1-1047 | 4,188
10-10-10-20 | 1-792 | 3,168
Third Charter, Date Back, Blue Seal
10-10-10-20 | 1-2200 | 8,800
Third Charter, Plain Back, Blue Seal
10-10-10-20 | 2201-6708 | 18,032
1929, Type I
6-10's | 1-941 | 5,646
6-20's | 1-242 | 1,452

Total amount of circulation issued = $916,520. Amount of large outstanding at close = $5,447. Amount of small outstanding at close = $44,550.

112,216 Large   7,098 Small   119,314 Total

Year		Denom	Plate	Ser	Ser2	Grade	Notes
2015	-	$2	ORIG 389	760 A	D221314	XF	
2015	-	$5	1875 401	1757 D	E675582	VG	pen Higgins Mus.
2015	-	$5	1875 401	5424 C	Z503907	VG	Higgins Mus.
2015	-	$5	1882BB 472	636 C	N917894	G/VG	pen/pen
2015	M	$10	1882BB 485	2219 B	V339908V	VF	pen/pen
2015	M	$20	1882BB 499	2185 A	V339874V	CU	pen Higgins Mus.
2015	M	$5	1882DB 533	540 E	B639160	VG	
2015	M	$10	1902DB 620	1052 A	R907722A	XF	pen Higgins Mus.
2015	M	$10	1902DB 620	1607 B	X487872A	VG	
2015	M	$20	1902DB 646	1976 A	M342522B	F	
2015		$10	1902PB 628	3737 A	?	?	
2015	-	$10	1902PB 628	5379 B	5379 B	F	
2015	-	$10	1902PB 628	5402 A	5402 A	G/VG	
2015	-	$10	1902PB 628	5692 B	5692 B	AU	gone/gone
2015	-	$10	1902PB 628	5692 C	5692 C	CU	gone Pin holes
2015	-	$10	1902PB 628	5693 A	5693 A	CU	
2015	-	$10	1902PB 628	5693 C	5693 C	CU	
2015	-	$10	1902PB 628	5694 A	5694 A	AU	gone Tight bottom
2015	-	$10	1902PB 628	5694 C	5694 C	CU	
2015	-	$10	1902PB 628	5695 A	5695 A	CU	gone/gone
2015	-	$10	1902PB 628	5695 C	5695 C	CU	
2015	-	$10	1902PB 628	5706 A	5706 A	CU	gone/gone
2015	-	$10	1902PB 628	5706 C	5706 C	CU	
2015	-	$10	1902PB 628	5707 A	5707 A	CU	
2015	-	$10	1902PB 628	5707 B	5707 B	CU	
2015	-	$10	1902PB 628	5707 C	5707 C	CU	
2015	-	$10	1902PB 628	5708 B	5708 B	CU	gone 2 pinholes
2015	-	$10	1902PB 628	5709 B	5709 B	CU	
2015	-	$10	1902PB 628	5710 B	5710 B	CU	
2015	-	$10	1902PB 628	5712 B	5712 B	CU	
2015	-	$10	1902PB 628	5713 B	5713 B	CU	
2015	-	$20	1902PB 654	5692 A	5692 A	CU	
2015	-	$20	1902PB 654	5693 A	5693 A	AU	gone 2 pinholes
2015	-	$20	1902PB 654	5706 A	5706 A	CU	
2015	-	$20	1902PB 654	5707 A	5707 A	CU	
2015	-	$20	1902PB 654	5710 A	5710 A	CU	fake sigs
2015	-	$20	1902PB 654	5711 A	5711 A	AU	
2015	-	$20	1902PB 654	6069 A	6069 A	VG	
2015		$10	1929T1	C000046A		F	
2015		$10	1929T1	C000094A		VF	
2015		$10	1929T1	E000409A		?	
2015		$10	1929T1	B000444A		AU	Higgins Mus.
2015		$10	1929T1	D000445A		XF	
2015		$10	1929T1	F000637A		VG	
2015		$10	1929T1	E000799A		VF	
2015		$10	1929T1	D000841A		F	
2015		$20	1929T1	E000024A		VG	
2015		$20	1929T1	F000037A		F	
2015		$20	1929T1	A000074A		F	UR corner torn
2015		$20	1929T1	B000106A		AU	
2015		$20	1929T1	E000225A		?	
2015		$20	1929T1	E000237A		?	

THE FIRST NATIONAL BANK OF WHAT CHEER   12 L   25 S
3192   KEOKUK

Organized on April 8, 1884 with a capital of $50,000. Succeeded The What Cheer Bank. Placed in conservation on March 24, 1933. Placed in receivership on January 18, 1934. Restored to solvency on May 18, 1934. Placed in voluntary liquidation on June 20, 1934; capital of $50,000. Succeeded by #14143.

Officers: Pres. Charles H Keck 1884, Joseph Keck 1885, Theodore Robison 1887-89, Edmund Jackson 1890-93, JH Leathers 1894-1903, JL Mitchell 1904-33; **VP** John Schott 1896-1909, Joseph Edgerton 1910-13, LS Cory 1914-33, John T Baylor 1929-33; **Cash.** Theodore Robison 1884-85, JL Mitchell 1887-1903, WT Bonsall 1904-18, Robert Schott 1919-33; **AC** Jas. L Mitchell 1885, WT Bonsall 1900-03, VB Whyle 1920-23

Second Charter, Brown Backs | Ser # | # Notes
10-10-10-20 | 1-2825 | 11,300
Third Charter, Red Seal
10-10-10-20 | 1-1700 | 6,800
Third Charter, Date Back, Blue Seal
10-10-10-20 | 1-3300 | 13,200
Third Charter, Plain Back, Blue Seal
10-10-10-20 | 3301-9264 | 23,856
1929, Type I
6-10's | 1-976 | 5,856
6-20's | 1-278 | 1,668

Total amount of circulation issued = $781,370. Amount of large outstanding at close = $4,070. Amount of small outstanding at close = $45,450.

55,156 Large   7,524 Small   62,680 Total

Bank		Denom	Plate	Ser	Ser2	Grade	Notes
3192	M	$10	1902PB 624	5596 E	Z984258D	VG	
3192		$10	1902PB 624	6441 D	B354623H	VG	
3192	-	$10	1902PB 624	7008 F	R940530N	G/VG	gone/gone
3192		$10	1902PB 624	7594 E	7594 E	VG	
3192	-	$10	1902PB 624	8056 E	8056 E	F	
3192	-	$10	1902PB 624	8433 E	8433 E	F	stamp/stamp
3192	-	$10	1902PB 624	8678 F	8678 F	F/VF	
3192	-	$10	1902PB 624	8793 E	8793 E	VF	
3192	M	$20	1902PB 650	5099 B	T396141D	VG	
3192		$20	1902PB 650	6508 B	B354690H	VG/F	Higgins Mus.
3192	-	$20	1902PB 650	7954 B	7954 B	F/VF	
3192	-	$20	1902PB 650	8193 B	8193 B	F	stamp/lt stamp
3192		$10	1929T1	?000001A		F	
3192		$10	1929T1	C000050A		F	
3192		$10	1929T1	E000096A		VG	
3192		$10	1929T1	E000382A		VG	
3192		$10	1929T1	A000384A		F+	
3192		$10	1929T1	A000415A		VF	
3192		$10	1929T1	C000539A		?	
3192		$10	1929T1	F000574A		F	
3192		$10	1929T1	B000590A		F	
3192		$10	1929T1	C000622A		F/VF	
3192		$10	1929T1	C000673A		F/VF	
3192		$10	1929T1	E000936A		G	
3192		$10	1929T1	D000966A		VF	
3192		$20	1929T1	B000001A		F	
3192		$20	1929T1	B000043A		F/VF	
3192		$20	1929T1	C000094A		VF	
3192		$20	1929T1	C000102A		F	
3192		$20	1929T1	A000126A		VG/F	
3192		$20	1929T1	A000140A		XF+	Higgins Mus.
3192		$20	1929T1	F000178A		F	
3192		$20	1929T1	E000208A		F	
3192		$20	1929T1	F000240A		F	
3192		$20	1929T1	C000261A		?	
3192		$20	1929T1	C000268A		VF	
3192		$20	1929T1	E000277A		CU	

THE FIRST NATIONAL BANK OF WHITING   11 L   7 S
10861   MONONA

Organized on May 2, 1916 with a capital of $25,000. Placed in conservatorship on March 30, 1933. Placed in receivership on October 31, 1933; capital of $25,000. On large-size notes the bank title is printed erroneously as First National Bank of Whiting. On Series of 1929 notes the bank title is printed as The First National Bank of Whiting. This is the only known case in Iowa of this kind of difference in bank titles on large and small notes from the same bank.

Officers: Pres. Lyman Whittier 1916-22, Geo H When 1923-33; **VP** GH When 1920-22, William Boyd 1922-33; **Cash.** JW Beggs 1916-33; **AC** BC Brous 1920-23, Eugene E Hopkins 1924-32, ML When 1933

Third Charter, Plain Back, Blue Seal | Ser # | # Notes
10-10-10-10 | 1-4827 | 19,308
1929, Type I
6-10's | 1-892 | 5,352
1929, Type II
10's | 1-130 | 130

Total amount of circulation issued = $247,900. Amount of large outstanding at close = $2,490. Amount of small outstanding at close = $22,510.

19,308 Large   5,482 Small   24,790 Total

Bank		Denom	Plate	Ser	Ser2	Grade	Notes
10861	M	$10	1902PB 632	1174 C	R581344	VF	Higgins Mus.
10861	M	$10	1902PB 632	1175 C	R581345	VF/XF	pen/pen

Charter	Denom	Type	Plate	Ser #	Treasury #	Grade	Notes
10861M	$10	1902PB	632	1182 D	R581352	VF+	
10861M	$10	1902PB	632	2012 C	U331402	VG/F	Edge nicks
10861M	$10	1902PB	632	2614 C	V344639	XF	Staining
10861 -	$10	1902PB	632	3620 D	3620 D	VG	
10861 -	$10	1902PB	632	3754 B	3754 B	F	
10861 -	$10	1902PB	632	3763 C	3763 C	VG/F	
10861 -	$10	1902PB	632	4264 A	4264 A	F/VF	pen/pen
10861 -	$10	1902PB	632	4599 D	4599 D	F	pen/pen
10861 -	$10	1902PB	632	4747 A	4747 A	XF	gone/pen vp
10861	$10	1929T1		D000012A		VG/F	
10861	$10	1929T1		F000314A		VG/F	
10861	$10	1929T1		B000492A		F+	Higgins Mus.
10861	$10	1929T1		D000492A		VF	
10861	$10	1929T1		C000522A		F	552 ?
10861	$10	1929T1		F000694A		?	
10861	$10	1929T2		A000076		F	Ink

THE FIRST NATIONAL BANK OF WILLIAMS 10 L 2 S
5585 HAMILTON
Organized on Sept. 13, 1900 with a capital of $25,000. Chartered on Sept. 24, 1900. Placed in receivership on July 1, 1930; capital of $25,000.
Officers: Pres. RJ Hurd 1900-07, John McCarley 1908-23, WJ Foran 1924-30; **VP** Warren Worthington 1900-07, LW Schroeder 1909-27, RJ Hurd 1909-22, WJ Foran 1923, Wm Whisler 1928-29, PW Petersen 1930; **Cash.** John McCarley 1900-07, CM Trumbauer 1908-14, EG Simpson 1915, LE Pound 1916-30; **AC** Lulu Hurd 1903-04, CM Trumbauer 1907, Ruth G Martinson 1920-30, Harold Wilkinson 1922-23, Millard L Riley 1924-26

	Ser #	# Notes
Second Charter, Brown Backs		
5-5-5-5	1-1200	4,800
10-10-10-20	1-860	3,440
Second Charter, Date Back		
5-5-5-5	1-1525	6,100
10-10-10-20	1-1160	4,640
Second Charter, Value Back		
5-5-5-5	1526-2545	4,080
10-10-10-20	1161-1762	2,408
Third Charter, Plain Back, Blue Seal		
5-5-5-5	1-2697	10,788
10-10-10-20	1-1629	6,516
1929, Type I		
6-5's	1-315	1,890
6-10's	1-140	840
6-20's	1-9	54

Total amount of circulation issued = $360,320. Amount of large outstanding at close = $6,510. Amount of small outstanding at close = $18,070.
42,772 Large 2,784 Small 45,556 Total

Charter	Denom	Type	Plate	Ser #	Treasury #	Grade	Notes
5585 M	$10	1882BB	490	488 C	R347275R	VG+	
5585 M	$5	1882DB	537	1455 E	N308842	VG+	Higgins Museum
5585 M	$20	1882DB	555	328 B	H149106	VG	Ink
5585 M	$5	1882VB	574	1976 F	T544713	F	gone Higg. Mus.
5585 M	$5	1882VB	574	2253 E	T813140	VF	
5585	$5	1902PB	607	1354 A	N987040H	VG/F	Pinholes
5585 -	$5	1902PB	607	1480 C	U867641H	VG	lt stamp sigs
5585 -	$5	1902PB	607	2131 C	2131 C	VG	gone/gone
5585	$10	1902PB	633	79 B	X667911D	VG	Higgins Mus.
5585 -	$20	1902PB	659	1228 A	1228 A	VG/F	Higgins Mus.
5585	$10	1929T1		E000016A		G	Higgins Mus.
5585	$10	1929T1		E000066A		VG/F	tear R margin

THE FARMERS NATIONAL BANK OF WINFIELD 15 L 14 S
10640 HENRY
Organized on May 4, 1914 with a capital of $50,000. Licensed after the banking holiday on March 22, 1933.
Officers: Pres. WI Huston 1915, RP Davidson 1916-28, CB Van Syoc 1929-35; **VP** William Carden 1920-35; **Cash.** OL Karsten 1915-28, TT Warren 1929-35; **AC** Harry E Olson 1920-35

	Ser #	# Notes
Third Charter, Date Back, Blue Seal		
5-5-5-5	1-1250	5,000
10-10-10-20	1-1000	4,000
Third Charter, Plain Back, Blue Seal		
5-5-5-5	1251-5134	15,536
10-10-10-20	1001-3291	9,164
1929, Type I		
6-5's	1-988	5,928
6-10's	1-486	2,916
6-20's	1-158	948
1929, Type II		
5's	1-194	194
10's	1-90	90
20's	1-50	50

Total amount of circulation issued = $347,860. Amount of large outstanding in 1935 = $1,180. Amount of small outstanding in 1935 = $23,820.
33,700 Large 10,126 Small 43,826 Total

Charter	Denom	Type	Plate	Ser #	Treasury #	Grade	Notes
10640M	$10	1902DB	623	1000 A	M496606B	VG	
10640M	$20	1902DB	649	844 A	M496450B	VF	
10640M	$5	1902PB	605	1352 D	A381288D	VF	stamp/stamp
10640M	$5	1902PB	605	1776 A	N197602D	VG	
10640 -	$5	1902PB	605	3548 B	T144884H	VG	stamp sigs vp
10640 -	$5	1902PB	605	4544 D	4544 D	F	vp Yellow stains
10640 -	$5	1902PB	605	4670 C	4670 C	?	
10640 -	$5	1902PB	605	4697 C	4697 C	XF/AU	stamp sigs vp
10640 -	$5	1902PB	605	4705 A	4705 A	F	stamp sigs vp
10640M	$10	1902PB	631	1701 B	H448193E	VG/F	stamp/pen
10640M	$10	1902PB	631	1781 B	N851833E	VG+	
10640M	$10	1902PB	631	1972 A	X170574E	VG	stamp/pen
10640M	$10	1902PB	631	2178 A	H100710H	F+	stamp/pen
10640 -	$10	1902PB	631	3122 C	3122 C	VG/F	Higgins Mus.
10640 -	$10	1902PB	631	3142 B	3142 B	VG	
10640	$5	1929T1		B000407A		VG	
10640	$5	1929T1		D000916A		XF	
10640	$5	1929T1		D000967A		VF	
10640	$10	1929T1		A000035A		VG	
10640	$10	1929T1		C000318A		VF	
10640	$10	1929T1		F000380A		F	
10640	$10	1929T1		E000484A		F+	
10640	$20	1929T1		E000025A		F	Tear
10640	$20	1929T1		E000110A		VG	Higgins Mus.
10640	$20	1929T1		F000110A		VG	
10640	$20	1929T1		A000128A		VF	
10640	$20	1929T1		A000137A		XF	
10640	$20	1929T1		E000154A		F/VF	
10640	$20	1929T2		A000018		F/VF	

THE CITIZENS NATIONAL BANK OF WINTERSET 21 L 60 S
2002 MADISON
Organized on May 11, 1872 with a capital of $50,000. Chartered on June 25, 1872. Absorbed #6852 on May 15, 1930 in conjunction with Madison County State Bank, Winterset and the Winterset Savings Bank. These three banks absorbed #6852. Placed in conservation on March 24, 1933. Placed in receivership on June 4, 1934; capital of $200,000.
Officers: Pres. Joseph J Hutchings 1872-87, Edward Brown 1888-89, JH Wintrode 1890-1909, JP Steele 1910-30, Chas T Koser 1931-34; **VP** SC Ruby 1896, 1902, JP Steele 1903-09, George M Pratt 1920-34; **Cash.** Daniel E Cooper 1872-73, Levi F Smith 1874-84, WJ Cornell 1885-1934; **AC** JW McKee 1920-34, J Robt. Cornell 1929-34

	Ser #	# Notes
First Charter, Original Issue		
1-1-1-2	1-1700	6,800
5-5-5-5	1-2375	9,500
First Charter, Series of 1875		
5-5-5-5	1-5908	23,632
Second Charter, Brown Backs		
50-100	1-390	780
Second Charter, Date Back		
50-100	1-54	108
Third Charter, Date Back, Blue Seal		
50-50-50-100	1-2760	11,040
Third charter, Plain Back, Blue Seal		
50-50-50-100	2761-3672	3,648
1929, Type I		
6-10's	1-721	4,326
6-20's	1-297	1,782
6-50's	1-376	2,256
6-100's	1-124	744

Total amount of circulation issued = $1,424,860. Amount of large outstanding at close = $21,800. Amount of small outstanding at close = $177,300.
55,508 Large 9,108 Small 64,616 Total

Charter	Denom	Type	Plate	Ser #	Treasury #	Grade	Notes
2002 -	$1	ORIG	382	709 B	D194893	F/VF	pen/pen
2002 -	$1	ORIG	382	1528 A	E56607	F	
2002 -	$5	1875	401	4593 B	V845122	F	Grinnell # 4009
2002 -	$5	1875	401	5168 A	X633344	XF/AU	Higgins Mus.
2002 M	$50	1902DB	671	577 C	A820029	F	
2002 M	$50	1902DB	671	1333 B		?	?
2002 M	$50	1902DB	671	1374 A	A901111	F	pen/pen
2002 M	$50	1902DB	671	1446 B	A901183	VG	pen/pen
2002 M	$50	1902DB	671	1520 C	A901257	F/VF	faded/pen
2002 M	$50	1902DB	671	1704 C	A947358	VG	
2002 M	$50	1902DB	671	1937 B	B26281	F	pen/pen light tear
2002 M	$50	1902DB	671	2397 B	B106521	F	
2002 M	$100	1902DB	693	808 A	A820260	VG	pen/pen
2002 M	$100	1902DB	693	2059 A	B26403	VG	pen/pen
2002 -	$50	1902PB	679	3188 A	3188 A	F/VF	pen/pen

2002	- $50	1902PB	679	3249 B	3249 B	VF	
2002	- $50	1902PB	679	3256 B	3256 B	F	
2002	- $50	1902PB	679	3454 C	3454 C	F/VF	Higgins Mus.
2002	- $50	1902PB	679	3547 B	3547 B	VG	pen/pen
2002	-$100	1902PB	702	2872 A	2872 A	VF+	
2002	-$100	1902PB	702	3084 A	3084 A	F/VF	
2002	$10	1929T1		A000213A		XF	
2002	$10	1929T1		B000218A		F	
2002	$10	1929T1		B000314A		F	Stain
2002	$10	1929T1		D000350A		VG+	
2002	$10	1929T1		B000494A		VF	
2002	$10	1929T1		D000549A		VG	
2002	$10	1929T1		B000683A		VF	
2002	$20	1929T1		?000066A		F/VF	
2002	$20	1929T1		F000097A		VF	
2002	$20	1929T1		D000101A		F	
2002	$20	1929T1		E000152A		AU	
2002	$20	1929T1		A000185A		AU	Higgins Mus.
2002	$20	1929T1		D000191A		VG	
2002	$20	1929T1		F000195A		F/VF	
2002	$20	1929T1		B000215A		VG/F	
2002	$20	1929T1		D000259A		VF	
2002	$20	1929T1		C000263A		VF	
2002	$20	1929T1		A000264A		F/VF	
2002	$50	1929T1		D000022A		F/VF	
2002	$50	1929T1		D000034A		VF	
2002	$50	1929T1		D000041A		VF	
2002	$50	1929T1		C000050A		F/VF	
2002	$50	1929T1		E000116A		VF	
2002	$50	1929T1		C000160A		VF	
2002	$50	1929T1		F000162A		VG	
2002	$50	1929T1		D000176A		VG/F	
2002	$50	1929T1		A000188A		F/VF	
2002	$50	1929T1		D000206A		AU	
2002	$50	1929T1		E000207A		F	
2002	$50	1929T1		F000209A		VG/F	
2002	$50	1929T1		E000274A		?	
2002	$50	1929T1		A000322A		F/VF	
2002	$50	1929T1		C000330A		F	
2002	$50	1929T1		F000335A		G/VG	UR corner gone
2002	$50	1929T1		D000339A		XF	Higgins Mus.
2002	$50	1929T1		C000343A		CU	
2002	$50	1929T1		A000353A		XF/AU	Replacement
2002	$50	1929T1		B000353A		AU	Replacement
2002	$50	1929T1		C000353A		CU	Replacement
2002	$50	1929T1		D000353A		CU	Replacement
2002	$50	1929T1		A000354A		VF+	
2002	$50	1929T1		C000354A		CU	
2002	$50	1929T1		D000355A		XF/AU	
2002	$50	1929T1		F000364A		XF	
2002	$50	1929T1		A000371A		VF	
2002	$50	1929T1		B000373A		VG/F	
2002	$100	1929T1		E000006A		F	
2002	$100	1929T1		E000009A		XF/AU	
2002	$100	1929T1		E000021A		F/VF	
2002	$100	1929T1		B000024A		F	
2002	$100	1929T1		A000031A		F	
2002	$100	1929T1		F000033A		VG/F	
2002	$100	1929T1		E000045A		F/VF	
2002	$100	1929T1		E000066A		VF	Ink on face
2002	$100	1929T1		?000071A		F	
2002	$100	1929T1		C000099A		XF	
2002	$100	1929T1		C000102A		CU	
2002	$100	1929T1		C000105A		VG	
2002	$100	1929T1		F000113A		VF	

THE NATIONAL BANK OF WINTERSET   **0 L**
1403 (FIRST TITLE)   **MADISON**
Chartered in 1865. Title changed to The First National Bank of Winterset on April 18, 1883.
Officers: Pres. Charles D Bevington 1867-1883; **Cash.** Frederick Mott 1867-69, William W McKnight 1870-75, Frederick Mott 1876, SG Bevington 1880-83; **AC** AH Adkison 1878-79

First Charter, Original Issue	Ser #	# Notes
5-5-5-5	1-3000	12,000
10-10-10-20	1-2115	8,460
First Charter, Series of 1875		
5-5-5-5	1-313	1,252
10-10-10-20	1-468	1,872
23,584 Large	0 Small	23,584 Total

THE FIRST NATIONAL BANK OF WINTERSET   **15 L**   **5 S**
1403 (SECOND TITLE)   **MADISON**
Succeeded The National Bank of Winterset on April 18, 1883. Placed in voluntary liquidation on February 20, 1930; capital of $50,000. Absorbed by The Winterset Savings Bank, Winterset.
Officers: Pres. Charles D Bevington 1883-1904, Frederick Mott 1904-08, PJ Cunningham 1909-29; **VP** SD Alexander 1907, EE Orris 1909-10, Guy A Lee 1909, Douglas Roy 1911, JE Hamilton 1913-29, SM Hamilton 1920-29; **Cash.** SG Bevington 1883-87, WS Whedon 1889-1908, WE Grismer 1909-14, Eugene Wilson 1915-17, HC Husted 1918-19, WE Grismer 1920, FS Nelson 1922-26, FS Hamilton 1927-29; **AC** AB Shriver 1896, FS Hamilton 1920-26, Will Cochran 1927-29, ST Lawler 1929

First Charter, Series of 1875	Ser #	# Notes
5-5-5-5	1-865	3,460
Second Charter, Brown Backs		
5-5-5-5	1-1000	4,000
50-100	1-633	1,266
Third Charter, Red Seal		
5-5-5-5	1-1575	6,300
10-10-10-20	1-1070	4,280
Third Charter, Date Back, Blue Seal		
5-5-5-5	1-2750	11,000
10-10-10-20	1-2300	9,200
Third Charter, Plain Back, Blue Seal		
5-5-5-5	2751-8745	23,980
10-10-10-20	2301-6215	15,660
1929, Type I		
6-10's	1-260	1,560
6-20's	1-40	240

Total amount of circulation issued = $918,710. Amount of large outstanding at close = $16,950. Amount of small outstanding at close = $20,400.
79,146 Large   1,800 Small   80,946 Total

1403	M	$10	1902RS	613	463 A	H590889	F+	Higgins Mus.
1403	M	$5	1902DB	590	2576 H	K548538B	XF	
1403	M	$20	1902DB	642	392 B	M232433	F+	stamp Higg. Mus.
1403	M	$20	1902DB	642	2008 B	?	G	Tears and stains
1403	M	$5	1902PB	598	4725 F	A810396C	VF	
1403	M	$5	1902PB	598	4876 E	A810547E	F	pen/faded
1403	-	$5	1902PB	598	6369 H	M631630H	F/VF	
1403	-	$5	1902PB	598	6763 G	T953699H	VF	pen/stamp
1403	-	$10	1902PB	624	4457 D	R143169H	VG/F	pen/stamp
1403	-	$10	1902PB	624	4683 D	V300355H	VG	Bayard
1403	-	$10	1902PB	624	5115 F	5115 F	F+	
1403	-	$10	1902PB	624	5253 D	5253 D	F	Fed. Res. Bk., San Francisco
1403	-	$10	1902PB	624	5556 F	5556 F	F	pen/gone
1403	M	$20	1902PB	650	3827 B	V505269E	VG	
1403	-	$20	1902PB	650	5250 B	5250 B	F	
1403		$10	1929T1		F000015A		VG/F	
1403		$10	1929T1		C000017A		F	
1403		$10	1929T1		B000151A		VG/F	Wallet stain
1403		$10	1929T1		A000159A		VG	
1403		$20	1929T1		A000037A		F/VF	Higgins Mus.

THE FIRST NATIONAL BANK OF WOODBINE   **31 L**   **25 S**
4745   **HARRISON**
Chartered in 1892. Succeeded The Commercial Banking Company.
Officers: Pres. Josiah Coe 1892-1914, HB Kling 1915-19, Dr. EJ Cole 1920-35; **VP** Geo A Mathews 1896-1909, HM Bostwick 1909, HB Kling 1910-14, AJ Coe 1920-35; **Cash.** HM Bostwick 1892-1905, Geo W Coe 1906-32, SR De Cou 1932-35; **AC** Geo W Coe 1902-04, SL Hull 1907-09, OH Perrin 1911-14, DE Brainard 1914, HL Haight 1920-35, CS King 1922-35

Second Charter, Brown Backs	Ser #	# Notes
5-5-5-5	1-4380	17,520
10-10-10-20	1-1798	7,192
Second Charter, Date Back		
5-5-5-5	1-1628	6,600
10-10-10-20	1-1050	4,200
Third Charter, Date Back, Blue Seal		
5-5-5-5	1-1650	6,600
10-10-10-20	1-1300	5,200
Third Charter, Plain Back, Blue Seal		
5-5-5-5	1651-7960	25,240
10-10-10-20	1301-5348	16,192
1929, Type I		
6-5's	1-1522	9,132
6-10's	1-784	4,704
6-20's	1-212	1,272
1929, Type II		

5's			1-1684	1,684		
10's			1-1013	1,013		
20's			1-285	285		

Total amount of circulation issued = $831,550. Amount of large outstanding in June 1935 = $4,590. Amount of small outstanding in June 1935 = $45,410.

88,656 Large   18,090 Small   106,746 Total

4745		$5 1882BB 472	2541 A	B659911B	VG	
4745		$20 1882BB 499	1143 A	N771264N	VF	Higgins Mus.
4745	M	$5 1882DB 533	4 G	A904099	F	pen/pen
4745	M	$20 1882DB 550	589 B	A908189	F	
4745	M	$5 1902DB 594	1 C	H344307A	CU	pen/pen vp
4745	M	$10 1902DB 620	1 A	K123286A	VF	vp Higgins Mus.
4745	M	$5 1902PB 602	2876 D	A230062D	VF/XF	stamp/stamp
4745	M	$5 1902PB 602	? D	V96678D	?	
4745	M	$5 1902PB 602	5511 D	D931047H	VG	gone/gone
4745		$5 1902PB 602	7220 A	?	VG	gone/gone
4745		$5 1902PB 602	7220 C	?	G/VG	
4745	-	$5 1902PB 602	7616 A	7616 A	VG	
4745	-	$5 1902PB 602	7748 C	7748 C	F	stamp/stamp
4745	M	$10 1902PB 628	1681 A	V638631B	VG/F	stamp/stamp
4745	M	$10 1902PB 628	2144 C	H826944D	VG+	
4745	M	$10 1902PB 628	2736 C	D951298E	XF	lt stamp sigs
4745	M	$10 1902PB 628	2736 C	D951298E	XF	faded stamps
4745	-	$10 1902PB 628	3832 C	X99754H	Fr/G	Y or X ?
4745	-	$10 1902PB 628	5233 A	5233 A	VF	
4745	M	$20 1902PB 654	1644 A	V638594B	XF	
4745	M	$20 1902PB 654	1651 A	V638601B	CU	
4745	M	$20 1902PB 654	1669 A	V638619B	CU	stamp/stamp
4745	M	$20 1902PB 654	1675 A	V638625B	CU	
4745	M	$20 1902PB 654	1676 A	V638626B	CU	stamp/stamp
4745	M	$20 1902PB 654	2908 A	N742560E	XF	
4745	M	$20 1902PB 654	3566 A	H490188H	CU	stamp/stamp
4745	M	$20 1902PB 654	3608 A	H490230H	VF	stamp/stamp
4745	-	$20 1902PB 654	3663 A	R98305H	CU	
4745	-	$20 1902PB 654	3904 A	X99826H	VF	
4745	-	$20 1902PB 654	3931 A	X99853H	VG	faded/gone Stains
4745	-	$20 1902PB 654	4526 A	4526 A	F	
4745		$5 1929T1	A000242A		AU	
4745		$5 1929T1	D000255A		F/VF	
4745		$5 1929T1	D000540A		G	
4745		$5 1929T1	C000801A		VF	
4745		$5 1929T1	D001116A		F	
4745		$10 1929T1	C000085A		F	
4745		$10 1929T1	E000117A		VG/F	
4745		$10 1929T1	D000333A		VG	
4745		$10 1929T1	E000455A		VF	
4745		$10 1929T1	C000486A		VG/F	
4745		$10 1929T1	A000611A		VG/F	
4745		$10 1929T1	A000704A		F	
4745		$10 1929T1	B000731A		VF	
4745		$20 1929T1	E000014A		?	
4745		$20 1929T1	F000020A		VF	
4745		$20 1929T1	A000079A		VF	
4745		$20 1929T1	C000083A		F+	Higgins Mus.
4745		$20 1929T1	F000130A		CU	
4745		$20 1929T1	A000137A		XF	
4745		$20 1929T1	A000201A		VG	
4745		$5 1929T2	A001225		F	
4745		$10 1929T2	A000016		F+	
4745		$10 1929T2	A000192		F/VF	
4745		$10 1929T2	A000600		VF	
4745		$20 1929T2	A000016		VG	

First Charter, Series of 1875

5-5-5-5	1-817	3,268
10-10-10-20	1-805	3,220

Second Charter, Brown Backs

5-5-5-5	1-1975	7,900
10-10-10-20	1-1340	5,360

Second Charter, Date Back

5-5-5-5	1-746	2,984
10-10-10-20	1-404	1,616

Third Charter, Date Back, Blue Seal

10-10-10-20	1-2400	9,600

Third Charter, Plain Back, Blue Seal

10-10-10-20	2401-7982	22,328

1929, Type I

6-10's	1-556	3,336
6-20's	1-144	864

Total amount of circulation issued = $727,950. Amount of large outstanding at close = $10,670. Amount of small outstanding at close = $39,330.

66,876 Large   4,200 Small   71,016 Total

1943	-	$10	1875 417	147 C	A934562	XF/AU	Blue end paper
1943	-	$10	1875 417	560 B	E971098	AG	pen/pen
1943	M	$10	1902DB 620	83 B	E590821A	F/VF	pen Higgins Mus.
1943	M	$10	1902DB 646	2400 A	B41306B	VG	Soiled
1943	M	$10	1902PB 628	2855 A	V641295B	XF	
1943	M	$10	1902PB 628	4471 A	A853133E	VF	
1943	-	$10	1902PB 628	6601 C	6601 C	F	pen/stamp
1943	-	$10	1902PB 628	7163 C	7163 C	F/VF	pen/stamp
1943	M	$20	1902PB 654	3093 A	A374390D	F/VF	Davenport B&T
1943	M	$20	1902PB 654	5035 A	M665932E	XF	
1943	M	$20	1902PB 654	5066 A	M665963E	VF	pen/lt stamp
1943	-	$20	1902PB 654	6366 A	B526088K	VG	
1943	-	$20	1902PB 654	6797 A	6797 A	F+	nice sigs
1943		$10	1929T1	F000042A		F+	
1943		$10	1929T1	A000288A		VG	
1943		$20	1929T1	E000070A		VG	Soiled back
1943		$20	1929T1	E000077A		VF	
1943		$20	1929T1	D000110A		XF+	
1943		$20	1929T1	E000116A		?	
1943		$20	1929T1	F000120A		VG	

THE FIRST NATIONAL BANK OF WYOMING   13 L   7 S
1943   JONES

Organized on January 27, 1872 with a capital of $50,000. Chartered on February 29, 1872. Placed in voluntary liquidation on March 3, 1931; capital of $50,000. Absorbed by The Citizens State Bank of Wyoming. Placed in receivership on October 11, 1932; reason of deficiency in assets sold.

Officers: Pres. Hiram Smith 1872-73, Wallace T Foote 1874-1901, JW Wherry 1902-03, John K Pixley 1903-04, Fred H Foote 1905-11, Park Chamberlain 1912-30, Wal. G. Wherry 1930-31; **VP** JA Bronson 1896, J Wm. Wherry 1900, Aaron M Loomis 1902-09, Park Chamberlain 1910-11, JT Wherry 1913-26, WG Wherry 1920-30, AA Vaughn 1922-30, EL Anderson 1930; **Cash.** John K Pixley 1872-1902, AA Vaughn 1903-20, Wallace E Schreiber 1922-25, Roy L Truesdell 1926-30; **AC** Arthur A Vaughn 1896-1902, LM Barrett 1903-04, B Tourtellot 1907, John S Robertson 1909-20

First Charter, Original Issue	**Ser #**	**# Notes**
5-5-5-5	1-1750	7,000
10-10-10-20	1-900	3,600

Chapter Four
Summary and Analysis of the Census

Introduction

The most popular method of collecting national banknotes today is by location. Collections are typically formed based on particular cities, counties, states, state capitols, etc. of interest to the collector. However, in addition to the bank location, many other identifying features are printed on each note. This information includes bank name, charter number, denomination, bank sheet serial number, Treasury serial number, series year identifier, Treasury signatures, bank officer signatures, plate position letter, Treasury seal, charter date, and vignette. Collections may be formed around any these features. Even if one's primary collection is location-based, other features of the notes may add desirability. This chapter will discuss several of these features of interest to collectors.

The census contains listings for 11,058 notes. This total is about 3,000 more than any previously published listing of Iowa notes. Thus, it is the most complete census of Iowa notes ever recorded and indeed one of the most complete in the nation.

Type Notes

Different note types are typically distinguished by differences in major design elements. These are usually specified by denomination and charter period. The number of notes of each type in the Iowa census is given in Table 1. The column labeled with a "?" indicates notes for which a serial number is known but the denomination is not recorded.

The $1 and $2 denominations were not issued after January 1879 when prohibited by legislation that permitted the redemption of currency for hard specie (gold and silver coin). High denomination Second Charter Value Backs and 1929 Type II notes were not issued simply because none of the eligible banks chose to provide them to their customers.

The totals of Table 1 reveal some interesting data. There are a total of 304 First Charter notes of all denominations known, equally split between Original Series and Series of 1875 notes. The number of Second Charter notes recorded is 984. This total is split between Brown Backs, Date Backs, and Value Backs in a ratio of about 3-to-2-to-1. The differences in availability do not appear to be reflected in the current valuations of these respective types. Third Charter notes number 4,573. Of these only 154 are Red Seals. Plain Backs outnumber Date Backs by 5-to-1. Small size notes total 5,197 with Type Is outnumbering Type IIs by 6-to-1.

The total number of $1 notes is 86. Lazy deuces are less common, with only 36 known. The most common First Charter denomination is the $5, with 113 notes. The First Charter $10 and $20 denominations were produced primarily on 10-10-10-20 sheets and have proportionate abundances of 41 and 13, respectively.

Counting the two versions of first charter notes separately, we see that there were 50 different types issued. Three

Table 1. The number of notes in census for each type

	$1	$2	$5	$10	$20	$50	$100	?	Total
1st Ch. Original Series	76	34	38	3	0	0	0	1	152
1st Ch. Series of 1875	10	2	83	36	14	5	1	1	152
2nd Ch. Brown Back	-	-	105	237	113	15	12	0	482
2nd Ch. Date Back	-	-	56	172	81	11	18	0	338
2nd Ch. Value Back	-	-	65	54	45	-	-	0	164
3rd Ch. Red Seal	-	-	18	78	47	2	9	0	154
3rd Ch. Date Back	-	-	69	412	195	62	38	0	776
3rd Ch. Plain Back	-	-	694	1926	963	27	32	1	3643
1929 Type I	-	-	520	1979	1706	170	63	4	4442
1929 Type II	-	-	195	416	144	-	-	0	755
Total	86	36	1843	5313	3308	292	173	7	11,058

Types marked "-" were not issued by any Iowa bank.

types were issued but not known to exist. These are the First Charter Original $20, $50, and $100. The Original $20 notes were issued by 49 Iowa banks, so it is unfortunate that none are presently known.

The high denomination First Charter notes present a different story. Only nine Iowa banks issued First Charter $50 and $100 notes. All high denomination First Charter notes were produced in two-note sheets of a $50 and a $100 bill. Currently five 1875 $50 notes are known. These include specimens from the Merchants National Bank of Cedar Rapids, #2511, the First National Bank of Villisca, #2766, the Des Moines National Bank, #2583 (which is in the Higgins Museum), and two notes from the First National Bank of Newton, #2644. One of the Newton $50s is impounded in the Federal Reserve Bank of Chicago. Only one 1875 $100 note is known. This is an extremely fine note from the Des Moines National Bank, #2583, which was owned for many years by a prominent dealer and collector and is now ensconced in the collection of the Higgins Museum. Because equal numbers of $50 and $100 notes were produced, a 5-to-1 survival rate for the $50 and $100 represents somewhat of an anomaly.

Although the First Charter $100 note is clearly the rarest Iowa type, several other types are notable for their scarcity. The $50 Red Seal has only two known examples and has long been recognized as one of the outstanding rarities. The Higgins Museum has a $50 Red Seal from the Merchants National Bank of Grinnell, #2953. The other note is from the First National Bank of Davenport, #2695. Another type of equal rarity, but which has not been widely recognized as such, is the Series of 1875 $2. Only two examples are known, one each from the First National Bank of Tama City, #1880, and the Marion County National Bank of Knoxville, #1986. The Original $10 and 1875 $50 types are also rare, with three and five known, respectively. The three original $10s are from the National State Bank of Burlington, #751, the Citizens National Bank of Davenport, #1671, and the First National Bank of Lyons, #66 (which may be seen in the Higgins Museum).

Certain other types are not excessively rare as Iowa types, but have a high valuation because of the scarcity of the type on a national scale. Leading this list are the $100 Red Seals. Although only about 100 of these notes are known from all banks in the nation, Iowa is blessed with nine of them. All of the nine were issued by the First National Bank of Davenport, #2695. At least four, and perhaps all, of them were found in the accumulation at the Davenport Bank and Trust in the 1990s. High denomination Second Charter Brown Backs and Date Backs are scarce nationally with about 200 or less known. Iowa is fortunate to have substantial numbers of each of these types, ranging from 11 to 18 as in Table 1. The majority of these notes are from big banks in Sioux City, Davenport, and Cedar Rapids.

Treasury Signatures and Friedberg Numbers
Every national banknote bears the engraved signatures of a Treasurer of the United States and a Register of the Treasury. These federal officers served at the pleasure of the President. Consequently the time served by each officeholder was usually a few years. During the 72-year period of national banknote issuance, 18 Registers and 17 Treasurers held office, producing 34 different signature combinations, which may be found in standard currency reference books. The note type and signature combination is usually denoted by its Friedberg number.

The signature combinations of Rosecrans/Morgan, Woods/White, Woods/Tate, and Jones/Woods are not found on any Iowa notes. On First Charter notes, all other signature combinations may be found except those of Bruce/Wyman and later signers. On Second Charter notes, Vernon/Treat and later signers are unknown. On Second Charter Value Backs, the only recorded signatures are Lyons/Roberts. On $5, $10, and $20 Third Charter notes, all signature combinations are known except for Napier/Thompson on $5 Plain Backs, Teehee/Burke on $20 Date Backs, and the universal exceptions listed above.

There are five known notes with Chittenden/Spinner signatures. These were issued by Iowa City, #18, Burlington, #351, Washington, #398, and Muscatine, #692. Jeffries/Spinner appears only on four notes from Council Bluffs, #1684. There are eight Bruce/Jordan notes from Fairfield, #1475 and Council Bluffs, #1479. Tillman/Roberts is represented by nine notes from Decorah, #5081 and Vinton, #5088. Five banks issued the nine Allison/Wyman notes, charters #493, 922, 1801, 1943, and 1982. Davenport, #1671, issued the five known Allison/Gilfillan notes. The 49 Napier/Thompson notes make that combination more available than Speelman/White, which is on only 39 notes.

There are 189 different Friedberg numbers recorded in the census. These are distributed with 32 different Friedberg numbers in First Charter notes, 66 in Second Charter notes, and 91 in Third Charter notes. None of the added Friedberg numbers with letter suffixes, such as 597-a, are found in Iowa notes. There are 21 Friedberg numbers that are represented by only a single example in the census. The city and charter for these unique numbers are given in Table 2. As expected, these numbers are concentrated in the scarce types discussed above.

Table 2. Unique Friedberg numbers in the census

381	Council Bluffs #1684	519	Davenport #2695
390	Tama City #1880	525	Spirit Lake #4758
391	Knoxville #1986	530	Creston #2586
403	Davenport #1671	536	Lake Mills #5123
412	Burlington #751	553	Decorah #5081
414	Davenport #1671	554	Lake Mills #5123
432	Mt. Pleasant #922	559	Estherville #4700
446	Cedar Rapids #2511	571	Cedar Rapids #2511
460	Des Moines #2583	597	Fredericksburg 10541
488	Decorah #5081	700	Clarion #3796
507	Davenport #2695		

Varieties

National bank notes exist in numerous variations from the standard types as discussed above. Some varieties are of widespread interest and others are currently relegated to the status of curiosities studied and collected by only a few individuals. Several of these varieties are discussed below, but their inclusion here should not be taken as an indicator of their relative importance. As new research appears and/or as collecting interests evolve, other varieties may very well come to the forefront.

Original Series with charter number: Initially, national bank notes were printed without an identifying charter number. In 1874, the Treasury started placing charter numbers on notes to aid in the sorting of redeemed notes. Only a small percentage of Original Series notes are found with charter numbers. (Examples of notes with and without the charter number are shown in the chapter of color illustrations.) See Peter Huntoon's book *United States Large Size National Bank Notes* for more details on these and other First Charter varieties.

Black charter number:. The first charter numbers on notes were overprinted in red ink. Late in 1873, the Treasury apparently experimented with the idea of having the charter numbers engraved on the plates and printed in black ink. This was done on $5 Original Series and Series of 1875 plates from the Continental Bank Note Co. that were dated between Nov. 15, 1873 and May 15, 1874. Only ten banks in the nation are known to have issued these notes (including two for which no notes have been reported) with four other banks probably issuing them. The First National Bank of Red Oak, #2130, is one of this elite group of issuing banks. Three black charter notes from Red Oak are known and are the three First Charter $5s listed in this census, one Original Series and two 1875 notes. (See the color illustration in Chapter Five.)

Blue end paper: Special paper, usually referred to as "blue end paper," was used to print the earliest Series of 1875 notes from September 1875 to at least the fourth quarter of 1877. The paper had a two to three inch wide vertical section stained a beautiful color. This blue band was usually positioned to the left of the note's center, but could be found in other positions. Sometimes it was readily visible on only one side, either the front or back. Our census lists 11 notes printed on blue end paper. Towns originating these notes were Charles City, Knoxville, Mt. Pleasant, Pella, Tama City, and Wyoming. Other 1875 notes in the census may also have blue end paper, but these have not been verified. (See the color illustrations for a spectacular Tama City note.)

Replacement notes: Replacement notes were not designated by a "star" as they are on more recent currency. Instead they can be distinguished only by a slightly irregular serial number overprinting. The census records only four Iowa replacement notes printed on one sheet. The Citizens National Bank of Winterset, #2002, issued a replacement sheet of $50 1929 Type I notes with serial numbers A-F000353A.

Circus poster layouts: The bank titles, or tombstones, on five dollar 1882 Brown Backs were printed with a large variety of type fonts and layouts, ranging in aesthetic quality from striking to ugly. One of the favorite layouts for collectors is known as the "circus poster layout." Its printing is reminiscent of the gaudy circus advertising posters of the day. The only bank in Iowa to issue notes with a circus poster layout was The Live Stock National Bank of Sioux City, #5022. Three of these notes are known, and one is shown in the color illustrations.

Fourth Charter notes: Banks that needed to extend their charters in late 1921 or 1922 issued notes that had a new date on the note to designate their changed status. The date was about twenty years after the date on their earlier Third Charter notes. Otherwise the notes were unchanged. These notes with a 1922 plate date are sometimes called "Fourth Charter" or "Series of 1922" notes. Banks in Shenandoah, #2679, and Lyons, #66, were the only Iowa banks to issue these notes.

Stolen notes: Before the Act of July 28, 1892, national bank notes were not redeemable by the Treasury until they were signed by the bank officers. Several batches of notes from various banks were stolen before they could be signed. If these were passed by the thieves and eventually returned to the Treasury for redemption, the Treasury would cancel them and return them to the bank that sent them in. This fate befell The Osage National Bank, #1618.

The bank was chartered in 1865 and commenced operations on February 1, 1866 in the former Treasurer's office of the county courthouse. Three months later on Saturday night May 5/6, 1866, robbers boldly broke open the vault door and used drill and gunpowder to blow the door of the Lillie's Patent chilled iron safe contained within the vault. They stole over $8,000 of money and securities (mostly compound interest notes and interest bearing notes). In addition, their haul included another $9,000 worth of unsigned national bank notes. The stolen notes were Original Series $5 bills with serial numbers in the range 1751-2200. Subsequently, at least some of the notes reappeared with forged bank signatures and processing to make them appear well circulated.

Thirteen stolen Osage notes have been preserved for collectors and appear in the census. The stolen notes comprise about a third of all known Iowa $5 Original Series notes. Some, but not all, have been cancelled by a receiving bank. (A canceled note is shown in the color illustrations.)

The First National Bank of Mason City, #2574, was the subject of an infamous robbery. On March 13, 1934, John Dillinger "Public Enemy No. 1" robbed the bank of $52,000 out of an estimated $300,000 that the bank had on hand. The bank must have had a considerable amount of its own and neighboring banks' currencies, but unfortunately no serial numbers of the stolen notes were available. Thus, collectors are left to dream about whether their Mason City or other Cerro Gordo county notes may have been part of the loot.

Counterfeit pieces: Counterfeiting has been a problem ever since the invention of paper currency. It was a severe epidemic before the Civil War during the era of obsolete bank notes and led to the publication and widespread use of Banknote Reporters to verify the legitimacy of questionable notes. The introduction of high quality federal notes produced a diminution but not an elimination of the problem. However, counterfeiting of national bank notes was primarily confined to notes from banks in the larger population centers. Collectors of Iowa notes are fortunate that there are no known contemporary counterfeit notes on any Iowa bank.

Banks, Towns, and Counties

Only one note has been identified from each of nine towns. Another ten towns are represented by just two notes. On the other end of the scale, 353 notes from Cedar Rapids have been found. Des Moines has 671 notes, while Sioux City leads the pack with 693 notes.

The Higgins Museum has one of the most complete collections of notes from a single state ever assembled. However, the musuem does not yet possess notes from nineteen towns in Iowa. The towns missing from the Higgins Museum's collection include Adair, Afton, Brighton*, Clutier, Coin*, College Springs, Fort Madison*, Garden Grove, Goldfield, Grafton, Harris, Holstein, Ireton, Jesup, Macksburg, Nashua, Orange City, Sanborn*, and Sutherland. Notes from all of these, except the four towns marked with an asterisk, are unreported. The Museum would be interested to hear of an opportunity to acquire notes from any of these towns.

Some collections are formed based on counties. Table 3 lists the number of notes recorded from counties that have smaller numbers known. Clarke county is the scarcest county, with only eight notes recorded. Osceola, the only issuing town in the county, is well known as a tough town from which to obtain a note. The next scarcest county is Shelby with nine notes. Shelby has only one note-issuing town, Harlan. For many years, Shelby was considered the scarcest county, but as more Harlan notes have surfaced, Shelby has lost its former title.

Table 3. Some scarcer counties and the total number of the notes and large and small subtotals

County	Total	Large	Small	County	Total	Large	Small
Clarke	8	8	0	Monona	18	11	7
Shelby	9	9	0	Davis	21	17	4
Ida	10	10	0	Winneshiek	23	15	8
Butler	12	12	0	Ringgold	25	12	13
Warren	12	12	0	Wright	27	12	15
Delaware	15	15	0	Adair	28	24	4
Emmet	15	15	0	Worth	28	7	21
Van Buren	15	11	4	Wayne	34	32	2
Osceola	17	8	9	Palo Alto	44	40	4
Iowa	18	18	0	Des Moines	83	80	3

Considering only large-size notes, the scarcest county is Worth, which has two issuing towns, Northwood and

Grafton. However, no notes are known from Grafton. That leaves just the seven large notes from Northwood available for seekers of a large-size note from Worth County. Several counties have no small-size notes. For those that do, Wayne County is the scarcest, with only two notes known from the First National Bank of Seymour and one of those is in the Higgins Museum. Although the large-size notes from Burlington are plentiful, the three small-size notes from the Merchants National Bank of Burlington are the only opportunities to find a small-size Des Moines County note.

Presented below is a summary of the census listing the total number of large and small size notes reported for each bank. The columns list in order the town name, charter number, large size total, and small size total.

Town	Charter	Large	Small
Ackley	8762	16	12
Adair	8699	0	-
Adel	8981	18	-
Afton	2326	0	-
Akron	7322	6	11
Albia	3012	0	-
Albia	1799	10	5
Albia	8603	14	11
Algona	3197	7	-
Allerton	9231	5	-
Allerton	2191	1	-
Alta	7126	7	-
Ames	10408	14	12
Ames	3017	18	10
Anamosa	4696	18	32
Anamosa	1813	1	-
Arlington	9664	8	22
Arlington	9664	3	-
Armstrong	5442	9	-
Atlantic	2762	21	19
Atlantic	1836	3	-
Audubon	4891	11	9
Aurelia	9724	13	19
Aurelia	7108	5	11
Ayrshire	5479	9	1
Bagley	6995	7	7
Bancroft	5643	14	-
Bedford	5165	22	22
Bedford	2298	0	-
Belle Plaine	4754	19	18
Belle Plaine	2012	20	-
Belmond	8748	2	-
Blanchard	4902	3	-
Blockton	8211	4	1
Bloomfield	1299	1	-
Bloomfield	9303	16	4
Bode	10371	2	2
Boone	6838	11	-
Boone	13817	-	19
Boone	2051	1	-
Boone	3273	24	46
Boone	3273	3	-
Brighton	2033	0	-
Brighton	5554	1	-
Britt	5020	5	-
Brooklyn	3284	2	-
Buffalo Center	5154	28	26
Burlington	351	5	-
Burlington	351	10	-
Burlington	1744	41	3
Burlington	751	24	-
Burt	5703	7	-
Burt	5685	18	3
Cambridge	9014	17	-
Carroll	3969	7	-
Casey	8099	24	0
Cedar Falls	3871	21	8
Cedar Falls	5507	1	-
Cedar Falls	2177	2	-
Cedar Rapids	3643	103	70
Cedar Rapids	5113	2	-
Cedar Rapids	483	2	-
Cedar Rapids	9168	4	-
Cedar Rapids	500	4	-
Cedar Rapids	2511	55	113
Centerville	2841	12	15
Centerville	2197	0	-
Centerville	337	11	-
Centerville	337	-	31
Chariton	13458	-	32
Chariton	9024	77	4
Chariton	6014	8	-
Chariton	1724	2	-
Chariton	9024	11	-
Charles City	2579	5	-
Charles City	4677	14	25
Charles City	5979	17	29
Charles City	1810	46	-
Charter Oak	4376	10	20
Chelsea	5412	10	19
Cherokee	3049	9	14
Cherokee	10711	12	6
Churdan	6737	6	15
Clarence	7682	11	8
Clarinda	3112	11	-
Clarinda	2028	4	-
Clarion	3796	7	15
Clarion	3788	0	-
Clear Lake	7869	9	26
Clearfield	9549	6	1
Clinton	66	3	-
Clinton	2469	86	128
Clinton	994	24	29
Clinton	3736	38	18
Clutier	5366	0	-
Coin	7309	2	1
Colfax	13686	-	5
Colfax	7114	7	10
College Springs	11295	0	-
Columbus Junction	2032	16	25
Conrad	9447	8	2
Coon Rapids	6080	1	-
Coon Rapids	5514	15	19
Corning	8100	8	-
Corning	2936	2	-
Corning	4268	0	-
Corning	8725	20	89
Corwith	5775	2	-
Corydon	10146	12	-
Council Bluffs	14028	-	22
Council Bluffs	9306	33	39
Council Bluffs	5838	11	-
Council Bluffs	3427	0	-
Council Bluffs	1479	69	47
Council Bluffs	1684	4	-
Cresco	4897	10	15
Creston	2833	18	3
Creston	12636	-	52
Creston	2586	2	-
Crystal Lake	9853	8	7
Crystal Lake	5305	3	-
Cumberland	7326	2	-
Davenport	1671	20	-
Davenport	848	1	-
Davenport	15	4	-
Davenport	2695	16	-
Davenport	15	69	127
Davenport	4022	39	-
Dayton	5302	11	22
De Witt	3182	28	34
Decorah	493	1	-
Decorah	5081	14	8
Deep River	6705	5	-
Denison	4784	30	69
Des Moines	13321	-	102
Des Moines	2307	-	230
Des Moines	1970	16	-
Des Moines	2583	113	-
Des Moines	389	0	-
Des Moines	2307	60	-
Des Moines	2631	1	-
Des Moines	950	0	-
Des Moines	485	0	-
Des Moines	2886	110	39
Dexter	10030	7	-
Diagonal	9125	6	12
Dike	5372	1	-
Doon	6764	14	11
Dougherty	5576	2	5
Dubuque	1801	4	-
Dubuque	2327	37	13
Dubuque	3140	11	-
Dubuque	317	65	71
Dubuque	846	0	-
Dubuque	1540	0	-
Dubuque	2327	17	-
Dunkerton	6722	10	13
Dunlap	4139	7	-

City				City				City			
Dyersville	9555	12	7	Hamburg	6017	4	-	Lawler	10599	12	-
Dysart	5934	13	-	Hamburg	2364	0	-	Lehigh	5868	6	9
Eagle Grove	4694	1	-	Hampton	13842	-	36	Lemars	2728	23	19
Eagle Grove	3439	0	-	Hampton	7843	23	40	Lemars	2818	0	-
Eagle Grove	4694	2	-	Hampton	2573	1	-	Lenox	14040	-	2
Eldon	5342	11	27	Harlan	5207	0	-	Lenox	5517	25	16
Eldora	5140	9	14	Harlan	10354	9	-	Leon	5489	12	-
Eldora	9233	18	23	Harris	6949	0	-	Leon	1696	1	-
Elkader	1815	20	12	Hartley	4881	8	-	Lime Springs	6750	6	20
Elliott	6857	4	6	Harvey	6936	14	18	Lineville	7261	1	-
Emmetsburg	8035	4	-	Havelock	7294	9	-	Linn Grove	7137	5	5
Emmetsburg	3337	14	-	Hawarden	13939	-	7	Lisbon	2182	2	-
Essex	5803	15	9	Hawarden	4594	5	14	Little Rock	8119	8	7
Essex	5738	17	26	Hawkeye	8900	13	9	Logan	6771	15	16
Estherville	4700	6	-	Hedrick	5540	4	-	Lorimor	12248	7	27
Everly	7828	11	6	Hedrick	12656	11	6	Lost Nation	5402	4	8
Exira	6870	7	5	Henderson	7382	6	10	Lyons	4536	1	-
Fairfield	8986	2	-	Holstein	4553	0	-	Lyons	66	3	-
Fairfield	1475	32	42	Hubbard	8970	6	14	Lyons	2733	4	-
Farmington	5579	7	-	Hudson	5659	2	-	Lyons	66	5	-
Farnhamville	11907	11	12	Hull	6953	6	11	Macksburg	6852	1	0
Farragut	6700	5	5	Humboldt	13766	-	11	Malvern	4834	0	-
Fayette	9592	5	-	Humboldt	8277	8	18	Malvern	2247	4	-
Floyd	9821	5	1	Ida Grove	3930	1	-	Malvern	8057	1	0
Fonda	6550	6	23	Imogene	8295	0	7	Manchester	4221	15	-
Fontanelle	7061	9	4	Independence	1581	0	-	Manilla	5873	7	15
Forest City	4889	10	-	Independence	3263	44	-	Manilla	6041	2	-
Forest City	5011	10	17	Independence	3263	2	-	Manning	3455	14	36
Fort Dodge	4566	35	11	Independence	2187	53	-	Maquoketa	999	6	12
Fort Dodge	1661	70	23	Indianola	1811	12	-	Marathon	4789	3	6
Fort Dodge	2763	51	53	Inwood	8257	12	9	Marcus	9819	2	-
Fort Dodge	1947	1	-	Inwood	7304	10	-	Marengo	2484	18	-
Fort Dodge	11304	9	-	Iowa City	18	1	-	Marion	117	2	-
Fort Madison	3974	1	-	Iowa City	2738	4	-	Marion	2753	0	-
Fort Madison	1611	1	-	Iowa City	18	26	32	Marion	117	20	26
Fredericksburg	10541	35	2	Iowa City	977	0	-	Marshalltown	4359	0	-
Galva	10501	9	-	Iowa City	2821	1	-	Marshalltown	2971	0	-
Garden Grove	5464	0	-	Iowa Falls	3252	12	27	Marshalltown	2115	1	-
Garner	8367	7	5	Iowa Falls	7521	14	13	Marshalltown	411	8	-
Garner	4810	12	-	Ireton	4794	0	-	Mason City	4587	10	-
George	9910	11	9	Jefferson	10123	2	-	Mason City	2574	55	68
Gilmore City	6611	1	-	Jefferson	8262	2	-	Mason City	10428	14	-
Gladbrook	5461	15	24	Jesup	2856	0	-	McGregor	323	21	19
Glenwood	1862	7	10	Jewell Junction	5743	2	10	Melvin	5616	4	-
Glidden	4814	19	22	Kanawha	9018	6	11	Milford	5539	7	-
Goldfield	5373	0	-	Keokuk	14309	-	0	Milford	9298	5	-
Gowrie	5707	10	12	Keokuk	80	0	-	Milford	9298	2	3
Graettinger	5571	6	3	Keokuk	1992	17	17	Milton	10243	4	4
Grafton	6610	0	-	Keokuk	1441	2	-	Missouri Valley	3189	12	17
Grand River	9737	9	7	Kimballton	9619	7	12	Monroe	2215	2	-
Greene	3071	0	-	Kingsley	9116	4	11	Monroe	7357	2	1
Greene	6880	6	-	Klemme	6659	7	16	Montezuma	2961	12	0
Greenfield	5334	15	-	Knoxville	12849	-	7	Monticello	2080	3	-
Grinnell	7439	10	2	Knoxville	4633	19	25	Montour	7469	10	16
Grinnell	1629	4	-	Knoxville	13707	-	12	Moulton	5319	5	-
Grinnell	2953	7	-	Knoxville	1871	29	-	Mount Pleasant	299	33	12
Grinnell	13473	-	31	Knoxville	12849	-	0	Mount Pleasant	922	15	-
Griswold	3048	0	-	Knoxville	1986	21	-	Muscatine	1577	6	84
Griswold	8915	17	0	La Porte City	4114	17	-	Muscatine	1577	1	-
Grundy Center	3225	14	-	Lake City	4966	15	7	Muscatine	692	1	-
Grundy Center	3396	12	15	Lake Mills	5123	8	-	Nashua	2411	0	-
Guthrie Center	7736	1	-	Lansing	405	2	-	Nevada	14065	-	4
Guthrie Center	5424	15	5	Laurens	4795	7	3	Nevada	2555	22	

New Hampton	2588	14	-	Rock Valley	5200	16	17	Swea City	5637	7	-
New Hampton	7607	25	14	Rockford	3053	6	-	Tabor	4609	8	-
New London	5420	1	-	Rockwell	10217	7	1	Tama	1880	9	-
New London	8352	7	10	Rockwell City	5185	27	-	Tama City	1880	4	-
New Sharon	8950	5	-	Rockwell City	11582	2	11	Terril	10238	49	-
Newell	10191	7	18	Roland	11249	5	28	Thompson	5054	11	19
Newton	650	3	-	Rolfe	4954	6	-	Thornton	8340	3	19
Newton	2644	23	10	Royal	10395	6	-	Tipton	6760	29	-
Newton	13609	-	31	Ruthven	5541	7	-	Tipton	2983	5	-
Nora Springs	4761	6	14	Sac City	4450	16	-	Tipton	13232	-	17
Northboro	9015	12	6	Saint Ansgar	10684	8	13	Titonka	5597	8	4
Northwood	8373	7	21	Sanborn	4824	1	-	Toledo	6432	20	-
Norway	7287	9	-	Seymour	8247	9	2	Toledo	13073	-	30
Odebolt	5817	1	-	Seymour	11210	4	-	Traer	5135	18	47
Odebolt	4511	27	43	Shannon City	9723	10	10	Valley Junction	5891	4	18
Oelwein	5778	53	20	Sheffield	12430	1	13	Villisca	2766	20	7
Olin	7585	6	-	Sheldon	3848	27	-	Villisca	14041	-	18
Orange City	6132	0	-	Sheldon	7880	15	16	Villisca	7506	6	20
Osage	4885	-	33	Shenandoah	12950	6	40	Vinton	5088	9	-
Osage	4885	5	-	Shenandoah	8971	0	-	Vinton	1593	0	-
Osage	1618	16	-	Shenandoah	11588	1	-	Washington	6122	1	-
Osceola	1776	1	-	Shenandoah	2363	5	-	Washington	398	2	-
Osceola	6033	7	-	Shenandoah	2679	9	-	Washington	2656	1	-
Oskaloosa	2895	0	-	Sibley	3320	4	9	Washington	1762	24	29
Oskaloosa	8076	10	-	Sidney	5145	20	13	Waterloo	6854	38	-
Oskaloosa	147	0	-	Sigourney	1786	32	5	Waterloo	2910	31	-
Oskaloosa	1101	1	-	Sioux Center	7369	2	13	Waterloo	792	16	-
Oskaloosa	2417	15	-	Sioux City	4510	18	11	Waterloo	5120	49	-
Ottumwa	107	25	23	Sioux City	3940	0	-	Waterloo	13702	-	24
Ottumwa	1726	6	11	Sioux City	1976	0	-	Waterloo	5120	22	44
Ottumwa	2621	29	16	Sioux City	7401	0	-	Waterloo	5700	4	-
Panora	3226	16	-	Sioux City	4630	0	-	Waukon	4921	19	-
Parkersburg	9846	6	-	Sioux City	4235	0	-	Waukon	10207	24	-
Pella	8047	8	-	Sioux City	1757	84	29	Waverly	3105	42	38
Pella	1891	2	-	Sioux City	3968	13	-	Webster City	3420	8	21
Pella	2063	19	30	Sioux City	5022	59	213	Webster City	1874	39	25
Perry	3026	9	-	Sioux City	4209	2	-	Webster City	2984	0	-
Perry	10130	4	-	Sioux City	10139	4	-	Wesley	5457	3	-
Perry	10130	9	-	Sioux City	4431	0	-	West Union	2015	38	14
Peterson	4601	10	15	Sioux City	4510	8	-	What Cheer	3192	12	25
Pleasantville	5564	3	-	Sioux City	3124	64	57	Whiting	10861	11	-
Pocahontas	12544	3	-	Sioux City	2535	2	-	Whiting	10861	-	7
Pocahontas	6303	8	-	Sioux City	10139	41	88	Williams	5585	10	2
Pomeroy	6063	16	3	Sioux Rapids	7189	0	-	Winfield	10640	15	14
Prairie City	6755	5	16	Sioux Rapids	13400	-	9	Winterset	2002	21	60
Prescott	5912	13	16	Sioux Rapids	9585	14	-	Winterset	1403	15	5
Preston	8273	6	5	Spencer	6941	20	-	Winterset	1403	0	-
Primghar	6650	0	-	Spencer	3898	5	-	Woodbine	4745	31	25
Primghar	4155	9	24	Spirit Lake	13020	5	18	Wyoming	1943	13	7
Radcliffe	6435	3	9	Spirit Lake	4758	20	-				
Rake	11735	-	14	Spirit Lake	8032	15	-				
Randolph	7833	5	4	Stanton	6434	4	5				
Red Oak	6056	17	1	State Center	8931	2	19				
Red Oak	2130	21	33	Storm Lake	10223	1	-				
Red Oak	3055	21	19	Storm Lake	10034	2	15				
Red Oak	2230	0	-	Storm Lake	10034	3	-				
Remsen	6975	16	21	Storm Lake	2595	6	-				
Renwick	7988	1	-	Story City	9017	24	34				
Riceville	8442	5	15	Story City	10222	3	-				
Richland	5611	2	-	Strawberry Point	9069	8	-				
Rippey	7609	12	12	Stuart	2721	8	4				
Rock Rapids	3153	29	11	Sumner	8198	30	53				
Rock Rapids	7089	21	13	Sutherland	3618	1	-				

Chapter Five
Illustrations of Iowa National Bank notes

This chapter supplies illustrations of Iowa National Bank notes. Images of all the known types of Iowa notes are provided as well as several interesting varieties. Notes from some scarce towns and banks are displayed. Also illustrated are rare U. S. consuls or bonds that banks purchased to provide backing for their notes.

left, First Charter, Original Series, $1, First National Bank of Dubuque, serial number 1, signed by Assistant Cashier and Vice-President

right, First Charter, Series of 1875, $1, First National Bank of Tama City, Blue End Paper, in the Higgins Museum

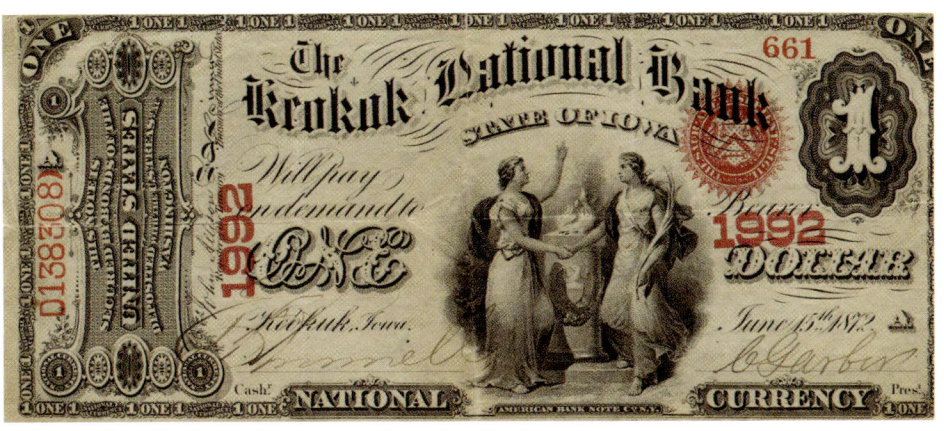

left, First Charter, Original Series, $1, Keokuk National Bank, with Charter Number, in the Higgins Museum

165

left, reverse of First Charter $1 notes, Tama City, reverses of Original Series and Series of 1875 were similar, Vignette is "Landing of the Pilgrims"

right, First Charter, Original Series, $2 Lazy Deuce, Monticello National Bank, serial number 1, in the Higgins Museum

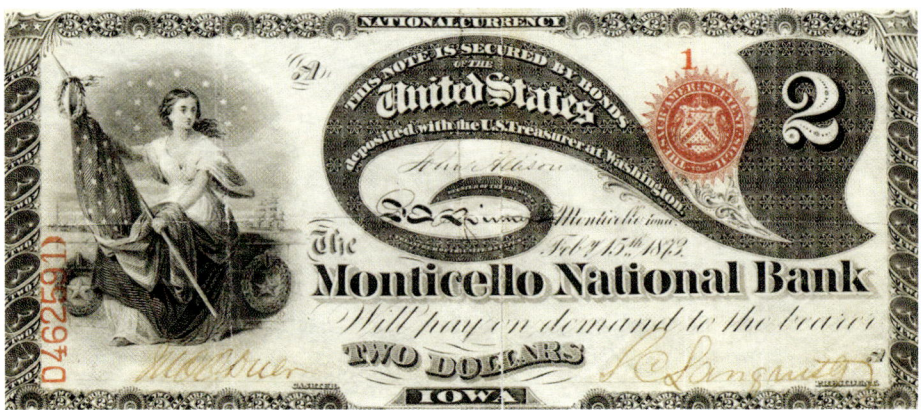

left, First Charter, Series of 1875, $2 Lazy Deuce, Marion County National Bank of Knoxville, one of two known Iowa notes of this type

right, reverse of First Charter $2 notes, Monticello, reverses of Original Series and Series of 1875 were similar, Vignette is Sir Walter Raleigh in England exhibiting corn and smoking tobacco from America

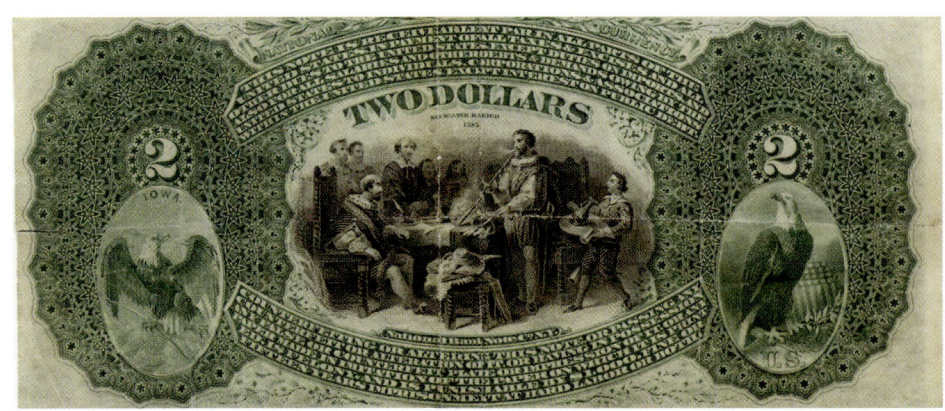

left, First Charter, Original Series, $5, Pacific National Bank of Council Bluffs, charter #1684, one of 18 banks in the nation to issue notes with the rare Jeffries-Spinner Treasury signatures, in the Higgins Musuem

right, First charter, Original Series, $5, First National Bank of Red Oak, engraved black charter number 2130, one of eight banks in the nation from which black charter notes are known, in the Higgins Museum

left, First Charter, Series of 1875, First National Bank of Elkader, charter number 1815, signed by President Wm. Larrabee, twelfth Governor of Iowa, in the Higgins Musuem

right, reverse of First Charter $5 notes, Original Series and Series of 1875 reverses were similar, Red Oak, Vignette is "The Landing of Columbus" by John Vanderlyn

167

left, First Charter, Original Series, $10, National State Bank of Burlington, only three Iowa notes of this type are known, This note was found in the Oat Bin Hoard.

right, First Charter, Series of 1875, $10, Pella National Bank, printed on blue end paper

left, First Charter, Series of 1875, $10, The only known note from the Merchants National Bank of Des Moines.

left, reverse of $10 First Charter notes, Pella, reverses of Original Series and Series of 1875 were similar, vignette is "DeSoto discovering the Mississippi, in 1541" by W.H. Powell

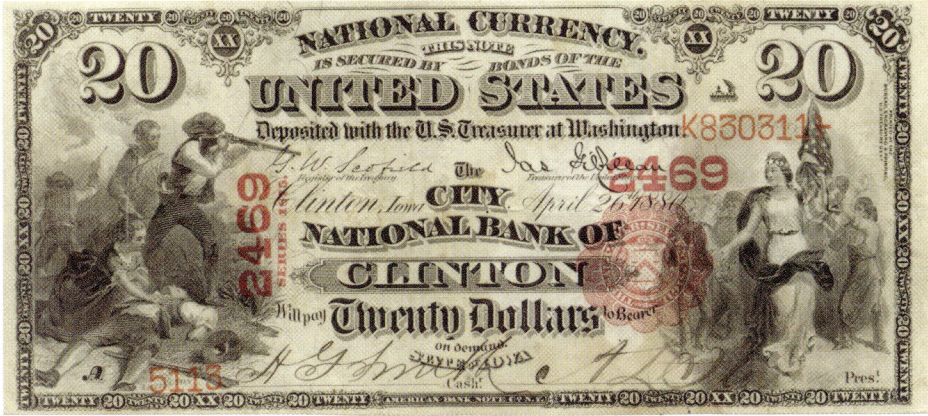

left, First Charter, Series of 1875, $20, City National Bank of Clinton

right, reverse of $20 First Charter notes. vignette is "The Baptism of Pocahontas" by John G. Chapman

left, First Charter, Series of 1875, $50, Des Moines National Bank, only five Iowa notes of this type are known, in the Higgins Museum

right, reverse of First Charter $50 notes, vignette is "Embarkation of the Pilgrims" by Robert W. Weir

Unique

The only known $100 First Charter note from Iowa.

First Charter, Series of 1875, $100, The Des Moines National Bank, Reverse vignette is "The signing of the Declaration of Independence" from a painting by John Trumball. The note is in the Higgins Museum.

left, Second Charter, Brown Back, $5, Union National Bank of Ames, vertically stacked Treasury signatures, Interesting "Geometric" bank name layout

right, reverse of Ames $5 Brown Back, an eagle in the left vignette of this early Brown Back

left, Second Charter, Brown Back, $5, City National Bank of Clinton, horizontally spaced Treasury signatures, more common later layout, serial number 1, in the Higgins Museum

reverse of Clinton $5 Brown Back, the Iowa state seal in the left vignette in this and most later Brown Backs

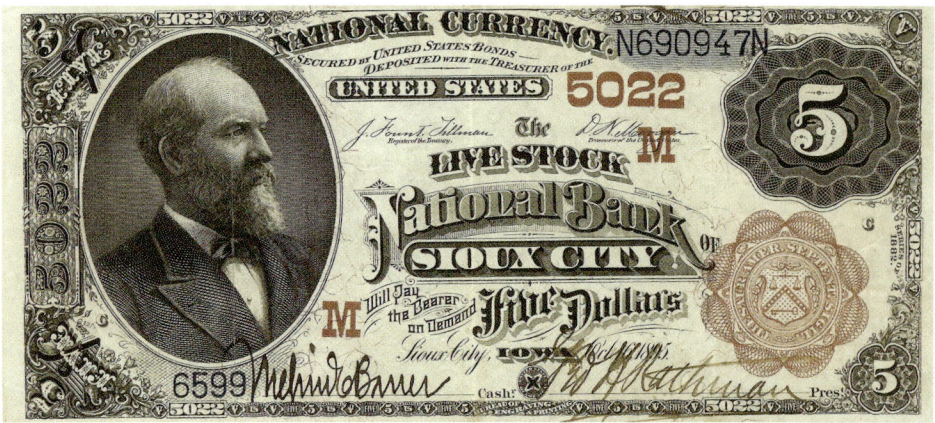

left, Second Charter, Brown Back, $5, Live Stock National Bank of Waterloo, This was the only Iowa bank to issue notes with the "Circus Poster" layout.

right, Second Charter, Brown Back, $5, Iowa State National Bank of Sioux City, $5 Brown Backs had many different bank name layouts, in the Higgins Museum

left, Second Charter, Brown Back, $5, the only known note from the Iowa City National Bank, an early layout with vertically stacked Treasury signatures, in the Higgins Museum

right, Second Charter, Brown Back, $5, Farmers National Bank of Hamburg, one of only four known notes from Hamburg, in the Higgins Museum

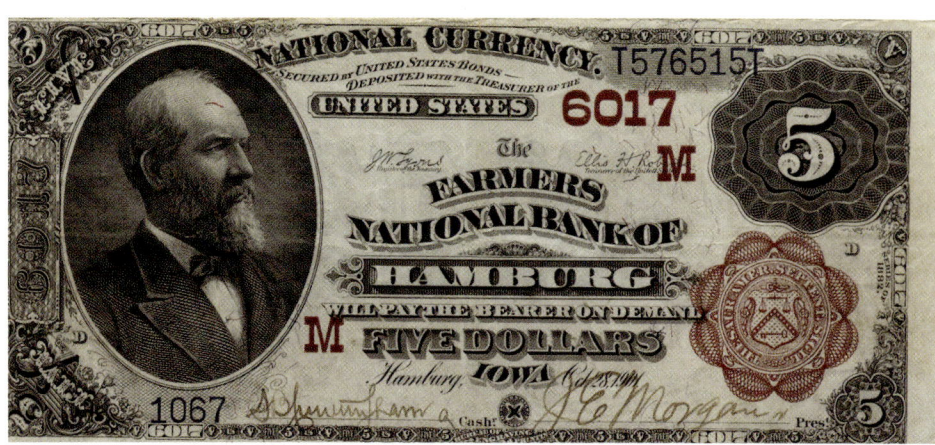

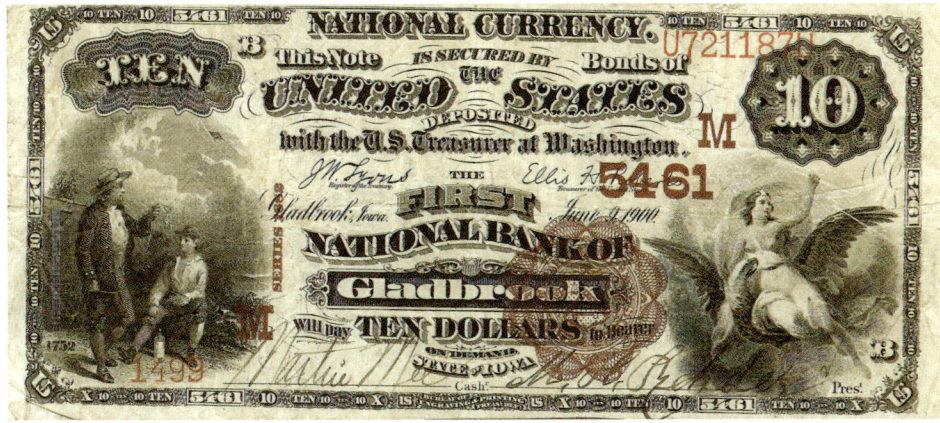

left, Second Charter, Brown Back, $10, First National Bank of Gladbrook, This note is treasured by an Iowa collector because it was signed by his great-grandfather.

right, Second Charter, Brown Back, $10, Cedar Falls National Bank

left, Second Charter, Brown Back, $10, National Bank of Brighton, the only known note from Brighton, from the Davenport Bank & Trust accumulation

right, reverse of the $10 Brown Back Gladbrook note above

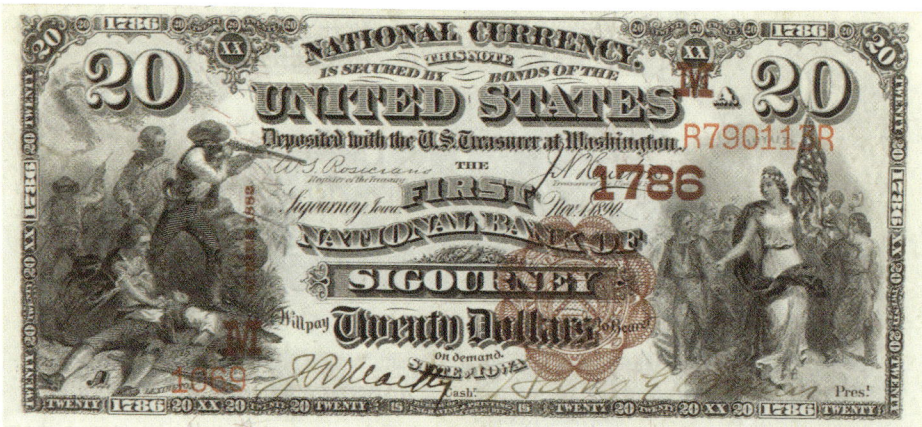

left, Second Charter, Brown Back, $20, First National Bank of Sigourney

right, Second Charter, Brown Back, $20, First National Bank of Dike, the only known note from the town of Dike, in the Higgins Museum

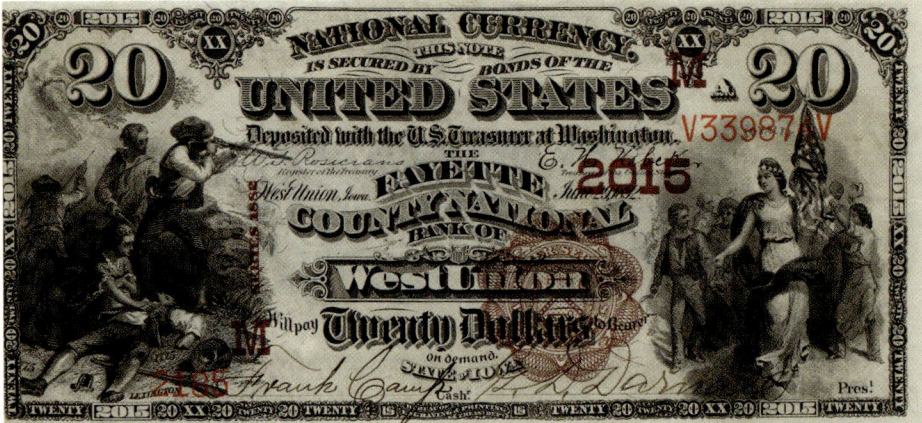

left, Second Charter, Brown Back, $20, Fayette County National Bank of West Union, in the Higgins Museum

right, reverse of $20 Brown Back Sigourney note above

left, Second Charter, Brown Back, $50, Des Moines National Bank, a scarce type nationally, in the Higgins Museum

right, reverse of the Des Moines $50 Brown Back above

left, Second Charter, Brown Back, $100, First National Bank of Spirit Lake, the inspiration for the William R. Higgins, Jr. collection, a scarce type nationally, in the Higgins Museum

right, reverse of the Spirit Lake $100 Brown Back above

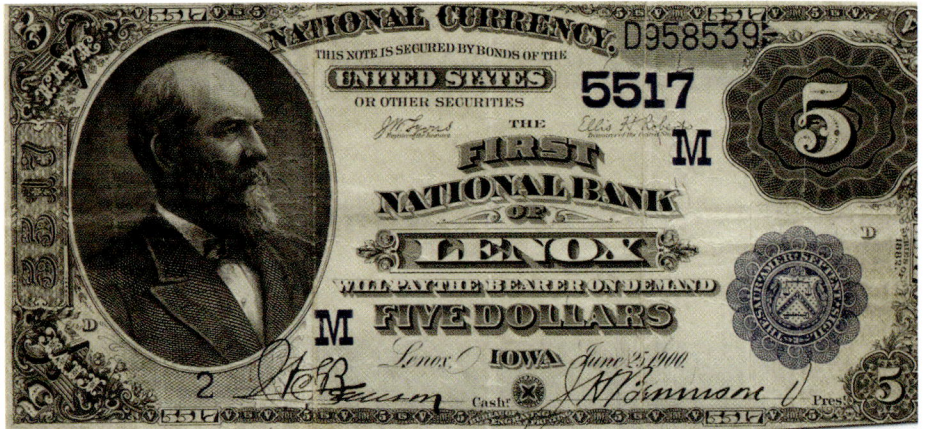

left, Second Charter, Date Back, $5, First National Bank of Lenox, serial number 2, signed by Cashier Walter S. Bennison, in the Higgins Museum

right, reverse of $5 1882 Date Back from Lenox above, inscribed from Cashier Walter S. Bennison to his nephew, Henry P. Bennison in 1928

left, Second Charter, Value Back, $5, Leavitt and Johnson National Bank of Waterloo, one of four private name banks in Iowa, in the Higgins Museum

right, reverse of the $5 Second Charter Value Back note from Waterloo above

left, Second Charter, Date Back, $10, National Bank of Decorah, one of only two Iowa banks to issue notes with the Tillman/Roberts Treasury signature combination, in the Higgins Museum

right, reverse of the $10 Date Back note from Decorah above

left, Second Charter, Value Back, $10, First National Bank of Dysart, in the Higgins Museum

right, reverse of the $10 Value Back note from Dysart above

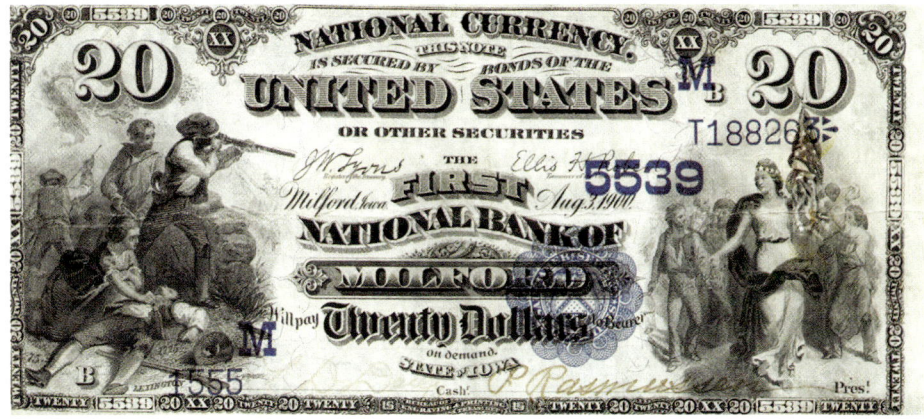

left, Second Charter, Date Back, $20, First National Bank of Milford, in the Higgins Museum

right, reverse of $20 Date Back note from Milford above

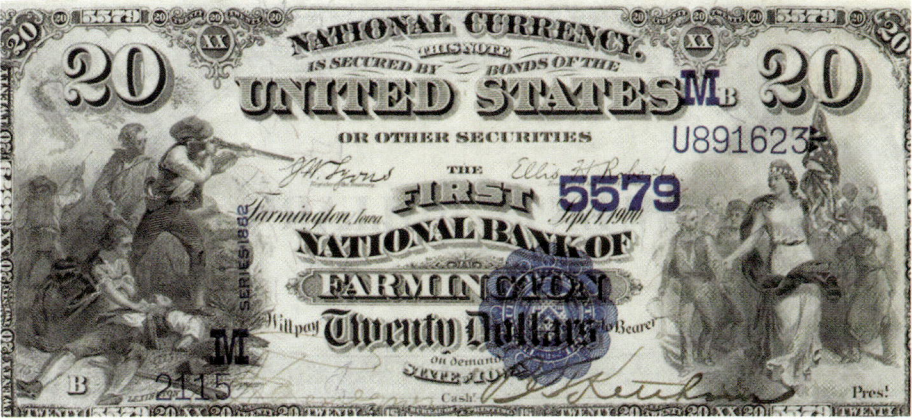

left, Second Charter, Value Back, $20, First National Bank of Farmington, in the Higgins Musuem

right, reverse of the $20 Value Back note from Farmington above

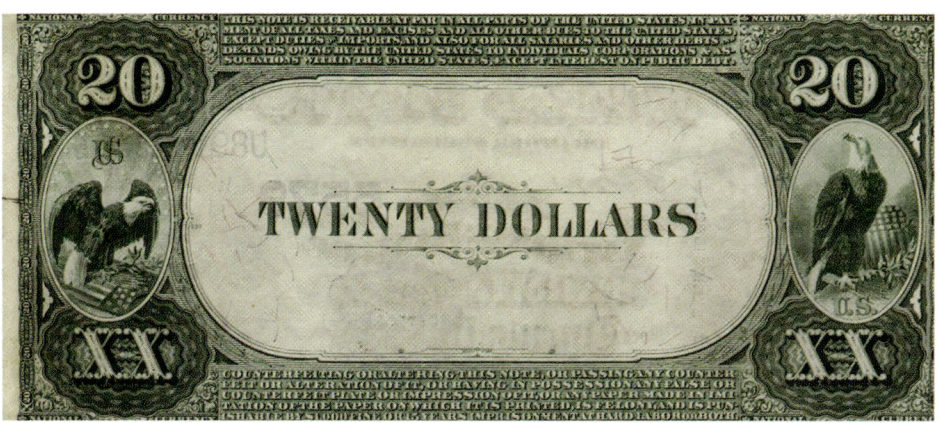

left, Second Charter, Date Back, $50, First National Bank of Nevada, a scarce type nationally

right, reverse of $50 Date Back from Nevada above

left, Second Charter, Date Back, $100, Live Stock National Bank of Sioux City, a scarce type nationally, in the Higgins Museum

right, reverse of $100 Date Back from Sioux City above

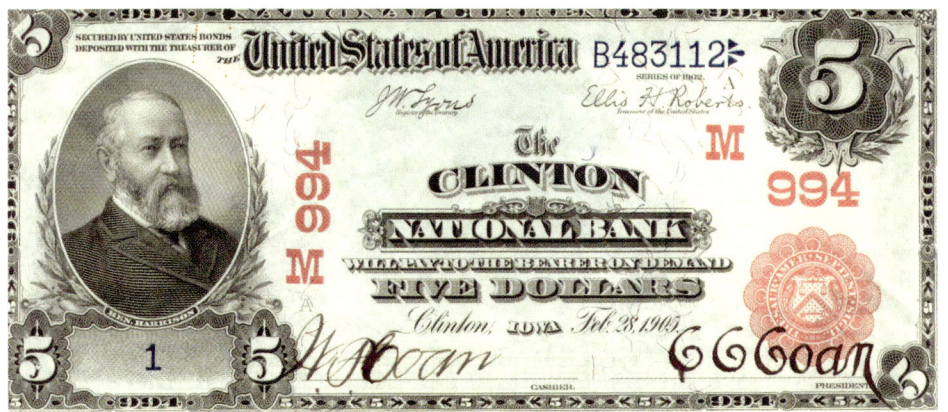

left, Third Charter, Red Seal, $5, Clinton National Bank, serial number 1

right, reverse of the $5 Red Seal from Clinton above, $5 reverses of Third Charter Plain Back notes are similar. Date Backs have "1902-1908" at top. The vignette is "The Landing of the Pilgrims".

left, Third Charter, Red Seal, $10, Second National Bank of New Hampton

right, reverse of $10 Red Seal note from New Hampton above, $10 reverses of Third Charter Plain Back notes are similar. Date Backs have "1902-1908" at top.

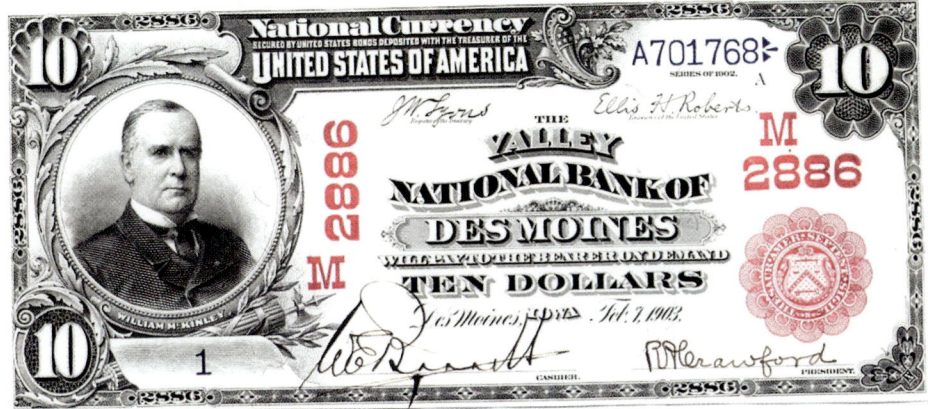

left, Third Charter, Red Seal, $10, Valley National Bank of Des Moines, serial number 1

right, Third Charter, Red Seal, $10, Merchants National Bank of Clinton, serial number 1

left, Third Charter, Red Seal, $20, First National Bank of McGregor

right, reverse of $20 Red Seal note from McGregor above. Reverses of $20 Third Charter Plain Back notes are similar. Date Backs have "1902-1908" at center top.

left, Third Charter, Red Seal, $50, First National Bank of Davennport, one of the scarcest Iowa types, only two Iowa notes of this type known, from the Davenport B&T accumulation

right, reverse of $50 Red Seal from Davenport above, Reverses of $50 Third Charter Plain Backs are similar. Date Backs have "1902-1908" at center top.

left, Third Charter, Red Seal, $100, First National Bank of Davenport, very scarce type nationally with about 100 known, all 9 known Iowa notes are from this bank, in the Higgins Museum

right, reverse of $100 Third Charter Red Seal from Davenport above, Reverses of $100 Third Charter Plain Backs are similar.

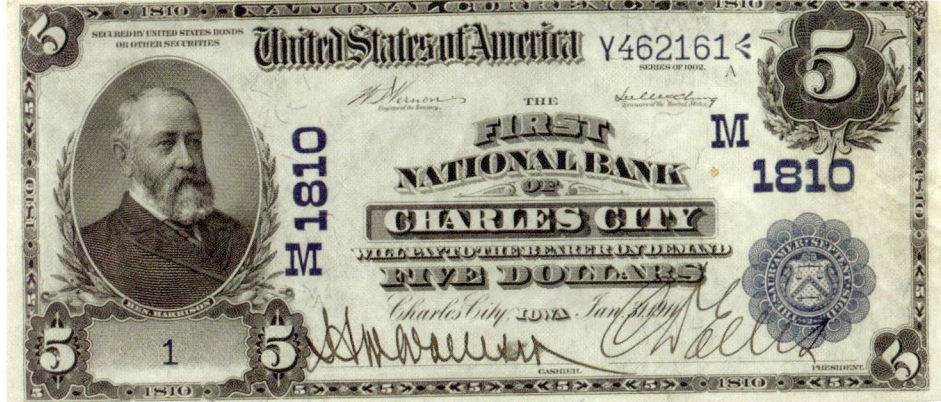

left, Third Charter, Date Back, $5, First National Bank of Charles City, serial no. 1

right, Third Charter, Plain Back, $5, Consolidated National Bank of Dubuque, one of only two Iowa banks to have the bank officers' signatures engraved on the printing plate, in the Higgins Museum

left, Third Charter, Date Back, $10, First National Bank of Sac City, in the Higgins Museum

right, Third Charter, Plain Back, $10, Exchange National Bank of Leon, in the Higgins Museum

left, Third Charter, Date Back, $20, First National Bank of Sumner

right, Third Charter, Plain Back, $20, Toy National Bank of Sioux City, named after President James F. Toy, one of four private name banks in Iowa, in the Higgins Museum

left, Third Charter, Date Back, $50, First National Bank of Marshalltown

left, Third Charter, Plain Back, $50, First National Bank of Clarion, in the Higgins Musuem

left, Third Charter, Date Back, $100, Osage National Bank, in the Higgins Musuem

right, reverse of $100 Date Back Osage note above

left, Third Charter, Plain Back, $100, Mills County Bank of Glenwood, in the Higgins Museum

right, reverse of the $100 Plain Back note from Glenwood above

left, Series of 1929, Type I, $5, First National Bank of Roland, in the Higgins Museum

right, Series of 1929, Type I, $10, First National Bank of Farifield

left, Series of 1929, Type I, $20, National Bank of Milton

right, Series of 1929, Type I, $50, Iowa National Bank of Ottumwa, in the Higgins Museum

left, Series of 1929, Type I, $100, Merchants National Bank of Cedar Rapids

right, Series of 1929, Type II, $5, Okey-Vernon National Bank of Corning, one of four private name national banks in Iowa, in the Higgins Museum

left, Series of 1929, Type II, $10, First National Bank of Creston, note the changed serial number and charter number overprint in this and all other Type II notes, in the Higgins Museum

right, Series of 1929, Type II, $20, Nodaway Valley National Bank of Villisca. No Type II $50 or $100 notes were issued by any bank in Iowa. in the Higgins Museum

left, reverse of Series of 1929 Type I and II, $5

right, reverse of Series of 1929 Type I and II, $10

left, reverse of Series of 1929 Type I and II, $20

right, reverse of Series of 1929, Type I, $50

left, reverse of Series of 1929, Type I, $100

left, First Charter, Original Series, $5, First National Bank of Washington, scarce Chittenden/Spinner Treasury signature combination, in the Higgins Museum

right, Third Charter, Plain Back, $20, First National Bank of Renwick, only known note from Renwick, in the Higgins Museum

left, Second Charter, Date Back, $20, First National Bank of Richland, one of two known notes from Richland

right, Third Charter, Plain Back, $10, First National Bank of Lineville, only known note from Lineville, in the Higgins Museum

left, Third Charter, Red Seal, $10, First National Bank of Deep River, from the Estherville hoard

right, Second Charter, Brown Back, $10, Citizens' National Bank of Lyons, only known note from this bank, only Iowa Bank to have an apostrophe in its name, in the Higgins Museum

left, Second Charter, Brown Back, $10, First National Bank of Ida Grove, only known note from Ida Grove, in the Higgins Museum

right, Third Charter, Plain Back, $20, First National Bank of Lost Nation, sought after nationally for its unusual town name, in the Higgins Museum

left, Third Charter, Plain Back, $20, German-American National Bank of Arlington, the only "ethnic" named bank in Iowa, in the Higgins Museum

right, First Charter, Series of 1875, Citizens National Bank of Davenport, the only Iowa bank with notes known to have the Allison/Gilfillan Treasury signature combination, in the Higgins Museum

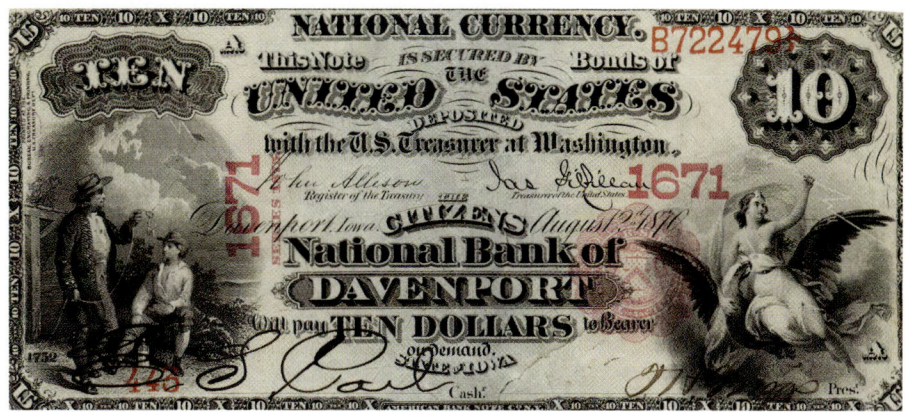

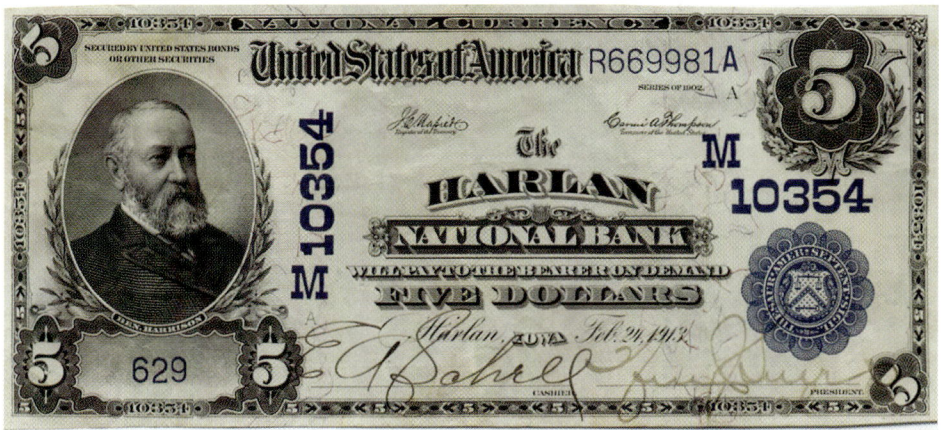

left, Third Charter, Date Back, $5, Harlan National Bank, once one of the most sought-after Iowa towns because there was only one known note from Shelby county, in the Higgins Museum

right, Third Charter, Date Back, $10, Story City National Bank, one of three known notes from this bank

left, Third Charter, Date Back, $10, First National Bank of Coin, only three notes known from this town, highly desirable for its unusual, numismatic town name

right, Third Charter, Plain Back, $20, First National Bank of What Cheer, sought after nationally for its unusual town name, in the Higgins Museum

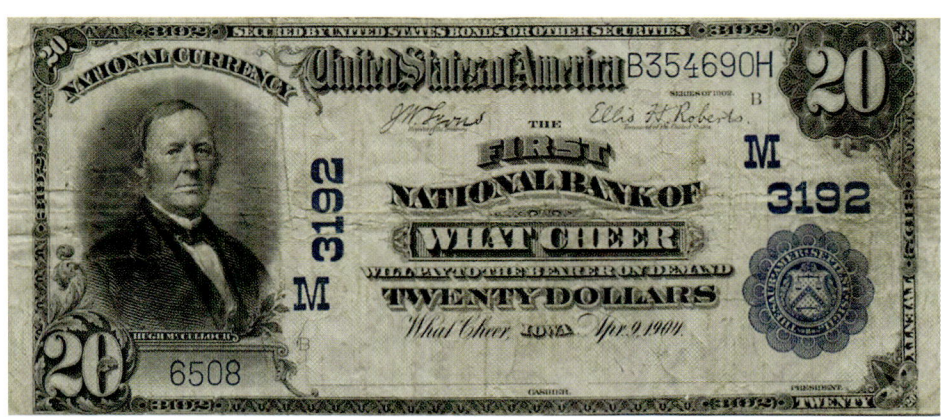

left, Second Charter, Brown Back, $10, First National Bank of Fairfield, one of two known banks to have issued notes with the Bruce/Jordan Treasury signature combination

right, $100 Two percent Consol of 1900-1930, a bond purchased by banks to provide security for their currency, very scarce

Uncut sheet
Live Stock National Bank of Sioux City
Third Charter $5 Plain Backs

Osage National Bank $5 Original Series
Stolen unsigned in 1866 Robbery
Distressed and signatures forged
Rejected by the Chase National Bank of New York on April 13, 1875
Stamped "S" and with original wrapper bearing rejection notice

$50 Four Per Cent Consols of 1877
A bond that national banks bought to back their notes.
Each coupon was for $0.50 quarterly interest on the $50 principal.
Very Scarce

First National Bank of Gladbrook
Stock Certificate

Ten shares of stock issued to founder and bank President William Mee on July 7, 1900
Certificate canceled with overscript on Dec. 29, 1909

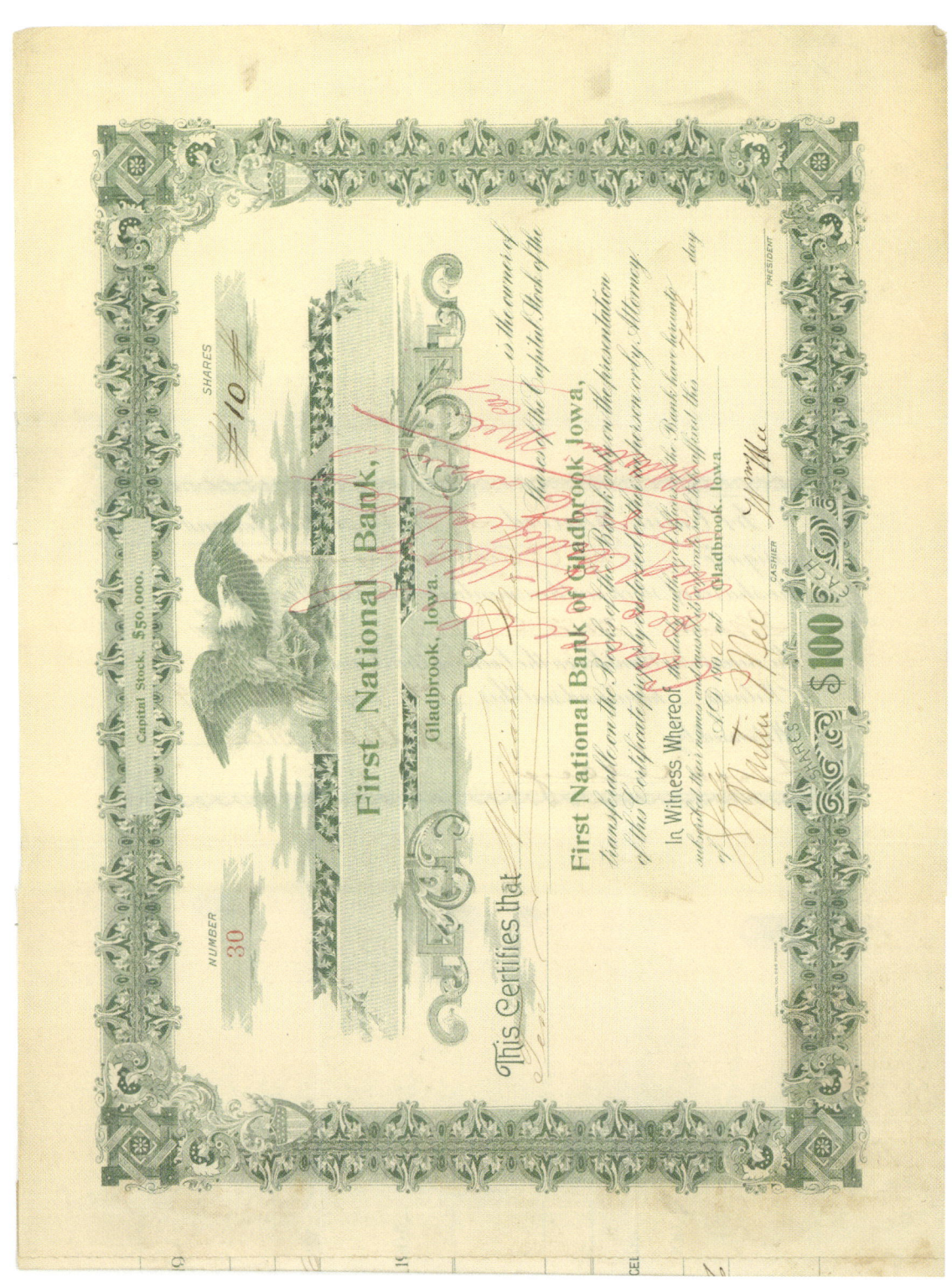

Chapter Six
The Abram Rutt National Bank of Casey

The Abram Rutt National Bank of Casey is one of only four "private name" banks chartered in Iowa. A "private name" bank is one in which the founder's name or surname is included in the name of the bank. The bank notes issued by these "private name" banks are quite fascinating to collect, as they are more readily identifiable with the early bankers of the state.

Abram Rutt

Abram Rutt was born on October 3, 1831 in Lancaster County, Pennsylvania. Lured by the fascinating stories of the great West, at the age of 22 he arrived in Iowa. In the spring of 1854 he settled in Adair County, helping to map out the town of Fontanelle, which became the first county seat. It was here that he made his home until 1876. At which time he moved his family to the town of Casey, just north into Guthrie County. After years of ill health, his wife Sarah of 19 years died August 25, 1885.

During October 1885, Abram Rutt founded the Farmers' Bank of Casey, which he operated as a private bank until it was merged into the newly chartered Abram Rutt National Bank in February 1906. Abram served as the new bank's first President. On January 6, 1913, at the age of 81, the life of Abram Rutt came to an end.

The Bank

Chartered February 17, 1906 with capital of $25,000, The Abram Rutt National Bank of Casey served as a continuation of the banking business established by Abram Rutt 20 years earlier. (A copy of the original charter, No. 8099, is illustrated at the end of this chapter.) This banking business grew along with the growth and prosperity of the local economy of Adair and Guthrie counties.

Unfortunately, like so many banks it succumbed to the agricultural depression of the 1920s and was placed in voluntary liquidation on February 1, 1930. Its assets were absorbed by the Citizens Savings Bank, which moved across the street into the Abram Rutt bank building. This bank was the predecessor to the Security State Bank, which is now a branch of MetaBank and still operates out of The Abram Rutt National Bank building.

Comparative Deposits

Jan. 1, 1886..........	$5,494.93
Jan. 1, 1890..........	20,469.25
Jan. 1, 1895..........	31,224.63
Jan. 1, 1900..........	47,418.20
Jan. 1, 1905........	121,617.12
Jan. 1, 1910.......	224,338.37
Jan. 1, 1915.......	354,403.00

The Building

In 1915, The Abram Rutt National Bank moved into its new building, which was erected as a memorial to its founder. The Lytle Company of Sioux City, Iowa served as the architect and builder.

As with many banks of the period, the quality of the building served as a reflection of the financial strength and integrity of the bank and its importance within the community. To this day, it stands as the most prestigious building in the town of Casey.

The exterior was of buff hytex enameled brick in Roman shape, trimmed in cream terra cotta in glazed finish. The interior was finished in Honduras mahogany, the lobby floor being of ceramic tile in decorative design, and the lower walls and fixtures in Italian and Verde antique marble. A notable feature was the farmers' and businessmen's room in the basement, so located to be accessible from the outside, from the public lobby, or from the bank space.

The Abram Rutt National Bank of Casey remains of personal interest of this author (S. Sweeney) as it was the issuer of the first Iowa national bank note he acquired and served to foster an ongoing interest in Iowa national banks.

The other Iowa "private name" banks are The Okey-Vernon National Bank of Corning, The Toy National Bank of Sioux City, and The Leavitt and Johnson National Bank of Waterloo.

Charter of The Abram Rutt National Bank of Casey, Charter #8099

ORGANIZATION DIVISION.
Form No. 1998.
(Ed. Jan. 14-05—5 vols.)

No. 8099

Treasury Department,

OFFICE OF COMPTROLLER OF THE CURRENCY,

Washington, D.C., February 17, 1906

Whereas, by satisfactory evidence presented to the undersigned, it has been made to appear that "The Abram Rutt National Bank of Casey," in the Town of Casey, in the County of Guthrie and State of Iowa, has complied with all the provisions of the Statutes of the United States, required to be complied with before an association shall be authorized to commence the business of Banking;

Now, THEREFORE, I, Thomas P. Kane, Deputy and Acting Comptroller of the Currency, do hereby certify that "The Abram Rutt National Bank of Casey," in the Town of Casey, in the County of Guthrie and State of Iowa, is authorized to commence the business of Banking as provided in Section Fifty-one hundred and sixty-nine of the Revised Statutes of the United States.

IN TESTIMONY WHEREOF, witness my hand and seal of office this Seventeenth day of February, 1906.

T. P. Kane
Deputy and Acting Comptroller of the Currency.

Chapter Seven
Nevada's Bank Holiday

Many Iowa banks had greater financial difficulties during the late 1920s and early 1930s. As an example of what the banks and their communities experienced, we present the story of the bank holiday in Nevada, Iowa.

On March 6, 1933 President Franklin D. Roosevelt declared a bank holiday, closing all banks in the United States. The purpose was to help stem a money panic spreading throughout the nation. Many banks had insufficient cash to cover depositor withdrawals and were forced to suspend payments.

The Banking Act of 1933 passed by Congress on March 9, 1933 allowed those banks with sufficient cash on hand to reopen on March 13, 1933. The availability of cash withdrawals helped restore public confidence in the banking system. A significant number of banks either did not survive the Bank Holiday or succumbed within the next few years.

The City of Nevada, Iowa had experienced banking uncertainty six years earlier when the Peoples Savings Bank and the First National Bank (charter #2555) failed in 1927 due to a local depression. On Monday, July 18, 1932 Mayor C. F. Wilson of Nevada, Iowa issued a proclamation which declared a four-day holiday for businesses in Nevada. This action was motivated by a desire to give the Farmers Trust and Savings Bank time to recover from its financial difficulties. The Nevada Community Club quickly met and passed the following proclamation at a mass meeting of citizens later that morning.

"Resolution of Confidence
Whereas, on this 18th day of July, 1932, the mayor of the City of Nevada has issued a proclamation publicly proclaiming and declaring the period of July 18 to July 21 inclusive as one of holiday; and recommending that business be closed during certain hours of each day, and Whereas the undersigned committee representing the Nevada Community Club are fully confident that in these strenuous times it is best for the people to counsel with each other for their mutual benefit, and being advised that the Farmers Trust and Savings Bank of Nevada, Iowa, is about to request the signing of depositors agreements on the part of their depositors, to the end that they may prevent further withdrawal of funds and thus conserve its assets for the benefit of the depositors, and,
Whereas the Nevada Community Club has the fullest confidence in the integrity, honesty and business ability of the officers and management of the Farmers Trust and Savings Bank, now we, as your committee do earnestly recommend the fullest cooperation of the members of the club and the people of the community at large expediting the signing of these depositors agreements, to the end that the bank may continue to function and be a benefit to the community in the future as it has been so many years in the past."

During the four-day holiday, practically all businesses in Nevada were closed with the exception of food stores, which were allowed to operate during certain hours. Two banking institutions, the Nevada National Bank and the Farmers Trust and Savings Bank, were affected by Mayor Wilson's proclamation.

Nevada National Bank
The Nevada National Bank was organized on May 17, 1927, received charter 13083, and elected not to issue national banknotes. Capitalization was in the amount of $40,000.

This bank had sufficient cash on hand to pay depositors. A 4 1/2" x 6" display advertisement appearing in the Monday, July 18, 1932 Nevada Evening Journal stated in bold type: "The Nevada National Bank is ready and in a position to Pay Any and All Depositors as soon as the Mayor Permits us to be open." The photograph below shows money stacked on the bank's counters prior to reopening in an attempt to reassure its patrons.

The Nevada National Bank reopened on Friday morning, July 22, 1932. It weathered this crisis easily, but entered a conservatorship on March 23, 1933 and suffered voluntary liquidation on May 1, 1934. Bank officers were S. M. McHose, President and H. F. Jones, Cashier.

Farmers Trust and Savings Bank
This was the oldest surviving bank in Story County. It was founded in 1870 by Otis Briggs, Sr. as a private bank. Mr. Briggs relinquished his interest to his son-in-law, Jay G. Dutton, and Dutton's partner, J. A. Mills, Sr. in 1897. The Farmers Bank reorganized, receiving a state charter on February 6, 1928, as the Farmers Trust and Savings Bank. It was capitalized at $100,000 and deposits exceeded $1,250,000.

A cash shortage forced the bank to adopt a waiver arrangement whereby if 100 % of the depositors agreed to leave their funds on deposit for three years, the bank would be permitted to reopen. Interest accrued at 3 % and was payable semiannually. Quite a task as depositors resided as far away as California. The waiver campaign was under the personal direction of Ray H. Emmert of Des Moines who was experienced in such matters. Community Club members and others contacted all depositors on behalf of the arrangement.

As Mayor Wilson's proclamation expired Thursday evening, July 21, an extension was necessary to protect the Farmers Trust and Savings Bank while waivers were solicited. A 3" x 3 1/2" display advertisement in the

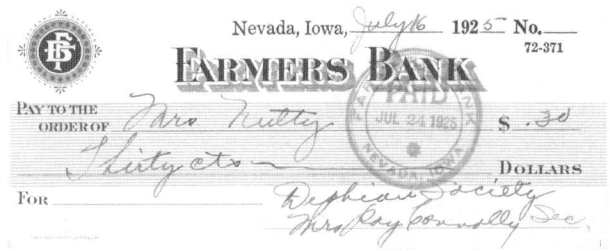

Wednesday, July 20 Nevada Evening Journal stated:
"A PLEDGE Nevada, Iowa, July 19, 1932. I hereby give you my personal pledge that, if the Depositor's Agreement Plan is accepted by this community, as it now appears that it will be, that I will myself continue in the management of the Farmers Trust and Savings Bank for at least three years, that the business of the bank will be managed as efficiently and economically as possible, and that there will be no reduction in the capital or in the stockholder's liability. (signed) Joseph A. Mills"

Several depositor meetings were held, culminating at the Knights of Pythias Hall at 8:00 pm on Saturday, July 23. At 8:30 pm it was announced that 97.5 % of the approximately $400,000 in deposits had been secured by waivers. The Farmers Trust and Savings Bank reopened for business on Monday, July 25, 1932 to the great relief of the town citizenry. At the hour of opening the banks that morning, the high school band played a concert in front of each of the banks. Unfortunately, the reprieve was only temporary as the bank's doors closed for good on June 7, 1933.

by Carl Allen

Chapter Eight
Non-issuing Iowa National Banks

The National Currency Act of February 25, 1863 created the system of national banks throughout the country. Among the many provisions of this act was the requirement that national banks purchase interest-bearing government bonds and deposit them with the Treasury. Each bank was entitled to circulate notes with a face value of 90% of the value of the bonds deposited. Originally for all but the largest banks, $50,000 worth of bonds were required to be deposited; and the bank could then issue $45,000 worth of national bank notes. Thus, essentially all banks chartered in the nineteenth century issued notes. The only exceptions to this rule were a few banks scattered throughout the nation that were unable to complete the process or raise the required funds. The Second National Bank of Ottumwa, charter #195, had the dubious distinction of being the earliest chartered bank in the nation that failed to issue notes. It could not raise sufficient capital and went in voluntary liquidation on May 2, 1864, shortly after its formation.

The Federal Reserve Act of 1913 produced major changes in the banking system. One provision of the act eliminated the requirement for national banks to issue currency. Several Iowa national banks that were chartered after this Act took advantage of this provision to operate their banking business without issuing any notes.

One interesting bank was The Citizens National Bank of Webb, Iowa charter # 11162. It was chartered on March 22, 1918. Following an order from the bank, $50,000 in currency (one thousand sheets of $10-10-10-20 notes) was printed. However, these were never issued and the sheets were later canceled on April 22, 1929. A $20 proof prepared for this printing is illustrated below.

Other banks had intentions of issuing notes, but circumstances prevented it. These were usually banks that had been organized to succeed a prior bank in financial trouble. The new bank took over the assets and assumed the existing circulation of the old bank. If the new bank was formed with a lower capital than the old one, a portion of the old bank's currency had to be retired before any new currency could be issued. If the new bank failed before it had retired enough of the old currency, no notes were ever issued from the new bank.

Ashton, #11644, the First National Bank of Ashton, chartered March 1920, capital of $25,000, voluntary liquidation Nov. 15, 1926 with a capital of $25,000, succeeded by #12883
Ashton, #12883, First National Bank, Ashton, organized January 15, 1926 with a capital of $25,000; conservatorship March 20, 1933; receivership October 31, 1933 capital $25,000
Belle Plaine, #14069, the Citizens National Bank at Belle Plaine, chartered March 1934, succeeded and assumed the circulation of #4754. At the end of the note-issuing period it was in the process of reducing the $50,000 capitalization of #4754 to $25,000 at which point it would have issued its own notes.
Bellevue, #12303, The First National Bank, in receivership June 25, 1934
Bellevue, #14158, First National Bank
Burlington, #13694, the First National Bank in Burlington, chartered May 1933
Cedar Falls, #14421, First National Bank, chartered 1935
Clear Lake, #14085, the First National Bank in Clear Lake, chartered March 1935, succeeded #7869

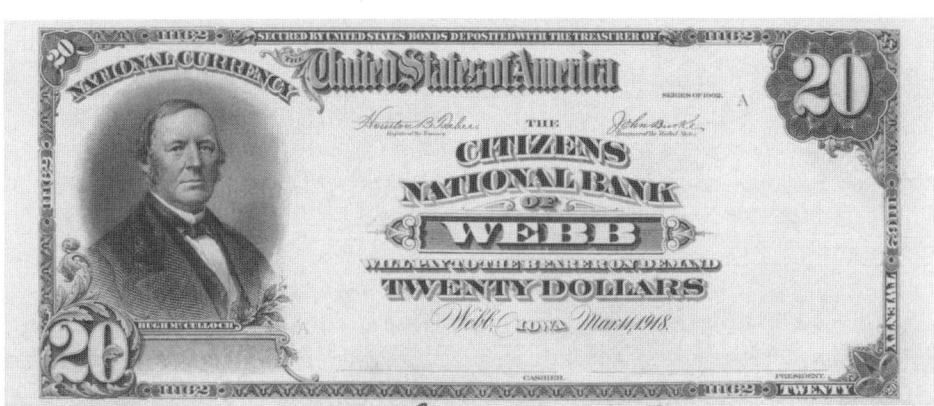

Corydon, #13109, the Commercial National Bank, chartered July 1927, voluntary liquidation Feb. 24, 1930 @ capitalization of $40,000. Absorbed by Corydon State Bank

Derby, #10848, First National Bank of Derby, organized March 23, 1916 with a capital of $25,000, in receivership Feb. 10, 1928, cause: local depression

Dyersville, #13508, Dyersville National Bank of Dyersville, chartered December 1930, succeeded #9555, title change to Dyersville National Bank on January 21, 1931.

Dysart, #5934 (Second Title), Dysart National Bank, Mar. 10, 1928.

Eldora, #14286, Hardin County National Bank in Eldora, chartered October 1934, succeeded and assumed the circulation of #9233, in process of reducing the $50,000 capital of #9233 to $35,000 at which point it would have issued.

Emmetsburg, #13059, the National Bank of Emmetsburg, organized Apr. 5, 1927 with $60,000 capital; succeeded # 3337, in receivership Mar. 15, 1929 with $60,000 capital; cause: local depression

Fairfield, #13991, First National Bank in Fairfield, chartered February 1934, succeeded #1475

Garner, #14036, Hancock County National Bank, chartered February 1934

Glidden, #14326, First National Bank in Glidden, chartered February 1935 with $50,000 capital; succeeded and assumed circulation of #4814

Grundy Center, #14066, Grundy National Bank of Grundy Center, chartered March 1934, succeeded #3396.

Hamburg, #12610, First National Bank in Hamburg, chartered Dec. 1924, with $50,000 capital; voluntary liquidation Nov. 13, 1931 at $50,000, absorbed by Iowa State Bank.

Independence, #13188, Buchanan County National Bank of Independence, organized Mar. 15, 1928 with $125,000 capital; in receivership Aug. 1, 1932 at $125,000.

Iowa City, #13697, First Capitol National Bank of Iowa City, chartered June 1933 with $100,000 capital.

Knoxville, #12849 (First Title), The Knoxville National Bank and Trust Company, no issue, succeeded by #12849 (Second Title) Knoxville-Citizens National Bank & Trust Company which did issue notes.

Lake Park, #12645, First National Bank of Lake Park, chartered Feb. 1925, with $25,000 capital.

Le Mars, #14253, First National Bank in Le Mars, chartered Aug. 1934, with $65,000 capital, succeeded and assumed circulation of #2778.

Mallard, #10562, First National Bank of Mallard, organized May 19, 1914 with $25,000 capital; in receivership Oct. 3, 1927 at $25,000, cause: local depression

Mapleton, #10701, The First National Bank

Merrill, #10889, The First National Bank of Merrill, organized Aug. 3, 1916 with $40,000 capital; in receivership Sep. 18, 1931 at $40,000 capital

Nevada, #13083, Nevada National Bank, liquidated May 1, 1934, succeeded by #14065

New Hampton, #12998, the First National Bank in New Hampton, chartered Oct. 1926

Newton, #10726, Clark National Bank of Newton, chartered Apr. 1915; in voluntary liquidation Oct. 20, 1926 with $50,000 capital; absorbed by Jasper County Savings Bank

Ogden, #11604, The First National Bank, liquidated April 16, 1935

Orange City, #10877, Orange City National Bank, organized June 7, 1916 with $25,000 capital; in conservatorship Mar. 25, 1933

Ottumwa, #195, the Second National Bank, attempted to organize in 1864; voluntary liquidation May 2, 1864; no capital, organization not completed.

Paullina, #10812, First National Bank, chartered Jan. 1916 with $25,000 capital.

Red Oak, #13875, Montgomery County National Bank of Red Oak, chartered Sep. 1928, with $50,000 capital; succeeded and assumed circulation of #3055.

Rembrandt, #10729, The First National Bank

Pella, #8047 (Second Title), The Farmers National Bank of Pella.

Rockwell City, #13890, The National Bank of Rockwell City, chartered Dec. 1933; succeeded #11582

Seymour, #13495, National Bank of Seymour, absorbed #8247 on December 17, 1930, in receivership December 30, 1931

Shenandoah, #14057, the City National Bank of Shenandoah, chartered Mar. 1934 with $100,000 capital; succeeded and assumed the circulation of #12950 (& #2679; capital reduction from $100,000 to $60,000 not reached by end of note-issuing period.

Sioux City, #10518, Continental National Bank of Sioux City, chartered Apr. 1914; voluntary liquidation Jan. 10, 1922 at $250,000 capital, absorbed by #4510.

Sioux City, #13538, First National Bank, chartered Apr. 1931

Spencer, #13112, Clay County National Bank of Spencer, chartered Aug. 1927 with $60,000 capital.

Traer, #14172, First National Bank in Traer, chartered May 1934, succeeded #5135.

Vinton, #13263, Farmers National Bank in Vinton, organized Nov. 23, 1928, with $75,000 capital, succeeded

#5088; in receivership July 2, 1932 at $75,000 capital.

Washington, #13849, The National Bank of Washington, chartered Nov. 1933, succeeded and assumed the circulation of #1762, capital reduction from $100,000 to $50,000 not reached by the end of the note-issuing period.

Webb, #11162, Citizens National Bank of Webb, chartered Mar. 22, 1918, with $50,000 capital.

West Union, #13978, First National Bank of West Union, chartered Jan. 1934, succeeded #2015

What Cheer, #14143, First National Bank, succeeded #3192

Winterset, #14129, Farmers and Merchants National Bank of Winterset, chartered May 1934 with $50,000 capital.

Chapter Nine
Index to Bank Officers

Some collectors enjoy searching for notes signed by bank officers who may be their relatives, have names similar to theirs, or have some other special interest. To aid in finding particular bank officers, we provide here an index of all the officers listed in the main section. Rather than index by page number, each individual is listed by the town and charter number of the bank in which he served. An individual is indexed only once for a specific bank even though he may have served in more than one office in the bank. If a person has served as an officer in more than one bank, he is indexed separately for each bank. The lists of bank officers were compiled from the handwritten notes of William Higgins who compiled them from official bank registers covering the entire span of national banknote issuance. Occasionally names were difficult to read and our best estimate was used. This may have produced a few errors in spelling, so use the list appropriately. Because it was compiled from annual bank reports, the list may not include officers that served a brief time between reporting periods. If you find a note with a signature not included here, please inform the authors so that the name may be listed at a later time. (A photocopy would be helpful.)

We believe that this is the largest and most comprehensive indexed list of National bank officers ever published for a state. Hopefully it will inspire additional study of officers from Iowa and other states. The list of officers for each bank makes it clear that banking frequently was a family business. A specific bank may have several officers with the same family name whose careers may be followed as they are promoted to higher offices, especially in smaller towns. An extreme example of a family bank is the First National Bank of Logan, charter # 6771. All six recorded officers of this bank from 1904 to 1935 bore the "Wood" surname.

Trolling the list of bank officers yields many names that would deserve investigation. For example, a history of the Toy family and their multitude of banking endeavors would be interesting. Another individual who may merit attention is W. I. Rosecrans, President of the First National Bank of Belmond, charter #8748, during 1914-1918. Was he related to William S. Rosecrans who served as Register of the Treasury from June 8, 1885 to June 19, 1893 and whose signature graces many Second Charter notes? For those who also enjoy Civil War or railroad history or who simply wonder how charter #1684 of Council Bluffs got its unique (for Iowa) name, the story of the Pacific National Bank would be interesting. This author would love to have one of its First Charter notes signed by co-founder and President Grenville M. Dodge, Major General, congressman, and Chief Engineer for the Union Pacific Railroad during the construction of the first transcontinental railroad. Was Charles Beiderbecke, the first president of the Iowa National Bank of Davenport, charter # 4022, the grandfather of the great Davenport jazz musician Bix Beiderbecke? If so, a banknote collector and jazz enthusiast would be delighted to find one of the early Second Charter notes signed by this gentleman. Can anyone top the tenure of Roger Leavitt who was Cashier and Vice-President of the Cedar Falls National Bank, #3871, for 45 years? An examination of the index will suggest many more subjects of possible inquiry.

Abbott HS	Milford 5539	Addicks MG	Newton 13609	Albee MPW	Spencer 3898
Abbott HS	Milford 9298	Addicks MG	Newton 2644	Albertson WE	Cedar Falls 5507
Abbott JH	Boone 13817	Addison MA	Fontanelle 7061	Albreti LE	Council Bluffs 5838
Abels BB	Melvin 5616	Addison WA	Fontanelle 7061	Alden CJ	Shenandoah 2679
Achorn CE	Sutherland 3618	Addison WA	Prescott 5912	Alders CH	Cambridge 9014
Ackerley AL	Grand River 9737	Adkins HB	Grinnell 2953	Aldrich EA	Creston 2833
Ackerley AL	Leon 5489	Adkison AH	Winterset 1403	Aldrich LP	Renwick 7988
Ackley PC	Ottumwa 107	Adsit R	Cherokee 10711	Aldrich WW	Tipton 2983
Adair RW	Montour 7469	Agena AF	Gladbrook 5461	Aldrich WW	Tipton 6760
Adams CB	Sac City 4450	Agnes MA	Akron 7322	Alexander A	Jewell Junction 5743
Adams CE	Riceville 8442	Ahmann AJ	Remsen 6975	Alexander CE	Jewell Junction 5743
Adams JR	Nora Springs 4761	Ahrens GR	Belle Plaine 2012	Alexander FH	Jewell Junction 5743
Adams RB	Odebolt 4511	Ainsworth TJ	Arlington 9664	Alexander GE	Webster City 3420
Adams W	Denison 4784	Aistrope TM, Jr.	Tabor 4609	Alexander JB	Sioux City 10139
Adams WP	Odebolt 4511	Aitchison RD	Colfax 7114	Alexander JB	Storm Lake 2595

Alexander JH	Akron 7322	Anderson WA	Clinton 2469	Bailey ES	Clinton 3736
Alexander JS	Marion 2753	Anderson WA	Washington 1762	Bailey GA	Glenwood 1862
Alexander S	Jewell Junction 5743	Anderson WE	Arlington 9664	Bailey GM	New Hampton 7607
Alexander SD	Winterset 1403	Anderson WG	Linn Grove 7137	Bailey JG	Dubuque 3140
Alford RT	Albia 1799	Anderson WG	Milford 9298	Bailey MW	Washington 1762
Alger MB	Villisca 2766	Anderson WG	Pocahontas 6303	Bailey P	Cedar Rapids 2511
Alger WS	Villisca 2766	Anderson WG	Royal 10395	Bailey PF	Cedar Rapids 3643
Allanson EA	Waukon 4921	Anderson WM	Iowa City 18	Bailey WH	Armstrong 5442
Allen AL	Gilmore City 6611	Andrew CO	Grand River 9737	Bailie AD	Storm Lake 10034
Allen BF	Atlantic 1836	Annis FW	Osage 4885	Baily CB	Bedford 5165
Allen BF	Des Moines 389	Annis JW	Osage 1618	Bainbridge M	New Sharon 8950
Allen BF	Des Moines 485	Antes WH	West Union 2015	Baird DS	McGregor 323
Allen BF	Des Moines 950	Apple B	Panora 3226	Baker AE	Odebolt 5817
Allen CS	Pocahontas 6303	Apple WM	Red Oak 3055	Baker CA	Coon Rapids 5514
Allen FE	Estherville 4700	Applegate EB	Corwith 5775	Baker ER	Decorah 493
Allen FH	Estherville 4700	Archer JH	Sheldon 3848	Baker ER	Keokuk 1992
Allen HB	Waterloo 792	Arent A, Jr.	Harlan 10354	Baker ES	Keokuk 1992
Allen JC	Prescott 5912	Argo GD	Centreville 337	Baker L	Essex 5803
Allen JH	Pocahontas 6303	Armbruster M	Eagle Grove 4694	Baker MF	Keokuk 1992
Allen WG	Columbus Junction 2032	Armistead RH	Doon 6764	Baker WF	Decorah 5081
Allen YE	Churdan 6737	Armour CC	Little Rock 8119	Bakeslee E	Anamosa 1813
Alley GR	Ames 10408	Armstrong EJ	Spencer 6941	Balch WD	Mason City 2574
Allfree HB	Newton 2644	Armstrong HC	Britt 5020	Baldwin G	Ruthven 5541
Allison EW	Grundy Center 3225	Armstrong HC	Titonka 5597	Baldwin HC	Charles City 1810
Allison GC	Grundy Center 3396	Armstrong LE	Fort Dodge 2763	Baldwin HC	Charles City 4677
Allison GC	Peterson 4601	Armstrong LG	Creston 2833	Baldwin JT	Council Bluffs 1684
Allison HH	Sac City 4450	Arnold F	Klemme 6659	Bales JH	Eldora 5140
Allison JE	Marathon 4789	Arnold FA	Klemme 6659	Ball E	Charles City 5979
Allison JE	Peterson 4601	Arnold HA	Audubon 4891	Ball FD	Creston 2586
Almquist CV	Stanton 6434	Arnold RL	Newton 2644	Ball FD	Prescott 5912
Alquist ER	Thompson 5054	Arrasmith AG	Griswold 8915	Ball GW	Iowa City 2738
Altick AT	Osage 4885	Arthur CH	De Witt 3182	Balliett CO	Waterloo 792
Ambrason AT	Forest City 4889	Arthur EB	Boone 3273	Ballord ES	Davenport 848
Amen JJ	Randolph 7833	Arthur T	Newton 650	Ballou FM	Boone 6838
Amick CH	Henderson 7382	Ashford TL	Boone 6838	Ballstadt RC	Buffalo Center 5154
Amidon JR	Cedar Rapids 483	Ashley CE	La Porte City 4114	Balluff AA	Davenport 1671
Amidon JR	Cedar Rapids 5113	Ashley LM	Sioux City 1757	Balster EH	Lost Nation 5402
Amos EH	Knoxville 1871	Ashley RE	La Porte City 4114	Bandler JF	Fontanelle 7061
Amstein H	Charter Oak 4376	Aten L	Garden Grove 5464	Bang LG	Carroll 3969
Ancraux I	Exira 6870	Atkinson DW	Ames 3017	Bangs WH	Fairfield 1475
Andereck LJ	Des Moines 2583	Aue FC	Sioux Center 7369	Bangs WH	New London 5420
Anderson A	Sioux City 4510	Auld JH	Knoxville 1871	Barber RH	Boone 13817
Anderson AE	Spencer 3898	Aulverson O	McGregor 323	Barbour GH	New Sharon 8950
Anderson AO	Linn Grove 7137	Auracher G	Lisbon 2182	Bardole C	Rippey 7609
Anderson AO	Peterson 4601	Ausharm C	Crystal Lake 9853	Barfoot G	Ayrshire 5479
Anderson C	Farragut 6700	Ausland M	Emmetsburg 8035	Barhydt TW	Burlington 1744
Anderson CE	Lime Springs 6750	Austin GW	Lorimor 12248	Bark TB	Sutherland 3618
Anderson CG	Blanchard 4902	Austin RE, Jr.	Montour 7469	Barlow FS	Spirit Lake 13020
Anderson CL	Red Oak 6056	Averill AT	Cedar Rapids 3643	Barnes BC	Strawberry Point 9069
Anderson DM	Albia 8603	Averill GM	Cedar Rapids 3643	Barnes CR	Strawberry Point 9069
Anderson EL	Wyoming 1943	Ayers CT	Osceola 6033	Barnes EH	Nashua 2411
Anderson GM	Inwood 8257	Babbage RA	Dubuque 846	Barnes F	Marcus 9819
Anderson GO	Inwood 8257	Bachman HE	Havelock 7294	Barnes FS	Marcus 9819
Anderson H	Swea City 5637	Bacon MG	Lorimor 12248	Barnes FS, Jr.	Marcus 9819
Anderson JH	Ottumwa 2621	Badeau WH	Glidden 4814	Barnes HF	Chariton 13458
Anderson JS	Stanton 6434	Badollet P	Council Bluffs 1479	Barnes HF	Chariton 9024
Anderson LC	Alta 7126	Baer W	Pella 2063	Barnes OM	Eldora 5140
Anderson N	Alta 7126	Baggs WL	Garner 8367	Barnes RC	Strawberry Point 9069
Anderson O	Oskaloosa 8076	Bagley WGC	Mason City 2574	Barnett GM	Centerville 2841
Anderson OE	Linn Grove 7137	Bailey A	Charles City 1810	Barnett GM	Centerville 2841
Anderson RC	Monroe 2215	Bailey A	Diagonal 9125	Barnt HS	Sac City 4450
Anderson RV	Lenox 5517	Bailey CO	Burt 5685	Barnum BB	Council Bluffs 5838
Anderson W	Webster City 1874	Bailey CO	Burt 5703	Barnum RB	Council Bluffs 5838

Name	Location	Name	Location	Name	Location
Barr CA	Des Moines 2583	Begalske AJ	Hawkeye 8900	Bieber JP	Waukon 10207
Barr JA	Greenfield 5334	Beggs JW	Whiting 10861	Biebesheimer C	Waterloo 5700
Barragar FL	Sheldon 3848	Behnke JA	Dubuque 2327	Bier CF	Klemme 6659
Barrett LM	Wyoming 1943	Behnke JA	Dubuque 3140	Bierwirth HC	Charter Oak 4376
Barrett WE	Des Moines 2886	Beiderbecke C	Davenport 4022	Bigelow AE	New Hampton 2588
Barringer EP	Ayrshire 5479	Bein LJ	Davenport 4022	Bigelow GM	New Hampton 2588
Barthell JM	Waukon 4921	Bekins P	Sioux City 3124	Billings E	Rockford 3053
Bartholowmew AL	Preston 8273	Belding N	Corning 8100	Billings LL	Jewell Junction 5743
Bartholowmew GE	Preston 8273	Bell DC	Washington 1762	Bilsborough HL	Little Rock 8119
Bartle GJ	Prescott 5912	Bell FG	McGregor 323	Bilsborough MD	Little Rock 8119
Bartlett HG	Osage 4885	Bell HE	Colfax 7114	Bing CS	Manchester 4221
Barz A	Klemme 6659	Bell HH	Colfax 13686	Bingham CE	Marengo 2484
Bascom AW	Terril 10238	Bell JM	Fort Dodge 1947	Binns HC	Red Oak 3055
Bash CW	Pocahontas 12544	Bell MH	Villisca 2766	Bird AJ	Cresco 4897
Bash CW	Pocahontas 6303	Bell RH	Griswold 8915	Birdsall CJ	Clarence 7682
Bash R	Pocahontas 12544	Bell RR	Griswold 8915	Birdsall CJ	Clarion 3796
Bassett LR	Nevada 14065	Bell TE	De Witt 3182	Bischell WH	Aurelia 7108
Bassett LR	Odebolt 4511	Bell TE	Iowa Falls 3252	Bisgard J	Harlan 10354
Batchelder DJ	Lyons 2733	Bell WH	Cumberland 7326	Bishop H	Rockford 3053
Bates CE	Stuart 2721	Bellman AE	Albia 8603	Bishop WF	Muscatine 1577
Bates JR	Stuart 2721	Belt EC	Oelwein 5778	Bitterley LJ	La Porte City 4114
Bates RA	Fontanelle 7061	Bender CC	Spencer 3898	Bixler F	Corning 8100
Bates S	Osceola 6033	Bender TP	Spencer 3898	Bjorenson PO	Milford 5539
Bauer JR	Keokuk 1992	Benedict EE	Iowa Falls 7521	Black FJL	Fairfield 1475
Bauer ME	Sioux City 5022	Benesh C	Toledo 13073	Black FJL	Fairfield 8986
Bauman GW	Sibley 3320	Benesh C	Toledo 6432	Black GW	Gilmore City 6611
Bauman GW	Melvin 5616	Benesh J	Chelsea 5412	Black J	Waterloo 792
Baumer C	Marengo 2484	Benesh W	Clutier 5366	Black TA	Sioux City 1757
Baumgardner IE	Cherokee 10711	Bennett AL	Akron 7322	Black TA	Sioux City 3124
Baumgardner IE	Galva 10501	Bennett AT	Manilla 5873	Blackburn HT	Des Moines 1970
Baur JR	Keokuk 14309	Bennett AT	Sioux City 7401	Blackburn HT	Des Moines 2307
Bawden SD	Davenport 848	Bennett JC	Chariton 6014	Blackford JC	Algona 3197
Baxter EW	Albia 8603	Bennett LP	Valley Junction 5891	Blackman JF	Stuart 2721
Bay WF	Odebolt 4511	Bennett SJ	Fort Dodge 4566	Blackstone FE	Garner 8367
Baylor CE	Sigourney 1786	Bennett TW	Lenox 5517	Blair CE	Clarinda 3112
Baylor JT	What Cheer 3192	Bennison JH	Lenox 5517	Blair JH	Des Moines 2307
Bayston AH	Ottumwa 2621	Bennison WS	Lenox 5517	Blair JH	Des Moines 2583
Beacham C	Farnhamville 11907	Benson PE	Swea City 5637	Blair W	Washington 2656
Beacham HW	Farnhamville 11907	Bentley L	Malvern 2247	Blake AH	Manchester 4221
Beal GM	Hamburg 6017	Bentley WC	Doon 6764	Blake CF	Ottumwa 1726
Beal WW, Jr.	Dunkerton 6722	Beresheim J	Council Bluffs 1684	Blake CK	Ottumwa 1726
Bean KH	Harvey 6936	Berg CH	Dubuque 3140	Blake JL	Perry 3026
Beans WI	Oskaloosa 8076	Berg HA	Fairfield 1475	Blake MT	Dunkerton 6722
Beard RR	Pella 2063	Berg JA	Ruthven 5541	Blake SA	Osceola 6033
Beard TC	Shenandoah 2363	Berggren CF	Swea City 5637	Blake WE	Burlington 1744
Beardsley LD	Laurens 4795	Bergman AH	Newton 2644	Blakeslee GW	Perry 3026
Beaty FJ	Tipton 6760	Bergman WC	Newton 2644	Blakeslee W	Perry 3026
Beck N	Cambridge 9014	Berkhimer JD	Humboldt 13766	Blanchard DA	Adel 8981
Becker DP	Cumberland 7326	Bernhardi GW	Council Bluffs 5838	Blanchard JL	Council Bluffs 5838
Beckjorden O	Forest City 4889	Berry JM	Pocahontas 6303	Blanchard WJ	Strawberry Point 9069
Beckman HD	Grundy Center 3396	Berry L	Bagley 6995	Bland FW	Sioux City 1757
Beckman HS	Grundy Center 3396	Bertrom EC	Peterson 4601	Blanden CG	Fort Dodge 1661
Beckwith HM	Preston 8273	Betz PT	Malvern 2247	Blanden L	Fort Dodge 1661
Bedfor LD	Waterloo 6854	Bever JB	Cedar Rapids 483	Bledsoe AF	Rockwell City 11582
Bedford CD	Hudson 5659	Bever JL	Cedar Rapids 483	Blenkiron JE	Missouri Valley 3189
Bedford CW	Hudson 5659	Bever JL	Cedar Rapids 5113	Blenn RJ	Olin 7585
Bedford WH	Cedar Falls 3871	Bever JL	Cedar Rapids 9168	Blinn LB	Toledo 6432
Beebe JT	Afton 2326	Bever JL, Jr.	Cedar Rapids 9168	Block H	Little Rock 8119
Beebe NW	Hampton 2573	Bever SC	Cedar Rapids 483	Block TA	Sioux City 2535
Beebe NW	Hampton 7843	Bevington CD	Winterset 1403	Blocklinger BF	Dubuque 317
Beecher JJ	Dougherty 5576	Bevington JC	Centerville 2841	Bloem D	Akron 7322
Beede C	Oskaloosa 1101	Bevington SG	Winterset 1403	Bloem D	Rock Valley 5200
Beem WP	Chariton 1724	Bickle CB	Clinton 3736	Bloem D	Sheldon 7880

Name	Location	Name	Location	Name	Location
Bloem D	Sioux City 3124	Bowland RR	Washington 398	Breheney TP	Atlantic 2762
Blomgren Q	Fort Dodge 4566	Bowlin A	Hedrick 5540	Breneman V	New London 5420
Bloom EE	Muscatine 1577	Bowman CO	Gowrie 5707	Brennaman B	Grand River 9737
Bloomer RH	Council Bluffs 5838	Bowman JH	Waverly 3105	Brennaman FE	Grand River 9737
Blosser GW	Moulton 5319	Bowman JW	Imogene 8295	Brennaman P	Grand River 9737
Blosser L	Moulton 5319	Bowman JW	Marion 117	Brennaman R	Grand River 9737
Blossom CA	Belle Plaine 4754	Bowman JW	Marion 2753	Brenton CE	Des Moines 2307
Blossom CH	Burt 5703	Boyd FE	Colfax 13686	Brenton CE	Grinnell 13473
Blossom WR	Belle Plaine 4754	Boyd FE	Colfax 7114	Brenton CE	Perry 3026
Blough I	Waterloo 5120	Boyd W	Whiting 10861	Brenton WH	Des Moines 2307
Bloxham FW	Sheldon 3848	Boyd WW	Mason City 2574	Brenton WH	Grinnell 13473
Blumenstiel AL	Rockford 3053	Boyer DA	Richland 5611	Brenton WH	Perry 3026
Blythe JE	Mason City 4587	Boyer RE	Creston 2833	Brewster C	Fort Madison 3974
Boardman HEJ	Marshalltown 2115	Boykin W	Titonka 5597	Brewster JC	Fort Madison 3974
Bockwitz J	Radcliffe 6435	Boynton CD	Carroll 3969	Brickey MO	Buffalo Center 5154
Boddy MD	Iowa Falls 7521	Boysen A	Cedar Falls 5507	Bridgman A, Jr.	Keokuk 1441
Bodeker AF	Waverly 3105	Boysen A	Exira 6870	Briggs AJ	Knoxville 1871
Bodholdt PC	Newell 10191	Boysen HJ	Dike 5372	Briggs S	Lyons 66
Boehmler JH	Hampton 13842	Boyson	Cedar Rapids 2511	Briggs S	Lyons 2733
Boehmler JH	Hampton 7843	Boyson HN	Cedar Rapids 2511	Brinkman D	Rolfe 4954
Boeke SH	Hubbard 8970	Bracewell B	Allerton 9231	Brinkman JH	Rolfe 4954
Boeyink J	Sioux Center 7369	Bracewell HB	Allerton 9231	Brintnall CH	Sutherland 3618
Bogart G	Shenandoah 2679	Bracewell JE	Allerton 9231	Brittain EA	Hamburg 6017
Bohlander A	Manilla 5873	Bracken JL	Tama City 1880	Britton CW	Sioux City 3124
Bohnson AF	Clinton 994	Bracken TJ	Tama City 1880	Brock CL	Jefferson 10123
Boies FS	Fairfield 1475	Braden J	Chariton 1724	Brockman JD	Davenport 4022
Boileah GC	Red Oak 6056	Braden JS	Goldfield 5373	Brodby FJ	Red Oak 2130
Boiler J	Griswold 8915	Bradford WT	Charter Oak 4376	Brodby FJ	Red Oak 6056
Boisot L	Dubuque 2327	Bradley AT	Centreville 337	Brodeen A	Essex 5738
Bolks A	Orange City 6132	Bradley DC	Centreville 337	Broders EF	Hartley 4881
Bolks HB	Sioux City 3124	Bradley DC	Eldon 5342	Broders HF	Hartley 4881
Bone F	Grand River 9737	Bradley DC	Fairfield 8986	Broders HT	Hartley 4881
Bonesteel VC	Sioux City 3124	Bradley DC	Seymour 8247	Brodt MD	Sibley 3320
Bonnifield WB	Ottumwa 107	Bradley JA	Centreville 337	Broeksmit JS	Cedar Rapids 2511
Bonnifield WB, Jr.	Ottumwa 107	Bradley JA	Eldon 5342	Broeksmit JS	Cedar Rapids 5113
Bonsall WT	What Cheer 3192	Bradley JA	Moulton 5319	Brogmus JH	Pomeroy 6063
Boomer BF	Waukon 4921	Bradley W	Albia 3012	Brogmus RC	Fonda 6550
Boone WA	Leon 5489	Bradley W	Allerton 2191	Brones CN	Crystal Lake 9853
Boorman HM	Atlantic 2762	Bradley W	Centreville 337	Bronson JA	Wyoming 1943
Boots JM	Hampton 7843	Bradley WL	Dubuque 2327	Brook CF	Burlington 751
Bopp CW	Hawkeye 8900	Bradley WS	Centreville 337	Brooks CE	Burlington 751
Bopp EL	Hawkeye 8900	Bradley WS	Seymour 8247	Brooks CE	Mason City 4587
Bopp JG	Hawkeye 8900	Bradt JH	Rockwell City 5185	Brooks FW	Burlington 751
Bopp LE	Hawkeye 8900	Brady EM	Sanborn 4824	Brooks JM	Newell 10191
Bopp WE	Hawkeye 8900	Brady JM	Hedrick 12656	Brooks JT	Hedrick 5540
Bordewick FC	Cherokee 3049	Brainard DE	Woodbine 4745	Brooks JW	Burlington 751
Bordewick FC	Primghar 4155	Bramwell DD	Hampton 13842	Brooks MR	Burlington 351
Bordewick JH	Hartley 4881	Bramwell WK	Hampton 13842	Brooks RL	Hawarden 4594
Borrusch MP	Bedford 5165	Branagan WI	Emmetsburg 8035	Brothers BL	Grand River 9737
Boston T	Clarinda 2028	Branagan WT	Emmetsburg 8035	Brothers JC	Grand River 9737
Bostwick HM	Woodbine 4745	Branch EW	Gladbrook 5461	Broulik LW	Cedar Rapids 2511
Boude CE	Ottumwa 2621	Branch JG	Gladbrook 5461	Brous BC	Whiting 10861
Bousquet HL	Pella 2063	Branch JH	Marengo 2484	Brown AB	Muscatine 692
Bousquet PH	Pella 2063	Brand WO	Belle Plaine 4754	Brown AB	Ruthven 5541
Bousquiet HL	Knoxville 1871	Brandan C	Dysart 5934	Brown CD	Clarinda 3112
Bowdish JW	Cedar Rapids 5113	Brandon WM	Davenport 15	Brown CE	Sibley 3320
Bowdish JW	Marion 117	Brandon WM	Des Moines 2307	Brown CH	Anamosa 4696
Bowen AB	Maquoketa 999	Braniger FC	Dunkerton 6722	Brown D	Inwood 8257
Bowen CW	Centreville 337	Brann DB	Des Moines 13321	Brown E	Ayrshire 5479
Bowen EE	Little Rock 8119	Bratnober CP	Gilmore City 6611	Brown E	Emmetsburg 8035
Bower E	Sigourney 1786	Bratnober CP	Waterloo 792	Brown E	Winterset 2002
Bowers HW	Nevada 14065	Breckenridge CL	Manilla 5873	Brown F	Corning 8100
Bowland RR	Washington 1762	Breed A	Perry 3026	Brown FA	Manilla 5873

Brown FL	Griswold 3048	Buck HH	Spirit Lake 8032	Bussard O	Essex 5803
Brown HG	Sigourney 1786	Buck HH	Terril 10238	Busselle LH	Chariton 13458
Brown HJ	Sigourney 1786	Buck NA	Arlington 9664	Busselle LH	Chariton 9024
Brown HW	Creston 2833	Buckey CP	Spencer 3898	Butcher FM	Knoxville 12849
Brown J	Grand River 9737	Buckey WD	Spencer 3898	Butcher FM	Knoxville 1871
Brown JF	Red Oak 6056	Buckley EF	Des Moines 2583	Butler AO	Davenport 1671
Brown JL	Clarinda 3112	Buckley EF	Des Moines 13321	Butler CF	Clarinda 3112
Brown JW	Sioux City 4630	Buckman FA	Council Bluffs 1479	Butler CL	Fontanelle 7061
Brown LE	Newton 2644	Bucknam FA	Inwood 7304	Butler EL	Oskaloosa 2417
Brown LH	Sioux City 4630	Buckwalter HH	Sioux City 3124	Butler HS	Des Moines 2307
Brown ML	Ayrshire 5479	Bucner JC	Clinton 994	Butler J	Muscatine 692
Brown ML	Emmetsburg 8035	Budlong E	Titonka 5597	Butler JB	Fort Dodge 11304
Brown ML	Graettinger 5571	Budlong J	Titonka 5597	Butterfield CD	Hamburg 6017
Brown ML	Milford 5539	Budlong R	Titonka 5597	Butterfield E	Knoxville 12849
Brown ML	Ruthven 5541	Buell HO	Burt 5685	Butterfield EM	Knoxville 12849
Brown PS	Emmetsburg 8035	Buell HO	Burt 5703	Butterfield EM	Knoxville 13707
Brown RD	Cedar Rapids 2511	Buffington BF	Glenwood 1862	Butterfield EM	Knoxville 1871
Brown RD	Cedar Rapids 3643	Buffington CR	Glenwood 1862	Butzloff FL	Tipton 6760
Brown RE	Sioux City 3124	Buffington FM	Glenwood 1862	Byam DE	Eldora 5140
Brown RH	Storm Lake 2595	Bulkley CG	Newton 650	Byers OR	Red Oak 3055
Brown RL	Griswold 3048	Bull HV	Mason City 2574	Byrkit FM	Blanchard 4902
Brown TH	Griswold 3048	Bull JH	Brighton 5554	Byrkit FM	Elliott 6857
Brown TL	Shenandoah 2363	Bullard CL	Creston 2586	Byrkit FM	Red Oak 2130
Brown TN	Muscatine 1577	Bumann RO	Hartley 4881	Cadwell CF	Elliott 6857
Brown TR	Pleasantville 5564	Bundy JA	Knoxville 12849	Cadwell PM	Coin 7309
Brown WD	Fayette 9592	Bundy OM	Knoxville 12849	Cain CW	Bagley 6995
Brown WE	Storm Lake 2595	Bunkers B	Remsen 6975	Cain HF	Ruthven 5541
Brown WJ	Emmetsburg 8035	Burch GB	Dubuque 2327	Cain RH	Bagley 6995
Brown WM	Shannon City 9723	Burch JM	Dubuque 2327	Cairns JH	Colfax 13686
Browne AR	Alta 7126	Burchett O	Grand River 9737	Cairns JH	Colfax 7114
Browne HH	Knoxville 1986	Burd HC	Grinnell 2953	Cairns JJ	Spencer 3898
Browne HP	Independence 1581	Burdick A	Davenport 2695	Calhoun JC	Seymour 8247
Browne M	Alta 7126	Burdick A	Davenport 15	Call AA	Algona 3197
Brownell EF	Keokuk 1992	Burdick TW	Decorah 493	Call GC	Sioux City 3124
Brownell WA	Keokuk 1992	Burgess CC	Cresco 4897	Call GC	Swea City 5637
Brownlee DM	Sioux City 3124	Burgess HC	Cresco 4897	Callanan J	Des Moines 1970
Brubacher IC	Fonda 6550	Burk AJ	Waterloo 792	Callen P	Moulton 5319
Brubacher RR	Sioux City 10139	Burk HL	Milford 9298	Calligan TJ	Gilmore City 6611
Brubacher RR	Storm Lake 10223	Burk IJ	Rippey 7609	Cameron JE	Lenox 14040
Bruce CW	Exira 6870	Burk LS	Rippey 7609	Camp F	West Union 2015
Bruce J	Pocahontas 6303	Burke JF	Clinton 3736	Camp JF	La Porte City 4114
Bruce JE	Exira 6870	Burke ME	Dougherty 5576	Camp RP	West Union 2015
Bruce RF	Rockford 3053	Burkett ER	Perry 3026	Campbell DC	Centerville 2197
Bruce WB	Rockwell 10217	Burlingame CH	Iowa Falls 3252	Campbell DC	Centerville 337
Bruckshaw JB	Centerville 337	Burmeister JE	Davenport 4022	Campbell ER	Fort Dodge 4566
Bruer RN	Bancroft 5643	Burnett MW	Lost Nation 5402	Campbell FT	Newton 2644
Brugman E	Everly 7828	Burns EE	Hartley 4881	Campbell JW	Fort Dodge 1661
Brummer EL	Aurelia 9724	Burnside AM	Boone 6838	Campbell JW	Fort Dodge 4566
Bruns M	Marcus 9819	Burnside GW	Harris 6949	Campbell JW	Clinton 66
Brunskill S	Hawarden 4594	Burnstedt JE	Webster City 3420	Campbell JW	Lyons 66
Brush A	Charles City 4677	Burr HG	Spirit Lake 13020	Campbell JW	Preston 8273
Brush A	Osage 1618	Burr HS	Waverly 3105	Campbell R	Independence 1581
Brush AL	Osage 1618	Burrell WW	Greenfield 5334	Campbell R	Independence 3263
Brush B	Osage 1618	Burrichter HF	Lost Nation 5402	Campbell RM	Independence 3263
Brush B	Osage 4885	Burroughs NT	Cherokee 3049	Canfield HH	Boone 6838
Brush JH	Osage 1618	Burson J	Des Moines 1970	Cannell TE	Maquoketa 999
Brush JP	Osage 1618	Burson J	Des Moines 2307	Canning JA	Albia 8603
Brust CA	La Porte City 4114	Burton WB	Little Rock 8119	Cannon AO	Alta 7126
Brutsche A	Coon Rapids 6080	Busch JD	Lost Nation 5402	Capper AF	Aurelia 9724
Buchan MA	Dike 5372	Buscher JP	Rock Rapids 3153	Capps JR	Des Moines 13321
Buchanan AG	Lime Springs 6750	Buser JD	Columbus Junction 2032	Capps JR	Des Moines 2307
Buchanan E	Independence 2187	Bush EJ	Creston 2586	Capron GF	Marshalltown 4359
Buchanan GS	Montour 7469	Bush FL	Kanawha 9018	Carden W	Winfield 10640

Carey RW	Shenandoah 2363	Chantry FR	Malvern 8057	Clark HH	Sioux City 3968
Carl ES	Davenport 1671	Charlton JH	Rolfe 4954	Clark IN	Leon 5489
Carleton JH	Iowa Falls 3252	Chase HV	Alta 7126	Clark J	Red Oak 3055
Carleton JJ	Iowa Falls 3252	Chase RL	Des Moines 2631	Clark L	Belle Plaine 4754
Carlson AR	Fairfield 1475	Chase RL, Jr.	Des Moines 2307	Clark PP	Red Oak 3055
Carlson JE	Boone 3273	Cheney JC	Fort Dodge 2763	Clark PP	Red Oak 6056
Carlson JGE	Essex 5738	Cheney JT	Fort Dodge 2763	Clark TC	Muscatine 1577
Carlson JM	Exira 6870	Cheyney CH	Glenwood 1862	Clark W	Red Oak 6056
Carlson WE	Swea City 5637	Cheyney HH	Glenwood 1862	Clark WA	Pleasantville 5564
Carlton CC	Clearfield 9549	Chicoine WR	Akron 7322	Clark WF	Boone 2051
Carmody J	Perry 10130	Chilcote AW	Washington 1762	Clark WH	Dubuque 317
Carmody ME	Perry 10130	Chilcote WE	Washington 1762	Clark WH	Sioux Rapids 9585
Carney BJ	Grinnell 2953	Child CE	Grinnell 13473	Clarke AF	Havelock 7294
Carney GA	Greene 6880	Child CE	Grinnell 7439	Clarke CF	Red Oak 2130
Carney JL	Marshalltown 4359	Childs CC	Alta 7126	Clarke FW	Creston 2586
Carpenter AJ	Elkader 1815	Childs CC	Sioux City 10139	Clarke HS	Creston 2586
Carpenter AW	Burlington 351	Childs FA	Lenox 5517	Clarke HS	Washington 398
Carpenter LM	Olin 7585	Childs JS	Rockford 3053	Clarke J	Leon 1696
Carpenter MW	Cedar Rapids 3643	Chipps F	Monroe 7357	Clarke JP	Eagle Grove 4694
Carpenter SB	Cresco 4897	Chisholm AD	Spirit Lake 8032	Clarke LJ	Eagle Grove 4694
Carr H	Manchester 4221	Christ WB	Perry 3026	Clarke RF	Independence 2187
Carroll J	Churdan 6737	Christensen AN	Audubon 4891	Claussen AD	Laurens 4795
Carry CE	Red Oak 3055	Christensen C	Kimballton 9619	Clayton CB	Hamburg 6017
Carson C	Thompson 5054	Christensen CN	Story City 10222	Clayton HH	Hamburg 6017
Carson M	Thompson 5054	Christensen CP	Audubon 4891	Clemens A	McGregor 323
Carson MH	Thompson 5054	Christensen LB	Aurelia 9724	Clemens RA	McGregor 323
Carson W	Burlington 351	Christensen LC	Graettinger 5571	Clemens RB	Galva 10501
Carter ED	Boone 6838	Christensen LE	Aurelia 9724	Clements CC	Marengo 2484
Carter ED	Perry 10130	Christensen VL	Harlan 10354	Cleophas HR	Forest City 5011
Carter FH	Elkader 1815	Christian J	Roland 11249	Clevenger U	Monroe 7357
Carter HB	Elkader 1815	Christians A	Little Rock 8119	Clifton WL	Webster City 1874
Cartwright FW	Conrad 9447	Christians C	Dougherty 5576	Clinton WE	Hampton 7843
Carver MS	Independence 2187	Christians C	Grafton 6610	Clothier WN	Fayette 9592
Casady S	Valley Junction 5891	Christians CH	Dougherty 5576	Cloud AM	Dyersville 9555
Cascaden T, Jr.	Waterloo 5120	Christians FL	Dougherty 5576	Coady JT	Albia 8603
Case A	Nashua 2411	Christians OH	Grafton 6610	Coan CC	Clinton 994
Case AG	Charles City 1810	Christians WJ	Dougherty 5576	Coan WF	Clinton 994
Case AG	Nashua 2411	Christianson CP	Norway 7287	Coburn RE	Carroll 3969
Case CD	Fort Dodge 1661	Christianson E	Bode 10371	Cochran W	Winterset 1403
Case CD	Rockwell City 5185	Christianson NT	Northwood 8373	Cochrane ER	Keokuk 14309
Case FM	Sioux City 3124	Christy CB	Malvern 2247	Cochrane ER	Keokuk 1992
Case JA	Charles City 1810	Christy CB	Malvern 8057	Cochrane JH	Pella 8047
Casey JR	Dysart 5934	Christy W	Osceola 1776	Cochrane W	Red Oak 3055
Casey O	Dysart 5934	Chubb CC	Burt 5703	Cochrane WH	Corning 8100
Casey WJ	Knoxville 12849	Church ZA	Jefferson 10123	Coder J	Glidden 4814
Cash FH	Sheldon 7880	Cilley PC	Spencer 6941	Coe AJ	Woodbine 4745
Cassatt ER	Pella 1891	Clagg WE	Sheldon 7880	Coe GW	Woodbine 4745
Cassill CB	Garner 4810	Clancy CJ	Storm Lake 2595	Coe J	Woodbine 4745
Casteel WL	Fort Dodge 4566	Claney JR	Clarence 7682	Coe VG	Clinton 3736
Cate CR	Linn Grove 7137	Clapham AW	Lawler 10599	Coffin FG	Columbus Junction 2032
Cavanaugh JA	Des Moines 2583	Clapp DC	Iowa City 18	Coffman AD	Aurelia 7108
Chamberlain DS	Des Moines 2886	Clapp DWC	Iowa City 2738	Coffman AD	Hawarden 4594
Chamberlain ER	Ames 3017	Clark BB	Red Oak 3055	Cokenower HL	Clarinda 3112
Chamberlain P	Anamosa 4696	Clark BL	Shannon City 9723	Colburn HJ	Pomeroy 6063
Chamberlain P	Wyoming 1943	Clark C	Pleasantville 5564	Coldren JN	Iowa City 2821
Chambers A	Inwood 8257	Clark CA	Waterloo 5120	Cole BR	Strawberry Point 9069
Chambers CB	Oelwein 5778	Clark CR	Montezuma 2961	Cole CT	Corning 4268
Chambers CB	Strawberry Point 9069	Clark DL	Newton 650	Cole CT, Jr.	Des Moines 2886
Chambers HC	Ottumwa 1726	Clark E	Iowa City 977	Cole EE	Independence 3263
Chandler BD	West Union 2015	Clark EW	Grinnell 2953	Cole EJ, Dr.	Woodbine 4745
Chandler CQ	Sioux City 4431	Clark EW	Mason City 10428	Cole HB	Renwick 7988
Chandler M	Red Oak 6056	Clark F	Malvern 2247	Coles E	Ida Grove 3930
Chantry AJ	Malvern 4834	Clark GN	Parkersburg 9846	Collier JC	Dubuque 317

Collins AW	Knoxville 1871	Cosgrove JJ	Titonka 5597	Crouse EA	Grundy Center 3225
Collins JC	Knoxville 12849	Cottrell MB	Clarence 7682	Crouse HJ	Storm Lake 10223
Collins JC	Knoxville 4633	Cottrell WDG	Clarence 7682	Crouse HT	Sioux City 10139
Collins JH	Chariton 9024	Couch GW	Waterloo 792	Crowe TH	Clarion 3796
Collins JL	Knoxville 13707	Countryman RA	Preston 8273	Crowell WH	Alta 7126
Collins JL	Knoxville 4633	Coutts JH	Tipton 2983	Crum NV	Bedford 5165
Collins LS	Albia 8603	Covey HH	Storm Lake 10223	Crum WE	Bedford 5165
Collins LS	Knoxville 4633	Covil WJ	Webster City 1874	Crum WE Jr.	Bedford 5165
Collins RH	Des Moines 2583	Cowles EC	Storm Lake 2595	Crummer JA	Pocahontas 6303
Collins S	Albia 8603	Cowles G	Swea City 5637	Cuddy OH	Maquoketa 999
Collins SL	Knoxville 4633	Cowles HM	Waterloo 792	Culbertson SC	Jefferson 10123
Collins T	Eagle Grove 4694	Cownie JH	Des Moines 2307	Culbertson SC	Jefferson 8262
Collins WL	Knoxville 1871	Cownie JH	Des Moines 2886	Culbertson W	Chariton 6014
Collman OC	George 9910	Cox GW	Allerton 9231	Culbertson WL	Carroll 3969
Collman WC	George 9910	Cox IM	Hubbard 8970	Cullen EA	Stuart 2721
Colton FM	Columbus Junction 2032	Cox JF	Keokuk 1441	Culver HJ	Garden Grove 5464
Colton WA	Columbus Junction 2032	Cox MA	Rock Rapids 7089	Cummings C	Sioux City 3124
Comstock JR	Prescott 5912	Cox MA	Sioux Center 7369	Cummings CH	Bedford 5165
Conklin JC	Davenport 1671	Cox TJ	Iowa City 977	Cummings RE	Colfax 13686
Conner A	Alta 7126	Coy JF	Independence 2187	Cummings RE	Colfax 7114
Conner E	Coon Rapids 6080	Cozad WT	Sidney 5145	Cunningham CC	Knoxville 12849
Conner WG	Washington 1762	Craig CO	Boone 3273	Cunningham CC	Knoxville 1871
Connor EE	Algona 3197	Craig CO	Des Moines 2886	Cunningham CC	Washington 1762
Conover FE	Clinton 2469	Cramer AB	Clarinda 2028	Cunningham JS	Knoxville 1871
Converse AB	Cresco 4897	Crandall FE	Red Oak 3055	Cunningham PJ	Winterset 1403
Converse AJ	Cresco 4897	Crandall HA	Webster City 3420	Cunningham SB	Hamburg 6017
Converse FA	Harvey 6936	Crandell AW	Marion 117	Currey EC	Sioux City 5022
Converse SA	Cresco 4897	Crane HH	Clear Lake 7869	Currier LB	Fontanelle 7061
Conway CL	Macksburg 6852	Crapser WV	Thornton 8340	Curtis AC	Stuart 2721
Conway EC	Garner 8367	Cravath SA	Grinnell 2953	Curtis EH	Waverly 3105
Conwell R	Gilmore City 6611	Cravens JF	Spirit Lake 4758	Curtis GL	Clinton 2469
Cook AE	Odebolt 5817	Cravens JW	Spirit Lake 4758	Curtis GM	Clinton 2469
Cook AL	Lost Nation 5402	Craver CF	Grinnell 1629	Curtis LJ	Independence 2187
Cook ES	Pella 2063	Crawford AD	Centreville 337	Curtis SC	Columbus Junction 2032
Cook F	Marengo 2484	Crawford CA	Cresco 4897	Cushman RE	Waterloo 6854
Cook GW	Guthrie Center 5424	Crawford JM	New London 8352	Cutler HO	Webster City 1874
Cook L	Burlington 351	Crawford RA	Colfax 7114	Cutler JG	Nora Springs 4761
Cook WA	Washington 1762	Crawford RA	Des Moines 2886	Cuttell CA	Spencer 6941
Cooke TF	Burt 5703	Crecelius WH	Davenport 4022	Cutts ME	Oskaloosa 2417
Coolbaugh WF	Burlington 751	Creglow C	Sioux Center 7369	Daggett P	Ottumwa 2621
Cooley DN	Dubuque 317	Crego CM	Centreville 337	Daggett W	Ottumwa 1726
Coons MF	Churdan 6737	Creps CI	Dysart 5934	Daggett WR	Mason City 4587
Cooper CC	Knoxville 12849	Criss E	Sac City 4450	Daggett WR	Ottumwa 1726
Cooper DE	Winterset 2002	Crissman MH	Klemme 6659	Dahl W	Montour 7469
Cooper G	Des Moines 1970	Crissman MH	Olin 7585	Dahl WE	Montour 7469
Cooper J	Boone 6838	Criswell RS	Malvern 8057	Dahlberg A	Marathon 4789
Cooper S	Grinnell 2953	Criswell RW	Malvern 8057	Daily JE	Ayrshire 5479
Cope PT	New Sharon 8950	Crocker FR	Chariton 1724	Daily JM	Ayrshire 5479
Copeland HD	Chariton 6014	Crockett FW	Iowa Falls 3252	Daily LD	Milford 5539
Copeland JC	Chariton 6014	Cronk AP	Everly 7828	Daily M	Ayrshire 5479
Copeland WC	Chariton 6014	Cronk CM	Everly 7828	Daily MZ	Cresco 4897
Coppage EM	Stanton 6434	Cronk ER	Montour 7469	Dake MH	Lost Nation 5402
Coquilette SE	Cedar Rapids 2511	Cronk GD	Everly 7828	Dale JO	Bode 10371
Cordes HH	Waterloo 792	Cronkelton GG	Dunlap 4139	Dalgliesh JJ	Grundy Center 3225
Core R	Pleasantville 5564	Cronkhite HC	Stuart 2721	Dalton EA	Le Mars 2728
Cornell JR	Spirit Lake 13020	Crooks WH	Boone 3273	Dalton GL	Titonka 5597
Cornell JR	Winterset 2002	Crookshank MM	Des Moines 2886	Dalton PF	Le Mars 2728
Cornell WJ	Winterset 2002	Crose AJ	Shenandoah 2363	Dalton RB	Le Mars 2728
Cornish JN	Hamburg 2364	Crosley VC	Webster City 3420	Daly JH	Sanborn 4824
Cornwell CM	Des Moines 2886	Cross CH	Iowa Falls 7521	Dalzell M	Maquoketa 999
Cornwell CM	Valley Junction 5891	Cross SR	Iowa Falls 7521	Dalziel GA	Alta 7126
Corson GE	Spirit Lake 4758	Crossan AW	Spirit Lake 8032	Dana SL	Fairfield 1475
Cory LS	What Cheer 3192	Crosson AW	Eldora 5140	Danforth LF	Lake City 4966

Daniels A	Burlington 1744	Denmead JL	Marshalltown 411	Donhowe PC	Story City 10222
Daniels CA	Burlington 1744	Denn LJ	Doon 6764	Donley L	Knoxville 1986
Daniels WT	Moulton 5319	Dennison M	Grinnell 7439	Donley LO	Knoxville 1986
Darling AB	Sioux City 10139	Dennison OT	Mason City 2574	Donlin WJ	Creston 2833
Darling AB	Sioux City 3124	Dent WH	Le Mars 2818	Donlon PH	Graettinger 5571
Darnall GD	West Union 2015	Derflinger LJ	Clinton 994	Donnan WG	Independence 3263
Darrow LE	Corning 2936	Derrough FO	Chariton 9024	Donnan WW	Independence 3263
Daubenberger WF	McGregor 323	Dersheid H	Eagle Grove 4694	Donovan T	Fredericksburg 10541
Daugenbaugh AF	Gowrie 5707	Dethlefs EA	Charter Oak 4376	Donovan T	Mason City 10428
Daugenbaugh AR	Gowrie 5707	Deur CH	Missouri Valley 3189	Donovan T	New Hampton 2588
Davenport D	Prescott 5912	Deutmeyer FH	Dyersville 9555	Dorland HH	Lake Mills 5123
Davenport EL	Inwood 8257	Devoe AB	Creston 2586	Dorn AE	Leon 5489
Davenport GL	Davenport 848	DeVries JH	Pella 2063	Dorn ED	Leon 5489
Davidson M	Marion 117	Dewess WA	Waterloo 5120	Dorow RF	Osage 4885
Davidson RP	Winfield 10640	Dewey MS	Milford 9298	Dorsey AL	Greenfield 5334
Davidson WA	Shenandoah 2363	Dewey RM	Indianola 1811	Dotson EE	Colfax 7114
Daviel J	Fairfield 1475	DeWitt FB	Griswold 8915	Dougherty CB	Columbus Junct. 2032
Davis AE	Seymour 8247	DeWitt FS	Griswold 8915	Dougherty JB	Muscatine 692
Davis AJ	Seymour 11210	DeWitt WL	Elliott 6857	Dougherty RE	Washington 1762
Davis BG	Fontanelle 7061	Dexter WA	Toledo 6432	Dougherty W	Columbus Junct. 2032
Davis DW	Lime Springs 6750	Dey PA	Iowa City 18	Douglas GB	Cedar Rapids 3643
Davis FP	Dunkerton 6722	Dey PA	Iowa City 2738	Douglass EF	Dysart 5934
Davis FW	Eldon 5342	Deyloff HH	Aurelia 7108	Dow JL	Davenport 2695
Davis GE	Rock Rapids 3153	Dickey CA	Hedrick 12656	Dow TT	Davenport 15
Davis JE	Harlan 10354	Dickey WP	Sioux City 5022	Dowd T	New Hampton 7607
Davis MT	Tabor 4609	Dickman FW	Lost Nation 5402	Downey VH	Milford 9298
Davis OE	Afton 2326	Diehl C	Des Moines 2307	Downs JL	Brighton 5554
Davis PS	Eldora 9233	Diehl CA	Des Moines 2583	Downs RA	Osceola 6033
Davis RK	Oskaloosa 8076	Diehl CH	Des Moines 2583	Dows J	Armstrong 5442
Davis RS	Milford 9298	Diehl FH	Eldora 9233	Doyle RJ	Sioux City 4510
Davis SD	Malvern 2247	Diercks FH	Sioux Rapids 13400	Draeger FW	Rockford 3053
Davis SD	Tabor 4609	Diercks FH	Sioux Rapids 9585	Drake CB	Albia 1799
Davis TJ	Marion 117	Diercks RJ	Muscatine 1577	Drake FM	Albia 1799
Davis TJ	Marion 2753	Dietrick FB	Waterloo 792	Drake FM	Centerville 2841
Davis WJ	Hartley 4881	Dillenberg E	Waukon 4921	Drake JH	Albia 1799
Dawson AF	Davenport 15	Dillin J	Nevada 2555	Drake MH	Lost Nation 5402
Day EG	Clarinda 3112	Dilworth CH	Des Moines 2886	Drake WH	Imogene 8295
Day EG	Essex 5803	Dimmitt F	Ottumwa 2621	Drape W	Fredericksburg 10541
Day GP	Sioux City 4209	Dinges CV	Bedford 5165	Draper GE	Sidney 5145
Day WH	Dubuque 2327	Dinkel CF	Charles City 4677	Drewelow WA	Wesley 5457
Daylor T	Corwith 5775	Dinkel HC	Floyd 9821	Drexler FL	Dyersville 9555
De Cou SR	Woodbine 4745	Dinwiddie JM	Cedar Rapids 2511	Drybread JE	Nevada 2555
De Haan JW	Hull 6953	Dirrim FM	Villisca 7506	Dudden CP	Grundy Center 3225
De Koster J	Hull 6953	Dixon A	Coon Rapids 5514	Duer JO	Monticello 2080
De Koster JM	Hull 6953	Dixon GH	Coon Rapids 5514	Dufur ET	Diagonal 9125
De Mots E	Orange City 6132	Dixon J	Coon Rapids 5514	Dufur ET	Lorimor 12248
Dean HL	Tipton 2983	Dixon JA	Coon Rapids 5514	Dufur ET	Shannon City 9723
Dean JF	Cedar Rapids 500	Dobbin FL	State Center 8931	Dugan D	Rippey 7609
Dearborn WN	Anamosa 4696	Dobbin JW	State Center 8931	Dugan LA	Kingsley 9116
Deardorff I	Malvern 8057	Dodds TA	Ames 3017	Duncan FH	Allerton 9231
Deardorff L	Malvern 8057	Dodge E	Milford 5539	Duncan HS	Clearfield 9549
Decker AM	Waterloo 5120	Dodge GM	Council Bluffs 1684	Duncan WB	Clearfield 9549
Decker HI	Clarence 7682	Doe AP	Davenport 4022	Dunfrund GE	Strawberry Point 9069
Deemer HE	Red Oak 2130	Doebel GA	Norway 7287	Dunham LB	Maquoketa 999
DeJong J	Des Moines 2307	Doerfler T	Wesley 5457	Dunigan J	Emmetsburg 3337
Deke AF	De Witt 3182	Donaldson EM	Ida Grove 3930	Dunkelberg EC	Hull 6953
DeLand JL	Storm Lake 10223	Donaldson EM	Sioux City 4510	Dunkerton CH	Dunkerton 6722
Deming AL	Council Bluffs 1479	Donhowe	Des Moines 13321	Dunkle SC	Glidden 4814
Deming JK	Dubuque 2327	Donhowe AT	Des Moines 13321	Dunlap JA	Keokuk 14309
Deming MH	Council Bluffs 1479	Donhowe AT	Story City 10222	Dunlap JA	Keokuk 1992
Denmead DT	Marshalltown 411	Donhowe HN	Story City 10222	Dunlop GW	Jefferson 10123
Denmead DT	Marshalltown 4359	Donhowe J	Story City 10222	Dunn EG	Mason City 4587
Denmead HK	Marshalltown 411	Donhowe M	Story City 10222	Dunn MS	Maquoketa 999

Name	Location	Name	Location	Name	Location
Dunton AG	Riceville 8442	Edwards WJ	Leon 5489	Erickson C, Jr.	Inwood 7304
Durand JA	Belle Plaine 2012	Edwards WL	Griswold 8915	Erickson EE	Sioux City 10139
Durbin F	Malvern 8057	Eells DT	Lyons 66	Erickson EJ	Bode 10371
Durbin J	Malvern 8057	Egbert H	Davenport 848	Erickson LA	Newell 10191
Duren CM	Eldora 9233	Eggen AJ	Charter Oak 4376	Erickson O	Crystal Lake 5305
Duroe CR	Sioux Rapids 9585	Eggert FS	Ackley 8762	Ericson CJA	Boone 2051
Duroe EM	Boone 6838	Eggert SY	Ackley 8762	Erwin AW	Cambridge 9014
Duroe EM	Linn Grove 7137	Ehlbeck FH	Spirit Lake 13020	Erwin CW	Cambridge 9014
Duroe EM	Sioux Rapids 13400	Ehlers EC	Boone 3273	Erwin RF	Cambridge 9014
Duroe EM	Sioux Rapids 9585	Eickhoff FE	Lawler 10599	Eschen H	Dubuque 2327
Duroe FM	Sioux Rapids 13400	Eighmey CH	Dubuque 317	Escher WV	Mason City 4587
Dutcher CM	Iowa City 2738	Eighmey FJ	Waterloo 792	Espeseth SE	Northwood 8373
Dutton FE	Manchester 4221	Eighmey PW	Waterloo 792	Estes LL	Clarion 3796
Dutton G	Knoxville 4633	Eikenberry WA	Chariton 13458	Estes LL	Webster City 1874
Dutton JG	Missouri Valley 3189	Eikenberry WA	Chariton 9024	Estes M	Sidney 5145
Dutton OB	Missouri Valley 3189	Ekeroth JF	Essex 5803	Euken E	Cumberland 7326
Dutton OE	Manning 3455	Ekeroth JJ	Essex 5803	Evans AM	Melvin 5616
Dye JH	Gladbrook 5461	Elbert BF	Albia 1799	Evans FT	Sioux City 4510
Dyer JR	Knoxville 12849	Elder EE	Albia 8603	Evans JF	Council Bluffs 1479
Dyer JR	Knoxville 13707	Elder JM	Garner 4810	Evans ML	Malvern 2247
Dyer JR	Knoxville 4633	Ellerbroek JJ	Melvin 5616	Evans O	Hartley 4881
Dykhouse JT	Rock Rapids 7089	Ellickson E	Thompson 5054	Evans W	Centreville 337
Eagan WR	Emmetsburg 8035	Ellickson J	Thompson 5054	Evans WD	Bloomfield 1299
Early HA	Britt 5020	Elliot JA	Des Moines 1970	Evans WM	Centreville 2841
Early HA	Cambridge 9014	Elliott JB	Knoxville 12849	Evans WM	Centreville 337
Eastman CL	Le Mars 2728	Elliott JB	Knoxville 1871	Evans WM	Malvern 4834
Eastman D	Diagonal 9125	Elliott TK	Essex 5803	Everest FF	Council Bluffs 1479
Eastman GH	Storm Lake 2595	Elliott TK	Waterloo 6854	Everett EE	Independence 2187
Eastman OK	Webster City 1874	Ellis AE	Charles City 1810	Everett H	Traer 5135
Eastman OK	Webster City 2984	Ellis CD	Charles City 1810	Everist HH	Sioux City 3124
Easton JD	Waterloo 5700	Ellis CL	Marcus 9819	Everson N	Washington 2656
Easton JH	Decorah 493	Ellis CL	Red Oak 6056	Everson N	Washington 398
Eaton CH	Blockton 8211	Ellis CS	Davenport 1671	Ewen EL	Milford 9298
Eaton FL	Sioux City 5022	Ellis DH	Greene 6880	Ewen JF	Milford 9298
Eaton HR	Boone 3273	Ellis JC	Maquoketa 999	Exeroth JJ	Essex 5738
Eaton SG	Sioux City 5022	Ellis JW	Bloomfield 1299	Eygabroad JA	Fredericksburg 10541
Eaton TH	Ottumwa 1726	Ellis MW	Charles City 1810	Faaborg F	Kimballton 9619
Ebersole EC	Toledo 6432	Ellis WC	Vinton 5088	Faber M	Remsen 6975
Eckardt F	Stuart 2721	Ellis WS	Red Oak 2130	Faber MR	Remsen 6975
Eckerson LE	Fonda 6550	Ellsworth EO	Iowa Falls 3252	Failing HJ	Randolph 7833
Eckert AC	Sioux City 3124	Ellsworth ES	Iowa Falls 3252	Fairbrother FF	Melvin 5616
Eckert OV	Lake Mills 5123	Else FW	New Sharon 8950	Falk GW	Oelwein 5778
Eckert OV	Northwood 8373	Elsenbast HA	Graettinger 5571	Fardal EG	Webster City 1874
Ecklund EO	Conrad 9447	Elston IC	Sioux City 5022	Farguhar LW	College Springs 11295
Ecklund OF	Newton 2644	Elston L	Burt 5703	Farguhar WS	College Springs 11295
Eddleman WH	Akron 7322	Emal O	Deep River 6705	Fariday FA	Creston 2586
Eddy WH	Primghar 6650	Emmel RG	Harvey 6936	Farmer HL	Laurens 4795
Edens RA	Aurelia 7108	Emmert HL	Melvin 5616	Farmer HL	Marathon 4789
Edgar JC	Holstein 4553	Emmert HL	Sibley 3320	Farmer JP	Havelock 7294
Edge T	Havelock 7294	Emry CN	Fairfield 8986	Farmer JP	Laurens 4795
Edgerly JW	Ottumwa 1726	Emry CU	Fairfield 8986	Farmer JP	Marathon 4789
Edgerton J	What Cheer 3192	Endicott AB	Brighton 5554	Farmer JP	Peterson 4601
Edgington CW	Gilmore City 6611	Engebretson M	Thornton 8340	Farmer JP	Rolfe 4954
Edgington DR	Sheffield 12430	Engebretson PR	Thornton 8340	Farmer JP	Tabor 4609
Edmundson JD	Council Bluffs 1479	Engel JH	Rolfe 4954	Farmer SC	Fairfield 1475
Edson HK	Grinnell 1629	Engel RM	Rock Rapids 3153	Farnham SF	Charles City 2579
Edwards AH	Clearfield 9549	Engeldinger EJ	Ames 3017	Farnsworth S	Council Bluffs 1479
Edwards AJ	Waterloo 2910	Engeldinger EJ	Arlington 9664	Farnsworth S	Washington 398
Edwards CW	Clearfield 9549	Engler EA	Dubuque 317	Farquhar RB	Pleasantville 5564
Edwards JL	Burlington 1744	Ennor MC	George 9910	Farquhar RB	Sidney 5145
Edwards JL	Burlington 1744	Enyart CW	Des Moines 2886	Farrell T	Iowa City 2738
Edwards LB	Albia 1799	Erdahl AM	Rake 11735	Farrow FC	Boone 6838
Edwards T	Independence 2187	Erickson C	Inwood 7304	Farwell CA	Waterloo 792

Fast BF	Villisca 2766	Fletcher TJ	Marshalltown 411	Freeman GA	Emmetsburg 3337
Fast NG	Knoxville 4633	Fletcher TJ	Oskaloosa 1101	Freeman WF	Harlan 5207
Fatland CO	Cambridge 9014	Flindt W	Royal 10395	Freese E	Adair 8699
Faurote ER	Fontanelle 7061	Flindt W	Spencer 6941	French AD	Glenwood 1862
Faurote GF	Fontanelle 7061	Floete F	Spencer 3898	French BT	Hawarden 13939
Fawcett EA	Nevada 2555	Floete F	Spencer 6941	French EA	Waterloo 6854
Fedderson AE	Belle Plaine 4754	Florea WG	Blockton 8211	French HA	Glenwood 1862
Fedderson CP	Dysart 5934	Focht LG	Eagle Grove 4694	French JC	Sioux City 4235
Feenan JH	Marengo 2484	Foft MJ	Kingsley 9116	Frescoln LN	Eldon 5342
Feeney WM	Kingsley 9116	Foley FC	Newell 10191	Freudenberg RE	Clarinda 3112
Felt AJ	Nashua 2411	Folsom	Cedar Rapids 2511	Frey OJ	Sheldon 3848
Felt ZC	Storm Lake 2595	Folsom RC	Cedar Rapids 2511	Frick PC	Cedar Rapids 2511
Felthous GH	Rockwell 10217	Foltz EM	Perry 3026	Frick SA	Rockwell City 11582
Feltus JB	Oelwein 5778	Foltz HA	Perry 3026	Fridolph CS	Red Oak 6056
Fenton WT	Ottumwa 107	Fonda ES	Osage 4885	Fridolph J	Essex 5803
Ferguson HI	Alta 7126	Foote CE	Iowa Falls 3252	Friend AM	Marshalltown 411
Ferguson WK	Algona 3197	Foote FH	Wyoming 1943	Friend BE	Coon Rapids 5514
Ferman KC	Cedar Rapids 3643	Foote RB	Keokuk 80	Frisbee F	Sheldon 3848
Ferner JD	Nevada 2555	Foote WT	Wyoming 1943	Frisbee FE	Sheldon 3848
Ferris BD	Diagonal 9125	Foran WJ	Williams 5585	Frisbee LD	Sheldon 3848
Ferris DV	Diagonal 9125	Forbes FJ	Jefferson 10123	Fritschel E	Strawberry Point 9069
Ferris ES	Shenandoah 2679	Forbes RT	Cedar Rapids 5113	Fritzson F	Sioux City 1757
Fichter AW	Randolph 7833	Ford EC	Garner 8367	Fry FR	Corydon 10146
Fichter CH	Randolph 7833	Foreseth RL	Belmond 8748	Fryer OF	Red Oak 6056
Fichter HJ	Randolph 7833	Fortune DH	Elliott 6857	Fuchs J	Odebolt 4511
Fidlar JB	Davenport 2695	Fosen CB	Kanawha 9018	Fuler QC	Milford 9298
Fidlar JB	Davenport 15	Foskett HI	Essex 5738	Fuller CC	Milford 9298
Field JB	Ottumwa 107	Foskett HI	Shenandoah 2679	Fuller LG	Des Moines 13321
Field JB	Ottumwa 1726	Foskett HI	Shenandoah 8971	Fuller WE	West Union 2015
Field WW	Odebolt 4511	Fosmire G	Clearfield 9549	Fulton CL	Burlington 1744
Fields CJ	Cedar Falls 2177	Fosnes H	Northwood 8373	Funk AB	Spirit Lake 8032
Fields WM	Cedar Falls 2177	Foss HF	Missouri Valley 3189	Funk BA	Spirit Lake 8032
Fiene PF	Charter Oak 4376	Foster CS	Guthrie Center 5424	Funk RW	Ottumwa 2621
Fierce JE	Grand River 9737	Foster CS	Guthrie Center 7736	Furrow	Cedar Rapids 2511
Fifer JL	Washington 1762	Foster CS	Stuart 2721	Furrow EH	Cedar Rapids 2511
Finch FE	Fayette 9592	Foster JW	Guthrie Center 5424	Gaass GG	Pella 2063
Finch GH	Fayette 9592	Foster JW	Guthrie Center 7736	Gabriel MJ	Clinton 2469
Finlayson HD	Grundy Center 3225	Foster JW	Stuart 2721	Gabriel MJ	Lyons 66
Finlayson RM	Grundy Center 3225	Foster LB	Sidney 5145	Gabriel MJ	Lyons 2733
Finlayson WK	Villisca 7506	Foster TD	Ottumwa 2621	Gabrielson FA	Crystal Lake 9853
Finney CW	Eldon 5342	Foster TG	Burlington 751	Gabrielson GG	Crystal Lake 9853
Finney KC	Eldon 5342	Foster TJ	Guthrie Center 5424	Gabrielson R	Crystal Lake 9853
Finney MH	Le Mars 2728	Foster TJ	Guthrie Center 7736	Gadd CW	Buffalo Center 5154
Fishbaugh EC	Shenandoah 2363	Foster WP	Burlington 351	Gadd CW	Fort Dodge 1661
Fisher CU	Glidden 4814	Foust J	Hubbard 8970	Gage JP	Lyons 66
Fisher FC	Charles City 5979	Fowler AJ	Osceola 6033	Gage LG	Davenport 15
Fisher HC	Mason City 2574	Fowler FJ	Waterloo 792	Gagle FM	Colfax 13686
Fisher SF	Independence 2187	Fowler ME	Ames 3017	Gagle FM	Colfax 7114
Fisher SJ	Independence 2187	Fowler PL	Osceola 6033	Galagan CH	Buffalo Center 5154
Fisher W	Pella 1891	Fowler SW	Des Moines 2307	Gale AH	Dougherty 5576
Fitch CB	Gilmore City 6611	Fox ME	Britt 5020	Gale AH	Mason City 4587
Fitchpatrick JA	Nevada 2555	Fracker CW	Marshalltown 411	Galligan CP	Lawler 10599
Fitzgerald RN	Marion 117	Francy WJ	New London 8352	Gamble A	Columbus Junction 2032
Fitzmaurice J	Eagle Grove 4694	Franke CF	Parkersburg 9846	Gamble JD	Knoxville 1986
Fitzpatrick J	Churdan 6737	Franken E	Sigourney 1786	Gamble RO	Coin 7309
Flanagan AS	Pleasantville 5564	Franklin BG	Hamburg 6017	Garber JF	Leon 5489
Flanagan RS	Pleasantville 5564	Franklin TN	Harlan 5207	Gardner GQ	Decorah 493
Flanery C	Guthrie Center 5424	Franks GL	Montour 7469	Gardner HG	Titonka 5597
Fleak LE	Hedrick 12656	Frazer WT	Sidney 5145	Garfield CW	Humboldt 13766
Fleming JJ	Burlington 751	Fredricksen CL	Sioux City 5022	Garfield CW	Humboldt 8277
Flemming VD	Milford 5539	Fredrickson CW	Essex 5803	Garlock CA	Fort Dodge 4566
Flesher MB	Farnhamville 11907	Freed V	Essex 5803	Garmoe J	Fort Dodge 4566
Fletcher J	Cedar Rapids 3643	Freeman EL	Gilmore City 6611	Garner GM	New Sharon 8950

Garner JW	Columbus Junction 2032	Gjermo LP	Armstrong 5442	Graves RE	Dubuque 317
Garratt JW	Allerton 9231	Glass JL	Gladbrook 5461	Graves WL	Washington 1762
Garretson AS	Sioux City 1757	Gleason JA	Imogene 8295	Greeley WM	Ames 3017
Garretson AS	Sioux City 2535	Glenn CP	Ottumwa 2621	Green BL	Rolfe 4954
Garrett HC	Burlington 1744	Glenn JB	Bloomfield 1299	Green HS	Primghar 4155
Garrettson GA	Muscatine 692	Glenn M	Havelock 7294	Green IJ	Davenport 15
Garrettson GN	Waterloo 5700	Glenny AE	Waterloo 6854	Green RO	Oskaloosa 1101
Garst WC	Des Moines 13321	Glenny ED	Waterloo 6854	Greene EM	Waterloo 5120
Gatens JE	Iowa City 2738	Glenny WJ	Hudson 5659	Greenlander J	Belmond 8748
Gates FA	Kingsley 9116	Glesne JO	Elkader 1815	Greenshields JP	Council Bluffs 1479
Gates MD	Kingsley 9116	Glick AG	Marshalltown 411	Greenwald WG	New Hampton 7607
Gaukel EA	Red Oak 6056	Glick G	Marshalltown 411	Greenwaldt AF	Coon Rapids 5514
Gay HD	Vinton 1593	Gloden LL	Dyersville 9555	Greenwalt FH	Nevada 2555
Gaylord JG	Nora Springs 4761	Glotfelty WA	Denison 4784	Grefstad O	Bode 10371
Gearke EM	Aurelia 9724	Glynn WW	Tabor 4609	Gregory JS	Moulton 5319
Gee HH	Anamosa 4696	Goettsch RM	Renwick 7988	Greiman F	Klemme 6659
Geelhoed HH	Pella 2063	Goldie WP	Cherokee 10711	Greiner TA	Hawarden 4594
Gehrmann WH	Davenport 4022	Goldthwaite FW	Marengo 2484	Gressler FJ	Strawberry Point 9069
Geiger RS	Newell 10191	Goldthwaite FW	New London 8352	Grieve JP	Royal 10395
Geiger WGW	Tipton 6760	Goltry ST	Marathon 4789	Griffin PK	Grand River 9737
Gemmel JM	Independence 3263	Gooch HA	Sioux City 1757	Griffith A	New Hampton 7607
George CS	Graettinger 5571	Gooch HA	Sioux City 3968	Griffith AS	Floyd 9821
Georgen AA	Davenport 15	Goodale R	Lenox 14040	Griffith GR	Iowa City 2738
Georingger JH	Boone 13817	Goodale R	Lenox 5517	Griffith T	Red Oak 2130
Gerberich FL	Vinton 5088	Goodell DE	Tama City 1880	Griggs FH	Davenport 1671
Gerberich JP	Atlantic 1836	Goodfellow J	Grinnell 7439	Grimes JM	Montezuma 2961
Gerdes IA	Wesley 5457	Goodhue SN	Marion 2753	Grimes JM	Perry 3026
Gerhardt VA	Iowa Falls 7521	Goodrich CW	Fort Dodge 11304	Grimes JM, Jr.	Perry 3026
Gerhart H	Marshalltown 411	Goodrich JC	Grinnell 2953	Grinnell JB	Grinnell 1629
Gettler A	Glenwood 1862J	Goodrich LD	Red Oak 6056	Grismer WE	Winterset 1403
Gfeller WT	Belmond 8748	Goodrich LD	Spirit Lake 4758	Groe TO	Northwood 8373
Gibbs MD	Hull 6953	Gookin EL	Chariton 13458	Groeltz FA	Cedar Rapids 2511
Gibson OJ	Red Oak 2130	Gookin EL	Chariton 6014	Groff LL	Milford 5539
Gibson OJ	Red Oak 6056	Gookin EL	Chariton 9024	Groninger A	Sioux City 1757
Gibson WD	Rockwell 10217	Gord ER	Grand River 9737	Gronstal BA	Estherville 4700
Gifford EG	Odebolt 4511	Gordon A	Oskaloosa 8076	Groote W	Grundy Center 3396
Gifford GM	Elkader 1815	Gordon LC	Seymour 11210	Gross JP	Hartley 4881
Gifford IM	Davenport 15	Gordon LC	Seymour 8247	Grummon PW	Rockwell 10217
Gilbert ES	Lorimor 12248	Gore FA	Sidney 5145	Guenther AF	Fort Dodge 2763
Gilbert FL	Waterloo 2910	Gorman P	Dougherty 5576	Guenther GO	Eldora 5140
Gilbertson GS	Forest City 5011	Goss J	Centerville 2841	Guenther TP	Eldora 9233
Gilbertson GS	Lake Mills 5123	Gossett CR	Sioux City 3124	Guenther TP	Hubbard 8970
Gilbertson GS	Titonka 5597	Goy RM	Sidney 5145	Guernsey OF	Dubuque 317
Gilchrist G	Randolph 7833	Grace MJ	Dubuque 2327	Gulemanson A	Alta 7126
Gilchrist GW	Pocahontas 6303	Gracey R	Cherokee 3049	Gullixson OT	Bode 10371
Gilcrest GG	Centerville 2841	Graham CB	Estherville 4700	Gunderman HR	Atlantic 2762
Gilkey HS	Cedar Falls 3871	Graham JM	Waterloo 13702	Gunderman LE	Villisca 2766
Gill SH	Havelock 7294	Graham JM	Waterloo 2910	Gunderson OE	Forest City 5011
Gillette WR	Milford 9298	Graham PR	Spencer 6941	Gunsul M	Sutherland 3618
Gilliland OS	Rippey 7609	Graham RD	Manchester 4221	Gurley H	New Hampton 2588
Gillis RS	New London 5420	Graham WR	Des Moines 2631	Gustofson H	Farnhamville 11907
Gilman DT	Sioux City 3968	Grangaard OH	Waukon 4921	Guyer JJ	Buffalo Center 5154
Gilman WS	Sioux City 3968	Granger HA	Manchester 4221	Gwynn JL	Imogene 8295
Gilmore C	Sioux Rapids 9585	Grant CE	Knoxville 1986	Gwynn RM	Shenandoah 2679
Gilmore HM	Mason City 4587	Grant DJ	Bedford 5165	Haas C	Holstein 4553
Gilroy JE	Lost Nation 5402	Grant J	Preston 8273	Haas GF	Dunlap 4139
Gingerich N	Seymour 8247	Grath TA	Saint Ansgar 10684	Haas L	Marengo 2484
Gingrich CB	La Porte City 4114	Gravatt A	Traer 5135	Haberer JA	Rippey 7609
Ginsberg JH	Des Moines 2886	Gravatt CC	Spirit Lake 8032	Hackworth JT	Ottumwa 2621
Ginthner A	Mason City 10428	Gravatt CC	Terril 10238	Haddock JB	Iowa City 18
Gish AH	Lost Nation 5402	Gravatt O	Traer 5135	Haddock JB	Iowa City 2738
Gittinger LB	Chariton 6014	Graves AC	Melvin 5616	Haga EC	Crystal Lake 5305
Gjellefald H	Forest City 5011	Graves RE	Dubuque 1801	Hager OJ	Waukon 4921

Haight HL	Woodbine 4745	Hanson H	Bode 10371	Harvey WE	Renwick 7988
Hainer JP	Sioux City 1757	Hanson H	Odebolt 4511	Harvey WG	Harvey 6936
Haines ER	Britt 5020	Hanson HJ	Inwood 7304	Harwood MF	Strawberry Point 9069
Haines JW	Seymour 8247	Hanson JW	Oelwein 5778	Hasbrouck IO	Ames 10408
Haines W	Seymour 8247	Hanson MC	Oelwein 5778	Hasenclever EF	New London 8352
Hale OC	Keokuk 1441	Hanson MC	Story City 9017	Haskell AE	Fort Dodge 2763
Hale WH	Waukon 10207	Hanson MO	Milford 5539	Haskell CD	Sioux City 5022
Hall BA	Tama City 1880	Hanson TL	Oelwein 5778	Haskins N	Atlantic 1836
Hall EE	Hartley 4881	Hanson WO	Forest City 4889	Hass AR	Chariton 13458
Hall J	Montezuma 2961	Hanson WO	Forest City 5011	Hass AR	Chariton 9024
Hall J, Jr.	Montezuma 2961	Harberts GD	Grundy Center 3225	Hasselbusch EC	Clarence 7682
Hall J, Sr.	Montezuma 2961	Harder RM	Clarence 7682	Hastings AC	Peterson 4601
Hall NC	Olin 7585	Hardin E	Harvey 6936	Hatch WT	Sioux City 4510
Hall PW	Sheldon 7880	Hardin E	Knoxville 1871	Hatswell LA	Red Oak 6056
Hall SB	Charles City 1810	Harding EL	Sibley 3320	Hattenhauer HC	Council Bluffs 5838
Hall WC	Columbus Junction 2032	Harding EL, Mrs.	Sibley 3320	Hatter HW	Deep River 6705
Hall WW	Hawarden 4594	Harker E	Sanborn 4824	Hatter HW	Deep River 6705
Hallam D	Indianola 1811	Harker W	Sanborn 4824	Hatterscheid HC	Corwith 5775
Hallam TW	Indianola 1811	Harlan JM	Indianola 1811	Hatterscheid P	Corwith 5775
Hallberg A	Essex 5803	Harlan TK	Ottumwa 107	Hauck AC	Akron 7322
Hallett DE	Sac City 4450	Harmon M	Waterloo 5120	Hauge AO	Belmond 8748
Halsrud OE	Bode 10371	Harmon MW	Independence 3263	Haugen GN	Forest City 5011
Halst AM	Kimballton 9619	Harnagel M	Farmington 5579	Haugen GN	Northwood 8373
Halvorson HN	Clear Lake 7869	Harold HH	Oskaloosa 2417	Haugen NE	Decorah 5081
Hamann FH	Clinton 2469	Harragan J	Dubuque 3140	Haugen NE	Northwood 8373
Hamann JG	Manilla 6041	Harragan JF	Dubuque 3140	Haugland WC	Forest City 4889
Hambright JE	Perry 10130	Harrell JT	Clarinda 3112	Hausberg W	Charles City 1810
Hamilton BH	Glenwood 1862	Harrington CO	Vinton 5088	Hausen H	Villisca 7506
Hamilton FS	Winterset 1403	Harrington TF	Sioux City 10139	Hauser AM	Charles City 5979
Hamilton FS	Winterset 1403	Harrington TF	Sioux City 4510	Hauswirth D	Havelock 7294
Hamilton HC	Nora Springs 4761	Harris A	Northboro 9015	Hauswirth F	Havelock 7294
Hamilton JE	Cedar Rapids 2511	Harris CAC	Montezuma 2961	Hauswirth L	Havelock 7294
Hamilton JE	Winterset 1403	Harris CH	Dubuque 1801	Hausz C	Lorimor 12248
Hamilton JM	Bagley 6995	Harris HH	Northboro 9015	Haven ML	La Porte City 4114
Hamilton JP	Leon 5489	Harris HH	Ottumwa 2621	Haviland WE	Fort Dodge 4566
Hamilton JT	Cedar Rapids 2511	Harris HM	Grinnell 7439	Haw G	Ottumwa 107
Hamilton SM	Winterset 1403	Harris JR	Northboro 9015	Hawk JW	Des Moines 13321
Hamlin GH	Grinnell 2953	Harris LE	Northboro 9015	Hawkins BF	Hull 6953
Hammer L	Council Bluffs 5838	Harris T	Montezuma 2961	Hawks SG	Clutier 5366
Hammond H	Tipton 2983	Harris WH	Havelock 7294	Hawley CW	Tipton 2983
Hamstreet CR	Clear Lake 7869	Harrison ID	Macksburg 6852	Hawley J	Ottumwa 107
Hamstreet CS	Clear Lake 7869	Harrison RJ	Knoxville 12849	Hayes G	Red Oak 3055
Hanf R	Floyd 9821	Harrod A	Kingsley 9116	Hayes JR	Centreville 337
Hanna AJ	Knoxville 4633	Harrow AG	Ottumwa 2621	Hayes OR	Shenandoah 2363
Hanna AJ, Jr.	Knoxville 4633	Harsh AF	Creston 2833	Hayes WR	Prairie City 6755
Hannan CR	Council Bluffs 1479	Harsh GS	Creston 2833	Haynes WI	Stuart 2721
Hannan CR, Jr.	Council Bluffs 9306	Harsh HF	Creston 12636	Hays JM	Le Mars 2728
Hanrahan JL	Fort Dodge 11304	Harsh HF	Creston 2833	Hays JR	Centreville 337
Hansen AF	Hartley 4881	Harsh JB	Creston 2833	Hays JR	Albia 3012
Hansen AW	Clinton 2469	Harstedt B	Forest City 4889	Hayward WC	Davenport 848
Hansen FM	Garner 4810	Harstedt L	Forest City 4889	Hazen WE	Des Moines 2583
Hansen G	Strawberry Point 9069	Hart EE	Council Bluffs 1479	Hazleton HW	Council Bluffs 5838
Hansen H	Exira 6870	Hart JF	Des Moines 2307	Hazlett J	Boone 3273
Hansen HP, Jr.	Exira 6870	Hart WH	Manilla 5873	Head A	Jefferson 8262
Hansen JE	Crystal Lake 9853	Hartman GS	Fayette 9592	Head MM	Jefferson 8262
Hansen P	Audubon 4891	Hartman MJ	Fayette 9592	Head RC	Jefferson 8262
Hanson A	Oelwein 5778	Hartness M	Greene 3071	Heald P	Tipton 2983
Hanson A	Strawberry Point 9069	Hartsock E	Clarion 3796	Heald P	Tipton 6760
Hanson AC	Fayette 9592	Hartsock K	Tama City 1880	Healy EP	Cambridge 9014
Hanson CE	Bode 10371	Harvey AL	Harvey 6936	Healy MF	Fort Dodge 11304
Hanson EM	Odebolt 5817	Harvey AW	Exira 6870	Heath AC	Montezuma 2961
Hanson GH	Odebolt 4511	Harvey RG	Harvey 6936	Heath JES	Waterloo 792
Hanson GW	Titonka 5597	Harvey RW	Missouri Valley 3189	Hecht H	Charles City 5979

Hecht WT	Dysart 5934	Hibbard EW	Missouri Valley 3189	Holmes AS	Perry 3026
Hedges DT	Sioux City 2535	High A	Rippey 7609	Holmes F	Rippey 7609
Heenan CC	Valley Junction 5891	High E	Rippey 7609	Holmes HJ	Perry 3026
Heffernan WJ	Rock Valley 5200	Higley MA	Cedar Rapids 2511	Holmes R	Waterloo 5700
Heflen GR	Creston 12636	Hildreth F	Terril 10238	Holmes R	Waterloo 6854
Hefling WS	Corning 4268	Hill AJ	Newell 10191	Holmes TJ	Brooklyn 3284
Heft J	Rockford 3053	Hill CW	Villisca 7506	Holmes W	Lyons 2733
Heggen WH	Cambridge 9014	Hill GW	Mason City 4587	Holmes W	Lyons 66
Hegland BT	Saint Ansgar 10684	Hill JK	Clear Lake 7869	Holmes W	Oskaloosa 2417
Heimke EA	Grafton 6610	Hill TJ	Cambridge 9014	Holst H	Clutier 5366
Heinsheimer DL	Glenwood 1862	Hill WS	Lost Nation 5402	Holstrop WN	Cedar Falls 3871
Heiny FW	Marathon 4789	Hilton J	Albia 1799	Holtz C	Alta 7126
Heitsman JB	New Sharon 8950	Himes EK	Oskaloosa 2417	Holyoke T	Grinnell 1629
Heldridge FA	Milford 9298	Himes GE	Lawler 10599	Homan GJ	Dubuque 3140
Helgerson O	Decorah 5081	Hinchman AC	Red Oak 2130	Hooker F	Blanchard 4902
Helgeson JE	Thompson 5054	Hinchman JV	Glenwood 1862	Hooker F	Shenandoah 2363
Helsell FH	Laurens 4795	Hinman R	Primghar 4155	Hooker W	Blanchard 4902
Helsell FH	Marathon 4789	Hinman R	Primghar 6650	Hoover IJ	Waterloo 5120
Hemenway VC	Spirit Lake 4758	Hinton AT	Riceville 8442	Hopkins EE	Whiting 10861
Hemmings JP	New London 8352	Hinton FL	Hedrick 5540	Hopkins FM	Guthrie Center 5424
Henderson AM	Story City 9017	Hinz H	Manning 3455	Horn JH	Grinnell 2953
Henderson CH	Coin 7309	Hitchcock A	Osage 1618	Horridge G	Vinton 5088
Henderson J	Goldfield 5373	Hixon OB	Macksburg 6852	Horton AD	Hawarden 4594
Henderson JW	Cedar Rapids 2511	Hjerleid HC	Decorah 5081	Horton HL	Des Moines 2307
Hendrick H	Waukon 4921	Hjerleid RC	Decorah 5081	Horton HL	Des Moines 2583
Hendricks BN	Riceville 8442	Hobson J	West Union 2015	Horton RL	Des Moines 2307
Hendricks J	Riceville 8442	Hochberger AJ	Hawkeye 8900	Horvel O	Lake Mills 5123
Hendrikson CR	Mason City 10428	Hockberger AJ	Hawkeye 8900	Hoskins EE	Milton 10243
Heneman FC	Mason City 2574	Hodges JT	Sidney 5145	Hosmer A	Keokuk 1441
Heney GL	Ackley 8762	Hodgkinson OW	Emmetsburg 3337	Hostrop WN	Cedar Falls 5507
Henn SC	Blanchard 4902	Hodgson CM	New London 8352	Houg MA	Saint Ansgar 10684
Henningsen BHA	Clinton 3736	Hoehn G	Davenport 2695	Houke FL	Burlington 1744
Henry AR	Indianola 1811	Hoeven B	George 9910	House GE	Milford 9298
Henry GL	Nevada 14065	Hoeven EA	Sheldon 7880	Housman CW	Belle Plaine 2012
Henry LH	Sioux City 1757	Hoffer HF	Waterloo 13702	Housman WJ	Davenport 15
Henryson HT	Story City 9017	Hofferd J	Norway 7287	Housman WJ	Davenport 2695
Henryson OT	Story City 9017	Hoffman AF	Webster City 1874	Howard OF	Imogene 8295
Henryson TT	Roland 11249	Hoffman AF	Webster City 3420	Howard R	Imogene 8295
Henryson TT	Story City 9017	Hoffman CD	Le Mars 2728	Howard WG	Webster City 3420
Hensley C	Exira 6870	Hoffman EA	Sioux City 10139	Howe CR	Spencer 3898
Hensley FM	Exira 6870	Hoffman JA	Le Mars 2728	Howe EA	Harlan 10354
Henson JE	Columbus Junction 2032	Hoffman PJ	Radcliffe 6435	Howe JR	Marathon 4789
Henstorf RO	Farragut 6700	Hoffman W	Radcliffe 6435	Howell A	Des Moines 2631
Herman JH	Boone 3273	Hoffman WM	Renwick 7988	Howell HR	Des Moines 2583
Herman JM	Boone 3273	Hoflund CE	Sioux City 4510	Howell JH	Eagle Grove 4694
Hermanson LT	Waukon 10207	Hoflund PE	Sioux City 4510	Hoyer RO	Clarence 7682
Herren FC	Macksburg 6852	Hogan JH	Des Moines 2583	Hoyt EH	Manchester 4221
Herrick AA	Estherville 4700	Hogan JJ	Corning 8100	Hoyt HB	West Union 2015
Herrmann R	Waverly 3105	Hogan M	Marengo 2484	Hoyt JC	Greenfield 5334
Hertsche JH	Hamburg 2364	Hogue WS	Ottumwa 2621	Hoyt JH	Greenfield 5334
Hesner EC	Manchester 4221	Hohenschuh WP	Iowa City 2738	Hoyt LL	Manchester 4221
Hesner JW	Strawberry Point 9069	Holbert GR	Moulton 5319	Hubbard A	Sioux City 1757
Hess AL	Odebolt 4511	Holcomb OC	Milford 5539	Hubbard A	Spencer 3898
Hesse H	Hartley 4881	Holderness M	Deep River 6705	Hubbard A	Spencer 6941
Hester TO	Exira 6870	Holdoegel PC	Rockwell City 5185	Hubbard AD	Eldora 9233
Hetherton EM	Dubuque 317	Holland D	Floyd 9821	Hubbard AW	Sioux City 1757
Hetherton W	Dubuque 317	Holland GE	Inwood 7304	Hubbard MA	Rockford 3053
Hetzler HB	Graettinger 5571	Hollander WJ	Sheldon 7880	Hubbard WH	Iowa City 18
Heuck JAM	Everly 7828	Hollingsworth HS	Des Moines 2886	Hubbell DM	Maquoketa 999
Heuser GF	Decorah 5081	Hollis FR	Hudson 5659	Hubbell FM	Des Moines 2583
Heyer WA	Sumner 8198	Holmes AL	Clinton 66	Huber GW	Olin 7585
Heyer WH	Sumner 8198	Holmes AL	Lyons 66	Huddleston HC	Milton 10243
Hiams HR	Hawkeye 8900	Holmes AL	Lyons 2733	Hudson GF	Muscatine 1577

Name	Location	Name	Location	Name	Location
Huff FP	Rockwell City 5185	Irwin NW	Panora 3226	Johns EE	Des Moines 13321
Huff HT	Rockwell City 5185	Isaacs CA	Forest City 5011	Johns G	Jefferson 10123
Hughes EE	Belle Plaine 4754	Isaacs NE	Thompson 5054	Johns GW	Cherokee 10711
Hughes EE	Boone 3273	Isaacs SE	Thompson 5054	Johns GW	Galva 10501
Hughes EE	Boone 6838	Isaacson TE	Thompson 5054	Johns WJ	Harvey 6936
Hughes RJ	Lime Springs 6750	Iverson I	Northwood 8373	Johnson AJ	Graettinger 5571
Hughes SM	Muscatine 1577	Iverson WP	Sheldon 7880	Johnson AJ	Roland 11249
Huglin AJ	Des Moines 2307	Iwert FJ	Columbus Junction 2032	Johnson AO	Northwood 8373
Huglin AJ	Des Moines 2583	Jackson DV	Muscatine 1577	Johnson AT	Essex 5803
Huizenga JA	Rock Valley 5200	Jackson E	What Cheer 3192	Johnson C	Prescott 5912
Hulbert JH	Fontanelle 7061	Jackson GH	Floyd 9821	Johnson CA	Sioux City 10139
Hulbert JS	Fontanelle 7061	Jackson HE	Rippey 7609	Johnson CB	Preston 8273
Hull OE	Leon 5489	Jackson JR	Charles City 4677	Johnson CC	Havelock 7294
Hull SL	Woodbine 4745	Jackson LH	Emmetsburg 8035	Johnson CJ	Essex 5803
Hume TH	Saint Ansgar 10684	Jackson LH	Primghar 4155	Johnson E	Waterloo 5120
Hummell C	Des Moines 2583	Jackson P	Muscatine 1577	Johnson E	Waterloo 792
Humphries ED	Sac City 4450	Jackson RC	Manilla 5873	Johnson E	Waverly 3105
Hungerford HJ	Burlington 1744	Jacobs A	Hawarden 4594	Johnson EL	Waterloo 2910
Hunnell JO	Eldon 5342	Jacobs C	Garner 4810	Johnson EL	Waterloo 5120
Hunt CR	Atlantic 2762	Jacobs EH	Hawarden 4594	Johnson EL	Waverly 3105
Hunt EA	Rock Rapids 3153	Jacobs W	Lake City 4966	Johnson F	Jefferson 8262
Hunt FR	Atlantic 2762	Jacobsen A	Nevada 14065	Johnson F	Pomeroy 6063
Hunt GE	Exira 6870	Jacobsen CC	Sioux City 3124	Johnson F	Rockwell 10217
Hunt J	Churdan 6737	Jacobsen M	Ayrshire 5479	Johnson FC	Tabor 4609
Hunt O	Exira 6870	Jacobson CC	Charter Oak 4376	Johnson FE	Thornton 8340
Hunter EH	Des Moines 2307	Jacobson LO	Story City 10222	Johnson G	Rake 11735
Huntington CH	Rock Rapids 3153	Jaeger WA	Coon Rapids 5514	Johnson GE	Indianola 1811
Huntington E	Doon 6764	James JJ	Moulton 5319	Johnson GW	Charles City 5979
Hurd A	Spirit Lake 8032	James JL	Thornton 8340	Johnson GW	Missouri Valley 3189
Hurd L	Williams 5585	James PL	Thornton 8340	Johnson H	Cedar Falls 3871
Hurd RJ	Williams 5585	Jamison RL	Hedrick 12656	Johnson H	Dike 5372
Hursey W	Hedrick 5540	Jandt JA	Sioux City 3968	Johnson H	Royal 10395
Hurst FP	Waterloo 792	Janssen AJ	Crystal Lake 9853	Johnson HW	Cedar Falls 3871
Husted HC	Winterset 1403	Jansson AR	Crystal Lake 9853	Johnson JA	Aurelia 9724
Husting J	Nora Springs 4761	Jasinsky S	Bagley 6995	Johnson JB	Bancroft 5643
Huston WI	Winfield 10640	Jasper C	Newton 2644	Johnson JB	Osage 1618
Hutchings JJ	Winterset 2002	Jay G	Shenandoah 11588	Johnson JH	Osage 4885
Hutchins DH	Algona 3197	Jayne SJ	Boone 3273	Johnson JOE	Northwood 8373
Hutchinson AM	Storm Lake 2595	Jenkins FH	Bagley 6995	Johnson JP	Crystal Lake 9853
Hutchinson LL	Leon 5489	Jenkins H	Preston 8273	Johnson KJ	Osage 4885
Hutchinson R	Clinton 994	Jenks G	Toledo 13073	Johnson MF	Webster City 3420
Hutchison GG	Lake City 4966	Jenks G	Toledo 6432	Johnson MJ	Forest City 5011
Hutchison JF	Rockwell City 5185	Jennings HP	Rock Rapids 3153	Johnson MO	Chariton 6014
Hutchison JG	Ottumwa 2621	Jensen AE	Creston 12636	Johnson MO	Chariton 9024
Hutchison MB	Ottumwa 107	Jensen E	Graettinger 5571	Johnson NW	Des Moines 2886
Hutchison MB	Ottumwa 2621	Jensen HA	Rock Rapids 3153	Johnson OC	Decorah 5081
Hutchison R	Oskaloosa 8076	Jensen HP	Dysart 5934	Johnson R	Toledo 6432
Hutchison RO	Waterloo 6854	Jensen JC	Council Bluffs 5838	Johnson RB	Mason City 2574
Hutchison ST	Lake City 4966	Jepson W	Sioux City 7401	Johnson S	Nora Springs 4761
Hydinger A	Hamburg 6017	Jertson JO	Graettinger 5571	Johnson WP	Bancroft 5643
Hyland DH	Traer 5135	Jertson JO	Ruthven 5541	Johnston CR	Tama City 1880
Iddings FR	Red Oak 2130	Jewett C	Tipton 2983	Johnston JC	Chelsea 5412
Ide FA	Creston 12636	Job EL	Knoxville 12849	Johnston JD	Seymour 8247
Igo H	Indianola 1811	Job EL	Knoxville 13707	Johnston P	Centerville 2841
Illingworth CW	Waterloo 2910	Job EL	Knoxville 1986	Johnston RS	Columbus Junct. 2032
Illingworth WL	Waterloo 2910	Job EL	Knoxville 4633	Johnston SE	New Hampton 7607
Inglis DD	Hampton 2573	Johannaber WF	Rockford 3053	Johnston WF	Fontanelle 7061
Ingwersen JH	Cedar Rapids 3643	Johannsen E	Clinton 2469	Joice PM	Britt 5020
Inman MO	Randolph 7833	Johannsen JB	Colfax 7114	Joice PM	Buffalo Center 5154
Inman P	Randolph 7833	Johannsen PE	Colfax 7114	Joice PM	Lake Mills 5123
Irick GB	Boone 6838	Johansen FW	Cherokee 3049	Joiner HR	Centerville 2841
Irvine HL	Emmetsburg 8035	John E	Nevada 2555	Joiner HR	Centreville 337
Irwin CE	Henderson 7382	John W	Nevada 2555	Jolliffe SM	Villisca 14041

Jones EW	Des Moines 2307	Keck CH	What Cheer 3192	King CS	Woodbine 4745
Jones FF	Villisca 14041	Keck CM	Richland 5611	King DE	Adel 8981
Jones FF	Villisca 7506	Keck CM	Washington 2656	King EF	Webster City 1874
Jones FR	Guthrie Center 7736	Keck CM	Washington 6122	King JE	Albia 8603
Jones FW	Spirit Lake 4758	Keck IA	Sigourney 1786	King JP	Seymour 8247
Jones H	Fort Dodge 1661	Keck J	Sigourney 1786	King JS	Grundy Center 3396
Jones HE	Everly 7828	Keck J	Washington 2656	King LL	Panora 3226
Jones JG	Oskaloosa 2895	Keck J	Washington 398	King RH	Cherokee 3049
Jones JM	Webster City 3420	Keck J	What Cheer 3192	King RM	Primghar 4155
Jones L	Oskaloosa 2417	Keeler FE	Mason City 2574	King TF	Prescott 5912
Jones L	Oskaloosa 8076	Keeline O	Council Bluffs 9306	Kingdon FB	Monroe 7357
Jones OL	Des Moines 2583	Keepf F	Hampton 13842	Kingdon RO	Monroe 7357
Jones OS	Spirit Lake 4758	Keiser S	New London 8352	Kingman A	Spirit Lake 4758
Jones RA	Storm Lake 10034	Keister MB	Coon Rapids 5514	Kingman HM	Dubuque 1801
Jones RE	Webster City 3420	Keller AH	Emmetsburg 3337	Kingsbury BH	Sioux City 4510
Jones S	Malvern 2247	Kelley C	Grand River 9737	Kingsbury K	Sioux City 4510
Jones TW	Cherokee 3049	Kelley CH	Forest City 5011	Kingsley AO	Strawberry Point 9069
Jones WF	Crystal Lake 9853	Kelley CH	Thompson 5054	Kingsley CL	Waterloo 5120
Jones WF	Indianola 1811	Kelley F	Gladbrook 5461	Kingston HA	Armstrong 5442
Jones WP	Crystal Lake 9853	Kelley M	Davenport 1671	Kinkade WH	Red Oak 2230
Jordahl JO	Rake 11735	Kelling JF	Renwick 7988	Kinnaird WA	Valley Junction 5891
Jordan AN	Dunlap 4139	Kelling JF	Renwick 7988	Kinnaird WR	McGregor 323
Jordan ER	Knoxville 12849	Kellogg GA	Missouri Valley 3189	Kinnick PH	Coon Rapids 5514
Jordan FC	George 9910	Kellogg LM	Missouri Valley 3189	Kinseth BN	Bode 10371
Jordan JC	Ottumwa 1726	Kelly A	Garner 8367	Kinsey RS	Grinnell 13473
Jordan JP	Lineville 7261	Kelly AE	Clarence 7682	Kinsey RS	Jefferson 8262
Jordan LE	Dunlap 4139	Kelly GC	Grinnell 13473	Kinsey RS	Perry 3026
Jordan TF	Dunlap 4139	Kelly GC	Perry 3026	Kirby DJ	Estherville 4700
Jorgensen HJ	Kimballton 9619	Kelly JM	Ayrshire 5479	Kirby JP	Estherville 4700
Joy CR	Keokuk 1992	Kelly T	Sigourney 1786	Kircher JF	Dubuque 317
Joy WL	Sioux City 2535	Kennedy WG	Osceola 1776	Kirchner W	Peterson 4601
Joyce D	Lyons 2733	Kennedy WH	Elliott 6857	Kirk FR	Sioux City 1757
Joyce WT	Clinton 3736	Kenney AR	Marcus 9819	Kirk Mrs. LV	Audubon 4891
Joyce WT	Lyons 2733	Kent EC	Graettinger 5571	Kirkpatrick E	Clarence 7682
Judisch G	Ames 3017	Kenyon CH	New Hampton 2588	Kirkpatrick W	Hedrick 5540
Junk MI	Sioux City 4510	Kenyon HD	Doon 6764	Kirkpatrick WT	Griswold 8915
Jurgemeyer LH	Norway 7287	Kenyon SJ	New Hampton 2588	Kirkwood SJ	Iowa City 2821
Kahuda CH	Greene 6880	Kepple WE	Floyd 9821	Kirsch P	Bode 10371
Kaiser HEW	Parkersburg 9846	Keppler JV	Dubuque 317	Kirsland WO	Bode 10371
Kakac J	Cresco 4897	Kergsen HW	Corning 8100	Kislingbury CG	Alta 7126
Kalbach WH	Oskaloosa 2417	Kerndt G	Lansing 405	Kittle NS	Eldon 5342
Kaliban WA	Toledo 13073	Kerndt M	Lansing 405	Klatt AC	New Hampton 2588
Kammann FW	Sioux City 10139	Kerr JC	Rockwell City 5185	Klaus MJ	Charles City 1810
Kammann FW	Sioux City 1757	Kershner FO	Clinton 994	Klaus PA	Manchester 4221
Kane FW	Sioux City 7401	Kerwick MF	Emmetsburg 3337	Klay JL	Hawarden 13939
Karlson WL	Kingsley 9116	Keseberg FH	Waverly 3105	Kleckner EJ	Dunkerton 6722
Karsten OL	Newton 13609	Kesl EW	Chelsea 5412	Kleckner GS	Dunkerton 6722
Karsten OL	Winfield 10640	Kessey N	Ireton 4794	Kliebenstein LF	Kingsley 9116
Kasemeier H	Waverly 3105	Ketcham BF	Farmington 5579	Kling HB	Woodbine 4745
Kass WJ	Remsen 6975	Ketelson FP	Everly 7828	Klingaman OE	Macksburg 6852
Kast CA	Rock Rapids 3153	Kettelsen P	Everly 7828	Klinkenborg JH	George 9910
Kaster RW	Allerton 9231	Keup FA	Crystal Lake 5305	Kloster H	Story City 10222
Kaster RW	Corydon 10146	Keys M	Lorimor 12248	Klove GA	Nevada 2555
Kaufman BP	Des Moines 2307	Kickels EP	Iowa Falls 7521	Kluver HR	Crystal Lake 9853
Kaufman FR	Fort Dodge 4566	Kiernan ES	Aurelia 7108	Knapp SA	Ames 3017
Kaufman TB	Belmond 8748	Kierulff GW	Montezuma 2961	Knebel EJ	Charter Oak 4376
Keane J	Dunkerton 6722	Kilgore L	Waterloo 13702	Knepper FC	Holstein 4553
Kearney EC	Fonda 6550	Kilmer JT	Panora 3226	Knepper HA	Sioux City 4510
Kearney N	Fonda 6550	Kilpatrick F	Randolph 7833	Knigge GA	Fort Dodge 4566
Kearney OA	Cedar Rapids 2511	Kimm SC	Waterloo 2910	Knight HB	Washington 1762
Kearney OA	Cedar Rapids 3643	Kimmel WC	Sheldon 7880	Knight RS	Estherville 4700
Keck CH	Washington 2656	Kimple L	Corydon 10146	Knoop CW	Garner 4810
Keck CH	Washington 6122	Kindig OC	Floyd 9821	Knoop CW	Waterloo 6854

Knox RM	Waterloo 5700	Lake JF	Shenandoah 2363	Laughlin R	Emmetsburg 3337
Knox WJ	Essex 5803	Lake JF	Shenandoah 2679	Lauman GC	Burlington 351
Knudsen FN	Kanawha 9018	Lake JF	Shenandoah 8971	Lawbaugh H	Stuart 2721
Knudson FN	Kanawha 9018	Lake RS	Shenandoah 12950	Lawler ST	Casey 8099
Knutson CA	Clear Lake 7869	Lally D	Dysart 5934	Lawler ST	Winterset 1403
Knutson EM	Rake 11735	Lalor WJ	Dougherty 5576	Lawrence HS	Marshalltown 411
Koester HA	Dubuque 317	Lamar AF	Spencer 3898	Lawrence HS	Marshalltown 4359
Kolling MC	Valley Junction 5891	Lamb L	Clinton 3736	Lawrence ME	Tabor 4609
Kolthoff JH	New Hampton 2588	Lambert TR	Coon Rapids 6080	Lawther W, Jr.	Dubuque 317
Konigmacher C	Council Bluffs 5838	Lamm C	Saint Ansgar 10684	Le Roy AR	Manchester 4221
Konigmacher F	Council Bluffs 5838	Lamm J	Elkader 1815	Le Roy MF	Manchester 4221
Koob F	Le Mars 2818	Lande JF	Greenfield 5334	Leach CE	Fredericksburg 10541
Koons VD	Eldon 5342	Lane BD	Grundy Center 3396	Leach E	Independence 3263
Korslund C	Lake City 4966	Lane CH	Guthrie Center 5424	Lease JA	Sumner 8198
Koser CT	Winterset 2002	Lane CH	Indianola 1811	Leathers JH	What Cheer 3192
Krag C	Hampton 7843	Lane CH	Red Oak 2130	Leavitt JA	Hudson 5659
Kramer A	Elkader 1815	Lane EC	Guthrie Center 5424	Leavitt JH	Waterloo 5120
Kramer HG	Clinton 2469	Lane EC	Indianola 1811	Leavitt R	Cedar Falls 3871
Krapfel JW	Waterloo 792	Lane HD	Oskaloosa 2417	Leavitt R	Grundy Center 3396
Krapfel WR	Centreville 337	Lane HL	Oskaloosa 2417	Lederer A	Des Moines 1970
Krause R	Davenport 1671	Lane JR	Davenport 15	Ledgerwood J	Osceola 6033
Kreps S	Greenfield 5334	Lane JR	Davenport 2695	Lee CW	Lime Springs 6750
Kriebs HJ	De Witt 3182	Lane ND	Oskaloosa 2417	Lee GA	Greenfield 5334
Kriege JF	Remsen 6975	Lane R	Indianola 1811	Lee GA	Winterset 1403
Krieger JW	New Hampton 2588	Lane WA	Guthrie Center 5424	Lee J	Coon Rapids 6080
Kroeger FC	Davenport 1671	Lane WA	Indianola 1811	Lee OM	Sioux Rapids 9585
Kroninger HJ	Fredericksburg 10541	Lane WA	Waterloo 2910	Lee QM	Renwick 7988
Krouth GS	Iowa City 2738	Lane WA	Waterloo 792	Lee W	De Witt 3182
Kruidenier L	Pella 8047	Langworthy SC	Monticello 2080	Leet FM	Exira 6870
Kruse AA	Audubon 4891	Lanphere HF	Grinnell 7439	Leet FM	Manilla 5873
Kruse FH	Malvern 2247	Lanther WM	Dubuque 317	Lehaw F	Riceville 8442
Kruse ND	Little Rock 8119	Large FA	Rock Valley 5200	Lehmann CO	George 9910
Kubicek H	Montour 7469	Large IS	Rock Valley 5200	Leighton H	Stuart 2721
Kucheman OC	Maquoketa 999	Large JJ	La Porte City 4114	Leland RD	Humboldt 13766
Kudje AJ	Klemme 6659	Large JJ	Rock Valley 5200	Leland RD	Humboldt 8277
Kuehl RJ	Grundy Center 3396	Large JJ	Sioux City 1757	Lemen EB	Rockwell City 11582
Kuehnle CF	Manilla 6041	Larimer GW	Chariton 6014	Lemen GB	Rockwell City 11582
Kuhl OB	Dubuque 3140	Larkin OF	Washington 1762	Lemon JK	Rolfe 4954
Kuhlmer EJ	Maquoketa 999	Larrabee F	McGregor 323	Lenander CJ	Swea City 5637
Kuhn H	Spirit Lake 8032	Larrabee W	Elkader 1815	Lenmann W	Aurelia 7108
Kuning CC	Cedar Rapids 3643	Larrabee W	McGregor 323	Leonard OH	Cedar Falls 5507
Kunz J	Wesley 5457	Larsen GM	Inwood 8257	Leonard RH	Sioux Rapids 9585
Kunz J	Wesley 5457	Larsen LC	Crystal Lake 5305	Leverett WJ	Council Bluffs 1479
Kupka L	Glenwood 1862	Larson AC	Bode 10371	Levong El	Crystal Lake 5305
Kurtz CH	Marion 2753	Larson CA	New Hampton 2588	Lewis AW	Odebolt 4511
Kurtz LC	Des Moines 2583	Larson CA	Waterloo 792	Lewis CP	Britt 5020
Kuyper AJ	Orange City 6132	Larson CL	Britt 5020	Lewis CW	Centreville 337
Kuyper AN	Pella 8047	Larson EF	Britt 5020	Lewis FR	Algona 3197
Kuyper H	Orange City 6132	Larson FW	Cambridge 9014	Lewis FR	Muscatine 1577
Kyhl JJ	Cedar Falls 3871	Larson HD	Britt 5020	Lewis HE	Harlan 10354
La Bam J	Waterloo 5120	Larson J	Rake 11735	Lewis JH	Marengo 2484
La Tourette WC	Cedar Rapids 9168	Larson L	Britt 5020	Lewis WJ	Harlan 10354
Lacey ER	Columbus Junction 2032	Larson LJ	Alta 7126	Lexvold HH	Radcliffe 6435
Lacolli PR	Marengo 2484	Larson SH	Lake Mills 5123	Lichty GE	Waterloo 2910
Lacy BW	Dubuque 317	Larson W	Gowrie 5707	Lichty JN	Toledo 6432
Ladd WJ	Traer 5135	Lashbrook WD	Waverly 3105	Lichty JW	Toledo 6432
Laffer E	Sigourney 1786	Lasheck J	Iowa City 2738	Lien RP	Waterloo 13702
LaFontaine LP	Spirit Lake 13020	Lathrop GE	Sibley 3320	Light F	Fairfield 1475
Laird CO	Tabor 4609	Latimer JF	Hampton 2573	Lightfoot J	Farmington 5579
Laird HA	Boone 13817	Lau A	Klemme 6659	Lightfoot JC	Alta 7126
Laird HR	Tabor 4609	Laubender HE	Audubon 4891	Liljedahl CJ	Essex 5738
Laird JO	Malvern 8057	Laufer HE	Fort Dodge 2763	Liljedahl GH	Essex 5738
Lake J	Independence 3263	Laughlin J	Imogene 8295	Lillie WG	Marion 117

Lind CG	Stanton 6434	Lorenzen J	Davenport 1671	Lyons WW	Des Moines 2583
Lindaman WJ	Little Rock 8119	Lorenzen L	Gilmore City 6611	Mabry JC	Albia 1799
Lindberg CT	Hedrick 12656	Lorge FJ	Akron 7322	Mabry NM	Albia 1799
Lindburg A	Essex 5803	Lorge FJ	Pocahontas 12544	MacEachron SA	Grinnell 2953
Lindburg Abe	Essex 5803	Lorimer G, Jr.	Estherville 4700	Mack CZ	Clarence 7682
Lindburg J	Essex 5803	Loucee FC	Council Bluffs 5838	Mack JH	Macksburg 6852
Lindeman F	Kingsley 9116	Louden RB	Fairfield 8986	Mackey J	Northboro 9015
Lindeman FW	Pocahontas 12544	Loudon JD	Clarinda 3112	Mackey JB	Northboro 9015
Lindeman FW	Pocahontas 6303	Loudon JD	College Springs 11295	Mackey JR	Sigourney 1786
Lindeman G	Kingsley 9116	Loudon VH	College Springs 11295	Mackey WA	Sigourney 1786
Lindenmayer FC	Marengo 2484	Loutzenheiser HC	Chelsea 5412	Mackovets A	Pocahontas 6303
Linder EG	Fairfield 1475	Loutzenheiser WR	Chelsea 5412	Maclagan GC	Le Mars 2818
Lindly ED	Oskaloosa 1101	Love HK	Des Moines 2307	Macomber HW	Carroll 3969
Lindly WA	Oskaloosa 1101	Love HK	Keokuk 80	Madden WH	Lenox 14040
Lindly WA	Oskaloosa 2417	Loving JG	Henderson 7382	Madden WH	Lenox 5517
Lindquist AE	Gowrie 5707	Lowe GO	Malvern 2247	Maddy WG	Harvey 6936
Lindquist FW	Gowrie 5707	Lowis G	Dexter 10030	Madison FE	Grand River 9737
Lindquist GG	Gowrie 5707	Lowry EP	Laurens 4795	Madison JC	Grand River 9737
Lindquist NA	Gowrie 5707	Lowry EP	Marathon 4789	Madsen A	Kimballton 9619
Linduski H	Denison 4784	Lucas CC	Kanawha 9018	Madsen H	Kimballton 9619
Linebarger HN	Greenfield 5334	Lucas WD	Des Moines 2886	Madsen HE	Kimballton 9619
Linebarger L	Greenfield 5334	Ludeking JC	Waukon 4921	Madsen S	Exira 6870
Linebarger WW	Clarion 3796	Ludemann JJ	Parkersburg 9846	Magdsick CC	Charles City 5979
Lippert B	Hawkeye 8900	Ludemann RA	Parkersburg 9846	Magoun CM	Sioux City 4510
Liston AW	Coin 7309	Ludemann S	Parkersburg 9846	Magoun JA, Jr.	Sioux City 4510
Little HG	Prairie City 6755	Ludwig H	Gladbrook 5461	Magowan SN	Fort Dodge 4566
Little J	Crystal Lake 5305	Ludwig P	Casey 8099	Mahon S	Ottumwa 1726
Little JH	Prairie City 6755	Ludy JC	Strawberry Point 9069	Maine HA	Waterloo 2910
Littler WF	Bode 10371	Luedtke AG	Belle Plaine 4754	Maine HA	Waterloo 792
Littleton AP	Greenfield 5334	Lukes CN	Sioux City 1757	Mains CA	Charter Oak 4376
Littleton VC	Greenfield 5334	Lukes CN	Sioux City 3124	Mains CA	Fonda 6550
Livingston CB	Monroe 7357	Lull CH	Anamosa 4696	Maish WW	Des Moines 1970
Lloyd WH	Brighton 2033	Lull JZ	Anamosa 4696	Major B	Corwith 5775
Locke FY	Harris 6949	Lumbarge HH	Clarion 3796	Maland O	Kanawha 9018
Locke FY	Melvin 5616	Lund AN	Saint Ansgar 10684	Malcolm TH	Belle Plaine 4754
Lockman TD	Albia 1799	Lund AS	Belmond 8748	Maley JF	Elkader 1815
Lockridge W	Nevada 2555	Lund AS	Northwood 8373	Mall WA	Belle Plaine 2012
Lockwood HF	Marion 117	Lund C	Laurens 4795	Mallory AL	Chariton 1724
Lodge AL	Milford 5539	Lund JP	Saint Ansgar 10684	Mallory SH	Chariton 1724
Loe EO	Linn Grove 7137	Lund V	Lyons 4536	Mallory SH	Creston 2586
Loepp AC	Gladbrook 5461	Lundberg AH	Odebolt 4511	Manker HE	Elliott 6857
Lofland CE	Oskaloosa 2417	Lundquist EL	Marcus 9819	Manker JJ	Elliott 6857
Logan JM	Elliott 6857	Lundy TC	Coon Rapids 6080	Manker JW	Elliott 6857
Logan WC	Waterloo 5120	Lunemann JH	Dysart 5934	Manley EP	Sioux City 3124
Lohr OC	Churdan 6737	Lunemann JH	La Porte City 4114	Manley LR	Sioux City 3124
Lomas DE	Villisca 2766	Lusch JC	Ackley 8762	Manley WP	Marcus 9819
Lomen EP	Marathon 4789	Lyday EE	Newton 2644	Manley WP	Sioux City 3124
Long GE	Cherokee 10711	Lyday JH	Newton 2644	Mann FJ	Burt 5685
Long GR	Hubbard 8970	Lyle ID	Armstrong 5442	Mann SM	Grafton 6610
Long HR	Hubbard 8970	Lyle RB	Kingsley 9116	Mannatt RW	Cedar Rapids 2511
Long HT	Seymour 8247	Lyman JP	Grinnell 1629	Manning C	Chariton 6014
Long J	Newton 650	Lynch CJ	Tipton 13232	Manning C	Ottumwa 1726
Long RF	Guthrie Center 5424	Lynch DR	West Union 2015	Manning E	Ottumwa 1726
Long RF	Guthrie Center 7736	Lynd EA	Des Moines 2583	Manson FS	Holstein 4553
Long WE	Hubbard 8970	Lynn HC	Hedrick 5540	Manson R	Waterloo 792
Longfellow JF	Bedford 5165	Lyon CR	Perry 3026	Mantor EL	Peterson 4601
Longman WH	Northboro 9015	Lyon EL	Marshalltown 2971	Mantor EL	Peterson 4601
Loomis AM	Wyoming 1943	Lyon EL	Nevada 2555	Manwaring GA	Inwood 8257
Loomis AR	Manchester 4221	Lyon GA	Rockford 3053	Manwaring GA	Rock Rapids 3153
Loonan J	Waterloo 6854	Lyon IM	Sioux City 4510	Marcy LJ	Fairfield 1475
Loonan T	Hudson 5659	Lyon OH	Rockford 3053	Mardis A	Lineville 7261
Loosbrock WA	Charles City 4677	Lyons LM	Glidden 4814	Markitan OE	Creston 12636
Lorensen J	Everly 7828	Lyons WW	Colfax 7114	Markley JEE	Mason City 4587

Marks GL	Eldora 5140	McBane A	Fort Dodge 1947	McElhinney BW	Renwick 7988
Marlow BH	Burt 5685	McBride PJ	Council Bluffs 9306	McElhinney FF	Waterloo 6854
Marmet JW	Galva 10501	McCabe WH	Seymour 11210	McElhinny BS	Fairfield 1475
Marquis CE	Jefferson 8262	McCall FC	Nevada 2555	McElroy GD	Vinton 5088
Marr TD	Richland 5611	McCammon DL	Rippey 7609	McEvoy JJ	Gilmore City 6611
Marsau JC	Dysart 5934	McCammon WH	Perry 10130	McEwen WD	Pocahontas 6303
Marschall F	George 9910	McCammon WH	Rippey 7609	McEwen WS	Pocahontas 6303
Marsh CA	Waterloo 792	McCammond RV	Charles City 1810	McFadon AA	Marshalltown 2971
Marsh EB	Macksburg 6852	McCardell HC	Newton 13609	McGarvey WF	Waterloo 5120
Marshman WA	Hubbard 8970	McCargill AC	Imogene 8295	McGavern JS	Missouri Valley 3189
Martens MP	Charles City 5979	McCarley J	Williams 5585	McGill FT	Rock Valley 5200
Martin AJ	Ames 3017	McCarthy D	Ames 3017	McGrew HL	New London 5420
Martin CG	Bedford 5165	McCarthy J	Jefferson 10123	McGrew N	Osceola 6033
Martin CJ	Churdan 6737	McCarthy TJ	New Hampton 2588	McGrew WA	Ottumwa 107
Martin JW	Fonda 6550	McCartney HH	Villisca 2766	McGuire JE	Exira 6870
Martin LJ	Knoxville 4633	McCarton CCB	Pocahontas 6303	McHaffey D	Eldon 5342
Martin LM	Fort Dodge 4566	McCarton TF	Pocahontas 6303	McHenry G	Denison 4784
Martin W	Webster City 1874	McCarty HL	Strawberry Point 9069	McHenry MS	Denison 4784
Martin WH	Renwick 7988	McCarty JH	Fairfield 8986	McHenry S	Denison 4784
Martinson HM	Lake Mills 5123	McCarty RE	Richland 5611	McHenry WA	Denison 4784
Martinson RG	Williams 5585	McCarty TF	Richland 5611	McHenry WH	Denison 4784
Marwick J	Story City 10222	McChesney WJ	Iowa City 2738	McHose SM	Nevada 14065
Marwick SJ	Story City 10222	McClary W	Newton 2644	McHose SM	Nevada 2555
Marz J	Richland 5611	McClelland WF	Rockwell 10217	McHugh J	Sioux City 1757
Mason AW	Cedar Falls 2177	McClure FH	Indianola 1811	McHugh J	Sioux City 3968
Mason BC	Webster City 1874	McColl DD	Perry 10130	McKean AJ	Marion 2753
Mason BS	Webster City 1874	McColl DD	Perry 3026	McKee EE	New London 8352
Mason EE	Webster City 1874	McColl EAB	Perry 3026	McKee JW	Winterset 2002
Mason HP	Webster City 1874	McConnell CR	Marcus 9819	McKelry WA	Corning 8100
Mast CA	Carroll 3969	McConnell SF	Bloomfield 9303	McKinnon GE	Laurens 4795
Mast CA	Davenport 2695	McConnell SF	Milton 10243	McKinstry CS	Waterloo 13702
Mast CA	Davenport 848	McCook N	Sumner 8198	McKinstry CS	Waterloo 2910
Mathews GA	Woodbine 4745	McCook RD	Sumner 8198	McKitterick E	Burlington 1744
Mathews JL	Odebolt 4511	McCord JH	Linn Grove 7137	McKlveen JH	Prairie City 6755
Mathews LW	Tipton 13232	McCord JH	Royal 10395	McKlveen S	Chariton 9024
Mathews LW	Tipton 6760	McCord JH	Spencer 6941	McKnight WW	Winterset 1403
Mathews RC	Rockford 3053	McCord JS	Seymour 8247	McLain RJ	Deep River 6705
Matless AE	Keokuk 1992	McCormick I	Tabor 4609	McLane WF	Grundy Center 3225
Matson N	Crystal Lake 9853	McCornack FA	Sioux City 1757	McLaughlin EJ	Dubuque 3140
Matson NT	Rake 11735	McCornack FA	Sioux City 3968	McLaury CS	Sheldon 3848
Mattert JF	Melvin 5616	McCoy J	Allerton 9231	McMahon JL	State Center 8931
Mattert JF	Sibley 3320	McCracken LS	Coin 7309	McMahan O	Lyons 2733
Mattes J	Odebolt 4511	McCracken LS	Imogene 8295	McMahon O	Lyons 66
Matthiesen EE	Clinton 66	McCue JW	Creston 2833	McMahon SE	Burt 5685
Matthiesen EE	Lyons 66	McCulley AW	Washington 1762	McManus JF	Adair 8699
Maurer WA	Council Bluffs 5838	McCulloch B	Waterloo 5120	McManus ML	Adair 8699
Mauss CF	Milford 5539	McCulloch RM	Pomeroy 6063	McMillan J	Knoxville 4633
Mauss ER	Spencer 6941	McCulloch WC	Pomeroy 6063	McMurray AR	Grinnell 13473
Mawdsley JR	Burt 5685	McCutchen EH	Holstein 4553	McMurray AR	Grinnell 7439
Maxfield R	Council Bluffs 14028	McDaniels C	Atlantic 2762	McMurray GH	Grinnell 7439
Maxfield R	Council Bluffs 1479	McDaniels J	Atlantic 2762	McMurray LA	Webster City 2984
Maxwell GE	Davenport 848	McDermott B	Buffalo Center 5154	McNary C	Terril 10238
Maxwell OW	Hampton 7843	McDermott OP	Des Moines 2583	McNaughton MN	Villisca 2766
May C	Dyersville 9555	McDonald BK	Montezuma 2961	McNee WA	Laurens 4795
May CD	Clinton 3736	McDonald CP	Coon Rapids 6080	McNeil JF	Oskaloosa 2417
May GE	Charles City 2579	McDonald E	Coon Rapids 5514	McNeill JF	Oskaloosa 2895
May GE	Charles City 5979	McDonald FP	Boone 3273	McNider CH	Dougherty 5576
May JF	Milford 9298	McDonald GW	Centerville 2841	McNider CH	Mason City 2574
Mayer C	Oskaloosa 2417	McDonald HW	Webster City 1874	McNider H	Mason City 2574
Mayer C	Oskaloosa 8076	McDonald OP	Des Moines 2583	McNulty CJ	Waterloo 5120
Mayne S	Swea City 5637	McDonald R	Grinnell 2953	McPherrin G	Clearfield 9549
McAllister C	Spencer 3898	McDowell CR	Doon 6764	McPherrin G	Des Moines 13321
McAnulty NR	Toledo 6432	McDowell F	Doon 6764	McWaid JA	Atlantic 2762

McWilliams JG	Hedrick 5540	Mickelwait G	Glenwood 1862	Miner FB	Corning 2936
Mead BN	Greene 6880	Mieke RA	Fayette 9592	Miner HD	Lake City 4966
Mead L	Eldon 5342	Miick E	Washington 1762	Missildine GE	Galva 10501
Means RB	Villisca 14041	Miles BF	Manchester 4221	Mitchell EH	Shenandoah 2679
Means RB	Villisca 7506	Miles JW	Manchester 4221	Mitchell GF	Coin 7309
Mee M	Gladbrook 5461	Miles WA	State Center 8931	Mitchell GL	Maquoketa 999
Mee W	Gladbrook 5461	Millard OL	Montour 7469	Mitchell JL	Sioux City 1757
Mee W, Jr.	Gladbrook 5461	Miller AA	Corwith 5775	Mitchell JL	Sioux City 5022
Meek K	Farmington 5579	Miller AB	Olin 7585	Mitchell JL	What Cheer 3192
Meggers F	Clutier 5366	Miller AG	Doon 6764	Mitchell P	Maquoketa 999
Mehan J	Jefferson 10123	Miller AG	Rock Rapids 7089	Mitchell SA	Rock Valley 5200
Mehrhoff SH	Centerville 2841	Miller AW	Spencer 3898	Mitchell SG	Leon 5489
Meinert FG	Remsen 6975	Miller BF	Webster City 3420	Mitchell T	Des Moines 2631
Meisgeier C	Arlington 9664	Miller CE	Havelock 7294	Mitchell WJ	Waukon 4921
Melberg A	Norway 7287	Miller CJ	Dysart 5934	Mitchell ZT	Rockford 3053
Melchior AP	Dubuque 2327	Miller DB	Red Oak 3055	Mitchell HL	Rockford 3053
Mellen WE	Akron 7322	Miller DB	Shenandoah 2363	Mittendorff LW	Primghar 4155
Mellor G	Malvern 2247	Miller EJ	Marion 117	Moe CK	Garner 8367
Melrose A	Hawarden 4594	Miller EL	Clinton 3736	Moeller CW	Milford 9298
Melter D	Marcus 9819	Miller EW	Waterloo 2910	Moeller E	Dysart 5934
Meltzer WD	Ames 10408	Miller FB	Cedar Falls 3871	Moeller FC	Fort Dodge 2763
Mengis W	Odebolt 4511	Miller FJ	Hubbard 8970	Moeller H	Rock Valley 5200
Mennenga B	Belmond 8748	Miller FL	Adair 8699	Mohl HA	Lost Nation 5402
Menor CE	Milford 9298	Miller FM	Garner 8367	Mohling E	Sumner 8198
Mentzer BF	Marion 117	Miller FS	Hamburg 6017	Mohling WH	Fredericksburg 10541
Mentzer BF	Marion 2753	Miller GB	Waterloo 6854	Mohr H	Clutier 5366
Mercer JH	Chelsea 5412	Miller GF	Cedar Rapids 2511	Moir A	Burlington 1744
Meredith CP	Atlantic 2762	Miller GF	Cedar Rapids 3643	Moir J	Burlington 1744
Meredith F	Blanchard 4902	Miller GF	Cedar Rapids 9168	Moir WJ	Eldora 5140
Merner WH	Cedar Falls 3871	Miller H	College Springs 11295	Moldenschardt WC	Gladbrook 5461
Merrell NA	De Witt 3182	Miller HA	Des Moines 2307	Molleston GW	Lineville 7261
Merrill GW	Columbus Junction 2032	Miller HA	Guthrie Center 5424	Molleston RE	Lineville 7261
Merrill HA	Mason City 4587	Miller HA	Eagle Grove 3439	Moncrief AS	Indianola 1811
Merrill HA	Rockford 3053	Miller HD	Olin 7585	Monel JB	Bancroft 5643
Merrill HW	Ottumwa 1726	Miller HF	Hamburg 6017	Monk I	Blanchard 4902
Merrill JH	Des Moines 1970	Miller J	Cedar Falls 3871	Monlux WL	Corwith 5775
Merrill JH	McGregor 323	Miller JE	Belle Plaine 4754	Monroe C	Leon 5489
Merrill JH	Ottumwa 1726	Miller JF	Belle Plaine 4754	Monroe EG	Leon 5489
Merrill LA	Mason City 4587	Miller LA	Anamosa 4696	Monroe PC	Dexter 10030
Merrill LJ	Des Moines 1970	Miller M	Terril 10238	Monserud NO	Linn Grove 7137
Merrill S	Des Moines 1970	Miller OJ	College Springs 11295	Montague JVW	Mason City 2574
Merrill S	McGregor 323	Miller OP	Doon 6764	Montgomery LJ	Keokuk 1992
Merrill SA	Des Moines 1970	Miller OP	Rock Rapids 7089	Montgomery WL	Sioux City 1757
Mertens C	Peterson 4601	Miller OP	Sioux Center 7369	Montzheimer OH	Primghar 4155
Meservey ST	Fort Dodge 1661	Miller RE	Iowa Falls 7521	Monzingo JF	Coin 7309
Metcalf E	Pleasantville 5564	Miller RE	Waterloo 5120	Moody JA	Hawarden 4594
Metcalf FT	Pleasantville 5564	Miller RH	Estherville 4700	Moody LW	Pomeroy 6063
Metcalf FT, Mrs.	Pleasantville 5564	Miller RH	Spencer 6941	Moody MR, Mrs.	Pomeroy 6063
Metcalf HC	Anamosa 1813	Miller VE	Eldora 5140	Moon JS	Albia 8603
Metcalf JM	Primghar 4155	Miller VM	Adel 8981	Moore	Sioux City 10139
Metcalf LJ	Storm Lake 2595	Miller WC	Ottumwa 1726	Moore BE	Prairie City 6755
Metelman AF	Sidney 5145	Miller WH	Boone 6838	Moore EH	Fort Dodge 1661
Metelman CA	Sidney 5145	Miller WH	Des Moines 2307	Moore GH	Panora 3226
Meyer CE	Stuart 2721	Miller WH	Fort Madison 3974	Moore HA	Dunlap 4139
Meyer CF	Davenport 15	Miller WP	Aurelia 7108	Moore HL	Bagley 6995
Meyer H	Elkader 1815	Miller WW	Waterloo 2910	Moore HL	Panora 3226
Meyer JW	Dubuque 2327	Mills CB	Linn Grove 7137	Moore HN	Charter Oak 4376
Meyers AP	Milford 9298	Mills CB	Sioux Rapids 13400	Moore HN	Red Oak 2230
Meyers WC	Milford 9298	Mills CB	Sioux Rapids 9585	Moore HW	Muscatine 1577
Meyne W	Greene 6880	Mills CB, Jr.	Sioux Rapids 9585	Moore IA	Fonda 6550
Michaelson J	Roland 11249	Mills FM	Des Moines 2631	Moore IA	Sioux City 10139
Michelson MA	Clarion 3796	Miner EF	Corning 2936	Moore KP	Traer 5135
Mickelson AR	Linn Grove 7137	Miner FB	Charles City 4677	Moore MH	Waterloo 792

Moore NB	Clarinda 2028	Murphy AW	Shenandoah 8971	Newcomer CS	Eldora 9233
Moore NM	Tipton 2983	Murphy G	Sioux City 1757	Newcomer JD	Eldora 9233
Moore RH	Traer 5135	Murphy RB	Northboro 9015	Newcomer M	Cedar Rapids 3643
Moore RW	Marcus 9819	Murphy TD	Red Oak 3055	Newell VF	Des Moines 2583
Moore SL	Boone 3273	Murray RH	Greenfield 5334	Newlon WW	Clarinda 3112
Moore TE	Boone 3273	Murray WJ	Eldora 5140	Newman LJ	Stanton 6434
Moore WJ	Tipton 2983	Murtagh CB	Titonka 5597	Newton RW	Garner 4810
Moore WJ	Tipton 6760	Murtagh EJ	Burt 5703	Newton RW	Garner 8367
Moorhouse A	Glidden 4814	Murtagh EJ	Swea City 5637	Nichols C	Vinton 5088
Moret HC	Sheldon 3848	Murtagh EJ	Titonka 5597	Nichols E	Belle Plaine 4754
Morgan DC	Council Bluffs 5838	Myatt G	Harlan 10354	Nichols FM	Atlantic 2762
Morgan EDG	Fort Dodge 1661	Myers	Cedar Rapids 2511	Nichols JC	Sidney 5145
Morgan EG	Fort Dodge 1661	Myers CD	Greenfield 5334	Nicolet R	Strawberry Point 9069
Morgan JP	Aurelia 7108	Myers DD	Dubuque 3140	Nieman HW	Randolph 7833
Morrill E	Greene 6880	Myers EB	Sheldon 7880	Nienstedt A	Clarinda 3112
Morris ER	Lime Springs 6750	Myers G	De Witt 3182	Nierling AT	Waukon 10207
Morris JR	Deep River 6705	Myers GW	Dubuque 2327	Nierling AT	Waukon 4921
Morris OL	Waterloo 792	Myers GW	Dubuque 3140	Niles LW	Atlantic 2762
Morris SE	Seymour 8247	Myers JW	Dubuque 3140	Nissager M	Kimballton 9619
Morrison DA	Fort Madison 3974	Myers JW	Le Mars 2728	Nissen JH	Clinton 2469
Morrison HG	Peterson 4601	Myers LB	Knoxville 4633	Nissley GL	Des Moines 13321
Morrison JB	Fort Madison 3974	Myers MJ	Cedar Rapids 2511	Nixon AB	Pomeroy 6063
Morrison RJ	Traer 5135	Myers MJ	Cedar Rapids 2511	Nokes LE	Lake City 4966
Morrison SE	Seymour 11210	Myers WA	Storm Lake 10034	Nollen J	Pella 2063
Morrison WC	Grundy Center 3225	Myers WH	Sheldon 7880	Nolterieke AH	Greene 6880
Morrow TF	Audubon 4891	Myers WR	Knoxville 4633	Nolting HC	Waverly 3105
Morse CR	Grinnell 2953	Myrick HD	Anamosa 4696	Nordling JC	Hartley 4881
Morse DE	Floyd 9821	Narey CE	Laurens 4795	Nordstrom F	Shenandoah 11588
Morsman MJ	Iowa City 18	Narey CE	Spirit Lake 13020	Norene AO	Red Oak 6056
Mortensen HM	Exira 6870	Narey CE	Spirit Lake 4758	Norgaard JJ	Harlan 10354
Morton R	Le Mars 2818	Natvig O	Cresco 4897	Norris JA	Linn Grove 7137
Mosely GA	Creston 12636	Neal JE	Knoxville 1986	Norris WH	Manchester 4221
Moser DM	Eldora 9233	Neal M	Charter Oak 4376	Norton CC	Corning 2936
Moser DM	Grundy Center 3396	Nearham JW	Ottumwa 2621	Norton CC	Corning 8100
Mosher C	Des Moines 389	Neiswanger TJ	Harvey 6936	Norton ER	Newell 10191
Mosher O	Perry 3026	Nelson C	Aurelia 9724	Norton H	Fort Dodge 4566
Mosnat JJ	Belle Plaine 4754	Nelson C	Bancroft 5643	Nothem SR	Remsen 6975
Mote WL	Griswold 3048	Nelson C	Crystal Lake 9853	Novak JP	Clutier 5366
Mott F	Winterset 1403	Nelson CE	Audubon 4891	Nowak FJ	Chelsea 5412
Mousel HP	Sheldon 7880	Nelson CH	Garner 8367	Nuckolls EW	Eldora 9233
Mouw N	Sioux Center 7369	Nelson EC	Burt 5703	Nuckolls J	Eldora 9233
Mouw PB	Sioux Center 7369	Nelson EN	Roland 11249	Nugen GW	New London 8352
Mowrey JB	Ottumwa 2621	Nelson EP	Crystal Lake 9853	Nutt CH	Des Moines 2307
Muckler HD	Toledo 6432	Nelson FS	Winterset 1403	Nye FT	Northboro 9015
Muckles R	Toledo 6432	Nelson JC	Crystal Lake 9853	Nye JP	Essex 5738
Mueller C	Davenport 2695	Nelson JH	Charles City 4677	O'Connor JM	Missouri Valley 3189
Mueller DH	Adair 8699	Nelson JS	Sioux City 4510	O'Dair KB	Guthrie Center 5424
Mueller DH	Marengo 2484	Nelson MB	Exira 6870	O'Donnell PE	Waukon 10207
Mullane JW	Valley Junction 5891	Nelson NC	Essex 5738	O'Malley GW	Perry 10130
Mullane JW	Valley Junction 5891	Nelson NP	Linn Grove 7137	O'Malley JC	Perry 10130
Mullin R	Dougherty 5576	Nelson PM	Iowa Falls 3252	O'Malley JP	Perry 10130
Mulroney JM	Fort Dodge 1661	Nelson WG	Sioux City 5022	O'Niel JF	Armstrong 5442
Mulroney JM	Fort Dodge 1947	Nelson WH	Decorah 493	Oasheim AJ	Bode 10371
Mummert CM	Aurelia 7108	Nerby CO	Forest City 5011	Obrecht AG	Havelock 7294
Mummert CM	Charter Oak 4376	Nervig EO	Humboldt 8277	Obrecht JG	Havelock 7294
Mummert M	Aurelia 7108	Nervig EO	Humboldt 13766	Obrecht WM	Havelock 7294
Munger TC	Cedar Rapids 5113	Nervig JT	Renwick 7988	Odens P	Little Rock 8119
Munson CA	Hawkeye 8900	Nettleton LJ	Tabor 4609	O'Donnell F	Dubuque 3140
Murdock FC	Boone 6838	Newcomb B	Corning 2936	Oehmke FJ	Pomeroy 6063
Murdock FW	Boone 6838	Newcomb B	Prescott 5912	Oehring CC	Elkader 1815
Murphey GS	Jesup 2856	Newcomb LS	Olin 7585	Ogan H	Indianola 1811
Murphy AW	Randolph 7833	Newcomb R	Corning 2936	Ogden DB	Clinton 66
Murphy AW	Shenandoah 2679	Newcomb R	Prescott 5912	Ohlschlager Z	Creston 2833

Ohlson TG	Aurelia 9724	Palmer CA	Algona 3197	Peck CA	Newton 13609
Okey AF	Corning 8725	Palmer EC	Sioux City 3124	Pedersen SC	Kimballton 9619
Okey CE	Corning 8725	Palmer FW	Des Moines 389	Peebler GL	Fairfield 1475
Okey FC	Corning 8725	Palmer MF	Dexter 10030	Peet FD	Iowa Falls 3252
Oldaker HE	Marengo 2484	Palmer RP	Greene 6880	Peet FD	Iowa Falls 7521
Oldfield CB	Sioux City 4235	Palmer RP	Mason City 4587	Pelletier FM	Sioux City 10139
Oldon FA	Alta 7126	Palmer WV	Goldfield 5373	Pellsbury FW	Eagle Grove 4694
Olds AL	Charles City 4677	Pankow CA	Aurelia 9724	Pendry LC	Indianola 1811
Olds HB	Charles City 4677	Panther L	Burlington 351	Penick HO	Chariton 6014
Olds RB	Charles City 4677	Parden JA	George 9910	Penick JA	Chariton 6014
Olenheimer AN	Eagle Grove 3439	Parden JA	Mason City 4587	Penick L	Chariton 6014
Oleson OM	Fort Dodge 1661	Parish FW	Clarinda 3112	Penick WC	Chariton 6014
Ollenburg HL	Garner 8367	Parizer J	Pocahontas 6303	Penne RL	Waterloo 13702
Olmsted JG	Prairie City 6755	Parker CA	Mason City 2574	Penne RL	Waterloo 2910
Olney HM	Clinton 2469	Parker CM	Lawler 10599	Pennington CW	Sumner 8198
Olson BJ	Villisca 2766	Parker E	Lawler 10599	Penrose EG	Tama City 1880
Olson E	Story City 10222	Parker FB	Rock Rapids 7089	Pentecost LJ	Panora 3226
Olson EJ	New London 8352	Parker GS	Sioux City 5022	Pentecost VR	Panora 3226
Olson FD	Armstrong 5442	Parker LF	Cherokee 3049	Perine AC	Spencer 3898
Olson HE	Winfield 10640	Parker LF	Grinnell 2953	Perisho LD	Kanawha 9018
Olson J	Forest City 4889	Parker LF	Newell 10191	Perkins CE	Burlington 351
Olson J	Forest City 4889	Parker MI	Klemme 6659	Perkins GB	Sac City 4450
Olson M	Forest City 4889	Parks CW	Council Bluffs 9306	Perkins RA	La Porte City 4114
Olson OC	Rake 11735	Parr WL	Charles City 5979	Perkins WG	Prescott 5912
Oltmann J	George 9910	Parrott RJ	Aurelia 9724	Perley DC	Elliott 6857
Opfer HS	Waukon 4921	Parslow HE	Clarinda 3112	Perrin C	Knoxville 1986
Opperman G	Strawberry Point 9069	Parsons H	Rockwell City 11582	Perrin J	Greene 3071
Orcutt GH	Monroe 7357	Parsons L	Iowa City 2738	Perrin OH	Woodbine 4745
Orcutt HL	Monroe 7357	Parsons OW	Spirit Lake 13020	Perrine D	Villisca 2766
Ormsby AL	Emmetsburg 3337	Parsons OW	Spirit Lake 8032	Perry C	Knoxville 1986
Ormsby ES	Emmetsburg 3337	Parsons RL	Iowa City 2738	Perry EH	Chariton 13458
Orr B	Shannon City 9723	Partch EL	Rock Rapids 3153	Perry EH	Chariton 6014
Orris EE	Winterset 1403	Pasche C	Davenport 4022	Perry EH	Chariton 9024
Osborn FH	Elliott 6857	Passig HE	Humboldt 13766	Peterman TB	Wesley 5457
Osborne AW	Spirit Lake 8032	Passig HE	Humboldt 8277	Peters JH	Clinton 66
Osborne JH	Sioux City 5022	Patrick OR	Cumberland 7326	Peters JH	Lyons 66
Osborne TR	New Sharon 8950	Pattee DJ	Perry 3026	Peters JH	Lyons 2733
Osgood JC	Burlington 351	Pattee HM	Perry 3026	Petersen PW	Williams 5585
Osgood PB	Jefferson 10123	Pattee LC	Pocahontas 6303	Peterson BG	Sioux Rapids 9585
Osgood PG	Boone 6838	Pattee WH	Perry 3026	Peterson E	Crystal Lake 9853
Osmundson JO	Crystal Lake 5305	Patterson GF	Fonda 6550	Peterson EE	Marathon 4789
Osness JL	Cambridge 9014	Patterson J	Burlington 1744	Peterson JE	New London 5420
Osness JS	Cambridge 9014	Patterson JH	Dunlap 4139	Peterson L	Stanton 6434
Ostrom P	Stanton 6434	Patterson P	New Sharon 8950	Peterson PH	Villisca 7506
Ostrus TE	Cumberland 7326	Patterson W	Keokuk 1992	Peterson S	Thornton 8340
Oughten RE	Centreville 337	Patterson WE	New Sharon 8950	Peterson WM	Albia 8603
Ouren CG	Council Bluffs 14028	Patton JA	Council Bluffs 1479	Petro B	Marion 117
Ouren FW	Harlan 10354	Paul AS	Henderson 7382	Pettinger P	Cumberland 7326
Ouren HW	Harlan 10354	Paul HE	Corwith 5775	Pettinger PH	Cumberland 7326
Outhier B	Prescott 5912	Paulsen F	Preston 8273	Pettinger WT	Cumberland 7326
Outhier FA	Prescott 5912	Paulson CE	Lake Mills 5123	Pettit OD	Sioux City 1757
Overbaugh JM	Clarion 3796	Paulson LJ	Lake Mills 5123	Pettit OD	Sioux City 3968
Overbeck HC	Essex 5803	Payne FS	Centerville 2841	Petty OP	Clinton 2469
Overocker HH	Milford 9298	Payne MM	Hamburg 6017	Petzinger S	New London 8352
Owen JH	Charles City 2579	Peacock JH	Rock Rapids 3153	Pfiffner AE	Lake Mills 5123
Owens AP	Ireton 4794	Pearsall GE	Des Moines 1970	Phelps A	Henderson 7382
Oxborrow CW	Des Moines 13321	Pearsall GE	Des Moines 2307	Phelps WA	Henderson 7382
Packard CA	Renwick 7988	Pearsall GE	Emmetsburg 8035	Phillipps JW	Seymour 8247
Packard RE	Centerville 2841	Pearsons JH	Fort Dodge 4566	Phillips CB	New Hampton 7607
Padden GM	Fredericksburg 10541	Pease TC	Sioux City 3940	Phillips RE	Corning 2936
Painter D	Spencer 3898	Peasley JC	Burlington 751	Phippin EF	Spirit Lake 4758
Painter RD	Sigourney 1786	Peatman CA	Centerville 2841	Pickett CE	Waterloo 5120
Palmer AW	Clarinda 3112	Peavey FH	Sioux City 3124	Piehn LH	Nora Springs 4761

Name	Location	Name	Location	Name	Location
Pierce GG	Pomeroy 6063	Price WB	Council Bluffs 5838	Read H	Shenandoah 2363
Pierce HS	Spirit Lake 8032	Priester A	Davenport 1671	Read TH	Coin 7309
Pike HL	Oskaloosa 8076	Prime EE	Osage 4885	Read TH	Farragut 6700
Pike WH	Oskaloosa 8076	Pritchard WS	Des Moines 389	Read TH	Imogene 8295
Pile WC	Webster City 1874	Pritchard WS	Des Moines 485	Read TH	Shenandoah 2363
Pillsbury LO	Milford 5539	Prizer JW	Brighton 2033	Reames GC	Richland 5611
Pillsbury SL	Spirit Lake 4758	Prouty GC	Des Moines 2307	Rechtfertig VJ	Waterloo 792
Pinckney EA	Forest City 4889	Pruess J	Clarence 7682	Recknor W	Creston 12636
Pingel LF	Sioux Rapids 13400	Purviance M	Shannon City 9723	Recknor W	Creston 2586
Pinkerton RI	Creston 12636	Putnam CE	Cedar Rapids 2511	Redden CL	Spirit Lake 4758
Pinkerton RI	Creston 2586	Putnam CE	Cedar Rapids 5113	Reddish JL	Albia 8603
Pirie HA	Norway 7287	Pylman FJ	Sheldon 7880	Redfearn I	New London 8352
Pitner H	Cedar Rapids 9168	Quackenbush BH	Rockford 3053	Redfield JM	Cherokee 3049
Pittman EH	Britt 5020	Quiner FE	Des Moines 13321	Reed WO	Hubbard 8970
Pixley JK	Wyoming 1943	Quinn CC	Boone 3273	Reed CW	Cresco 4897
Place AM	Waterloo 2910	Quist DL	Essex 5738	Reed D	Coon Rapids 6080
Place AM	Waterloo 792	Rachut HE	Titonka 5597	Reed JR	Council Bluffs 5838
Plank JU	Iowa City 2738	Rademacher BW	Gilmore City 6611	Reed SS	Rolfe 4954
Platt EC	Eagle Grove 4694	Raffety ER	New Sharon 8950	Reed WC	Pleasantville 5564
Platt FC	Waterloo 2910	Raffety ER	Oskaloosa 8076	Reed WL	Guthrie Center 5424
Platt JD	Waterloo 2910	Rainbow J	Henderson 7382	Reeder HF	Alta 7126
Plumer MJ	Forest City 4889	Raines RB	Independence 3263	Reeder HF	Aurelia 9724
Plumer RC	Forest City 4889	Rake AA	Rake 11735	Reese CA	Red Oak 3055
Plummer BA	Forest City 4889	Rake TA	Rake 11735	Reese HC	Prescott 5912
Poley IJ	Clarinda 3112	Ramsey CL	Sibley 3320	Reese N	Belmond 8748
Pollard JAS	Fort Madison 3974	Ramsey E	Fairfield 8986	Reeves H	McGregor 323
Pollock MR	Garner 8367	Ramsey HI	Melvin 5616	Rehder MH	Gladbrook 5461
Pollock RI	Nora Springs 4761	Ramsey JN	Anamosa 4696	Rehder RH	Dike 5372
Pond SP	Keokuk 1992	Rand ED	Burlington 751	Rehnstrom JM	Alta 7126
Pope L	Havelock 7294	Rand RN	Lyons 66	Reibsamer G	Titonka 5597
Porter HW	Glidden 4814	Rand SC	Clinton 66	Reid EF	Laurens 4795
Porter AJ	Monroe 7357	Randall PE	Spencer 3898	Reigart H	Maquoketa 999
Porter DC	Davenport 15	Randall WS	Hawarden 4594	Reihman JW	Cumberland 7326
Porter GE	Fort Dodge 4566	Ranous GN	Richland 5611	Reilly J	New Hampton 7607
Porter JH	Montezuma 2961	Ransom HJ	Des Moines 2631	Reimers H	Inwood 7304
Porter MR	Stuart 2721	Rasch AE	Fort Dodge 4566	Reiniger RG	Charles City 2579
Porter SL	Stuart 2721	Rasmussen EC	Exira 6870	Remey JT	Burlington 751
Porter VA	Bagley 6995	Rasmussen P	Milford 5539	Remien WR	Atlantic 2762
Post A	Moulton 5319	Rath JW	Waterloo 792	Remsburg MC	Spencer 3898
Potgeter J	Crystal Lake 9853	Rathbone WE	Eldora 5140	Renesh LF	Toledo 6432
Potter LF	Harlan 5207	Rathbun MF	Kingsley 9116	Reno QP	Marengo 2484
Pound LE	Williams 5585	Rathburn AB	Clinton 994	Renshaw E	Inwood 7304
Powell OJ	Elliott 6857	Rathke M	Glenwood 1862	Renshaw H	Inwood 7304
Powers FW	Waterloo 6854	Rathke WC	Glenwood 1862	Repass FC	Dexter 10030
Powers HS	Iowa Falls 7521	Rathman GH	Sioux City 5022	Reynolds A	Des Moines 2583
Pratt GM	Winterset 2002	Rauscher CF	Ottumwa 1726	Reynolds A	Panora 3226
Prechel AJ	Spencer 3898	Rawson GL	Arlington 9664	Reynolds AB	Conrad 9447
Preston HL	Dunlap 4139	Ray CA	Boone 6838	Reynolds AD	Pleasantville 5564
Preston JC	Crystal Lake 5305	Ray DA	Humboldt 8277	Reynolds CR	Farnhamville 11907
Preston WT	Dunlap 4139	Ray WH	Waverly 3105	Reynolds EJ	Panora 3226
Prettyman WR	Coon Rapids 6080	Rayburn AF	Montezuma 2961	Reynolds GM	Des Moines 2583
Preussner DA	Manchester 4221	Rayburn ED	Montezuma 2961	Reynolds GM	Panora 3226
Preussner DE	Manchester 4221	Raymond HC	Charles City 1810	Reynolds HR	Bedford 5165
Price AM	De Witt 3182	Raymond MM	Charles City 1810	Reynolds JL	Alta 7126
Price CE	Council Bluffs 5838	Raymond MM	Floyd 9821	Reynolds JL	Jefferson 10123
Price EW	De Witt 3182	Raymond SR	Grundy Center 3396	Reynolds MM	Panora 3226
Price FR	Eldora 5140	Rea GM	Grundy Center 3396	Reynolds TL	Northboro 9015
Price H	Davenport 15	Read CE	Clarence 7682	Rhenberg KH	Cedar Rapids 3643
Price JH	De Witt 3182	Read DW	Belle Plaine 2012	Rhode RH	Rock Rapids 3153
Price LA	Spirit Lake 13020	Read EA	Coin 7309	Rhynsburger JS	Pella 8047
Price LA	Spirit Lake 4758	Read EA	Imogene 8295	Rice EW	Sioux City 4209
Price RE	Elkader 1815	Read EA	Shenandoah 2363	Rice HB	Sioux City 1757
Price VT	Elkader 1815	Read GM	Cumberland 7326	Rice UG	Milton 10243

Rich CS	Burlington 351	Roberts LR	Adel 8981	Ross AGF	Little Rock 8119
Rich EH	Clear Lake 7869	Roberts MI	Shannon City 9723	Ross E	Independence 2187
Rich EH	Fort Dodge 1661	Roberts R	Osage 4885	Ross HE	Shenandoah 12950
Rich EH	Fort Dodge 1947	Roberts RM	Newton 2644	Ross HE	Shenandoah 2679
Rich EH	Rockwell City 5185	Roberts RM	Red Oak 2230	Ross HE	Shenandoah 2679
Rich GL	Fort Dodge 1661	Roberts RR	Osage 4885	Roth GW	Burlington 751
Rich GL	Fort Dodge 1947	Roberts W	Adel 8981	Rothe LA	Fonda 6550
Rich JF	Fort Dodge 1661	Roberts WJ	Des Moines 2583	Rounds JG	Des Moines 1970
Rich WF	Fort Dodge 1661	Roberts WJ	Red Oak 2130	Rouse HA	Perry 3026
Rich WF	Rockwell City 5185	Robertson AJ	Des Moines 2307	Rouse R	Waterloo 5120
Richards BB	Dubuque 3140	Robertson C	Charter Oak 4376	Rouze LS	Pleasantville 5564
Richards BL	Rock Rapids 3153	Robertson JS	Wyoming 1943	Rowe AH	Bancroft 5643
Richards CB	Fort Dodge 1661	Robertson SA	Des Moines 2307	Rowe CW	Marcus 9819
Richards EA	Rockwell City 5185	Robinson BF	Armstrong 5442	Rowe DM	Milton 10243
Richards FS	McGregor 323	Robinson ES	Sioux City 10139	Rowe M	Macksburg 6852
Richards JR	Washington 1762	Robinson FH	Primghar 4155	Rowe SE	Bloomfield 9303
Richards S	Oskaloosa 1101	Robinson FS	Armstrong 5442	Rownd CA	Cedar Falls 3871
Richardson CA	Renwick 7988	Robinson LC	Hampton 7843	Roy D	Winterset 1403
Richardson E	Dysart 5934	Robinson RR	Manchester 4221	Royce CH	Harris 6949
Richardson G	Ames 3017	Robinson SM	Indianola 1811	Royer M	Fonda 6550
Richardson GH	Belmond 8748	Robinson T	Adair 8699	Rozema JH	Spirit Lake 4758
Richardson J	Muscatine 692	Robinson TJB	Hampton 7843	Ruby JC	Manilla 6041
Richardson JV	Creston 2586	Robinson WL	Hampton 7843	Ruby SC	Winterset 2002
Richardson M	Elkader 1815	Robinson WL, Jr.	Hampton 7843	Ruehl RJ	Grundy Center 3396
Richardson S	Moulton 5319	Robinson WT	Hampton 7843	Rugg AE	Sioux City 5022
Richardson SW	Creston 2586	Robinson WT	Newton 13609	Rugg HE	Waterloo 6854
Richmond CB	Iowa Falls 7521	Robison T	What Cheer 3192	Rugg M	Dike 5372
Richmond LT	Albia 1799	Rockhold G	Lineville 7261	Ruggeberg E	Lost Nation 5402
Ricker BJ	Grinnell 2953	Rockrohr O	Clinton 66	Rule FS	Oelwein 5778
Ricker RE	Northboro 9015	Rockrohr O	Lyons 66	Rule J	Mason City 4587
Ridge RA	Perry 3026	Rodamar E	Waterloo 5120	Rule JP	Belmond 8748
Ridgeway P	Lenox 5517	Rodamar I	Waterloo 5120	Rule JT	Belmond 8748
Rief H	Manilla 5873	Rodda A	Havelock 7294	Rumble AE	Tipton 13232
Rief JG	Manilla 5873	Rodenbach CH	Cedar Falls 3871	Rumsey HE	Des Moines 2583
Riekman AW	Council Bluffs 1479	Rodman RG	Cherokee 3049	Runge BH	Charter Oak 4376
Rietveld H	Harvey 6936	Rodskial E	Traer 5135	Runyon WW	Corning 2936
Rikansrud OT	Kanawha 9018	Roe OO	Story City 9017	Rusch JH	Marengo 2484
Riley BM	Rippey 7609	Roenfanz A	Clear Lake 7869	Rush JF	Leon 5489
Riley ML	Williams 5585	Roenfanz A	Clear Lake 7869	Russell CE	Adel 8981
Rines RB	Toledo 6432	Rogers CL	Corning 8725	Russell GM	Garden Grove 5464
Ringham TL	Northwood 8373	Rogers CT	Grundy Center 3225	Russell H	Sioux City 3940
Ringland GS	Bancroft 5643	Rogers FL	Clear Lake 7869	Russell HH	Bagley 6995
Ringland GS	Clarion 3796	Rogers FM	Clear Lake 7869	Russell JW	Adel 8981
Ripley AC	Garner 4810	Rogers H	Farragut 6700	Russell LA	Newton 2644
Risk RC	Brighton 2033	Rogers JT	Corydon 10146	Russell S	Nora Springs 4761
Risser FS	Prairie City 6755	Rogers MS	Clear Lake 7869	Rutenbeck WC	Lost Nation 5402
Ritchie JC	Columbus Junction 2032	Rogers RR	Clear Lake 7869	Ruthven J	Ruthven 5541
Ritz HE	Eldon 5342	Rogers W	Farragut 6700	Rutt A	Casey 8099
Ritz MH	Eldon 5342	Rohe AJ	Bancroft 5643	Rutt SL	Casey 8099
Rivard PL	Pocahontas 12544	Roland SE	Marengo 2484	Ryan JW	Chelsea 5412
Rixon F	Clinton 3736	Rolston CH	Rolfe 4954	Ryburn WH	Rockwell 10217
Roach J	Corning 8100	Romey GA	Melvin 5616	Rye HN	Forest City 5011
Roach JW	Rock Rapids 3153	Rood JM	Bode 10371	Sabin AC	Glenwood 1862
Roadman MW	Dike 5372	Roof FS	Blockton 8211	Sackett OA	Arlington 9664
Robb ED	Eldora 9233	Roof ME	Blockton 8211	Sage FR	Brighton 5554
Robbins CH	Grand River 9737	Roovaart JB	Harvey 6936	Sage FR	Washington 6122
Roberts CM	Independence 2187	Roovaart JVD	Pella 8047	Sam AG	Sioux City 5022
Roberts DR	Adel 8981	Rorebeck WC	Northboro 9015	Sampson J	Storm Lake 2595
Roberts F	Oskaloosa 2417	Rorem ET	Radcliffe 6435	Sampson LW	Fredericksburg 10541
Roberts FC	Guthrie Center 7736	Rose EF	Clarinda 3112	Samson JF	Indianola 1811
Roberts JJ	Knoxville 12849	Rosecrans WI	Belmond 8748	Sandburg WA	Rockwell City 5185
Roberts JJ	Knoxville 1871	Rosendall AP	Royal 10395	Sanderson HA	Shannon City 9723
Roberts LGD	Shannon City 9723	Rosiersz J	Pella 2063	Sanderson HO	Shannon City 9723

Sanderson RA	Essex 5738
Sanderson RA	Essex 5803
Sandine K	Marathon 4789
Sandschulte LF	Rock Valley 5200
Sandusky JW	New Hampton 2588
Sandy JG	Indianola 1811
Sanford GP	Council Bluffs 1479
Sanford WA	Cherokee 3049
Sanford WA	Primghar 6650
Sargent EM	Grundy Center 3396
Sargent FD	Centerville 2841
Sargent WC	Grundy Center 3225
Sartorius CH	Everly 7828
Saunders CD	Denison 4784
Saunders CW	Clarence 7682
Saunders E	Manilla 5873
Saunders JA	Manilla 5873
Saverbry RB	Strawberry Point 9069
Sawyer RH	Shenandoah 12950
Sawyers FL	Centerville 2841
Sawyers JD	Centerville 2841
Sawyers JL	Centerville 2841
Sax JB	Ottumwa 107
Sayler WA	Clarinda 3112
Sayre CH	Guthrie Center 5424
Sayre RM	Guthrie Center 7736
Sayre RM	Stuart 2721
Sayre RW	Odebolt 5817
Sayre SB	Odebolt 5817
Sayre WM	Odebolt 5817
Scarcliff T	Independence 2187
Scarr FM	Council Bluffs 1479
Schaap CB	Hull 6953
Schadel FS	Red Oak 2130
Schaefer EA	Waterloo 6854
Schaffer FB	Floyd 9821
Schakel L	Prairie City 6755
Schaller F	Storm Lake 10034
Schaller GJ	Storm Lake 10034
Schaller HW	Storm Lake 10034
Schaller P	Sac City 4450
Scharfenberg A	Traer 5135
Scharnberg EF	Everly 7828
Scharnberg L	Everly 7828
Schee GW	Sheldon 3848
Scheffield ES	Ottumwa 1726
Schell EA	Harlan 10354
Schemmel L	Inwood 8257
Schenck CT	Monroe 7357
Schenck CT	Red Oak 2130
Schenck T	Monroe 2215
Schenk WC	Sioux City 5022
Schick JF	Coin 7309
Schimelfenig AF	Indianola 1811
Schlegel V	New Sharon 8950
Schleiter FH	Galva 10501
Schmidt CF	Davenport 15
Schmidt FH	Dysart 5934
Schmidt H	Davenport 15
Schmidt H	Davenport 1671
Schmidt JA	Sioux City 1976
Schmidt JG	Nora Springs 4761
Schmidt LC	Dysart 5934
Schmidt W	Galva 10501
Schmidt WH	Elkader 1815
Schnedler HF	Nora Springs 4761
Schnedler JG	Nora Springs 4761
Schneider FM	Shenandoah 12950
Schneider FM	Shenandoah 2679
Schneider SA	Mason City 10428
Schneider SA	Milford 5539
Schneider SA	Titonka 5597
Schnurr G	Fort Dodge 2763
Schoenmann GA	Blockton 8211
Scholte HP	Pella 2063
Scholte P	Pella 2063
Scholz HCW	Dubuque 317
Schoonover GL	Anamosa 4696
Schoonover GL	Olin 7585
Schoonover L	Anamosa 4696
Schott J	What Cheer 3192
Schott R	What Cheer 3192
Schrader OV	Maquoketa 999
Schreiber EW	Charter Oak 4376
Schreiber WE	Wyoming 1943
Schroeder H	Dysart 5934
Schroeder HE	Muscatine 1577
Schroeder LW	Williams 5585
Schroeder R	Dysart 5934
Schroeder WF	Preston 8273
Schrup NJ	Dubuque 3140
Schultz HA	Charter Oak 4376
Schultz HC	Waterloo 2910
Schultz JJ	Dike 5372
Schultz WB	Toledo 13073
Schultz WJ	Lost Nation 5402
Schuster LJ	Clinton 994
Schuyler AL	Clinton 994
Schwendemann WT	Tipton 13232
Schwind JW	Dubuque 3140
Scofield EJ	Osage 4885
Scott AJ	Linn Grove 7137
Scott AV	Creston 2833
Scott BF	Cambridge 9014
Scott DC	Grundy Center 3396
Scott EM	Cedar Rapids 3643
Scott H	Corning 8100
Scott HB	Sioux City 1757
Scott HB	Sioux City 5022
Scott HJ	Northboro 9015
Scott J, Jr.	Sioux City 4510
Scott JB	Fort Dodge 1661
Scott OB	Royal 10395
Scott OB	Spencer 6941
Scott SC	Corning 8100
Scott WA	Belle Plaine 2012
Scott WD	Prairie City 6755
Scott WW	Des Moines 2307
Scribner RH	Cherokee 3049
Seaman C	Charles City 5979
Seaman HW	Clinton 2469
Sebern WB	Marion 117
Secor E	Forest City 4889
Sederburg ML	Essex 5803
Sedgwick JE	Waterloo 5120
Sedgwick LM	Iowa City 18
Seeley WB	Farmington 5579
Seeman L	Denison 4784
Seerley HH	Cedar Falls 3871
Seevers WH	Oskaloosa 2417
Seifert EF	Elkader 1815
Selby WL	Centerville 2841
Selden MR	Cedar Rapids 2511
Selden MR	Cedar Rapids 3643
Senior CF	Centerville 337
Senneff JA	Mason City 10428
Sessler AL	Davenport 15
Sevareid EE	Story City 9017
Sever PL	Stuart 2721
Severin LH	Cedar Falls 5507
Severson DB	Sioux City 3124
Severson SJ	Cambridge 9014
Severson TJ	Lake Mills 5123
Seward LC	Algona 3197
Sewell RH	Waverly 3105
Sewell RH	Waverly 3105
Sewell VL	New Hampton 7607
Sexton HM	Macksburg 6852
Sexton L	New Sharon 8950
Seymour FE	Fort Dodge 2763
Shadbolt A	Grinnell 7439
Shade C	Inwood 8257
Shade C	Rock Rapids 3153
Shade J	Rock Rapids 3153
Shade JJ	Rock Rapids 3153
Shaffer AH	New Hampton 7607
Shaffer FB	Lawler 10599
Shaffer LC	New Hampton 7607
Shaffer WG	New Hampton 7607
Shaffer WH	New Hampton 7607
Shaible JF	Mason City 10428
Shaible JF	Mason City 4587
Shaler JW	Chelsea 5412
Shambaugh IW	Clarinda 3112
Shane FE	Villisca 2766
Shaner MW	Laurens 4795
Shapely TW	Anamosa 1813
Shattuck W	Garner 4810
Shaw DL	Harlan 10354
Shaw DW	Manilla 6041
Shaw EB	West Union 2015
Shaw FE	Le Mars 2728
Shaw LM	Manilla 6041
Shaw LW	Manilla 6041
Shear GE	Rockford 3053
Sheets E	Shenandoah 2363
Sheffield FWH	Dubuque 846
Sheffield RE	Storm Lake 10034
Sheldon DM	Sutherland 3618
Sheldon JA	Rake 11735
Sheldon NL	Lake Mills 5123
Sheldon OJ	Lake Mills 5123
Shelton JM	Allerton 9231
Shenkberg F	Sioux City 10139
Shepardson JB	Greene 6880
Shepardson WS	Greene 6880
Sheppard GW	Oskaloosa 147
Sherlock J	Ayrshire 5479
Sherman GA	Fairfield 1475

Name	Location	Name	Location	Name	Location
Sherman JJ	Bancroft 5643	Sleeper WH, Jr.	Everly 7828	Snow H	Albia 1799
Sherman LW	Clear Lake 7869	Slimmer A	Greene 3071	Snyder CA	Tipton 2983
Sherman LW	Mason City 4587	Sloan E	Fredericksburg 10541	Snyder IN	Charles City 5979
Sherman OB	New Hampton 2588	Sloanaker C	Newton 2644	Snyder M	Spirit Lake 13020
Sherman T	Bancroft 5643	Slocum CH	Primghar 4155	Snyder M	Spirit Lake 8032
Shields HS	Allerton 9231	Slocum GR	Primghar 4155	Snyder SN	Charles City 5979
Shields VH	New London 5420	Smeby EO	Sioux City 3124	Soe P	Kimballton 9619
Shimon T	Pocahontas 6303	Smith AC	Clinton 2469	Soenke H	Little Rock 8119
Shinn WP	Prescott 5912	Smith AG	Clinton 2469	Soesbe CW	Greene 6880
Shipp G	Webster City 3420	Smith AK	Parkersburg 9846	Soesbe EW	Greene 6880
Shipp JH	Webster City 3420	Smith AR	Spencer 3898	Sofer EB	Estherville 4700
Shoecraft S	Clinton 3736	Smith AR	Spencer 6941	Sofholm SO	Armstrong 5442
Shoemaker RE	Red Oak 3055	Smith AW	Sioux City 5022	Sogard S	Webster City 1874
Shoemaker TJ	Marshalltown 411	Smith C	Webster City 2984	Sollenbarger DT	Allerton 9231
Shore WG	Chariton 9024	Smith CD	Algona 3197	Sollenbarger DT	Lineville 7261
Shors ET	Pocahontas 6303	Smith CD	Burt 5685	Soper EB	Emmetsburg 3337
Shoulberg H	Akron 7322	Smith DH	Marcus 9819	Soper EB	Titonka 5597
Shove WF	Glidden 4814	Smith EH	Cedar Rapids 3643	Sorg PM	Sumner 8198
Show CB	Kanawha 9018	Smith ES	Montour 7469	Sowers WE	Henderson 7382
Shriver AB	Winterset 1403	Smith FC	Osage 4885	Spaanum LB	Osage 1618
Shuler C	Davenport 4022	Smith FH	Washington 1762	Spaethe FC	Columbus Junction 2032
Shuler CC	Grundy Center 3225	Smith FN	New London 8352	Spalla JP	Britt 5020
Shuler JA	Indianola 1811	Smith FW	Cedar Rapids 2511	Spalla JP	Forest City 5011
Shumaker FL	Charter Oak 4376	Smith GJN	Sioux City 1757	Spaulding EB	Sioux City 4209
Shumaker JG	Charter Oak 4376	Smith H	Sioux Rapids 13400	Spaulding HW	Grinnell 7439
Shutts E	Centreville 337	Smith H	Sioux Rapids 9585	Spaulding JD	Sioux City 3124
Siebel J	Oskaloosa 2895	Smith H	Wyoming 1943	Spencer CH	Grinnell 1629
Siedentopf WM	Council Bluffs 1684	Smith HC	Cedar Falls 3871	Spencer CM	Des Moines 2583
Siegfried FC	Rockwell 10217	Smith HC	Jewell Junction 5743	Spencer HC	Grinnell 1629
Siegmund P	De Witt 3182	Smith HE	Casey 8099	Spencer HL	Oskaloosa 2417
Siemen GD	Sioux Center 7369	Smith HI	Mason City 2574	Sperbeck CH	Spirit Lake 8032
Sievers H	Newell 10191	Smith HN	Spencer 3898	Sperbeck L	Spirit Lake 8032
Sievers WG	Remsen 6975	Smith J	Hawarden 4594	Spicer VA	Red Oak 6056
Sigler DS	Corning 4268	Smith JA	Osage 4885	Spieker C	Swea City 5637
Sigler HC	Osceola 1776	Smith JS	Jewell Junction 5743	Spielman JA	Fairfield 1475
Sigler LP	Leon 1696	Smith JT	Norway 7287	Spies F	Graettinger 5571
Silliman RJ	Nevada 2555	Smith JW	Coon Rapids 6080	Spindler JJ	Council Bluffs 1479
Silsby HM	Missouri Valley 3189	Smith K	Burt 5685	Spindler JJ	Linn Grove 7137
Sime S	Toledo 13073	Smith LC	Burt 5685	Spinharney JH	Cherokee 10711
Simmon CT	Ames 10408	Smith LF	Winterset 2002	Spinney LB	Ames 10408
Simmons CF	Waukon 4921	Smith MD	Creston 2586	Sponheim EA	Saint Ansgar 10684
Simmons CT	Burlington 351	Smith RG	Carroll 3969	Spooner GF	Council Bluffs 1479
Simmons WG	Washington 2656	Smith RK	Muscatine 1577	Spooner R	Dexter 10030
Simmons WG	Washington 398	Smith RP	Mason City 2574	Springer EE	Charter Oak 4376
Simpson CE	Norway 7287	Smith SE	Montezuma 2961	Sprole JN	Garner 8367
Simpson E	La Porte City 4114	Smith SF	Davenport 848	Spry HR	Clarinda 3112
Simpson EG	Williams 5585	Smith T	Oelwein 5778	Spry MC	Shenandoah 11588
Simpson JD	Le Mars 2818	Smith WH	Primghar 4155	Spurgin W	Panora 3226
Singmaster CF	Richland 5611	Smith WM	Hartley 4881	Spurgin WC	Panora 3226
Sipe CL	Sioux Rapids 9585	Smith WM	Sheldon 3848	Squires JE	Maquoketa 999
Sipe FM	Sioux Rapids 9585	Smith WM	Sheldon 3848	St. Clair CC	Marshalltown 411
Sitzmann V	Kingsley 9116	Smock GV	Dubuque 2327	St. Clair CC	Marshalltown 4359
Siver CC	Charles City 1810	Smorenberg C	Pella 2063	St. John ER	Riceville 8442
Siverly CL	Ames 3017	Smouse AR	Cedar Rapids 3643	St. John JH	Arlington 9664
Sivright HH	Des Moines 2307	Smouse W	Washington 1762	St. John RT	Riceville 8442
Skinner S	Creston 2833	Smyth JJ	Marion 117	Staak H	Davenport 4022
Skinner S	Prescott 5912	Smyth JJ	Marion 2753	Staat WC	Grinnell 2953
Skrable J	Clutier 5366	Snakenberg D	Hedrick 5540	Stackhouse EM	Deep River 6705
Skrovig MO	Radcliffe 6435	Snakenberg FD	Cedar Rapids 9168	Stafford CW	Ames 10408
Slade JL	Eagle Grove 4694	Snell RW	Hawarden 4594	Stafford HW	Ames 10408
Slayman P	Knoxville 1986	Snodgrass G	Indianola 1811	Stahr HP	Crystal Lake 9853
Sleeper AW	Everly 7828	Snover J	Boone 6838	Stahr TM	Crystal Lake 9853
Sleeper AW	Sheldon 7880	Snow E	Grinnell 1629	Stair JB	Red Oak 6056

Stamp J	Strawberry Point 9069	Stone EJ	Sioux City 1757	Sweney MC	Lost Nation 5402
Standley SS	Bloomfield 9303	Stone MR	Hawarden 13939	Swenson HL	Elkader 1815
Stansberry JP	Moulton 5319	Stone TJ	Sioux City 1757	Swenson LR	Waterloo 792
Stansbury BE	Fayette 9592	Stonebraker BE	Rockwell City 11582	Swetting EV	Algona 3197
Stanton EW	Ames 3017	Storm WA	Coon Rapids 6080	Swetting EV	Titonka 5597
Staples CH	Peterson 4601	Stoufer DB	Council Bluffs 14028	Swinehart LE	Knoxville 12849
Stapleton T	Marengo 2484	Stout HL	Dubuque 1801	Swisher L	Iowa City 2738
Starker C	Burlington 751	Stout Z	Independence 3263	Switzer JC	Iowa City 2821
Starkey EJ	Terril 10238	Strahan JM	Malvern 2247	Tabor LV	Independence 3263
Starr AP	Tama City 1880	Strahan OA	Malvern 2247	Talbot WH	De Witt 3182
Starr WP	Fairfield 1475	Straight LS	Fonda 6550	Talbott AB	Brooklyn 3284
States F	Rippey 7609	Strauser MF	Coon Rapids 6080	Talbott BM	Brooklyn 3284
Stayman C	Fort Dodge 2763	Streater WA	Estherville 4700	Talbott EH	Brooklyn 3284
Stearns CS	Garden Grove 5464	Streator LC	Emmetsburg 3337	Talle A	Northwood 8373
Stearns FE	Garden Grove 5464	Streib JW	Clinton 3736	Talley JN	Diagonal 9125
Stearns JW	Garden Grove 5464	Strohl GW	Malvern 8057	Tallman B	Creston 12636
Stearns ML	Atlantic 2762	Strong H	Fort Dodge 1947	Tallman B	Creston 2586
Stebbins GE	La Porte City 4114	Stroud SR	Hedrick 12656	Tapager JM	Lake Mills 5123
Steckmest F	Peterson 4601	Struble GH	Toledo 6432	Taplin AB	Montour 7469
Steel WO	Centreville 337	Struyk LP	Sheldon 3848	Tauck JH	Renwick 7988
Steele A	Grinnell 1629	Stubenrauch JH	Pella 1891	Taylor BW	Valley Junction 5891
Steele CW	Corydon 10146	Stuckslager H	Lisbon 2182	Taylor EC	Rolfe 4954
Steele CW	Lineville 7261	Studer N	Wesley 5457	Taylor FE	Forest City 4889
Steele JP	Winterset 2002	Studley CE	Cumberland 7326	Taylor GC	Spirit Lake 8032
Steffen J	Traer 5135	Studley HH	Cumberland 7326	Taylor HC	Bloomfield 9303
Stein SG	Muscatine 1577	Stukenberg F	Radcliffe 6435	Taylor HS	Perry 3026
Stein SG, Jr.	Muscatine 1577	Sullivan C	Cherokee 3049	Taylor HT	Milton 10243
Steiner WT	Melvin 5616	Sullivan JJ	Dubuque 2327	Taylor JB	Centerville 2841
Steiner WT	Sibley 3320	Sullivan JJ	Dubuque 3140	Taylor JC	Malvern 4834
Steinmetz AH	Muscatine 1577	Sullivan JW	Bancroft 5643	Taylor JP	Charles City 2579
Stelle MC	Burlington 351	Sullivan JW	Swea City 5637	Taylor OB	Lawler 10599
Stelle MC	Burlington 751	Sullivan JW	Titonka 5597	Taylor OJ	Sioux City 3940
Stephens LB	Marion 2753	Sullivan NC	Osage 4885	Taylor OJ	Sioux City 4431
Stephens RD	Cedar Rapids 2511	Sullivan VC	Osage 4885	Taylor T	Jesup 2856
Stephens RD	Marion 117	Summers WL	Malvern 2247	Taylor WB	Bloomfield 9303
Stephensen OJ	Algona 3197	Summerwill WJ	Odebolt 4511	Taylor WS	Rolfe 4954
Stephenson CH	Des Moines 2307	Sunderman LJ	Clarinda 3112	Te Paske A	Sioux Center 7369
Stephenson GA	Waverly 3105	Sutherland DW	Manning 3455	Temple EA	Chariton 1724
Stephenson RW	Forest City 5011	Sutherland ED	Manning 3455	Temple GD	Fairfield 1475
Stephenson WB	Corning 8725	Sutherland LC	Manning 3455	Tennis SM	Shannon City 9723
Stevens CT	Milford 9298	Sutherland RG	Manning 3455	Tenny RM	Montour 7469
Stevens FB	Titonka 5597	Swab GW	Cedar Rapids 3643	Terry MC	Brighton 5554
Stevens LE	Ottumwa 2621	Swain EN	Perry 3026	Terry WE	Denison 4784
Stevenson EC	Rockwell City 5185	Swalin H	Pomeroy 6063	Terwilliger CS	Garner 8367
Stevenson WB	Independence 3263	Swan CM	Sioux City 3968	Thatcher JH	Ruthven 5541
Stevenson WG	Independence 3263	Swan FC	Sioux City 3124	Thatcher O	Fort Dodge 11304
Stewart B	Primghar 4155	Swan GN	Sioux City 4209	Thatcher OM	Fort Dodge 11304
Stewart JB	Des Moines 389	Swanson CW	Stanton 6434	Thayer JM	Chariton 1724
Stewart R	Waterloo 5120	Swanson EC	Osage 4885	Theobald E	Manilla 6041
Stewart WR	Conrad 9447	Swanson TR	Panora 3226	Thiel L	Dysart 5934
Stich JF	Clinton 3736	Swanson WK	Clarinda 3112	Thoma L	Fairfield 8986
Stickney EL	Moulton 5319	Swartzlender C	Tipton 13232	Thoma RP	Fairfield 8986
Stickney WC	Moulton 5319	Swartzlender C	Tipton 6760	Thomas BH	Forest City 5011
Stiger HG	Montour 7469	Swartzlender RD	Tipton 13232	Thomas BH	Iowa Falls 7521
Stiger HJ	Toledo 6432	Swartzlender RD	Tipton 6760	Thomas BH	Lake Mills 5123
Stiles DG	Fort Dodge 11304	Swayze WF	Nevada 2555	Thomas DH	Lime Springs 6750
Stoakes WM	Terril 10238	Sweesy WE	Manning 3455	Thomas EJ	Cresco 4897
Stock ER	Storm Lake 10034	Sweet CA	Belle Plaine 2012	Thomas GF	Swea City 5637
Stock TB	Waukon 10207	Sweet LT	Belle Plaine 2012	Thomas GW	Red Oak 6056
Stockwell CH	Coon Rapids 6080	Sweet SS	Belle Plaine 2012	Thomas HL	Perry 3026
Stoll GF	Sheffield 12430	Sweetser GN	Charter Oak 4376	Thomas HS	Conrad 9447
Stone AL	Clinton 2469	Sweigard CR	Garner 8367	Thomas JW	Lansing 405
Stone CE	Nevada 2555	Sweigard I	Garner 8367	Thomas NA	Norway 7287

Thompson AR	Des Moines 2886
Thompson B	Sutherland 3618
Thompson BJ	Buffalo Center 5154
Thompson CJ	Forest City 5011
Thompson FW	Thompson 5054
Thompson GD	Des Moines 2583
Thompson HA	Burt 5685
Thompson HE	Tipton 6760
Thompson HJ	Floyd 9821
Thompson J	Davenport 2695
Thompson JB	Buffalo Center 5154
Thompson JB	Jewell Junction 5743
Thompson JF	Casey 8099
Thompson JKP	Doon 6764
Thompson LM	Renwick 7988
Thorn RE	Clarinda 3112
Thornton LC	Pocahontas 6303
Thurn AR	Clinton 2469
Tilden GH	Ames 3017
Tilden JG	Ames 3017
Timm EW	Charter Oak 4376
Tincknell GF	Marathon 4789
Tincknell GF	Sioux Rapids 9585
Tipp DC	Graettinger 5571
Todd CW	Titonka 5597
Toepfer EA	Charles City 4677
Toft PJ	Peterson 4601
Tolander HL	Washington 1762
Tollerton JJ	Cedar Falls 3871
Tomkins LA	Shenandoah 2363
Tomkins NC	Grundy Center 3396
Tool RE	Kingsley 9116
Tornquist PA	Davenport 15
Torstenson C	Milford 5539
Tourtellot B	Wyoming 1943
Tourtellott FB	Rockwell 10217
Town JJ	Des Moines 2886
Townsend CH	Exira 6870
Townsend EB	Melvin 5616
Townsend HM	Randolph 7833
Townsend JA	Clinton 994
Townsend LT	Macksburg 6852
Townsend R	Milton 10243
Townsend WA	Randolph 7833
Toy CB	Sioux City 10139
Toy JF	Akron 7322
Toy JF	Alta 7126
Toy JF	Aurelia 7108
Toy JF	Charter Oak 4376
Toy JF	Fonda 6550
Toy JF	Orange City 6132
Toy JF	Sheldon 7880
Toy JF	Sioux City 10139
Toy JF	Sioux City 1757
Toy JF	Sioux City 4510
Toy JF	Storm Lake 10223
Toy ME	Sioux City 10139
Toy PC	Sioux City 10139
Toy PC	Storm Lake 10223
Tracey V	Corning 8100
Tracy AH	Clarion 3796
Tracy AL	Clarion 3796
Tracy GS	Burlington 1744
Tracy UB	Clarion 3796
Tracy V	Clarion 3796
Trainer FE	Ackley 8762
Trainer SS	Ackley 8762
Trautwein AW	Ottumwa 107
Treat CL	Webster City 1874
Tredway OC	Sioux City 1976
Troeger GE	Garner 8367
Trotter GF	Chariton 6014
True JW	Columbus Junction 2032
Truesdell RL	Wyoming 1943
Trukken VH	Kimballton 9619
Trumbauer CM	Williams 5585
Trumbauer JO	Waterloo 5120
Tucker E	Shenandoah 2679
Tupper BO	Spencer 6941
Turner FC	Prairie City 6755
Turner HH	Eldora 9233
Turner J	Marshalltown 2115
Turner MC	Henderson 7382
Turner RD	Henderson 7382
Turner RDM	Council Bluffs 9306
Turner RW	Council Bluffs 9306
Turner TG	Atlantic 2762
Turner TG	Council Bluffs 1479
Turner TG	Council Bluffs 9306
Turney E	Fairfield 8986
Tuttle H	Norway 7287
Tuttle RR	Fontanelle 7061
Twedt OE	Roland 11249
Tweedy OA	Centreville 337
Twyford CA	Osceola 6033
Tyler CJ	Anamosa 4696
Tymeson A	Storm Lake 10223
Tymeson A, Jr.	Linn Grove 7137
Tyner OH	New London 8352
Ulch A	Chelsea 5412
Ulch JR	Chelsea 5412
Ulm JW	Des Moines 1970
Ulve G	Lake Mills 5123
Underwood FL	Muscatine 692
Underwood N	Perry 3026
Ungerer JF	Hawkeye 8900
Untendorfer JD	Sioux City 10139
Updegraff T	McGregor 323
Upton JJ	Garner 4810
Utley LM	New Hampton 7607
Utter MF	Coin 7309
Vale LW	Ottumwa 1726
Valentine W	Casey 8099
Van Alstine RL	Gilmore City 6611
Van Buskirk D	Shenandoah 2679
Van De Berg J	Hull 6953
Van der Meide A	Sioux Center 7369
Van Der Stoep H	Hawarden 13939
Van Dyke BR	Chariton 13458
Van Dyke BR, Jr.	Chariton 9024
Van Dyke CD	Sioux City 4510
Van Dyke CD	Sioux City 5022
Van Dyke JT	Sioux City 10139
Van Dyke JW	Sioux City 10139
Van Dyke SP	Belle Plaine 4754
Van Dyke SR	Belle Plaine 4754
Van Dyke W	Sioux City 10139
Van Gorder C	Audubon 4891
Van Gorder ES	Audubon 4891
Van Gorder ES, Jr.	Audubon 4891
Van Gorp PH	Pella 8047
Van Houweling AC	Pella 8047
Van Keuren RS	Sioux City 3968
Van Kuran RC	Clinton 3736
Van Patten CL	Charter Oak 4376
Van Patten JE	Sheldon 3848
Van Patten JP	Davenport 2695
Van Rhee ED	Rock Rapids 7089
Van Scoy H	Rippey 7609
Van Scoy J	Rippey 7609
Van Scoy JH	Rippey 7609
Van Scoy M	Rippey 7609
Van Slyke FL	Manilla 6041
Van Spanckeren A	Pella 8047
Van Spanckeren BH, Jr.	Pella 8047
Van Steenbergen J	Inwood 8257
Van Steenbergen J	Prairie City 6755
Van Steenburg BB	Spirit Lake 4758
Van Steenburg BB	Spirit Lake 8032
Van Steenburg BB	Terril 10238
Van Syoc CB	Winfield 10640
Van Vechten GF	Cedar Rapids 3643
Van Vechten R	Cedar Rapids 3643
Vander Stoep DH	Inwood 8257
Vanderploeg WH	Pella 8047
Vargaa S	Leon 5489
Vaughan JR	Waterloo 5120
Vaughan W	Newton 650
Vaughan WB	Crystal Lake 5305
Vaughn AA	Wyoming 1943
Vaughn EA	Marion 2753
Vaughn JR	Waterloo 5700
Vaughn WW	Marion 117
Vaughn WW	Marion 2753
Vaux GB	Bagley 6995
Veiths DH	Davenport 4022
Vernon CH	Corning 8725
Vernon EM	Corning 8725
Vernon WGH	Sioux City 4235
Versteeg J	Sheldon 3848
Vest SL	Ottumwa 107
Vincent EL	Algona 3197
Vincent W	Britt 5020
Vincent W	Estherville 4700
Vincent W	Fort Dodge 1661
Vincent W	Fort Dodge 1947
Virtue SK	Webster City 3420
Visha L	Cedar Rapids 3643
Visser H	Hawarden 13939
Visser H	Rock Rapids 7089
Vogel HA	Newell 10191
Vogl AL	Dyersville 9555
Vogt HJ	Leon 5489
Vogt WF	Grinnell 7439
Volberding AF	Pomeroy 6063
Von Lackum HJ	Dysart 5934
Von Oven HA	Manchester 4221
Von Schrader B	Maquoketa 999
Von Schrader C	Maquoketa 999

Name	Location	Name	Location	Name	Location
Voorhees A	Exira 6870	Warner HL	Sioux City 4431	Wellik C	Garner 8367
Voss CN	Davenport 4022	Warnick FR	Prescott 5912	Wells AA	Marathon 4789
Vrba JFW	Garner 4810	Warnke AJ	Des Moines 2307	Wells G	Grundy Center 3225
Wacholz FL	Forest City 4889	Warren AG	Monroe 7357	Wells L	Council Bluffs 1479
Wadhams WH	Tabor 4609	Warren FC	Tama City 1880	Wells WP	Washington 1762
Wadleigh LB	Lyons 4536	Warren GH	Tama City 1880	Wells WW	Marathon 4789
Wadsworth JG	Council Bluffs 9306	Warren GL	Spirit Lake 13020	Wells WW	Washington 1762
Wadsworth JW	Burt 5685	Warren JH	Oskaloosa 147	Wellslager RT	Des Moines 2583
Wadsworth WC	Davenport 1671	Warren JH	Oskaloosa 2895	Weltner KH	Sheffield 12430
Wadsworth WS	Forest City 5011	Warren JW	Rolfe 4954	Welton MH	Adair 8699
Wagner HA	Buffalo Center 5154	Warren TT	Hedrick 12656	Welton RR	Adair 8699
Wagner J	Dubuque 2327	Warren TT	Winfield 10640	Wenck FJ	Renwick 7988
Wagner W, Jr.	Sioux City 5022	Wasson WB	Lineville 7261	Wennes OL	Decorah 5081
Wagoner WD	La Porte City 4114	Waterman CG	Klemme 6659	Wenstrand A	Essex 5803
Waite OJ	Webster City 1874	Waterman HL	Ottumwa 107	Wenstrand CA	Shenandoah 11588
Waitt AH	Storm Lake 2595	Watkins FE	Hawarden 4594	Wenstrand DA	Shenandoah 11588
Wakeman F	Akron 7322	Watland GO	Grinnell 7439	Wente HW	Waterloo 2910
Walden TP	Allerton 2191	Watson BB	Humboldt 13766	Wenzel C	Manilla 6041
Waldron DE	Glidden 4814	Watson BB	Humboldt 8277	Wernli GL	Le Mars 2728
Waldruff CH	Coin 7309	Watson BB	New Sharon 8950	Wertheim S	Belle Plaine 4754
Walker CE	New London 8352	Watson FB	Sioux City 1757	West A	Council Bluffs 1684
Walker DJ	Waterloo 5120	Watson JJ	Emmetsburg 3337	West AP	Villisca 7506
Walker FE	Bedford 5165	Watson JS	Council Bluffs 1479	West C	Seymour 8247
Walker FP	Clear Lake 7869	Watson LL	Bode 10371	West FR	Des Moines 950
Walker FW	Clarion 3796	Watson SH	Vinton 1593	West FS	Fairfield 8986
Walker G	Randolph 7833	Wattles CL	Carroll 3969	West RT	Churdan 6737
Walker HE	New London 5420	Wattles GW	Carroll 3969	West S	Clarinda 2028
Walker J	New London 8352	Watts FS	Audubon 4891	West SK	Fairfield 8986
Walker MB	Macksburg 6852	Watts TR	Jefferson 8262	Westergaard HC	Adair 8699
Walker RH	Macksburg 6852	Waugh NE	Roland 11249	Westergaard MI	Adair 8699
Walker RS	Greene 6880	Way SX	Titonka 5597	Westlake HB	Grinnell 2953
Walker RS	Waterloo 792	Way SX	Wesley 5457	Weston FJ	Renwick 7988
Walker SL	Knoxville 12849	Way TA	Corwith 5775	Weston JC	Clinton 994
Walker WC	Cambridge 9014	Way TA	Wesley 5457	Wettengel F	Dunlap 4139
Walker WW	Cedar Rapids 500	Weare EE	Cedar Rapids 500	Wettengel RW	Dunlap 4139
Walker WW	Macksburg 6852	Weare G	Sioux City 3968	Wettengel WJ	Dunlap 4139
Walkinshaw JH	Blanchard 4902	Weare HG	Sioux City 1757	Wetterholm H	Red Oak 6056
Wallace AH	Independence 3263	Weare HG	Sioux City 3968	Wettstein FE	La Porte City 4114
Wallace AH	Washington 1762	Weare J	Cedar Rapids 500	Wetzel JL	Grundy Center 3225
Wallace AH	Washington 2656	Weaver JF	Chelsea 5412	Wetzeler HH	Akron 7322
Wallace ME	Coon Rapids 5514	Weaver TC	Sigourney 1786	Wever CR	Fort Madison 1611
Wallaser HM	Charles City 1810	Webb CE	Montour 7469	Wharton A	Dubuque 2327
Wallbridge LC	Burlington 351	Webber JT	Sigourney 1786	Wharton GR	Aurelia 9724
Walleser HM	Charles City 4677	Webbles E	Anamosa 4696	Whedon WS	Winterset 1403
Wallsworth ED	Fontanelle 7061	Webbles E	Burlington 351	Wheeler GB	Fort Dodge 2763
Walston CE	Olin 7585	Webcott F	Sumner 8198	Wheeler GB	Lake City 4966
Walter HB	Tipton 13232	Weber JF	Ottumwa 2621	Wheeler JF	Conrad 9447
Walter JJ	Lenox 5517	Weber NF	Clarion 3796	Wheeler JL	Villisca 14041
Walter JW	Hartley 4881	Weberg BH	Inwood 7304	Wheeler JL	Villisca 7506
Walter JW	Lenox 5517	Webster WE	Clarinda 2028	Wheeler JS	Mason City 4587
Walters CE	Council Bluffs 5838	Wegersley JH	Marathon 4789	Wheelock BM	Ames 3017
Walters G	Harlan 10354	Wehrmacher WH	Waverly 3105	Whelan MK	Estherville 4700
Walters RC	Anamosa 4696	Weiditschka W	Waverly 3105	When GH	Whiting 10861
Walters RC	Olin 7585	Weir AS	Peterson 4601	Wherry AT	Swea City 5637
Walton JS	Clearfield 9549	Weiser CJ	McGregor 323	Wherry JR	Churdan 6737
Wanberg JF	Cherokee 10711	Welch CS	Iowa City 18	Wherry JT	Wyoming 1943
Wankel L	Sidney 5145	Welch ES	Shenandoah 12950	Wherry JW	Wyoming 1943
Wanless OG	Cresco 4897	Welch WB	Farmington 5579	Wherry WG	Wyoming 1943
Ward TF	Le Mars 2818	Welden JL	Iowa Falls 3252	Whetstone LA	Keokuk 14309
Warden FR	Des Moines 13321	Weldin CP	Hedrick 12656	Whetstone LA	Keokuk 1992
Warne GB	Independence 1581	Weldin PH	Washington 1762	Whinery AJ	Aurelia 7108
Warne GB	Independence 3263	Welik C	Garner 8367	Whinery HM	Ida Grove 3930
Warner HA	Oskaloosa 8076	Welle PC	Toledo 13073	Whinnery AJ	Aurelia 9724

Whisenand JD	Prairie City 6755
Whisler W	Williams 5585
White A	Knoxville 1986
White HR	Sigourney 1786
White J	Oskaloosa 1101
White J	Oskaloosa 147
White SA	Washington 2656
White SH	Washington 1762
White TL	New London 8352
Whitehall WJ	State Center 8931
Whitehead F	Monroe 7357
Whitehead SW	Sioux Rapids 9585
Whiting JT	New London 5420
Whitmer GR	Primghar 6650
Whitmer GR	Sioux City 10139
Whitney D	Hawarden 4594
Whitney DE	Churdan 6737
Whitney DR	Aurelia 7108
Whitney EA	West Union 2015
Whitney ET	Deep River 6705
Whitney FH	Atlantic 1836
Whitney JM	Aurelia 7108
Whitney LB	Decorah 5081
Whittier L	Whiting 10861
Whyle VB	What Cheer 3192
Wichhart EW	Burlington 1744
Wichman JE	Garner 4810
Wichman JE	Kanawha 9018
Wick AO	Lake City 4966
Wick CR	Colfax 7114
Wick MI	Osceola 6033
Wickham EA	Council Bluffs 1479
Widner FM	Corning 2936
Widner FM	Prescott 5912
Wiegman CH	Klemme 6659
Wiegner EH	Farmington 5579
Wiemer CG	Radcliffe 6435
Wiemer EE	Hubbard 8970
Wiemer EE	Radcliffe 6435
Wiemer W	Radcliffe 6435
Wiese WC	Gladbrook 5461
Wieting PG	Toledo 6432
Wiewel WK	Fonda 6550
Wiggins JM	Jefferson 10123
Wightman TM	Sidney 5145
Wilcockson KE	Sigourney 1786
Wilcox CH	Greene 3071
Wilcox DO	Chelsea 5412
Wilcox H	Griswold 8915
Wilcox JF	Council Bluffs 5838
Wild G	Shenandoah 11588
Wildberger A	Sidney 5145
Wilde GF	Fonda 6550
Wilder EA	Humboldt 8277
Wilder RM	Macksburg 6852
Wiley CA	Council Bluffs 1479
Wiley DG	Creston 12636
Wiley DG	Creston 2586
Wiley RE	Mason City 2574
Wilharm FJ	Sumner 8198
Wilhite RP	Deep River 6705
Wilke GH	Strawberry Point 9069
Wilken FC	Exira 6870
Wilken JC	Arlington 9664
Wilkenson LP	Chelsea 5412
Wilkin F	Lenox 5517
Wilkinson F	Albia 1799
Wilkinson FA	Albia 1799
Wilkinson HW	Williams 5585
Wilkinson MJ	Nora Springs 4761
Will RP	Cherokee 10711
Willem AA	Burlington 1744
Willenborg HB	Dyersville 9555
Willey EP	Chelsea 5412
Williams AC	Oskaloosa 1101
Williams AF	Osceola 6033
Williams B	Stuart 2721
Williams CH	Greene 6880
Williams D	Tabor 4609
Williams DE	Allerton 9231
Williams EB	Montezuma 2961
Williams FC	Cumberland 7326
Williams FD	Sheffield 12430
Williams FS	Marshalltown 4359
Williams GC	Des Moines 2583
Williams JA	Lime Springs 6750
Williams JC	Lake Mills 5123
Williams JL	Marshalltown 4359
Williams L	Fairfield 1475
Williams L	Osceola 6033
Williams L	Pleasantville 5564
Williams LN	De Witt 3182
Williams OD	Guthrie Center 7736
Williams WW	Lime Springs 6750
Williamson CC	Sigourney 1786
Williamson TL	Tama City 1880
Willig IM	Hubbard 8970
Willimack V	Lost Nation 5402
Wills IW	Keokuk 1992
Willson UI	Blockton 8211
Wiloth KJ	Gladbrook 5461
Wilson AC	Oelwein 5778
Wilson AD	Clinton 3736
Wilson AJ	Boone 6838
Wilson AJ	Sioux City 7401
Wilson BA	Webster City 3420
Wilson CE	Lorimor 12248
Wilson E	Macksburg 6852
Wilson E	Winterset 1403
Wilson EB	Council Bluffs 1479
Wilson FB	Manchester 4221
Wilson FT	Sioux City 7401
Wilson GE	Clinton 3736
Wilson GE, Jr.	Clinton 3736
Wilson H	Ames 3017
Wilson H	Malvern 2247
Wilson HF	Shenandoah 2679
Wilson HG	Des Moines 2307
Wilson J	Traer 5135
Wilson JC	Hull 6953
Wilson JF	Clinton 3736
Wilson JF	Fairfield 1475
Wilson JF	Grinnell 2953
Wilson JH	Emmetsburg 8035
Wilson JJ	Malvern 2247
Wilson JL	Lyons 66
Wilson JS	Hull 6953
Wilson JW	Macksburg 6852
Wilson L	Burlington 351
Wilson LB	Lenox 5517
Wilson MA	Sioux City 5022
Wilson MH	Seymour 11210
Wilson P	Clearfield 9549
Wilson R	Shannon City 9723
Wilson RF	Fairfield 1475
Wilson RJ	Fairfield 1475
Wilson SG	Emmetsburg 8035
Wilson VH	Grundy Center 3396
Wilson WD	Grundy Center 3396
Wilson WF	Washington 1762
Wilson WP	Grinnell 13473
Winden AW	Buffalo Center 5154
Winden AW	Lake Mills 5123
Winders C	Tama City 1880
Windsor L	Des Moines 13321
Wine PD	Aurelia 9724
Wine WW	Coon Rapids 6080
Wingert FD	Tipton 6760
Winks LP	Sumner 8198
Winsell FF	Dexter 10030
Winslow FS	Marion 117
Winslow JW	Atlantic 2762
Winterbotham JH	Fort Madison 1611
Winterbotham JR	Fort Madison 1611
Winterfield LL	Iowa Falls 3252
Wintrode JH	Winterset 2002
Wiseman LE	Sac City 4450
Wissink DH	Hull 6953
Wissler WE	Exira 6870
Witt G	Elkader 1815
Witter G	Storm Lake 10223
Wiwali JW	Dubuque 317
Wolcott ES	Richland 5611
Wolcott JE	Richland 5611
Wold SS	Rock Rapids 3153
Wolf BM	Cedar Rapids 3643
Wolf CM	Alta 7126
Wolf RG	Sheffield 12430
Wolfe F	Shannon City 9723
Wollenhaupt GE	Cumberland 7326
Wollenhaupt LM	Cumberland 7326
Wooch V	Coin 7309
Wood BH	Perry 3026
Wood BJ	Logan 6771
Wood CN	Logan 6771
Wood EJ	Logan 6771
Wood FQ	Logan 6771
Wood JW	Logan 6771
Wood L	Traer 5135
Wood LE	Traer 5135
Wood LM	Logan 6771
Wood WC	Havelock 7294
Wood WH	Logan 6771
Woodard RO	West Union 2015
Woodbury GM	Marshalltown 411
Woodbury JP	Marshalltown 411
Woodcock CC	Albia 8603
Woodcock JW	Buffalo Center 5154
Woodin GD	Sigourney 1786

Woods GW	Council Bluffs 14028	Young WH	Hedrick 5540
Woods N	Coin 7309	Young WJ, Jr.	Clinton 994
Woods W	Tipton 2983	Young WW	Hedrick 5540
Woods WH	Iowa Falls 3252	Zalesky FE	Belle Plaine 2012
Woodward BB	Davenport 848	Zbanek EB	Cedar Rapids 2511
Woodworth JM	Perry 3026	Zbanek EB	Cedar Rapids 9168
Woodworth JM	Rippey 7609	Zeigler SB	West Union 2015
Wormhoudt A	Pella 8047	Zigrang EV	Bancroft 5643
Wormhoudt GH	Pella 8047	Zuerrer EH	Fort Dodge 2763
Wormhoudt HD	Pella 8047	Zwart AJ	Des Moines 2583
Worth GA	Indianola 1811	Zwilling EP	Nevada 2555
Worthington W	Williams 5585		
Worthington WS	Eagle Grove 4694		
Wray FH	Waterloo 5120		
Wright CL	Sioux City 3124		
Wright IV	Blockton 8211		
Wright L	Knoxville 1871		
Wright L	Knoxville 1986		
Wright LE	Dunlap 4139		
Wright NH	Brooklyn 3284		
Wright OL	Knoxville 1986		
Wright OP	Knoxville 1986		
Wright OP	Pella 1891		
Wright R	Iowa Falls 7521		
Wright RM	Fort Dodge 4566		
Wright SW	Centerville 2197		
Wright TH	Fort Dodge 4566		
Wright US	Blockton 8211		
Wright W	Hedrick 12656		
Wright WM	Blockton 8211		
Wright WV	Blockton 8211		
Wurster BF	Lenox 5517		
Wyatt HH	Hull 6953		
Wyman J	Des Moines 2583		
Wynkoop OG	Jefferson 8262		
Yager JF	Milford 9298		
Yaggy LJ	Davenport 2695		
Yaggy LJ	Davenport 15		
Yeliner EE	Traer 5135		
Yerger FS	Hedrick 5540		
Yerger JP	Sigourney 1786		
Yetter FB	Davenport 4022		
Yeutter CE	Spirit Lake 13020		
Yokum EL	Aurelia 9724		
Yokum OE	Aurelia 9724		
York GH	Colfax 7114		
Yost DE	Chariton 13458		
Yost DE	Chariton 9024		
Young C	Clarion 3788		
Young CD	Clarion 3788		
Young CH	Clinton 994		
Young EA	Clinton 994		
Young FS	Shenandoah 2363		
Young HR	Arlington 9664		
Young HS	Washington 1762		
Young JA	Washington 1762		
Young JA	Waterloo 5120		
Young JL	Corydon 10146		
Young JL	Leon 1696		
Young JP	Buffalo Center 5154		
Young JW	Webster City 1874		
Young K	Webster City 1874		
Young TK	New Hampton 7607		

Notes

Notes

Notes

Notes

Notes

Notes